GEORGE GERSHWIN

George Gershwin. (Photograph by Emmett Schoenbaum. Copyright©RKO Radio Pictures, June 1937. Courtesy of Marc George Gershwin and the Library of Congress Gershwin Collection.)

GEORGE GERSHWIN

A Bio-Bibliography

NORBERT CARNOVALE

Bio-Bibliographies in Music, Number 76
Donald L. Hixon, Series Adviser

GREENWOOD PRESS
Westport, Connecticut • London

Library of Congress Cataloging-in-Publication Data

Carnovale, Norbert, 1932–
    George Gershwin : a bio-bibliography / Norbert Carnovale.
        p.   cm.—(Bio-bibliographies in music, ISSN 0742–6968 ; no. 76)
    Discography: p.
    Includes index.
    ISBN 0–313–26003–6 (alk. paper)
    1. Gershwin, George, 1898–1937—Bibliography.   2. Gershwin, George,
1898–1937—Discography.   I. Title.   II. Series.
ML134.G29 C37 2000
780′.92—dc21
    [B]   99–046018

British Library Cataloguing in Publication Data is available.

Library of Congress Catalog Card Number: 99–046018
ISBN: 0–313–26003–6
ISSN: 0742–6968

First published in 2000

Greenwood Press, 88 Post Road West, Westport, CT 06881
An imprint of Greenwood Publishing Group, Inc.
www.greenwood.com

Printed in the United States of America

The paper used in this book complies with the
Permanent Paper Standard issued by the National
Information Standards Organization (Z39.48–1984).

10 9 8 7 6 5 4 3 2

To Jo and my three children:
Phylanne, Noranne, and Norman,
with affection

"He is as simple, as unaffected, as modest and as charming a youth as one would desire to meet. There is nothing about him that is forbidding. He wears his unprecedented celebrity as lightly as if it were a cane—that cane which one can hear swinging so jauntily in the opening rhythms of *An American in Paris* . . ."

—Isaac Goldberg, *George Gershwin: A Study in American Music*

Contents

Part II

Preface

This volume consists of seven main sections, in two parts, as follows:

Part I

(1) An overview of George Gershwin's life in the form of a ***Brief Biography.***

(2) A list of ***Works and Performances***, arranged by genre, and arranged chronologically by title. Following many titles are listings of premiere and other selected performances.

Cross-references to citations about the work in the ***Bibliography*** chapters, many times referring to essays about the work, reviews of its performances, and to recordings of the work listed in the ***Discography,*** are included in the ***Works and Performances*** list. Each work in the Works and Performances chapter is preceded by the mnemonic **"W"** and the appropriate number **W1, W2,** etc., and each selected performance of that work is listed in ascending chronological order and identified by successive lowercase letters (**W1a, W1b,** etc.) Works are listed first in their original version (e. g., *Rhapsody in Blue* in the composer's holographs) with subsequent versions following. This section does *not* include overtures for musicals. The symbol * indicates that a listed song is thought to have been published in sheet music format. Details of instrumentation (and dedication) are generally given for the Orchestral Works as is the location of holographs when known.

(3) ***Individual Songs*** are given a section, listing the songs in alphabetical order. Readers so interested will find the name(s) of performers who introduced the songs originally and the names of the stage shows in which they were introduced.

(4) The ***Discography*** includes a wide selection of sound recordings, both old and new, in all formats as of 1999. Each recorded work or composite recording is preceded by the mnemonic **"D"** (**D1, D2, D3,** etc.) References (*See*: **"B924,"** e. g.) are made to commentaries about the recordings made in the ***Bibliography about Discography*** chapter, and listings of original compositions and arrangements in this section include the **"W"** number of the work for ease in referring back to the ***Works and Performances*** chapter. **"F"** references are to the ***Filmography.***

(5) A ***Filmography*** of works which included significant use of Gershwin's music, listed by title in chronological order.

Part II

(6) *Bibliography by the Gershwins,* including an annotated bibliography of fifteen writings by George which is followed by an annotated bibliography of thirteen writings by Ira.

(7) The classified section *Bibliography about George Gershwin* includes the sections "Biographies"; "Bibliography about Biographies"; "Bibliography about Works"; "Bibliography about Discography"; "Other General Information Sources about the Gershwins"; "Bibliography about Filmography"; "Bibliography about Orchestra Tours"; and "Bibliography about Dissertations and Theses."

Appendix A affixes copies of *Whiteman and Reisman Orchestra Tour Itineraries.*

An **Index** concludes the volume.

Because Gershwin bibliography and discography continued to appear during the final stages of producing this book, I deemed it necessary to insert selected items by using supplementary numbers such as **W52.1** rather than renumber the entire bibliography. The work of a Gershwin bibliographer will truly never be finished!

Acknowledgements

I am indebted to all of the Gershwin scholars who have preceded me, the work of many, some of whose names are acknowledged in the first sentence of the **Brief Biography.**

The University of Southern Mississippi, Hattiesburg, assisted in several ways: leaves, grants, and near the end of the work, release time. I am indebted to Charles Elliott, presently Director of the School of Music, for the latter. The University of Southern Mississippi's Vice President for Research Donald R. Cotten and his predecessor Karen Yarbrough both provided generous grants over the protracted period of work. The National Endowment for the Humanities awarded a Travel to Collections grant; numerous mini-grants from the Speakers Bureau of the Mississippi Humanities Council allowed me to present my lecture on Gershwin, a talk which derived much of its substance from this book.

My friends John D. W. Guice and Charles T. Harrison were omnipresent with words of encouragement and support. James W. Pruett, formerly Chief, Music Division, Library of Congress, was my gracious host on one of my several visits to the Music Division. Raymond A. White helped guide me through the George and Ira Gershwin Collection there. Sylvia B. Kennick of Williams College provided valuable information on Paul Whiteman and his bands.

George Marc Gershwin, brother Arthur Gershwin's son, granted an interview and provided insights, as well as permission to use some of the materials in the Collection at the Library of Congress.

Miles Kreuger of the Institute for the American Musical, Los Angeles allowed me full access to his files. Don Hixon, Series Adviser for the Greenwood Press Bio-Bibliographies in Music series, helped and inspired in innumerable ways. Marilyn Brownstein, Alicia Merritt, Pamela St. Clair, and Jane Lerner, Editors at Greenwood, demonstrated remarkable patience and help during the twelve years I worked on this book.

The staffs of libraries at Tulane University; Louisiana State University; the University of California at Los Angeles; the Kenneth Spencer Research Library, Special Collections, University of Kansas; the Academy for Motion Picture Arts and Sciences; the Library of Congress; the Theatre Library at the Goodspeed Opera House; the Library of the City Museum of New York; and the New York Public Library at Lincoln Center were consistently cordial and efficient. Karolyn Thompson; interlibrary-loan coordinator at USM's Cook library; was of substantial assistance in locating materials not present in our local library.

Annette Farrington sent me a very useful and thorough inventory of Gershwin sound recordings. These are the recordings contributed by Carol and Frank Tuit and housed among the holdings of the rich and   fascinating Goodspeed Library of Musical Theatre at the Goodspeed Opera House in East Haddam, Connecticut. During the course of my research I was given permission to photocopy a list of recordings that were in Gershwin's library at the time of his death and given to the Library of Congress by Ira Gershwin; Ronald L. Blanc, attorney for the Ira Gershwin estate, granted the needed approval.

Early on, Robert Sherman of WQXR in New York supplied a tape copy for study of the impressive *Gershwin Tribute* aired over that station on March 1st, 1987. Selected newspapers throughout the United States enthusiastically provided me with copies of reviews from a number of cities where concerts were given during the Whiteman and Reisman (1934) tours.

Southern Mississippi assigned me several graduate assistants through the years of the research; all of them were helpful; the last one, Cheryl Morris, deserves special thanks for assisting in bringing the volume to fruition.

Errors or omissions are mine alone and should not reflect on any of the persons or institutions named above.

Abbreviations

Works:

AiP-*An American in Paris*
Cake-*Let 'Em Eat Cake*
Concerto-Concerto in F
OTIS-*Of Thee I Sing*
P&B-*Porgy and Bess*
RiB-*Rhapsody in Blue*

Libraries:

AMPAS-Academy of Motion Picture Arts and Society, Margaret Herrick Library, Los Angeles
DLC-Music Division, Library of Congress
GOH-Goodspeed Opera House Library, East Haddam, CT
NN-L-New York Public Library at Lincoln Center
NNMus-Museum of the City of New York
UCLA-Film and Television Archive, University of California in Los Angeles

Place names:

LA-Los Angeles
NY-New York

Names:

GG-George Gershwin
G-Gershwin
IG-Ira Gershwin

Periodicals:

ARG-*American Record Guide*
LATimes-*Los Angeles Times*

NY Herald Tribune- New York Herald Tribune
NYTimes-The New York Times

Miscellaneous:

AA- An Academy award
DAI- *Dissertations Abstract International*
DVD- Digital Video Disc
pa. or pf- piano
q. v.- which see
VC- Videocassette, currently available
*: The song was published in sheet music format.
+: Song published as part of a piano/vocal score

Part I

Brief Biography

More than seventy biographies and thousands of words have been written about George Gershwin. Jablonski, Schwartz, Ewen, Crawford and Schneider, Rosenberg, Peyser, Krasker and Kimball, and Gilbert, among many others, have provided students of the Gershwins, both George and Ira, with a wealth of information.(1) Because of easy access to the Gershwin family, not to mention their industriousness, Jablonski and Kimball, in particular, have provided much inside information. My biography of Gershwin, consistent with all of those in the Greenwood Press series of bio-bibliographies of musicians, is provided primarily to give the user convenient reference to the basics of the composer's life and music.

1898–1919

George Gershwin was born on September 26, 1898, in Brooklyn, New York, after his parents, Russian-Jewish emigrants, Rose and Gershovitz had moved to this country. George's older brother, Ira, was born two years earlier, on December 6, 1896; Arthur became the third Gershwin boy (and father of Marc George) born about eighteen months after George, on March 14, 1900, and finally, George's baby sister, Frances ("Frankie," mother of Leopold Godowsky, III and three girls), was born December 6, 1906, and passed away on January 18, 1999, at age 92.

After George was born, the family moved back to Manhattan, to a second-story flat at 91 Second Avenue, in New York's Lower East Side. George spent his preadolescent years in and about this polyglot neighborhood. During his time at the New York school P. S. 25 at ten years old, he met Max Rosen, violinist (1900-1956), who exerted considerable influence on him musically. In 1910, Mother Rose Gershwin felt that the Gershwin household should have a piano, which she purchased with Ira in mind. Ira was not interested, but George amazed the family with what he could already do on the keyboard (he had the opportunity to tinker on a friend's player piano). Lessons commenced with the neighborhood piano teacher, a Miss Green. George learned so quickly that he soon exhausted what Miss Green had to offer, and moved on to a man named Goldfarb, ultimately to Charles Hambitzer (1881–1918), a well-trained musician, whom George credited with a significant influence upon his life in music.

---

1. Full bibliographical information on the contributions of these scholars is given under their names in the appropriate subsection of Part II "Bibliography about George Gershwin."

Early influences were composers Jerome Kern and Irving Berlin, and pianists such as Lucky Roberts. Kern influenced Gershwin throughout his career as is corroborated by George's own statement: "Incidentally, I believe Kern's *Showboat* score to be the finest light opera achievement in the history of American music," a statement made when he was a guest performer on the Rudy Vallee Hour radio broadcast on November 10, 1932.

George's first attempts at composition resulted in two songs: "Since I Found You" and "Raggin' the Traumeri," neither of which was published. In May 1914, at age 15, George dropped out of school to go to work full time as a song plugger at Jerome H. Remick's music publishing firm in Tin Pan Alley. An advertisement in the May 27, 1914, edition of *Music Trades* gives Remick's address as 131 West 41st Street. Thus this is probably where George first worked, rather than at the oft-pictured building at 45 West 28th Street. Incidentally, Remick's moved further uptown shortly after that, to 219 West 46th Street.**(2)** "Pounding" the piano all day, along with transposing songs to various keys to suit the performers who came to Remick's in search of material, helped develop George's piano technique in a remarkably short time.

Toward the end of 1915, George began making piano rolls as a means to supplement his income. The rolls include instrumental renderings of songs written by his contemporaries, as well as, later, many of his own compositions. Among the rolls that Gershwin cut are "When You Want 'Em, You Can't Get 'Em," *Rialto Ripples,* and *Rhapsody in Blue.* Through the efforts of Artis Wodehouse (about which more at the end of this biography), it is possible to hear these rolls recorded on compact disc today.

In 1916, George and Will Donaldson wrote *Rialto Ripples,* which combined elements of the traditional ragtime piano piece with those of a piano novelty work—Jablonski calls it his "first instrumental piece."**(3)** Gershwin's first published song was "When You Want 'Em, You Can't Get 'Em, When You've Got 'Em, You Don't Want 'Em," with lyrics by Murray Roth, produced by publisher Harry Von Tilzer.

Gershwin left Remick's after nearly three years on Friday, March 17, 1917. Unemployed, he worked meanwhile as the relief pianist at the City Theater on 14th Street.

George became rehearsal pianist for *Miss 1917,* a Kern-Victor Herbert show, to which he contributed no songs. Vivienne Segal was in the cast. On February 1, 1918, at age nineteen, George became a member of the staff at music publisher T. B. Harms, as a salaried songwriter working for Max Dreyfus. George had published "You-oo, Just You" with lyrics by Irving Caesar with Remick, but Harms' first published Gershwin song was "Some Wonderful Sort of Someone" in 1918. Nora Bayes, outstanding vaudeville performer, became acquainted with George. She asked him to accompany her in a song recital in the middle of her then current show, *Look Who's Here* (retitled *Ladies First*).

According to Irving Caesar, he and Gershwin composed "Swanee" in fifteen minutes after plotting it out during a bus ride from downtown Manhattan up to Gershwin's apartment. By this time the show *Demi-Tasse* had opened. "Swanee" was used in the show, but was not a success in this setting. It wasn't until Al Jolson heard the song at a party, interpolated it into his own already successful touring show *Sinbad,* and most importantly recorded it. Only then did the song became a hit, bringing Gershwin about $10,000 in royalties the first year.

---

2. *See:* the Remick advertisement in *Music Trades,* July 14, 1914, and the Appendix in David A. Jasen, *Tin Pan Alley* (New York: Donald I. Fine, 1988), p. 291.

3 . Edward Jablonski, *Gershwin: A Biography.* (New York: Doubleday, 1987), p. 18.

"Swanee" provided Gershwin the exposure he needed to insure success and subsequent demand as a writer of complete Broadway shows.

George became involved with the show *Half Past Eight* (1918), a flop for which he wrote five original songs. An Alex Aarons' produced musical *La-La-Lucille!* (1919) became the first show for which he provided the entire score (*See:* **W9a**). Although the music for the show attracted little attention, Max Dreyfus of T. B. Harms saw fit to publish six of its songs.

Gershwin had been studying with Edward Kilenyi (1884–1968). During the year 1919 he wrote *Lullaby* for string quartet as part of his studies with Kilenyi. George and Irving Caesar had two songs interpolated into *Good Morning, Judge*, which had its premiere in February of 1919. The tunes were "There's More to a Kiss Than the X-X-X" and "I Was So Young (You Were So Beautiful)."

1920–1923

A key junction for Gershwin in terms of his career came in 1920 with the beginning of his association with *George White's Scandals,* starting that year. Probably because of the success of "Swanee," George was hired to compose all of the music for the *Scandals* beginning in 1920, at a salary of fifty dollars per week during the run of the show.   The *Scandals,* for which George wrote the music through the fifth edition of 1923, were in competition with Florenz Ziegfeld's *Follies.* I know of no better description of the *Scandals* than that given by Edward Jablonski:

> The prime feature of the *Scandals* was its dancing, along with its
> washroom humor, skits parodying Prohibition, the always reliable
> bedroom farce and scantily clad beauties. One theater historian
> observed that Ziegfeld had glorified the American girl and White
> undressed her.**(4)**

During his tenure with the *Scandals,* two of George's songs achieved popularity: "I'll Build a Stairway to Paradise" and "Somebody Loves Me." "Somebody Loves Me" has been recorded countless times and, like so many Gershwin songs, the tune has become a standard for jazz improvisations. Five consecutive years of working with White's *Scandals* also cemented George's place on Broadway as a composer to be reckoned with.

George collaborated with Ira (then writing under the pseudonym Arthur Francis) on the tune "Waiting for the Sun to Come Out" (1920) for a show titled *The Sweetheart Shop.* "Waiting for the Sun to Come Out" was the first *published* song on which George and Ira collaborated. *Piccadilly to Broadway,* including songs by the Gershwin brothers and others, was a show from 1920 that toured but never made it to Broadway. This show was followed by *A Dangerous Maid* (1921). "Do It Again," with lyrics by Buddy DeSylva, was interpolated into *The French Doll* and made a success in 1922 by Irene Bordoni.

Blue Monday (135th Street), a short thirty-minute operatic presentation, was composed for but dropped from the 1922 *Scandals.* Perhaps the most significant thing about *Blue Monday,* apart from the fact that it might be considered a progenitor of *Porgy and Bess,* is that it attracted the attention of Paul Whiteman. Paul was the dance band leader who led the

---

4. Jablonski, *Gershwin,* 43.

pit orchestra for the *Scandals* that year.

In 1923, George traveled for the first time to London to work on a show titled *Silver Lining*, which ultimately became titled *The Rainbow*. The soprano Eva Gauthier and George appeared in recital on November 1, 1923, at Aeolian Hall—a very successful concert including the songs "I'll Build a Stairway to Paradise," "Innocent Ingenue Baby," "Swanee," and as an encore, sung twice incidentally, "Do It Again." This recital was Gershwin's debut on the New York concert stage.

1924–1933

1924 was an incredibly fruitful year for George: the annual *Scandals*, the shows *Sweet Little Devil, Primrose,* and *Lady, Be Good!* all took place that year. And, this is not to mention the premiere of the now ubiquitous *Rhapsody in Blue*!

George had completed work on the musical *Sweet Little Devil* by January of 1924. He was awaiting its January 21st Broadway premiere when, at a Times Square billiards/pool hall, Ira read an announcement in the *New York Tribune* of January 4, to the effect that "George Gershwin is at work on a jazz concerto . . ." The "concerto" was to be but one number on a concert dubbed **"An Experiment in Modern Music"** featuring the Paul Whiteman Palais Royale Jazz Band and novelty pianist Zez Confrey (1895-1972).

Gershwin contacted Whiteman by telephone after hearing of the announcement, tried to beg off writing the "concerto" only to be talked into doing so by the insistent, convincing Whiteman. Thus, the creation of the work was begun on January 7, 1924, as indicated on the holograph manuscript. Because time was short, a mere five weeks before the concert, and because he was so familiar with the abilities of the various members of Whiteman's regular personnel, Ferde Grofé was called upon to orchestrate for the slightly expanded Whiteman band. Grofé began his work, literally scoring behind Gershwin pages at a time. The orchestration was completed on February 4, 1924, and rehearsals had already begun at the Palais Royale during the daytime prior to that date.**(5)** An unofficial premiere took place at the Palais Royale, while the official premiere performance was held at 3:00 p.m. on Tuesday, February 12, 1924, at Aeolian Hall in New York. Competition for the audience that day in New York was keen:

> Theatergoers had the choice of such plays as *Abie's Irish Rose* and
> *Wildflower. St. Joan*—George Bernard Shaw's latest work—and
> Kaufman and Connelly's *Beggar on Horseback* were scheduled
> to open later in the week . . . A new edition of the *Ziegfeld Follies*
> starred comedian Fanny Brice and dancer Ann Pennington. The
> Hippodrome offered its usual potpourri, which currently included the
> Albert Rasch Ballet, singers Nellie and Sara Kouns, the Vincent Lopez
> Orchestra, trained seals, champion ropers, clowns, and equestrians.

---

5. A brief announcement regarding the beginning of these rehearsals appeared in the
   New York Times on January 22, 1924, alongside a review of the New York premiere
   of *Sweet Little Devil*. This announcement states that the first rehearsal was to be on
   the day of the article, January 22, and this fact suggests that at least parts of the
   work were orchestrated by that date.

Cecil B. DeMille's *The Ten Commandments* [movie] was shown twice a day.**(6)**

It is also interesting to note that on the printed program for the premiere performance, Gershwin took second billing to Zez Confrey, thus attesting to Gershwin's comparative lack of fame prior to the launching of the first rhapsody on that occasion.

1924 was indeed a busy year for Gershwin because, besides the premiere of the rhapsody on February 12th, there was a concert with Eva Gauthier in Boston on January 29, fifteen days before the premiere of the rhapsody; a repeat performance of the rhapsody at Aeolian Hall on March 7 and a performance in Carnegie Hall on April 21; the *Rhapsody in Blue* tour beginning on May 15 in Rochester, New York, with George leaving the tour after May 21 in Saint Louis; the first recording of the rhapsody on June 10 and the appearance of other Gershwin melodies on record; the June 30 opening of George White's *Scandals* in New York; George's departure for London on July 8 to work on *Primrose*; the September 11 opening of *Primrose* in London; another Carnegie Hall performance of the rhapsody with Whiteman on November 15; the opening of *Lady, Be Good!* in Philadelphia on November 17; a performance of the rhapsody at Philadelphia's Academy of Music (with Whiteman) on November 27; *Lady Be Good*'s opening in New York on December 1; and finally the first performance of the rhapsody in Boston at Symphony Hall on December 4.

While the performances in the East and the recordings certainly contributed to the spread of the fame of the *Rhapsody in Blue*, I believe that the tours of Paul Whiteman and his Orchestra contributed a great deal more than has previously been acknowledged. Whiteman toured the U. S. several times beginning in 1924. His band played the rhapsody on most every concert covering every major city as well as many minor cities in the U. S. and in Canada . (*See* Appendix A). It must be kept in mind that for many people, these tour appearances were the first opportunity to hear the rhapsody live. An example from a review of a concert attended by more than 2,000 people in the Deep South city of Jacksonville, Florida: ". . . The Rhapsody in Blue, by Gershwin, much heralded and rather well known through the phonograph records widely sold and played, was the great, big number of the concert, and parts of it were very beautiful . . ."**(7)**

As stated above, *Primrose* was premiered on September 11, 1924, in London. In 1989, the marvelous singer Maureen McGovern recorded one of the songs from this show, "Naughty Baby," in her All-Gershwin album of the same name **(D900)**. This song was also chosen for use in the "new" (1990s) Gershwin show, *Crazy for You.*

The next important event, mentioned above, was the opening of *Lady, Be Good!*—first at its November tryout in Philadelphia, and later in New York, on December 1, 1924. Three very important songs emerged from this show: "The Man I Love," which was removed from the show before New York, "Fascinating Rhythm," and of course, "Oh, Lady Be Good!" Further, in the words of Edward Jablonski, the show *Lady, Be Good!* marked "the

---

6. Thomas A. DeLong, *Pops: Paul Whiteman, King of Jazz.* (Piscataway, NJ: New
    Century, 1983), p. 4.

7. George Boyt Smith, "Paul Whiteman and His Jazz Orchestra Scored Hit Here, Big
Audience [over 2,000] Enjoyed Program Yesterday in Duval County—Orchestra Includes
Splendid Musicians." *Times-Union* [Jacksonville, FL], January 12, 1925.

advent of *the* Gershwin musical."**(8)**

Tell Me More opened in New York on April 13, 1925, and in London on May 26. Before the show opened in London, Eva Gauthier and Gershwin repeated their "From Java to Jazz" concert at London's Aeolian Hall on May 22.

By this time, Gershwin had been commissioned by Harry Harkness Flagler, at the request of Walter Damrosch, conductor of the New York Symphony Society, to write a concerto for piano and orchestra. He began work on the concerto in mid-July of 1925, the completed manuscript bearing the date November 25, 1925. The world premiere took place at Carnegie Hall on December 3, 1925, with Gershwin at the piano, and Damrosch conducting the New York Symphony. Initial reaction to the concerto was mixed as typified by a review by the well-known New York critic Olin Downes:

> In essence this is a more ambitious and less original piece of
> music than the one which first brought Mr. Gershwin to the
> attention of the orchestral public. It is not only immature—which
> need be no crime—but it is self-conscious, lacking the esprit and felicity
> of touch that he shows when he is truly in the creative vein. **(9)**

Despite mixed reviews such as that cited above, the concerto has become a popular repertory piece, recorded many times in its various versions, and performed regularly on symphony concerts. Before the completion of the concerto in the latter part of the summer of 1925, Gershwin was working on the shows *Tip-Toes* and *Song of the Flame*. On July 20, George was honored by having his picture on the cover of *Time* magazine.

The very successful show *Tip-Toes* made its New York premiere on December 28th, 1925; *Blue Monday*, by then retitled *135th Street*, was revived in a concert presentation, with a new orchestration by Ferde Grofé, at Carnegie Hall on the 29th; and on the 30th, *Song of the Flame* opened in New York—three premieres for George in three nights! In late 1925, Gershwin met Oscar Levant—pianist, composer, author, raconteur—who was to become a close friend and interpreter of G's music.

Audience acceptance of *Song of the Flame* was good.   According to Jablonski, *Song of the Flame* had a longer run (219 performances) than the "more Gershwinesque*" Tip-Toes* (194 performances). **(10)** It is not surprising then that it was made into a movie in 1930 by First National-Warner Bros. **(F6.1)**. Interestingly, the motion pictures *Song of the Flame* and *King of Jazz*, the latter featuring Paul Whiteman and His Orchestra playing the first rhapsody, played New York theaters concurrently during the week of May 11, 1930. **(11)**

On January 21, 1926, George traveled to Derby, CT for another concert with Eva Gauthier. Later in 1926, he went to England to supervise the British productions of *Lady*,

---

8. Jablonski, *Gershwin*, p. 87.

9. Olin Downes, "Music: The New York Symphony." *New York Times,* Dec. 4, 1925, p. 26.

10. Jablonski, op. cit., p. 116.

11. Mordaunt Hall, "Murray Anderson's Sparkling Film: Pastel Shaded 'King of Jazz' Possesses Wonderful Photography And Smart Skits—Einstein's Old and New . . . An Operetta . . ." *New York Times,* May 11, 1930, p. 5. *See:* **B1970**

Be Good! and *Tip-Toes*. *Lady, Be Good!* opened at the Empire in London on April 14 and was a resounding success with the English audiences. On April 19 and 20 of 1926 Gershwin and

the Astaires recorded "Hang On to Me," "Fascinating Rhythm," "Half of It Dearie Blues" (George and Fred Astaire), "Swiss Miss" (the Astaires only), and "I'd Rather Charleston" (the Astaires with George) for English Columbia. These recordings have been made available in an LP recording through the efforts of the Smithsonian Institution **(D459,** Original cast, with Fred & Adele Astaire).

In preparation for the premiere of *Tip-Toes* in London, to be on August 31, George recorded songs from that show after his return to London in July. He also recorded songs from *Oh, Kay!* for British Columbia: "Maybe," "Clap Yo' Hands," "Do, Do, Do," and "Someone to Watch Over Me."

Oh, Kay! was premiered in New York at the Imperial Theatre on November 8, 1926, after a tryout in Philadelphia. Starring Gertrude Lawrence, one of its memorable songs was "Someone to Watch Over Me," which she sang to a rag doll. George had purchased the doll for her after spotting it in a toy store window during the trial run in Philadelphia. According to Edward Jablonski, *Oh, Kay!* serves well "as the typical Gershwin musical of the twenties."**(12)** That the plot concerned lawbreaking in the form of rum-running on Long Island comes as no surprise during this period of the prohibition of alcohol in the United States (1920–1933). As was the custom, *Oh, Kay!* moved to London to open a run there on September 21, 1927, at His Majesty's Theatre. Only Gertrude Lawrence remained from the original cast.

The year 1926 proved to be more fruitful for Gershwin because the Peruvian contralto Marguarite D'Alvarez, whom George had met through his friend Carl Van Vechten, engaged George to be her accompanist in a group of popular songs during her 1926–1927 recital tour. She also asked him to perform a two-piano version of the *Rhapsody in Blue* on these concerts, and to compose a new piano piece for the programs. The "new piano piece" became what we know as the preludes today. According to Gershwin scholar, Robert Wyatt, "there is a distinct possibility that six preludes were performed" at the concert where the preludes were premiered, at the Hotel Roosevelt in New York on the afternoon of December 4, 1926.**(13)** Of these, as is well known in Gershwin circles, only the three listed in the "Works" section of this book were published under the titles "Preludes." An unknown copyist prepared the versions for Gershwin's approval prior to publication of the Harms editions, and these copies are in the Gershwin Collection at the Library of Congress. While these copies do not specify composition dates, they are interesting for what appear to be Gershwin's own penciled–in corrections. It is clear, for example, in the case of the second slow prelude, that Gershwin did not want the piece played too slowly. He (or someone) scratched through the original tempo marking "Slowly," replacing it with what appears in the published edition: "Andante con moto e poco rubato." This intent is further clarified by a comment from Kay Swift, who said, referring to the three preludes: "They're easy to ruin, you know. Most people

12. Jablonski, *Op. cit.*, *p.* 131.

13. Robert Wyatt, "The Seven Jazz Preludes of George Gershwin: A Historical Narrative." *American Music* 7/1 (Spring 1989): 83.

play the fast ones too fast and the slow one too slow."**(14)** Gershwin and D'Alvarez repeated the performance at which the preludes were premiered in NY on December 15, 1926, as well as in Boston, on January 16, 1927.

By April of 1927, the Gershwins had begun work on *Strike Up the Band*. On April 21, George made his second recording—this one by the more modern electric method as compared to the previous acoustical recording of June 1924—of *Rhapsody in Blue* with Paul Whiteman, for the Victor Talking Machine Company at Liederkranz Hall in New York. According to Edward Jablonski, "The earlier recording . . . is superior not only because of the presence of most of the original musicians, including clarinetist Ross Gorman, but because Gershwin's performance is freer, more relaxed . . . [An] argument with Whiteman [at the second recording session] had disturbed him.."**(15)** By the middle of June 1927, the score for *Strike Up the Band* was in shape to begin rehearsals, in preparation for an August 1927 tryout opening in Long Branch, NJ, followed by a second trial in Philadelphia beginning on September 5. The show was not a success and closed in Philadelphia after only two weeks. It was brought back to Broadway in 1930 and was then a success. Both the 1927 and 1930 versions have been revived several times to varying degrees of critical appraisal, and the show is one of those that has been recorded **(D564)** in the Leonore Gershwin/Library of Congress recording project, about which more later.

Prior to the Philadelphia opening in September, George had made his first appearance at a concert in New York's Lewisohn Stadium, on July 26, 1927. He played the *Rhapsody in Blue* for this occasion.

The Gershwin's next musical theatre project was *Funny Face*, originally titled *Smarty*, which opened under that title for its trial in Philadelphia at the Shubert on October 11, 1927. An additional six weeks of work and a second tryout in Wilmington, DE ultimately led to its premiere as *Funny Face* in New York on November 22, 1927. Critical appraisal was uniformly good; the distinguished critic and Algonquin hotel roundtable member Alexander Woollcott wrote for the *New York World* calling the Gershwin music "a clever, sparkling, teasing score."**(16)**

Edward Jablonski calls the next Gershwin musical score, *Rosalie*, a "musical hodgepodge," and that it was, being made up of old tunes dug up out of the trunk. Sigmund Romberg also contributed "stock operetta numbers" (Jablonski's term) to the show.

During the time that George was involved with *Strike Up the Band* and *Rosalie*, he began the solo piano version of *An American in Paris*. On the way to Paris he stopped off in London to see Gertrude Lawrence on the closing night of *Oh, Kay!* During this visit to the French city, friend Mabel Schirmer helped George to find the now-famous taxi horns used in *An American in Paris*. While in Paris, they heard the first rhapsody performed poorly by pianists Jean Wiener and Clement Doucet at the Théâtre Mogador, conducted by one Rhené-Baton.

From Paris, the Gershwin party (including George, Ira, Leonore, and Frankie**)**

---

14. *Op cit.*, p. 74.

15. Jablonski, *Op cit.*, 140.

16. Alexander Woollcott, "The Stage." *New York World*, Nov. 23, 1927.

moved on to Berlin, then to Vienna. In Vienna, George met Alban Berg and heard his string quartet. After Vienna, George returned to Paris where the next major event was to be the European premiere of the *Concerto in F*, on May 29, 1928, at the Théâtre de l'Opéra, with Dmitri Tiomkin as soloist and Vladimir Golschmann conducting.

George then went to London to meet with Gertrude Lawrence who was to be the star of the Gershwin's next show, *Treasure Girl*. On June 8, 1928, before leaving London on the way back home to the states, George recorded the three published piano preludes and the slow theme of the first rhapsody for the Columbia Gramophone Company.

On August 1st , George completed the solo piano version of *An American in Paris*, leaving only the two-piano version, and the important orchestration to complete. Concurrently he was working on the songs for *Treasure Girl* with its tryout opening planned for Philadelphia on October 15, and a New York opening on November 8. *American* was scheduled for its premiere at Carnegie Hall on December 13, 1928. *Treasure Girl* was a failure; Robert Littell, writing in the *New York Post*, summed it up: ". . . It comes down to a certain canned, made-to-order quality which suggests that too many people worked over it too hard and without enjoying themselves. 'Treasure Girl' simply isn't much fun . . ."**(17)**

However, it should be pointed out that *Treasure Girl* produced the song "I've Got a Crush on You" now sung at a slower tempo than originally intended. The likes of Lee Wiley, Linda Ronstadt, Frank Sinatra and many others have recorded this great song.

Walter Damrosch, conductor of the New York Symphony, who had commissioned the *Concerto in F*, had decided to conduct the premiere of *An American in Paris*, and was inquiring about George's progress with this piece as early as late summer of 1928. As mentioned above, the premiere took place on December 13, 1928. As usual with Gershwin's "serious" music, a variety of critical assessments appeared. When one considers that *American* has become a repertory piece, perhaps Eugene Bonner's contemporaneous evaluation of 1929, was the most forward-looking:

> "Gershwin has written a delightful, clever and extremely amusing
> little work . . . The thematic material if not of startling originality [?]
> . . . is quite adequate and although not developed to any great extent,
> is cleverly, even expertly, handled. The orchestration throughout is
> pungent, witty or sentimental as the situation demands . . ."**(18)**

The year of the stock market crash, 1929, a disaster for many, did not adversely affect Gershwin; in fact, it was a very productive year for him. George and Ira moved from their previous residence at 103rd Street to 33 Riverside Drive, where the brothers took adjoining apartments. It was during this period that George began dabbling in art, both purchasing art works and doing some painting himself. George's first portrait, a watercolor, was of Margaret Wolfe, the Countess Ricci, titled *Margaret*, that portrait is archived at the

17. Robert Littell, *New York Post*, Nov. 9, 1928.

18. Eugene Bonner, "George Gershwin's Latest." *Outlook and Independent* 151 (Jan. 2, 1929): 34.

Museum of the City of New York. **(19)**

J. P. McEvoy's *Show Girl*, an attempt to glorify Florenz Ziegfeld's girls, became the next project for the Gershwins. Because of an obligation on producer Ziegfeld's part and shortness of time, Gus Kahn served as co-lyricist. The show opened in New York on July 2, 1929. This show is notable for several reasons: among these, its inclusion of a ballet choreographed by Harriet Hoctor, based on *An American in Paris*; the composition of the song *Liza*; the presence of the Duke Ellington Orchestra; and Jimmy Durante in the cast. Moreover, the Dixie Dugan in the cast was the comic strip character drawn by artist John H. Striebel, inspired by the face of silent film star Louise Brooks and based on the character in McEvoy's earlier magazine serial (1927) called *Show Girl*. **(20)**

In late 1929 and 1930, *Strike Up the Band* was revived with a book, originally by George S. Kaufman, worked over by Morrie Ryskind. By toning down the original "sting" of the Kaufman libretto, the show became a success. "I've Got a Crush on You," written for the unsuccessful *Treasure Girl*, was interpolated into the new version. John Mason Brown wrote about it in the *New York Evening Post*:

> "Strike Up the Band" is by no means just one more musical comedy.
> It comes in truth as a welcome and almost completely enjoyable
> escape from the moldy formulas on which most musical comedies
> are built . . . By no means least among it pleasures are the lyrics
> and the music that the Gershwins have supplied. **(21)**

Before settling down to work on their next show, to be the successful *Girl Crazy*, George agreed to appear on stage at New York's Roxy Theatre for one week. He played the first rhapsody with the Paul Whiteman band in connection with the showing of Whiteman's feature film *The King of Jazz*. Incidentally, the movie was not a success, audiences having tired of the variety show it was.

George made his debut as conductor of a symphony orchestra on the occasion of a performance of *An American in Paris* by the New York Philharmonic at Lewisohn Stadium on August 26, 1929 (*See* **W3b**).

The show *Girl Crazy* included one of the Gershwin's most exceptional songs. Ethel Merman's rendition of "I Got Rhythm" made her a star overnight; and the underlying harmonies for *Rhythm* became the basis for countless improvisations by jazz musicians, second only to the twelve–bar blues progression. Gershwin was in the pit conducting on opening night in New York, October 14, 1930, as was Red Nichols and his Orchestra.

On the heels of the success of *Girl Crazy* came the beckoning call of the new

---

19. Cat. No. 68.1.4, **NNMus.**

20. Barry Paris, *Louise Brooks*. (Alfred A. Knopf, 1989), p. 204.

21. John Mason Brown, "'Strike Up the Band' at Times Square . . . The Play." *New York Evening Post*, Jan. 15, 1930, p. 14.

"talkie" movies from Hollywood. George and Ira had contracted to compose music for the film *Delicious* to be released the week of December 25, 1931. *(22)*

George's baby sister, Frances, married Leopold Godowsky, Jr. on Sunday, November 2, 1930, before George, Ira (and Leonore), and Guy Bolton left for Hollywood by train on November 5.

As stated above, the purpose of the Gershwin's temporary move to California was to provide music for the film *Delicious*, starring Janet Gaynor and Charles Farrell. Guy Bolton wrote the screen play. The song "Blah, Blah, Blah" had been written originally for a show idea of Florenz Ziegfeld, *East is West*; it was revised for *Show Girl* but not used there either, ultimately finding its niche in *Delicious*. Perhaps the most famous music created for *Delicious* was called variously the *Manhattan Rhapsody, New York Rhapsody* or *Rhapsody for Rivets*—which ultimately became the *Second Rhapsody for Orchestra with Piano*.

The Gershwins began working seriously on their score for the political satire *Of Thee I Sing* toward the latter part of their first stay in California. After opening on Broadway the day after Christmas 1931, the show ran for 441 performances. The libretto and lyrics by George Kaufman, Morrie Ryskind, and Ira Gershwin, respectively, were awarded the Pulitzer Prize for 1931, a first for a music theater piece. Isaac Goldberg summed up well: "We have had nothing like it in the history of our stage; after this event in our Theatre musical comedy can never be the same. Overnight, as it were, our musical stage . . . has come of age . . ." *(23)* A second company of *Of Thee I Sing* toured, beginning in Chicago.

Of Thee I Sing has been the subject of revivals, a particularly notable one being the concert version presented in March of 1987 at the Brooklyn Academy of Music in connection with the commemorative observance of the fiftieth anniversary of George's death. Historian Arthur M. Schlesinger, Jr. wrote about these performances: "The Gershwin Celebration that closed last Sunday (March 29, 1987) at the Brooklyn Academy of Music was a public service. The double-feature bill of 'Of Thee I Sing' and 'Let 'Em Eat Cake' offered a new generation the chance to hear great Gershwin songs and to sample two classics of American musical comedy . . ."*(24)*

The premiere of the *Second Rhapsody* was to be the next significant event in George's life. The conductor Serge Koussevitzky was the protagonist that brought the new work its premiere, in Boston on January 29, 1932. Inevitably, the critics compared the piece to the first rhapsody, to the second rhapsody's detriment.

After the premiere of the *Second Rhapsody* in New York on February 5, 1932, Gershwin took a well-deserved vacation to Havana, Cuba. While in Cuba, he bought a bongo drum, gourd, and some maracas and claves, which were later to be used in *Cuban Overture*. The colorful overture was no doubt inspired somewhat by the rhumba bands he heard there.

Upon his return to New York he was restless and again wrote to DuBose Heyward about his idea of turning *Porgy* into an opera. Getting to work on the opera, however, was

---

22. For more information about the Gershwins and film, see the section "Filmography."

23. Isaac Goldberg, "American Operetta Comes of Age: Annotations Upon 'Of Thee I   Sing' and Its Merry Makers." *Disques* 3 (March 1932): 7.

24. Arthur M. Schlesinger, Jr., "Theater: How History Upstaged the Gershwins."
NY Times, Apr. 5, 1987, p. H6. This version was recorded by the cast of that show
(D467, CBS Masterworks 42522).

delayed because the Gershwins took on a new Aarons and Freedley musical, *Pardon My English*. George's father died rather unexpectedly after a brief illness with lymphatic leukemia on May 14, 1932. Although his father's death saddened him immensely, George's busy state of affairs prevented him from dwelling on his grief too long. His first All-Gershwin concert with the summer New York Philharmonic at Lewisohn Stadium was scheduled for August 16, 1932. He had promised to compose his new "rumba" for that occasion.

Gershwin had been in touch with DuBose Heyward by mail in March of 1932 indicating to Heyward his continued interest in making *Porgy* an opera. The distractions of the events of the remainder of 1932 prevented him from beginning the work on the opera, a postponement that was to extend to two years.

The publication of the first printing of the *Song Book* in May of 1932 was one of these distractions. The book contains a range of songs from "Swanee" (1919) through "Who Cares?" (1932). In one of his few prose writings, George provided an introduction for the song book. What is most important about the song book is that it contained the original published version of each song, followed side by side with George's "improvised" versions of the songs.

From the spring of 1932 until the summer of 1936 when he moved to California the second time, Gershwin studied in New York with the composer/mathematician Joseph Schillinger (1895–1943). *Cuban Overture* (1932), the Broadway shows *Pardon My English* (1932) and *Let 'Em Eat Cake* (1933), "*I Got Rhythm*" *Variations* (1934), and the "folk opera" *Porgy and Bess (1935)* are works composed after George came under the influence of Schillinger. According to Steven E. Gilbert, "Schillinger's role was pervasive," particularly in regard to *Porgy and Bess*. **(25)** Evidence of more understanding of counterpoint and generally a more mature musical approach can be found in Gershwin's work beginning with the rhythm variations.

Gershwin first appeared as featured guest on the famed band leader/entertainer Rudy Vallee's radio show on November 10, 1932. He played "Fascinating Rhythm," "Liza," the second of the three piano preludes, and a portion of "I Got Rhythm" on this show which may be heard on the LP recording Mark 56 667, "Gershwin Conducts Excerpts from Porgy and Bess" **(D716)**.1929 (Aug. 26): He and brother Ira were working on *Pardon My English* at the time of this broadcast. The show was a failure; the Library of Congress revived it in what appears to have been a successful concert performance on May 15, 1987. Tim Page wrote about *Pardon My English*: ". . . 'Pardon My English' . . . a product of the Gershwin's full maturity, is sheer ecstasy . . . The melodies are tough, visceral, creative and irresistible; the lyrics are often hilarious . . ."**(26)** The show has been recorded as part of *The Leonore S. Gershwin-Library of Congress Recording and Publishing Project* (*See:* **D492**).

After the failure of *Pardon My English* in 1933, George and Ira's next commitment was to *Let 'Em Eat Cake*, the sequel to *Of Thee I Sing*. George moved to 132 East 72nd St., to be his last New York home, while Ira and Lee moved across the street.

This was a most trying time in America. Herbert Hoover was displaced by Franklin D. Roosevelt as president in March of 1933, a time when the Depression had millions unemployed; Prohibition (1920–1933) and the concomitant crime continued. Hitler was on the rise in Germany. Wayne J. Schneider provided a good assessment of *Let 'Em Eat Cake*:

25. Steven E. Gilbert, *The Music of Gershwin*. (Yale University Press, 1995), p. 6.

26. *Newsday*, Long Island, NY, May 18, 1987, from *Newsbank*, PER — 10:E9.

OTIS's [*Of Thee I Sing*'s] sequel *CAKE* and its bleak vision
of America's political future failed, and it, too marked a
cadence in the composer's life. *CAKE*'s caustic book and lyrics,
coupled with GG's new 'acidic' musical style, simply did not
appeal to Depression audiences who wanted to forget their
troubles at the theater, not be reminded of them. Moreover
. . . the real failure of *CAKE* was not a literary one, but a
musical one: G's music, technically splendid, failed to put the
show over. In fact, G's music is uncomfortable-sounding. **(27)**

1934–1937

After the failure of *Let 'Em Eat Cake*, with only ninety performances on Broadway, George could turn his attention to creating *Porgy and Bess*, **(28)** interrupted only by his tour in 1934 with the Leo Reisman orchestra and the "Music by Gershwin" radio shows of 1934. The CBS radio shows, sponsored by the laxative Feen-A-Mint, were in two series, the first ran from February 19 to May 31, 1934, being fifteen minute shows on Mondays and Fridays; the second was for a full half hour on Sunday nights, from September 30 to December 23.

To celebrate the tenth anniversary of *Rhapsody in Blue*, a tour with the Leo Reisman orchestra was developed, to twenty-eight cities in twenty-eight strenuous days (See Appendix A for the itinerary of this tour). Although the tour was not a financial success, it undoubtedly contributed to the further spread of Gershwin's fame as well as providing the motivation for the composition of the "*I Got Rhythm*" *Variations*. The program for the tour included the *Concerto in F*, *Rhapsody in Blue*, *An American in Paris*, the newly composed variations, "Wintergreen for President" from *Of Thee I Sing*, some Gershwin songs, and other small pieces. Reisman was unable to make the tour due to a leg injury, and was replaced by Broadway veteran conductor Charles Previn, André's uncle.

Meanwhile, DuBose Heyward and Gershwin were working on parts of *Porgy and Bess*. On June 16, 1934, George set out from New York by rail for Charleston (and Folly Island) to compose, work with Heyward and absorb the local color. Indeed, he did just that even attending a prayer meeting at a church on a nearby island. He returned to New York around July 21 in anticipation of the second series of his radio shows; nonetheless, he continued work on the opera. Gershwin left a careful record of the progress of the work by dating, the last comment entered on the score being "Orchestration begun late 1934—finished Sept. 2, 1935." The tryout run in Boston was scheduled to open September 30, 1935. It was well received in Boston, but since members of the sponsoring Theatre Guild and director Rouben Mamoulian felt it was too long, cuts had to be made before the historic New York opening on October 10, 1935. Audience reception in New York was good, but the reviews, by both music

27. Schneider, Wayne J. *George Gershwin's Political Operettas 'Of Thee I Sing'* (1931) and *'Let 'Em Eat Cake'* (*1933*), *and Their Role in Gershwin's Musical and Emotional Maturing*, 2 vols. Ph. D. dissertation, Cornell University, 1985, II, p. 816.

28. For the best attempt at a well-researched history of *Porgy and Bess*, see Hollis Alpert, *The Life and Times of Porgy and Bess* (New York, Alfred A. Knopf, 1990).

and drama critics, were mixed. It ran at the Alvin in New York for 124 performances, a comparatively short run for a Broadway show, but a long one for opera. On October 14, 1935, four days after the New York premiere, Victor Records recorded "Highlights from Porgy and Bess." Metropolitan stars Lawrence Tibbett and Helen Jepson were chosen for the roles of Porgy and Bess; their version of "Bess, You Is My Woman Now" can be heard on Victrola America AVM1-1742 (**D521**). Their interpretation presumably is an authentic one since Gershwin himself was present at the recording session.

With no immediate projects in sight, George took an unsatisfactory vacation to Mexico in November after the opening of *Porgy and Bess*. He was hoping to be inspired by the Mexican music as he had been on the Cuban trip in 1932; Instead, he found the Mexican music less exciting and inspirational.

In an effort to recoup some of the losses in New York, a short tour of *Porgy and Bess* was planned to begin in Philadelphia on January 27, 1936, ending in Washington on March 21, 1936. To help promote the tour, Gershwin agreed to appear in Philadelphia performing the *Concerto in F*, and premiering the orchestral suite he extracted from *Porgy* (later to be named *Catfish Row*).

By 1936, sound in the movies was well established and the Hollywood moguls were continually looking for songwriters to provide them with material for the movie musicals market. By the end of June 1936, after much negotiating, George and Ira agreed to work for the RKO studio on Fred Astaire–Ginger Rogers musicals under a sixteen–week contract for $55,000, with an option for a second film for $75,000.

Ira, Leonore, and George boarded the plane for California on August 10, 1936. Their departure must have been particularly painful for Kay Swift, with whom George had become very close. Swift and James Warburg were by this time divorced, so that she was available to George for more than a casual relationship. Apparently, George made no commitment, and it is apparent from his later flirtations in California (Simone Simon and Paulette Goddard, among others) that he was not ready for the kind of commitment required for a successful marriage.

Early on, while getting settled in Hollywood, the Gershwin's wrote "Hi-Ho," as an opener for the Astaire–Rogers musical, but not used there, and the waltz "By Strauss," for Vincente Minnelli and the Broadway revue *The Show is On*. In the meantime, they had found an appropriate house in the lovely Beverly Hills neighborhood, at 1019 North Roxbury Drive.

While waiting to wrap up the work for what became the film *Shall We Dance?*, George agreed to some concertizing: at Seattle with their orchestra, on December 15, 1936, and in San Francisco on January 15, 16, and 17, of 1937, under Pierre Monteux. An unnamed reviewer commented on the performance in Seattle:

> The songs were over but the melody lingered on in the
> humming of several thousand Seattle Symphony Orchestra
> patrons whom George Gershwin sent home last evening from
> the Civic Auditorium swaying to the tunes of "I've Got Rhythm,"
> "Man I Love," and "I Got Plenty O' Nuttin" . . . He played his
> "Rhapsody in Blue," and forever after thousands of Seattleites will
> be spoiled—they won't be able to bear hearing anyone else's

fingers, however nimble, slip through the melody . . . **(29)**

He flew to Detroit, MI for a performance there on January 20, 1937. On the second of two concerts, February 10 and 11, 1937, he experienced a short blackout and hit a few clinkers in *Concerto in F.* He had a physical examination after the incident, but the examination revealed nothing serious.

The next film scheduled was *Damsel in Distress*, which inspired two of the greatest of Gershwin songs: "Nice Work If You Can Get It" and "A Foggy Day." The scene in which Fred Astaire introduced "A Foggy Day" is a genuine classic. In a few years, both "Nice Work" and "Foggy Day" became standards in the repertory that singers sang, jazz arrangers arranged, and instrumentalists improvised upon.

Without a break, the Gershwins were scheduled to start right away on the Samuel Goldwyn film *The Goldwyn Follies*. From time to time, George was complaining of vertigo and headaches. For this film, George and Ira produced the unforgettable "Love Walked In" and George's last song "Love Is Here to Stay." By the 12th of June, his headaches had increased, both in frequency and intensity. On June 23, he was admitted to Cedars of Lebanon Hospital, where a series of tests was undertaken, but once again no symptoms of serious disease were found. It was suggested, however, that he undergo a spinal tap during this hospital stay; George refused, having heard that the procedure was most painful. It was S. N. Behrman, the playwright, who, not having seen George for a while, noticed the most change in him, about July 3rd. On Friday the 9th, after rising from sleep and faltering, his doctors were called, and after being examined he was readmitted to Cedars of Lebanon. Gershwin sunk into a deep coma. Dr. Carl Rand, a neurosurgeon, and Dr. Eugene Ziskind were suspicious that George was the victim of a brain tumor, despite the fact that none was visible on the x-ray (Of course, this was in the days before the CAT-scan.)

Attempts to get Dr. Walter E. Dandy, the country's leading neurosurgeon, to the West Coast were not successful. A second prominent surgeon, Dr. Howard C. Naffziger, was located and flown in. Dr. Rand operated, with Naffziger consulting. What they found was glioblastoma, one of the most malignant types of tumors. Gershwin was returned to his room around seven in the morning after five hours of surgery, still in a coma. He expired at 10:35 a.m. that Sunday, July 11, 1937, at thirty-eight years of age. **(30)** Despite its unfortunate ending, it should be noted that Gershwin maintained his zest for life right up to the last. According to author Barry Paris, he danced and flirted with the beautiful silent film star Louise Brooks at Los Angeles' Clover Club "a few nights before he died."**(31)**

1987 marked the fiftieth anniversary of George's death. The lasting appeal of George and Ira's work is perhaps most recently attested to by the opening of a new Gershwin musical on Broadway: *Crazy for You*, in 1992. This show was inspired by the 1930's *Girl Crazy* but modernized, with basically the only concept retained being that of the "Easterner

---

29. "Gershwin Has Musical Treat At Auditorium." *Seattle* [WA] *Daily Times,* Dec. 16, 1936, p. 18.

30. Readers wishing more complete details on Gershwin's final illness are referred to Jablonski, *Gershwin,* pp. 316-325.

31. Barry Paris, *Louise Brooks* (New York: Alfred A. Knopf, 1989), p. 378.

going out West." The show contains an assemblage of Gershwin standards, including "rediscovered Gershwin songs." It opened on Broadway on February 19, 1992, and has had a very successful run there. In fact, it has been successful enough to justify touring companies: to London, the United States, and Japan, as well as two cast recordings (New York and London, **D429** and **D439,** respectively).

Successors to George Gershwin have done much to perpetuate his contribution to American music. Before his death on August 17, 1983, Ira Gershwin organized a great deal of Gershwiniana, depositing it to the Gershwin collection at the Library of Congress. Leonore Gershwin passed away on August 20, 1991, but not before she had made substantial contributions to the Gershwin legacy through the Leonore Gershwin-Library of Congress Recording and Publishing project and by other means. Marc George Gershwin, son of brother Arthur, and Leopold Godowsky, III, son of sister Frances, **(32)** have monitored Gershwin activity from New York where they live. On March 16, 1994, Seattle, WA opened yet another new production of *Porgy and Bess* shared with the Houston Opera.

As of April 6,1994, the Leonore S. Gershwin-Library of Congress Recording and Publishing Project has begun work on a series to be scholarly printed editions of Gershwin's musicals, as a second phase of a project begun in 1989. The series of printed editions will result in assemblages of piano-vocal editions of the classic Gershwin scores.

Since the initiation of the first phase of the Gershwin-Library of Congress Project, complete recordings of five musicals have been prepared: *Girl Crazy* **(D450)**, *Oh, Kay!* **(D490),** *Strike Up the Band* **(D564)**, *Lady, Be Good!* **(D456)**, and *Pardon My English,* **(D492).**

Pianist/musicologist Artis Wodehouse has achieved considerable well-deserved attention because of her realizations of the Gershwin piano rolls via 3.5 inch computer disk. The information on the disks has been read and performed on the Yamaha Disklavier and recorded to albums (**D1122** and **D1131**).

The Library of Congress honored the Gershwins March 13-16, 1998, with a conference entitled "The Gershwins and Their World," held at the Coolidge Auditorium. The Centennial of George's birth, 1898-1998, seemed a fitting time for such a celebration. Only a month later, on April 14th, the Pulitzer Prize committee announced a special award bestowed posthumously on George, commemorating the Centennial at the same time recognizing his "distinguished and enduring contributions to American music." From October 28-November 8, the Institute for Studies in American Music & the Arts at Brooklyn College sponsored an excellent festival, "The Gershwins at 100." The Festival included an exclusive, rare screening of Otto Preminger's 1959 film classic *Porgy and Bess* (**F25**). The *Newsletter* of the Institute for Fall 1998 (28/1) was devoted to incisive articles about Gershwin and the present state of Gershwin scholarship. Hence, with all this continued activity, it should be apparent that the insouciance of the Gershwin's music, both serious and otherwise, will allow it to continue to be heard, probably for generations to come. One has only to look in the bins of contemporary record outlets to observe the persistent issues and reissues of recorded Gershwin music in a multiplicity of configurations. George Gershwin was a sincere musician who thoroughly enjoyed his work and whatever perks came with it; his contribution to American music is inestimable.

---

32. Frankie and her husband Leopold Godowsky, II, had four children: Leopold III, Alexis, Georgia, and Nadia.

Works and Performances

The compositions are listed by title, in chronological order by date of composition. Works are listed first in their original version (e. g., *An American in Paris* in the composer's holograph) with subsequent versions following. This section does *not* include overtures for musicals. Dates of premiere performances are given when available. The symbol * indicates that the song is thought to have been published in sheet music format.

Since it would be impossible to list all performances of Gershwin's oeuvre, the other performances given here are selective. "*See*" references, e. g., *See*: **B100**, identify citations in the "Bibliography" sections; "**D**" references are to the "Discography" sections; "**F**" references to the "Filmography" section; "**T**" references to the tour itineraries in Appendix A. **Abbreviations** are defined on page xiii. Note that abbreviations for some of the works, RiB for *Rhapsody in Blue*, e. g., are used to save space. Abbreviations for libraries are generally standard, **DLC** for the Library of Congress, e. g., and are also given on p. xiii.

ORCHESTRAL WORKS

W1. *RHAPSODY IN BLUE* **for piano and jazz band**. (January 25, 1924); New World (Warner); timings vary greatly, ranging from about 12 min. to about 18 min.

Abbreviation: RiB

Holograph two-piano sketch by the composer
Original orchestration by Ferde Grofé for solo piano and jazz band: Bb cl (double bscl, ob, Eb sop sax, Eb alto sax).al sax (double Bb sop sax).ten sax (double Bb sop sax, bari sax)/2.2.2.tuba & string bass/timp/traps (incl. brush or fly swatter)/vlns(8)/banjo/piano acc./celeste, dated Feb. 4, 1924 (This version was published with score & parts in 1925 by Harms).
Rev. orchestration for full orchestra by Grofé, Feb. 23, 1926: 2.2.3(bscl).2.al sax(2).ten sax./4.3.3.1/timp/perc/pf/banjo/strings
Commemorative facsimile edition of Grofé's 1924 holograph score, with historical notes, 64 pp.(cat. no. FS0004, Warner, 1987, notes by Jeff Sultanof)
Miniature score, solo piano & Orchestra, Harms [Warner Brothers M00013], 1942 *See*: **B255**
Arr. for two pianos (Harms, 1925 [Warner])
Arr. for piano, four hands by Henry Levine (Harms, 1943 [Warner])

Modified version for piano solo by Herman Wasserman (New World, 1924, 1940 [Warner])

Version for concert band without solo piano, arr. by Ferde Grofé, Harms, 1938, Plate no. 19902; duration 16 min.: Score at **NN**; Standard band instrumentation: Condensed score/2.1picc.2.1EngH.2bsns.Eb cl.Bb cls.2 al cls.2bs cls.sop sax.2 al sax.2 ten sax.bari sax/6cnts.2tpts.4hns. 3trbs.baritone.tuba/string bass/harp-piano/perc

Version for string Orchestra, arr. by James Curnow, Warner Bros. (Distributed by Jenson Publications), © 1987. 1 score (8 p.) + 41 parts

LC Call No.: M1420 .G

"New" version for solo piano ed. by Alicia Zizzo, Warner Bros.,1995

For more information about editions, *See*: David Schiff, *Gershwin: Rhapsody in Blue* (**B260**)

Holographs at DLC: Gershwin's sketch score in pencil with emendations in colored pencil, GC microfilm no. MUSIC 1350; Gershwin's piano score in ink, GC microfilm no. MUSIC 1036; Grofé's full score for solo piano & jazz band, GC microfilm no. MUSIC 1351 or 1037, Item 1; Grofé score for piano & symphony orchestra in ink, with emendations in pencil, GC microfilm no. MUSIC 1352 or MUSIC 1037, Item 2; jazz band part (arr.) trans. for second piano, first edition (Harms, 1924), GC Box 9, *Item 3

Commissioned by & dedicated to Paul Whiteman

See: **B88, B149, B151, B152, B153, B154, B155, B156, B158, B159, B163, B166, B167, B168, B170, B179, B180, B181, B189, B194, B209, B216, B219, B220, B221, B226, B239, B248, B250, B253, B257, B258, B259, B260, B262, B263, B264, B270, B271 (story of the clar. glissando), B272, B273, B275, B276, B277, B278, B279, B290, B1548, B1634, B1671, B1730, B1824, B1838, B2114, B2115, B2116, B2118, B2120, B2121, B2124, B2125, B2126, B2127, B2128, B2129, B2131, B2133, B2134, B2135, B2138, B2141, B2142, B2143, B2144, B2145, B2148, B2150, B2151, B2153, B2154, B2155, B2161, B2163, B2165, B2167**

Premieres

W1a. 1924 (Feb. 12): NY; Aeolian Hall; GG, piano; Paul Whiteman and His Orchestra (World premiere and first formal performance in NY) **Personnel for Whiteman Jazz Band on the day of the Aeolian Hall premiere:** Ross Gorman: E-flat & B-flat soprano saxophones, alto saxophone, multiple woodwinds; Hale Byers: B-flat soprano saxophone, tenor & baritone saxophone, flute?; Donald Clark: B-flat soprano saxophone, alto & baritone saxophone; Henry Busse & Frank Siegrist: trumpet & Flugelhorns; Trombones: Roy Maxon (& Euphonium) & James Casseday (& bass trombone); horns: Arthur Cerino & Alfred Corrado; Tuba & string bass: Gus Helleberg & Albert Armer; Banjo: Mike Pingatore; Piano: Ferde Grofé & Henry Lange (celeste); Drums, timpani, & traps: George Marsh; Violins: Alex Drasein (concertmaster); George Tjorde, Robert Berchad, Kurt Dieterle, Joseph Streisof, Jack East, Bert Hirsh, Mario Perry (& accordian) [deriv. from Warner Bros. facsimile score] *See*: **B234, B236, B237, B245, B246, B249, B251, B253, B265, B269, B270, B274, B276, B922, B1411**

Other Selected Performances

W1b. 1924 (Mar. 7): NY: Aeolian Hall; repeat performance

W1c. 1924 (Apr. 21): NY: Carnegie Hall; "for the American Academy in Rome"; Gershwin, piano; Paul Whiteman and His Orchestra

W1d. 1924 (May 15–June 1): Paul Whiteman Spring tour *See*: **T1-T15, B2119**

W1e. 1924 (Sept. 19): Paul Whiteman Fall tour, beginning in Cumberland, MD

W1f. 1924 (Nov. 14); NY: Earl Carroll Theatre, afternoon; special invitation performance prior to Carnegie Hall performance the next evening

W1g. 1924 (Nov. 15): NY: Carnegie Hall; repeat performance with Whiteman *See*: **B2132, B233**

W1h. 1924 (Nov. 27): Philadelphia; Academy of Music; repeat performance with Whiteman

W1i. 1924 (Dec. 4): Boston; Symphony Hall; repeat performance with Whiteman

W1j. 1926 (Apr. 12): London; The Midnight Follies at the Hotel Metropole; Performed as a ballet **CAST:** Jeanne Aubert; Madge Elliot; Vera Bryer; Quentin Tod; Cyril Richard; Elsa Macfarlane

W1j.1. 1927 (July 27): NY, Lewisohn Stadium; George Gershwin, piano *See*: **B217**

W1k. 1928 (April 4): Paris; Mogador; Jean Wiener & Clement Doucet, pianists; Pas de Loup Orchestra; Rhené-Baton, conducting *See*: **B231**

W1l. 1928 (Apr. 16): Paris Théâtre des Champs-Élysées; Dance version, choreographed by Anton Dolin; Dolin & Vera Nemchinova, dancers

W1l.1 1930 (Week of May 2): NY; Roxy Theatre; George Gershwin, piano, with Paul Whiteman Orchestra *See*: B240, F6

W1m. 1930 (Aug. 28): NY; Lewisohn Stadium; George Gershwin, piano & conductor on RiB, AiP, & Concerto; New York Philharmonic; William van Hoogstraten, conducting *See*: **B252**

W1n. 1934 (Jan. 14.-Feb. 10); Leo Reisman ten-year anniversary tour *See*: Tour itinerary in Appendix A; Many of these performances constituted premieres of works in the cities of the tour *See also*: **W2d**

W1o. 1936 (Dec. 15): Seattle, WA; George Gershwin, piano; Seattle Symphony Orchestra; Basil Cameron, conducting *See*: **B1483, B1551**

W1p. 1938 (Feb. 20): NY; Carnegie Hall; American Guild of Musical Artists is

sponsor; José & Amparo Iturbi, pianists (Iturbi's arr. for two pianos)
See: **B244**

W1q. 1938 (July 12): NY; Lewisohn Stadium; New York Philharmonic Symphony Orchestra; Paul Whiteman Orchestra; Maxine Sullivan, vocals; Lyn Murray Chorus **PROGRAM**: RiB; Second Rhapsody; AiP; Hollywood Medley: They Can't Take That Away From Me, Nice Work if You Can Get It, Love Walked In; Summertime; Do It Again (chorus); Dawn Of a New Day

W1r. 1942 (Nov. 1): NY; Studio H, Radio City (Broadcast); Benny Goodman, clarinet; Earl Wild, piano; NBC Symphony; Arturo Toscanini, conducting *See*: **B247**, **B266**, **B268**

W1s. 1942 (Dec. 24, 25, 27): NY; The Philharmonic-Symphony Society of New York *See*: **B228**

W1t. 1943 (July 4): Hollywood, CA; Hollywood Bowl; Ray Turner, piano, Hollywood Bowl Symphony Orchestra; Paul Whiteman, conducting *See*: **B267**

W1u. 1951 (Feb. 16): Cincinnati, OH *See*: **B256**

W1v. 1954 (Dec. 25): NY; Carnegie Hall; All-Gershwin program; Eugene List, piano; NY Philharmonic-Symphony; André Kostelanetz, conducting

W1w. 1955 (Feb. 12): NY; Carnegie Hall; Anniversary benefit concert; Bruce Steeg (15 years old), piano; Paul Whiteman & His Orchestra *See*: **B1477**

W1x. 1963 (June 5): NY; Philharmonic Hall; All-Gershwin program; New York Philharmonic; George Gershwin via piano rolls; Veronica Tyler, soprano & Henry Boatwright, bass-baritone, with two dozen members of the NY Schola Cantorum (in excerpts from P&B); Agustin Anievas, piano (in RiB); New York Philharmonic; André Kostelanetz, conducting *See*: **B230**, **B235**

W1y. 1970 (Oct. 29): Miami, FL; Miami Beach Auditorium, final concert of three-day Gershwin Festival; George Roth, piano; University of Miami Symphony Orchestra; Frederick Fennell, conducting *See*: **B1456, B1457**

W1z. 1984 (Feb. 12): NY; Town Hall; reenactment of the original Paul Whiteman Aeolian Hall concert; Maurice Peress, conducting

W1aa. 1987 (Nov. 15): Chicago; Orchestra Hall; David Golub, piano; members of the Chicago Symphony Orchestra; Mitch Miller, conducting *See*: **B254.1**

W1bb. 1987 (Nov.30): NY; Merkin Hall; Artis Wodehouse, piano *See*: **B232**

W1cc. 1988 (Feb. 28): Chicago; Auditorium Theatre; Dick Hyman & Ivan Davis, piano; Free lance NY musicians; Maurice Peress, conducting *See*: **B254**

W2.   *CONCERTO IN F* **for piano and orchestra.** (Original orchestration: October-November, 1925, holograph of full score completed November 25, 1925; Warner; 16 min)

Abbreviation: Concerto

Holograph: solo piano/3(picc).3(EngH).3(bscl).3(cbsn)/3.3.3.1/timp/
   perc/hp/strings
Commemorative facsimile edition of holograph score with historical notes,
   200 pp. (cat. no FS0002, Warner, 1987)
Orig. pubd as 2-piano score
Version for solo piano and jazz band (for Paul Whiteman) by Ferde Grofé [Paul
   Whiteman Collection, Williams College, MA and DLC] *See*: recordings
   by Whiteman, **D780,** and Schuller, **D765**
Pubd orchestral version rev. F. Campbell-Watson: solo piano/3(picc).
   3(EngH).3(bscl).2/4.3.3.1/ timp/perc/bells/xylo/strings (Chappell also)
Concert transcription for pf solo by Grace Castagnetta (Chappell, London
   [1955])
Commissioned by Harry Harkness Flagler, at the request of Walter
   Damrosch for the New York Symphony Society
Miniature score (Warner, MO0003)

Holographs at DLC: Full score in ink, GC microfilm no. MUSIC 1341; sketch
score in pencil, title page title: New York Concerto, GC microfilm no. MUSIC
1342; orchestration (incomplete) in ink with additional notations in pencil, 8 pp.,
GC microfilm no. MUSIC 1339; sketches in pencil, 12 leaves, GC microfilm no.
MUSIC 1340; orchestra part (arr.) trans. for second piano, first edition (Harms,
1927), GC Box 9, item 2.

See: **B88, B149, B151, B154, B158, B166, B170, B179, B180, B181, B189,
   B194, B197, B199, B200, B203, B204, B205, B206, B207, B209, B213-215**
   (all three of the latter 200 no. articles by Wayne Shirley); **B216, B217-B223,
   B258, B263, B264, B270, B290, B1614, B1838, B1841, B2150, B2153,
   B2154, B2163, B2165, B2174**

Premieres

W2a. 1925 (Dec. 3): NY; Carnegie Hall; NY Symphony; GG, piano; Walter Damrosch,
   conducting (world premiere) Perf. also scheduled for Washington,
   Philadelphia, Baltimore *See*: **B201, B202, B208, B211, B251**

W2b. 1928 (May 29): Paris; Dmitri Tiomkin, piano; Vladimir Golschmann,
   conducting (premiere in Europe) *See*: **B222**

W2c. 1930 (May): New Haven, CT; Yale School of Drama; With choreographed
   dance, first movement only **CAST:** Dancers: six men, six women, and **soloist:**
   Elizabeth Elsom; **Other dancers:** Gertrude Kurath; Virginia Roediger; Roy
   Stransky; Harriet Meyer; **Choreography:** Gertrude Kurath *See*: **B210**

W2d. 1934 (Jan. 14): Boston; Symphony Hall; George Gershwin, piano; Leo

Reisman Orchestra; Charles Previn, conducting This was the opening concert of the Leo Reisman tour of 1934. Presumably, Concerto was played in every city on the tour, the itinerary of which can be seen in Appendix A.

W2e. 1936 (Dec. 15): Seattle, WA; George Gershwin, piano; Seattle Symphony Orchestra; Basil Cameron, conducting *See:* **B1483**

Other Selected Performances

W2f. 1927 (July 26): NY; Lewisohn Stadium; George Gershwin, piano *See:* **B217**

W2g. 1930 (Aug. 28): NY; Lewisohn Stadium; George Gershwin, piano on RiB & Concerto; New York Philharmonic; William van Hoogstraten, conducting *See:* **B252**

W2h. 1937 (Sept. 8): Hollywood; Hollywood Bowl, Memorial concert; Southern California Symphony Association; various conductors *See:* **B1423, D510**

W2h.1. 1944: NY: radio debut; Oscar Levant, piano; NBC Symphony Orchestra; Arturo Toscanini, conducting See: **B212, B1583**

W2i. 1946 (Jan. 6): NY; The Philharmonic-Symphony Society of New York *See:* **B196**

W2j. 1946 (Aug. 8): NY; Oscar Levant, piano; NY Phiharmonic; Artur Rodzinski, conducting *See:* **B1583**

W2k. 1949 (Jan. 27): NY; Carnegie Hall; [NY] Philharmonic-Symphony Orchestra; Byron Janis, piano soloist; Leopold Stokowski, conducting *See:* **B218**

W2l. 1951 (Dec. 6): Chicago; Chicago Symphony Orchestra *See:* **B198**

W2m. 1956 (Feb. 14): Brooklyn, NY; Brooklyn Academy of Music; Philippa Schuyler, piano; Brooklyn Philharmonic; Siegfried Landau, conducting

W2n. 1962 (July 10): NY; Lewisohn Stadium; All-Gershwin program; Earl Wild, piano (in Concerto & RiB), Camilla Williams & Lawrence Williams, singers (in excerpts from P&B); New York Philharmonic; Franz Allers, conducting

W2o. 1970 (Oct. 28): Miami, FL; Dade County Auditorium; University of Miami, "The George Gershwin Festival"; Univ. of Miami Symphony Orchestra; Ivan Davis, piano; F. Fennell, conducting *See:* **B1456, B1457**

W2p. 1985 (June 30): Cuyahoga Falls, OH; Blossom Center, All-Gershwin concert; Cleveland Orchestra (summer)

W2q. 1987 (Nov. 15): Chicago; Orchestra Hall; David Golub, piano; Gail Nelson, soprano; Members of the Chicago Symphony Orchestra; Mitch Miller, conducting **PROGRAM:** Concerto, RiB, AiP, Medley of show tunes *See*: **B254.1**

W3. *AN AMERICAN IN PARIS*, **a tone poem.** (November 18, 1928;
New World (Warner, 1930); 16 min); min. score (Warner, 1930)

Abbreviation: AiP

Composer's holograph: 3(picc).3(EngH).3(bscl).al sax(sop sax).tn sax(al
sax).bari   sax(al   sax).2/4.3.3.1/taxi   horns(4)/timp/perc/bells/xylo/
cel/strings
Edition, rev. by F. Campbell-Watson: 3(picc).3(EngH).3(bscl).al sax.tn
sax.bari sax.2/4.3.3.1/timp/perc/bells/xylo/taxi-horns(4)/cel/strings
(Full) miniature score (Harms, 1930), now available as MO0001, Warner
Commemorative facsimile edition of holograph score, 112 pp. (Cat. no. FS 0001,
Warner, 1987)
Arr. by Bowen (unpublished): 1.1.1.sax(4).0/2.3.3.0/timp/perc/hp/pf/strings
Trans. & arr. for symphonic band by John Krance; Score (28 pp.), condensed
score (12 pp.) & 78 parts; (New World, 1959; 5 min., 45 sec)
Arr. by Jim Curnow for young concert band; Score (15 pp.) & parts
(Warner Bros., arr. © 1987, distrib. by Hal Leonard Publishing, by
arrangement w/ Warner/Jenson Distribution, 1988)
Arr. by John Moss for symphonic band
Arr. two pianos by the composer, unpubd
Arr. two pianos, revised by G. Stone, (pubd?)
Paraphrased for piano solo ("In Miniature") by Maurice Whitney
(Chappell, London, 1951)
Transcription for piano by William Daly

Holographs at DLC: full orchestral score, GC microfilm no. MUSIC 1338;
arr. for two pianos by the composer, in ink, GC microfilm no. MUSIC
85/20240<MUS>;sketch score, in pencil, GC microfilm no. MUSIC
1337; transcription for piano by William Daly (first edition, Harms
1935), GC Box 9, Item 1
See: **B88, B149, B151, B152, B154, B155, B158, B163, B170, B179, B180,
B181, B182, B183, B184, B186, B188, B189, B193, B194, B195, B219,
B220, B221, B223, B226, B258, B263, B270, B380, B2166**

Premieres

W3a. 1928 (Dec. 13): NY; Carnegie Hall; NY Philharmonic; Walter Damrosch,
conducting (world premiere) *See*: **B173, B175, B177, B185, B187, B191,
B192**

Other Selected Performances

W3b. 1929 (Aug. 26): NY; Lewisohn Stadium of City College of NY;
NY Philharmonic; George Gershwin, piano (on RiB), Gershwin (conducting
on AiP) & Willem van Hoogstraten (other pieces), conducting (Gershwin's
conducting debut)

W3c. 1929 (Nov. 10): NY; Mecca Auditorium; Manhattan Symphony

Orchestra; George Gershwin (on AiP) and Henry Hadley, conducting

W3d. 1930 (Aug. 28): NY; Lewisohn Stadium; George Gershwin, piano & conductor on RiB, AiP, & Concerto; New York Philharmonic; William van Hoogstraten, conducting *See*: **B252**

W3e. 1937 (Aug. 9): NY; Lewisohn Stadium; New York Philharmonic-Symphony Orchestra; Alexander Smallens & Ferde Grofé, conducting *See*: **B919**

W3f. 1938 (July 10): Hollywood; Hollywood Bowl, Southern California Symphony Association, Memorial Concert; Nathaniel Shilkret, conducting

W3g. 1938 (July 12): NY; Lewisohn Stadium, memorial concert; Oscar Levant, piano; Maxine Sullivan, vocalist; Lyn Murray Chorus; New York Philharmonic & Paul Whiteman Orchestras *See*: **B1474**, **B1583**

W3h. 1946 (Apr. 18): NY; Carnegie Hall; Philharmonic-Symphony Orchestra, Pension Fund Benefit Concert; Anne Brown, soprano; Todd Duncan, baritone; Oscar Levant, piano; Artur Rodzinski, conducting *See*: **B166, B1583**

W3i. 1949 (July 7): NY; Lewisohn Stadium; Oscar Levant, piano; New York Philharmonic; Alexander Smallens, conducting *See*: **B1516, B1583**

W3i.1. 1951 (Nov. 2): San Francisco, CA; San Francisco Symphony Orchestra [Program]. Also in program of Nov. 18, 1954 *See*: **B176**

W3j. 1954 (Mar. 13): NY; The Philharmonic-Symphony Society of New York *See*: **B178**

W3k. 1954 (Dec. 25): NY; Carnegie Hall; All-Gershwin program; NY Philharmonic-Symphony; André Kostelanetz, conducting

W3l. (Feb. 14): Brooklyn, NY; Brooklyn Academy of Music; Brooklyn Philharmonic; Siegfried Landau, conducting

W3m. 1973 (Dec.): Boston; Jordan Hall, New England Conservatory; NEC Symphony; Gunther Schuller, conducting *See*: **B190**

W3n. 1985 (Jan. 6): Virginia Beach, VA; Pavilion, "Gershwin and Company Salute;" The Virginia Symphony Pops; Newton Wayland, guest conducting

W3o. 1985 (Feb. 8): Raleigh, NC; Memorial Auditorium; Penelope Jensen, soprano; Paul Tardif, piano; NC Symphony, James Ogle, conducting

W3p. 1985 (June 30): Cuyahoga Falls, OH; Blossom Center, All-Gershwin concert; Cleveland Orchestra (summer)

W3q. 1987 (July 5): London; The Barbicon; London Symphony Orchestra; Michael

Tilson Thomas, conducting

W3r. 1987 (Nov. 15): Chicago; Orchestra Hall; David Golub, piano; Gail Nelson, soprano; Members of the Chicago Symphony Orchestra; Mitch Miller, conducting *See*: **B254.1**

W4. *SECOND RHAPSODY* for piano and orchestra. (March 14, 1931; New World (Warner); 12 min., 30 sec.)

Original manuscript unpubd; pubd rev. version by Robert McBride [same instrumentation as G's original orchestration, *See*: **B942**]: solo piano/3(picc). 3(EngH).3(bscl).2/4.3.3(bstrb).1/timp/perc(6)/hp/strings. (According to Youngren, the McBride version has been withdrawn from circulation as of May, 1986)
Version for 2 pianos-four hands (New World [Warner])
Dedicated to Max Dreyfus
Holographs at DLC: Full score in ink, with emendations in pencil, GC microfilm no. MUSIC 1353; full score (photocopy) with emendations in colored pencil and ink; sketches in pencil, GC microfilm no. MUSIC 1354
As of this writing (1998), a critical edition of this work has been proposed by the Committee on Publications of American Music (COPAM) of the American Musicological Society
See: **B88, B152, B158, B216, B263, B264, B280, B281, B285, B290, B1915-B1917, B2163, B2165, F7**

Premieres

W4a. 1932 (Jan. 29): Boston; Symphony Hall; GG, piano; Boston Symphony Orchestra; Serge Koussevitzky, conducting (world premiere) *See*: **B282, B283, B284 (program notes), B286**

W4b. 1932 (Feb. 5): New York; Carnegie Hall; GG, piano; Boston Symphony Orchestra; Serge Koussevitzky, conducting (New York premiere) *See*: **B288**

Other Selected Performances

W4c. 1938 (July 12): NY; Lewisohn Stadium, memorial concert; Oscar Levant, piano; Maxine Sullivan, vocalist; Lyn Murray Chorus; New York Philharmonic & Paul Whiteman Orchestras *See*: **B1583**

W4d. 1949 (July 7): NY; Lewisohn Stadium; Oscar Levant, piano; New York Philharmonic; Alexander Smallens, conducting (First performance in

Lewisohn Stadium) *See*: **B1583**

W4e. 1970 (Oct. 27): Miami, FL; Dade County Auditorium; University of Miami, "The George Gershwin Festival"; George Roth, piano; Univ. of Miami Symphony Orchestra; Frederick Fennell, conducting *See*: **B1456, B1457**

W4f. 1985 (June 13): Chicago; Chicago Symphony Orchestra; Michael Tilson Thomas, conducting *See*: **B289**

W5. *CUBAN OVERTURE* (originally titled *RUMBA*). (original orchestration manuscript: July-August, 1932 [orchestration: Aug. 1-9]; New World (Warner & Chappell); 10 min)

> *Holograph*:   3(picc).3(EngH).3(bscl).3(cbsn).saxophones/4.3.3.1/timp/ perc/bells/xylo/wood block/Cuban sticks/gourd/maracas/bongos/strings
> Pubd versions: same instrumentation excluding saxophones (New World [Warner])
> Arr. by G. Ritchie *See*: **B1125**
> Commemorative facsimile edition of holograph score with historical notes, 72 pp., comments by Jeff Sultanof (Warner, 1987)
> Editions as piano duet (one piano, four hands) & 2 pianos, four hands (New World [Warner])
>
> *Holographs* at DLC: full score in ink with additional notation in pencil, title page: Rumba, GC micro-film no. MUSIC 1334; sketch score in pencil (32 pp.), GC Box 8, Item 2; sketches in pencil (39 pp.), with yellow introductory sheet, GC microfilm no. MUSIC 1343
> *See*: **B88, B152, B158, B1841, B2171**

Premieres

W5a. 1932 (Aug. 16): NY; Lewisohn Stadium; All-Gershwin concert; NY Philharmonic; Albert Coates, conducting (world premiere) *See*: **B224, B225**

Other Selected Performances

W5b. 1932 (Nov. 1): NY: Metropolitan Opera House; Cuban Overture and AiP (GG conducting); Concerto (GG, piano), Bill Daly, conducting

W5c. 1954 (Dec. 25): NY; Carnegie Hall; All-Gershwin program; NY Philharmonic-Symphony; André Kostelanetz; conducting

W5d. 1970 (Oct. 27): Miami, FL; Dade County Auditorium; University of Miami, "The George Gershwin Festival"; Univ. of Miami Symphony Orchestra; Frederick Fennell, conducting *See*: **B1456, B1457**

W5e. 1987 (Mar 27 & 28): NY; Carnegie Hall; The New York Pops; Skitch Henderson, conducting

W6. **"*I GOT RHYTHM*" VARIATIONS for solo piano and orchestra.** (holograph score dated January 6, 1934; New World, 1934, 1953 [Warner]; 8-1/2 min)

> Written for tour with the Leo Reisman Orchestra, Jan. 14–Feb. 10, 1934 (*See*: Appendix A for the itinerary)
>
> *Holograph* score: 1(picc).1(EngH).al sax(2-double clar).tn sax(double clar).bari sax(double clar).1/3.3.2.1/drums/bells/pf/strings

Pubd score: orchestra version revised by William C. Schoenfeld, 2(picc).3(EngH).4(bscl).2.al sax(2).ten sax.bari sax/4.3.3.1/ timp/perc/bells/xylo/cel/strings

2 pianos-four hands version (New World, 1932 [Warner]) dedicated to "my brother Ira"

Holographs at DLC: orchestra score in ink with emendations in pencil & colored pencil, GC microfilm no. MUSIC 1348; copyist's ms. of piano part in ink, with emendations by the composer in pencil & holograph sketches in pencil laid in, GC microfilm no. MUSIC 1347; program outline (1p.) in pencil, GC Box 11, Item 3 *See*: **B88, B226, B1841, B2148, B2147.1, B2149, B2151, B2148, B2150, B2163, B2164, B2165, T16, T36, T40, T42**

Premieres

W6a. 1934 (Jan 14): Boston; Symphony Hall; GG, piano solo; Leo Reisman Orchestra; Charles Previn, conducting (world premiere) *See*: **T16**

Having been composed especially for the Leo Reisman tour of Jan. 14–Feb. 10, 1934, the piece was played at every concert on the tour. Hence, these performances could each be considered premieres for the cities on the tour. *See*: **B2147.2** & the 1934 tour itinerary in Appendix A.

Other Selected Performances

W6b. 1955 (Feb. 12): NY; Carnegie Hall, 31st Anniversary of RiB benefit concert; Buddy Weed, piano; Paul Whiteman & His Orchestra

W6c. 1970 (Oct. 29): Miami, FL; Miami Beach Auditorium, final concert of three-day Gershwin Festival; George Roth, piano; University of Miami Symphony Orchestra; Frederick Fennell, conducting *See*: **B157, B1456, B1457, B1482**

W6d. 1985 (Feb. 8): Raleigh, NC; Memorial Auditorium; Paul Tardif, piano; NC Symphony; James Ogle, conducting

W6e. 1987 (May 15): NY; Alice Tully Hall, "Gershwin/Jazz Celebration"; Leonard Pennario, piano; Harmonie Ensemble; Steven Richman, conducting (First NY performance in 50 years)

W7.   *CATFISH ROW: SUITE FROM PORGY AND BESS.* (1935-1936) Chappell; 26 min; also available from Rodgers & Hammerstein, rental.

Ira Gershwin retitled this suite *Catfish Row* in 1958.
2(picc).2(EngH).4(bscl).1/3.3.2.1/timp/perc/pf/banjo/strings

Holograph at DLC: photostatic copy with emendations in pencil & ink, & additions/deletions taped in, GC Box 8, Item 3

Five movements: **1.** Catfish Row **2.** Porgy Sings **3.** Fugue **4.** Hurricane **5.** Good Morning, Brother

See: **B88, B1838, B2171**

Premieres

W7a. 1936 (Jan. 21): Philadelphia, Academy of Music; Philadelphia Orchestra; Alexander Smallens, conducting (world premiere)

W7b. 1936 (Dec. 15): Seattle, WA; Civic Auditorium; Seattle Symphony Orchestra; *See*: **B1483**

STAGE SHOWS

Broadway musicals customarily had overtures, but since they are not "songs" per se, they are not listed here. Song lists were derived from Jablonski, **B53**, Schwartz, **B86,** and Kimball, **B21,** and Krasker & Kimball, **B291.** There are discrepancies between these sources. For more information on the current availability of performance materials, *See*: Krasker & Kimball. In the lists of songs, the symbol * indicates that the song is thought to have been published.

W8.   *HALF PAST EIGHT* (1918)
Revue, lyrics by Fred Caryll (Edward B. Perkins). Music mostly by G. Produced by Edward B. Perkins

Premiere

W8a. 1918 (Dec. 9): Syracuse, NY; Empire Theater; never reached Broadway
CAST: Joe Cook, Sybil Vane, Roy Stever, Mildred Lovejoy, Ruby Loraine, & the Famous Original Clef Club Jazz Band.

SONGS: There's Magic in the Air (IG)*;   Hong Kong;   Cupid; Half Past Eight; Little Sunbeam

W9.   *LA-LA-LUCILLE!* (1919)
Performance materials currently unavailable

Premiere

W9a. 1919 (April 21): Atlantic City, NJ (World premiere & out-of-town tryout); (May 26): NY premiere; Henry Miller's Theatre; 104 performances
CAST: Johnathon Jaynes: J. Clarence Harvey; **Lucille Jaynes Smith:** Janet Velie; **John Smith:** John E. Hazzard; **Oyama:** M. Rale; **Nicholas Grimsby:** Maurice Cass; **Thomas Brady:** Sager Midgely; **Mrs. Thomas Brady:** Cordedlia MacDonald; **Allan Brady:** John Lowe; **Reginald Blackwood:** Alfred Hall; **Fanny:** Eleanor Daniels; **Mlle. Victorine:** Marjorie Bentley; **Britton Hughes:** Lorin Raker; **Mrs. Britton Hughes (Peggy):** Helen Clark; **A Bellboy:** Edward DeCamp; **A Waiter:** Harold D. Millar; **Duffey:** George W. Callahan; **Colonel Marrion, Peggy's father:** Stanley H. Forde; **A Stranger:** Estar Banks; **Bill Collectors, heiresses, etc.:** The Misses Morgan, Jarvis, Hamilton, Devere, Irving, Miles, Wilson, Harden, Harrison, Cotton, Cullen, and Edwardy. **Heirs,**

etc.: The Misses DeCamp, Joslyn, Millar, and Daly
Book: Fred Jackson; **Lyrics:** Arthur Jackson & B. G. DeSilva [sic];
Staged by: Herbert Gresham & Julian Alfred (choreography); **Producers:**
Alex A. Aarons & George B. Seitz; Charles Previn, **conducting** (NY
premiere)

SONGS:

Unless otherwise indicated, all lyrics were by Arthur J. Jackson & B. G.
DeSylva; When You Live in a Furnished Flat; The Best of Everything*;
From Now On*; It's Hard to Tell; Tee-Oodle-Um-Bum-Bo*; Nobody But
You*; It's Great to Be in Love; There's More to a Kiss than the Sound
(Irving Caesar)—issued in separate edition, revised lyric for There's More to
a Kiss than the X-X-X*; Somehow It Seldom Comes True*; Ten
Commandments of Love (same song as There's Magic in the Air), *See also:*
B1602, Robert Kimball, *The Complete Lyrics of Ira Gershwin,* p. 6).

Dropped after the opening in NY: Money, Money, Money!; Oo, How I Love
to Be Loved by You (Lou Paley)
Dropped before NY: The Love of a Wife*; Our Little Kitchenette (Later
redone for *Sweet Little Devil, q. v.* at **W19,** but dropped from that show
before it opened in NY)

W10. *MORRIS GEST'S MIDNIGHT WHIRL* (1919)

Premiere

W10a.1919 (Dec. 27): Century Grove; Century Theatre; 110 performances
  CAST: Bessie McCoy Davis, Bernard Granville, Helen Shipman, Rath
  Brothers
  Lyrics: B. G. DeSylva & John Henry Mears; **Book:** DeSylva and Mears
  Producer: Morris Gest; Frank Yours, **conducting**

  SONGS: The League of Nations; Doughnuts; Poppyland*; I'll Show You a
  Wonderful World; Limehouse Nights*; Let Cutie Cut Your Cuticle; Baby
  Dolls

1919: Swanee (A second edition, known as the *Sinbad* edition as "Successfully introduced by
Al Jolson").* Picture of Jolson is on cover. A third sheet music edition of Swanee appeared
along with the biographical film of G, *Rhapsody in Blue* (1945).

1920:
Interpolated into *Dere Mable*: We're Pals (Irving Caesar)*; Back Home (Arthur Francis); I
Don't Know Why (Irving Caesar); I Want To Be Wanted by You (IG)

Interpolated into *The Ed Wynn Carnival*: Oo, How I Love to be Loved By You (Lou Paley)*

W11. *GEORGE WHITE'S SCANDALS OF 1920*, Second Annual Production

  Lyrics by Arthur Jackson; book by Andy Rice and George White. **Produced
  by** White, **Directors:** White and Willie Collier; **Orchestrations:** Frank
  Saddler *See:* **B150**

Premiere

W11a.1920 (June 7); NY; Globe Theatre; 134 performances. *See*: **B327**

> **CAST**: Ann Pennington, Lou Holtz, "Doc" Rockwell, Ethel Delmar, Lester Allen, George White, the Yerkes Happy Six; Alfred Newman, conducting

> *SONGS*: Idle Dreams (Jackson)*; My Lady (Jackson)*;   Everybody Swat the Profiteer*;   On My Mind the Whole Night Long (Jackson)*;   Tum On and Tiss Me (Jackson)*;   Scandal Walk (Jackson)*;   The Songs of Long Ago (Jackson)*

Not used: Queen Isabella (Jackson); My Old Love Is My New Love

W12. *A DANGEROUS MAID* (1921)
Performance materials currently not available

> *SONGS*: Anything for You;   Just to Know You Are Mine (A. Francis [IG])*;   Boy Wanted (A. Francis [IG])*;   The Simple Life (A. Francis [IG])*;   The Sirens (same as Four Little Sirens, used in *Primrose*);   Dancing Shoes (A. Francis [IG])*;   True Love (A. Francis [IG]); Some Rain Must Fall (A. Francis [IG])*

Not used: Pidgee Woo; Every Girl Has a Way

Premieres

W12a.1921 (Mar. 21): Nixon's Apollo Theatre, Atlantic City, NJ (closed in

> Pittsburgh at the Nixon, Apr. 30, 1921) **CAST:** Vivienne Segal, Amelia Bingham, Johnnie Arthur, Vinton Freedley, Juanita Fletcher, Creighton Hale; Juliette Day (replaced by Vivienne Segal); **Lyrics:** Arthur Francis [IG]; **Book:** Charles W. Bell; **Producer:** Edgar MacGregor

W13 . *GEORGE WHITE'S SCANDALS OF 1921*, Third Annual Production

> **Book:** Bugs Baer & George White; **Lyrics:** Arthur Jackson; **Entire Production Staged By:** George White; Alfred Newman, **conducting** (First performance in NY) *See*: **B150**, **B328**, **B329**

> SONGS: Mother Eve (Opening); I Love You (Jackson)*; South Sea Isles (Jackson)*; Drifting Along with the Tide (Jackson)*; She's Just a Baby (Jackson)*; Where East Meets West at Panama (Jackson)*

Premieres

W13a.1921 (July 4): Atlantic City, NJ; Nixon's Apollo Theatre (Out-of-town tryout)

W13b.1921 (July 11): NY; Liberty Theatre; 97 perfs. **CAST:** Ann
Pennington;   Theresa   Gardella   (**Aunt   Jemima**);   Olive

Vaughn; Victoria Herbert; Gene Ford; Myra Cullen; Christine Welford; Darry Welford; Geraldine Alexander; Phoebe Lee; George White; George LeMaire; Lou Holtz; Lester Allen; Charles King; George Bickel; Harry Rose; Bert Gordon; Lloyd Garrett; James Miller

W14. *GEORGE WHITE'S SCANDALS OF 1922*, Fourth Annual Production

SONGS: Argentina (DeSylva)*;   Just A Tiny Cup of Tea; Oh, What She Hangs Out (Also titled She Hangs Out in Our Alley) (DeSylva only)*; Cinderelatives (DeSylva)***;** I Found a Four Leaf Clover (DeSylva)***;** I Can't Tell Where They're From When They Dance; I'll Build a Stairway to Paradise (DeSylva & A. Francis)*; Across the Sea*; Where Is the Man of My Dreams?*; *Blue Monday, q. v.,* below (used in the show for one night only) *See*: **B150**

Premieres

W14a.1922: New Haven, CT; Shubert Theatre (Out-of-town tryout)

W14b.1922 (Aug. 28): NY; Globe Theatre; "George White's Scandals," Fourth Annual Production; 88 perfs.
  CAST: W. C. Fields; Jack McGowan; Winnie Lightner; Pearl Regay; Lester Allen; Richard Bold; Coletta Ryan; George White; Dolores Costello; Paul Whiteman and His Palais Royal Orchestra **Book:** Andy Rice, George White, & W. C. Fields; **Lyrics:** B. G. De Sylva & E. Ray Goetz; **Music:** George Gershwin; **Orchestrations:** Maurice De Pack; **Scenes Designed by:** John Wenger & Herbert Ward; **Entire Production Staged By:** George White; Max Steiner, conducting (First performance in NY)

1922: Interpolated into *The French Doll*: Do It Again! (B. G. DeSylva, also used in the motion picture *Thoroughly Modern Millie*, starring Julie Andrews)*

W15. *BLUE MONDAY* (retitled *135th Street* by Paul Whiteman in 1925) (1922)

Opera Ala Afro-American, never published (Orig. Orch. by Will Vodery, a second orchestration by Ferde Grofé for Paul Whiteman band); **Lyrics:** B. G. De Sylva

Sketch score by GG, in pencil, 41 leaves, at **DLC** (Bound)
Full score by Will Vodery at **DLC**, Vodery's holograph in ink, with holograph notations by the composer in pencil, 156 pp, description of history of *135th Street Blues* orchestrations laid in (Box 8, Item 1)
Photocopy of Grofé's orchestration at **NN-L**
Photocopy of a "vocal score and adaptations by George Bassman" (1976) at **DLC** as copyright copy

  Arr. for piano solo by Alicia Zizzo, incl. introductory notes on the historical significance of the piece and performance notes (Warner Bros., no. 0375)

SONGS: Blue Monday Blues; Has Anyone Seen My Joe?; I'm Going to See My Mother

See: **B1838,** and an excellent essay by **John Andrew Johnson** in **Schneider,**
                                                                B 162.1, pp. 111-141.

Premieres

W15a.1922 (Aug. 28, one performance only): NY; Globe Theatre, in George White's *Scandals* of 1922, Act 2; four preview perfs. in New Haven, CT

Other Selected Performances

W15b.1925 (Dec. 29): NY; Carnegie Hall, 2 concert performances as part of Paul Whiteman's second "Experiment in Modern Music"
    CAST: Blossom Seeley, Benny Fields, & Charles Hart, *et al See*: **B296**

W15c.1953 (Mar. 29): NY; CBS Television's "Omnibus" **CAST: Vi:** Etta Warren; **Sweetpea:** Lorenzo Fuller; **Sam:** Jimmy Rushing; **Joe:** Raun Spearman; **Bartender:** Warren Coleman; 15 dancers; **Staging & Choreography:** Valerie Bettis; **Executive Producer of Omnibus:** William Spier; **Music score reconstruction:** George Bassman
    Video of the production is at **DLC** *See*: **F33, B292, B296, D365**

W15d.1975 (Nov.): New York; under title *Blue Monday Blues*; concert presentation by the Composers Showcase; Gregg Smith, conducting (Ewen)

W15e.1978 (Feb 25-26): NY; Marymount Manhattan College, Third World Club; The Harlem Opera Society

W15f.1982 (Jan. 29): Cheverly, MD; Prince George's Civic Opera, Third Annual Operafest; **CAST: Joe:** Alburtt Rhodes; **Vi:** Elizabeth Lyra Ross; **Tom:** Warren Price; **Mike:** Reginald Evans; **Lou:** Marvin Mills; **Sam:** Gordon Hawkins; *See*: **B293**

W15g.1987 (July 6): Warwick, England; Cameo Opera at St. Nicholas's Church; **Joe:** Paul Farrington; **Vi:** Mary Truelove; **Tom:** Darron Moore; Ronnie Binnie, **arrangements & conducting** *See*: **B297**

W16. OUR NELL (original title: *HAYSEED*) (1922)
Performance materials currently not available

SONGS:
    Gol-Durn! (mus: G & Wm. Daly, lyrics: Hooker); Innocent Ingenue Baby (G & Daly/Hooker)*; The Cooney County Fair (Hooker); Names I Love to Hear (mus: G & Daly, ly: Hooker); By and By (G/Hooker)*; Madrigal (G & Daly/Hooker); We Go to Church on Sunday (Hooker); Walking Home with Angeline (Hooker)*; Oh, You Lady! (G & Daly/Hooker); Little Villages (G & Daly/Hooker); Barn Dance (G &/or Daly)

Dropped before NY: The Custody of the Child (G/Hooker), dropped during the tryout

Premieres

W16a.1922 (Nov. 20): Stamford, CT (Out-of town tryout)

W16b.1922 (Dec. 4): NY; Nora Bayes Theatre; 40 performances **CAST: Malvina Holcombe:** Mrs. Jimmy Barry; **Mortimer Bayne:** John Merkyl; **Peleg Doolittle:** Jimmy Barry; **Joshua Holcombe:** Frank Mayne; **Frank Hart:** Thomas Conkey; **Deacon Calvin Sheldrake:** Guy Nichols; **Helen Ford:** Eva Clark; **Angeline Weems:** Emma Haig; **Chris Deming:** Olin Howland; **Mrs. Rogers:** Lora Sonderson; **Lyrics:** Brian Hooker; **Book by:** Hooker & A. E. Thomas; **Producers:** Ed. Davidow & Rufus LcMaire **Directors:** Edgar MacGregor & W. H. Gilmore; Charles Stieger, **conducting** *See*: **B507**

W17. *THE RAINBOW* **(The New Empire Revue, London)** (1923)
   Performance materials not currently available
   See: **B150**
   SONGS: All lyrics by Clifford Grey except for Innocent Lonesome Blue Baby, in which Grey was assisted by Hooker, w/ music by G and Wm. Daly, this is the same tune as Innocent Ingenue of 1922*; Sweetheart (I'm So Glad That I Met You)*; Good-Night, My Dear*; Any Little Tune; Moonlight in Versailles*; In the Rain*; Beneath the Eastern Moon*; Oh! Nina*; Strut Lady with Me*; Sunday in London Town*; All Over Town (same melody as Come to the Moon)*

Not used: Give Me My Mammy (advertised but not published)

Premiere

W17a.1923 (Apr. 3): London; Empire Theatre; 113 performances
   CAST: Daphne Pollard; Grace Hayes, Stephanie Stevens. Earl Rickard, Ernest Thesiger, Lola Raine, Fred A. Leslie; Elsie Mayfair; Elaine Lettor; Clifford Cobe; Jerry & Co.; Alec Kellaway; Cecil Mannering; Frances Grant & Ted Wing; The Fayre Four; Gaston & Andrée; **In "Plantation Days" number:** James P. Johnson with his Syncopated Orchestra and Entire Company, **staged by** Leonard Harper, **music by** James P. Johnson; Ladies & gentlemen of the chorus & sixteen Empire Girls; **Lyrics by:**

   Clifford Grey; **Book by:** Albert de Courville, Edgar Wallace & Noel Scott; **Dances & ensembles:** Allan K. Foster; **Scenery:** Marc Henri, Oliver Bernard, Robert H. Law; **Costumes designed by:** Hugh Willoughby; **Gentlemen's costumes by:** Pope & Bradley, Morris Angel & Sons, W. Clarkson, M. Berman; **Produced by:** de Courville; Kennedy Russell, **conducting**

W18. *GEORGE WHITE'S SCANDALS OF 1923*, Fifth Annual Production

   See: **B150**

SONGS: Little Scandal Dolls; You and I (music by G & Jack Green/lyrics by DeSylva, Goetz, & B. MacDonald)*; Katinka; Lo-La-Lo (DeSylva only)*; There Is Nothing Too Good for You (DeSylva & Goetz)*; Throw Her in High! (DeSylva & Goetz)*; Let's Be Lonesome Together (De Sylva, Goetz)*; The Life of a Rose (DeSylva)*; Look in the Looking Glass; Where Is She? (DeSylva)*; Laugh Your Cares Away; (On the Beach at) How've-You-Been (DeSylva)*; Garden of Love

CAST: James Miller; Winnie Lightner, Tom Patricola, Lester Allen, Richard Bold, Beulah Berson, Johnny Dooley, Marga Waldron; Olive Vaughn, Helen Hudson; Newton Alexander; Tip Top Four; London Palace Girls and Scandal Beauties; and others; **Book:** George White & William K. Wells; **Lyrics:** B. G. De Sylva & E. Ray Goetz, with additional lyrics by Ballard McDonald; **Orchestrations:** Maurice De Pack; **Entire Production Staged By:** George White; Charles Drury, **conducting**

W18a.1923 (June 5): Atlantic City, NJ; Nixon's Apollo Theatre (Out-of-town tryout)

W18b.1923 (June 18): NY; Globe Theatre, "George White's Scandals," Fifth Annual Edition; 168 perfs.

W19. *SWEET LITTLE DEVIL* (*A Perfect Lady*) (1924)
Performance materials currently unavailable
Scripts at Amherst College and **DLC** (without lyrics)

SONGS:

Strike, Strike, Strike; You're Mighty Lucky; Virginia (Don't Go Too Far)*; Someone Who Believes in You***;** The Jijibo*; Quite a Party; Under a One-Man Top*; The Matrimonial Handicap; Just Supposing; Hey! Hey! Let 'Er Go!*; Pepita (Rosita)*; Hooray for the U.S.A.

Added for post-Broadway tour: Sweet Little Devil
Dropped: System; The Same Old Story; Our Little Kitchenette (IG & De Sylva); Not Used: Mah-Jongg*; My Little Duckie; Be the Life of the Crowd

Premieres

W19a.1923 (Dec. 20): Boston; Shubert Theatre; (Out-of-town tryout) *See*: **B249**

W19b.1924 (Jan. 21): NY; Astor Theatre (later moved to the Central Theatre); 120 perfs. **CAST: Rena:** Rae Bowdin; **Joyce West:** Marjorie Gateson; **May Rourke:** Ruth Warren; **Sam Wilson:** Franklyn Ardell; **Virginia Araminta Culpepper:** Constance Binney; **Tom Nesbitt:** Irving Beebe; **Fred Carrington:** William Wayne; **Jim Henry:** O. J. Vanasse; **Susette:** Mildred Brown; **Joan Edward:** Bobbie Breslaw;

Richard Brook: William Holbrook; **Marian Townes:** Olivette

Book By: Frank Mandel & Laurence Schwab; **Lyrics:** B. G. De Sylva; **Staged by:** Edgar MacGregor; **Musical numbers Staged by:** Sammy Lee; **Stage Settings by:** Lee Simonson; **Miss Binney's ballet arranged by:** Michel Fokine; **Produced by** Schwab; **Director:** Edgar MacGregor & Sammy Lee; **Producer:** Laurence Schwab; Ivan Rudisill, **conducting** See: **B249, B381**

W20. *GEORGE WHITE'S SCANDALS OF 1924*, Sixth Annual Edition
See: **B150, D911**

> *SONGS:* All lyrics by DeSylva, except Somebody Loves me, *q. v.* below; Just Missed the Opening Chorus; I Need a Garden*; Night Time in Araby*; I'm Going Back*; Year After Year*; Somebody Loves Me (DeSylva & Ballard MacDonald)*; Tune In (to Station J.O.Y.)*; Mah-Jongg*; Lovers of Art; Rose of Madrid*; I Love You, My Darling; Kongo Kate*

Premiere:

W20a.1924 (June 30): NY; Apollo Theatre; 192 performances **CAST:**
Winnie Lightner, Tom Patricola, the Elm City Four, the Williams Sisters, Will Mahoney, Richard Bold, Helene Hudson, Helene & Dolores Costello; **Lyrics by:** B. G. DeSylva; **book by:** William K. Wells & George White; **Producer:** White; William Daly, **conducting**

W21. *PRIMROSE* (1924)
Piano/vocal score, London: Chappell, NY: Harms, 1924, at **NN-L, classmark**
***MS-Amer.**
Performance materials not currently available
See: **B1348**

SONGS

The symbol + indicates songs published in the piano/vocal score;

Leaving Town While We May, opening chorus of Act I (Desmond Carter)+; Till I Meet Someone Like You (Carter)+; Isn't It Wonderful?*; This Is the Life for a Man (Carter)*; When Toby Is Out of Town (Carter)+; Some Far-away Someone (Gershwin & B.

G. DeSylva; same melody as Half Past Seven)*; The Mophams (Carter)+; Can We Do Anything?+*; Roses of France (Carter)+; Four Little Sirens (Gershwin)+; Berkeley Square and Kew (Carter)+; Boy Wanted (IG & Carter)*; Wait a Bit, Susie (IG & Carter)*; Isn't It Terrible What They Did to Mary, Queen of Scots? (Carter); Naughty Baby (music: GG; lyrics: IG & Carter), orchestration by GG+; It Is the Fourteenth of July [Finale Act II] (Carter)+; Ballet; I Make Hay While the Moon Shines (Carter)+; That New-Fangled Mother of Mine (Carter)*; Beau Brummel (Carter)+

Not Used: Pep! Zip! and Punch! [alternate title: The Live Wire (both Carter)] When You're Not at Your Best

Premieres

W21a.1924 (Sept. 11-closing April 25, 1925): London, Winter Garden; 255 performances, **CAST: Jason:** Ernest Graham; **Freddie Falls:** Claude Hulbert; **May Rooker:** Vera Lennox/Dorothy Field; **Sir Benjamin Falls:** Guy Fane; **Joan:** Margery Hicklin; **Hilary Vane:** Percy Heming; **Toby Mopham:** Leslie Hensen; **Michael:** Thomas Weguelin; **Pinky Peach:** Heather Thatcher/Vera Lennox (Margaret Moore); **Lady Sophia Mophum:** Muriel Barnhy; **Pritchard:** Sylvia Hawkes; **Villagers, River Girls, Sports Girls, Sportsmen, visitors, etc.: Post Girl:** Mignon Morenza; **Flower Girl:** Esme de Vayne; **Ballet Girl:** Winifred Shotter; **First bather:** Kathleen Burgis; **Second bather:** Beryl Murray; **Third bather:** Lelia Farmar; **Fourth baker:** Molly Vere; **Lady Kitty:** Dorothy Deane; **Lady Katy:** Yvonne O'Beare; **Hon. Dilly:** Phyllis Swinburne; **Hon. Dally:** Margaret Moore; **Miss Tishy:** Geraldine Aylmer; **Miss Toshy:** Phyllis Garton; **Marie:** Dorothy Daw; **Cutex:** Sybil Eastley; **Blush:** Bubbles Ryan; **Witch Hazel:** Estelle Dudley; **First ballerina:** Elaine Ferrars; **Second ballerina:** Daisy Dalziel; **Third ballerina:** Audrey Carlyon; **Artist:** Leslie French; **Turk:** Guy Saunders; **Tom:** Ralph Rutland; **Jerry:** George Hamilton; **Alvanley:** Frank Wilson Barrett; **Jorrocks:** Fred Whitlock; **De Travers:** Frank Brown; **Agent de Police:** Jack Morgan; **Colonel:** Jackson Werndley; **Captain:** John Redmond

Book: George Grossmith & Guy Bolton; **Lyrics:** Desmond Carter & IG; **Producers:** Grossmith & Ja. A. E. Malone; **Director:** George Grossmith; **Choreography:** Laddie Cliff, Carl Hyton, & Dyta Morena; **Scenery:** Joseph & Phil Harker; **Costumes:** Comelli; **Additional lyrics:** B. G. DeSylva; **Producers:** George Grossmith & J. A. E. Malone; **Orchestrations:** George Gershwin & Frank Saddler; **Stage Direction:** Charles A. Maynard; **Musical Direction** and **conducting:** John Ansell *See*: **B883**

W21b.1987 (May 15): Washington, D. C.; Coolidge Auditorium of the Library of Congress, under the auspices of the Gertrude Clarke Whittall Foundation and the Ira and Leonore Gershwin Charitable Foundation; **CAST**: **Pinkie/May:** Kim Criswell; **Freddie/Turk/Village Boy:** George Dvorsky; **Hilary/Artist:** Cris Groenendaal; **Joan/Postal Girl/ Flower seller:** Rebecca Luker; **Toby:** John Sinclair; Norman Scribner Choir; John McGlinn, **conducting** (First complete concert performance in America) *See*: **B512, B515**

W22. *LADY, BE GOOD!* **(Originally titled** *Black Eyed Susan***) (1924)**

Typescript of undated libretto at **NN-L.** classmark **NCOF, p.v. 282.**

+

Performance materials available for rent from Tams-Witmark, *See*: Krasker/Kimball, **B1615**, p. 83, **B162**, **B50**

Recordings at: D456 (Roxbury), D459 (Smithsonian)

SONGS: Hang on to Me (Two editions)*; A Wonderful Party; The End of a String; We're Here Because; Fascinating Rhythm (Two editions)*; So Am I*; Oh, Lady Be Good! (Two editions)*; The Robinson Hotel; The Half of It, Dearie, Blues (Two editions)*; Juanita; Little Jazz Bird*; Carnival Time instrumental, Orchestration by Grant; Swiss Miss [The Cab-Horse Trot] (Lyrics by Arthur Jackson & IG)*

Added after NY opening: Linger in the Lobby

Not Used: Seeing Dickie Home; The Man I Love*; Will You Remember Me?; Singin' Pete; Evening Star; The Bad, Bad Men; Weather Man; Rainy Afternoon Girls; Laddie Daddie; Leave It to Love

Added to London production of 1926: Something About Love (Lou Paley)*; I'd Rather Charleston (Desmond Carter)*; Buy a Little Button (Carter)

Premieres

W22a.1924 (Nov. 17): Philadelphia (World premiere & out-of-town tryout)

W22b.1924 (Dec.1): NY; Liberty Theatre (NY Premiere); 330 perfs. **CAST: Dick Trevor:** Fred Astaire; **Susie Trevor:** Adele Astaire; **Jack Robinson:** Alan Edwards; **Josephine Vanderwater:** Jayne Auburn; **Daisy Parke:** Patricia Clark; **Bertie Bassett:** Gerald Oliver Smith; **J. Watterson Watkins:** Walter Catlett; **Shirley Vernon:** Kathlene Martyn; **Jeff:** Cliff Edwards; **Manuel Estrade:** Bryan Lycan; **Flunkey:** Edward Jephson; **Victor Arden:** Victor Arden; **Phil Ohman:** Phil Ohman; **Rufus Parke:** James Bradbury; **Ladies of the Ensemble; Gentlemen of the Ensemble; Book:** Guy Bolton & Fred Thompson; **Lyrics:** IG; **Orchestrations by:** Stephen Oscar Jones, Robert Russell Bennett, Charles N. Grant, Paul Lannin, Max Steiner, William Daly **Book Staged by:** Felix Edwardes; **Dances and Ensembles Staged by:** Sammy Lee; **Set designs:** Norman Bel-Geddes; **Producers:** Alex. A. Aarons & Vinton Freedley; Paul Lannin, **conducting** See: **B346, B350**

W22c.1926 (March 29): Opening tryout in Liverpool, England

W22d.1926 (Apr. 14—for nine months, followed by a tour of Britain): Old Empire Theatre, Leicester Square (Premiere in London) 326 performances **CAST: Bertie Bassett:** Ewart Scott; **Daisy Parke:** Glori Beaumont; **Dick Trevor:** Fred Astaire; **Susie Trevor:** Adele Astaire; **Jack Robinson:** George Vollaire; **Flunkey:** Alec Johnstone; **Josephine Vanderwater:** Sylvia Leslie; **J. Watterson Watkins:** William Kent; **Shirley Vernon:** Irene Russell; **Jeff:** Buddy Lee; **Manuel Astrada:** Roy Emerton; **Rufus Parke:** Denier Warren; **Presented by:** Alfred Butt, Alex. A. Aarons & Vinton Freedley; **Dances & Ensembles staged by:** Max Scheck;

Producer: Felix Edwardes

Other Selected Performances

W22e.1925? (Nov. 16-23): Atlanta, GA; Atlanta Theatre

W22f.1926 (Sept.-December): from Newark, NJ to Boston

W22g.1927 tour of Britain until Spring of 1927

W22h.1956 (May 28-June 2): London; Golders Green Hippodrome; Sonnie Hale, male lead *See*: **B352**

W22i.1974 (June 3-July 6): East Haddam, CT; Goodspeed Opera House **CAST: Shirley:** Leilani Johnson; **Dick Trevor:** Richard Cooper Bayne; **Bertie Bassett:** Hal Shane; **Susie Trevor:** Bonnie Schon; **Jack Robinson:** David Chaney; **Buck Benson:** Joel Craig; **Josephine Vanderwater:** Jeanne Walsh; **Watty Watkins:** John Remme; **Daisy:** Valena Westmoreland; **Estrada:** Milton Tarver; **Rufus Parke:** Milton Tarver; **Ladies & Gentlemen of the Singing & Dancing Ensemble:** Wendy Lamoreaux, Bonnie Simmons, Valena Westmoreland, Chuck Beard, Tedd Carrere, & Hal Shane; Lynn Crigler, **conducting;**
Lyrics: IG; **Book:** Guy Bolton & Fred Thompson; **Producer:** Michael P. Price; **Costumes:** David Toser; **Scenic production:** Fred Voelpel; **Lighting:** Peter M. Ehrhardt; **Production associate:** Michael T. Brooks; **Production stage manager:** Don Judge; **Technical director:** Jim Waters; **Choreographer:** Bick Goss; **Special consultant:** Robert Kimball; **Director:** Neal Kenyon; **Producer:** Michael P. Price *See*: **B355**

W22j.1987 (Jan. 5): New Orleans; Saenger Performing Arts Center
(The Goodspeed Opera House production on tour); "Pickup" orchestra of New Orleans musicians; **CAST: Same as 1987 Goodspeed Opera House production above except for: Daisy Parke:** Lorraine Goodman; **Bertie Bassett:** Michael Kay; **Shirley Vernon:** Rebecca Spencer; **Ladies and Gentleman of the Ensemble:** Bobby Clark, Ron Crofoot, Richard Dodd, Alain Freulon, Pixley Lewis, Patricia Lockery, David Monzione, Lori Oaks, Ann-Marie Rogers, Tara Tyrell; **Swing Singer/Dancers:** Dana Lewis, Alan Onickel

W22k.1987 (July 8-Oct. 2): East Haddam, CT; Goodspeed Opera House;

CAST: Susie Trevor: Nikki Sahagen; **Moving Man:** Bobby Clark; **Dick Trevor:** Ray Benson; **Jack Robinson:** Steve Watkins; **Policeman:** Bryan Harris; **Jeff White:** Richard Stillman; **Delivery Boy:** Bobby Clark; **Daisy Parke:** Iris Revson; **Bertie Bassett:** Christopher Seppe; **Josephine Vanderwater:** Marlena Lustik; **Watty Watkins:** Russell Leib; **Vanderwater Waiter:** Allain Freulon; **Shirley Vernon:** Karen Culliver; **Manuel Estrada:** Bryan Harris; **Rufus Parke:** Bryan Harris; **Hotel Waiter:** Ron Crofoot; **Ladies and Gentleman of the**

Ensemble: Bobby Clark, Ron Crofoot, Janice Cronkhite, Richard Dodd, Alain Freulon, Patricia Lockery, David Monzione, Dana Pinchera, Ann-Marie Rogers, Tara Tyrell; Stage Manager: Michael Brunner; Assistant Stage Manager: Dave Harris; Book by: Guy Bolton & Fred Thompson; Lyrics: IG; Scenery designed by: Eduardo Sicangco; Costumes designed by: John Carver Sullivan; Lighting designed by: Curt Ostermann; Dance Arrangements by: Russell Warner; Additional orchestrations by: Lynn Crigler & Russell Warner; Choreography & Musical Staging by: Dan Siretta; Technical director: Daniel Renn; Dramaturg: Tommy Krasker; Special consultant: Alfred Simon; Director: Thomas Gruenewald; Associate Artistic Director: Dan Siretta; Associate Producer: Sue Frost; Producer: Michael P. Price; Lynn Crigler, conducting *See*: B354

W22l.1987? (July 8): London; Guildhall School of Music and Drama CAST:
Jeff the Entertainer: Nigel Richards; Watty Watkins: Clive Rowe; Dawn Lisell; Simon Waters; Anika Bluhm; Andrew Nymen; Shirley: Teresa McElroy; Jack: Robin Fritz; Choreography: Gerry Tebbett; Director: Martin Conner; Big band in the pit; Michael Ohmer, conducting *See*: B351

W23. *TELL ME MORE* (1925)
Performance materials not currently available *See*: B883

SONGS

Most lyrics by B. G. DeSylva & IG; Tell Me More (DeSylva & IG)*; Shop Girls and Mannikins; Mr. and Mrs. Sipkin; When the Debbies Go By (DeSylva & IG); Three Times a Day (DeSylva & IG)*; Why Do I Love You? (DeSylva & IG)*; How Can I Win You Now?— replaced in NY opening by Once; Kickin' the Clouds Away (DeSylva & IG)*; Love Is in the Air; My Fair Lady (DeSylva & IG)*; In Sardinia; Baby! (DeSylva & IG)*; Ukulele Lorelei; Oh Sole, Oh Me!

Not used: I'm Somethin' on Avenue A; The He-Man; Gushing

New for London production, 1925: Murderous Monty (and Light-Fingered Jane) (Desmond Carter)*; Love, I Never Knew (Desmond Carter); Have You Heard? (Hulbert)

Premieres

W23a.1925 (Apr. 6): Atlantic City, NJ (Out of town tryout)

W23b.1925 (Apr. 13): NY; Gaiety Theater; 100 performances CAST:
Gertrude: Ruth Raymond; Harry: Eddie Dowling, Jr.; Kenneth Dennison: Alexander Gray; Peggy Van De Leur: Phyllis Cleveland; Billy Smith: Andrew Tombes; Bonnie Reeves: Emma Haig; Estelle: Charlotte Esmone; Lucy: Nita Jacques; Heather: Marion Mueller;.

Toots: Dolla Harkins; **Edith:** Vivian Glenn; **Mrs. Pennyfeather:** Florence Auer; **Monty Sipkin:** Lou Holtz; **Jane Wallace:** Esther Howard; **Mrs. Wallace:** Maud Andrew; **George B. Wallace:** Robert C. Ryles; **Monsieur Cerise:** Eugene Redding; **Cashier:** Cecil Brunner;

Waiters: Covan & Ruffin; **Doorman:** Morton McConnachie; **Book:** Fred Thompson & William K. Wells; **Book Staged by:** John Harwood; **Lyrics:** B. G. de Sylva & IG; **Additional music & lyrics by:** William Daly, Lou Holtz, Desmond Carter, & Claude Hulbert; **Dances and Ensembles staged by:** Sammy Lee; **Costumes and Gowns designed by:** Chas. LeMaire; **Producer:** Al. Aarons (New York premiere); Max Steiner, musical direction

W23c.1925 (May 26): London; Winter Garden; 263 performances

CAST: **Gertrude:** Dorothy Field; **Kenneth Dennison:** Arthur Margetson; **Billy:** Claude Hulbert; **Peggy van de Leur:** Elsa MacFarlane; **Bonnie Reeves:** Vera Lennox; **Mrs. Pennyfeather:** Ada Palmer; **Monty Sipkin:** Leslie Henson; **Jane Wallace:** Heather Thatcher; **Mamie:** Sylvia Hawkes; **Mrs. Wallace:** Muriel Barnby; **Manager of Hotel:** George de Warfaz; **George B. Wallace:** Guy Fane; **Cyrus P. Tyler:** Ernest Graham; **Book:** Fred Thompson & William. K. Wells; **Lyrics:** IG, B. G. de Sylva, Desmond Carter; **Presented by:** George Grossmith & J. A. E. Malone by arrangement with Alex. A. Aarons; **Dances & Ensembles:** Sammy Lee; **Produced by:** Felix Edwarde

W24. *TIP-TOES* (1925)

Tams-Witmark rents performance material. Typescript of libretto at **NN-L,** no date, classmark **NCOF, p. v. 277,** and script at **DLC.** *See*: **B291** (Krasker/ Kimball), p. 95, for more information. *Also See*: **B162**

SONGS

Waiting for the Train; Nice Baby!*; Looking for a Boy*; Lady Luck; When Do We Dance?*; These Charming People*; That Certain Feeling*; Sweet and Low-Down*; Our Little Captain; It's a Great Little World*; Nightie-Night*; Tip-Toes

Dropped before NY run: Harlem River Chanty (first published in 1968 non show choral arr.)*; Gather Ye Rosebuds; Dancing Hour; Life's Too Short to Be Blue; Harbor of Dreams; Not used: We

Premiere

W24a.1925 (Nov. 24): Washington, DC (Out-of-town tryout); According to Jablonski, there were also tryouts in Newark, Nov.29 and Philadelphia, Dec. 7.

W24b.1925 (Dec.28): NY; Liberty Theater (NY premiere); 194 performances

CAST: Sylvia Metcalf: Jeannette MacDonald; **Rollo Metcalf:** Robert

Halliday; **Peggy Schuyler:** Amy Revere; **Al Kaye:** Andrew Tombes; **Hen Kaye:** Harry Watson, Jr.; **"Tip-Toes" Kaye:** Queenie Smith; **Steve Burton:** Allen Kearns; **Binnie Oakland:** Gertrude McDonald; **Denise Marshall:** Lovey Lee; **Steward:** Edwin Hodge; **Detective Kane:** Seldon Bennett; **Telephone Operator:** Lillian Michell; **Ladies of the Ensemble; Gentlemen of the Ensemble; Lyrics:** IG; **Book:** Guy Bolton & Fred Thompson; **Producers:** Alex. A. Aarons & Vinton Freedley; **Book Staged by:** John Harwood; **Dances & Ensembles staged by:** Sammy Lee; **Settings Designed and Painted by:** John Wenger; Victor Arden & Phil Ohman at the pianos *See:* **B385, B389**

W24c.1925 (Opened Aug. 31): London

Other Selected Performances

W24d.1978 (Apr. 11-June 17): East Haddam, CT; Goodspeed Opera House
CAST: Stationmaster: Peter Boyden; **Rollo Metcalf:** W. M. Hunt; **Sylvia Metcalf (His wife):** Marti Rolph; **Miss Peggy Revere**: Sally O'Donnell; **Hen Kaye:** Jerry Jarrett; **Al Kaye:** Tony Aylward; **Tip-Toes Kaye:** Georgia Engel; **Steve Burton (Sylvia's brother):** Russ Thacker; **Hodge (Attendant at the surf club):** Peter Boyden; **Sam Fisher:** Eric Geier; **Miss Binnie Jones:** Kim Morgan; **Miss Denise Miller:** Carol Wade; **Miss Mitchell:** Dawn Le Ann Herbert; **Miss Wright:** Laura Ackermann; **Miss Hart:** Teri Corcoran; **Mr. Otto:** Brad Witsger; **Mr. Shay:** Michael Hamilton; **Mr. Quinn:** Quin Baird; **Mr. O'Brien:** Jonathan Aronson; **Mr. Walker:** Rick Pessagno; **Second Attendant at Surf Club:** Michael Hamilton **Steward:** Rick Pessàgno; **Detective:** Peter Boyden; **Lyrics:** IG; **Scenery:** John Lee Bailey; **Costumes:** David Toser; **Lighting:** Peter M. Ehrhardt; **Music Research Consultant:** Alfred Simon; **Production Stage Manager:** John J. Bonanni; **Technical Director:** Jim Crossley; **Assistant Musical director:** Russell Warner; **Assistant Choreographer:** Larry McMillian; **Choreography & Musical Staging:** Dan Siretta; **Director:** Sue Lawless; **Producer:** Michael P. Price; Lynn Crigler, **conducting** *See:* **B382, B384, B386, B387, B1502**

W24e.1979 (opened Mar 25): Brooklyn, NY; Helen Carey Playhouse, Brooklyn Academy of Music; **CAST: Stationmaster:** Ronn Robinson; **Rollo Metcalf:** Bob Gunton; **Sylvia Metcalf (his wife):** Jana Robbins; **Hen Kaye:** Haskell Gordon; **Al Kaye:** Michael Hirsch; **Tip Toes Kaye:** Georgia Engel; **Steve Burton:** Russ Thacker; **Hodge:** Ronn Robinson; **Sam Fisher:** Erik Geier; **Miss Binnie Jones:** Sally O'Donnell; **Miss Denise Miller:** Nicole Barth; **Miss Peggy Revere:** Gwen Hillier Lowe;

Miss Lucille Wright: Susan Danielle; **Miss Mitchell:** Dawn Le Ann Herbert; **Miss Hart:** Jill Owens; **Mr. Otto:** Brad Witager; **Mr. Shay:** Bobby Longbottom; **Mr. Quinn:** Rodney Pridgen; **Second Attendant at Surf Club:** Jon Engstrom; **Steward:** David Monzione; **Detective:** Ronn Robinson; **Lyrics:** IG; **Book:** Guy Bolton & Fred Thompson; **Producer for BAM:** Warren Pincus, originally produced Spring 1978 by Goodspeed Opera House, East Haddam, CT; **Executive Producer:** Michael P. Price; **Staging:** Sue

Lawless; **Choreography & musical staging:** Dan Siretta; **Costumes:** David Toser; **Lighting:** Peter M. Ehrhardt; **Music research consultant:** Alfred Simon; **Musical direction:** William Cox *See:* **B383, B385, B388, B390, B391, B392**

W25. *SONG OF THE FLAME,* **A Romantic Opera** (1925)

Performance materials not currently available; Piano/vocal score at Tams-Witmark *See:* **F6.1** (the film)

SONGS

All lyrics by Otto Harbach/Oscar Hammerstein II; Prelude; Far Away; Song of the Flame*; Woman's Work Is Never Done; The Signal (music: G only)*; The Cossack's Love Song (Don't Forget Me)*; Tartar; Vodka*; Midnight Bells (G only)* Dropped: You Are You*
(Songs by Stothart only not listed above)

Premiere

W25a.1925 (Dec. 9): Wilmington, DE (Out-of-town tryout)

W25b.1925 (Dec. 14): NY; 44th Street Theatre; 219 performances

CAST: Konstantin: Edmund Fitzpatrick; **Aniuta:** Tessa Kosta; **Grusha:** Dorothy MacKaye; **Nicholas:** Neil Moore; **Boris:** Bernard Gorcey; **Nadya:** Alice Weaver; **Natasha:** Emily Sherman; **Volodya:** Guy Robertson; **A Dancer:** Leonard St. Leo; **Olga:** Marye Carney; **Alexis:** Paul Wilson; **An Avenger:** George Delaney; Russian Art Singers, Alexander U. Fine, **conducting;** American Ballet; Gentleman of the Ensemble; **Book & Lyrics:** Otto Harbach & Oscar Hammerstein, 2nd; **Music:** Herbert Stothart & GG; **Book staging:** Frank Reicher; **Scenery:** Joseph Urban; **Orchestra arrangement** (according to printed program): Russell Bennett; **Costumes:** Mark Mooring; **Producer:** Arthur Hammerstein; Herbert Stothart, conducting *See:* **B393, B394, B395, B396, B397**

AMERICANA, a revue in two acts, was produced in 1926 (July 26 for 224 perfs.): New York; Belmont Theatre; Book by J. P. McEvoy, but with only one G song: *The Lost Barbershop Chord* (Lyrics by Ira)*

W26. *OH, KAY!* (1926)

Performance materials available from Tams-Witmark; Script at **DLC**; *See:* **B151, B162, D478, D481, D482, D483, D490** (Roxbury)

SONGS:

Dear Little Girl* (First publication upon use in 1968 film titled *Star!*); The Woman's Touch* (first published in the *Oh, Kay!* vocal selections, published by Warner Bros., 1984); Maybe*; Don't Ask!* (in Vocal Selections, WB,

1984); Clap Yo' Hands*; Do-Do-Do*; Bride and Groom*; Someone to Watch Over Me*; Fidgety Feet*; Heaven on Earth (G, music, lyric by IG & Howard Dietz)*; Oh, Kay! (G and IG & Dietz)*

Not used: Show Me the Town*; What's the Use?; When Our Ship Comes Sailing In (IG & Dietz); The Moon Is on the Sea (or titled: The Sun Is on the Sea); Stepping with Baby; Guess Who (Same melody as Don't Ask!); Ain't It Romantic? (Duet intended for Kay & Shorty); Bring on the Ding Dong Dell

Premieres

W26a.1926 (Oct. 18): Philadelpia, PA (out-of town tryout, world premiere)

W26b.1926 (Nov. 8–July 18, followed by tour w/ some cast changes, and a
return to NY for two-week engagement in Jan. 1927): NY; Imperial Theatre; 256 perfs. **CAST: Molly Morse:** Betty Compton; **Peggy:** Janette Gilmore;**The Duke:** Gerald Oliver Smith; **Larry Potter:** Harland Dixon; **Phil Ruxton:** Marion Fairbanks; **Dolly Ruxton:** Madeleine Fairbanks; **"Shorty" McGee:** Victor Moore; **Constance Appleton:** Sascha Beaumont; **Jimmy Winter:** Oscar Shaw; **Kay:** Gertrude Lawrence; **Revenue Officer Jansen:** Harry T. Shannon: **Mae:** Constance Carpenter: **Daisy:** Paulette Winston; **Judge Appleton:** Frank Gardiner; **Ladies of the Ensemble; Gentlemen of the Ensemble**
Book: Guy Bolton & P. G. Wodehouse; **Lyrics:** IG; **Book Staged by:** John Harwood; **Dances & Ensembles Staged by:** Sammy Lee; **Settings Designed & Painted by:** John Wenger; **Producers:** Alex A. Aarons & Vinton Freedley; Victor Arden & Phil Ohman at the pianos; William Daly, **conducting** *See:* **B418, B421, B424, D483**

W26c.1927 (Sept. 21): London; His Majesty's Theatre, 213 performances
CAST: Molly: Rita McLean; **Peggy:** Cecile Maule-Cole; **Dolly Ruxton:** Beth Dodge; **Phillipa Ruxton:** Betty Dodge; **Larry Potter:** Eric Coxon; **The Duke of Datchet:** Claude Hulbert; **Revenue Officer Jansen:** Percy Parsons; **Chauffeur:** Jack Dalmayne; **Jimmy Winter:** Harold French; **Constance Appleton:** April Harmon; **"Shorty" McGee:** John Kirby; **Kay:** Gertrude Lawrence; **Judge Appleton:** Charles Cautley; **Daisy:** Phillis Dawn; **Director:** William Ritter; **Choreographer:** Elsie Neal; Arthur Wood, **conducting**

Other Selected Performances

W26d.1960 (Apr. 16): NY; East 74th St. Theatre; Off-Broadway revival, 89 performances; with songs interpolated from other Gershwin shows & certain new lyrics by P. G. Wodehouse **CAST: The Cotton Tails; Phil:** Rosemarri Sheer; **Izzy:** Linda Lavin; **Polly:** Penny Fuller; **Jean:** Francesca Bell; **Odile:** Lynn Gay Lorino; **Molly:** Sybil Scotford; **Larry Potter:** Eddie Phillips; **Earl of Blandings:** Murray Matheson; **McGee:** Bernie West; **Chauffeur:** James Sullivan; **Jimmy Winters:** David Daniels; **Constance:** Edith Bell; **Revenue officer:** Mike Mazurki; **Kay:** Marti Stevens; **Judge Appleton:** Joseph Macaulay; **Director:** Bertram Yarborough; **Musical & Dance numbers by:** Dania Krupska; **Costumes:** Pearl Somner; **Lighting:** Richard Nelson; **At the twin pianos:** Dorothea Freitag & Reginald

Beane;   **Producers: Musical Direction, orchestrations, & vocal arrangements by:** Freitag

Songs added with lyrics by P. G. Wodehouse: The Twenties are Here to Stay; The Pophams; You'll Still Be There; List of other songs given under the cast album recording, **D483**

W26e. 1960 (Opened Apr. 16, 1960, this version is a continuation of above from May 1960, reflecting cast changes): NY; East 74th St. Playhouse

CAST: Phil: Rosemarri Sheer; **Izzy:** Linda Lavin; **Polly:** Penny Fuller; **Jean:** Francesca Bell; **Odile:** Lynn Gay Lorino; **Mollie:** Sybil Scotford; **Larry Potter:** Eddie Philips; **Earle of Blandings:** Murray Matheson; **McGee:** Bernie West; **Chauffeur:** James Sullivan; **Jimmy Winters:** David Daniels; **Constance:** Edith Bell; **Revenue Officer:** Mike Mazurki; **Kay:** Marti Stevens; **Judge Appleton:** Len Mence; **Asst. Revenue Officer:** James Sullivan; **Choreography:** Dania Krupska; Dorothea Freitag, **Musical Direction** *See:* **B419, B421**

W26f. 1978 (opened July 18): Toronto, Canada; Royal Alexandra Theatre;

CAST: Shorty McGee: Jack Weston; **Lady Kay Wellington:** Jane Summerhays; **Jimmy Winter:** David-James Carroll; **Tommy Potter:** Gene Castle; **Constance Washburn:** Marie Cheatham; **Agent Baldwin:** David Cromwell; **Duke of Argylle:** Reno Roop; **Velma Delmar:** Alexandra Korey; **Sen. Washbrook:** Thomas Ruisinger; **Polly & Molly:** Janet & Louise Arters;
    Minister & M. C.: Joe Palmieri; **Singers & Dancers:** Barbara Hanks, Holly Jones, Jean McLaughlin, Annette Michelle, Diana Lee Mirras, Dana J. Moore, Terry Reiser, Yveline Semiria, Dorothy Stanley; Roxanna White, Stephen Bray, Jameson Foss, Tom Garrett, Peter Heuchling, Timothy R. Kratoville, Michael Lichtefeld, Dick Lumbard, Bob Morrisey, Richard Parrot, Danny Robins, J. Thomas Smith, Thomas J. Stanton; Linda Kinnaman, Bob Heath; **Producer:** Cyma Rubin; **Book:** Guy Bolton & P. G. Wodehouse, rev. by Thomas Meehan; **Lyrics:** IG; **Staging & Choreography:** Donald Saddler; **Associate Choreography:** Mercedes Ellington; **Scenery & Costumes:** Raoul Pene DuBois; **Lighting:** Beverly Emmons; **Sound:** Richard Fitzgerald; **Dance Music Arrangements:** Wally Harper; **Orchestrations:** Bill Byers; **Vocal Arrangements:** William Elliott *See:* **B417**

W26g. 1989 (Sept. 27 through Dec. 23): East Haddam, CT; Goodspeed Opera House; **CAST, in order of appearance:** [All black performers], **Duke:** Stanley Wayne Mathis; **Larry Potter:** Marion J. Caffey; **Jimmy Winters:** Ron Richardson; **Constance DuGrass:** Brenda Pressley; **Shorty:** Helmar Augustus Cooper; **Kay Jones (Ladie Katy):** Pamela Isaacs; **Janson:** Mark Kenneth Smaltz; **Reverend DuGrass:** Alexander Barton; **Dolly:** Lynn Sterling; **Phil:** Denise Heard; **Jill:** Lynise Heard; **Nightclub Performers, Bootlegger, and Others:** Tracey M. Bass, Keith Robert Bennett, Yvette Curtis, Denise Heard, Lynise Heard, Larry Johnson, Dexter Jones, Beth Lane, Sharon Moore, Ken Leigh Rogers, Lynn Sterling, & Horace Turnbull; **Orchestra: Woodwinds:** Michael Schuster, Elizabeth Smith, John Pytel; **Trumpet:** Nancy Brown; **Trombone:** Steve Jackson; **Banjo/Guitar:** Susan Burkhart; **Percussion:** Eugene Bozzi; **Violin:** Perry Eliot; **Bass:** Roy Wiseman; **Original book by:** Guy Bolton & P. G. Wodehouse; **Concept:**

Dan Siretta; **Adaptation by:** James Racheff; **Scenery designed by:** Kenneth Foy; **Costumes designed by:** Judy Dearing; **Lighting design:** Craig Miller; **Artistic consultant:** Sheldon Epps; **Assistant choreo-grapher:** Keith Savage; **Dance arrangements & orchestrations:** Donald W. Johnston; **Additional orchestrations by:** Larry Moore & Danny Troob; **Technical director:** John Hugh Minor; **Resident dramaturg:** Tommy Krasker; **Associate artistic director:** Dan Siretta; **Associate producer:** Sue Frost; **Casting director:** Warren Pincus; **Choreography & musical staging:** Dan Siretta; **Directed by:** Martin Conner; **Produced for the Goodspeed Opera House by:** Michael P. Price, co-produced with the Birmingham Theatre, Birmingham, Michigan, Jay Brooks, **Executive producer**; **Musical direction:** David Evans *See:* **B420, B422**

W26h. 1990 (Previews beginning Sept. 29, opening October 25): NY; Richard Rodgers Theatre (46th St. Theatre); David Merrick's production (which did not survive on Broadway)

CAST: Bill Lyles: Gregg Burge; **Dolly Greene:** Kyme; **Duke:** Stanley Wayne Mathis; **Nick and Sam:** David Preston Sharp; **Joe:** Fracaswell Hyman; **Walter and Jake:** Frantz Hall; **Larry Potter:** Kevin Ramsey; **Shorty:** Helmar Augustus Cooper; **B. J.:** Keith Robert Bennett; **Floyd:** Frederick J. Boothe; **Zeke:** Ken Roberson; **Jimmy Winter:** Brian Mitchell; **Constance DuGrasse:** Tamara Tunie Bouquett; **Chauffeur:** Byron Easley; **Kay Jones:** Angela Teek; **Janson:** Mark Kenneth Smaltz; **Rev. Alphonse DuGrasse:** Alexander Barton

Direction & Choreography: Dan Siretta; **Adaption by:** James Racheff; **Concept by:** Mr. Siretta; **Scenery:** Kenneth Foy; **Costumes:** Theoni V. Aldredge; **Lighting:** Craig Miller; **Musical director, vocal & additional dance arrangements:** Tom Fay; **Ochestrations:** Arnold Goland; **Dance arrangements:** Donald Johnston; **Sound:** Jan Nebozenko; **Hair design:** Robert DiNiro; **Assistant choreographer:** Ken Leigh Rogers; **Executive Producer:** Natalie Lloyd; **Associate Producer:** Leo K. Cohen; **Presented by:** David Merrick *See:* **B423, B425, B426, B428, B429**

W27. *STRIKE UP THE BAND* (1927 version)

A script (without lyrics) is at **NN-L**, cat. no. NCOF. Newly prepared "authentic" vocal score published 1999 by Warner Bros. *See also:* **B384, D564**

SONGS

Fletcher's American Cheese Choral Society; 17 & 21*; A Typical Self-made American; Meadow Serenade; The Unofficial Spokesman; Patriotic Rally* in 1930 pa./vocal score only; The Man I Love (The Girl I Love)*, composed earlier for *Lady, Be Good!*, later to be used for *Rosalie,* but dropped from both shows; Yankee Doodle Rhythm*; Strike Up the Band!*; Oh, This Is Such a Lovely War (The Knitting Song); Hoping That Someday You'd Care; Military Dancing Dancing Drill*; How About a Man Like Me?; Homeward Bound; The War That Ended War; Sing Carry On!

Not used: Bring On the Ding Dong Dell (Revision of a song orig. written for *Oh, Kay!*)

Premieres

W27a. 1927 (Aug. 29): Long Branch, NJ; Broadway Theater (world premiere)

W27b. 1927 (Sept. 2): Philadephia, PA; Shubert Theater **CAST:** Vivian
Hart, Roger Pryor, Edna May Over, Morton Downey, Lew Hearn, Jimmy
Savo; **Book by** George S. Kaufman; R. H. Burnside, **Director; Produced by**
Edgar Selwyn; William Daly, **conducting**
The 1927 version of the show closed out-of-town, not reaching Broadway until revised in 1930
Piano/vocal score of 1927 version reconstructed by Eric Salzman, copy at **DLC**, 312 leaves
Piano/vocal score from 1930 version was published

Other Selected Performances

1927 version:

W27c. 1984 (June 27 to July 29): Philadelphia, PA; Walnut Street Theatre,
American Music Theater Festival; **Reconstructed & adapted by:** Eric
Salzman; **Orchestrations, Dance & Vocal arrangements prepared under
the supervision of:** Maurice Peress; **CAST: George Spelvin:** Bill Irwin;
Timothy Harper: Kevin Daly; **Sloane:** Robert Schlee; **Horace J. Fletcher:**
David Sabin; **Mrs. Draper:** Marge Redmond; **Anne Draper:** Kim Criswell;
Joan Fletcher: Katherine Buffaloe; **Jim Townsend:** David Carroll; **Colonel
Holmes:** Robert Trebor; **Scenery & Costume design:** Ronald Chase

Lighting design: Peter Kaczorowski; **Production conceived by:** Frank
Corsaro & Ronald Chase; **Choreography:** Randolyn Zinn; **Directed by:**
Frank Corsaro; **Producing Director:** Marjorie Samoff; **Artistic Director:**
Eric Salzman; Maurice Peress, **Musical Director & Conductor** *See:*
B398, B401, B402, B406

W27d. 1988 (Aug. 4-14): Pasadena, CA; Pasadena Civic Auditorium
CAST: Timothy Harper: Kirby Ward; **Edgar Sloane:** Donald Most;
Horace J. Fletcher: Tom Bosley; **George Spelvin:** Bobby Herbeck; **Mrs.
Draper:** Faye DeWitt; **Anne Draper:** Beverly Ward; **Joan Fletcher:** Roxann
Parker; **Jim Townsend:** Michael Magnusen; **Colonel Holmes:** Avery
Schreiber
Original Orchestrations: William Daly; **Additional Orchestrations:** Larry
Moore; **Script and Score revised by:** Tommy Krasker; **Drama Director:**
Gary Davis; **Choreographer:** Randy Skinner; Steven Smith, **Music Director**
See: **B399, B404, B405, B1541**

This version also played the Orange County Performing Arts Center, Aug. 18-24 and
Dorothy Chandler Pavilion in L. A., Aug. 26–Sept. 11.

W27e. 1995 (Prior to Dec. 17, 1995, and running through that date);
East Haddam, CT; Goodspeed Opera House
CAST: Ron Holgate; Emily Loesser; Jason Danieley, and others; **Director:**
Charles Repole *See:* **B403**

W27f. 1998 (Sept. 18): London; Barbican Center

W28. *FUNNY FACE* (Original title: *Smarty*] (1927)

Tams-Witmark has the original book & pa./vocal score, as well as an orchestration. Persons interested in performing the work should write to them regarding availability. *See:* **F23**

SONGS

Birthday Party; Once; Funny Face*; High Hat*; 'S Wonderful!*; Let's Kiss and Make Up*; In the Swim (not published at time of original show, later published as part of One and Only selections, Warner, 1983); He Loves and She Loves*; Tell the Doc*(published in a vocal arr. only); My One and Only*; Sing a Little Song: The Babbitt and the Bromide*; Look at the Damn Thing Now (added for 1928 London version)

Dropped during out-of-New York tryout: Your Eyes! Your Smile! (Those Eyes); When You're Single; The World Is Mine*; How Long Has This Been Going On?*; Aviator (We're All A-Worry, All Agog); The Finest of the Finest; Dancing Hour; Dance Alone with You (Why Does Everybody Have to Cut In?)*; Astaire's Nut Dance

Dropped in NY: Blue Hullaballoo

Not used: Come Along, Let's Gamble; Acrobats; Bluebeard; Invalid Entrance

Premieres

W28a. 1927 (Oct.11): Philadelphia, PA (World premiere, out-of-town tryout) Sam S. Shubert Theatre [under the title *Smarty*]

W28b. 1927 (Nov 14): Wilmington, DE (out-of-town tryout)

W28c. 1927 (Nov 22): NY; Alvin Theatre (First show in that theatre); 244 perfs. **CAST: Jimmy Reeve:** Fred Astaire; **"Frankie":** Adele Astaire; **"Dugsie" Gibbs:** William Kent; **Herbert:** Victor Moore; **Peter Thurston:** Allen Kearns; **June:** Gertrude McDonald; **Dora:** Betty Compton; Phil Ohman & Victor Arden at the pianos; **Ritz Quartette:** Ritz Quartette; **Book:** Fred Thompson & Paul Gerard Smith; **Lyrics:** IG; **Director:** Edgar MacGregor; **Dances Staged by:** Bobby Connolly; **Producers:** Alex. A. Aarons & Vinton Freedley; Alfred Newman, **conducting** (First performance in NY) *See:* **B322, B326**

W28d. 1928 (Nov. 8): London; Princes Theater; 263 performances

CAST: Dora Wynne: Rita Page; **June Wynne:** Renée Gadd; **Dugale Gibbs:** Leslie Hensen; **Jimmy Reeve:** Fred Astaire; **"Frankie:"**Adele Astaire; **Crooks:** JohnMcNally & Sidney Howard; **Presentors**: Alfred Butt & Lee Ephraim & Alex A. Aarons & Vinton Freedley; **Dances & Ensembles created by** Robert Connolly; **Producer:** Felix Edwardes *See:* **B323**

Other Selected Performances

W28e. 1981 (June 17–Sept. 12): East Haddam, CT; Goodspeed Opera House;
CAST: Dora: Carolyn Casanave; **Margie:** Eva Grant; **Peaches:** Mollie Smith; **Georgia:** Kitty Kuhn; **Lucy:** Deirdre Kane; **Blossom:** Karen Ziemba; **Squiffy:** Meredith Murray; **June:** Lora Jeanne Martens; **Frankie Reeve:** Karen Jablons; **Dougsie Gibbs:** Mark Frawley; **Jimmy Reeve:** James J. Mellon; **Police Sergeant:** Frank Kosik; **Stretcher Bearers:** David Brownlee, Richard Dodd; **Chester:** Lou Criscuolo; **Herbert:** Dennis Warning; **Peter Thurston:** Joel Stedman; **Binky Davis:** Scott Evans; **Hotel Manager:** Dennis Angulo; **Bellhop:** Scott Evans; **Boyfriends:** Dennis Angulo, David Brownlee, Richard Dodd, Scott Evans, Erik Geier, Frank Kosik, Wade Laboissonniere, Gary Sullivan
Lyrics: IG; **Book:** Fred Thompson & Paul Gerard Uhry; **Adapted by:** Alfred Uhry; **Scenery & Lighting:** Michael J. Hotopp & Paul DePass; **Costumes:** David Toser; **Dance Arrangements & Additional Orchestrations:** Russell Warner; **Production Stage Manager:** John J. Bonanni; **Technical Director:** Jim Crossley; **Assistant Choreographer:** Carol Marik; **Associate Producer:** Warren Pincus; **Music Research Consultant:** Alfred Simon; **Choreography & Musical Staging:** Dan Siretta; **Director:** Will Mackenzie; **Producer:** Michael P. Price; Lynn Crigler, **conducting**
See: **B324, B325**

W29.   *ROSALIE* (1927–28)

Tams-Witmark has an approximate version for rental
Music by GG and Sigmund Romberg; Lyrics by IG and P. G. Wodehouse; Book by William Anthony McGuire and Guy Bolton. Produced by Florenz Ziegfeld,
CAST: Marilyn Miller, Jack Donahue, Gladys Glad, Frank Morgan, Bobbe Arnst, Oliver McLennan, Margaret Dale. **Conducted by** Oscar Bradley

See: **B162, B421** NOTE: Some music by Sigmund Romberg for songs and ballet

SONGS (Only George Gershwin music listed here; lyric writers given in parentheses)

Show Me the Town (Gershwins only, orchestration by Spialek)*; Say So! (IG & Wodehouse)*; Let Me Be a Friend to You (IG); Oh Gee! Oh Joy! (IG & Wodehouse)*; New York Serenade (IG, orchestration by DePackh); Ev'rybody Knows I Love Somebody (Gershwin; same melody as Dance Alone with You [Funny Face]); Follow the Drum (Gershwin); How Long Has This Been Going On?*; Setting-up Exercises (instrumental, orchestration by W. Daly, published separately as "Merry Andrew")*

Dropped before the NY opening: Rosalie (Gershwin)*; Beautiful Gypsy (Gershwin; same melody as Wait a Bit, Susie)*; Yankee Doodle Rhythm (IG)*; When Cadets Parade (IG); I Forgot What I Started to Say (IG); The Man I Love (IG)

Not used: You Know How It Is (Wodehouse & IG); True to Them All; When the Right One Comes Along; Under the Furlough Moon (GG & Romberg/IG); At the Ex-King's Club

Premieres

W29a. 1927 (Dec. 5): Boston; World premiere, out-of-town tryout

W29b. 1928 (Jan. 10): NY; New Amsterdam Theatre; 327 perfs. **CAST:**
Carl Rabisco: Halford Young; **Michael O'Brien:** Clarence Oliver; **Mary O'Brien:** Bobbe Arnst; **Prince Rabisco,** Chancellor of Romanza: A. P. Kaye; **His Royal Highness King Cyril:** Frank Morgan; **Her Royal Highness Queen:** Margaret Dale; **Ladies in Waiting: Rosita:** Claudia Dell, **Marcia:** Gladys Glad, **Alla:** Jeanne Audree; **Xenia:** Hazel Forbes; **Mariza:** Yvonne Gray; **Sister Angelica:** Katherine Burke; **Bill Delroy,** of the West Point Corps: Jack Donahue; **Lt. Richard Fay, U.S.A:** Oliver McLennan; **Princess Rosalie:** Marilyn Miller; **Marinna**: Antonina Lalaew; **Steward,** on the S. S. Isle de France: Charles Gotthold; **Corps Lieutenant:** Jack Bruns; **Superintendent of West Point:** Charles Gotthold; **Captain Banner:** Clay Clement; **The Ex-King of Portugal:** Charles Davis; **Ex-King of Bulgaria**: Clarence De Silva; **Ex-King of Prussia:** Henri Jackin; **Ex-King of Greece:** Mark Shull; **Ex-King of Bavaria:** Harry Donaghy; **Ex-Sultan of Turkey:** Edgar Welch; Eight Estelle Liebling Singers;
Music: Sigmund Romberg & GG; **Lyrics:** IG & P. G. Wodehouse; **Book:** William Anthony McGuire & Guy Bolton; **Dances:** Seymour Felix; **Scenes:** Joseph Urban; **Dialogue Staged by:** Wm. Anthony McGuire; **Costumes designed by:** John W. Harkrider; **Producer:** Florenz Ziegfeld; **Orchestrations:** Emil Gerstenberger, Bill Daly, & Maurice DePakch [sp?]; **Orchestra Vocal Arrangements:** Arthur Johnson; Oscar Bradley, conducting *See* **B884.2**

Other Selected Performances

W29c. 1957 (June 25): NY, Wollman Memorial Rink, Central Park
CAST: Captain Banner: Harold Gary; **Corporal Applewaite:** Robert Shawley; **The King:** Henny Youngman; **Captain Rabisco:** Chet O'Brien; **Mary O'Brien**: Helen Wood; **Mr. O'Brien:** Lou Nova; **The Queen:** Ruth McDevitt; **Bill Delroy:** Kelly Brown; **Princess Rosalie:** Mimi Benzel; **Dick Fray:** David Brooks; **Senator Muggs:** Jack Davis; **Music:** Sigmund Romberg & GG; **Lyrics:** IG & P. G. Wodehouse; **Book:** William Anthony McGuire & Guy Bolton, adapted by Stella Unger; **Additional songs**: Cole Porter; **Director:** Felix Brentano; **Choreography:** Geoffrey Holder; **Costumes & Scenary:** Raoul Pene du Bois; **Producers:** Michael Grace & Chris Anderson; Arthur Lief, conducting *See*: **B884.1**

W29d. 1983 (Apr. 18): NY; Town Hall, The New Amsterdam Theatre Company, a concert version **CAST: Captain Carl Rabisco:** Ed Dixon; **Mary O'Brien:** Alexandra Korey; **King of Romanza:** George S. Irving; **Queen of Romanza:** Paula Laurence; **Bill Delroy:** Russ Thacker; **Dick Fay:** Richard Muenz; **Princess Rosalie:** Marianne Tatum; **Music:** GG & Sigmund Romberg; **Lyrics:** IG & P. G. Wodehouse; **Book:** Wm. Anthony McGuire & Guy Bolton; **Hosted by:** Dina Merrill & Cliff Robertson; **Stage Direction:** Jason Buzas; The New York City Gay Men's Chorus Chamber Choir; The New Amsterdam Theatre Company Orchestra and

Women's chorus; Evans Haile, **conducting**

W30.   *TREASURE GIRL* (1928)
Performance materials not currently available
Copies of the original script with all lyrics are at DLC & NN-L

SONGS

Skull and Bones; I've Got a Crush on You, not published until included in
1930 version of *Strike Up the Band**; According to Mr. Grimes; Place in the
Country*; K-ra-zy for You*; I Don't Think I'll Fall in Love Today*; Got a
Rainbow*; Feeling I'm Falling*; Treasure Island; What Causes That?; What
are We Here For?*; Where's the Boy? Here's the Girl!*; Oh, So Nice*

Dropped before the NY opening: Dead Men Tell No Tales; This Particular Party; Goodbye
to the Old Love, Hello to the New; A-Hunting We Will Go; I Want to Marry a Marionette

Premieres

W30a. 1928 (Nov. 8): NY; Alvin Theatre; 68 perfs. **CAST:**
Mary Grimes: Virginia Franck; **Kitty:** Peggy O'Neill; **"Nat" McNally:**
Clifton Webb; **Polly Tees:** Mary Hay; **Mortimer Grimes:** Ferris Hartman;
Neil Forrester: Paul Frawley; **Footman:** Frank G. Bond; **Larry Hopkins:**
Walter Catlett; **Ann Wainwright:** Gertrude Lawrence; **Bunce:** Norman
Curtis; **Postman:** Edwin Preble; **"Slug" Bullard:** Stephen Francis; **First
Mate:** John Dunsmure; Ladies of the Ensemble; Gentlemen of the Ensemble;
Producers: Alex. A. Aarons & Vinton Freedley; **Book:** Fred Thompson and
Vincent Lawrence; **Lyrics:** IG; **Book Staged by:** Bertram Harrison; **Dances
& Ensembles:** Bobby Connolly; **Costumes designed by:** Kiviette; **Settings:**
Joseph Urban; Victor Arden & Paul Ohman at the pianos; Alfred Newman,
conducting See: **B416**

W31.   *SHOW GIRL* (1929)
Performance materials not currently available

SONGS

All lyrics by IG & Gus Kahn, unless otherwise indicated. Happy Birthday; My
Sunday Fella (orchestration: DePackh); How Could I Forget; Lolita, My
Love; Do What You Do!*; One Man; So Are You! (The Rose is Red—
Violets are Blue)*; I Must Be Home by Twelve O'Clock*; Harlem
Serenade*; Blues Ballet (from AiP), instrumental. According to
Krasker/Kimball, the score and parts for this version are missing. See: **B291**,
p. 139; Home Blues; Follow the Minstrel Band; Liza (All the Clouds'll Roll
Away)*

Dropped before NY: Feeling Sentimental*; Tonight's the Night

Unused: At Mrs. Simpkin's Finishing School; Adored One; I Just Looked at You (Eventually
this became Blah, Blah, Blah, and was published under that title; I'm Just a Bundle of
Sunshine; Minstrel Show; Somebody Stole My Heart Away; Someone's Always Calling a

Rehearsal; I'm Out for No Good Reason Tonight; Home Lovin' Gal (Man)

Premieres

W31a. 1929 (June 24): Boston; World premiere and out-of-town tryout

W31b. 1929 (July 2): NY; Ziegfeld Theater; 111 performances **CAST**:
Ruby Keeler; Eddie Foy, Jr.; Frank McHugh; Jimmy Durante; Lou Clayton;
Eddie Jackson; Barbara Newberry; Harriet Hoctor; **Duke Ellington and
his Orchestra**; William Daly, **conducting**; **Book by** William Anthony
McGuire and J. P. McEvoy; **Director:** William A. McGuire; **Produced
by** Florenz Ziegfeld, Jr.(NY premiere) *See:* **B376, B379, B380**

W32. *STRIKE UP THE BAND* (Second version, 1930)

Typescript of the libretto for the 1930 version at the Times Square Theatre in
NY, prepared by Rialto Service Bureau, NY, at **NN-L** includes property plot,
chorus roster, and other notes inserted. Piano/vocal score of second, 1930 version,
published by New World, 1930, at **NN-L & DLC**. Newly prepared "authentic"
vocal score published 1999 by Warner Bros. *See:* **D564 , B1509**

SONGS (+ indicates published in piano/vocal score)
Fletcher's American Chocolate Choral Society Workers (Fletcher's American
Cheese Choral Society in 1927 show)+; I Mean To Say*; A Typical Self-
Made American+; Soon* +; The Unofficial Spokesman+; Patriotic Rally+; If
I Became the President+; Hangin' Around with You* +; He Knows Milk+;
Strike Up the Band!* +; In the Rattle of the Battle+; Military Dancing Drill*
+; Mademoiselle in New Rochelle* +; I've Got a Crush on You* +; How
About a Boy Like Me?+; Official Résumé; Ring a Ding a Ding Dong Dell+;
I   Want to be a War Bride*; A Man of High Degree+; Three Cheers for the
Union!+; This Could Go on for Years+; Official Résumé: First There Was
Fletcher+; Soldiers' March+

Not used: There Was Never Such a Charming War; Thanks to You

Premieres

W32a. 1929 (Dec. 25, 1929): Boston premiere and tryout *See:* **B414**

W32b. 1930 (Jan. 14): NY; Times Square Theatre; 191 perfs. **CAST:**
In the Story: Timothy Harper: Gordon Smith; **Richard K. Sloane:**
Robert Bentley; **Horace J. Fletcher:** Dudley Clements; **Myra Meade:**
Ethel Kenyon; **Mrs. Grace Draper:** Blanche Ring; **Anne Draper:** Doris
Carson; **Joan Fletcher:** Margaret Schilling; **Jim Townsend:** Jerry Goff;
Two Men About Town: Bobby Clark & Paul McCullough; **Doctor:**
Maurice LaPue; **In the Dream: Doris Dumme:** Marion Miller; **Suzette:**
Ethel Britton; **Soisette:** Virginia Barnes; **Sergeant Doax:** Walter Fairmont;
Premiere Danseuse: Joyce Coles; **Book:** Morrie Ryskind, based on a
libretto by George S. Kaufman, **Lyrics:** IG; **Staging:** Alexander Leftwich;
Dances & Ensembles: George Hale; **Settings:** Raymond Sovey; **Director**

      & Producer: Edgar Selwyn; Red Nichols and His Orchestra; Hilding Anderson, **conducting** *See*: **B407, B409, B410, B411, B413, B32b**

Toddlin' Along (same melody as World Is Mine) interpolated into *Nine-Fifteen Revue*

W33. *GIRL CRAZY* (1930)
      Piano/vocal score at **NN, DLC**, published by New World, NY, 1954
Current availability of performance materials: Available, contact Tams-Witmark
See: **B332, B384, B1838, B1509, B2164, F8, F15, F27, W50** (*Crazy for You*)

      SONGS (+Indicates songs published in the pa./vocal score)

      Bidin' My Time* +; The Lonesome Cowboy+; Could You Use Me?* +; Broncho Busters+; Barbary Coast+; Embraceable You* +; Goldfarb! That's I'm+; Sam and Delilah* +; I Got Rhythm* +; Land of the Gay Caballero+; But Not for Me* +; Mexican Dance (instrumental); Treat Me Rough (First published after use in 1943 motion picture version)* +; Boy! What Love Has Done to Me!* +; When It's Cactus Time in Arizona+; You've Got What Gets Me (Written for 1932 motion picture version)*

Dropped before NY: You Can't Unscramble Scrambled Eggs; The Gambler of the West; And I Have You; Not used: Something Peculiar (IG & Lou Paley); Are You Dancing?

    Premieres

W33a. 1930 (Sept. 29): Philadelphia (World premiere & tryout)

W33b. 1930 (Oct. 14): NY; Alvin Theatre; 272 performances **CAST:**
      Danny Churchill: Allen Kearns; **Molly Gray:** Ginger Rogers; **Pete:** Clyde Veaux; **Lank Sanders:** Carlton Macy; **Gieber Goldfarb:** Willie Howard; **Flora James:** Eunice Healy; **Patsy West:** Peggy O'Connor; **Kate Fothergill:** Ethel Merman; **Slick Fothergill:** William Kent; **Sam Mason:** Donald Foster; **Tess Parker:** Olive Brady; **Jake Howell:** Lew Parker; **Eagle Rock:** Chief Rivers; **Hotel Proprietor:** Jack Classon; **Lariat Joe:** Starr Jones; **The Foursome:** Marshall Smith, Ray Johnson, Del Porter, & Dwight Snyder; **Staging:** Alexander Leftwich; **Dances & Ensembles:** George Hale; **Costumes:** Kiviette; **Dancers:** Antonio & Renee Demarco; **Book:** Guy Bolton & John McGowan; **Lyrics:** IG; **Producers:** Alex Aarons & Vinton Freedley; "Red" Nichols and his Orchestra (Benny Goodman, Glenn Miller, Jimmy Dorsey, Jack Teagarden, Gene Krupa, Al Siegel at the piano [later, Roger Edens]; GG, **conducting** on opening night *See*: **B331, B334, B335, B337, B342, B343, B349**

    Other Selected Performances

W33c. 1971 (July 19-Aug. 14): East Haddam, CT; Goodspeed Opera House
      CAST: Jake: Ray Baron; **Joe:** George Connolly; **Jack:** Kevin Daly; **Pete:** Harold Lubin; **Danny:** Martin Ross; **Gieber Goldfarb:** Bill McCutcheon; **Lank:** Richard Bonelle; **Molly Gray:** Eileen Rogosin; **Tess:** Ann Hodapp; **Flora:** Sherry Lynn Diamant; **Brenda:** Carol Culver; **Barbara:** Cynthia

Wells; **Bette:** Sheila Bowe; **Patsy:** Mary Jo Catlett; **Kate:** Janie Sell;
Slick: John Remme; **Sam:** Noel Craig; **Señora Gracia Maria Consuelo
Pearl:** Ida Mae McKenzie; **Sheriff:** Kevin Daly; **Lyrics:** IG; **Book:** Guy
Bolton & John McGowan; **Costumes:** David Toser; **Scenic production:**
Raymond T. Kurdt; **Production manager:** A. Brian Liddicoat;
Choreographer: Voight Kempson; **Lighting:** Peter M. Ehrhardt;
Technical director: Peege Stevens; **Director:** William Gile; **Producer:**
Michael P. Price; Lynn Crigler, **conducting**

W34. *OF THEE I SING* (1931)

Performance materials available from Samuel French
(Abbreviation: OTIS)
Lyrics by IG; book by George S. Kaufman and Morrie Ryskind. **Original
Orchestrations:** Robert Russell Bennett & William Daly; **Director:**
Kaufmann; **Produced by** Sam H. Harris

Piano/vocal score and an acting edition of the libretto have been available
from The **Drama Book Shop**, 723 Seventh Avenue (at 48th Street, 2nd
Floor), NY 10019, Phone 212-944-0595. Published version of script in
MANTLE, R. B., and **J. GASSNER, eds.,** *A Treasury of the Theatre*, NY:
1935, pp. 29-80; also in *Famous Plays of 1933*, London, 1933, pp. 581-702;
and *Ten Great Musicals of the American Theatre*, ed. by Stanley Richards.
Radnor, PA: Chilton, 1973, pp. 1-74, & published separately
See: **B151, B159, B162, B248, B384, B432, B468, B472, w36B1509, B1548,
B1659, B1665, B1838, B2170, W2173**

SONGS (+Indicates songs published in pa./vocal score)

Wintergreen for President+; Who Is the Lucky Girl to Be?+; The Dimple on
My Knee+; Because, Because* +; Never Was There a Girl so Fair+; Some
Girls Can Bake a Pie (Corn Muffins)+; Love Is Sweeping the Country* +; Of
Thee I Sing * +; Hello, Good Morning+; Who Cares?* +; The Illegitimate
Daughter* +; The Senator from Minnesota+; The Senate (Includes Jilted,
Jilted!)+; Prosperity Is Just Around the Corner+; Trumpeter, Blow Your
Golden Horn!+; On That Matter No One Budges **(**Finale ultimo)**+; Here's a
Kiss for Cinderella+; I Was the Most Beautiful Blossom+; Garçon, S'il Vous
Plait+; I'm About to Be a Mother

Not used: Call Me Whate'er You Will

Premieres

W34a. 1931 (Dec. 8): Boston (World premiere, out-of-town tryout) *See:* **B469, B477**

W34b. 1931 (Dec. 26): NY; Music Box; 441 perfs. **CAST: Louis Lippman:**
Sam Mann; **Francis X. Gilhooley:** Harold Moffet; **Maid:** Vivian
Barry; **Matthew Arnold Fulton:** Dudley Clements; Senator Robert E.
Lyons: George E. Mack; **Senator Carver Jones:** Edward H. Robins;
Alexander Throttlebottom: Victor Moore; **John P. Wintergreen:** William
Gaxton; **Sam Jenkins:** George Murphy; **Diana Devereaux:** Grace Brinkley;

Mary Turner: Lois Moran; **Miss Benson:** June O'Dea; **Vladimir Vidovitch:** Tom Draak; **Yussef Yussevitch:** Sulo Hevonpaa; **The Chief Justice:** Ralph Riggs; **Scrubwoman:** Leslie Bingham; **The French Ambassador:** Florenz Ames; **Senate Clerk:** Martin Leroy; **Guide:** Ralph Riggs; **Photographers, Policemen, Supreme Court Justices, Secretaries, Sight-seers, Newspapermen, Senators, Flunkeys, Guests,** etc.; **Orchestrations:** Robert Russell Bennett, William Daly, & GG; **Book:** George S. Kaufman & Morrie Ryskind; **Lyrics:** IG; **Book staged by:** George S. Kaufman; **Singing & Dancing Ensembles staged by:** Georgie Hale; **Settings:** Jo Mielziner; **Producer:** Sam H. Harris; The Jack Linton Band; **Orchestra under the direction of:** Eugene Fuerst (First performance in NY); **Musical Direction:** Charles Previn *See:* **B430, B431, B433, B434, B437, B438, B453, B454, B456, B458, B471, B473, B1665, B1874**

W34c. 1987 (Mar. 18 & ending Mar. 29, several performances on odd nights): Brooklyn, NY; Brooklyn Academy of Music, Opera House **CAST**: **Alexander Throttlebottom:** Jack Gilford; **John P. Wintergreen:** Larry Kert; **Mary Turner:** Maureen McGovern; **Diana Devereaux:** Paige O'Hara; **French Ambassador:** Jack Dabdoub; **Sam Jenkins & Clerk:** George Dvorsky; **Miss Benson & Mrs. Fulton:** Louise Edeiken; **Louis Lippman:** Merwin Goldsmith; **Senator Robert E. Lyons:** Walter Hook; **Francis X. Gilhooley:** Frank Kopyc; **The Chief Justice:** Casper Roos; **Matthew Arnold Fulton:** Raymond Thorne; **Senator Carver Jones:** Mark Zimmerman; **Wives of the Committee members, Supreme Court Justices, Paraders, Flunkeys, Radicals, Salesgirls, Customers, Members of the Union League Club, Soldiers, Sailors, League of Nations, etc.:** New York Choral Artists; **Orchestrations** by Robert Russell Bennett, William Daly, and George Gershwin; **Performing editions** reconstructed by John McGlinn [through the generosity of Mrs. Ira Gershwin]; **Scenic design:** Eduardo Sicangco; **Lighting design:** Jeff Davis; **Sound design:** Otts Munderloh; Orchestra of St. Luke's (Michael Feldman, Artistic Director) with New York Choral Artists (Joseph Flummerfelt, Director); Michael Tilson Thomas, **conducting** these concert presentations (With a performance of *Let 'Em Eat Cake* the same evenings, constitutes a world premiere of these versions) *See:* **B499, B500, B501, B502, B503, B504, B505, B1713, D467**

Other Selected Performances

W34d. 1937 (Aug. 10-17): Jones Beach, Long Island, NY; Marine Stage at Zach's Bay; **An abridged version; CAST: Wintergreen:** John Cherry; **Alexander Throttlebottom:** Jack Sheehan; **Diana Devereaux:** Vivienne Segal; **Mary Turner:** Diana Gaylen; **Presented by Shubert Productions,** Fortune Gallo, **Producer**
See: **B481, B919, B923, B1709**

W34e. 1952 (opening night: May 5): NY; Ziegfeld Theatre
CAST: Francis X. Gilhooley: J. Pat O'Malley; **Louis Lippman:** Robert F. Simon; **Chambermaid:** Louise Carlyle; **Matthew Arnold Fulton:** Loring Smith; **Senator Carver Jones:** Howard Freeman; **Senator Robert E. Lyons:** Donald Foster; **Alexander Throttlebottom:** Paul Hartman; **John P.**

Wintergreen: Jack Carson; **Beauty Contestant**: Jean Bartel; **Mary Turner**: Betty Oakes; **Sam Jenkins**: Jonathan Lucas; **Diana Devereaux**: Lenore Lonergan; **Emily Benson**:Joan Mann; **Announcer**: Mort Marshall; **Vladimir Vidovitch**: Abe Stein; **Yussef Yussevitch**: Bob Oran; **The Chief Justice**: Jack Whiting; **Guide**: Jack Whiting; **A Sightseer**: Parker Wilson; **The French Ambassador**: Florenz Ames; **Chief Senate Clerk**: Mort Marshall; **Senator from Massachusetts**: Jack Whiting; **Attache**: Tom Wells; **Chief Flunkey**: Al McGranary; **Flunkies**: William Krach, Michael King, Ken Ayers; **Ensemble**; **Director**: George S. Kaufman; **Musical Numbers and Ensembles staged by**: Jack Donohue; **Musical Director**: Maurice Levine; **Orchestrations**: Don Walker; **Dance Arrangements**: David Baker *See*: **B482, B483, B484, B485, B486, B487, B489, B491, B492, B493**

W34f. 1965 (twenty-four performances): Dallas, TX; Kalita Humphreys Theatre
See: **B1665**

W34g. 1968: NY; Equity Library Theatre *See*: **B1665**

W34g.1. 1969: NY; New Anderson Theatre
    CAST: Alexander Throttlebottom: Lloyd Hubbard; **John P. Wintergreeen:** Hal Holden; **Diana Devereaux:** Katie Anders; **Mary Turner:** Joy Franz; et al
    Entire Production Directed and Staged by: Marvin Gordon
    See: **B495, B496**

W34h. 1972: NY; CBS Television network; **John P. Wintergreen:** Carroll O'Conner *See*: **B497**

W34i. 1984 (Aug. 16): Hartford, CT; Hartford Stage Company Youth Theater
    CAST: President John Wintergreen: Richard Luciano; **Matthew Fulton:** Warren Boyd; **Vice President Throttlebottom:** Luis Robles; **Diana Devereaux:** Sandra G. Murphy; **Mary:** Karen Sevenoff; **Stage Direction:** Clay Stevenson *See*: **B498**

W34j. 1987 (May): Washington; Opera House, John F. Kennedy Center for the Performing Arts; Brooklyn Academy of Music production of a concert presentation; **CAST: John P. Wintergreen:** Larry Kert; **Alexander Throttlebottom:** Jack Gilford; **MaryTurner:** Maureen McGovern; **Diana Devereaux (OTIS) & Trixie Flynn (*Let 'Em*):** Paige O'Hara; **Kruger (*Let 'Em*):** William Parry; **French Ambassador (OTIS) & General Adam Snookfield (*Let 'Em*):** Alan Kass; **Sam Jenkins & Clerk (OTIS) & Lieutenant (*Let 'Em*):** George Dvorsky; **Louis Lippman:** William McCauley; **John P. Twiddledee (*Let 'Em* only):** Haskell Gordon; **Senator Robert E. Lyons:** Don Wonder; **Francis X. Gilhooey:** Frank Kopyc; **Miss Benson (OTIS only):** Betty Joslyn; **The Chief Justice:** Caspar Roos; **Matthew Arnold Fulton:** Raymond Thorne; **Senator Carver Jones:** Rodne Brown; **Wives of the Committee Members, Supreme Court Justices, Paraders, Flunkeys, Radicals, Salesgirls, Customers, Members of the Union League Club, Soldiers, Sailors, League of Nations, etc.:** Norman Scribner Chorale; *Of Thee I Sing* orchestrations: Robert Russell Bennett,

William Daly, & George Gershwin; *Let 'Em Eat Cake* **orchestrations:** Russell Warner; **Performing Editions reconstructed by** John McGlinn; **Scenic Design**: Eduardo Sicangco; **Lighting Design:** Jeff Davis; **Sound Design:** Otts Munderloh; **Executive Producers**: Harvey Lichtenstein & Morton Gottlieb; **Concert Narration & Direction:** Maurice Levine; The Kennedy Center Opera House Orchestra; Robert Fisher, **Music Director & Conductor**

W34k. 1988 (July 11,18, 24, & 25): Bloomington, IN; Indiana University, School of Music; Indiana University Opera Theater
CAST (in order of appearance): **Louis Lippman**: David Azar; **Francis X. Gilhooley:** Gary Jankowski; **Maid**: Gilda McClure; **Matthew Arnold Fulton**: Frank Martinez; **Sen. Robert E. Lyons**: Eric James; **Alexander Throttlebottom**: John Wilmes; **Waiter**: Greg Snow; **John P. Wintergreen**: Randal Turner; **Sam Jenkins**: Michael McVey; **Diana Devereaux**: Patricia Dewey; **Mary Turner**: Melanie Galloway; **Miss Benson**: Heather Hertling; **The Chief justice**: Brian Horne; **Guide**: Walter Ulrich; **The French Ambassador**: Steven Peeler; **Scrubwoman**: Rita DiCarlo; **Senate Clerk**: David Lamb; **Chief of Staff**: Walter Ulrich; **Doctor**: David Lamb; **Stage Director:** Vincent Liotta; **Musical Director**: Robert E. Stoll; **General Manager**: Dean Charles H. Webb; **Stage Director**: Vincent Liotta

W34l. 1990 (Mar. 29–Apr. 15): NY; Symphony Space; NY Gilbert & Sullivan Players; Keith Jurosko, starring; Other principals: Del-Bouree Bach, Kate Egan, Jayne Lynch; **Stage direction:** Kristin Garver *See*: **B506**

W34m. 1998 (Nov. 7): Chicago; Orchestra Hall; A concert staging of OTIS
A reprise series OTIS will be held at Freud Hall in Los Angeles, Nov. 11-22.

W35. *PARDON MY ENGLISH* (1933)

Lyrics by IG; book by Herbert Fields (et al.).
Currently unavailable for rental
See: **B162, B150, B1509, D492**

SONGS

In Three-Quarter Time; The Lorelei*; Pardon My English; Dancing in the Streets; So What?*; Isn't It a Pity?*; My Cousin in Milwaukee*; Hail the Happy Couple (or, Bride and Groom); The Dresden Northwest Mounted; Luckiest Man in the World*; What Sort of Wedding Is This? (Finale, Act I); Tonight (also includes thematic material for *Two Waltzes in C,* under which title it was published in 1971 as a piano solo); Where You Go, I Go*; I've Got to Be There*; He's Not Himself

Dropped before NY: Freud and Jung and Adler (used in 1987 revival at **DLC**); He's Oversexed (also used in 1987 **DLC** performance); Watch Your Head; Together at Last; Luckiest Boy in the World; No Tickee, No Washee; Poor Michael! Poor Golo!; Fatherland, Mother of the Band

See: **B158**

Premieres

W35a. 1932 (Dec. 2): Philadelphia. PA (World premiere, out-of-town tryout) *See*:
B514

W35b. 1933 (Jan. 20): NY; Majestic Theatre; 46 perfs. **CAST**: **Mr. Preston:**
Tony Blair; **Mrs. Preston:** Eleanor Shaler; **Robin:** Jack Davis; **Schultz:** Cliff
"Charlie"Hall; **Johnny Stewart:** Carl Randall; **Gerry Martin:** Barbara
Newberry; **McCarthy:** Harry T. Shannon; **Gita:** Lyda Roberti; **Michael
Bramleigh:** George Givot; **Commissioner Bauer:** Jack Pearl; **Dr. Richard
Carter:** Gerald Oliver Smith; **Ilse Bauer:** Josephine Huston; **Book:** Herbert
Fields; **Lyrics:** IG; **Director:** John McGowan, **Staging:** Vinton Freedley;
Producers: Alex E. Aarons & Vinton Freedley; **Director:** Vinton Freedley,
Orchestrations: variously, by William Daly, Robert Russell Bennett, &
Adolph Deutsch ; Earl Busby, **conducting** GG, **conducting** for this
performance (First performance in NY) *See*: **B508, B510, B511, B513,
B1874**

W35c. 1987 (May 15): Washington; Coolidge Auditorium of the Library of
Congress, under the auspices of the Gertrude Clarke Whittall Foundation
and the Ira and Leonore Gershwin Charitable Foundation; **CAST**: **Gita:**
Kim Criswell; **Commissioner Bauer:** Jack Dabdoub; **Karl/Johnny:**
George Dvorsky; **Michael:** Cris Groenendaal; **Ilse:** Rebecca Luker; **Dr.
Steiner/Innkeeper/Katz:** John Sinclair; Norman Scribner Choir; John
McGlinn, **conducting** *See*: **B512, B514 , B515**

W36. *LET 'EM EAT CAKE* (1933)
The script was published in 1933 by Alfred A. Knopf; **Performance materials
exist, but have been unavailable**
(Abbreviation: Cake) Lyrics by IG; book by George S. Kaufman and Morrie
Ryskind. Produced by Sam H. Harris *See*: **B361, B369, B370, B384, B468,
B472, B1509, B1665, B1838, B2170**

SONGS (*indicates published song)

Wintergreen for President (Tweedledee for President); Union Square* (not
a song, per se, *See*: Schneider, **B2170**, p. 608); Store Scene (includes three
tunes: Shirts by the Millions, Comes the Revolution, & Mine*. Of these only
Mine was published); Climb Up the Social Ladder (The New Blue
D.A.R.)—this song was dropped soon after the opening in NY, but it has
since been put back into the show, at the Brooklyn Academy of Music in 1987
(**W36d**), e. g.; Our Hearts Are in Communion; Down with Everything That's
Up; The Union League (Cloistered from the Noisy City); On and On and
On*; I've Brushed My Teeth; Double Dummy Drill; The General's Gone to
a Party; All the Mothers of the Nation; Let 'Em Eat Cake*; Blue, Blue,
Blue*; Who's the Greatest?, League of Nations (includes: *No Comprenez, No
Capish, No Versteh!;* Why Speak of Money?); Up and At 'Em!; Oyez, Oyez,
Oyez dropped before opening in NY, but included in Pa./voc. score and

restored for BAM 1987 performances (**W34c**); That's What He Did; I Know a Foul Ball; Throttle Throttlebottom; It Isn't What You Did But What You Didn't; A Hell of a Hole; Let 'Em Eat Caviar (not extant, replaced in pa./voc. score by First Lady and First Gent); Hanging Throttlebottom in the Morning

According to Jablonski, *et al*: The following songs were also in the show: Orders, Orders; What More Can a General Do?; What's This/Where's the General?; He's a Bachelor (to the melody of Union League); There's Something We're Worried About; What's the Proletariat?; The Welcome; No Better Way to Start a Case; On to Vict'ry; We're in a Hell of a Jam; I'm About to Be a Mother

Not used (according to Schwartz): First Lady and First Gent; Till Then

Premieres

W36a. 1933 (Oct. 2); Boston (World Premiere) *See*: **B371, B372**

W36b. 1933 (Oct. 21): NY; Imperial Theatre; 90 perfs. **CAST: Gen. Adam Snookfield:** Florenz Ames; **Trixie Flynn:** Grace Worth; **A Flunkey:** David Lawrence; **Francis X. Gilhooley:** Harold Moffet; **Mrs. Gilhooley:** Alice Burrage; **Louis Lippman:** Abe Reynolds; **Mrs. Lippman:** Grenna Sloan; **Senator Carver Jones:** Edward H. Robins; **Mrs. Jones:** Vivian Barry; **Senator Robert E. Lyons:** George E. Mack; **Mrs. Lyons:** Consuelo Flowerton; **Matthew Arnold Fulton:** Dudley Clements; **Mrs. Fulton:** Mary Jo Matthews; **Mary Wintergreen:** Lois Moran; **John P. Wintergreen:** William Gaxton; **Chief Justice of the Supreme Court:** Ralph Riggs; **Alexander Throttlebottom:** Victor Moore; **Kruger:** Philip Loeb; **The President of the Union League Club:** Ralph Riggs; **Uncle William:** J. Francis Robertson; **Pete:** Hazzard Newberry; **Lieutenant:** George Kirk; **John P. Tweedledee:** Richard Temple; **Secretary:** Charles Conklin; **Paraders, Flunkeys, Supreme Court Justices, Radicals, Salesgirls, Members of the Union League Club, Soldiers, Sailors, League of Nations, etc.; The Misses; The Messrs.; Policeman:** Don Hudson; **Customers:** Terry Lawlor & Pat Hastings; **Snodgrass:** Charles Fowler; **Passersby:** Michael Forbes, Leon Dunar; **Dignitaries:** Robert Burton, Robert Lewis, & Martin Leroy; **Nurse:** Evelyn Hannons; **Photographers:** David Lawrence & Charles Fowler; **Vendor:** Martin Leroy; **Finn:** Edward Loud; **Russian:** Morris Tepper; **Prison Guards:** Vance Elliott & Bruce Barclay; **Orchestrations**: Edward Powell; **Book:** George S. Kaufman & Morrie Ryskind; **Lyrics:** IG; **Book staged by:** George S. Kaufman; **Costumes designed by:** Kiviette and John Booth; **Dances & Ensembles staged by:** von Grona & Ned McGurn; **Settings:** Albert R. Johnson; **Producer**: Sam H. Harris; William Daly (later Harry S. Levant), **conducting** (First performance in NY) *See*: **B357, B356, B358, B363, B364, B366, B367 (The book, published), B368, B369, B374, B1874**

W36c. 1934 (Week beginning Jan 8, 1934): Washington; National Theatre; **CAST: Gen. Adam Snookfield:** Florenz Ames; **Trixie Flynn:** Grace Worth; **Francis X. Gilhooley:** Harold Moffet; **Mrs. Gilhooley:** Ruth Adams;

Louis Lippman: Abe Reynolds; Mrs. Lippman: Irma Philbin: Senator Carver Jones: Edward H. Robins; Mrs. Jones: Gail Darling; Senator Robert E. Lyons: George E. Mack; Mrs. Lyons: Consuelo Flowerton; Matthew Arnold Fulton: Dudley Clements; Mrs. Fulton: Grace Garnett; Mary Wintergreen: Lois Moran; John P. Wintergreen: William Gaxton; The Chief Justice: Ralph Riggs; Alexander Throttlebottom: Victor Moore; Kruger: Philip Loeb; The President of the Union League Club: Ralph Riggs; Uncle William: J. Francis Robertson; Lieutenant: George Kirk; John P. Twiddledee: Richard Temple; Flunkey: David Lawrence; Policeman: Don Hudson; Snodgrass: Martin Sheppard; Passersby: Michael Forbes & Leon Dunar; Dignitaries: Robert Burton, Robert Lewis, & Martin Leroy; Secretary: Charles Conklin; Nurse: Rosalind Shaw; Photographers: David Lawrence & Martin Sheppard; Vendor: Martin Leroy; Finn: Edward Loud; Russian: Morris Tepper; Prison Guards: Vance Elliott & Bruce Barclay; Paraders, Flunkeys, Supreme Court Justices, Radicals, Salesgirls, Customers, Members of the Union League Club, Soldiers, Sailors, League of Nations, etc.; The Misses; The Messrs.; Orchestrations: Edward Powell; Book: George S. Kaufman & Morrie Ryskind; Lyrics: IG; Book staged by: George S. Kaufman; Costumes designed by: Kiviette and John Booth; Dances & Ensembles staged by: von Grona & Ned McGurn; Settings: Albert R. Johnson; Producer: Sam H. Harris; Harry S. Levant, conducting

W36d. 1987 (Mar. 18 & ending Mar. 29, several performances): Brooklyn, NY; Brooklyn Academy of Music, Opera House   CAST: Alexander Throttlebottom: Jack Gilford; John P. Wintergreen: Larry Kert; Mary Turner: Maureen McGovern; Kruger: David Garrison [Mark Zimmerman, understudy]; Trie Flynn: Paige O'Hara; General Adam Snookfield: Jack Dabdoub; Lieutenant: George Dvorsky; John P. Tweedledee: Haskell Gordon; Louis Lippman: Merwin Goldsmith; Senator Robert E. Lyons: Walter Hook; Francis X. Gilhooley: Frank Kopyc; The Chief Justice: Casper Roos; Matthew Arnold Fulton: Raymond Thorne; Senator Carver Jones: Mark Zimmerman; Wives of the Committee members, Supreme Court Justices, Paraders, Flunkeys, Radicals, Salesgirls, Customers, Members of the Union League Club, Soldiers, Sailors, League of Nations, etc; New York Choral Artists; Orchestrations: Russell Warner; Performing editions reconstructed by John McGlinn [through the generosity of Mrs. Ira Gershwin]; Producer: Morton Gottlieb; Scenic design: Eduardo Sicangco; Lighting design: Jeff Davis; Sound design: Otts Munderloh; Orchestra of St. Luke's (Michael Feldman, Artistic Director) with New York Choral Artists (Joseph Flummerfelt, Director); Michael Tilson Thomas, conducting these concert presentations (With a performance of *Of Thee I Sing* the same evenings, constitutes a world premiere of these versions) *See*: B499-505

Other Selected Performances

W36e. 1978 (July): Stockbridge, MA; Berkshire Theatre Festival

CAST: Tony Roberts; Arnold Stang; **Trixie Flynn:** Suzanne Lederer; **Book:** George S. Kaufmann & Morrie Ryskind; **Lyrics:** IG; **Stage Direction:** Allan Albert; ? **conducting** *See:* **B360**

W36f. 1978 (May 20): New York; Alice Tully Hall of Lincoln Center; partial concert performance; Gregg Smith Singers; Gregg Smith, **conducting** *See:* **B365**

W36g. 1981: Coral Gables, FL; University of Miami

W36h. 1995 (Mar. 13): Washington; Arena Stage; Benefit performance for the Living Stage Theatre Company
CAST: Included, among others, Sen. Alan Simpson, Rep. Pat Schroeder, Rep. Barney Frank, Rep. Kweisi Mfume; **Director:** Laurence Maslon

W37. *PORGY AND BESS* (1935). Originally produced by the Theater Guild (NY), opera in three acts. Lyrics by DuBose Heyward and Ira Gershwin; libretto by Heyward

Prompt copy of the vocal score at **NN-L,** including property plot, ground plans, light cue sheet, & key to switchboard inserted for the 1935 Alvin theatre production.
Abbreviation: P&B
Typescript of the libretto of the version presented at the Ziegfeld, Mar. 10, 1953, is at **NN-L,** classmark **NCOF p. v. 504**
Pa./Vocal score edited by Albert Sirmay, published by Gershwin Publishing (Chappell), 1935
Libretto, in English and French. Paris: Edicion Mensuel, 1987
Current Performance materials available from: Tams-Witmark Music Library, Inc., 560 Lexington Ave., NY 10022

See: **B30, B121, B149, B151, B152, B153, B154, B158, B159, B516, B156, B162, B163, B166, B167, B168, B170, B179, B180, B181, B263, B384, B590, B1509, B1548, B1552, B1627, B1837, B1838, B2022, B2023, B2154, B2156, B2159, B2160, B2168, B2171, B2173, B2175**

MUSICAL NUMBERS (+indicates published in pa./vocal score)

Introduction (orchestra)+; Instrumental: Jazzbo [also spelled Jasbo] Brown Blues (piano, piano & orchestra, chorus)+

ACT I, SCENE 1

Summertime* + (Heyward); A Woman Is a Sometime Thing (Heyward)+; Here Come de Honey Man (Street Cry)+; Evenin' Ladies (entrance of Porgy); They Pass By Singin'! (Heyward)+; Crap Game: Yo' Mammy's Gone . . . Crown Cockeyed Drunk . . . Oh Little Stars . . *Robbins murder* (Orchestra)

SCENE 2

Gone, Gone, Gone (Heyward)+; Overflow (Heyward)+; My Man's Gone Now (Heyward)+; Leavin' fo' the Promis' Land (Train Song) (Heyward)+;

ACT II SCENE 1

> It Take a Long Pull to Get There (Heyward); I Got Plenty O' Nuttin'* (IG &
> Heyward); Buzzard Song (Heyward); I Hates Yo' Struttin' Style; Mornin',
> Lawyer (Entrance of Frazier) (Heyward); Lord, Lord, Listen What She Say;
> 'Course I Sells Divorce; Woman to Lady; Bess, You Is My Woman Now (IG
> & Heyward)*+; Oh, I Can't Sit Down (IG)+

SCENE 2

> *Allegretto barbaro* (percussion) I Ain't Got No Shame+; It Ain't Necessarily So
> (IG)*;   Shame on All of You Sinners; What You Want Wid Bess? (Heyward)+

SCENE 3

> It Take a Long Pull to Get There (reprise) (Heyward)+; De White Folks Put Me
> In; Oh, Doctor Jesus (Time and Time Again) (Heyward)+; Street Cries; Strawberry
> Woman; Crab Man (Heyward)+; I Loves You, Porgy (IG) [First published in sheet
> music version when used in 1959 movie version]*; *Hurricane* (orchestra)

SCENE 4

> Prayers, for Six Voices, Oh, Hev'n-ly Father (IG)+; Oh, de Lord Shake de
> Heavens (Heyward)+; Summertime (reprise) [Lonely Boy. a duet for Bess and
> Serena, was originally composed for this spot]; Oh, Dere's Somebody Knockin'
> at de Do'+; A Red Headed Woman (IG) +

ACT 3

> Clara, Clara, Don't You Be Downhearted (Heyward)+; Summertime (reprise by
> Bess)*; *Fugue* (the death of Crown, orchestra)

SCENE 2

> There's a Boat Dat's Leavin' Soon for New York (IG)+; *Moderato commodo*
> (Occupational humoresque); Good Mornin', Sistuh!+; Sure to Go to Heaven;
> How Are You Dis Mornin'?; Thank Gawd, I's Home Again! (Return of Porgy);
> Here, boy look what I brought for you/Here gal, hol' up yo' head/Here Mingo,
> what's de matter wid you all?; Oh Bess, Oh Where's My Bess? (IG)+; Oh Lawd,
> I'm on My Way (Heyward)+

Premieres

W37a. 1935 (Sept. 30): Boston; Colonial Theatre (Out-of-town tryout) *See*: **B564, B565,
B571, B572, B581, B585, B2175**

W37b. 1935 (Oct. 10): NY; Alvin Theatre (New York premiere) 124 performances
CAST: Porgy: Todd Duncan; **Bess:** Anne Wiggins Brown; **Crown:** Warren
Coleman; **Serena:** Ruby Elzy; **Clara:** Abbie Mitchell; **Maria:** Georgette
Harvey; **Jake:** Eddie Matthews; **Sporting Life:** John W. Bubbles; **Mingo**:
Ford L. Buck; **Robbins**: Henry Davis; **Peter:** Gus Simons; **Frazier (& Asst.
chorus conductor):** J. Rosamond Johnson; **Annie:** Olive Ball; **Lily &**

Strawberry Woman: Helen Dowdy; **Jim:** Jack Carr; **Undertaker:** John Garth; **Nelson and Crab Man:** Ray Yeats; **Mr. Archdale:** George Lessey; **Detective:** Alexander Campbell; **Policeman:** Harold Woolf; **Coroner:** George Carleton; **Scipio:** Scipio; **Settings:** Sergei Soudeikine; **Director:** Rouben Mamoulian; The Eva Jessye Choir; The Charleston Orphans' Band; Alexander Smallens, **conducting** *See:* **B516, B542, B551, B553, B555, B559, B561, B562, B563, B565, B568, B569, B570, B571, B573, B574, B578, B579, B580, B584, B586, B587, B588, B590, B591, B2156, B2175**

W37c. 1936 (Jan. 27–Mar. 21): **THEATRE GUILD TOUR:** (Initial performances are all premieres) (Jan. 27–Feb. 8): Philadelphia, Pa.; Forrest Theatre; (Feb. 10–Feb. 15): Pittsburgh, Pa.; Nixon Theatre; (Feb. 17–Mar. 7): Chicago, Ill.; Erlanger Theatre *See:* **B552**; (Mar. 9–Mar. 14): Detroit, MI; Cass Theatre; (Mar. 16–Mar.21): Washington, D. C.; National Theatre

W37d. 1938 (Feb. 3–Mar. 8): **MERLE ARMITAGE PRODUCTIONS Tour:** [All premieres] (Feb. 3): Pasadena, CA; Municipal Auditorium; (Feb. 4–19): Los Angeles; Philharmonic Auditorium; (Feb. 21–Mar.8): San Francisco; Curran Theatre

W37e. 1941 (Oct.13): Maplewood, NJ (premiere); Cheryl Crawford, **Producer** *See:* **B167, B524, B547, B604**

W37f. 1942 (Jan., for three weeks): Boston, MA; Cheryl Crawford, **Producer**

W37g. 1942 (Jan. 22–Sept.26): NY; Majestic Theatre; Cheryl Crawford, **Producer**, 286 performances *See:* **B592, B593, B594, B597, B606**

W37h. 1942–1944 (Sept. 28, 1942–Apr. 4, 1944): CHERYL CRAWFORD TOUR *See:* **B603, B605, B844** (Initial performances are all premieres, except Philadelphia, Pittsburgh, Chicago, Detroit, Los Angeles, Pasadena, San Francisco, Boston): (September 28–30, 1942): Rochester, NY; Masonic Auditorium; (Oct.1–3): Buffalo, NY; Erlanger Theatre; (Oct. 5–10): Cleveland, OH; Hanna Theatre: (Oct. 12–24): Detroit, MI; Cass Theatre; (Oct. 26–31): Cincinnati, OH; Taft Auditorium; (Nov. 2, 1942–Jan. 16, **1943**): Chicago, IL; Studebaker Theatre; (Jan. 18–Jan. 30): St. Louis, MO; American Theatre; (Feb. 3–6): Kansas City, MO; Municipal Auditorium; (Feb. 8–11): Minneapolis, MN; Lyceum Theatre; (Feb. 12–13): St. Paul, MN; Auditorium; (Feb. 15–20: Milwaukee, WI; Davidson Theatre; [According to the unsigned article in *Theatre Arts* 27/11 (Nov. 1943), there was a performance in Toledo, OH]; (Feb. 22–27): Detroit, MI; Cass Theatre; (Mar. 2–6): Indianapolis, IN; English Theatre; (Mar. 8–13): Toronto, Canada; Royal Alexander Theatre; (Mar. 15–27): Pittsburgh, PA; Nixon Theatre; (Mar. 29–Apr. 17): Philadelphia, PA; Forrest Theatre; (Apr. 26–May 8): San Francisco, CA; Curran Theatre; [According to the unsigned article in *Theatre Arts* 27/11 (Nov. 1943), there were also performances in (May 25–29): Portland, OR; Auditorium; Seattle, WA, & Sacramento, & (June 9–13): Oakland, CA; Auditorium; (June 16–19): Denver, CO; Auditorium]; & New York, NY, as:

W37i. 1943 (Sept. 13, 1943–Oct. 2, 1943—24 performances) NY; Forty-fourth

Street Theatre **CAST:** Maria: Georgette Harvey; **Lily:** Catherine Ayers; **Annie:** Musa Williams; **Clara:** Harriett Jackson; **Jake:** Edward Matthews; **Sportin' Life:** Avon Long; **Mingo:** Jerry Laws; **Robbins:** Henry Davis; **Serena:** Alma Hubbard; **Jim:** William C. Smith; **Peter:** George Randol; **Porgy:** Todd Duncan; **Crown:** Warren Coleman; **Bess:** Etta Moten; **Policeman:** Kenneth Konopka; **Detective:** Richard Bowler; **Undertaker:** Cowal McMahon; **Lawyer Frazier:** Charles Welch; **Nelson:** Charles Colman; **Strawberry Woman:** Catherine Ayers; **Crab Man:** Edward Tyler; **Coroner:** Don Darcey; **Staging:** Robert Ross; **Scenery:** Herbert Andrews; **Costumers supervised by** Paul du Pont; **Producer:** Cheryl Crawford; Alexander Smallens, **conducting** *See:* **B599, B602**

W37j. 1943: **Tour:** (Oct. 4–9): Baltimore, MD; Ford's Theatre; (Oct. 11–23): Boston, MA; Colonial Theatre; (Oct. 27–30): New Haven, CT; Shubert Theatre; (Nov. 3): Springfield, MA; Court Sq. Theatre; (Nov. 4–6): Hartford, CT; Bushnell Auditorium; (Nov. 10): Williamsport, PA; Karlton Theatre; (Nov. 11): Harrisburg, PA;. State Theatre; (Nov.12– 13): Trenton, NJ; War Memorial Auditorium; (Nov. 17):Greensboro, NC; State Theatre; (Nov. 18): Raleigh, NC; Carolina Theatre; (Nov. 19): Columbia, SC; Auditorium; (Nov. 20): Asheville, NC; Plaza Theatre; (Nov. 24): Louisville, KY;. Memorial Auditorium; (Nov. 25–27): Columbus, Ohio; Hartman Theatre; (Nov. 29–Dec. 4): St. Louis, MO; American Theatre; (Dec. 8): Memphis, TN; Auditorium; (Dec. 9): Jackson, MS; Municipal? Auditorium; (Dec. 11): Fort Worth, TX; Auditorium; (Dec. 15): Austin, Texas; Paramount Theatre; (Dec. 16–17): San Antonio, TX; Texas Theatre; (Dec. 18): Dallas, TX; Auditorium; (Dec. 29): Oklahoma City, OK; Shrine Auditorium; (Dec. 30–31): Tulsa, OK; Convention Hall; (Jan. 5, **1944**): Dayton, OH; Victory Theatre; (Jan. 6–8, second appearance): Columbus, OH; Hartman Theatre; (Jan. 12); Saginaw, MI; Temple Theatre;(Jan. 13): Lansing, MI; Michigan Theatre; (Jan. 14–15): Grand Rapids, MI; .Keith Theatre; (Jan. 17–19, second appearance): Buffalo, NY: Erlanger Theatre; (Jan. 20): Erie, PA; Shea Theatre; (Jan. 20–21): Youngstown, OH; Park Theatre; (Jan. 27–29, second appearance): Cincinnati, OH; Taft Auditorium; (Jan. 31–Feb. 5, second appearance): Baltimore, MD; Ford's Theatre; (Feb. 21–26): Newark, NJ; Mosque Theatre

W37k. 1943 (Mar. 23, for twenty-two performances): Copenhagen, Denmark; Royal Danish Opera; all-white cast (First performance in Europe); 22 performances *See:* **B596, B598**

W37l. 1944 (Feb. 7–Feb. 19): New York, NY; City Center, (sixteen performances); (Feb. 28–Apr. 8): New York, NY, City Center, (forty-eight performances) *See:* **B601**

W37m. 1945 (May 14): Moscow; Actor's House; Stanislavsky Players and Chorus of the Moscow Theatrical Society; No orchestra, score played by a pianist assisted by Latsy Olakh, drummer; **Staging** by Konstantin Popov; A. Khessin, **conducting** *See:* **B600**

W37n. 1948 (Feb. 10): Gothenburg, Sweden; Lyriskateatern (First perf. in Sweden)

W37o. 1949 (Apr. 1): Stockholm, Sweden; Oscarsteatern

1952 United States Tour

W37p. 1952 (June 9): Dallas, TX; State Fair Auditorium
    CAST: Bess: Leontyne Price & Urylee Leonardos; **Porgy:** William Warfield &
    LaVern Hutcherson; **Sportin' Life:** Lorenzo Fuller; **Maria:** Georgia Burke;
    Clara: Helen Colbert; **Crown:** John McCurry *See*: **B701, B2156**

W37q. 1952 (June 25): Chicago, IL; Civic Opera House; **CAST:** Cab Calloway took over
    as **Sportin' Life;** (July 22): Pittsburgh, PA; .Nixon Theatre; (Aug. 6): Washington,
    DC; National Theatre *See*: **B631, B703, B2156**

1952–1953, Europe

W37r. 1952: (Opened Sept. 7 for 9 performances, to Sept. 12): Vienna; Staats-
    theater inthe Volksoper (European premiere) *See*: **B615, B618, B641, B632,
    B636, B637, B638, B641, B650, B653, B692, B695, B711, B712, B718,
    B723, B726, B784**

W37s. 1952: (Sept. 17, 12 performances, to Sept. 27): Berlin; Titania Palast (First perform-
    ance in Germany) *See*: **B607, B619, B621, B661, B696, B697, B700, B705,
    B713, B720, B721**

W37t. 1952–1953: (Oct. 9, 1952–Feb. 10, 1953): London; Stoll Theatre
    See: **B616, B622, B630, B642, B648, B652, B655, B657, B658, B659,
    B673, B699, B710, B715, B719, B724**

W37u. 1953 (Feb. 16–Mar. 1): Paris; Empire Theatre (First perf. in Paris) *See*: **B664**

W37v. 1953 (Official opening March 10, with an invited preview performance on March
    9, to Nov. 28); **Blevins Davis and Robert Breen production**; NY; Ziegfeld
    Theatre; 305 performances **CAST** (in order of appearance): **Clara:** Helen
    Colbert; **Mingo:** Jerry Laws; **Sportin' Life**: Cab Calloway; **Serena**: Helen
    Thigpen; **Jake**: Joseph James; **Robbins**: Howard Roberts; **Jim**: Sherman
    Sneed; **Joe**: Hugh Dilworth; **Peter: (The Honey Man)**; Joseph Crawford;
    Lily (The Strawberry Woman): Helen Dowdy; **Maria**: Georgia Burke;
    Porgy: LeVern Hutcherson or Leslie Scott or Irving Barnes; **Crown**: John
    McCurry; **Annie**: Catherine Van Buren; **Bess**: Leontyne Price or Urylee
    Leonardos; **Policeman**: Sam Kasakoff; **Detective**: Walter Riemer;
    Undertaker: William Veasey; **Frazier**: Moses Lamarr; **Ruby**: Elizabeth
    Foster; **Crab Man:** Ray Yeates; **Coroner:** Sam Kasakoff; **Policeman**: Willis
    Daily; **Porgy's Goat**: Jebob; **Residents of Catfish Row**; **Dramatic
    Direction:** Robert Breen; **Sets:** Wolfgang Roth; **Musical Director:**
    Alexander Smallens; **Choral Director:** Eva Jessye *See*: **B547, B612, B613,
    B626, B640, B643, B663, B844, B884**

1953–1954, United States and Canada

W37w. 1953 (Dec. 1–19, 1953): Philadelphia, PA; Forrest Theatre; (Dec. 21–Jan. 16,
    1954, second appearance): Washington, DC; National Theatre; (Jan. 18–23):
    Richmond, VA; Mosque Theatre; (Jan. 25–30, second appearance):

Pittsburgh, PA; Nixon Theatre; (Feb. 1–6): Cincinnati, OH; Taft Theatre; (Feb. 8–20): St. Louis, MO; American Theatre; (Feb. 22–28): Kansas City, MO; Music Hall; (Mar. 2–20, second appearance): Chicago, IL; Civic Opera House; (Mar. 24–Apr. 23): Minneapolis, MN; Lyceum Theatre; (Apr. 6–17): Toronto, Ontario; Royal Alexandra Theatre; (Apr. 19–May 8): Detroit, MI; Cass Theatre; (May 10–22): Cleveland, OH; Hanna Theatre; (May 24–29): Columbus, OH; Hartman Theatre; (June 1–5): Denver, CO; Denver Auditorium; (June 14–July 10): San Francisco, CA; Curran Theatre; (July 12–Aug. 14): Los Angeles, CA; Philharmonic Auditorium; (Aug. 20–28): Boston; Shubert Theatre; (Aug. 31–Sept. 11, second appearance): Toronto, Ontario; Royal Alexandra Theatre; (Sept. 13–18): Montreal, Quebec; Her Majesty's Theatre

1954–55 Europe and Middle East

W37x. 1954 (Sept. 22–25): Venice, Italy; Teatro Fenice (premiere) *See*: **B651, B654, B683**

W37y. 1954 (Sept. 30– Dec. 4): Paris, France; Empire Theatre (second appearance in Paris) **CAST: Bess:** Irene Williams, Gloria Davy, & Fredye Marshall; **Sportin' Life:** Lorenzo Fuller, James Attles, & Earl Jackson

W37z. 1954 (Dec. 11–14): Zagreb, Yugoslavia; Théâtre de l'Opéra (premiere); (Dec. 16–18): Belgrade, Yugoslavia; National Theatre (premiere); *See*: **B614, B698**

W37aa. 1954 (Dec. 31–Jan. 2, **1955**): Alexandria, Egypt; Théâtre Mohamed Aly; (Jan. 7–12): Cairo, Egypt ; Théâtre de l'Opéra; (Jan. 17–22): Athens, Greece; Royal National Theatre *See*: **B610, B687**; (Jan. 26–Jan. 30): Tel Aviv, Israel; Habimah Theater (First perf. in Israel) *See*: **B679**; (Jan. 31): Casablanca (concert for Nouasseur Air Depot); (Feb. 3–13): Barcelona, Spain; Gran Teatro del Liceo and Windsor Palace *See*: **B656, B680**

W37bb. 1955 (Feb. 15–17): Naples, Italy; Teatro di San Carlo *See*: **B691**

W37cc. 1955 (Opened Feb. 22, for a week): Milan, Italy; Teatro Alla Scala; (First perf. at La Scala) **CAST:** (on opening night) **Porgy:** Leslie Scott; **Bess:** Gloria Davy; **Sportin' Life:** Earl Jackson *See*: **B627, B628, B686**

W37dd. 1955: (Mar. 1–6): Genoa, Italy; Teatro Carlo Felice

W37ee. 1955: (Mar. 9–13): Florence, Italy; Teatro Comunale; *See*: **B708**

W37ff. 1955 (Mar. 16–23): Lausanne, Switzerland; Théâtre de Beaulieu; (Mar. 26–Apr. 3): Marseilles, France; Opéra Municipal; (Apr. 9–13): Turin, Italy; Teatro Alfieri; (Apr. 21–May 14): Rome; Teatro Quattro Fontane *See*: **B675**; (June 3–12): Zurich, Switzerland; Hallenstadion; (June 15–21): Brussels, Belgium; Théâtre de la Monnaie; (June 23–30): Antwerp, Belgium; Théâtre de l'Hippodrome

1955, Latin America

W37gg. 1955 (July 7–13): Rio de Janeiro, Brazil; Teatro Municipal; *See*: **B676**

W37hh. 1955 (July 16–24): São Paulo, Brazil; Teatro Santana; (July 26–31): Montevideo, Uruguay; Teatro Solis; (Aug. 3–21): Buenos Aires, Argentina; Teatro Astral; (Aug. 25–30): Santiago, Chile; Teatro Municipal; (Sept. 3–7): Lima, Peru; Teatro Municipal; (Sept. 13–18); Bogotá, Colombia; Teatro Colombia; (Sept. 21–23): Cali, Colombia; Teatro Municipal; (Sept. 27–Oct. 3): Caracas, Venezuela; Teatro Municipal; (Oct. 6–7): Panama City, Panama; Teatro Nacional; (Oct. 11–25): Mexico City, Mexico; Teatro Bellas Artes

1955–1956, Europe

W37ii. 1955 (Nov. 9–16): Antwerp, Belgium; Théâtre de l'Hippodrome (second appearance); (Nov. 18–Nov. 22): Dusseldorf, Germany; Apollo Theater;1955 (Nov. 25–27): Frankfort, Germany; 5 performances at Grosses Haus der Städtischen Bühnen See **B717**; (Dec. 1–6): Munich, Germany; Deutsches Theatre; (Dec. 9–15): Berlin, Germany; Titania Palast (second appearance)

W37jj. 1956 (Dec. 26–Jan. 5): Leningrad, USSR; Palace of Cultural and Industrial Cooperatives See: **B609**, **B625**, **B639**, **B645**, **B685**, **B714**, **B716**

W37kk.1956 (Jan. 10–17): Moscow; Stanislavsky & Nemirovich-Danchenka Theatre; See: **B639**, **B644**, **B669**, **B678**, **B714**, **B716**

W37ll. 1956 (Jan. 24–Feb. 1): Warsaw, Poland; National Opera House; (Feb. 4–8): Stalinograd, Poland; Wyspianski Theatre; (Feb. 11–19): Prague, Czechoslovakia; Karlin Theatre; (Feb. 22–29): (Mar. 1–4): Munich, Germany; Deutsches Theatre (second appearance); Stuttgart, Germany; (Mar. 7–11, seven performances): Hamburg, Germany; Staatsoper; (Mar. 16–22): Dusseldorf, Germany; Apollo Theater (second appearance) See: **B649**; (Mar. 25–31): Brussels, Belgium; Théâtre de la Monnaie (second appearance); (Apr. 2–10): The Hague, Holland; Gebouw Voor Kunsten En Wetenschappen; (Apr. 13–20): Rotterdam, Holland; Luxor Cinema Theatre; (Apr. 25–May 6): Oslo, Norway; Volks Theatre; (May 9–16): Aarhus, Denmark; Aarhushallen; (May 9–June 3): Amsterdam, Holland; Theatre Carre See: **B646**

W37mm. 1961 (opened May 17): NY; City Center **CAST: Clara:** Billie Lynn Daniel; **Mingo:** Jerry Laws; **Sportin' Life:** Rawn Spearman; **Jake:** Irving Barnes; **Serena:** Barbara Webb; **Robbins:** Ned Wright; **Jim:** Scott Gibson; **Peter:** Joseph Crawford; **Lily:** Edna Ricks; **Maria:** Carol Brice; **Porgy:** William Warfield; **Crown:** James Randolph; **Bess:** Martha Flowers; **Policemen:** Harry Bessinger & Howard Poyro; **Detective:** William Coppola; **Police Sergeant:** Norman Grogan; **Undertaker:** Wanza King; **Annie:** Alyce Webb; **Frazier:** Eugene Brice; Nelson: Arthur Williams; **Strawberry Woman:** Doreese Duquan; Crabman: Clyde Turner; **Coroner:** Eugene Wood; **Residents of Catfish Row, fisherman, children, stevedores, etc.; Settings: Costumes**: **Stage Director:** William Ball; City Center Orchestra, Julius Rudel, **conducting** See: **B728**, **B745**

W37nn. 1964 (opened May 6): NY; City Center, New York City Center Light Opera Company; **CAST: Clara:** Marie Young; **Mingo:** Tony Middleton; **Sportin' Life:** Robert Guillaume; **Jake:** Irving Barnes; **Serena:** Gwendolyn Walters;

Robbins: Eugene Edwards; Jim: Garwood Perkins; Peter: Garrett Morris; Lily: Frances Haywood; Maria: Carol Brice; Porgy: William Warfield; Crown: William Dillard; Bess: Veronica Tyler; Policeman: David Hicks & John Smith; Detective: Walter Riemer; Undertaker: Wanza King; Annie: Alyce Webb; Frazier: Al Fann; Strawberry Woman: Kay Barnes; Crabman: Clyde Turner; Scipio: William Harris; Pearl: Lillian Hayman; Residents of Catfish Row, fisherman, children, stevedores, etc.; Settings: Stephen O. Saxe; Costumes: Stanley Simmons; Stage Director: John Fearnley; City Center Orchestra, Julius Rudel, conducting See: B741

W37oo. 1965 (Dec.): Vienna; Volksoper; CAST: Porgy: William Warfield; Bess: Olive Moorefield; Crown: James Randolph; Sportin' Life: Robert Guillaume; Supporting cast: Annette Meriweather, Daniel Camagys, Gwendolyn Walters, Robert C. Battle, Debria Brown, Irene Oliver, William Ray, Walker Wyatt, & Albert Clipper; Sets & Costumes: Robert O'Hearn; Choreography: Archie Savage; Choral direction: Nathaniel Merrill; Volksoper chorus; Orchestra, Lee Schaenen, conducting See: B733, B734, B753, B749, B754

W37pp. 1966–1967: New Zealand & Australia; All premieres: (In NZ: Christ-church, Invercargill, Dunedin, Palmerston North, Wellington, Hastings, Napier, New Plymouth, Hamilton, & Aukland; In Australia: Brisbane & other principal cities)
CAST (In order of appearance): Clara: Isabel Cowan; Mingo: Sam Stevens; Sportin' Life: Toni Williams; Jake: Mark Metekingi; Serena: Delores Ivory; Robbins: Peter Keiha; Ruby: Newha Taiaki; Jim: Don Selywn; Scipio: Api Taylor; Peter, the Honeyman: Bob Hirini; Lily: Celeste Barker; Annie: Diana Winterburn; Maria: Hannah Tatana; Porgy: Inia Te Wiata; Bess: Martha Flowers; Crown: John McCurray; Detective: Eric Wood; Policeman: Bernard Reid; Undertaker: Bill Mataira; Frazier: Tuta Kainamu; Strawberry woman: Peti Rei; Crabman: Edward Huriwai; Coroner: John Roberts; Residents of Catfish Row (Fisherman/Stevedores): Thelma Grabmaier, Margaret Kimura, Peti Rei, Mary Reid, Melva Puki, Polly Tarawhiti, Hera Wainohu, Loraine Bristowe, Ann Baird, Ngaire Karaka, Newha Taiaki, Josh Gardiner, Rangi Hopi, Kahu Karaitiana, Sid Reweti, George Henare, John Denny, Edward Huriwai, Tuta Kainamu, Bill Mataira, Down Selwyn, Ross Waters, George Wikaira, Peter Dowan; Children: Mark & Jessica Metekingi, Api Taylor; Productions manager: Barry Leighton; Entire production directed by: Ella Gerber; Designer: John Brayden; Resident producer: John Thompson; The New Zealand Theatre Ensemble (Leader, Ruth Pearl), with The Christchurch Civic Orchestra in Christchurch, Invercargill, & Dunedin, & The Auckland Symphonia in Auckland & Hamilton; Chorus Master: Harry Brusey; Chief repetiteur: Patrick Flynn; Repetiteur: Gwyneth Brown; Resident producer: John Thompson; Overall music director: Dobbs Franks See: B748

W37qq. 1967: Tallin, Estonia, Soviet Union; Estonia Opera and Ballet Theatre
CAST: Porgy: George Ots; Bess: Haili Sammelseld; Stage settings: Lembit Rooz; Stage Director: Udo Vilyoats (sp?); H. Neeme Yarvi,

conducting *See*: **B744**

W37rr.   1968 (Sept. 7): Oslo, Norway **CAST: Porgy:** John Fleming; **Bess:** Irene Oliver; **Sportin' Life:** Clyde Williams; **Crown:** George Goodman; **Scenary:** Wolfgang Vollhard; **Costumes:** Ivar Karlsen; **Produced by:** Anne Brown; Arvid Fladmore, conducting *See*: **B735**

W37ss.   1970 (Jan. 24): East Berlin; Komische Oper; **in a German translation** by Horst Seeger & Götz Friedrich **CAST**: **Porgy:** Cullen Maiden; **Bess:** Caroline Smith-Meyer; **Crown:** Vladimir Bauer; **Robbins:** John Moulson; **Serena:** Christa Noack; **Clara:** Ingrid Czerny; **Sportin' Life:** Manfred Krug; **Director:** Götz Friedich; **Set designs:** Reinhart Zimmermann; **Choreography:** Michael Boyle; **Costume design:** Susanne Raschig; Gerd Bahner, **conducting** *See*: **B755,**   **B773, B780, B782, B787, B789, B791, B792, B796**

W37tt.   1970 (June 25–July 8 for 15 performances): Charleston, SC; Municipal Auditorium, presented by the Tricentennial Commission & Charleston Symphony Orchestra Association **CAST: Porgy:** Reuben Wright; **Bess:** Annette McKenzie Anderson; **Sportin' Life:** Eugene Pinson; **Crown:** Kent Byas, Jr.; **Supporting Roles:** John E. Dowling; LeRoy Singleton; Ruth Gibson; James Fields; Sarah Reese; Rebecca Sherman; Ermine Seabrook; Anthony Burke; James Edwards; Eugene Hunt; Helen Mikell; Juanita Greene; Maria L. Roper; Madeline Fields; Villicia Grant; and children; **Stage direction:** Ella Gerber; **Scenery designer:** Emmett Robinson; **Lighting:** Norman Weber; **Choral director:** James Edwards; **Producers for the symphony orchestra:** Fitzhugh Hamrick & Louis Condon; Lucien De Groote, **conducting** (First performance in Charleston, S. C.) See: **B800**

W37uu.   1970 (Oct. 3): Gelsenkirchen, then W. Germany **CAST: Porgy:** Wolfe Hacke; **Bess:** Ursula Schröder-Feinen; **Crown:** Roderick Ristow; **Robbins:** Willi Kunzmann; **Serena:** Anna Green; **Jake:** Gerhard Faulstich; **Clara:** Petra Kollakowsky; **Maria:** Ingrid Karrasch; **Sportin' Life:** Dale Goss; **Mingo:** Jan Thompson; **Honigverkäufer:** Wolfram Assmann; **Lily:** Elke Estlinbaum; **Frazier:** Albert Zell; **Staging:** Günter Roth; **Sets:** Otto-werner Meyer; **Costumes:** Ingeborg Ketterer; **Chorus:** Julius Aspeck; Ljubomir Romansky, **conducting** (First performance in what was then West Germany) *See*: **B761, B777, B799**

W37vv.   1970; Hanau

W37ww.   1970: Frankfort/Nordwestadt. Swiss Theater Company-Basel; Schweizer Turness-Theater; **Seeger/Friedrich German translation CAST: Porgy:** John Swift; **Bess:** Marjorie Vance; **Crown:** Joel Thomas; **Sportin' Life:** Kosto Kilroy; H. Trikolidis, **conducting**

W37xx.   1971 (Opened in Interlaken, Switzerland Sept. 3, completed a two-month run toward the end of March in then West Berlin); Under the auspices of the Swiss Theatre Touring Company **CAST: Porgy**: George Goodman or John Swift; **Bess:** Colette Warren or Vivian Martin; **Serena**: Bennie Jean Gilette;

Clara: Elzar Levister; **Sportin' Life**: Eugene Edwards *See*: **B756**, **B772**, **B797**

W37yy.   1973: Leningrad; Maly Opera and Ballet Theatre; **Drama direction:** Emil Pasynkov; Yury Temirkanov, **conducting** *See*: **B788**

W37zz.   1975: Ann Arbor, MI; Michigan Opera Theatre; University of Michigan Musical Society; **CAST: Porgy:** Robert Mosley & Benjamin Matthews; **Bess:** Irene Oliver & Leona Mitchell; **Crown:** Leonard Parker; **Sportin' Life:** Robert Monroe; **Honey Man:** Melvyn Hardiman; **Sets:** Paul Norrenbrock; **Stage direction:** Ella Gerber *See*: **B795**

W37aaa. 1975 (Opened Oct. 3): Detroit, MI; Music Hall; Michigan Opera Theatre **CAST: Bess:** Leona Mitchell & Irene Oliver; **Porgy:** Robert Mosley; **Crown:** Leonard Parker; **Sportin' Life:** Robert Munroes; **Stage Direction:** Ella Gerber; **Sets:** Paul Norrenbrock; **Rhemi Ghilespi,** conducting *See*: **B731**

W37bbb. 1975 (July 1): Houston; Houston Grand Opera; **Producer**: Sherwin M. Goldman; **Stage Direction:** Jack O'Brien

W37ccc. 1975 (Aug. 16): Cleveland, OH; Blossom Music Center; Cleveland Orchestra, chorus, and soloists; Lorin Maazel, conducting (Source: Ewen)

W37ddd. 1976 (Mar. 17): Camden Festival; St. Pancras Town Hall (England); A concert performance; Chelsea Opera Group; **CAST: Porgy:** Willard White; **Bess:** Laverne Williams; **Serena:** Dorothy Ross; **Clara:** Dinah Harris; **Maria:** Grace Dives; **Sportin' Life:** Zack Matalon; **Jake:** Richard Heyman; **Crown:** John O'Flynn; **Strawberry Woman:** Hilary Weston; Simon Rattle, **conducting** *See*: **B778**

W37eee. 1976-1977 Tour of **Sherman M. Goldman-Houston Grand Opera** production; Performances in Houston, TX; Boston, Cleveland, Chicago, Montreal; Los Angeles (Pantages Theatre); San Francisco, CA; New York *See*: **B759**, **B785**, **B790**

W37fff.   1976 (July 30): Philadelphia; Academy of Music; **CAST:** Houston Grand Opera; Porgy: Donnie Ray Albert; **Bess**: Clamma Dale; **Clara**: Betty Lane; **Serena**: Wilma Shakesnider; **Maria**: Carol Brice; **Crown**: Andrew Smith; **Sportin' Life:** Larry Marshall; **Producer:** Sherwin M. Goldman;. **Staging:** Jack O'Brien; **Sets:** Robert Randolph; **Costumes:** Nancy Potts; **Lighting:** Gilbert V. Hemsley; Jr., John DeMain, **conducting** *See*: **B767**

W37fff.1. 1976 (Aug. 24–26): Wolf Trap, VA; Houston Grand Opera production *See*: **B783**

W37ggg. 1976 (Opened Sept. 25): New York; Uris Theatre (moved to Mark Hellinger Dec. 7) **CAST: Houston Grand Opera; Jassbo Brown:** Ross Reimueller; **Clara:** Betty D. Lane; **Mingo**: Bernard Thacker; **Jake:** Curtis Dickson; **Sportin' Life:** Larry Marshall; **Robbins:** Glover Parham; **Serena:** Wilma Shakesnider (Delores Ivory-Davis); **Jim:** Hartwell Mace; **Peter:** Mervin

Wallace; **Lily:** Myra Merritt; **Maria:** Carol Brice; **Scipio:** Alex Carrington; **Porgy:** Donnie Ray Albert (Abraham Lind-Oquendo, Robert Mosley, alternates); **Crown:** Andrew Smith (George Robert Merritt, alternate); **Bess:** Clamma Dale (Esther Hinds, Irene Oliver, alternates); **Detective;** Hansford Rowe; **Policeman:** William Gammon; **Undertaker:** Cornel Richie; **Annie:** Shirley Baines; **Frazier:** Raymond Bazemore; **Mr. Archdale:** Kenneth Barry; **Strawberry Woman:** Phyllis Bash; **Crab Man:** Steven Alex-Cole; **Coroner:** John B. Ross; **Vocal Ensemble; Staging:** Jack O'Brien; **Settings:** Robert Randolph; **Costumes:** Nancy Potts; **Lighting:** Gilbert V. Hemsley, Jr.; **Choreography:** Mabel Robinson; **Producer:** Sherwin M. Goldman; **Musical director and chorus master:** John DeMain *See:* **B763, B764, B766, B775, B790, B794**

W37ggg.1. 1977 (Jan. 29): Czechoslovakia *See:* **B793**

W37hhh. 1977: Zürich **CAST: Porgy:** Simon Estes; **Bess:** Laverne Williams; **Crown:** Allan Evans; **Sportin' Life:** Charles Williams; **Serena:** Gwendolyn Walters; **Clara:** Diane Bolden; **Maria:** Carol Smith; Charly Schneider, **conducting** *See:* **B769, B770**

W37iii. 1980 (Feb. 2, 9, 15, 16, 23): Bloomington, IN; Indiana University Opera Theater **CAST:** in order of appearance: **Clara:** Luvenia Garner, Roberta Gumbel; **Jake:** Philip Craig, William Johnson; **Sportin' Life:** Ben Barnes, Virgil Vaughn; **Mingo:** Samuel Cook, Leslie Jackson; **Serena:** Pamela Jones, Denise Myers; **Robbins:** Jay Poindexter; **Jim:** Essic Parker; **Peter (the Honey Man):** Albert Neal; **Lily:** Regina Falker, Alicia Helm; **Scipio:** Borden Addai; **Porgy:** Michael Smartt, Martin Strother; **Maria:** Paula Redd; **Crown:** James Mumford, Alvy Powell; **Bess:** Julia Blair, Diane J. Johnson; **Annie:** Joy Clarice Heath; **Nelson:** Ronald House; **Detective:** Mark Lundberg; **Policeman:** Ted Adkins; **Undertaker:** Philip Craig, William Johnson; **Frazier:** Moses Braxton, Jr., Colenton Freeman; **Strawberry Woman:** Johnna McCullough; **Crab Man:** Colenton Freeman; **Coroner:** Dennis Leach; **Little Girls:** Eboni Neal, Elán Neal; **Residents of Catfish Row:** 48 members including 26 from the Afro-American Choral Ensemble, Mellonee Burnim, **conductor; Production staff: Lighting design:** Allen R. White; **Choral directors:** Michael Dixon & Mellonee Burnim; **Stage Designer:** Max Röthlisberger; **Stage Director:** Ross Allen; **General Manager & Conductor:** Charles H. Webb *See:* **B850**

W37iii.1. 1981(Oct. & Nov.): Norfolk & Richmond, VA; The Virginia Opera Association resident company *See:* **B813**

W37jjj. 1983 (opened Feb. 16): Chicago; Arie Crown Theatre **CAST: Jasbo Brown:** George Darden or Eddie Strauss; **Porgy:** Jonathan Sprague or Robert Mosley; **Bess:** Naomi Moody or Daisy Newman or Henrietta Elizabeth Davis; **Serena:** Veronica Tyler or Wilma Shakesnider; **Clara:** Luvenia Garner or Priscilla Baskerville; **Jake:** Alexander Smalls or James Tyeska; **Sportin' Life:** Damon Evans or Larry Marshall; **Crown:** George Baker or George Robert Merritt; **Mingo:** Timothy Allen; **Robbins:** Tyrone Jolivet; **Jim:** Donald Walter Kase; **Peter:** Mervin Bertrel Wallace; **Lily:** Y. Yvonne Matthews;

Maria: Loretta Holkmann or Gwendolyn Shepherd; **Scipio:** Akili Prince; **Detective:** Larry Storch; **Policeman:** William Moize; **Undertaker:** Michael V. Smartt; **Annie:** Lou Ann Pickett; **Frazier:** Raymond H. Bazemore; **Strawberry Woman:** Denice Woods; **Crab Man:** Thomas J. Young; **Nelson:** Everett McCorvey; **Coroner:** Richard Easley; Ensemble; **Producer:** Sherwin F. Goldman; **Staging:** Jack O'Brien; **Choreography:** George Faison; **Sets:** Douglas W. Schmidt; **Lighting:** Gilbert V. Hemsley, Jr.; **Costumes:** Nancy Potts; C. William Harwood, **conducting** *See*: **B843**

W37kkk. 1983 (Apr. 7–May 15): New York; Radio City Music Hall
  CAST:Porgy: Michael V. Smartt or Robert Mosley; **Bess:** Naomi Moody or Daisy Newman or Henrietta Elizabeth Davis; **Serena:** Veronica Tyler; **Clara:** Luvenia Garner or Priscilla Baskerville; **Jake:** Alexander Smalls; **Sportin' Life:** Larry Marshall; **Crown:** George Baker; **Producer:** Sherwin F. Goldman; **Staging:** Jack O'Brien; **Choreography:** George Faison; **Sets:** Douglas W. Schmidt; **Lighting:** Gilbert V. Hemsley, Jr.; C. William Harwood, **conducting** (April 7); John Miner, **conducting** (April 16) *See*: **B809, B816, B819, B828, B829, B833, B863**

W37lll. 1985 (Oct. 10–20): Charleston, SC; Gaillard Auditorium; The Catfish Row Company, Richard Lewine, **Producer CAST: Porgy:** James Tyeska & Arthur Woodley; **Bess:** Daisy Newman & Vanessa Shaw; **Crown:** Ivan Thomas; **Serena:** Barbara Moore; **Sportin' Life:** Damon Evans; **Jake:** Alexander Smalls; **Clara:** Harolyn Blackwell; **Robbins & Choral Director:** James C. Edwards, Jr.; **Stage Director:** John Fearnley; **Choral direction by** James C. Edwards, Jr.; Charleston Symphony Orchestra, David Stahl, **conducting** *See*: **B842, B858**

W37mmm. 1985 (Feb. 6): NY: Metropolitan Opera (Premiere at the Met):
  CAST: Bess: Grace Bumbry; **Clara:** Myra Merritt; **Serena:** Florence Quivar; **Porgy:** Simon Estes; **Sportin' Life:** Charles Williams; **Crown:** Gregg Baker; **Jake:** Bruce Hubbard; **Strawberry Woman:** Isola Jones; **Maria:** Barbara Conrad; **Lily:** Priscilla Baskerville; **Mingo:** John Freeman-McDaniels; **Robbins:** Donald Osborne; **Peter:** Mervin Wallace; **Crabman:** Jay Aubrey Jones; **Undertaker:** Milton B. Grayson, Jr.; **Frazier:** John D. Anthony; **Jim:** Michael Smartt; **Mr. Archdale:** Gary Drane; **Scipio:** Clinton Chinyelu Ingram; **Detective:** Larry Storch; **Coroner:** Hansford Rowe; **Jasbo Brown:** Joseph Joubert; **Policeman:** Andrew Murphy; James Levine, **conducting**; Workshop Ensemble of the Dance Theater of Harlem *See*: **B823, B825, B826, B831, B832, B834, B844, B849, B852, B857, B864, B865, B884**

W37nnn. 1985 (A perf. in Dec.): New York; Metropolitan Opera   **CAST: Jasbo Brown:** Joseph Joubert; **Clara:** Gwendolyn Bradley; **Jake:** David Arnold; **Mingo:** Jerrod Sanders; **Sportin' Life:** Bernard Thacker; **Maria:** Elvira Green; **Serena:** Karen Williams; **Robbins:** Donald Osborne; **Jim:** Michael Lofton; **Peter:** Mervyn Wallace; **Lily:** Hillary Johnson; **Scipio:** Clinton Chinyelu Ingram; **Porgy:** Robert Mosley; **Crown:** Arthur Thompson; **Bess:** Roberta Alexander; **Detective:** Jack Sims; **Police-man:** Andrew Murphy; **Undertaker:** Milton B. Grayson, Jr.; **Frazier:** John D. Anthony; **Mr. Archdale:** Osie Hawkins; **Strawberry Woman:** Isola Jones; **Crabman:** Jay

Aubrey Jones; **Coroner:** Gary Drane; Porgy & Bess Chorus; Workshop Ensemble of Dance Theatre of Harlem; **Chorus master:** David Stivender; **Production:** Nathaniel Merrill; **Sets & Costumes:** Robert O'Hearn; **Staging of Dance Sequences & Consultant to the Production:** Arthur Mitchell; **Lighting Designer:** Gil Wechsler; **Stage Director:** David Sell; James Levine, **conducting**

W37ooo. 1986 (July 5): Glyndebourne, England **CAST: Porgy:** Willard White; **Bess:** Cynthia Haymon; **Clara:** Harolyn Blackwell; **Sportin' Life:** Damon Evans; **Jake:** Bruce Hubbard; **Serena:** Cynthia Clarey; **Maria:** Marietta Simpson; **Crown:** Gregg Baker; **Mingo:** Barrington Coleman; **Robbins:** Johnny Worthy; **Jim:** Curtis Watson; **Peter, The Honey Man:** Mervin Wallace; **Lily:** Dorothy Ross; **Undertaker:** Autris Paige; **Annie:** Paula Ingram; **Frazier:** William Johnson; **Scipio:** Nana Antwi-Nyanin; **Nelson/Crab Man:** Colenton Freeman; **Strawberry Woman:** Maureen Brathwaite; **Jasbo Brown:** Wayne Marshall; **Producer:** Trevor Nunn; **Directors:** John Gunter & Sue Blane; **Choreographer:** Charles Augins; **Conductor:** Simon Rattle; **Substitute conductor:** Richard Bradshaw See: **B803, B804, B810, B839, B817, B820, B823, B824, W841.1, B851, B853, B862, B874, B2058-59.1**

W37ppp. SHERWIN M. GOLDMAN PRODUCTIONS, HOUSTON GRAND OPERA COMPANY TOUR, 1986-1987: (Dec. 29-31, 1986; Jan. 2, 3, 1987 (mat & eve): Miami, FL; Dade County Auditorium (Greater Miami Opera Assoc.); (Jan. 15, 1987-preview, 16, 17 (mat & eve), 18 (mat & eve), 20-23, 24 (mat & eve), 25 (mat): Houston, TX; Jones Hall for the Performing Arts (Houston Grand Opera Assoc.)

W37qqq. 1987: (Feb. 4-6, mat & eve): Austin, TX; Grand Concert Hall (Univ. of Texas Performing Arts) See: **B840**

W37rrr. 1987: (Feb. 11-13, 14 (mat & eve), 15 (mat & eve): Costa Mesa, CA; Orange County Performing Arts Centre (Opera Pacific) See: **B805, B818, B830**

W37sss. 1987: (Feb. 19-22, 25-28, Mar. 1 (mat): Los Angeles, CA; Wiltern Theatre; (L. A. Music Center Opera Association) See: **B860**

W37ttt. 1987: (Mar. 5-6, 7 & 8 (mat & eve): San Diego, CA; Civic Theatre (San Diego Opera) See: **B811, B812**

W37uuu.1987: (Apr. 7-11, 12 (mat & eve): Seattle (WA) Opera House (Seattle Opera); (Apr. 15-17, 18 (mat & eve), 19 (mat): Portland, OR; Portland Civic Auditorium (Portland Opera); (Apr. 23-24, 25 (mat & eve), 26 (mat): Omaha, NB; Orpheum Theatre (Opera Omaha); (Apr. 30, May 1, 2 (mat & eve), 3 (mat): Boston, MA (Boston Opera Assoc.); (May 6-8, 9 (mat & eve), 10 (mat): Louisville, KY: Robert S. Whitney Hall (Kentucky Opera Assoc.)

W37vvv. 1987 (May 13-15, 16 (mat & eve), 17 (mat & eve): Dallas, TX; Music Hall (Fair Grounds) (The Dallas Opera) **CAST: Porgy:** Donnie Ray Albert, Terry Cook; **Bess:** Carmen Balthrop, Henrietta Davis; **Crown:** Gregg Baker, William Bradley-Johnson; **Serena:** Priscella Baskerville, Patricia Miller;

Clara: Rita McKinley; **Maria:** Marjorie Wharton; **Jake:** Jubilant Sykes; **Sportin' Life:** Larry Marshall, Krister St. Hill; **Drama Director:** Jack O'Brien; **Choreographer:** George Faison; **Music Director and Conductor:** John DeMain *See:* **B802, B803, B827**

W37www. 1987 (May 21-22, 23 (mat & eve), 24 (mat): Minneapolis, MN; Northrup Memorial Auditorium (Metropolitan Opera in the Upper Midwest); (May 27-29, 30 (mat & eve), 31 (mat & eve): Cleveland, OH; State Theatre (Cleveland Opera); (June 3-5, 6 (mat & eve), 7 (mat & eve): Detroit, MI; Masonic Temple Auditorium (Michigan Opera Theatre); (June 11-12, 13 (mat & eve), 14 (mat & eve), 16-19, 20 (mat & eve): Denver, CO; Auditorium Theatre (Opera Colorado); June 24-27, 28 (mat & eve), 30, July 1-3, 5 (mat & eve): San Francisco, CA; War Memorial Opera House (San Francisco Opera); 1987 (June 28): London; Barbicon Hall; Concert performance; London Symphony Orchestra; Michael Tilson Thomas, conducting *See:* Full entry at **W54n**

W37xxx. 1987 (Nov. 10–Dec. 13): Paris; Le Théatre musical de Paris/Chatelet
CAST: **Porgy:** Mic Bell, Michael Smartt; **Bess:** Henrietta Davis, Naomi Moody; **Crown:** William Bradley-Johnson, Ivan Thomas; **Serena:** Priscilla Baskerville, Patricia Miller; **Clara:** Rita McKinley; **Maria:** Marjorie Wharton; **Jake:** Jubilant Sykes; **Sportin' Life:** Larry Marshall; **Mingo:** Ronn K. Smith; **Robbins:** Irwin Reese; **Peter:** Mervin Wallace; **Frazier:** Russell Saint John; **Annie:** Jan Forney-Davis; **Lily:** Yvette Matthews; **Strawberry Woman:** Denise Woods; **Jim:** Jerry Godfrey; **Undertaker:** Robert Vaucresson, Jr.; **Nelson:** Robert McDaniel; **Crab Man:** Cornelius White; **Detective:** Alfred J. Kiggins; **Coroner:** Ted Bouton; **Scipio:** Kiah Jackson; **Jasbo Brown (piano):** Fryderyk Babinski; **Habitants of Catfish Row; Dancers:** Karen Eubanks, Linda James, Jo Ann Harris Ingram, Cliff Hicklen, Reggie Leon, Stephen Semien; **Sets:** Douglas W. Schmidt; **Costumes:** Nancy Potts; **Lighting:** John McLain; **Choreography:** Mabel Robinson; **Producer:** Sherwin M. Goldman; **Associate Producer:** Peter Weicker; **Stage director:** Jack O'Brien; **Assistant conductor:** Chris Nance; **Conductor:** Michael Fardink

W37yyy. 1988 (Feb. 4, Feb. 7): London; Royal Festival Hall, in concert; (Feb. 10–15): Calgary, Alberta, Canada; Calgary Jubilee Auditorium; (Apr. 26–May 8): Palermo, Sicily; Teatro Politeama di Palermo; (May 11–June 13): Munich, West Germany; Deutsches Theatre *See:* **B845**

W37zzz. 1988 (May 28–July 31): West Berlin, Germany; Theater des Westens;
CAST: **(partial):** Clamma Dale; Wilhemenia Fernandez; Donnie Ray Albert; **Sets:** Hans Shavernoch; **Director:** Friedrich Götz *See:* **B795, B806, B821**

W37aaaa. 1988 (June 16–19): Messina, Sicily; Teatro Vittoria Emanuels

W37bbbb. 1988 (July 11–17): St. Louis, MO (USA); Muny Theatre, Forest Park
CAST: **Porgy:** Michael Smartt & Robert Mosley; **Bess:** Naomi Moody & Vanessa Shaw; **Crown:** Ivan Thomas & William Bradley-Johnson; **Sportin' Life:** Larry Marshall; **Serena:** Theresa Hamm; **Clara:** Alma Johnson; **Jake:**

Cedric Cannon; **Maria:** Linda F. Thompson; **Lawyer Frazier:** Autris Page; **Strawberry Woman:** Denise Woods; **Sets:** Paul Wonsek; Chris Nance, **conducting** *See*: **B848**

W37cccc. 1989 (Mar. 5–Apr.16): West Berlin, Germany; Theater des Westens *See*: **B807**

W37dddd.1989 (Sept. 29 & 30): Liverpool, England; Liverpool Philharmonic Hall, in concert *See*: **B877**

W37eeee. 1989 (Oct. 6): England; Huddersfield Civic Hall, in concert; (Oct. 7): England; Leeds Town Hall, in concert

W37ffff. 1989 (Apr. 21 & Apr. 23): Syracuse, NY; Syracuse Opera with Syracuse Symphony Orchestra **CAST: Porgy:** Alvy Powell; **Bess:** Roberta Laws; **Crown:** William Drake; **Clara:** Claudette Brown-McCargo; **Serena:** Lou Ann Pickett; **Sportin' Life:** Charles Williams; **Honeyman:** Leslie Childs; **Strawberry Woman:** Tiron Anderson; **Crab Man:** H. Bernard Alex; **Set:** Merrill Stone; **Costumes:** Zach Brown; **Stage direction:** Roman Terleckyj; Chris Nance, **conducting** *See*: **B841**

W37gggg.1990 (Apr. 11–May 20): West Berlin, Germany; Theater des Westens *See*: **B866**

W37hhhh.1995 (opened on Jan. 27, through Feb. 10): Houston, Brown Theater, Wortham Center **CAST** (for the Jan.–Feb. 1995 performances in Houston; the cast varied during the subsequent tour): **Porgy:** Terry Cook & Alvy Powell; **Bess**: Roberta Laws & Marquita Lister, on tour: Isabelle Kabatu; **Crown:** Lester Lynch & Stacey Robinson; **Serena,** Robbins' wife: Luvenia Garner & Angela Simpson; **Clara,** Jake's wife: Kimberly Jones; **Maria,** keeper of the cookshop: Ann Duquesnay; **Jake**: Elex Lee Vann; **Sportin' Life**: Larry Marshall; **Mingo**: Barron Coleman; **Robbins**: Richard Taylor; **Peter,** the honey man: Richard Smith; **Frazier,** a "lawyer:" Keith Crawford; **Annie**: Sabrina Carten; **Lily**: Lou Ann Pickett; **Strawberry Woman**: Sherry Dukes Williams; **Jim**: Matthew J. Minor; **Undertaker**: Henry Jones; **Nelson**: Stanley Jackson; **Crab Man**:David Lee Brewer; **Detective**: Charles Sanders; **Coroner**: Russell Johnson; **African Drummer**: Richard Taylor; **Ensemble**: Residents of Catfish Row, Scipio, fishermen, children, stevedores, etc.; **Drama Director and Choreographer:** Hope Clarke; **Assistant Choreographer:** Tanya Gibson; **Assistant Director:** Amy Hutchison; **Set Designer:** Ken Foy; **Costume Designer:** Judy Dearing; **Lighting Designer:** Ken Billington; **Sound Designer:** Steven Canyon Kennedy; **Assistant Conductor:** Douglas Fisher; **Chorus Preparation:** Richard Bado; **Musical Preparation:** Leticia Austria & Jennifer Walsh; **Music Director and Conductor**: John DeMain *See:* **B 872, B882.** This was a "Broadway-oriented production" in a touring co-production with nine other North American companies, namely:

W37iiii. 1995: (opened Feb. 15): Dallas, TX; Dallas Opera; The Music Hall at Fair Park

W37jjjj.1995 (Mar. 8-12): San Diego, CA; San Diego Opera, Civic Theatre *See*: **B868**

W37kkkk. 1995 (Mar. 16-25): Seattle, WA; Seattle Opera; (Apr. 5-9): Cleveland,

OH; Cleveland Opera State Theatre

W37llll.   1995 (Apr. 26-29): Minneapolis, MN; The University of Minnesota's Northrop Auditorium

W37mmmm.   1995 (May 10-14): Miami, FL; Florida Grand Opera; Dade County Auditorium; (May 24-June 3): San Francisco, CA; San Francisco Opera

W37nnnn. 1995 (June 7-18): Los Angeles, CA; The Los Angeles Music Center Opera; Dorothy Chandler Pavilion *See*: **B867**, **B873, B875;** (June 21-25): Costa Mesa, CA; Orange County Performing Arts Center; Segerstrom Hall

W37oooo.   1995 (July 19-29): Portland, OR; Houston Grand Opera, Portland Opera; Civic auditorium *See*: **B881** Performances at Milan's La Scala and Paris' Bastille Opera were planned.

W37pppp.   1996 (Jan. 31-Feb. 12): Tokyo, Japan; Bunkamura Orchard Hall *See*: **B878**; (Feb. 14–15): Nagoya, Japan; Aichi Arts Theater; (Feb. 17–18): Osaka, Japan; Festival Hall

W37qqqq.   1998 (Dec. 17): NY; Avery Fisher Hall; concert performance; New York Philharmonic; Bobby McFerrin, conducting

OTHER ORIGINAL GERSHWIN WORKS

W38.   *LULLABY,* string quartet, *ca.* 1919-20 (© 1963, pub. 1968) New World; miniature score, 1968. *See*: **B1837**

   Premieres

   W38a. 1963 (Aug. 29) Scotland Edinburgh Festival; Larry Adler, in his arrangement for harmonica & string quartet *See*: **B902**

   W38b. 1967 (Oct. 19): Washington; Juilliard String Quartet

   W38c. 1968 (Apr. 14): NY; Hotel Pierre; Juilliard String Quartet

W39.   *SHORT STORY,* Orig. for pf, arr. S. Dushkin For Violin, pf, *ca.* 1923-25 Orig. published 1925 by Schott; also known as *PRELUDE*, **G MAJOR arr. for violin & piano (*SHORT STORY*),** by Samuel Dushkin, it is a previously unpublished piano prelude; Associated, 1945, at **NN-L, Classmark *MYK-Amer. box**   *See*: **B152**

   Premiere

   W39a. 1925 (Feb. 8): NY; University Club; Samuel Dushkin, Gershwin at the piano

W40.   *RIALTO RIPPLES,* for piano, *ca.* 1916, co-written with Will Donaldson

W41.   *THREE-QUARTER BLUES (Irish Waltz),* for piano, early 1920s

W42. *PRELUDES FOR PIANO,* [5] ca. 1923-26; (Only three were published in 1927)
    See: **B152, B890, B899, B900, B901, B2165, B899, B900, B2154**

Premieres

W42a. 1926 (Dec. 4, 2:30 pm): NY; Hotel Roosevelt, Grand Ballroom;
Marguerite d'Alvarez, contralto, GG, piano *See:* **B886, B887, B888, B892, B896, B898**

W42b. 1927 (Jan.16): Boston; Symphony Hall; Repeat of **W42a.** According to
Jablonski, G played a sixth prelude at this concert. *See:* **B889, B891, B893, B894, B895**

W43. *IMPROMPTU IN 2 KEYS,* for piano, ca. 1924

W44. *MERRY ANDREW* [orig. dance piece in *Rosalie*, 1928, **W29**]

W45. *GEORGE GERSHWIN'S SONG-BOOK,* 18 arrs. of refrains from Gershwin's
songs, orig. published by Random House (1932)
Includes Constantin Alazalov's illlustrations depicting the eighteen songs in the
collection; The volume printed the original sheet music of the songs, plus G's
own arranged party versions. Dedicated to Kay Swift *See:* **B8, B1841, B2157**

SONGS included:

Swanee; Nobody But You; I'll Build a Stairway to Paradise; Do It
Again; Fascinating Rhythm; Oh, Lady Be Good!; Somebody Loves Me;
Sweet and Low-Down; That Certain Feeling; The Man I Love; Clap Yo'
Hands; Do-Do-Do; My One and Only; 'S Wonderful; Strike Up the
Band; Liza; I Got Rhythm; Who Cares? In May a limited, signed edition
was published (300 copies); this included a copy of Mischa, Yascha,
Toscha, Sascha. The transcriptions have been in print in a folio entitled
Gershwin at the Keyboard.

W46. *SLEEPLESS NIGHT,* Gershwin Melody No. 17, ca. 1936. pf piece
Recorded by Michael Tilson Thomas *See:* **D357**

W46.1 *TWO WALTZES IN C,* ca. 1933
Orig. as 2-pf piece in *Pardon My English*, 1933, arr. pf solo by I. Gershwin, S.
Chaplin; (1933; pub. 1971)

W46.2. *NOVELETTE IN FOURTHS* [Prelude No. 5] (*ca.*.1919), "salon piano solo"
Published in ed. by **Alicia Zizzo** by Warner Bros., 1997. *See:* **D610**

W47. *PROMENADE* (1937)
Originally the inst. interlude called *Walking the Dog*, in the movie *Shall We Dance?*,
1937, transcr. pf solo by H. Borne, copy of transcr. at **DLC** (pub. 1960 by the
Gershwin Publishing Co.); orchestral arrangements exist also.
See: **D357, B157**

DERIVATIVE WORKS

W48. *MY ONE AND ONLY* (1983)

Out-of-town tryout given below; Libretto, May 1983. **[NN-L]** Call no. NCOF+84-1034 *See*: **B905**

SONGS

I Can't Be Bothered Now; Blah, Blah, Blah; Boy Wanted; Soon; High Hat; Sweet and Low Down; He Loves and She Loves; 'S Wonderful; Strike Up the Band; In the Swim; Nice Work If You Can Get It; My One and Only; Funny Face; How Long Has This Been Going On?; Kickin' the Clouds Away

Premieres

W48a. 1983 (Feb. 9): Boston; Colonial Theatre; **CAST: Ritz Quartet:** Casper Roos, Paul David Richards, Carl Nicholas, Will Blankenship; **Bishop Wellington St. Kings:** Roscoe Lee Browne; **Deacons:** Adrian Bailey, David Jackson, Alde Lewis, Jr., Bernard Manners, Ken Leigh Rogers, Roderick Spencer Sibert; **Captain Billy Buck Chandler:** Tommy Tune; **Lotus:** Denny Dillon; **Prince Nicolai:** Bruce McGill; **Edythe Herbert:** Twiggy; **Prawn:** Nana Visitor; **Kipper:** Stephanie Eley; **Haddie:** Susan Hartley; **Roe:** Jill Cook; **La Beluga:** Karen Tamburrelli; **Mr. Footbridge, Man in Red Shoes, Baron Saturday:** Charles "Honi" Coles; **Producers:** Paramount Theatre Productions-Francine LeFrak & Kenneth Mark Productions; **Book:** Timothy S. Mayer, based on 1927 show *Funny Face*, with music by GG, lyrics by IG; **Staging & Choreography:** Thommie Walsh & Tommy Tune; **Scenery:** Adrianne Lobel; **Costumes:** Rita Ryack; **Lighting:** Marsha Madeira; **Sound:** Otts Munderloh; **Orchestrations:** Michael Gibson; **Dance Music Arrangements:** Wally Harper, Peter Larson; Jack Lee, conducting *See*: **B914**

W48b. 1983 (Opened May 1): New York; St. James Theatre; **CAST: New Rhythm Boys:** David Jackson, Ken Leigh Rogers, Ronald Dennis; **Captain Billy Buck Chandler:** Tommy Tune; **Mickey:** Denny Dillon; **Prince Nicolai:** Bruce McGill; **Flounder:** Nana Visitor; **Sturgeon:** Susan Hartley; **Minnow:** Stephanie Eley; **Prawn:** Jill Cook; **Kipper:** Niki Harris; **Anchovie:** Karen Tamburelli; **Edith Herbert:** Twiggy; **Rt. Rev. J. D. Montgomery:** Roscoe Lee Browne; **Reporter:** Jill Cook; **Mr. Magix:** Charles "Honi" Coles; Ritz Quartet: Casper Roos, Paul David Richards, Carl Nicholas, Will Blankenship; **Policeman/Stage Doorman:** Paul David Richards; **Mrs. O'Malley:** Ken Leigh Rogers; **Achmed:** Bruce McGill; **Dancing Gentlemen:** Adrian Bailey, Bar Dell Conner, Ronald Dennis, David Jackson, Alde Lewis, Jr., Bernard Manners, Ken Leigh Rogers; **Producers:** Paramount Theatre Productions-Francine LeFrak & Kenneth Mark Productions; **Book:** Peter Stone & Timothy S. Mayer, based on 1927 show *Funny Face*, with music by GG, lyrics by IG; **Staging & Choreography:** Thommie Walsh & Tommy Tune; **Scenery:** Adrianne Lobel; **Costumes:** Rita Ryack; **Lighting:** Marsha Madeira; **Sound:** Otts Munderloh; **Musical Concept & Dance Arrangements:** Wally Harper; **Orchestrations:** Michael Gibson; **Dance Arrangements:** Peter Larson; **Musical and Vocal Direction:** Jack Lee; Associate choreographer: Baayork Lee; **Associate director:** Philip Oesterman; **Musical consultant:** Jonathan Feinstein; Adrian Bailey, conducting *See*: **B908,**

B915, B903 (with different cast), **B1751**; Not the prem.: **B909, B912, B911**

Other Selected Performances

W48c. 1985 (limited run in July): Los Angeles; Ahmanson Theatre; **CAST: Edith Herbert:** Sandy Duncan; **Billy Buck Chandler:** Tommy Tune; **Mr. Magix:** Charles "Honi" Coles; **Prince Nicolai:** Don Amendolia; **Mickey:** Peggy O'Connell; **The Rev. Montgomery:** Tiger Haynes; John Dorrin; Mark East; Walter Hook; Adam Petroski; David Jackson; Ken Leigh Rogers; Glenn Turner; Susan Hartley; Debi A. Monahan; Sandra Menhart; Karen Prunczik; Niki Harris; Elleen Casey; Adrian Bailey; Shaun Baker-Jones; James Ervin; Luther Fontaine; Jan Mickens; **Directors & Choreographers:** Thommie Walsh & Tommy Tune; **Set Design:** Adrianne Lobel & Tony Walton; **Lighting Design:** Marc B. Weiss; **Costumes:** Rita Ryack; **Sound Design:** Otts Munderloh; **Orchestration:** Michael Gibson; **Musical & Vocal Direction:** Jack Lee *See:* **B906, B910, B913**

W49. *REACHING FOR THE MOON,* **A New Musical.** (1987; unpublished?; full evening) **Book by John Mueller**
A new musical based on Gershwin music, in two acts
The Eastman School of Music/University of Rochester contribution to the 1987 commemoration marking the 50th anniversary of G's death. The performances were dedicated to the memory of Fred Astaire

> **Musical numbers:** *Act I*, Overture/Nice Work if You Can Get It; Put Me to the Test ; A Foggy Day; For You, For Me, Forever More; The World Is Mine; Nice Work if You Can Get It (reprise); He Loves And She Loves; I Don't Think I'll Fall In Love Today; These Charming People; I Can't Be Bothered Now; *Act II*, Prelude (orchestra); Sing of Spring; Let's Call the Whole Thing Off; Things Are Looking Up; Pay Some Attention to Me; Love Is Here To Stay; Stiff Upper Lip; Love Walked In; Put Me To The Test (reprise); They All Laughed; But Not For Me; Love Walked In (reprise); Finale

Premieres

W49a. 1987 (Oct 30-Nov 3, 6 perfs.): Rochester, NY; Kilbourn Hall, Eastman School of Music, University of Rochester; Eastman Opera Theater; **CAST: Lady Jessica:** Nancy R. Allen; **Keggs:** Brad Fullagar; **Steve Riker:** Ronald Watkins; **Billie Dore:** Kimberly Jajuan; **Mac:** Steven Scheschareg; **Policeman:** Derrick Smith; **Lady Caroline:** Sonya Raimi; **Thomas:** Todd Greer; **Lord Marshmoreton:** Robert Aberdeen; **Albertina:** Caroline Scimone; **Alice Faraday:** Lynn Matthews; **Reggie:** Kevin A. Tarte; **Captain Plummer:** James Dalfonso; **Walter Jordan:** Terry Stoneberg; **A Cockney Man:** Brian Chilton; **Lyrics** by IG; **Book** by John Mueller; Based on *A Damsel in Distress*, a play by Ian Hay & P. G. Wodehouse & a novel by P. G. Wodehouse; **Choreographer:** Teddy Kern; **Set design:** Peter Harvey; **Costumes:** John Deering & Lare Schultz; **Lighting design:** Michael W. Powell; **Director:** Richard Pearlman; **Musical arrangements & orchestrations:** Rayburn Wright, **conducting** *See:* **B884**

W50. *CRAZY FOR YOU* (1992; full evening)
See: **B298, B300, B303, B304 Typescript** of script at **NN-L**

Premieres

W50.1. 1991 (Dec. 12): Washington; National Theatre; Out-of-town tryout?

W50a. 1992 (Feb. 19): New York; Shubert Theatre; Tryout run was in Washington,
National Theatre, December, 1991 prior to NY opening, *See:* **B315**; This show also
played London during 1993, *See:* **B299, B306, B307, B311;** and Japan, *See:* **B309,
B310** (Casts varied)

    CAST for NY prem.: **Tess:** Beth Leavel; **Patsy:** Stacey Logan; **Bobby Child:**
Harry Groener (the leading man); **Bela Zangler:** Bruce Adler; **Sheila:** Judine
Hawkins Richard; **Mitzi:** Paula Leggett; **Susie:** Ida Henry; **Louise:** Jean Marie;
Betsy: Penny Ayn Maas; **Margie:** Salomé Mazard; **Vera:** Louise Ruck; **Elaine:**
Pamela Everett; **Irene Roth:** (Bobby's jealous fiancée) Michele Pawk; **Mother:**
Jane Connell; **Perkins:** Gerry Burkhardt; **Moose, Mingo, & Sam:** Manhattan
Rhythm Kings (Brian M. Nalepka, Tripp Hanson, & Hal Shane); **Junior:** Casey
Nickolaw; **Custus:** Gerry Burkhardt; **Pete:** Fred Anderson; **Jimmy:** Michael
Kubala; **Billy:** Ray Roderick; **Wyatt:** Jeffrey Lee Broadhurst; **Harry:** Joel
Goodness; **Polly Baker:** Jodi Benson (the leading lady); **Everett Baker:** Ronn
Carroll; **Lank Hawkins:** John Hillner; **Eugene:** Stephen Temperly; **Patricia:**
Amelia White; **The Ensemble**

    Swings Choreography: Susan Stroman; **Sets:** Robin Wagner; Dance &
Incidental music arranged by: Peter Howard; **Musical consultant:** Tommy
Krasker; **Sound design:** Otis Munderloh; **Orchestrations:** William D. Brohn;
Playwright: Ken Ludwig; **Director:** Mike Ockrent; **Musical direction:** Paul
Gemignani; **Producers:** Roger Horchow & Elizabeth Williams
See: **B298, B301, B302, B303, B305 (B1139), B308, B312, B313,
B316, B317, B318, B319, B320**

    SONGS:

    18 Gershwin standards and 5 rediscovered songs, including: in order of
presentation:
Act I: K-ra-zy for You; I Can't Be Bothered Now; Bidin' My Time; Things
Are Looking Up; Could You Use Me?; Shall We Dance?; Someone to Watch
Over Me; Slap That Bass; Embraceable You; Tonight's the Night; I Got
Rhythm; **Act II:** The Real American Folksong; What Causes That?; Naughty
Baby; Stiff Upper Lip; They Can't Take That Away From Me; But Not For
Me; Nice Work If You Can Get It; Finale

Other Selected Performances

W50b. 1994 (Opening night: Jan. 18): New Orleans, LA; Saenger Performing Arts
Center; 1994 Touring Company
    CAST: (in order of appearance) **Tess:** Cathy Susan Pyles; **Patsy:** Sally Boyett;
Bobby Child: James Brennan; **Bela Zangler:** Stuart Zagnit; **Sheila:** Sharon
Ferrol; **Mitzi:** Heather Douglas; **Susie:** Caitlin Carter; **Louise:** Angie L.
Schworer; **Betsy:** Kay Perry; **Vera:** Jenny Gruby; **Irene Roth:** Belle Calaway;
Mother: Ann B. Davis; **Perkins:** Noel Parenti; **Moose:** John Boswell; **Cody:**

Bobby Clark; **Sam:** Alan Gilbert; **Bud:** Gary Kirsch; **Custus:** Noel Parenti; **Mingo:** Jackie J. Patterson; **Jimmy:** Keith Savage; **Billy:** Bill Brassea; **Wyatt:** Stephen Reed; **Johnny Joe:** Michael Lord; **Polly Baker:** Karen Ziemba; **Everett Baker:** Carleton Carpenter; **Lank Hawkins:** Christopher Coucill; **Eugene:** Geoffrey Wade; **Patricia:** Jeanette Landis

> **The Ensemble:** John Boswell; Bill Brassea; Caitlin Carter; Bobby Clark; Heather Douglas; Sharon Ferrol; Alan Gilbert; Jenny Gruby; Gary Kirsch; Michael Lord; Noel Parenti; Jackie J. Patterson; Kay Perry; Stephen Reed; Keith Savage; Angie L. Schworer
> **Swings:** Deanna Dys; Stacey Todd Holt; Mia Malm; Dean Stroop

W50c. 1994 (Nov. 8-13): San Antonio, TX; Majestic Theatre; 1994 Touring Company
> **CAST:** Same as above except: **Bobby Child:** Kirby Ward; **Bela Zangler:** Paul Keith; **Sheila:** Sharon Ferrol; **Mitzi:** Heather Douglas; **Susie:** Caitlin Carter; **Louise:** Jennifer Paige Chambers; **Betsy:** Tony Georgiana; **Vera:** Jenny Gruby; **Irene Roth:** Belle Calaway; **Mother:** Ann B. Davis; **Perkins:** Scott Willis; **Moose:** Tom Sardinia; **Cody:** Jack Doyle; **Sam:** Alan Gilbert; **Bud:** Gary Kirsch; **Custus:** Scott Willis; **Mingo:** Jackie J. Patterson; **Jimmy:** Franz C. Alderfer; **Billy:** Matt Baker; **Wyatt:** Stephen Reed; **Johnny Joe:** Jeff Shade; **Polly Baker:** Beverly Ward; **Everett Baker:** Al Checco; **Lank Hawkins:** Daren Kelly; **Eugene:** John Curless; **Patricia:** Not listed in San Antonio cast

> **The Ensemble:** Franz C. Alderfer; Matt Baker; Caitlin Carter; Jennifer Paige Chambers; Heather Douglas; Jack Doyle; Sharon Ferrol; Alan Gilbert; Toni Georgiana; Jenny Gruby; Gary Kirsch; Jackie J. Petterson; Stephen Reed; Tom Sardinia; Jeff Shade; Scott Willis

> **Swings:** Same as in New Orleans, above

W50d. 1995: continuing New York run; Sam S. Shubert Theatre **CAST:** (*in order of appearance)*: **Tess:** Melinda Buckley; **Patsy**: Rebecca Downing; **Bobby Child:** James Brennan; **Bela Zangler:** Bruce Adler; **Sheila**: Judine Richard; **Mitzi**: Wendy Waring; **Susie:** Angie L. Schworer; **Louise:** Jean Marie; **Betsy:** Leigh Zimmerman; **Margie:** Kimberly Hester; **Vera**: Shannon Lewis; **Elaine**: Elizabeth Mills; **Irene Roth**: Pia Zadora; **Mother**: Ann B. Davis; **Perkins:** James Young; **Moose:** Gary Douglas; **Mingo**: Branch Woodman; **Sam**: Alan Gilbert; **Junior**: John M. Wiltberger; **Custus**: James Young; **Pete**: James Doberman; **Jimmy**: Michael Kubala; **Billy**: Ray Roderick; **Wyatt:** Stephen Reed; **Harry**: Joel Goodness; **Polly Baker:** Karen Ziemba; **Everett Baker:** John Jellison; **Lank Hawkins:** Daren Kelly; **Eugene**: Stephen Temperley; **Patricia**: Colleen Smith Wallnau

> **The Ensemble**: James Doberman, Gary Douglas, Rebecca Downing, Alan Gilbert, Joel Goodness, Kimberly Hester, Michael Kubala, Shannon Lewis, Penny Ayn Maas, Jean Marie, Elizabeth Mills, Stephen Reed, Judine Hawkins Richard, Ray Roder, Angie L. Schworer, John M. Wiltberger, Branch Woodman, James Youn, Leigh Zimmerman

Swings: William Alan Coats, Angelique Ilo, Stacey Todd Holt, Scott Taylor, Leigh-anne Wencker

MUSICAL CREDITS:
Scenes and Musical Numbers

Scene 1: Backstage at the Zangler Theatre, New York City, in the 1930s
K-ra-zy for You, Bobby
Scene 2: 42nd Street, outside the theatre
I Can't Be Bothered Now, Bobby and the Girls
Scene 3: Main Street, Deadrock, Nevada
Bidin' My Time Mingo, Moose and Sam
Things Are Looking Up, Bobby
Scene 4: Lank's Saloon
Could You Use Me?, Bobby and Polly
Scene 5: In the Desert
Shall We Dance?, Bobby and Polly
Scene 6: The Gaiety Theatre
Scene 7: Main Street, Deadrock, three days later
Entrance to Nevada, The Company
Someone To Watch Over Me, Polly
Scene 8: The Lobby of the Gaiety Theatre, two weeks later
Scene 9: The Stage of the Gaiety Theatre
Slap That Bass *, Bobby, Moose, Tess, Patsy and Company
Embraceable You, Polly and Bobby
Scene 10: The Gaiety Theatre Dressing Room, opening night
Tonight's the Night**, The Company
Scene 11: Main Street, Deadrock
I Got Rhythm Polly and the Company

Act II
Scene 1: Lank's Saloon, later that evening
The Real American Folk Song (Is a Rag), Mingo, Moose and Sam
What Causes That?, Bobby and Bela
Scene 2: Lank's Saloon, the next morning
Naughty Baby***, Irene, Lank and Boys
Scene 3: The Gaiety Theatre, backstage
Scene 4: The Auditorium of the Gaiety Theatre
Stiff Upper Lip, Bobby, Polly, Eugene, Patricia and Company
They Can't Take That Away From Me, Bobby
But Not for Me, Polly
Scene 5: New York, six weeks later
Nice Work If You Can Get It, Bobby and Girls
Scene 6: Main Street, Deadrock, six days later
Finale, The Company
*__Orchestration__ by Sid Ramin; **__Lyric__ by Ira Gershwin and Gus Kahn;
***__Lyric__ by Ira Gershwin and Desmond Carter
ADDITIONAL PRODUCTION CREDITS:
Roger Horchow and Elizabeth Williams present the new Gershwin musical comedy "Crazy for You"; Music and Lyrics by George and Ira Gershwin; **Book by** Ken Ludwig; **Co-Conceived by** Ken Ludwig and Mike Ockrent;

Inspired by material by Guy Bolton and John McGowan; Scenic Design by Robin Wagner; Costume Design by William Ivey Long; Lighting Design by Paul Gallo; Dance & Incidental Music arranged by Peter Howard; Musical Consultant: Tommy Krasker; Sound Design by Otis Munderloh; Fight Staging by B.H. Barry; Conducted by Pam Drews Phillips; Orchestrations by William David Brohn; Musical Direction by Paul Gemignani; Choreography by Susan Stroman; Directed by Mike Ockrent

PLOT:

A new musical comedy inspired by the 1930 musical "Girl Crazy," with a cornucopia of Gershwin songs set in a new book by Ken Ludwig. Young banker sets out to foreclose on an old theater in Arizona, but winds up falling for the owner's feisty daughter. Mistaken identities and lots of fancy dancing keep things hopping.

MISC. DATA: Best Musical Tony Award, 1992;. 1993 Olivier Award Winner.

W51.   *THE GEORGE AND IRA GERSHWIN SONG BOOK.* (1960)

Foreword by Ira Gershwin, Illustrations by Milton Glaser, Arrangements by Albert Sirmay. New York: Simon & Schuster, 1960.

The foreword by IG is primarily biographical. Included with the set is an elucidating section "Marginalia on Most of the Songs," also by Ira. Alfred Simon compiled the excellent appendix "List of Songs by George Gershwin with Lyrics by Ira Gershwin and Others," together with the facts about the shows and motion pictures in which these songs were used.

CONTENTS: Fascinatin' Rhythm [sic]; The Half of It, Dearie, Blues; The Man I Love; Oh, Lady, Be Good!; Looking for a Boy; Do, Do, Do; Maybe; Someone to Watch Over Me; Funny Face; How Long Has This Been Going On?; 'S Wonderful; Strike Up the Band; I've Got a Crush on You; Soon; Bidin' My Time; But Not for Me; Could You Use Me?; Embraceable You; I Got Rhythm; Blah, Blah, Blah; Delishious; Love Is Sweeping the Country; Of Thee I Sing; Who Cares; Isn't It a Pity?; The Lorelei; Mine; It Ain't Necessarily So; By Strauss; Let's Call the Whole Thing Off; They All Laughed; They Can't Take That Away from Me; A Foggy Day (In London Town); Nice Work If You Can Get It; Things Are Looking Up; Love Walked In; Our Love Is Here to Stay; Swanee; Somebody Loves Me; Summertime

Derivative Ballet

W52. *WHO CARES?* (1970) ballet based on Gershwin music

See: B1712; *Also see*: Review by W. Terry, *Saturday Review* 53 (Mar. 7, 1970):41.

Premiere

W52a . 1970 (Feb. 5): NY State Theater; NY City Ballet; Pianist on opening night (orchestration had been completed only for *Strike Up the Band* and *I Got Rhythm*): Gordon Boelzner; *Clap Yo' Hands* played by GG, recorded; CAST: Karin von Aroldingen, Patricia McBride, Marnee Morris, Jacques d'Amboise; 15 women, 5 men; Program: Strike Up the Band: Ensemble;

Sweet And Low Down: Ensemble; **Somebody Loves Me:** Deborah Flomine, Susan Hendl, Linda Merrill, Susan Pilarre, Bettijane Sills; **Bidin' My Time:** Deni Lamont; Robert Maiorano, Frank Ohman, Richard Rapp, Earle Sieveling; **'S Wonderful!:** Pilarre, Rapp; **That Certain Feeling:** Flomine, Lamont, Sills, Sieveling; **Do, Do, Do:** Hendl, Ohman; **Lady, Be Good!:** Merrill, Maiorano; **Repeat:** Ensemble; **The Man I Love:** McBride, d'Amboise; **I'll Build A Stairway To Paradise:** von Aroldingen; **Embraceable You:** Morris, d'Amboise; **Fascinating Rhythm:** McBride; **Who Cares?:** von Aroldingen, d'Amboise; **My One and Only:** Morris; **Liza:** d'Amboise; **Clap Yo' Hands:** von Aroldingen, McBride, Morris, d'Amboise; **I Got Rhythm:** Entire cast; **Orchestrations:** Hershy Kay; **Choreography:** George Balanchine; First presented with costumes (by Karinska) but without décor; from November, 1970. with **scenery** by Jo Mielziner; Robert Irving, **conducting**

Other Selected Performances

W52b. Revisions: (1976): NY; NY City Ballet; Clap Yo' Hands eliminated

W52c. Stagings: (1980): Zürich; 1982: Chicago City (excerpts)

W52d. Television: (1971): CBC, Montreal; 1975, The Man I Love, NBC

W52e. Videorecording: at **NN-L,** Call # *MGZIA 4-1378; Imprint 1971.
  1 cassette. 39 min. : sd. b&w NTSC. ; 1/2 in. (VHS)
  Note: Excerpt from Le New York City Ballet, produced by Radio-Canada and telecast by the Canadian Broadcasting Corporation in 1971.
  For the complete telecast, see: *MGZHB 12-583.
  Choreography: George Balanchine. Music: George Gershwin.
  Scenery: Jo Mielziner. Costumes: Karinska.
    Performed by members of the New York City Ballet: Patricia McBride, Marnee Morris, Karin von Aroldingen, Jean-Pierre Bonnefous, and ensemble. Cast: Strike up the band, perf. by ensemble. Sweet and low down, perf. by ensemble. Somebody loves me, perf. by five women. Bidin' my time, perf. by five men. 'S wonderful, perf. by couples. The man I love, perf. by McBride and Bonnefous. I'll build a stairway to paradise, perf. by von Aroldingen. Embraceable you, perf. by Morris and Bonnefous. Fascinatin' rhythm, perf. by McBride. Who cares?, perf. by von Aroldingen and Bonnefous. My one and only, perf. by Morris. Liza, perf. by Bonnefous. Clap yo'hands, perf. by McBride, Morris,von Aroldingen, and Bonnefous. I got rhythm, perf. by entire cast.

W52f. Videorecording at **NN-L,** Call # *MGZIA 4-2072; Imprint 1992.
  Performed by Pacific Northwest Ballet ; choreography by George Balanchine; staging by Susan Hendl and Christine Redpath; music, George Gershwin.
  Tape location: in Performing Arts-Dance   *MGZIA 4-2072
    1 videocassette (42 min.) : sd., col. NTSC ; 1/2 in. (VHS)
  Note: Title from container and accompanying program.
  CONTENTS and PERFORMERS: Strike up the band / performed by Theresa Goetz, Linnette Hitchin, Karen Meisenholder, Lauri-Michelle

Rohde, Melanie Skinner, Uko Gorter, Charles Newton, Brad Phillips, Daniel Wong, Yu Xin, Marisa Albee, Catherine Baker, Amara Balthrop-Lewis, Leah Belliston, Kristen Brackman, Rachel Butler, Bryce Jaffe, Gavin Larsen, Jennifer Sax, and Lisa Williamson -- Sweet and low down/ performed by Albee, Baker, Balthrop-Lewis, Belliston, Brackman, Butler, Jaffe, Larsen, Sax, and Williamson --Somebody loves me / performed by Goetz, Hitchin, Meisenholder, Rohde, and Skinner -- Bidin' my time/ performed by Gorter, Newton, Phillips, Wong, and Yu -- 'S wonderful / performed by Goetz and Yu -- That certain feeling / performed by Skinner and Gorter -- That certain feeling (second time) / performed by Rohde and Wong -- Do do do / performed by Meisenholder and Newton -- Lady be good / performed by Hitchin and Phillips, with Skinner, Gorter, Rohde, Wong, Goetz, Yu, Meisenholder, and Newton -- The man I love / performed by Patricia Barker and Phillip Otto -- I'll build a stairway to paradise / performed by Lucinda Hughey -- Embraceable you / performed by Ariana Lallone and Otto -- Fascinatin' rhythm / performed by Barker -- Who cares? / performed by Hughey and Otto -- My one and only / performed by Lallone -- Liza / performed by Otto -- I got rhythm / performed by entire cast

Scenery: Tony Walton ; costumes, Patricia Zipprodt; lighting, Randall G. Chiarelli

Videotaped in performance at Seattle Center Opera House, Seattle, Washington, on November 21, 1992.

W52.1. *AT WIT'S END* (1987), a play by **Joel Kimmel**

Premiere

W52.1.aa. (1987): Jupiter, FL; Burt Reynolds Theatre (world premiere) *See:*
B918.3, B1583, B1571

CAST: Oscar Levant: Stan Freeman, pianist
Book by Joel Kimmel
Directed by: Charles Nelson Reilly
The play was given in other locations in Florida after its premiere

Other Selected Performance

W52.1.bb. (1989); Los Angeles, Coronet Theatre
CAST: Stan Freeman, playing Oscar Levant
Set Design: Patrick Hughes and Christopher Mandick
Tuxedo Design: Noel Taylor
Book by Joel Kimmel
Directed by: Charles Nelson Reilly
Associate Producer: Richard Thomas Hart
Producers: Lawrence Kasha & Ronald A. Lachman

MUSIC:

RiB; Second Rhapsody; Three Preludes; AiP; Concerto; Swanee; Somebody Loves Me; Lady Play Your Mandolin (Oscar Levant, Irving Caesar); True Blue Lou (Whiting, Spier & Coslow); That Old Feeling (Sammy Fain, Lew

Brown); Wacky Dust (Levant, Stanley Adams); Blame It On My Youth (Levant, Edward Heyman); That's Entertainment (Howard Dietz, Arthur Schwartz)

See: **B918.2, B918.3, B1571, B1583**

MISCELLANEOUS PUBLICATIONS OF GERSHWIN MATERIAL

W53. WODEHOUSE, Artis. *Gershwin's Improvisations for Solo Piano transcribed from the 1926 and 1928 disc recordings*. Secaucus, NJ: Warner Bros. #PF0471, 1987.
CONTENTS: (Dates are the original recording dates), Clap Yo' Hands (Dec. 11, 1926); Looking for a Boy (July 6, 1926); Maybe (Dec. 11, 1926); My One and Only (Aug. 6, 1928); Someone to Watch Over Me (Aug. 11, 1926); Sweet and Lowdown (July 6, 1926); 'S Wonderful!/Funny Face (June 12, 1928); That Certain Feeling (July 6, 1926) *See:* **B916, B917, B918, D1056, B1856, B1857, B1858, D1134**

Selected Performance:

W53a. 1988 (Dec. 10): Stanford, CA; Stanford University, Dinkelspiel Auditorium, presented by Department of Music, Archive of Recorded Sound; Gershwin and Friends," Alex Hassan & Artis Wodehouse, solo & duo-pianists **Program:** Gershwin trans. by Wodehouse, and performed by her: Looking for a Boy, Maybe, Someone to Watch Over Me, So Am I (1926 piano roll), 'S Wonderful!/Funny Face; From 1926 piano rolls, trans. & arr. by Wodehouse, and performed by Alex Hassan & Wodehouse: That Certain Feeling, Sweet and Low-Down, Kickin' the Clouds Away; other period pieces by Roy Bargy, Saul Sieff, Billy Mayerl, Frank Banta, Rolph Bolton, & Joy Gorney

OTHER PERFORMANCES AND
SELECTED ALL-GERSHWIN CONCERTS

There have been innumerable performances of Gershwin music as well as All-Gershwin concerts of varying historical importance. A selection of these performances follows:

W54a. 1937 (Sept. 8): Hollywood; Hollywood Bowl, Southern California Symphony Association, **Memorial Concert**; **Program:** Prelude, Otto Klemperer, conducting; AiP, Nathaniel Shilkret, conducting; Speaker, George Jessel; Song Group: Swanee, Al Jolson; The Man I Love, Gladys Swarthout; They Can't Take That Away From Me, Fred Astaire, Victor Young, conducting; Concerto, Oscar Levant, piano, Charles Previn, conducting; Anthology: The Man I Love, Liza, Lady Be Good, Somebody Loves Me, Do It Again, I Got Rhythm, Wintergreen, Strike Up the Band, Nathaniel Finston, conducting; P&B excerpts: Summertime, Lily Pons; My Man's Gone Now, Ruby Elzy & Hall Johnson Choir; Buzzard Song, Todd Duncan; The Train Song, Anne Brown & Hall Johnson Choir; I Got Plenty of Nuttin', Todd Duncan & Hall Johnson Choir; Bess You Is My Woman Now, Todd Duncan & Anne Brown with Hall Johnson Choir; I'm On My Way, Todd Duncan & Hall Johnson Choir, Alexander Steinert, conducting; RiB, José Iturbi, piano, and conducting *See:* **D749, B1252**

W54b. 1937 (Aug. 9): New York; Lewisohn Stadium; Harry Kaufman, piano (On Concerto & RiB), Ethel Merman, Todd Duncan, Anne Brown, Eva Jessye

Chorus; New York Philharmonic-Symphony Orchestra; Alexander Smallens & Ferde Grofé, conducting; **Program:** Excerpts from OTIS; Concerto; Summertime (Anne Brown), My Man's Gone Now (Ruby Elzy), The Train Song (Brown), I Got Plenty of Nuttin', repeated (Duncan), Bess, You Is My Woman Now (Duncan & Brown), Buzzard Song & I'm On My Way (Duncan); Short extract from Strike Up the Band; AiP; The Man I Love; Strike Up the Band, They Can't Take That Away From Me; I Got Rhythm, repeated (the latter four songs by Merman); RiB *See*: **B919, B923, B1709**

W54c. 1938 (July 12): NY; Lewisohn Stadium; New York Philharmonic Symphony Orchestra; Paul Whiteman Orchestra; Maxine Sullivan, vocals; Lyn Murray Chorus **Program**: RiB; Second Rhapsody; AiP; Hollywood Medley: They Can't Take That Away From Me, Nice Work if You Can Get It, Love Walked In; Summertime; Do It Again (chorus); Dawn Of a New Day

W54d. 1942 (Aug. 31): NY; "The Telephone Hour"; Oscar Levant, piano soloist; Bell Telephone Orchestra & Chorus; Donald Voorhees, conducting
Program: Medley (Swanee, Somebody Loves Me, Embraceable You) Chorus & Orchestra; Preludes II & III for piano; Medley (Someone to Watch Over Me, Fascinating Rhythm) Orchestra; Concerto, 2nd Movement; Medley (Lady Be Good, Do It Again, Liza, Wintergreen for President) Levant, Chorus, & Orchestra *See*: **B1583**

W54d.1. 1943 (Nov. 17, 19, 21): NY; New York Philharmonic
Program: Included AiP *See*: **B172**

W54e. 1946 (Apr. 18): NY; Carnegie Hall; Philharmonic-Symphony Orchestra, Pension Fund Benefit Concert; **Soloists:** Anne Brown, soprano; Todd Duncan, baritone; Oscar Levant, piano soloist; Artur Rodzinski, conducting **Program:** AiP; Concerto; Excerpts from P&B: Buzzard Song; Summertime, I Got Plenty O' Nuttin'; My Man's Gone Now; It Ain't Necessarily So; Bess, You Is My Woman Now; RiB *See*: **B166, B1583**

W54f. 1948 (July 17) Los Angeles; Hollywood Bowl; Hollywood Bowl Orchestra; Oscar Levant, Piano soloist; Eugene Ormandy, conducting
Program: AiP, Concerto; Cuban Overture; Suite from P&B (Bennett); RiB *See*: **B1583**

W54g. 1949 (July 7): NY; Lewisohn Stadium; Oscar Levant, piano; New York Philharmonic; Alexander Smallens, conducting
Program: Concerto; Second Rhapsody; RiB; Two of the three Piano Preludes; Strike Up the Band selections; AiP; P&B medley arr. by Robert Russell Bennett *See*: **B1583**

W54h. 1966 (Jan. 23): NY; Philharmonic Hall, "George Gershwin's Theatre"
CAST: Soloists: Jack Cassidy; Barbara Cook; Stan Freeman, **piano;** Eileen Rodgers; Veronica Tyler; William Walker; **Producer:** Music Theater of Lincoln Center; **Commentator:** Garry Moore; **Commentary by:** Judy Crichton; **Staging:** Roger Ellender; **Orchestra & Chorus conducted by:** Jay Blackton

W54i. 1970 (Oct. 27, 28, 29): Miami; Dade County Auditorium (first two concerts)

& Miami Beach Auditorium (third concert), sponsored by University of Miami School of Music, **"The George Gershwin Festival;"** **Oct 27:** University of Miami Symphony Orchestra; Frederick Fennell, conducting: *Strike Up the Band* (not on the program), *Cuban Overture*, *Second Rhapsody*, *Promenade*, & AiP. **Oct 28:** University of Miami Symphony Orchestra, Frederick Fennell, conducting: *Symphonic Syntheses of Song Classics*, Ivan Davis, piano: *Preludes for Piano*, University of Miami Student String Quartet: *Lullaby*, Mary Henderson Buckley, soprano, & George Roth, piano: *In A Mandarin's Orchid Garden*, George Zazofsy, violin, & George Roth, piano: *A Short Story*, & Ivan Davis, piano: *Concerto*. **Oct 29:** George Roth, piano; University of Miami Symphony Orchestra; Frederick Fennell, conducting: *"I Got Rhythm" Variations* & *Rhapsody in Blue*; Orchestral Excerpts from *135th Street*; **Porgy:** Eugene Holmes, baritone; **Bess:** Rebecca Langstroth; Chamber Singers; Lee Kjelson, conducting: P&B (Concert version, arr. and abridged for concert performance by Robert Russell Bennett) *See*: **B157, B1667, B1782**

W54j. 1981 (Dec. 14): Los Angeles; Academy of Motion Picture Arts and Sciences; Samuel Goldwyn Theatre, sponsored by the Academy Foundation; **"A Salute to Ira Gershwin"**; Introduction by **Arthur Hamilton,** Chairman, Executive Committee of the Music Branch of the Academy; Hosted and moderated by **Ronald Haver,** Director of Film Programs at the Los Angeles County Museum of Art **Program:** "Blah, Blah, Blah," from *Delicious* (1931); "Bell Telephone Hour—The Music of Gershwin" (1959); Title Song from *Lady Be Good* (1941); "The Man I Love" from *The Helen Morgan Story* (1957); "Clap Yo' Hands" from *Funny Face* (1957); "But Not For Me" & "Embraceable You" from *Girl Crazy* (1943); "By Strauss" from AiP (1951); "Delicious" from *Delicious* (1931); "I Got Rhythm" from AiP; "Nice Work if You Can Get It" from *A Damsel in Distress* (1937); "Let's Call The Whole Thing Off" from *Shall We Dance?*; "They Can't Take That Away From Me" from *Shall We Dance?* (1937); "A Foggy Day" from *A Damsel in Distress*; "Love Walked In" from *The Goldwyn Follies* (1937); Oscar Levant/Fred Astaire T. V. Show (1958); "Our Love Is Here to Stay" from AiP; Trailer from *Shocking Miss Pilgrim* (1946); "The Saga of Jennie" from *Lady in the Dark* (1944); "Nina, Pinta and the Santa Maria" from *Where Do We Go From Here?* (1947); "Who's Complaining?" from *Cover Girl* (1944); "Long Ago (and Far Away)" from *Cover Girl*; "Island in the West Indies" from *The Judy Garland Show* T. V. (1963); "Weekend in the Country" from *The Barkleys of Broadway* (1949); "Dissertation on a State of Bliss" from *The Country Girl* (1954); "Calypso Commercial," "Gotta Have Me Go with You," & "The Man That Got Away" from *A Star is Born* (1954); "'S Wonderful!" from AiP; **Program coordinated by** Douglas Edwards, Michael Feinstein, & Ronald Haver; **Film Prints courtesy of:** Columbia, UA, UA Classics, UCLA Film & Television Archives; Universal, 20th Century-Fox, MGM, Goldwyn Studios, Warner Bros. Films, Inc., RKO, Paramount, Los Angeles County Museum of Art, Sid Luft, & USC Special Collections

W54k. 1985 (Jan.6): Virginia Beach, VA; Pavilion, **"Gershwin and Company Salute;"** Jan Curtis, mezzo-soprano & George Gershwin, Duo-Art pianist (recording of piano roll); The Virginia Symphony Pops; Newton Wayland, guest conducting; **Program:** Overture to Strike Up the Band; Gershwin on Broadway medley: I Got Rhythm, Someone to Watch Over Me, The Man I Love, Stairway to Paradise, Swanee, My Ship; AiP; RiB; Tchaikovsky (Weill); The Man That

Got Away

W54l. 1981 (Dec. 14): Los Angeles; Academy of Motion Picture Arts and Sciences, Samuel Goldwyn Theatre, sponsored by the Academy Foundation; **"A Salute to Ira Gershwin"** *See*: Full entry at **B54j.**

W54m. 1987 (Mar. 11): NY; Brooklyn Academy of Music, Opera House, "The Gershwin Gala: A Tribute to the musical collaboration of George and Ira Gershwin in celebration of the 125th Anniversary of the Brooklyn Academy of Music." **Stage Director:** Patricia Birch; **Performers:** Leonard Bernstein; (performing the Prelude II for piano); American Ballroom Theater; Drew Barrymore; Mikhail Baryshnikov; Gregg Burge; Rosemary Clooney; The Copasetics; Damon Evans; Cynthia Haymon; Ruby Hinds; Bob Dylan; Madeline Kahn; Larry Kert; Manhattan Rhythm Kings; Julia Migenes; Maureen McGovern; Erie Mills; Harold Nicholas; Chita Rivera; Bobby Short; Tommy Tune; Christopher Walken; **Choreography:** Walter Painter & Dan Siretta; **Scenery & Costumes:** Eduardo Sicangco; **Producer:** Arthur Whitelaw; Johnny Green with big band; The Orchestra of St. Luke's; Michael Tilson Thomas, conducting *See*: **B921, B1530, B1719, B1866**

W54n. 1987 (June 28): London; Barbican Hall; Concert performance; London Symphony Orchestra; Michael Tilson Thomas, conducting; **CAST: Porgy:** Willard White; **Bess:** Cynthia Haymon; **Sportin' Life:** Bernard Thacker; Alteouise DeVaughn; Camellia Johnson; Barrington Coleman; This performance included "Lonely Boy," the newly-restored duet orchestrated by Gregg Smith and first performed in NY earlier this year. *See*: **B1809**

W54o. 1987 (July 2): London; The Barbicon; Larry Adler, harmonica; Peter Donohue, piano; London Symphony Orchestra; Michael Tilson Thomas, conducting; **Program**: Overture to Cake (Don Rose, arr.); Lullaby (Adler); Concerto; With music by Kurt Weill

W54p. 1987 (July 5): London; The Barbicon; Nigel Kennedy, violin; Cleo Laine, vocals; LSO chorus; London Symphony Orchestra; Michael Tilson Thomas, conducting; **Program:** Three Piano Preludes (Kennedy playing Heifetz's arrangements); Overture to OTIS (Don Rose arr.); AiP; Songs (Laine); Swanee (chorus)

W54q. 1987 (July 17 & 18): Hollywood, CA; Hollywood Bowl, **"A Memorial Tribute;"** Michael Feinstein, piano; Andrew Litton, conducting

W54r. 1988 (May 7): New Orleans, LA; Orpheum Theater, sponsored by The Omega Foundation; **"Shirley Verrett Sings Gershwin;"** Shirley Verrett, vocals; Moses G. Hogan & John Nauman, duo-pianists; Pickup orchestra basically from New Orleans Symphony; Warren George Warren, conducting
Eighteen Songs, including: Our Love Is Here To Stay; Do It Again; Stairway To Paradise; For You, For Me, Forever More; Someone to Watch Over Me; They Can't Take That Away From Me; Love Walked In; Embraceable You; Fascinating Rhythm; Let's Call The Whole Thing Off; But Not For Me; They All Laughed; The Man I Love; RiB (Hogan & Nauman); Arrangements by Pat Holley

W54s. 1988 (June 23): Washington; Library of Congress, Coolidge Auditorium;
"**A Program of Music by George and Ira Gershwin Celebrating the Presentation of the Congressional Gold Medal Honoring George and Ira Gershwin's Contributions to American Music**"; **Performers:** Rebecca Luker; Chris Groenendaal; John McGlinn, conducting the Musicrafters; **Program:** Overture from OTIS; Embraceable You; How Long Has This Been Going On?; Love Walked In; Isn't It a Pity?; The Man I Love; Love Is Sweeping the Country

W54t. 1988 (Dec. 10): Stanford, CA; Stanford University, Dinkelspiel Auditorium, presented by Department of Music, Archive of Recorded Sound; "**Gershwin and Friends,**" Alex Hassan & Artis Wodehouse, solo & duo-pianists **Program:** Gershwin trans. by Wodehouse, and performed by her: Looking for a Boy, Maybe, Someone to Watch Over Me, So Am I (1926 piano roll), 'S Wonderful!/Funny Face; From 1926 piano rolls, trans. & arr. by Wodehouse, and performed by Alex Hassan & Wodehouse: That Certain Feeling, Sweet and Low-Down, Kickin' the Clouds Away; other period pieces by Roy Bargy, Saul Sieff, Billy Mayerl, Frank Banta, Rolph Bolton, & Joy Gorney *See:* **W53**

W54u. 1989 (May 22 & 23): Washington; Coolidge Auditorium, Library of Congress,
"**A Program of Music by George and Ira Gershwin Celebrating the Inauguration of the Leonore Gershwin/Library of Congress Recording and Publishing Project**"
CAST and Program: **Act I:** Overture from *Girl Crazy*, orchestrated by Robert Russell Bennett; Our Little Kitchenette from *La-La-Lucille!*, orchestrated by Maurice DePackh: Paige O'Hara & David Garrison; Isn't It Wonderful? from *Primrose*, orchestrated by GG: Rebecca Luker & men; Somebody Loves Me from *George White's Scandals of 1924*, orchestrated by DePackh: Christine Andreas; You're Mighty Lucky from *Sweet Little Devil*, orchestrator unknown: Richard Muenz & Luker; From *Tip-Toes*: Looking for a Boy: Luker; That Certain Feeling: Muenz & Luker; When Do We Dance?: Garrison & O'Hara; Sweet and Low-Down: Damon Evans & company; *Pardon My English*: My Cousin in Milwaukee, orchestrated by Adolph Deutsch: O'Hara; Isn't It a Pity?, orchestrated R. R. Bennett: Garrison & Luker; I've Got to Be There, orchestrated by Adolph Deutsch: Evans; 'S Wonderful! from *Funny Face*, orchestrated by R. R. Bennett, restored in 1989 by Dale Kugel: Muenz & Andreas; Oh, So Nice from *Treasure Girl*, orchestrated by William Daley: O'Hara & Evans; Strike Up the Band [1927 & 1930]: Yankee Doodle Rhythm, orchestrated in 1989 by Larry Moore: Garrison; Soon, orchestrated in 1989 by Russell Warner: Muenz & Andreas; Hanging Around With You, orchestrated in 1989 by Russell Warner: Luker & Garrison; Homeward Bound, orchestrated in 1988 by Larry Moore: Evans; Strike Up the Band [1927 & 1930], orchestrated in 1989 by Russell Warner: Muenz & company;/ **Act Two,** Overture from *Oh, Kay!*, orchestrated by Hilding Anderson, restored in 1987 by Larry Moore; "**A Selection of Songs By G & I Gershwin:**" Michael Feinstein; "**A Tribute to Ira Gershwin:**" Oh Me! Oh My! Oh You! from *Two Little Girls in Blue* [1921], Vincent Youmans/IG, orchestrated by Stephen O. Jones: Feinstein & Andreas; This is New from *Lady in the Dark* [1941], Kurt Weill/IG, orchestrated by Kurt Weill: Muenz & Luker; My Ship from *Lady in the Dark*, orchestrated by Kurt Weill: Andreas; **A selection of songs featuring the lyrics of IG:** Feinstein; Fun to be Fooled from *Life Begins at 8:40* [1934], Harold Arlen/IG & E. Y. Harburg, orchestrated by Hans Spialek; Weekend Cruise from *Life Begins at 8:40*,

orchestrator unknown: Morrow & company; I Can't Get Started from *Ziegfeld Follies of 1936*, Vernon Duke/IG, orchestrated by Don Walker: Feinstein; *Girl Crazy*, all orchestrations by R. B. Bennett, Bidin' My Time: Evans & women; Barbary Coast: O'Hara; Embraceable You: Muenz & Morrow; Treat Me Rough: Garrison; I Got Rhythm: Morrow & company; Of Thee I Sing from *Of Thee I Sing*, orchestrator unknown: Entire company; **Duo-pianists:** Michael Barrett & Steve Blier; **Supervising Producer:** Tommy Krasker; the **Musicrafters Orchestra**, Robert Fisher, conducting *See*: **B930, B935, B1662**

SELECTED CENTENNIAL COMMEMORATIVE EVENTS

W54v. 1998 (Mar. 13-16): Washington; Coolidge Auditorium at Library of Congress; **"The Gershwins and Their World;"** Robert Kimball and Elizabeth H. Auman, Coordinators

W54w. 1998 (Sept. 8): NY; Oak Room of the Algonquin Hotel. The cabaret singer Mary Cleere Haran opened a month long Gershwin engagement at the Oak Room in the Algonquin Hotel in Manhattan. *See*: **D855.1, D1164.1**

W54x. 1998 (Sept. 10-12): Washington; Kennedy Center;   The Kennedy Center presents the premiere of a new ballet choreographed by Hope Clark, to the 1958 Miles Davis and Gil Evans landmark jazz recording of *Porgy and Bess.*

W54y. 1998 (Sept. 18): Paris; Outdoor "Popular Ball" featuring the Claude Bolling Big Band. All the lights of the Place de l'Hôtel will be turned blue for the occasion

W54z. 1998 (Sept. 20): Kilgore, TX opening of "American Rhapsody," a concert tour that will bring Gershwin to more than 30 towns across the American West

W54aa. 1998 (Sept. 23): NY; Carnegie Hall opens its 108th season with **"Gershwin at 100,"** a gala conducted by Michael Tilson Thomas, featuring the San Francisco Symphony, the mezzo soprano Frederica von Stade along with Audra McDonald and Brian Stokes Mitchell, co-stars of *Ragtime*, the popular musical currently running on Broadway. Sept. 26: **"Gershwin at 100"** will be reprised at the Kennedy Center

W54bb. 1998 (Sept. 26): National Public Radio observed the actual birthday with 24 hours of Gershwin programing. At the Carnegie Recital Hall, "A Birthday Toast to Gershwin" will be offered by the Eaken Piano Trio, with the actress Dana Ivey reading excerpts from Gershwin-related writings.

W54cc. 1998 (Oct. 24): Paris; The Cité de la Musique in Paris will play host to **"Gershwin Non-Stop,"** a three-day marathon.

W54dd. 1998: (Oct. 28-Nov. 8): Brooklyn, NY; **"The Gershwins at 100,"** sponsored by the Institute for Studies in American Music & the Arts at Brooklyn College; Included symposiums and performances at Brooklyn College and CUNY Graduate Center (Manhattan), including a screening of the rarely seen Samuel Goldwyn-produced 1959 movie *Porgy and Bess.*

W54ee. 1998 (Nov. 12): NY; Sylvia Fine and Danny Kaye Playhouse; The New York Festival of Song offers a concert led by Audra McDonald

W54ff. 1998 (Nov. 19): NY; The Metropolitan Museum of Art presents a Gershwin recital by the composer William Bolcom and his wife, the vocalist Joan Morris

W54gg. 1998 (Dec. 10-19): The New York Philharmonic contributes its tribute—three programs, featuring André Previn as piano soloist, Sylvia McNair as vocal soloist and the singer Bobbie McFerrin conducting a concert performance of *Porgy and Bess*

W54hh. 1998: Paris; Théâtre Champs-Elysée; Orchestre National de France; Seiji Ozawa conducting, performing in concert with the jazz pianist Marcus Roberts and the singer-songwriter James Taylor

Addendum to Ballets:

W55. 1940 (Oct. 18): NY; 51st Street Theater; Ballet Russe de Monte Carlo presented a new ballet *The New Yorkers,* with G music adapted and orchestrated by David Raksin (World Premiere)

Individual Songs

This list is based on the work of Wayne Schneider (*New Grove Dictionary of American Music*, 6th ed., **B40**), Robert Kimball and Alfred Simon (*The Gershwins*, **B62**) Kimball's *The Complete Lyrics of Ira Gershwin*, **B21**, and that of Deena Rosenberg *(Fascinating Rhythm*, **B80**). Readers so interested will find the name(s) of performers who introduced the songs and the names of the shows in which they were introduced. Songs by composers other than GG, with lyrics by IG in whole or in part are not included here as they are in Kimball and Simon. Music written by GG in collaboration with other composers is listed and so indicated. In the interest of saving space, names of lyric writers are not given here. Readers needing names of lyric writers may find them under the listings of the shows in Chapter II, Works and Performances, or in Rosenberg's *Fascinating Rhythm*. Songs thought to be published as separate sheet music are marked with an asterisk (*). Songs thought to be published as parts of piano/vocal scores are marked with a cross (+). Dates are those of the year of first performance. Readers with a special interest in a study of the songs may find Jon Conrad's study of 132 of the songs **(B2158)**, helpful; Conrad points out discrepancies between the various lists.

A

According to Mr. Grimes, Ferris Hartman and ensemble, *Treasure Girl*, 1928; **Acrobats,** unused, *Funny Face*, 1927; **Across the Sea*,** Richard Bold and Pearl Regay, *George White's Scandals*, 1922; **Adored One,** unused, *Show Girl*, 1929; **A Foggy Day*** (See under"F"); **A-Hunting We Will Go,** unused, *Treasure Girl*, 1928; **Ain't It Romantic,** unused, *Oh, Kay!,* 1926; **All Over Town,** unused, *The Rainbow*, 1913; **All the Livelong Day (and the Long, Long Night)*,** Roy Walston, *Kiss Me, Stupid*, 1964; **All the Mothers of the Nation,** Lois Moran and ensemble, Cake, 1933; **And I Have You,** unused, *Girl Crazy*, 1930; **Any Little Tune,** Fred A. Leslie and ensemble, *The Rainbow*, 1923; **Anything for You,** Vinton Freedley and Juanita Fletcher, *A Dangerous Maid*, 1921; **A Red Headed Woman*,** Warren Coleman, *Porgy and Bess*, 1935; **Aren't You Kind of Glad We Did?*,** Dick Haymes and Betty Grable, *The Shocking Miss Pilgrim*, 1946; **Argentina*,** Jack McGowan and ensemble, *George White's Scandals*, 1922; **Ask Me Again,** written *ca.* 1930, considered for *Goldwyn Follies*, 1938; **At Half Past Seven*,** may have been sung by Hazel Dawn and Joe Schenck in *Nifties*, 1923 (Same melody used in *Primrose* song: "Some Far-Away Someone"); **At Mrs. Simpkin's Finishing School,** unused, *Show Girl*, 1929; **At the Ex-King's Club,** A. P. Kaye and ensemble, *Rosalie*, 1928; **Aviator,** unused, *Funny Face*, 1927; **A Woman Is a Sometime Thing*,** Edward Matthews and ensemble, *Porgy and Bess*, 1935

B

The Babbitt and the Bromide*, Fred and Adele Astaire, *Funny Face*, 1927; **Baby!***, Emma Haig, Andrew Tombes, and ensemble, *Tell Me More*, 1925; **The Baby Blues,** Delyle Alda and ensemble, *Snapshots*, 1921; **Baby Dolls,** Helen Shipman and ensemble, *Morris Gest Midnight Whirl*, 1919; **The Back Bay Polka***, Allyn Joslyn, Charles Kemper, Elizabeth Patterson, Lillian Bronson, Arthur Shields, Betty Grable, *The Shocking Miss Pilgrim*, 1947; **Back Home,** unused, *Dere Mable*, 1920; **The Bad, Bad Men,** unused, *Lady, Be Good!*, 1924; **Barbary Coast***, Ginger Rogers, Olie Brady, and Eunice Healy, *Girl Crazy*, 1930; **Bauer's House,** unused, *Pardon My English*, 1933; **Beau Brummel+,** Percy Hemming and ensemble, *Primrose*, 1924; **Beautiful Bird,** 1918; **Beautiful Gypsy***, unused, *Rosalie*, 1928 (same music as "Wait a Little Bit, Susie," from *Primrose)*; **Because, Because***, Grace Brinkley, George Murphy, and ensemble, OTIS, 1931; **(I've Got) Beginner's Luck***, Fred Astaire, *Shall We Dance*, 1937; **Beneath the Eastern Moon***, Lola Raine and ensemble, *The Rainbow*, 1923; **Berkeley Square and Kew+,** Claude Hulbert and Margery Hicklin, *Primrose*, 1924; **Bess, You Is My Woman Now***, Todd Duncan and Anne Brown, *Porgy and Bess*, 1935; **The Best of Everything***, John E. Hazzard and ensemble, *La, La, Lucille*, 1919; **Be the Life of the Crowd,** unused, *Sweet Little Devil*, 1924; **Bidin' My Time***, The Foursome, *Girl Crazy*, 1930; **Birthday Party,** Betty Compton, Gertrude McDonald, and ensemble, *Funny Face*, 1927; **Black and White,** ensemble, *Show Girl*, 1929; **Blah, Blah, Blah***, *Delicious*, 1931 (Previous titles: see "I Just Looked at You" and "Lady of the Moon."); **Bluebeard,** unused, *Funny Face*, 1927; **Blue, Blue, Blue***, ensemble, Cake, 1933; **Blue Hullabaloo,** unused, *Funny Face*, 1927; **Blue Monday Blues,** Jack McGowan and ensemble, *George White's Scandals*, 1922; **Boy Wanted***, ensemble, *A Dangerous Maid*, 1921, same melody with revised lyrics by IG and Desmond Carter sung by Heather Thatcher and ensemble, *Primrose*, 1924; **Boy! What Love Has Done to Me!***, Ethel Merman, *Girl Crazy*, 1930; **Bride and Groom***, Sascha Beaumont, Oscar Shaw, Frank Gardiner, and ensemble, *Oh, Kay!*, 1926; **Bring On the Ding Dong Dell,** unused, *Oh, Kay!*, unused, *Strike Up the Band* (first version), 1927; **Bronco Busters***, ensemble, *Girl Crazy*, 1930; **But Not For Me***, Ginger Rogers and Willie Howard, *Girl Crazy*, 1930; **But Not in Boston,** unused, *The Shocking Miss Pilgrim*, 1947; **Buy a Little Button From Us,** ensemble, *Lady, Be Good!*, (London production), 1926; **Buzzard Song***, *Porgy and Bess*, 1935; **By and By***, Thomas Conkey and Eva Clark, *Our Nell*, 1922; **By Strauss***, Gracie Barrie and ensemble, *The Show is On*, 1936

C

Cadet Song, *Rosalie*, 1928; **Can We Do Anything?+***, *Primrose*, 1924; **Carnival Time,** ensemble, *Lady, Be Good!*, 1924; **Changing My Tune***, Betty Grable, *The Shocking Miss Pilgrim*, 1946; **China Girl,** unused, unproduced musical, *Ming Toy*, 1929; **Cinderelatives***, ensemble, *George White's Scandals*, 1922; **Clap Yo' Hands***, Harland Dixon, Betty Compton, Paulette Winston, Constance Carpenter, Janette Gilmore, and ensemble, *Oh, Kay!*, 1926; **Clara, Don't You Be Downhearted***, ensemble, *Porgy and Bess*, 1935; **Climb Up the Social Ladder,** Lois Moran and ensemble, Cake, 1933; **Cloistered from the Noisy City,** Ralph Riggs and ensemble, Cake, 1933; **Come Along, Let's Gamble,** unused, *Funny Face*, 1927; **Comes the Revolution,** Victor Moore and ensemble, Cake, 1933; **Come to the Moon***, Paul Frawley and Lucille Chalfont, *Capitol Revue* ("Demitasse"), 1919; **Cooney County Fair,** Olin Howland, Emma Haig, and ensemble, *Our Nell*, 1922; **Cossack Love Song (Don't Forget Me)*** (music by GG and Herbert Stothart), Tessa Kosta, Guy Robertson, and ensemble, *Song of the Flame*, 1925; **Could You Use Me?***, Ginger Rogers and Allen Kearns, *Girl Crazy*, 1930; **The Countryside (This is the Life for a Man),** Percy Heming, *Primrose*, 1924; **Crab Man***, *Porgy and Bess*, 1935; **Crap Game Fugue,** ensemble, *Porgy and Bess*, 1935; **Cupid,**

probably sung by Sibyl Vane, *Half Past Eight*, 1918; **The Custody of the Child,** unused, *Our Nell*, 1922

D

Dance Alone with You (Why Does Ev'rybody Have to Cut In)*, unused, *Funny Face*, 1927 (same music as "Ev'rybody Knows I Love Somebody" from *Rosalie*); **Dancing Hour,** unused, *Tip-Toes*, 1925; unused, *Funny Face*, 1927; **Dancing in the Streets,** ensemble, *Pardon My English*, 1933; **Dancing Shoes*,** Vinton Freedley and Juliette Day, *A Dangerous Maid*, 1921; **Dawn of a New Day*,** 1938, song for the New York World's Fair, 1939; **Dead Men Tell No Tales,** unused, *Treasure Girl*, 1928; **Dear Little Girl (I Hope You've Missed Me)*,** Oscar Shaw and ensemble, *Oh, Kay!*, 1926; **Delishious*,** Raul Roulien, *Delicious*, 1931; **Demon Rum,** ensemble, *The Shocking Miss Pilgrim*, 1947; **The Dimple on My Knee,** ensemble, OTIS, 1931; **Dixie Rose*,** Featured by Al Jolson, 1921 (Same music as Swanee Rose); **Do, Do, Do*,** Oscar Shaw and Gertrude Lawrence, *Oh, Kay!*, 1926; **Do It Again!*,** Irene Bordoni, *The French Doll*, 1922; **Don't Ask!,** Harland Dixon and the Fairbanks Twins, *Oh, Kay!* 1926; **Double Dummy Drill,** Cake, 1933; **Doughnuts,** Annette Bade and ensemble, *Morris Gest Midnight Whirl*, 1919; **Do What You Do*!,** Ruby Keeler and Frank McHugh, *Show Girl*, 1929; **Dream Sequence ('We're from the *Journal*, the *Wahrheit*, the *Telegram*, the *Times*),** Raul Roulien, Marvin(e) Maazel, and ensemble, *Delicious*, 1931; **The Dresden Northwest Mounted,** Jack Pearl and ensemble, *Pardon My English*, 1933; **Drifting Along with the Tide*,** Lloyd Garrett and Victoria Herbert, *George White's Scandals* (1921)

E

Embraceable You*, Ginger Rogers, *Girl Crazy*, 1930, **End of a String,** ensemble, *Lady, Be Good!*, 1924; **Entrance of the French Ambassador,** OTIS, 1931; **Entrance of the Supreme Court Judges,** ensemble, OTIS, 1931; **Evening Star,** unused, *Lady, Be Good!*, 1924; **Everybody Swat the Profiteer,** Myra Cullen, Anna Green, Sascha Beaumont, Eleanor Dana, Ruth Grey, and Vera Colburn, *George White's Scandals*, 1920; **Every Girl Has a Way,** unused, *A Dangerous Maid*, 1921; **Ev'rybody Knows I Love Somebody*,** Bobbe Arnst and Jack Donahue, *Rosalie*, 1928 (Added after opening. Same music as "Dance Alone with You," dropped from *Funny Face)*

F

Far Away, Greek Evans and the Russian Art Choir, *Song of the Flame*, 1925; **Fascinating Rhythm*,** Fred and Adele Astaire and Cliff Edwards, *Lady, Be Good!*, 1924; **Fatherland, Mother of the Band,** unused, *Pardon My English*, 1933; **Feeling I'm Falling*,** Gertrude Lawrence and Paul Frawley, *Treasure Girl*, 1928; **Feeling Sentimental*,** unused, *Show Girl*, 1929; **Fidgety Feet*,** Harland Dixon, Marion Fairbanks and ensemble, *Oh, Kay!*, 1926; **The Finest of the Finest,** unused, *Funny Face* (1927); **First Lady and First Gent,** unused, Cake, 1933; **The Flapper** (music by GG and William Daly), non-production, 1922; **Fletcher's American Cheese Choral Society,** Herbert Corthell, Max Hoffman, Jr., Robert Bentley, and ensemble, *Strike Up the Band* (first version), 1927; **Fletcher's American Chocolate Choral Society*,** Dudley Clements, Robert Bentley, Gordon Smith, and ensemble, *Strike Up the Band* (second version), 1930; **A Foggy Day (In London Town)*,** Fred Astaire, *A Damsel in Distress*, 1937; **Follow the Drum,** Marilyn Miller and ensemble, *Rosalie* (added after opening), 1928; **Follow the Minstrel Band,** Eddie Jackson and band, *Show Girl*, 1929; **For You, For Me, For Evermore*,** Dick Haymes and Betty Grable, *The Shocking Miss Pilgrim*, 1947; **Four Little Sirens+,** ensemble, *Primrose*, 1924; **French Ballet Class,** *Shall We Dance*, 1937; **Freud and Jung and Adler,** unused, *Pardon My English*, 1933; **From Now On*,** Janet Velie and John E. Hazzard, *La, La, Lucille*, 1919; **Funny Face*,** Fred and Adele Astaire, *Funny Face*,

1927; **Futuristic Melody,** Leo Henning, Ruth White, Gertrude McDonald, Violet Vale, Inez and Florence Courtney, and Gilda Gray, *Snapshots,* 1921

G

Gambler of the West, The, unused, *Girl Crazy,* 1930; **Garçon, S'il Vous Plait*,** OTIS, 1931; **Garden of Love,** Helen Hudson and the Tip Top Four, *George White's Scandals,* 1923 (added on tour); **Gather Ye Rosebuds,** unused, *Tip-Toes,* 1925; **General's Gone to a Party, The,** George Kirk, William Gaxton, Richard Temple, and ensemble, Cake, 1933; **Girl I Love, The,** Morton Downey, *Strike Up the Band* (first version), 1927 (rewritten lyric of "The Man I Love"); **Give Me My Mammy,** unused, *The Rainbow,* 1923; **Gol-Durn!** (Music by GG and William Daly), Jimmie Barry and ensemble, *Our Nell,* 1922; **Gone, Gone, Gone*,** ensemble, *Porgy and Bess,* 1935; **Goodbye to the Old Love, Hello to the New,** unused, *Treasure Girl,* 1928; **Good Little Tune,** non-production, *ca.* 1918; **Good Mornin', Sistuh!*,** chorus, *Porgy and Bess,* 1935; **Good Night, My Dear*,** Grace Hayes, *The Rainbow,* 1923; **Got a Rainbow*,** Walter Catlett, Peggy O'Neill, Virginia Franck, and ensemble, *Treasure Girl,* 1928; **Guess Who?,** unused, *Oh, Kay!,* 1926; **Gush-Gush-Gushing,** non-production, 1918

H

Hail the Happy Couple, Carl Randall, Barbara Newberry, and ensemble, *Pardon My English,* 1933; **The Half of It, Dearie, Blues*,** Fred Astaire and Kathlene Martyn, *Lady, Be Good!,* 1924; **Hangin' Around with You*,** Doris Carson and Gordon Smith, *Strike Up the Band!* (second version), 1930; **Hanging Throttlebottom in the Morning,** ensemble, Cake, 1933; **Hang On to Me*,** Fred and Adele Astaire, *Lady, Be Good!,* 1924; **Happy Birthday,** ensemble, *Show Girl,* 1929; **Harbor of Dreams,** unused, *Tip-Toes,* 1925; **Harlem River Chanty*,** unused, *Tip-Toes,* 1925; **Harlem Serenade*,** Ruby Keeler and ensemble, *Show Girl,* 1929; **Has Anyone Seen My Joe?,** Coletta Ryan, *George White's Scandals,* 1922 (Music adapted from "Lullaby' for string quartet written in 1919); **Have You Heard?,** Leslie Henson and Claude Hulbert, *Tell Me More* (London production, 1925; **Heaven on Earth*,** Oscar Shaw, Betty Compton, Constance Carpenter, *Oh, Kay!,* 1926; **He Knows Milk*,** Jerry Goff, Margaret Schilling, Robert Bentley, Dudley Clements, Bobby Clark and ensemble, *Strike Up the Band* (second version), 1930; **A Hell Of a Hole,** William Gaxton and ensemble, Cake, 1933; **Hello, Good Morning*,** ensemble, OTIS, 1931; **He Loves and She Loves*,** Adele Astaire and Allen Kearns, *Funny Face,* 1927; **He-man, The,** unused, *Tell Me More,* 1925; **Here Come De Honey Man*,** *Porgy and Bess,* 1935; **Here's a Kiss for Cinderella,** William Gaxton and ensemble, OTIS, 1931; **He's Not Himself,** entire company, *Pardon My English,* 1933; **He's Oversexed,** *Pardon My English,* 1933; **Hey! Hey! Let 'er Go!*,** William Wayner and ensemble, *Sweet Little Devil,* 1924; **High Hat*,** Fred Astaire and ensemble, *Funny Face,* 1927; **Hi-Ho*,** written for Fred Astaire but unused, *Shall We Dance,* 1937; **Home Blues** (Lyrics by IG and Gus Kahn, set to Homesickness Theme from *An American in Paris),* Joseph Macauley, *Show Girl,* 1929; **Home Lovin' Gal,** unused, *Show Girl,* 1929; **Home Lovin' Man,** unused, *Show Girl,* 1929; **Homeward Bound,** Morton Downey and ensemble, *Strike Up the Band* (first version), 1927; **Hong Kong,** thought to have been sung by Sibyl Vane, *Half Past Eight,* 1918; **Hooray for the U. S. A.,** Franklyn Ardell, Ruth Warren, and ensemble, *Sweet Little Devil,* 1924; **Hoping That Someday You'll Care,** Vivian Hart and Roger Pryor, *Strike Up the Band,* (first version), 1927; **How About a Boy like Me?*,** Bobby Clark, Paul McCullough, Dudley Clements, and Blanche Ring, *Strike Up the Band* (second version), 1930; **How About a Man Like Me?,** Herbert Corthell, Lew Hearn, and Edna May Oliver, *Strike Up the Band* (first version), 1927; **How Beautiful*,** ensemble, *If Thee I Sing,* 1933; **How Can I Win You Now?,** Emma Haig and Andrew Tombes, *Tell Me More!,* 1925 (Replaced after opening by "Once"); **How Could I Forget?,** Blaine Cordner and Barbara Newberry, *Show*

Girl, 1929; **How Long Has This Been Going On?***, unused, *Funny Face*, 1927; Bobbe Arnst, *Rosalie*, 1928; **(On the Beach At) How've-You-Been?**, Helen Hudson and ensemble, *George White's Scandals*, (Same music as "Lo-La-Lo"), 1923

I

I Ain't Got No Shame*, *Porgy and Bess*, 1935; **I Can't Be Bothered Now***, Fred Astaire, *A Damsel in Distress*, 1937; **I Can't Tell Where They're From When They Dance,** George White; danced by Mary Reed and Myra Cullen, *George White's Scandals*, 1922; **Idle Dreams***, Lloyd Garrett, Ann Pennington, and ensemble, *George White's Scandals*, 1920; **I Don't Know Why (When I Dance with You),** unused, *Dere Mable*, 1920; **I Don't Think I'll Fall in Love Today***, Gertrude Lawrence and Paul Frawley, *Treasure Girl*, 1928; **I'd Rather Charleston***, Fred and Adele Astaire, *Lady, Be Good!* (London production), 1926; **If I Became the President***, Bobby Clark and Blanche Ring, *Strike Up the Band* (second version), 1930; **I Forgot What I Started to Say,** unused, *Rosalie*, 1928; **I Found a Four Leaf Clover,** Colleta Ryan and Richard Bold, *George White's Scandals*, 1922; **If You Only Knew,** 1918; **If You Will Take Our Tip,** unused, *Funny Face*, 1927; **I Got Plenty o'Nuthin'***, Todd Duncan and ensemble, *Porgy and Bess*, 1935; **I Got Rhythm***, Ethel Merman, the Foursome, and ensemble, *Girl Crazy*, 1930; **I Know a Foul Ball,** Victor Moore, Cake, 1933; **I Love to Rhyme***, Phil Baker, Edgar Bergen, and "Charlie McCarthy," *Goldwyn Follies*, 1938; **I Love You***, Harry Rose, *George White's Scandals*, 1921; **I Love You, My Darling,** Will Mahoney, *George White's Scandals*, 1924; **I Loves You, Porgy***, Anne Brown and Todd Duncan, *Porgy and Bess*, 1935; **I'll Build a Stairway to Paradise***, Winnie Lightner, Pearl Regay, Coletta Ryan, Olive Vaughn, George White, Jack McGowan, Richard Bold, Newton Alexander, and ensemble, with Paul Whiteman's Orchestra, *George White's Scandals*, 1922; **Illegitimate Daughter, The***, Florenz Ames and ensemble, OTIS, 1931; **I'll Show You a Wonderful World,** Helen Shipman and Bernard Granville, *Morris Gest Midnight Whirl*, 1919; **I'm About to Be a Mother***, Lois Moran and ensemble, OTIS, 1931; **I'm a Poached Egg***, Cliff Osmand and Ray Walston, *Kiss Me Stupid*, 1964; **I Make Hay While the Moon Shines+**, Heather Thatcher, *Primrose*, 1924; **I'm Going Back,** Will Mahoney, *George White's Scandals*, 1924; **I'm Just a Bundle of Sunshine,** unused, *Show Girl*, 1929; **I'm On My Way,** (See Oh Lawd, I'm On My Way); **I'm Out for No Good Reason Tonight,** unused, *Show Girl*, 1929; **Impromptu in Two Keys***, Instrumental possibly intended for unproduced *Ming Toy*, 1929, Amerigrove (*New Grove DAM*) says *ca.* 1924; **I'm Somethin' on Avenue A,** *Tell Me More*, 1925; **I Just Looked at You,** unused, *Show Girl*, 1929 (Same music as "Blah, Blah, Blah" in *Delicious*, 1931, and "Lady of the Moon" in the unproduced *Ming Toy*, 1929; **I Mean to Say***, Doris Carson and Gordon Smith, *Strike Up the Band* (second version), 1930; **I Must Be Home by Twelve O'clock***, Ruby Keeler and ensemble, *Show Girl*, 1929; **I Need a Garden***, Helen Hudson and Elm City Four, *George White's Scandals*, 1924; **Innocent Ingenue Baby***, John Merkyl and ensemble, *Our Nell*, 1922; **Innocent Lonesome Blue Baby*** (Music by GG and William Daly, revised version of "Innocent Ingenue Baby"), Stephanie Stephens and Alec Kellaway; danced by Ted Grant and Frances Wing, *The Rainbow*, 1923; **In Sardinia,** Lou Holtz and ensemble, *Tell Me More*, 1925; **In the Heart of a Geisha***, 1921; **In the Mandarin's Orchid Garden***, written for the unproduced *Ming Toy*, 1929 (Introduced in recital by Eleanor Marum with Carroll Hollister at piano, Blackstone Theatre, Chicago, November 10, 1929); **In the Rain***, Fred A. Leslie, Stephanie Stephens, and ensemble, *The Rainbow*, 1923; **In the Rattle of the Battle***, ensemble, *Strike Up the Band* (second version), 1930; **In the Swim,** ensemble, *Funny Face*, 1927; **In Three-Quarter Time,** Ruth Urban, John Cortez, and ensemble, *Pardon My English*, 1933; **Invalid Entrance,** unused, *Funny Face*, 1927; **Isn't It a Pity?***, George Givot and Josephine Houston, *Pardon My English*, 1933; **Isn't It Terrible What They Did to Mary Queen of Scots,** Leslie Henson and Claude

Hulbert, *Primrose,* 1924; **Isn't It Wonderful?+*,** Margery Hicklin and ensemble, *Primrose,* 1924; **It Ain't Necessarily So*,** John W. Bubbles and ensemble, *Porgy and Bess,* 1935; **It is the Fourteenth of July+,** ensemble, *Primrose,* 1924; **It Isn't What You Did,** William Gaxton and ensemble, Cake, 1933; **It's a Great Little World*,** Allen Kearns, Jeanette MacDonald, Andrew Tombes, and Gertrude McDonald, *Tip-Toes,* 1925; **It's Great to Be in Love,** Helen Clark, John Lowe, and ensemble, *La, La, Lucille,* 1919; **It's Hard to Tell,** Janet Velie, John E. Hazzard, Sager Midgely, Cordelia MacDonald, Maurice Cass, and ensemble, *La, La, Lucille,* 1919 (added after opening); **It Take a Long Pull to Get There*,** Edward Matthews and ensemble, *Porgy and Bess,* 1935; **I Want to Be a War Bride*,** Doris Carson, Gordon Smith, and ensemble, *Strike Up the Band* (second version), (deleted soon after New York opening), 1930; **I Want to Marry a Marionette,** unused, *Treasure Girl,* 1928; **I Was Doing Alright*,** Ella Logan, *Goldwyn Follies,* 1938; **I Was So Young (You Were So Beautiful)*,** Mollie King and Charles King, *Good Morning, Judge,* 1919; **I Was the Most Beautiful Blossom*,** Grace Brinkley, OTIS, 1931; **I Won't Give Up Till You Give In to Me,** Written in 1936; **I Won't Say I Will, But I Won't Say I Won't*,** Irene Bordoni, *Little Miss Bluebeard,* 1923; **I've Brushed My Teeth,** Florenz Ames and ensemble, Cake, 1933; **I've Got a Crush on You*,** Clifton Webb, Mary Hay, and ensemble, *Treasure Girl,* 1928, Gordon Smith and Doris Carson, *Strike Up the Band* (second version), 1930; **(I've Got) Beginner's Luck*,** Fred Astaire, *Shall We Dance,* 1937; **I've Got to Be There*,** Carl Randall, Barbara Newberry, and ensemble, *Pardon My English,* 1933

J

Jasbo Brown Blues*, *Porgy and Bess,* 1935; **The Jijibo*,** Ruth Warren, William Wayne, and ensemble, *Sweet Little Devil,* 1924; **Jilted, Jilted!*,** Grace Brinkley, Florenz Ames, and ensemble, OTIS, 1931; **The Jolly Tar and the Milkmaid*,** Fred Astaire, with Jan Duggan, Mary Dean, Pearl Amatore, Betty Rone, and ensemble, *A Damsel in Distress,* 1937; **Juanita,** Adele Astaire and ensemble, *Lady, Be Good!,* 1924; **Just Another Rhumba*,** unused, *Goldwyn Follies,* 1938; **Just a Tiny Cup of Tea,** Pearl Regay, Richard Bold, and ensemble, *George White's Scandals,* 1922; **Just Missed the Opening Chorus,** The Williams Sisters (Dorothy and Hannah), *George White Scandals,* 1924; **Just Supposing,** Constance Binney and Irving Beebe, *Sweet Little Devil,* 1914; **Just to Know You Are Mine*,** Juliette Day, *A Dangerous Maid,* 1921

K

Katinka, Lester Allen and ensemble, *George White's Scandals,* 1923; **Katinkitschka*,** Mischa Auer and Manya Roberti, *Delicious,* 1931; **Kickin' the Clouds Away*,** Phyllis Cleveland, Esther Howard, Lou Holtz, and ensemble, *Tell Me More,* 1925; **King of Swing*,** Ford L. Buck, and John W. Bubbles, Radio City Music Hall stage show, 1936; **Kiss for Cinderella, A*,** William Gaxton and ensemble, OTIS, 1931; **Kongo Kate*,** Winnie Lightner, Tom Patricola, and ensemble, *George White's Scandals,* 1924; **K-ra-zy for You*,** Clifton Webb, Mary Hay, and ensemble, *Treasure Girl,* 1928

L

Lady Luck, ensemble, *Tip-Toes,* 1925; **Lady of the Moon,** written for the unproduced *Ming Toy,* 1929, same music as "I Just Looked at You," dropped from *Show Girl,* 1929, and "Blah, Blah, Blah" in *Delicious,* 1931; **Land of the Gay Caballero*,** ensemble, *Girl Crazy,* 1930; **Laugh Your Cares Away,** entire company, *George White's Scandals,* 1923; **Leave It to Love** (lyrics missing), *Lady, Be Good!,* 1924; **Leavin' For De Promise' Lan'*,** Anne Brown and ensemble, *Porgy and Bess,* 1935; **Leaving Town While We May+,** ensemble, *Primrose,* 1924; **Let Cutie Cut Your Cuticle,** Annette Bade and ensemble, *Morris Gest Midnight Whirl,* 1919;

Let 'Em Eat Cake*, William Gaxton, Cake, 1933; **Let 'Em Eat Caviar,** Phillip Loeb and ensemble, Cake, 1933; **Let Me Be a Friend to You,** Marilyn Miller and Jack Donahue, *Rosalie,* 1928; **Let's Be Lonesome Together,** Richard Bold and Delyle Alda, *George White's Scandals,* 1923; **Let's Call the Whole Thing Off***, Fred Astaire and Ginger Rogers, *Shall We Dance,* 1937; **Let's Kiss and Make Up***, Fred and Adele Astaire and ensemble, *Funny Face,* 1927; **Life of a Rose, The***, Richard Bold and Marga Waldron, *George White's Scandals,* 1913; **Life's Too Short to Be Blue,** unused, *Tip-Toes,* 1925; **Limehouse Nights***, Bessie McCoy Davis with Mae Leslie, Margaret Morris, Peggy Fears, and Helen Lovett, *Morris Gest Midnight Whirl,* 1919; **Linger in the Lobby,** ensemble, *Lady, Be Good!,* 1924; **Little Jazz Bird***, Cliff Edwards, *Lady, Be Good!,* 1924; **Little Scandal Dolls,** Olive Vaughn and ensemble, *George White's Scandals,* 1923; **Little Theatre of Our Own,** written *ca. 1919;* **Little Villages** (music by GG and William Daly), John Merkyl and Mrs. Jimmie Barry, *Our Nell,* 1922; **The Live Wire,** unused, *Primrose,* 1924; **Liza (All the Clouds'll Roll Away)***, Nick Lucas, Ruby Keeler, and ensemble, *Show Girl,* 1929; **Lo-la-lo***, Richard Bold, Olive Vaughn, Tom Patricola, and ensemble, *George White's Scandals,* 1923 (same music as "[On the Beach at] How've-You-Been"); **Lolita, My Love,** Joseph Macaulay, *Show Girl,* 1929; **The Lonesome Cowboy***, The Foursome and ensemble, *Girl Crazy,* 1930; **Look at the Damn Thing Now,** Leslie Henson, Rita Page, and ensemble, *Funny Face* (London production), 1928; **Looking for a Boy***, Queenie Smith, *Tip-Toes,* 1925; **Look in the Looking Glass,** Helen Hudson and ensemble, *George White's Scandals,* 1923; **Lorelei, The***, Carl Randall, Barbara Newberry, and ensemble, *Pardon My English,* 1933; **Love, I Never Knew,** Elsa McFarlane, *Tell Me More* (London production), 1925; **Love Is Here to Stay***, Kenny Baker, *Goldwyn Follies,* 1938; **Love Is in the Air,** ensemble, *Tell Me More!,* 1925; **Love Is Sweeping the Country***, George Murphy, June O'Dea, and ensemble, OTIS, 1931; **Love of a Wife, The,** unused, *La, La, Lucille,* 1919; **Lovers of Art,** Elm City Four and ensemble, *George White's Scandals,* 1924; **Love Walked In***, Kenny Baker, *Goldwyn Follies,* 1938; **Luckiest Boy in the World,** unused, *Pardon My English,* 1933; **Luckiest Man in the World***, George Givot and ensemble, *Pardon My English,* 1933; **Lu Lu***, Edith Hallor and ensemble, *Broadway Brevities,* 1920

M

Mademoiselle in New Rochelle*, Bobby Clark, Paul McCullough, and girls, *Strike Up the Band* (second version), 1930; **Madrigal** (Music by GG and William Daly), ensemble, *Our Nell,* 1922; **Magnolia Finale,** unused, *Show Girl,* 1929; **Mah-Jongg***, unused, *Sweet Little Devil,* Richard Bold and ensemble, *George White's Scandals,* 1924; **Making of a Girl*** (music by Sigmund Romberg and GG), Jack Boyle and ensemble, *The Passing Show,* 1916; **The Man I Love***, unused in New York. Introduced by Adele Astaire in *Lady, Be Good!* (tryout 1924); sung by Vivian Hart and Roger Pryor in *Strike Up the Band* (first version) 1927, rewritten for Marilyn Miller in *Rosalie,* but unused (alternate title "The Girl I Love"); **Man of High Degree, A***, Bobby Clark, Paul McCullough, Dudley Clements, and ensemble, *Strike Up the Band* (second version), 1930; **Matrimonial Handicap, The,** Marjorie Gateson, Ruth Warren, William Wayne, Irving Beebe, and ensemble, *Sweet Little Devil,* 1924; **Maybe***, Gertrude Lawrence and Oscar Shaw, *Oh, Kay!,* 1926; **Meadow Serenade,** Vivian Hart and Roger Pryor, *Strike Up the Band,* (first version), 1927; **Merry-Andrew** (Instrumental), danced by Marilyn Miller and Jack Donahue, *Rosalie,* 1928; **Mexican Dance** (See Tamale, I'm Hot for You), **Midnight Bells***, Tessa Kosta, *Song of the Flame,* 1925; **Midnight Blues,** Lola Raine and ensemble, *The Rainbow,* 1923; **Military Dancing Drill***, Max Floffman, Jr. and Dorothea James, *Strike Up the Band* (first version), 1927, ensemble, *Strike Up the Band* (second version), 1930; **Mine***, William Gaxton, Lois Moran, and ensemble, Cake, 1933; **Minstrel Show,** unused, *Show Girl,* 1929; **Mischa, Yascha, Toscha, Sascha***, written, *ca. 1921;*

Molly-on-the-Shore, Written *ca.* 1921; **Money, Money, Money,** Janet Velie, John E. Hazzard, J. Clarence Harvey, Sager Midgely, Cordelia MacDonald, Maurice Cass, and ensemble, *La, La, Lucille,* (subsequently replaced by "It's Hard to Tell"), 1919; **The Moon is on the Sea,** unused, *Oh, Kay!,* 1926; **Moonlight in Versailles*,** Grace Hayes; danced by Ted Grant, Frances Wing, and ensemble, *The Rainbow,* 1923; **The Mophams+,** Leslie Henson, Heather Thatcher, and Thomas Weguelin, *Primrose,* 1924; Mr. and Mrs. Sipkin, Lou Holtz and ensemble, *Tell Me More!,* 1925; **Murderous Monty (and Light-fingered Jane)*,** unused, *Tell Me More* (London production), 1925; **My Cousin in Milwaukee*,** Lyda Roberti and ensemble, *Pardon My English,* 1933; **My Fair Lady*,** Phyllis Cleveland, Esther Howard, and ensemble, *Tell Me More!,* 1925; **My Lady*,** Lester O'Keefe, *George White's Scandals,* 1920, also in *Mayfair and Montmartre,* London, 1922; **(You're Mighty Lucky) My Little Ducky,** unused, *Sweet Little Devil,* 1924, Cyril Ritchard and Madge Elliott in *The Midnight Follies* at Hotel Metropole (London), 1926; **My Log-Cabin Home*,** singer not credited, *The Perfect Fool,* 1921; **My Man's Gone Now*,** Ruby Elzy and ensemble, *Porgy and Bess,* 1935; **My Old Love Is My New Love,** unused, *George White's Scandals,* 1920; **My Old New England Home*,** 1922; **My One and Only (What Am I Gonna Do)*,** Fred Astaire, Betty Compton, Gertrude McDonald, and ensemble, *Funny Face,* 1927; **My Runaway Girl** (music by Sigmund Romberg and GG, unused, *The Passing Show,* 1916; **My Sunday Fella,** Barbara Newberry and ensemble, *Show Girl,* 1929

N

Names I Love to Hear (music by GG and William Daly), Olin Howland, Emma Haig, Mr. and Mrs. Jimmie Barry, and Guy Nichols, *Our Nell,* 1922; **Nashville Nightingale*,** Performer not credited, may have been sung by Jane Greene, *Nifties,* 1923; **Naughty Baby+*,** Margery Hicklin and ensemble, *Primrose,* 1924; **Never Was There a Girl So Fair*,** ensemble, OTIS, 1931; **New York Serenade,** Bobbe Arnst and ensemble, *Rosalie,* 1928; **Nice Baby*,** Jeanette MacDonald, Robert Halliday, and ensemble, *Tip-Toes,* 1925; **Nice Work If You Can Get It*,** Fred Astaire, Jan Duggan, Mary Dean, Pearl Amatore, and ensemble, *A Damsel in Distress,* 1937; **Nightie-night*,** Queenie Smith and Allen Kearns, *Tip-Toes,* 1925; **Night of Nights,** unused film song; **Night Time in Araby*,** Richard Bold and ensemble, *George White's Scandals,* 1924; **No Better Way to Start a Case,** Ralph Riggs and ensemble, *Cake,* 1933; **Nobody But You*,** Helen Clark and Lorin Raker, *La, La, Lucille,* 1919 (added after opening); **No Comprenez, No Capish, No Versteh!,** ensemble, *Cake,* 1933; **No One Else But That Girl of Mine*,** performer not credited, *The Perfect Fool,* 1921, (Later rewritten as "That American Boy of Mine" in *The Dancing Girl),* 1923; **No Tickee, No Washee,** unused, *Pardon My English,* 1933

O

Official Resume*, ensemble, *Strike Up the Band* (second version), 1930; **Off With the Old Love,** unused, *Treasure Girl,* 1928 (Also known as "Goodbye to the Old Love"); **Of Thee I Sing (Baby)*,** William Gaxton, Lois Moran, and ensemble, OTIS, 1931; **Oh Bess, Oh Where's My Bess?*,** Todd Duncan, Ruby Elzy, and Helen Dowdy, *Porgy and Bess,* 1935; **Oh, De Lawd Shake De Heaven*,** ensemble, *Porgy and Bess,* 1935; **Oh, Dere's Somebody Knockin' at de Door*,** *Porgy and Bess,* 1935; **Oh, Doctor Jesus*,** principals and ensemble, *Porgy and Bess,* 1935; **Oh Gee! Oh Joy!*,** Marilyn Miller and Jack Donahue, *Rosalie,* 1928; **Oh, Hev'enly Father*,** *Porgy and Bess,* 1935; **Oh, I Can't Sit Down*,** ensemble, *Porgy and Bess,* 1935; **Oh, Kay!*,** Gertrude Lawrence and ensemble, *Oh, Kay!,* 1926; **Oh, Lady, Be Good!*,** Walter Catlett and ensemble, *Lady, Be Good!,* 1924; **Oh Lawd, I'm on My Way*,** Todd Duncan, *Porgy and Bess,* 1935; **Oh Little Stars*,** 1935; **Oh! Nina,** Earl Rickard, the Fayre Four, and ensemble, *The Rainbow,* 1923; **Oh, So Nice*,** Gertrude Lawrence and Paul

Frawley, *Treasure Girl*, 1928; **Oh, This Is Such a Lovely War,** ensemble, *Strike Up the Band* (first version), 1927; **Oh, What She Hangs out (She Hangs Out in Our Alley)*,** Lester Allen and ensemble, *George White's Scandals*, 1922 (also published under title in parentheses); **Oh, You Lady!** (music by GG and William Daly), Lora Sonderson and ensemble, *Our Nell*, 1922; **O Land of Mine, America*,** One of fifteen winners in a song contest conducted by the *New York American*, 1919; **On and On and On*,** William Gaxton, Lois Moran, and ensemble, *Cake*, 1933; **Once*,** unused, *Tell Me More*, 1925, William Kent, Betty Compton, and ensemble, *Funny Face*, 1927; **One Man,** Barbara Newberry and ensemble, *Show Girl*, 1929; **One, Two, Three*,** Dick Haymes and ensemble; danced by Betty Grable and Dick Haymes, *The Shocking Miss Pilgrim*, 1946; **On My Mind the Whole Night Long*,** Lloyd Garrett, *George White's Scandals*, 1920; **On That Matter No One Budges*,** OTIS, 1931; **On the Beach at How've-You-Been*** (see **How've-You-Been**), 1923; **On the Brim of Her Old-fashioned Bonnet,** Delyle Alda and ensemble, *Snapshots*, 1921; **Oo, How I Love to Be Loved by You*,** Helen Clark and Lorin Raker, *La, La, Lucille*, 1919 (subsequently replaced by "Nobody But You," unused, Ed Wynn's *Carnival*, 1920; **Our Little Captain,** Queenie Smith and ensemble, *Tip-Toes*, 1925; **Our Little Kitchenette,** unused, *La, La, Lucille*, 1919; **Overflow*,** ensemble, *Porgy and Bess*, 1935; **Oyez,! Oyez! Oyez!,** unused, Cake, 1933

P

Pardon My English, Lyda Roberti and George Givot, *Pardon My English*, 1933; **Patriotic Rally*,** ensemble, *Strike Up the Band*, both versions, 1927 & 1930; **Pay Some Attention to Me,** unused, *A Damsel in Distress*, 1937; **Pepita*,** unused, *Sweet Little Devil*, 1924; **Pep! Zip! And Punch!,** unused, *Primrose*, 1924; **Phoebe,** written in August 1921; **Pidgee Woo,** unused, *A Dangerous Maid*, 1921; **Place in the Country,** Paul Frawley, Norman Curtis, and ensemble, *Treasure Girl*, 1928; **Poetry of Motion, The,** Willie Covan and Leonard Ruffin, *Tell Me More!*, 1925; **Poor Michael! Poor Golo!,** unused, *Pardon My English*, 1933; **Poppyland*,** Bernard Granville, Helen Shipman, and ensemble, *Morris Gest Midnight Whirl*, 1919; **Posterity Is Just Around the Corner*,** William Gaxton and ensemble, OTIS, 1931; **Put Me to the Test** (this version by GG with unused lyrics by IG), danced by Fred Astaire, George Burns, and Gracie Allen, *A Damsel in Distress*, 1937

Q

Queen Isabella, unused, *George White's Scandals*, 1920; **Quite a Party,** ensemble, *Sweet Little Devil*, 1924

R

Ragging the Traumerei, written *ca.* 1913 or 1914; **Rainy Afternoon Girls,** ensemble, *Lady, Be Good!*, 1924; **The Real American Folk Song (Is a Rag)*,** Hal Ford, *Ladies First*, 1918 (Nora Bayes sang the song on the tryout tour); **Ring a Ding a Ding Dong Dell*,** ensemble, *Strike Up the Band* (Second version), 1930; **Rosalie*,** unused, *Rosalie*, 1928; **Rose of Madrid*,** Richard Bold and ensemble, *George White's Scandals*, 1924; **Roses of France+,** Esme de Vayne and ensemble, *Primrose*, 1924

S

Sam and Delilah*, Ethel Merman and ensemble, *Girl Crazy*, 1930; **Same Old Story, The,** Constance Binney and ensemble, *Sweet Little Devil*, 1924; **Say So!*,** Marilyn Miller and Oliver McLennan, *Rosalie*, 1928; **Scandal Walk*,** Ann Pennington and ensemble, *George White's Scandals*, 1920; **Seeing Dickie Home,** unused, *Lady, Be Good*, 1924; **Senatorial Roll Call*, The,** Victor Moore and ensemble, OTIS, 1931; **Seventeen and Twenty-one*,** Dorothea James and Max Hoffman, Jr., *Strike Up the Band* (first version), 1927; **Shall We Dance?*,** Fred

Astaire; danced by Astaire, Ginger Rogers, and ensemble, *Shall We Dance?*, 1937; **She Hasn't a Thing Except Me** (listed in Rosenberg), **She's Just a Baby***, Ann Pennington and ensemble, *George White's Scandals*, 1921; **Shirts by the Millions,** Lois Moran and Florenz Ames, Cake, 1933; **Shop Girls and Mannikins,** unused, *Tell Me More!*, 1925; **Show Me the Town***, unused, *Oh, Kay!*, 1926, Bobbe Arnst and ensemble, *Rosalie*, 1928; **Signal*, The,** Tessa Kosta, Guy Robertson and ensemble, *Song of the Flame*, 1925; **The Simple Life***, Juliette Day, *A Dangerous Maid*, 1921; **Since I Found You,** George Gershwin's earliest song, *ca.* 1915; **Sing a Little Song,** Ritz Quartet, Phil Ohman and Victor Arden, and ensemble, *Funny Face*, 1927; **Singin' Pete,** unused, *Lady, Be Good!*, 1924; **Sing of Spring,** Jan Duggan and ensemble, *A Damsel in Distress*, 1937; **Sing Song Girl,** unused in the unproduced *Ming Toy*, 1929; **The Sirens,** ensemble, *A Dangerous Maid*, 1921; **Skull and Bones,** ensemble, *Treasure Girl*, 1928; **Slap That Bass***, Fred Astaire and unidentified singer, *Shall We Dance*, 1937; **Snow Flakes***, Edith Hallor, *Broadway Brevities*, 1920; **So Am I***, Alan Edwards and Adele Astaire, *Lady, Be Good!*, 1924; **So Are You!***, Eddie Foy, Jr., and Kathryn Hereford, *Show Girl*, 1929; **Soldiers' March (Unofficial March of General Holmes)***, (instrumental), *Strike Up the Band* (second version), 1930; **Somebody from Somewhere***, Janet Gaynor, *Delicious*, 1931; **Somebody Loves Me***, Winnie Lightner to Tom Patricola; ensemble, *George White's Scandals*, 1924; **Somebody Stole My Heart Away,** unused, *Show Girl*, 1929; **Some Far-away Someone*** (same melody as **At Half Past Seven**), Percy Heming and Margery Hicklin, *Primrose*, 1914, (same melody as "At Half Past Seven" from *Nifties)*, 1923; **Some Girls Can Bake A Pie***, William Gaxton, Grace Brinkley, and ensemble, OTIS, 1931; **Somehow It Seldom Comes True***, Janet Velie, *La, La, Lucille*, 1919; **Someone***, Helen Ford, Vinton Freedley, and ensemble, *For Goodness Sake*, 1922; **Someone Believes in You***, Constance Binney and Irving Beebe, *Sweet Little Devil*, 1924; **Someone's Always Calling a Rehearsal,** unused, *Show Girl*, 1929; **Someone to Watch Over Me***, Gertrude Lawrence, *Oh, Kay!*, 1926; **Some Rain Must Fall***, Juliette Day, *A Dangerous Maid*, 1921; **Something about Love***, Adele Rowland and Donald MacDonald, *The Lady in Red*, 1919, (Also in British production of *Lady, Be Good!*, 1924); **Something Peculiar,** written *ca.* 1921; **Something Peculiar,** unused, *Girl Crazy*, 1930; **Some Wonderful Sort of Someone***, Nora Bayes, *Ladies First*, 1918; **Song of the Flame***, Tessa Kosta, Greek Evans, and Russian Art Choir, *Song of the Flame*, 1925; **Songs of Long Ago*, The,** Lester O'Keefe and ensemble, *George White's Scandals*, 1920; **Soon***, Jerry Goff and Helen Gilligan, *Strike Up the Band* (second version), 1930; **Sophia***, Ray Walston; reprised by Dean Martin and ensemble, *Kiss Me, Stupid*, 1964, (music adapted from "Wake Up Brother and Dance"); **South Sea Isles (Sunny South Sea Islands)***, Charles King and Ann Pennington, *George White's Scandals*, 1921 (also used in *Mayfair and Montmartre*, London, 1922); **So What?***, Jack Pearl and Josephine Huston, *Pardon My English*, 1933; **Spanish Love***, Hal van Rensellaer, *Broadway Brevities*, 1920; **Stand Up and Fight,** Anne Revere, Betty Grable, Dick Haymes, and ensemble, *The Shocking Miss Pilgrim*, 1946; **Stepping with Baby,** unused, *Oh, Kay!*, 1926; **Stiff Upper Lip***, Gracie Allen; danced by Fred Astaire, George Burns, and Gracie Allen, *A Damsel in Distress*, 1937; **Street Cries (Strawberry Woman, Crab Man)***, Helen Dowdy and Ray Yeates, *Porgy and Bess*, 1935; **Strike, Strike, Strike,** Marjorie Gateson, Rae Bowdin, and ensemble, *Sweet Little Devil*, 1924; **Strike Up the Band!***, Max Hoffman, Jr. and ensemble, *Strike Up the Band* (first version, 1927), Jerry Goff and ensemble, *Strike Up the Band* (second version, 1930); **Strike Up the Band for U.C.L.A.***, Special lyrics, rewritten in 1936; **Strut Lady with Me***, Grace Hayes; danced by Jack Edge, Ted Grant, Frances Wing, Fred A. Leslie, and ensemble, *The Rainbow*, 1923; **Suffragetes,** unused, *The Shocking Miss Pilgrim*, 1947; **Summertime***, Abbie Mitchell, *Porgy and Bess*, 1935; **The Sun Is On The Sea,** unused, *Oh, Kay!*, 1926; **Sunday in London Town***, unused, *The Rainbow*, 1923; **The Sunshine Trail***, Theme song to promote the silent film *The Sunshine Trail*, 1923; **Swanee***, Muriel DeForrest, *Capitol Revue*

("Demi-Tasse"), 1919, (Subsequently, Al Jolson popularized "Swanee" in a Sunday-night show at the Winter Garden, New York, and then in a touring company of his revue *Sinbad* during 1920); **Swanee Rose***, Featured by Al Jolson, 1921 (Same music as "Dixie Rose"); **Sweet and Low-down***, Harry Watson, Lovey Lee, Amy Revere, and ensemble, *Tip-Toes,* 1925; **Sweetheart (I'm So Glad That I Met You)***, Lola Raine and Elsie Mayfair, *The Rainbow,* 1923; **Sweet Little Devil,** unused, *Sweet Little Devil,* 1924; **Sweet Packard,** ensemble, *The Shocking Miss Pilgrim,* 1946; **Swiss Miss,** Fred and Adele Astaire, *Lady, Be Good!,* 1924; **'S Wonderful***, Adele Astaire and Allen Kearns, *Funny Face,* 1927; **System,** Constance Binney, Marjorie Gateson, and Ruth Warren, *Sweet Little Devil,* 1924

T

Tamale (I'm Hot for You),* retitled **Mexican Dance** by G, 1921; **Tango,** GG performed this as a piano solo in his first appearance as pianist-composer at the Finley Club, Christadora House, New York, March 21, 1914; **Tartar** (music by GG and Herbert Stothart), Greek Evans and the Russian Art Choir, *Song of the Flame,* 1925; **Tee-oodle-um-bum-bo***, Janet Velie, J. Clarence Harvey, and ensemble, *La, La, Lucille,* 1919; **Tell Me More!***, Alexander Gray and Phyllis Cleveland, *Tell Me More!,* 1925; **Tell the Doc,** William Kent and ensemble, *Funny Face,* 1927; **Thanks to You,** unused, *Delicious,* 1931; **That American Boy of Mine***, Sally Fields, *The Dancing Girl,* 1923 (rewritten version of "No One Else But That Girl of Mine" in *The Perfect Fool,* 1921); **That Certain Feeling***, Queenie Smith and Allen Kearns, *Tip-Toes,* 1925; **That Lost Barber Shop Chord***, Louis Lazarin and male quartet, *Americana,* 1926; **That New-Fangled Mother of Mine***, Leslie Henson, *Primrose,* 1924; **That's What He Did,** Victor Moore, Philip Loeb, and ensemble, Cake, 1933; **There Is Nothing Too Good for You***, Richard Bold, Helen Hudson, and ensemble, *George White's Scandals,* 1923; **There's a Boat Dat's Leavin' Soon for New York***, John W. Bubbles and Anne Brown, *Porgy and Bess,* 1935; **There's Magic in the Air,** probably sung by Sibyl Vane, *Half Past Eight,* 1918; **There's More to the Kiss Than the X-X-X***, Mollie King, *Good Morning, Judge,* 1919, (Same song, retitled "There's More to the Kiss than the Sound," was sung by Helen Clark and ensemble in *La, La, Lucille,* 1919); **There Was Never Such a Charming War,** unused, *Strike Up the* Band (second version), 1930; **These Charming People***, Queenie Smith, Andrew Tombes, and Harry Watson, Jr., *Tip-Toes,* 1925; **The Ten Commandments of Love** (Lyrics by Edward B. Perkins), this version probably sung by Sibyl Vane, *Half Past Eight,* 1918; **The Ten Commandments of Love** (Lyrics by Arthur J. Jackson and B. G. De Sylva), John E. Hazzard, Janet Velie, and ensemble, *La, La, Lucille,* 1919; **They All Laughed***, Ginger Rogers, *Shall We Dance,* 1937; **They Can't Take That Away from Me***, Fred Astaire, *Shall We Dance,* 1937 (also presented by Fred Astaire in *The Barkleys of Broadway,* 1949); **They Pass By Singin'***, Todd Duncan, *Porgy and Bess,* 1935; **Things Are Looking Up***, Fred Astaire, danced by Fred Astaire and Joan Fontaine, *A Damsel in Distress,* 1937; **This is the Life for a Man+***, 1924; **This Particular Party,** unused, *Treasure Girl,* 1928; **Those Eyes,** unused, *Funny Face,* 1927; **Three-quarter Blues,** Instrumental, written in the late 1920s; **Three Times a Day***, Alexander Gray and Phyllis Cleveland, *Tell Me More!,* 1925; **Throttle Throttlebottom,** Phillip Loeb and ensemble, Cake, 1933; **Throw 'er In High***, Winnie Lightner and Lester Allen, *George White's Scandals,* 1923; **Till I Meet Someone Like You+,** Claude Hulbert and Vera Lennox, *Primrose,* 1924; **Till Then***, non-production, 1933; **Time and Time Again,** Ruby Elzy and ensemble, *Porgy and Bess,* 1935; **Tip-Toes,** Queenie Smith and ensemble, *Tip-Toes,* 1925; **Toddlin' Along,** Nan Blackstone, *9:15 Revue,* 1930 (same song as "The World Is Mine" from *Funny Face);* **Together At Last;** unused, *Pardon My English,* 1933;, featured by Al Jolson, 1921; **Tonight,** George Givot and Josephine Huston, *Pardon My English,* 1933 (one of the *Two Waltzes in C* for piano); **Tonight's the Night!,** unused, *Show Girl,* 1929; **Tour Of The Town,** unused, *The Shocking Miss Pilgrim,* 1946;

Tra-La-La*, Marjorie Gateson and John E. Hazzard, *For Goodness Sake,* 1922 (also presented by Gene Kelly and Oscar Levant in the movie *An American in Paris*); **Treasure Island,** unused, *Treasure Girl,* 1928; **Treat Me Rough*,** William Kent and ensemble, *Girl Crazy,* 1930; **True Love,** Juliette Day and Vinton Freedley, *A Dangerous Maid,* 1921; **True to Them All,** unused, *Rosalie,* 1928; **Trumpeter, Blow Your Golden Horn*,** ensemble, OTIS, 1931; **Tum On and Tiss Me*,** Ann Pennington and ensemble, *George White's Scandals* 1920; **Tune In (to Station J.O.Y.)*,** Winnie Lightner and ensemble, *George White's Scandals,* 1924; **Tweedledee for President,** ensemble, Cake, 1933; **A Typical Self-made American*,** Herbert Corthell, Roger Pryor, and ensemble, *Strike Up the Band* (first version), 1927, Dudley Clements, Jerry Goff, and ensemble, *Strike Up the Band* (second version), 1930

U

Ukulele Lorelei, Emma Haig and ensemble, *Tell Me More!,* 1925; **Under a One-man Top*,** Ruth Warren and William Wayne, *Sweet Little Devil,* 1924; **Under the Furlough Moon,** (Music by GG and Sigmund Romberg), unused, *Rosalie,* 1928; **Union Square*,** ensemble, Cake, 1933; **The Unofficial Spokesman*,** Lew Hearn, Herbert Corthell, and ensemble, *Strike Up the Band* (first version), 1927, Bobby Clark and ensemble, *Strike Up the Band* (second version), 1930; **Up and At 'Em,** Ralph Riggs and ensemble, Cake, 1933

V

Virginia (Don't Go Too Far)*, Constance Binney and ensemble, *Sweet Little Devil,* 1924; **Vodka*** (Music by GG and Herbert Stothart), Dorothy Mackaye and ensemble, *Song the Flame,* 1925

W

Wait a Bit, Susie*, Margery Hicklin, Percy Heming, and ensemble, *Primrose,* 1924; same music as "Beautiful Gypsy" dropped from *Rosalie,* 1928; **Waiting for the Sun to Come Out*,** Helen Ford, Joseph Lertora, and ensemble, *The Sweetheart Shop,* 1920; **Waiting for the Train,** ensemble, *Tip-Toes,* 1925; **Wake Up, Brother, and Dance,** unused, *Shall We Dance,* 1937; **Walking Home with Angeline*,** Olin Howland, Emma Haig, and ensemble, *Our Nell,* 1922; **Walking the Dog* (published as Promenade),** Instrumental, performed by Fred Astaire and Ginger Rogers as walk on deck in *Shall We Dance,* 1937; **Waltzing Is Better Sitting Down,** Dick Haymes and Betty Grable, *The Shocking Miss Pilgrim,* 1946; **The War That Ended War,** ensemble, *Strike Up the Band* (first version), 1927; **Watch Your Head,** unused, **We,** unused, *Tip-Toes,* 1925; **We Are Visitors,** written for the unproduced *Ming Toy,* 1929, some of the music (with new lyrics) was used in the patter chorus of "Love Is Sweeping the Country" in OTIS, 1931; **Weather Man,** ensemble, *Lady Be Good!,* 1914; **Welcome Song,** unused, *The Shocking Miss Pilgrim,* 1946; **Welcome to the Melting Pot,** ensemble, *Delicious,* 1931; **We're All A-Worry, All Agog,** unused, *Funny Face,* 1927; **We're Here Because,** Patricia Clarke, Gerald Oliver Smith, and ensemble, *Lady, Be Good!,* 1924; **We're Pals*,** Louis Bennison, *Dere Mable,* 1919; **What Are We Here For?*,** Gertrude Lawrence, Clifton Webb, and ensemble, *Treasure Girl,* 1928; **What Causes That?,** Clifton Webb, Mary Hay, and ensemble, *Treasure girl,* 1928 (added after New York opening); **What Sort of Wedding is This?,** ensemble, *Pardon My English,* 1933; **What You Want Wid Bess?*,** Anne Brown and Warren Coleman, *Porgy and Bess,* 1935; **What's the Big Idea?,** written in mid-1920s; **What's the Use?,** unused, *Oh, Kay!,* 1926; **When Cadets Parade,** unused, *Rosalie,* 1928; **When Do We Dance?*,** Allen Kearns, Gertrude McDonald, and Lovey Lee, *Tip-Toes,* 1925; **When It's Cactus Time in Arizona*,** Ginger Rogers and ensemble, *Girl Crazy,* 1930; **When Our Ship Comes Sailing In,** unused, *Oh, Kay!,* 1926; **When The Armies Disband,** written for Henry Ford's Peace Ship during World War I, *ca.* 1918; **When**

the **Debbies Go By;** Esther Howard and ensemble, *Tell Me More!*, 1925; **When the Judges Doff the Ermine,** Ralph Riggs and ensemble, Cake, 1933; **When the Right One Comes Along,** unused, *Rosalie*, 1928; **When There's a Chance to Dance,** written in 1919; **When Toby is Out of Town+,** Leslie Henson and ensemble, *Primrose*, 1924; **When You Live in a Furnished Flat,** Janet Velie, J. Clarence Harvey, and M. Rale, *La, La, Lucille*, 1919; **When You Want 'Em, You Can't Get 'Em (When You Got 'Em, You Don't Want 'Em)*,** GG's first published song, 1916; **When You're Single,** unused. *Funny Face*, 1927; **Where East Meets West*,** Charles King and Victoria Herbert, *George White's Scandals*, 1921 (also used in *Mayfair and Montmartre*, London, 1922); **Where Is She?*,** Tip Top Four and ensemble, *George White's Scandals*, 1923; **Where Is the Man of My Dreams?*,** Winnie Lightner, *George White's Scandals*, 1922; **Where's the Boy? Here's the Girl!*,** Gertrude Lawrence, Phil Ohman, Victor Arden, and ensemble, *Treasure Girl*, 1928; **Where You Go, I Go*,** Lyda Roberti and Jack Pearl, *Pardon My English*, 1933; **Who Cares?*,** William Gaxton and Lois Moran, OTIS, 1931; **Who Is the Lucky Girl to Be?,** Grace Brinkley and ensemble, OTIS, 1931; **Who's the Greatest?,** William Gaxton and ensemble, Cake, 1933; **Why Do I Love You?*,** Esther Howard, Lou Holtz, and ensemble, *Tell Me More!*, 1925; **Why Speak of Money?*,** Cake, 1933; **Will You Remember Me?,** unused, *Lady, Be Good!*, 1924; **Wintergreen for President*,** ensemble, OTIS, 1931; **Woman's Touch*, The,** Betty Compton, Constance Carpenter, and ensemble, *Oh, Kay!*, 1926; **Woman's Work Is Never Done** (Music by GG and Herbert Stothart), Dorothy Mackaye and ensemble, *Song of the Flame*, 1925; **Woman to Lady** (Lyrics by Du Bose Heyward), Todd Duncan, Anne Brown, J. Rosamond Johnson, and ensemble, *Porgy and Bess*, 1935; **Wonderful Party, A,** ensemble, *Lady, Be Good!*, 1924; **World Is Mine*, The,** unused, *Funny Face*, 1927 (same song as "Toddlin' Along" in *9:15 Revue*, 1930)

Y

Yankee*, written in 1920; **Yankee Doodle Blues, The,** Georgie Price, *Spice*, 1922; **Yankee Doodle Rhythm*,** Jimmy Savo, Ruth Wilcox, Max Hoffman, Jr., and Dorothea James, *Strike Up the Band* (first version, 1927), unused, *Rosalie*, 1928; **Year after Year*,** Richard Bold and Helen Hudson, *George White's Scandals*, 1924; **You and I,** Beulah Berson and ensemble, *George White's Scandals*, 1923; **You Are You*** (Music by GG and Herbert Stothart), unused, *Song of the Flame*, 1925; **You Can't Unscramble Scrambled Eggs,** unused, *Girl Crazy*, 1930; **You Know How It Is,** unused, *Rosalie*, 1928; **You Started It,** unused, *Delicious*, 1931; **You-oo Just You!*,** Adele Dixon, *Hitchy-Koo*, 1918; **You've Got What Gets Me*,** Eddie Quillan and Arlene Judge, *Girl Crazy* (first film version), 1932.

Discography

Works are listed by title, in alphabetical order. Because of the impracticality of listing all recordings of Gershwin's oeuvre, the recordings given here are selective. Efforts have been made to provide a good balance between older and newer recordings. "*See*" references, e. g., *See*: **B100**, identify citations under the section labeled "Bibliography about Discography." "**W**" references are to the works in their original listings in the "Works and Performances" chapter. "**F**" references are to the "Filmography" section.

Abbreviations for works are defined on page xiii. Abbreviations for some of the works, RiB for *Rhapsody in Blue,* e. g., are used to save space. Abbreviations for libraries, place names, personal names, periodicals, and miscellaneous items are also given on page xiii.

Recordings are listed without concern for whether they are in- or out-of-print; the thought is that interested collectors are willing to search for rare recordings, at the same time taking into consideration the current trend of record companies to produce remastered compact discs (or any formats of the future) of recordings which have been out-of-print. This discography includes items listed in the *Schwann Opus* catalogue as of Summer, 1991, and selected items after that date. For an excellent listing of recordings issued between 1972 and 1979 see Carol J. Oja, *American Music Recordings: A Discography of 20th-Century U. S. Composers*, pp. 112-126 (**B935.1**). The journal *Show Music* provides good information for those wishing to keep up with new releases of Gershwin material. For the admittedly subjective opinions of one Gershwin expert regarding some of the recordings, the reader may wish to consult Edward Jablonski's "Selected Discography" in his *Gershwin: A Biography*, pp. 402-415. (**B53**). Walter Rimler has provided a thorough discography through 1984: *A Gershwin Companion (***B936**). Rimler's work is particularly strong in popular and jazz recordings, both vocal and instrumental; it includes no compact discs.

It is very near impossible to account for all of the Gershwin discography considering all the old records from the 1920s and '30s, coupled with the fact that there is a constant flow of newly produced discs as well as digitally remastered versions of the older ones. Hence, if the reader does not find a desired recording listed in this selected list, she/he is well advised to check the bins at major record outlets or specialty stores such as may be found in New York, or an appropriate Internet site.

The abbreviation **[GOH]** in the entry indicates that the recording is listed in an inventory, prepared by Annette Farrington when she worked at the Goodspeed Library of

Musical Theatre at the Goodspeed Opera House in East Haddam, CT

The materials in the Discography are organized under the following headings:

- **Orchestral Works**

- **Stage Shows**

- **Piano Music [works for piano alone]**

- **Chamber Music**

- **Anthologies**

- **Songs: a) Vocal treatment b) Instrumental treatment**

- **Overtures to Musicals**

- **Music Used in Films**

- **Recordings by Gershwin**

- **Recordings of a Biographical Nature**

- **Miscellaneous Recordings**

ORCHESTRAL WORKS
(in alphabetical order)

AN AMERICAN IN PARIS (1928) (W3)

D1.   American Radio Symphony Orchestra; M. Brown, conducting
Allegro ACS 8034, cassette (1980); also Vox STPL 513.030 (19--?)
With RiB

D2.   Austrian Symphony Orchestra; George Roessler, conducting
Masterseal 1840 (1957)
With RiB
Program notes by Marty Ostrow on container

D3.   BBC Philharmonic Orchestra: conducted by Yan Pascal Tortelier
Chandos Chan 9325 **[DDD]**
With Girl Crazy: **Overture** (Orchestra Don Rose); Variations on "I Got
Rhythm"; Symphonic Suite: Catfish Row (G's version); Strike Up the Band:
Overture (Orchestra Don Rose).
Produced by Brian Pidgeon. (Distributed by Koch International.) *See*: **B1322**

D4.   Boston Pops Orchestra; Arthur Fiedler, conductor
RCA Victor LM 2367 (1960)
With RiB
Program notes by Deems Taylor on slipcase

LC card no. r60-188 *See:* **B971, B1071, B1090**

D5.   Boston Pops Orchestra; Arthur Fiedler, conducting
RCA Victor LM 2702 (1964)
With **D. Milhaud:** A Frenchman in New York
Program notes by Robert Taylor on container; 15 min., 57 sec. (AiP)
LC card no. r64-146 *See:* **B991**

D6.   Boston Pops; Arthur Fiedler, conducting
RCA Victrola VICS 1423 (1969)
With **Ferde Grofé:** Grand Canyon Suite; 15 min, 53 sec (AiP)
Program notes on container
LC card no. 71-750195

D7.   Boston Pops; Earl Wild, piano; Arthur Fiedler, conducting
RCA Red Seal CSC-0605, 2 discs (1969?)
"The Best of Gershwin"
With RiB; Concerto; "I Got Rhythm" Variations; Cuban Overture
Program notes, in part by Deems Taylor or Carl Bosler, on container

D8.   Boston Pops; Earl Wild, pa.; Arthur Fiedler, conducting
RCA (Papillon Collection) 6519-2 RG, CD [ADD]; 6519-4 RG, cassette
With RiB, Concerto, "I Got Rhythm" Variations *See:* **B988, B1036, B1063,
B1105, B1264**

D9.   Boston Pops Orchestra; Arthur Fiedler, conducting
Chesky RC-8
With RiB

D10.   Boston Pops; Arthur Fiedler, conducting
RCA AGL1-5215; AGK1-5215, cassette
With RiB

D11.   Boston Pops Orchestra, Arthur Fiedler, conducting
RCA Red Seal LSC 3319 (1972)
"The World's Favorite Gershwin"
With RiB & Concerto
A Basic Library of the Music America Loves Best
Program notes on container
LC card no. 72-750302

D12.   Chicago Symphony Orchestra; James Levine, piano and conducting
Deutsche Grammophone 4316252 GH (in Schwann, Spring 1994)
With Cuban, RiB, & G's Catfish Row *See:* **B968, B1089, B1132**

D13.   Cincinnati Symphony Orchestra; Erich Kunzel, conducting
Telarc CD-80058 **[DDD]** (© 1984? p 1981)
With RiB
Recorded in Music Hall, Cincinnati, Jan. 5, 1981

D14.   Cleveland Orchestra; Riccardo Chailly, conducting

       London CD 417326-2 LH **[DDD]**; 417326-4 LH, cassette
       With Cuban Overture; Lullaby; RiB

D15.   Cleveland Orchestra; Ivan Davis, piano (RiB); Lorin Maazel, conducting (1985)
       London (Decca) 414 067-1 (1985); London 417098-4 LT; 414067-4 LJ,
         cassette
       With RiB; Cuban Overture *See:* **B1060**

D16.   Cleveland Orchestra; Lorin Maazel, conducting
       London 417716-2 LM, CD **[ADD]**
       With Cuban; RiB; & **Copland:** Appalachian Spring; Fanfare

D17.   Dallas Symphony Orchestra; Eduardo Mata, conducting
       RCA Red Seal RCD1, CD (1981)
       With Cuban Overture; **Robert R. Bennett:** P&B, A Symphonic Picture
       Program notes by Edward Jablonski & John Pfeiffer (2 pp.) on container;
       Recorded Mar. 28, May 11-12, 1981, Cliff Temple Baptist Church

D18.   Dallas Symphony; Eduardo Mata, conducting
       Victrola 7726-2-RV **[DDD]** ; 77264-RV3, cassette
       With Cuban; **R. R. Bennett:** Porgy and Bess (symphonic picture)

D19.   Denver Symphony Pops; Newton Wayland, conducting
       Pro Arte CDD-352, CD **[DDD]**; PCD-352, cassette
       With Piano Music; RiB (G piano roll, 1925)

D20.   Elite Concert Orchestra; Gerhard Stein, piano (in RiB); Max Marschner,
       conducting
       Allegro 3063 (195-?)
       With RiB
       Recorded in Europe

D21.   English Chamber Orchestra; Bedford
       Angel CDB-62022
       With Concerto; RiB

D22.   Feder & Gilgore (2-piano arr.)
       Chandos ABRD-1199
       With Cuban; Music by Barber & Copland

D23.   Gewandhausorchester Leipzig; Kurt Masur, conducting
       Eterna (Berlin) 8 26 779
       With Porgy and Bess, A Symphonic Picture (Bennett, arr.); Cuban Overture

D24.   Morton Gould, piano; with orchestra
       RCA Victor LM 6033, 2 discs (1955)
       "The Serious Gershwin"
       With P&B, piano solo, from act 1, scene 1; Suite from P&B arr. by M.
         Gould; RiB; Concerto; Three Preludes for Piano
       Program notes by Arthur Schwartz [24 pp.] laid in container
       LC card no. r55-581 *See:* **B1021**

D25.   Hollywood Bowl Symphony Orchestra; Felix Slatkin, conducting
Capitol P-8343 (1956)
With RiB
Program notes by Alex North on container
LC card no. r56-584

D26.   Hollywood Bowl Symphony; Slatkin, conducting
Seraphim 4XG-60174, cassette
With RiB

D27.   Kingsway Symphony Orchestra; Camarata, conducting
Decca DL 8519, 2 discs (195-?)
With RiB
LC card no. r62-534

D28.   Kingsway Symphony Orchestra; Camarata, conductor
Decca DCM 3206 (1962)
With RiB
Notes on the Age of Jazz (Series G) on slipcase
Program notes (1 p.) inserted
Chronicle of Music, Ser. G: Music of the Jazz Age, no. 1

D29.   Leipzig Gewandhaus Orchestra; K. Masur, conducting
DG413851-4 GW,cassette
With RiB; Concerto; **L. Bernstein:** West Side Story

D30.   London Symphony; A. Previn, conducting
Angel CDC-47161; 4AM-34760, cassette; AXS 36810, cassette
With Concerto; RiB

D31.   London Philharmonic Orchestra; John Pritchard, conducting
Musical Heritage Society MHS 7088, 7088H, 9088K (1985, 1976)
With **Copland:** El Salón México; **Robert R. Bennett:** P&B, A Symphonic
    Picture
Recorded Feb. 1975 in Fairfield Hall, Croydon

D32.   London Symphony Orchestra; David Golub, piano; Mitch Miller, conducting
Arabesque Z6587, CD (1987) **[DDD]**
With RiB, Concerto
Producer: Ward Botsford

D33.   London Festival Orchestra; Stanley Black, conducting
London 421 025-4, cassette
"Weekend Classics"
With Cuban Overture (Cleveland Orchestra), RiB (S. Black, piano), & Variations
    (IGR-D. Parkhouse, piano)

D34.   Mantovani & his orchestra (Katchen, piano)
London LL.1262 (195-?)
With RiB
Recorded in Europe *See:* **B1017, B1021, B1041, B1101**

D35. Minneapolis Symphony Orchestra; Antal Dorati, conducting
Mercury MG50071, Olympian Series (1957)
With **Robert R. Bennett,** arr.: Porgy & Bess, A Symphonic Picture
Recorded in the Northrup. Auditorium, University of Minnesota
LC card no. r60-562 *See:* **B943, B948, B975, B1130**

D36. Minneapolis Symphony Orchestra; Antal Dorati, conducting
Mercury SR 90290 **"Curtain Up! George Gershwin Favorites"** **[GOH]**
CONTENTS & PERFORMERS: An American in Paris (Gershwin)
1928--Minneapolis Symphony Orchestra, A. Dorati, conducting;
Rhapsody in Blue, Eugene List, piano; Cuban Overture—Eastman-
RochesterOrchestra; H. Hanson, conducting

D37. Monte Carlo Philharmonic; L. Foster, conducting
Erato ECD-55031 **[DDD]**; MCE-55031, cassette
With Concerto; RiB

D38. National Philharmonic; Morton Gould, conducting
Pro-Arte Records, SDS 627 (1987?)
With music by **Barber** and **Gould**
See: **B983**

D39. NBC Symphony Orchestra; Arturo Toscanini, conducting (Rec. 5/18/1945)
RCA Victor LM 9020 (1952)
With **Prokofiev:** Classical Symphony
LC card no. r63-1889 *See:* **B993**

D40. New York Philharmonic; Leonard Bernstein, conducting
CBS MT-31804, cassette
With RiB *See:* **B1071**

D41. New York Philharmonic; Leonard Bernstein, conducting
CBS CD MYK-37242 **[ADD]**; MYT-37242, cassette
With RiB (Columbia SO)

D42. New York Philharmonic; Leonard Bernstein, conducting
CBS Masterworks MK 42264; CBS CD MK-42264 **[ADD]**
With RiB; **Grofé:** Grand Canyon Suite
See: **B992, B1121**

D43. New York Philharmonic; Leonard Bernstein, conducting
CBS CD MK-42516 **[ADD/DDD]**; FMT-42516, cassette
With Preludes; Porgy and Bess (selections); RiB *See:* **B1264**

D44. Philharmonia Orchestra of Hamburg, Hans-Jurgen Walther, cond.
MGM E 3253
An American in Paris; Porgy and Bess, Symphonic Suite
(arr. Robert Russell Bennett)

D45. Philharmonic-Symphony of New York; André Kostelanetz, conducting
Columbia 4879, mono, Columbia Masterworks (1954)
With Concerto; RiB (Oscar Levant, piano)
Program notes by Charles Burr on slipcase
LC card no. r54-522 *See*: **B1583**

D46. New York Philharmonic; Zubin Mehta, conducting
Teldec 2292-46318-2, CD **[DDD]**
With excerpts from P&B & Cuban Overture

D47. Philharmonic-Symphony Orchestra of New York; Artur Rodzinski, conducting
Columbia 12106-D, 12107-D, 2 discs, 78 mono, 4026, (194?)
Program notes, in part by Paul Affelder, on container *See*: **B972**

D48. New York Philharmonic (AiP); Buffalo Philharmonic (overtures); Michael
Tilson Thomas, conducting
CBS Masterworks MK 42240 (1976); DIDC 70127, reissue as a CD
[ADD] (1987)
With RiB (Columbia Jazz Band); Broadway Overtures to Oh, Kay!, Funny
Face, Girl Crazy, Strike Up the Band, OTIS, Cake (Arr. by Don Rose)
RiB recorded at 30th St. Studios, NY, 1976; AiP at Philharmonic Hall, NY,
1974; Broadway Overtures at Kleinhans Hall, Buffalo, NY, 1976
Program notes in English, German, & French by Andrew Kazdin on insert
in container Durations on back of insert
Produced by Andrew Kazdin & Steven Epstein *See*: **B1331, B1116**

D49. Philadelphia Orchestra; Eugene Ormandy, conducting
Columbia Masterworks, Columbia MGT 30073, 2 cassettes; CBS Masterworks
40-79024, cassette (© 1983)
In **"The Gershwin Album"**
With RiB, Concerto, and Porgy and Bess: A Symphonic Picture (**Robert
R. Bennett,** arr.)

D50. Philadelphia Orchestra; Ormandy, conducting
CBS MLK-39454, CD; PMT-39454, cassette
With Music; Preludes; Rhapsody

D51. Philadelphia Orchestra; Ormandy, conducting
Odyssey YT-35496, cassette
With RiB

D52. Philadelphia Orchestra; Ormandy, conducting
Columbia MS 7258, Columbia Masterworks (1969)
With **Robert R. Bennett:** P&B, A Symphonic Picture
Program notes by Phillip Ramey on container

D53. Pittsburgh Symphony; William Steinberg, conducting
Command CC 11037 (1967)
With **Robert R. Bennett:** P&B, A Symphonic Picture
Program notes by F. B. Weille on container
LC card no. r68-1848 *See*: **B959**

D54. Pittsburgh Symphony Orchestra; [Jesús Sanromá] William Steinberg, conducting
Everest Record Group WRC4 2024, cassette, analog, Dolby (19--?); Everest
3067, cassette (198-?)
With RiB
See: **B1000, B1098**

D55. Pittsburgh Symphony Orchestra; André Previn, conductor
Philips 412611-2 PH **[DDD]** (1984); 412611-4 PH, cassette
With RiB & Concerto
Recorded in Pittsburgh, May, 1984
Durations and album notes (with German & French translations) by Max
Harrison on container

D56. RCA Victor Symphony Orchestra; George Gershwin, celeste; Nathaniel Shilkret,
conducting
RCA ALK1-7114, cassette ; other version on RCA Victor 27-0111 (AiP & RiB
only)
"Gershwin Plays Gershwin"
With RiB (GG, piano; Whiteman & Orchestra, version of Apr. 21, 1927); Three
Piano Preludes (GG, piano); Songs (GG, piano)
AiP recorded Feb. 4, 1929 *See*: **B993, B1331**

D57. RCA Victor Symphony Orchestra; Leonard Bernstein, conducting
RCA Camden CAL 439 (1958)
"Leonard Bernstein Conducts"
With **A. Copland**: Billy the Kid Suite *See*: **B947**

D58. David Rose and His Orchestra
M-G-M E 3123-A & B "Love Walked In—The Music of George Gershwin"
[GOH]
With songs and RiB; *See* full entry under **"Anthologies"**

D59. Royal Concert Orchestra; Louis Shankson, conducting
Allegro 1609 (n.d.)
With Prelude No. 2; I Got Plenty O' Nuttin'; **Grofé:** Mississippi Suite,
Grand Canyon Suite
Recorded in Europe

D60. Royal Philharmonic Orchestra; Henry Lewis, conducting; Janis Vakarelis, piano
RPO Records MCAD-6229 (1988?); MCA Classics MCA-6229; MCAD-6229,
CD **[DDD]**; MCAC-6229, cassette
With Concerto
See: **B1019**

D61. Royal Promenade Orchestra; of London (on AiP & RiB); Russell Sherman, piano;
Orchestra of St. Luke's; Gunther Schuller, conducting; et al
Pro Arte CDM 814 **[DDD]**
First movement of Concerto only (Sherman); With RiB; Lullaby; "Gershwin
in Hollyood"

D62. Saint Louis Symphony Orchestra; Leonard Slatkin, conducting

Vox CT-2101, cassette
With Catfish Row; Promenade

D63. Saint Louis Symphony Orchestra; Leonard Slatkin, conducting; Barbara Liberman,
solo piano & David Mortland, solo banjo (in Catfish Row Suite); George
Silfies, solo clarinet (Promenade)
Moss Music Group MMG MCD 10035, digitally remastered (1988, 1974)
With Catfish Row Suite; Promenade; "I Got Rhythm" Variations
Durations & **Program notes** by Edward Jablonski on insert in container
See: **B952, B955**

D64. Saint Louis Symphony Orchestra; Leonard Slatkin, conducting
Angel CDC-49278 **[DDD]**; 4DS-49278, cassette
With Cuban Overture; Lullaby; Catfish Row Suite

D65. San Francisco Symphony; Seiji Ozawa, conducting (AiP)/ Robert Szidon,
piano; London Philharmonic Orchestra; Downes, conducting (Concerto)/
Siegfried Stöckigt, piano; Leipzig Gewandhaus Orchestra; Kurt Masur,
conducting (RiB)
DG Walkman 413 851-4 GW, cassette
With Concerto; RiB; **L. Bernstein:** West Side Story: Symphonic Dances
See: **B926**

D66. Seattle Symphony; Charles Butler, trumpet; Gerard Schwarz, conducting
Delos DE 3078, CD **[DDD]**
With music by **L. Bernstein; S. Barber**
First recording of the original uncut score which includes about three minutes
of music excised by G before the first performance
Producer: Adam Stern
See: **B989**

D67. Slovak Philharmonic Orchestra; Dennis Burkh, conducting
Musical Heritage Society MHC 4158, cassette (1979)
"Music by George Gershwin"
With RiB

D68 . Slovak Philharmonic Orchestra; (AiP); Richard Hayman, conducting
Kathryn Selby, piano; CSR Symphony Orchestra (Bratislava) (Concerto & RiB),
Naxos 8.550295 **[DDD],** CD
With Concerto; RiB
Producers: Karol Kopernicky & Hubert Geschwantder
Reviewed, *Fanfare*, Jan.-Feb. 1992, by Peter J. Rabinowitz, 216-217

D69. Slovak Philharmonic Orchestra; Libor Pesak, conducting (RiB & AiP)
Madacy BC-4-3609, cassette; avail. on CD
With RiB; Selections from P&B (Vienna Phil., Simon Gale, conducting); Songs
(Kuno Alexander's Sound Orchestra); piano selections (Eugen Cicero, pa.)

D70. Utah Symphony; Maurice Abravanel, conducting
Vanguard VCS 10017 (1967)
With Concerto

Vanguard Cardinal Series
Program notes by Martin Bookspan *See*: **B984**

D71.   Utah Symphony; Maurice Abravanel, conducting
Vanguard CD VBD-10017; C-10017, cassette
With Concerto & RiB

D72.   Utah Symphony; Maurice Abravanel, conductor
Westminster XWN 18686 (XTV 27137) (196-?)
With Concerto
Program notes by James Lyons on container *See*: **B998, B1002**

D73.   Utah Symphony; Reid Nibley, piano; Maurice Abravanel, cond.
Westminster XWN 18687 **[GOH]**
With RiB
See: **B950, B1015**

D74.   Victor Symphony Orchestra, N. Shilkret, conducting; Gershwin on celeste
Smithsonian Recordings, POB 2122, Colchester, VT 05449-2122 (As of 1995)
"I Got Rhythm: The Music of George Gershwin," 4 CDs or cassettes
With RiB and Variations on "I Got Rhythm" with G performing; and 60
G selections performed by various artists, An informative 64-page booklet is
included with the set *See*: Full entry under **"Anthologies," D1267**

D75.   Warner Brothers Orchestra; Bert Shefter, piano; Ray Heindorf, conducting
Warner Brothers BS 1243 (1959?)
With RiB
See: **B944, B949, B1067, B1068, B1296**

D76.   Orchestra with Paul Whiteman conducting
Capitol P-303 (1952?)
With RiB
Program notes on container

Arrangements of *American in Paris*

D77.   Anognoson & Kinton (original 2-piano version)
Pro Arte CDD-367 **[DDD]**
With I Got Rhythm; RiB

D78.   Jeffrey Reid Baker, synthesizers
"Rhapsody in Electric Blue"
Newport Classic CD NC-60042
With Concerto; 3 Preludes; RiB; music by Baker *See*: **B1111**

D79.   First Piano Quartet (originated by Edwin Fadiman)
RCA Victor LM 125, mono, 10 in. (19--?)
AiP arr. for piano quartet
With RiB; Summertime; Bess, You Is My Woman Now; I Got Plenty O'
Nuttin'; The Man I Love; Strike Up the Band

D80 . Gershwin (6 Duo-Art piano rolls)
Pro Arte CDD-352, CD **[DDD]**; PCD-352, cassette
With RiB; Songs

D81. George Gershwin, piano rolls realized by Artis Wodehouse
Elektra\Nonesuch 79287-2 CD; 79287-4 cassette
"Gershwin Plays Gershwin: The Piano Rolls"
With Songs, Full entry under **"Recordings by Gershwin"**

D82. Grierson & Kane, pianos (duo-piano arrangement)
"'S Wonderful!"
Angel CDM-69119
With Preludes, etc.; *See*: Full entry under **"Anthologies"**

D83. Katia & Marielle Labèque, pianos; Cleveland Orchestra; Riccardo Chailly,
conducting [2 pianos, arr. Katia & Marielle Labèque]
London 417326-1, available in all three formats (© 1986)
With RiB; Lullaby; Cuban Overture
Recorded in Masonic Auditorium, Cleveland, OH, November, 1985
Program notes in English, French, & German inserted in container

D84. Katia & Marielle Labèque, pianos
Angel CDC-47044 **[DDD]**; DS-38130, cassette (1984)
With **Percy Grainger's** Fantasy on GG's Porgy & Bess arr. for Two Pianos
Program notes by Michael Feinstein on container *See*: **B963**, **B964**

D85. Milne and Leith, piano rolls
in album: **"Gershwin Plays Gershwin: The Piano Rolls"**
Elektra/Nonesuch 79287-2, CD
With songs from G's own performances on rolls
See: Full entry under **"Recordings by Gershwin"**

D86. The New York Banjo Ensemble
Kicking Mule Records KM 224 (1982)
"The New York Banjo Ensemble Plays Gershwin"
With RiB, arr.; Swanee; I'll Build A Stairway to Paradise; Strike
Up the Band; Oh, Lady Be Good!; 'S Wonderful!; Sweet and
Low-Down; Clap Yo' Hands; Prelude No. 2; Impromptu in Two
Keys; Rialto Ripples

D87. Jean-Pierre Rampal, flute; John Steele Ritter, piano; Randy Kerber,
synthesizer; James Walker, alto flute; Los Angeles Philharmonic; Michel
Colombier, arranging & conducting
CBS FM 39700 (1985)
"Fascinatin' Rampal"
With Songs; Excerpts from P&B; Piano Preludes
See: **B1250**

D88. Frances Veri & Michael Jamanis, pianos
Book-of-the-Month Records 61-5426, 3 discs (1981)
"The Complete Piano Music"

AiP is a transcription for two pianos by Frances Veri, with other works for piano, *See:* complete entry under **"Piano Music"**

D89.   Paul Whiteman and His Concert Orchestra; Rosa Linda, piano
Decca 29054, Brunswick 0142, Capitol P-303 (1938)
AiP (Part 1); With Cuban Overture (Part 3)

D90.   Paul Whiteman and His Concert Orchestra
Decca 29055, Brunswick 0143 (1938)
AiP (Parts 2 & 3)

D91.   Paul Whiteman and His Concerto Orchestra
Decca DL 8024
With RiB (Roy Bargy, piano); Cuban Overture; Second Rhapsody (Roy Bargy, piano)

CATFISH ROW: SUITE FROM PORGY AND BESS (1935-1936) **(W7)**

D92.   BBC Philharmonic Orchestra: conducted by Yan Pascal Tortelier
CHANDOS CHAN 9325 **[DDD]**
With Girl Crazy: Overture (orchestration Don Rose); Variations on "I Got Rhythm"; An American in Paris.; Strike Up the Band: Overture (orchestration Don Rose)
See: Full entry at **D1088**

D93.   Berlin Philharmonic Orchestra; Karl Leister, clarinet; Alexis
Weissenberg (in RiB), Elaine Donohoe (in Catfish Row), pianos;
Seiji Ozawa, conducting
EMI/Angel DS 38050, disc; 4DS 38050, cassette; CDC 7 47152 2, CD **[DDD]** (c 1984)
With RiB; Variations on "I Got Rhythm"
Program notes by Max Harrison on container
Producer: Robert Woods
See: **B1080**

D94.   Chicago Symphony Orchestra; James Levine, Piano and conducting
Deutsche Grammophone 4316252 GH (in Schwann, Spring 1994)
With AiP, Cuban, & RiB *See:* **B1089**, **B1132**

D95.   Cincinnati Pops; William Tritt, piano (on Jazzbo Brown music & Hurricane scene); Erich Kunzel, conducting
Telarc CD-80086 **[DDD]** (1987)
With music by **Grofé**

D96.   Hamilton Philharmonic Orchestra; W. Tritt, piano; B. Brott, conducting
CBS Records SMCD 5111 **[DDD]**
With Second Rhapsody; RiB

D97.   André Kostelanetz & His Orchestra; Kostelanetz, conducting
Columbia CL-2133/CS-8933

D98.   Saint Louis Symphony; Slatkin, conducting
Vox CT-2101, cassette
With AiP; Promenade

D99.   Jeffrey Siegel, piano; Saint Louis Symphony Orchestra,; Leonard Slatkin,
conducting
Murray Hill Records 932520, 4 discs (n.d.)
With Concerto; Cuban Overture; Lullaby (Version for String Orchestra);
AiP

D100. Saint Louis Symphony Orchestra; Leonard Slatkin, conducting
Angel CDC-49278 **[DDD]**
With AiP; Cuban; Lullaby

D101. Saint Louis Symphony Orchestra; Slatkin, conducting; Barbara Liberman, solo
piano & David Mortland, solo banjo (in Catfish Row Suite); George Silfies,
solo clarinet (Promenade)
Moss Music Group MMG MCD 10035, digitally remastered (1988, 1974)
With AiP; Promenade; "I Got Rhythm" Variations
Durations & **Program notes** by Edward Jablonski on insert in container
See: **B955, B980, B981**

D102. Utah Symphony Orchestra; Maurice Abravanel, conducting
Westminster WST 14063 (1970, 1975)
With **Copland:** El Salón México

D103. Utah Symphony Orchestra; Maurice Abravanel, conducting
Westminster XWN-18850; Music Guild MS-167
With F. Grofé: Grand Canyon Suite
First recording made of the original suite by Gershwin
See: **B997**

CONCERTO IN F for Piano and Orchestra (1925) (W2)

D104. Roy Bargy, piano; Paul Whiteman and His Orchestra
Columbia 50139-40-41-D, 12", 7170-71-72-M, 9665-66-67 (Sept. 15, 17, &
Oct. 5, 1928, NY)
Grofé orchestration *See*: **B1044**

D105. Roy Bargy, piano; Paul Whiteman and His Concert Orchestra
Decca 29056-29057, Brunswick 0145-0146 (Apr. 18, 1939, NY)

D106. Roy Bargy, piano; Bix Beiderbecke, cornet; William Daly, conducting
Concerto, arr. By Ferde Grofé (1928)
Preamble PRCD 1785
"Whiteman Plays American Classics"
With **Grofé** Grand Canyon Suite
Entry continued on next page

Interesting **notes** by John Lasher in jewel box
Sonic restoration by Lane Audio *See*: **B1025, B1040, B1044**

D107. Leon Bates, piano; Basel Symphony; Matthias Bemert, conducting (Gershwin);
Volker Banfield, piano; Swiss Radio Symphony; Klauspeter Seibel,
conducting (Martin)
RCA 60852; 55 min.
With **MARTIN:** Piano Concerto 2   Classic Visions, Vol. 4

D108. D. Blumenthal, piano; English Chamber Orchestra; Bedford, conducting
Angel CDB-62022; also Classics for Pleasure CFP 9012, CD **[ADD]**
With AiP; RiB

D109. [Various] Bulgarian orchestras and soloists
AVM AVZ-3006, budget CD **"George Gershwin's Best"**
CONTENTS: Cuban Overture; Concerto; RiB; Porgy and Bess (Introduction &
Summertime); Three Preludes for Piano (3-90); Same entry as:
Simfonichen orkestur na bulgarskoto radio i televiziia
DCC Compact Classics AVZ-3005, CD (p 1990)

D110. Alexander Cattarino, piano; Slovak Philharmonic Orchestra (Bratislava); Bystri
Rezucha, conducting
Opus LC 5969, CD **[DDD]** (1988?) [distrib. by Koch Import Service]
With **Addinsell:** Warsaw Concerto
See: **B1018**

D111. Peter Donohue, piano; Michael Collins, clarinet; Harvey and the Wall-
bangers; London Sinfonietta conducted by Simon Rattle
EMI Angel CDC7 47991-2 or EMI Classics CDC 54280
"THE JAZZ ALBUM" With RiB; Song
See: **B1084, B1102**

D112. Phillipe Entremont, piano; Philadelphia Orchestra; Eugene Ormandy, conducting
Columbia ML 6413 oir MS 7013
With RiB *See*: **B958, D1075**

D113. Phillipe Entremont, piano; Philadelphia Orchestra; Eugene Ormandy, conducting
2-CBS LPs MGT-30073
"The Gershwin Album"
With American; P&B: A Symphonic Picture; RiB

D114. Phillipe Entremont, piano; Philadelphia Orchestra; Eugene Ormandy,
conducting
CBS Masterworks 40-79024, cassette (© 1983)
"The Gershwin Album"
With RiB (complete, uncut version); AiP; R. R. Bennett: P&B:
A Symphonic Picture

D115. Phillipe Entremont, piano; Philadelphia Orchestra; Eugene Ormandy, conducting
(Concerto); Entremont; Cleveland Orchestra; Pierre Boulez, conducting (in
Ravel concertos)

Essential Classics (Sony Classical) SBT 46338 (c 1972, 1990 Sony), cassette
With Ravel Concerto in G & Concerto for Left Hand in D
Program notes by Uwe Kraemer, trans. Gery Bramell in container
Previously recorded material

D116. George Gershwin, piano ·
Mark 56 Records 641-A-D **"Gershwin By Gershwin" [GOH]**
CONTENTS:
Sides A & B: Concerto—from radio broadcast April 7, 1935; Fragment
from Concerto, second mvt.—from radio broadcast April 7, 1935;
Rhapsody in Blue (Performed on Duo-Art reproducing piano); Variations
on "I Got Rhythm"; Second Rhapsody—from rehearsal recording June 26,
1931; **Sides C & D:** Of Thee I Sing—from radio broadcast Feb. 19,
1934; The Man I Love—from radio broadcast Feb. 19, 1934; I Got
Rhythm—from radio broadcast Feb. 19, 1934; Swanee—from radio
broadcast Feb. 19, 1934; Mine/I Got Rhythm—from radio broadcast
April 30, 1934; Also from same broadcast: Variations; Love Is Sweeping
the Country & Wintergreen for President; Hi-Ho (I. Gershwin, vocal &
Harold Arlen, piano)

D116.1. Leopold Godowsky, III, piano (nephew of George); Royal
Scottish National Orchestra; José Serebrier, conducting (debut record-
ing for Godowsky)
"Gershwin: Centennial Edition"
Dinemec Classics
With Three Preludes and Lullaby arr. for Orchestra by Serebrier

D117. David Golub, piano; London Symphony; Mitch Miller, conducting
Arabesque Z-6587, CD **[DDD]**; ABQC-6587, cassette
With AiP; RiB *See:* **B987**

D118. Morton Gould, piano; Morton Gould and his orchestra
RCA Victor Red Seal LM 2017 (1956)
With RiB; Three Preludes for piano
Program notes, based on an essay by Arthur Schwartz, on container
LC card no. r56-693

D119. Morton Gould, piano; with orchestra
RCA Victor LM 6033, 2 discs (1955)
"The Serious Gershwin"
With P&B, piano solo, from act 1, scene 1; Suite from P&B arr. by M.
Gould; RiB; AiP; Three Preludes for Piano
Program notes by Arthur Schwartz [24 pp.] laid in container
LC card no. r55-581 *See:* **B1021**

D120. W. Haas, piano; Monte Carlo Opera Orchestra; De Waart, conducting
Philips 420492-2 PM, CD **[ADD]**
With American; RiB

D121. Peter Jablonski, piano; Royal Philharmonic Orch; V. Ashkenazy, cond.
London 430542 **[DDD]** *See:* Full entry at **D743**

D122. Julius Katchen, piano; Mantovani & his orchestra
London LL 1262 (195-?)
With RiB
Recorded in Europe *See*: **B1017, B1021, B1101**

D123. S. Knor, piano; Prague Symphony; Vaclav Neumann, conducting
Supraphonet 11 1105-2 **[AAD]**
With Cuban Overture; **Milhaud:** Création

D124. Piano ?; Prague Symphony Orchestra; Vaclav Smetbaicek & Vaclav Neumann,
conducting
Supraphon SUA ST 50479 (1963)
In **"Musical Gems of the Twentieth Century"**
With **I. Stravinsky**, Feux d'artifice; **A. Roussel**; **D. Milhaud**, La création
du monde
LC card no. 79-761605/R

D125. K. & M. Labèque (2 pianos), Cleveland Orchestra; Riccardo Chailly, conducting
Philips 400022-2 PH, CD; 400022-4 PH, cassette
With RiB *See*: **B1082**

D126. Oscar Levant, piano; NBC Symphony; A. Toscanini, conducting
Hunt Productions CD-534 (monaural) **[AAD]**
With American; RiB (Rec. 1942-44) *See*: **B1583**

D127. Oscar Levant, piano (Concerto); Earl Wild, piano (RiB); Benny Goodman,
clarinet; NBC Symphony Orchestra; Arturo Toscanini, conducting
Ark 4 (1981)
"Toscanini dirige Gershwin"
With AiP; RiB
Recorded in New York Nov. 1, 1942, Nov. 14, 1943, & Mar. 2, 1944,
respectively
Program notes by Riccardo Risaliti in Italian with English translation by
Gabriele Dotto on container *See*: **B1331, B1583**

D128. Oscar Levant, piano; Philharmonic-Symphony of New York; André Kostelanetz,
conducting
Columbia 4879, mono, Columbia Masterworks (1954)
With RiB; AiP
Program notes by Charles Burr on slipcase
LC card no. r54-522 *See*: **B1583**

D129. Oscar Levant, piano; New York Philharmonic; A. Kostelanetz, conducting
(Concerto) (Rec. 1942); Morton Gould Orchestra (Second Rhapsody & "I Got
Rhythm"); Philadelphia Orchestra, Eugene Ormandy, conducting (RiB)
"Levant Plays Gershwin" (consists of previously recorded material)
CBS MK-42514 (monaural), CD **[ADD]**; FMT-42514, cassette (compilation
p 1987)
With "I Got Rhythm" Var.; Preludes; RiB; Second Rhapsody
Producers: Goddard Lieberson, Richard Gilbert, & Howard Scott *See*:

B1237, B1583

D130. Oscar Levant, piano; Philadelphia Orchestra; Eugene Ormandy, conducting;
Philharmonic-Symphony Orchestra of New York; Artur Rodzinski & André
Kostelanetz, conducting
Columbia CS-8641 (19--?)
With AiP & RiB *See:* **B1583**

D131. Raymond Lewenthal, piano; Metropolitan Symphony Orchestra; Oscar Danon,
conducting
Quintessence PMC 7115 (1979)
With RiB
Recorded Feb., 1962 at Walthamstow Town Hall, London
Program notes by Steven Vining on container *See:* **B1100**

D132. Eugene List, piano; Berlin Symphony; Samuel Adler, conducting
Turnabout CT-4457, cassette
With Preludes; RiB *See:* **B1120**

D133. Eugene List, piano; Eastman-Rochester Orchestra; Howard Hanson, conducting
Mercury MG 50138, SR 90002, Olympian Series (1957)
With RiB
Recorded in the Eastman Theater, Rochester, NY, May 4, 1957
LC card no. r60-639 *See:* **B999, B1004, B1023, B1094**

D134. Andrew Litton, piano & conductor; Bournemouth Symphony Orchestra
Virgin Classics SICS VC 90780-2, CD **[DDD]**
With **Ravel:** Concerto in G
Producer: Andrew Keener
See: **B1014**

D135. Jerome Lowenthal, piano; Utah Symphony, Maurice Abravanel, conducting
Vanguard VBD-10017, CD; Everyman Classics VBD-10017; C-10017,
cassette
With AiP; RiB
Program notes by Martin Bookspan on insert in container
See: **B966**

D136. Peter Nero, piano; Boston Pops Orchestra; Arthur Fiedler, cond.
RCA Red Seal LSC 3025
With Fantasy and Improvisations (Blue fantasy) (Nero) for piano, jazz bass,
& drums & Symphony orch; Gene Cherico, bass; Joe Cusatis, drums

D137. Peter Nero, piano; Boston Pops Orchestra; Arthur Fiedler, conducting
RCA LSC-3319

D138. Reid Nibley, piano; Utah Symphony; Maurice Abravanel, conducting
2-MCA Classics MCAD2-9800, CD
With American; P&B Symphony Pictures (Bennett); **Copland:** Appalachian;
Billy; Rodeo; Salón

D139. Reid Nibley, piano; Utah Symphony; Maurice Abravanel, conducting
Westminster XWN 18685 **[GOH]**
With RiB *See:* **B1095**

D140. Reid Nibley, piano; Utah Symphony, Maurice Abravanel, conductor
Westminster XWN 18686 (XTV 27135, 27137) (196-?)
With AiP

D141. Pyotr Pechersky & Alexander Tsvassman, pianos; Moscow Philharmonic
Orchestra, Kiril Kondrashin, conducting & U. S. S. R. Symphony
Orchestra; Gennady Rozhdestvensky, conducting
Westminster Gold/Melodiya WG 8355 (1980)
With RiB
Producers: Alexander Griva & David Gaklin
See: **B962, B1011, B1078**

D142. Piano?; Simfonichen orkestur na bulgarsradio i televiziia.
Bulgarian Broadcasting Symphony Orchestra ; various soloists and conductors
DCC Compact Classics AVZ-3005, CD (p 1990)
With Rhapsody in blue - Three preludes for piano - Cuban overture - Porgy
and Bess (Introduction and Summertime)

D143. André Previn (piano & conductor); London Symphony
Angel CDC-47161; 4AM-34760, cassette
With AiP & RiB *See:* **B965**

D144. André Previn, piano; André Kostelanetz and His Orchestra
Columbia CL 1495; CS 8286
With RiB
See: **B1000**

D145. André Previn, piano; André Kostelanetz and His Orchestra
"Gershwin's Greatest Hits"
CBS MLK-39454, CD; PMT-39454, cassette
Concerto-finale (Previn, Kostelanetz, Orchestra); With Porgy & Bess, a
symphonic picture-excerpts (Ormandy, Philadelphia Orchestra); AiP; Preludes;
RiB

D146. A. Previn (piano & cond.); Pittsburgh Sym.
Philips 412611-1; Philips 4126ll-2, CD **[DDD]**; 412611-4 PH, cassette
With AiP & RiB
Recorded in Pittsburgh, May, 1984
Durations & **album notes** (with German and French translations) by Max
Harrison on container

D147. Harry Reims, piano; Philharmonic Symphony Orchestra (for Concerto)
Allegro ALG-3096, mono (1953)
With RiB (piano excerpts)
Recorded in Europe

D148. Jesús Sanromá, piano; Boston Pops Orchestra; Arthur Fiedler, conducting
RCA Camden CAL 304 (19--?)
With RiB

D149. Kathryn Selby, piano; CSR Symphony Orchestra (Bratislava) (Concerto & RiB),
Slovak Philharmonic Orchestra (AiP); Richard Hayman, conducting
Naxos 8.550295 **[DDD]**, CD
With Concerto; AiP
Producers: Karol Kopernicky & Hubert Geschwantder
Reviewed, *Fanfare*, Jan.-Feb. 1992, by Peter J. Rabinowitz, pp. 216-217

D150. Shelly, H., piano; Philharmonia Orchestra; Yan Pascal Tortelier, conducting
Chandos CHAN 9092 [DDD]
With Second Rhapsody; RiB

D151. Russell Sherman, piano; Orchestra of St. Luke's; Gunther Schuller,
conducting (Grofé arrangement)
Pro Arte PCD, cassette, digital; CDD 244, CD **[DDD]** [dist. by Intersound]
(1986)
With Three Preludes; Fascinating Rhythm; The Man I Love; Somebody
Loves Me
American Artists Series
See: **B1038, B1042, B1044**

D152. Russell Sherman, piano; Orchestra of St. Luke's; Gunther Schuller, conducting
Pro Arte CDM 814 **[DDD]**
First movement of Concerto only; With RiB; Lullaby; AiP; "Gershwin in
Hollywood" by other orchestras

D153. Jeffrey Siegel, piano; St. Louis Symphony; Leonard Slatkin, conducting
Vox CT-2122, cassette
With Cuban & RiB

D154. Jeffrey Siegel, piano; St. Louis Symphony Orchestra; Leonard Slatkin,
conducting; Susan Slaughter, solo trumpet in Concerto
Vox Cum Laude MMG MCD 10011, CD
"Works for Piano and Orchestra"
With Second Rhapsody & RiB
Program notes by Edward Jablonski in English, French, & German inserted
See: **B955**

D155. F. Sosina, piano; USSR Radio Orchestra; A. Yansons, conducting
D 5674/5 (Soviet) [in *Melodiya*]

D156. Leslie Stifelman, piano; Marin Alsop, conducting Concordia
Angel CDC 7 54851 2 7 **[DDD]**
CONTENTS: Concerto (Orchestrated Grofé?); Oscar Levant: Caprice for
Orchestra; Blue Monday (arr. Bassman)
Producer: Karen Chester *See*: **B1040, B1138, B1583**

D157. Siegfried Stöckigt, piano; Leipzig Gewandhaus Orch.; Kurt Masur, conducting

> DG 413851-4 GW, cassette
> With RiB; AiP; **L. Bernstein:** West Side Story

D158. Robert Szidon, piano; London Philharmonic Orchestra; Downes, conducting
(Concerto); San Francisco Symphony; Seiji Ozawa, conducting (AiP); Siegfried
Stöckigt, piano; Leipzig Gewandhaus Orchestra; Kurt Masur, conducting (RiB)
DG Walkman 413 851-4
With AiP; RiB; **L. Bernstein:** West Side Story: Symphonic Dances
See: **B926**

D159. Gabriel Tacchino, piano; Monte Carlo Philharmonic; Lawrence Foster,
conducting
Erato ECD-55031 **[DDD]**; MCE-55031, cassette
Collection Bonsai
With AiP; RiB *See:* **B956**

D160. Alec Templeton, piano; Cincinnati Symphony Orchestra; Thor Johnson,
conducting
Remington R-199-184, mono (1954) *See:* **B1008, B1013, B1029, B1041**

D161. Wm. Tritt, piano; Cincinnati Pops; Eric Kunzel, conducting
Telarc CD-80166 **[DDD]**
With "I Got Rhythm" Var.; RiB; Rialto Ripples

D162. Janis Vakarelis, piano; Royal Philharmonic Orchestra; Henry Lewis,
conducting; Raymond Simmons (solo trumpet in second movement of
Concerto)
RPO Records MCAD-6229 (1988?); MCA Classics MCA-6229;
MCAD-6229, CD **[DDD]**; MCAC-6229, cassette
With AiP *See:* **B1019**

D163. Vodenicharov, piano; Bulgarian Radio Sym.; Alfidi, conducting
Sound CD-3447
With RiB

D164. Earl Wild, piano; Boston Pops; Arthur Fiedler, conducting
RCA (Papillon Collection) 6519-2 RG, CD **[ADD]**; 6519-4 RG, cassette
With AiP; "I Got Rhythm" Variations; RiB *See:* **B988, B1036, B1063, B1105**

D165. Earl Wild, piano; Boston Pops; Arthur Fiedler, conducting
RCA Red Seal LM-2586 (19-?); also available as RCA Victrola ALK1-4636
Cassette series (© 1983)
With "I Got Rhythm" Variations, Cuban Overture
See: **B1001, B1005, B1006, B1016, B1036, B1125**

D166. Earl Wild, Des Moines, IA Symphony; Joseph Giunta, conducting
Chesky 98 - 55 minutes (1994)
With **Wild:** Variations on an American Theme *See:* **B1040, B1034, B1138**

D167. Alicia Zizzo, piano; George Gershwin Festival Orchestra; Michael Charry,
conducting

Pro Arte CDD 514 **[DDD]**
With Cuban Overture (orch. only); Lullaby (pa. solo); RiB
Producer: Eugene Simon
See: **B1020, B1022, B1049**

Arrangements of Concerto
(Other than Grofé's)

D168. Jeffrey Reid Baker (synthesizers)
Newport Classic NC-60042, CD **[DDD]**
With AiP; Preludes; RiB; Music by **Baker**

D169. Gisela Binz & Thomas Thomassen, pianos; Orchestra; Hans Bund, conducting
Telefunken E 1808, 78, 12" **[GOH]**
With RiB

D170. Norman Krieger
Stradivari Classics SCD-8000, CD **[DDD]**; SCD-8000, cassette
With Preludes; RiB (Gershwin arr. for solo piano); Concerto is the solo piano
arr. by Grace Castagnetta
Producer: Laura Harth Rodriguez
See: **B1012, B1085**

D171. K. & M. Labèque (2 pianos)
Philips 400022-2 PH, CD **[ADD]**; 400022-4 PH, cassette
With RiB

CUBAN OVERTURE (originally titled *RUMBA*). (1932) **(W5)**

D172. Boston Pops Orchestra; Arthur Fiedler, conducting
RCA Red Seal LM-2586 (19-?); also available as RCA Victrola ALK1-4636
Cassette series (© 1983)
With "I Got Rhythm" Variations; Concerto

D173. Boston Pops; Earl Wild, piano; Arthur Fiedler, conducting
RCA Red Seal CSC-0605, 2 discs (1969?)
"The Best of Gershwin"
With AiP; RiB; Concerto; "I Got Rhythm" Variations
Program notes, in part by Deems Taylor or Carl
Bosler, on container

D174. Boston Pops Orchestra; Arthur Fiedler, conducting
RCA Gold Seal (Papillon Collection) 6806-2-RG, CD
[ADD]; 6806-4-RG6, cassette
With **Bernstein:** Fancy Free; **Copland:** Salón; & music
by **Gould, Grofé, Rodgers**

D175. [Various] Bulgarian orchestras and soloists
AVM AVZ-3006, CD
"Gershwin's Best"

With Concerto; RiB; Porgy & Bess (Introduction & Summertime); Three
Preludes for Piano

D176. Chicago Symphony Orchestra; James Levine, piano and conducting
Deutsche Grammophon 4316252 GH (in Schwann, Spring 1994)
With AiP, Catfish Row, & RiB *See:* **B968, B1048, B1089, B1132**

D177. Cleveland Orchestra; Labèque sisters (Katia & Marielle); Riccardo Chailly
London 417326-2 LH, CD **[DDD]**
With AiP; Lullaby; RiB *See:* **B1083**

D178. Cleveland Orchestra; Ivan Davis, piano (RiB); Lorin Maazel, conducting (1985)
London (Decca) 414 067-1 (1985); London 417098-4 LT;
414067-4 LJ, cassette
With RiB; AiP *See:* **B1077**

D179. Cleveland Orchestra; Lorin Maazel, conducting
London 417716-2 LM, CD
With AiP; RiB; **Copland:** Appalachian Spring; Fanfare for the Common Man

D180. Cleveland Pops Orchestra; Louis Lane, conducting
Epic LC-3626/BC-1047

D181. Dallas Symphony Orchestra; Eduardo Mata, conducting
RCA Red Seal RCD1, CD (1981)
With AiP; **Robert R. Bennett:** P&B, A Symphonic Picture
Program notes by Edward Jablonski & John Pfeiffer (2 pp.) on container;
Recorded Mar. 28, May 11-12, 1981, Cliff Temple Baptist Church

D182. Dallas Symphony; Eduardo Mata, conducting
Victrola 7726-2-RV, CD **[DDD]**, also avail. on cassette
With AiP; P&B Symphonic Picture (**R. R. Bennett**)

D183. Eastman-Rochester Orchestra, Howard Hanson, conducting
Mercury MG 50166
With **McBride:** Mexican Rhapsody; **Gould:** Latin-American Symphonette
See: **B1045, B1050**

D184. Eastman-Rochester Orchestra; Howard Hanson, conducting
"Curtain Up! George Gershwin Favorites"
Mercury MG-50290/SR-90290
With AiP (Minneapolis Orchestra, Dorati, conducting); RiB (Eugene List, piano)

D185. Gewandhausorchester Leipzig; Kurt Masur, conducting
Eterna (Berlin) 8 26 779
With P&B; A Symphonic Picture (**Bennett,** arr.); AiP

D186. George Gershwin Festival Orchestra; Alicia Zizzo, piano; Michael
Charry, conducting
Pro Arte CDD 514 **[DDD]**
With Concerto (Alicia Zizzo, piano); Lullaby (pa. solo); RiB (Zizzo)

Producer: Eugene Simon
See: **B1020, B1022, B1049**

D187. Hollywood Bowl Symphony Orchestra; Leonard Pennario, piano; Alfred Newman,
conducting
Capitol P 8581
"Gershwin By Starlight"
With Second Rhapsody; P&B Medley; Variations on "I Got Rhythm" (Shelly
Manne, drums, & Russ Cheevers, clarinet) *See:* **B1125, B1058**

D188. André Kostelanetz and His Orchestra
Columbia Masterworks ML 4481, LP, 12"
With Mine; Highlights from PORGY AND BESS (1935): I Got Plenty O'
Nuttin'; Bess, You Is My Woman Now; Summertime; I'm On My Way;
Love Walked In

D189. London Festival Recording Ensemble; Stanley Black, conducting
London 417098-4 LT, cassette
With AiP; RiB

D190. London Symphony; André Previn, conducting
Angel CDC-47021, CD **[DDD]**
With **Bennett:** P&B: A Symphonic Picture; Second Rhapsody *See:* **B1131**

D191. Orchestre national de l'Opera de Monte-Carlo; Edo de Waart, conducting
Philips 416 220-4, cassette (198-?)
With Selections from Porgy & Bess; AiP; RiB; "I Got Rhythm" Var.; Three
Preludes

D192. New York Philharmonic; Z. Mehta, conducting
Teldec 2292-46318-2, CD **[DDD]**
With excerpts from P&B & AiP

D193. Piano?; Simfonichen orkestur na bulgarskoto radio i televiziia.
Bulgarian Broadcasting Symphony Orchestra ; various soloists
and conductors (Same as **D196**)
DCC Compact Classics AVZ-3005, CD (p 1990)
With Rhapsody in blue - Three preludes for piano - Porgy and Bess
(Introduction and Summertime) - Concerto

D194. Prague Symphony; Vaclav Neumann, conducting
Supraphonet 11 1105-2, CD **[AAD]**
With Concerto; **Milhaud:** Création du monde

D195. Prague Symphony Orchestra; Vaclav Neumann, conducting
Everest SDBR 3405
With Concerto

D196. Simfonichen orkestur na bulgarskoto radio i televiziia. Bulgarian Broadcasting
Symphony Orchestra ; various soloists and conductors
DCC Compact Classics AVZ-3005, CD (p 1990)

"George Gershwin's best"
With other G works; *See*: Full entry under **"RiB"**

D197. St. Louis Symphony Orchestra; L. Slatkin, conducting
Vox CT-2122, cassette
With Concerto; "I Got Rhythm" Var.; RiB

D198. St. Louis Symphony Orchestra; Slatkin, conducting
Angel CDC-49278 **[DDD]**; 4DS-49278, cassette
With AiP; Lullaby; Catfish Row Suite

Arrangements of *Cuban Overture*

D199. Feder & Gilgore (2-piano arrangement)
Chandos ABRD-1199
With AiP; Music by **Barber** & **Copland**

D200. Frances Veri and Michael Jamanis, pianos
Connoisseur Society CS 02067 (Quadrophonic)
With Variations on "I Got Rhythm"; The Man I Love; Do It Again; Somebody
Loves Me; Second Rhapsody; Preludes for Piano

D201. Frances Veri & Michael Jamanis, pianos
Connoisseur Society 30-5663, 2 discs (1974)
"Fascinating Piano Music of George Gershwin"
Cuban Overture orig. for orchestra, arr. for piano, 4 hands; With 1) RiB;
    2) Piano Introduction to P&B; 3) "I Got Rhythm" Variations; 5) Two
    Waltzes in C; 6) The Songbook; 7) Second Rhapsody; 8) Three Preludes
The Classics Record Library; The 1st (RiB) & 7th works in original piano
    version; the 2nd, 5th, & 8th works for piano; the 3rd work originally for
    orchestra, arr. for two pianos

D202. Frances Veri & Michael Jamanis, pianos
Book-of-the-Month Records 61-5426, 3 discs (1981)
"The Complete Piano Music"
Cuban Overture trans. for one piano, four hands; With other works for solo
piano, *See*: Complete entry under **"Piano Music"**

D203. Paul Whiteman and His Concert Orchestra; Rosa Linda, piano
Decca DL 8024
With RiB (Ray Bargy, piano); AiP; Second Rhapsody (Ray Bargy, piano)

D204. Paul Whiteman and His Concert Orchestra
Decca 29053, 29092, 40114, Brunswick 0141 (Oct. 21, 1938, NY), 78
Cuban Overture (Parts 1 & 2)

D205. Paul Whiteman and His Concert Orchestra; Rosa Linda, piano
Decca 29054, Brunswick 0142 (1938)
Cuban Overture (Part 3); AiP (Part 1)

D206. Paul Whiteman and His Concert Orchestra

Decca 29055, Brunswick 0143 (1938)
AiP (Parts 2 & 3)

"I GOT RHYTHM" VARIATIONS **for solo piano and orchestra** (1934) **(W6)**

D207. Sondra Bianca, piano; Pro Musica Orchestra of Hamburg; Hans-Jurgen Walther,
conducting
MGM 3E-1, 3 discs *See:* **B1051**

D208. George Gershwin, piano
Mark 56 Records 641-A-D "Gershwin By Gershwin" **[GOH]**
With other serious works & songs, *See:* Full entry under **"Recordings by
Gershwin"**

D209. Werner Haas, piano; National Opera Orchestra of Monte Carlo; Edo de Waart,
conducting
Phillips 6500.118 (1971) *See:* **B1010**

D210. Werner Haas, piano; Orchestre national de l'Opera de Monte-Carlo; Edo de
Waart, conducting
Philips 416 220-4, cassette (198-?)
With Selections from Porgy & Bess; AiP; Cuban Overture; Three Preludes

D211. Oscar Levant, piano; Orchestra; M. Gould, conducting (Rec. 1949)
CBS MK-42514 (m), CD **[AAD]**, FMT-42514, cassette (m)
With Concerto; Preludes; RiB; Second Rhapsody *See:* **B1583**

D212. Lincoln Mayorga, piano; Moscow Philharmonic; Kitayenko, conducting
Sheffield Lab CD-28; LP & cassette versions avail.
With Lullaby; Preludes; Promenade; RiB

D213. Moussov, piano; TVR Orchestra; Vladigerov, conducting
Monitor MCS-2153
With RiB; Second Rhapsody

D214. David Parkhouse, piano; London Festival Recording Ensemble; Bernard
Herrmann, conducting
London SPC-21077/4-SPC-21007, also on cassette: London 421 025-4 as
"Weekend Classics"
With RiB (London Festival Orch., S. Black, piano & cond.); AiP (LFO, Black);
Cuban Overture (Cleveland Orchestra, Lorin Maazel cond.)

D215. Leonard Pennario, piano; Hollywood Bowl Symphony Orchestra; Alfred Newman,
conducting
Capitol P 8581
"Gershwin By Starlight"
With Second Rhapsody; P&B Medley; Cuban Overture *See:* **B1125**

D216. Leonard Pennario, piano; Hollywood Bowl Symphony Orchestra; Alfred
Newman, conducting
Angel S-36062

D217. Artur Rodzinski, conducting; pianist?
Penzance Records 43 Gershwin: 135th Street [Blue Monday] **[GOH]**
CONTENTS & PERFORMERS: Variations on "I Got Rhythm," pianist?,
Rodzinski, cond., 10/8/44; 135th Street; Skitch Henderson, conducting, perf.
at Philharmonic Hall, NY, May 20, 1968; Rhapsody in Blue; Earl Wild,
piano; Benny Goodman, clar.; cond. by Toscanini, Nov. 1, 1942; Mischa,
Jascha, Toscha, Sascha; Bobby Short, vocal and piano; Nov. 14, 1971

D218. J. Siegel, piano; St. Louis Symphony; L. Slatkin, conducting
Vox CT-2122
With Concerto; Cuban; RiB

D219. Wm. Tritt, piano; Cincinnati Pops; Kunzel, conducting
Telarc CD-80166
With Concerto; RiB; Rialto Ripples

D220. Alexis Weissenberg, piano; Berlin Philharmonic; Seiji Ozawa, conducting
Angel CDC-47152, CD **[DDD]**
With Catfish Row Suite; RiB *See:* Full entry at **D93**

D221. Earl Wild, piano; Boston Pops Orchestra; Arthur Fiedler, conducting
RCA Red Seal LM-2586 (19-?); also available as RCA Victrola ALK1-4636
Cassette series (c 1983)
With Cuban Overture; Concerto

D222. Earl Wild, piano; Boston Pops; Fiedler, conducting
RCA (Papillon Collection) 6519-2 RG, CD **[ADD]**
With AiP; Concerto; RiB *See:* **B988, B1036, B1063, B1105**

D223. Earl Wild, piano; Paul Whiteman Orchestra; Paul Whiteman, conducting
Coral 57021

Arrangements of *"I Got Rhythm" Variations*

D224. Anognoson & Kinton (original 2-piano version)
Pro Arte CDD-367, CD **[DDD]**
With AiP; RiB

D224.1. Ofra Harnoy, cello
Mastersound DFCDI-020 (dist. Allegro Imports), **CD [DDD]**
"Ofra Harnoy and Friends Play George Gershwin" p1990, ©1992
Includes Prelude No. 2 *See:* Full entry at **D735**

D225. Frances Veri & Michael Jamanis, pianos, playing Gershwin's arr. for two
pianos
Connoisseur Society CSQ-2067-SQ

D226. Frances Veri & Michael Jamanis, pianos
Book-of-the-Month Records 61-5426, 3 discs (1981)
"The Complete Piano Music"
"I Got Rhythm" Variations (trans. for two pianos); With other music for

piano, See complete entry under **"Piano Music"**

PORGY AND BESS: CATFISH ROW SUITE, see under "Catfish Row"

PORGY AND BESS: A SYMPHONIC PICTURE, arr. by Robert Russell Bennett

D227. Dallas Symphony Orchestra; Eduardo Mata, conducting
Victrola 7726-2-RV, CD **[DDD]**; 7726-4-RV3, cassette

D228. Dallas Symphony Orchestra; Eduardo Mata, conducting
RCA digital 150282, CD
With RiB; Cuban Overture

D229. Detroit Symphony; Antal Dorati, conducting
London 410110-1 LH (avail. in CD & cassette also)
With music by **F. Grofé**

D230. Gewandhausorchester Leipzig; Kurt Masur, conducting
Eterna (Berlin) 8 26 779
With Cuban Overture; AiP

D231. Indianapolis Symphony Orchestra; Victor Sevitzky, conducting
Columbia Set 999 (1945)
See: **B1092**

D232. London Philharmonic Orchestra; John Pritchard, conducting
Musical Heritage Society MHS 7088, 7088H, 9088K (1985, 1976)
With AiP; **Copland:** El Salón México

D233. London Symphony Orchestra; Cristina Ortiz, piano; André Previn, conducting
Angel S-37773 (1981)
"Previn Conducts Gershwin"
With Second Rhapsody; Cuban Overture

D234. London Symphony; Previn, conducting
Angel CDC-47021
With Cuban; Second Rhapsody

D235. Minneapolis Symphony Orchestra; Antal Dorati, conducting
Mercury Olympian MG 50394 **[GOH]**
With Latin-American Symphonette **(Gould)** 1940

D236. Philharmonia Orchestra of Hamburg, Jurgen Walther, cond.
MGM E 3253
An American in Paris; Porgy and Bess, Symphonic Suite
(arr. Robert Russell Bennett) See: **B1135**

D237. Philharmonic Symphony Orchestra of New York; André Kostelanetz,
conducting
Columbia ML-4904 (1954); Columbia CL-721 (1955); Columbia A-1102, 45, 7
in.; Columbia A-1921, 45, 7 in.; Philips (English) NBL-5020, 10 in. *See*: **B1134**

D238. Philadelphia Orchestra; Phillipe Entremont, piano (in 1st & 2nd works); Eugene
Ormandy, conducting
CBS Masterworks 40-79024, cassette (© 1983)
"The Gershwin Album"
With Concerto; RiB (complete, uncut version); AiP

D239. Philadelphia Orchestra; Eugene Ormandy, conducting
2-CBS MGT-30073, cassette
With American; Piano Con.; RiB

D240. Philadelphia Orchestra; Eugene Ormandy, conducting
Columbia MS 7258, Columbia Masterworks (1969)
With AiP

D241. Pittsburgh Symphony Orchestra; William Steinberg, conducting
Command CC 11037 (1967); Command/ABC Records 11037S (1972)
CONTENTS: With (Side II): AiP
LC card no. r68-1848 (CC 11037) *See:* **B959**

D242. Pittsburgh Symphony Orchestra; William Steinberg, conducting
Command CC 11027 S **[GOH]**
CONTENTS: Porgy and Bess - A Symphonic Picture (Gershwin-Bennett,
arr.); AiP

D243. Pittsburgh Symphony Orchestra; Fritz Reiner, conducting
Columbia 12118-20D (in set M-572), 78, 3 discs (1945); Columbia 12121-23D
(in set MM-572), 78, 3 discs (1945); Columbia ML-2019, 10 in. *See:* **B1092**

D244. RCA Symphony; R. R. Bennett, conducting
Victrola ALK1-4505, cassette
With **Bernstein:** West Side Story

D245. Royal Farnsworth Symphony Orchestra; Alfonso D'Artega, conducting
Design DLP-44/DCF-33 (1959)

D246. Symphony of the Air Pops Orchestra; Alfonso D'Artega, conducting
Epic LN-3621-22 (in set SN-6034)/BSN-549-50 (in set
BSN-104) (1959); Epic LN-3651/BN-552
"The Gershwin Story"
CONTENTS: Medleys of material from RiB, AiP, Concerto, "Gershwin on
Broadway" and "Gershwin in Hollywood" *See:* **B1257, B1306**

D247. Utah Symphony Orchestra; Maurice Abravanel, conducting
Vanguard Cardinal VCS-10023; Vanguard SRV-345-SD

D248. Utah Symphony; Maurice Abravanel, conducting
2-MCA Classics MCAD2-9800, CD
With AiP; Concerto; **Copland:** Appalachian; Billy; Rodeo; Salón

D249. Utah Symphony; M. Abravanel, conducting
Vanguard VCD-72009; CSRV-345, cassette (same, except with other works

only by Kern) **Copland:** Our Town; works by **J. Kern & K. Weill**

D250. Victor Symphony Orchestra; Robert Russell Bennett, conducting
RCA LM-2340/LSC-2340; RCA-Victrola VlCS-1491; RCA-Victrola
VlCS-1669(e)

PORGY AND BESS [Suite] (arr. for orch. by Morton Gould)

D251. Morton Gould and his Orchestra; Morton Gould, conducting
RCA LM-6033, 2 discs; RCA LM-2002
With Concerto, AiP, RiB, Piano Preludes *See:* **B973, B997, B1021, B1030**

RHAPSODY IN BLUE **(1924) (W1)**

D252. Frank Banta, piano
Mark 56 Records 800 Songs of George & Ira Gershwin 1920s-Vol. II **[GOH]**
An original Thomas Alva Edison Re-recording
With songs, *See:* Full entry under **"Anthologies"**

D253. Ray Bargy & W. Gross, pianos; Paul Whiteman Orchestra; Lyn Murray Chorus;
M. Sullivan vocals
Mark 56 Records 761-A & B **[GOH]**
"Paul Whiteman: A Tribute to George Gershwin" July 10, 1938 Original
Radio Broadcast
With Deems Taylor introduction; Second Rhapsody; Songs; *See:* Full entry in
"Anthologies"

D254. T. Barto, piano; London Philharmonic.; A. Davis, conducting
Angel CDC-49495 **[DDD]**; 4DS-49495, cassette
With **Prokofiev:** Piano Con. 3; **Ravel:** Piano Con. in G

D255. Leonard Bernstein, piano; New York Philharmonic; Bernstein, conducting;
John Corigliano, Sr., violin (In **Grofé**)
CBS Masterworks MK 42264, CD **[ADD]**
With AiP; **Grofé:** Grand Canyon Suite
See: **B992, B1121**

D256. Leonard Bernstein, piano; Los Angeles Philharmonic; Leonard Bernstein,
conducting
DG 410025-2 GH, CD **[DDD]**
With Prelude for Piano No. 2; and **Bernstein:** Symphonic Dances from West
Side Story
Program notes by Jack Gottlieb and technical notes on the recording in English,
German, French, and Italian inserted in container (12 pp.)

D257. Leonard Bernstein, Los Angeles Philharmonic
DG 423168-4 GH, cassette
With **Copland:** Appalachian Spring

D258. Leonard Bernstein, piano soloist & conducting; Los Angeles Philharmonic

Deutsche Grammophon 3302 084, cassette (1983)
"Bernstein Conducts Copland and Gershwin"
With Prelude No. 2 for piano; **Copland**: Appalachian Spring

D259. Leonard Bernstein (piano & conductor); Columbia Symphony
CBS MYK-37242, CD **[ADD]**; MYT-37242, cassette   **"Great Performances"**
With AiP (NY Philharmonic)

D260. Leonard Bernstein (piano & conductor); Columbia Symphony
CBS MLK-39454, CD; PMT-39454, cassette
With AiP; Preludes; other music

D261. Stanley Black, piano & conducting; London Festival Orchestra
London 417098-4 LT, cassette
With AiP; Cuban; Variations (IGR) *See: See:* **B990, B1114**

D262. D. Blumenthal, piano; English Chamber Orchestra; Bedford, conducting
Angel CDB-62022; also Classics for Pleasure CFP 9012, CD **[ADD]**
With AiP; Concerto

D263. [Various] Bulgarian orchestras and soloists
AVM AVZ-3006, CD
"Gershwin's Best"
CONTENTS: With Concerto; Cuban Overture; Porgy & Bess (Introduction &
Summertime); Three Preludes for Piano

D264. Ivan Davis, piano (in RiB); Cleveland Orchestra; Lorin Maazel, conducting
London (Decca) 414 067-1 (1985)
With AiP; Cuban Overture

D265. Ivan Davis, piano; Cleveland Orch.; Maazel, conducting
London 417716-2 LM, CD
With AiP; Cuban; **Copland:** Appalachian; Fanfare

D266. Ivan Davis, piano (Rhapsody); Dick Hyman, piano on other pieces
Maurice Peress, conductor
Musicmasters LP 20113X/14T; CD 60113-4 2 discs; 40113W, 40114M, 2
cassettes (1985?)
"The Birth of Rhapsody in Blue"
Performed from scores from the Paul Whiteman collection at Williams College
Recreation of the entire Feb. 12, 1924, Aeolian Hall concert
Album notes by Maurice Peress *See:* **B1042, B1107, B1108, 1110, B1119**

D267. Misha Dichter, piano; Philharmonia Orchestra; Neville Marriner, conducting
Philips 411 123-2, CD (1983)
With works by **Addinsell, Litolff, Chopin, & Lizst**
Recorded in London, July, 1983
Program notes by Max Harrison in English, French, & German on
    container
*See:***B1250**

D268. Peter Donohue, piano; Michael Collins, clarinet; Harvey and the Wall-
bangers; London Sinfonietta conducted by Simon Rattle
EMI Angel CDC7 47991-2 or EMI Classics CDC 54280
"THE JAZZ ALBUM" With Concerto; Song
See: **B1084, B1102**

D269. S. Dorensky, piano; USSR Ministry of Culture Symphony;
A. Dmitriyev, conducting
Mobile Fidelity/Melodiya MFCD-866
With **Rachmaninoff:** Rhapsody *See:* **B1117**

D270. Phillipe Entremont, piano; Philadelphia Orch.; Eugene Ormandy, conducting
Columbia ML 6413 or MS 7013
With Concerto *See:* **B958, B1009**

D271. Philippe Entremont, piano (in Concerto & RiB); Philadelphia Orchestra; Eugene
Ormandy, conducting
2-CBS Masterworks MGT-30073, cassette; Odyssey YT-35496, cassette
(1970); CBS Masterworks 40-79024, cassette (© 1983)
"The Gershwin Album"
With Concerto; AiP; **R. R. Bennett:** P&B: A Symphonic Picture

D272. Frank Fernandez, piano, with Orquesta Sinfonica Nacional (Cuba);
Manuel Duchesne Cuzan, conducting)
LD-4283 Areito, Havana, Cuba : Areito : Distribuido por
EGREM (198-?), LP
CONTENTS: Danzas para piano: Ante el Escorial ; Y la negra bailaba ; Danza
negra ; La comparsa ; A la antigua ; En tres por cuatro ; Danza de los nanigas
; Interrumpida ; Malaguena / Ernesto Lecuona; Rapsodia en blue / George
Gershwin (with Orquesta Sinfonica Nacional)

D273. Brian Gatchell, piano; The Heidelberg Ensemble
Coronet LPS 3126 (1984?)
With Song Book (18 original compositions)
Program notes by J. Mann on container

D274. George Gershwin, piano; Paul Whiteman and his Orchestra
Victor Talking Machine 55225, 78, 12 in. (June 10, 1924)
Arrangement for piano & jazz band by Ferde Grofé

D275. George Gershwin, piano; Paul Whiteman and His Concert Orchestra
Victor 55225, also His Majesty's Voice HMV C-1171, 78 (NY, June 10, 1924)

D276. George Gershwin, piano; Paul Whiteman & His Concert Orchestra
Victor 35822, His Majesty's Voice (British) HMV C-1395, 78 (Camden, NJ,
Apr. 21, 1927)

D277. George Gershwin, piano; Paul Whiteman & Orchestra; RCA Victor Symphony
Orchestra, George Gershwin, celeste (on AiP); Nathaniel Shilkret, conducting
RCA ALK1-7114, cassette

"**Gershwin Plays Gershwin**"
With AiP; Three Piano Preludes (GG, piano); Songs (GG, piano) *See:* **B1096**

D278. George Gershwin, piano; Paul Whiteman and his concert orchestra
RCA Victor LPT 29, 10 in.
With AiP

D279. George Gershwin, piano (Duo-Art piano rolls on RiB)
Distinguished Recordings 107 (1962)
"**Gershwin Plays** *Rhapsody in Blue*" *See:* Full entry under
"**Anthologies**"

D280. George Gershwin, Piano (Rhapsody); Zez Confrey, piano; Paul Whiteman
and his Orchestra [various personnel given in album notes]
The Smithsonian Collection RCA Special Products R028, 2 discs (1981)
"**An Experiment in Modern Music: Paul Whiteman at Aeolian Hall.**"
Recorded reconstruction from period records of the Feb. 12, 1924,
Aeolian Hall concert; RiB is the version recorded June 10, 1924
Produced by Martin Williams and J. R. Taylor
Has been available from: Smithsonian Customer Service
P. O. Box 10230, Des Moines, IA 50336
See: Full entry under "**Anthologies**" at **D780**

D281. George Gershwin, piano; Orchestra with Paul Whiteman conducting
Capitol P-303 (1952?)
With AiP

D282. Gershwin (1925 piano roll)
CBS MK-42516, CD; FMT-42516, cassette
Columbia Jazz Band; Michael Tilson Thomas, conducting
With AiP; Porgy and Bess (selections); Preludes; & other G music *See:* **B987,**
B1088

D283. George Gershwin, piano roll, with the Columbia Jazz Band (RiB);
New York Philharmonic (AiP); Buffalo Philharmonic (overtures); Michael Tilson
Thomas, conducting
CBS Masterworks MK 42240 (1976); DIDC 70127, reissue as a CD **[ADD]**
(1987)
With AiP; Broadway Overtures to Oh, Kay!, Funny Face, Girl Crazy, Strike
Up the Band, OTIS, Cake (Arr. by Don Rose)
The legendary 1925 piano roll of RiB combined with Columbia Jazz Band
RiB recorded at 30th St. Studios, NY, 1976
Program notes in English, German, and French by Andrew Kazdin on insert in
container
Produced by Andrew Kazdin & Steven Epstein *See:* **B1116**

D284. George Gershwin, piano roll
Klavier KS 124 (1974)
"**Gershwin Plays Rhapsody in Blue**"
With Swanee; That Certain Feeling; & songs by **Berlin, Shilkret, Gold,**
Whiting, & Kern

"A re-enacted performance from Steinway Duo-Art reproducing piano"
Program notes by Lawrence D. Stewart on container *See*: **B1330**

D285. George Gershwin, piano roll
Mark 56 Records 641-A-D, 2 discs "Gershwin By Gershwin" **[GOH]**
Rhapsody in Blue (Performed on Duo-Art reproducing piano); With
Concerto–from radio broadcast April 7, 1935; Variations on "I Got Rhythm";
Second Rhapsody, et al; *See*: Full entry under **"Recordings by Gershwin"**

D286. George Gershwin (1925 piano roll); Denver Symphony Pops; Wayland,
conducting
Pro Arte CDD-352, CD **[DDD]**; PCD-352, cassette
With Piano Music; AiP

D287. George Gershwin, Duo-Art piano
Telarc SE-1001 (1982)
"Gershwin Plays Gershwin"
With So Am I; That Certain Feeling; Swanee; Sweet and Low-Down;
    Kickin' the Clouds Away; I Was Young, You Were So Beautiful;
    Tee-oodle-um-bum-bo; Drifting Along with the Tide (From George White's
    Scandals of 1921)
Program notes by Albert Petrak on container

D288. George Gershwin at the piano; George Gershwin, Duo-Art piano **[GOH]**
Twentieth (20th) Fox FOX 3013-B
RiB on A side; With other material, *See*: Full entry under **"Recordings by
    Gershwin"**

D289. David Golub, piano (on RiB & Concerto); London Symphony Orchestra; Mitch
Miller, conducting
Arabesque Z6587, CD **[DDD]**; cassette, ABQC 6587 (1988)
With Concerto; AiP

D290. Isador Goodman, piano; Melbourne Symphony Orchestra; Patrick Thomas,
conducting
Philips 6527 092 (1981)
With music by **R. Addinsell, H. Litolff, F. Lizst**

D291. Morton Gould, piano; Morton Gould and his orchestra
RCA Victor Red Seal LM 2017 (1956)
With Three Preludes for piano; Concerto
Program notes, based on an essay by Arthur Schwartz, on container
LC card no. r56-693

D292. Morton Gould, piano; with orchestra
RCA Victor LM 6033, 2 discs (1955)
"The Serious Gershwin"
With P&B, piano solo, from act 1, scene 1; Suite from P&B arr. by M. Gould;
AiP; Concerto; Three Preludes for Piano
Program notes by Arthur Schwartz [24 pp.] laid in container
LC card no. r55-581 *See*: **B1021**

D293. Werner Haas, piano; Monte Carlo Opera Orchestra; Edo de Waart, conducting
   Philips 6500 118 (1971)
   With Concerto; "I Got Rhythm" Variations (rev. William C. Schoenfeld)
   See: **B1010, B1120**

D294. Werner Haas, piano; Orchestre national de l'Opera de Monte-Carlo; Edo de
   Waart, conducting
   Philips 416 220-4, cassette (198-?)
   With Selections from Porgy & Bess; AiP; Cuban Overture; I Got Rhythm;
   Three Preludes

D295. Werner Haas, piano; Monte Carlo Opera Orchestra; Edo de Waart, conducting
   Philips 420492-2 PM, CD **[ADD]**
   With AiP; Concerto

D296. Kamil Haba, piano; Slovak Phil. Orch.; Libor Pesak, conducting (RiB & AiP)
   Madacy BC-4-3609, cassette; avail. on CD
   With AiP; Selections from P&B (Vienna Philharmonic, Simon Gale, conducting);
   Songs (Kuno Alexander's Sound Orch.); piano selections (Eugen Cicero)

D297. Josef Hala, piano; Slovak Philharmonic Orch.; Dennis Burkh, conducting
   Musical Heritage Society MHS 4158, cassette (1979)
   "Music by George Gershwin"
   With AiP

D298. David Haynes, piano; Hamburg Philharmonia Orchestra; Hans
   Jurgen-Walter, conducting RiB; Heinrich Alster, conducting other work
   Somerset SF-1800 (195-?)
   "George Gershwin's Immortal Rhapsody in Blue"
   With **Joseph Kuhn:** Symphony for Blues

D299. Byron Janis, piano; Hugo Winterhalter, conducting
   RCA Victor LPM 1429, mono, (1957); also Bluebird Classics LBC 1045
   With **F. Grofé**: Grand Canyon Suite

D300. Julius Katchen, piano; Montovani & his orchestra
   London LL.1262 (195-?); also London CS 6633 (1970)
   With AiP
   Recorded in Europe *See*: **B1017, B1021, B1022, B1041, B1101**

D301. Hyperion Knight, piano and conductor, with chamber orchestra
   Stereophile No. ? (avail. from P. O. Box 1702, Sante Fe, NM 87504, USA)
   See: Full entry at **D744** under **"Anthologies," B1109**

D302. James Levine, piano and conducting; Chicago Symphony Orchestra
   Deutsche Grammophone 431625-2 GH (in *Schwann*, Spring 1994)
   With Aip, Catfish Row, & Cuban *See*: **B968, B1089, B1132**

D303. Oscar Levant, piano; Philadelphia Orchestra; Eugene Ormandy, conducting
   Columbia MX-251, 2 discs, 78, mono, 12 in. (194-?) *See*: **B1092, B1583**

D304. Oscar Levant, piano; The Philadelphia Orchestra; Eugene Ormandy,
conducting (in RiB)
Columbia MM 1076, 2 discs, 78, Columbia Masterworks (195-?)
With Preludes Nos. 2 & 3 (for piano solo)
Program notes by Paul Affelder on inside of container *See:* **B1583**

D305. Oscar Levant, piano; Philharmonic-Symphony of New York; André
Kostelanetz, conducting
Columbia 4879, mono, Columbia Masterworks (1954)
With Concerto; AiP
Program notes by Charles Burr on slipcase
LC card no. r54-522 *See:* **B1583**

D306. Oscar Levant, piano; New York Philharmonic; A. Kostelanetz, conducting
(Concerto) (Rec. 1942); Morton Gould Orchestra (Second Rhapsody & "I Got
Rhythm"); Philadelphia Orchestra, Ormandy, conducting (RiB)
"Levant Plays Gershwin" (consists of previously recorded material)
CBS MK-42514 (monaural), CD **[ADD]**; FMT-42514, cassette (compilation
p 1987)
With "I Got Rhythm" Var.; Preludes; Concerto; Second Rhapsody
Producers: Goddard Lieberson, Richard Gilbert, & Howard Scott *See:*
B1237, B1583

D307. Raymond Lewenthal, piano; RCA Victor Symphony (*Concerto)*, Metropolitan
Symphony Orchestra **(RiB)**; Royal Philharmonic Orchestra (**Enesco &
Prokofieff**); Oscar Danon, conducting all three orchs.
Chesky CD56 With Concerto; **Enesco:** Romanian Rhapsody No. 1, Op. 11, No.
1 & **Prokofieff**: The Love for Three Oranges Suite, Op. 33-b
Producer: Charles Gerhardt
Reviewed by Michael Ullman in *Fanfare*, Jan.-Feb. 1992, p. 217 *See also:*
B1026

D308. Raymond Lewenthal, piano; Metropolitan Symphony Orchestra; Oscar
Danon, conducting
Quintessence PMC 7115 (1979)
With Concerto
Recorded Feb. 1962 at Walthamstow Town Hall, London
Program notes by Steven Vining on container *See:* **B1100**

D309. Eugene List, piano; Eastman-Rochester Orchestra; Howard Hanson, conducting
Mercury MG 50138, SR , Olympian Series (1957)
With Concerto
Recorded in the Eastman Theater, Rochester, NY, May 4, 1957
LC card no. r60-639 *See:* **B951, B998, B1002, B1037, B1094**

D310. Eugene List, piano; Rhapsody in Blue, Cuban Overture—Eastman-
Rochester Orchestra; Howard Hanson, conducting
Mercury SR 90290 Curtain Up! George Gershwin Favorites **[GOH]**
With An American in Paris, Minneapolis Symphony Orchestra, Antal Dorati,
conducting

D311. Eugene List, piano; Cincinnati Symphony Orchestra; Erich Kunzel, conducting
Telarc CD-80058 (1981)
With AiP
Recorded at Music Hall, Cincinnati, OH, Jan. 5, 1981
Program notes by Deena Rosenberg & notes on the pianist & technical
information on the recording (12 pp.) inserted in container

D312. Eugene List, piano; Berlin Symphony Orchestra, Samuel Adler, conducting
Vox CT-4457, cassette (1972)
With Concerto; Three Preludes *See:* **B1071, B1120, B1055**

D313. Andrew Litton (piano & conductor); Royal Philharmonic
MCA Classics MCA-6216; MCAD-6216, CD **[DDD]**; MCAC-6216 cassette
With George Gershwin Songbook; Music by **H. Kay** *See:* **B1268**

D314. Jerome Lowenthal, piano; Utah Symphony; Abravanel, conducting
Vanguard VBD-10017, CD; C-10017, cassette
With AiP; Concerto

D315. W. Marshall, piano; City of London Sinfonia (playing the original Grofé arr.);·
R. Hickox, conducting
Virgin Classics VC 7 -2, CD **[DDD]**
With **Barber:** Adagio; Knoxville; **Copland:** Appalachian Spring Suite;
Quiet City *See:* **B987**

D316. Mayorga, piano; Moscow Philharmonic; Kitayenko, conducting
Sheffield Lab CD-28; LP & cassette versions avail.
With Lullaby; Preludes; Promenade; "I Got Rhythm" Var.

D317. Theodor Moussov, piano; Orchestre Symphonique de la Radio-TV
Bulgare; Alexandre Vladigerov, conducting
Harmonia Mundi France HM 40.126, cassette (1979); also Monitor MCS
2153
With Rhapsody No. 2; "I Got Rhythm" Variations
Recorded 1973 in Sofia by Balkanton
Program notes in French on inlay card

D318. Peter Nero, piano; Boston Pops Orchestra; Arthur Fiedler, conducting
RCA ANL1-1970 **"Nero Goes 'Pops'"**
With (Our) Love is Here To Stay; Embraceable You; The Man I Love; They
Can't Take That Away From Me; Bidin' My Time; I Got Rhythm

D319. Peter Nero, piano (in RiB & Concerto); Boston Pops Orchestra, Arthur
Fiedler, conducting
RCA Red Seal LSC 3319 (1972)
"The World's Favorite Gershwin"
With AiP & Concerto
A Basic Library of the Music America Loves Best

D320. Reid Nibley, piano; Utah Symphony Orchestra; Maurice Abravanel,

conducting
Sina Qua Non C 7746, cassette (1980)
LC card no. 72-750302

D321. Reid Nibley, piano (On RiB); Utah Symphony; Maurice Abravanel,
conducting
Westminster Gold (ABC/Dunhill Records) WGS-8122 (1970)
With AiP

D322. Reid Nibley, piano; Utah Symphony; Maurice Abravanel, conducting
Westminster WST 14002 (19--?)
With AiP
Program notes by James Lyons on container

D323. Reid Nibley, piano; Utah Symphony; Maurice Abravanel, cond.
Westminster XWN 18687 **[GOH]**
With AiP *See:* **B950, B998, B1015, B1024**

D324. Piano?; Philharmonic-Symphony of New York; André Kostelanetz, conducting
Columbia 4879, mono, Columbia Masterworks (1954)
With Concerto; AiP
Program notes by Charles Burr on slipcase
LC card no. r54-522

D325. Piano?; Gershwin's Greatest Hits
CBS MLK-39454, CD; PMT-39454, cassette
With Concerto-finale (Previn, Kostelanetz, Orch.); Porgy & Bess, a symphonic
picture-excerpts (Ormandy, Philadelphia Orch.) AiP; Preludes

D326. Piano?; Simfonichen orkestur na bulgarskoto radio i televiziia.
Bulgarian Broadcasting Symphony Orchestra ; various soloists and conductors
DCC Compact Classics AVZ-3005, CD (p 1990)
"George Gershwin's best"
CONTENTS: Rhapsody in blue; Three preludes for piano; Cuban overture;
Porgy and Bess (Introduction and Summertime); Concerto in F

D327. Pyotr Pechersky & Alexander Tsvassman, pianos; Moscow Philharmonic
Orchestra, Kiril Kondrashin, conducting & U. S. S. R. Symphony
Orchestra; Gennady Rozhdestvensky, conducting
Westminster Gold/Melodiya WG 8355 (1980)
With Concerto
Producers: Alexander Griva & David Gaklin *See:* **B1011, B1078**

D328. Leonard Pennario, piano (in RiB); Orchestra with Paul Whiteman conducting
Capitol P-303 (1952?)
With AiP

D329. Leonard Pennario, piano; Hollywood Bowl Symphony Orchestra; Felix
Slatkin, conducting
Capitol P-8343 (1956)
With AiP

Program notes by Alex North on container
LC card no. r56-584

D330. Leonard Pennario, piano; Hollywood Bowl Orch.; Felix Slatkin, conducting
Seraphim 4XG-60174, cassette
With AiP

D331. Leonard Pennario, piano; Hollywood Bowl Symphony Orchestra;
Carmen Dragon, Miklos Rozsa, conducting
Angel 4XS-36062, cassette, 4-track, stereo (19--?)
"Warsaw Concerto & Other Favorite Showpieces for Piano & Orchestra"
With music by Addinsell (Warsaw Concerto); Litolff; Rachmaninoff; Bath;
Lizst; Rozsa (Spellbound Concerto)

D332. K. Perkins, piano; American Radio Symphony Orchestra; M. Brown,
conducting
Vox STPL 513.030 (19--?)
With AiP

D333. Ralph Potapek, piano; Michigan State University Band; Stanley De Rusha,
conducting
Mark Records PC 23700, 2 discs
"Midwestern Conference 1983"
Arr. for band
With music by E. Toch; K. Husa; N. Dello Joio
Recorded in Ann Arbor, MI, Jan. 20, 1983

D334. André Previn, piano; A. Kostelanetz and His Orchestra
Columbia CL 1495; CS 8286
With Concerto

D335. André Previn, piano; A. Kostelanetz and His Orchestra (Rec. 1960)
Odyssey MBK 46270, CD [ADD]; YT 46270, cassette
With Concerto; P&B sels. See: B1118, B1264

D336. Previn, piano; London Symphony Orchestra; André Previn, conducting
Angel AXS 36810, cassette (197-?)
"Previn Plays Gershwin"
With AiP; Concerto See: B960, B1010

D337. André Previn (piano & conductor); London Symphony
Angel CDC 47161; 4AM-34760, cassette
With AiP; Concerto

D338. André Previn (piano & conductor); Pittsburgh Symphony
Philips 412611-2, CD [DDD]; 412611-4 PH, cassette
With AiP; Concerto

D339. Arthur Sandford, piano; Kingsway Symphony Orchestra; Camarata,
conducting
Decca DL 8519, 2 discs (195-?)

With AiP
LC card no. r62-534

D340. Jesús Sanromá, piano; Boston Pops Orchestra; Arthur Fiedler, conducting
RCA Camden CAL 304 (19--?)
With Concerto

D341. Jesús Sanromá, piano; Boston Pops Orchestra; Arthur Fiedler, conducting
RCA Victor DM 358, 2 discs, 78, 12 in. (19--)
With Strike Up the Band

D342. Jesús Sanromá, piano; Pittsburgh Symphony Orchestra; William Steinberg,
conducting
Everest Record Group WRC4 2024, cassette, analog, Dolby (19--?)
With AiP

D343. Jesús Sanromá, piano; Pittsburgh Symphony Orchestra; William Steinberg,
conducting
Everest 3067, cassette (198-?)
With AiP
See: **B1000, B1098**

D344. Kathryn Selby, piano; CSR Symphony Orchestra (Bratislava) (Concerto & RiB),
Slovak Philharmonic Orchestra (AiP); Richard Hayman, conducting
Naxos 8.550295 **[DDD]**, CD
With AiP
Producers: Karol Kopernicky & Hubert Geschwantder
Reviewed, Fanfare, Jan.-Feb. 1992, by Peter J. Rabinowitz, 216-217

D345. Bert Shefter, piano; Warner Brothers Orchestra; Ray Heindorf, conducting
Warner Brothers BS 1243 (1959?)
With AiP *See:* **B944, B949, B1067, B1068, B1296**

D346. H. Shelly, piano; Philharmonia Orchestra; Yan Pascal Tortelier, conducting
Chandos CHAN 9092 **[DDD]**
With Concerto; Second Rhapsody

D347. Jeffrey Siegel, piano; St. Louis Symphony; Leonard Slatkin, conducting
Vox CT-2122, cassette
With Concerto; Cuban; "I Got Rhythm" Var.

D348. Jeffrey Siegel, piano; Saint Louis Symphony Orchestra; Leonard Slatkin,
conducting
Vox CBX 5132, 3 cassettes (1974, 1979)
With Concerto; Lullaby for String Quartet; Cuban Overture; Catfish Row
(Suite from P&B); Second Rhapsody; "I Got Rhythm" Variations; AiP;
Promenade
Cassette Library of Recorded Music
Biographical notes on performers on container; **Program notes** by Edward
Jablonksi (12 pp.) inserted; Durations on labels
Complete orchestral works available in 1991 as Vox Box 2 CDX 5007

[ADD] *See:* **B994, B1129,** and mention of Vox Box CDX 5007 at **B987**

D349. Jeffrey Siegel, piano; Saint Louis Symphony Orchestra; Leonard Slatkin, conducting; Susan Slaughter, solo trumpet in Concerto
Vox Cum Laude MMG MCD 10011, CD
"Works for Piano and Orchestra"
With Second Rhapsody & Concerto
Program notes by Edward Jablonski in English, French, & German inserted
See: **B955**

D350. Nigel Simpson; piano; Royal Promenade Orch. of London (on RiB & AiP)
Pro Arte CDM 814 **[DDD]**
With Concerto in F, 1st movement (Russell Sherman, piano); AiP;
"Gershwin in Hollywood"; and Lullaby *See:* complete entry under
"Anthologies"

D351. Vladimir Sokoloff, piano; Al Goodman and his Orchestra (in RiB); Camilla
Williams, soprano; Guild Choristers (Summertime)
RCA Victor 46-0004, 78, mono, (194-?)
With Summertime (C. Williams)

D352. Gerhard Stein, piano (in RiB); Elite Concert Orchestra; Max Marschner,
conducting
Allegro 3063 (195-?)
With AiP
Recorded in Europe

D353. Siegfried Stöckigt, piano; Leipzig Gewandhaus Orch.; Kurt Masur, conducting
DG 413851-4 GW, cassette
With AiP; Concerto; **L. Bernstein:** West Side Story

D354. Siegfried Stöckigt, piano; Leipzig Gewandhaus Orch.; Kurt Masur,
conducting (RiB); San Francisco Symphony; Ozawa, conducting (Russo); Boston
Pops Orch.; Fiedler, conducting (Rags)
Deutsche Grammophon [Musikfest] DG 413258-4 GMF, cassette
"Rhapsody in Blue"
With music by **William Russo** (Street Music, Op. 65, Pt. 3); Rags by
Joplin, E. Blake, Berlin, & Bowman

D355. Siegfried Stöckigt, piano; Leipzig Gewandhaus Orchestra; Kurt
Masur, conducting (RiB) / San Francisco Symphony; Seiji Ozawa,
conducting (AiP)/ Robert Szidon, piano; London Philharmonic Orchestra;
Downes, conducting (Concerto)
DG Walkman 413 851-4
With Concerto; AiP; **L. Bernstein:** West Side Story; Symphonic Dances
See: **B926**

D356. Gabriel Tacchino, piano; Monte Carlo Philharmonic; Lawrence Foster, conducting
Erato ECD-55031 **[DDD]**; MCE-55031, cassette
With AiP; Concerto

D357. Michael Tilson Thomas, pianist and conductor; Los Angeles Philharmonic

CBS Masterworks M 39699 (© & p 1985); IMT-39699, cassette
With Preludes for Piano; Short Story; Violin Piece; Second Rhapsody; For
   Lily Pons; Sleepless Night; Promenade
Program notes in English, German, & French on container
Album dedicated to IG
See: **W46, W47, B1081, B1091, B1124, B1250**

D358. William Tritt, piano; Cincinnati Jazz Orchestra; Erich Kunzel, conducting ("performing the original jazz band orchestration of 1924, including 48 bars, mostly solo
piano, cut prior to the premiere")
Telarc CD-80166 **[DDD]**
With Concerto; "I Got Rhythm" Var.; Rialto Ripples

D359. William. Tritt, piano; Hamilton Philharmonic Orchestra; B. Brott, conducting
CBS Records SMCD 5111 **[DDD]**
With Second Rhapsody; P&B (Catfish)

D360. Ilana Vered, piano (Gershwin, Honegger); Volker Banfield (d'Albert); Brigitte
Engerer (Strauss); Swiss Radio Symphony; Matthias Bamert, conducting
RCA 60853; 65 min.
CONTENTS: With **d'ALBERT**: Piano Concerto in E; **STRAUSS**: Burleske;
HONEGGER: Concertino
   Classic Visions, Vol. 5

D361. Alexis Weissenberg (in RiB); Elaine Donohoe (in Catfish Row), pianos; Karl
Leister, clarinet; Berlin Philharmonic Orchestra; Seiji Ozawa, conducting
EMI/Angel DS 38050, disc; 4DS 38050, cassette; CDC 47152 2 **[DDD]**
   (1984)
With Variations on "I Got Rhythm;" Catfish Row: Suite from P&B
Program notes by Max Harrison on container *See:* **D93, B1080**

D362. Sunny White, piano; Austrian Symphony Orchestra; George Roessler,
conducting
Masterseal 1840 (1957)
With AiP
Program notes by Marty Ostrow on container

D363. Earl Wild, piano; Boston Pops Orchestra; Arthur Fiedler, conducting
RCA Victor AGL1-5215 (1983?)
With AiP

D364. Earl Wild, piano; NBC Symphony; Arturo Toscanini, conducting (Rec. 1942)
Hunt Productions CD-534, monaural
With AiP; Concerto

D365. Earl Wild, piano; NBC Symphony; Arturo Toscanini, conducting (RiB); New York
Philharmonic, Morton Gould, conducting ("I Got Rhythm" Variations);
   Arthur Schwarz (on song)
PR 42-A (Music Masters, NY)
With 135th Street (Blue Monday); "I Got Rhythm" Variations; Mischa,
   Jascha, Toscha, Sascha

Omnibus T. V. performance of *Blue Monday* of Mar. 29, 1953, *See:* **W15c**

D366. Earl Wild, piano; NBC Symphony; Benny Goodman, clarinet.; conducted by
   by Arturo Toscanini, Nov.1, 1942
   Penzance Records 43 **[GOH]**
   OTHER CONTENTS & PERFORMERS: Variations on "I Got Rhythm,"
      Gould?, piano; Rodzinski, cond., 10/8/44; 135th Street; Skitch
      Henderson, conducting, perf. at Philharmonic Hall, NY, May 20, 1968;
      Mischa, Jascha, Toscha, Sascha; Bobby Short, vocal and piano; Nov. 14,
      1971

D367. Earl Wild, piano (RiB); Benny Goodman, clarinet; Oscar Levant, piano; Harry
      Glantz, trumpet (Concerto); NBC Symphony Orchestra; Arturo Toscanini,
      conducting
   Ark 4 (1981)
   "Toscanini dirige Gershwin"
   With AiP; Concerto
   Recorded in New York Nov. 1, 1942, Nov. 14, 1943, & Mar. 2, 1944,
      respectively
   Program notes by Riccardo Risaliti in Italian with English translation by
      Gabriele Dotto on container
   See: **B1043, B1583**

D368. Earl Wild, piano; Boston Pops; Arthur Fiedler, conducting
   RCA (Papillon Collection) 6519-2 RG, CD **[ADD]**; 6519-4 RG, cassette
   With AiP; Concerto; "I Got Rhythm" Variations *See:* **B988, B1036, B1063,**
      B1105

D369. Earl Wild, piano; Boston Pops; Arthur Fiedler, conducting
   Chesky RC-8
   With AiP *See:* **B978, B979, B981**

D370. Earl Wild, piano; Paul Whiteman and His Orchestra
   Signature GP-1 (20001, 20002), 2 discs, 78, 12", mono (195-?)

D371. Roger Williams, piano; Symphony of the Air; Willis Page, conducting
   "Roger Williams Plays Gershwin"
   Kapp KL 1088, mono (195-?)
   With Someone to Watch Over Me; Liza; Love Walked In; Bidin' My Time;
      Maybe; I Got Rhythm
   Program notes by George T. Simon on container

D372. Arthur Young and the Youngsters
   Liberty Music Shop MK 1568 (Regal), 78, 10" **[GOH]**
   "A Bouquet for George Gershwin"
   With Oh, Lady Be Good!; Fascinating Rhythm; Do, Do, Do;
      'S Wonderful!; That Certain Feeling; Looking for a Boy; I'd Rather
      Charleston

D373. (Number inadvertently omitted)

D374. Alicia Zizzo, piano; George Gershwin Festival Orchestra; Michael Charry, conducting
Pro Arte CDD 514 **[DDD]**
With Cuban Overture; Concerto; Lullaby (pa. solo)
Producer: Eugene Simon
See: **B1020, B1022, B1049**

Arrangements of *Rhapsody in Blue* (Various)

D375. Larry Adler, harmonica virtuoso; Pro Arte orchestra; Francis Chagrin & Eric Robinson, conducting
Everest SDBR 3494 (19--?)
CONTENTS: RiB; With works by **Chagrin; Enesco; Bizet; Ravel; Granados; Benjamin**

D376. Larry Adler, harmonica, w/ various singers
Mercury (Phonogram, London) 522 727 - 2, CD (1994)
"The Glory of Gershwin"
Various Artists and CONTENTS: Adler & George Martin (RiB); With songs by pop artists
See: Full entry at **D695** under **"Anthologies"**

D377. Anognoson & Kinton (original 2-piano version)
Pro Arte CDD-367 **[DDD]**
With AiP; "I Got Rhythm" Variations

D378. Jeffrey Reid Baker (synthesizers)
Newport Classic A NC-60042, CD **[DDD]**
With AiP; Concerto; Preludes *See:* **B1228**

D379. First Piano Quartet (originated by Edwin Fadiman)
RCA Victor LM 125, mono, 10 in. (19--?)
RiB arr. for piano quartet
With AiP and songs; *See:* Full entry under **"Anthologies"**

D380. Gershwin (6 Duo-Art piano rolls)
Pro Arte CDD-352, CD **[DDD]**; PCD-352, cassette
With AiP; Songs

D381. Leonid Hambro, piano; Gershon Kingsley, electronic keyboard synthesizer
Avco AV 11004-598; Avco Embassy AVE 33021
With I Got Rhythm; P&B introduction & opening scene I; Summertime; My Man's Gone Now; It Ain't Necessarily So; Clara, Clara; Crown's Killing

D382. Earl "Fatha" Hines, piano **"Earl Hines Plays George Gershwin"** (October 16, 1973)
Classic Jazz CJ 31 **[GOH]**
With songs; *See:* Full entry under **"Songs, Instrumental Treatment"**

D383. José & Amparo Iturbi, duo-pianists; RCA Victor Symphony Orchestra; José
Iturbi, conducting
RCA Victor LM 23, 78?, mono, 10 in. (19--)
With work by **J. C. Chambers**

D384. José & Amparo Iturbi, duo-pianists
RCA Victor DM 517 (18446, 18447), 2 discs, 78, mono, 12 in. (194--?)
Transcribed & arranged for two pianos by José Iturbi

D385. Norman Krieger, piano (G's solo piano arrangement)
Stradivari Classics SCD-8000 **[DDD]**; SCD-8000, cassette
With Concerto; Preludes *See:* **B1085**

D386. Katia & Marielle Labèque, pianos; Cleveland Orchestra; Riccardo Chailly,
conducting
London 417326-1, available in all three formats (©1986)
[2 pianos, arr. Katia & Marielle Labèque]
With AiP; Lullaby; Cuban Overture
1st work on album (RiB) originally for piano and jazz band arr. for 2 pianos
with orchestra; Lullaby originally for string quartet arr. for string
orchestra
Recorded in Masonic Auditorium, Cleveland, OH, November, 1985

D387. Katia & Marielle Labèque, pianos
Philips (Polygram) 400 022-2 (1980); 400022-2 PH, CD
RiB arr. for two pianos; With Concerto
Previously released as 9500 917, Recorded in Paris, May 1980
Program notes by David Hogarth in English with German & French
translations on container

D388. L. Lortie (playing Gershwin's solo piano arrangement)
Chandos ABRD-1373, LP; CHAN-8733, CD **[DDD]**; ABTD-1373, cassette
With **Prokofiev:** Romeo; **Ravel:** La Valse; **Stravinsky:** Petrouchka, 3
Scenes   *See:* **B1112**

D389. Adam Makowicz, piano; Dave Holland & Charlie Haden, bass; Al Foster, drums
RCA (Novus) 3022-2-N, CD, digital (1987)
"Adam Makowicz—Naughty Baby Honoring George Gershwin"
CONTENTS: RiB (6:13 version, arr. Makowicz); With songs
Recorded at Radio City, Studio B, June 25, 26, 27, 1987
Producer: Edith Kiggen *See:* **B1318**

D389.1. Glenn Miller and His Orchestra with Bobby Hackett, trumpet soloist
Bluebird 9785-2-RB (1941)
Arranged by Bill Finegan

D390. New American String Ensemble
Sine Qua Non 74810-4
"Gershwin On Broadway"
CONTENTS: RiB arr.; With songs. *See:* Full listing under **"Anthologies"**

D391. The New York Banjo Ensemble
Kicking Mule Records KM 224 (1982)
"The New York Banjo Ensemble Plays Gershwin"
With AiP, arr.; Swanee; I'll Build A Stairway to Paradise; Strike
Up the Band; Oh, Lady Be Good!; 'S Wonderful!; Sweet and
Low-Down; Clap Yo' Hands; Prelude No. 2; Impromptu in Two
Keys; Rialto Ripples

D392. David Rose and His Orchestra
M-G-M E 3123-A & B **"Love Walked In—The Music of
George Gershwin" [GOH]**
With AiP and Songs; *See:* Full entry at **D764** under **"Anthologies"**

D393. Edward Tarr (Trumpet); Westenholz (Piano), arr. for trumpet & piano
Bis LP-152
With orig. music for trpt. & piano: **Carl J. Alexius:** Sonatine;
Hindemith: Trumpet Sonata; **Martinu:** Sonatina

D394. François-Joël Thiollier, piano; no orchestra
RCA RL 37590 (1981)
With Preludes; Song Book
Made in France from master recordings owned & controlled by RCA

D395. François-Joël Thiollier, piano; no orchestra
Musical Heritage Society MHS 4865 (© 1983)
"The Works for Solo Piano"
CONTENTS: RiB (orig. version for piano solo) With Piano Preludes;
Song Book
Also available as cassette on Musical Heritage Society MHC 6865Y;
Recorded Nov. 9-10, 1981, Notre-Dame du Liban, Paris
Program notes by Neal Campbell in container
LC card no. 83-743319/R

D396. F.-J. Thiollier (solo piano arrangement)
Thésis THC 82001, CD
With AiP; George Gershwin Song Book; Piano Music; Preludes

D397. Bradley Tinflow, piano with the University of Illinois Symphonic Band,
Harry Begian, conducting (1980?)
"In Concert with University of Illinois Symphonic Band"
Bradley Tinflow, piano (RiB); Edmund Williams, oboe (Haydn); University
of Illinois Band; Harry Begian, conducting
CONTENTS: RiB, arr. for piano & band; **J. Haydn,** Concerto in C for
oboe; **J. P. Sousa,** University of Illinois March

D398. Frances Veri & Michael Jamanis, pianos
Connoisseur Society 30-5663, 2 discs (1974)
"The Fascinating Piano Music of George Gershwin"
With Piano Introduction to P&B; "I Got Rhythm" Variations; Cuban
Overture; Two Waltzes in C; The Songbook; Second Rhapsody; Three
Preludes

D399. Frances Veri & Michael Jamanis, pianos
Book-of-the-Month Records 61-5426, 3 discs (1981)
"The Complete Piano Music"
With other works for solo piano, see complete entry under **"Piano Music"**

D400. André Watts (solo piano version)
CBS MT-34221
With other music; Preludes *See:* **B1331**

SECOND RHAPSODY for piano and orchestra. (1931) **(W4)**

D401. Roy Bargy & W. Gross, pianos; Paul Whiteman, Orchestra; Lyn Murray Chorus;
M. Sullivan vocals
Mark 56 Records 761-A & B **[GOH]**
"Paul Whiteman: A Tribute to George Gershwin" July 10, 1938 Original
Radio Broadcast
With Deems Taylor introduction; Songs, & RiB; *See:* Full entry in
"Anthologies"

D402. Roy Bargy, piano; Paul Whiteman Orchestra; Whiteman, conducting
Decca DL-8024
With RiB; AiP; Cuban (Rosa Linda at the piano)

D403. Sondra Bianca, piano; Pro Musica Orchestra of Hamburg; Hans-Jurgen Walther,
conducting
MGM E-3307 *See:* **B1128**

D404. George Gershwin, piano
Mark 56 641, 2 discs (1973)
"Gershwin by Gershwin"
CONTENTS: side 2: Second Rhapsody (rehearsal, June 25, 1931);
Produced by George Garabedian, in commemoration of the 75th
anniversary of the birth of GG; a recorded documentary; "Rare,
rediscovered historic recordings of G compositions as performed and
discussed by the composer himself"
See: Full entry under **"Recordings by Gershwin "**

D405. George Gershwin, et al
MusicMasters 5062-4-C, cassette; also available in CD (1991)
"Gershwin Performs Gershwin Rare Recordings, 1931-1935"
CONTENTS: *Second Rhapsody* **Rehearsal Performance,** June 26, 1931/
"Music by Gershwin" Radio Program, Feb. 19, 1934: Signature, OTIS
Overture, The Man I Love, I Got Rhythm, Commercial, Swanee, Sign-Off/
"Music by Gershwin" Radio Program, Apr. 30, 1934: Signature, Mine,
Variations on "I Got Rhythm," Love Is Sweeping the Country, Commercial,
Wintergreen for President, Sign-Off/ **Rudy Vallée "Fleischmann Hour"
Radio Program,** Nov. 10, 1932: Variations of Fascinating Rhythm,
Variations on Liza, Piano Prelude II, Interview (Vallée & GG), I Got Rhythm/
P&B Rehearsal, July 19, 1935: Introduction, Summertime (Abbie Mitchell),
A Woman Is a Sometime Thing (Edward Matthews), Act I, Scene 1: Finale;

My Man's Gone Now (Todd Duncan & Anne Brown)--GG, pianist and
conductor
Notes by Edward Jablonski, inserted
Producer: Russell L. Caplan/American Classics, Inc.

D406. Stewart Goodyear, piano (on Second Rhapsody) ; Cincinnati Pops Orchestra; Eric
Kunzel, conducting
Telerc CD 80112 **[DDD]**
"American Piano Classics"
With music by **L. Anderson; Gottschalk & H. Kay; Euday Bowman;
S. Joplin; M. Gould**

D407. Oscar Levant, piano; Orch.; Morton Gould, conducting (Rec. 1949)
CBS MK-42514, CD **[ADD]**; FMT-42514, cassette
With Concerto; "I Got Rhythm" Variations; Preludes; RiB *See:* **B1583**

D408. Wayne Marshall, piano; Hollywood Bowl Orchestra; John Mauceri,
conducting; Gregory Hines & Patti Austin, vocals
Philips 434 274-4, cassette (1991)
"The Gershwins in Hollywood"
CONTENTS: Side 1: Overture: Gershwin in Hollywood (pub. Chappell);
New York Rhapsody, piano solo Wayne Marshall; With songs *See:* Full
entry under **"Anthologies"**

D409. Teodor Moussov, piano; TVR Orchestra; Vladigerov, conducting
Monitor MCS-2153
With RiB; "I Got Rhythm" Variations

D410. C. Ortiz, piano; London Symphony; André Previn, conducting
Angel CDC-47021
With Cuban; P&B suite

D411. Leonard Pennario, piano; Hollywood Bowl Symphony Orchestra; Alfred
Newman, conducting
Capitol P 8581
"Gershwin By Starlight"
With Cuban Overture; P&B Medley; Variations on "I Got Rhythm" (Shelly
Manne, drums, & Russ Cheevers, clarinet) *See:* **B1125**

D412. Leonard Pennario, piano; Hollywood Bowl Symphony Orchestra; Alfred Newman,
conducting; Angel S-36070

D413. H. Reims, piano; Berlin Symphony Orchestra; Gerd Rubahn, conducting
Allegro-Royale 1512

D414. H. Shelly, piano; Philharmonia Orchestra; Yan Pascal Tortelier, conducting
Chandos CHAN 9092 [DDD]
With Concerto; RiB

D415. Jeffrey Siegel, piano; Saint Louis Symphony Orchestra; Leonard Slatkin,
conducting; Susan Slaughter, solo trumpet in Concerto

Vox Cum Laude MMG MCD 10011, CD
"Works for Piano and Orchestra"
With RiB & Concerto
Program notes by Edward Jablonski in English, French, & German inserted
See: **B955**

D416. Jeffrey Siegel, piano with St. Louis, Leonard Slatkin, conducting
Vox CBX 5132, 3 cassettes (1974, 1979)
With RiB; Concerto; Lullaby for String Quartet; Cuban Overture; Catfish
Row (Suite from P&B); "I Got Rhythm" Variations; AiP; Promenade
Cassette Library of Recorded Music
Biographical notes on performers on container; **Program notes** by Edward
Jablonksi (12 pp.) inserted; Durations on labels
Complete orchestral works available in 1991 as Vox Box 2 CDX 5007
[ADD] *See:* **B980, B986, B1129**

D417. Michael Tilson-Thomas (piano & cond.); L. A. Philharmonic
CBS MK-39699 **[DDD]**; IMT-39699, cassette
With Preludes; RiB *See:* **B1081, B1091, B1124**

D418. William Tritt, piano; Hamilton Philharmonic Orchestra; B. Brott, conducting
CBS Records SMCD 5111 **[DDD]**
With P&B (Catfish); RiB

D419. William Tritt, piano; Cincinnati Pops; Erich Kunzel, conducting
Telarc CD-80166 **[DDD]**
CONTENTS: Rialto Ripples Rag, arr. by E. Kunzel for Piano &
Orchestra; With Concerto; "I Got Rhythm" Variations; RiB

D420. Ralph Votapek, piano; Boston Pops Orchestra; Arthur Fiedler, conductor
"Fiedler conducts Gershwin, I Got Rhythm"
London SPC-21185 (1979)
With Girl Crazy Suite; Oh, Kay! Overture; Funny Face Overture; Let 'Em
Eat Cake Overture; Of Thee I Sing Overture; Wintergreen for President;
[3] Preludes (arr. for orch.)
Orchestrations of overtures by Rose
Program notes by Tim McDonald & durations on container
See: **B1126, B1325**

Arrangements of *Second Rhapsody*

D421. Frances Veri & Michael Jamanis, pianos
Connoisseur Society 30-5663, 2 discs (1974)
"The Fascinating Piano Music of George Gershwin"
With 1) RiB; 2) Piano Introduction to P&B; 3) "I Got Rhythm" Variations;
4) Cuban Overture; 5) Two Waltzes in C; 6) The Songbook; 8) Three
Preludes
The Classics Record Library; The 1st (RiB) & 7th (2nd Rhapsody) works
in original piano version; the 2nd, 5th, & 8th works for piano; the 3rd
work originally for orchestra, arr. for two pianos; the 4th work orig. for
orchestra, arr. for piano, 4 hands; the 6th work consists of eighteen of

the composer's songs transcribed by the composer for piano

D422. Frances Veri & Michael Jamanis, pianos
Book-of-the-Month Records 61-5426, 3 discs (1981)
"The Complete Piano Music"
CONTENTS: Second Rhapsody (original version for two pianos); With
other music for piano, *See*: Full entry under **"Piano Music"**

D423. Frances Veri & Michael Jamanis, pianists; Bands 3-5, side 1, played by Veri;
Band 2, side 2, played by Jamanis; All others played as piano duo
Connoisseur Society CSQ 2067 (1974)
CONTENTS: "I Got Rhythm" Variations (trans. by the composer for 2 pianos);
Cuban Overture (trans. by the composer for 1 piano, 4 hands); The Man I
Love; Do It Again; Somebody Loves Me; Second Rhapsody (trans. by the
composer for 2 pianos, 4 hands); Three Preludes
Program notes by E. Jablonski on container; Durations on labels

SHORT STORY, orig. for piano (ca. 1923-1925) **(W39),** arr. for Orchestra

D424. Richard Stoltzman, clarinet; London Symphony Orchestra; Michael
Tilson Thomas and Eric Stern, conductors
RCA Victor Red Seal 09026-61790-2 (BMG Classics), CD **[DDD]**
CONTENTS: Short Story arr. by Don Sebesky With GG: Bess, You Is My
Woman Now, Promenade, & Three Preludes; music by **Copland, G. Jenkins, &
Bernstein**

STAGE SHOWS

The shows are listed in alphabetical order. The abbreviation **GOH** indicates that an archival
copy of the recording is owned by the Library at the Goodspeed Opera House in East
Haddam, CT.

BLUE MONDAY **(retitled *135th Street* by Paul Whiteman in 1925)** (1922) **(W15)**
See: **B292-B294, B296, B297**

D425. Marin Alsop, conducting Concordia Orchestra; Leslie Stifelman, piano
CAST: (Blue Monday): Amy Burton, soprano; Gregory Hopkins, tenor;
William Sharp & Arthur Woodley, baritones; Jamie J. Offenbach, bass-
baritone
Angel CDC 7 54851 2 7 **[DDD]**
CONTENTS: Blue Monday (arr. Bassman); Concerto in F (orch. Grofé);
Levant: Caprice for Orchestra
Producer: Karen Chester *See*: **B1040, B1583, B294**

D425.1. Cincinnati Pops Orchestra, Erich Kunzel, conducting
Gershwin: Porgy and Bess (Selections) /Blue Monday (Original Version)
Telarc CD 80434
Performers: Cincinnati Pops Orchestra; Gregg Baker, baritone; Sebronette
Barnes, soprano; Harolyn Blackwell, soprano ("Summertime"); Angela
Brown, soprano; William Henry Caldwell, baritone; Cab Calloway, baritone;
Larence Craig, baritone; Marquita Lister, soprano; Kirk Walker, baritone;
Thomas Young, tenor; Central State University Chorus, William Henry

Caldwell, director

CONTENTS: PORGY AND BESS (Selections) Act I: Introduction;
A Woman Is a Sometime Thing; Gone, Gone, Gone; Overflow;
My Man's Gone Now; Leavin' for the Promise Lan'; Act II: I Got
Plenty O' Nuttin'; Bess, You Is My Woman Now; Oh, I Can't Sit
Down; I Ain't Got No Shame; It Ain't Necessarily So (Cab Calloway);
I Loves You, Porgy

Act III: Opening Scene; Lonely Boy; Oh, Bess, O Where's My Bess?;
Oh, Lawd, I'm On My Way

Notes from Telarc: "In honor of the Gershwin centennial year, conductor
Erich Kunzel worked in cooperation with Gershwin scholar Edward
Jablonski, the Music Division of the Library of Congress, and John Andrew
Johnson at Harvard University to create his own performing edition of the
one-act opera Blue Monday, heard here for the first time with its original
orchestration by Will H. Vodery. Kunzel's sources included the original
piano sketches by Gershwin, the Vodery orchestration, and the original
Buddy De Sylva text, all of which are housed in the Library of Congress.
The recording of legendary performer Cab Calloway singing 'It Ain't
Necessarily So,' was made about one year before he died [d. 1994]. This is
the only *available* [italics mine] performance on disc of him singing a
selection from his signature role [*See*: **D451** in re: an out-of-print disc].
Maestro Kunzel also discovered, at the Library of Congress, previously
unrecorded dialogue from Act III, Scene I of Porgy and Bess, which leads
into the duet between Bess and Serena, "Lonely Boy," also never before
recorded. Gershwin discarded the duet for reasons of length (and thus
never orchestrated it), substituting the aria,"Summertime" . . . The duet is
heard in an orchestration provided by Steven Reinke." *See*: **B294**

D426. Skitch Henderson, conducting

Penzance Records 43 Gershwin: 135th Street [Blue Monday] **[GOH]**

CONTENTS: 135th Street; Skitch Henderson, conducting, perf. at Philharmonic Hall, NY, May 20, 1968 *See*: Full entry under **"'I Got Rhythm'
Variations," D217** *See*: **B1137**

D427. Omnibus T. V. performance of Mar. 29, 1953

NBC Symphony, Arturo Toscanini, conducting (RiB); New York
Philharmonic,

Morton Gould, conducting ("I Got Rhythm" Variations); Arthur Schwarz
(on song)

PR 42-A (Music Masters, NY)

"Gershwin—135th Street (Blue Monday)"

CONTENTS: 135th Street (Blue Monday, arr.); RiB; "I Got Rhythm"
Variations; Mischa, Jascha, Toscha, Sascha

D428. The Gregg Smith Singers; Oresta Cybriwsky, piano; Gregg Smith, conducting;
Rosalind Rees, soprano, **Vi:** Joyce Andrews; **Mike:** Patrick Mason; **Joe:** Thomas
Bogdan; **Sam:** Walter Richardson; **Tom--The Jolly Tar:** Jeffrey Meyer; **The
Jolly Tar:** Catherine Aks

Vox Turnabout TV-S 34638 (1976?)

With Two Madrigals: The Jolly Tar & Sing of Spring; Two Art Songs: In the
Mandarin's Garden & By Strauss; Choral Scene from Let 'Em Eat Cake;

Orders, Orders & Mine
Recorded Spring 1976 *See*: **B1137**

CRAZY FOR YOU, based on Gershwin songs (1992) **(W50)**

D429. Original Broadway cast recording
Angel ANG 54618 (May 1992), available in CD or cassette
CAST: Tess: Beth Leavel; **Patsy:** Stacey Logan; **Bobby Child:** Harry
Groener; **Bela Zangler:** Bruce Adler; **Sheila:** Judine Hawkins Richárd;
Mitzi: Paula Leggett; **Susie:** Ida Henry; **Louise:** Jean Marie; **Betsy:**
Penny Ayn Maas; **Margie:** Salomé Mazard; **Vera:** Louise Ruck; **Elaine:**
Pamela Everett; **Irene Roth:** Michele Pawk; **Mother:** Jane Connell;
Perkins: Gerry Burkhardt; **Moose, Mingo, & Sam (The Manhattan
Rhythm Kings):** Brian M. Nalepka, Tripp Hanson, & Hal Shane;
Junior: Casey Nicholaw; **Custus:** Gerry Burkhardt; **Pete:** Fred
Anderson; **Jimmy:** Michael Kubala; **Billy:** Ray Roderick; **Wyatt:** Jeffrey
Lee Broadhurst; **Harry:** Joel Goodness; **Polly Baker:** Jodi Benson;
Everett Baker: Ronn Carroll; **Lank Hawkins:** John Hillner; **Eugene:**
Stephen Temperley; **Patricia:** Amelia White
Book by Ken Ludwig; **Co-conceived by**: Ken Ludwig & Mike Ockrent, inspired
by material by Guy Bolton & Keith McGowan; **Scenic design:** Robin
Wagner; **Costume design by:** William Ivey Long; **Orchestrations:** William
D. Brohn & Sid Ramin; **Dance & incidental music arranged by:** Peter
Howard; **Music consultant:** Tommy Krasker; **Sound design:** Otis
Munderloh; **Choreography:** Susan Stroman; **Stage direction:** Mike Ockrent;
Musical direction: Paul Gemignani
Producers of the show: Roger Horchow & Elizabeth Williams**; Producer for
the album:** Thomas Z. Shepard
CONTENTS: Overture; K-ra-zy for You; I Can't Be Bothered Now;
Bidin' My Time; Things Are Looking Up; Someone to Watch Over
Me; Could You Use Me?; Shall We Dance?; Entrance to Nevada
(Stairway to Paradise, Bronco Busters, K-ra-zy for You); Slap That Bass;
Embraceable You; Tonight's the Night; I Got Rhythm; The Real American
Folksong; What Causes That?; Naughty Baby; Stiff Upper Lip; They Can't
Take That Away From Me; But Not For Me; New York Interlude (Concerto
in F); Nice Work If You Can Get It; Bidin' My Time (French reprise); Finale
Recorded at BMG Studio A March 2, 8, 10, 1992 *See*:**B1139, B1140**

D430. Original 1992 London cast of *Crazy for You*
RCA 09026-61993 **"MUSIC BY GERSHWIN"** 11/93, avail. for CD or
cassette
Ruthie Henshaw; Kirby Ward

FUNNY FACE (Original title: *Smarty*) (1927) **(W28)**

D431. Archival reconstruction of the 1927 and 1928 productions
The Smithsonian Collection RCA Special Products R019
CONTENTS & PERFORMERS: Side One: 'S Wonderful! & Funny
Face(Victor Arden & Phil Ohman & their Orch.); Funny Face (Fred & Adele
Astaire with orch. conducted by Julian Jones); High Hat (Fred Astaire and

chorus with orch. conducted by Julian Jones); 'S Wonderful! (Adele Astaire & Bernard Clifton, with orch. conducted by J. Jones); A Few Drinks (Leslie Henson & Sidney Howard); **Side Two:** Entr'acte medley: 'S Wonderful!, My One & Only, He Loves & She Loves, Funny Face (Arden & Ohman and their Orch. with the Revelers and James Melton, tenor soloist); He Loves & She Loves (Adele Astaire & Bernard Clifton, with orch. conducted by J. Jones); Tell the Doc (Leslie Henson & male quartet with orch. conducted by J. Jones); My One & Only (GG, piano); My One & Only (F. Astaire [vocal & tap dancing] with unidentified duo pianists); The Babbitt & the Bromide (F. & A. Astaire with orch. conducted by J. Jones); Reprise: Funny Face; 'S Wonderful (GG, piano)

Informative Program Notes by: Deena Rosenberg
Production coordination: Bill Bennett
Part of **The Smithsonian American Musical Theater Series**

D432. 1927 records by Arden and Ohman, pianists from original production of Funny Face, with their orchestra; Johnny Marvin, vocalist
JJA Records 1974-1 (Music Masters, NY)
Includes Funny Face & 'S Wonderful!

D433. The Revelers
His Master's Voice C-1586 (British), 78 (1927)
Funny Face, Selections
CONTENTS: Introduction; 'S Wonderful!; My One and Only; He Loves and She Loves; Funny Face
Recorded NY, Apr. 5, 1928

D434. Jacques Fray & Mario Braggiotti, pianos
His Master's Voice B 2910, 78, 10" **[GOH]** FUNNY FACE-medley
CONTENTS: Funny Face; 'S Wonderful!; My One and Only; Let's Kiss and Make Up

D435. New Mayfair Orchestra
His Master's Voice C 1588-A, 78, 12". FUNNY FACE - selections 1928 (London) **[GOH]**
CONTENTS: 'S Wonderful!; Let's Kiss and Make Up; He Loves and She Loves; My One and Only

D436. Original Cast, featuring GG at the piano
World Record Club SH 144, LP, 12" FUNNY FACE 1928 (London)
CONTENTS: Funny Face; The Babbit and the Bromide; He Loves and She Loves; 'S Wonderful!; My One and Only; High Hat; A Few Drinks (Fred Thompson) —sketch; Tell the Doc; Funny Face and 'S Wonderful!; My One and Only; Looking for a Boy; Sweet and Low Down; That Certain Feeling;Oh Gee! Oh Gosh! (Daly-Lanin); The Whichness of the Whatness (Daly-Lanin)

D437. 1952 record of original cast of Funny Face with Fred Astaire
Verve (England) VSP-23/24
Includes 'S Wonderful!

D438. 1952 record of original cast of Funny Face with Fred Astaire
Verve MGV-2010
"Mr. Top Hat"
Includes 'S Wonderful!

D439. Original cast, 1963 Studio production
World Record Club (England) T-191
CAST: Scott Peters; Patricia Lynn; Maggie Fitzgibbon; Chorus; Orchestra,
Bobby Richards, conducting

D440. Lee Wiley, with Bushkin,-Joe; Kaminsky,-Max
Liberty Music Shop L 281 (WP 26268 A, WP 26272 A), 78, 10" (194-)
"My one and only"
CONTENTS: Funny face; My one and only; How long has this been going on?;
Funny Face
Excerpts from "Funny Face" (1927).
Personnel: Lee Wiley, vocal ; Joe Bushkin's Orchestra (side A) ;
Max Kaminsky's Orchestra (side B). [Max Kaminsky, trumpet; Bud
Freeman, tenor sax; Joe Bushkin, piano/celeste; Artie Shapiro, bass;
George Wettling, drums] - *Cf. 60 years of recorded jazz* / Bruynincx.
Recorded in New York, Nov. 13 (side A) and 15 (side B), 1939 -
Cf. Bruynincx.
Liberty Music Shop: L 281 (WP 26268 A (matrix), WP 26272 (matrix)).

GEORGE WHITE'S SCANDALS OF 1922 (W14)

D441. Joseph C. Smith & His Orchestra
Brunswick 2328-A, 78, 10" **[GOH]**
CONTENTS: GEORGE WHITE'S SCANDALS 1922: Where is tbe Man Of
My Dreams? (G-DeSylva-Goetz); Cinderelatives (G-DeSylva); Side B is
songs by Von Tilzer
Very rare recording of Cinderelatives

D442. Paul Whiteman and His Orchestra
Victor 18949-A, 78, 10" **[GOH]** WHITE'S SCANDALS of 1922
I'll Build a Stairway to Paradise

D443. Paul Whiteman and His Orchestra
Victor 18950-A, 78, 10" **[GOH]** WHITE'S SCANDALS of 1922
I Found a Four Leaf Clover

GEORGE WHITE'S SCANDALS OF 1923 (W18)

D444. Charles Dornberger and His Orchestra
Victor 19151-B, 78, 10" **[GOH]** WHITE'S SCANDALS 1923
The Life of a Rose'

D445. Paul Whiteman and His Orchestra
Victor 19024-A, 78, 10" **[GOH]** in THE DANCING GIRL 1923, not the
Scandals: That American Boy of Mine

GEORGE WHITE'S SCANDALS OF 1924 **(W20)**

D446. Paul Whiteman and His Orchestra
Victor 19414-A, 78, 10" **[GOH]** GEORGE WHITE'S SCANDALS 1924
Somebody Loves Me

GIRL CRAZY (1930) **(W33)**

D447. Ruby Braff and the Shubert Alley Cats
Warner Bros. WS 1273, LP, 12" **"Ruby Braff Goes 'Girl Crazy'"**
CONTENTS: Embraceable You; Treat Me Rough; But Not For Me; Boy!
What Love has Done for Me; I Got Rhythm; Bidin' My Time; Could You Use
Me?; Barbary Coast

D448. Jackie Cain and Roy Kral
Roulette R-25278

D449. Center for Cassette Studies 884, cassette (1971?)
"Girl Crazy: George and Ira Gershwin's Smash Musical Comedy"
Notes and bibliography inserted in container

D450. Elektra Nonesuch (Roxbury Recordings) 9 79250-2, CD (1990)
"George & Ira Gershwin Girl Crazy"
CAST: John Mauceri, **conducting**; **Kate:** Lorna Luft; **Danny:** David
Carroll; **Molly:** Judy Blazer; **Gieber Goldfarb**: Frank Gorshin; **Slick:**
David Garrison; **Patsy:** Vicki Lewis; **Cowboy:** Eddie Korbich; **Sam:**
Rex Hays; **Vocal Quartet;** Guy Stroman (Lead), Stan Chandler, Larry
Raben, David Engel
CONTENTS: Overture; Bidin' My Time #1; The Lonesome Cowboy;
Could You Use Me?; Bidin' My Time #2; Bronco Busters; Barbary
Coast; Embraceable You; Embraceable You (Encore); Goldfarb! That's
I'm!; Bidin' My Time #3; Sam and Delilah; I Got Rhythm; I Got
Rhythm (Encore); Finale Act I/Entra'acte, Act II; Land of the Gay
Caballero; But Not For Me; But Not For Me (Comic reprise); Treat Me
Rough; Boy! What Love Has Done to Me!; Cactus Time in Arizona;
Finale Ultimo
Orchestra of NY free-lance instrumentalists
Orchestrations: Robert Russell Bennett
Orchestrations edited by Larry Moore & Russell Warner
Performing edition restored by: Tommy Krasker, Larry Moore, Keith
Wiggs
Recorded Feb. 26-28, 1990, at BMG Studio C, NY
Program notes in 96 pp. booklet in package; includes 6 excellent essays
by Miles Krueger, Edward Jablonski, Jon Alan Conrad, Tommy Krasker,
Robert Kimball, Richard M. Sudhalter, and Lee Davis, as well as a plot
synopsis and complete lyrics
Produced by Tommy Krasker & Leroy Parkins, Jr.
Executive Producers: Robert Kimball (for Roxbury Recordings) & Robert
Hurwitz (for Elektra Nonesuch)
Representative from the Library of Congress: Elizabeth H. Aumen

Vocal direction & additional arrangements: Paul Trueblood
Musical consultant: Dick Hyman
First recording in the Leonore Gershwin-Library of Congress Recording and
Publishing Project
See: **B1139, B1142, B1143, B1144, B1145, B1146, B1147, B1148, B1149,
B1150, B1151, B1152, B1153, B1426, B1509, B1662**

D451. Hejlen Gallagher, Lisa Kirk, Edith Adams, vocals; Milton Rosenstock,
conducting (on Side A); Cab Calloway, Helen Thigpen, Leslie Scott, vocals; Jay
Blackton, conducting (on Side B)
RCA Victor LPM 3156-A & B, 10"   Songs from GIRL CRAZY & P&B
CONTENTS: Side A: Embraceable You; But Not For Me; I Got
Rhythm; Bidin' My Time; **Side B:** It Ain't Necessarily So; Summertime;
I Got Plenty O' Nuttin'; Bess, You Is My Woman Now

D452. Mary Martin, et al
Columbia CL-822
1951 studio production of Girl Crazy
CAST: Mary Martin; Louise Carlyle; Eddie Chappell; Orchestra; Lehman
Engel, conducting

D453. Mary Martin, Louise Carlyle, Eddie Chappell; Chorus & Orchestra;, Lehman Engel,
conducting
Columbia COS 2560, 2 discs, stereo (1964); Columbia OL 7060, monaural
(1964); Columbia Broadway Masterworks Sony Classical/olumbia/Legacy SK
60704, CD
Girl Crazy Selections
Synopsis available
CONTENTS: Overture (orchestra), Opening Chorus (Male chorus & orches-
tra), Bidin' My Time (Martin & male quartet), Could You Use Me? (Chappell
and Carlyle), Bronco Busters (chorus & orchestra), Barbary Coast (chorus &
orchestra), Embraceable You (Martin), Sam and Delilah (Carlyle), I Got
Rhythm (Martin), But Not For Me (Martin), Treat Me Rough (Chappell),
Boy! What Love Has Done To Me (Martin with chorus), Cactus Time
(Carlyle with male chorus), Finale (Martin with chorus), Bonus track on CD:
But Not for Me
Produced by Goddard Lieberson *See:* **B928**

D454. Time-Life Records STL-AM09, 3 discs (1982)
"Oh, Kay!; Girl Crazy; Of Thee I Sing"
CONTENTS: Girl Crazy: Overture, Opening Chorus, Could You Use
Me?; Bidin' My Time; Bronco Busters; Barbary Coast, Embraceable
You, Sam & Delilah, I Got Rhythm, But Not For Me, Treat Me Rough,
Boy! What Love Has Done to Me!; When It's Cactus Time in Arizona,
Finale; With a selection of songs from Oh, Kay! & OTIS
Pamphlet (48 pp.) LC card no. 81-750256

HALF PAST EIGHT (1918) **(W8)**

No recordings were found

LA-LA-LUCILLE! (1919) **(W9)**

D455. Barbara Cook, Anthony Perkins, Elaine Stritch, and Bobby Short
Painted Smiles PS 1357
There's More to the Kiss Than the X-X-X

LADY, BE GOOD! (Originally titled *Black Eyed Susan*) (1924) **(W22)**

D456. Elektra Nonesuch (Roxbury Recordings) 79308-2 CD (1992)
"George & Ira Gershwin Lady, Be Good!"
CAST: Dick Trevor: Lara Teeter; **Susie Trevor:** Ann Morrison; **Watty Watkins:** Jason Alexander; **Jack Robinson:** Michael Maguire; **Jeff White:** John Pizzarelli (ukelele); **Daisy Parke:** Ivy Austin; **Shirley Vernon:** Michelle Nicastro; **Bertie Bassett:** Robin Langford; **Josephine Vanderwater:** Carol Swarbrick; Steven Blier and John Musto and the pianos
SONGS: Overture; Hang On to Me; A Wonderful Party; End of a String; We're Here Because; Fascinating Rhythm; So Am I; Oh, Lady, Be Good!; Linger in the Lobby; The Half of It, Dearie, Blues; Juanita; I'd Rather Charleston; Little Jazz Bird; Carnival Time (orchestra); Swiss Miss Orchestra of free-lance Los Angeles musicians
Orchestrations: Larry Wilcox, Russell Warner, and Robert Russell Bennett, William Daly, Charles Grant, Stephen O. Jones, Paul Lannin, & Max Steiner
Recorded August 12-14, 1992 at The Todd-AO Scoring Stage, Studio City, CA
Program notes in 60 pp. booklet in CD package: "A Wonderful Party: *Lady, Be Good!*" by Tommy Krasker, "The Gershwins and the Astaires" by John Mueller, and "Fascinating Rhythms" by Deena Rosenberg
Restored by Tommy Krasker
Produced by John McClure and Tommy Krasker
Vocal director: Carol Weiss
Eric Stern, **conducting** A Leonore S. Gershwin-Library of Congress Recording and Publishing Project Production; **For the Library of Congress:** James W. Pruett, Chief, Music Division & Elizabeth H. Auman, Advisor *See:* **B1154, B1157, B1426**

D457. Jack Hylton and his orchestra
His Master's Voice C 1261, 78, 12" **[GOH]** LADY BE GOOD
CONTENTS: Oh, Lady Be Good!; So Am I; I'd Rather Charleston; Hang On To Me; The Half Of It, Dearie, Blues; Little Jazz Bird; Fascinating Rhythm

D458. Kenneth "Red" Norvo and His Swing Sextette; Herbie Haymer, vocal
Decca 3884-B, 78, 10" **[GOH]**
Oh, Lady Be Good! Album 244, Side 8

D459. Original cast, with Fred & Adele Astaire
Smithsonian Collection R 008
In New York and London with the composer and members of the 1924 cast, including Fred & Adele Astaire, Cliff Edwards (Ukelele Ike), & duo pianists Arden & Ohman

CONTENTS: Prologue: Fascinating Rhythm (Gershwin, piano, with orchestra, 1934 broadcast); Hang on to Me (Fred & Adele Astaire, GG, piano, recorded by English Columbia, 1926); Fascinating Rhythm (Fred & Adele Astaire, GG, piano, recorded by English Columbia, 1926); So Am I (GG, from a 1924 Duo Art piano roll) & So Am I (Adele Astaire & George Vollaire with the Empire Theatre Orch.); Oh, Lady, Be Good! (William Kent with the Empire Theatre Orch.); Entr'acte: Fascinating Rhythm & So Am I (Carl Fenton's Orch. featuring Arden & Ohman, recorded for Brunswick in 1924); The Half of It Dearie, Blues (Astaire, singing & dancing, with GG, piano); The Man I Love (GG, piano, 1934 broadcast); Insufficient Sweetie by Wells/Edwards (Cliff Edwards, ukelele & vocal); Reprise: Oh, Lady Be Good! (Cliff Edwards, ukelele & vocal); Swiss Miss (F. & A. Astaire with Empire Theatre Orch.); I'd Rather Charleston (Fred & A. Astaire with GG, piano, recorded by English Columbia in 1926)

Program notes by Edward Jablonski *See:* **B348, B937, B1155, B1156, B1271**

D460. Original 1926 London cast
World Record Club SH 124, mono (197--?) **[GOH]**
Lady, Be Good! Selections
CONTENTS: On Lady, Be Good!: Fred and Adele Astaire, with Empire Theatre Orch.: Oh, Lady Be Good!; So Am I; Fascinating Rhythm; I'd Rather Charleston; Hang On to Me; Swiss Maid; The Half of It Dearie, Blues
With other songs by Porter, Berlin, Youmans, etc.
Lady, Be Good! recorded in London, ca. 1926, with members of the 1926 London cast; George Gershwin, piano
Program notes by Peter Orchard on container

D461. Original cast with Fred and Adele Astaire
Monmouth-Evergreen MES 7036 (1971?)
Lady, Be Good! Selections
Recorded in London, ca. 1926
LC card no. 72-760373 *See:* **B928**

D462. Paul Whiteman and His Orchestra
Victor 19682, 78, 10" **[GOH]** LADY BE GOOD! 1924
CONTENTS: Fascinating Rhythm; Oh, Lady Be Good!; So am I

LET 'EM EAT CAKE (Abbreviation: *Cake*) (1933) **(W36)**

D463. Brooklyn Academy of Music production (With 0TIS)
CBS Records Masterworks SM 42638 & 42639, 2 LP records (1987);
CBS-2 M2K 42522 CD **[DDD]**
CAST: Alexander Throttlebottom: Jack Gilford; **John P. Wintergreen:** Larry Kert; **Mary Turner:** Maureen McGovern; **Kruger:** David Garrison; **Trixie Flynn:** Paige O'Hara; **General Adam Snookfield, France, China:** Jack Dabdoub; **Speaker, Lieutenant, & Dignitary:** George Dvorsky; **Louis Lippman:** Merwin Goldsmith; **Senator Robert E. Lyons:** Walter Hook; **Francis X. Gilhooley:** Frank Kopyc; **The Chief Justice:** Casper Roos; **Matthew Arnold Fulton:** Raymond Thorne; **Senator Carver Jones:** Mark

Zimmerman; **Supreme Court Justices, Boys & Girls, etc.:** New York
Choral Artists; Orchestra of St. Luke's (Michael Feldman, Artistic Director)
with New York Choral (Joseph Flummerfelt, Director); Michael Tilson
Thomas, **conducting; Producer:** Steven Epstein
See: **B1042, B1139, B1159, B1160**

D464. Bob Lawrence, Romana, & The Rhythm boys; Paul Whiteman Orchestra
JJA Records 1977-6 (Music Masters)
"Musical Comedy Medleys, 1928-1934"

D465. Victor Young & Orchestra; Dick Robertson, vocal
Brunswick 6691, 78, 10" **[GOH]**
CONTENTS: Let 'Em Eat Cake; Mine

MY ONE AND ONLY (1983) **(W48)**

D465.1. Atlantic 80110-1-E, LP (1983)
My One and Only Original 1983 cast recording
CAST: The New Rhythm Boys: David Jackson, Ken Leigh Rogers,
Ronald Dennis; Tommy Tune; Denny Dillon; Bruce McGill; Nana
Visitor; Susan Hartley; Stephanie Eley; Jill Cook; Niki Harris; Karen
Tamburrelli; Sandra Menhart; Twiggy; Roscoe Lee Browne; Jill Cook;
Charles "Honi" Coles; Ritz Quartet: Casper Roos, Carl Nicholas, Adam
Petroski, Will Blankenship; Adrian Bailey; Bruce McGill; **Arranger:**
Michael Gibson; Jack Lee, **conducting**
CONTENTS: Side 1: Overture; I Can't Be Bothered Now; Blah, Blah,
Blah; Boy Wanted; Soon; Sweet 'N Low Down; He Loves and She
Loves; 'S Wonderful!; Strike Up the Band; Side 2: Entr'acte; In the
Swim; Nice Work if You Can Get It; My One and Only; Little Jazz Bird;
Funny Face; Kickin' the Clouds Away; How Long Has This Been Going
On?
Program notes by Peter Stone on record jacket inserted in container
Recorded at RCA Studios, NY, Sept. 20-23, 1983
Producers: Ahmet Ertegun & Wally Harper; **Executive Producer:** Mike
Berniker
Songs selected from Broadway productions; Lyrics by Ira Gershwin
LC card no. 84-758134/R/r86 *See:* **B1216, B1217**

OF THEE I SING (Abbreviation: OTIS) (1931) **(W34)**

D466. Victor Arden & Phil Ohman & Their Orchestra
Victor 22911, 10"
CONTENTS: Of Thee I Sing; Who Cares?

D467. Brooklyn Academy of Music production (with Cake)
CBS Records Masterworks SM 42638 & 42639, 2 records (1987);
CBS-2 M2K 42522 CD
CAST: Alexander Throttlebottom: Jack Gilford; **John P. Wintergreen:** Larry
Kert; **Mary Turner:** Maureen McGovern; **Diana Devereaux:** Paige O'Hara;
French Ambassador: Jack Dabdoub; **Sam Jenkins & Doctor:** George

Dvorsky; **Miss Benson:** Louise Edeiken; **Louis Lippman:** Merwin Goldsmith; **Senator Robert E. Lyons:** Walter Hook; **Francis X. Gilhooley:** Frank Kopyc; **The Chief Justice:** Casper Roos; **Matthew Arnold Fulton:** Raymond Thorne; **Senator Carver Jones:** Mark Zimmerman; **Beauty contestant girls, photographers, judges, supreme court judges, boys & birls, etc.:** New York Choral Artists; Orchestra of St. Luke's (Michael Feldman, Artistic Director) with New York Choral Artists (Joseph Flummerfelt, Director); Michael Tilson Thomas, **conducting; Producer:** Steven Epstein *See:* **B1139, B1159, B1161, B1163**

D468. Jane Froman & Sonny Schuyler, vocals; chorus; Orchestra, Nathaniel Shilkret, conducting
JJA Records 19778 (Music Masters, NY)
"The Music of Broadway: 1931"

D469. Indiana University Opera Theater. Wilmes,-John; Turner,-Randal; Dewey,-Patricia; Galloway,-Melanie; Peeler,-Steven; Stoll,-Robert-E
"Of Thee I Sing"
6 sound tape reels (131 min.): analog, 7 1/2 ips, 2 track, stereo. ; 7 in Tape reel
Program / Indiana University School of Music ; 1987-1988, no. 22
Indiana Unversity, Bloomington. School of Music. Program ; 1987-1988, no. 22.
CAST: John Wilmes as **Alexander Throttlebottom**; Randal Turner as **John P. Wintergreen** ; Patricia Dewey as **Diana Devereaux** ; Melanie Galloway as **Mary Turner** ; Steven Peeler as the **French Ambassador** ; supporting soloists: Indiana University Opera Theater ; Robert E. Stoll, **conductor**
Recorded on July 25, 1987.
Program ([12] p.) and cast list ([1] leaf) laid in containers.

D470. Hal Kemp and Orchestra
Brunswick 6416-A, 78, 10" **[GOH]**
Wintergreen for President
See: Rimler, pp. 252–253, for more listings on Wintergreen

D471. The Knickerbockers
Victor C-2598, 10"
Of Thee I Sing; Who Cares?

D472. Abe Lyman & His California Orchestra
Victor B-20103
CONTENTS: Of Thee I Sing; Who Cares?; Love Is Sweeping the Country

D473. Abe Lyman and His California Orchestra; Vocals by Phil Neely, Frank Sylvano, & Dick Robertson
Brunswick 20103 A & B **[GOH]**
CONTENTS: Side B: OTIS; Who Cares?; Love Is Sweeping the Country; **Side A:** Music from THE LAUGH PARADE 1931 by Warren-Dixon-Young

D474. Original cast of 1952 production of OTIS with one interpolated G song

Capitol S-350; T-11651

CAST: Jack Carson; Paul Hartman; Betty Oakes; Lenore Lonergan; Jonathan Lucas; Florenz Ames; Loring Smith; Jack Whiting; Donald Foster; **Orchestrations:** Don Walker; Maurice Levine, conducting

D475. Original cast of 1952 TV production with one interpolated G song
Columbia S-31763

CAST: Carroll O'Connor; Jack Gilford; Cloris Leachman; Michele Lee, Garrett Lewis; **Orchestrations:** Peter Matz; Peter Matz, conducting

CONTENTS: Wintergreen for President/Overture; Who Is the Lucky Girl?/Because; Mine; Love Is Sweeping the Country; OTIS; Tap Drill; I Was the Most Beautiful Blossom; It's Great to Be a Secret'ry/Who Cares?; The Senator From Minnesota/Jilted/I'm About to Be a Mother

D476. Time-Life Records STL-AM09, 3 discs (1982)

"Oh, Kay!; Girl Crazy; Of Thee I Sing"

CONTENTS: Of Thee I Sing: Prelude, Wintergreen for President, Who Is the Lucky Girl to Be?, Never Was There a Girl So Fair, Love Is Sweeping the Country, Of Thee I Sing, Finaletto, Hello, Good Morning, Mine, Who Cares?, Garçon, s'il vous plaît, The Senate Roll Call, Trumpeter, Blow Your Horn, Finale; With selections from Oh, Kay! and Girl Crazy

Pamphlet (48 pp.) LC card no. 81-750256

OH, KAY! (1926) (W26)

D477. Columbia Light Opera Co. with Constance Mering & Frank Banta, pianos
Columbia 50031 D-B, 78, **[GOH]**

"Vocal Gems from Oh, Kay!"

CONTENTS: Introduction; Oh, Kay!; Maybe; Do Do Do!; Someone to Watch Over Me; Clap Yo' Hands

D478. David Daniels, Marti Stevens, Bernie West, Linda Lavin, Penny Fuller, and Murray Matheson as The Earl; Dorothea Freitag & Reginald Beane, piano; Pat Harrison, percussion; Original cast of 1960 revival
DRG Records DS15017 (1960, 1980)

CONTENTS: Overture; The Woman's Touch; The Twenties Are Here to Stay; Home; Stiff Upper Lip; Maybe; The Pophams; Do, Do, Do; Clap Yo' Hands; Someone to Watch Over Me; Fidgety Feet; You'll Still Be There; Little Jazz Bird; Oh, Kay!; Finale

Program notes by Edward Jablonski on container

D479. Edgar Fairchild & Ralph Rainger, pianos
Victor 20435, 78, 10" **[GOH]** OH, KAY! medley 1926

CONTENTS: Fidgety Feet; Maybe; Clap Yo' Hands; Do, Do, Do; With music by Gensler-DeSylva

D480. Linda Lavin, George Segal, & Penny Fuller; Original cast of 1960 Off-Broadway revival
Stet CDXP-15017, CD (As of 1995)

With Leave It to Jane

D481. Gertrude Lawrence, with orchestra

Monmouth Evergreen MES 7043 (1972) **[NN-L]** LSRX 6384

"Gertrude Lawrence in Songs from George & Ira Gershwin's Oh Kay! & Cole Porter's Nymph Errant"

CONTENTS: From **Oh, Kay!:** Someone to Watch Over Me; Do-Do-Do; Maybe; From Cole Porter, **Nymph Errant:** Experiment; It's Bad for Me; How Could We Be Wrong?; Medley of Song Successes

Discographical information on original issues on container

Program notes by Stanley Green on container

LC card no. 73-760883/R *See:* **B928**

D482. Original Cast, 1926

RCA Records DPL 1-0310, Smithsonian American Musical Theater Series (1978)

Gertrude Lawrence; Arden & Ohman, duo-pianists; in New York & London with the composer & members of the 1926 cast *See:* **B421, B1156, B928**

D483. Original cast, 1926

Smithsonian Collection R 011, **[NN-L]** LRX 6450 (1978)

In New York and London, with the composer and members of the 1926 cast *See:* **W26b, B427, B937**

D484. Original cast of 1957 Studio production

Columbia CL-1050 **[NN-L]** LRXP 852 (1957); Columbia OS 2550, stereo, **[NN-L]** LSRX 687 (1964); Columbia Broadway Masterworks Sony Classical/Columbia/Legacy SK 60703

CAST: Barbara Ruick; Jack Cassidy; Allen Case; Roger White; Cy Walter & Bernie Leighton, pianos; Orchestra & chorus; Lehman Engel, **conducting**

CONTENTS: Overture/The Woman's Touch; Dear Little Girl; Don't Ask; Maybe; Clap Yo' Hands; Bride and Groom; Do, Do, Do; Fidgety Feet; Someone to Watch Over Me; Heaven On Earth; ; Oh, Kay!; Finale; CD has three bonus tracks: Maybe; Someone to Watch Over Me; & Clap Yo' Hands

PRODUCER: Goddard Lieberson

D485. Original cast of 1960 revival

Twentieth-Century Fox 4003, mono **[NN-L]**; also DRG Records DS 15017 (1960, 1980)

"Oh, Kay!"

CAST: David Daniels; Marti Stevens; Bernie West; Eddie Phillips; Edith Bell; Joe Hill; Joseph Macaulay; Murray Matheson; Linda Lavin; Penny Fuller; Dorothea Freitag & Reginald Beane, piano; Pat Harrison, percussion; **Director:** Bertram Yarborough; **Musical & Dance numbers by:** Dania Krupska; **Costumes:** Pearl Somner; **Lighting:** Richard Nelson; **Recorded production:** Henry Onorati & Hugo Montenegro; **At the twin pianos:** Dorothea Freitag & Reginald Beane; **Musical Direction, orchestrations, & vocal arrangements by:** Freitag

CONTENTS: Oh, Kay! Overture; The Woman's Touch; The Twenties Are Here To Stay; Home; Stiff Upper Lip; Maybe; The Pophams; Do, Do,

Do; Clap Yo' Hands; Someone to Watch Over Me; Fidgety Feet; You'll
Still Be There; Little Jazz Bird; Oh, Kay You're Okay; Finale to Oh,
Kay *See*: **B1167**

D486. The Revelers
Victor 35811; His Master's Voice C-1396 (British) (1927)
"Oh, Kay! Vocal Gems"
CONTENTS: Introduction; Clap Yo' Hands; Someone to Watch Over
Me; Maybe; Do, Do, Do; (With Gladys Rice & extra pianist, Adam
Carroll)
Recorded NY, Jan. 14, 1927

D487. Nat Shilkret and the Victor Orchestra; Jesse Crawford, Wurlitzer organ
Victor 2O392, 78, 10" **[GOH]** OH, KAY! 1926
CONTENTS: Maybe; Someone to Watch Over Me (perf. by George
Olsen and His Music)

D488. The Sylvians at the Savoy Hotel, London Selections from Oh, Kay!
His Master's Voice B 2606, 78, 10" **[GOH]**

D489. Time-Life Records STL-AM09, 3 discs (1982)
"Oh, Kay!; Girl Crazy; Of Thee I Sing"
CONTENTS: Oh, Kay!: Overture; The Woman's Touch; Don't Ask;
Dear Little Girl; Maybe; Clap Yo' Hands; Do; Do; Do; Bride & Groom;
Fidgety Feet; Heaven On Earth; Oh; Kay!; Finale; Includes songs from
the other two musicals named
Pamphlet (48 pp.) LC card no. 81-750256

D490. Dawn Upshaw, Kurt Ollmann, Patrick Cassidy, Adam Arkin, Liz Larsen,
Robert Westenberg, Stacy A. Logan, Fritz Weaver, Susan Lucci with Orch.
of St. Luke's, Eric Stern, conducting, and duo-pianists Kevin Cole and Joseph
Thalken
Nonesuch 79361 (Roxbury Recordings)
CONTENTS: Someone To Watch Over Me; Clap Yo' Hands; Do, Do,
Do; The Moon is On the Sea, When Our Ship Comes Sailing In, and Ain't It
Romantic (the latter three songs resurrected); and others
Producers: Tommy Krasker and John McClure
See: **B1164, B1166, B1426**

OUR NELL (original title: *HAYSEED*) (1922) (W16)

D491. Bobby Short, piano and vocal
Atlantic SD 2-608
Innocent Ingenue Baby

PARDON MY ENGLISH (1933) (W35)

D492. Elektra Nonesuch (Roxbury Recordings) 79338-2, CD (1994)
"George and Ira Gershwin *Pardon My English*"
CAST: Golo/Michael Bramleigh: William Katt; **Commissioner Bauer:**
John Cullum; **Gita:** Arnetia Walker; **Ilse Bauer:** Michelle Nicastro; **Karl**

Blau: Philip A. Chaffin; **Innkeeper:** Patty Tiffany; **Magda:** Roberta
Wall; **Katz:** Peter Kevoian; **Schultz:** David Engel; Arnetia Walker;
CONTENTS: Overture; Fatherland, Mother of the Band; The Lorelei; I
Three-Quarter Time; Dancing in the Streets; So What?; Isn't It a Pity?;
Freud and Jung and Adler; He's Oversexed; Watch Your Head; My
Cousin in Milwaukee; Luckiest Man in the World; Hail the Happy
Couple; Dresden Northwest Mounted; Tonight; Opening Act II; Where
You Go, I Go; I've Got to be There; Reprises; Finale: He's Not Himself
Orchestra of NY free-lance instrumentalists
Conductor: Eric Stern
Orchestrations: Robert Russell Bennett; William Daly; Adolph Deutsch;
and Russell Warner
Vocal Director & Vocal Arrangements: Robert Webb
Performing edition restored by: Tommy Krasker
Recorded June 9-11, 1993 at Todd-AO Scoring Stage, Studio City, CA
Program notes in 60 pp. booklet in package; includes 3 excellent essays by
Tommy Krasker, Edward Jablonski, and Michael Kuchwara, and a plot
synopsis and complete lyrics
Produced by John McClure and Tommy Krasker
Executive Producer: Robert Hurwitz
Representatives from the Library of Congress: Elizabeth H. Aumen &
James W. Pruett *See:* **W35, B1426, B1662**

D493. Lyda Roberti of the original cast
Epic LZN-6072
"Encores from the 30s: Volume I, 1930–1935"
Includes My Cousin in Milwaukee

D494. Lyda Roberti
Totem 1026
"The Thirties Girls"
Includes My Cousin in Milwaukee

PORGY AND BESS (Abbreviation: P&B) (1935) **(W37)**
(Complete)

D495. Cleveland Orchestra & Chorus, with Mitchell, White, Boatwright, Quivar, Lorin
Maazel, conducting
3-London 414559-2 LH3, CD; also London OSA 13116, **[NN-L]**, KSRX 2363
See: **B1168, B1170, B1173, B1176, B1187**

D496. Columbia Odyssey (A product of CBS–originally OSL-162, 1951) 32 36 0018,
3 LP records
"Gershwin: Porgy and Bess (Complete)"
CAST: **Porgy:** Lawrence Winters; **Bess:** Camilla Williams; **Serena:** Inez
Matthews; **Sportin' Life:** Avon Long; **Crown:** Warren Coleman; **Clara:**
June McMechen; **Maria, Lily, & Strawberry Woman:** Helen Dowdy;
Jake: Eddie Matthews; **Mingo:** William A. Glover; **Robbins:** Irving
Washington; **Peter:** Harrison Cattenhead; **Frazier:** J. Rosamund Johnson;
Annie: Sadie McGill; J. Rosamund Johnson Chorus & Orchestra; Lehman

Engel, **conducting**
CONTENTS: Act I, Scene 1, Catfish Row, Act I, Scene 2, Serena's
room/ Act II Scene 1, Catfish Row, a month later, Act II, Scene 2,
Kittiwah Island, Scene 3, Catfish Row, Before dawn a week later, Scene
4, Serena's room, dawn of the following day/ Act III, Scene 1, Catfish
Row, the next night, Scene 2, Catfish Row, the next afternoon, Scene 3,
Catfish Row, A Week later (the Conclusion)
Producer: Goddard Lieberson *See*: **B565, B928, B1171, B1176, B1186** (new
release of same)

D497. Glyndebourne Festival Opera production; The London Philharmonic, Simon
Rattle, conducting; The Glyndebourne Chorus, Craig Rutenberg, chorus
master
EMI CDS 749568-2, 3 CDs **[DDD]**; 4D3S-49568, cassettes (1989)
"Gershwin: Porgy and Bess"
CAST: Porgy: Willard White; **Bess:** Cynthia Haymon; **Clara:** Harolyn
Blackwell; **Sportin' Life:** Damon Evans; **Jake:** Bruce Hubbard; **Serena:**
Cynthia Clarey; **Maria:** Marietta Simpson; **Crown:** Gregg Baker; **Mingo:**
Barrington Coleman: **Robbins:** Johnny Worthy; **Jim:** Curtis Watson; **Peter,
The Honey Man:** Mervin Wallace; **Lily:** Maureen Brathwaite; **Undertaker:**
Autris Paige; **Annie:** Paula Ingram; **Frazier:** Johnson; **Scipio:** Linda
Thompson; **Nelson/Crab Man:** Colenton Freeman; **Strawberry Woman:**
Camellia Johnson; **Detective:** Alan Tilvern; **Coroner:** Billy J. Mitchell; **Mr.
Archdale:** Ted Maynard; **Policeman:** Ron Travis; **Jasbo Brown:** Wayne
Marshall
Extensive **notes** by Robert Kimball & Michael Stegemann, biographical
notes on performers, and **libretto** in English, German, & French printed
on booklet in container
Recorded February, 1988, No. 1 Studio, Abbey Road, London
Producer: David R. Murray
See: **B1172, B1182, B1188 , B1189**

D498. Glyndebourne Production: EMI 77754, 3 laser discs or EMI 77757-3, 2
VHS videocassettes (Available from: WNET, 19 Gregory Drive, So. Burlington,
VT 05403 and **Sound Delivery,** P.O. Box 2213, Davis, CA 95617-2213, 1-800-
888-8574)
CAST: Porgy: Willard White; **Bess:** Cynthia Haymon; **Crown:** Gregg Baker;
Sportin' Life: Damon Evans; Glyndebourne Chorus; London Philharmonic;
Simon Rattle, conducting
See: **B1178**

D499. Houston Grand Opera (Sherwin M. Goldman) production
3-RCA ARL3-2109; RCD3-2109; 3-2109, 3 cassettes (© 1977)
CAST: Porgy: Donnie Ray Albert; **Bess:** Clamma Dale; **Crown:** Andrew
Smith; **Serena:** Wilma Shakesnider; **Clara:** Betty Lane; **Maria:** Carol
Brice; **Jake:** Alexander B. Smalls; **Sportin' Life:** Larry Marshall;
Mingo: Bernard Thacker; **Robbins:** Glover Parham; **Peter:** Mervin
Wallace; **Frazier:** Raymond Bazemore; **Annie:** Shirley Baines; **Lily:**
Myra Merritt; **Strawberry Women:** Phyllis Bash; **Jim:** Hartwell Mace;
Undertaker: Cornel Richie; **Nelson & Crab Man:** Steven Alex-Cole;

Mr. Archdale: Kenneth Barry; **Detective:** Hansford Rowe; **Police-
man:** William Gammon; **Coroner:** John B. Ross; **Scipio:** Alex
Carrington; **Jasbo Brown:** Dick Hyman Orchestra; Ensemble; Children's
chorus, Janice Campbell, Director; John DeMain, **Music Director**
Biographies of principals, The History of P&B by Robert Kimball, The
story and libretto printed in booklet included in container
Produced for Records by Thomas Z. Shepard
Recorded in RCA's Studio A (NY) Nov. 22, 23, 24, 1976 *See:* **B1177, B1179,
B1180, B1184, B1185**

D500. (excerpts of above) RCA ARK1-4680

D501. Opera Society Chorus and Orchestra; Paul Belanger, conducting
Concert Hall CHS 1247 (1956?) (Almost complete)
CAST: Porgy: Brock Peters; **Bess:** Margaret Tynes; **Serena:** Miriam Burton;
Sportin' Life: Joseph Crawford; **Crown:** William Dillard; **Clara &
Strawberry Woman:** Theresa Merritte (s); **Jake:** Charles Coleman; *See:*
B1199

D502. Original cast and orchestra
MCA-10520 (digitally restored) (1992)
Original cast including: Todd Duncan; Anne Brown; Plus a reissue
bonus track: Avon Long's I Got Plenty O' Nuttin'

D503. Swedish cast & orchestra
SR Records SR 40-2, SRLP 1337/8, 2 discs (p 1979) [Scarce, by mail order
from **Svala & Söderlund,** Box 3231, 103 64 Stockholm, Sweden]
"Opera av George Gershwin: Porgy och Bess"
CAST: Porgy: Bernhard Sönnerstedt; **Bess:** Gurli Lemon-Bernhard;
Crown: Sven-Erik Jacobsson; **Jake:** Hugo Hasslo; **Clara:** Birgit
Stenberg; **Sportin' Life:** Gösta Kjellertz; **Robbins:** Herbert Krantz;
Serena: Inga Sundström; **Maria:** Göta Allard; **Mingo:** Gösta Bäckelin;
Peter: Folke Rydberg; **Frazier:** Simon Edwardsen
Program notes in Swedish by Nils Castegren on container; Durations by
scenes printed on container

Selections from *Porgy & Bess*

D504. Roberta Alexander, soprano; Diane Curry, mezzo-soprano; Simon Estes, bass;
Rundfunkchor Berlin; Rundfunk-Sinfonie-Orchester Berlin; Leonard
Slatkin, conducting
Philips 412 720-1; 412 720-2 PH, CD **[DDD]**; 412720-4-PH, cassette
(1985)
"Highlights from Gershwin's 'Porgy and Bess'"
CONTENTS: Introduction; Jazzbo Brown Blues; Summertime; My Man's
Gone Now; I Got Plenty O' Nuttin'; Buzzard Keep On Flyin'; Bess, You
Is My Woman Now; Oh, I Can't Sit Down; I Ain't Got No Shame; It
Ain't Necessarily So; Now De Time, Oh Gawd; Tell Me Quick Where's
Bess; Oh Lawd, I'm On My Way
Co-production with VEB Deutsche Schallplatten, Berlin/DDR

LC card no. 85-752997/R *See*: **B1201, B1203, B1250**

D505. Roberta Alexander; Gregg Baker; New York Phil.; Z. Mehta, conducting
Teldec 2292-46318-2, CD **[DDD]**
CONTENTS: Introduction & Summertime; A Woman Is a Sometime
Thing; Overflow; Since I Lose My Man; The Promise' Land; Oh, I Can't
Sit Down; It Ain't Necessarily So; There's a Boat Dat's Leavin' Soon
for New York; Oh, Lawd, I'm On My Way; With AiP & Cuban Overture

D506. "Pearl Bailey sings Porgy & Bess and other Gershwin melodies"
Roulette SR-25063, LP, (© 1958)
See: Full entry at **D524**

D507. Cab Calloway; Helen Thigpen; Leslie Scott; Jay Blackton, conducting
RCA LPM-3156, 10 in. (1953)
With selections from Girl Crazy
CONTENTS: on Side B: It Ain't Necessarily So; Summertime; I Got Plenty
O' Nuttin'; Bess, You Is My Woman Now

D507.1. Cincinnati Pops Orchestra, Erich Kunzel, conducting
Gershwin: Porgy and Bess (Selections) /Blue Monday (Original Version)
Telarc CD 80434 *See*: Full entry at **D425.1**

D508. Cheryl Crawford 1942 production; Todd Duncan; Anne Brown; Edward
Matthews; Helen Dowdy; Georgette Harvey; William Woolfolk; Avon
Long; Harriet Jackson; Gladys Good; Alexander Smallens, conducting
Decca 8042 (Various numberings) *See*: **B1176**

D509. [1942] Cheryl Crawford Broadway revival cast recording; Brown, Matthews,
Jackson, Todd Duncan; Orchestra, A. Smallens, conducting
MCA MCAC-1631, cassette (monaural)

D510. Citadel CT 7025 (Available Jem Music Corp. USA (212) 684-6768)
"George Gershwin Memorial Concert September 8, 1937"
Live radio broadcast from the Hollywood Bowl
CONTENTS: Side B: Hall Johnson Choir & Los Angeles Philharmonic
cond. by Alexander Steinert: Excerpts from PORGY AND BESS:
Introduction and Summertime, Lily Pons, vocal; My Man's Gone Now,
Ruby Elzy, vocal; Buzzard Song, Todd Duncan, vocal; The Train Song,
Anne Brown, vocal; I Got Plenty O' Nuttin', Todd Duncan, vocal;
Bess, You Is My Woman Now, Todd Duncan and Anne Brown, vocals;
I'm On My Way, Todd Duncan, vocal
Side A: (Accompanied by the Los Angeles Philharmonic Orchestra):
Prelude No. 2; arr. and cond. by Otto Klemperer; Concerto in F (first
movement) Oscar Levant, piano; Charles Previn, cond.; Swanee, Al
Jolson, vocal; Victor Young, cond.; The Man I Love, Gladys Swarthout,
vocal; Victor Young, cond.; They Can't Take That Away from Me; Fred
Astaire, vocal; Victor Young, conducting *See*: **W2h, B1423**

D511. Helen Jepson, soprano; Lawrence Tibbett, baritone; Alexander Smallens &
Nathaniel Shilkret, conducting

RCA Camden CAL 500 (1959); CAK 500, cassette (reissue 1986)
P&B, selections
Program notes by Stanley Green on container
See: **B1181, B1200**

D512. Janet A. Jordan; Ethelouise Banks; Warren F. Michon
Eva-tone 49812, 1 soundsheet, mono (1981)
"The Suppressed Scene from Porgy & Bess"
Issued with: *The Quarterly Journal of the Library of Congress* 38/3
(Summer 1981) to accompany an article "Reconciliation on Catfish Row"
by Wayne D. Shirley

D513. Claudia Lindsey, soprano; Benjamin Matthews, bass-baritone; Slovak
Philharmonic Orchestra; Ettore Stratta, conducting
Moss Music Group D-MMG 103 A & B (1981, 1980) P&B in
Concert **[GOH]**
CONTENTS: Side A: Selections from P&B: Introduction; Summertime;
A Woman Is a Sometime Thing; My Man's Gone Now; I Got Plenty O'
Nuttin'; Bess, Yo' Is My Woman Now; It Ain't
Necessarily So; I Loves You, Porgy, arr. by Jim Tyler; There's A Boat Dat's
Leavin' Soon for New York; Oh, Lawd, I'm On My Way; Girl Crazy
Overture arranged as a symphonic potpourri by Don Rose
Finale recorded in Czechoslovakia under co-production of OPUS
Czechoslovakia, in Aug. 1980
Program notes, synopsis of the opera, & biographical notes on the performers
on container

D514. London Festival Orchestra; Stanley Black & Robert Farnon, conducting
London Weekend Classics 425 508 4, cassette
CONTENTS: Suite from P&B, arr. by Farnon: Overture; Summertime;
A Woman Is a Sometime Thing; Honey Man; My Man's Gone Now; I
Got Plenty O' Nuttin'; Bess, You Is My Woman Now; It Ain't
Necessarily So; Strawberry Woman; Crab Man; I Loves You, Porgy;
There's a Boat Dat's Leavin' Soon for NY; Oh, Where's My Bess; Oh
Lawd, I'm On My Way; With **F. Grofé:** Grand Canyon Suite

D515. Metropolitan Opera Box CBS P15931 (1981)
"Porgy and Bess"
CONTENTS: Introduction, Act I (Orch.); Summertime; A Woman is a
Sometime Thing; Overflow, Overflow (Chorus, Porgy); My Man's Gone
Now; I Got Plenty O' Nuttin'; Bess, You Is My Woman Now;
Conclusion, Act II, Scene 1, Oh I Can't Sit Down!; Introduction, Act II,
Scene 2 (Orch.); It Ain't Necessarily So; Act II, Scene 4 (Hurricane
Scene) Excerpt; There's a Boat That's Leavin' Soon for New York;
Opening, Act III, Scene 3, Good Mornin'; Oh Bess, Oh, Where's My
Bess?; Conclusion of the Opera
Producer: Goddard Lieberson
This recording is included in the **Metropolitan Opera Box**, which has been
available from the Education Department of the Metropolitan Opera Guild,
1865 Broadway, NY 10023. The box also includes a sound filmstrip, a
poster-size sheet for bulletin board display, and thirty student handouts in

addition to the teacher's manual.

D516. Original cast: Todd Duncan, baritone; Anne Brown, soprano; Eva Jessye Choir;
Decca Symphony Orchestra; Alexander Smallens, conducting
Decca 29067-29070, 4 discs, 78
"Selections from George Gershwin's Folk Opera Porgy & Bess" Personality
Series

D517. Original cast album
MCA-2035 (date?)
Anne Brown; Todd Duncan; and other members of the original New York
cast; Decca Symphony Orchestra; Alexander Smallens, conducting
P&B selections

D518. Original cast; Todd Duncan; Anne Brown; The Eva Jessye Choir; Decca
Symphony Orchestra; Alexander Smallens, conducting
Decca DL 79024, simulated stereo, **[NN-L]** (1959)
**"Porgy and Bess, selections from George Gershwin's folk opera, featuring
members of the original New York cast"**
Program notes by L. Untermeyer on container

D519. Brock Peters, baritone; Margaret Tynes, soprano; Opera Society Chorus &
Orchestra; Paul Belanger, conducting
Musical Masterpiece Society M2035-OP22, mono, **[NN-L]** (19--?)
Program notes on container; Libretto (4 pp.) inserted

D520. Leontyne Price, soprano; John W. Bubbles, tenor; William Warfield, McHenry
Boatwright, baritones; supporting solists; RCA Victor Orchestra & Chorus;
Skitch Henderson, conducting
RCA Gold Seal AGL1-5234 (1984), 5234-2-RG, CD **[ADD]**; also as RCA
Victor R8S 1065, cartridge (1970, 1979)
"Great Scenes from Porgy and Bess"
Legendary Performers, vol. 34; Previously released as AGL1-3654;
Program notes by Edward Jablonski, and biographical notes, on container
See: **B1197, B1204, B1206**

D521. RCA Victrola America AVM1-1742 (© 1976)
"A Collector's Porgy & Bess" Historic Recordings
CONTENTS & PERFORMERS: Summertime (Eleanor Steber, rec. Jan.
15, 1946); A Woman Is a Sometime Thing (Robert Merrill, Robert Shaw
Chorale, rec. Sept. 13, 1950); Gone, Gone, Gone (Robert Shaw Chorale,
rec. Sept. 13, 1950); My Man's Gone Now (Rise Stevens, Robert Shaw
Chorale, rec. Sept. 13, 1950); I Got Plenty O' Nuttin' (Lawrence
Tibbett, rec. Oct. 23, 1935); Buzzard Song (Lawrence Tibbett with
Chorus rec. Oct. 23, 1935); Bess, You Is My Woman Now (Lawrence
Tibbett & Helen Jepson, rec. Oct. 14, 1935); It Ain't Necessarily So
(Cab Calloway, rec. May 5, 1953); Bess, Oh Where's My Bess? & Oh
Lawd, I'm On My Way (Robert Merrill, Robert Shaw Chorale, rec.
Sept. 12, 1950); Jay Blackton, R. R. Bennett, or Alexander Smallens,
conducting
Reissue produced by Peter Dellheim

Program notes by Edward Jablonski and durations on container

D522. RCA Victor Red Seal LM 11224 (date?)
"Highlights from Porgy and Bess"
Risë Stevens; Robert Merrill; Robert Shaw Chorale; Robert Shaw,
conducting; RCA Victor Orchestra; Robert Russell Bennett, conducting
CONTENTS: Summertime; A Woman Is a Sometime Thing; Gone, Gone,
Gone; My Man's Gone Now; I Got Plenty O' Nuttin'; Bess, You Is My
Woman Now; It Ain't Necessarily So; Where Is My Bess?

D523. **"Ed Sullivan Presents Porgy and Bess."**
National Academy 7
No other credits given

D524. Vienna Symphonic Pop Orchestra; Simon Gale, conducting
ZYX Classic CLS 4120
CONTENTS: P&B Selections: I Got Plenty O' Nuttin'; Summertime;
I Loves You, Porgy; It Ain't Necessarily So; Bess, You Is My Woman
Now; There's a Boat Dat's Leavin' Soon for New York; With selections
from **L. Bernstein's** West Side Story

D525. Lawrence Winters (Porgy); Isabelle Lucas, Ray Ellington, and others, singing;
Chorus & Orchestra; Kenneth Alwyn, conducting
Heliodor HS 25052, **[NN-L]** (1967)
"Porgy and Bess Highlights"
LC card no. R 67-1021

Arrangements of *Porgy and Bess* Material

D526. Pearl Bailey with the Voices of the Ambassadors; Orchestra cond. by Buddy
Baker
Forum SF 9024-A & B; also Roulette R-25063 (1958) **[GOH]**
"Pearl Bailey Sings PORGY AND BESS and other Gershwin Melodies"
CONTENTS: I Got Plenty O' Nuttin'; I Got Rhythm; Summertime; Oh,
Lady Be Good!; A Foggy Day; Our Love Is Here to Stay; Bess, You Is
My Woman Now; They Can't Take That Away from Me; Someone to
Watch Over Me; It Ain't Necessarily So; A Woman Is a Sometime Thing;
Clap Yo' Hands *See*: **B1196, B1212**

D527. Harry Belafonte and Lena Horne; Arrangements & musical direction by
Lennie Hayton & Robert Corman
RCA Victor LSC 1507, mono (1959)
CONTENTS: A Woman Is a Sometime Thing; Summertime; I Got Plenty
O' Nuttin'; I Wants To Stay Here; Bess, You Is My Woman Now; It
Ain't Necessarily So; Street Calls; Strawberry Woman; The Honey Man;
Crab Man; My Man's Gone Now; Bess, Oh, Where's My Bess?; There's
A Boat That's Leavin' Soon For New York
See: **B1196, B1212**

D528. Canadian Brass
RCA 6490-2-RC, CD **[DDD]** (1987)

"Strike Up the Band" album
CONTENTS: Suite from P&B (arr. by Luther Henderson):
Introduction/Jasbo Brown Blues/Summertime; It Ain't Necessarily So;
Bess, You Is My Woman Now; I Loves You, Porgy; A Woman is a
Sometime Thing/I Got Plenty O' Nuttin'; Oh, Lawd, I'm on My Way;
plus other G music, *See:* Full entry in **"Anthologies"**

D529. Empire Brass Quintet: Rolf Smedvig & Charles A. Lewis, Jr., trumpets;
David Ohanian, horn; Donald Sanders, trombone; Samuel Pilafian, tuba
Digitech DIG 104, dist. by Sina Qua None Productions (1980); Telarc CD-
80159 **[DDD]** CS-30159; cassette
CONTENTS: Suite from Porgy & Bess: Overture, Summertime, A Woman
a Sometime Thing; I Got Plenty O' Nuttin', My Man's Gone Now, Bess,
You Is My Woman, It Ain't Necessarily So; **Leonard Bernstein**: Suite
from West Side Story; **J. P. Sousa:** Washington Post March; **S. Joplin:**
Paragon Rag; The CD version includes **L. Bernstein**: Mass (excerpts)
& West Side Story (excerpts) done by Michael T. Thomas
All arrangements by Jack Gale
Program notes by M. C. Conley on container

D530. Carroll Gibbons & the Savoy Hotel Orpheans; Anne Ziegler & Webster Booth,
vocals
Columbia (English) DX 824, 78 **[GOH]**
CONTENTS: Summertime; Bess, You Is My Woman Now; It Ain't
Necessarily So; I Got Plenty O' Nuttin'; There's a Boat Dat's Leavin'
Soon for New York

D531. Hollywood Bowl Symphony Orchestra; Alfred Newman, conducting; Leonard
Pennario, piano;
"Leonard Pennario Plays Gershwin"
Angel S 36070, **[NN-L]** (1974)
CONTENTS: P&B medley (arr. McRitchie); Cuban Overture (arr.
McRitchie); Second Rhapsody; Variations On I Got Rhythm
Previously recorded on Capitol Records SP 8581
Program notes and durations on container; LC card no. 73-751160
See: **B1125**

D532. Monty Kelly and Orchestra   PORGY AND BESS: Stereorchestrations
Carlton STLP 12-111-A & B **[GOH]**
CONTENTS: Side A: Opening and Summertime; A Woman is a
Sometime Thing; My Man's Gone Now; I Got Plenty O' Nuttin'; Bess,
You Is My Woman Now; Oh, I Can't Sit Down; **Side B:** I Ain't Got
No Shame; It Ain't Necessarily So; I Wants to Stay Here;
There's a Boat Dat's Leavin' Soon for New York; Oh, Bess, Oh Where's My
Bess?; I'm On My Way

D533. André Kostelanetz and Orchestra
Columbia 7362 M, 78   Highlights from PORGY AND BESS
CONTENTS: Summertime; I'm On My Way; I Got Plenty O' Nuttin'; Bess,
You Is My Woman Now

D534. Avon Long & Helen Dowdy, vocalists; Leo Reisman Orchestra
JJA 19845-A (Music Masters, NY)
"Gershwin for Dancing"
1942 P&B revival recordings (originally on Decca 351, 78)
CONTENTS: It Ain't Necessarily So; A Woman Is a Sometime Thing;
Summertime; There's A Boat That's Leavin' Soon for New York; I Got
Plenty O' Nuttin'; Bess, You Is My Woman Now

D535. Anna Moffo; Urylee Leonardos; Billie Daniel; Valentine Pringle; Avon Long;
Andrew Frierson; **Orchestrations:** Henri Rene; Lehman Engel, conducting
Reader's Digest 40-8
With The Vagabond King
Studio production

D536. Earl Wild, piano
Arr. for Piano by Earl Wild
Quintessence PMC-7060
Recorded Oct. 18-20, 1976

Specifically Jazz Treatments of Material from P&B

D537. Ralph Burns, piano; jazz orchestra
Decca DL-9215
"Gershwin's Porgy and Bess in Modern Jazz"
Arr. for Jazz Orchestra and Piano by Ralph Burns
CONTENTS: Summertime; My Man's Gone Now; It Takes a Long Pull to Get
There; I Got Plenty O' Nuttin'; Bess You Is My Woman Now; It Ain't
Necessarily So; I Loves You Porgy; A Red-headed Woman; There's a Boat
Dat's Leavin' Soon for New York; Oh Bess, Oh Where's My Bess?
Descriptive notes on container.

D538. Bob Crosby & His Bobcats
Dot DLP 3193, mono, (n. d.) **[NN-L; GOH]**
"Porgy and Bess selections"
CONTENTS: Oh, I Can't Sit Down; Bess, You Is My Woman Now; It
Ain't Necessarily So; It Takes A Long Pull To Get There; I Loves You,
Porgy; I Got Plenty O' Nuttin'; There's A Boat Dat's Leavin' Soon For
New York; Oh Bess, Oh Where's My Bess?; My Man's Gone Now;
Summertime

D539. Jim Cullum Jazz Band **"Porgy & Bess"**
CBS Records FM 42517; MK 42517, CD **[DAD]** (1987)
Personnel: Jim Cullum, cornet, Allan Vaché, clarinet, Randy
Reinhart & Ed Hubble, trombones, Howard Elkins, guitar & banjo, John
Sheridan, piano, Ed Torres, drums, Jim Hunter & Jack Wyatt, bass
CONTENTS: Jasbo Brown Blues; Summertime; A Woman Is a Sometime
Thing; They Pass By Singin'; Oh Little Stars; My Man's Gone Now; It
Take a Long Pull to Get There; I Got Plenty O' Nuttin'; Buzzard Song;
Bess, You Is My Woman Now; It Ain't Necessarily So; Strawberry
Woman; Honey Man; Crab Man; I Loves You, Porgy; Oh, De Lawd
Shake De Heavens; Oh, Dere's Someboy Knockin' At De' Do'; A Red-

Headed Woman; Clara, Clara; There's a Boat Dat's Leavin' Soon for
New York; Oh, Bess, Oh Where's My Bess; Oh Lawd, I'm On My Way
Arrangements by John Sheridan, Allan Vaché, & Randy Reinhart
Recorded digitally at Dallas Sound Lab's Studio A, Dallas, TX, Dec. 1985
& Jan. 1987
Producer: Jim Cullum
Program notes by Jim Cullum inserted in jewel box; Durations on back of
notes *See:* **B1209, B1211, B1633**

D540. "Miles Davis—Porgy and Bess"
Under the direction of Gil Evans
Columbia CK 40647, CD; Sony SON 65141 (re-issue w/ 2 alternate takes)
Personnel: Miles Davis (trumpet and flugelhorn); Louis Mucci, Ernie Royal,
John Coles, Bernie Glow (Trumpets); Jimmy Cleveland, Joseph Bennett,
Richard Hixon, Frank Rehak (Trombones); Jullian (Cannonball) Adderly,
Daniel Banks (Saxophones); Philip Bodner (Flute, replaced by Jerome
Richardson on 8/4/58 date); Willie Ruff, Julius B. Watkins, Gunther Schuller
(French horns); Romeo Penque (Flute); Danny Bank (alto flute, bass clarinet);
John "Bill" Barber (tuba); Paul Chambers (Bass); Philly Joe Jones (replaced by
Jimmy Cobb at 7/29/58 date)
CONTENTS: The Buzzard Song; Bess, You Is My Woman Now; Gone; Gone,
Gone Gone; Summertime; Bess, Oh Where's My Bess; Prayer (Oh Doctor
Jesus); Fisherman, Strawberry and Devil Crab; My Man's Gone Now; It Ain't
Necessarily So; Here Come De Honey Man; I Loves You, Porgy; There's a
Boat That's Leavin' Soon for New York
Arrangements: Gil Evans
Original Program Notes by Charles Edward Smith
Recorded: 7/22/58, 7/29/58, 8/4/58, 8/18/58 at 30th St. Studio in New York
Producers: Cal Lampley and Teo Macero *See:* **B1194, B1208, B1212**

D541. Sammy Davis, Jr. & Carmen McRae; chorus & orchestra
Decca DL 8854 (1959)
CONTENTS: Summertime; A Woman Is A Sometime Thing; My
Man's Gone Now; I Got Plenty O' Nuttin'; Bess, You Is My Woman;
It Ain't Necessarily So; I Loves You, Porgy; There's A Boat Dat's Leavin'
Soon For New York; Oh Bess, Oh Where's My Bess?; Oh Lawd, I'm On My
Way
Program notes by Miles Kreuger on container
LC card no. 59-1112 *See:* **B1200, B1212**

D542. Ella Fitzgerald & Louis Armstrong, singers; Armstrong, trumpet solos, with
orchestra; Russ Garcia, conducting
Verve Records MG 4011-2 (1958); Verve 827 475-2, CD **[AAD]** (198?)
CONTENTS: P&B, selections: Overture; Summertime; I Wants to Stay; My
Man's Gone Now; I Got Plenty O' Nuttin'; Buzzard Song; Bess, You Is My
Woman Now; It Ain't Necessarily So; What You Want Wid Bess?; A Woman Is
a Sometime Thing; Oh, Doctor Jesus; Medley: (Here Come De Honey Man,
Crab Man, Oh, Dey's So Fresh and Fine); There's a Boat Dat's Leavin' Soon For
New York; Bess, Oh Where's My Bess?; Oh Lawd, I'm On My Way
Synopsis & program notes by Lawrence D. Stewart & Norman Granz
bound in LP album & inserted in container of CD

Producer: Norman Granz *See:* **B1200, B1210, B1212**

D543. Joe Henderson **"The Gershwins Porgy and Bess"**
Verve 314 539 046-2 (1997)
Performers: Joe Henderson (Tenor Sax), Conrad Herwig (Trombone), John
Scofield (Electric Guitar), Stefon Harris (Vibes), Tommy Flanagan (piano),
Dave Holland (Bass), Jack DeJohnette (Drums), Chaka Khan (Vocal on
Summertime), Sting (vocal on It Ain't Necessarily So)
CONTENTS: Introduction: Jassbo Brown Blues, Summertime; Here Come de
Honeyman/They Pass By Singin'; My Man's Gone Now; I Got Plenty O'
Nuttin'; Bess, You Is My Woman Now; It Ain't Necessarily so; I Loves You
Porgy; There's a Boat Dat's Leavin' Soon for New York; Oh Bess, Oh
Where's My Bess
See: **B1192**

D544. Monty Kelly and Orchestra   PORGY AND BESS: Stereorchestrations
Carlton STLP 12-111-A & B **[GOH]**
CONTENTS: Side A: Opening and Summertime; A Woman Is a Sometime
Thing; My Man's Gone Now; I Got Plenty of Nuttin'; Bess, You is My
Woman Now; Oh, I Can't Sit Down; **Side B:** I Ain't Got No Shame; It
Ain't Necessarily So; I Wants to Stay Here; There's a Boat Dat's Leavin'
Soon for New York; Oh, Bess, Oh Where's My Bess?; I'm On My Way

D545. Cleo Laine & Ray Charles
RCA 1831-2-R, CD; 1831-4-R, cassette *See:* **B1207, D1210**

D546. Mundell Lowe, guitar & his All Stars: George Duvivier, bass; Don Elliot,
mellophone & vibes; Art Farmer, trumpet; Osie Johnson, drums; Tony Scott
& Ben Webster, sax; Ed Shaughnessy, drums/vibes
Camden CDN 132; RCA Camden CAS 490 (1959)
CONTENTS: P&B, selections: Summertime; Bess, You Is My Woman
Now; I Loves You, Porgy; I Got Plenty O' Nuttin'; Oh Bess, Oh,
My Bess?; Red Headed Woman; My Man's Gone Now; It Take
A Long Pull To Get There; It Ain't Necessarily So; There's A Boat
Dat's Leavin' Soon For New York
Program notes by Frank Talmadge on container
Recorded in New York, July 16 & 17, & Oct. 3, 1958
See: **B1212**

D547. **"The Modern Jazz Quartet Plays George Gershwin's Porgy & Bess"**
Atlantic 1440 (1965)
CONTENTS: Summertime; Bess, You Is My Woman Now; My Man's
Gone Now; I Loves You, Porgy; It Ain't Necessarily So; Oh Bess, Oh
Where's My Bess?; There's a Boat Dat's Leavin' Soon for New York
Recorded in New York, April 26 & July 23-24, 1964

D548. Oscar Peterson, clavichord; Joe Pass, guitar
Pablo 2310-779
Arr. for Clavichord and Guitar   **Recorded** Jan. 26, 1976

D549. Oscar Peterson, piano Verve 314-519807-2, CDh

"Oscar Peterson Plays Porgy and Bess"
CONTENTS: It Ain't Necessarily So, etc.

D550. Bill Potts, conducting various jazz greats
United Artists UAL 4032-A & B **"The Jazz Soul of PORGY AND BESS"**
[GOH]
CONTENTS: Summertime; A Woman Is a Sometime Thing; My Man's Gone
Now; It Take a Long Pull to Get There; I Got Plenty O' Nuttin'; Bess, You Is
My Woman Now; It Ain't Necessarily So; Medley: Minor themes, Prayer,
Street cries; I Loves You, Porgy; Clara, Don't You be Downhearted; There's
a Boat Dat's Leavin' Soon for New York; Oh Bess, Oh Where's My Bess?;
I'm On My Way
Arrangements by Bill Potts

D551. Mel Tormé as Porgy, Frances Faye as Bess, & supporting singers, choruses,
& music ensembles; Al "Jazzbo" Collins, narrator; Russ Garcia, arranger-
conductor
Bethlehem BCP-6040 (1970, 1979); Bethlehem 3BP 1 **[GOH]**; Bethlehem
EXLP-1, 3 LPs, **[NN-L]** LRXPA (1957?)
CONTENTS: Excerpts of a jazz version of the opera; The Bethlehem
Orchestra; Duke Ellington & His Orchestra; Australian Jazz Quintet; Pat
Moran Quartet; Stan Levey Group; Russ Garcia, conducting; Al "Jazzbo"
Collins, narrator
Studio version adapted for Bethlehem Records
Narration written by Al Moritz *See:* **B1202, B1205**

D552. Sarah Vaughan and jazz trio with the Los Angeles Philharmonic, Michael Tilson
Thomas, conducting
CBS MK-42516, CD **[ADD/DDD]**; FMT-42516, cassette
CONTENTS: Overture and song medley arr. by Marty Paich; With AiP;
Preludes; RiB; and other G music *See:* **B1266**

D553. When People Were Shorter and Lived Near the Water (Rock Music group)
Shimmy-Disc SHIMMY-44, LP (1991?)
Rock version of the opera, Porgy and Bess, performed by the group
CONTENTS: Intro/Summertime - Roll Dem Bones - A Woman Is
a Sometime Thing - Happy Dust - Gone, Gone, Gone - My Man's Gone
Now - It Takes a Long Pull to Get There - I Got Plenty O' Nuttin' - I
Hates Yo' Guts - Buzzard Song - Bess, You Is My Woman Now - Oh, I
Can't Sit down - Plenty (Reprise) - I Ain't Got No Shame - It Ain't
Necessarily So - The Rape - Serena's Prayer - Strawberry Woman -
Honey Man - Crab Man - I Loves You Porgy - Somebody Knockin' on
De Door - Red Headed Woman - Summertime (Reprise) - There's a Boat
Dat's Leavin' Soon for New York - Oh Lawd, I'm on My Way

D554. Cootie Williams, trumpet (Porgy); Hilton Jefferson, alto sax (Bess); Rex
Stewart, cornet (Sportin' Life); Lawrence Brown, trombone (Serena &
Clara)
DRG/Swing SW 8414 (1986)
"Porgy and Bess Revisited"
Reissue of Warner Bros.' 1959 album

Miscellaneous Treatments

D555. Georgia Brown, vocal with the Mike Sammes Singers; orch. cond. by Ian Fraser
London LL 3331-A **"Georgia Brown Loves Gershwin" [GOH]**
CONTENTS: Summertime; It Ain't Necessarily So; I Loves You, Porgy;
I Got Plenty O' Nuttin'; My Man's Gone Now; I'm On My Way

D556. Various performers with symphony orchestra using the original Broadway full
pit-band orchestrations
MMO Pocket Songs PS 21, cassette (c 1986) [Available in U. S. in retail
music stores]
"You Sing the Shows"
CONTENTS: Summertime; A Woman Is a Sometime Thing; Gone, Gone,
Gone; My Man's Gone Now; I Got Plenty O' Nuttin'; Bess, You is My
Woman Now; Oh, I Can't Sit Down; It Ain't Necessarily So; Strawberry
Woman; Crab Man; I Loves You, Porgy; Hev'nly Father; Oh, Bess, Oh
Where's My Bess?; Oh Lawd, I'm on My Way
Program notes & plot synopsis by Rob Lesser printed on insert in container
Producer and recording: Dennis McCorkle
This is a "sing along" album. The songs are presented with the lyrics and
vocal; by turning off the right channel, the listener can sing along, or on
side 2, the accompaniment is present without the vocals
For more recordings of P&B, *See:* **B 936**, Walter Rimler, *A Gershwin
Companion,* pp. 307-344.

PRIMROSE (1924) **(W21)**

D557. JJA Records 19794 (Music Masters)
"British Musical Comedies By American Composers (1912-1935)"
Orchestra
Medley

D558. Monmouth Evergreen MES 7071 (196-?)
George Gershwin, piano, on the piano solos; The original London cast on
Primrose
"An American in London" CONTENTS: Primrose: This is the Life for a
Man; When Toby is out of Town; Some Far Away Someone; The Mophams;
Berkeley Square and Kew; Boy Wanted; Mary, Queen of Scots; Wait A Bit,
Susie; Naughty Baby; Ballet Music; That New Fangled Mother of Mine; I
Make Hay When the Sun Shines; **George Gershwin Piano Solos:** Andante
from RiB; Preludes Nos. 1, 2, & 3; Oh, Kay!; Do, Do, Do; Maybe; Someone
to Watch Over Me; Clap Yo' Hands

D559. World Records (England) SH-214 (1924)
"Primrose"
Original London cast, John Ansell, conducting
CONTENTS: Percy Heming: The Countryside, Wait A Bit, Susie;
Heather Thatcher: Boy Wanted, I Make Hay When The Moon Shines;
Heming, Margery Hicklin: Some Far Away Someone; Hicklin, Claude
Hulbert: I'll Have A House In Berkeley Square; Leslie Henson: That

New-Fangled Mother Of Mine, When Toby Is Out Of Town; Hicklin: Naughty Baby; Henson, Hulbert: Mary, Queen Of Scots; Henson, Thatcher, Thomas Weguelen: "The Mophams" Orchestra: "Ballet Music"
With additional music

THE RAINBOW [The New Empire Review] (1923) (W17)

D560. World Records SH 451-A **[GOH]**
"The Great British Dance Bands Play George Gershwin 1920–1928"
Innocent Lonesome Blue Baby

D560.1. Courtney Kenny, vocalist
No label, LMSYS 2, cassette (available from Mr. Kenny, 14 Grange Grove, London N1 2NP, England @ $15.00 in 1991)
"The Great Mr. Gershwin"
CONTENTS: 18 songs, including Strut Lady With Me; In the Rain; Innocent Lonesome Blue Baby [the latter three songs from *The Rainbow* **(The New Empire Revue)** *See:* Full entry at **D881**

ROSALIE (1928) (W29)

See: Rimler, pp. 187–192

SHOW GIRL (1929) (W31)

D561. Leo Reisman and Orchestra
Victor 22069, 78, 10" **[GOH]** SHOW GIRL 1929
CONTENTS: Liza; Do What You Do
See: Rimler, pp. 202–208

SONG OF THE FLAME (1925) (W25)
See: Information about the film at **F6, B2107-2109**.

D562. International Novelty Orchestra
Victor 19965-A, 78, 10" **[GOH]** SONG OF THE FLAME 1925
CONTENTS: Cossack Love Song; Vodka

D563. Roger Wolfe Kahn (son of millionaire & G's friend, Otto Kahn) & Orch.
Victor 19935
CONTENTS: Song of the Flame
See: Rimler, pp. 150–151

STRIKE UP THE BAND (1927) (W27) and (1930) (W32)

D564. Elektra/Nonesuch (Roxbury Recordings) 79273-4, 2 cassettes; also available on CD (1991)
"George and Ira Gershwin Strike Up the Band [1927 & 1930]"
CAST: Jim Townsend: Brent Barrett; **Horace J. Fletcher:** Don Chastain; **Joan Fletcher:** Rebecca Luker; **Timothy Harper:** Jason Graae; **Mrs. Draper:** Beth Fowler; **Colonel Holmes:** Charles Goff; **Anne**

Draper: Juliet Lambert; **Spelvin/Gideon:** Jeff Lyons; **Soldier:** Dale Sandish; **Sloane:** James Rocco; Singing Chorus

Vocal director: Paul Trueblood; **Orchestrations by:** Russell Warner, William D. Brohn, Steven D. Bowen, William Daley, Dick Hyman, Donald Johnston, Sid Ramen, & Larry Wilcox; **Musical supervisor:** Steven D. Bowen

Restored by Tommy Krasker; **Conducted by** John Mauceri

CONTENTS: Cassette 1, Side 1: Overture; Fletcher's American Cheese Choral Society; 17 & 21; Typical Self-made American; Meadow Serenade; Unofficial Spokesman; Patriotic Rally/**Cassette 1, Side 2:** The Man I Love; Yankee Doodle Rhythm; 17 & 21 (reprise); Finaletto Act I; Strike Up the Band

Cassette 2, Side 1: Oh This is Such a Lovely War; Hoping That Someday You'd Care; Come-Look-At-The-War Choral Society; Military Dancing Drill; How About a Man?; Finaletto Act II; Homeward Bound/The Girl I Love (reprise); The War That Ended War; Finale Ultimo/**Cassette 2, Side 2: appendix, Strike Up the Band (1930);** Interlude: Strike Up the Band (orchestra); I Mean to Say; Soon; If I Became the President; Hangin' Around With You; Mademoiselle in New Rochelle; I've Got a Crush on You

The CD includes a booklet which has six essays: "What Price Cheese?" by Tommy Krasker; "The Gershwins Go to War" by Edward Jablonski; "George S. Kaufman: The Gloomy Dean of American Comedy" by Laurence Maslon; Preaching to the Masses: *Strike Up the Band* and War by John Mueller; "Two Strikes, Two Hits, and One 'Man' Out" by Tommy Krasker; "Let the Drums Roll Out" by Jon Alan Conrad; a plot synopsis and copy of the lyrics

Recorded Dec. 13-20, 1990 at BMG Studio A, NY

For the Library of Congress: James W. Pruett, former Chief, Music Division & Elizabeth H. Auman, advisor; Robert Kimball Artistic Advisor to Roxbury

Producers: John McClure & Tommy Krasker *See:* **B1139, B1214, B1215, B1426, B1662**

D565. JJA Records 19777 (Music Masters)
   "The Music of Broadway 1930"
   Includes newsreel soundtrack of a 1929 stage rehearsal of *Strike Up the Band* with Bobby Clark & Paul McCullough and GG, piano; Mademoiselle from New Rochelle, Strike Up the Band, GG, piano; Red Nichols orch. of original production, its versions of Soon and Strike Up the Band, with uncredited vocals

D566. Marion Harris, comedienne with violin, guitar, & piano
   Victor 21116-B, 78, 10" **[GOH]** STRIKE UP THE BAND   1927
   The Man I Love

D567. Red Nichols and His *Strike Up the Band* Orchestra
   Brunswick 4695, 78, 10 in. STRIKE UP THE BAND 1930 **[GOH]**
   CONTENTS: Strike Up the Band featuring Tommy Dorsey; Soon
   Also See: Rimler, pp. 170–174, 209–231

SWEET LITTLE DEVIL (1924) **(W19)**

See: Rimler, pp. 75–79

TELL ME MORE! (also known as *My Fair Lady* (1925) **(W23)**

D568. Columbia, 78 368-D
"Tell Me More!"
Alexander Gray
CONTENTS: Three Times A Day; Tell Me More!

D569. Paul Whiteman and His Orchestra
Victor 19682, 78, 10 in. **[GOH]** TELL ME MORE 1925
CONTENTS: Tell Me More!; Baby!; Why Do I Love You?; Kickin' the
Clouds Away

Also See: More selections under **"Songs, Instrumental Treatment" (D1064**,
e. g.) and Rimler, pp. 127-133

TIP-TOES (1925) **(W24)**

D570. Dorothy Dickson, supporting singers, chorus, and orchestra (Tip-toes)
World Records SH 185 (1970, 1979)
"George Gershwin in London, Tip-toes and other Gershwin Successes"
Buddy Lee, Gilt Edged Four (Lady, Be Good!); Gertrude Lawrence,
supporting singers, chorus, and orchestra (Oh, Kay!)
CONTENTS: **Tip-toes**: These Charming People, That Certain Feeling,
It's A Great Little World, Looking for a Boy, When Do We Dance?,
Night-Light, Sweet and Low-Down; **Lady, Be Good!**: Lady, Be
Good!, Fascinating Rhythm; **Oh, Kay!**: Someone to Watch Over Me,
Do-Do-Do, Clap Yo' Hands
Retrospect Series
Program notes by Peter Myers on container
LC card no. 80-760736

D571. Roger Wolfe Kahn and His Orchestra
Victor 19939-A, 78, 10" **[GOH]** TIP-TOES 1925
Looking for a Boy

D572. Original Cast
Monmouth Evergreen MES 7052-A & B (Re-mastered from original 78
discs) Performers: Original London cast of TIP-TOES 1926 (London)
[GOH]
CONTENTS: **Side A:** These Charming People; That Certain Feeling;
It's a Great Little World; Looking For a Boy; Nice Baby; Nightie-night;
Sweet and Low Down; **Side B:** Music from WILDFLOWER (Youmans-
Stothart-Harbach-Hammerstein II) 1926 (London) *See*: **B928**

D573. The Revelers
Victor 35772; His Master's Voice C-1293 (British) (1926)
"Tip-Toes, Vocal Gems"

CONTENTS: Introduction; Charming People; That Certain Feeling; When Do We Dance?; Looking For a Boy; Sweet and Low Down (with Gladys Rice)
Recorded NY, Feb. 12, 1926

D574. Paul Whiteman and His Orchestra
Victor 19920, 78, 10" **[GOH]** TIP-TOES 1925
CONTENTS: That Certain Feeling; Sweet and Low Down
Also See: Rimler, pp. 138-147

TREASURE GIRL (1928) **(W30)**

D575. JJA Records 1974-1 (Music Masters)
Records by members of the original production of Treasure Girl
Arden and Ohman, pianists, with their orchestra, 1928
Feeling I'm Falling; Got A Rainbow

D576. Decca 8673
"Lawrence: A Remembrance"
Records by members of the original production of Treasure Girl
Gertrude Lawrence, in 1952
I've Got A Crush On You

D577. Åva Records A/AS-26, **[NN-L]** *LSRX 4828 (1963)
"Remember These," Vol. I
Betty Comden, singing; Arranged & played by Richard Lewine (piano)
CONTENTS: Treasure Girl: I Don't Think I'll Fall In Love Today; What Are We Here For?; Feeling I'm Falling; Oh, So Nice; Where's The Boy? (Here's The Girl); With **R. Rodgers/Lorenz Hart**: Chee-Chee
Also See: Rimler, pp. 192-199

D578. *See*: **D465.1**

PIANO MUSIC

General

D579. Dag Achatz (complete works composed or arranged by Gershwin for solo piano)
Bis CD404 **[DDD]**
CONTENTS: The George Gershwin Song Book; RiB: Three Preludes; Impromptu in Two Keys; Rialto Ripples; Merry Andrew; Three-Quarter Blues; Promenade

D580. Victor Arden, piano roll
Biograph 1022
"The Music of George Gershwin"
1924 Piano roll
CONTENTS: Fascinating Rhythm

D581. **"Richard Rodney Bennett Plays George Gershwin Solo Piano Works"**
IMP Classics IMPPCD 1058 **[DDD]; EMI EMD 5538 (1981)**

CONTENTS: Promenade; Merry Andrew; Impromtu in Two Keys; Two Waltzes; Three Quarter Blues; Rialto Ripples; Little Jazz Bird (arr. Bennett); Bess, Oh Where's My Bess (arr. Bennett); Someone to Watch Over Me (arr. Bennett); and others

Program notes by Max Harrison on container

D582. Paul Bisaccia, piano.

CPD942 Vista Records, CD (p 1994)

"Rhapsody in blue : Gershwin's Complete Solo Piano Music"

CONTENTS: Rhapsody in Blue (15:23) - 3 Preludes (7:28) - 2 Waltzes in C (4:27) - Rialto Ripples (2:45) - Merry Andrew (2:21) - Three-quarter Blues (1:00) - Promenade (3:03) - Impromptu in 2 Keys (1:17) - the George Gershwin Songbook: Swanee (1:07) - Somebody Loves Me (1:26) - My One and Only (1:07) - Who Cares (1:34) - I'll Build a Stairway to Paradise (1:00) - the Man I Love (3:40) - Strike up the Band (1:12) - Sweet and Low down (1:05) - Do it Again (2:05) - Fascinatin' Rhythm (0:57) - 'S Wonderful! (3:04) - Lady Be Good (1:25) - Do-do-do (1:25) - Nobody But You (0:46) - That Certain Feeling (1:41) - Clap Yo' Hands (0:57) - Liza (3:11) - I Got Rhythm (1:24).

Recorded at Studio Works, North Stonington, CT.

D583. William Bolcom, piano

Elektra/Nonesuch N5-71284; H-71284, cassette; 79151-2, CD **[AAD]**

CONTENTS: Rialto Ripples; Three Preludes; Impromptu in Two Keys; Three-Quarter Blues; Merry Andrew; Piano Playin' Jazzbo Brown; Promenade; George Gershwin Song Book; Songs *See:* **B928**

D584. Richard & John Contiguglia, duo-pianists

MCA Classics MCAD-6226, digital CD (1988)

"Gershwin: The Legendary Transcriptions of Percy Grainger"

CONTENTS: Arrangements for two pianos by Percy Grainger, unless otherwise noted: Fantasy on P&B (Suite) [for two pianos]; Rhapsody in Blue [arr. for two pianos by GG]; Cuban Overture [arr. for four hands by GG]; The Man I Love (Richard, soloist); Love Walked In (John, soloist); Embraceable You [arr. from Maurice C. Whitney's paraphrase for four hands by Grainger]

Recorded at Hirsch Hall, Elias Cohn Institute, New York, 1987

Program notes by John Bird in container

Produced by Thomas Frost   *See:* **B1224**

D585. N. Coxe, piano

"Showstoppers"

Titanic Ti 170, CD **[DDD]**

CONTENTS: Girl Crazy & Lady, Be Good overtures; Ballet from Primrose; Jasbo Brown; Merry Andrew; George Gershwin Songbook; With Blake: Piano Music & Grainger: Piano Music

D586. Brian Gatchell, piano; The Heidelberg Ensemble

Coronet LPS 3126 (1984?)

With RiB

Program notes by J. Mann on container; Durations: 22:50 (Songbook); 16:00 (RiB)

D587. Gershwin (6 Duo-Art piano rolls)
> Pro Arte CDD-352, CD **[DDD]**; PCD-352, cassette
> **CONTENTS:** Kicking the Clouds Away; Drifting Along with the Tide;
> Tweeoodle-um-bum-bo; So Am I; That Certain Feeling; Sweet and Low
> Down; AiP; RiB   .

D588. Gershwin, et al. (12 Duo-Art, QuartetS, Imperial, and Perfection piano rolls)
> Biograph BCD-106, CD **[DDD]**
> **CONTENTS:** Gershwin: RiB, rec. on 2 rolls; Swanee; Walkin' the Dog;
> Frank Milne & Ernest Leith: AiP, piano duet version rec. on two rolls);
> J. Lawrence Cook: Let's Call the Whole Thing Off; 'S Wonderful!,
> Embraceable You, Oh, Lady Be Good!; Victor Arden & Max Kortlander:
> Somebody Loves Me; Rudy Marlin: Our Love Is Here To Stay

D589. Jack Gibbons, piano
> P-ASV 2077 (Koch), or ASV WHL 2077, CD
> **"The Authentic GERSHWIN: Volume 2: 1925-1930"**
> **CONTENTS:** *Tip-Toes*: Sweet and Low-Down, That Certain Feeling,
> Looking for a Boy; When Do We Dance?; Three-Quarter Blues; *Oh,
> Kay*: Do, Do, Do; Someone to Watch Over Me; Clap Yo' Hands;
> Maybe; Three Preludes; *Strike up the Band* Overture; Meadow
> Serenade; *Funny Face*: My One and Only; 'S Wonderful; He Loves
> and She Loves; An American in Paris (transcr. William Daly, arr. Gibbons);
> *Show Girl*: Liza; *Girl Crazy*: Embraceable You; I Got Rhythm (two versions)
> *See*: **B1261**

D590. Jack Gibbons, piano
> ASV White Line CD WHL 2082 **[DDD]** (distr. Koch International)
> **"GERSHWIN: The Authentic George Gershwin, Volume 3: 1931–1937"**
> **CONTENTS:** OTIS: Overture; Jilted; Second Rhapsody; For You, For
> Me, For Evermore; Cuban Overture; Isn't It a Pity?; Variations on "I Got
> Rhythm;" P&B Suite (Catfish Row); They Can't Take That Away From Me;
> Let's Call the Whole Thing Off; Our Love Is Here To Stay
> **Producer:** Jack Gibbons
> *See*: **B1235**

D591. Leonid Hambro, piano
> Walden WL 220, mono, (1950?)
> **CONTENTS:** Songs in the Songbook: Swanee, Nobody But You, I'll Build a
> Stairway to Paradise, Do It Again, Fascinating Rhythm, Oh, Lady Be Good!,
> Somebody Loves Me, Sweet and Low-down, That Certain Feeling, The Man I
> Love, Clap Yo' Hands, Do, Do, Do, My One and Only, 'S Wonderful!, Strike
> Up the Band, Liza, I Got Rhythm, Who Cares?
> **Program notes** by Edward Jablonski & Edith Garson on container

D592. Leonid Hambro, piano; Gershon Kingsley, keyboard & electronic synthesizer
> Avco Embassy AVE 33021
> **"Gershwin: Alive & Well & Underground"** (1970)
> **CONTENTS:** RiB; I Got Rhythm; PORGY AND BESS Introduction and
> opening scene; Summertime; My Man's Gone Now; It Ain't Necessarily So;

Clara, Clara, Don't You be Downhearted; Crown's Killing

D593. Norman Krieger, solo piano
Stradivari Classics SCD-8000, CD, digital, SMC 8000 cassette (1988)
CONTENTS: Three Preludes & RiB (Gershwin arr. for solo piano); Concerto,
is the solo piano arr. by Grace Castagnetta
Produced by Laura Harth Rodriguez
See: **B1012, B1085, B1221**

D594. Litton (4 selections-Swanee; Nobody But You; Do It Again; Clap Yo' Hands)
MCA Classics MCA-6216; MCAD-6216, CD **[DDD]**
With RiB; music by **H. Kay**

D595. Clive Lythgoe, piano
Concerto 0016 (Allegro Import)
See: **B1239**

D596. **"Midora Matsuya Plays George Gershwin"**
Camerata 32CM-169, available from Koch Imports
CONTENTS: Songbook; RiB (piano arr.); Three Preludes for Piano

D597. J. Miltenberger (piano) *(aleatoric improvisations)*
ACA digital Recording CM 20021
CONTENTS: Nice Work If You Can Get It; Embraceable You; The Man
I Love; But Not for Me; Our Love Is Here to Stay; Fascinating Rhythm; With
Aguila: Son. 2; **Ginastera:** Son. 1; **S. Green:** Onata-say; **Morillo**: Son. 4;
solo piano version of Promenade

D598. Musical Heritage Society 4865 (© 1981 by RCA Records, France)
"The Works for Solo Piano"
CONTENTS: RiB (orig. version for piano solo); Piano Preludes; **Song Book:**
The Man I Love, Swanee, Nobody But You, I'll Build a Stairway to Paradise,
Do It Again, Fascinating Rhythm, Oh, Lady Be Good!, Somebody Loves Me

D599. L. Pennario, piano
Angel CDC-47418, CD **[DDD]** Includes Preludes

D600. Leonard Pennario, piano
Angel CDM 64668-2 **[ADD/DDD]**
CONTENTS: Promenade, from 'Shall We Dance'; 2 Waltzes In
C; Merry-Andrew; Ballet from 'Primrose'; Three-Quarter Blues; Rialto
Ripples (Gershwin-Donaldson); Three Preludes; With Piano Music by **Joplin**
& Gottschalk

D601. Leonard Pennario, piano
Angel 4DS-37359, cassette (1986)
"George Gershwin's Song Book & Other Music for Piano Solo"
CONTENTS: Jasbo Brown Blues; George Gershwin's Song Book
(1932); Three Preludes; Promenade; Two Waltzes in C; Merry-Andrew; Ballet
from Primrose; Three-quarter Blues; Rialto Ripples

Recorded in Bridges Hall of Music, Pamona College, Claremont, CA
Program notes by Michael Feinstein included
See: **B1218, B1229, B1230**

D602. Robert Phillips and Franco Renzulli, pianos
Crystal Clear CCS 6002, LP, 12" Gershwin Fantasia **[GOH]**
CONTENTS: Fantasy on P&B (P. Grainger, arr.); George Gershwin
Song Fantasy (Phillips & Renzulli, arr.)

D603. Piano?; Simfonichen orkestur na bulgarskoto radio i televiziia.
Bulgarian Broadcasting Symphony Orchestra ; various soloists and conductors
DCC Compact Classics AVZ-3005, CD (p 1990)
CONTENTS: Rhapsody in blue; Three Preludes for piano; Cuban overture;
Porgy and Bess (Introduction and Summertime); Concerto

D604. Paul Posnak (**"Gershwin's Piano Improvisations"**): Posnak plays his
own note-for-note reconstructions of improvisations recorded by Gershwin in
1916, 1926 and 1928 studio recordings and in 1932 and 1934 radio broadcast
performances)
Stradivadi Classics SCD-6039
See: Full entry under **"Songs, Instrumental Treatment"**

D605. Anna-Stella Schic, piano
Discques FY et du Solstice SoCD 114 **[DDD]** (distr. Allegro)
"GERSHWIN: Piano Music"
CONTENTS: Rialto Ripples; Song Book; Jasbo Brown; Merry Andrew;
Three-Quarter Blues; Promenade; Impromptu in Two Keys; Two Waltzes in
C; Sleepless Night; Three Preludes; RiB
Producer: Yvette Carbou
See: **B1236**

D606. F.-J. Thiollier, solo piano
Thésis THC 82001
CONTENTS: Impromptu in Two Keys; Rialto Ripples; American in Paris;
George Gershwin Song Book; Preludes; Rhapsody

D607. Frances Veri and Michael Jamanis, pianos
Connoisseur Society CS 02073
CONTENTS: George Gershwin's Songbook; Two Waltzes in C
(Gershwin) cut from PARDON MY ENGLISH 1932; The Entertainer (Joplin)
1902; Maple Leaf Rag (Joplin) 1899; The Easy Winners (Joplin) 1901; Solace
(Joplin) 1909; Bethena (Joplin) 1905?; Pineapple Rag (Joplin) 1908; Jasbo
Brown Blues (GG)

D608. Frances Veri & Michael Jamanis, pianos
Book-of-the-Month Records 61-5426, 3 discs (1981)
"The Complete Piano Music"
CONTENTS: Concerto (Original version for two pianos); AiP (trans. for
two pianos by Frances Veri); RiB (original version for two pianos); Piano
intro. to P&B; "I Got Rhythm" Variations (trans. for two pianos); Cuban
Overture (trans. for one piano, four hands); Two Waltzes in C; George

Gershwin's Song Book (trans. for solo piano); Second Rhapsody (original version for two pianos); Preludes
Classics Record Library
"About George Gershwin" by Mary M. Anderberg and "Notes on the Music" by Edward Jablonski & Mary M. Anderberg (13 pp.) laid in container
Jablonski gave this recording a positive review in his 1987 *Gershwin*, p. 404

D609.   Earl Wild, piano (plays his own transcriptions of works by Gershwin)
Chesky CD-32 **[DDD]**
CONTENTS: Fantasy on Porgy and Bess; Improvisation in the form of a Theme and Three Variations on Someone To Watch Over Me; Seven Virtuoso Etudes (I Got Rhythm, Oh, Lady Be Good!, Liza; Embraceable you; Somebody Loves Me, Fascinating Rhythm, The Man I Love)
See: **B1022**

D610.   Alicia Zizzo, piano
Carlton Classics LC 8747 (Allegro), CD (© 1996)
"Gershwin rediscovered." ("The Gershwin Manuscripts") Researched, restored, and performed by Zizzo
CONTENTS: PIANO PRELUDES: Prelude I in B-flat; PRELUDE NO.2, Melody No. 17 (1925-1926); PRELUDE NO.3 "Rubato" (1923); PRELUDE NO.5, "Novelette in Fourths" (1919); PRELUDE No. 4, Prelude II; PRELUDE NO.6, Prelude III "Spanish Prelude"; PRELUDE NO.7, Fragment (later used for the opening of the last movement of the Concerto); BLUE MONDAY Piano Suite
SEVEN MINIATURES IN GERSHWIN'S HAND: "Irish Waltz"; Original Impromptu in Two Keys (manuscript form); Melody No. 36 "Three Note Waltz;" Melody No. 55 "Romantic;" "Machinery Going Mad;" "Sleepless Night (As arr. By Kay Swift); Melody No. 59 "Sutton Place" RIB for Piano Solo **Album notes** by Zizzo in English, French, & German *See*: **W46.2, B259, B1223**

PRELUDES FOR PIANO (1923–1926) **(W42)**

This listing represents only a sampling of the many recordings. The category can include one, two, or all three of the published preludes, or in the case of the Zizzo recording above (**D610**), additional Preludes beyond the three published ones. Other recordings of the Preludes may be found scattered about the Discography, in the sections **Piano Music, Anthologies,** and **Recordings by Gershwin**. *See* other listings at: **D395, D396, D421, D558, D716, D719, D723, D730, D742, D1129, 1130, 1133, 1137, 1145**

D611.   Dag Achatz (complete works composed or arranged by Gershwin for solo piano)
Bis CD404 **[DDD]**
With other G Piano Music

D612.   Leon Bates, piano
Naxos 8.550341
CONTENTS: Three Preludes; six G songs: Fascinating Rhythm; Somebody Loves Me; Liza; The Man I Love; I Got Rhythm; Strike Up the Band; and **Chick Corea**: Twenty Children's Songs
See: **B1226, B1234, B1240**

D613. Jeanne Behrend, piano
Victor 17910 (in set M-764), 78

D614. Leonard Bernstein, piano (in 1st & 2nd works); Los Angeles Philharmonic;
Leonard Bernstein, conducting
DG 410025-2 GH, CD **[DDD]**
CONTENTS: RiB; Prelude for Piano No. 2; and Bernstein: Symphonic
Dances from West Side Story

D615. Sondra Bianca, piano
MGM E-3307; MGM 3E-1 *See:* **B1128**

D616. William Bolcom, piano
Elektra/Nonesuch H-71284; 79151-2, CD **[AAD]**; N5-71284, cassette
CONTENTS: Rialto Ripples; Impromptu in Two Keys: Three-Quarter Blues;
Merry Andrew; Piano Playin' Jazzbo Brown; Promenade; George Gershwin
Song Book; Songs *See:* **B1218, B1315**

D617. Walter Chodack, piano
Ades (French) 14.002; LP (1976)

D618. Percy Faith and His Orchestra
Harmony Headliner KH 31538-A & B, Vol.2 **[GOH]**
CONTENTS: Preludes II & III with songs; *See* full entry under **"Songs,
Instrumental Treatment"**

D619. George Gershwin, piano
Columbia C-50107D, 78; Columbia 7192M, 78 (London, June 8, 1928)
Preludes I, II, & III; With Andante from RiB

D620. Gershwin, piano
RCA ALK1-7114, monaural cassette
With AiP; RiB

D621. Jack Gibbons, piano
P-ASV 2077 (Koch), CD
"The Authentic GERSHWIN: Volume 2: 1925-1930"
Includes the Three Preludes; With songs from shows from 1925-1930:
See: Full entry at **D589**

D622. Frank Glazer, piano
Concert-Disc M-1217/CS-217

D623. Morton Gould, piano; with orchestra
RCA Victor LM 6033, 2 discs (1955)
"The Serious Gershwin"
With Concerto; P&B, piano solo, from act 1, scene 1; Suite from P&B
arr. by M. Gould; RiB; AiP
See: **B1021**

D624. Morton Gould, piano; Morton Gould and his orchestra
RCA Victor Red Seal LM 2017 (1956)
With RiB; Concerto
Program notes, based on an essay by Arthur Schwartz, on container

D625. Werner Haas, piano; Orchestre national de l'Opera de Monte-Carlo; Edo
de Waart, conducting
Philips 416 220-4, cassette (198-?)

D625.1. Peter Jablonski, piano; V. Ashkenazy, cond.; Royal Philharmonic Orch.
London 430542 **[DDD]**
CONTENTS: Concerto; 3 Preludes, etc. *See:* Full entry at **D743**

D626. Norman Krieger, solo piano
Stradivari Classics SCD-8000, CD **[DDD]**; SCD-8000; SMC 8000, cassette
(1988)
With Concerto (solo piano arr. by Grace Castagnetta); Rhapsody
See: **B1012, B1085**

D627. E. Leichner, piano *See:* **D628,** below

D628. E. Leichner, piano
Supraphon 1 11 1721-1 11 1722, 2 discs (p 1975); Supraphonet 11 1117-2, CD
[AAD]
With music by: **Auric:** Adieu; **Copland:** Four Piano Blues; **Debussy:**
Children's Corner; **Hindemith:** Suite; **Satie:** Jack in the Box;
Schulhoff: Esquisses de jazz
Recorded June 1972–March 1973, Supraphon Domoniva Studio, Prague
Durations with **program notes** in English, German, and French by
J. Kotek on container

D629. Oscar Levant, piano; Morton Gould and his orchestra
Columbia Masterworks ML 2073, 10 in. (1950)
With Second Rhapsody for piano & orchestra; Variations on "I Got Rhythm"
Program notes by Morris Hastings on container *See:* **B1583**

D630. Oscar Levant, piano (mono. recording)
CBS MLK-39454 (mono), CD; PMT-39454, cassette; CBS MK-42514,
CD **[ADD]**; FMT-42514, cassette
With American; RiB; O. Levant (Rec. 1949); Concerto; "I Got Rhythm"
Var.; Second Rhapsody *See:* **B1237, B1583**

D631. Eugene List, piano
Turnabout CT-4457, cassette
With Concerto; RiB

D632. "Midora Matsuya Plays George Gershwin"
Camerata 32CM-169, available from Koch Imports
CONTENTS: RiB (piano arr.); Three Preludes for Piano; Songbook

D633. L. Mayorga, piano

Sheffield Lab CD-28; available in all three formats
With "I Got Rhythm" Variations; Lullaby; Promenade; RiB

D634. L. Mayorga, piano
Town Hall M-4
With **Brahms**: Piano Music; **Chopin**: Polonaises

D635. Eric Parkin, piano
Preamble PRCD 1776, CD (1987?)
"American Piano Music, Volume One"
With piano music by **Antheil; Barber:** Excursions; **Copland:** Our Town; **H. Stevens; Waxman**
Produced by Tony Bremner & John Lasher
See: **B1220**

D636. G. & S. Pekinel (2-piano arrangement by Gregory Stone)
Teldec 243719-2 ZK, CD **[DDD]**; available in all three formats
With **Bartók:** 2-Piano Son.; **Bernstein:** West Side Story
(symphonic dances)

D637. Leonard Pennario, piano
Angel CDC-47418 **[DDD]**
With George Gershwin Song Book *See*: **B1229, B1230**

D638. Leonard Pennario, piano
Angel CDC 7474182; Angel 4DS-37359, cassette (1986)
"George Gershwin's Song Book & Other Music for Piano Solo"
See: Full entry at **D601, B1229, B1230**

D639. Leonard Pennario, piano
Angel CDM 64668-2 **[ADD/DDD]**
With Promenade from 'Shall We Dance'; 2 Waltzes In C; Merry-Andrew; Ballet from 'Primrose'; Three-Quarter Blues; Rialto Ripples (Gershwin-Donaldson); Piano Music by **Joplin & Gottschalk**

D640. André Ratusinski, piano
Trax Classique TRXCD-111
With George Gershwin Songbook
Program notes by Robert Matthew-Walker on insert in jewel case
Producer: Stanislaw Dybowski

D641. Anna-Stella Schic, piano
Discques FY et du Solstice SoCD 114 **[DDD]** (distr. Allegro)
"GERSHWIN: Piano Music"
CONTENTS: Three Preludes, with other Piano Music
See: Full entry at **D605**

D642. Stepan, piano
Sonic 10 (Direct to disc)

D643. François-Joel Thiollier, piano
    Thésis THC 82001, CD
    With AiP; George Gershwin Song Book; Piano Music; RiB

D644. François-Joel Thiollier, piano
    Musical Heritage Society MHS 4865 (c 1983)
    "The Works for Solo Piano"
    With Song Book; RiB
    Recorded Nov 9-10, 1981, Notre-Dame du Liban, Paris

D645. Michael Tilson Thomas, pianist and conductor; Los Angeles Philharmonic
    CBS Masterworks M 39699 (© & p 1985); IMT-39699, cassette
    CONTENTS: RiB; Preludes for Piano; With other G compositions
    See: Full entry under **"Anthologies"**

D646. Michael Tilson Thomas, piano
    Columbia MK 42516, CD (1988?)
    CONTENTS & ARTISTS: Three Preludes (M. T. Thomas); RiB (M. T.
    Thomas & Columbia Jazz Band); AiP (Bernstein & NY
    Philharmonic); Liza (Jean Pierre Rampal); A Foggy Day (John
    Williams, guitar); Embraceable You (Cleo Laine); Medley from
    Woody Allen Film Manhattan (Zubin Mehta & NY
    Philharmonic); Overture to P&B; Medley from P&B (Sarah
    Vaughan)
    See: **B1088, B1120, B1266**

D647. Frances Veri & Michael Jamanis, pianos
    Book-of-the-Month Records 61-5426, 3 discs (1981)
    "The Complete Piano Music"
    With other music for piano, *See:* Full entry at **D608**

D648. André Watts, piano
    CBS MT-34221, cassette
    With RiB & other music *See:* **B1331**

D649. Ken Werner, piano
    Finnadar 9019, cassette
    ". . . Plays music of Beiderbecke, Ellington, Gershwin, Johnson"

D650. Alicia Zizzo, piano
    Carlton Classics LC 8747 (Allegro), CD (© 1996)
    "Gershwin rediscovered." ("The Gershwin Manuscripts") Researched,
    restored, and performed by Zizzo *See:* Full entry at **D610**

Preludes, Arranged for Instruments Other Than Piano

D651. Mimi Allen, Harp
    Virtuosity Records NR 7656 (197-?)
    "Mimi Allen Plays Gershwin"
    CONTENTS: Prelude II & G songs: Summertime; It Ain't Necessarily So;

I Got Plenty of Nothin'; Bess, You Is My Woman Now; Our
Love Is Here to Stay; AiP/Fascinating Rhythm; etc.

D652. Baker (synthesizers)
Newport Classic A NC-60042, CD **[DDD]**
With AiP; Concerto; Rhapsody

D653. Carlos Barbosa-Lima, guitar
Concord Records CC-2005 (1982)
**"Carlos Barbosa-Lima Plays the Music of Antonio Carlos Jobim and
George Gershwin"**
CONTENTS: Preludes 1 & 2 with compositions by G & others

D653.1. Joshua Bell, violin; London Symphony Orchestra; John Williams, piano
and conductor
Sony Classical SK 60659
"Gershwin Fantasy" (Includes Three Preludes, arr. Heifetz) *See:* Full entry at
D701.1.

D654. Canadian Brass
RCA 6490-2-RC, CD **[DDD]**
"Strike Up the Band" album
Three Preludes arr. for brass quintet by Luther Henderson, plus other G
music
See: Full entry at **D704** under **"Anthologies"**

D655. Eroica Trio
EMI classics- 56482 2 8 [DDD] (1997)
Performers: Adela Peña, violin; Sara Sant' Ambrogio, cello; Erica Nickrenz,
piano
Three Preludes arr. For violin, pa. & cello
With music by Ravel, Godard, & Schoenfeld
Contact **www.emiclassics.com** for more information

D656. Percy Faith and His Orchestra
Harmony Headliner KH 31538-A & B, Vol.2 **[GOH]**
CONTENTS: Preludes for piano 2 & 3; With songs

D657. **"Fiedler Conducts Gershwin, I Got Rhythm"**
Ralph Votapek, piano (on Second Rhapsody); The Boston Pops; Arthur
Fiedler, conducting
London Phase-4 SPC 21185 (1979)
CONTENTS: Three Preludes (arr. Gregory Stone); Girl Crazy, suite (arr.
Leroy Anderson); **Overtures** (all arr. by Don Rose): Oh, Kay!,
Funny Face, OTIS, Cake; Wintergreen for President (arr.
Walter Paul); Second Rhapsody (rev. Robert McBride)
LC card no. 79-750381
See: **B1122, B1126, B1219, B1325**

D657.1 Leopold Godowsky, III, piano (nephew of George); Royal
Scottish National Orchestra; José Serebrier, conducting (debut record-

ing for Godovsky)
"Gershwin: Centennial Edition"
Dinemec Classics *See:* Full entry at **D116.1**

D658. Grierson & Kane (duo-piano arrangement)
Angel CDM-69119, CD
With AiP

D658.1. Ofra Harnoy, cello
Mastersound DFCDI-020 (dist. Allegro Imports), **CD [DDD]**
"Ofra Harnoy and Friends Play George Gershwin" p1990, ©1992
Includes Prelude No. 2 *See:* Full entry at **D735**

D658.2. Jascha Heifetz, violin; Emanuel Bay, piano
Decca DLP 7003, 10 in., mono (orig. 1946, 1949)
"Heifetz Playing the Music of Gershwin"
CONTENTS: Includes Prelude No. 1; Prelude No. 2; Prelude No. 3
Arrangements by Heifetz *See:* Full entry at **D737**

D659. John Holmquist & Daniel Estrem, guitars
ProArte PCD 226, cassette (1985)
"Gershwin by Guitar"
Favorite melodies of Gershwin played in arrangements for two guitars;
works transcribed & arranged by Daniel Estrem
See: Full entry under **"Anthologies"**

D660. Los Angeles Philharmonic; various conductors
Citadel CT 7025 (1981, 1937)
"George Gershwin Memorial Concert, September 8, 1937"
CONTENTS: Prelude No. 2 (arr. & cond. by Otto Klemperer)
See: Full entry at **D749**

D661. Adam Makowicz, piano; Dave Holland & Charlie Haden, bass; Al Foster,
drums
RCA (Novus) 3022-2-N, CD, digital (1987)
"Adam Makowicz—Naughty Baby Honoring George Gershwin"
CONTENTS: Prelude II; RiB (6:13 version); With songs [all arrangements
by Makowicz]

D662. The New York Banjo Ensemble
Kicking Mule Records KM 224 (1982)
"The New York Banjo Ensemble Plays Gershwin"
CONTENTS: RiB, arr.; Swanee; I'll Build a Stairway to Paradise;
Strike Up the Band; Oh, Lady Be Good!; 'S Wonderful!; Sweet and
Low-Down; Clap Yo' Hands; Prelude No. 2; AiP; Impromptu in Two Keys;
Rialto Ripples

D663. **"Fascinatin' Rampal: Jean-Pierre Rampal Plays Gershwin"**
CBS Records BL 39700 (1985)
With songs and AiP

D663.1 Russell Sherman, piano; Orchestra of St. Luke's; Gunther Schuller,

conducting
Pro Arte CCD 244, completely digital (1986) *See*: Full entry at **D765**

D664. Sonus Brass Quintet: Allan Cox & Michael Tunnel, trumpets; Bruce Heim,
horn; Lawrence Borden, trombone; Mark Moore, tuba
Mark Records MCD-1067
"Sonus Brass Captured"
Prelude II (arr. Norbert Carnovale); With early music, arranged,
& contemporary quintets

D665. Richard Stoltzman, clarinet; London Symphony Orchestra; Michael Tilson Thomas
and Eric Stern, conductors
RCA Victor Red Seal 09026-61790-2 (BMG Classics), CD **[DDD]**
Three Preludes arr. by Don Sebesky
With GG: Promenade, Bess, You Is My Woman Now, and Short Story;
music by **Copland, Gordon Jenkins,** and **L. Bernstein**
Producer: Max Wilcox

D666. Yo Yo Ma, cello, trans. by Yo Yo Ma from J. Heifetz transcriptions (1992)
Sony Classical SK 53126 **[DDD]**
Three Preludes with music by **Bernstein, Ives,** and **L. Kirchner**

CHAMBER MUSIC

LULLABY FOR STRING QUARTET (1919) **(W38)**

D667. Alexander String Quartet
Analekta CLCD 2009
With music by **S. Barber** & **Copland**

D668. Dickermann Quartett Frankfurt ; with Timm J. Trappe, double bass
Thorofon Capella MTH 275. LP 12" Wedemark/Hannover [West Germany] :
[1984?]
With Streichquartett op. 11 / **Samuel Barber** & Deuxißeme quintette /
Darius Milhaud
LC Call No.: M178
Recorded Apr. 23-27, 1984 at the Festeburgkirche, Frankfurt am Main.
See: **B1241**

D669. Juilliard String Quartet
CBS Records MP 39553 & Columbia M 32596 (1984, 1974); Resissue
of Columbia M 32596 (1974)
"Miniatures"
With music by **J. Haydn; F. Schubert; F. Mendelssohn; G. Puccini;** and **H.
Wolf**
"Digitally re-mastered from newly re-mixed master analog tapes"—container

D670. Kohon Quartet
Vox SVBX 5305, 3 discs
"American String Quartets, Vol. II: 1900-1950"
The Kohon Quartet: Harold Kohon & Isadora Kohon, violins; Eugenie Dengel,

viola; W. Ted Hoyle, cello
With works by **Copland; Piston; Thomson; Schuman; Sessions; Hanson; Mennin**; & **Ives**
Program notes & biographical notes by Donald Chittum laid in container

D671. Manhattan String Quartet
Newport Classic NC-60033, CD **[DDD]**

D672. Philarte [string] quartet (from Philadelphia Orch.); Royal Promenade Orch. of London (on AiP & RiB); Russell Sherman, piano; Orchestra of St. Luke's; Gunther Schuller, conducting; et al
Pro Arte CDM 814 **[DDD]**
With First movement of Concerto only (Sherman, pa.); RiB; AiP; "Gershwin in Hollywood" (Rochester Pops; E. Kunzel, conducting)

LULLABY, ARRANGED

D673. Larry Adler; harmonica; Morton Gould & His Orchestra
RCA LM-2986/LSC-2986 (Original release); later released as RCA AGK1-3791,
CONTENTS: Arr. of Lullaby is called Lullabye Time

D674. Cleveland Orchestra; Riccardo Chailly, conducting
London 417326-2 LH, CD **[DDD]** (available also as LP or cassette)
Arr. for string orchestra
With AiP; Cuban; RiB

D674.1. Leopold Godowsky, III, piano (nephew of George); Royal Scottish National Orchestra; José Serebrier, conducting (debut recording for Godowsky)
"Gershwin: Centennial Edition"
Dinemec Classics *See*: Full entry at **D116.1**

D674.2. Ofra Harnoy, cello
Mastersound DFCDI-020 (dist. Allegro Imports), **CD [DDD]**
"Ofra Harnoy and Friends Play George Gershwin" p1990, ©1992
Includes Lullaby *See*: Full entry at **D735**

D675. Moscow Philharmonic Strings; D. Kitayenko, conducting
Lab TLP-27; CD-27
With music by **Glazunov, Copland, Griffes, Ives,** & **Shostakovich**

D676. Moscow Philharmonic Strings; Mayorga, piano; D. Kitayenko, conducting
Sheffield Lab TLP-28; CD-28; CS-28, cassette
With "I Got Rhythm" Var.; Preludes; Promenade; RiB; & other music
See: **B1099**

D677. St. Louis Symphony Orchestra; Leonard Slatkin, conducting
Murray Hill Records 932520, 4 discs (n.d.)

"Complete Concert Music of George Gershwin"
Version for string orchestra
With Concerto; Cuban Overture; Catfish Row Suite from P&B; AiP

D678. St. Louis Symphony; Leonard Slatkin, conducting
Angel CDC-49278, CD **[DDD]**
With AiP; Cuban; P&B suite

D679. Alicia Zizzo, piano; George Gershwin Festival Orchestra; Michael Charry,
conducting
Pro Arte CDD 514 **[DDD]**
Lullaby is a solo piano version
With RiB; Concerto; Cuban Overture (orch. only)
Producer: Eugene Simon
See: **B1020, B1022, B1049**

PROMENADE (WALKING THE DOG) (1937) **(W47)**

Orchestral versions

D680. **"The Gershwins in Hollywood: 1931–1964"** album
JJA Records 19773 Box Office label (Music Masters, NY)
Includes orig. *Walking the Dog* version from *Shall We Dance* movie soundtrack
See: **B1243,** Full entry at **D1097**

D681. Moscow Philharmonic; L. Mayorga, piano; Dmitri Kitayenko, conducting
Sheffield Lab TLP-28; CD-28; CAS-28, cassette (1989)
With "I Got Rhythm" Var.; Lullaby; Preludes; RiB; the CD includes Rialto
Ripples; Impromptu in Two Keys, & Summertime *See:* **B1099**

D682. St. Louis Symphony; Leonard Slatkin, conducting
Vox CT-2101, cassette; also avail. in Vox Box CDX-5007
"Complete Works . . ."
In Vox CT-2101 With AiP; Porgy
See: **B1269**

Promenade, arranged

D683. Jeanne Baxtresser (flute); Eric Robertson Trio
Pro Arte/Fanfare CDD-4D4 **[DDD]**; PCD-404, cassette
CONTENTS: Impromptu in Two Keys/Promenade; Swanee; With Bolling
Suite

D684. Ella Fitzgerald, vocals; Orchestra cond. by Nelson Riddle
Verve EP V 5069, LP, 7" **[GOH] "Ella Fitzgerald Sings the George and Ira
Gershwin Songbook"**; also avail. as deluxe ed. Verve MG V-4029-5
(1959)
CONTENTS: Ambulatory Suite, including: Promenade
(Walkin' the Dog arr. by Riddle); March of the Swiss Soldiers; Fidgety Feet;
With Preludes for piano

D685. J. Miltenberger (piano) (*aleatoric improvisations*)
    ACA digital Recording CM 20021
    CONTENTS: Nice Work If You Can Get It; Embraceable You; The Man I
    Love; But Not for Me; Our Love Is Here to Stay; Fascinating Rhythm;
    With **Aguila:** Son. 2; **Ginastera:** Son. 1; **S. Green:** Onata-say; **Morillo:** Son.
    4; **Solo piano version of Promenade**; With songs and works of other
    composers *See:* Full entry under **"Piano Music"**

D686. Leonard Pennario, piano
    Angel CDM 64668-2 **[ADD/DDD]**
    See: Full entry under **"Piano Music"**

D687. Leonard Pennario, piano
    Angel 4DS-37359, cassette (1986)
    "George Gershwin's Song Book & Other Music for Piano Solo"
    See: Full entry under **"Piano Music"**

D688. Richard Stoltzman, clarinet; London Symphony Orchestra; Michael
    Tilson Thomas and Eric Stern, conductors
    RCA Victor Red Seal 09026-61790-2 (BMG Classics), CD **[DDD]**
    Promenade arr. by Stanley Silverman
    See: Full Entry under **"Anthologies"**

SHORT STORY (1925) **(W39)**

D689. Samuel Dushkin, violin
    Gramophone Record Shop GP-794
    Violin/piano arr. by Dushkin

D690. Michael Tilson Thomas, piano
    CBS Masterworks IM 39699; MK 39699, CD
    Reconstructed version for solo piano *See:* **B1081, B1091, B1124**

D691. Kevin Cole
    Fanfare DFL-7007
    Original published version
    See: Full **CONTENTS** under **"Songs, Instrumental Treatment"**

ANTHOLOGIES

Some record labels and printed sources call these "Collections" or "Compilations" which terms seem apt because many times the selections are compiled from a number of different sources. The entries in this section include anthologies of Gershwin's classical and song production mixed on the same album, as well as compilations of works by Gershwin and other composers on the same recording. Gershwin songs only will be included under the sections **"Songs, Vocal Treatment"** and **"Songs, Instrumental Treatment."** Mixtures of vocal and instrumental treatment on the same album are included in this section. Compilations of Gershwin's classical compositions will generally be found under their respective titles, with a few exceptions (as in **D781**, e.g) listed here.

D692. Ron Abel and the S.T.A.G.E. Orchestra with an all star cast

MCAD2-10865 (2 CD Set) (1994)

"George and Ira Gershwin: A Musical Celebration"

SELECTED CONTENTS & PERFORMERS: Overture (Excerpts from RiB, AiP, P&B, & Concerto); Kickin' the Clouds Away **(Patty Tiffany)**; Could You Use Me? **(Betty Garrett & Dale Conyea)**; Somebody Loves Me **(Mary Gordon Murray)**; I Got Plenty O' Nuttin' **(Sam Harris)**; Embraceable You **(Mara Getz)**; I Love to Rhyme/Blah, Blah, Blah **(Christine Ebersole)**; But Not for Me **(Holly Near)**; They Can't Take That Away from Me **(Loretta Devine)**; Some Rain Must Fall **(Brian L. Green)**; How Long Has This Been Going On? **(Betty Buckley)**; Sam and Delilah **(Debbie Shapiro Gravitte)**; Strike Up the Band **(Carol Cooke)**; Heaven On Earth **(Davis Gaines)**; and performers **William Katt, Shaun Cassidy, Sherry Hursey, Jane Carr, Roger Rees, Linda Purl, Mariette Hartley, Billy Porter, Obba Bobatunde, Mary Jo Catlett, Shirley Jones, Bill Hutton, Lucie Arnaz, Kay Cole, Penny Fuller, Gogi Grant, Susan Johnson, Michelle Nicastro,** and others

Features I Got Rhythm and the 76-voice show capper, Our Love Is Here to Stay

An Aids Project Los Angeles tribute; Recorded live at the S.T.A.G.E. (Southland Theatre Artists Goodwill Event) benefit show, Feb. 6, 1993

See: Review in *Show Music,* Fall, 1994

D693. Larry Adler, harmonica virtuoso; Pro Arte orchestra; Francis Chagrin & Eric Robinson, conducting

Everest SDBR 3494 (19-?)

CONTENTS; RiB; With works by **Chagrin; Enesco; Bizet; Ravel; Granados; Benjamin**

D694. Larry Adler, harmonica

"Larry Adler Plays Gershwin, Porter, Kern, Rodgers, Gould, Arlen"

RCA AGK1-3791

Orchestra conducted by Morton Gould

CONTENTS: Three-Quarter Blues; Lullabye Time (Lullaby); Merry Andrew; With songs by the composers named above

Producer: Howard Scott

D695. Larry Adler, harmonica, w/ various singers

Mercury (Phonogram, London) 522 727 - 2, CD (1994)

"The Glory of Gershwin"

Various Artists and CONTENTS: Adler & George Martin (RiB); **Sting** (Nice work If You Can Get It); **Elton John** (Our Love Is Here To Stay & Someone To Watch Over Me); **Courtney Pine** (Summertime); **Carly Simon** (I've Got A Crush On You); **Lisa Stanfield** (They Can't Take That Away From Me); **Meat Loaf** (Somebody Loves Me); **Robert Palmer** (I Got Rhythm); **Issy Van Randwyck** (I'll Build a Stairway to Paradise); **Oleta Adams** (Embraceable You); **Kate Bush** (The Man I Love); **Cher** (It Ain't Necessarily So); **Peter Gabriel** (Summertime); **Elvis Costello** (But Not for Me); **Sinead O'Conner** (My Man's Gone Now); **Jon Bon Jovi** (How Long Has This Been Going On?)

Producer: George Martin; **Presented by** Jonathan Shalit

D696. Mimi Allen, Harp
Virtuosity Records NR 7656 (197-?)
"Mimi Allen Plays Gershwin"
CONTENTS: Summertime; It Ain't Necessarily So; I Got Plenty of
Nothin'; Bess, You Is My Woman Now; Our Love Is Here to Stay;
AiP/Fascinating Rhythm; Prelude II; I Got Rhythm; Love Walked In;
'S Wonderful!

D697. F. & A. Astaire (vocals); G. Gershwin (piano)
Pearl PEA 9483 **[AAD]**
CONTENTS: Hang on to Me; Fascinating Rhythm; The Half of It Dearie
Blues; I'd Rather Charleston ('G. Gershwin Plays') (rec. 1926) With
Concerto; Piano Music; Porgy (selections); RiB

D698. Atlantic Brass Quintet
Music Masters 01612-67104-2, CD (1994?)
"By George—Gershwin's Greatest Hits"
PERFORMERS: Joseph Damian Foley and Jeffrey Luke, trumpets; Kevin
Owen, horn; John Faieta, trombone, John Manning, tuba
CONTENTS: Foley, arr.: RiB, AiP, They Can't Take That Away from Me;
J. Luke, arr.: Someone To Watch Over Me, Strike Up the Band, A Foggy
Day, Fascinating Rhythm; Gale, arr.: Selections from Porgy and Bess *See*:
B1247

D699. Carlos Barbosa-Lima, guitar
Concord Records CC-2005 (1982)
**"Carlos Barbosa-Lima Plays the Music of Antonio Carlos Jobim and
George Gershwin"**
CONTENTS: Gershwin: Prelude No. 2; Prelude No. 1; Promenade;
Summertime; Swanee; 'S Wonderful!; Merry Andrew; The Man I Love;
With music by Carlos Barbosa-Lima

D700. Leon Bates, piano
Naxos 8.550341 **[DDD]**
CONTENTS: Three Preludes; Songs arr. Bates: Fascinating Rhythm;
Somebody Loves Me; Liza; The Man I Love; I Got Rhythm; Strike Up the
Band. Chick Corea: Twenty Children's Songs
Produced by Karol Kopernicky & Hubert Geschwandtner
See: **B1226, B1234, B1240**

D701. Jeanne Baxtresser (flute); Eric Robertson Trio
Pro Arte/Fanfare CDD-4D4 **[DDD]**; PCD-404, cassette
CONTENTS: Impromptu in Two Keys/Promenade; Swanee; With **Bolling**
Suite

D701.1 Joshua Bell, violin; London Symphony Orch.; John Williams, piano & conductor
Sony Classical SK 60659
"Gershwin Fantasy"
CONTENTS: Fantasy for Violin and Orchestra on Porgy and Bess (arr.
Alexander Courage): Prologue; It Ain't Necessarily So; I Got Plenty of
Nuttin'; My Man's Gone Now, Summertime; There's a Boat That's Leavin'

Soon for New York; Bess, You Is My Woman Now; Oh Bess, Oh, Where's
My Bess (cadenza written by Joshua Bell); Oh Lawd, I'm On My Way; **Three
Preludes** (Joshua Heifetz' transcriptions for Violin & Piano); **Songs for
Violin & Orch.:** I Got Rhythm; Embraceable You; Nice Work If You Can
Get It; Liza; But Not For Me; Sweet and Low Down (Gershwin piano roll);
Our Love Is Here to Stay
Producer & Recording Engineer: Shawn Murphy
Recorded at: Abbey Road Studio, No. 1, London Mar. 24, 26 & 28, 1998

D702. Leonard Bernstein, piano (in 1st & 2nd works); Los Angeles Philharmonic;
Leonard Bernstein, conducting
DG 410025-2 GH, CD **[DDD]**
CONTENTS: RiB; Prelude for Piano No. 2; and **Bernstein:** Symphonic
Dances from West Side Story
Program notes by Jack Gottlieb and technical notes on the recording in
English, German, French, and Italian inserted in container (12 pp.)

D703. Boston Pops Orchestra **"Fiedler Conducts Gershwin, I Got Rhythm"**
Ralph Votapek, piano (on Second Rhapsody); The Boston Pops; Arthur
Fiedler, conducting
London Phase-4 SPC 21185 (1979)
CONTENTS: Girl Crazy, suite (arr. Leroy Anderson); **Overtures** (all arr.
by Don Rose): Oh, Kay!, Funny Face, OTIS, Cake; Three Preludes (arr.
Gregory Stone); Wintergreen for President (arr. Walter Paul); Second
Rhapsody (rev. Robert McBride)
Excellent program notes by Tim McDonald & durations on container
Recorded June 15 & 17, 1979 *See*: **B1126, B1325**

D704. The Canadian Brass Quintet
RCA 6490-2-RC, CD **[DDD]**
"Strike Up the Band, The Canadian Brass Plays George Gershwin"
CONTENTS: Strike Up the Band; Someone to Watch Over Me; "The
Rhythm Series" (Medley): Clap Yo' Hands, Fidgety Feet, Fascinating
Rhythm, I Got Rhythm; A Foggy Day/Nice Work If You Can Get
It; The Man I Love; **P&B Suite:** Introduction/Jasbo Brown
Blues/Summertime, It Ain't Necessarily So, Bess, You Is My Woman
Now, I Loves You, Porgy, A Woman Is a Sometime Thing/I Got
Plenty O' Nuttin', Oh, Lawd, I'm On My Way; Rialto Ripples; 3 Piano
Preludes

D704.1. Matt Catingub, arranger, alto saxophone, piano, vocals
Concord Jazz CCD-4797-2 (1998)
"Gershwin 100"
With special guests: Louie Bellson - drums (The Man I Love); Rosemary
Clooney vocals (I've Got A Crush On You); Michael Feinstein - vocals &
piano (Home & Slap That Bass); John Pizzarelli- vocals & guitar (Lady Be
Good) and: Albert Alva, Gary Foster, Rusty Higgins, Sal Lozano,
Don Shelton - saxophones; Wayne Bergeron, George Graham,
Steve Huffsteter, Frank Szabo - trumpets; Andy Martin, Bob McChesney,
Chauncey Welsch -trombones; Tom Garvin - piano/Kevin Axt - rhythm
bass/Kevin Winard - drums & percussion, Big Band

CONTENTS: Blues For Mr. G; I Got Rhythm; They Can't Take That Away From Me; Soon; I've Got a Crush On You; Summertime; Your Eyes Your Smile!; Fascinating Rhythm; Home Blues; But Not For Me; Lady Be Good; Slap That Bass; How Long Has This Been Going On?; The Man I Love; There's a Boat That's Leavin' Soon for New York

D704.2 Cincinnati Pops Orchestra; Erich Kunzel, conducting
Telarc 2CD-80445 **"Gershwin Centennial Edition: The Complete Orchestral Collection"**
Performers: Cincinnati Pops Orchestra; Timothy Berens, banjo; Stewart Goodyear, piano; Richard Hawley, clarinet; William Tritt, piano; Central State University Chorus, William Henry Caldwell, director
CONTENTS: O Land Of Mine, America; Rhapsody in Blue; Second Rhapsody for Piano and Orchestra; Concerto; Variations on "I Got Rhythm"; Rialto Ripples Rag; An American in Paris; Cuban Overture; Lullaby; Walking The Dog; Mexican Dance; Catfish Row Suite
Notes from Telarc: "Erich Kunzel worked in cooperation with the Music Division of The Library of Congress to find the never-before-recorded 'O Land of Mine, America,' a work for chorus and orchestra written in 1919 as an entry in a magazine contest. *The New York American* offered a prize of $5,000 to the winning composer of an American anthem. Gershwin's entry (with lyrics by Michael E. Rourke of England) won honorable mention and a prize of $50.00. The other previously unrecorded piece, Mexican Dance, is based on the song 'Tamale (I'm Hot for You),' written in 1921. It was retitled by Gershwin when it was transcribed by Broadway orchestrator Frank Sadler."

D705. Frank Chacksfield & His Orchestra & Chorus; Kenny Baker, trpt.;
Michael Reeves, piano
London Phase 4 SW 95146-A & B **"The Glory That Was Gershwin"**
[GOH]
CONTENTS: PORGY AND BESS: Introduction; Rhapsody in Blue (abridged); With songs *See:* Full entry under **"Songs, Instrumental Treatment"**

D706. Frank Chacksfield and His Orchestra
London LL 1203-A & B **"The Music of George Gershwin"** [GOH]
CONTENTS: RiB; With songs *See:* Full entry under **"Songs, Instrumental Treatment"**

D707. Cincinnati Pops Orchestra; Erich Kunzel, conducting
Vox/Turnabout TV 34749 (1979)
"A Portrait of George"
CONTENTS: Gershwin Overtures: Oh, Kay!; Girl Crazy; Tiptoes; Of Thee I Sing; Our Love Is Here to Stay; Love Walked In; Nice Work If You Can Get It; Foggy Day; Strike Up the Band
Program notes by Richard Freed on container

D708. Denver Symphony Pops, Wayland, conducting
Pro Arte CDD-352, CD **[DDD]**;
CONTENTS: Swanee; Strike Up The Band Overture; AiP; Piano Music;

RiB

D709. Percy Faith and His Orchestra
Columbia Special Products EN2 13719-A, B, C, D, LP, 12" **[GOH]**
"The Columbia Album of George Gershwin"
CONTENTS: Side A: Fascinating Rhythm; A Foggy Day; Soon; I Got
Plenty O' Nuttin'; Embraceable You; Somebody Loves Me: **Side B:** I Got
Plenty O' Nuttin'; Summertime; Bess, You Is My Woman Now; My Man's
Gone Now; Nice Work If You Can Get It; For You, For Me, For Evermore;
Liza (All the clouds'll roll away); **Side C:** 'S Wonderful!; (Our) Love is Here
To Stay; They Can't Take That Away From Me; The Man I Love; Love
Walked In; Oh, Lady Be Good!; **Side D:** Preludes for Piano, Nos. 2 & 3;
Maybe; Someone to Watch Over Me; They All Laughed; Bidin' My Time; I
Got Rhythm

D710. Percy Faith and His Orchestra
Harmony Headliner KH 31538-A & B, Vol.2 **[GOH]**
CONTENTS: Preludes for piano 2 & 3; Fascinating Rhythm; A Foggy Day;
I Got Plenty O' Nuttin'; Embraceable You; Somebody Loves Me;
Summertime; Nice Work If You Can Get It; Bess, You Is My Woman Now;
My Man's Gone Now

D711. Wilhelmenia Fernandez, soprano, et al.; St. Louis Symphony Orchestra
Milan A249 & A250, 2 discs
"Gershwin in the Movies"
CONTENTS: RiB; Second Rhapsody; AiP; Medley from P&B; **Fernandez
singing:** Embraceable You, Our Love Is Here to Stay; Strike Up the Band,
But Not for Me; Somebody Loves Me, & 'S Wonderful! *See:* **B1283**

D712. George Feyer, piano; T. Lucas, guitar; G. Mell, bass; Sy Salzberg, drums **[GOH]**
Vanguard VSD 61-A & B **"George Feyer Plays the Essential George
Gershwin"** Also avail. in 1994 as OVC 6002, CD **[ADD]**
CONTENTS: Someone to Watch Over Me; Love Walked In; Let's Call
the Whole Thing Off; Somebody Loves Me; Soon; Fascinating Rhythm; Love
is Here to Stay; Mine; That Certain Feeling; Liza (All the clouds'll roll away);
An American in Paris [excerpts]; I'll Build a Stairway to Paradise; How Long
Has This Been Going On?; Bidin' My Time; I Got Rhythm; Clap Yo' Hands;
I've Got a Crush On You; Oh, Lady Be Good!; The Man I Love;
Summertime; It Ain't Necessarily So; Bess, You Is My Woman Now; I Got
Plenty O' Nuttin'; They Can't Take That Away From Me; He Loves and She
Loves; Of Thee I Sing (baby); Strike Up the Band; Preludes for piano [no. 2];
Who Cares?; Swanee; Love Is Sweeping the Country; Embraceable You; But
Not for Me; Do, Do, Do; Funny Face; Maybe; 'S Wonderful!; A Foggy Day;
Themes from Concerto in F; Rhapsody in Blue [excerpts]

D713. First Piano Quartet (originated by Edwin Fadiman)
RCA Victor LM 125, mono, 10 in. (19--?)
CONTENTS: RiB; AiP; Summertime; Bess, You Is My Woman Now; I Got
Plenty O' Nuttin'; The Man I Love; Strike Up the Band

D713.1. "Ella [Fitzgerald] and Louis [Armstrong] Sing Gershwin: Our Love is

Here to Stay"
Verve (Polygram) 314 539 679-2, CD (This Version © 1998)
CONTENTS: I Got Plenty O' Nuttin'; He Loves and She Loves; A Woman Is a Sometime Thing; They Can't Take That Away From Me; Let's Call the Whole Thing Off; Strike Up the Band; Things are Looking Up; They All Laughed; A Foggy Day; How Long Has This Been Going On?; Summertime; Love Is Here to Stay; There's a Boat Dat's Leavin' Soon for New York; 'S Wonderful!; I Was Doing Alright; Oh, Lady Be Good!
Original recordings were **produced by** Norman Granz

D714. Erroll Garner, piano
EmArcy 826 224-4 (1976)
"Erroll Garner Plays Gershwin and Kern"
Garner, Baldwin piano; Eddie Calhoun, bass; Kelly Martin, drums, on all selections except I Got Rhythm, where Calhoun and Martin are replaced by Charles "Ike" Isaacs, bass; Jimmy Smith, drums, & Jose Mangual, congas
CONTENTS: Strike Up the Band; Love Walked In; I Got Rhythm; Someone to Watch Over Me; A Foggy Day; Nice Work if You Can Get It; With songs by **Kern**

D715. "The George and Ira Gershwin Songbook"
RCA 9613-2-R, CD digitally remastered (© 1989 by BMG Music, recorded before 1972)
CONTENTS & PERFORMERS: They Can't Take That Away From Me (Perry Como, Mitchell Ayres and His Orchestra); Nice Work if You Can Get It (Dinah Shore, Harry Zimmerman's Orchestra & the Skylarks); Let's Call the Whole Thing Off (Norman Luboff Choir); A Foggy Day (John Gary, arr. and conducted by Marty Gold); 'S Wonderful! (Della Reese, Orchestra, John Cotter, conducting); Wintergreen for President (Hugo Winterhalter and His Orchestra); He Loves and She Loves (Julie Andrews, Irwin Kostal and His Orchestra); Who Cares? (Benny Goodman Quartet); Bidin' My Time (June Valli, Hugo Winterhalter and His Orchestra); Embraceable You (André Previn with voices); Strike Up the Band (Sid Ramin and His Orchestra); Love Walked In (Gogi Grant, Dennis Farnon and His Orchestra); Of Thee I Sing, Baby (Tommy Leonetti, Orchestra conducted by Van Alexander; I Was Doing All Right (Helen Humes, Red Norvo and His Orchestra); They All Laughed (Jaye P. Morgan, Hugo Winterhalter and His Orchestra); But Not for Me (Frankie Carle and His Orchestra); I've Got a Crush on You (Lou Monte, Joe Reisman and His Orchestra); Aren't You Kinda Glad We Did? (The Ames Brothers, Sid Ramin and His Orchestra); Looking for a Boy (Eartha Kitt, Henri Rene's Orchestra and Chorus); I Got Rhythm (Peter Nero, piano and arranger, Boston Pops Orchestra, Arthur Fiedler, conducting)
Program notes by Patrick Snyder and durations on insert in container
Digitally mastered at RCA Recording Studios, New York, December, 1988
Digital producer: Chick Crunpacker

D716. "Gershwin Conducts Excerpts from Porgy & Bess"
Mark 56 Records LP 667 (1974)

George Gershwin, piano including piano rolls; Abbie Mitchell, soprano; Edward Matthews, baritone; Ruby Elzy, soprano; Todd Duncan, bass-baritone; Anne Brown, soprano

CONTENTS: Piano roll medley: Rialto Ripples, On My Mind the Whole Night Long, Tee-Oodle-Um-Bum-Bo; Fascinating Rhythm; Liza; Second Prelude; I Got Rhythm; Porgy & Bess rehearsal of July 19, 1935: Introduction & Summertime (A. Mitchell); A Woman is a Something Thing (Matthews); My Man's Gone Now (Elzy); Bess, You is My Woman Now (Duncan & Brown)

Program notes by E. Jablonski on container *See:* **B928**

D717. George Gershwin, piano

Mark 56 Records 641-A-D **"Gershwin By Gershwin" [GOH]**

CONTENTS: Sides A & B: Rhapsody in Blue (Performed on Duo-Art reproducing piano); Concerto—from radio broadcast April 7, 1935; Variations on "I Got Rhythm"; Second Rhapsody—from rehearsal recording June 26, 1931; **Sides C & D:** Of Thee I Sing—from radio broadcast Feb. 19, 1934; The Man I Love—from radio broadcast Feb. 19, 1934; I Got Rhythm—from radio broadcast Feb. 19, 1934; Swanee—from radio broadcast Feb. 19, 1934; Fragment from Concerto, second mvt.—from radio broadcast April 7, 1935; Mine/I Got Rhythm—from radio broadcast April 30, 1934; Also from same broadcast: Variations; Love Is Sweeping the Country & Wintergreen for President; Hi-Ho (I. Gershwin, vocal & Harold Arlen, piano)

Produced by George Garabedian, in commemoration of the 75th anniversary of the birth of GG, a recorded documentary

See: **B280, B928, B1120, B1332**

D718. George Gershwin, piano rolls realized by Artis Wodehouse

Elektra\Nonesuch 79287-2 CD; 79287-4 cassette

"Gershwin Plays Gershwin: The Piano Rolls"

CONTENTS: *See:* Full entry under **"Recordings by Gershwin" D1122**

D719. George Gershwin, piano, on the piano solos; The original London cast of Primrose

Monmouth Evergreen MES 7071 (196-?)

"An American in London"

CONTENTS: Primrose: This is the Life for a Man; When Toby is out of Town; Some Far Away Someone; The Mophams; Berkeley Square and Kew; Boy Wanted; Mary, Queen of Scots; Wait A Bit, Susie; Naughty Baby; Ballet Music; That New Fangled Mother of Mine; I Make Hay When the Sun Shines; **George Gershwin Piano Solos:** Andante from RiB; Preludes Nos. 1, 2, & 3; Oh, Kay!; Do, Do, Do; Maybe; Someone to Watch Over Me; Clap Yo' Hands

Electronically adapted to simulate stereo

D720. George Gershwin, piano (Duo-Art piano rolls on RiB)

Distinguished Recordings 107 (1962)

"Gershwin Plays *Rhapsody in Blue*"

CONTENTS: RiB; Gershwin, 3 songs from 1925: Kickin' the Clouds Away, That Certain Feeling, Sweet and Low-Down; J. Kern: Left All Alone Again

Blues, Whose Baby Are You?; R. Whiting: Ain't You Coming Back to
Dixie?; Sam Coslow, Grieving For You

**D721. "The Gershwin Collection, A Historical Treasury of the Music of George
Gershwin"**
Teledisc USA TD 10, 5 discs, LP (1987)
Various performers, see below
CONTENTS & PERFORMERS: **Side 1-A:** When You Want 'Em You
Can't Get 'Em, When You've Got 'Em You Don't Want 'Em (George
Bassman); Love Is Sweeping the Country (Ella Fitzgerald); I've Got
Beginner's Luck (Fred Astaire/Johnny Green); Aren't You Kind of Glad
We Did? (Judy Garland/Dick Haymes); Liza (All the Clouds Will Roll
Away (Art Tatum); Clap Yo' Hands (Doris Day); **Side 1-B:** Fascinating
Rhythm (The Hi-Lo's); I've Got a Crush on You (Lee Wiley/Bobby
Hackett); I Was Doing All Right (Artie Shaw); 'S Wonderful (Dinah
Shore/Buddy Clark); I Loves You, Porgy (Diana Ross); Bess, You is My
Woman Now (Roger Williams); **Side 2-A:** Maybe (Bing Crosby); Who
Cares? (Helen O'Connell/Jimmy Dorsey); Bidin' My Time (The
Foursome); But Not For Me (Helen Forrest/Harry James); That Certain
Feeling (Bob Hope); A Foggy Day (Oscar Peterson); **Side 2-B:** Let's Call
the Whole Thing Off (Billie Holiday); The Man I Love (Lena Horne);
Mine (Percy Faith Orchestra); Oh, Lady Be Good! (Benny Goodman
Trio); My Man's Gone Now (Sarah Vaughan/Hal Mooney); OTIS
(Andrews Sisters); **Side 3-A:** Someone to Watch Over Me (Willie
Nelson); He Loves and She Loves (Julie Andrews/Irwin Kostal); Nice
Work if You Can Get It (Tommy Dorsey/Edythe Wright); There's a
Boat Dat's Leavin' Soon for New York (John Bubbles); For You, For
Me, Forever More (Judy Garland/Dick Haymes); Soon (Les Brown &
His Band of Renown); They All Laughed (Tony Bennett); **Side 3-B:** It
Ain't Necessarily So (Ella Fitzgerald/Louis Armstrong); Looking for a
Boy (GG); Love Walked In (The Hilltoppers); Swanee (Al Jolson);
Strike Up the Band (Arthur Fiedler/Boston Pops); Summertime (Billie
Holiday); **Side 4-A:** I Got Plenty O' Nuthin' (Sammy Davis, Jr.); Do, Do,
Do (Tommy & Jimmy Dorsey); The Real American Folk Song (Is A
Rag) (Ella Fitzgerald/Nelson Riddle); Slap That Bass (Fred Astaire/Johnny
Green); Do It Again (Judy Garland); Wintergreen For President (André
Kostelanetz); Somebody Loves Me (Four Lads); **Side 4-B:** They Can't Take
That Away From Me (Louie Prima/Keely Smith); How Long Has This Been
Going On? (Peggy Lee/Benny Goodman); I'll Build a Stairway to Paradise
(Paul Whiteman); Embraceable You (Johnny Mathis); I Got Rhythm (Ethel
Merman); [Our] Love is Here to Stay (Andy Williams); **Side 5-A:** Concerto
(André Previn/London Symphony Orch.); **Side 5-B:** AiP (NY Philharmonic,
Leonard Bernstein, conducting); RiB (GG, piano; Paul Whiteman Orchestra;
Nathaniel Shilkret, conducting; Recorded Apr. 21, 1927)
Program notes with many photographs (17 pp.) by Edward Jablonski in
attractive booklet inserted
The above collection available from: **Teledisc USA**, 300 Park Avenue, New
York, NY 10022
See: **B977, B1245, B1270, B1295**

D722. "Gershwin's Greatest Hits"

Performers: Nigel Simpson, piano; Royal Promenade Orchestra of London
(RiB, AiP); Russell Sherman, piano; Orchestra of St. Luke's; Gunther
Schuller, conducting (Concerto only); Rochester Pops, Erich Kunzel,
conducting; (Philarte [string] Quartet, from Philadelphia Orchestra)
Pro Arte CDM-814
CONTENTS: RiB; AiP; Concerto, 1st movement only; "Gershwin in
Hollywood" (Rochester Pops); Lullaby (Philarte [string] Quartet)

D723. "Gershwin's Greatest Hits"
CBS MLK-39454, CD; PMT-39454, cassette
CONTENTS: Concerto-finale (Previn, Kostelanetz, Orch.); Porgy & Bess,
a symphonic picture-excerpts (Ormandy, Philadelphia Orchestra) AiP;
Preludes; RiB

D724. "Gershwin Performs Gershwin: Rare Recordings 1931-1935"
MusicMasters 5062-4-C
See: Full entry under **"Recordings by Gershwin"**

D725. "George Gershwin Plays George Gershwin"
Pavilion Records Pearl GEMM CDS 9483, 2 CDs **[AAD]** (p 1991)
CONTENTS: *See:* Full entry under **"Recordings by Gershwin"**

D726. "George Gershwin Plays Rhapsody in Blue"
Klavier KCXD, CD (1989)
CONTENTS: Rhapsody in Blue; That Certain Feeling; Tee-Oodle-Um-
Bum-Bo; Kickin' the Clouds Away; Sweet and Low-Down; So Am I;
Drifting Along with the Tide; I Was So Young, You Were So Beautiful; Left
All Alone Blues; Whip-Poor-Will; Whose Baby Are You?; Rock-A-Bye
Lullaby Land; **Berlin:** For Your Country and My Country; **Kern:** Land
Where the Good Songs Go; **Whiting:** Ain't You Comin' Back to Dixie? and
Some Sunday Morning

D727. "Gershwin Revisited"
Painted Smiles 1357

D728. "The Gershwin Years"
Decca DXSZ 7160, DL 78910-78912 (1959) 3 discs
Paula Stewart, Richard Hayes, Lynn Roberts, singers; chorus and orchestra,
George Bassman, selector, arranger, coordinator, and conductor
See: Full entry at **D808, B1288, B1293, B1296**

D729. Jack Gibbons, **"The Authentic Gershwin,"** Vol. I
ASV 2074
CONTENTS: Come to the Moon; I Was So Young; Tee-Oodle-Um-Bum-
Bo; Nobody But You; Drifting Along With the Tide; RiB

D730. Richard Glazier, piano
Centaur Records CRC, CD 2271 **[DDD]**
"Gershwin: Remembrance and Discovery"
Release Date: February 10, 1996
CONTENTS: Embraceable You (Earl Wild); Somebody Loves Me (Earl Wild);

Jilted (from OTIS); Meadow Serenade (from *Strike up the Band);* Love Walked In (Percy Grainger); The Man I Love (Percy Grainger); Impromptu in 2 keys (from the unpublished song file of Ira Gershwin -- the original version which is different than the published version); Sleepless Night (unpublished song file); Three Preludes; Three Quarter Blues (unpublished song file); They Can't Take That Away From Me (based on the original orchestrations from the movie *Shall We Dance*); Promenade (from *Shall We Dance*); Ballet Music (from the musical Primrose); Sixteen Bars Without a Name (dedicated to Beryl Rubinstein)

Rubinstein was a friend of Gershwin. Dr. Glazier discovered the following "Porgy" transcriptions at the Cleveland Institute of Music where Rubinstein taught from 1924-1952:

Bess You Is My Woman (Rubinstein transcription); Summertime (Rubinstein transcription); I Got Plenty O' Nuttin' (Rubinstein transcription); Melody #40 (Sylvia Rabinof transcription, commissioned by Dr. Glazier)

D731. Stewart Goodyear, Keith Lockhart, and William Tritt, piano.
American Piano Classics: Anderson, Joplin, Gould, Bowman, Gottschalk, Gershwin. Cincinnati Pops Orchestra; Erich Kunzel, conductor; Telarc CD-80112 (1993)
CONTENTS: Second Rhapsody is 1931 version; With piano music by Leroy Anderson: Louis Moreau Gottschalk/Hershy Kay; Euday Bowman; Scott Joplin; and Morton Gould; *See:* Full entry under **"Piano Music"**
Review in *American Music* 13/2 (Summer 1995): 260

D732. **"The Great Vocalists Sing the Gershwin Songbook."**
Blue Note CDP 80506-2
CONTENTS AND ARTISTS: Sixteen previously recorded tunes, including: Embraceable You (**Nat King Cole**); Summertime (**Nina Simone**); But Not for Me (**Chet Baker**); The Man I Love (**Carmen McRae**); I Was Doing All Right (**Annie Ross**); I Got Rhythm (**Sarah Vaughan**); Someone to Watch Over Me (**Nancy Wilson**); They Can't Take That Away From Me (**June Christy**); They All Laughed (**David Allyn**); Do Do Do (**Mel Tormé**); Aren't You Kind of Glad We Did? (**Peggy Lee**); How Long Has This Been Going On? (**Johnny Hartman**); RiB, et al.

D733. Grierson & Kane, pianos
Angel CDM-69119
"'S Wonderful!"
CONTENTS: Oh, Lady Be Good!; Embraceable you; Fascinating Rhythm; The Man I Love; Strike Up the Band; 'S Wonderful!; AiP; Preludes (duo-piano arrangements)

D734. Dave Grusin, piano
GRP Records GRC-2005, cassette; also avail. as CD with informative booklet (1991)
"The Gershwin Connection"
Personnel: Dave Grusin and Friends: Chick Corea, piano; Lee Ritenour, guitar; Gary Burton, vibes; Eddie Daniels, clarinet; John Patitucci, bass; Dave Weckl, drums; Don Grusin, T-3 Clavinet; Eric Marienthal, alto & soprano sax; Sal Marquez, trumpet; Sonny Emory, drums; David Nadien, concertmaster of

string section, conducted by Ettore Strata; (Personnel varies on the different songs)

CONTENTS: That Certain Feeling (perf. by GG from piano roll); Soon (w/ Eddie Daniels, clar.); Fascinating Rhythm; Prelude II (for clarinet & rhythm section); How Long Has This Been Going On?; There's a Boat Dat's Leavin' Soon for New York; Maybe; My Man's Gone Now; Our Love Is Here to Stay; 'S Wonderful! (Corea & Grusin); I've Got Plenty O' Nuttin'; Nice Work If You Can Get It; Medley: Bess, You Is My Woman/I Loves You Porgy

Executive Producers: Dave Grusin & Larry Rosen *See*: **B1320**

D735. Ofra Harnoy, cello

Mastersound DFCDI-020 (dist. Allegro Imports), **CD [DDD]**

"Ofra Harnoy and Friends Play George Gershwin" p1990, ©1992

Performers: Ofra Harnoy, cello; Helena Bowkun, Michael Dussek, Catherine Wilson, piano; Paul Brodie, saxophone; Shauna Rolston, cello; Orford String Quartet; Canadian Piano Trio; Trio Vivant. Recorded in Toronto.

CONTENTS: Porgy and Bess. Summertime (2:11); Variations on Summertime (2:01); It Ain't Necessarily So (2:43); Bess, You Is My Woman Now (5:00); Clara, Clara (3:51); Reprise : Bess You Is My Woman Now (3:41); I Got Plenty O' Nothin' (2:41); There's a Boat Dat's Leavin' Soon for New York (4:41); O Gee, O Joy (2:24); Love Is Sweeping the Country (2:40); Lullaby (6:59); Stairway to Paradise (3:30); The Man I Love (4:39); Prelude No. 2 (3:20); Variations on "I Got Rhythm" (8:30)

D736. Leonid Hambro, piano; Gershon Kingsley, keyboard & electronic synthesizer

Avco Embassy AVE 33021

"Gershwin: Alive & Well & Underground" (1970)

CONTENTS: RiB; I Got Rhythm; PORGY AND BESS Introduction and opening scene; Summertime; My Man's Gone Now; It Ain't Necessarily So; Clara, Clara, Don't You be Downhearted; Crown's Killing

D736.1. Herbie Hancock, leader and piano

Verve 314557797-2, CD (1998)

"Gershwin's World"

Performers: Herbie Hancock, Eddie Henderson, Kathleen Battle, Chick Corea, Joni Mitchell, Wayne Shorter, Stevie Wonder, and the Orpheus Chamber Orchestra, et al.

CONTENTS: 1. Overture (Fascinating Rhythm-Hancock) :55; 2. It Ain't Necessarily So (Eddie Henderson, trumpet, et al) 4:43 ; 3. The Man I Love (Joni Mitchell, vocal) 5:56; 4. Here Come de Honey Man (Henderson, tpt, et al) 3:58; 5. St. Louis Blues (W. C. Handy-Stevie Wonder, vocal) 5:49; 6. Lullaby (Hancock w/ Orpheus)11:04; 7. Blueberry Rhyme (Corea & Hancock) 3:29; 8. It Ain't Necessarily So (Interlude-Henderson) 1:23; 9. Cotton Tail (Duke Ellington-Wayne Shorter) 4:42; 10. Summertime (Joni Mitchell, vocal) 4:41; 11. My Man's Gone Now (Hancock) 1:56; 12. Prelude in C# minor (Kathleen Battle) 4:42; 13. Concerto for Piano and Orchestra in G, 2nd movement (Maurice Ravel-Hancock) 9:11; 14. Embraceable You (Hancock) 4:38

Producer: Robert Sadin

Executive Producers: Herbie & David Passock

Reviewed (positively) by Bill Milkowski in *JazzTimes* 28/10
(December 1998): 137-138.

D737. Jascha Heifetz, violin; Emanuel Bay, piano
Decca DLP 7003, 10 in., mono (orig. 1946, 1949)
"Heifetz Playing the Music of Gershwin"
CONTENTS: Summertime; A Woman Is a Sometime Thing; My Man's
Gone Now; It Ain't Necessarily So; Tempo de Blues; Bess, You is My
Woman Now; Prelude No. 1; Prelude No. 2; Prelude No. 3
Arrangements by Heifetz

D738. Jascha Heifetz, violin; Brooks Smith, piano
RCA LSC 2856 (1965)
"Heifetz Plays Gershwin" "Heifetz Plays Music of France"
CONTENTS: Three Preludes; P&B selections: Summertime, A Woman
is a Sometime Thing; My Man's Gone Now; It Ain't Necessasrily So;
Bess, You Is My Woman; Tempo di Blues; With music of Debussy,
Ravel, Poulenc, Saint-Saens, & Ibert
Program notes by Francis Robinson on container *See*: **B1246, B1254,
B1255, B1265**

D739. **"Earl Hines Plays the Music of George Gershwin"**
Classic Jazz TCJ 31, cassette (1981)
Earl 'Fatha' Hines, piano
CONTENTS: RiB; A Foggy Day; Love is Here to Stay; They All Laughed;
Somebody Loves Me; Embraceable You; Let's Call the Whole Thing
Off; They Can't Take That Away from Me; Love Walked In; Summetime
Recorded in Milan, Italy, on Oct. 16, 1973

D740. Hollywood Bowl Orchestra; John Mauceri, conducting; Gregory Hines & Patti
Austin, vocals
Philips 434 274-4, cassette (1991)
"The Gershwins in Hollywood"
CONTENTS: Side 1: Overture: Gershwin in Hollywood (pub. Chappell);
New York Rhapsody, piano solo by Wayne Marshall; Walking the Dog;
With various songs written for movies
See: Full entry under **"Music Used in Films"**

D741. John Holmquist & Daniel Estrem, guitars
ProArte PCD 226, cassette (1985)
"Gershwin by Guitar"
CONTENTS: Promenade; Merry Andrew; Three-quarter Blues; A Foggy
Day; Do It Again; Somebody Loves Me; Summertime; Rialto Ripples;
Three Preludes; Jasbo Brown Blues; I Was Doing All Right; Oh, Lady
Be Good!; Sweet & Low Down; Love Is Here To Stay; My One and
Only; The Man I Love; Nobody But You; Who Cares?; I Got Rhythm
Favorite melodies of Gershwin played in arrangements for two guitars;
works transcribed & arranged by Daniel Estrem *See*: **B1319**

D742. **"I Got Rhythm: The Music of George Gershwin,"** 4 CDs or cassettes
BMG-RCA 1247-1-4 (This compilation © 1995)
The Smithsonian Collection of Recordings, POB 2122, Colchester, VT 05449-

2122 (As of 1995)

CONTENTS: Over 60 G selections performed by various artists, including AiP, RiB, Variations on "I Got Rhythm", and the three Piano Preludes, all with G performing; The material is divided on the four CDs among the following categories: **"Gershwin and the Popular Song;"; "Gershwin on Stage and Screen"; "Gershwin in the Concert Hall;" and "Gershwin and Jazz."** An informative 64-page booklet is included with the set.

Performers: Among the many performers included in addition to Gershwin himself are: Alleen Stanley (Somebody Loves Me), Ethel Waters (I've Got Rhythm), Lee Wiley (Someone to Watch Over Me), Vaughn Monroe (Aren't You Kinda Glad We Did?), Sarah Vaughan (Isn't It a Pity?), Tony Bennett ([Our] Love is Here to Stay), Irene Bordoni (I Won't Say I Will), NBC Radio Orchestra (Overture to OTIS), Lyda Roberti (My Cousin in Milwaukee), Todd Duncan (I Got Plenty o' Nuttin'), Ella Logan (I Was Doing All Right), John W. Bubbles (It Ain't Necessarily So), Billie Holiday (Summertime), Benny Goodman & His Orchestra (Somebody Loves Me), Chet Baker (Love Walked In), Gertrude Lawrence (Someone to Watch Over Me), Fred Astaire, Judy Garland, Lena Horne, and more
See: **B1267**

D743. Peter Jablonski, piano; V. Ashkenazy, cond.; Royal Philharmonic Orchestra
London 430542 **[DDD]**
CONTENTS: Concerto in F; 3 Preludes; **Barber:** Ballade; **Copland:** Four Piano Blues & El Salón México for Piano *See:* **B1027, B1039, B1227**

D744. Hyperion Knight, piano and conductor, with chamber orchestra
Stereophile No. ? (avail. from P. O. Box 1702, Sante Fe, NM 87504, USA)
With *Three Preludes*, arr. for pa./orch by Joe Cea; *Four Songs*, transcr. by Earl Wild: Fascinatin' Rhythm; The Man I Love; I Got Rhythm (Etude No.6); Embraceable You (Etude No. 4)
Five Songs, transcr. by Joe Cea and Hyperion Knight:
Let's Call the Whole Thing Off; Someone to Watch Over Me; They Can't Take That Away from Me; Love is Here to Stay; A Foggy Day
Porgy and Bess Fantasy, by Earl Wild
Recorded at: First United Methodist Church, Albuquerque, MN, Mar. 10-12, 1997
Engineer: John Atkinson
Executive Producer: Gretchen Grogan *See:* **B1109**

D745. André Kostelanetz, conducting; Orchestra
Columbia CL 2133 (1964)
"Gershwin Wonderland"
CONTENTS: Principally excerpts from musical comedies, arranged, based on live Kostelanetz concert at Lincoln Center, 1963
Program notes by IG on container
LC card no. 64-23 *See:* **B1253**

D746. Oscar Levant, piano; André Kostelanetz, conducting (RiB)
Medallion MK-130
"Oscar Levant—For the Record" *See:* **F19, D1096, B1583**
CONTENTS: Levant's recollections and performances of G music; Four

songs cut from the soundtrack of AiP, including My Cousin from
Milwaukee; Abbreviated version of RiB; **O. Levant**: Piano Concerto

D747. Oscar Levant, piano; Alfred Wallenstein, Samuel Kayien, André Kostelanetz,
  conducting
  Medallion ML 310   **"Oscar Levant: For the Record"**
  CONTENTS: Piano Concerto (Levant) 1942; Four Sequences (Levant);
    Charlie Chan at the Opera 1936 film; Gershwin: A portrait by Levant
    (Levant) n.d. *See*: **B1583**

D748. Claudia Lindsey, soprano; Benjamin Matthews, bass-baritone;
  Slovak Philharmonic Orchestra; Ettore Stratta, conducting
  Moss Music Group D-MMG 103 (1981, 1980)
  CONTENTS: Girl Crazy Overture arranged as a symphonic potpourri by
    Don Rose; Selections from P&B: Introduction; Summertime; A Woman Is a
    Sometime Thing; My Man's Gone Now; I Got Plenty O' Nuttin'; Bess, You
    Is My Woman Now; Oh, I Can't Sit Down; It Ain't Necessarily So; I Loves
    You, Porgy; There's A Boat Dat's Leavin' Soon for New York; Oh, Lawd,
    I'm On My Way
  Finale recorded in Czechoslovakia under co-production of OPUS
    Czechoslovakia, in Aug. 1980
  Program notes, synopsis of the opera, & biographical notes on the performers
    on container

D749. Los Angeles Philharmonic; various conductors
  Citadel CT 7025 (1981, 1937)
  "George Gershwin Memorial Concert, September 8, 1937"
  CONTENTS: Prelude No. 2 (arr. & cond. by Otto Klemperer); Concerto,
    Allegro (Oscar Levant, piano; Charles Previn, conducting); Swanee (Al
    Jolson); The Man I Love (Gladys Swarthout); The Can't Take That
    Away from Me (Fred Astaire); Excerpts from the Opera Porgy & Bess
    (Lily Pons, Anne Brown, Ruby Elzy, Todd Duncan; Hall Johnson Choir;
    Los Angeles Philharmonic, Alexander Steinert, conducting)
  "The historic recordings in this album were made available by . . . Mr. Ira
    Gershwin"
  Program notes by Michael Feinstein & Celia Grail on container
  See: **B1252, W54a**

D750. Adam Makowicz, piano; Dave Holland & Charlie Haden, bass; Al Foster,
  drums
  RCA (Novus) 3022-2-N, CD, digital (1987)
  "Adam Makowicz—Naughty Baby Honoring George Gershwin"
  CONTENTS: Prelude II; RiB (6:13 version); With songs [All arrangements
    by Makowicz] *See*: Full entry under **"Songs, Instrumental Treatment"**

D751. Mark 56 Records 800 **"Songs of George & Ira Gershwin 1920s"**-Vol. II
  [GOH] An original Thomas Alva Edison Re-recording
  CONTENTS: Fascinating Rhythm; Liza & Do What You Do!; Song of the
    Flame; Say So; Tell Me More; Somebody Loves Me; The Man I Love;
    Rhapsody in Blue, Frank Banta, piano

D752. "Midora Matsuya Plays George Gershwin"
Camerata 32CM-169, available from Koch Imports
CONTENTS: RiB (piano solo arr.); Three Preludes for Piano; Songbook

D753. Lincoln Mayorga, piano; Moscow Philharmonic; Dmitri Kitayenko, conducting
Sheffield Lab CD-28 (1989)
CONTENTS: RiB; "I Got Rhythm" Variations; Promenade; Three Preludes;
Rialto Ripples; Impromptu in Two Keys; Lullaby; Summertime
See: **B1099**

D754. "Memorial Album to George Gershwin"
Jane Froman; Sonny Schuyler; Felix Knight; Nathaniel Shilkret; The Victor
Salon Group
Recorded from the Magic Key Gershwin Memorial Program of July 10,
1938
RCA Victor C29 (12332-12336), 5 discs, 78, 12 in. (194-?)
CONTENTS: Gems from OTIS, Girl Crazy, P&B, Oh, Kay!, Lady, Be
Good!, Tip-Toes, including: Wintergreen for President; Who Cares?;
Of Thee I Sing; Love Is Sweeping the Country; I Got Rhythm; Bidin' My
Time; Embraceable You; The Man I Love; RiB (middle movement, arr.
Shilkret); Gems from P&B: Introduction; I Got Plenty of Nuttin'; My
Man's Gone Now; Summertime; Bess, You Is My Woman Now; Oh, I
Can't Sit Down; It Ain't Necessarily So

D755. Munich Brass (Richard Steuart & Josef Bierlmeyer, trumpets; Michael Lösch,
horn; Michael Stöhr & Richard Roblee, trombones; Finn Schumacker, tuba;
Giuseppe Solera, flute, clarinet, & saxophone; Norman Shetler, piano)
"George Gershwin: Rhapsody in Brass"
Orfeo C306 931 A **[DDD]** (Qualiton Imports)
CONTENTS: Arrangements of AiP; RiB; The Man I Love; Cuban
Overture; Somebody Loves Me; I Got Fascinating Rhythm - Medley (I
Got Fascinating Rhythm, Love Walked In, Someone to Watch Over Me,
But Not for Me, I Got Rhythm, Fascinating Rhythm)

D756. Musical Heritage Society 4865 (© 1981 by RCA Records, France)
"The Works for Solo Piano"
CONTENTS: RiB (orig. version for piano solo); Piano Preludes; **Song
Book**: The Man I Love, Swanee, Nobody But You, I'll Build a Stairway
to Paradise, Do It Again, Fascinating Rhythm, Oh, Lady Be Good!,
Somebody Loves Me

D757. NBC Symphony; Arturo Toscanini, conducting
RCA Victor Gold Seal 09026-60207-2 **[DDD]**, CD
CONTENTS: AiP; **Sousa:** El Capitan & Stars & Stripes Forever; **Grofé:**
Grand Canyon Suite; **Barber:** Adagio for Strings; **Smith:** The Star
Spangled Banner
Producer: John Pfeiffer
Part of the RCA Toscanini Reissue series *See*: **B1244**

D758. NBC Symphony, Arturo Toscanini, conducting (RiB); New York Philharmonic,
Morton Gould, conducting ("I Got Rhythm" Variations); Arthur Schwarz

(on song)
PR 42-A (Music Masters, formerly of NY)
"Gershwin—135th Street (Blue Monday)"
CONTENTS: 135th Street (Blue Monday); RiB; "I Got Rhythm"
Variations; Mischa, Jascha, Toscha, Sascha
Omnibus T. V. performance of Mar. 29, 1953

D759. Peter Nero, piano; Boston Pops Orchestra; Arthur Fiedler, conducting
RCA ANL1-1970 Nero Goes "Pops"
CONTENTS: RiB; (Our) Love is Here To Stay; Embraceable You; The Man I
Love; They Can't Take That Away From Me; Bidin' My Time; I Got Rhythm

D760. New American String Ensemble
Sine Qua Non 74810-4
"Gershwin On Broadway"
CONTENTS: RiB arr.; Embraceable You; A Foggy Day; Oh, Lady Be
Good!; But Not For Me; Someone to Watch Over Me; Summertime; I
Got Plenty of Nuttin'; It Ain't Necessarily So; Portrait of You

D761. The New York Banjo Ensemble
Kicking Mule Records KM 224 (1982)
"The New York Banjo Ensemble Plays Gershwin"
CONTENTS: RiB, arr.; Swanee; I'll Build A Stairway to Paradise; Strike
Up the Band; Oh, Lady Be Good!; 'S Wonderful!; Sweet and
Low-Down; Clap Yo' Hands; Prelude No. 2; AiP; Impromptu in Two
Keys; Rialto Ripples

D762. Ricardo Odnoposoff, violin; Hans Richter-Haaser, Jean Antonietti, & Hans
Priegnitz, piano accompanists
Bayer BR 200004, CD **[ADD]** monaural
Porgy & Bess (suite arr. by Jascha Heifetz for Violin & Piano); With
other works by Kreisler, Albéniz-Heifetz, Tartini, Mozart, Falla, &
Paganini

D763. **"Fascinatin' Rampal: Jean-Pierre Rampal Plays Gershwin"**
CBS Records BL 39700 (1985)
CONTENTS: AiP; Preludes; and Songs
See: Full entry under **"Songs, Instrumental Treatment," D1060**

D764. David Rose and His Orchestra
M-G-M E 3123-A & B **[GOH]**
"Love Walked In—The Music of George Gershwin"
CONTENTS: **Side A:** Embraceable You; Someone to Watch Over Me;
(Our) Love is Here to Stay (Gershwin) Goldwyn Follies 1938 film; Liza (All
the clouds'll roll away) G. & I. Gershwin-Kahn) SHOW GIRL 1929; Love
Walked In; Fascinating Rhythm; **Side B:** Somebody Loves Me; AiP;
Summertime; RiB; I've Got a Crush On You; The Man I Love

D765. Russell Sherman, piano; Orchestra of St. Luke's; Gunther Schuller,
conducting
Pro Arte CCD 244, completely digital (1986)

CONTENTS: Concerto (F. Grofé arr. for Paul Whiteman); Three
Preludes; The Man I Love; Somebody Loves Me; Fascinating Rhythm
"American Artists Series"
Program notes by David Eagle & durations on insert in container
Recorded June 19-20, 1985, at Masonic Hall, NY *See*: **B1038, B1042**

D766. Slovak Phil. Orch.; Kamil Haba, piano; Libor Pesak, conducting (RiB & AiP)
Madacy BC-4-3609, cassette; avail. on CD
CONTENTS: RiB; AiP; Selections from P&B (Vienna Philharmonic, Simon
Gale, conducting); Songs (Alexander's Sound Orchestra); piano selections
(Eugen Cicero, pa.)

D767. Leo Smit, piano
Dot DLP 3111 (1958?)
**"The Masters Write Jazz (Stravinsky, Hindemith, Gershwin, Copland,
Milhaud, Tansman)"**
Works of the composers named above *See*: **B1263**

D768. **"'S Wonderful! 'S Marvelous! 'S Gershwin!"**
Daybreak DR 2009 (1972) **[NN-L] [GOH]**
Performers: Jack Lemmon, Fred Astaire, Leslie Uggams, Peter Nero;
Larry Kert; Linda Bennett; Robert Guillaume; Alan Johnson; Elliot
Lawrence Orchestra, with chorus
An original soundtrack recording of the television special originally
presented by the Bell System Family Theatre
CONTENTS: 'S Wonderful!/Mose Gumbel comment (all comments,
except one by Jimmy Fidler, read by Jack Lemmon); RiB (finale)/Max
Dreyfus comment; Someone to Watch Over Me/My One and Only/The
Man I Love (Uggams); (Our) Love is Here to Stay (Kert)/Stairway to
Paradise (Guillaume)/But Not For Me (Bennett); I've Got a Crush on
You/Looking for a Boy (Lemmon); AiP/Concerto in F/RiB (Nero with
orch./Paul Whiteman comment, Jimmy Fidler comment/'S Wonderful!/Oh,
Lady Be Good!/They All Laughed/Fascinating Rhythm/A Foggy Day/Let's
Call the Whole Thing Off/They Can't Take That Away from Me (Astaire);
P&B medley: Summertime (Uggams)/comment/A Woman Is a Sometime
Thing (Kert)/ Bess, You Is My Woman Now (Guillaume);/I Got Plenty O'
Nuttin' (Nero)/It Ain't Necessarily So (Lemmon)/Strawberry (Guillaume)/I
Loves You Porgy (Uggams)/There's a Boat Dat's Leavin' Soon for New
York (Guillaume & Kert)/I'm On My Way (entire company); **Finale:**
Embraceable You (entire company)/Obituary (Jack Lemmon)
Musical arrangements by Elliot Lawrence
Program notes by Sonny Burke on container
Produced by Sonny Burke
LC card no. r72-760225 *See*: **B922**

D769. Marcus Roberts, piano, with members of the Orchestra of St. Luke's and
the Lincoln Center Jazz Orchestra, Robert Sadin, conducting
Sony SK-68488, CD
"Marcus Roberts: Portraits in Blue"
CONTENTS: RiB, in a new interpretation/improvisation by Roberts;
Yamekraw (James P. Johnson); "I Got Rhythm" Variations, also in a new

version by Roberts
See: **B1249,** and a negative review in *ARG* (Nov./Dec. 1996): 127

D770. Stöckigt, piano; Leipzig Gewandhaus Orchestra; K. Masur, conducting (RiB);
San Francisco Symphony; Ozawa, conducting (Russo); Boston Pops Orchestra;
Fiedler, conducting (Rags)
Deutsche Grammophon [Musikfest] DG 413258-4 GMF, cassette
"Rhapsody in Blue"
With music by **William Russo** (Street Music, Op. 65, Pt. 3); Rags by
Joplin, E. Blake, Berlin, & Bowman

D771. Richard Stoltzman, clarinet; London Symphony Orchestra; Michael
Tilson Thomas and Eric Stern, conductors
RCA Victor Red Seal 09026-61790-2 (BMG Classics), CD **[DDD]**
CONTENTS: Promenade arr. by Stanley Silverman; Bess, You Is My Woman
Now, Short Story, and Three Preludes; music by **Copland, Gordon Jenkins,**
and **L. Bernstein**
Producer: Max Wilcox

D772. Tashi
RCA 7901-2-RC, CD **[DDD]**; 7901-4-RC, cassette
CONTENTS: Bess, You Is My Woman; I Got Rhythm; Promenade; Who
Cares?; With music by **Foss, Hindemith, & Shulman**

D773. Michael Tilson Thomas, pianist and conductor; Los Angeles Philharmonic
CBS Masterworks M 39699 (© & p 1985); IMT-39699, cassette
CONTENTS: RiB; Preludes for Piano; Short Story; Violin Piece; Second
Rhapsody; For Lily Pons; Sleepless Night; Promenade
Program notes in English, German, & French on container
Album dedicated to IG
See: **B1081, B1091, B1124, B1127, B1243, B1250**

D773.1. Michael Tilson Thomas, conductor & pa; San Francisco Symphony
BMG68931 (Release date 9/15/1998)
"George Gershwin: The Hundreth Birthday"
CONTENTS: Porgy and Bess: Suite "Catfish Row"; Rhapsody for Piano and
Orchestra no 2; Concerto; An American in Paris; Porgy and Bess:
Summertime; Bess, You Is My Woman Now; My Man's Gone Now; There's
a Boat Dat's Leavin' Soon for New York.
Performers: Audra McDonald, soprano; Brian Stokes Mitchell, baritone;
Garrick Ohlsson, piano

D774. Various artists
CBS 66369 CBS; CBS 80194 CBS; CBS 85197 CBS; CBS 80196 CBS (1974) 3
LP discs
"A George Gershwin anthology"
CONTENTS & PERFORMERS: Swanee (Al Jolson); Someone to
Watch over Me (George Gershwin); I Got Rhythm (Louis Armstrong);
Somebody Loves Me (Jack Teagarden); I Got Rhythm (Glenn Miller); They
All Laughed (Fred Astaire); The Man I Love (Billie Holiday); How Long Has
this Been Going On? (Peggy Lee with Benny Goodman); Liza (Benny

Goodman Sextet); Bidin' My Time (The Modernaires); Nice Work If You Can Get it (Sarah Vaughan); Embraceable You (Harry James); Swanee (Judy Garland) ; But Not for Me (Erroll Garner) ; Oh! Lady Be Good (Percy Faith); 'S Wonderful! (Ray Conniff); Soon (Percy Faith) ; Love Walked in (Johnny Mathis); I Loves You Porgy (Miles Davis with Gil Evans); Of Thee I Sing (The Hi-Lo's); Fascinating Rhythm (Tony Bennett with Count Basie); I've Got a Crush on You (Teddy Wilson); Clap Your Hands (Doris Day); It Ain't Necessarily So (Aretha Franklin); Summertime (Duke Ellington); A Foggy Day (André Previn); Love Is Here to Stay (Andy Williams) ; They Can't Take That Away from Me (Steve Lawrence); Isn't it a Pity? (Mel Torme); I Got Plenty O' Nuthin' (Barbra Streisand); Hi-ho (Tony Bennett); Concerto in F for Piano and Orchestra (Paul Whiteman and His Concert Orchestra); Rhapsody in Blue (Oscar Levant, Piano, with the Philadelphia Orchestra, Eugene Ormandy, Conductor); An American in Paris (Arthur Rodzinski, Conductor, Philharmonic-Symphony Orchestra of New York). *See:* **B1092 (Rodzinski)**

D775. Various artists, St. Johnsbury, VT: 1003 Vintage Recording Co.
   "Vintage George Gershwin" cassette, analog (198-)
   Recorded 1920-1928.
   CONTENTS: Yan-kee (Marion Harris) - Scandals of 1920 Medley (Van Eps Specialty Four) - Swanee (Al Bernard & Frank Kamplain) - Oh, Lady Be Good (Imperial Dance Orchestra) - Yankee Doodle Blues (Billy Murray and Ed Smalle) - I'll Build a Stairway to Paradise (Paul Whiteman's Orchestra) - Somebody Loves Me (Isabelle Patricola, Assisted by Tom Patricola) - Nashville Nightingale (Waring's Pennsylvanians) - Looking for a Boy (Roger Wolfe Kahn and His Orchestra) - Three Times a Day (Alexander Gray) - Why Do I Love You So? (The Clover Gardens Orchestra) - Sweet and Low down (The Singing Sophomores) - That Certain Feeling (Phil Ohman, Victor Arden & Their Orchestra) - Song of the Flame (Victor Light Opera Company) - Clap Yo' Hands (Phil Ohman, Victor Arden & Their Orchestra) - Maybe (Viginia Rea And Franklyn Baur With Ohman and Arden) - Do-do-do (Phil Ohman, Victor Arden and Their Orchestra) - My One and Only (Clicquot Club Eskimos) - 'S Wonderful! (Victor Arden, Phil Ohman & Their Orchestra) - The Man I Love (Ben Bernie & His Hotel Roosevelt Orchestra).
   Cf. Rimler listings

D776. Various artists
   CSP P2 15974-A-D **"Vintage Gershwin" [GOH]**
   CONTENTS: **Side A:** Oh, Lady Be Good; Looking For a Boy; My One and Only; 'S Wonderful!; The Man I Love; **Side B:** I Got Rhythm; My Cousin in Milwaukee; Mine; Let 'Em Eat Cake; Mischa, Jascha, Toscha, Sascha; **Sides C & D:** Liza (All the clouds'll roll away); Who Cares?; Swanee; Sweet and Low Down; Wintergreen for President; Concerto in F (Roy Bargy, piano, with Paul Whiteman Orchestra)

D777. Various artists **"Classic Gershwin"**
   Columbia MK 42516, CD (1988?)
   CONTENTS & ARTISTS: RiB (M. T. Thomas & Columbia Jazz Band); AiP (Bernstein & NY Philharmonic); Three Preludes (M. T. Thomas); Liza (Jean

Pierre Rampal); A Foggy Day (John Williams, guitar); Embraceable You
(Cleo Laine); Medley from Woody Allen Film Manhattan (Zubin Mehta & NY
Philharmonic); Overture to P&B; Medley from P&B (Sarah Vaughan)
See: **B1088, B1266**

D778. Frances Veri & Michael Jamanis, pianists; Bands 3-5, side 1, played by Veri;
Band 2, side 2, played by Jamanis; All others played as piano duo
Connoisseur Society CSQ 2067 (1974)
CONTENTS: "I Got Rhythm" Variations (trans. by the composer for 2
pianos); Cuban Overture (trans. by the composer for 1 piano, 4 hands);
The Man I Love; Do It Again; Somebody Loves Me; Second Rhapsody
(trans. by the composer for 2 pianos, 4 hands); Three Preludes
Program notes by E. Jablonski on container; Durations on labels

D779. Westside Strutters ['Disco']
Parachute RRLP 9013 Gershwin '79 **[GOH]**
CONTENTS: Medley: The Man I Love; Embraceable You; Strike Up the
Band; RiB; Medley: I Got Rhythm & Fascinating Rhythm

D780. Paul Whiteman and His Orchestra [various personnel of Whiteman Orchestra
given in album notes] and other orchestras
The Smithsonian Collection RCA Special Products R028A, 2 LP discs (1981)
"An Experiment in Modern Music, Paul Whiteman at Aeolian Hall"
RiB is the June 10, 1924, version with the following suggested personnel:
GG, piano soloist; Henry Busse & Frank Seigrist (trumpets); Roy Maxon
& Wilbur Hall (trombones); Ross Gorman, Edward Stannard, Charles
Strickfadden, Lyle Sharpe, and "possibly" Hale Byers (woodwinds) Phil
Boutelje (piano, celeste); Milton Rettenberg (piano, cello); Mike
Pingatore (banjo); Al Armer & Gus Helleberg (bass); George Marsh
(drums); Arthur Cerino & Alfred Corrado (French horns); "Violinists
may include: George Tjorde, Perry, Jack Eaton, Edmund Carradi, John
Bowman, Max Barr, Oscar Alder; Aldo Ricci"
CONTENTS: A reconstruction of the Aeolian Hall concert, collected from
Whiteman recordings (dates of which are noted after the titles). This
first list of pieces is in chronological order by date of the recording, and
includes only those recordings by the Paul Whiteman Orchestra present
on this album:
Whispering (8/23/20); Song of India (5/31/21); Say It With Music
(8/30/21); Ka-Lu-A (11/4/21); Stumbling (3/30/22); I'll Build a Stairway
to Paradise (9/1/22); Lonely Nest (10/27/22); Chansonette (9/12/23); I
Love You (9/20/23); An Orange Grove in California (10/9/23); Mama
Loves Papa (10/29/23); Raggedy Ann (10/30/23); So This is Venice!
(1/11/24); Limehouse Blues (1/22/24); What'll I Do? (3/18/24); Pale
Moon (4/8/24); RiB (First issue Victor 55225, 6/10/24); Meditation from
"Thais" (6/11/24); A Suite of Serenades, Cuban/Oriental/Spanish/Chinese
[Victor Herbert] (6/11/24)
CONTENTS by album side: Side One: Livery Stable Blues (ODJB);
Mamma Loves Papa (Whiteman Orch.); Yes! We Have No Bananas
(The Great White Way Orchestra); So This is Venice! (Whiteman
Orch.); Whispering (Whiteman Orch.); Whispering excerpt (Art Hickman
& His Orchestra); Limehouse Blues, I Love You, & Raggedy Ann

(Whiteman Orch.); **Side Two:** Humorestless (Zez Confrey & His Orchestra); Kitten on the Keys (Z. Confrey); Nickel in the Slot (Z. Confrey & His Orchestra); Stumbling (Whiteman Orch.); Russian Rose (Broadway Dance Orchestra); Say It With Music, What'll I Do, & An Orange Grove in California [I. Berlin] (Whiteman Orch.); **Side Three:** Suite of Serenades: Cuban/Oriental/Spanish/Chinese [V. Herbert] (Whiteman Concert Orch.); Pale Moon (Whiteman Orch.); Fox Trot Classique (Jean Goldkette & His Orchestra); Chansonette & (Whiteman Orch.); RiB (Gershwin with Whiteman Concert Orch.); Pomp and Circumstance (No. 1 in D Major, excerpt [E. Elgar (Gino Marinuzzi & His Symphony Orch.); **Side Four:** Barnyard Blues (Original Dixieland Jazz Band); Wang Wang Blues (Whiteman Orch.); How to Write a Popular Song, excerpt of Yes! We Have No Bananas (Clarence Senna); Song of India, Meditation from "Thais" [Massenet], & Ka-Lu-A (Whiteman Orch.); Mississippi Shivers (Z. Confrey & His Orch.); Lonely Nest & I'll Build a Stairway to Paradise (Whiteman Orch.)

Extensive **program notes** by Thornton Hagert in container, 10 pp.

Executive Producer: Bill Bennett

Produced by: Martin Williams & J. R. Taylor

D780.1 "Paul Whiteman Conducts Gershwin."

Music and Arts CD-1042

CONTENTS and Performers: (Live performances from New York & Los Angeles, 1934-1948): RiB (Roy Bargy, piano, July 10, 1938); Dawn of a New Day (Lyn Murray Chorus, July 10, 1938; Medley: They Can't Take That Away From Me, Nice Work If You Can Get It, Love Walked In (Maxine Sullivan, vocal, July 10, 1938); Second Rhapsody (Roy Bargy, piano, July 10, 1938); Medley: Clap Yo' Hands, Do It Again (Lyn Murray Chorus), I Got Rhythm (Jack Teagarden, trombone), Somebody Loves Me (Murray chorus & The Modernaires), July 10, 1938; Mischa, Jascha, Toscha, Sascha (The Modernaires, July 10, 1938); AiP (Whiteman Orch., Dec. 6, 1934); Medley: Swanee, Do It Again, OTIS, Someone To Watch Over Me (1948); They Can't Take That Away From Me (Kay Armen, vocal, 1948); Cuban Overture (1948); Summertime (Al Galladoro, sax, 1948); RiB (Earl Wild, May 6, 1945

Liner notes: Scott Yanow

D781. Paul Whiteman, Orchestra; Roy Bargy & W. Gross, pianos; Lyn Murray Chorus; M. Sullivan vocals

Mark 56 Records 761-A & B **[GOH]**

"Paul Whiteman: A Tribute to George Gershwin" July 10, 1938 Original Radio Broadcast   Radio show soundtrack of the same title

CONTENTS: Side A: Deems Taylor introduction; Second Rhapsody; Song medley: Clap Yo' Hands/Do It Again/I Got Rhythm/Somebody Loves Me; Summertime; Mischa, Yascha, Toscha, Sascha; **Side B:** Medley: They Can't Take That Away From Me/Nice Work If You Can Get It/Love Walked In; Piano medley: Someone To Watch Over Me/Somebody Loves Me/Fascinating Rhythm; Dawn of a New Day; Rhapsody in Blue

D782. Roger Williams, piano; Symphony of the Air; Willis Page, conducting
"Roger Williams Plays Gershwin"
Kapp KL 1088, mono (195--?)
CONTENTS: RiB; Someone to Watch Over Me; Liza; Love Walked In;
Bidin' My Time; Maybe; I Got Rhythm
Program notes by George T. Simon on container *See:* **B1248**

D783. The World's Greatest Brass cond. by Jack Saunders
Everest LP BR 5047-A & B   **"Gershwin in Brass" [GOH]**
CONTENTS: Side A: Fascinating Rhythm; But Not for Me; American in
Paris; The Man I Love; Summertime; Liza (All the clouds'll roll away);
Side B: Strike Up the Band; Embraceable You; Rhapsody in Blue; I
Got Plenty O'Nuttin'; Someone to Watch Over Me; Clap Yo' Hands
Arrs. by Charlie Margulis & Bobby Byrne with Jack Saunders *See:* **B1258**

SONGS, VOCAL TREATMENT

D784. Larry Adler, harmonica, w/ various singers
Mercury (Phonogram, London) 522 727 - 2, CD (1994)
"The Glory of Gershwin"
CONTENTS and Singers: Summertime (Peter Gabriel); Do What You
Do (Chris DeBurgh); Nice Work If You Can Get It (Sting); They Can't Take
That Away From Me (Lisa Stansfield); Someone To Watch Over Me/Love Is
Here To Stay (Elton John); I've Got a Crush On You (Carly Simon); But Not
For Me (Elvis Costello); It Ain't Necessarily So (Cher); The Man I Love
(Kate Bush); How Long Has This Been Going On? (Jon Bon Jovi);
Embraceable You (Oleta Adams); Bidin' My Time (Willard White); My Man's
Gone Now (Sinead O'Connor); I Got Rhythm (Robert Palmer); Somebody
Loves Me (Meat Loaf); I'll Build a Stairway to Paradise (Issy Van
Randwyck); Summertime (Courtney Pine); RiB (Larry Adler & George
Martin)
Produced by George Martin; **Executive Producer:** Jonathan Shalit

D785. **"AMERICAN POPULAR SONG"** Album
Smithsonian Collection 1500 (© 1983)
7-LP boxed set
CONTENTS: Various singers and songs, among them: **Fred Astaire**:
Puttin' On The Ritz & They Can't Take That Away From Me; **Mildred
Bailey:** Georgia On My Mind; **Tony Bennett:** I'll Be Around; **Nat "King"
Cole:** Lush Life & Star Dust; **Bing Crosby:** Out Of Nowhere; **Ella
Fitzgerald:** Blues In The Night; **Helen Forrest:** Day In, Day Out; **Judy
Garland**: But Not For Me; **Dick Haymes:** You Are Too Beautiful; **Billie
Holiday:** More Than You Know; **Lena Horne:** Just One Of Those Things;
Al Jolson: April Showers; **Peggy Lee:** As Time Goes By; **Gordon McRae:**
All The Things You Are; **Carmen McRae:** Baltimore Orioles; **Mabel
Mercer:** Hello, Young Lovers; **Frank Sinatra:** I've Got You Under My
Skin; **Mel Tormé**: Nice Work If You Can Get It; **Sarah Vaughan:** Autumn
in New York; and others
Includes 148-page booklet, art work on booklet and container commissioned
from **Al Hirshfield**

D786. The Andrews Sisters
Decca 1562, Brunswick 02552 (British), 78, 10" **[GOH]**
Nice Work if You Can Get It

D787. Victor Arden, Phil Ohman and Orch.; Lewis James, vocal; Arr. by Frank J. Black
Victor 21795, 78, 10" **[GOH]** TREASURE GIRL 1928
CONTENTS: Feeling I'm Falling; Got a Rainbow

D788. Robert Ashley & Elisabeth Welch, vocals, with New Mayfair Orchestra
His Masters Voice C 2992, 78   Gershwin Medley-Part 3 & 4 **[GOH]**
CONTENTS: The Man I Love; Oh, Lady Be Good!; Do, Do, Do; Someone
to Watch Over Me; Swanee; That Certain Feeling; Tell Me More;
Fascinating Rhythm

D789. Adele Astaire and Bernard Clifton with Orchestra, Julian Jones, conducting
Columbia 5175 (English), 78, 10" **[GOH]**
CONTENTS: 'S Wonderful!; He Loves and She Loves

D790. Fred Astaire and chorus
Columbia 5173 (English), 78, 10" **[GOH]**
CONTENTS: High Hat; My One and Only
Includes actual dancing by Astaire

D791. Fred Astaire with Johnny Green and Orchestra; Johnny Green, piano
Brunswick 7855, 78, 10" **[GOH]**
CONTENTS: They Can't Take That Away From Me; (I've Got) Beginner's
Luck

D792. Fred Astaire, vocal & tap dancing with Johnny Green and His
Orchestra, Green at the piano
Brunswick 7856, 78, 10" **[GOH]**
CONTENTS: Slap That Bass; They All Laughed

D793. Fred Astaire, vocal & tap dancing with Johnny Green and His Orchestra
Brunswick 7857, 78, 10" **[GOH]**
CONTENTS: Let's Call the Whole Thing Off; Shall We Dance?

D794. Fred Astaire, vocal & tap dancing with Ray Noble and His Orchestra
Brunswick 7982, 78, 10" **[GOH]**
CONTENTS: A Foggy Day; I Can't Be Bothered Now

D795. Fred Astaire, vocal & tap dancing with Ray Noble and His Orchestra
Brunswick 7983, 78, 10" **[GOH]**
CONTENTS: Things Are Looking Up; Nice Work If You Can Get It

D796. Fred Astaire accompanied by various orchestras
Columbia C44234, 2 discs (1989)
"Starring Fred Astaire" (A Columbia Years Series Release)
CONTENTS: They Can't Take That Away from Me; They All Laughed;

Beginner's Luck; Let's Call the Whole Thing Off; Shall We Dance?; Slap That Bass; A Foggy Day; Things are Looking Up; Nice Work if You Can Get It; I Can't Be Bothered Now; Who Cares? (**Acc. by Benny Goodman & His Orchestra**, including Jimmy Maxwell, Ziggy Elman, Irving Goodman (Trumpets); Red Ballard, Vernon Brown, Ted Vesely (Trombones); Toots Mondello, Les Robinson (Alto saxes); Bus Bassey, Jerry Jerome (Tenor saxes); Johnny Guarnieri (Piano); Charlie Christian (Electric guitar); Artie Bernstein (Bass); Nick Fatool (Drums); With songs by **I. Berlin, J. Kern, J. Mercer,** & one by **Astaire**
Original 78s from the collections of Robert Altshuler & Michael Brooks
Program notes by Michael Brooks inside container
Producer: Michael Brooks
See: **B1251, B1310**

D797. Fred & Adele Astaire, vocals; George Gershwin, piano
Monmouth Evergreen MES 7036-A & B, re-mastered from Columbia 78 discs **[GOH]**
CONTENTS: Side A: Fascinating Rhythm; Hang On To Me; Oh, Lady Be Good!; I'd Rather Charleston; So Am I; The Half Of It, Dearie, Blues; Swiss Maid (Yodel Song); **Side B**: Fred Astaire, vocals & dancing with orchestra: Not My Girl (Astaire-Van Phillips-Carter?) 1929?; Louisiana (Johnson-Schafer-Razaf) 1928; Puttin' On the Ritz (Berlin) Puttin' On the Ritz 1929 film; Crazy Feet (Conrad-Gottler-Mitchell) Happy Days 1930 film; Night and Day (Porter); After You (Porter); Flying Down to Rio (Youmans-Eliscu-Kahn) Flying Down to Rio 1933 film; Music Makes Me (Youmans-Eliscu-Kahn) Flying Down to Rio 1933 film

D798. Fred & Adele Astaire, vocals; George Gershwin, piano
Monmouth Evergreen MES 7037-A & B FUNNY FACE 1928 (London), re-mastered from the original discs **[GOH]**
CONTENTS: Side A: Funny Face; He Loves and She Loves; High Hat; A Few Drinks (Fred Thompson) [sketch perf. by L. Henson & S. Howard]; 'S Wonderful!; My One and Only; Tell the Doc; The Babbit and the Bromide; **Side B:** Looking For a Boy; Sweet and Low Down; That Certain Feeling; When Do We Dance?; Oh Gee! Oh Gosh! (Daly-Lannin) STOP FLIRTING 1923 (London); The Whichness of the Whatness (Daly-Lannin) STOP FLIRTING 1923; My One and Only (Gershwin) FUNNY FACE 1928 (London); Medley: Funny Face and 'S Wonderful! [G at the piano on the original discs]

D799. Fred & Adele Astaire with George Gershwin at the piano
Columbia 3970 (English), 10" **[GOH]**
CONTENTS: Hang On to Me; I'd Rather Charleston

D800. Fred & Adele Astaire, vocals; George Gershwin, piano; Empire Theatre Orch.
World Record Club SH 124 (remastered from 78 discs), LP, 12" **[GOH]**
LADY, BE GOOD! 1926 (London)
CONTENTS: Oh, Lady Be Good!; So Am I; Fascinating Rhythm; I'd Rather Charleston; Hang On to Me; Swiss Maid (Yodel song); The Half of It, Dearie, Blues; With music by **Porter, Berlin, Youmans, Astaire, & Johnson**

D801. Fred and Adele Astaire with Orchestra, Julian Jones, conducting
Columbia 5174 (English), 78, 10" **[GOH]**
CONTENTS: Funny Face; The Babbitt and the Bromide

D802. Ben Bagley assembled the cast; Directed by Dick Hyman
Painted Smiles PS 1353-A & B   **"Ira Gershwin Revisited" [GOH]**
CONTENTS: On My Mind the Whole Night Long (GG-Jackson) G. WHITE
SCANDALS 1920; Boy Wanted (GG-Francis) A DANGEROUS MAID
1921; I Don't Think I'll Fall In Love Today (GG-I. Gershwin) TREASURE
GIRL 1928; With songs by other composers and lyrics by IG

D803. Ben Bagley, Barbara Cook, Bobby Short, Elaine Stritch, Anthony Perkins
M-G-M 4375 **"George Gershwin Revisited" [GOH]**
The New American Theatre Series
Cast assembled by Ben Bagley; Directed & arr. by Norman Paris
CONTENTS: **Side A**: There's More to the Kiss Than the X-X-X (Gershwin-C-
aesar); Under a One Man Top; Feeling Sentimental; Tra-la-la; Nashville
Nightingale; Drifting Along With the Tide; Virginia (Don't go too far);
(Gershwin-DeSylva) SWEET LITTLE DEVIL 1924; **Side B:** Back Bay
Polka; Changing My Tune; Rose of Madrid; Oh Gee! Oh Joy!; Three Times a
Day; Scandal Walk (Gershwin-Jackson) G. WHITE'S SCANDALS 1920
See: **B1673**

D804. Mildred Bailey, vocalist; Red Norvo & His Orchestra
Brunswick 8068 (British), 78, 10" **[GOH]**
CONTENTS: I Was Doing All Right; Love Is Here to Stay
Recorded in NY, Jan. 21, 1938

D805. Kaye Ballard, David Craig, Nancy Walker, Louise Carlyle, W. Galjour,
B. Gillett; David Baker & John Morris, piano; The John Morris Trio
Citadel CT 7017-A & B   **"Gershwin Rarities, Vol. I" [GOH]**
CONTENTS (different from those on Walden 302, below): Side A:
Blah, Blah, Blah; Soon; My One and Only (what am I gonna do); Let's
Kiss and Make Up; Isn't It a Pity?; I Want to be a War Bride; Seventeen and
Twenty-one; **Side B:** I Don't Think I'll Fall In Love Today; Where's the Boy?
Here's the Girl; Stiff Upper Lip; Shall We Dance?; Aren't You Kind of Glad
We Did? **Now (1999) avail. as Harbinger CD 1603**

D806. Kaye Ballard, David Craig, Warren Galjour, B. Gillett; David Baker & John
Morris, piano; The John Morris Trio; Now (1999) avail. as Harbinger 1603 CD
Walden 302 **"Gershwin Rarities, Vol. I"** (1953)
CONTENTS: Aren't You Kinda Glad We Did?; Funny Face; Isn't It a Pity?;
Kickin' the Clouds Away; Seventeen and Twenty-One; Shall We Dance?;
Soon; Stiff Upper Lip; They All Laughed; Things Are Looking Up
Cover Art by Hirschfeld
Producers: Edward Jablonski and Leon Seidel
Now (1999) avail. as Harbinger CD 1603, including **D807,** below
See: **B1301, B1309,** and *Show Music* 15/1 (1999): 30.

D807. Louise Carlyle, Warren Galjour, John Morris, piano; The John Morris Trio
Walden Records 303; **Harbinger CD 1603 "Gershwin Rarities, Vol. II"**
CONTENTS: Side 1: Where's the Boy?; That Certain Feeling; Let's Kiss and
Make Up; Oh, So Nice; I Want to be a War Bride **Side 2:** Nice Work If You
Can Get It; A Foggy Day; How Long Has This Been Going On?; Nightie
Night; Sweet and Low Down *See:* **B1309** and *Show Music* 15/1 (1999).

D808. George Bassman, selector, arranger, coordinator, and conductor; Paula Stewart,
Richard Hayes, Lynn Roberts, singers; chorus and orchestra
Decca DXZ-160 (mono?); DXSZ 7160; DL 78910-78912 (1959) 3 discs
"The Gershwin Years"
CONTENTS: Selections from musical comedies, motion picture scores, and
P&B: When You Want 'Em, You Can't Get 'Em, When You Got 'Em,
You Don't Want 'Em; Rialto Ripples; Some Wonderful Sort of Someone;
I Was So Young; Nobody But You; Do It Again; I'll Build a Stairway to
Paradise; I Won't Say I Will, But I Won't Say I Won't; Somebody Loves Me;
Oh, Lady, Be Good!; Fascinating Rhythm; So Am I; The Man I Love; Sweet
and Low-Down; Looking for a Boy; That Certain Feeling; Maybe; Clap Yo'
Hands; Do-Do-Do; Someone to Watch Over Me; High Hat; He Loves and
She Loves; 'S Wonderful!; My One and Only; How Long Has This Been
Going On?; Oh, So Nice; I Don't Think I'll Fall In Love Today; Where's the
Boy? Here's the Girl!; Feeling I'm Falling; Do What You Do!; Liza; Swanee;
I've Got a Crush on You; Soon; Strike Up the Band; Embraceable You;
Could You Use Me?; But Not For Me; Bidin' My Time; I Got Rhythm; Of
Thee I Sing; Who Cares?; Love Is Sweeping the Country; The Lorelei; Isn't It
a Pity?; My Cousin in Milwaukee; Mine; The Man I Love; Maybe; Do, Do,
Do; **Porgy and Bess—Selections**: Introduction, Summertime; There's a Boat
Dat's Leavin' Soon for New York; Bess, You Is My Woman Now; Let's Call
the Whole Thing Off; They Can't Take That Away from Me; They All
Laughed; A Foggy Day; Nice Work If You Can Get It; Love Walked In; Our
Love Is Here to Stay; Love Walked In
Program notes by L. Untermeyer, E. Jablonski, & S. M. Saget, and list of
the composer's musical comedies & film scores by Miles Krueger, and
reproduction of a self-portrait by the composer on the back cover of the
booklet.
LC card no. r59-1252
See: **B1288, B1293, B1296, B1304, B1305, B1306, B1309**

D809. Linda Bennett, mezzo-soprano; Michael McMahon, piano
Radio Canada International RCI 642, cassette (198?)
"George Gershwin: The Canadian Connection"
CONTENTS: Recreation of the Eva Gautier/Gershwin recital of Nov. 1,
1923: I'll Build A Stairway To Paradise; Innocent Ingenue Baby; Do It
Again; Swanee; **Songs from the Thirties:** Just Another Rhumba; Love
Walked In; The Lorelei; Isn't It a Pity?; They All Laughed; Love Is Here To
Stay; By Strauss
This program is excerpted from a special tribute to GG produced by the
Canadian Broadcasting Corporation in cooperation with the faculty of
music at McGill University
Program notes on insert in container; Durations on same insert, total time:
34 min.

Producer: Frances Wainwright
Available from RCI, P. O. Box 6000, Montreal, Canada

D810. Rose Blaine, vocal; Abe Lyman and His Californians
Decca 1225, 78, 10" (1937) **[GOH]**
CONTENTS: Shall We Dance?; I've Got Beginner's Luck

D811. Irene Bordoni, comedienne, acc. by violin & piano (from original and 1925
London casts)
Victor 19199, His Master's Voice B-2011, 78, 10" **[GOH]**
From the show *Little Miss Bluebird*
I Won't Say I Will, But I Won't Say I Won't
Recorded NY, Nov. 5, 1923

D812. Connie Boswell with Victor Young and His Orchestra
Decca 2879, 78, 10", Album 97, Sides 1 & 2 - George Gershwin Songs,
Vol. 2 **[GOH]**
CONTENTS: Soon; They Can't Take That Away from Me

D813. Georgia Brown, vocal with the Mike Sammes Singers; orch. cond. by Ian Fraser
London LL 3331-B **"Georgia Brown Loves Gershwin" [GOH]**
CONTENTS: Fascinating Rhythm; But Not for For Me; Blah, Blah, Blah;
Slap That Bass; How Long Has This Been Going On?; Strike Up the Band

D814. Georgia Brown (early 1960s Decca recordings w. Ian Fraser, arranger
& conductor & the Mike Sammes Singers)
Pearl SHE CD 9617 **[AAD]**
CONTENTS: Summertime; It Ain't Necessarily So; I Loves You, Porgy, I
Got Plenty O' Nuthin'; My Man's Gone Now; Oh Lord, I'm on My Way;
Fascinating Rhythm; But Not for Me; Blah-blah-blah; Slap That Bass; How
Long Has this Been Going On; Strike up the Band; With **Weill**: Songs

D815. Billy Butterfield and his Orchestra, with various vocalists
Capitol BD 10 (20025 - 20028), 78, 4 10" mono discs
"Gershwin featuring Billy Butterfield" {1945?)
Program and biographical notes on container.
CONTENTS: [Disc 1]. Someone to Watch over Me : from "Oh Kay" /
George and Ira Gershwin (Margaret Whiting, Vocal); Oh Lady Be Good :
from "Lady Be Good" / George & Ira Gershwin - [Disc 2]. Somebody Loves
Me from "George White's Scandals" / Gershwin, Desylva, Mcdonald
(Tommy Taylor, Vocal) ; Nice Work If You Can Get it : from "Damsel in
Distress" / George & Ira Gershwin (Sue Allen, Vocal) - [Disc 3]. It Ain't
Necessarily So from "Porgy and Bess" George & Ira Gershwin (Johnny
Mercer, Vocal) ; Maybe : from "Oh Kay" / George & Ira Gershwin (Tommy
Taylor, Vocal) - [Disc 4]. Do it Again : from "The French Doll" / Gershwin,
Desylva (Sue Allen, Vocal) ; They Can't Take That Away from Me : from
"Shall We Dance" / George & Ira Gershwin.

D816. George Byron, vocal; Bobby Tucker, piano
General 4011, 78, 10" **[GOH]**
"George and Ira Gershwin Specials"

CONTENTS: By Strauss; Blah-blah-blah   DELICIOUS 1932 film
Album G-13

D817. George Byron, vocal; Bobby Tucker, piano
General 4012, 78, 10" **[GOH]**
"George and Ira Gershwin Specials"
CONTENTS: The Lorelei; Isn't It a Pity?
Album G-13

D818. George Byron, vocal; Bobby Tucker, piano
General 4013, 78, 10" **[GOH]**
"George and Ira Gershwin Specials"
CONTENTS: Three Times a Day TELL ME MORE 1925; I Love to Rhyme
TELL ME MORE is also known as MY FAIR LADY

D819. George Byron, vocal; Bobby Tucker, piano
General 4014, 78, 10" **[GOH]**
"George and Ira Gershwin Specials"
CONTENTS: The Half of It, Dearie, Blues; The Jolly Tar and the Milk Maid

D820. George Byron, baritone; Dick Hyman, piano
Atlantic ALS 410 (1952)
CONTENTS: Back Bay Polka; Blah, Blah, Blah; Lorelei; By Strauss; The Half
of It Dearie Blues
See: **B1300**

D821. Irving Caesar performing
Coral 57083 (1956)
"Irving Caesar: And Then I Wrote"
CONTENTS: Swanee & Yankee Doodle Blues

D822. George Chakiris, voice; Ted Heath Band; arr. & cond. by Norman Stenfalt
Horizon WP 1610 **[GOH]**
"The Gershwin Songbook"
CONTENTS: But Not for Me; It Ain't Necessarily So; Love Walked In; My
One and Only; They All Laughed; I'll Build a Stairway to Paradise;
Embraceable You; Things Are Looking Up; Do It Again; For You, For Me,
For Evermore; I Got Rhythm

D822.1. Rosemary Clooney, vocal with jazz combo
Concord Jazz CJ 112 A & B **[GOH]**
"Rosemary Clooney Sings the Lyrics of Ira Gershwin"
CONTENTS: **Side A:** But Not For Me; Nice Work If You Can Get It; How
Long Has This Been Going On?; Fascinating Rhythm; (Our) Love Is Here
to Stay; **Side B:** Strike Up the Band; Long Ago (and far away); They All
Laughed; The Man That Got Away (Arlen-IG) A STAR IS BORN 1954 film;
The Can't Take That Away From Me

D823. Betty Comden, vocal; Richard Lewine, piano; George Duvivier, bass; Mundell
Lowe, guitar

äva AS 26 A & B Remember These, Vol. I (1963) **[GOH]**
CONTENTS: **Side A:** I Don't Think I'll Fall In Love Today; What Are
We Here For?; Feeling I'm Falling; Oh, So Nice; Where's the Boy? Here's
the Girl; **Side B:** Songs by Rodgers & Hart

D824. **"Chris Conner Sings the George Gershwin Almanac of Song"**
Atlantic 2-601, 2 discs, mono (n.d.)
Chris Conner, vocals; Instrumental accompaniment by seven different
ensembles, including such performers as Joe Newman, trumpet; Al
Cohn, tenor sax; Ralph Sharon, piano; Milt Hinton, bass; Johnny Rodriguez,
bongo; Osie Johnson, drums; Herbie Mann, flute & alto flute; Barry Galbraith
& Mundell Lowe, guitars; Oscar Pettiford, bass; Doc Severinsen, etc.
CONTENTS: Somebody Loves Me; Fascinating Rhythm; Little Jazz Bird;
That Certain Feeling; The Man I Love; Looking For a Boy; Clap Yo'
Hands; 'S Wonderful!; My One and Only; How Long Has This Been Going
On?; Liza; I've Got A Crush On You; Strike Up the Band; Soon; I Got
Rhythm; Embraceable You; Blah Blah Blah; Of Thee I Sing; Love Is
Sweeping the Country; Medley from P&B: Summertime, There's a Boat
That's Leaving Soon for New York, I Loves You, Porgy; I've Got Beginner's
Luck; A Foggy Day; Slap That Bass; They Can't Take That Away From Me; I
Can't Be Bothered Now; Nice Work if You Can Get It; Love is Here To Stay;
Love Walked In; I Was Doing All Right; For You, For Me, Forever More
See: **B1292**

D825. **"Crazy for Gershwin"** (Original versions of Gershwin's songs) with various
artists
Memoir CDMOIR 502 **[AAD]**
CONTENTS and Performers: Opening music; I Can't Be Bothered Now;
Things Are Looking Up; Shall We Dance?; Slap that Bass; They Can't
Take That Away from Me; Nice Work If You Can Get It (Fred Astaire);
Bidin' My Time (The Foursome); I'll Build a Stairway to Paradise (Paul
Whiteman & his Orchestra); Someone to Watch Over Me (Gertrude
Lawrence); Embraceable You (Judy Garland); I Got Rhythm; Embraceable
You (Red Nichols & his Orch.); Naughty Baby (Margery Hicklin); Stiff Upper
Lip (Gracie Allen); But Not for Me (Helen Forrest); Someone to Watch over
Me; I Got Rhythm (George Gershwin); Sam & Delilah (Duke Ellington & his
Cotton Club Orch.); Boy, What Love Has Done for Me (Jane Froman); Do
What You Do! (Zelma O'Neal); Hang on to Me (Fred & Adele Astaire); That
Certain Feeling (Dorothy Dickson & Allen Kearns); So Am I (Adele Astaire
& George Vollaire) (rec. between 1922-1941)

D826. Bing Crosby with Victor Young and Orchestra
Decca 806, 78, 10" **[GOH]**
CONTENTS: It Ain't Necessarily So; I Got Plenty O' Nuttin'

D827. Bing Crosby, vocal; Matty Malneck & His Orchestra
Decca 2147, 24542; Decca DL-5081; Brunswick 02746 (British), 78
Summertime
Recorded in Los Angeles, July 8, 1938

D828. Bing Crosby with orchestra; John Scott Trotter, Matty Malneck, or

Victor Young, conducting
Decca A-702 (24541, 24542, 25409, 25410), 4 discs, 78 mono, 10 in. (© 1949)
"Bing Crosby Sings Songs by George Gershwin"
CONTENTS: Embraceable You; They Can't Take That Away from
Me; Love Walked In; Summertime; It Ain't Necessarily So; I Got Plenty O'
Nuttin'; Somebody Loves Me; Maybe
Program notes, in part by Irving Kolodin, on container

D829. Bing Crosby, vocals; Victor Young & His Orchestra
Decca 2874, 25410, DL-5081; Brunswick 02986 (British), 78
Maybe; Somebody Loves Me
Recorded in Los Angeles, June 14, 1939

D830. Vaughn DeLeath, vocal, with Fred Rich & Hotel Astor Orchestra
Columbia 1241 D-A, 78, 10" **[GOH]**
CONTENTS: The Man I Love

D831. Alice Delysia, from original London cast of *Mayfair and Montmartre,* 1933
recording
World Record Club 164   Do It Again

D832. Bob Eberle, Don Matteson, vocals; Jimmy Dorsey Orchestra
Coral CRL 56033, LP, 10" **[GOH]**
CONTENTS: I Got Rhythm; Love Walked In; Let's Call the Whole Thing Off;
(Our) Love is Here to Stay; I Was Doing All Right; They Can't Take That Away
From Me; Shall We Dance?; Slap That Bass; They All Laughed

D833. Bob Eberle, vocal; Jimmy Dorsey and Orchestra
Decca 1203, Brunswick 02433, 78, 10" **[GOH has the Decca]** (1937)
CONTENTS: They Can't Take That Away from Me; Slap That Bass

D834. Bob Eberle, vocal; Jimmy Dorsey and Orchestra
Decca 1724 (1938)
Love Walked In

D835. Bob Eberle, vocal; Jimmy Dorsey and Orchestra
Decca 1660, 78, 10" **[GOH]**
CONTENTS: (Our) Love is Here to Stay; I Was Doing All Right

D835.1. "Michael [Feinstein] & George"
CONCORD JAZZ CON4849 (9/98)
Personnel includes: Michael Feinstein (vocals, piano, Fender Rhodes); Gary
Foster (flute, alto flute, alto saxophone); George Gershwin (piano roll); Chuck
Berghofer (bass); David Lasley, Arnold McCuller, Bruce Roberts
(background vocals).
CONTENTS: Comes the Revolution; Delishious; Do it Again; Embraceable
You; Funny Face; Lonely Boy; Love Is Here to Stay; Love Walked In;
Nobody but You; Of Thee I Sing; Oh Gee!-Oh Joy!; Shall We Dance?; Soon;
Stairway to Paradise, (I'll Build A); Swanee
Producers: Bruce Roberts, David Tobocman, John Burk.
Recorded at Mad Hatter Studios and Bomec Studios, Los Angeles, California.

Album notes by Michael Feinstein.

D836. Michael Feinstein, vocals and piano
Atlantic 82833 (1996) avail. as CD & cassette
"Nice Work If You Can Get It: Songs By The Gershwins"
Performers: Michael Feinstein (vocals, piano); Rob Fisher, Don Sebesky, Bill
Elliot, Mort Lindsey, Larry Blank (conductor); Gerry Vinci, Endre Granat
(concertmaster); Bill Watrous (trombone); Armen Guzelimian, Stan Freeman,
Tom Ranier (piano); Chuck Berghofer (bass); Jeff Hamilton (drums).
L.A. Voices: Gene Merlino, Don Shelton, Med Flory, Sue Raney,
Melissa McKay.
CONTENTS: Anything for You; Ask Me Again; Fascinating Rhythm Medley;
Foggy Day (In London Town); For You, for Me, Forevermore; I Got
Rhythm; Love Is in the Air; Luckiest Man in the World; Nice Work If You
Can Get It; Some Wonderful Sort of Someone; Somebody Stole My Heart
Away; Someone to Watch over Me; They Can't Take That Away from Me;
Things Are Looking Up; Who Cares?; Will You Remember Me?
Liner notes by Michael Feinstein. *See:* **B1469**

D837. Michael Feinstein, solo voice and piano; David Ross, extra piano; Jim Hughart;
Ted Hawke, drums; Guest vocalist, Rosemary Clooney
"Pure Gershwin"
Elektra 60742; Parnassus PR 0100, also avail. on CD & cassette (1987)
CONTENTS: 'S Wonderful!; Embraceable You; The Girl I Love; He Loves
and She Loves; How Long Has it Been Going On?; Isn't It a Pity? - (With
Rosemary Clooney); Let's Call the Whole Thing off; Liza; Our Love Is Here
to Stay; Someone to Watch over Me; They All Laughed; They Can't Take
That Away from Me; What Causes That?; The World Is Mine *See:* **B1274,
B1281, B1469**

D838. Wilhemenia Fernandez, vocals; George Darden, piano
Milan A-215 [French?] (1984?)
CONTENTS: Fascinating Rhythm; I'll Build a Stairway to Paradise; They All
Laughed; The Man I Love; 'S Wonderful!; By Strauss; Love Is Here to Stay;
Embraceable You; Someone to Watch Over Me; Somebody Loves Me; Strike
Up the Band; But Not For Me; Soon *See:* **B1291, B1298**

D839. Ella Fitzgerald, vocals; André Previn, piano
Pablo Today PACD-2312-140-2 **[DDD]** (p 1983)
"Nice work if you can get it: Ella Fitzgerald & André Previn do Gershwin"
CONTENTS: A Foggy Day (3:58); Nice Work If You Can Get it (5:23);
But Not for Me (3:58); Let's Call the Whole Thing off (2:54); How Long Has
this Been Going on (4:58); Who Cares (4:39); They Can't Take That Away
from Me (3:36) – Medley: I've Got a Crush on You (1:23); Someone to
Watch over Me (1:39) ; Embraceable You (2:06).
Recorded May 23, 1983, at RCA Studios, New York City *See:* **B1277**

D840. Ella Fitzgerald, vocalist; Nelson Riddle, arranger & conductor
Verve Records 2615 063 (2367 431--2367 435), 5 LP discs (1982, 1959); CD
release by **Polygram (three-disc package, no. 825 024-2)**
"Ella Fitzgerald Sings the George and Ira Gershwin Song Book"

CONTENTS: **Vol. I:** Sam & Delilah; But Not For Me; My One and Only; Let's Call the Whole Thing Off; Beginner's Luck; Nice Work if You Can Get It; Things Are Looking Up; Just Another Rhumba; How Long Has This Been Going On?; **Vol. 2:** 'S Wonderful!; The Man I Love; That Certain Feeling; By Strauss; Someone to Watch Over Me; The Real American Folk Song; Who Cares?; Looking for a Boy; They All Laughed; My Cousin from Milwaukee; Somebody from Somewhere; **Vol. 3:** A Foggy Day; Clap Yo' Hands; For You, For Me, Forever More; Stiff Upper Lip; Boy Wanted; Strike Up the Band; Soon; I've Got a Crush On You; Bidin' My Time; Aren't You Kind of Glad We Did?; Of Thee I Sing, Baby; **Vol. 4:** The Half of It Dearie, Blues; I Was Doing All Right; He Loves & She Loves; Love is Sweeping the Country; Treat Me Rough; Love is Here to Stay; Slap That Bass; Isn't It a Pity?; Shall We Dance?; Love Walked In; You've Got What Gets Me; **Vol. 5:** They Can't Take That Away from Me; Embraceable You; I Can't Be Bothered Now; Boy! What Love Has Done to Me!; Fascinating Rhythm; Funny Face; Lorelei; Oh, So Nice; Let's Kiss and Make Up; I Got Rhythm Recorded Jan.–July, 1959

Conceived and Produced by Norman Granz with cover painting by Bernard Buffet   *See*: **B1279 (CD release), B1287, B1289, B1305, B1307, B1308, B1673, B1791**

D841. Ella Fitzgerald; Ellis Larkin, piano
Decca DL 5300 **"Ella Sings Gershwin"**
CONTENTS: Someone to Watch Over Me; My One and Only (what am I gonna do); But Not For Me; Looking for a Boy; I've Got a Crush on You; How Long Has This Been Going On?; Maybe; Soon

D842. Ella Fitzgerald, vocals; Orchestra cond. by Nelson Riddle
Verve EP V 5069, LP, 7" **[GOH] "Ella Fitzgerald Sings the George and Ira Gershwin Songbook"**
CONTENTS: Ambulatory Suite: Promenade, Shall We Dance, March of the Swiss Soldiers; Fidgety Feet; Preludes for Piano

D843. The Foursome
Decca 2880, 78, 10", Album 97, Sides 3 & 4 - George Gershwin Songs, Vol.2 **[GOH]**
CONTENTS: Bidin' My Time; Oh, Lady Be Good!

D844. Jane Froman, Sonny Schuyler, Felix Knight vocals; RCA Victor Salon Group, Nathaniel Shilkret, conducting
RCA Victor LPT 3055, 10" **[GOH]**, reissue on CD BMG/RCA Victor 63275 **"Gems from Gershwin"**
CONTENTS: Gems from GIRL CRAZY—I Got Rhythm; Bidin' My Time; Embraceable You; Medley of Gershwin Tunes—Oh Gee! Oh Joy!; 'S Wonderful!; Do It Again; Strike Up the Band; Gems From OF THEE I SING—Wintergreen for President; Who Cares; Of Thee I Sing; Love is Sweeping the Country; The Man I Love STRIKE UP THE BAND 1927; Gems From OH, KAY!—Maybe; Do, Do, Do; Clap Yo' Hands; Someone to Watch Over Me; Gershwin Medley—Swanee; South Sea Isle; That Certain Feeling; Somebody Loves Me; Gems From PORGY AND BESS—I Got Plenty of Nuttin'; My Man's Gone Now; Summertime; Gems From LADY,

BE GOOD! and TIP-TOES—Oh, Lady Be Good!; Sweet and Low Down; So
Am I; Fascinating Rhythm   Reviewed in *Show Music* 15/1 (1999): 30.

D845. Jane Froman, S. Schuyler, F. Knight vocals; Victor Salon Group, N. Shilkret,
cond.
Victor Red Seal 12334, 78, 12"
Memorial Album to George Gershwin
CONTENTS: I Got Plenty of Nuttin'; My Man's Gone Now; Summertime;
Bess, You Is My Woman Now; Oh, I Can't Sit Down; It Ain't Necessarily
So; Swanee; South Sea Isles; That Certain Feeling; Somebody Loves Me;
Maybe; Do, Do, Do; Clap Yo' Hands; Someone to Watch Over Me

D846. Jane Froman, S. Schuyler, F. Knight vocals; Victor Salon Group, N. Shilkret,
conducting
Victor Red Seal 12336 Same material as **D844** CD
Memorial Album to George Gershwin
CONTENTS: Oh, Lady Be Good!; Sweet and Low-down; So am I;
Fascinating Rhythm; Oh Gee! Oh Joy!; 'S Wonderful!; Do It Again; Strike Up
the Band

D847. Judy Garland with Victor Young and His Orchestra
Decca 2881, 78, 10", Album 97, Sides 5 & 6 - George Gershwin Songs,
Vol. 2 **[GOH]**; also Brunswick 02993 (British); Coral CP-54, 78 (1939)
CONTENTS: Embraceable You; Swanee
Recorded in Los Angeles, July 29, 1939

D848. Judy Garland
Decca 18543, 78 (1939)
Fascinating Rhythm
Recorded Los Angeles, July 29, 1939

D849. Judy Garland & Mickey Rooney with Georgie Stoll and Orchestra
Decca DL 5412, LP, 10"
CONTENTS: Embraceable You; Could You Use Me?; But Not For Me;
Treat Me Rough; Bidin' My Time (featuring the Leo Diamond Harmonica
Quartet); I Got Rhythm

D850. Mitzi Gaynor, vocal; Arr. and dir. by Russell Garcia
Verve MG V 2115 **"Mitzi Gaynor Sings the Lyrics of Ira Gershwin"**
[GOH]
CONTENTS: Soon; The Half of It, Dearie, Blues; There's a Boat Dat's
Leavin' Soon for New York; Isn't It a Pity? (G. Gershwin-I. Gershwin)
PARDON MY ENGLISH 1933; With other non-GG songs, lyrics by IG
See: **B1296, B1306**

D851. Frances Gershwin (1906-1999), vocals; Alfred Simon or Jack Easton, piano
Monmouth-Evergreen MES/7060, SH 208 (1973); reissue Audiophile 116

"Frances Gershwin: For George & Ira"
CONTENTS: Oh Gee, Oh Joy! Oh Joy!; Someone to Watch Over Me; My
One and Only; Let's Kiss and Make Up; Isn't It a Pity?; That Certain Feeling;

I've Got Beginner's Luck; The Man I Love; Sweet and Low-Down; Embraceable You; Oh, So Nice; Fascinating Rhythm; How Long Has This Been Going On?; When Do We Dance? & Shall We Dance?; Where's the Boy? Here's the Girl!; I've Got A Crush On You; Do It Again!; My Cousin in Milwaukee; Love is Here to Stay
Recorded at Nola Penthouse Sound Studios on June 19, 20, and 21st, 1973
Produced by Bill Borden & Alfred Simon *See:* **B1294**

D852. **"The George and Ira Gershwin Songbook"**
RCA 9613-2-R, CD digitally remastered (© 1989 by BMG Music, recorded before 1972)
See: Full entry under **"Anthologies"**

"George & Ira Gershwin / Standards & Gems" by Nonesuch (1998) *See:* **D945.17**

D853. Ira Gershwin & Kurt Weill, et al, vocals; Kurt Weill, piano
Mark 56 Records 721 A-D **[GOH]**
"Ira Gershwin Loves to Rhyme"
CONTENTS: No GG songs, but many with lyrics by IG

D854. GLAD
Light 51416 5166 2 (Distr. BMG), **CD** (©1995)
"A Cappella Gershwin"
CONTENTS: I Got Rhythm; The Girl I Love; Our Love Is Here to Stay; Embraceable you; The Gershwin Medley (AiP; Strike Up the Band; How Long Has This Been Going On?); Summertime; They Can't Take That Away From Me; RiB); They All Laughed; A Foggy Day; Little Jazz Bird; But Not for Me; They Can't Take That Away from Me; Someone To Watch Over Me
Produced by: Ed Nalle

D855. Charles Goodman, vocal; Horace Heidt & His Musical Knights
Brunswick 8318-A, 78, 10" **[GOH]**
Dawn of a New Day

D855.1. Mary Cleere Haran, vocals, with Richard Rodney Bennett, piano/vocals
Managra Music MMI 100199-2 [Orchard] (1999)
"The Memory of All That" A selection of 19 songs

D856. Marion Harris, comedienne
Columbia 3353-A, 78, 10" **[GOH]**
CONTENTS: Yan-Kee (1920)

D857. Barbara Hendricks, soprano; Katia & Marielle Lebèque
Philips 416460-2 PH, CD; 9500 987; 7300 987, cassette (1981)
"Barbara Hendricks Sings Gershwin"
CONTENTS: The Man I Love; They Can't Take That Away From Me; (Our) is Here to Stay; But Not For Me; Embraceable You; Nice Work if You Can Get It; I Got Rhythm; Summertime; Has Anyone Seen Joe?; I Loves You, Porgy; Songs with two pianos; Text of the songs inserted *See:* **B1139**

D858. Margery Hicklin & Claude Hulbert with Winter Garden Theatre Orchestra;

J. Ansell, conducting

Columbia 9004 PRIMROSE 1924 (London) **[GOH]**

CONTENTS: I'll Have a House in Berkeley Square (Gershwin-Carter);
   Naughty Baby (Gershwin-Carter)

D859. Hildegard

Columbia FB-1712 (British), 78 (1937)

CONTENTS: Let's Call the Whole Thing Off & They Can't Take That Away
   from Me

Recorded London, May 20, 1937

D860. Hildegard

Columbia FB-1992 (British), 78 (1938)

Love Walked In

Recorded London, July 1, 1938

D861. (Number inadvertently omitted)

D862. Hildegarde, vocalist; Larry Adler, harmonica

Columbia (English) number ? (1937)

"Gershwin—King of Rhythm"

CONTENTS: The Man I Love (Hildegarde); et al

D863. Hildegard with Carrol Gibbons Orchestra

Columbia 296 M, 78, 10" **[GOH]**

CONTENTS: Let's Call the Whole Thing Off; They Can't Take That Away
   From Me

D864. **"Hildegard Looks Back** - Part 2"

Columbia FB-1541 (British), 78 (1936)

CONTENTS: 'S Wonderful! & I Got Rhythm

Recorded London, July 3, 1936

D865. **"The Honey Dreamers Sing Gershwin: With The Elliot Lawrence Band"**

Fantasy 3-207, LP (1959?)

CONTENTS: Do It Again; I Was Doing All Right; Lady Be Good; A Foggy
   Day; How Long Has this Been Going On?; Stairway to Paradise: Things
   Are Looking Up; But Not for Me; Mine; Summertime; Little Jazz Bird; My
   One and Only Love.

D866. Lena Horne, vocal; Orchestra with Lou Bring, conducting; Arr. by Ned Freeman

Victor 27818-A, Album P 118, 78, 10" (1941) **[GOH]**; also on digitally
   remastered LP album: **"Stormy Weather"** Bluebird 9985-1-RiB (BMG,
   1990)

The Man I Love

Recorded Hollywood, Dec. 15, 1941

D867. The Ink Spots

Decca 1251 **[GOH]**; Brunswick 02440 (British), 78 (1937)

CONTENTS: Let's Call the Whole Thing Off & Slap That Bass

Recorded NY, Apr. 9, 1937

D868. Ipana Troubadours; Smith Ballew, vocals
Columbia 1903 D, 78, 10" (1929) **[GOH]**
CONTENTS: Do What You Do!; Liza

D869. Ipana Troubadours, Harold Lambert, voc./Clicquot Club Eskimos, Tom Stacks, voc.
Columbia 12l3 D, 78, 10" **[GOH]**
CONTENTS: 'S Wonderful!; My One and Only

D870. Joni James, vocal; Orchestra cond. by Paul Smith
M-G-M E 4255-A & B
"Joni James Sings the Gershwins" [GOH]
CONTENTS: **Side A:** How Long Has This Been Going On?; 'S Wonderful!; A Foggy Day; Embraceable You; They Can't Take That Away From
Me; (Our) Love is Here to Stay; **Side B:** Bidin' My Time; But Not For Me; Love Walked In; Nice Work If You Can Get It; Soon

D871. Lewis James, vocal with Ben Selvin & Orchestra
Columbia 1285 D, 78, 10" **[GOH]**
CONTENTS: Oh Gee! Oh Joy!; Say So!

D872. Anne Jamison with Victor Young and His Orchestra
Decca 2876, 78, 10", Album 96, Sides 5 & 6 - George Gershwin Songs, Vol. I **[GOH]**
CONTENTS: Summertime; Looking for a Boy

D873. Jack Jones, singer
"The Gershwin Album"
Columbia/Legacy CK 48511, CD (1991)
CONTENTS: 13 G tunes, including: Embraceable You; Who Cares?; #Love Walked In; But Not for Me; Nice Work if You Can Get It; Someone to Watch Over Me; #'S Wonderful; I've Got a Crush on You; Soon; #I Loves You, Porgy; He Loves and She Loves; How Long Has This Been Going On?; Aren't You Kind of Glad We Did? # indicates piano interludes by Fred Hersch

D874. Al Jolson
Audio Fidelity 708, 45 (1920)
"The Actual Voices of My Pals," packaged with George Jessel: **"Songs My Pals Sang"**
Audio Fidelity 1708
CONTENTS: Swanee

D875. Al Jolson
Columbia A-2884, 2974, 78 (1920)
Swanee; With That Wonderful Kid from Madrid (not G)
Recorded NY, Jan. 9, 1920

D876. **"A Tribute to Al Jolson"**
Audio Rarities 2285 (1920)

CONTENTS: Swanee

D877. Judy Kaye, soprano; William Sharp, baritone; Steven Blier, piano
Koch International Classics KIC 7028, CD & cassette
"He Loves and She Loves" New York Festival of Song
CONTENTS: How Long Has This Been Going On?; Nice Work If You Can
Get It; Hi-Ho!; Feeling I'm Falling; Yankee Doodle Rhythm; He Loves and
She Loves; Innocent Ingenue Baby; Hangin' Around With You; Isn't It
Wonderful?; Till Then; My Cousin in Milwaukee; Liza; Fascinating Rhythm;
Little Jazz Bird; Oh, De Lawd Shake de Heavens/Leavin' Fo' de Promis'
Lan'; The Half of It Dearie, Blues; Oh, Lady Be Good!; The Man I Love; Oh,
So Nice; Who Cares?
Produced by Michael Fine & Karen Chester
See: **B1139, B1276**

D878. Linda Keene, vocal; with Henry Levine & His Strictly from Dixie Jazz Band
Victor 27829-B, Album P 119, 78, 10" **[GOH]** GIRL CRAZY 1930
Embraceable You

D879. Linda Keene, vocal; with Henry Levine & His Strictly from Dixie Jazz Band
Victor 27831-A, Album P 119, 78, 10" **[GOH]** WHITE'S SCANDALS 1924
Somebody Loves Me

D880. Linda Keene
Victor 27832
Someone to Watch Over Me; Mound Bayou (not G)

D881. Courtney Kenny, vocalist
No label, LMSYS 2, cassette (available from Mr. Kenny, 14 Grange Grove,
London N1 2NP, England @ $15.00 in 1991)
"The Great Mr. Gershwin"
CONTENTS: 18 songs, including I Love to Rhyme; Mischa, Jascha, Toscha,
Sascha; Nobody But You; The Half of It, Dearie, Blues; When Toby is Out of
Town [*Primrose*]; Nashville Nightingale; Isn't It a Pity?; Strut Lady With Me;
In the Rain; Innocent Lonesome Blue Baby [the latter three songs from *The
Rainbow*]

D882. Bobby King, vocal; Johnny Messner & Orchestra
Bluebird B 10101-A, 78, 10" **[GOH]**
CONTENTS: Dawn of a New Day (GG-I. Gershwin-Kay Swift)
Official march of the 1939 New York World's Fair

D883. Teddi King, vocal; Dave McKenna, piano
Inner City 1C 1044 **[GOH]**
"This Is New"
CONTENTS: Isn't It a Pity?; How Long Has This Been Going On?; But Not
For Me; I Can't be Bothered Now; Soon; For You, For Me, For Evermore
With other non-GG songs with IG lyrics

D884. Dorothy Kirsten with Percy Faith and Orchestra
Columbia 52 G-A & B, 78, 10" **[GOH]**

CONTENTS: Soon; (Our) Love is Here to Stay

D885. Dorothy Kirsten with Percy Faith and His Orchestra & Chorus
Columbia Masterworks ML 2189, LP, 10" (1950?) **[GOH]**
"Dorothy Kirsten Sings Songs of George Gershwin"
CONTENTS: Someone to Watch Over Me; Love Walked In; I've Got
a Crush On You; Mine; Embraceable You; Soon; (Our) Love Is Here To
Stay; Do, Do, Do
Program notes on container

D886. Eartha Kitt, Dinah Shore, et al. (20 songs)
RCA 9613-2-R, CD; 9613-4-R, cassette

D887. The Knickerbockers
Columbia 2598 D, 78, 10" **[GOH]**
CONTENTS: Who Cares?; Of Thee I Sing

D888. Dorothy Lamour
Bluebird B 10302-B; His Master's Voice B-8963 (British), 78 (1939) **[GOH]**
The Man I Love
Recorded Hollywood, Apr. 26, 1939

D889. Frances Langford with Victor Young and His Orchestra; Arthur Schutt, piano
Decca 2882, 78, 10", Album 97, Sides 7 & 8 **[GOH];** also Brunswick 02994
(British), 78 (1939)
CONTENTS: The Man I Love; Someone to Watch Over Me
Recorded Los Angeles, June 30, 1939

D890. Gertrude Lawrence, comedienne
Victor 20331, 78, 10" **[GOH]** OH, KAY! 1926
CONTENTS: Do, Do, Do; Someone to Watch Over Me

D891. (Number inadvertently omitted)

D892. "Steve [Lawrence] & Eydie [Gorme] and Friends Celebrate Gershwin."
New Horizons NH 01:59:39 (1987?)
20 Gershwin songs *See:* **D1282**

D893. Ella Logan, vocal with Orchestra conducted by Bill Harty
Brunswick 8064, 78, 10" **[GOH]**
CONTENTS: (Our) Love Is Here to Stay; I Was Doing All Right

D894. Avon Long & Helen Dowdy, vocalists; Leo Reisman Orchestra, & others
JJA 19845-A (Music Masters, NY)
"Gershwin for Dancing"
CONTENTS & PERFORMERS: Say So! (Ben Selvin); Oh Gee! Oh Joy!
(Johnny Johnson); Somebody from Somewhere/Delishious (Nat Shilkret);
You've Got What Gets Me (Roy Fox); Mine (Emil Coleman); Till Then
(Don Bestor); 'S Wonderful!/My One and Only (Henry King); A Foggy
Day/Nice Work if You Can Get It (Bob Crosby); Shall We Dance?/

Beginner's Luck (Abe Lyman); They Can't Take That Away from Me/Slap That Bass (Jimmy Dorsey); Excerpts from 1942 revival of P&B recordings

D895. Mirth Mack, vocal with Milton Charles, pipe organ
Columbia 1363 D-B, 78, 10" **[GOH]**
The Man I Love

D896. Mark 56 Records 799-A & B
"Songs of George & Ira Gershwin 1920s"-Vol. I **[GOH]**
An original Thomas Alva Edison Re-recording
CONTENTS: **Side A:** Oh, Lady Be Good!; Clap Yo' Hands; Do, Do, Do;
'S Wonderful!; Nashville Nightingale; **Side B:** Do It Again; Drifting Along
With the Tide; The Life of a Rose; Argentina; He Loves and She Loves;
Swanee

D897. Tony Martin with Victor Young and His Orchestra
Decca 2883, 78, 10" **[GOH]**; also Brunswick 02995 (British), 78 (1939)
CONTENTS: Song of the Flame; Cossack Love Song (Don't forget me)
Recorded Los Angeles, July 14, 1939
Album 97, Sides 9 & 10

D898. Johnny Marvin, vocal; Victor Arden, Phil Ohman and Orchestra
Victor 21114, 78, 10" **[GOH]** FUNNY FACE 1927
CONTENTS: 'S Wonderful!; Funny Face

D899. Don Mattison, vocal; Jimmy Dorsey and Orchestra
Decca 1204, Brunswick 02434 (1937)
CONTENTS: They All Laughed; Let's Call the Whole Thing Off

D900. Maureen McGovern, vocals; Jeff Harris, piano & conductor; Jay Leonhart,
acoustic bass; Grady Tate, drums; Lou Marini, reeds; Mark Sherman,
percussion & vibes
CBS FMT 44995, cassette (1989)
"Naughty Baby, Maureen McGovern Sings George Gershwin"
Arrangements by Mike Renzi & Jeff Harris
CONTENTS: Stiff Upper Lip; Things Are Looking Up; I've Got Beginner's
Luck; How Long Has This Been Going On?; By Strauss; Naughty Baby; Love
Walked In; Embraceable You; A Corner of Heaven With You (1918, Lyrics
by Lou Paley, premiere recorded performance); Somebody Loves Me; Little
Jazz Bird; My Man's Gone Now; Porgy, I Is Your Woman Now; The Man I
Love; Piano Prelude II/Summertime; **Gershwin Tribute:** Strike Up the Band;
Fascinating Rhythm; Clap Yo' Hands; They Can't Take That Away from Me;
'S Wonderful!; They All Laughed; I Got Rhythm; Love Is Here to Stay
(verse)/OTIS refrain
Recorded at a live concert Nov. 20, 1988, at Studio A at Clinton Recording
Studio, NY
Program notes by Tommy Krasker & Ron Barron in container
Producer: Ron Barron *See:* **B1139, B1310**

D901. James Melton, vocal; Arr. and cond. by Hugo Montenegro
Mayfair 960595 A & B **[GOH]**

"James Melton Sings Cole Porter and George Gershwin"
CONTENTS: Side B: A Woman Is a Sometime Thing; Summertime; Love Walked In; I Got Plenty O' Nuttin'; (Our) Love Is Here to Stay; Bess, You Is My Woman Now; Side A: Songs by Cole Porter

D902. James Melton, vocal; Barbara Meister, on duets; Arr. and cond. by Hugo Montenegro
Tops L 1609-B [GOH]
"James Melton Sings Cole Porter and George Gershwin"
CONTENTS: A Woman Is a Sometime Thing; Summertime; Love Walked In; I Got Plenty O' Nuttin'; (Our) Love Is Here to Stay; Bess, You Is My Woman Now; With music by Cole Porter

D903. The Merry Macs
Decca 2877, 78, 10", Album 96, Sides 7 & 8 - George Gershwin Songs, Vol. I [GOH]
CONTENTS: Clap Yo' Hands; I Got Rhythm

D904. Helen Morgan, vocal, with Chick Endor & Paul Reese; Leslie A. "Hutch" Hutchinson, piano
Brunswick 129, 78 (1927)
CONTENTS: Do, Do, Do & Maybe
Recorded London, September, 1927

D905. Julia Migenes-Johnson, vocals
"Julia Migenes-Johnson Sings Gershwin"
RCA ARK 1-5323, cassette (1982)
Performers: Migenes, vocals; Big Band and the Great Radio Orchestra of Cologne; Gershon Kingsley, conductor
CONTENTS: Somebody Loves Me; The Man I Love; They Can't Take That Away From Me; Embraceable You; Love is Here To Stay; By Strauss; Nice Work If You Can Get It; How Long Has This Been going On?; Summertime; Someone to Watch Over Me; But Not For Me; I Got Plenty O' Nuttin'
Produced by Gershon Kingsley See: B1275

D906. Joan Morris, vocals; W. Bolcom, piano
Elektra/Nonesuch 79151-2, CD [AAD]
CONTENTS: George Gershwin Song Book; piano music

D907. Joan Morris, vocals; William Bolcom, piano
Elektra/Nonesuch H-71358; N5-71358, cassette (p 1978)
"Songs by Ira & George Gershwin"
CONTENTS: I'll Build A Stairway To Paradise; Love Walked In; How Long Has This Been Going On?; My Cousin In Milwaukee; Nice Work If You Can Get It; The Man I Love; By Strauss; Just Another Rhumba; Someone to Watch Over Me; The Lorelei; Fascinating Rhythm; Isn't It A Pity?; They All Laughed; Love Is Here To Stay See: B1673

D908. Marni Nixon, vocals; Lincoln Mayorga, piano

Reference RR-19, digital; RR-19CD **[DDD]**
"Marni Nixon Sings Gershwin"
CONTENTS: Eighteen songs, including: The Real American Folk Song; By
Strauss; I've Got a Crush On You; But Not for Me; Someone to Watch
Over Me; Embraceable You; The Man I Love; Soon; Maybe; Looking for
a Boy; OTIS; Blah, Blah, Blah; Blue, Blue, Blue; The Babbit and the
Bromide
Program notes by Michael Feinstein
See: **B1042, B1280**

D909. Helen O'Connell, vocal; Jimmy Dorsey & His Orchestra
Decca 3928-A, 78, 10" **[GOH]**
Embraceable You

D910. George Olsen and His Music; Bob Borger, Frank Frey, & Bob Rice, vocals;
Victor 2O327, 78, 10" **[GOH]**
CONTENTS: Do, Do, Do; Clap Yo' Hands (perf. by Roger Wolfe Kahn
Orchestra) OH, KAY! 1926

D911. Isabelle Patricola, with original cast
Vocalian 14866, 78 (1924)
"George White's Scandals of 1924"
Somebody Loves Me *See:* **W20**

D912. The Pied Pipers with Paul Weston and His Orchestra
Capitol 10065-B, 78, 10" **[GOH]**
Embraceable You
Album CD-36

D913. "The Popular Gershwin"
RCA Victor LPM 6000, LP 2 discs (1955)
Performers: Various soloists and orchestra
CONTENTS: Somebody Loves Me; Of Thee I Sing; Love Walked In; Looking
for a Boy; Strike Up the Band; Someone to Watch Over Me; Nice Work If
You Can Get It; But Not For Me; Wintergreen for President; They Can't
Take That Away From Me; Fascinating Rhythm; Who Cares?; I'll Build a
Stairway to Paradise; Lady, Be Good!; A Foggy Day; Love Is Sweeping the
Country; I've Got a Crush on You; Do It Again; Let's Call the Whole thing
Off; Embraceable You; I Got Rhythm; Mine; Song of the Flame; Swanee;
How Long Has This Been Going On?; Liza; Bidin' My time; They All
Laughed; 'S Wonderful!
Biographical Notes on GG by Arthur Schwartz in 24 pp. booklet in container
See: **B1273**

D914. Martha Raye
Columbia 35394 (1939)
It Ain't Necessarily So
Recorded Los Angeles, Sept. 17, 1939

D915. Virginia Rea & Franklyn Baur, vocals; Phil Ohman & Victor Arden, pianos
Brunswick 3381, 78, 10" **[GOH]**

CONTENTS: Maybe; Someone to Watch Over Me

D916. Virginia Rea & Franklyn Baur with Brunswick Hour Orchestra, Walter Haenschen, conducting
Brunswick 3053, 78, 10" **[GOH]**
CONTENTS: Looking for a Boy; Nightie-night

D917. The Revelers
Victor 22401, 78 (1930)
Strike Up the Band
Recorded NY, March 31, 1930

D918. The Revelers, vocalists
Victor 35772-A, 78, 12" **[GOH]** Gems from TIP-TOES 1925
CONTENTS: Those Charming People; That Certain Feeling; When Do We Dance?; Looking for a Boy; Sweet and Low-Down

D919. The Revelers, vocalists
Victor 35811-A, 78, 12" **[GOH]** Gems from OH, KAY! 1926
CONTENTS: Clap Yo' Hands; Someone to Watch Over Me; Maybe; Do, Do, Do

D920. The Revelers, vocalists
Victor 22308, 78 (1930)
Strike Up the Band
Recorded NY, Jan. 31, 1930

D921. Dick Robertson, vocal; Red Nichols and Orchestra
Brunswick 4957, 78, 10" **[GOH]**
CONTENTS: Embraceable You; I Got Rhythm

D922. Dick Robertson, vocal; Victor Young and Orchestra
Decca 426-B, 78, 10" **[GOH]**
That Certain Feeling

D923. Dick Robertson & Lou Sherwood, vocals; Eddie Duchin & His Central Park Orchestra
Brunswick 6476, 78, 10" **[GOH]**
CONTENTS: My Cousin in Milwaukee; Isn't It a Pity?

D924. Rondoliers Quartet (vocal refrain); Emil Coleman and His Riviera Orch.
Columbia 2831 D, 78, 10" **[GOH]**
CONTENTS: Let 'Em Eat Cake; Mine

D925. Shirley Ross and the Foursome; cond. by Victor Young
Decca 2878, 78, 10", Album 96, Sides 9 & 10 - George Gershwin Songs, Vol. I **[GOH]**
CONTENTS: Mine; That Certain Feeling

D926. Jane Russell, vocal; Orchestra cond. by Lou Bring

Columbia 37917-B, 78, 10" **[GOH]** THE FRENCH DOLL 1922
Do It Again
Album C 157, Side 4

D927. Nathaniel Shilkret and His Orchestra with Soloists
RCA Camden CAL 177-A **"Music by George Gershwin/Victor Herbert"**
CONTENTS: **Side A:** Wintergreen for President; Who Cares?; Of Thee I
Sing; Love Is Sweeping the Country; I Got Rhythm; Bidin' My Time;
Embraceable You; The Man I Love; Introduction to P&B; I Got Plenty O'
Nuttin'; My Man's Gone Now; Summertime; Bess, You Is My Woman
Now; Oh, I Can't Sit Down; It Ain't Necessarily So; Maybe; Do, Do, Do;
Clap Yo' Hands; Someone to Watch Over Me; Oh, Lady Be Good!; Sweet
and Low Down; So Am I; Fascinating Rhythm; **Side B:** Songs by Victor
Herbert *See*: **B1309**

D928. Dinah Shore, vocal with Buddy Clark Orchestra
Columbia 38253-B, 78, 10" **[GOH]**
'S Wonderful!
Album C 166-4

D929. Dinah Shore, B. Clark, M. Marlowe, J. Russell, H. Ward, L. Wiley, K. Smith, F.
Sanders, with performances by the Modernaires
Harmony HL 7050-A & B   **"The Music of George Gershwin" [GOH]**
CONTENTS: The Man I Love; 'S Wonderful!; Do It Again; Bidin' My Time;
Nice Work If You Can Get It; Summertime; I've Got a Crush on You; How
Long Has This Been Going On?; They Can't Take That Away from Me;
Somebody Loves Me

D930. Dinah Shore, vocal; Orchestra; Leonard Joy, conducting
Bluebird B-10978; His Majesty's Voice BD-1092 (British), 78 (1940)
Somebody Loves Me
Recorded NY, Dec. 10, 1940

D931. Dinah Shore, vocals; Orchestra with Albert Sack, conducting
Victor 20-1650, 78, 2-10" (194?) **[GOH]**
"Victor Showcase presents Dinah Shore in Gershwin Show Hits"
CONTENTS: The Man I Love; Do It Again; Love Walked In; Someone to
Watch Over Me

D932. Dinah Shore, vocals; Al Hirt, trumpet; Eartha Kitt, vocalist, et al
RCA 9313-2-R, CD
The George and Ira Gershwin Songbook

D933. Bobby Short, vocalist; Second piano on Hi-Ho is by Kay Swift; Beverly Peer,
bass; Richard Sheridan, drums
Atlantic 608-2, CD; Atlantic CS2-608. cassette
"Bobby Short Is K-Ra-Zy for Gershwin"
This is the CD version of the original 1972 double-LP set
Bonus tracks on the CD: I've Got Beginner's Luck, Here's a Kiss for
Cinderella, & I Love to Rhyme, recorded in 1956-1957
CONTENTS: 'S Wonderful!; Love Is Here To Stay; I Must Be Home By

Twelve O'Clock; Love Walked In; They Can't Take That Away From Me;
Embraceable You; (I've Got) Beginner's Luck; Kickin' The Clouds Away;
I've Got A Crush On You; I Was So Young (You Were So Beautiful);
Hi-Ho; Innocent Ingenue Baby; Do What You Do; Delishious; High Hat;
I've Got To Be There; Comes The Revolution; The Lorelei; Feeling I'm
Falling; That Certain Feeling; Drifting Along With The Tide; P&B medley
(instrumental): Clara; Oh De Lawd Shake De Heavens; They Pass By
Singin'; Oh Bess, Where's My Bess; I Loves You Porgy; There's A Boat
Dat's Leavin' Soon For New York; A Foggy Day; Mine; But Not For Me;
Let's Kiss And Make Up; Feeling Sentimental; Shall We Dance?; K-ra-zy
  For You
Produced by Lew Hahn; Recorded at Atlantic Studios, NY
Program notes by Bobby Short & durations on container
LC card no. 73-762940 *See*: **B1294, B1469, B1673**

D934. Frank Sinatra, vocal
Columbia 38191-A, 78, 10" **[GOH]**
I've Got a Crush On You; a later duet version (with Barbara Streisand) is
available on Capitol cassette C4 0777 7, **"Frank Sinatra Duets"** (1993),
which album includes They Can't Take That Away from Me

D935. The Singing Sophomores
Columbia 568 D-B, 78, 10" **[GOH]**
Sweet and Low Down

D936. The Singing Sophomores (also known as The Revelers, vocal quintet/quartet);
Frank Black, piano accompanist
Columbia 838-D, 4619, 78 (1926) **[GOH]**
Clap Yo' Hands
Recorded NY, Nov. 30, 1926

D937. Paul Small, vocals; Fred Rich and His Orchestra
Columbia 2328 D, 78, 10" (1930) **[GOH]**
CONTENTS: I Got Rhythm; Embraceable You

D938. Buddy Stewart & Carolyn Grey, vocal; Gene Krupa and Orchestra
Columbia 37158-B, 78, 10" **[GOH]**
CONTENTS: Aren't You Kinda' Glad We Did?

D939. Gladys Swarthout, vocal; Orchestra; Al Goodman, conducting
Victor 10-1039, 78 (1942)
The Man I Love
Recorded NY, July 30, 1942

D940. Kiri Te Kanawa, vocals; New Princess Theater Orch.; John McGlinn, conducting
Angel CDC-47454 **[DDD]**
"Kiri Sings Gershwin!"
CONTENTS: Somebody Loves Me; Embraceable You; Love Walked In; The
Man I Love; I Got Rhythm; & ten more of G's best loved songs
See: **B1042, B1284, B1290, B1299, B1303, B1370, B1541**

D941. Heather Thatcher, Leslie Henson & Claude Hulbert with Winter Garden Theatre
Orchestra; J. Ansell, conducting Columbia 9002 PRIMROSE 1924 (London)
[GOH] CONTENTS: Boy Wanted; Mary, Queen of Scots

D942. "These Charming People"
RCA Victor ARL 1-2491
CONTENTS: These Charming People, The Half of It Dearie, Blues, Feeling
I'm Falling, I Don't Think I'll Fall in Love Today, Hang On To Me, and
The Babbitt and the Bromide, and other songs *See:* **B1271**

D943. Mel Tormé
M-G-M 10874, 78, 10" **[GOH]**
CONTENTS: Until the Real Thing Comes Along (Chaplin-Nichols-Cahn-
Holiner-Freeman); A Foggy Day (Side B)

D944. Mel Tormé, vocal; The Marty Paich Dek-Tette
Bethlehem BCP 6022 A & B **[GOH]**
"Mel Tormé Loves Fred Astaire" (1956)
CONTENTS: Side A: Nice Work If You Can Get It; Something's
Gotta Give (Mercer); A Foggy Day; A Fine Romance (Kern-Fields)
SWING TIME 1936 film; Let's Call The Whole Thing Off; Top Hat, White
Tie and Tails (Berlin) TOP HAT 1935 film; **Side B:** They Can't Take That
Away From Me; They All Laughed; With songs by Irving Berlin

D945. Sophie Tucker, vocalist; Orchestra; Ted Shapiro, piano
Okeh 41010; Parlophone R-100 (British), Parlophone R-3181; Columbia SEG-
7766 (1928)
The Man I Love
Recorded NY, Mar. 9, 1928

D945.1. Dawn Upshaw/Audra McDonald/JudyBlazer/John Pizzarelli,et al
Nonesuch Non79498 (9/98) **"G. & I. Gershwin / Standards and Gems"**
CONTENTS: Barbary Coast (Vicki Lewis); But Not for Me (Judy Blazer);
Could You Use Me? (David Carroll/Judy Blazer); Fascinating
Rhythm (John Pizzarelli/Ann Morr); How Long Has this Been Going On?
(Audra Mcdonald); I Don't Think I'll Fall in Love Today (Dawn); I've Got a
Crush on You (Jason Graae/Juliet); Isn't it a Pity? (William Katt/Michelle
Nica); Little Jazz Bird (John Pizzarelli); Maybe (Dawn Upshaw/Kurt
Ollmann); Meadow Serenade (Brent Barrett/Rebecca Luker); My Cousin in
Milwaukee (Arnetia Walker); Somebody Loves Me (Judy Blazer); Someone
to Watch over Me (Dawn Upshaw); When Our Ship Comes Sailing In (Robert
Weste)
Producers: John McClure, Tommy Krasker, Leroy Parkins Jr.
Compilation producer: Tommy Krasker.
Album notes by Edward Jablonski.
This is part of the Nonesuch Gershwin Series.

D946. Various singers
AEI 1160 (AEI Sales, 7348 Matilija Ave., Van Nuys, CA 91404) (1986?)
"Lyrics by Ira Gershwin"
Reissues of Walden Records albums from the 1950s

D947. Various singers

"Fascinatin' Rhythm: Capitol Sings George Gershwin"

Capitol C21S-96792, CD; C41H-96792, cassette

CONTENTS: A Foggy Day (Dorothy Donegan); Embraceable You (Nat King Cole trio); I Got Rhythm (Ann Richards); It Ain't Necessarily So (Ella Mae Morse); Let's Call the Whole Thing Off (Marian McPartland); Nice Work If You Can Get It (Jeri Southern); Strike Up the Band (Tony Bennett & Count Basie); They All Laughed (Dakota Staton); How Long Has This Been Going On? (June Christy); RiB for dancing (Freddy Martin Orch.); But Not For Me (Margaret Whiting); They Can't Take That Away From Me (Peggy Lee); Swanee (Judy Garland); I'll Build a Stairway to Paradise (Liza Minelli); Summertime (Gordon McRae); That Certain Feeling (Jo Ann Greer); I've Got a Crush on You (Anna Maria Alberghetti)

D948. Various singers

"Great American Songwriters" Vol. I—*George and Ira Gershwin*

Rhino Records CD R2 71503 (CODE: RHR-6)

CONTENTS: How Long Has This Been Going On? (Tony Bennett); Embraceable You (Jo Stafford); But Not For Me (Chris Conner); They All Laughed (Ella Fitzgerald & Louis Armstrong); Somebody Loves Me (Bing Crosby); Love Walked In (Sylvia Sims); et al.

D949. Various singers

Smithsonian Collection 048-2, available in all formats

"American Songbook" subscription series—**George Gershwin**

CONTENTS: Swanee (1920 recording by Jolson); I'll Build a Stairway to Paradise (Paul Whiteman); The Man I Love (Lee Wiley); Embraceable You (Nat King Cole and his trio's 1943 recording); But Not For Me (Judy Garland's Decca *Girl Crazy* recording); Changing My Tune (Mel Torme and the Meltones); How Long Has This Been Going On? (Ella Fitzgerald's 1950 Decca recording); A Foggy Day (Chris Conner); My Cousin in Milwaukee (Nancy Walker's 1955 Dolphin recording); Soon (Kaye Ballard from Walden's 1955 collection); 'S Wonderful! & My Man's Gone Now (Sarah Vaughan's recordings for Mercury); Isn't It a Pity? (Mabel Mercer); Someone to Watch Over Me (Lena Horne on RCA); Somebody Loves Me (Maureen McGovern from her all-G album, **D900**)

D950. Sarah Vaughan, vocal; Hal Mooney & His Orchestra

Mercury MG 20310   **"Sarah Vaughan Sings George Gershwin"** -Vol. I **[GOH]**

CONTENTS: **Side A:** Isn't It a Pity?; Of Thee I Sing; I'll Build a Stairway to Paradise; Someone to Watch Over Me; Bidin' My Time; The Man I Love; **Side B:** How Long Has This Been Going On?; My One and Only (what am I gonna do); The Lorelei; I've Got a Crush On You; Summertime

See: **B1292**

D951. Sarah Vaughan, vocal; Hal Mooney & His Orchestra

Mercury MG 20311   **"Sarah Vaughan Sings George Gershwin"**-Vol.2 **[GOH]**

CONTENTS: **Side A:** Aren't You Kinda Glad We Did?; They All Laughed; Looking For a Boy; He Loves and She Loves; My Man's Gone Now; **Side B:** I Won't Say I Will, But I Won't Say I Won't; A Foggy Day; Let's Call the Whole Thing Off; Things Are Looking Up; Do It Again; Love Walked In

D952. Sarah Vaughan, vocals, Los Angeles Philharmonic; Michael Tilson Thomas, conducting
CBS FMT 37277, cassette (1982)
"Gershwin Live!"
CONTENTS: Overture: P&B; Medley: Summertime/It Ain't Necessarily So/I Loves You, Porgy; Medley: But Not For Me/Love is Here to Stay/ Embraceable You/Someone to Watch Over Me; Sweet & Low Down; Fascinating Rhythm; Do It Again; My Man's Gone Now; The Man I Love; Medley: Nice Work If You Can Get It/They Can't Take That Away from Me/'S Wonderful!/Swanee/Strike Up the Band; Encore: I've Got A Crush On You/A Foggy Day

D953. Sarah Walker, mezzo-soprano; Roger Vignoles, piano
Meredian CDE 84167 **[AAD?]**, CD (198?); Distributed by Harmonia Mundi (USA)
"Cabaret Songs"
CONTENTS: Songs by **Britten, Gershwin** (nine songs), **Dankworth, Vernon Duke, Margaret Mallory, Noël Coward, & Geoffrey Wright**, 27 cuts in all
See: **B1285**

D954. Kay Weber and Bob Crosby, vocals; Bob Crosby and Orchestra
Decca 1539 **[GOH]**
CONTENTS: A Foggy Day; Nice Work If You Can Get It

D955. Elisabeth Welch, vocalist; Benny Carter and His Swing Quartet
Vocalion 515, side 2, 78 (1936)
The Man I love
Recorded London, Oct. 13, 1936

D956. Margaret Whiting, vocal; Orchestra cond. by Jerry Gray
Capitol 294-B, 78, 10" **[GOH]** THE SHOCKING MISS PILGRIM 1947 film
For You, For Me, For Evermore *See:* p. 275

D957. Ronny Whyte & Travis Hudson, vocals and piano
Monmouth Evergreen MES 7061-A & B **"We Like a Gershwin Tune"**
[GOH]
CONTENTS: **Side A:** I Mean To Say; Bidin' My Time; The Real American Folk Song (is a Rag); I Don't Think I'll Fall In Love Today; Vodka (Gershwin-Stothart- Harbach-Hammerstein II) SONG OF THE FLAME 1925; Hang On to Me; How Long Has This Been Going On?; I Must Be Home By Twelve O'clock; **Side B:** Tell Me More!; Do What You Do!; That New Fangled Mother Of Mine; Medley: Something About Love (Gershwin-Paley) THE LADY IN RED 1919; He Loves and She Loves; Fidgety Feet; Hangin' Around With You; Kickin' the Clouds Away; I'd Rather Charleston

See: **B1294**

D958. Lee Wiley with Joe Bushkin's Orchestra & Max Kaminsky's Orchestra
Liberty Music Shop L 281, 78, 10"   Lee Wiley album **[GOH]**
CONTENTS: My One and Only; How Long Has This Been Going On?

D959. Lee Wiley with Joe Bushkin Orchestra
Liberty Music Shop L 283 (WP 26267 A, WP 26269 A), 78, 10" (194-?)
Girl Crazy. Sam and Delilah
Excerpt from "Girl crazy" (1930) (side A); excerpt from "Funny face" (1927).
Lee Wiley, vocal ; Joe Bushkin's Orchestra [Max Kaminsky, trumpet; Bud
Freeman, tenor sax; Joe Bushkin, piano/celeste; Artie Shapiro, bass; George
Wettling, drums] - *Cf.* 60 years of recorded jazz / Bruynincx.
Recorded in New York, Nov. 13, 1939 - *Cf.* Bruynincx.

D960. Lee Wiley with Max Kaminsky and Joe Bushkin orchs.
Liberty Music Shop L 284 (WP 26266 A, WP 26273 A), 78, 10" (194-?) **[GOH]**
CONTENTS: Sweet and Low down (Tip Toes); But Not for Me. (Girl
Crazy)
Personnel: Lee Wiley, vocal ; Max Kaminsky's Orchestra, [Max
Kaminsky, trumpet; Bud Freeman, tenor sax; Pee Wee Russell, clarinet
(side B); Joe Bushkin, piano/celeste; Eddie Condon, guitar (side B); Artie
Shapiro, bass; George Wettling, drums] - *Cf.* 60 years of recorded jazz /
Bruynincx.
Recorded in New York, Nov. 13 (side A) and 15 (side B), 1939 -
Cf. Bruynincx.

D961. Lee Wiley with Eddie Condon, vocals & instrumentals
New York, Decca DL 5137 [1949] LP
"George Gershwin jazz concert [sound recording]"
CONTENTS: 'S Wonderful!, Somebody Loves Me, My One and Only, Oh,
Lady Be Good!, Someone to Watch over Me, The Man I Love, Swanee, I'll
Build a Stairway to Paradise
Performed by Eddie Condon and his orchestra; featuring Lee Wiley, vocals
and instrumental solos
RECORD ID: LC01-046650
DATABASE: LIBRARY OF CONGRESS

D962. Lee Wiley with Max Kaminsky's Orchestra, featuring Pee Wee Russell,
Bud Freeman, Eddie Condon, Fats Waller, Artie Shapiro, George Wettling, Joe
Bushkin
"Lee Wiley Sings George Gershwin and Cole Porter"
Monmouth Evergreen MES 7034 (1972) from the original 78's released by
Liberty Music Shop in 1939 & 1940; Audiophile AP-1; CD: ACD-1
CONTENTS: How Long Has This Been Going On?; My One and Only; Sweet
and Low Down; 'S Wonderful! I've Got a Crush on You; Someone to Watch
Over Me; Sam and Delilah; But Not For Me; With songs by C. Porter
Program notes by Bill Borden on early slipcase ; on CD: samples of orig. notes
& notes by Larry Carr & Frank Driggs *See*: **B1278**

D962.1 Julie Wilson, vocals, with William Roy

"Julie Wilson Sings the Gershwin Songbook"
DRG 5251 (1999)
CONTENTS: Sweet and Low-Down; Oh, Lady Be Good!; He Loves and She
Loves; My One and Only; That Certain Feeling; They All Laughed; Someone
to Watch Over Me; Treat Me Rough; Do, Do, Do; Isn't It a Pity?; Funny
Face; Soon; A Foggy Day; :Love Walked In; Lorelei; It Ain't Necessarily So;
Sam and Delilah; They Can't Take That Away From Me; But Not for Me;
Nice Work If You Can Get It; Could You Use Me?; Let's Call The Whole
Thing Off; I've Got a Crush On You; Embraceable You; How Long Has This
Been Going On?; The Man I Love; OTIS; 'S Wonderful!

D963. Bill Wright, vocals
B.A.S.E. 9001, CD & cassette (avail. from Wright, POB 2032, New York,
NY 10011; cassette @ $12, CD $15 as of 1991)
CONTENTS: All-G program, including, among others: There's More to a
Kiss Than the X-X-X; Nashville Nightingale; Someone to Watch Over Me;
How Long Has This Been Going On?; Here's a Kiss for Cinderella; (Our)
Love Is Here to Stay

D964. Edythe Wright, vocal; Tommy Dorsey & His Clambake Seven
Victor 26595-B, 78, 10" **[GOH]** A Damsel in Distress 1937 film
Nice Work If You Can Get It

SONGS, INSTRUMENTAL TREATMENT

D965. American Classics String Quartet
AmCam ACR 10304
CONTENTS: (Gershwin & Kern: Together Again) (five G songs, newly
arranged by John Stephens for string quartet): By Strauss; The Man I Love: A
Foggy Day; For You, For Me, Forever More; Nice Work If You Can Get It;
With Kern Songs

D966. George Bassman and His Orchestra
Decca DL 74468, **"Gershwin from Broadway to Hollywood" [GOH]**
CONTENTS: OF THEE I SING-selections; PARDON MY ENGLISH-
Selections; PORGY AND BESS-selections; Shall We Dance?-selections;
A Damsel In Distress-selections; Goldwyn Follies-selections

D967. **"Beatrice, Nicolas, & Maurice André Jouent Gershwin."**
EMI CLASSICS 7243 5 55620 2 9, CD (1996)
Beatrice, oboe; Nicolas & Maurice, trumpet
CONTENTS: They Can't Take That Away from Me; AiP (Opening & Blues);
Swanee; Bess, You Is My Woman and other songs

D968. Ran Blake, piano
Therwil, Switzerland, Hat Hut, ART CD 6077 (1991)
"That Certain Feeling"
CONTENTS: Ouverture I; Mine; It Ain't Necessarily So; The Man I
Love; Oh Where's My Bess; Blues; Strike up the Band; What Do
You Want Wid Bess; I Got Rhythm; That Certain Feeling; Someone to
Watch Over Me; But Not for Me; Who Cares; Liza; Clara Clara; Oh Where's

My Bess; 'S Wonderful! That Certain Feeling

D969. Hill Bowen, arrs. & conducting
RCA Camden CAL 675-A & B Living Strings and Living Voices in Music of
George Gershwin
CONTENTS: **Side A:** The Man I Love; Love Walked In; But Not For Me;
Embraceable You; (Our) Love Is Here To Stay; Summertime; Somebody Loves
Me; They Can't Take That Away From Me; A Foggy Day; Someone to Watch
Over Me

D970. Ruby Braff, tpt.; George Barnes, guitar; Wayne Wright, gtr.;
Michael Moore, bass
Concord Jazz CJ 5-A & B **[GOH]**
"The Ruby Braff/George Barnes Quartet Plays Gershwin" (July 26, 1974)
CONTENTS: **Side A:** 'S Wonderful!; I Got Rhythm; They Can't Take That
Away from Me; Nice Work If You Can Get It; Somebody Loves Me;
Side B: But Not For Me; Summertime; Bidin' My Time; Love Walked In;
Embraceable You; Liza (All the clouds'll roll away)

D971. Ruby Braff and the Shubert Alley Cats
Warner Bros. WS 1273 **"Ruby Braff Goes 'Girl Crazy'"** **[GOH]**
CONTENTS: Embraceable You; Treat Me Rough; But Not For Me; Boy!
What Love Has Done for Me; I Got Rhythm; Bidin' My Time; Could You
Use Me?; Barbary Coast

D972. Les Brown and his Band of Renown
Columbia CS 8479 (196-?)
CONTENTS: 'S Wonderful! (3:07); Somebody Loves Me (2:31); Soon (2:32);
I Was Doing All Right (3:21); Love Walked in (3:12); Oh, Lady Be Good
(2:48); Liza (2:33); Summertime (3:37); They All Laughed (3:09); Nice Work
If You Can Get it (3:16); But Not for Me (2:15); A Foggy Day (3:30)
Program notes by Curtis F. Brown on container
Arrangements by Jay Hill
RECORD ID: LC01-036857; DATABASE: LIBRARY OF CONGRESS

D973. Billy Butterfield and His Orchestra
Capitol 20025-26-27-28, Album BD-10, 78, 10" **[GOH]**
CONTENTS: Oh, Lady Be Good!; Someone to Watch Over Me; Somebody
Loves Me; Nice Work If You Can Get It; Maybe; It Ain't Necessarily So; Do It
Again; They Can't Take That Away From Me

D974. George Cables, piano; John Heard, bass; Ralph Penland, drums
Contemporary Records 5C 14030, cassette (1987)
"By George: George Cables Plays the Music of George Gershwin"
CONTENTS: Bess, You Is My Woman Now; My Man's Gone Now; I Got
Rhythm; Embraceable You; Someone to Watch Over Me; A Foggy Day
Program notes by Cables in container
Producer: George Cables
Recorded at Fantasy Studios (CA?) Feb. 27, 1987

D975. Al Caiola and Orchestra, arrs. by Caiola

Time Series 2OOO S 2010, LP, 12" **"Gershwin and Guitars" [GOH]**
CONTENTS: The Man I Love; Fascinating Rhythm; I'll Build a Stairway to
Paradise; Mine; But Not for Me; A Foggy Day; Strike Up the Band;
Swanee; Oh, Lady Be Good!; Nice Work If You Can Get It; Soon;
Embraceable You

D976. The Canadian Brass Quintet
RCA 6490-2-RC, CD **[DDD]**
"Strike Up the Band, The Canadian Brass Plays George Gershwin"
CONTENTS: Strike Up the Band; Someone to Watch Over Me; "The Rhythm
Series" (Medley): Clap Yo' Hands, Fidgety Feet, Fascinating Rhythm, I Got
Rhythm; A Foggy Day/ Nice Work If You Can Get It; The Man I Love; **P&B**
Suite: Introduction/Jasbo Brown Blues/Summertime, It Ain't Necessarily So,
Bess, You Is My Woman Now, I Loves You, Porgy, A Woman Is a
Sometime Thing/I Got Plenty O' Nuttin'; Oh, Lawd, I'm On My Way; With
other pieces by G, *q. v.* in full entry under **"Anthologies"**

D977. Frankie Carle, piano with rhythm accompaniment
RCA Victor LPM 3083, 10" Song Hits From the Broadway Shows PAL JOEY
& OF THEE I SING **[GOH]**
CONTENTS: Songs from PAL JOEY (Rodgers-Hart) 1940; OTIS; Wintergreen
For President; Who Cares?; Love Is Sweeping the Country

D978. Barbara Carroll Trio (Joe Schulman, bass; Joe Petti, drums) **[GOH]**
Verve MGV 2063   Selections from Funny Face 1957 film & other tunes
See: Full entry under **"Music Used in Films"**

D979. Frank Chacksfield & His Orchestra & Chorus; Kenny Baker, trpt.; Michael Reeves,
piano
London Phase 4 SW 95146-A & B **"The Glory That Was Gershwin" [GOH]**
CONTENTS: PORGY AND BESS: Introduction; I Got Rhythm; The Man I
Love; Embraceable You; Rhapsody in Blue (abridged); Fascinating Rhythm;
But Not For Me; Strike Up the Band; Liza (All the clouds'll roll away); Suite
from PORGY AND BESS: Introduction; Summertime; It Ain't Necessarily
So; A Woman Is a Sometime Thing; I Got Plenty O' Nuttin'; Bess, You Is My
Woman Now; I'm On My Way
Arrangements by Roland Shaw

D980. Frank Chacksfield and His Orchestra
London LL 1203-A & B **"The Music of George Gershwin" [GOH]**
CONTENTS: Fascinating Rhythm; Someone to Watch Over Me; (I've Got)
Beginner's Luck; The Man I Love; Do, Do, Do; They Can't Take That Away
From Me; Embraceable You; Oh, Lady Be Good!; Bidin' My Time; I Got
Rhythm; Love Walked In; Somebody Loves Me; Rhapsody in Blue

D981. Kevin Cole, piano
Fanfare DFL 7007 (Canada) **[GOH]**
"The Unknown George Gershwin"
CONTENTS: LADY, BE GOOD! overture; Yankee; The World is Mine
(Gershwin) FUNNY FACE 1927 (unused); Waltz medley: Roses of France
(PRIMROSE 1924); I'm About to be a Mother (OF THEE I SING 1931); By

Strauss (THE SHOW IS ON 1936); Short Story; Till Then; Just Another
Rhumba; Wake Up, Brother, and Dance; Dance Alone With You; All the
Livelong Day (Gershwin) 1921—used in KISS ME, STUPID movie1964;
Dawn of a New Day; GIRL CRAZY overture *See*: **B1313, B1321**

D982. Kevin Cole, piano
Pro Arte CDD-365 **[DDD]**
"Lady Be Good!: The Unknown George Gershwin" playing recently
discovered original piano scores of 13 selections)
CONTENTS: Oh, Lady Be Good!; Yan-Kee; The World is Mine; Waltz
Medley; Short Story; Till Then; Just Another Rhumba; Wake Up, Brother,
and Dance; Primrose Medley; Dance Alone With You; All the Livelong day;
Dawn of a New Day; Girl Crazy (overture)

D983. Eddie Condon & his Orchestra
"George Gershwin Jazz Concert"
Decca DL 5137, 10 in., (1949)
CONTENTS: 'S Wonderful!; Somebody Loves Me; My One and Only;
Oh, Lady Be Good!; Someone to Watch over Me; The Man I Love; Swanee;
I'll Build A Stairway to Paradise

D984. Eddie Condon & his Orch; Bobby Hackett, et al
Decca A-398 (23430 - 23433), 4 discs, 78, 10"
"George Gershwin jazz concert"
CONTENT:. [Disc 1]. 'S Wonderful! / George Gershwin, Ira Gershwin ;
Somebody Loves Me / G. Gershwin, Ballard Macdonald, B.G. Desylva (Jack
Teagarden, Vocal) - [Disc 2]. My One and Only / G. Gershwin, I. Gershwin
(Bobby Hackett, Trumpet Solo) ; Oh, Lady Be Good! / G. Gershwin, I.
Gershwin - [Disc 3]. Someone to Watch over Me / G. Gershwin, I. Gershwin
(Lee Wiley, Vocal; B. Hackett, Trumpet; J. Teagarden, Trombone) ; the Man
I Love / G. Gershwin, I. Gershwin (Lee Wiley, Vocal; B. Hackett, Trumpet) -
[Disc 4]. Swanee / G. Gershwin, Irving Caesar ; I'll Build a Stairway to
Paradise / G. Gershwin, B.G. Desylva, Arthur Francis.
Personality series.   Principally instrumental fox trots.
Title from container.
Recorded in New York, Dec. 12, 1944 (side 1), Dec. 14, 1944 (sides 2, 5-6),
May 17, 1945 (sides 3, 8) and June 14, 1945 (sides 4, 7) - Cf. *60 years of
recorded jazz* / Bruynincx.
Program and biographical notes ([12] p. : ill., ports.) laid in container.

D985. Decca Band with the American Eight; Harry Sosnik, director
Decca 3373-A, 78, 10" **[GOH]**
CONTENTS: Strike Up the Band
Album 156, Side 1

D986. Buddy DeFranco, clarinet; Oscar Peterson, piano; Orch. cond. by Russell Garcia
Verve MGV 2022
"The George Gershwin Song Book"
CONTENTS: I Wants to Stay Here; I Was Doing All Right; 'S Wonderful!;
Bess, You Is My Woman Now; Strike Up the Band; They Can't Take That
Away from Me; The Man I Love; Someone to Watch Over Me; It Ain't

Necessarily So

D987. **"Buddy DeFranco & Oscar Peterson Play George Gershwin"**
Norgran MGN-1016 (date ?)

D988. Jimmy Dorsey and Orchestra; Toots Camarata, arranger
Decca 1508, 3861, Brunswick 02481 (1937)
I Got Rhythm

D989. Eddie Duchin & His Central Park Orch.; Dick Robertson & Lou Sherwood, vocals
Brunswick 6476, 78, 10" **[GOH]**
CONTENTS: My Cousin in Milwaukee; Isn't It a Pity?

D990. Eddie Duchin, piano, with drums and bass
Columbia C-52
"A Natural: Duchin-Gershwin"
CONTENTS: The Man I Love; Someone to Watch Over Me; Love Walked In;
Embraceable You; Swanee; Somebody Loves Me; Summertime; They Can't
Take That Away from Me

D991. Dan Estrem & John Holmquist
ProJazz CDJ-607; MM-607
"Gershwin By Guitar"
Two-guitar arrs. of G melodies

D992. Percy Faith and His Orchestra
Columbia Special Products EN2 13719-A, B, C, D, LP, 12" **[GOH]**
"The Columbia Album of George Gershwin"
CONTENTS: **Side A:** Fascinating Rhythm; A Foggy Day; Soon; I Got Plenty
O' Nuttin'; Embraceable You; Somebody Loves Me; **Side B:** I Got Plenty O'
Nuttin'; Summertime; Bess, You Is My Woman Now; My Man's Gone Now;
Nice Work If You Can Get It; For You, For Me, For Evermore; Liza (All the
clouds'll roll away); **Side C:** 'S Wonderful!; (Our) Love is Here To Stay;
They Can't Take That Away From Me; The Man I Love; Love Walked In;
Oh, Lady Be Good!; **Side D:** Preludes for Piano, Nos. 2 & 3; Maybe;
Someone to Watch Over Me; They All Laughed; Bidin' My Time; I Got
Rhythm

D993. Percy Faith and His Orchestra
Harmony Headliner KH 31537-A & B, Vol. I **[GOH]**
CONTENTS: 'S Wonderful!; The Man I Love; Mine; They Can't Take That
Away from Me; Love Walked In; Oh, Lady Be Good!; Someone to Watch
Over Me; I Got Rhythm; Bidin' My Time; Maybe

D994. Percy Faith and His Orchestra
Harmony Headliner KH 31538-A & B, Vol.2 **[GOH]**
CONTENTS: Fascinating Rhythm; A Foggy Day; I Got Plenty O' Nuttin';
Embraceable You; Somebody Loves Me; Summertime; Nice Work If You
Can Get It; Bess, You Is My Woman Now; Preludes for piano 2 & 3; My
Man's Gone Now

D995. Carl Fenton and Orchestra
Brunswick 4808, 78, 10" SONG OF THE FLAME 1925 **[GOH]**
CONTENTS: Cossack Love Song (Don't forget me); Song of the Flame
From the 1930 First National movie

D996. Carl Fenton's Orchestra with piano passages by Arden & Ohman
Brunswick 2790, 78, 10" **[GOH]**
CONTENTS: Oh, Lady Be Good!; Fascinating Rhythm; So Am I

D997. Frederick Fennell conducting his orchestra
Mercury SRI 75127, previously released in 1961 as Mercury SPS 6006, q.v.
below (1979?)
"Music of George Gershwin"
CONTENTS: I Got Rhythm; Love Is Sweeping the Country; Love Walked In;
'S Wonderful!; Bidin' My Time; Oh, Lady Be Good!; Fascinating Rhythm;
Liza; Embraceable You; The Man I Love; Someone to Watch Over Me; But
Not for Me
Durations & program notes by Edward Jablonksi & Frederick Fennell on
container

D998. Frederick Fennell conducts Gershwin
Mercury PPS-2006, LP (1961?); Perfect presence sound series
"Frederick Fennell conducts Gershwin"
Arranged for orchestra by Rayburn Wright
CONTENTS: I Got Rhythm (3:01); Love Is Sweeping the Country (2:33);
Love Walked in (3:27); 'S Wonderful (2:38); Bidin' My Time (2:45); Oh, My
Lady by Good (3:25); Fascinating Rhythm (1:55); Liza (All the Clouds'll Roll
Away) (3:44); Embraceable You (2:35); The Man I Love (3:25); Someone to
Watch over Me (3:10); But Not for Me (3:14)
Recorded in Studio A at Fine Recording Studios, New York, NY
Program notes by Edward Jablonski, Fennell, and Wright on container *See*:
B1259, B1262

D999. First Modern Piano Quartet: Dick Marx, Eddie Costa, Hank Jones, Johnny
Costa, pianos; w/ Orchestra, Manny Albam, conducting
Coral CRL 759102-A & B, LP, 12"
"A Gallery of Gershwin By the First Modern Piano Quartet"
CONTENTS: Side A: Fascinating Rhythm; Love Walked In; Clap Yo' Hands;
The Man I Love; Someone to Watch Over Me; Mine; **Side B:** Liza (All the
clouds'll roll away); Bess, You Is My Woman Now; (Our) Love Is Here To Stay;
Somebody Loves Me; Soon

D1000. Jacques Fray and Mario Braggiotti, pianos
Decca 2875, 78, 10", Album 96, Sides 3 & 4 - George Gershwin Songs, Vol. I
[GOH]
CONTENTS: 'S Wonderful!; My One and Only; Who Cares?; Wintergreen for
President

D1001. Jacques Fray & Mario Braggiotti, pianos
His Master's Voice B 2910, 78, 10" **[GOH]** FUNNY FACE-medley 1928
London

CONTENTS: Funny Face; 'S Wonderful!; My One and Only; Let's Kiss and Make Up

D1002. Jacques Fray & Mario Braggiotti, pianos
Disque Gramophone K 5309-B, 78, 10" **[GOH]**
The Man I Love

D1003. Jacques Fray & Mario Braggiotti, pianos
Disque Gramophone K 5310-A, 78, 10" **[GOH]**
The World is Mine

D1004. Erroll Garner, piano
EmArcy 826 224-4 (1976)
"Erroll Garner Plays Gershwin and Kern"
Garner, Baldwin piano; Eddie Calhoun, bass; Kelly Martin, drums, on all selections except I Got Rhythm, where Calhoun and Martin are replaced by Charles "Ike" Isaacs, bass; Jimmy Smith, drums, & Jose Mangual, congas
CONTENTS: Strike Up the Band; Love Walked In; I Got Rhythm; Someone to Watch Over Me; A Foggy Day; Nice Work if You Can Get It; With songs by **Kern**
Program notes by George Wein on container; durations on container
Producer: Martha Glaser

D1005. Carroll Gibbons Orchestra; Christopher Stone, narr.; Larry
Adler, harmonica; (for D-D, for D-A): Carroll Gibbons & the Savoy Hotel Orpheans; Anne Ziegler & Webster Booth, vocals; Carroll Gibbons Orchestra; Hildegarde & Christopher Stone, narr.
Columbia 70546 D-A through D, Columbia Masterworks Set X-95, 78, **[GOH]**
CONTENTS: **(D-A):** The Man I Love; Do, Do, Do; My One and Only; 'S Wonderful!; **(D-D):** It Ain't Necessarily So; I Got Plenty O' Nuttin'; There's a Boat Dat's Leavin' Soon For New York; **(D-B):** The Half of It, Dearie, Blues; Sweet and Low Down; The Man I Love; **(C):** Summertime; Bess, You Is My Woman Now

D1006. Carroll Gibbons Orchestra; Larry Adler, harmonica; Hildegarde & Christopher Stone, narr.
Columbia (English) DX 786-A, 78 **[GOH]**
CONTENTS: **Side A:** The Man I Love; Do, Do, Do; My One and Only; 'S Wonderful!; **Side B:** The Half Of It, Dearie, Blues; Fascinating Rhythm; Sweet and Low Down; The Man I Love
Includes extracts of records by GG & Fred Astaire; Columbia Masterworks Set X-95

D1007. Lou Gold & Orchestra
Harmony 314-H, 78, 10" (1926) **[GOH]**
CONTENTS: Clap Yo' Hands; Do, Do, Do

D1008. Benny Goodman & His Orchestra
Okeh 6544 A & B 78, 10" **[GOH]**

CONTENTS: Clarinet a la King (Eddie Sauter); How Long Has This Been Going On?

D1009.   George Greeley and His Piano
Harmony HS 11309 **"Greeley Plays Gershwin" [GOH]**
CONTENTS: RiB [themes]; The Man I Love; Someone to Watch Over Me; Mine; An American in Paris [themes]; But Not For Me; Summertime; Bess, You Is My Woman Now

D1010.   Johnny Green, piano
Brunswick 7892, 78, 10" **[GOH]**
CONTENTS: Let's Call the Whole Thing Off; Beginner's Luck; Slap That Bass; They All Laughed; They Can't Take That Away From Me; Shall We Dance?

D1011.   Phil Green and His Rhythm on Reeds
London 243-A, 78, 10" **[GOH]**
CONTENTS: Fascinating Rhythm (on A side); Moonglow (Hudson-Mills-DeLange) (on B side)

D1012.   Ralph Grierson and Artie Kane, pianists.
Angel S 36083, LP
"'S Wonderful!"
CONTENTS: An American in Paris; Three Preludes ; 'S Wonderful!; The Man I Love; Strike up the Band; Embraceable You; Oh, Lady, Be Good; Fascinating Rhythm
Orchestral works, piano works and songs arr. for 2 pianos by G. Stone and others
Durations and program notes by R. Guy on slipcase.

D1013.   Bobby Hackett, cornet, and Orchestra
Okeh 4877-A & B, 78, 10" **[GOH]**
CONTENTS: Ain't Misbehavin' (Waller-Brooks-Razaf); Embraceable You

D1014.   Hamburg Radio Dance Orchestra; Benjamin Thomson, conducting
Summit, LP (p 1977)
"The very best of Gershwin"
CONTENTS: Fascinating rhythm; 'S Wonderful!; Summertime; Embraceable You; Foggy Day; Liza; It Ain't Necessarily So; Nice Work if You Can Get It; The Man I Love; Somebody Loves Me; They Can't Take That Away From Me; I Got Rhythm; Let's Call the Whole Thing Off; Someone to Watch Over Me; But Not for Me

D1015.   **"Ofra Harnoy and Friends Play Gershwin"**
Mastersound DFCI-020
Ofra Harnoy, cello
CONTENTS: Songs *See*: Full entry at **D735**

D1016.   Ted Heath and His Music   London LL 1217A & B **[GOH]**
"Gershwin for Moderns" CONTENTS: The Man I Love; Love Walked In; Nice Work If You Can Get it; (Our) Love is Here to Stay; Clap Yo' Hands; I

Got Rhythm/ But Not For Me; Someone to Watch Over Me; That Certain Feeling; Embraceable You; Changing My Tune (THE SHOCKING MISS PILGRIM) 1947 film; Soon *See*: p. 275

D1017. Ted Heath and His Music
London 1324-A, 78, 10" STRIKE UP THE BAND 1927/30 **[GOH]**
CONTENTS: Strike Up the Band

D1018. Leslie Henton with Orchestra
Columbia 9592, 78 FUNNY FACE 1928 (London) **[GOH]**
CONTENTS: Tell the Doc (G. Gershwin-Carter-I. Gershwin);
A few drinks—a comedy sketch by Leslie Henton & Sydney Howard

D1019. Skitch Henderson and His Orchestra
Capital 15234-B, 78, 10" **[GOH]**
Maybe

D1020. Skitch Henderson and His Orchestra
Capitol 15136-A, 78, 10" **[GOH]**
Mine

D1021. John Hicks plays selections from Crazy for You
Red Baron AK 52761 (1992)
Crazy for you [sound recording]/ songs by George & Ira Gershwin
CONTENTS: K-ra-zy for you (part 1); K-ra-zy for you (part 2);
Embraceable You; I Got Rhythm; They Can't Take That Away from Me;
Bidin' My Time; Someone to Watch over Me; Nice Work If You Can Get
It; But Not for Me; I Got Rhythm (Reprise)
RECORD ID: LC01-050021
DATABASE: LIBRARY OF CONGRESS

D1022. "Earl Hines Plays George Gershwin" Earl Hines, piano
South Yarra, Vic., Australia, Swaggie S1338. LP (1981)
CONTENTS: Liza; I've Got a Crush on You; Nice Work If You Can Get It;
But Not for Me; The Man I Love; Love Walked In; It Ain't
Necessarily So; Love Walked In; 'S Wonderful!
Recorded Aug. 27, 1973, at Edd Kalehoff Studios, New York City

D1023. Earl 'Fatha' Hines, piano **"Earl Hines Plays George Gershwin"** October
16, 1973
Classic Jazz CJ 31 **[GOH]**
CONTENTS: RiB; A Foggy Day; (Our) Love is Here To Stay; They All
Laughed; Somebody Loves Me; Embraceable You; Let's Call the Whole
Thing Off and They Can't Take That Away From Me; Love Walked In;
Summertime; RiB

D1024. Jack Hylton and Orchestra
Disque Gramophone K 3317, 78, 10" **[GOH]**
CONTENTS: So Am I; Hang On to Me; Fascinating Rhythm; Oh, Lady Be
Good!; Little Jazz Bird

D1025.   Dick Hyman, piano
MusicMasters 01612-65094-2.
"THE GERSHWIN SONGBOOK: Jazz Variations"
CONTENTS: 18 Gershwin arrangements & 18 improvisations including
Nobody But You, Stairway to Paradise, Who Cares?, Sweet and
Low-Down, My One and Only.

D1026.   Ida James and Ellis Larkins Trio
Decca 11004-A & B, 78, 10" **[GOH]**
CONTENTS: (A): You Must Be Blind (Lorenzo Pack-Milton Nelson)
(B): I Won't Say I Will, But I Won't Say I Won't (1923)

D1027.   Roger Wolfe Kahn and Orchestra
Brunswick 4479, 78, 10" **[GOH]**
CONTENTS: Liza (all the clouds'll roll away); Do What You Do!

D1028.   Hal Kemp and Orchestra
Brunswick 6416-A, 78, 10" **[GOH]**
Wintergreen for President

D1029.   Orchestra; André Kostelanetz, conducting
Columbia CL 2133 (1964)
"Gershwin Wonderland"
CONTENTS: Principally excerpts from musical comedies, arranged
Program notes by IG on container

D1030.   André Kostelanetz and his orchestra
Columbia CL 770, mono (195-?)
"Music of George Gershwin"
CONTENTS: Fascinating Rhythm; Mine; The Man I Love; Embraceable
You; Soon; I Got Rhythm; Bess, Oh Where's My Bess?; 'S Wonderful!;
Maybe; Someone to Watch Over Me; Oh, Lady Be Good!; Strike Up the
Band
Biographical & **program notes** by Paul Affelder on container

D1031.   Louis Levy and His Concert Orchestra
London B 12010, 78, 12" **("George Gershwin Suite"**-Part 1) **[GOH]**
CONTENTS: Strike Up the Band; Embraceable You; Do, Do, Do; But Not
For Me; Somebody Loves Me; Of Thee I Sing
Album LA 64, Sides 1 & 4

D1032.   Louis Levy and His Concert Orchestra
London B 12011, 78, 12" **("George Gershwin Suite"**-Part 2) **[GOH]**
CONTENTS: Love Walked In; Swanee; Someone to Watch Over Me;
'S Wonderful!; I Got Rhythm; Bidin' My Time
Album 64, Sides 2 & 3

D1033.   Longines Symphonette Society/American Music Makers Program
Longines Symphonette LW 227-A & B **"A George Gershwin Festival"**
[GOH]

CONTENTS: **Side A:** They All Laughed; Shall We Dance?; My Man's Gone Now; A Foggy Day; Nice Work If You Can Get It; Changing My Tune, THE SHOCKING MISS PILGRIM 1947 film; Till Then (1933); **Side B**: Medley: Aren't You Kind Of Glad We Did?/By Strauss; They Can't Take That Away From Me; Love Walked In; Let's Call the Whole Thing Off; Dawn of a New Day

D1034.   Longines Symphonette Society/American Music Makers Program
Longines Symphonette LW 228-A & B **"A George Gershwin Festival"**
CONTENTS: **Side A:** I Was Doing Alright; Medley: It Ain't Necessarily So & I Loves You Porgy; Love is Here to Stay; Shall We Dance; Bess, You Is My Woman Now; **Side B:** Summertime; For You, For Me, Forevermore; I Got Plenty O' Nuttin'; Medley: Things Are Looking Up & I've Got Beginner's Luck; A Woman Is a Sometime Thing

D1035.   Longines Symphonette
Longines Symphonette LWS GF1-A & B **"A George Gershwin Festival"** **[GOH]**
CONTENTS: **Side A:** Summertime; They Can't Take That Away From Me; Nice Work If You Can Get It; Let's Call the Whole Thing Off; I Got Plenty O'Nuttin'; **Side B:** A Foggy Day; Love Walked In; Shall We Dance?; I Was Doing All Right; They All Laughed

D1036.   Louisiana Rhythm Kings
Brunswick 4845-B, 78, 10" (1930?) **[GOH]**
Swanee

D1037.   Louisiana Rhythm Kings
Brunswick 4706-A & B, 78, 1O" **[GOH]**
CONTENTS: **A:** Oh, Lady Be Good!; **B**: I Have to Have You (Whiting-Robin)

D1038.   Music Minus One MMO 1023 (197-?)
"The Gershwin-Porter Songbook"
Unidentified orchestra conducted by Bob Dorough
CONTENTS: Popular songs, in recorded accompaniments
Printed music (12 pp.) inserted

D1039.   Marcus Roberts, piano; Reginald Veal, bass; Herlin Riley, Jr., drums
Columbia CK 66437, CD
"Gershwin for Lovers"
CONTENTS: A Foggy Day; The Man I Love; Our Love Is Here to Stay; Summertime; Someone to Watch Over Me; It Ain't Necessarily So; Nice Work If You Can Get It; They Can't Take That Away From Me; How Long Has This Been Going On?; But Not For Me
Produced By: Marcus Roberts *See also*: **D769**

D1040.   Symphonic Portrait of George Gershwin, arr. and cond. by Guy Luypaerts
Capitol L-252, LP, 10" **[GOH]**
CONTENTS: Medley Introduction; Fascinating Rhythm; The Man I Love; Embraceable You; Somebody Loves Me; Summertime; I Got Plenty O'

Nuttin'; Someone to Watch Over Me; Oh, Lady Be Good!; They Can't
Take That Away From Me; A Foggy Day; Do It Again; I Got Rhythm;
Finale

D1041.   Clive Lythgoe, piano
Tioch Digital TD 1006-A & B **"Gershwin's Fascinating Rhythms"**
CONTENTS: Fascinating Rhythm; The Man I Love; I'll Build a Stairway to
Paradise; Somebody Loves Me; Strike Up the Band; Clap Yo' Hands; Oh,
Lady Be Good!; Liza (All the clouds'll roll away); Do It Again; 'S
Wonderful!; Who Cares?; My One and Only; Do, Do, Do; That Certain
Feeling; Sweet and Low Down; I Got Rhythm

D1042.   Percival Mackey, piano
Columbia 4000 (English), 10" **[GOH]**
CONTENTS: Fascinating Rhythm; Oh, Lady Be Good!; So Am I

D1043.   Adam Makowicz, piano; Dave Holland, bass; Charlie Haden, bass;
Al Foster, drums
Novus 3022-4-N9 (1987)
**"Adam Makowicz Naughty Baby Honoring George Gershwin
(1898-1937)"**
CONTENTS: Somebody Loves Me; They All Laughed; Prelude 2; Maybe;
Fascinating Rhythm; Naughty Baby; Oh Bess, Oh, Where's My Bess?;
Embraceable You; RiB; My Man's Gone Now; Summertime
Arrangements by Makowicz
Recorded at RCA Studio B, NY, June 25, 26, & 27, 1987
Producer: Edith Kiggen *See*: **B1541**

D1044.   Shelly Manne Quintet and Big Band
Manne,-Shelly; Williams,-John, b. 1932, Musical Director
Capitol T 2313, LP (1965) [earliest release]; DS-909 Discovery Records
"Manne - That's Gershwin!"
CONTENTS: By Strauss (2:53); My Man's Gone Now (3:30); Mine (3:55);
Love Is Here to Stay (2:31); Summertime (3:55); The Real American Folk
ng (Is a Rag) (2:45); The Man I Love (5:23); Prelude #2 (2:37); How
Long Has this Been Going On? (2:33); Theme from Concerto in F (2:55)
Recorded 2/24-2/26/65 in Studio A, the Capitol Tower, Hollywood, CA.
Program notes on container; by Harvey Siders on Discovery release

D1045.   **"Yehudi Menuhin & Stephane Grappelli play Gershwin"**
I Records CDM 7 69218 2 EMI , CD (p 1988)
Yehudi Menuhin & Stephane Grappelli, violins; with other instrumentalists.
CONTENTS: Fascinating Rhythm (2:18); Soon (3:47); Summertime (4:22);
Nice Work If You Can Get it (2:30); Embraceable You (3:10); Liza
(3:39); A Foggy Day (3:45); 'S Wonderful! (2:44); The Man I Love
(4:42); - I Got Rhythm (2:57); He Loves and She Loves (2:53); They
Can't Take That Away (4:47); They All Laughed (2:58); Funny Face
(3:20); [Our] Love Is Here to Stay (3:57); Lady Be Good (3:37). **Program
notes** by John W. Duarte on booklet inserted in container.
Recorded 1972-1981.

D1046. Peter Nero, piano; Boston Pops Orchestra; Arthur Fiedler, conducting
RCA ANL1-1970 **"Nero Goes 'Pops'"**
CONTENTS: RiB; (Our) Love Is Here To Stay; Embraceable You; The Man
I Love; They Can't Take That Away From Me; Bidin' My Time; I Got
Rhythm

D1047. Red Nichols and His *Strike Up the Band* Orchestra
Brunswick 4695, 78, 10" STRIKE UP THE BAND 1930 **[GOH]**
CONTENTS: Strike Up the Band; Soon

D1048. Kenneth "Red" Norvo and His Swing Sextette
Decca 779-A & B, 78, 10" **[GOH]**
CONTENTS: I Got Rhythm; Oh, Lady Be Good!

D1049. Phil Ohman & Victor Arden with Orchestra
Brunswick 3035, 78, 10" **[GOH]**
CONTENTS: Looking for a Boy; Sweet and Low Down; That Certain
Feeling; When Do We Dance?

D1050. Phil Ohman & Victor Arden with Orchestra
Brunswick 3377, 78, 10" **[GOH]**
CONTENTS: Clap Yo' Hands; Fidgety Feet; Do, Do, Do; Someone to
Watch Over Me

D1051. Joe Pass, guitar; Shelly Manne, drums; John Pisano, rhythm guitar; Jim
Hughart, bass
"Ira, George, and Joe: Joe Pass Loves Gershwin"
Pablo Today 2312-133 (1982)

D1052. Oscar Peterson, piano; Ray Brown, bass; Irving Ashby, guitar
Mercury 89009, 78, 10", Album C 119 **"Oscar Peterson Plays Pretty"**
[GOH]
CONTENTS: Blue Moon (Rodgers-Hart) 1935; They Can't Take That Away
from Me

D1053. Oscar Peterson, piano; Barney Kessel, guitar; Ray Brown, bass
Mercury MG C 605-A & B **"Oscar Peterson Plays George Gershwin"**
[GOH]
CONTENTS: **Side A:** The Man I Love; Fascinating Rhythm; It Ain't
Necessarily So; Somebody Loves Me; I've Got a Crush On You;
Side B: I Was Doing All Right; 'S Wonderful!; Oh, Lady Be Good!;
A Foggy Day

D1054. Oscar Peterson, piano; Barney Kessel, guitar; Ray Brown, bass
Polygram 823-249-4, cassette (1985, 1952); Verve 823 249-1
"The George Gershwin Songbook"
Verve Great American Songbooks
Recorded in Los Angeles, November & December, 1952; this version is a re-
mastering *See*: **B1232**

D1055.   Emile Petti and His Cosmopolitans
　　　　　　Liberty Music Shop L 243, 78, 1O" **[GOH]**
　　　　　　"Melody Bouquet of George Gershwin"
　　　　　　CONTENTS: Embraceable You; That Certain Feeling; Swanee; Do, Do, Do;
　　　　　　Soon; Clap Y,o' Hands

D1056.   Paul Posnak, piano
　　　　　　Stradivari Classics SMC-6039, cassette; SCD-6039 CD **[DDD]** (1989)
　　　　　　"Gershwin's Piano Improvisations"
　　　　　　CONTENTS: Improvisations recorded by GG in 1916, 1926, 1928
　　　　　　(studio recordings) and in 1932 and 1934 (the latter two being radio
　　　　　　broadcasts), **S=songbook, T=transcription, S + B=songbook &**
　　　　　　broadcasts: Clap Yo' Hands (S); Clap Yo' Hands' (T); 'S Wonderful! (S);
　　　　　　'S Wonderful!/Funny Face (T); My One & Only (S); My One & Only (T);
　　　　　　Someone to Watch Over Me (T); Sweet & Lowdown (S); Sweet &
　　　　　　Lowdown (T); Rialto Ripples (piano roll); That Certain Feeling (S); That
　　　　　　Certain Feeling (T); Swanee (S); Stairway to Paradise (S); Liza (S);
　　　　　　Fascinating Rhythm (S + B); I Got Rhythm (S + B)
　　　　　　Producer: Julian Kreeger *See*: **B1314, W53**

D1057.   André Previn, piano; A. Hendrickson, gtr., Robert Bain, gtr., on songs
　　　　　　marked *; A. Shapiro, bass; I. Gettier, drums
　　　　　　RCA Victor LPM 1011-A & B, LP, 12" **"André Previn Plays Gershwin"**
　　　　　　GOH]
　　　　　　CONTENTS: **Side A:** Love Walked In; Maybe; How Long Has This Been
　　　　　　Going On?; (Our) Love is Here to Stay*; They All Laughed; **Side B:**
　　　　　　There's a Boat Dat's Leavin' Soon For New York; Lookin' For a Boy;
　　　　　　Nice Work If You Can Get It*; I've Got a Crush On You*; Strike Up the
　　　　　　Band

D1058.   André Previn, piano, with trio incl. Finck, bass
　　　　　　"We Got Rhythm: A Gershwin Songbook" (© 1998)
　　　　　　DG or Polygram 289-453-493-2
　　　　　　Contents: They All Laughed; Someone to Watch over Me; Oh, Lady, Be
　　　　　　Good!; A Foggy Day; Soon; Do It Again; I Got Rhythm; Embraceable
　　　　　　You; He Loves and She Loves; Love Is Here to Stay; Fascinating Rhythm;
　　　　　　Isn't t a Pity; Boy! What Love Has Done to Me!; I've Got a Crush on
　　　　　　You; Love Walked In; The Man I Love; 'S Wonderful!
　　　　　　Recorded at Tanglewood Music Festival, Lenox, MA

D1059.   Don Ralke and His Orchestra
　　　　　　Warner Bros. W 1360, LP, 12" **[GOH]**
　　　　　　"But You've Never Heard Gershwin With Bongos"
　　　　　　CONTENTS: Fascinating Rhythm; How Long Has This Been Going On?;
　　　　　　(Our) Love is Here to Stay; Summertime; My One and Only; They All
　　　　　　Laughed; Love Walked In; They Can't Take That Away from Me;
　　　　　　Maybe; A Foggy Day; I Got Rhythm *See*: **B1316**

D1060.   **"Fascinatin' Rampal: Jean-Pierre Rampal Plays Gershwin"**
　　　　　　CBS Records BL 39700 (1985)

Performers: Jean-Pierre Rampal, flute & alto flute; James Walker, alto flute; John Steele Ritter, piano, flute/piano arranger; Michael Colombier, synthesizer arranger, Randy Kerber, synthesizer player; Robbie Buchanen, synthesizer piano; Vince Colaiuta, drums; Neil Stubenhaus, bass; Paul Jackson, Jr., guitar; in part accompanied by members of the Los Angeles Philharmonic (in last two works, A Foggy Day & AiP, Michel Colombier, **conducting**); **Arrangements** by Michel Colombier

CONTENTS: Fascinating Rhythm; I Got Rhythm; Someone to Watch Over Me; Nice Work If You Can Get It; The Man I Love; Bess, You Is My Woman Now; My Man's Gone Now; Summertime; Liza; Preludes for Piano; A Foggy Day; AiP

Recorded at Evergreen Studios, Burbank, CA

Producer: Thomas Mowrey

See: **B1250**

D1061. Harry Ray's Tiger-Ragamuffins
Decca 1118, 78, 10" **[GOH]**
CONTENTS: Oh, Lady Be Good!; 'S Wonderful!; Looking for a Boy; Fascinating Rhythm; Clap Yo' Hands; That Certain Feeling

D1062. Leo Reisman and his Orchestra
Victor 22069, 78, 10" (1929)
CONTENTS: Liza: fox trot : (All the clouds'll roll away) : from Ziegfeld production, "Show Girl"; Do What You Do!; No importa lo que hagas; Show girl
Vocal refrains; excerpts from musical.
Performers: [Lew Conrad] (side A), [Smith Ballew] (side B), vocals ; Leo Reisman and his orchestra, performers. [Side B: Leo Reisman, violin/director; John Jacobson, Louis Shaffrin, trumpet; Ernie Gibbs and another (Possibly Chuck Campbell), trombone; Burt Williams, alto sax/baritone sax; Andrew Quenze, clarinet/C-melody sax/alto sax; Bill Tronstein, clarinet/soprano sax/alto sax/tenor sax; Lew Conrad, violin; Eddie Duchin, piano; Ned Cola, banjo; Harry Atlas, brass bass; Harry Sigman, drums] - *Cf. The American dance band discography* / Rust, 1975.
Recorded in New York, July 9 (side A) and July 31 (side B), 1929

D1063. Gene Rodemich and his orchestra.
Brunswick, 78, 10" (1919?)
Piano; Trumpet; Trombone; Saxophone; Violin; Other; Tuba; Drum
Swanee: one step, for dancing on side 2 of 1 disc
With: Roberts, L. S. Patches
Gene Rodemich's Orchestra. [Includes Gene Rodemich, piano.]-*cf.* B. Rust, *American Dance Band Discography*, 1975
Probably recorded in St. Louis ca. Oct. 1919
Acoustic recording

D1064. The Riviera Orchestra
Wing SRW 11012, LP, 12" **[GOH] "The Best of George Gershwin"**
CONTENTS: A Foggy Day; But Not For Me; Embraceable You; Fascinating Rhythm: I've Got a Crush On You; (Our) Love Is Here to Stay; Somebody Loves Me; The Man I Love; Someone to Watch Over Me; Summertime

D1065.   David Rose and His Orchestra
    M-G-M E 3123-A & B **[GOH] "Love Walked In—The Music of George Gershwin"**
    CONTENTS: **Side A:** Embraceable You; Someone to Watch Over Me; (Our) Love is Here to Stay (Gershwin) Goldwyn Follies 1938 film; Liza (All the clouds'll roll away) G. & I. Gershwin-Kahn SHOW GIRL 1929; Love Walked In; Fascinating Rhythm; **Side B**: Somebody Loves Me; AiP; Summertime; RiB; I've Got a Crush On You; The Man I Love

D1066.   Savoy Havan Band at the Savoy Hotel, London; B. L. Ralton, conducting
    Columbia 3289-A (English), 78, 10" **[GOH]**
    I'll Build a Stairway to Paradise

D1067.   **"Don Shirley plays Gershwin"**
    Cadence CLP 3032, LP (1956)
    CONTENTS: Porgy and Bess Suite: My Man's Gone; I Got Plenty of Nuttin'; It Ain't Necessarily So; Strawberry Song; Summertime; I Love You Porgy; Bess You Is My Woman; Love Is Here to Stay; But Not for Me; The Man I Love; Someone to Watch Over Me; They Can't Take That Away from Me
    Recorded in New York City, 1955-1956.
    Program notes on container

D1068.   Don Shirley, piano
    Picadilly PIC-3425 (1980)
    CONTENTS: Porgy & Bess medley; But Not for Me; The Man I Love; Someone to Watch Over Me; They Can't Take That Away From Me

D1069.   Nat Shilkret and the Victor Orchestra, 78, 10"
    Victor 22902, His Majesty's Voice B-6156 (1931)
    CONTENTS: Delishious; Somebody From Somewhere

D1070.   Allen Toussaint Orchestra
    Holland : MCR Productions MCR 2668272 (1988), CD
    "Twenty great Gershwin themes: 'S Wonderful!"
    CONTENTS: Rhapsody in Blue; I Got Rhythm; Swanee; Our Love Is Here to Stay; Summertime; Let's Call the Whole Thing off ; Embraceable You; But Not for Me; I Got Plenty of Nothing; The Man I Love; A Foggy Day; Someone to Watch over Me; It Ain't Necessarily So; Somebody Loves Me; Oh, Lady Be Good; They Can't Take That Away from Me; I've Got a Crush on You; They All Laughed; 'S Wonderful!; Strike up the Band

D1071.   Zoot Sims, tenor sax; Oscar Peterson, piano; Joe Pass, guitar; G. Mraz, bass; G. Tate, drums
    Orig. LP: Pablo 2310-744; Original Jazz Classics 444; **CD:** Pablo OJCCD 444-2
    "Zoot Sims and the Gershwin Brothers"
    CONTENTS: The Man I Love; How Long Has This Been Going On?; Oh, Lady Be Good!; I've Got a Crush On You; I Got Rhythm; 'S Wonderful!;

Someone to Watch Over Me; Isn't It a Pity?; Summertime; They Can't
Take That Away From Me (Additional track not on original LP)
Recorded at RCA Recording Studios, NY, June 6, 1975
Producer: Norman Granz

D1072. Joseph C. Smith & His Orchestra
Brunswick 2328-A, 78, 10" **[GOH]**
CONTENTS: GEORGE WHITE SCANDALS 1922: Where is the Man
Of My Dreams? (G-DeSylva-Goetz); Cinderelatives (G-DeSylva);
Side B is songs by Von Tilzer
**Very rare recording of Cinderelatives

D1073. Van Eps Banta Trio
Emerson 503-B, 78, 12" **[GOH]**
CONTENTS: Tee-oodle-um-bum-bo; Nobody But You LA, LA, LUCILLE

D1074. Various artists
Verve 314 525 361-2, CD (p1995)
"'S Paradise: the Gershwin Songbook"
CONTENTS: Fascinating Rhythm (Louis Bellson); My Man's Gone Now
(Bill Evans and Jim Hall); Mine (Buddy DeFranco); How Long Has this
Been Going On? (Coleman Hawkins); Somebody Loves Me (Oscar
Peterson); Prelude II (Henry Burrell); They All Laughed (George
Shearing); Nice Work If You Can Get it (Stan Getz and Bob Brookmeyer);
I Loves You Porgy (Bill Evans); Love Is Here to Stay (Jimmy Cleveland);
The Man I Love (Toshiko Akiyoshi); A Foggy Day (Tal Farlow); Strike up
the Band (Oscar Peterson); Embraceable You (Clifford Brown); 'S
Wonderful! (Don Elliot); Someone to Watch over Me (Art Tatum).

D1075. Various Jazz bands
World Records SH 452, Remastered from original 78 recordings, Album
SHB 45 **"The Great British Dance Bands Play George Gershwin
1920-1928" [GOH]**
CONTENTS: **Side A:** Fascinating Rhythm; Oh, Lady Be Good!; I'd
Rather Charleston; The Half of It, Dearie, Blues; That Certain Feeling;
Looking for a Boy; When Do We Dance? and Nice Baby; Nashville
Nightingale; **Side B:** Someone to Watch Over Me; Clap Yo' Hands; Do,
Do, Do; The Man I Love; 'S Wonderful!; My One and Only (what am I
gonna do?); Funny Face; He Loves and She Loves

D1076. Various Jazz Bands
World Records SH 451, LP, 12" Remastered from original 78 recordings,
Album SHB 45 **"The Great British Dance Bands Play George Gershwin"
1920-1928" [GOH]**
CONTENTS: Swanee; Drifting Along With the Tide; Do It Again; The
Yankee Doodle Blues; I'll Build a Stairway to Paradise; Sweetheart (I'm
So Glad That I Met You) THE RAINBOW; Innocent Lonesome Blue
Baby THE RAINBOW; Someone (Gershwin-Francis) FOR GOODNESS
SAKE; Virginia (don't go far) (Gershwin-DeSylva) SWEET LITTLE
DEVIL; Wait a Bit, Susie (G. & I. Gershwin-Carter) PRIMROSE;
Somebody Loves Me; Why Do I Love You? (G. & I. Gershwin-DeSylva)

TELL ME MORE!; Tell Me More! (G. & I. Gershwin-DeSylva) TELL
ME MORE!; My Fair Lady (G. & I. Gershwin-DeSylva) TELL ME
MORE!; Hang On to Me; So Am I

D1077.   Joe Venuti, violin; Gottuso, gtr; Zimmerman, bs.; Donaldson, drums;
Larkins, piano
Golden Crest Jazz Classic CR 3100
"Joe Venuti Plays Gershwin"
CONTENTS: Clap Yo' Hands; Someone to Watch Over Me; Fascinating
Rhythm; Embraceable You; Summertime; I Got Rhythm; Do, Do, Do; It
Ain't Necessarily So; Somebody Loves Me; 'S Wonderful!; Oh, Lady Be
Good!; Liza (All the Clouds'll Roll Away)

D1078.   Viennese Symphonic Orchestra
Plymouth PI2-67 George Gershwin Favorites and Other Popular Favorites
[GOH]
CONTENTS: George Gershwin Favorites: The Man I Love; Somebody
Loves Me; Oh, Lady Be Good!; Cavalleria Rusticana highlights (Mascagni)
1890; Tosca highlights (Puccini) 1900

D1079.   Westside Strutters ['Disco']
Parachute RRLP 9013 Gershwin '79 **[GOH]**
CONTENTS: Medley: The Man I Love; Embraceable You; Strike Up the
Band; RiB; Medley: I Got Rhythm & Fascinating Rhythm

D1080.   Paul Whiteman and His Orchestra
Victor 19414, on side 1 of 1 disc, acoustic recording, 78, mono, 10 in.
(1924?)
Personnel: Henry Busse & Frank Siegrist, trumpets; Roy Maxon &
possibly Wilbur Hall, trombones; Ross Gorman, clarinet or alto sax; Don
Clark, clarinet, sop sax or alto sax; Ed Stannard, clarinet or alto sax; Paul
Whiteman, violin; Mario Perry, violin or accordion; Ferdie Grofé and
Henry Lange, piano; Mike Pingitore, banjo; Al Armer or Carl Wagner,
tuba; George Marsh, drums. *Cf.* B. Rust, *American Dance Band
Discography,* 1975
Somebody Loves Me; With **G. Buck:** Lonely Little Melody
Recorded in NY, July 11, 1924

D1081.   Paul Whiteman and His Concert Orchestra
Victor 25552, His Majesty's Voice BD-5221 (1937), 78, 10"
Shall We Dance?

D1082.   Earl Wild, piano solo
Ouintesseance PMC 7060 **"Wild About Gershwin!"** **[GOH]** or:
"Earl Wild Plays His Transcriptions of Gershwin" Chesky Records CD32
(1990?)
CONTENTS: Grand fantasy on airs from PORGY AND BESS
(Gershwin- Wild); Seven virtuoso etudes on popular songs
(Gershwin-Wild)—songs are: Liza; Somebody Loves Me; Oh, Lady Be
Good!; The Man I Love; Fascinating Rhythm; Embraceable You; I Got
Rhythm

D1083. Teddy Wilson & His Trio
Columbia CL2539, **[NN-L]** *LRXP 1379 (1959)
"Mr. Wilson and Mr. Gershwin"
CONTENTS: Liza; Nice Work if You Can Get It; Oh, Lady Be Good!;
Somebody Loves Me; But Not For Me; I Got Rhythm; The Man I Love;
Bess, You Is My Woman Now; Embraceable You; Love Is Here To Stay;
I've Got A Crush On You; Summertime
Matrix nos. XLP45391/2

D1084. Teddy Wilson, piano
Brunswick 7563-A, 78, 10" **[GOH]**
Liza

D1085. The World's Greatest Brass cond. by Jack Saunders
Everest LP BR 5047-A & B **"Gershwin in Brass" [GOH]**
CONTENTS: **Side A:** Fascinating Rhythm; But Not for Me; American in
Paris; The Man I Love; Summertime; Liza (All the clouds'll roll away);
Side B: Strike Up the Band; Embraceable You; Rhapsody in Blue; I Got
Plenty O' Nuttin'; Someone to Watch Over Me; Clap Yo' Hands
Arrs. by Charlie Margulis & Bobby Byrne with Jack Saunders *See:* **B1258**

D1086. The World's Greatest Jazzband: Yank Lawson & Billy Butterfield, trumpets;
Carl Fontana & George Masso, trombones; Eddie Miller, tenor sax; Peanuts
Hucko, clarinet; Roger Kellaway, piano; Bob Haggart, bass; Nick Fatool,
drums
World Jazz Records WJLP-S-11 (1977)
**"The World's Greatest Jazzband of Yank Lawson & Bob Haggart Plays
George Gershwin"**
CONTENTS: Liza; I've Got a Crush on You; But Not for Me; How Long
Has This Been Going On?; Embraceable You; Strike Up the Band; Who
Cares?; Maybe; Fascinating Rhythm; Soon; 'S Wonderful!
Program notes by Leonard Feather

D1087. George Wright, Wurlitzer pipe organ
Dot DLP 25612-A & B **"George Wright Plays George Gershwin" [GOH]**
CONTENTS: **Side A:** I Got Rhythm; Embraceable You; 'S Wonderful!;
Mine; I'll Build a Stairway to Paradise; OTIS; Wintergreen for President;
Side B: Swanee; Bidin' My Time; How Long Has This Been Going On?;
But Not For Me; The Man I Love

OVERTURES TO MUSICALS

Albums are included here only if they *feature* overtures, i. e., they have more
than one Gershwin overture present on the album. Items like the complete recording of *Girl
Crazy* (**D450**) by the Library of Congress present the overture but are not included here.

D1088. BBC Philharmonic Orchestra: conducted by Yan Pascal Tortelier
CHANDOS CHAN 9325 **[DDD]**
CONTENTS: *Girl Crazy:* **Overture** (orch. Don Rose); Strike Up the Band:
Overture (orch. Don Rose); With Variations on "I Got Rhythm"; An
American in Paris; Symphonic Suite: Catfish Row (G's version)

Produced by Brian Pidgeon. (Distributed by Koch International.) *See*: **B1322**

D1089.   Boston Pops Orchestra; Arthur Fiedler, conductor; Ralph Votapek, piano
"Fiedler conducts Gershwin, I Got Rhythm"
London SPC-21185 (1979)
CONTENTS: Girl Crazy Suite (arr. Leroy Anderson); **Overtures:** (arr.
by Don Rose): Oh, Kay! Overture; Funny Face Overture; Let 'Em Eat
Cake Overture; Of Thee I Sing Overture; Wintergreen for President; [3]
Preludes (arr. for orch. Gregory Stone); Second Rhapsody (rev. Robert
McBride)
Program notes by Tim McDonald & durations on container
See: **B1126, B1219, B1325**

D1090.   Buffalo Philharmonic (Overtures); Michael Tilson Thomas, conducting;
George Gershwin, piano roll, with the Columbia Jazz Band (RiB); New York
Philharmonic (AiP)
CBS Masterworks MK 42240 (1976); DIDC 70127, reissue as a CD **[ADD]**
(1987)
CONTENTS: Broadway Overtures to Oh, Kay!, Funny Face, Girl
Crazy, Strike Up the Band, OTIS, Cake (Arr. by Don Rose); RiB; AiP;
The legendary 1925 piano roll of RiB
RiB recorded at 30th St. Studios, NY, 1976; AiP at Philharmonic Hall, NY,
1974; Broadway Overtures at Kleinhans Hall, Buffalo, NY, 1976
Program notes in English, German, and French by Andrew Kazdin on insert
in container; Durations on back of insert
Produced by Andrew Kazdin & Steven Epstein *See*: **B1072, B1323, B1326**

D1091.   Cincinnati Pops; Erich Kunzel, conducting
Turnabout CT-2250, cassette
CONTENTS: Oh, Kay!; Girl Crazy; Tip-toes; Of Thee I Sing- arrangements
by Don Rose); With music by Proto

D1092.   Cincinnati Pops Orchestra; Erich Kunzel, conducting
Vox/Turnabout TV 34749 (1979)
"A Portrait of George"
CONTENTS: Gershwin Overtures: Oh, Kay!; Girl Crazy; Tiptoes; Of Thee I
Sing; Our Love Is Here to Stay; Love Walked In; Nice Work if You Can
Get It; Foggy Day; Strike Up the Band

D1093.   Kevin Cole, piano
Pro Arte CDD-365 **[DDD]**; Fanfare DFL 7007 (Canada)
"The Unknown George Gershwin"
CONTENTS: LADY, BE GOOD! & GIRL CRAZY Overtures, with other
G compositions

D1094.   N. Coxe
Titanic Ti-170 **[DDD]**
"Showstoppers"
CONTENTS: Girl Crazy & Oh, Lady Be Good! Overtures; With other G
compositions & piano music by Blake & Grainger

D1095.   New Princess Theater Orchestra; John McGlinn, conducting
Angel-EMI digital CDC-7 47977-2; 4DS-47977, cassette
"Gershwin Overtures"
CONTENTS: A Damsel In Distress (1937 film) - Suite from the film;
Overtures to: Girl Crazy; Of Thee I Sing; Tip-toes; Primrose; Oh, Kay!;
Stiff Upper Lip ("Fun House") Dance sequence from A Damsel In Distress
1937 film *See:* **F11, B1139, B1324, B1327, B1370**

MUSIC USED IN FILMS

Items are alphabetized by title of the film and by label name, beneath the name of the film.

AN AMERICAN IN PARIS (1951), **F19**

D1096.   CBS Special Products AK 45391 (CD) (p 1990)
Original soundtrack
Featuring Gene Kelly, Georges Guetary, Oscar Levant *See:* **B1583**

D1097.   JJA Records 19773 (Music Masters)
"Gershwins in Hollywood, 1931-1964" 2 LP discs [Complete Entry]
CONTENTS: SIDE FOUR: *American in Paris***:** Nice Work If You Can
Get It (Georges Guetary); By Strauss (Georges Guetary, Gene Kelly); *My
Cousin From Milwaukee/A Foggy Day/The Half of It, Dearie Blues/But
Not For Me (Oscar Levant); *But Not For Me (Georges Guetary); Tra-La-
La (Gene Kelly, Oscar Levant); I Don't Think I'll Fall In Love Today
(Oscar Levant); *Love Walked In (Georges Guetary); Bidin' My Time
(Oscar Levant); Do-Do-Do/Bidin' My Time/I've Got a Crush On You/Our
Love Is Here To Stay (Benny Carter and Jazz Combo) *=cut from film
Somebody Loves Me from Somebody Loves Me (1952) (Betty Hutton
[LP]); I've Got a Crush On You from Three For The Show (1955 (Betty
Grable and Jack Lemmon), unused version; Changing My Tune from The
Shocking Miss Pilgrim (1947)(Louise Carlyle) [1971 live performance
introduced by Arthur Schwartz and Kay Swift); They Can't Take That
Away From Me from Shall We Dance (1937) [Ginger Rogers(1976
Nightclub Act)]
   SIDE ONE: *Delicious* (1931): l. Main Title/Delishious (Raul Roulian);
2.Welcome To The Melting Pot (Chorus); 3.Somebody From Somewhere
(Janet Gaynor); 4. Katinkitschka (Mischa Auer, Manya Roberti);
5. Blah, Blah, Blah (El Brendel, Manya Roberti); 6.New York Rhapsody
(Orchestra)
   Girl Crazy (1932): 7.Main Title/Bidin' My Time (Male Quartet);
8.You've Got What Gets Me (Bert Wheeler, Dixie Lee);
9.But Not For Me (Eddie Quillan, Arline Judge, Mitzi Green (Age 12); 10.
I Got Rhythm/Finale (Kitty Kelly and Chorus);
   SIDE TWO: 1. Walking The Dog from Shall We Dance 1937 (Orchestra);
2. Fascinating Rhythm from Lady Be Good (1941) (Connie Russell, danced
by Eleanor Powell); 3. Lady Be Good (Ann Sothern, Robert Young, Red
Skelton, John Carroll, Virginia O'Brien, Eleanor Powell); *Goldwyn Follies*
(1938): 4. Love Walked In (Kenny Baker, Andrea Leeds); 5.Our Love Is

Here To Stay from Follies (Kenny Baker); 6. I Love To Rhyme (Phil Baker, Charlie MaCarthy); 7. I Was Doing All Right (Ella Logan [78]); 8.Our Love Is Here To Stay (Ella Logan [78]); 9.Love Walked in/Finale (Andrea Leeds, Kenny Baker, Helen Jepson)

SIDE THREE:

1. The Man I Love from *The Man I Love* (1946) Ida Lupino [Peg La-Centra] 2.'S Wonderful! from *Starlift* (1951) (Doris Day); 3.Liza from *Starlift* (Patrice Wymore) *Rhapsody in Blue* (1945): 4.Main Title (Orchestra); 5. Swanee (Joan Leslie, Robert Alda, Al Jolson); 6.Somebody Loves Me (Joan Leslie, Tom Patricola); 7.Blue Monday (Unidentified Soloists); 8.The Man I Love/Clap Yo' Hands/ Fascinating Rhythm/I Got Rhythm(Hazel Scott); 9.Embraceable You (Joan Leslie [Sally Sweetland]); 10.Someone To Watch Over Me/I Got Rhythm (Oscar Levant); 11.Delishious (Joan Leslie [Sally Sweetland]); 12.Mine/Finale (Robert Alda, Oscar Levant)

*Cut From Film. All *American In Paris* selections from Original Studio Recordings.

Note: Additional soundtrack recordings from *Shall We Dance, A Damsel In Distress, Funny Face,* the 1943 *Girl Crazy, The Shocking Miss Pilgrim, An American In Paris, Rhapsody in Blue,* and *Porgy and Bess* have been available on other labels. *See*: **F14, B1243**

A DAMSEL IN DISTRESS (1937), **F11**

D1098.   Curtain Calls 100/19 **[GOH]**
Original soundtrack
Fred Astaire, et al
CONTENTS: Also includes "The Sky's the Limit" (Arlen-Mercer), 1943 film

D1099.   Decca DL 74468
"Gershwin from Broadway to Hollywood" [GOH]
George Bassman and His Orchestra
CONTENTS: OF THEE I SING: selections; PARDON MY ENGLISH: selections; PORGY AND BESS: selections; Shall We Dance?: selections; A Damsel In Distress: selections; Goldwyn Follies: selections

D1100.   Decca Personality 29195-A, 78, 1211 **[GOH]**
Frankie Carle, piano solo
George Gershwin Selections from Damsel in Distress
CONTENTS: Nice Work If You Can Get It; A Foggy Day; Things Are Looking Up; I Can't Be Bothered Now

DELICIOUS (1931), **F7**

D1101.   Crown 3252-B, 78, 10" Delicious 1931 film **[GOH]**
Lou Gold & Orchestra
CONTENTS: Intro: Somebody from Somewhere/Delishious

D1102.   JJA Records 19773 (Music Masters)
"Gershwins in Hollywood, 1931-1964"

CONTENTS: **Side 1:** Main Title/Delishious (Raul Roulian); Welcome To The Melting Pot (Chorus); Somebody From Somewhere (Janet Gaynor); Katinkitschka (Mischa Auer, Manya Roberti); Blah, Blah, Blah (El Brendel, Manya Roberti); New York Rhapsody (Orchestra) *See:* Full entry at **D1097**

FUNNY FACE (1957), **F23**

D1103. Verve MGV 2063   Selections from Funny Face 1957 film & other tunes
Barbara Carroll Trio (Joe Schulman, bass; Joe Petti, drums) **[GOH]**
CONTENTS: Let's Kiss and Make Up; Funny Face; He Loves and She Loves; 'S Wonderful!; How Long Has This Been Going On?; Clap Yo' Hands; Let's Call the Whole Thing Off; Someone to Watch Over Me; Who Cares?; They Can't Take That Away from Me; (Our) Love Is Here to Stay; They All Laughed

D1104. Verve MG V 15001 or Stet DS-15001 (dist. by DRG Records) and
on Verve 31231 (CD) Original soundtrack
CONTENTS: Overture/Funny Face; 'S Wonderful!; Think Pink! (Edens-Gershe); How Long Has This Been Going On? [with instrumental reprise];   Funny Face; Bonjour, Paris! (Edens-Gershe); Clap Yo' Hands; He Loves and She Loves; Instrumental reprise: Bonjour, Paris! (Eden); On How to be Lovely (Eden-Gershe); Basal Metabolism (How long has this been going on? & Funny Face); Let's Kiss and Make Up; 'S Wonderful!
Orchestrations by A. Courage, C. Salinger, V. Cleave, & S. Martin
See: **B1328**

GIRL CRAZY (1938, 1943, & 1965), **F8, F15, and F27**

D1105. DRG Records SL-5187 **"Judy Garland: The Beginning"** 1943 album by Judy Garland & Mickey Rooney of the 1943 film cast, George Stoll, conducting

D1106. Hollywood Soundstage HS 5008, LP, mono; Sandy Hook CSH 2114 (digital compact cassette); Curtain Calls 100/9-10 **[GOH]**
The 1943 soundtrack of the film
CAST: Judy Garland; Mickey Rooney; June Allyson; Rags Ragland; George Stoll & Tommy Dorsey, conducting

D1107. Howards International Hollywood Soundstage HS 5008 (1982)
"Girl Crazy"
CAST: Judy Garland, June Allyson, Nancy Walker, Mickey Rooney & Rags Ragland, singers; Tommy Dorsey's Orchestra; The King's Men, Chorus
CONTENTS: Overture, Treat Me Rough, Bidin' My Time; Could You Use Me?; Broncobusters; Happy Birthday, Ginger; Embraceable You; Comedy Routine; Fascinating Rhythm; But Not for Me; I've Got Rhythm
Original motion picture soundtrack

D1108. JJA Records 19773 (Music Masters)

"Gershwins in Hollywood, 1931-1964"
1932 film soundtrack from Girl Crazy
CONTENTS: Side 1: Orchestra: main title; Male quartet: Bidin' My
Time; Bert Wheeler & Dixie Lee: You've Got What Gets Me; Eddie
Quilan, Arline Judge, Mitzi Green: But Not For Me; Kitty Kelly & chorus:
I Got Rhythm/Finale *See*: Full entry at **D1097**

D1109.   MGM 4334
Soundtrack of the 1965 film called When The Boys Meet The Girls
CAST: Connie Francis; Harve Presnell; Louis Armstrong; Sam the Sham and the
Pharoahs; Herman's Hermits; Fred Karger & Ernie Freeman, conducting

D1110.   Unnamed label mx CC-1190-1
"Who Could Ask For Anything More" Industrial show
Includes five songs from Girl Crazy
CAST: Bill Hayes; Florence Henderson; Chorus; Orchestrations: Glenn
Osser; Luther Henderson; Sherman Frank, conducting

GOLDWYN FOLLIES (1938), **F12**

D1111.   Brunswick 8068 (B 22323, B 22325), 78, 10" (1938)
CONTENTS: I was doing all right: from "The Goldwyn follies" / Love is
here to stay
Personnel: Mildred Bailey, vocals ; Red Norvo and his orchestra,
performers. [Red Norvo, xylophone/director; Jimmy Blake, Zeke Zarchy,
Barney Zudecoff, trumpet; Al Mastren, Wes Hein, trombone; Hank
d'Amico, clarinet; Len Goldstein, alto sax; Charles Lamphere, alto
sax/tenor sax; Jerry Jerome, tenor sax; Bill Miller, piano; Alan Hanlon,
guitar; Pete Peterson, string bass; George Wettling, drums] - Cf. *Jazz
records, 1897-1942* / Rust, c1978.
Recorded in New York, Jan. 21, 1938

D1112.   Decca DL 74468, Gershwin from Broadway to Hollywood **[GOH]**
George Bassman and His Orchestra
Selections from the film, with other G music

D1113.   JJA Records 19773 (Music Masters)
"Gershwins in Hollywood, 1931-1964"
CONTENTS: Love Walked In (Kenny Baker, Andrea Leeds); Our Love
Is Here To Stay (Kenny Baker); I Love To Rhyme *See*: Full entry at
D1097

THE HELEN MORGAN STORY (1957), **F24**

D1114.   Gogi Grant, vocals; Orchestra; Ray Heindorf, conducting
RCA Victor LOC 1030 (1957) **[NN-L]** LXRP 815
"The Helen Morgan Story" (1957), Original soundtrack
CONTENTS: Someone to Watch Over Me; Do, Do, Do; The Man
I Love; I've Got a Crush On You

MANHATTAN (1979) Woody Allen film, **F29**

D1115.   Columbia CK-36020, CD; JST 36020, cassette (1979)
New York Philharmonic; Z. Mehta, conducting; Gary Graffman, piano
MANHATTAN soundtrack
CONTENTS: RiB; Gay Cabellero/Someone to Watch Over Me; I've Got
a Crush on You; Do, Do, Do; Mine; He Loves & She Loves; Bronco
Busters; Lady Be Good!; 'S Wonderful!; Love is Here to Stay; Sweet &
Low-Down; Blue, Blue, Blue; Embraceable You; He Loves and She
Loves; Love Is Sweeping the Country; Cabellero/Strike Up the Band; But
Not for Me *See:* **B2008**

PORGY AND BESS (1959), **F25**

D1116.   Porgy and Bess an original sound track recording, the Samuel Goldwyn
motion picture production / words by DuBose Heyward and Ira Gershwin ;
music by George Gershwin.
Columbia OL 5410 & OS 2016, LP Series: Columbia Masterworks (1959)
Performers: Sidney Poitier, as Porgy, sung by Robert McFerrin;
Dorothy Dandridge, as Bess, sung by Adele Addison ; Sammy Davis, Jr.,
as Sportin' Life, sung by Cab Calloway; with chorus and orchestra ; André
Previn, arranger & conductor
CONTENTS: Selections: Overture; Summertime; A Woman Is a Sometime
Thing; The Wake: Gone, Gone, Gone; Porgy's Prayer -- My Man's Gone
Now; I Got Plenty O' Nuttin'; Bess, You Is My Woman Now; Morning,
Catfish Row; Oh, I Can't Sit Down; It Ain't Necessarily So; I Ain't Got
No Shame; What You Want with Bess?; Street Cries: Strawberry Woman;
Crab Man; I Loves You, Porgy; A Red Headed Woman; Clara, Clara;
There's a Boat That's Leavin' Soon for New York; Oh, Where's My
Bess?; I'm on My Way.
Program notes on container *See:* **B1196, B1198, B1200, B1213, B1329,**
B2022

RHAPSODY IN BLUE (1945), **F16**

D1117.   JJA Records 19773 (Music Masters)
"Gershwins in Hollywood, 1931-1964"
CONTENTS: Main Title, Rhapsody In Blue (Orchestra); Swanee [Lyric by
Irving Caesar] (Joan Leslie, Robert Alda, Al Jolson); Somebody Loves Me
(Joan Leslie, Tom Patricola); Blue Monday (Unidentified Soloists); The
Man I Love/Clap Yo Hands/Fascinating Rhythm/I Got Rhythm (Hazel
Scott); Embraceable You (Joan Leslie-Sally Sweetland); Someone To
Watch Over Me/I Got Rhythm (Oscar Levant); Delishious (Joan Leslie-
Sally Sweetland); Mine/Finale (Robert Alda, Oscar Levant) *See:* Full entry
at **D1097**

D1118.   Titania 512
"Rhapsody in Blue" soundtrack
Cast from the film except for Sally Sweetland for Joan Leslie

SHALL WE DANCE (1937), **F10**

D1119.   JJA Records 19773 (Music Masters)
"Gershwins in Hollywood, 1931-1964"
Walking the Dog (Original version) *See*: **B1243,** Full entry at **D1097**

D1120.   Meritt Record Society [producer] 11 Meritt; M-287-2 Master, LP (p1980)
on track 2 side 2 of 1 sound disc : 33 1/3 rpm, mono. ; 12 in.
Adrian Rollini and his orchestra
Performers: Bunny Berigan, trumpet; Adrian Rollini, bass sax or vibraphone;
Sid Stoneburn, clarinet; Fulton McGrath, piano; Dick McDonough, guitar;
George Hnida, string bass; Al Sidell, drums; unknown vocalist and other
unidentified musicians.
CONTENTS: Shall we dance? Slap that bass. Reed album, volume two
Limited ed.; Dance orchestra; Voices, unspecified
Recorded in New York on March 20, 1937 for Master, matrix no. M-287-2.
Discographical notes on container.
Labels on disc are replicas of rare 1920's Meritt label.

THE SHOCKING MISS PILGRIM (1947), **F17**
See: **D956, D1016**

D1121.   Betty Grable, Dick Haymes
Classic Int'l Filmusicals LP CIF 3008
1947 Soundtrack
With Mother Wore Tights

D1121.1.   Longines Symphonette Society/American Music Makers Program
Longines Symphonette LW 227-A & B **"A George Gershwin Festival"**
[GOH]
Includes Changing My Tune *See*: Full Entry at **D1033**

Miscellaneous

D1122.   Hollywood Bowl Orchestra; John Mauceri, conducting; Gregory Hines &
Patti Austin, vocals
Philips 434 274-4, cassette (1991)
"The Gershwins in Hollywood"
CONTENTS: Side 1: Overture: Gershwin in Hollywood (pub.
Chappell); New York Rhapsody, piano solo by Wayne Marshall;
Walking the Dog; I've Got Beginner's Luck (Hines & Austin); Slap
That Bass (Hines); They All Laughed (Austin); Let's Call the Whole Thing
Off (Hines & Austin); A Foggy Day (Hines); **Side 2:** Watch Your Step!
final ballet for film *Shall We Dance?*; Nice Work If You Can Get It
(Hines); An American in London, ed. by John Mauceri & Tommy Krasker
(pub. Gershwin Bros. Music); Love Walked In (Austin); (Our) Love is
Here to Stay (Austin); For You, For Me, For Evermore (Hines & Austin)
Producer: Michael Gore; **Associate producer:** T. Krasker
Musical supervision: Steven D. Bowen
Essay on "The Gershwins in Hollywood" by Krasker inserted *See*: **B1139**

RECORDINGS BY GERSHWIN

D1123.   Biograph BCD-106, CD **[DDD]**
Gershwin, et al. (12 Duo-Art, QuartetS, lmperial, and Perfection piano rolls)

CONTENTS: Gershwin: RiB, rec. on 2 rolls; Swanee; Walkin' the Dog;
Frank Milne & Ernest Leith: AiP, piano duet version rec. on two rolls;
J. Lawrence Cook: Let's Call the Whole Thing Off; 'S Wonderful!,
Embraceable You, Oh, Lady Be Good!; Victor Arden & Max Kortlander:
Somebody Loves Me; Rudy Marlin: Our Love Is Here To Stay

D1124. Biograph BLP 10220-A & B "The Music of George Gershwin" From the
original piano rolls
CONTENTS: Fascinating Rhythm; The Man I Love; Oh, Lady Be
Good!; Somebody Loves Me; Swanee; Embraceable You; I Got Rhythm;
Let's Call the Whole Thing Off; A Foggy Day; But Not For Me;
Summertime; I Got Plenty Of Nuttin'; My Man's Gone Now; It Ain't
Necessarily So; Bess, You Is My Woman Now

D1125. Capitol P-303 (1952?)
Orchestra with Paul Whiteman conducting
AiP & RiB

D1126. CBS Masterworks MK 42240 (1976); DIDC 70127, reissue as a CD
[ADD] (1987)
George Gershwin, piano roll, with the Columbia Jazz Band (RiB); New
York Philharmonic (AiP); Buffalo Philharmonic (overtures); Michael
Tilson Thomas, conducting
CONTENTS: RiB; AiP; Broadway Overtures to Oh, Kay!, Funny Face,
Girl Crazy, Strike Up the Band, OTIS, Cake (Arr. by Don Rose)
The legendary 1925 piano roll of RiB combined with Columbia Jazz Band
RiB recorded at 30th St. Studios, NY, 1976
Program notes in English, German, and French by Andrew Kazdin on insert
in container; Durations on back of insert
Produced by Andrew Kazdin & Steven Epstein *See:* **B1116**

D1127. CBS MK-42516, CD; FMT-42516, cassette
Gershwin (1925 piano roll)
Columbia Jazz Band; M. T. Thomas, conducting
CONTENTS: RiB; AiP; Porgy and Bess (selections); Preludes; & other
G music *See:* **B1088**, **B1116**

D1128. Columbia 809-D **[GOH]**, 4538, 78, 10" (NY, Nov. 8 & 12, 1926)
CONTENTS: Do, Do, Do; Clap Yo' Hands from Oh, Kay!

D1129. Columbia 812-D **[GOH]**, 4539, 78, 10" (Nov. 8 & 12, 1926)
CONTENTS: Someone to Watch Over Me; Maybe from Oh, Kay!

D1130. Columbia 4065, 78 (London, July 6, 1926)
CONTENTS: Looking for a Boy; Sweet and Low-Dow from Tip-Toes

D1131. Columbia 4066, 78 (London, July 6, 1926)
CONTENTS: That Certain Feeling from Tip-Toes; When Do We Dance?
From Tip-Toes

D1132. Columbia 5109 (English, London, June 8 & 12, 1928), 78, 10" **[GOH]**

D1133.   Columbia 50107-D, Matrix nos. WAX-3758/3759, 78 (London, June 8, 1928)
CONTENTS: Preludes I, II, & III for piano; Andante from RiB

D1134.   Elektra\Nonesuch 79287-2 CD; 79287-4 cassette
"Gershwin Plays Gershwin: The Piano Rolls" [Vol. I]
Piano rolls realized by Artis Wodehouse
CONTENTS: Sweet & Lowdown; Novelette in Fourths; That Certain Feeling; So Am I; RiB; Swanee; When You Want 'Em You Can't Get 'Em; Kickin' the Clouds Away; Idol Dreams; On My Mind the Whole Night Long; Scandal Walk; AiP *See:* **B933, B1233, B1317, B1412, B1702, W3**

D1135.   Elektra/Nonesuch 7930 CD
"The Piano Rolls, Vol. 2" (*ca.* 1995)
George Gershwin, piano rolls realized by Artis Wodehouse
CONTENTS: Havanola (Have Another) (Frey) - 2:15; Singin' the Blues (Till My Daddy... (Conrad/Lewis/Robinson/Young) - 4:32; From Now On (DeSylva/Gershwin/Jackson) - 3:08; Jaz-O-Mine (Akst) - 2:26; Just Snap Your Fingers at Care (Silvers) - 2:17; Whip-Poor-Will (DeSylva/Kern) - 3:13; Rialto Ripples (Donaldson/Gershwin) - 1:54 Waitin' for Me (Green/McCoy/Pinkard) - 3:07; Buzzin' the Bee (Wells/Wendling) - 2:12; Darling (Jackson/Schonberg) - 2:31; For Your Country and My Country (Berlin) - 2:33; Kangaroo Hop (Morris) - 1:57; Pastime Rag No. 3 (Matthews) - 2:15; Chinese Blues (Gardner/Moore) - 2:08; Whispering (Schonberger/Schonberger) - 3:11; Arrah Go on I'm Gonna Go Back to... (Grant/Lewis/Young) - 1:51
Producer/Engineer: Max Wilcox
Liner notes: Artis Wodehouse

D1136.   Klavier KCXD, CD (1989)
"George Gershwin Plays Rhapsody in Blue"
CONTENTS: Rhapsody in Blue; That Certain Feeling; Tee-Oodle-Um-Bum-Bo; Kickin' the Clouds Away; Sweet and Low-Down; So Am I; Drifting Along with the Tide; I Was So Young, You Were So Beautiful; Left All Alone Blues; Whip-Poor-Will; Whose Baby Are You?; Rock-A-Bye Lullaby Land; **Berlin**: For Your Country and My Country; **Kern:** Land Where the Good Songs Go; **Whiting:** Ain't You Comin' Back to Dixie? and Some Sunday Morning

D1137.   Klavier KC-122, cassette (1989)
"George Gershwin Plays Gershwin & Kern"
CONTENTS: Sweet and Low-Down; Kickin' the Clouds Away; I Was So Young; Tee-Oodle-Um-Bum-Bo; Drifting Along With the Tide; So Am I; Left All Alone Blues; Whip-Poor-Will; Whose Baby Are You?; Rock-a-Bye Lullaby Land *See:* **B1332, B928**

D1138.   Klavier KC-124, cassette (1989)
"Gershwin Plays Rhapsody in Blue"
CONTENTS: Swanee; That Certain Feeling; Berlin: For Your Country and My Country; Shilkret: Make Believe; Whiting: Some Sunday Morning;

Kern: Land Where the Good Songs Go; Gold: Grieving for You; Whiting: Ain't You Comin' Back to Dixie? *See:* **B1330**

D1139.   Klavier KC-133, cassette (1989)
"Manhattan: George Gershwin at the Piano"
CONTENTS: Kickin' the Clouds Away; Swanee; Sweet and Low-Down; So Am I; Drifting Along With the Tide; I'll Build a Stairway To Paradise; Do It Again; Yankee Doodle Blues; I Was So Young; That Certain Feeling; Rhapsody in Blue (Andante)

D1140.   Mark 56 Records 641-A-D, 2 discs (1973) **"Gershwin By Gershwin"**
[GOH]
CONTENTS: Sides A & B: Rhapsody in Blue (Performed on Duo-Art reproducing piano); Concerto—from radio broadcast April 7, 1935; Variations on "I Got Rhythm"; Second Rhapsody—from rehearsal recording June 26, 1931; **Sides C & D:** Of Thee I Sing—from radio broadcast Feb. 19, 1934; The Man I Love— from radio broadcast Feb. 19, 1934; I Got Rhythm—from radio broadcast Feb. 19, 1934; Swanee—from radio broadcast Feb. 19, 1934; Fragment from Concerto, second mvt.—from radio broadcast April 7, 1935; Mine/I Got Rhythm—from radio broadcast April 30, 1934; Also from same broadcast: "I Got Rhythm" Variations; Love Is Sweeping the Country & Wintergreen for President; Hi-ho (I. Gershwin, vocal & Harold Arlen, piano)
Produced by George Garabedian *See:* **B1120**

D1141.   Mark 56 Records 680
"Gershwin . . . From Tin Pan Alley to Broadway"
Gershwin piano roll from 1920
Includes Kickin' The Clouds Away from Tell Me More; Swanee

D1142.   Musicmasters 5062-4-C, cassette; also available on CD (1991)
"Gershwin Performs Gershwin: Rare Recordings 1931-1935"
Music Masters in cooperation with Library of Congress
CONTENTS: "Music by Gershwin" Radio Program, Feb. 19, 1934: Signature, OTIS Overture, The Man I Love, I Got Rhythm, Commercial, Swanee, Sign-Off/ **"Music by Gershwin" Radio Program,** Apr. 30, 1934: Signature, Mine, Variations on "I Got Rhythm," Love Is Sweeping the Country, Commercial, Wintergreen for President, Sign-Off/ **Rudy Vallée "Fleischmann Hour" Radio Program,** Nov. 10, 1932: Variations of Fascinating Rhythm, Variations on Liza, Piano Prelude II, Interview (Vallée & GG), I Got Rhythm/ **Second Rhapsody Rehearsal Performance,** June 26, 1931/ **P&B Rehearsal,** July 19, 1935: Introduction, Summertime (Abbie Mitchell), A Woman Is a Sometime Thing (Edward Matthews), Act I, Scene 1: Finale; My Man's Gone Now (Todd Duncan & Anne Brown)—GG, pianist and conductor
Notes by Edward Jablonski, inserted
Producer: Russell L. Caplan/American Classics, Inc.

D1143.   Pavilion Records Pearl GEMM CDS 9483, 2 CDs **[AAD]** (p 1991)
"George Gershwin Plays George Gershwin"
CONTENTS: CD #1: RiB (version of Oct. 10, 1924, with GG, piano &

Paul Whiteman Orch.); **With Fred & Adele Astaire:** Hang On to Me, Fascinating Rhythm, The Half of It Dearie Blues, I'd Rather Charleston (the latter with only Astaire, vocalist, and "actual dancing"); **Gershwin as soloist:** *Sweet and Low Down (London, July 6, 1926, Col. 4065), *That Certain Feeling (London, July 6, 1926, Col. 4066), *Looking for a Boy (London, July 6, 1926, Col. 4065), Then Do We Dance (London, July 6, 1926, Col. 4066), Do-Do-Do (London, Nov. 8, 1926, Col. 4538), *Someone to Watch Over Me (London, Nov. 8, 1926, Col. 4539), *Clap Yo' Hands (London, Nov. 12, 1926, Col. 4539), *Maybe (London, Nov. 12, 1926, Col. 4539), *My One and Only (London, June 8, 1928, Col. 5109), Three [piano] Preludes (London, June 8, 1928, Col. 50107D), Andante from RiB; *'S Wonderful! & Funny Face (London, June 12, 1928, Col. 5109); RiB (version of Apr. 21, 1927, GG, piano, with Paul Whiteman Orch.); **CD #2:** AiP (Victor Symphony Orch., Nat Shilkret, conducting, Feb. 4, 1929); Selections from P&B;Concerto in F, third movement (arr. by Eliot Jacobi, performed by GG, piano, from live broadcast of Rudy Vallee show of Nov. 9, 1933; Song Medley w/ chorus & orchestra: I Got Rhythm & Of Thee I Sing, from live broadcast of Rudy Vallee show of Nov. 9, 1933

Songs marked with an * appear in A. Wodehouse's published set of transcriptions: *Gershwin's Improvisations for solo piano* **(W53),** published by Warner Bros.; complete entry given under **"Anthologies"**
Program notes by Charles Levin on insert in container

D1144.   PianoSoft 00501196, $34.95 Disc for Disklavier; Available directly from Music Dispatch (800) 637-2852
"Gershwin Plays Gershwin: The Piano Rolls," realized by Artis Wodehouse
CONTENTS: Sweet & Lowdown; Novelette in Fourths, That Certain Feeling, So Am I, RiB, Swanee, When You Want 'Em You Can't Get 'Em, Kickin' the Clouds Away, Idol Dreams, On My Mind the Whole Night Long, Scandal Walk, AiP; Nobody But You, Poppyland, Come to the Moon, Rialto Ripples, and From Now On. *See:* **B1333, B1412**

D1145.   Pro Arte CDD-352, CD **[DDD];** PCD-352, cassette
Gershwin (6 Duo-Art piano rolls)
CONTENTS: Kicking the Clouds Away; Drifting Along with the Tide; Twee-oodle-um-bum-bo; So Am I; That Certain Feeling; Sweet and Low Down; AiP; RiB

D1146.   RCA ALK1-7114, monaural cassette
Gershwin, piano
Preludes; AiP; RiB

D1147.   RCA Victrola AVM 1-1740
Gershwin, George: "Gershwin Plays Gershwin"
See: **B1120, B1331**

D1148.   RCA Special Products R028A, 2 discs (1981)
GG, piano; Paul Whiteman and His Orchestra [various personnel given in album notes]

"An Experiment in Modern Music, Paul Whiteman at Aeolian Hall"
RiB is the June 10, 1924, recorded version.
CONTENTS: A reconstruction of the Aeolian Hall concert; RiB; With
other pieces played on the concert by Whiteman (& various orchestras)
See: Full entry given under **"Anthologies"** at **D780**

D1149. RCA Victor LPT 29, 10 in.
With Paul Whiteman and his concert orchestra
AiP & RiB

D1150. RCA Victrola ALK1-7114, monaural, cassette
George Gershwin, piano; Paul Whiteman & His Concert Orchestra; RCA
Victor Symphony Orchestra, George Gershwin, celeste; Nathaniel Shilkret,
conducting
"Gershwin Plays Gershwin"
CONTENTS: RiB (GG, piano; Whiteman & Orch.); AiP (RCA Victor
Orch.); Three Piano Preludes (GG, piano); Songs (GG, piano) *See:* **B1096**

D1151. Smithsonian Recordings, POB 2122, Colchester, VT 05449-2122 (As of 1995)
"I Got Rhythm: The Music of George Gershwin," 4 CDs or cassettes
CONTENTS: AiP, RiB and Variations on "I Got Rhythm" with G
performing; With 60 other selections performed by various artists, A 64-
page booklet is included with the set *See:* Full entry under **"Anthologies,"**
D738

D1152. Telarc SE-1001 (1982)
"Gershwin Plays Gershwin"—Duo-Art piano
CONTENTS: RiB; So Am I; That Certain Feeling; Swanee; Sweet and
Low-Down; Kickin' the Clouds Away; I Was Young, You Were So
Beautiful; Tee-oodle-um-bum-bo; Drifting Along with the Tide (From
George White's Scandals of 1921)
Program notes by Albert Petrak on container; 37 min., 20 sec. total

D1153. Twentieth (20th) Fox FOX 3013-B **[GOH]**
George Gershwin, Duo-Art piano
CONTENTS: RiB on A side; That Certain Feeling (G. Gershwin-
I. Gershwin) TIP-TOES 1925; Left All Alone Again Blues (Kern-Caldwell)
THE NIGHT BOAT 1920; Grieving For You (Gibson-Ribaud-Gold); I'm
a Lonesome Little Raindrop (Hanley-Goodwin-Roth) G. VILLAGE
FOLLIES 1920; Just Snap Your Fingers At Care (Silvers-DeSylva) G.
VILLAGE FOLLIES 1920; *STRIKE UP THE BAND Rehearsal, Dec.
1929: Hangin' Around With You; Mademoiselle in New Rochelle (G. & I.
Gershwin); *I Got Rhythm—perf. by Gershwin for opening of Manhattan
Theatre, 8/5/31
*Recorded by Fox Movietone News cameras *See:* **B1225, B1256**

D1154. Victor test, un-numbered, 78 (NY, July 28, 1920)
The Gershwin Trio: Bert Ralton, clarinet & organ?; GG, piano; Eddie King,
banjo
CONTENTS: Kismet; Chica

D1155.   Victor 35822, His Majesty's Voice (British) HMV C-1395, 78 (Camden, NJ,
          Apr. 21, 1927)
          George Gershwin, piano; Paul Whiteman & His Concert Orchestra

D1156.   Victor 55225, His Majesty's Voice HMV C-1171, 78 (NY, June 10, 1924)
          George Gershwin, piano; Paul Whiteman and His Concert Orchestra
          RiB, Arrangement for piano & jazz band by Ferde Grofé

RECORDINGS OF A BIOGRAPHICAL NATURE

Listed alphabetically by Record Label name

D1157.   Educational Audio Visual LE 7761? (1972)
          "George Gershwin: His Story and His Music"
          Musical illustrations from the composer's works
          Written by Alfred Simon; Narrated by Arthur Hanes
          Music Master Series

D1158.   Facet FCD 8100, CD, **[AAD]**, distributed by Delos International
          [1-800-HI-DELOS, or 1-800-443-3567] (1987)
          "George Gershwin Remembered"
          Interviews with IG; Alfred Newman; Fred Astaire, who also sings; Arthur
              Schwartz; Paul Whiteman, Selections from Paul Whiteman's original
              recording of RiB; Oscar Levant, who also plays; Performance of the
              Prelude II by GG [These are important primary sources]
          Program notes by Tony Thomas in container; Total playing time: 58:30
          Written and narrated by Tony Thomas, based on the Original Spring 1961
              Radio Documentary produced by the Canadian Broadcasting Company
          Producer: Jack Vance

D1159.   London/Decca Compact Disc Video 071-211-1 LHG (Laser disc)
          "George Gershwin Remembered"
          An interesting film on G & IG, told through the eyes of friends and colleagues.

D1160.   National Recording Co. DD-8840, cassette (1972)
          **"George Gershwin, His Life Story; Ralph Waldo Emerson, His Life
          Story"**
          Recorded from radio programs made in 1939 & 1949.
          GG meets Fred Astaire & others as his story progresses.

D1161.   SQN Productions MC-330 (© 1979)
          "George Gershwin: His Story & His Music" In "Meet the Classics"
          Fully narrated with excerpts from his most important works; Biographical
          notes & chronology on slipcase

D1162.   Vox MM 3700 (1964)
          "George Gershwin: His Story and His Music" written by Alfred Simon
          George Gershwin, piano; Arthur Hannes, narrator
          Survey of the career of George Gershwin interspersed with excerpts for
          orchestra from his works; includes transcriptions from the original player

piano rolls by Gershwin

Vox Music Masters series; Chronology of Gershwin's life juxtaposed against major historical events of the day on container

LC card no. r64-1685

MISCELLANEOUS RECORDINGS

Listed alphabetically by artist's name

D1163.   Boxer, Harold; Ewen, David

INST. AUTHOR: Voice of America Music Library Collection (Library of Congress)

"[Talks about George Gershwin] [sound recording]" [19--]; 1 sound tape reel

Title supplied by cataloger. Interviewed by Harold Boxer of Voice of America, no date given

Recorded for use by the Voice of America

Copied from VOA 7 in. tape no. 532

D1164.   Bob Dorough, conducting

Music Minus One MMO 1023 (197-?)

"The Gershwin-Porter Songbook"

Unidentified orchestra conducted by Dorough

CONTENTS: Popular songs, in recorded accompaniments

Printed music (12 pp.) inserted

D1164.1 Kay DUKE-INGALLS, Mary Cleere HARAN, vocals; Richard Rodney BENNETT, piano. Music by **Vernon DUKE,** 1903-1969, and **George GERSHWIN.**

Library of Congress Music Division concert, Mar. 14, 1998.

Sound tape reels : analog, 7 1/2 ips, 2 track, mono. ; 10 in. + 1 program

NOTES: This is a tape recording of the live performance given on the evening of the date above, during **"The Gershwins and Their World"** conference held at the Library of Congress. The final medley is by George Gershwin. Concert given under the auspices of the Music Division and the Ira and Leonore Gershwin Trust for the benefit of the Library of Congress.

Produced by the Music Division and the Recording Laboratory of the Library of Congress. Library of Congress also holds version edited for broadcast.

Cataloged from printed program; actual tape contents may vary

Recorded in the Coolidge Auditorium of the Library of Congress, Washington, D.C.

CONTENTS: K-o-e; the Germ; the Ant; the Seagull; the Sparrow; The Mouse; Cabin in the Sky; What Is There to Say? ; Medley, A Penny for Your Thoughts/now; Taking a Chance on Love; Round About; Not a Care in the World; Autumn in New York; That's What Makes Paris Paree; April in Paris; I Like the Likes of You; Medley, Lady Be Good/Somebody Loves Me

D1165.   Artis Wodehouse, speaker & piano.

"George Gershwin, His Recordings, His Performance Style"

Association for Recorded Sound Collections Tape no. 83-5 [price?]

Obtain from **ARSC, % Conference Tapes, 8 Woodburn Drive, Ottawa Ontario K1B 3A7**

A paper presented by Ms. Wodehouse at the 1983 ARSC Conference held in Nashville, TN.

D1166.   Robert Wyatt, speaker & piano, with Ellen Williams, voice.

"The Unpublished Works of George Gershwin," paper presented to the national convention of the Music Teachers National Association in Salt Lake City, UT held March 19-24, 1988. Tape #MTNA 507 available from **Meetings Internationale, 1200 Delor Ave. Louisville, KY 40217.**

Filmography

The films are listed in chronological order. Films may be found alphabetically through the Index. There are movies and television advertisements not listed here which include Gershwin music. Warner Bros./Lorimar Film Entertainment's *See You in the Morning* (1989), e.g., makes tasteful, interesting use of two Gershwin songs (*Embraceable You* and *Our Love Is Here to Stay*), but that film is not listed here. Hence, this is a selected list of films chosen for their overall or historical significance to the saga of Gershwin's music.

Because of space limitations, it was not possible to digest all of the reviews of films listed in *Film Review Index*, 2 vols., by Patricia King HANSON and Stephen L. HANSON, Oryx Press, 1986. A judicious selection of reviews was chosen and annotated in the **"Bibliography about Filmography"** chapter.

Abbreviations in this chapter are: **AA**: An Academy award; **AMPAS**: Academy of Motion Picture Arts and Sciences, Los Angeles; **DVD**: Digital Video Disc; **UCLA**: The UCLA Film and Television Archive, University of California in Los Angeles; **VC**: Videocassette, currently available; *: The song was published in sheet music format.

F1. *THE SUNSHINE TRAIL* 1923 (Silent feature film), 5 reels; © Thomas H.
Ince, Apr. 25, 1923
   CAST: Douglas MacLean, William Wallace Cook; Adaptation: Bradley King;
James W. Horne, Director

   SONG: The title song, *The Sunshine Trail*, was especially written to accompany
this film; Ira's lyrics were written under his pseudonym, Arthur Francis

F2. *TIP-TOES* (British National in England, Paramount in U. S.)
© Paramount Famous- Lasky Corp., May 14, 1927 (Silent film), 7 reels; From
the play by Fred Thompson and Guy Bolton **CAST:** Dorothy Gish; Will Rogers;
Nelson Keys; **Director:** Herbert Wilcox

F3. *LADY, BE GOOD!* (First National, 1928) 7 reels, bw, silent, © First National,
April 24, 1928
   CAST: Jack: Jack Mulhall; **Mary:** Dorothy Mackaill; **Murray:** John Miljan;

   Madison: Nita Martin; **Texas West:** Dot Farley; **Trelawney West:** James

Finlayson; **Landlady:** Aggie Herring; **Dancers:** Jay Eaton & Eddie Clayton;
Assistant: Yola D'Avril; **Producer:** Charles R. Rogers; **Script writers:**
Adelaide Heilbron & Jack Wagner (based on the book by Guy Bolton & Fred
Thompson, music by GG, Lyrics by IG); **Photography:** George Folsey;
Director: Richard Wallace
See: **B1880**

F4.   *OH, KAY!* (First National, 1928, © August 17, 1928, 7 reels)
CAST: Colleen Moore; Lawrence Gray; Alan Hale; Ford Sterling; Claude
Gillingwater; **Directed by** Mervyn Leroy; **Presented by** John McCormick

F5.   [NEWSREEL] *HEARST METROTONE NEWS,* Vol. I, No. 225, distributed by Metro-Goldwyn-Mayer, 1929-10-26. **UCLA** has. Newsreel
reconstructed from story fragments by UCLA newsreel archivists based on
available documentation. "Behind the Scenes with Metrotone" is the title of the
film, and it includes four clips, no. 4 being of a *Strike Up the Band* Broadway
rehearsal called "Here's How a Show is Whipped into Shape," featuring GG, and
the comedians Clark & McCullough. Rights held by UCLA Film and Television
archive.

F6.   *THE KING OF JAZZ; FEERIE DU JAZZ.* (© Universal Pictures, May
17, 1930) 98 min. Premiere: May 2, 1930: NY: Roxy Theatre; **VC:** MCA Home
Video VHS 55119
This film is listed here only for its featuring the RiB played by the Whiteman
band; GG performed the RiB live on stage at the Roxy during the week of the
premiere with the Whiteman band
Stars: Paul Whiteman and His Orchestra; Roy Bargy on piano in the Rhapsody;
Bing Crosby & the Rhythm Boys; **Arrangements:** Ferde Grofé
See: **B240, B260, B1970-B1980**

F6.1. *SONG OF THE FLAME* (First National-Warner Bros., © June 12, 1930,
9 reels, color
See: **F9**, The Flame Song; *Premiere:* 1930 (May): NY; Warner's Theater
CAST: **Prince Volodya:** Alexander Gray; **Aniuta, the Flamey:** Berniyce
Claire; **Konstantin:** Noah Beery, Sr.; **Natasha:** Alice Gentle; **Count Boris:**
Bert Roach; **Grusha:** Inez Courtney; **Officer:** Shep Camp; **Konstantin's Pal:**
Ivan Linow; **Dancer:** Janina Smolinska; **Screenplay:** Gordon Rigby (based on
the book and lyrics by Oscar Hammerstein II & Otto Harbach, and music by
Herbert Stothart & GG); **Photography:** Lee Garmes (Technicolor); **Sets:**
Anton Grot; **Costumes:** Edward Stevenson; **Choreography:** Jack Haskell;
Director: Alan Crosländ; **Musical Director:** Leo F. Forbstein *See:* **B1880**

MUSIC:
Song of the Flame*; Cossack Love Song*; (These songs were published with
sheet music covers both for the Broadway musical and the film)

F7.   *DELICIOUS* (Fox, 1931) 71 min. *Premiere:* NY: Roxy, Week of Dec. 25, 1931;
© December 3, 1931.
Final shooting script, mimeograph typescript, 98 pp. at Gershwin Collection,
DLC, date on cover: Jan. 16, 1931 (Box 6, Item 7)

CAST: **Heather Gordon:** Janet Gaynor; **Jerry Beaumont:** Charles Farrell; **Jansen:** El Brendel; **Sascha:** Raul Roulien; **O'Flynn:** Lawrence O'Sullivan; **Olga:** Manya Roberti; **Diana Van Bergh:** Virginia Cherrill; **Mrs. Van Bergh:** Olive Tell; **Mischa:** Mischa Auer; **Tosha:** Marvin(e) Maazel **Screenplay by:** Guy Bolton & Sonya Levien; **Cinematographer:** Ernest Palmer; **Sound Engineer:** Joseph E. Aiken; **Art Direction:** Joe Wright; **Costumes:** Guy Duty; **Editor:** Irene Morra; **Asst. Director:** Ad Schaumer; **Director:** David Butler

Solo piano parts played by Marvin(e) Maazel

MUSIC:

Delishious*(Roulien sang, piano dubbed by **Marvin(e) Maazel**), reprised instrumentally later; Welcome to the Melting Pot—Dream Sequence (Gaynor, chorus); Somebody from Somewhere*(Gaynor); Katinkitschka* (Auer, Roberti, danced by Roulien, Maazel, Roberti, Auer, Gaynor); Blah-Blah-Blah*(Brendel, Roberti); Somebody from Somewhere (vocal group); Second Rhapsody, also known as Rhapsody in Rivets or New York Rhapsody (narration, piano by Roulien, pantomime by Gaynor, ensemble, [Hugo Friedhofer collaborated with G on the version used for the film]; You Started Something (underscore) Not used: Just Another Rhumba
See: **D1102, B280, B1871, B1874, B1915-B1923**

F8.   *GIRL CRAZY.* (RKO Radio Pictures, 1932; Release date: Mar. 25, 1932); © Mar. 26, 1932; 75 min. *See*: **B1874, B1941-B1942**
CAST: **Jimmy Deegan:** Bert Wheeler; **Slick Foster:** Robert Woolsey; **Danny Churchill:** Eddie Quillan; **Patsy:** Dorothy Lee; **Tessie Deegan:** Mitzi Green; **Kate Foster:** Kitty Kelly; **Molly Gray:** Arline Judge; **Lank Sanders:** Stanley Fields; **Mary:** Lita Chevret; **Pete:** Chris Pin Martin

Screenplay by: Tim Whelan and Eddie Welch; based on Herman J. Mankiewicz's adaptation of the stage play by John McGowan and Guy Bolton; **Dialogue:** Tim Whelan, Herman J. Mankiewicz, Edward Welch, Walter DeLeon; **Cinematographer:** J. Roy Hunt; **Art Direction:** Max Ree; **Editor:** Arties Roberts; **Sound Recording:** Hugh McDowell; **Producer:** David O. Selznick; **Director:** William A. Seiter

SONGS: One new song, based on pre-existing material: *You've Got What Gets Me** by the Gershwin brothers. According to Miles Krueger, *I Got Rhythm* was probably dubbed for Kitty Kelly by Barbara Van Brunt.

F9.   *THE FLAME SONG.* (The Vitaphone Corp., 1934) 2 reels © Nov. 24, 1934 Based on *The Flame* by Otto Harback, Oscar Hammerstein II, GG, & Herbert Stothart. **Director:** Joseph Henabery; **Adaptation:** Cyrus Wood. **DLC** has a copy in the Motion Picture, Broadcasting, & Recorded Sound Division.

F10.   *SHALL WE DANCE?* (RKO Radio, 1937) 116 min.

Premiere: 1937 (May 13): NY; Radio City Music Hall; © May 7, 1937; **UCLA**

has 16 mm. safety print; **VC:** Republic Pictures Home Video VHS 7730 & Nostalgia Merchant VHS NM8077 *See:* **B1871, B1881, D1097**

CAST: **Jeffrey Baird:** Edward Everett Horton; **Delivery boy:** not known; **Doorman:** not known; **Ballet masters:** Marek Windheim & Rolfe Sedan; **Peter P. Peters (Petrov):** Fred Astaire; **Linda Keene:** Ginger Rogers; **Rogers' rhumba partner:** Pete Theodore; **Rogers' show manager:** not known; **Rogers' maid (Tai):** Emma Young; **Arthur Miller (Rogers' manager):** Jerome Cowan; **Denise (Lady Tarrington):** Ketti Gallian; **Ship announcer:** not known; **Newspaper photographers:** not known; **English steward:** Douglas Gordon; **Singer in** *Slap That Bass:* Dudley Dickerson; **Ship's waiter:** Leonard Mudie; **Radio officer:** Henry Mowbray; **Purser:** not known; **Bar stewards:** not known; **Mrs. Fitzgerald:** Ann Shoemaker; **Other passenger:** Helena Grant; **Dispatcher:** Sam Hayes; **Ship steward:** George Magrill; **Cecil Flintridge:** Eric Blore; **Jim Montgomery: Rogers' fiance:** William Brisbane; **Rooftop Headwaiter:** not known; **Rooftop bandleader:** Ben Alexander; **Charlie:** Sam Wren; **Newsboy:** Sherwood Bailey; **Policeman in Central Park:** Charles Coleman; **Justice of the Peace:** William Burress; **Hotel desk clerk:** Jack Rice; **Hotel carpenter:** Harry Bowen; **Flower seller on ferry:** Tiny (Elizabeth) Jones; **Bellhop:** not known; **Process server:** Frank Moran; **Police officer in jail:** not known; **Ballet soloist in** *Shall We Dance?:* Harriet Hoctor; **Rogers' attorney:** Richard Tucker; **Producer:** Pandro S. Berman; **Director:** Mark Sandrich; **Ballet staged by:** Hermes Pan & Harry Losee; **Arrangements & orchestrations:** Nathaniel Shilkret; **Additional arrangements:** Robert Russell Bennett; **Screenplay:** Allan Scott, Ernest Pagano (based on the story *Watch Your Step* by Lee Loeb & Harold Buchman, adapted by P. J. Wolfson); **Director of photography:** David Abel; **Special effects:** Vernon Walker; **Art director:** Van Nest Polglase; **Associate art director:** Carroll Clark; **Set decoration:** Darrell Silvera; **Ginger Rogers' gowns:** Irene Sharaff; **Editor:** William Hamilton; **Recording:** Hugh McDowell, Jr.; **Musical director and conductor:** Nathaniel Shilkret *See:* **B1243, B1874**

MUSIC:

French Ballet Class (Orchestra, danced by girls); Dance of the Waves (Orchestra, danced by girls, Horton); Ginger Rhumba (orchestra); I've Got Beginner's Luck*(danced by Astaire); Graceful and Elegant (orchestra); Slap That Bass*(Black chorus, Dudley Dickerson?, Astaire); Walking the Dog (Solo clarinet with chamber orchestra, walking pantomime by Astaire & Rogers--later retitled Promenade and published as piano solo); I've Got Beginner's Luck, reprise (Astaire); They All Laughed (Rogers, second time danced by Astaire and Rogers); Balloon Ballet (orchestra); Let's Call the Whole Thing Off*(Astaire & Rogers); They Can't Take That Away from Me* (Astaire); Hoctors Ballet (orchestra); Wake Up, Brother, and Dance (Danced by Astaire, Hoctor, girls); Shall We Dance*(Astaire, danced by Astaire, girls, & Rogers); reprise of They All Laughed (Astaire, Rogers)

Not Used: Hi-Ho!; At Last

F11. *A DAMSEL IN DISTRESS* (RKO Radio, 1937) 98 min. *Premiere:* 1937
(Nov. 24): NY; Rivoli Theatre © Nov. 19, 1937; **VC:** RKO 2045 *See:* **B421,
B1507, D1098, D1099, B1871, B1874, B1881**

> **CAST: Butler (Keggs):** Reginald Gardiner (singing dubbed by Mario Berini);
> **Page (Albert):** Harry Watson; **Footman (Thomas):** John Blood(?); **Cook:**
> Mary Gordon; **Maid:** Violet Seton(?); **George Burns:** George Burns;
> **Gracie Allen:** Gracie Allen; **Jerry Halliday:** Fred Astaire; **Lady Alyce
> Marshmorton:** Joan Fontaine; **Woman in street:** not known; **English
> bobby:** Frank Moran; **Cockney street dancer & Halliday impersonator:**
> Joe Niemeyer; **Man in street:** not known; **Lord John Marshmorton:**
> Montagu Love; **Reggie:** Ray Noble; **Lady Caroline Marshmorton:**
> Constance Collier; **Footman (Henry):** Clive Moran(?); **Madrigal singers:**
> Pearl Amatore, Betty Rone, Jac George, and others; **Barker at carnival:**
> Charles Bennett; **Drunks in fun house:** Jack Walklin; James Clemens,
> Kenneth Terrell, James Fawcett; **Female singing trio in "Nice Work If You
> Can Get It":** Betty Rone, Jan Duggan, Mary Dean; **Chauffeur:** Bill O'Brien;
> **Sightseers:** Ralph Brooks, Fred Kelsey; **Dance Extra:** Major Sam Harris;
> **Dance Director:** Hermes Pan; **Additional musical aria:** Friedrich van
> Flotow; **Arrangements & orchestrations:** Robert Russell Bennett;
> **Additional arrangements:** Ray Noble & George Bassman; **Screenplay:** P.
> G. Wodehouse, Ernest Pagano, S. K. Lauren (from the novel by P. G.
> Wodehouse and the play by Wodehouse & Ian Hay); **Director of
> photography:** Joseph H. August; **Special effects:** Vernon Walker; **Art
> director:** Van Nest Polglase; **Associate art director:** Carroll Clark; **Set
> decoration:** Darrell Silvera; **Editor:** Henry Berman; **Recording:** Earl A.
> Wolcott; **Assistant director:** Argyle Nelson; **Producer:** Pandro S. Berman;
> **Director:** George Stevens; **Musical director & conductor:** Victor Baravelle

MUSIC

> I Can't Be Bothered Now*(Astaire); The Jolly Tar and the Milkmaid*
> (chorus, Astaire, Duggan, Dean, Amatore, Rone); Put Me to the Test (whisk
> broom dance, instrumental, danced by Astaire, Burns, & Allen); Stiff Upper
> Lip*(Allen, danced by Astaire, Burns, Allen, & dancers, won the **AA** for the
> best staged musical number of 1937); Things Are Looking Up* (Astaire,
> danced by Astaire, Fontaine); Sing of Spring (chorus, Duggan); Things Are
> Looking Up (Noble's orch.); A Foggy Day*(Astaire); Nice Work If You Can
> Get It* (Duggan, Dean, Rone, Astaire, chorus); Nice Work If You Can Get
> It—Drum Dance (reprise, danced by Astaire); Not Used: Pay Some Attention
> To Me

F12. *THE GOLDWYN FOLLIES* (Goldwyn-United Artists, released on Feb.
23, 1938) 115 min. © Feb. 23, 1938; Technicolor; **VC:** Embassy Home
Entertainment VHS 3043, Classic Musical Comedy *See:* **B1871, B1874, B1954-
B1969**

> **CAST: Oliver Merlin:** Adolphe Menjou; **Ritz Brothers:** Ritz Brothers; **Olga
> Samara:** Vera Zorina; **Danny Beecher:** Kenny Baker; **Hazel Dawes:** Andrea

Leeds; **Leona Jerome:** Helen Jepson; **Michael Day:** Phil Baker; **Glory Wood:** Ella Logan; **A. Basil Crane, Jr.:** Bobby Clark; **Lawrence:** Jerome Cowan; **Ada:** Nydia Westman; **Alfredo:** Charles Kullman; **Edgar Bergen & Charley McCarthy:** Edgar Bergen & Charley McCarthy; **Dancers:** American Ballet of the Metropolitan Opera

Screenplay by: Ben Hecht; **Cinematographer:** Gregg Toland; **Editor:** Sherman Todd; **Orchestrations:** Edward Powell; **Costumes:** Omar Kiam; **Ballets conceived & staged by:** George Balanchine; **Art direction:** Richard Day; **Producer:** Samuel Goldwyn; **Associate producer:** George Haight; **Assistant director:** Frank Shields; **Director:** George Marshall; **Musical direction:** Alfred Newman

SONGS:

Love Walked In* (Kenny Baker, sung twice, later repeated a third time with Andrea Leeds, who was dubbed by Virginia Verrill); I Was Doing Alright* (Ella Logan); (Our) Love Is Here To Stay* (K. Baker), Spring Again*; I Love To Rhyme*(Phil Baker, McCarthy, Bergen); Finale: Love Walked In (K. Baker, Jepson, Leeds); The remainder of the score was completed by Vernon Duke

F13.   *STRIKE UP THE BAND* (Metro-Goldyn-Mayer, 1940) 119 min. **VC:** MGM/ UA Home Video VHS MV400565
   Director: Busby Berkeley; **Producer:** Arthur Freed; **Stars:** Mickey Rooney, Judy Garland, Paul Whiteman; **Musical director:** Georgie Stoll

   This film should not be considered a Gershwin musical. It does, however, use the song "Strike Up the Band" as its title song and as a feature for a big production number at the conclusion of the film. The story bears no resemblance to the earlier 1927 and 1930 stage versions.

F14.   *LADY, BE GOOD!* (Metro, 1941) 110 mins. *Premiere:* 1941 (?): NY: Capitol; **VC avail.**
   Stars: Ann Southern; Eleanor Powell; Dan Dailey, Jr.; Lionel Barrymore; Red Skelton; John Carroll; Phil Silvers; Robert Young & others; Jimmy Dorsey Orchestra; **Director:** Norman McLeod; **Screenplay:** Jack McGowan, Kay Riper, & John McLain, based on a story by Jack McGowan; **Vocals & Orchestrations:** Lou Arnaud, George Bassman, & Conrad Salinger; **Musical numbers directed by:** Busby Berkeley; **Gowns:** Adrian; **Film Editor:** Frederick Y. Smith; **Musical presentation:** Merrill Pye; **Producer:** Arthur Freed; **Musical direction:** Georgie Stoll *See:* **D1097, B1999-2007**

   SONGS: Not based on the famous musical, has only three G songs, the title song: Lady, Be Good!; Fascinating Rhythm (instrumental danced by Eleanor Powell); Hang On to Me (according to Charles Schwartz); With additional songs by Kern, Hammerstein II, Arthur Freed, & Roger Edens

F15.   *GIRL CRAZY.* (MGM, July, 1943) 99 minutes; **VC:** MGM/UA Home Video MV300567 *See:* **B1874, B1943-B1949, W50**

CAST: **Danny Churchill, Jr.:** Mickey Rooney; **Ginger Gray:** Judy Garland;
Bud Livermore: Gil Stratton; **Henry Lathrop:** Robert E. Strickland; **Rags:**
Rags Ragland; **Specialty:** June Allyson; **Polly Williams:** Nancy Walker;
Dean Armour: Guy Kibbee; **Tommy Dorsey:** Himself; **Marjorie Tait:**
Frances Rafferty; **Mr. Churchill, Sr.:** Henry O'Neill; **Governor's Secretary:**
Sarah Edwards; **Radio Man:** William Bishop; **Maitre d' Hotel:** Charles
Coleman; **Reception Clerk:** Irving Bacon; **Blonde:** Kathleen Williams; **Boy:**
Don Taylor; **Boy:** Peter Lawford; **Committee Woman:** Bess Flowers;
Governor Tait: Howard Freeman; **Vocal arrangements:** Hugh Martin &
Jack Blane; *I Got Rhythm* number **directed by Bush Berkeley**; **Dances:**
Charles Walters; **Screenplay:** Fred F. Finklehoffe (based on the musical play
and book of the same name by Guy Bolton & Jack McGowan); **Musical
adaptation:** Roger Edens; **Cinematographers:** William Daniels and Robert
Planck; **Editor:** Albert Akst; **Art direction:** Cedric Gibbons; **Set
decorations:** Edwin B. Willis, Mac Alper; **Musical presentation:** Merrill
Pye; **Sound technician:** William Steinkamp; **Choreography:** Charles
Walters; **Orchestrations:** Conrad Salinger, George Bassman, Georgie Stoll,
Axel Stordahl, Sy Oliver; **Vocal arrangements:** Hugh Martin, Ralph Blane;
Asst. director: Joseph Boyle; **Director:** Norman Taurog; **Producer:** Arthur
Freed; **Musical direction:** Georgie Stoll *See:* **B1943-B1949**

SONGS:

I Got Rhythm*& Embraceable You*, under opening titles; Sam and
Delilah*(Tommy Dorsey & band); Treat Me Rough* (Allyson, girls, Rooney,
Dorsey's orch.); Bidin' My Time* (Garland, male quartet); Could You Use
Me?* (Rooney, Garland); Embraceable You (sung by Garland to a long table
of men at the ranch, interestingly staged, later danced by unidentified male &
Garland, then Garland and men; later sung by soloists & chorus); Instrumental
reprise: Embraceable You, as underscore to dialogue between Rooney &
Garland; Fascinating Rhythm* (Dorsey Band); But Not for Me*(Garland); I
Got Rhythm Finale (Garland singing with chorus & Dorsey band, then Rooney
joins singing, followed by a dance with Rooney & Garland & the whole
company)

F16. *RHAPSODY IN BLUE.* (Warner Bros.-First National, 1945) 130 min. **UCLA**
has three-reel, 35 mm. print of the original; Shooting script at **NN-L**
Premiere: 1945 (June 26): Hollywood & NY **VC:** MGM/UA 301149
See: **B1403, B1874, B1583 (Levant bio)**
CAST: **George Gershwin:** Robert Alda; **Julie Adams:** Joan Leslie, a fictional
show girl, songs dubbed by **Sally Sweetland**; **Christine Gilbert** (a fictional
artist in Paris—Alexis Smith; **Max Dreyfus:** Charles Coburn; **Lee Gershwin:**
Julie Bishop; **Professor Frank:** Albert Basserman; **Poppa Gershwin:** Morris
Carnovsky; **Momma Gershwin:** Rosemary De Camp; **Oscar Levant:** Oscar
Levant; **Paul Whiteman:** Paul Whiteman; **Al Jolson:** Al Jolson; **George
White:** George White; **Hazel Scott:** Hazel Scott; **Anne Wiggins Brown
(Bess, singing Summertime):** Anne Wiggins Brown; **Christine's escort
(American man):** Robert Shayne; **Ira Gershwin:** Herbert Rudley;
Commentator: John B. Hughes; **George Gershwin** (as a boy): Mickey Roth;
Ira Gershwin (as a boy): Darryl Hickman; **Mr. Kast:** Charles Halton; **Mr.**

Milton: Andrew Tombes; **Mr. Katzman:** Gregory Goluhoff; **Mr. Muscatel:** Walter Soderling; **Buddy DeSylva:** Eddie Marr; **William Foley:** Theodore Von Eltz; **Herbert Stone:** Bill Kennedy; **American Man:** Robert Shayne; **Ravel:** Oscar Loraine; **Dancer:** Johnny Downs; **Otto Kahn:** Ernest Golm; **Jascha Heifetz:** Martin Noble; **Walter Damrosch:** Hugo Kirchhoffer; **Rachmaninoff:** Will Wright; <u>**Bit parts:**</u> **Comic:** George Riley; **Cashier:** Virginia Sale; **Ragged bum:** Tom Stevenson; **Three song pluggers:** Harry Seymour, Joe Sullivan, Clarence Badger; **Prima donna:** Yola d'Avril; **Receptionist:** Claire DuBrey; **Swedish janitor:** Christian Rub; **Housewife:** Esther Michelson; **Piano mover:** Robert Wilbur; **Night club guest:** Ivan Lebedeff; **Madame DeBreteuil:** Odette Myrtil: **Guests:** Frank Reicher, Georges Renavent, Lynne Baggett, Elsa Basserman; **Orchestra leader:** Jay Novello; **Bootblack:** LeRoy Antoine; **Painter:** Oliver Prickett; **Painter:** Carl Neubert; **Ravel:** Oscar Lorraine; **Headwaiter:** Jack Chefe; **Doctor:** Charles Waldron; **Telephone operator:** Lillian Bronson; **Newsboy:** John Henry Morton; **Man in Turkish bath:** Clay Womack; **Man in Turkish bath:** Frank Pharr; **Masseur:** Sam Savitsky; **Party guests:** Constance Purdy, Caroline Burke, Milton Mack, Joan Winfield, Ralph McColm; **Butler:** Broderick O'Farrel; **Sport:** Robert Johnson; **Porgy:** William Gillespie; **Music teacher:** Kate Harrington; **Music teacher:** Walter White; **Other woman:** Nellie Nichols; **Customer in bakery:** Ernie Adams; **Music critic:** John Dilson; **Hotel clerk:** Armand Cortez; **Taxi driver:** Jacques Lory; **Porter:** Bernard Deroux; **Porter:** Fred Dosh; **Theatre manager:** Edward Harvey; **Tall man:** Ben Moroz; **Coachman:** Jesse Graves; **Singer:** Mark Stevens (dubbed by **Bill Days**)

Musical Direction: Leo F. Forbstein; **Lyrics by:** Ira Gershwin, Buddy DeSylva, & Irving Caesar; **Arrangements:** Ray Heindorf; **Vocal arrangements:** Dudley Chambers; **Music adapted by:** Max Steiner; **Choreography:** Leroy Prinz; **Sound:** David Forest & Stanley Jones; **Art Directors:** John Hughes & Anton Grot; **Montages:** James Leicester; **Dialogue director:** Felis Jacoves; **Special effects:** Roy Davidson, director & Williard van Enger; **Set decorations:** Fred M. MacLean; **Makeup artist:** Perc Westmore; **Gowns by:** Milo Anderson; **Screenplay by:** Howard Koch & Elliot Paul; based on an original story by Sonya Levien;
Cinematographers: Sol Polito, Merritt Gerstad, Ernest Haller, James Leicester, Roy Davidson, & William Van Enger; **Editor:** Folmer Blangsted; **Director:** Irving Rapper; **Producer:** Jesse L. Lasky

Musical Numbers (Only music by G listed):

When You Want 'Em, You Can't Get 'Em, When You Got 'Em, You Don't Want 'Em (Brief excerpt by Alda, played by **Ray Turner**?, to demonstrate to hoofer at Remick's); Swanee (Leslie, dubbed by **Sally Sweetland**, accompanied by Alda played by **Turner**, then Jolson); 'S Wonderful! (Alda, then Leslie dancing, then chorus); Somebody Loves Me (Patricola & Leslie); I'll Build a Stairway to Paradise (chorus) & Lady Be Good (Leslie, dancing & singing with chorus); Blue Monday excerpt (Unidentified soloists); RiB (Alda, Whiteman's orch.); The Man I Love (in French, Hazel Scott); Medley: Clap Yo' Hands (eight measures only), Fascinating Rhythm, I Got Rhythm (Scott);

Yankee Doodle Blues (Scott); Liza (Alda); Somebody Loves Me (Alda, Levant); Someone to Watch Over Me (Levant?); "I Got Rhythm" Variations (Alda, Levant); Bidin' My Time (chorus); My One and Only (Alda); Embraceable You (Leslie, dubbed by **Sweetland**); The Man I Love (underscore); AiP (under scenes of Paris, later, ballet dancers); Cuban Overture (orch.); Mine (sung duet by Alda & Levant); Delishious (Leslie, dubbed by **Sweetland**); Summertime (chorus, then Brown with chorus); It Ain't Necessarily So (underscore); Concerto (First movement only, Alda-Turner); Love Walked In (Alda); Love Walked In (Stevens, dubbed by **Bill Days);** Concerto (Last movement, Levant); RiB, abridged (Levant, Whiteman conducting) *See:* **D1097, D1117**

Piano for Alda played by Ray Turner. Sally Sweetland dubbed for Joan Leslie. Bill Days dubbed for Mark Stevens.

F17.   *THE SHOCKING MISS PILGRIM.* (20th Century-Fox, 1946, released Jan. 1947); 87 min.; **UCLA** has a 35 mm. nitrate, studio print *See:* **B1257, B1871, B1874, B2099-2106, D1121** (1947 soundtrack)
   CAST: Cynthia Pilgrim: Betty Grable; **John Pritchard:** Dick Haymes; **Alice Pritchard:** Anne Revere; **Leander Woolsey:** Allyn Joslyn; **Saxon:** Gene Lockhart; **Catherine Dennison:** Elizabeth Patterson; **Mrs. Pritchard:** Elisabeth Risdon; **Michael Michael:** Arthur Shields; **Herbert Jothan:** Charles Kemper; **Mr. Foster:** Roy Roberts; **Office clerk:** Tom Moore; **Lookout in office:** Stanley Prager; **Quincy:** Ed Laughton; **Office boy:** William Frambes; **Peabody:** Hal K. Dawson; **Viola Simmons:** Lillian Bronson; **Mr. Packard:** Raymond Largay; **Sarah Glidden:** Constance Purdy; **Miss Nixon:** Mildred Stone; **Wendell Paige:** Pierre Watkin; **Mr. Carter:** Junius Matthews; **Conductor:** William Halligan
   Screenplay by: George Seaton, based on a story by Ernest & Frederic Maas; **Cinematographer:** Leon Shamroy; **Editor:** Robert Simpson; **Non-Gershwin Music:** Alfred Newman; **Dances:** Hermes Pan; **Director:** George Seaton; **Producer:** William Perlberg
   Josyln, Kemper, Patterson, Bronson, & Shields were dubbed.

SONGS:

Sweet Packard (chorus); Changing My Tune* (Grable); Stand Up and Fight (chorus, Revere, Grable, Haymes, unidentified principals); Aren't You Kinda Glad We Did?* (Haynes, Grable); But Not In Boston (Joslyn, Kemper, Patterson, Bronson, Shields, Grable); One, Two, Three*(Chorus, Haymes, danced by Haymes, Grable, dancers); Waltzing Is Better Sitting Down (Haymes, Grable); Waltz Me No Waltzes (Grable, Haymes); For You, For Me, Forevermore* (Haymes, Grable); Finale: Aren't You Kinda Glad We Did? (Haymes, Grable); Back Bay Polka*; Demon Rum; Not used: Tour of the Town; Welcome Song

F18.   *THE BARKLEYS OF BROADWAY.* (MGM, 1949) 109 mins. © Mar. 15, 1949
   Premiere: 1949 (May 4): NY; Loew's State Theatre
   Stars: Fred Astaire, Ginger Rogers, Oscar Levant, Billie Burke, et al. For full details of cast, *See:* **B1881, B1902-1904, B1583**

SONG:

    This film employs only one Gershwin song: *You Can't Take That Away From Me*, interpolated. The other songs are by Harry Warren, hence they are not listed here. The movie is listed in this chapter by virtue of its being the last of the Astaire-Rogers films, and the only one in color.

F19.   *AN AMERICAN IN PARIS.* (Metro-Goldwyn-Mayer **(AA)**, 1951)
    113 minutes; MGM/UA Home Video MV600006; **UCLA** has a 35 mm. version and the videocassette; **VC:** MGM/UA Home Video MV 600006 MGM/UA ML 102803 **Deluxe Laser Disc** including several audio outtakes of Levant which were not included in the film. **DVD** version: 906273**DVD** (4/99)

    Premiere: 1951 (Oct. 4): NY; Radio City Music Hall *See*: **D746, D1096, B1871, B1887-B1900-(AA** indicates Academy Award winners)

    CAST: Jerry Mulligan: Gene Kelly; **Lise Bourvier:** Leslie Caron; **Adam Cook:** Oscar Levant; **Milo Roberts:** Nina Foch; **Henri Baurel:** Georges Guetary; **Georges Mattieu:** Eugene Borden; **Mathilde Mattieu:** Martha Bamattre; **Old Woman Dancer:** Mary Young; **Therese:** Ann Codee; **Francola:** George Davis; **Tommy Baldwin:** Hayden Rorke; **John McDowd:** Paul Maxey; **Ben Macrow:** Dick Wessel; **Honeymooner (wife):** Adele Coray; **Honeymooner (husband):** Don Quinn; **Boys with bubble gum:** Lucian Planzoles, Christian Pasques, Anthony Mazola; **Smiling young man:** Charles Bastin; **Nun:** Jeanne Lafayette; **Nun:** Louise Laureau; **Man at shutters:** Captain Garcia; **Man with books:** Charles Millsfied; **Woman with cats:** Louise Colombat; **Young man at mirror:** Leonard Mazola; **Postman:** Alfred Paix; **American Girl:** Noel Neill; **Maid:** Nan Boardman; **Jack Jansen:** John Eldredge; **Kay Jansen:** Anna Q. Nilsson; **Woman at table:** Louise E. Lareau; **Man at table:** Albert Pollet; **Edna Woman on phone:** Wanda Lucienne; **Mae Bestram (customer):** Madge Blake; **Driver:** Art Dupuis; **Man:** Charles Mauu; **Waiter:** Albert d'Arno; **Artist:** Greg McClure; **Dancing Partner:** André Charisse; **News Vendor:** Marie Antoinette Andrews; Benny Carter's Orch.; **Story & Screenplay by:** Alan Jay Lerner **(AA)**; **Photography:** Alfred Gilks; **Ballet photography:** John Alton [specially lensed the ballet] **(AA)**; **Technicolor consultants:** Henri Jaffa & James Gooch; **Editor:** Adrienne Fazan; **Art direction:** Cedric Gibbons & Preston Ames **(AA)**; **Set decoration:** Edwin B. Willis & Keogh Gleason **(AA)**; **Costume design:** Orry-Kelly; **Hair stylist:** Sydney Guilaroff; **Makeup:** William Tuttle; **Beaux-Arts ball costumes by:** Walter Plunkett; **Ballet costumes by:** Irene Sharaff **(AA)**; **Choreography:** Gene Kelly; **Asst. Choreographer:** Carol Haney; **Music direction:** Johnny Green & Saul Chaplin **(AA)**; **Adaption of AiP for ballet:** Saul Chaplin; **Producer:** Arthur Freed; **Asst. Director:** Al Raboch; **Director:** Vincente Minnelli

MUSIC:

    How Long Has This Been Going On?*(piano by Levant); Nice Work if You

Can Get It* (Guetary, piano by Levant); Embraceable You*(Danced by Caron); Fascinating Rhythm* (Levant); By Strauss* (Guetary, Kelly, & Levant, Chorus, danced by Kelly, Bammatre, & Young); I Got Rhythm* (Kelly, children); **Medley:** But Not For Me*, Do Do Do*, Bidin' My Time*, I've Got a Crush on You*, Our Love Is Here To Stay*, Someone to Watch Over Me*(Carter's orch.); Tra La La* (Kelly, Levant); Our Love Is Here to Stay* (Kelly, danced by Kelly & Caron); I'll Build a Stairway to Paradise* (Guetary, girls); I Don't Think I'll Fall in Love Today*(Levant); Concerto, 3rd movement only*(Levant); 'S Wonderful!* (Guetary, Kelly); Strike up the Band (beneath crowd scene at party, as instrumental)*; Liza*(Levant); ; An arrangement of excerpts from AiP (Concluding ballet, danced by Kelly, Caron & dancers)

Special AA went to Gene Kelly for his performance as actor, singer, dancer, & choreographer in the film. *See:* **B1583, bio of Levant)**

F20. *STARLIFT* (1951) 103 min. Studio? Source: p. 1003, Maltin, 1989 ed.
   CAST: Janice Rule; Dick Wesson; Ron Hagerthy; Richard Webb; Cameos by Warner Bros. people like James Cagney; Virginia Mayo; Ruth Roman; Doris Day; Gordon McRae, etc.; **Director:** Roy Dell Ruth

   SONGS:

   'S Wonderful! (Doris Day) *See:* **D1097**
   Liza (Patrice Wymore) *See:* **D1097**

F21. *THREE FOR THE SHOW.* (Columbia, 1955) 93 min.; CinemaScope/Technicolor
   Stars: Betty Grable, Marge Champion, Gower Champion, Jack Lemmon
   Music Director: Morris Stoloff

   SONGS:
   Someone to Watch Over Me (Marge & Gower Champion, dancing); I've Got a Crush on You (Grable & Lemmon, singing)
   See: **B1880**

F22. *THAT CERTAIN FEELING.* (Paramount Pictures, 1956) 103 min.; **UCLA** has an incomplete version
   Stars: Bob Hope, Eva Marie Saint, George Sanders, Pearl Bailey

   SONG: The title song is the only G song used.

F23. *FUNNY FACE.* (Paramount, 1957) Technicolor VistaVision 103 mins.;
   © Mar. 28, 1957 *Premiere:* 1957 (Mar. 28): NY; Radio City Music Hall; **VC:** Paramount 5608; laserdisc restoration available from Paramount (Summer, 1992) *See:* **B1874**, **B1881, B1924-1940, D1103, D1104** (orig. soundtrack)

   CAST: Receptionists: Marilyn White, Dorothy Colbert; **Lettie (Thompson's secretary):** Ruta Lee; **Maggie Prescott:** Kay Thompson; **Babs:** Virginia Gibson; **Laura:** Sue England; **Junior Editors:** Louise Glenn, Heather Hopper, Cecile Rogers; **Models in "Think Pink" number:** Suzy Parker,

Sunny Harnett; **Dovitch:** Alex Gerry; **Dick Avery:** Fred Astaire; **Steve (Astaire's Assistant):** Paul Smith; **Marion (Model):** Doima; **Jo Stockton:** Audrey Hepburn; **French tour man:** not known; **Male Dancers in "Bonjours, Paris!" number:** not known; **Paul Duval:** Robert Flemyng; **Sidewalk cafe patrons:** Baroness Ella van Heemstra, Roger Edens; **Gigi:** Karen Scott; **Man in cafe:** not known; **Man standing on head:** Jerry Chiat; **Man nearby:** Gabriel Curtiz; **Drinking companions:** George Dee, Marcel de LaBrosse, Albert Godderis; **Mimi:** Diane du Bois; **Dancers in "Basal Metabolism:"** not known; **Marcel (Astaire's assistant):** not known; **Priest:** not known; **French woman:** not known; **Professor Emile Flostre:** Michael Auclair; **Woman at door of Flostre's:** not known; **Bouncer:** Jerry Lucas; **Singer at Flostre's:** Elizabeth Slifer; **Woman crying at Flostre's:** Jan Bradley; **Mr. Barker:** Nesdon Booth; **Mrs. Barker:** Fern Barry; **Announcer at fashion show:** not known; **Clerk at hotel:** not known; **Telephone operator at hotel:** not known; **TWA clerk:** Donald Lawton; **Airport announcer:** not known; **Man buyer:** Peter Camlin; **Woman buyer:** Elsa Petersen

Producer: Roger Edens; **Director:** Stanley Donen; **Choreography:** Eugene Loring & Fred Astaire; **Songs staged by:** Stanley Donen; **Dance Assistants:** Dave Robel & Pat Denise; **Arrangements & Orchestrations:** Conrad Salinger, Mason Van Cleave, Alexander Courage, Skip Martin; **Screenplay:** Leonard Gershe (from his unproduced stage play *Wedding Day)*; **Director of Photography:** Ray June; **Color consultant:** Richard Mueller; **Special visual consultant and main title backgrounds:** Richard Avedon; **Special effects:** John P. Fulton; **Process photography:** Farciot Edouart; **Art directors:** Hal Pereira & George W. Davis; **Set decoration:** Sam Comer & Ray Moyer; **Costumes:** Edith Head; **Audry Hepburn's Paris wardrobe:** Hubert de Givenchy; **Makeup:** Wally Westmore; **Hair:** Nellie Manley; **Editor:** Frank Bracht; **Recording:** George & Winston Leverett; **Assistant director:** William McGarry; **Additional songs:** Roger Edens; Adolph Deutsch, **Musical director & conductor**

SONGS:

Funny Face (Astaire); 'S Wonderful!*(chorus); Think Pink! (non-G song, Thompson, chorus); How Long Has This Been Going On?*(Hepburn); reprise Funny Face (Astaire, danced by Astaire, Hepburn); Bonjour, Paris! (non-G song, Astaire, Thompson, Hepburn, men); Medley: How Long Has This Been Going On? (in avant garde modern jazz instrumental arr.) & Funny Face (danced by Hepburn, two unidentified dancers); Let's Kiss and Make Up*(Astaire); He Loves and She Loves*(Astaire, danced by Hepburn, Astaire); Clap Yo' Hands* (Thompson, Astaire); Finale: Funny Face (Astaire) & 'S Wonderful! (Astaire, Hepburn)

Songs other than those by the Gershwins: Think Pink; Bonjour Paris!; On How To Be Lovely; bridge for Clap Yo' Hands; music by Roger Edens; lyrics by Leonard Gershe; Marche Funébre: music by Roger Edens; lyrics by Lela Simone; **Additional music:** Bullfight Dance, Alexander Courage; Dance music for Clap Yo' Hands, Skip Martin; Basal Metabolism, Alexander Courage

F24. *THE HELEN MORGAN STORY.* (1957) 118 mins.
Stars: Ann Blyth (dubbed by Gogi Grant); Paul Newman; Richard
Carlson; Gene Evans; Alan King; Cara Williams; **Director:** Michael Curtiz

SONGS: Do, Do, Do; Someone to Watch Over Me; I've Got a Crush on You;
The Man I Love

F25. *PORGY AND BESS.* (Goldwyn-Columbia, 1959) Technicolor, produced
in Todd-AO 146 min. **UCLA** has three 35 mm. film versions, one complete and
uncut; *Premiere*: 1959 (June 24): NY; Warner Theatre *See*: **B844, B874, B1874,
B2023, D1116**

CAST: Porgy: Sidney Poitier (**dubbed** by Robert McFerrin); **Bess:** Dorothy
Dandridge (**dubbed** by Adele Addison); **Sportin' Life:** Sammy Davis, Jr.;
Maria: Pearl Bailey; **Crown:** Brock Peters; **Jake:** Leslie Scott;
Clara: Diahann Carroll (**dubbed** by Loulie Jean Norman); **Serena:** Ruth
Attaway; **Peter:** Clarence Muse; **Annie:** Everdinne Wilson; **Robbins:** Joel
Fluellen; **Mingo:** Earl Jackson; **Nelson:** Moses La Marr; **Lily:** Margaret
Hairston; **Jim:** Ivan Dixon; **Scipio:** Antoine Durousseau; **Strawberry
woman:** Helen Thigpen; **Old man:** Vince Townsend, Jr.; **Undertaker:**
William Walker; **Frazier:** Roy Glenn; **Coroner:** Maurice Manson; **Detective:**
Claude Akins
Screenplay by: N. Richard Nash; **Cinematographer:** Leon Shamroy; **Film
editor:** Daniel Mandell; **Art direction:** Serge Krizman & Joseph Wright;
Set design: Oliver Smith; **Libretto:** DuBose Heyward; **Choreography:**
Hermes Pan; **Costumes:** Irene Sharaff. **Orchestrations:** Alexander
Courage, Conrad Salinger, Robert Franklin, & Al Woodbury; **Director:**
Otto Preminger; **Producer:** Samuel Goldwyn, **Associate Music Director:**
Ken Darby; **Music Director:** André Previn

SONGS:

Part I: Summertime*(Carroll-Norman, chorus); Crap Game (Fluellen,
Carroll, chorus); A Woman is a Sometime Thing*(Scott, Jackson, Davis,
chorus, Carroll); Honey Man's Call (Muse); They Pass By Singin'*(Poitier-R.
McFerrin); Yo' Mammy's Gone (Jackson); Oh Little Stars*(Poitier); Gone,
Gone, Gone* (chorus, Scott); Porgy's Prayer (Poitier); My Man's Gone
Now* (Attaway-Matthews); The Train is at the Station (Dandridge-Addison,
chorus); I Got Plenty O' Nuttin'* (Poitier); Bess, You Is My Woman
Now*(Poitier, Dandridge); Oh, I Can't Sit Down*(Bailey, chorus, Davis); I
Ain't Got No Shame*(chorus); It Ain't Necessarily So*(Davis, chorus);
reprise I Ain't Got No Shame (chorus); What You Want Wid
Bess?*(Dandridge, Peters)

Part II: It Take a Long Pull to Get There*(Scott, men); De Police Put Me In
(Muse); Time and Time Again (Attaway); Strawberry Woman's Call
(Thigpen); Crab Man's Call (Townsend); I Loves You, Porgy*(Dandridge,
Poitier); Oh, De Lawd Shake De Heavens*(chorus); reprise Summertime
(Carroll, chorus); Dere's Somebody Knockin' at De Door (Jackson, chorus);
A Red Headed Woman*(Peters, chorus); Clara, Don't You Be Downhearted

(chorus); reprise Summertime (Dandridge); There's a Boat That's Leavin'
Soon for New York* (Davis); Good Mornin' Sistuh*(chorus); Bess, Oh
Where's My Bess?*(Poitier); Finale: I'm On My Way*(Poitier, chorus)

F25.1. *PORGY AND BESS.* Video of Glyndebourne Festival Opera Production,
staged. EMI 77757, 2 VHS (Video); EMI 77754, 3 Laser Discs (Available
From: WNET, 19 Gregory Drive, So. Burlington, VT 05403)

CAST: Porgy: Willard White; **Bess:** Cynthia Haymon; **Crown:** Gregg Baker;
Sportin' Life: Damon Evans; **Clara:** Paula Ingram (sung by Harolyn
Blackwell); **Jake:** Gordon Hawkins (sung by Bruce Hubbard); **Maria:**
Marietta Simpson; Glyndebourne Chorus; London Philharmonic; Simon
Rattle, conducting; this video based on the original Glyndebourne Festival
Opera stage production **directed by**: Trevor Nunn; **Adapted for the screen
by:** Trevor Nunn with Yves Baigneres; Original sound recording by EMI
Records Ltd., remixed for screen production; **Producers;** Greg Smith &
Stephany Marks; **Executive producers:** Richard Price (Primetime) & Dennis
Marks (BBC)
Recorded at: Shepperton Studios, London, Nov./Dec. 1992 Rv by
HERMAN, Justin R. *American Record Guide* (Nov.-Dec. 1993): 266-267.
See: **B874, B2059.1**

F26. *KISS ME, STUPID.* (Mirisch presentation of a Phalanx film, 1964) 126 min.
Premiere: 1964 (Dec. 22): NY; Astor & Trans-Lux East; **VCR:** Beta &
VHS, MGM-UA 202362 *See:* **B1981-1998**
CAST: Dino: Dean Martin; **Polly:** Kim Novak; **Orville J. Spooner:** Ray
Walston; **Zelda Spooner:** Felicia Farr; **Barney Millsap:** Cliff Osmond; **Big
Bertha:** Barbara Pepper; **Milkman:** James Ward; **Mrs. Pettibone:** Doro
Merande; **Mr. Pettibone:** Howard McNear; **Waitress:** Bobo Lewis; **Johnny
Mulligan:** Tommy Nolan; **Reverend Carruthers:** John Fiedler; **Bartender:**
Bern Hoffman; **Truck driver:** Henry Beckman; and Alice Pearce; A. Stuart;
Cliff Norton; Mel Blanc; Eileen O'Neal; Susan Wedell; Henry Gibson; Alan
Dexter?; A parrot named Sam

Art Director: Robert Luckhardt; **Set decoration:** Edward G. Boyle; **Film
editor:** Daniel Mandell; **Sound:** Robert Martin; **Music editor:** Richard
Carruth; **Re-recording:** Clem Portman; **Production manager:** Allen K.
Wood; **Assistant director:** C. C. Coleman, Jr.; **Casting:** Lyn Stalmaster;
Screenplay by: Billy Wilder and I. A. L. Diamond, based on the play "L'Ora
della Fantasia" by Anna Bonacci; **Cinematographer:** Joseph LaShelle;
Editor: Daniel Mandell; **Score:** André Previn; **Director:** Billy Wilder;
Producer: Mirisch presentation of a Phalanx film

SONGS:

Sophia*; I'm A Poached Egg*; All the Livelong Day*; supplied with
special lyrics provided by IG.

F27. *WHEN THE BOYS MEET THE GIRLS.* (Third film version of *Girl Crazy*). 100
min.; MGM Released Dec. 6, 1965.

CAST: Harve Presnell; Connie Francis; Liberace; Louis Armstrong; Fred Clark; Sue Ane Langdon; Frank Faylen; Joby Baker; Davis & Reese; Hortense Petra; Stanley Adams; Romo Vincent; Herman's Hermits; Sam the Sham (British Rock group); The Pharoahs; **Producer:** Sam Katzman; **Screenplay:** Robert E. Kent; **Photography:** Paul C. Vogel; **Art Direction:** George W. Davis, Eddie Imazu; **Set Decoration:** Henry Grace, Keogh Gleason, **Director:** Alvin Ganzer; **Sound:** Franklin Milton; **Film editor:** Ben Lewis; **Music scored & conducted by:** Fred Karger

SONGS:

Bidin' My Time; But Not For Me; Embraceable You; I Got Rhythm, plus six other songs by composers other than Gershwin.

F28. *GEORGE GERSHWIN—RHAPSODY IN BLUE.* 35 mm. film strip, with audio cassette (1/2 track, monaural, 11 min.), with program guide. South Yarmouth, MA: Aids of Cape Cod, 1977.
In series "Americans Who Changed Things [a biographical study]." LC card no. 77-730922.

F29. *MANHATTAN.* (United Artists, 1979) Black & white; 96 minutes; **UCLA** has a 35 mm. safety print; **VC:** MGM/UA MV 800469 *Premiere:* 1979 (Apr. 25): NY; The Baronet, The Little Carnegie, & other theaters
See: **B260, B2008-B2020**

CAST: Isaac Davis: Woody Allen; **Mary Wilke:** Diane Keaton; **Tracy:** Mariel Hemingway; **Yale:** Michael Murphy; **Jill:** Meryl Streep; **Emily:** Anne Byrne; **Party Guest:** Victor Truro; **Party Guest:** Tisa Farrow; **Party Guest:** Helen Hanft; **Guest of Honor:** Bella Abzug; **Pizza Waiter:** Ray Serra; **Connie:** Karen Ludwig; **Dennis:** Michael O'Donahue; **Television Director:** Gary Weiss; **Television Producer:** Kenny Vance; **TV Actor No. 1:** Charles Levin; **TV Actor No. 2:** Karen Allen; **TV Actor No. 3:** David Rasche; **Willie:** Damion Sheller; **Jeremiah:** Wallace Shawn; **Shakespearean Actor:** Mark Linn Baker; **Shakespearean Actress:** Frances Conroy; **Porsche Owner No. 1:** Bill Anthony; **Porsche Owner No. 2:** John Doumanian

Screenplay: Woody Allen & Marshall Brickman; **Cinematographer:** Gordon Willis; **Film editor:** Susan E. Morse; **Set decorator:** Robert Drumheller; **Costumes:** Albert Wolsky; **Music adapted and arranged by:** Tom Pierson; **Music performed by:** New York Philharmonic, Zubin Mehta, conducting & the Buffalo Philharmonic, Michael Tilson Thomas, conducting; **Producer:** Charles H. Joffe for United Artists; **Director:** Woody Allen

SONGS: The music used in the film is all Gershwin; it is, however, used as background underscore. The opening scene, including a monologue about G read by Woody Allen, employs RiB—under a marvelous scene of the Hudson River and New York city scenes. The RiB music is performed majestically by the New York Philharmonic under Zubin Mehta, with the opening cadenza played by **Stanley Drucker**, principal clarinetist of the

Philharmonic. The pianist is **Gary Graffman.**

RiB (underscore to opening scenes); Gay Cabellero/Someone to Watch Over
Me; I've Got a Crush on You; Do, Do, Do; Mine; He Loves & She Loves;
Bronco Busters; Lady Be Good!; 'S Wonderful; Love is Here to Stay; Sweet
· & Low-Down; Blue, Blue, Blue; Embraceable You; He Loves and She Loves;
Love is Sweeping the Country; Cabellero/Strike Up the Band; But Not for Me
See: **D1115 (Soundtrack)**

F30.   *AMERICAN POP.* (Columbia, 1981) *ca.* 95 minutes *See*: **B1901**
CAST: **Tony/Pete:** Ron Thompson; **Frankie:** Marya Small; **Louie:**
Jerry Holland; **Bella,** Lisa Jane Persky; **Zaimie:** Jeffrey Lippa; **Eva
Tanguay:** Roz Kelly; **Crisco:** Frank De Kova; **Benny:** Richard Singer;
Hannele: Elsa Raven; **Nicky Palumbo:** Ben Frommer; **Nancy:** Amy Levitt;
Leo: Leonard Stone; **Little Pete:** Eric Taslitz; **Izzy:** Gene Borkan; **Poet:**
Richard Moll; **Prostitute:** Beatrice Colen

Screenplay by: Ronnie Kern; **Animation direction:** Ralph Bakshi,
Animators: Lillian Evans, Carl Bell, Craig Armstrong, Debbie Hayes, Steve
Gordon, Brenda Banks, Jesus Cortes, James A. Davis, Robert Laduca,
Chrystal Russell, George Scribner, Paul Smith, Tom Tataranowicz, Robert
Carr Xeni; **Editor:** David Ramirez; **Music:** Lee Holdridge; **Producers:**
Ralph Bakshi & Martin Ransohoff; **Director:** Ralph Bakshi

SONGS:

I Got Rhythm; Swanee; Somebody Loves Me; Our Love Is Here to Stay;
Summertime (Janice Joplin)

F31.   *GEORGE GERSHWIN REMEMBERED,* **VC:** London Videocassette
440 071 211-3. **Written & Produced by**: Peter Adam.   90:26. Copy of TV
show of the same name, (from American Masters show of 1987, PBS). *See*: **B920,
B1950-B1953**

F32.   *THE GERSHWINS ON BROADWAY*, VHS **VC,** *CONVERSATION
PIECE,* featuring **Michael Feinstein** (1993). Feinstein introduces 1927 version
of *Strike Up the Band,* OTIS, and Cake (available from: Music Theatre
International, 545 Eighth Avenue, New York, NY 10018, 212-868-6668, or
FAX 212-643-8465)

F33.   *BLUE MONDAY,* **VC** (retitled *135th Street* by Paul Whiteman in 1925)
From "Omnibus. I", vol. 21 / the TV-Radio Workshop of
the Ford Foundation ; executive producer, Robert Saudek ; producer, William
Spier ; director, Andrew McCullough. Host: Alistair Cooke.
CBS Television Network, 1953-03-30.
2 videocassettes of 2 (90 min.) : sd., b&w ; 3/4 in. viewing copy.
1 videoreel of 1 (90 min.) : sd., b&w ; 1 in. master.
LC Call No.:   VBD 5926-5927 (viewing copy)
VCA 0321 (master) *See*: **W15c, W15g, B292, B296**

F33.1 *WHO CARES* **ballet, VC** (1970)

See: **W52e & W52f**

F34.   *MINE* (2000?)
A new projected film bio. *See*: **B2021**

Note: Laserdisc or DVD restorations of some of these films may become available after publication of this book. *An American in Paris* **(F19)** is already available in the DVD format.

Part II

Part II

Bibliography
by the Gershwins

This section includes writings by both George and Ira Gershwin. Those by George are listed first, followed by items by Ira. The items listed are alphabetized chronologically by date of publication within the two categories.

WRITINGS BY GEORGE GERSHWIN

B1. **GERSHWIN, George.** "Does Jazz Belong to Art? Foremost Composer of Syncopated Music Insists on Serious Appraisal." *Singing* 1/7 (July 1926): 13-14. [Reprinted in *Second Line* 14 (Sept.-Oct. 1965): 120-123]

G wrote this essay in defense of jazz six months before the premiere of his piano preludes at the now famous recital with Marguerite D'Alvarez, contralto, on December 4, 1926, at New York's Roosevelt Hotel. G stated that he was "now working" on these "two or three jazz 'Preludes,'" and voiced a prophetic prediction about the future of jazz: ". . . Every musician who has studied modern music knows that jazz already has made a real contribution to our art. How much this contribution will mean in the next decade nobody can predict, but assuredly its part will be large and important . . ." A list of "Eleven Jazz Songs Suitable for Concert Use" selected by G is appended.

B2. _____. "Mr. Gershwin Replies to Mr. Kramer." *Singing* 1/10 (Oct. 1926): 17-18.

G's brief response to Kramer's article "I Do Not Think Jazz 'Belongs.'"(**B1614**). In a very polite manner, G proceeds to point out Kramer's errors, particularly as regards the orchestration of the concerto. Alluding again to the piano preludes, this article states ". . . His [G's] real reply to critics of his position regarding jazz will be made, he avers, in musical notation, through a group of 6 [?] new piano preludes . . ." *See*: **B1614, B1619**

B3. _____. "The Composer in the Machine Age," in Oliver Sayler, ed., *Revolt in the Arts; A Survey of the Creation, Distribution and Appreciation of Art in America,* NY: Brentano's, 1930, pp. 264-269; reprinted in *George Gershwin,* Merle Armitage, ed. (NY: 1938, reprint Da Capo Press, 1995, pp. 225-230); also in: **Gilbert CHASE,** ed., *The American Composer Speaks: A Historical Anthology, 1770–1965* (Baton Rouge, LA: Louisiana State University Press, 1966), pp. 139-145.

Printing of G's essay. A brief excerpt: ". . . Originality is the only thing that counts. But, the originator uses material and ideas that occur around him and pass through him. And out of his experience comes this original creation or work of art, unquestionably influenced by his surroundings which include very largely what we call the Machine Age . . . Jazz is the result of the energy stored up in America. It is a very energetic kind of music . . . Jazz has contributed an enduring value to America in the sense that it has expressed ourselves. It is an original American achievement which will endure . . . [leaving] its mark on future music in one form or another . . .”

B4.   **GERSHWIN, George.** “Introduction,” in *Tin Pan Alley: A Chronicle of the American Popular Music Racket* by Isaac Goldberg. New York: John Day Co., 1930, vii-xi.

Includes G’s personal thoughts about the process of songwriting. “. . . I can think of no more nerve-racking, no more mentally arduous task than making music. There are times when a phrase of music will cost many hours of internal sweating. Rhythms romp through one’s brain, but they’re not easy to capture and keep; the chief difficulty is to avoid reminiscence.

Out of my entire output of songs, perhaps two—or at most, three—came as a result of inspiration. We can never rely on inspiration. When we most want it, it does not come. Therefore the composer does not sit around and wait for an inspiration to walk up and introduce itself. What he substitutes for it is nothing more than talent plus his knowledge. If his endowment is great enough, the song is made to sound as if it were truly inspired . . . Composing at the piano is not a good practice . . . However, it is possible to give the mind free rein and use the piano only to try what you can hear mentally . . . When I get a phrase which I am not sure I will remember the following day I set it down on paper at once. Occasionally compositions come in dreams, but rarely can they be remembered when you wake. On one occasion I did get out of bed and write a song. That number, incidentally, is one of my recent compositions, ‘Strike Up the Band!’ . . . the song writer must try to write something every day. I know that if I don’t do any writing for several weeks I lose a great deal of time in catching my stride again. Hence I am always composing.

My work is done almost exclusively at night, and my best is achieved in the fall and winter months . . . Many of us have learned to write music by studying the most successful songs published. But imitation can go only so far. The young song writer may start by imitating a successful composer he admires, but he must break away as soon as he has learned the maestro’s strong points and technique. Then he must try to develop his own musical personality, to bring something of his own invention to his work . . .”

B5.   Letters from George Gershwin to Isaac Goldberg (1930?), Isaac Goldberg Collection, Pusey Library, Harvard University, Cambridge, MA.

B6.   **GERSHWIN, George.** “Gershwin Sings Score of Praise for Hollywood; Composer Back After Four month’s Visit, Commends Workings of Film Capital.” *NY Herald Tribune*, Mar. 3, 1931, p. 22.

B7.   “Our Music Leads, Gershwin Asserts; American Popular Compositions Now ‘Most Vital’ in the World, He Holds; Finds Development Weak; Harlem Ideas Not Well Worked Out, He Says—New ‘Song Book’ to Be Published To-morrow.” *NYTimes*, Sept. 25, 1932, p. 17.

B8.   **GERSHWIN, George.** “Gershwin at the Keyboard, Arranged by the Composer,” in **JABLONSKI, Edward**, and **Lawrence D. STEWART**. *Introduction to The New York Times Gershwin Years in Song*. NY: Quadrangle/The NY Times Book Co., 1973, pp. 279-280.

A reprinting of the original Introduction GG prepared for his *George Gershwin Song Book* (1932). Gershwin’s thoughts are relevant to his beliefs about the performance practices in keyboard music of the era. G indicated some of the pianists who had influenced him, among them: ". . . Mike Bernard, Les Copeland, Melville Ellis, Lucky Roberts, Zez Confrey, Arden and Ohman, and others . . . Each of these was responsible for the popularization of a new technique, or a new wrinkle in playing . . . Confrey's contribution has been of a more permanent nature, as some of his piano figures found their way into serious American composition. To all of these predecessors I am indebted; some of the effects I use in my transcriptions derive from their style of playing . . . One chief hint as to the style best adapted in performance of these pieces is in order. To play American popular music most effectively one must guard against the natural tendency to make too frequent use of the sustaining pedal. Our study of the great romantic composers has trained us in the method of the *legato,* whereas our popular music asks for *staccato* effects, for almost a stenciled style. The rhythms of American popular music are more or less brittle; they should be made to snap . . . The more sharply the music is played, the more effective it sounds . . . Most pianists with a classical training fail lamentably in the playing of our ragtime or jazz because they use the pedaling of Chopin when interpreting the blues of Handy . . ." *See:* **W45**

B9. **GERSHWIN, George**. "The Relation of Jazz to American Music," in Henry Cowell, ed., *American Composers on American Music: A Symposium.* Palo Alto, CA: Stanford University Press, 1933, p. 187; reprint with a new introduction, NY: Frederick Ungar, 1962, p. 187.
". . . I believe that it [Jazz] can be made the basis of serious symphonic works of lasting value, in the hands of a composer with talent for both jazz and symphonic music [as in Gunther Schuller's Third Stream music?] . . ."

B10. _____. "Talented Children Need Help; To the Editor of The New York Times." *NYTimes,* Sept. 22, 1934, p. 14.

B11. _____. "Rhapsody in Catfish Row: Mr. Gershwin Tells the Origin and Scheme for His Music in That New Folk Opera Called 'Porgy and Bess.'" *NYTimes,* Oct. 20, 1935, Section 10, pp. 1-2. Also in **Merle ARMITAGE,** ed., *George Gershwin,* pp. 72-77.

B12. **JABLONSKI, Edward.** "Gershwin on Music."*Musical America* 82/7 (July 1962): 32-35.
A lengthy article based predominantly on the precious few statements written or spoken by G himself about music and his work.

B13. **GERSHWIN, George**. *Gershwin Remembered.* Portland, OR: Amadeus Press (an imprint of Timber Press), 1992.
Includes an appendix, "Gershwin on Music," which gives excerpts from twenty-nine well known writings by G.

B14. **AMIS, John, and Michael Rose.** *Words About Music.* Paragon House, 1992.
"A treasury of writings by over 500 celebrated figures including George Gershwin, Jane Austen, Bach, W. H. Auden, George Sand, Bernard Shaw, [etc.] . . ."

WRITINGS BY IRA GERSHWIN

B15. **GERSHWIN, Ira.** "Words and Music." *NYTimes,* Nov. 9, 1930, Section 9, p. 4.

B16. _____. "My Brother," in Merle Armitage, ed., *George Gershwin.* NY: Longmans, Green, 1938.

B17. _____. "Works of George Gershwin," in Merle Armitage, ed. *George Gershwin*. NY: Longmans, Green, 1938, reprint Da Capo, 1995, pp. 248-249 in the latter.

B18. _____. "Gershwin on Gershwin." *Newsweek* 24 (Oct. 23, 1944): 14.

B19. _____. "Twenty Years After." *New Yorker* 28/13 (May 17, 1952): 26-27.

B20. _____. ". . . But I Wouldn't Want to Live There." *Saturday Review* 41/42 (Oct. 18, 1958): 26-27, 48. Full bibliography of title: **LYONS, Leonard.** "New York is a Great Place to Be . . ." and **GERSHWIN, Ira,** ". . . But I Wouldn't Want To Live There."

Ira's statement concerning why he preferred to live in Los Angeles. The essay contains a number of small biographical details about his early life in Manhattan's Lower East Side.

B21. _____. *Lyrics on Several Occasions: A Selection of Stage and Screen Lyrics Written for Sundry Situations; And Now Arranged in Arbitrary Categories. To Which Have Been Added Many Informative Annotations & Disquisitions on Their Why & Wherefore, Their Whom-For. Their How And Matters Associative,* NY: Alfred A. Knopf, 1959. Reprinted by Omnibus, London, New York, Sydney, & Cologne, 1988. Reprinted in paperback by Limelight, London, with a new preface by John Guare and L'Envoi by Lawrence Stewart, 1997.

This gem by Ira includes the lyrics for 104 of the songs, but even more important, Ira's priceless discussion of the genesis of the songs. A sequel to this book was published in 1994 by Robert Kimball, currently (1990s) artistic advisor to the estate of IG . *See:* **B110, B123, B1367, B1461, B1538**

B22. **GERSHWIN, Ira.** "Which Came First?" *Saturday Review* 42/35 (Aug. 29, 1959): 31-33, 45.
Excerpts from *Lyrics on Several Occasions*

B23. _____. "Foreword," in *The George and Ira Gershwin Song Book*. NY: Simon & Schuster, 1960.

B24. _____. "Marginalia on Most of the Songs," in the *George and Ira Gershwin Song Book*. NY: Simon & Schuster, 1960.

B25. _____. "Frederick Loewe: Four Scores (and Seven Years Ago)." *NYTimes*, Mar. 27, 1960, XI, p. 5.

B26. _____. "That Inevitable Question: Which Comes First?" *Variety* 225/7 (Jan. 10, 1962): 187.
Ira on whether words or music come first.

B27. _____. "Euterpe and the Lucky Lyricist." *Variety* 233/7 (Jan. 8, 1964): 198.

B28. _____. "André Kostelanetz and a Gathering of Gershwiniana," liner notes for Columbia record CS 8933, *André Kostelanetz and His Orchestra*: "Gershwin Wonderland," n. d.

Bibliography about
George Gershwin

BIOGRAPHIES

B29. **ALTMAN, Frances.** *George Gershwin: Master Composer* (Men of Achievement Series). Minneapolis: T. S. Denison, 1968.

B30. **ARMITAGE, Merle.** *George Gershwin: Man and Legend*, with a note on the author by John Charles Thomas (Biography index reprint series). NY: Duell, Sloan, & Pierce, 1958; Freeport, NY: Books for Libraries Press, © 1958, 1970.
Includes works list and discography; brief bibliography. Appendix lists productions of P&B worldwide to 1958. *See:* **W37, B103, B111, B112**

B31. "The Ascendant Gershwin; Being the Story of His Rise from Piano Player to Carnegie Hall." *NYTimes*, Nov. 14, 1926, Section 8, p. 4.
Accurate and detailed biographical article to 1926, when G was 28 years old, up to the premiere of *Oh, Kay!* on November 8, 1926.

B32. **BACKERS, Cor.** *Het leven van George Gershwin, 1898-1937* (Musica-serie; kleine boeken over grote mannen, 19). Den Haag: J. P. Kruseman, 195?. 31 pp. **[DLC]**
Very brief biography with only 24 pp. of text. Works list, pp. 29-31.

B33. **BORDON, Furio**, 1943- . *Il favorito degli dei : una biografia immaginata di George Gershwin*. Pordenone: Edizioni dello Zibaldone, 1987. Series: Collezione Arabeschi ; 1. ISBN: 8-876-92183 4

B34. **BRYANT, Bernice Morgan.** *George Gershwin, Young Composer*. (Childhood of Famous Americans). Illustrated by Nathan Goldstein. Indianapolis: Bobbs-Merrill, 1965. 200 pp. **[DLC]**
Children's book. Bibliography, p. 198. *Also See* other children's books at **B71, B94, B95**

B35. **BUTTERWORTH, Neil.** "American Composers." Music: The *Official Journal of the Schools Music Association* 1/4 (1967): 25-26.

B36. _____ "American Composers." *Music: The Official Journal of the Schools Music Association* 2/1 (1967): 38-40.

B37.   CHALUPT, René. *Gershwin, a cura di Roberto Leydi* (Le Vite dei musicisti).
Milano: Nuova accademia editrice, 1959. 211 pp. **[DLC]**
In Italian. Works list, pp. 177-191. "Discografia essenziale," pp. 193-198. *See:* **B113**

B38.   _____. *George Gershwin, le musicien de la "Rhapsody in Blue."* Paris: Amiot-
Dumont, 1948. 175 pp. Italian translation by Robert Leydi as:
Gershwin. Milan: Nuova Accademia, 1959. 211 pp.

B39.   CRAWFORD, Richard, "Gershwin, George." *New Grove Dictionary of Opera,*
4 vols., ed. by Stanley Sadie. London: MacMillan, 1982, II, 393-395.
A short biography of G. by the distinguished American musicologist, Crawford. The article serves well for a quick reference on the basic facts of G's life and music, along with providing Crawford's unique, but objective perceptions. Crawford also recently wrote a significant article "Rethinking the Rhapsody" for the important, celebratory issue of the *Newsletter* of the *Institute for Studies in American Music* 28/1 (Fall 1998).

B40.   _____. (text) and **Wayne SCHNEIDER** (work list). "Gershwin, George."
New Grove Dictionary of American Music, 4 vols., ed. by H. Wiley Hitchcock and
Stanley Sadie. London & New York: Macmillan, 1986, II, 199-211. Also published
separately as Chapter 5 in *The New Grove Twentieth-Century American Masters.*
NY & London: W. W. Norton, 1988, pp. 137-179. (The type in this latter version
is larger than in Grove, thus is easier to read).
An excellent, substantial article. In addition to biographical details, Crawford's analysis of the music is enlightening and exemplary. A useful bibliography is appended, as are accurate chronological & alphabetical works lists. A new edition of this article is in press as of September, 1997, to be an article in the full set of the (new) New Grove, 7th edition.

B41.   DE SANTIS, Florence S. *Gershwin* (Portraits of Greatness Series). NY: Trevas,
a division of Elite, 1987.
This book is built around over 100 magnificent illustrations, all carefully annotated.

B42.   EWEN, David. *A Journey to Greatness: The Life and Music of George Gershwin.*
NY: Henry Holt, 1956. *See:* **B108, B115, B116**

B43.   _____. *George Gershwin: His Journey to Greatness,* 2nd enlarged ed. New
York: Ungar, 1970, 1986. *See:* **B108, B117, B118, B1448**

B44.   _____. "A Master of Symphonic Jazz: The Fourth Article in the Series "The
Jews in Music" Dealing with George Gershwin, Formerly of Tin Pan Alley." *The
Jewish Tribune* 91 (Oct. 7, 1927): 16.
A biographical article recounting the events of G's career to 1927.

B45.   EWEN, David. *The Story of George Gershwin,* Illustrated by Graham Bernbach.
New York: H. Holt, 1943. 211 pp. [Has been translated at least 10 times, each to
a different language, including Vietnamese, Japanese, Spanish, Italian, etc.].
Biography intended for children. Has a chronology of musical and non-musical events, covering the time from 1885-1937, on pp. 196-206, as well as a discography giving Victor, Columbia, Decca, and Gramophone record numbers as of *ca.* 1943, pp. 187-195. Bibliography, p. 185; "Musical comedies, revues, and films for which Gershwin wrote music," p. 186. *Also See* other children's books at **B34, B71, B94, B95, B114** (review).

B46.   GÁL, György Sándor. *Amerikai rapszdia: Gershwin élete.* Budapest: Gondolat,
1971. 268 pp. **[NN-L]**
In Hungarian. No works-list, bibliography, discography, or index.

B47.   GARSON, Edith. "Supplements," in: **Isaac GOLDBERG,** *George Gershwin;*
A Study in American Music (NY: Frederick Ungar, 1958), pp. 297-356.
Six new chapters by Garson added to the original Goldberg book of 1931 (q. v. at
B49)

B48.   GAUTHIER, André. *George Gershwin (Musiciens de notre temps).* Paris:
Hachette, 1973. 153 pp. **[NN-L]**
In French. No works list, discography, or index.

B49.   GOLDBERG, Isaac. *George Gershwin: A Study in American Music,* new edition,
supplemented by Edith Garson, with foreword and discography by Alan Dashiell.
New York: Frederick Ungar, 1958. [First published in 1931, while G was still alive,
by Simon & Schuster]
This is the first biography written about G, completed during his lifetime, when he was
only thirty-three years old. It includes a substantial amount of first-hand information about G,
as well as reviews from the 1924-1930 period (according to Charles Schwartz). *See:* **B108**

B50.   _____."Gebrüder Gershwin." *Vanity Fair* 38/4 (June 1932): 46-47, 62.
Biography of G and I to 1932. Among other things, the reader is informed that *Lady
Be Good* was Ira's "first important commission for a full production." *See:* **W22**

B50.1. GREENBERG, Rodney. *George Gershwin.* London, Phaidon, 1998.
A more recent life and works which includes the basics of G's life. *Crazy fpr You* gets
some coverage.

B51.   GRIGOŘEV, Lev Grigofevich. *Dzhordzh Gershvin.* Moscow, 1956. 43 pp. **[DLC]**

B52.   JABLONSKI, Edward, with an introduction by **Harold Arlen.** *George Gershwin*
(Lives to Remember). New York: G. P. Putnam's Sons, 1962. Works list, 151-159;
Selected discography, 161-177; Selected bibliography, 179-180.
Biography for young adults.

B53.   JABLONSKI, Edward. *Gershwin: A Biography, Illustrated.* Garden City, NY:
Doubleday, 1987, xv, 436 pp.
An indispensable source. Jablonski's years of study of the Gershwins, coupled with his
close association with and concomitant access to the family, enabled him to present a
remarkably complete and objective picture, caring without being maudlin. A forty-four page
chapter titled "*Epilogue:* The Myths of Ira Gershwin" contributes much towards bringing Ira's
role in the Gershwin successes into sharper focus (along with books like Robert Kimball's *The
Complete Lyrics of Ira Gershwin,* **B1602**, and Philip Furia's *Ira Gershwin: The Art of the
Lyricist,* **B1463).** A chronological list of compositions by George and Ira Gershwin, giving the
names of the Broadway shows and Hollywood films, along with the songs they included (or
dropped) is appended. Jablonski's "Selected [and informatively annotated] Discography"
serves as a guide for the student of Gershwin who is trying to wade through the thousands of
recordings which have been made. *See:* **B123-B131**

B54.   _____, and Lawrence D. STEWART. *The Gershwin Years,* with an introduction by Carl Van Vechten. Garden City, NY: Doubleday, 1973. 1st ed., 1958., reprint of 2nd ed. by DaCapo Press in paperback, 1996.

This is an important earlier bio by Jablonski with Stewart, rich in detail and photographs. The appendix of the DaCapo edition has updated information not present in the earlier editions, including a listing and useful evaluation of books about the Gershwins, the latter by Lawrence Stewart. *See*: **B102, B103, B104, B105, B106, B108, B109, B110, B112, B119, B120, B121, B122, B147**

B55. JEAMBAR, Denis. *George Gershwin,* suivi d'une presentation de son oeuvre par Maryvonne de Saint-Pulgent. Paris: Mazarine, 1982. 222 pp. **[NN-L]**
In French. Includes discography for RiB, Concerto, AiP, and P&B. Bibliography.

B56. JUHÁSZ, Elod. *George Gershwin.* Budapest, 1964. 225 pp. List of works, pp. 204-223. Bibliography: pp. 224-225.

B57. KANTER, Kenneth Aaron. *The Jews on Tin Pan Alley: The Jewish Contribution to American Popular Music, 1830-1940.* NY: KTAV Publishing House; Cincinnati, OH: American Jewish Archives, 1982, pp. 147-160.
Part II, No. 12 is devoted to biography of GG. No new information here. Playbill for *Sinbad* (re: Al Jolson and *Swanee*) reproduced on book jacket.

B58. KART, Larry. "Cover Story: An American ingenious, 50 years after his death, George Gershwin's music is here to stay." *Chicago Tribune,* February 15, 1987, Arts, Section 13, p. 4.
Lengthy tribute in the form of a biographical review of G's life.

B59. KENDALL, Alan. *George Gershwin: A Biography.* NY: Universe Books, 1987. Catalogue of works, pp. 181-188. Very brief bibliography, p. 189.
A unique feature of this book is the printing of the programs of G musicals performed in London (on the end papers).

B60. KENNEDY, John B. "Words and Music." *Collier's* 82 (Sept. 22, 1928): 13.
Some biography, quotes from G, all written during his lifetime.

B61. KILENYI, Edward. *Gershwiniana: Recollections and Reminiscences of Times Spent With My Student George Gershwin.* (Unpublished typescript). 89 pp. **[DLC]**

B62. KIMBALL, Robert, and **Alfred SIMON.** Designed by **Bea FEITLER.** *he Gershwins.* New York: Atheum, 1973.
A handsome and factual cocktail table book, profusely illustrated. Includes a "Chronology of Shows with their Songs," and a "Piano Rollography," the latter by Mike Montgomery, excellently updated in **B1735.1**, pp. 225-253. *Also See*: **B102, B104, B105, B106, B109, B110, B135**

B63. KOLODIN, Irving. *The Musical Life.* NY: Knopf, 1958.

B64. KRELLMANN, Hanspeter, 1935- . *George Gershwin:* mit Selbstzeugnissen und Bilddokumenten / dargestellt von Hanspeter Krellmann. Reinbek bei Hamburg: Rowohlt, 1988. Series: Rowohlts Monographien. ISBN: 3499504189 Erratum sheet

laid in, List of Gershwin's works: p. 134-149. Includes bibliographical references.
See: **B136**

B65. **KRESH, Paul.** *An American Rhapsody: The Story of George Gershwin.* Jewish
Biography Series. NY: E. P. Dutton, 1988, x,166 pp. Bibliography: pp.
153-154, good recommended listening list up to about 1987, pp. 145-152.

B66. **KYDRŃSKI, Lucjan.** *Gershwin.* Kraków: Polskie Wydawn, Muzyczne, 1962. 202
pp. **[DLC]** Polish. Works list, pp. 190-192. Discography, p. 195-196.
Bibliography, pp. 196-197.

B67. **LACOMBE, Alain.** *George Gershwin: une chronique de Broadway* (Les
Musiciens du spectacle). Paris: F. van de Velde, 1980. 204 pp. Chronological
works list, 2 pp. Bibliography, pp. 201-204. Selective discography, pp. 185-200.
Filmography, 2 pp.

B68. **LIPMANN, Eric.** *L'Amerique de George Gershwin.* Paris: Messine, Diffusion
Vilo, 1981. 223 pp. **[NN-L]**
In French. Heavily illustrated and including Discography, Filmography, and a
translation of the libretto of P&B from English into French, side by side. Usefulness limited
by lack of an index.

B69. **LONGOLIUS, Christian.** *George Gershwin.* Berlin/Halensee: Max Hesse Verlag,
1959.

B70. **MINGOTTI, Antonio.** *Gershwin: Eine Bildbiographie.* Munich: Kindler, 1958.
143pp.

B71. **MITCHELL, Barbara.** *America, I Hear You: A Story About George Gershwin*
[A Carolhoda creative minds book]. Illustrations by Jan Hosking Smith.
Minneapolis, MN: Carolhoda Books, 1987. 56 pp.
Accurate biography for children. The author consulted the George and Ira Gershwin
Collection at the Library of Congress. Cf. to other children's books at **B34, B45, B94, B95**

B72. **MORBELLI, Riccardo.** *Vita di George Gershwin.* Milano: Radio Record Ricordi,
1960. 22 pp. **[DLC]**
A brief biography.

B73. **PASI, Mario.** *George Gershwin.* Parma: Guanda, 1958. Czech translation as:
George Gershwin. Prague: Statni hudebni vyd, 1964.

B74. **PAYNE, Pierre Stephen Robert.** *Gershwin.* NY: Pyramid Books, 1960, London:
Robert Hale, 1960. 128 pp.
Straightforward biography, based on help received from Henry Cowell, Isamu Noguchi,
Carl Van Vechten, Jules Glaenzer, Irving Caesar, John Farrar, Vinton Freedley, Patrick Farrel,
Kay Swift, Edgar Varèse, Sholom Secunda, Robert Downing, Vernon Duke, and Dorothy
Heyward. *See:* **B108** *Also see:* Review in *Musical Times* 103 (Nov. 1962).

B75. **PEYSER, Joan.** *The Memory of All That.* NY: Simon & Schuster, 1993.
Peyser, eminent musicologist, who from 1977 to 1984 was editor of *The Musical
Quarterly,* spends considerable space in this psychobiography presenting the plausible theory

that one Alan Schneider is George's son by Mollie Charleston Schneider, an actress and showgirl. One of her other notions, among other theories of hers, is that Ira's lyrics represented "a sort of coded biography of George's life, complete with references to the women with whom he was having affairs [from dust jacket]." Critical opinion about the book has been mixed. Despite its publication date, there is no mention of the 1990s Gershwin musical *Crazy for You*. *See*: **B140, B141, B142, B143, B1473, B1590**

B76.   **POOL, Rosey E.** *Een nieuw lied voor Amerika; het leven van George Gershwin (1898-1937).* Amsterdam: Tilburg-Nederlands Boekhus, 1951. 155 pp.

B77.   **PUGLIARO, Maria Vittoria.** *Rapsodia in blue, l'arte e l'amore nella vita di George Gershwin.* Turin: S.A.S., 1952. 135 pp. **[DLC]**

B78.   **REIS, Claire.** "George Gershwin," in her: *Composers in America: Biographical Sketches of Living Composers, with a Record of Their Works, 1912-1937.* NY: Macmillan, 1938, p. 112.

B79.   *Rhapsody in Blue; screen play by Howard Koch and Elliot Paul, based on original screen story by Sonya Levien.* [Shooting script] Hollywood, CA: Warner Bros. Pictures, 1945. **[NN-L**

B80.   **ROSENBERG, Deena.** *Fascinating Rhythm: The Collaboration of George and Ira Gershwin.* NY: Dutton, 1991. 516 pp.
A substantial, important book by a theatre professor as well as a cultural and music historian, concerning both G brothers. Emphasis is on the songs, with little mention of the instrumental works, excepting RiB. Good bibliography, song list, and some discography. Short review by Wayne Schneider in the *Newsletter* of the Institute for Studies in American Music, 21/1 (November 1991): 5. *See*: **B144, B145**

B81.   **RUSHMORE, Robert.** *The Life of George Gershwin.* NY: Crowell-Collier, 1966.
A routine biography which seems to have been intended for young adults, requiring a reading comprehension level of approximately 11th-grade (based on the American twelve-grade system.). *See*: Review in *School Musician* 38 (Mar. 1967): 323.

B81.1   **SCHEBERA, Jürgen,** 1940- . *George Gershwin : eine Biographie in Bildern, Texten und Dokumenten.* Leipzig : G. Kiepenheuer, 1994, 181 p. : ill; Discography: p. 177-181. Includes bibliographical references (p.173-175).

B82.   **SCHIPKE, Brigitte.** *George Gershwin und die Welt seiner Musik.* Freiburg: Drei Ringe Musikverlag. 1958. 31 pp.**[NN-L]**
Very brief 32-page biography in German. Works list, pp. 31-32.

B83.   **SCHOORL, Bob.** *George Gershwin: van Broadway tot Carnegie-Hall.* Amsterdam: A. J. G. Strengholt, 1952. 251 pp. **[NN-L]**

B84.   **SCHWARTZ, Charles M.** "Gershwin," in: *Dictionary of Contemporary Music,* ed. by John Vinton. NY: E. P. Dutton, 1974.

B85.   _____. "Gershwin, George." *New Grove Dictionary of Music and Musicians,* 6th ed., 20 vols., ed. by Stanley Sadie. London: Macmillan, 1980, VII, pp. 302-304. [The new *New Grove* will have an article about Gershwin, *ca.* 2001]

About four columns of biography, with a classified works list (in chronological order) and a highly selective bibliography of twenty entries. Like some of his other work on G., this article carries the same condescending tone; one wonders if Schwartz is not envious of G's successes. Schwartz labels the *Lullaby* for string quartet "naive." This article should be compared to that in the NGDAM by Crawford and Schneider (**B40**).

B86. _____. *Gershwin: His Life and Music*. Indianapolis: Bobbs-Merrill, 1973.
Reprinted in paperback by Da Capo, 1979.
David Horn (**B148**) commented perceptively about Schwartz' book: "Clearly much of the detail gathered is of value; other portions . . . are less likely to be rewarding in the long-term. (Gershwin frequented prostitutes—so did Schubert. Are we expected to think less of Gershwin, and does it make *any* difference to the music of either?) . . ." *See:* **B101, B102, B104, B106, B107, B108, B109, B110, B121, B147, B148**

B87. SCHWARTZ, Charles M. *George Gershwin: A Selective Bibliography and Discography*. Detroit: Information Coordinators (for College Music Society), 1974.
This publication about Gershwin, following Schwartz' dissertation on the orchestral works (1969) and his major life and works of 1973 is a concise 118 pages (exclusive of front matter). In addition to "Highlights of Gershwin's Life," a chronology, the bibliography includes 654 citations, most of them not annotated. A comprehensive list of recordings to *ca.* 1973 arranged under titles of the works is included. Lists of musicals and movies of which recordings were made are appended. "Only a few doctoral dissertations . . . have been given, and only a relative sampling of contemporary reviews of Gershwin's works have been cited." There is no index.

B88. _____. *The Life and Orchestral Works of George Gershwin*. Ph.D. dissertation, Musicology, New York University, 1969. 2 parts, 466 pp.
A very lengthy study of Gershwin's life, along with a study of the orchestral works, excluding of course *Porgy*. More often than not, Schwartz seems deprecating to Gershwin, both in terms of his personal life and the music: ". . . Unquestionably the immediate success of the *Rhapsody* at its Aeolian Hall premiere was due in part to the 'good honest job' of Grofé's 'orchestral translation,' completed in approximately ten days . . . [p. 258] . . . Gershwin could hardly be considered an intellectual on any level. Moreover, considering the speed with which the *Rhapsody* was written and Gershwin's lack of compositional experience at the time, it is reasonable to assume that examples of sophisticated motivic transformation in the work did not result from premeditation and intellectualization on the composer's part, but wholly from instinct. . . . [fn. 40, pp. 269-270]" This dissertation includes considerable musical analysis of the orchestral works. A very lengthy bibliography to 1969 is appended.*See:* **W1-W7**

B89. SCHWINGER, Wolfram. *Er komponierte Amerika: George Gershwin, Mensch und Werk*. Berlin: Buchverlag Der Morgen, 1960. 222 pp. **[NN-L]**
A 2nd ed. pub. in Munich by Goldman is reviewed in *Buehne*, March 1984.

B90. SIMON, Alfred. *See:* **Robert KIMBALL, B62.**

B91. "The Story of George Gershwin, 1898-1937." *Music Journal* [Summarized from the *NYHerald Tribune* of July 12, 1937] 8/4 (Apr. 1955): 17-18, 36.
Biographical obituary.

B91.1. SURIANO, Gregory R. (With foreword by **Marvin HAMLISCH**). *Gershwin in* his Time: A Biographical Scrapbook, 1919-1937. New York: Gramercy Books, 1998.

I found this attractive book (140 pp.) helpful. Significant reviews or essays spanning GG's career from La, La, Lucille! to his death in Los Angeles are reprinted. Many of the reviews have been listed and briefly annotated here in the various bibliography sections of this book. Liberal use of color photos of sheet music covers, movie theater ads, record labels, book covers, and black and white photos of individuals add to the attractiveness of Suriano's work. The materials are presented in chronological order.

B92.   "Trade Winds: In Memory of George Gershwin . . ." *Saturday Review of Literature* 26/29 (July 7, 1943): 14-15.

Memorial taking the form of a biography with anecdotes, written six years after G's death.

B93.   **VALLANCE, Tom.** *The American Musical*, Screen Series. London: A. Zwemmer; NY: A. S. Barnes, 1970. 192 pp.

A biographical dictionary of the personalities involved in the American musical. Emphasis is on motion pictures, and titles are accessed through the index. No new information on G here.

VAUGHN, Genevieve. *See:* **B96**

B94.   **VENEZIA, Mike.** *George Gershwin* / written and illustrated by Mike Venezia consultants, Donald Freund, Amelia S. Kaplan. Chicago: Children's Press, 1994. Series: Getting to know the world's greatest composers ISBN: 0516045369.

For children in kindergarten through 3rd grade. *Also See* other children's books at **B34, B45, B71, B95**

B95.   **VERNON, Roland.** *Introducing Gershwin*. Silver Bur, 1996. 32 pp.

A recommended children's book, profusely illustrated. Should be compared to Barbara Mitchell's book and the other bios intended for children. *See:* **B34, B45, B71, B94**

B96.   **VAUGHN, Genevieve.** "Gershwin, George." *Encarta '95.* [CD-ROM] Microsoft & Funk & Wagnall's, 1994.

Short encyclopedia article.

B97.   **WARNER BROS. PICTURES, INC.** *Rhapsody in Blue, the Jubilant Story of George Gershwin and His Music*, published as a public service of Warner Bros. pictures. New York: 1945. 20 pp. **[DLC]**

Includes short articles by Walter Damrosch, Deems Taylor, Paul Whiteman, and others. "Rhapsody in Blue (the story of GG) a musical study outline of the motion picture by Warner Bros. for music clubs and classes, by Sigmund Spaeth" (4 pp.) is inserted.

B98.   **WINSTANLEY, Harry.** *George Gershwin: His Music and his Musicals*, foreword by Leopold Godowsky [III]. London: Toccata Press, 1990, ©1989. ISBN 0-907689-23-X (pbk)

B99.   **WOOD, Ean.** *George Gershwin: His Life & Music.* London: Sanctuary, 1996, 268 pp.

B100. WÜRZ, Anton. "George Gershwin," in: **Friedrich BLUME,** ed., *Die Musik in Geschichte und Gegenwart,* 17 vols. Kassel: Bärenreiter, 1949-1986, IV, cols. 1828-1831.

BIBLIOGRAPHY ABOUT BIOGRAPHIES

The list immediately below generally includes reviews which pertain to more than one book. Otherwise, the reviews are listed under the book titles, below the "General" section, in alphabetical order by author of the review.

General

B101. "Book Reviews: Music, Poems, Stories for Yuletide, **Gershwin: His Life and Music By Charles Schwartz** . . . [and] **The New York Times Gershwin Years in Song** . . ." *America* 129/21 (Dec. 23, 1973): 487.
Review of the two above-named books. In re: the first book, ". . . Schwartz has not captured Gershwin alive. He has shown us the warts without the face. His work is still very much the dissertation, its style homely and pregnant beyond term with facts . . ." In re: the New York Times anthology: ". . . It would be mean-spirited to question the selection of songs, but certainly not out of place to mention the sloppy editing . . . There are printing errors and some misleading, even false, harmonic indications over the vocal line . . ." *See:* **B86**
CHASE, Gilbert. *See:* **B147**

B102. CLEMONS, Walter. "The songwriter who was a composer: *The Gershwins . . . The Gershwin Years . . . Gershwin: His Life and Music . . . Lyrics on Several Occasions . . . The New York Times Gershwin Years in Song . . ."* *New York Times Book Review,* Sept. 23, 1973, p. 3+.
A detailed and lengthy review-article covering the books above by **Robert Kimball** and **Alfred Simon; Edward Jablonski** and **Lawrence D. Stewart; Charles Schwartz; Ira Gershwin;** and Quadrangle/The New York Times Book Company, respectively. Among many other comments by the reviewer, he made the following observation about the milieu in which G prospered: ". . . The famous first performance of the 'Rhapsody in Blue' . . . was a key moment in a general movement in all the American arts of the period: the revolt against the genteel tradition in literature, the fashionable discovery of Harlem, the search for a native idiom, a self-conscious, impatient desire for 'greatness' . . ." About Jablonski and Stewart's book, Clemons commented: "[It] is also a pictorial biography—with a fuller, though rather too fond and defensive narrative text . . ." Clemons evaluated each of the other books, concluding with the article with comments about selected songs and the estimate that ". . . As a songwriter, Gershwin's place is secure . . ." *See:* **B62, B54, B86, B21**

B103. FREEDLEY, Vinton. "Personalities: Porgy and Always the Best." *Saturday Review* 41/42 (Oct. 18, 1943): 14.
Review of **Jablonski** and **Stewart's** *The Gershwin Years* and **Merle Armitage's** *George Gershwin: Man and Legend.* Concerning the latter, Freedly observed: ". . . This work . . . is principally concerned with George's position in classical music, his admiration for the masters of his time—Schoenberg, Ravel, Berg, and Stravinsky—and intense devotion to the problems of orchestration . . ." *See:* **B54, B30**

B104. HAMILTON, David. "Will We Be Ready for the Gershwin Centenary?" *High Fidelity* 24/7 (July 1974): 44-48.

Of the three biographical volumes published in 1973 (**Kimball/Simon, Jablonski/Stewart**, and **Charles Schwartz**), the reviewer found the Kimball/Simon "the most enjoyable," and, among other comments, described Schwartz' book as "tiresome" and "exasperating." *See*: **B62, B54, B86**

B105. "**JABLONSKI, Edward** and **Lawrence D. Stewart**. The Gershwin Years . . . [and] **KIMBALL, Robert** and **Alfred Simon**. The Gershwins . . .[Book Reviews]." *Choice* 10/12 (Feb 1974): 1878.

A review which raised some questions about both books. ". . . Jablonski-Stewart has the better text of the two and more of the amenities of serious use . . . As documentary histories, both help us to gather impressions but fail to ask what there was about the man . . . that made the songs seem so basic a part of American life style around 1930. Those who seek to analyze and question the evidence will want to look at other books, such at Alec Wilder's . . ." *See*: **B54, B62**

B106. **LEVANT, Lorna.** "Remembering Gershwin." *Opera News* 38/6 (Dec. 8, 1973): 12-13.

The article recounts the events which transpired during the 75th anniversary year of G's birth, 1973. Considerable space is devoted to the biographies which appeared that year: those of **Robert Kimball/Alfred Simon, Edward Jablonski/Lawrence Stewart,** and **Charles M. Schwartz.** *See*: **B62, B54, B86, B1583**

B107. **MATTHEWS, Peter.** "Book Reviews: Music, Poems, Stories for Yuletide, **Gershwin: His Life and Music By Charles Schwartz** . . . [and] **The New York Times Gershwin Years in Song** . . ." *America* 129/21 (Dec. 23, 1973): 487.

Review of the two above-named books. In re: the first book, ". . . Schwartz has not captured Gershwin alive. He has shown us the warts without the face. His work is still very much the dissertation, its style homely and pregnant beyond term with facts . . ." In re: the *New York Times* anthology: ". . . It would be mean-spirited to question the selection of songs, but certainly not out of place to mention the sloppy editing . . . There are printing errors and some misleading, even false, harmonic indications over the vocal line . . ." *See*: **B86**

B108. "Of Books, Christmas Gift Books: Benny Green on the Gershwin Years." *Spectator* 233/7639 (Nov. 23, 1974): 662.

Calling it "the most useful biography so far" while reviewing the **Jablonski-Stewart** *The Gershwin Years*, the writer (Benny Green) takes the opportunity to give a masterful and trenchant account of some of the previous biographies. ". . . [F]or all the Gershwin chroniclers, being either insuperably unmusical or congenitally unliterary, have been reduced either to poking around among the dirty underwear, or burbling conservatory quackery about unresolved discords . . . **Isaac Goldberg**'s *A Study in American Music*, despite its breathless paternalism, remains the clearest picture of the composer at work, and is at any rate light years ahead of **David Ewen**'s *Journey to Greatness*, a work whose oversights of observation are surpassed only by the incoherence of its judgements . . . There is the book by **Robert Payne**, who, apparently being deaf to the march of harmony, falls back on the racial heritage flapdoodle so persistently as to read the entire Pentateuch into 'Swanee' . . . Earlier this year there were two further volumes, an unfortunate outburst of crazed Pinkertonian scopophilia from a Mr: **Schwartz** . . . In a sense the best Gershwin book of all remains the utterly charming compromise between primer, notebook, diary, and reminiscence achieved by Ira himself with *Lyrics on Several Occasions* . . ." *See*: **B43, B49, B54, B74, B86, B21**

B109. **PLEASANTS, Henry.** "Edward Jablonski and Lawrence D. Stewart *The Gershwin*

Years . . . Robson Books . . ." *Books and Bookmen* 21/5 (Feb. 1956): 58-59.
In a review comparing this book with the biographies by **Schwartz** and **Kimball** and **Simon**, Pleasants expressed his preference for the Jablonski-Stewart work. *See*: **B54, B62, B86**

B110. _____."Gershwin Season." *Stereo Review* 32 (Jan. 1974): 16-17.
An article which included a review of the "spate of books" which appeared during 1973, among them those by **Edward Jablonski and Lawrence Stewart, Robert Kimball and Alfred Simon, Charles Schwartz,** plus *The New York Times Gershwin Years in Song,* and **Ira G's** *Lyrics on Several Occasions.* ". . . All these books contribute to our understanding of the personal phenomenon [of GG]. Indeed—and this is surely symptomatic—they are all more intimately concerned with the personality than with the music . . ." This statement was followed by a perceptive assessment of each of the books and some other writings about G as well. *See*: **B54, B62, B86, B21**

ARMITAGE, Merle. *George Gershwin: Man and Legend,* **B30.**

B111. BUSH, Geoffrey. "George Gershwin by Isaac Goldberg (Constable, 16s)." *Music in Education* 26 (Nov. 15, 1962): 189.
Review in essay form of the second edition of Isaac Goldberg's biography. ". . . It is written in a very mannered American style (*brash* is perhaps the word), which begins by being irritating and ends by convincing one of its aptness for the subject . . ."

B112. FREEDLEY, Vinton. "Personalities: Porgy and Always the Best." *Saturday Review* 41/42 (Oct. 18, 1958): 14-15.
Review of **Jablonski and Stewart's** *The Gershwin Years* and **Merle Armitage's** *George Gershwin: Man and Legend.* Concerning the latter, Freedly observed: ". . . This work . . . is principally concerned with George's position in classical music, his admiration for the masters of his time—Schoenberg, Ravel, Berg, and Stravinsky—and intense devotion to the problems of orchestration . . ." *See*: **B54**

CHALUPT, Rene. *George Gershwin, le Musicien de la 'Rhapsody in Bleu,'* **B37.**

B113. PIRONTI, Alberto. "George Gershwin, le Musicien de la 'Rhapsody in Bleu.'" *La Rassegna Musicale* 21/2 (Apr. 1951): 178-179.

EWEN, David. *The Story of George Gershwin,* 1943, **B45.**

B114. CADMAN, B. Meredith. "Gershwin 'Algerized.'" *Etude* 64/9 (Sept. 1946): 491.

EWEN, David. *A Journey to Greatness: The Life and Music of George Gershwin,* 1956, **B42.**

B115. KOLODIN, Irving. "Paradox in Blue." *Saturday Review* 39/8 (Feb 25, 1956): 37-60, 61.
Review of David Ewen's first edition of the biography *Journey to Greatness.* While recognizing that ". . . Ewen has researched his subject thoroughly, interviewed or corresponded with virtually anyone who might have anything of value to say, straightened out a number of factual points, provided a budget of information more amply than previously available . . ." Kolodin was concerned that Ewen failed to see ". . . a sense of man seen whole as well as admiringly . . ." The reviewer further found fault with Ewen's view of G as a "composer of jazz," which, of course, he was not in the purist's sense. ". . . What Ewen has accomplished in

'Journey to Greatness' is less a definition of Gershwin than the exposition of a lot of things about him . . . [it] has added much to the sum of knowledge about Gershwin, but not very much to a comprehension of him . . ."

B116. SCULLY, Frank. "Scully's Scrapbook." *Variety* 201, Feb. 15, 1987 (dateline: Palm Beach, CA, 73.
    Lengthy review of the first edition. While the material here is largely a rehash of biographical material, Scully points out that he believes that P&B has been performed more often since 1935 than Mozart's *Marriage of Figaro* of 1786.

EWEN, David. *George Gershwin: His Journey to Greatness,* 2nd ed., 1970, B43.

B117. "October 1: *GEORGE GERSHWIN: His Journey to Greatness. David Ewen* . . ." *Publisher's Weekly* 198/5 (August 3,1970): 55.
    A very brief, highly complimentary review of Ewen's biography of 1970. The unsigned review calls it ". . . graceful, lucid, painstakingly researched . . ."

B118. "[Review]." *Reprint Bulletin Book Reviews* 32/1 (1987): 10.

JABLONSKI, Edward and Lawrence D. STEWART. *The Gershwin Years*, B54. *See:* **CHASE** at **B147.**

B119. ELLSWORTH, Ray. "Our Own Mr. Jablonski and Mr. Stewart: *The Gershwin Years* . . ." *American Record Guide* 24 (Dec. 1958): 232, 295.
    Review of Jablonski-Stewart's 1958 biography. ". . . This lavishly handsome labor of love . . . is much the best [of the biographies] so far . . ."

B120. FREEDLEY, Vinton. "'Porgy' and Always the Best." *Saturday Review* 41/42 (Oct. 18, 1958): 14.

B121. HARRISON, John. "The Gershwin Years. By Edward Jablonski and Lawrence D. Stewart . . . second edition . . . Gershwin: His Life and Music. By Charles Schwartz . . ." *Opera Journal* 9/2 (1976): 47-50.
    As might be expected in an opera journal, considerable attention is focused on P&B in this detailed comparative review of two Gershwin biographies from 1973. ". . . Both books are more biographical than musical, but Schwartz pays more attention to the music and has a number of good insights; a few of them are in a fine set of notes and require digging . . . The finer book is Schwartz's, but both are valuable and have separate merits . . ." *See:* **B86, W37**

B122. "The Instrumentalist's Bookshelf." *The Instrumentalist.* 13/4 (Dec. 1958): 12+.

JABLONSKI, Edward. *Gershwin: A Biography, Illustrated*, B53.

B123. BOWEN, Meirion. "Gershwin Remembered: Gershwin by Edward Jablonski . . . [and] Lyrics on Several Occasions by Ira Gershwin . . ." *Musical Times* 129/1749 (Nov. 1988): 599-602.
    Lengthy, descriptive review of Jablonski's biography, along with a shorter coverage of a paperback reprint by Omnibus (London) of IG's *Lyrics on Several Occasions*. . . . In re: Jablonski's book, the reviewer drew the following conclusion: "The curious thing about Gershwin is that despite all the books, films and television programmes about him, he remains an elusive figure, personally and creatively . . ." *See:* **B21**

B124. CARNOVALE, Norbert. "Edward Jablonski. *Gershwin: A Biography, Illustrated* [Review]." *Bulletin of the Council for Research in Music Education* 100 (Spring 1989): 100-102.
A generally complimentary review of Jablonski's 1987 bio.

B125. DAVIS, Francis. "[Review of book]." *NYTimes Book Review*, Sept. 27, 1987, p. 14.
". . . A wealth of pertinent detail and fresh musicological insight makes Mr. Jablonski's the definitive Gershwin biography. It is the book to which all subsequent Gershwin scholars will have to turn first."

B126. FOX, Gerald S. "Books: Gershwin, Edward Jablonski . . ." *American Record Guide* 51/5 (Sept.-Oct. 88): 123.
". . . [W]riting a first rate documentation of Gershwin's musical life is praiseworthy in itself, and Jablonski's detailed and accurate account of this will, I am sure, be deemed definitive for many years to come . . . The book is replete with interesting trivia . . ."

B127. KANFER, Stefan. "Books: Up Tunes." *Time* 130/12 (Sept 21, 1987): 76.
Kanfer summarized Gershwin's life, and called Jablonski's book "an amiable study."

B128. SULLIVAN, Mark H. "[Review of book]." *Library Journal* 112 (Sept. 15, 1987): 77.

B129. WIERZBICKI, James. "The Arts & Entertainment: Genius Wasn't Enough for George Gershwin: He Wanted To Do It All; Music." *St Louis Post-Dispatch,* Aug. 2, 1987, Section D, pp. 3+.
A substantial article reviewing Jablonski's biography. Wierzbicki takes the subjective view that Gershwin's orchestrations of his works after RiB are *not* "infinitely superior to the versions [those by Campbell-Watson, et al] familiar to most listeners today."

B130. WILLIS, Thomas, editor. "Book Reviews." *Musical America* 108/2 (May 1988): 20-22.
Brief review. ". . . Edward Jablonsky [sic] lets us in on all dimensions of the genius-subject he knows so well. This is one of those comparatively few cases where 'definitive' is the polar opposite of 'dull' . . ."

B131. YOUNGREN, William H. "[Review of book]." *Commentary* 84 (Dec. 1987): 69.
Positive review.

KENDALL, Alan. *George Gershwin: A Biography,* **B59.**

B132. CUSHMAN, Robert. "Books: Lords of the lyric . . ." *The Spectator* 259 (Aug. 29, 1987): 24-25.
A negative review of Kendall's work. ". . . George's latest biographer seems to dislike his subject, though Alan Kendall writes so clumsily that it is difficult to be sure . . ."

B133. "[Review]." *Punch* 293 (Oct. 14, 1987): 72.

B134. "[Review]." *British Book News* (May 1987): 303.

KIMBALL, Robert and Alfred SIMON. *The Gershwins,* **B62.**

B135. KOLODIN, Irving. "Jubilee in Blue." *SR World* (Oct 9, 1973): 17.
Article commemorating the seventy-fifth anniversary of G's birth, along with a review of the Kimball-Simon book.

KRELLMANN, Hanspeter. *George Gershwin*, **B64**.

B136. ARNOLD, Holger. "Hanspeter Krellmann George Gershwin . . ." *Neue Zeitschrift für Musik* 150 (Apr. 1989): 52.
One-column review of this biography.

KRESH, Paul. *An American Rhapsody,* **B65**.

B137. "An American Rhapsody: The Story of George Gershwin (book reviews)." *NYTimes Book Review*, July 31, 1988, p. 33.

B138. BUSH, Margaret A. "An American Rhapsody: The Story of George Gershwin. (book reviews)." *Horn Book Magazine* 64 (Nov.-Dec. 1988): 799.

MITCHELL, Barbara. *America, I hear you: A story about George Gershwin*, **B71**.

B139. WEISCHEDEL, Elaine Fort. "[Review of *America, I hear you: a story about George Gershwin]*." *School Library Journal* 34 (Dec. 1987): 96.

PEYSER, Joan. *The Memory of All That: The Life of George Gershwin*, **B75**.

B140. BLOCK, Geoffrey. [Review] "The Memory of All That: The Life of George Gershwin. By Joan Peyser . . ." M. L A. *Notes* 51/1 (Sept. 1994); 195-197.
An in-depth, well argued and insightful review of Peyser's book making the review necessary reading for G scholars and aficionados. Block rightfully concluded that "a well-documented and elegantly argued Gershwin biography . . . is still long overdue."

B141. KOZINN, Allan. "The Arts; Music Notes; Probing the Inner Life of Gershwin the Man." *NYTimes*, Jan. 19, 1993, p. C13, C17.
Article announcing the then forthcoming publication of Joan Peyser's "psychobiography" *The Memory of All That: The Life of George Gershwin,* announced for publication in May, 1993, by Simon & Schuster. The article includes insights gained from an interview of Peyser conducted by the reviewer. Kozinn gave clues as to some of the contents of the book especially regarding the reputed existence of Alan Gershwin ("whose original name was Albert Schneider"), son of "an actress named Molly Charleston."

B142. LUCAIRE, Ed. "In Short . . . NonFiction . . . **THE MEMORY OF ALL THAT** . . . by Joan Peyser . . ." *NYTimes Book Review*, Apr. 18, 1993, p. 22.
A brief, positive review in which Lucaire states that "Joan Peyser has written an iconoclastic book about George Gershwin that provides new insights into the man . . . All told . . . [this book] is a provocative new look at one of America's musical geniuses."

B143. YARDLEY, Jonathan. "It Ain't Necessarily So. **THE MEMORY OF ALL THAT** By Joan Peyser . . ." *Washington Post Book World,* Apr. 11, 1993, p. 3.
A thoughtful, negative review which gets to the core of Joan Peyser's biography. Among other things, the reviewer points out that "*The Memory of All That* is a very dirty book

. . . The pervasive meanness of this book is startling . . . her analysis of his popular songs is barely perfunctory . . ." Yardley concluded that the book is "merely mean, trivial and, in the deepest sense of the word, cynical." *See*: **B1473**

ROSENBERG, Deena. *Fascinating Rhythm,* **B80.**

B144. FLATOW, Sheryl. "Books . . . Fascinating Rhythm . . . by Deena Rosenberg . . ." *Opera News* 56/10 (Feb. 1, 1992): 45.
Short and complimentary review.

B145. SCHNEIDER, Wayne. "Book Nook I . . . Going Into the Gershwins." *I. S. A. M. Newsletter* 21/1 (Nov. 1991): 5.
Brief review. Gershwin scholar Schneider considered that the "best bits" of the book were "her comments on the social themes of Ira's song lyrics as America chugs from the post-World War I era into the roaring '20s and depressed '30s .'. ." Rosenberg's discussion of the music was found to be "disappointing" and "unsophisticated."

RIMLER, Walter. *A Gershwin Companion: A Critical Inventory and Discography,* **B936.**

B146. STARR, Larry. "Book Reviews Edited by Mark Germer and Marjorie Hassen . . . American Music . . . **A Gershwin Companion: A Critical Inventory and Discography** . . . by Walter Rimler . . ." M. L. A. *Notes* 49/4 (June 1993): 1489-1490.
Informative and complimentary review in which the reviewer calls Rimler's book "a thoroughly remarkable one." While this book is basically a discography, it contains biographical information within the annotations. It appears to be a labor of love for the music.

B146.1 _____. "A Gershwin Companion - a Critical Inventory and Discography, 1916-1984 - Rimler, W. [**Book review**]." (Reprint) Univ. Washington, Seattle, WA. 98195, 1993.

SCHWARTZ, Charles M. *George Gershwin: His Life and Music,* **B86.**

B147. CHASE, Gilbert. "[Reviews]: George Gershwin: His Life and Music. By **Charles M. Schwartz** . . . The Gershwin Years. By **Edward Jablonski and Lawrence D. Stewart** . . . **The New York Times Gershwin Years in Song** . . ." M. L. A. *Notes* 31/2 (December 1974): 297-298.
Chase's review of the triumvirate named above. About Schwartz: "[The author expressed] . . . 'the hope of bringing Gershwin's life and music into better focus.' His camera . . . is no respector of privacy or decorum. The better the focus, the worse for Gershwin, as the camera repeatedly zooms in on his inflated ego, his boorish behavior, his brothel escapades, and his troublesome digestive tract . . . Withal, this is the most heavily documented book on Gershwin to appear thus far . . . But this is not the definitive biography Gershwin deserves . . . Chase was generally positive about *The Gershwin Years* and called the *Gershwin Years in Song* "a welcome companion volume" to the former. ". . . [T]hese transcriptions are utterly delightful and truly artistic creations . . . ." *See*:   **B86, B54**

B148. HORN, David. *The Literature of American Music in Books and Folk Music Collections: A Fully Annotated Bibliography.* Metuchen, NJ, Scarecrow, 1977.
Horn commented perceptively about Schwartz' book: "Clearly much of the detail gathered is of value; other portions . . . are less likely to be rewarding in the long term.

(Gershwin frequented prostitutes—so did Schubert. Are we expected to think less of Gershwin, and does it make *any* difference to the music of either?) . . ."

BIBLIOGRAPHY ABOUT WORKS

GENERAL BIBLIOGRAPHY

When more than one work or individual songs are discussed in a reference, said reference is included under the **General Bibliography** section of this chapter, immediately below. Otherwise, the works are listed alphabetically under the appropriate category (**Orchestral Works**, e. g.) and title heading (*An American in Paris,* e. g.)

B149. BAGAR, Robert C., and **Louis BIANCOLLI.** *The Concert Companion.* NY
   & London: McGraw-Hill, 1947, pp. 273-78.
  Program notes for AiP, Concerto, selections from P&B, and RiB, said notes originally written for program booklets of the Philharmonic-Symphony Society of New York. *See:* **W3, W2, W37, W1**

B150. BARAL, Robert. *Revue: The Great Broadway Period.* Introduction by
   Robert J. Landry. New York & London: Fleet Press, 1962, pp. 39, 76, 109, 136-
   138, *et passim,* reprint ed. 1970.
  References to G here and there throughout this history of the musical revue. *George White's Scandals,* for which GG wrote 26 songs, are covered. Activity in London is also considered: GG's *The Rainbow.* e.g. A helpful feature of the book is an Appendix listing the shows by title, in chronological order, with their casts and lengths of their runs. *See:* **W11, W13, W14, W17, W18, W20**

B151. BERNSTEIN, Leonard. *The Joy of Music.* NY: Simon & Schuster, 1959, pp. 52-64:
   "Why Don't You Run Upstairs and Write a Nice Gershwin Tune?" reprint from
   Atlantic Monthly, and other references at pp. 169-172.
  Includes the essay, in mock interview form, of a conversation with a music- publishing executive discussing Gershwin's AiP, Concerto, P&B, and RiB. Referring to RiB, the imaginary interviewer called **P. M.**, states ". . . [I]t breathes America—the people, the urban society that George knew deeply, the pace, the nostalgia, the nervousness, the majesty . . ." Even though Bernstein admitted to adoring the rhapsody, he nonetheless pointed out what he considers to be its faults. There is also discussion of *Oh, Kay!* and OTIS (pp. 169-172). *See:* **W3, W2, W37, W1, W26, W34**

B152. CAMPBELL, Frank C. "Some Manuscripts of George Gershwin (1898-1937):
   a modern master is pictured in his manuscripts now in the Library of Congress."
   Manuscripts 6 (Winter 1954): 66-75.
  While announcing "the new Gershwin Collection" at the Library of Congress, this highly informative article also provides biographical details. Especially beneficial for those unable to visit the Library of Congress is the documentation of completion dates of six scenes from the P&B manuscripts (five other undated scenes are listed). Works discussed in detail include RiB, AiP, Second Rhapsody, Cuban Overture, the piano Preludes, Short Story, and P&B. A summary of the critic's opinions following the premieres of all the big works is also given. *See:* **W1, W3, W4, W5, W42, W39, W37**

B153. CHASE, Gilbert. *America's Music from the Pilgrims to the Present,* 3rd revised
   ed. Urbana & Chicago: Univ. of Illinois Press, 1987 (first published in 1955).

Has discussion of P&B and RiB. *See*: **W37, W1**

B154. CROSS, Milton, & David EWEN. *Milton Cross' Encyclopedia of the Great Composers and Their Music*, 2 vols., rev. ed. Garden City, NY: Doubleday, 1962. 1st ed, 1953.
Includes program notes for AiP, Concerto, P&B, and RiB *See*: **W3, W2, W37, W1**

B155. DOWNES, Edward. *Adventures in Symphonic Music*, Decorations by John O'Hara Cosgrove II. NY: Farrar & Rinehart, 1944.
Program notes for AiP and RiB. *See*: **W3, W1**

B156. DOWNES, Irene, ed. *Olin Downes on Music: A Selection from His Writings during the Half-Century from 1906 to 1955*. (Preface by Howard Taubman). New York: Simon & Schuster, 1957.
Includes three significant pieces from Downes' criticism for the *New York Times*: "*Rhapsody in Blue* Introduced in a Historic Whiteman Concert" (1924), "*Porgy and Bess* and the Future of American Opera" (1935), and "On the Passing of George Gershwin" (1937). *See*: **W1, W37**

B157. EWEN, David. "Miami: A Festival of George Gershwin: From an unknown early opera to a six-minute sequence for Ginger Rogers, Gershwin's music packs the house." *High Fidelity/Musical America* 21/1 (Jan. 1971): MA 24-25, 29.
Calling himself "Gershwin's definitive biographer" and "the one who conceived this festival," Ewen reported on the Gershwin Festival held in Miami, October, 1970. The origins of *Promenade* in its Kostelanetz orchestration, are covered. Ewen commented upon what he called G's "art song," *In a Mandarin's Garden*: ". . . what is most interesting in this number is the unusual intervallic structure of the melody, more in the idiom of serious modern music of the late 1920s than of Broadway or Gershwin . . ." Mention is made of an arrangement by Rayburn Wright and Richard Lieb, titled *Symphonic Settings for Orchestra*, and including *Love Is Sweeping the Country, Oh, Lady Be Good!, 'S Wonderful!; Love Walked In*; and *Liza*: ". . . These were more than transcriptions; they were re-creations which neatly combined Gershwin melodies and harmonies with appropriate orchestral settings . . ." An article concerning this Festival by Evelyn Spitalny appears in *Variety*, November 11, 1970, p. 46. *See also*: **W6c, W54i, W47**

B158. GILBERT, Steven E. *The Music of Gershwin*. New Haven & London: Yale University Press, 1995.
A very serious study focusing on G's music. Larry Starr commented on the book on its jacket: "This book—the first thorough and systematic treatment of Gershwin's work from a theoretical perspective—will serve to establish to music scholars Gershwin's 'legitimacy' as one of our most central and accomplished, as well as popular, American composers . . ." The result of more than ten years of work on Gilbert's part, the book applies Schenkerian techniques of analysis to such works as RiB, Concerto, AiP, P&B, *Second Rhapsody, Cuban Overture, Pardon My English,* as well as a selection of the songs. The book is a major accomplishment regarding the music of G; familiarity with the language of Schenkerian analysis will aid the reader's comprehension. It will be interesting to observe the impact of this study upon teachers and students using more traditional repertoire for courses in the analysis of music. I don't believe the book would be understood by non-musician laymen. *See*: **W1, W2, W3, W37, W4, W5, W35, B226**

B159. HYLAND. William G. *The Song Is Ended: Songwriters and American Music, 1900–*

1950. New York: Oxford University Press, 1995, 53, 56-57, 92, 95, 98, 122, 145, 180, 181, 226, 231, *et passim*.

Examination of the index to this book reveals many references to the Gershwins. The book is intended to treat principally the music of five composers: Berlin, Kern, Gershwin, Cole Porter, and Richard Rodgers. Seven chapters deal with Gershwin matters, titled: *Swanee, Fascinating Rhythm, Rhapsody in Blue, Lady, Be Good!, Of Thee I Sing, Porgy and Bess,* and *Foggy Day*. Hyland, presently Research Professor at Georgetown University's School of Foreign Affairs, has perceptive insights about the Gershwin legend, as well as that of the other composers discussed. *See*: **W1, W34, W37**

B160. LIBRARY OF CONGRESS. "The Gershwins and Their World." *See*: **B1637**

B161. LONGMIRE, John. *John Ireland: Portrait of a Friend*. London: John Baker, 1969. Some discussion of "The Man I Love."

B162. LYNCH, Richard Chigley. *Musicals! A Directory of Musical Properties Available for Production*. Chicago: American Library Association, 1984.

This useful source lists *Girl Crazy; Lady, Be Good!*; OTIS; *Oh, Kay!*; P&B; *Rosalie*; and *Tip-Toes*, giving a synopsis of the plots, along with other information necessary for production, such as whether or not a piano-vocal score is published, the licensing agent, available recordings, and cast requirements. The instrumentation requirements of the pit orchestra are *not* given, and, due to the recent revivals of *Primrose* and *Pardon My English*, it is somewhat out-of-date. Nonetheless, it is an excellent source to 1984. *See*: **W34, W22, W35, W26, W37, W29, W24**

B162.1. SCHNEIDER, Wayne J., ed. *The Gershwin Style: New Looks at the Music of George Gershwin*. NY: Oxford University Press, 1999.

Unfortunately, this indispensable book arrived too late to afford a full annotation. It is highly recommended to Gershwin researchers, including twelve essays by leading Gershwin experts *ca*. 1998. *See*: More complete entry at **B1735.1**

B163. SLONIMSKY, Nicolas. *Lexicon of Musical Invective*. NY: Coleman-Ross, 1953, p. 105; paperback second edition: Seattle & London: University of Washington Press, 1965, p. 105.

Includes derogatory reviews of *An American in Paris, Porgy and Bess, & Rhapsody in Blue*, by critics **Lawrence GILMAN, Herbert F. PEYSER**, and **Oscar THOMPSON**, respectively *See*: **W3, W37, W1**

B164. SLONIMSKY, Nicolas. *Music Since 1900*, 4th. ed. NY: Charles Scribner's, 1971, pp. 111, 294, 384-85, 395, 404, 422-423, 439, 462, 484, 487, 512, 515, 535, 541, 543, *et passim*. 1st, 2nd & 3rd ed. published by Coleman-Ross; 5th ed. covers to 1991, Schirmer Books, 1993.

Documents numerous first performances of Gershwin works & quotes from several reviews; *See*: **Olin DOWNES** (No. 123), **Lawrence GILMAN** (Nos. 229-30), **Herbert PEYSER** (No. 437), **Deems TAYLOR** (No. 572), & **Oscar THOMPSON** (No. 582).

B165. STRUNK, Steven. "The Harmony of Early Bop: A Layered Approach." *Journal of Jazz Studies* 6/1 (Fall-Winter 1979): 4-53.

A lengthy and in-depth analytical article treating the G tunes *Somebody Loves Me* and *Embraceable You*, among other songs of other composers exploited during the early bebop (jazz) era.

B166. THOMSON, Virgil. *The Art of Judging Music.* NY: Alfred A. Knopf, 1948, pp. 55-
  56, 126, 127, 131, 203-204, 306.
  A compendium of reprints of articles and reviews originally written for the *NYHerald-
Tribune.* Brief references to GG are scattered through the book as noted above, along with one
review: the April 18, 1946, All-Gershwin concert by the NY Philharmonic under Artur
Rodzinski. This review, printed in the Trib on April 19, was titled "Gershwin Black and Blue"
and discusses AiP, Concerto, excerpts from P&B, and RiB with Oscar Levant as soloist.
See: **W54e, W2, W3h, W37, W1, B1583**

B167. _____. *The Musical Scene.* NY: A. A. Knopf, 1945, pp. 18-19, 27-28, 118, 132,
  167-169, *et passim.*
  A collection of essays and reviews which, with one exception, originally appeared
in the *NYHerald Tribune.* Do It Again, P&B, an RiB are treated and the essays "It's About
Time," "Landscapes with Music," and "Porgy in Maplewood" are included. *See:* **W37, W37e,
W1**

B168. VINAY, G. "Gershwin and the Impertinent Analysis ('Rhapsody in Blue' And
  'Porgy and Bess') [Italian]." *Rivista Italiana di musicologia* 26/1 (1991): 59-78.
  See: **W1, W37**

B169. WILDER, Alec. "George Gershwin (1898-1937)," in his: *American Popular Song.*
  NY: Oxford University Press, 1972, pp. 121-162.
  Comments on the songs by a unique song writer himself, whom Gunther Schuller has
called "a somewhat enigmatic and still far-too-little appreciated figure in twentieth-century
American music [as of 1995]." Wilder evaluated and analyzed sixty-eight selected G songs.
Among many other comments, Wilder synthesized about G: ". . . He was an aggressive writer.
His was the 'hard sell,' as opposed to the softer, gentler persuasiveness of, say, Kern or Irving
Berlin. If I were to compare his songs with Kern's, I'd say Gershwin's were active and Kern's
passive. The constant, and characteristic, repeated note found throughout Gershwin's songs
is a basic attestation of this aggressiveness . . ." Wilder concluded: ". . . Probably with no other
writer is the personal character of this [Wilder's] book more apparent. Upon rereading my
words, I find I jump from enthusiasm to critical reservation like the lines on a fever chart . . .
No other writer of songs causes such disparate attitudes from me. For however excitingly
native his writing may have been, I feel that there was a scrim—a vaguely transparent theater
curtain—between him and what he sought musically. I'm trying to say that, for me, there is one
step missing in his restless movement toward a totally American expression . . ."

B170. YOUNGREN, William. "Gershwin." *New Republic* 176 (Apr. 23, 1977), 21-24;
  (Apr. 30, 1977), 27-30; (May 7, 1977), 23-26; (May 14, 1977), 23-27. *See:* **W1,
  W2, W3, W37**

ORCHESTRAL WORKS
(In alphabetical order)

W3. *AN AMERICAN IN PARIS,* a tone poem. (November 18, 1928)

B171. "American in Paris." *New York Philharmonic Program Notes* (March 13, 1954).

B172. BAGAR, Robert C. "An American in Paris." *The Philharmonic-Symphony Society* *of New York* [Program] (Nov. 17, 19, 21, 1943): 5-7. *See:* **W54d.1**

B173. BONNER, Eugene. "George Gershwin's Latest." *The Outlook and Independent*
151/1 (Jan. 2, 1929): 34.
General discussion of AiP shortly after its premiere. Includes quotes from Deems
Taylor's program notes for the work. *See:* **W3a**

B174. BOOKSPAN, Martin. "The Basic Repertoire: Gershwin's An American in Paris."
HiFi Stereo Review 14/5 (May 1965): 39-40.

B175. DOWNES, Olin. "Gershwin's New Score Acclaimed." *NYTimes,* Dec. 14, 1928,
p. 37. *See:* **W3a**

B176. FRANKENSTEIN. Alfred. "An American in Paris." *San Francisco Symphony
Orchestra* [Program]. (Nov. 2, 1951): 93. Also in program of Nov. 18, 1954, 63+.
See: **W3i.1**

B177. "Jazzed Homesickness in Paris." *Literary Digest* 100/1 (Jan. 5, 1929): 23-24.
Brief reference to AiP, including a compressed version of Deems Taylor's program
notes for the premiere. *See:* **W3a**

B178. KOLODIN, Irving. "An American in Paris." *The Philharmonic-Symphony Society
of New York* [Program] 111 (Mar. 13, 1954), p. 7.

B179. KRAMER, Jonathan D. "Program Notes." *San Francisco Symphony Program
Notes* (Mar. 1967): 22-23.
Notes for *An American in Paris, Concerto in F, Porgy and Bess,* & *Rhapsody in Blue.*
See: **W3, W2, W37, W1**

B180. LIEBERSON, Goddard. *The Columbia Book of Musical Masterworks,* introduction
by Edward Wallerstein. NY: Allen, Towne & Heath, 1947.
Program notes for *An American in Paris, Concerto in F, Porgy and Bess,* and
Rhapsody in Blue; [formerly appeared in Columbia Masterwork albums.] *See:* **W3, W2, W37,
W1**

B181. LOGAN, Charles G. *A Stylistic Analysis of George Gershwin's An American in
Paris.* Master of Music thesis (Music theory), Texas Christian University, 1949, v,
149 pp.
Analysis of AiP, with comparisons to RiB, Concerto, and P&B. The harmonic analysis
includes tables such as "Percentages of Chord Frequencies," "Table of 7th Chords," "Table of
9th Chords," and "Table of 11th Chords," each table breaking the types of chords down into
frequencies of occurrence. Logan employed the same approach as part of his melodic analysis.
Logan also subjected G's orchestration to analysis. Chapter six includes a comparison of AiP
with RiB, Concerto, and P&B. Overall, although there are no profound revelations, this is a
good master's study. *See:* **W3, W1, W2, W37**

B182. NILES, Abbe. "A Note on Gershwin." *The Nation* 128/33 (Feb. 13, 1929): 193-194.
An assessment of G's accomplishment by early 1929, focusing on AiP. " . . . 'An
American in Paris' represents an advance in Gershwin's ability both to get what he wants out
of a symphony orchestra (no mean problem), and so to transform and combine his themes as

to make a living organism of the sum total. It has a personality apart from Gershwin's own, which his concerto has not . . ."

B183. O'CONNELL, Charles. *The Victor Book of Overtures, Tone Poems, and Other Orchestral Works.* NY: Simon & Schuster, 1950.
A source of program notes for AiP.

B184. PALMER, Geoffrey, and **Noel LLOYD.** *Music Tells the Tale, A Guide to Programme Music.* London/NY: Frederick Warne, 1967.
Program notes.

B185. PEYSER, Herbert F. "[Review of the premiere of AiP]." *NYTelegram,* Dec. 14, 1928. *See* also: **B163** (Slonimsky *Lexicon*)
"An American in Paris is nauseous claptrap, so dull, patchy, thin, vulgar, long-winded and inane, that the average movie audience would be bored by it . . ." *See:* **W3a**

B186. ROSCOE, Burton. "Contemporary Reminiscences; In Memory of Elinor Wylie: An American in Paris Set to Music: and the Literary Censor at Work." *Arts and Decorations* 30 (Mar. 1929): 77, 116.

B187. SANDOW, Hyman. "Gershwin Presents a New Work; Getting in Step with 'American in Paris.'" *Musical America* 48/18 (Aug. 18, 1928): 5, 12.
Gives pre-premiere information on AiP. *See:* **W3a**

B188. _____. "Gershwin to Write New Rhapsody." *Musical America* 47/18 (Feb. 18, 1928): 5.
Refers to G's plan for composing AiP.

B189. SEAMAN, Julian. *Great Orchestral Music: A Treasury of Program Notes.* NY: Rinehart, 1950. (The Field of Music Series, Vol. 5)
Includes program notes for *American in Paris, Concerto in F,* and *Rhapsody in Blue.* *See:* **W3, W2, W1**

B190. STEINBERG. Michael. "Schuller and NEC Symphony provide a treat." *Boston Globe* A. M., Dec. 11, 1973.
Review of a concert conducted by Gunther Schuller of the New England Conservatory Symphony Orchestra including AiP. The review is included for the reviewers' interesting comments: ". . . It [AiP] is an enshrinement of two cliches, but it is funny and touching, the big, slow tune in the middle is a lovely indulgent squeeze, it is all put together neatly and without strain, and the sound has a captivating flash and richness to it . . . G extracts astonishingly varied and vivid colors. Schuller certainly did a superb job at sorting all that out. He knows, as few do, the language G. uses and plays with . . . the special pleasure of Schuller's performance was its straightness. And the straighter G's music is played, with uncomplicated grace and no tricks, the more directly it will come across as funny, touching, and musical . . ." *See:* **W3m**

B191. TAYLOR, Deems. [AiP] *The Philharmonic-Symphony Society of New York Program,* Dec. 13, 1928, pp. 5-8.
Includes the written program for the premiere concert. *See:* **W3a**

B192. THOMPSON, Oscar. "Gershwin's 'An American in Paris' Played for the First Time by the Philharmonic Symphony Orchestra." *NY Evening Post*, Dec. 14, 1928, p. 15.

Review of the world premiere. In an article for the same paper dated December 21st, Thompson commented: ". . . To conceive of a symphonic audience listening to it with any degree of pleasure or patience twenty years from now . . . is another matter . . ." *See*: **W3a**

B193. THOMSON, Virgil. "Expert and Original," in his: *Music Right and Left*. NY: Henry Holt, 1951, pp. 14-16.

Manuel Rosenthal's (b. 1904) *Magic Manhattan* is compared to AiP in a review reprint of a St. Louis Symphony Orchestra concert (from the original appearing in the *NY Herald Tribune* March 9, 1950).

B194. ULRICH, Homer. *Symphonic Music: Its Evolution Since the Renaissance*. NY: Columbia University Press, 1952.

Brief coverage of AiP, Concerto, and RiB by a distinguished musicologist. *See*: **W3, W2, W1**

B195 . YOUNGREN, William. "Gershwin, Part III: An American in Paris." *New Republic* (May 7, 1977): 23-26.

Discussion and analysis of AiP. ". . . One's first impression on looking at the score of *An American in Paris* is that here, in contrast to the *Concerto*, we have a work that was orchestrally conceived from the beginning . . . It is perhaps worth adding that while the original published score was almost exactly the same as Gershwin's manuscript score, the score one buys and hears today is quite different. It was edited [very heavily] . . . by Frank Campbell-Watson . . ."

W7. *CATFISH ROW: SUITE FROM PORGY AND BESS*. (1935-1936)

See: **B1838, B2171**

W2. *CONCERTO IN F* for piano and orchestra. (1925)

B196. BAGAR, Robert C. "Concerto for Piano and Orchestra in F Major." *The Philharmonic-Symphony Society of New York* [Program] (Jan. 6, 1946): 4-5. *See*: **W2i**

B197. BARNES, P. "Gershwin Concerto (Jerome Robbins Latest Creation for New-York-City-Ballet)." *Dance & Dancers* 390 (1982). *See*: **B200**

B198. BOROWSKI, Felix. "Concerto in F, for Piano and Orchestra." *Chicago Symphony Orchestra* [Program] (Dec. 6, 1951): 67-68. *See*: **W2l**

B199. BUCHANAN, Charles L. "Gershwin and Musical Snobbery." *The Outlook* 145 (Feb. 2, 1927): 146-148.

A provocative essay about *Concerto*, based on a second hearing a year after the world premiere. Buchanan maintained that the work ". . . shows an increasingly clear title to be ranked the one composition of indubitable vitality, originality, and authentic progressiveness that this country has produced . . ." Referring to reviews by critics Lawrence Gilman, Olin Downes, Henderson, and Peyser, Buchanen presented a convincing argument for a less snobbish, objective view of G's talent and accomplishment.

B200. CROCE, Arlene. "Dancing: This Space and That Jazz and These Dancers." *New Yorker* 58/1 (Feb. 22, 1982): 99-103.

Lengthy review principally of two 1982 ballets based on the *Concerto*: ". . . [one] by Billy Wilson for the Alvin Alley company [which] is in a jazz-wrenched modern-dance idiom; [and] the other is in the sleekly upholstered classicism of Jerome Robbins and New York City Ballet . . ." Croce had mixed feelings about the success of the ballets based on G's music, Robbins' being named "The Gershwin Concerto." *See:* **B197**

B201. DOWNES, Olin. "A Piano Concerto in the Vernacular To Have Its Day With Damrosch." *NYTimes*, Nov. 29, 1925, section 8, p. 6.

Substantial article announcing the upcoming premiere of the Concerto, to be on Dec. 3, 1925. In the article, Downes raised some questions, ". . . Is it for his [G's] best good . . . for a young man of native musical invention and dexterity in the lighter, smaller forms, to attempt to don the garb of a symphonist. The performance of the concerto will be a twofold test. It will tell us how far and how rapidly Mr. Gershwin is developing along the lines of orchestra composition, and it will provide a new and important trial of the availability of jazz as symphonic material." *See:* **W2a**

B202. DOWNES, Olin. "Music: The New York Symphony." *NYTimes*, Dec. 4, 1925, p. 26.

Negative review of the world premiere of the *Concerto*, December 3, 1925. Downes summarized his feelings: ". . . In essence this is a more ambitious and less original piece of music than the one which first brought Mr. Gershwin to the attention of the orchestral public. It is not only immature—which need be no crime—but it is self-conscious, lacking the espirit and the felicity of touch that he shows when he is truly in the creative vein . . ." *See:* **W2a**

B203. E[NGEL], C[arl]."Views and Reviews." *Musical Quarterly* 12/2 (Apr.1926): 299-314.

Discusses the concerto.

B204. _____."Views and Reviews." *Musical Quarterly* 12/3 (July 1926): 303-304.

". . . Mr. Gershwin has written not only a very courageous, but also a very creditable work—creditable especially because his jazz-concerto does not contain a trace of the vulgar. There are inevitably stretches that reveal a lack of experience and resourcefulness, others that are uninteresting and made of stuff as mediocre as any well-behaved and dry-as-dust conservative can roll off by the yard. The merit and promise of this composition lie in the portions that are distinctly poetical; in the orchestral coloring, that is often piquant without ever being offensive; but chiefly in the general tenor, which is unquestionably new of a newness to be found nowhere except in the United States . . ."

B205. FRANKENSTEIN, Alfred. *A Modern Guide to Symphonic Music.* NY: Meredith Press, 1966, pp. 244-246.

Frankenstein's notes for the concerto originally appearing in the San Francisco Symphony Orchestra Program.

B206. GRABBE, Paul. *The Story of One Hundred Symphonic Favorites.* NY: Grosset & Dunlap, 1940.

Program notes.

B207. HAMM, Charles. "A Blues for the Ages," in *A Celebration of American Music*, ed. by Richard Crawford, R. Allen Lott, and Carol J. Oja. Ann Arbor: University of

Michigan Press, 1990, pp. 346-355.

An insightful essay based on the second "blues" movement of the concerto. ". . . Unless new evidence comes to light, we must conclude that Gershwin's knowledge of the blues in 1925 came from performances and recordings by dance bands of a standard blues repertory built around pieces by W. C. Handy, who autographed a copy of *Blues: An Anthology* (1926) owned by Gershwin . . ." Through analysis presented in a table, Hamm shows those sections in the movement based on twelve-bar-blues harmonic progressions. Essential reading for those interested in understanding Gershwin's amalgamation of the blues into his serious work.

B208. "A Jazz Concerto." *The Outlook* 141/16 (Dec. 16, 1925): 582-583.

Review of the world premiere of Concerto, Dec. 3 and 4, 1925. ". . . Its long-awaited performance at Carnegie Hall was received enthusiastically—and with very good cause, for, in spite of obvious shortcomings, the concerto displayed freshness, vitality, and audacious originality. It brimmed to overflowing with ideas, some good and some poor, and with a feverish delight in rhythm . . . Gershwin's originality lies in something more than rhythm; it is an originality of language . . ." *See:* **W2a**

B209. KONSULOVA, V. "Plodiv: 'Gershwin-67.'" *Bulgarska Muzika* 29/3 (Mar.1968): 62-64.

Review of Concerto and RiB. *See:* **W2, W1**

B210. KURATH, Gertrude Prokosch. "George Gershwin's Concerto in F at the Yale School of Drama, Introduction by Joann W. Kealiinohomoku." *Dance Research Journal* 20/1 (Summer 1988): 43-46.

Article about the use of the concerto with a dance performance at the Yale School of Drama in May 1930. The author choreographed the dance and the choreography is printed with the article. *See:* **W2c**

B211. LA PRADE, Ernest. "Program Notes," in [The New York] *Symphony Society Bulletin* 29/6 (Dec. 2, 1925): 1-2.

Comments on Concerto. *See:* **W2a**

B212. MORGAN, Alfred Lindsay. "A Famous Radio Debut." *Etude* 62/4 (Apr. 1944): 202, 252.

Concerns Toscanini's performance of the concerto by the NBC Symphony Orchestra, with Oscar Levant as soloist. *See:* **W2h.1, B1583**

B213. SHIRLEY, Wayne D. "George Gershwin Learns to Orchestrate." *Sonneck Society Bulletin* 16/3 (Fall 1990): 101-102.

Typical for Shirley, a thought-provoking article. The essay focuses on G's study of orchestration before the appearance of the RiB (1924), and between it and the writing of the Concerto (1925). ". . . Gershwin's music studies had included orchestration for several years before he wrote Rhapsody in Blue. A brief look at the history of his involvement with instrumentation will dispel the idea that he had no idea of orchestration whatever before he undertook the scoring of the Concerto in F . . ."

B214. SHIRLEY, Wayne D. "Scoring the Concerto in F: George Gershwin's First Orchestration." *American Music* 3/3 (Fall 1985): 277-298.

A detailed article, the purpose of which "is not to judge the quality of Gershwin's orchestration . . . but merely to establish whether the notes as printed and performed are in fact what Gershwin wrote." Shirley provides the reader with a meticulous "Table of Variants" between the currently published full score of the Concerto in F and George Gershwin's manuscript full score. Shirley concluded ". . . His technique is occasionally a bit shaky in the Concerto in F, but it does win through, in fact, much of the piece is quite beautiful as sound . . ."

B215. _____. "The 'Trial Orchestration' of Gershwin's Concerto in F." M.L.A. *Notes* 39/3 (March 1983): 570-579.

Shirley studied the manuscripts of the concerto which are in the Gershwin Collection in the Music Division of the Library of Congress. This paper focused on the "initial sketched orchestration of the opening of the concerto." A "table of variants" showing "Differences between the Trial Orchestration and the Final Manuscript of Gershwin's *Concerto in F*" is included as in the article above.

B216. SPAETH, Sigmund. *A Guide to Great Orchestral Music.* NY: Modern Library, 1943.

Includes program notes for Concerto, RiB, and Second Rhapsody. *See:* **W2, W1, W4**

B217. "Stadium Throng Gives Gershwin A Welcome." *NYTimes*, July 27, 1927, Amusements section.

Review of G's first appearance at the summer City College Lewisohn Stadium concerts, on July 26, 1927. G performed the RiB and Concerto. After mentioning that the premiere of the Concerto met with "reservations as to its lack of technical resource," the reviewer predicted: ". . . Last night's repetition of the concerto was rapturously received by the vast audience, and it was evident that the applause was spontaneous and sincere. It is a work that grows with repeated hearings, has characteristics of solid musical worth, and may well achieve a place among the significant works of contemporary American composers."*See:* **W1j.1, W2f**

B218. THOMSON, Virgil. "English Landscape," in *Music Right and Left.* NY: Henry Holt, 1951, p. 111-112.

A review of the performance of the concerto in this collection of Thomson's reviews for the *NYHerald Tribune*. ". . . George Gershwin's Concerto in F is not an ugly piece . . . but it is a pretty empty one. Even treated to so loud and so irregularly metered a reading as it was given by Byron Janis and Stokowski, it failed to fill with afflatus, though the last movement did move along. All the sweet rapture and ease of the Gershwin style got lost . . ." *See:* **W2k**

B219. ULRICH, Homer. *Symphonic Music: Its Evolution Since the Renaissance.* NY: Columbia University Press, 1952.

Brief coverage of AiP, Concerto, and RiB by a distinguished musicologist. *See:*

W3, W2, W1

B220. VAN VECHTEN, Carl. *Victor Book of Concertos.* NY: Simon & Schuster, 1948.

Program notes for Concerto and RiB. *See:* **W2, W1**

B221. VEINUS, Abraham. *The Concerto.* Double, Doran, 1945, (reprint NY: Dover, 1964), pp. 289-291.

Concerto and RiB are given attention in discussion of the concerto genre. *See:* **W2, W1**

B222. VUILLERMOZ, Emile. "Gershwin's Concerto in Paris." *Christian Science Monitor*, July 7, 1928.

Review of the first performance in France (at the Paris Opéra on May 29, 1928) with

Dmitri Tiomkin, piano soloist, and Vladimir Golschmann conducting. ". . . Gershwin's Concerto will greatly help to dissipate the last prejudices attaching to the new technique that has emerged from the novelties of jazz. By the character of his style . . . this very characteristic work made even the most distrustful musicians realize that jazz, after having renewed the technique of dancing, might perfectly well exert a deep and beneficent [sic] influence in the most exalted spheres. There is, in this mixture of balance and suppleness, a whole series of indications from which the most serious music might reap advantage . . ." *See:* **W2b**

B223. YOUNGREN, William. "Gershwin, Part II, Concerto in F." *New Republic* (Apr. 30, 1977): 27-30.
Youngren concluded that ". . . the *Concerto* is a transitional work, formally unstable and orchestrated without particular distinction. It is no accident that three years later Gershwin, his skill at orchestration and musical construction enormously increased, returned in *An American in Paris* to the episodic form of *Rhapsody in Blue.*" *See:* **W2, W3, W1**

W5. *CUBAN OVERTURE* **(originally titled** *RUMBA***).** (original orchestration manuscript: July-August, 1932)

B224. "Gershwin to Lead Musicians Concert; Composer to Conduct for His 'Cuban' Overture' and Appear as Piano Soloist Nov. 1; Event at Metropolitan; Sandor Harmati and William Daly Also to Direct Symphony Group in Opening Performance." *NYTimes*, Oct. 8, 1932, p. 15. *See:* **W5a**

B225. T., H. "Music; 17,000 Hear Gershwin." *NYTimes,* Aug. 17, 1932, Amusements Section, p. 13.
Review of the All-G Lewisohn Stadium concert that included the premiere of the overture, then called *Rumba*. Basically, this was a negative review of Gershwin, the Cuban Overture being somewhat obscured by the rest of the program. The reviewer did comment on the piece, calling it "merely old Gershwin in recognizable form . . ." *See:* **W5a**

W6. *"I GOT RHYTHM" VARIATIONS* for solo piano and orchestra. (holograph score dated January 6, 1934)

B226. GILBERT, Steven E. "Gershwin's Art of Counterpoint." *Musical Quarterly* 70/4 (Fall, 1984): 423-456.
Harmonic and melodic analysis following a modified Schenkerian procedure of excerpts from RiB, AiP, and of the variation technique and counterpoint in "*I Got Rhythm*" *Variations*. In the latter, Gilbert points out the use of the first four notes of the chorus to *I Got Rhythm* (c', d', f', and g') as an "abstraction" (*See:* Ex. 7, a through d, in *The Schillinger System of Musical Composition*, and elsewhere in that Schillinger book). This scholarly article is abundantly illustrated with musical examples and Schenkerian diagrams. *See:* **W1, W3, W6, B158**

W1. *RHAPSODY IN BLUE* for piano and jazz band. (January 25, 1924)

B227. ANTRIM, Doran K. "Fortunes in Melody." *Etude* 60/1 (Jan. 1942): 11-12.

B228. BAGAR, Robert C. "Rhapsody in Blue." *The Philharmonic-Symphony Society of New York* [Program] (Dec. 24, 25, 27, 1942): 6-7. *See:* **W1s**

B229. "Barnet's 'Rhapsody' Arrangement Ordered Destroyed by Harms." *Variety* 173/13 (Mar. 9, 1949), 48.

Publisher Harms did not like bandleader Charlie Barnet's arrangement of the rhapsody and ordered its destruction.

B230. BENDER, William. "Gershwin Playing? Yes, It Was." *NYHerald Tribune*, June 6, 1963.

Review of the June 5, 1963, concert conducted by André Kostelanetz. *See:* **W1x**

B231. BIRKHEAD, May. "Parisians Favor Gershwin's Music: Critics Praise 'Rhapsody in Blue,' Leading to American Programs by Famous Orchestra. *NYTimes* (dateline: Paris, April 5, 1928), April 8, 1928, Section 2, p. 6.

Brief review of the performance of the RiB on April 4, 1928, by the two pianists Jean Wiener and Clement Doucet, with the Pas de Loup Orchestra. Commenting on the Rhapsody, ". . . [W]ith its ingenious development of modern American tonalities, [it] left the French critics interested and the audience delighted . . ."*See:* **W1k**

B231.1. CRAWFORD, Richard. "Rethinking the Rhapsody." *Institute for Studies in American Music Newsletter* 28/1 (Fall 1998): 1+.

This feature article includes the thoughtful perceptions on RiB from a major G scholar. Also included in this special issue of the newsletter issued during G's centennial year are the following fine articles: "A Centenary Moment," by Stephen Banfield; "Gershwin on Disc," by Edward A. Berlin; "Time to Remember Zez Confrey," by Artis Wodehouse; and "Porgy and Bess–The Film."

B232. CRUTCHFIELD, Will. "Piano: Artis Wodehouse In Gershwin." *NYTimes*, Dec.3, 1987.

Review of Wodehouse's Merkin Hall concert of November 30, 1987, at which she performed three of her transcriptions of G's improvisations and her new transcription for solo piano of the RiB. Speaking about the three song transcriptions. Crutchfield stated: ". . . They were delightful . . ." And of the RiB transcription: ". . . It was not simply a fresh piano arrangement of the familiar score, but an interpreter's version drawing on the surviving broadcasts of Gershwin himself playing it. It is teasing in places where we are used to flashiness, it swings in places where we are used to even, strutting rhythyms, it is witty in places where we are used to brashness . . ." *See:* **W1bb**

B233. DOWNES, Olin. "Opera . . . Paul Whiteman and His Orchestra . . ." *NYTimes*, Nov. 16, 1924, Section 1, p. 30, col. 4.

Review of the November 15, 1924, Carnegie Hall concert by the Whiteman band. Gershwin performed the *Rhapsody*. The gist of Downe's thoughts is that just because of the February 12th successful concert, not everything subsequently done by Whiteman is good. However, Downes had praise for Gershwin's work: ". . . Gershwin's Rhapsody is a different case. It suffers from a rather flimsey and unduly extended form, from unnecessary repetitions, and a piano style dictated by reminiscences of Lizst. But it has ideas; it has impudence, the swagger and tiff of Broadway . . . the orchestration is novel and of a kind peculiar to American dance orchestras . . ." *See:* **W1g, B2132**

B234. DOWNES, Olin. *"Rhapsody in Blue* Introduced in a Historic Whiteman Concert," in *Olin Downes on Music: A Selection of His Writings during the Half-Century 1906 to 1955*, ed. by Irene Downes). New York: Simon and Schuster, 1957, pp. 83-85. [This review by Downes originally appeared in the *New York Times*, February

13, 1924, p. 16].

Review of the world premiere at the Aeolian Hall concert of 1924. "This composition shows extraordinary talent, just as it shows a young composer with aims that go far beyond those of his ilk, struggling with a form of which he is far from being master. It is important to bear both these facts in mind in estimating the composition. Often Mr. Gershwin's purpose is defeated by technical immaturity, but in spite of that technical immaturity, a lack of knowledge of how to write effectively for piano alone or in combination with orchestra, an unconscious attempt to rhapsodize in the manner of Lizst, a naiveté which at times stresses something unimportant while something of value and effectiveness goes by so quickly that it is lost—in spite of all this, he has expressed himself in a significant and, on the whole, highly original manner. . . .There was tumultuous applause for Mr. Gershwin's composition. There was realization of the irresistable vitality and genuineness of much of the music heard on this occasion . . . The audience packed a house that could have been sold out twice over." *See*: **W1a**

B235. ERICSON, Raymond. "Gershwin Night Evokes 'Ghosts;' Piano Roll of 1926
  Is Played at Promenades Concert." *NYTimes*, June 6, 1963.
  Review of the June 5, 1963, concert. "That Certain Feeling" and "Tip-Toes" were played by G via piano rolls. The reviewer called the effect "a wonderful, spooky moment." *See*: **W1x**

B236. FARRINGTON, James. *Ferde Grofé: An Investigation into His Musical Activities and Works.* Master of Music thesis. Tallahassée, FL: Florida State University, 1985, pp. 60-71. 193 pp.
  This is an excellent life and works approach to Grofé by music librarian Farrington. The above-cited pages contain specific information on the RiB and the "Whiteman Experiment." Farrington took advantage of the Ferde Grofé Tape Archive housed at Florida State University. The archive comprises 152 reel-to-reel tapes including pieces composed or arranged by Grofé, as well as interviews with Grofé. According to Farrington, based on the Florida State tape no. 121, "Grofé was most influential in his advice to Gershwin concerning the inclusion of the E-major melody of the andante section" in the *Rhapsody. See:* **W1a**

B236.1. FLEMING, Shirley. "Music in Concert: [RiB] BROOKVILLE, NY **Sahan Arzruni, piano: Gershwin originals."** *American Record Guide* 61/2 (March-April 1998): 44-45.

B237. GILMAN, Lawrence. "Music: Paul Whiteman and the Palais Royalists Extend Their Kingdom; Jazz at Aeolian Hall." *NY Tribune*, Feb. 13, 1924, p. 9.
  Gilman's mixed review of the premiere. "Let it be happily chronicled . . . that Mr. Whiteman's 'experiment' was an uproarious success . . . But it seems to us that this music is only half alive. Its gorgeous vitality of rhythm and of instrumental color is impaired by melodic and harmonic anaemia of the most pernicious kind . . . The rhythmical structure of these pieces, and the manner in which they are scored for the small orchestra of so many wind and percussion instruments and so few strings, cannot but delight the observant musician. Here are daring, and imagination, and ingenuity, and the trail of an adventurous spirit . . . Recall the most ambitious piece on yesterday's program, the 'Rhapsody in Blue' . . . and weep over the lifelessness of its melody and harmony, so derivative, so stale, so inexpressive. And then recall, for contrast, the rich inventiveness of the rhythms, the saliency and vividness of the orchestral color . . ." *See*: **W1a**

B238. GREENE, Bob. "United Airlines Faces the Music." *Chicago Tribune,* Feb. 16, 1988,

Section 5, p. 1.

B239. GROFÉ, Ferde. "Gershwin's *A Rhapsody in Blue*: A Manuscript and its Provenance
——As told by the scribe and donor, Mr. Ferde Grofé." Typescript at DLC in the
Recorded Sound Reference Center of the Music Division.

A typed transcript of a taped conversation with Grofé made on the occasion of his visit
to the Library of Congress to contribute the holograph score of the RiB on July 1, 1946. The
transcript contains a brief historical introduction to the *Rhapsody* by Edward N. Waters, then
Assistant Chief of the Music Division, followed by a brief description, in interview style, by
Grofé of his role in the creation of the work. According to Grofé, it was he and IG who
convinced GG to use the E Major melody of the slow theme, in place of a 6/8 melody George
was originally planing to use for that section. *See*: **B272**

B240. HENDERSON, W. J. "Gershwin's 'Rhapsody in Blue' Again." *NY Sun* **[NN]** May
3, 1930.

Short review of a May 2, 1930, performance of the RiB at the Roxy theater in New
York in connection with the playing of the *King of Jazz* film featuring Paul Whiteman. ". . . Mr.
Gershwin performed his share of the work with facility and in the cantabile section the Roxy
chorus was introduced with more or less success. Altogether it was a bright night for American
music of the jazz type . . ." *See*:**W1l.1, F6**

B241. "It's About Time," in **THOMSON, Virgil.** *The Musical Scene*. NY: Alfred A.
Knopf, 1945, pp. 17-19. *See*: **B266**

B242. MAISEL, Arthur. *Talent and Technique: George Gershwin's "Rhapsody in Blue."*
Phd. dissertation., City University of New York, 1989.
See: Annotation under "**Theses and Dissertations**" at **B2167**

B243. _____. "Talent and Technique: George Gershwin's 'Rhapsody in Blue,'" in
Trends in Schenkerian Research, ed. By Allen Cadwallader. NY: Schirmer
Books, 1990, pp. 51-69.

B244. "Many Stars Heard on Guild Program . . . Miss Jepson and Tibbett Sing Gershwin
Airs . . ." *NYTimes*, Feb. 21, 1938, p. 15.

Brief review of the concert at Carnegie Hall on February 20, 1938. The program
included José Iturbi's two-piano arrangement of RiB, but the review has no judgement of the
arrangement. *See*: **W1p**

B245. MAREK, George. "The Rhapsody in Blue—twenty-five years later." *Good Housekeeping* 128 (Feb. 1949): 4, 180-181.

Story of the Aeolian Hall concert of Feb. 12, 1924, at which the first rhapsody received
its premiere along with an assessment of how the reputation of the work stood on its twenty-
fifth anniversary. ". . . Well, how does the *Rhapsody* measure up after twenty-five years?
Remarkably well. Much better than other sensational compositions of the period, such as
Honegger's *Pacific 231* (composed the same year as the *Rhapsody*) and Ravel's *Bolero*
(1928). And this in spite of the fact that the *Rhapsody* has been played so often it has led nine
lives, and has been hacked to pieces . . ." *See*: **W1a**

B246. MOORE, Macdonald Smith. *Yankee Blues: Musical Culture and American
Identity*. Bloomington, IN: Indiana University Press, 1985, pp. 70-71, 94, 96, 98,
130-131, 134, 135-139, 141, *et passim*.

Brief references to GG here and there. There is a concise biography along with coverage of the Aeolian Hall concert at which the first rhapsody was premiered. *See:* **W1a**

B247. MORGAN, Alfred Lindsay. "New Musical Heights in Radio." *Etude* 60/12 (Dec. 942): 806.
Brief announcement about the radio broadcast of the rhapsody by the NBC Symphony under Toscanini. *See:* **W1r**

B248. MURPHY, George, and **Victor LASKY.** "*Say. . . Didn't You Used To Be George Murphy?*"Bartholomew House, 1970, pp. 50, 109, 134.
Significant references to GG, including a brief reference to the first *private* performance of the RiB, "before a group of invited friends at the Palais Royale after hours several nights before." Murphy was a original cast member in OTIS, 1931. *See:* **W1, W34**

B249. "Music Notes." *NYTimes* or *Herald*, Jan. 22, 1924, on same page as review of *Sweet Little Devil.*
Announcement of commencement of the rehearsals for the February 12, 1924, Aeolian Hall concert. "Paul Whiteman will hold three Tuesday rehearsals, beginning today, at the Palais Royale, for his program . . . on Lincoln's birthday . . ." *See:* **W1a, W19b**

B250. OSGOOD, H[enry] O[sborne]. "The Arts and Sciences, Music: The Jazz Bugaboo." *American Mercury* 6 (Nov. 1925): 328-330.
Article in defense of jazz and with high praise for the RiB.

B251. _____. *So This Is Jazz.* Boston: Little, Brown, 1926.
Concerns the development and first performances of Concerto and RiB; Charles Schwartz recommends seeing chapters 11-17, "which provide many details about Rhapsody in Blue and 'Gershwin, the White Hope.'" *See:* **W2a, W1a**

B252. P., F. D. "Gershwin in Two Roles During Stadium Concert; Soloist and Conductor as His Three Works Played." *NYHerald Tribune* **[NN]**, Aug. 29, 1930.
Review of the Lewisohn Stadium concert of August 28, 1930. ". . . The senior Gershwin work, the Rhapsody, remains the most colorful and the most effective in realizing the atmosphere of the best jazz in a non-Broadway form. The concerto, a more transitional work, has its interesting features, although the composer is not entirely at home in this form, with which he was dealing for the first time. 'An American in Paris' remains amusing, but its interest is not consistently maintained . . ." *See:* **W1m, W2g, W3d**

B253. PERSICE, Joseph E. "Gershwin's Flawed Jewel: The Story behind 'Rhapsody in Blue.'" *Modern Maturity* 26/6 (Dec. 1983-Jan. 1984): 26-30.
The story of the birth of the rhapsody along with considerable biographical detail about Gershwin.

B254. REICH, Howard. "'Rhapsody' rebirth: A legendary concert returns to the stage." *Chicago Tribune,* Feb. 21, 1988, Arts, Section 13, p. 12.
Announcement of a reconstruction by Maurice Peress' group of New York free-lance musicians of the original Aeolian Hall concert performed at Chicago's Auditorium Theatre, on February 28, 1988. The genesis of the RiB is reviewed and the article is enhanced by quotes from the violinist Kurt Dieterle (currently 89 years old), who was concertmaster at the original performance. *See:* **W1aa**

B254.1._____. "Music: Mitch's new pitch, Miller preaches the virtues of authentic Gershwin." *Chicago Tribune,* Nov. 15, 1987, p. 16.

A three-column article prefatory to Miller's conducting the Chicago Symphony in a concert including Gershwin music and some "sing-a-longs." *See:* W2q, W3r

B255. "Rhapsody in Blue." *Musical Opinion* 80 [=No. 956] (June 1957): 537.

Concerns the miniature score of Grofé's arrangement of Rhapsody for symphony orchestra, published in England by Chappell. *See:* **W1**

B256. "Rhapsody in Blue, for Piano and Orchestra." *Cincinnati Symphony Orchestra Program Notes,* Feb. 16, 1951, pp. 509-511. *See:* **W1u**

B257. "Rhapsody in Blue, for Piano and Orchestra." *Philadelphia Orchestra Program Notes,* Dec. 7, 1951, p. 211. *See:* **W1**

B258. ROSENFELD, Paul. "Aaron Copland: George Gershwin," in *An Hour with American Music.* Westport, CT: Hyperion Press, 1979, reprint of the 1929 edition published by J. P. Lippincott, Chap. VI, pp. 126-143.

Written when Copland was only twenty-nine years old, the author had high praise for him. Gershwin was thirty-one but Rosenfeld was less kind to him: ". . . Gershwin's Rhapsody in Blue, Piano Concerto, and An American in Paris have found a good deal of popular favor; and Gershwin himself is assuredly a gifted composer of the lower, unpretentious order; yet there is some question whether his vision permits him an association with the artists. The Rhapsody in Blue is circus-music, pre-eminent in the sphere of tinsel and fustian . . ." Rosenfeld continued his negative assessment, covering the Concerto and AiP in the same sarcastic tone. *See:* **W1, W2, W3**

B259. SCHIFF, David. "In 'Rhapsody in Blue,' Much Ado About Plenty o' Nuttin.'" *NYTimes,* Arts & Leisure Section., June 29, 1997, pp. 24-25.

"The 'Rhapsody in Blue' of George Gershwin is the most familiar, most performed and . . . highest-grossing piece of 20th-century music. It is also the most protean. Since its premiere, in 1924, it has taken ever-changing forms, from multiple concert versions of varied lengths and orchestrations to 15-second commercial sound bites. So when the Boston Pops recently announced the premiere of an 'authentic' version, restoring 50 measures of Gershwin's music to the score, critics and orchestra managers rushed to hear it. In a burst of irrational exuberance one writer claimed that the new version added four minutes to the piece and that the restored passages were 'rich with jazzy blues interpolations.' Perhaps the Pops was giving free beer to the critics. On sober inspection, the expanded version, edited by Alicia Zizzo, a concert pianist and composer, is neither new nor improved . . ." *See:* **W1, D610**

B260. _____. *Gershwin: Rhapsody in Blue* (Cambridge Music Handbooks). Cambridge, UK: Cambridge University Press, 1997. 126 pp.

The blurb on the back cover of this excellent book states that David Schiff "traces the history of the *Rhapsody's* composition, performance, and reception, placing it within the context of American popular song and jazz and the development of modernism. He also provides a full account of the different published and [a selection of the] recorded versions of the work and explores many stylistic sources of Gershwin's music." In Chapter 5, "Inception: The Aeolian Hall Concert," Schiff discusses each piece on the historic concert, based upon his listening to the two recent recorded reconstructions of the concert (**D266** and **D280**). In his penultimate chapter, eminent scholar Schiff includes brief discussions of Concerto, Ravel's

Piano Concerto in G, James P. Johnson's *Yamekraw*, the Ellington *Creole Rhapsody*, and G's *Second Rhapsody* and *"I Got Rhythm" Variations*. I noted that while Schiff cites the use of the RiB in the late eighties as a commercial for United Airlines, he omitted mention of its prominent use in *King of Jazz* (1930) and in the introduction to Woody Allen's well known movie *Manhattan* in (1979). *See*: **W1, F6, F29**

B261. SEAMAN, Julian. *Great Orchestral Music: A Treasury of Program Notes.* NY: Rinehart, 1950. (The Field of Music Series, Vol. 5)
Includes program notes.

B262. SHAW, Arnold. *The Jazz Age: Popular Music in the 1920's.* New York & Oxford Oxford University Press, 1987, 24, 39, 43-44, 47-56, 76-78, 86-87, *et passim.*
The title is somewhat misleading in that there is a great deal of jazz history here. G is also amply treated (thirty-five index references). Among these, there is a lengthy discussion of RiB, including a summary of the critic's opinion of its premiere (pp. 47-53). The 1924 premiere of RiB is covered, replete with quotations from the newspaper reviews, concluding ". . . It has been estimated that royalties from the sale of sheet music, records, and performances have mounted to a figure of almost $1 million since its introduction in 1924 . . ." An extensive bibliography, discography, and *Variety*'s list of "Golden 100 Tin Pan Alley Songs" are in the back matter of the book. In re: G's piano rolls: ". . . It is said that George Gershwin was inspired to make piano rolls as a result of listening to [Felix] Arndt [the composer of *Nola*] . . ." Good bibliography and discography. *See*: **W1**

B263. SMITH, Warren Storey. "'Rhapsody'" Gershwin Classic, The News of the World of Music." *Boston Post,* July 18, 1937.
Writing only a week after G's death, Smith considered the RiB the best of the "classical" compositions. He felt that the Concerto, *Second Rhapsody*, AiP, and P&B failed because in them "Mr. Gershwin tried to reconcile the irreconcilable." *See*: **W1, W2, W3, W4 W37**

B264. SPAETH, Sigmund. *A Guide to Great Orchestral Music.* NY: Modern Library, 1943.
Includes program notes for Concerto, RiB, and *Second Rhapsody*. *See*: **W2, W1, W4**

B265. STRAUS, Henrietta. "Jazz and 'The Rhapsody in Blue.'" *The Nation* 118/3061, (Mar. 5, 1924): 263.
Review of the Aeolian Hall premiere. ". . . In 'The Rhapsody in Blue' . . . one heard a dialogue between American slang and expressions as elemental as the soil. This work was indeed an extraordinary concoction gathered together during the month preceding its performance. It began with a braying, impudent, laughing cadenza on the clarinet and ended with its initial motive, a broad and passionate theme worthy of a Tchaikovsky. In between were orchestral interludes as fantastic and barbaric as any of a Rimsky-Korsakoff or Stravinsky, and piano passages whose intricate and subtle rhythms might have been danced in the rites of Astarte. The form was haphazard, and the playing often ineffectual, but its substance marked a new era . . ." *See*: **W1a**

B266. THOMSON, Virgil. "It's About Time," in his: *The Musical Scene.* NY: A. A. Knopf, 1945, pp. 17-19.
Reprint of the review from the *NYHerald Tribune*, dated November 2, 1942, accounting for the NBC Symphony concert of November 1. ". . . Gershwin's *Rhapsody in Blue*

is a modern classic . . . It got tough treatment yesterday, from Mr. [Benny] Goodman's opening lick to Mr. Toscanini's final wallop . . . He [Earl Wild] leaned on it [RiB] heavily and then began building up a Warner Bros. finale. It all came off like a ton of bricks   . . . [I]t was as far from George's own way of playing the piece as one could imagine . . ." *See*: **W1r**

B267. _____. "Landscape with Music," in his: *The Musical Scene*. NY: A. A. Knopf, 1945, pp. 25-28.

Reprint of a review dated July 11, 1943, of the July 4, 1943, performance, from the *NYHerald Tribune*. ". . . [Paul Whiteman] . . . did more than accompany a soloist for Gershwin's *Rhapsody in Blue*. He gave the work shape and ease, in spite of Mr. Ray Turner's rather poundy piano-playing. Spontaneity is the charm of that piece, and spontaneity is about the last quality one ever encounters nowadays in its performance . . ." Thomson was critical of Ussher's program notes. *See*: **W1t**

B268. "Toscanini, All-American."*News-Week* 20/19 (Nov. 9, 1942): 78.

Concerning Toscanini performing RiB on radio. *See*: **W1r**

B269. "The Twenty-Fifth Anniversary of the Premiere Performance." *Southwestern Musician* 15/8 (Apr. 1949): 31+. *See*: **W1a**

B270 . **ULRICH, Homer**. *Symphonic Music: Its Evolution Since the Renaissance*. NY: Columbia University Press, 1952.

Brief coverage of AiP, Concerto, and RiB by a distinguished musicologist. *See*: **W3, W2, W1**

B271. **WALKER, Ray.** "Down the Scale of Musical Memories." *Variety* 196, Oct. 20, 1954, p. 50.

Lengthy article of anecdotes by Walker, who was a charter member of ASCAP. Concerning the origins of the clarinet glissando at the opening of RiB: "GG did not write all of 'RiB.' The glissando effect was written by Ross Gorman, by accident. Gorman was playing sax [and clarinet] in Paul Whiteman's orchestra and one day, while rehearsing the 'Rhapsody,' Gorman and G had an argument before rehearsal. To get G mad, Gorman played the glissando at the beginning of the number—and George rushed over to him and exclaimed, 'That stays in!' . . ."

B272. **WATERS, Edward N.** "Gershwin's *Rhapsody in Blue*." *The Library of Congress Quarterly Journal of Current Acquisitions* 4/3 (May 1947): 65-66.

Waters described the visit of Ferdé to the Library of Congress on July 1, 1946, to present his original copy of the autograph manuscript of RiB to the collection there. On that occasion Grofé recorded ". . . a fascinating story of the work's origin and its rapid, almost desperate, approach to completion . . ." A transcript of that statement is available from the Library of Congress and excerpted at **B239**

B273. **WHITEMAN, Paul.** "George and the Rhapsody," in: **Merle ARMITAGE**, ed., *George Gershwin*. NY: Longmans, Green, 1938, pp. 24-26.

B274. _____. "The Gershwin I Knew." *Music Journal* (Apr. 1955): 19-21.

Article reminiscing about the success of the RiB, including short quotes from a selection of the critics present at the Aeolian Hall concert. **W1a**

B275. _____. "Rhapsody in Blue," in: *Rhapsody in Blue; the Jubilant Story of George Gershwin and His Music*. Hollywood: Warner Bros, 1945, pp. 5-6.

Chapter in the booklet issued concurrently with the film biography of 1945.

B276 . WHITEMAN, Paul, & Mary Margaret McBRIDE. *Jazz*. NY: J. H. Sears, 1926.

Includes Whiteman's account of his role in the premiere of *Rhapsody in Blue*. *See:*
W1a

B277. WOLFF, Hellmuth Christian. „Aspekte des ‚sinfonischen' Jazz Zu Gershwins Rhapsody in Blue." *Beiträge zur Musikwissenschaft* 20/2 (1978): 132-136.

An attempt to make a comparison between RiB and Beethoven's *Klavierkonzert* G-Dur, Op. 58.

B278. YOUNGREN, William. "Gershwin, Part I: Rhapsody in Blue." *New Republic* (Apr. 23, 1977): 21-24.

B279. ZILCZER, J. "Synaesthesia and Popular Culture: Arthur Dove, George Gershwin and the 'Rhapsody in Blue.'" *Art Journal* 44/4 (Winter 1984): 361-366.

A discussion of synaesthesia as it relates to two of Arthur Dove's "little known" jazz paintings, both inspired by and titled *Rhapsody in Blue* (Part I and Part II). A scholarly article; extensive explanatory footnotes with corresponding bibliography are appended.

W4. *SECOND RHAPSODY* for piano and orchestra. (March 14, 1931)

B280. ATKINS, Irene Kahn. *Source Music in Motion Pictures*. Rutherford, Madison, & Teaneck, NJ: Fairleigh Dickinson University Press, 1983, pp. 100-108.

Gives the genesis of the second rhapsody and its use in the film *Delicious*. ". . . George Gershwin's Second Rhapsody is generally considered by music critics to be one of his lesser works. So why be excited about the fact that the rhapsody was an important piece of source music for *Delicious*? There are some important reasons . . . [T]he rhapsody *does* represent a development in Gershwin's compositional technique and, if not the widely acclaimed piece that *Rhapsody in Blue* was, is an interesting, highly underrated composition . . . [I]n the film, what was at the time of the picture's production the full-length version of the rhapsody is heard. (The film version is 7 minutes long; the published orchestral score runs 12.5 minutes.) At least two books about George Gershwin's life and music state that only one minute of the rhapsody is heard . . . Obviously the authors have not seen the film . . . Marvin Maazel, who played the piano solo in the film recording . . . has stated that when the music was being recorded, the piano was placed at the rear of the orchestra. He blames the director David Butler for this arrangement. Butler, Maazel said 'feared the music would be distracting to the action.' Hugo Friedhofer, who worked closely with Gershwin on the orchestration of the rhapsody, has told how the sequence in which the music is heard was put together . . ." The author goes on to describe Janet Gaynor's scene and how the rhapsody was used under it. ". . . That Gershwin felt encouraged enough to continue working on the composition after his assignment on the film was finished, that he completed the work to his satisfaction, and that the early version of it remains on the Fox film sound track, are all historically important to the study of Gershwin and his music . . ." The book also points out that the recording of a studio performance of the rhapsody at NBC in NY, with Gershwin at the piano, has been duplicated and is available on the "Gershwin by Gershwin" album, Marc 56 Records 641 **(D717)** *See also:* **W4, F7**

B281. BLITZSTEIN, Marc. "Forecast and Review: Premieres and Experiments, 1932."
    Modern Music 10/3 (Mar.-Apr. 1932): 122.
        ". . . The point about George Gershwin's new *Rhapsody* . . . is that it is no better and
no worse than the earlier one, but that it is a repetition, in rather more pretentious terms. There
are to be found the same 'war-horse' pianisms of Lizst; the same evidence of thinking from one
four-measure phrase to another, of enough breath for the broad melodies, and too little for the
patchwork-padding; the same excessive climaxes; and the same talent for easy, and extremely
catchy tunes . . ."

B282. DOWNES, Olin. "George Gershwin Plays His Second Rhapsody for First Time
    Here with Koussevitsky and Boston Orchestra." *NYTimes*, Feb. 6, 1932, p. 14.
    See: **W4a**

B283. "Gershwin's 2d Rhapsody, Song of Rivets, Is Heard: Boston Applauds Composer
    Himself at the Piano." *NY Herald Tribune*, Jan. 30, 1932 (dateline: Boston, Jan. 29).
        Positive review of the premiere in Boston. "Written originally to be used with a motion
picture, the composition as it was played today was a greatly expanded work. The staccato
note of the riveter tinkled loudly from the treble clef of the keyboard as Gershwin's dynamic
fingers went into action and the orchestra took it up . . ." *See*: **W4a**

B284. HALE, Philip. "Rhapsody, No. 2 for Orchestra."*Boston Symphony Orchestra
    Programmes* 51/14 (Jan. 29-30, 1932): 838-854.
        Program notes for the world premiere, in part biographical. No new information here.
See: **W4a**

B285. JOHNSON, Harold Earle. *Symphony Hall, Boston.* Boston: Little, Brown, 1950,
    126-27, 339, 405.
    Includes information about the *Second Rhapsody*.

B286. KERNOCHAN, Marshall. "Notable Music: Gershwin's 'Second Rhapsody' and
    'Robin Hood.'" *The Outlook* 159-160/6 (Mar. 1932): 196.
        Negative review of the premiere of the second rhapsody. Referring first to RiB, the
reviewer exposed his lack of foresight: ". . . From the purely musical viewpoint, the germs of
its decay lie in its inherent monotony and lack of variety; its narrow possibilities have now
probably been well-nigh exhausted . . . Mr. Gershwin's new *Rhapsody* must be termed
disappointing in all respects. Almost totally devoid of ingratiating melodic material, it offers
us nothing but rhythms grown trite . . ." The reviewer continues in that manner, concluding
. . . the *Rhapsody* is a mere hash of conventional jazz rhythms and harmonies. Mr. Gershwin
played the piano in hum drum style . . ." *See*: **W4a**

B287. (Number inadvertently omitted)

B288. GILMAN, Lawrence. "Mr. Gershwin Plays His New Rhapsody With the Boston
    Symphony Orchestra." *NY Herald Tribune*, Feb 6, 1932. **[NN-L]**
        Positive review of the NY premiere of *Second Rhapsody*. "Only Mr. Paderewski,
perhaps, could have drawn a gathering comparable in numbers if not in kind . . ." *See*: **W4b**

B289. RHEIN von, John. "CSO closes season on a noisy note." *Chicago Tribune*, June
    14, 1985.
        Concerning a program by the Chicago Symphony Orchestra, June 13, 1985, including
the *Second Rhapsody*, conducted by Michael Tilson Thomas, von Rhein found fault with the

work: "For a long time the piece has been considered a musical poor-relation to the familiar 'Rhapsody in Blue,' despite its greater sophistication, and I am afraid its episodic structure makes this verdict seem not unfair. . ." *See:* **W4f**

B290. SPAETH, Sigmund. *A Guide to Great Orchestral Music.* NY: Modern Library, 1943.
    Includes program notes for Concerto, RiB, and Second Rhapsody. *See:* **W2, W1, W4**

STAGE SHOWS

General Bibliography

B291. KRASKER, Tommy, and **Robert KIMBALL.** *Catalog of the American Musical: Musicals of Irving Berlin, George & Ira Gershwin, Cole Porter, Richard Rodgers & Lorenz Hart.* National Institute for Opera and Musical Theater, 1988, pp. 57-164.

The Shows in Alphabetical Order

W15. *BLUE MONDAY* **(retitled** *135th Street* **by Paul Whiteman in 1925)** (1922)

B292. GOULD, Jack. "Television in Review: `135th Street', Written by Gershwin at 22, Is Offered by 'Omnibus' in Local Premiere." *NYTimes,* Mar. 30, 1953, p. 18.
    Review of the "first local production" of the operetta as produced over CBS's "Omnibus" series television program. ". . . As an interesting sidelight on Mr. Gershwin's career, the operetta undoubtedly had a certain curiosity value, but otherwise the work proved most ordinary and pedestrian . . ." *See:* **W15c, F33**

B293. MOTT, M. "[135th Street] Cheverly, Maryland." *Opera News* 46 (June 1982): 40.
    See: **W15f**

B294. SHIRLEY, Wayne D. "Notes on George Gershwin's First Opera." *I. S. A. M. Newsletter* 11/2 (May 1982): 8-10.
    Like all of Shirley's writings, this article bears his stamp of thoroughness, authenticity, and excellence. It is, therefore, indispensable to anyone planning to study and/or perform the work. Descriptions of the various arrangements are included, and the following is a typical, classic Shirley remark: ". . . The libretto [by B. G. (Buddy) De Sylva] does, in fact, read somewhat like freeze-dried *Pagliacci,* complete with a microscopic sung prologue admonishing the listeners that they are about to see an opera about lowlife . . ." *See:* **D425, D425.1, F33**

B295.   (Number inadvertently omitted)

B296. "The Live Art of Music." *Outlook* 142/2 (Jan. 13, 1926): 47-48.
    Review. "George Gershwin's . . . jazz opera . . . is not likely to add to his reputation." Article includes brief comparison of Concerto with Ottorino Respighi's *Piano Concerto in the Mixolydian Mode. See:* **W15b, F33**

B297. WARRACK, John. "British Opera Diary: **Blue Monday** . . ." *Opera* (Eng.) 38/9 (Sept. 1987): 1080-1081.
    Review of a performance by the Cameo Opera at St. Nicholas's Church, Warwick, England, on July 6, 1987. ". . . The actual numbers are not among Gershwin's most

distinguished, though 'Has anyone seen Joe?' and 'I'm gonna see my mother' are both vintage, and the entry of the customers into Mike's tavern has the authentic Gershwin strut . . ." *See:* **W15g**

W50. *CRAZY FOR YOU* (1992)

B298. DUNNING, Jennifer. "Crazy for Dance, a Broadway Gypsy Creates Her Own." *NYTimes*, Feb. 16, 1992, Arts & Leisure section, pp. 5, 23.
   Article prior to the opening of the show on Broadway, February 19, 1992. ". . . 'Crazy for You' is a show about dancing, whether a waltz for two across a desert under a wide-open Western sky or a scene in which miners and chorus girls dance with and on every loose prop in sight . . . The new musical . . . incorporates 18 Gershwin standards, 5 rediscovered Gershwin songs . . ." Much emphasis is given in the article to the role of Susan Stroman, superb choreographer for the show. *See:* **W50a**

B299. "London hit filling *Crazy* coffers." *Variety* 350 (Apr. 26, 1993):73. *See:* **W50a**

B300. EVANS, G. "Selling the crop of new Broadway shows." *Variety* 346 (Jan. 20, 1992):145+.

B301. FEINGOLD. M. "Theater: Progress reports (Shubert Theatre)." *The Village Voice* 37 (Mar. 3, 1992): 89. *See:* **W50a**

B302. GERARD, J. "'90s are crazy for unforgettable past." *Variety* 346 (Mar. 2, 1992): 61+. *See:* **W50a**

B303. INGRAM, B. "Horchow hopes B'way loves new *Girl Crazy;* Gershwin classic will get brand-new book, look." *Variety* 342 (Mar. 25, 1991): 91+. *See:* **W50a**

B304. "Lughnasa, *Crazy* win nods from Outer Circle." *Variety* 347 (May 4, 1992): 297.

B305. MORDDEN, Ethan. "When the Go-Everywhere Song Grew Exclusive; The Gershwin style continues to develop as the new 'Crazy for You' and other recordings show." *NYTimes,* May 17, 1992, Arts & Leisure section, pp. 1, 8. *See:* Full entry at **B1139** under **"Bibliography About Recordings."**

B306. MORLEY, S. "West End *Crazy* rakes in raves." *Variety* 350 (Mar. 8, 1993): 67+. *See:* **W50a**

B307. [NIGHTINGALE, Benedict]. "Theatre: . . . Souped-up Gershwin goes like crazy." *The Times* [London], March 4, 1993, Arts section, p. 1.
   Detailed, rave review of the then current London cast of *Crazy for You* playing the Prince Edward theatre. ". . . Super choreography, imaginative spectacle, a spirited cast, a story almost more preposterous than the original one, and songs from all over Georgetown and Iraville . . ." *See:* **W50a**

B308. "On stage (Shubert Theatre, New York)." Billboard 104 (Mar. 21, 1992): 122. *See:* **W50a**

B309. REGELMAN, K. "*Crazy* sells out to Japanese auds." *Variety* 350 (Feb. 15, 1993):

90. *See:* **W50a**

B310. _____. "Gershwin tuner headed for Japan." *Variety* 349 (Dec. 21, 1992): 67.
See: W50a

B311. "Reviews: abroad (Prince Edward Theater, London)." *Variety* 350 (Mar. 8, 1993):
70. *See:* W50a

B312. "Reviews: Broadway (Shubert Theater)." *Variety* 346 (Feb. 24, 1992): 256. *See:*
W50a

B313. "Reviews: B'way followup (Shubert Theater)." *Variety* 349 (Jan. 18, 1993): 83
See: W50a

B314. "Reviews: road (Music Hall in Fair Park, Dallas)." *Variety* 351 (May 24, 1993): 53.

B315. "Reviews: tryout (*Crazy for You* at Natl. Theater, DC)." *Variety* 345 (Dec. 23, 1991):
48. *See:* **W50a**

B316. RICH, Frank. "Crazy for You." *NYTimes,* Feb. 20, 1992.
    "When future historians try to find the exact moment at which Broadway finally rose
up to grab the musical back from the British, they just may conclude that the revolution began
last night. The shot was fired at the Shubert Theater, where a riotously entertaining show called
'Crazy for You' uncorked the American musical's classic blend of music, laughter, dancing,
sentiment and showmanship with a freshness and confidence rarely seen during the 'Cats'
decade. Arriving within days of the enchanting production of 'The Most Happy Fella,' its
next-door neighbor in Shubert Alley, and a few weeks before three other eagerly anticipated
American musicals promised for this season ('Guys and Dolls,' 'Jelly's Last Jam' and
'Falsettos'), 'Crazy for You' could not be a more celebratory expression of a long-awaited shift
in Broadway's fortunes . . . The miracle that has been worked here—most ingeniously, though
not exclusively, by an extraordinary choreographer named Susan Stroman and the playwright
Ken Ludwig—is to take some of the greatest songs ever written for Broadway and Hollywood
and reawaken the impulse that first inspired them . . . When the curtain rises, it is to the
elevating opening bars of 'Stairway to Paradise,' a song that is never sung in 'Crazy for You'
but, in a typical example of the evening's cunning, is used more than once as an incidental motif
to pump up the audience's pulse rate before springing the next theatrical surprise . . . in the
secular land of Broadway, starved musical-theater audiences can't be blamed for at least
dreaming that 'Crazy for You' heralds a second coming . . . ." Mr. Rich's positive review of
the show is lengthy, must reading for fans of 'Crazy,' bristling with facts about the show and,
indeed, the current state of American musical theater in general. *See:* **W50a**

B317. RICHARDS, David. "'Crazy for You" Is Splashy, But Magical Would Be Better."
    NYTimes, March 1, 1992, Arts & Leisure, Section 2, pp. 1, 5.
    Calling it "pretty much a top-to-bottom remake of 'Girl Crazy,'" Richards was on the
whole dissatisfied with this show, commenting in the opening sentence of this review: "'Crazy
for You' has everything a 1930's-style musical comedy could want, except a leading man and
a leading lady." While Richards lays most of the blame on Harry Groener and Jodi Benson, the
leading man and lady, respectively, he has high praise for choreographer Susan Stroman, whose
work is "not to be missed." *See:* **W50a**

B318. SHENTON, Mark. "Crazy For You." *Plays International* 8/6 (Jan. 1, 1993): 10.

When the Gershwin musical *Crazy For You* opened on Broadway a year ago, some of the most enthusiastic reviews for the show went to its choreographer, Susan Stroman, who was hailed as a new Agnes de Mille. What is the background to this Broadway newcomer and what persuaded her to give up being a dancer to devise dance for others? *See:* **W50a**

B319. VITARIS, Paula. "Crazy for Harry Groener." *Show Music* 8/4 (Winter 1992/93): 13-15.

Biographical story about the leading man Groener, who is pictured on the cover of this issue, along with description of his role in the show. *See:* **W50a**

B320. WITCHEL, Alex. "'If I Lost Every Single Penny, We Would Never Look Back.'" *NYTimes,* Feb. 16, 1992, Arts & Leisure section, pp. 23.

Interesting article about Roger Horchow, former owner of the Horchow Collection catalogue mail order house and co-producer of *Crazy for You. See:* **W50a**

B321. "Yank shows flag Olivier noms." *Variety* 350 (Mar. 15, 1993): 69+.

W12. *A DANGEROUS MAID* (1921)

I did not locate any worthwhile bibliography for this show.

W28. *FUNNY FACE* (Original title: Smarty) (1927)

B322. ATKINSON, J. Brooks "The Play: Astaires and Others." *NYTimes* (*NYTimes Theater Reviews*), Nov. 23, 1927, section 2, p. 28.

Review of the November 22, 1927, premiere at the newly opened Alvin Theatre in New York. ". . . Mr. Gershwin, maker of tunes, has composed several good songs for 'Funny Face,' the best of which bears the same title as the play. ''S Wonderful, 'S Marvelous,' 'Let's Kiss and Make Up,' and 'The Babbitt and the Bromide' manage successfully to avoid the old song banalities . . ." *See:* **W28c**

B323. "'Funny Face' A London Hit: Patrons Wait 30 Hours in Line to See Gershwin Musical Comedy." *NYTimes* (Special cable to the Times) (*NYTimes Theater Reviews*), Nov. 9, 1928, section 3?, p. 22.

Brief, but very complimentary, review of the London premiere, November 8, 1928, at the Princess Theatre. *See:* **W28d**

B324. "[Funny face] Resident Legit Review (Goodspeed Opera House)." *Variety* 303 (July 15, 1981): 78. *See:* **W28e**

B325. "[Funny Face] Theater: How Long Has This Been Going On? (Goodspeed Opera House)." *Village Voice* 26 (Sept. 2, 1981): 74. *See:* **W28e**
Review of a revival at **GOH.**

B326. WOOLLCOTT, Alexander. "The Stage." *NYWorld,* Nov 23, 1927.

Review of the premiere of *Funny Face* at the new Alvin Theatre, November 22, 1927. ". . . Gershwin has written a clever, sparkling, teasing score. I can imagine that there are many who would find such a *sauce piquante* of odd dissonances and stumbling measures a little tiring as steady fare, like a whole meal made out of Worcestershire sauce. But it is tickling music, all of it . . ." *See*: **W28c**

W11. *GEORGE WHITE'S SCANDALS OF 1920*, Second Annual Production

B327. "'Scandals' of 1920 Has All Essentials For Summer Hit." *NY Clipper* 68 (June 9, 1920): 18.
Review of George White's production, summer of 1920. ". . . The score which George Gershwin has composed for the show is not only superior to last year's music in the same show, but it is easily one of the most tuneful now being played on Broadway. Its colorful melodies and piquant jazz strains will not fail of popular rendition in the various cafes and places where orchestras hold forth. Arthur Jackson wrote the lyrics . . ." *See*: W11a

W13. *GEORGE WHITE'S SCANDALS OF 1921*, Third Annual Production

B328. "White's 'Scandals' A Fine Spectacle: Effective Scenes and Broad Comedy in the New Revue at the Liberty . . ." *NYTimes (NYTimes Theater Reviews)*, Jan. 12, 1921, 14:1.
Review of the 1921 version of the Scandals. Only one comment about the music: ". . . 'The Flying Dutchman' is one of the best numbers, both scenically and musically . . ."

B329. "'White's Scandals' Dancers Third Revue Is The Best Of All." *The New York Clipper*, July 21, 1921.
Review predominantly of the revue, with small mention of the music: ". . . the music by George Gershwin was melodious and colorful . . ."

B330. (Number inadvertently omitted)

W14. *GEORGE WHITE'S SCANDALS OF 1922*, Fourth Annual Production

See: John Andrew Johnson's essay in **SCHNEIDER, B1735.1**

W33. *GIRL CRAZY* (1930)

B331. ATKINSON, J. Brooks. "'Girl Crazy' A Lively and Melodious Show: George Gershwin's Music Set to Fresh and Amusing Lyrics by His Brother Ira." *NYTimes*, October 15, 1930, p. 27.
Review of the New York premiere, October 14, 1930, at the Alvin Theatre. ". . . Not the least important item in these tidings is the part played by the brothers Gershwin. . . ." *See*: **W33b**

B332. ATKINSON, J. Brooks.. "They Say It with Music." *NYTimes*, Dec. 28, 1930, Section 3, p. 1.
A commentary written some two months after the October opening. Calling the show "a thoroughly organic musical comedy," Atkinson concluded: ". . . George Gershwin has written a score full of gusto and merriment, and Ira Gershwin has written the most soundly comic lyrics this student of levity has heard in an American musical show . . ." *See:* **W33**

B333. [BEACH, Stewart]. "The Editor Goes to the Play." *Theatre Magazine* 52 (Dec. 1930): 26-28, 64, 66.

B334. BOEHNEL, William. "'Girl Crazy' Makes Hit as Diverting New Show."
NY Telegram, Oct. 30, 1930. **[NNMus]**
Referring to the premiere performance: ". . . It is a big and breathless musical show, full
of excellent tunes by George Gershwin . . . It is an excellent score, one of his best, and if I
know my radio as well as I think I do you will hear 'Embraceable You,' 'I Got Rhythm,' and
'But Not for Me' being played and sung about the same time this report appears, if not sooner
. . ." *See:* **W33b**

B335. "'Girl Crazy' a Lively and Melodious Show; George Gershwin's Music Set to
Fresh and Amusing Lyrics by His Brother Ira." *NYTimes,* Oct. 15, 1930, p. 27.
See: **W33b**

B336. "Keeping Custerville on the Map." *NYTimes,* May 10, 1931, Section VIII, p. 3.

B337. LEVY, Newman. "Drama: Three Shows with Music." *The Nation* 131/3408 (Oct.
29, 1930): 479-480.
Generally positive review. ". . . 'Girl Crazy' (Alvin) is the new Gershwin show, and to
those of us who would rather listen to a song by Gershwin than a symphony by Mahler a new
Gershwin show is an event . . . Ira Gershwin has demonstrated that he is the most skillful
versifier writing for the American stage . . " *See:* **W33b**

B338. LÜTTWITZ, Heinrich von. "Musica-Bericht: Ein Musical von Gershwin (dateline:
Düsseldorf) ." *Musica* 17 (1963): 281-282.
Review of a revival of *Girl Crazy* in Düsseldorf.

B339. MARTENS, Anne Coulter, Newt MITZMAN, and **William DALZELL,** adapters.
Girl Crazy, A Straight Play Version from the Musical Comedy. Chicago: Dramatic
Publishing Co., 1930, 1954.
The published play script based on the original libretto for the musical by Guy Bolton
and John McGowan.

B340. MERMAN, Ethel. *Who Could Ask For Anything More, as told to Pete Martin.* NY:
Doubleday, 1955.
Reference to Merman's role in *Girl Crazy* of 1930, and her audition for the part.

B341. MILNES, R. *"Girl Crazy:* Guildhall School of Music and Drama." *Opera* (Eng)
39 (Sept.1988):1140-1141.

B342. RATHBUN, Stephen. "'Girl Crazy' Scores: New Musical Makes a Hit at the Alvin."
NYSun, Oct. 15, 1930. **[NNMus]**
Review of the NY premiere of October 14, 1930. "With delightful melodies by George
Gershwin, who conducted the orchestra last night, 'Girl Crazy' is a 1930 pattern of a musical
comedy success . . ." *See:* **B33b**

B343. RUHL, Arthur. "'Girl Crazy' Gershwin Melodies Offered in New Musical Comedy
at Alvin." *NYTribune,* Oct. 15, 1930. **[NNMus]**
Positive review of the NY premiere. ". . . George Gershwin himself led an orchestra
in his own music most of the time, and several of his numbers were far above the average of
routine musical comedy. One song, 'Sam and Delilah,' sung by Miss Ethel Merman . . . was
especially interesting . . . the chorus droned their accompaniment, and in the high spots raised

their arms and their voices much after the manner of the Negro chorus in 'Porgy' [the stage play] . . . Another song, 'I Got Rhythm,' also sung by Miss Merman, was somewhat along the same line . . ." *See*: **W33b**

B344. "Seen on the Stage: 'Girl Crazy.'" *Vogue* (Dec. 8, 1930?): 136.
Brief review.

VON LÜTTWITZ, Heinrich. *See*: **B338.**

B345. WALDORF, Wilella. "Stage and Screen New . . 'Girl Crazy' Arrives; The Hilarious New Musical Comedy at the Alvin Boasts One of George Gershwin's Best Scores." *NYPost*, Oct. 15, 1930.
Review of the New York opening. ". . . Mr. Gershwin , who conducted last night's performance amid much applause, was probably the outstanding star of the evening . . . The Gershwin score is so uniformly tuneful that it is hard to select outstanding numbers without reeling off the entire song list . . . Miss Merman's three offerings, 'Sam and Delilah, 'I Got Rhythm' and 'Look What Love Has Done for Me,' created considerable excitement . . . 'Embraceable You,' sung by Allen Kearns and Ginger Rogers, has a nice lilt to it . . ." *See*: **W33b**

W22. *LADY, BE GOOD!* (1924)

B346. "Astaires Renew Lively Hold on Broadway: Dancers Welcomed Back in New Musical Comedy. Lady, Be Good, at the Liberty Theatre, Also Offers Lively Score, Abundant Humor and Colorful Stage Settings." *Journal of Commerce* [NY], Dec. 2, 1924. **[NN-L]**
Review of the premiere, December 1, 1924. ". . . 'Lady, Be Good' is also favored with an excellent score, the work of George and Ira Gershwin . . ." *See*: **W22b**

B347. GIDDINS, G. "Riffs: Reconstructing the Great White Way (Smithsonian Collection Recordings)." *Village Voice* 23, Jan. 9, 1978, p. 49.

B348. JABLONSKI, Edward. "[Album Notes for] George and Ira Gershwin's Lady, Be Good!" *Smithsonian American Musical Theater Series*, R 008, P14271, 1977, 4 pp.
Excellently researched and informative album notes for the Smithsonian Collection album named above. *See*: **D459**

B349. KRESH, P. "Musical Comedy Archives (recordings)." *Stereo Review* 40 (May 1978): 146-147.

B350. "'Lady Be Good' is Among the Best." *NYCommercial*, Dec. 2, 1924. **[NN-L]**
Review of the December 1, 1924, premiere at the Liberty Theatre.   ". . . The piece has a whistleable score by George Gershwin. Several of the songs will doubtless develop into real song hits, among them 'So Am I' and 'Juanita.' Indeed, 'Lady Be Good' may be said to glorify the great American jazz . . ." *See*: **W22b**

B351. MILNES, Rodney. "At the Musical: Lady Be Good." *Opera* (Eng.), 1987?
Critique of a student production at the Guildhall School of Music and Drama, given July 8, 198?. ". . . It would be hard to stand at the bar of heaven and swear hand on heart that the

Gershwins' . . . musical of 1924 is an immortal work of art, but a show that contains the title song 'Fascinating Rhythm' and the exquisite 'So Am I' has got a head start in that direction. The trouble is the book, which is huge fun but totally inconsequential . . ." *See*: **W22l**

B352. MITCHELL, Donald. "Concerts and Opera." *Musical Times* 97 (July 1956): 373-375.

Includes review of the revival of 1956 in London. ". . . It would not be possible . . . to sit out the text without the relief of Gershwin's music which, in the majority of numbers, is vibrant with melody so inspired that I was lured to the theatre thrice in one week. There is ample . . . to engage the serious musician's attention, not least the highly original invention and organization of the most popular 'hits' and the masterful ease with which Gershwin varies his tunes and builds them up into extended ensembles . . . No amount of repetition . . . can exhaust the oddly haunting impact of his leading themes . . ." *See*: **W22h**

B353. (Number inadvertently omitted)

B354. PAVLAKIS, Christopher. "THE BULLETIN BOARD: Performances of American Music, 'Lady, Be Good!' Revival." *Sonneck Society Bulletin* 13/3 (Fall 1987): 105.

Brief but informative report on the Fall 1987 revival at the Goodspeed Opera House in East Haddam, CT. ". . . At the time the revival was proposed, Tommy Krasker was working with Leonore Gershwin . . . on a report on all the Gershwin book musicals from 1919 to 1933. He began working with four scripts, two of them from the Library of Congress. One was dated December 6, 1924, nearly a week after the show opened. The second was from the fall of 1925, and showed considerable change. The third script was a version written sometime in the late 1940s, with references to contemporary celebrities and altered dialogue. The fourth, from 1963, was a revision by Guy Bolton, who wrote the original libretto with Fred Thompson. Krasker used all four versions to produce the restoration of the original story, as much as possible as it was when it was first performed more than sixty years ago . . ." *See*: **W22k**

B355. SNYDER, Louis. "'Lady, Be Good!' is lively as ever in Goodspeed revival." *Christian Science Monitor* 66 (June 12, 1974 [dateline: East Haddam, CT]): 6.

Review of the revival in June-July 6, 1974. ". . . It's as lively, tuneful, and care-dispelling as ever it was, and the joyous production here at Goodspeed Opera House . . . is enough to prove it . . ." *See*: **W22i**

W9. *LA-LA-LUCILLE!* (1919)

See: pp. 216-217, 240-242 in **SCHNEIDER, 1735.1**

W36. *LET 'EM EAT CAKE* (1933)

B356. ATKINSON, Brooks. "'Let 'Em Eat Cake: Being a Few Further Considerations of the Sequel to 'Of Thee I Sing' Based on a Second Visit." *NYTimes*, Nov. 12, 1933, Section IX, pp. 1, 3.

Review, based on attending the performance ten days after the NY opening. ". . . Still the impression persisted that, brilliant as 'Let 'Em Eat Cake' is in every show detail, it does not yield a thoroughly enjoyable evening. There is a rasp in the humor; it rubs off the ecstasy of complete delight . . . Make no mistake about the quality of this sequel . . . It is a brilliant technical job . . . [therefore] it might seem hypercritical to insist that it lacks fullness of enjoyment . . . The task of writing political satire in terms of a blaring show has taxed the strength of the authors to a point where the simple-hearted fun of the music hall has disappeared . . ." *See*: **W36b**

B357. _____. "The Play; Further Adventures of Wintergreen and Throttlebottom in 'Let 'Em Eat Cake.'" *NYTimes*, Oct. 23, 1933, section 1, p. 18.
Review of the NY premiere at the Imperial theatre, on October 21, 1933. ". . . Most of Mr. Gershwin's score is an amorphous labor, with nothing so robustly enjoyable as the election march and the Supreme Court fanfare that are repeated. but he has written in an amusing light vein . . . 'Let 'Em Eat Cake' is a first-rate job of music show-making. But, in this column's opinion, it is not the hearty, guffawing burlesque than began the legend . . ." *See*: **W36b**

B358. CALDWELL, Cy. "To See or Not to See: 'Let 'Em Eat Cake.'" *New Outlook* 162 (Dec. 1933): 46-47.
Short negative review, critical mainly of "the grim Kaufman-Ryskind book." ". . . This unhappy sequel to *Of Thee I Sing* is no merry song and dance around the Washington political Maypole. It is a shrill, strident wail about Facism, dictatorships, revolutions: a savage, labored, over-wordy, under-musical snarl which fairly could be named *Of Thee I Screech*." *See*: **W36b**

B359. CROWTHER, Bosley. "Throttlebottom Says:" *NYTimes*, Oct. 29, 1933, Section 9 p. 2.

B360. FOX, Terry Curtis. "Aced in the Berkshires [*Let 'Em Eat Cake*]." *Village Voice* 23, (July 17, 1978): 77-78.
Negative review of a 1978 Berkshire Theatre Festival revival of *Let 'Em Eat Cake*. ". . . Alas, in hiring himself to direct . . . [Allan] Albert may have buried *Let 'Em Eat Cake* instead of resurrecting it . . ." *See*: **W36e**

B361. GOLDBERG, Isaac. "Music in the Air: Let Us Eat Cake." *The Musical Record* 1/6 (Nov. 1933): 216-219.

B362. GOTTFRIED, Martin. "Theatre: Gershwin Revived and Well." *Saturday Review* 5 (Sept. 16, 1978): 35.

B363. HAMMOND, Percy. "The Theaters: 'Let 'Em Eat Cake; Bulls in a China Shop." *NYHerald Tribune*, Oct. 23, 1933, p. 12.
Review of the NY premiere show at the Imperial. Hammond concluded: ". . . 'Let 'Em Eat Cake' is a funnier, prettier, and crueller conspiracy against Washington, D. C. than was its parent, 'Of Thee I Sing' . . . Mr. Gershwin's music—to ears that are attuned to harmonies less expressive and discordant—suits the acid attitude of the play, while adding little to melody's gentle inflammations . . ." *See*: **W36b**

B364. _____. "The Theaters: Quieting Fears for the Finish of Mr. Moore on the Block." *NYHerald Tribune*, Oct. 29, 1933, Section 5, p. 1. *See*: **W36b**

B365. JENKINS, Speight. "Rare Gershwin with bite and vinegar." *New York Post*, May 22, 1978.
Review of a performance at Alice Tully Hall by the Gregg Smith Singers, Smith conducting, on May 20, 1978. Only about half of the work was presented using a new orchestration by Smith. *See*: **W36f**

B366. KASHIN, Bella. "Wintergreen for Commissar?" *NYTimes*, Jan. 6, 1935, Section 9, p. 3.

B367. KAUFMAN, George S., and **Morrie RYSKIND**. *Let 'Em Eat Cake*. NY: A. A. Knopf, 1933.

B368. KRUTCH, Joseph Wood. "Review." *The Nation* 137/3566 (Nov. 8, 1933): 550.
Short review of Cake as seen at the Imperial in 1933. Krutch took issue with the libretto and the conclusion of the work: ". . . They [Kaufman and Ryskind] have, however, allowed themselves to go so far in some of the scenes, and so clearly implied so deep a scorn for conservative and radical alike, that the trifling conclusion seems almost an evasion of the issues they themselves have raised . . ." *See*: **W36b**

B369. _____. "Drama: Three Good Plays." *The Nation* 137/3566 (Nov. 8, 1933): 548-550.
". . . As for 'Let 'Em Eat Cake' . . . several hundred people are probably . . . debating whether or not it is as good as or better than its predecessor . . . I shall not take sides but content myself with reporting that these further adventures of Wintergreen and Throttlebottom are vastly amusing during many moments even if they are also occasionally dull. The music seems to me better than in the previous instalment [sic] of this epic and the general smartness beyond criticism . . ." *See*: **W36b**

B370. MANTLE, Burns, ed. *The Best Plays of 1933-34; And the Year Book of the Drama In America*. NY: Dodd, Mead, 1934.

B371. P., H. T. [PARKER, H. T.] "From Beans to Cake, An Account of Those Mad Doings Down By the Common." *NYTimes* [(dateline: Boston, Oct. 6, 1933), Section 10, p. 2.
Mixed review of the Boston tryout based on Parker's second hearing. "The alterations in 'Let 'Em Eat Cake' began promptly. Before the second performance there were material cuts. More are to come. Several of the conversational scenes are also to be revised to bring about what Mr. Kaufman calls 'a dictator approach.' By the middle of next week, well before the transfer to New York, the piece should be close to final form. Meanwhile, a wide public is flocking to see and hear; but obviously of two opinions . . ." *See*: **W36a**

B372. _____. "'Let 'Em Eat Cake' Cheered in Boston; 200 New Yorker's See Opening of Gershwin-Kaufman-Ryskind Musical Revue; Mayor Curley on Stage; Greets Authors at Conclusion of Continuation of Story of Wintergreen and Cohorts." Special to the *NYTimes*, Oct. 3, 1933 [dateline, Boston, Oct. 2], p. 26.
Descriptive commentary about the premiere tryout in Boston, Oct. 2. ". . . It [Cake] is less sequel [to OTIS] than independent piece . . . Ira Gershwin's play of words, rhyme and humor give an edge to the lyrics. George Gershwin has written a more or less satirical music, built up into long scenes shary-rhythmed and modernist enough for a musical play. In recent years he has done nothing better . . ." *See*: **W36a**

B373. SKINNER, Richard Dana. "The Play." *Commonweal* 19 (Nov. 10, 1933): 47.

B374. "Theatre . . . Let 'em Eat Cake . . ." *Time* (Oct. 30, 1933): 29-30.
This is *Time's* negative review of the first Manhattan production. ". . . [W]hen the curtain fell . . . there was an embarrassing dearth of applause. Critics and spectators went out grumbling that the nation's great musicomedy quadrivirate had lain down on their job, had

served a poorly warmed-over dish . . . their [Kaufman and Ryskind's] libretto wanders dreamily away into demented unreality . . . The jokes . . . fall flat. So do George Gershwin's antiphonal choral numbers which have grown longer and more tedious since he first used them in *Strike Up the Band* (1927). Brother Ira Gershwin's flair for writing silly repetitive lyrics no longer seems a sprightly burlesque of all lyric-writing . . ." *See*: **W36b**

B375. WYATT, Euphemia Van Rensselaer. "The Drama: Royal Humor." *Catholic World* 138 (Dec. 1933): 336-344.

W31. *SHOW GIRL* (1929)

B376. ATKINSON, J. Brooks. "The Play: Behind the Scenes With Ziegfeld." *NYTImes,* July 3, 1929.
Atkinson gave a mixed review of the NY premiere. ". . . The task of blending materials that are episodic and individual makes 'Show Girl' the least notable of the recent Ziegfeld productions . . . Although Mr. Gershwin's spray of notes does not result in a first-rate score, it has moments of vividness or melody . . ." *See*: **W31b**

B377. _____. "Summer: In Theatrical Memorial." *NYTimes* (*NYTimes Theater Reviews*), Aug. 25, 1929, VIII, 1:1.
Atkinson's report on the show a month after its July opening. ". . . Although Mr. Gershwin's score is not one of his most brilliant, it improves upon second hearing—especially his 'An American in Paris,' a turbulent, exotic rhapsody in red. Unlike most popular song writers, Mr. Gershwin composes with most flexibility when he is serious and ambitious . . ."

B378. BELLAMY, Francis R. "The Theatre." *Outlook and Independent* 152/13 (July 24, 1929): 515.
Review of *Show Girl*. ". . . In reporting to you on Ziegfeld's 'Show Girl,' . . . we must confess that we are only slightly enthusiastic . . . Also, George Gershwin has written the music; and we think so much of Gershwin that it's pretty hard for him to come up to our expectations . . . As for George Gershwin's music, with the exception of the 'American in Paris,' it is only fair, considered as the product of any good Broadway musical from Mr. Gershwin. Considered as melody from Mr. Gershwin, it's much below par . . ."

B379. HAMMOND, Percy. "The Theaters: 'Show Girl' is Mr. Ziegfeld and His Associates in Their Best Form." *NYHerald Tribune*, July 3, 1929, p. 12. **[NN-L]**
Highly complimentary review of the New York premiere, July 2nd. The reviewer was especially pleased with Ruby Keeler (Al Jolson's then new bride) as Dixie Dugan and Jimmy Durante. *See*: **W31b**

B380. "The New Plays; A Splendid Show." *The World* [NY], July 3, 1929.
Review. "To his own theatre last night Florenz Ziefeld brought a musical comedy of the first rank . . . Taking this unpretentious saga and decking it with the music of George Gershwin, the scenic wizardry of Joseph Urban, elegant ensembles and his own unquestionable good taste . . . Mr. Ziegfeld has transmuted it into a glamorous fable, without letting any heavy hand too thickly sugarcoat its incisive ironie . . As the curtain rises for the second act the orchestra suddenly breaks into the raveling and unraveling rhythms of George Gershwin's newest symphonic piece 'An American in Paris' . . . This is one of the high spots of the evening . . ." *See*: **W31b, W3**

W19. *SWEET LITTLE DEVIL* (A Perfect Lady) (1924)

B381. "Miss Binney Returns in a Musical Comedy." *Telegram* [NY], Jan. 22, 1924.
Review of the show. ". . . There are at least two songs, 'Virginia' and 'Someone Believes in You,' that will be distinct hits . . ." *See:* **W19b**

W24. *TIP-TOES* (1925)

B382. CROCE, Arlene. "Dancing: Soundtracks." *New Yorker* 55/8 (Apr. 9, 1979): 147-153.
Focusing on the dance in an extensive column, Croce reviewed the 1979 Goodspeed Opera House revival of *Tip-Toes* while it was playing at NY's Brooklyn Academy of Music. ". . . The production is an especially faithful one: many of the original musical arrangements were used; there is only one interpolated number ('Why Do I Love You?'); and the chorus reappears for the 'Sweet and Low-Down' encore carrying kazoo trombones, as in the original production . . ." *See:* **W24d**

B383. FEINGOLD, Michael. "Theatre: Burbling White Sugar." *Village Voice* 24, Apr. 9, 1979, pp. 91-92.
Mixed review of the 1979 revival at the Brooklyn Academy of Music (based on the revival originally produced at the Goodspeed Opera House). ". . . The songs and the dances, along with Ms. Engel and Mr. Thacker, make *Tip-Toes* something to love, and a lovable bad show is always much more fun than a show which is point perfect but stone cold . . ." *See:* **W24e**

B384. GOTTFRIED, Martin. "Theater: Gershwin Revived and Well." *Saturday Review* 5/24 (Sept. 16, 1978): 35.
This article is intended as a review of the 1978 revival of *Tip-Toes* at the Goodspeed Opera House, but is actually an essay about G and a selection of his works for the theatre. ". . . Gershwin carved out a niche for himself. His musical comedy scores made theater music; he wrote with a sense of the stage . . . Others have written great melodies, but the harmonies and rhythms of our theater are Gershwin's own. He practically invented the Broadway overture as we know it." Other shows mentioned in the article include: *Girl Crazy, Strike Up the Band, Of Thee I Sing, Let 'Em Eat Cake,* and P&B. *See:* **W24d, W33, W27, W34, W36, W37**

B385. GUSSOW, Mel. "Stage: 'Tip-Toes' of '25 By the Gershwins Opens." *NYTimes,* March 2?, 1979.
Generally a positive review of the 1979 revival at the Brooklyn Academy of Music. *See:* **W24e**

B386. MADD. "New Shows in Stock: Tip-Toes." *Variety* 291, May 24, 1978, p. 98.
Negative review of a revival opening May 30, 1978. "The Goodspeed Opera House [East Haddam, CT] has begun its 1978 season with a revival of G and IG's pleasant but unexciting 1925 Broadway musicomedy, 'Tip-Toes.' Except for the spirited choreography by Dan Siretta, there's very little else to recommend . . . The fault lies with a tired script, miscasting of several leading roles, and mostly uninspired staging . . ." *See:* **W24d**

B387. "New Shows in Stock (Goodspeed Opera House)." *Variety* 291, May 24, 1978, p. 98. *See:* **W24d**

B388. OLIVER, E. "[Tip-Toes] Off Broadway (Brooklyn Academy of Music)." *New Yorker* 55 (Apr. 9, 1979): 99-100. *See:* **W24e**

B389. "'Tip-Toes' Here With Tunes: Gershwins Please in New Musical Play, Aided by
Queenie Smith." *NYTimes (NYTimes Theater Review)*, Dec. 29, 1925, 20:2.
"... [The audience] found pleasure ... in everything with which Mr. Gershwin
provided it ... To at least one in last night's audience... the Gershwin score seemed to be
good but not irresistible in its just demands for cheers. There are two or three tunes—'Looking
for a Boy, 'Sweet and Low Down,' and 'It's a Great Little World,' one ventures to guess—
that may be destined to be restaurant pests this Winter. For the rest, the tunes seemed to be
average pretty-pretty ..." *See:* **W24b**

B390. [Tip-Toes] "Resident Legit Review (Brooklyn Academy of Music)." *Variety* 294
(Apr. 4, 1979): 124. *See:* **W24e**

B391. WATT, Douglas. "A Delightful 'Tip-Toes.'" *Daily News* [NY], Mar 27, 1978.
"'Tip-Toes,' a handsome revival of a 1925 Gershwin show at the Brooklyn Academy
of Music's lovely Carey Playhouse ... is exhilarating ... The score is one of George's finest,
brimming with the distinctive melodic, harmonic and rhythmic vitality of the young and
seasoned composer ..." *See:* **W24e**

B392. WOOLLCOTT, Alexander. "The Stage, Mr. Gershwin's Latest [*Tip-Toes*]."
NY World, Dec. 29, 1925.**[NNMus]**
Review of the New York premiere. "... The new musical comedy ... last night is made
altogether captivating by the pretty ... infectious music of George Gershwin ... It was ...
Gershwin's evening, so sweet and sassy are the melodies he has poured out ... so fresh and
unstinted the gay, young flood of his invention. The new tunes range from the seductive,
almost cloying waltz he wrote called 'Looking for a Boy' to the hot, panting, exuberant
Charleston tune, that 'Sweet and Low Down'—to say nothing of the pert ditty entitled 'These
Charming People' ..." *See:* **W24e**

W25. *SONG OF THE FLAME*, A Romantic Opera (1925)

B393. ATKINSON, Brooks. "THE PLAY: An Operatic Spectacle, Song of the Flame."
NYTimes, Dec 31, 1925.
Review of the premiere, December 30, 1925, at the Forty-Fourth Street Theatre.
"... In spite of the generous quantity of music composed by Mr. Stothart and Mr. Gershwin,
some of it pretentious in form and technique ... nothing is so striking as the samovar room
scene of the final act ..." *See:* **W25b**

B394. GABRIEL, Gilbert W. "Sumptuous Song of the Flame: Mr. Hammerstein Goes
One Grander With a Glorified Revolutionary Romance." *NYSun*, Dec 31, 1925.
[NNMus]
Positive review of the premiere describing the lavishness of the production, including
"a company of 200" and "an orchestra of grand operatic size," but with no particular comment
about the music. *See:* **W25b**

B395. HAMMOND, Percy. "The Theaters, 'Song of the Flame,' a Large, Lovely and
Solemn Semi-Grand Opera." *NYTribune*, December 31, 1925. **[NNMus]**
A not altogether complimentary review of the premiere. "...The costly George
Gershwin is one of his [Oscar Hammerstein's] composers, and Herbert Stothart, who is no
mean bourgeoise in matters of stipend ... is another. Hammond conceded that the work

represented " a large, beautiful and serious feast . . ." *See*: **W25b**

B396. R., W. "The New Play; Mr. Hammerstein Goes Russian." *The World* [NY], Dec. 31, 1925.

Review. ". . . George Gershwin and Herbert Stothart obliged with a score of richness and variety. The title song is a battle cry of the Four Hundred Million, much in the character of 'The Song of the Vagabond' in 'The Vagabond King.' There were comic songs, and love songs in the approved style, and a swinging waltz called 'You May Wander Away' . . ." *See*: **W25b**

B397. VREELAND, Frank. "'Song of the Flame.' In Hammerstein's Dazzling New Operetta, with Tessa Kosta, New Yorkers See More Russians—Yes, and Like It!" *NYTelegram*, Dec. 31, 1925.

Glowing review of the NY premiere, December 30, 1925. ". . . The operetta was further emblazoned on Broadway because it made this Gershwin Week just as much as Christmas Week. Even after falling under the enticement of his tripping tunes in the new 'Tip-Toes' the night before we still had admiration left over for his gadding, prodding music . . . swelling, now and then to rich proportions that must have echoed down to the Metropolitan Opera House . . . Gershwin does not seem to be striving so urgently to be mischievous as in 'Tip-Toes.' The syncopation is insidious but never obtrusive . . ." *See*: **W25b**

W27. *STRIKE UP THE BAND* (1927)

B398. COLLINS, William B. "Theater: Striking up a lost 'Band.'" *Philadelphia Inquirer* [*Newsbank* PER 5:G8], June 29, 1984.

Negative review of this revival, based on attendance at opening night, June 27. ". . . [L]ong stretches of simple-minded dialogue and stage action filled in the spaces between numbers. A generally first-rate cast acquitted itself with honor, giving full value to some superior songs by George and Ira Gershwin and heroically showing no embarrassment at the labored jokes and progressively incoherent book . . ." *See*: **W27c**

B399. DICKMANN, Ken. "Strike Up The Band Lights The Stage: Pasadena's California Music Theater revives the lost Gershwin and Kaufman musical satire." *Theater Week* 2/4 (Sept. 5, 1988): 32-37.

Background story on this revival including discussion of Tommy Krasker's role in reconstructing the 1927 version and quotes from the cast members. *See*: **W27d**

B400. PIRIE, Joan. "Winning the Battle and Losing the War: The 1927 'Strike Up the Band.'" *Sonneck Society Newsletter* 7 (Fall 1981): 12, also reprinted in **Loney-Glenn** (ed.), *Musical Theatre in America*. Westport, CT: Greenwood Press, 1984.

B401. RICHARDS, David. "Bringing Back the Band; Philadelphia Revives Gershwin's Musical." *Washington Post* (dateline: Philadelphia), July 6, 1984, Style section. A generally complimentary, descriptive review. *See*: **W27c**

B402. ROSENBERG, Deena. "Theater: A 'Lost' Musical By The Gershwins Makes a Comeback." *NYTimes*, June 24, 1984, pp. H4, H13.

This highly informative and long article announces the revival which opened on June 27, 1984, at the Walnut Street Theater in Philadelphia, the first performance since 1930. Two versions of the script and most of the lyrics were found at the New York Public Library.

According to Eric Salzman, "the 1927 version is much the zanier version, more cutting and more interesting . . . Mr. Salzman decided to stay close to the early version in his adaptation, with some additions from the 1930 score." *See*: **W27c**

B403. SNEAD, Elizabeth. "'Strike up the Band': No Longer in Tune with Times."*USA TODAY*, Oct. 31, 1995.

EAST HADDAM, Conn. "1927 version of Strike Up the Band has long had a mysterious, subversive mystique . . . As resurrected through Dec. 17 at the Goodspeed Opera House, which specializes in problem musicals, it seems like a rebuttal to a long-lost argument. That's not the only problem: The show's melding of George S. Kaufman's Marx Brothers-style humor and the score's jazz-age answer to Gilbert and Sullivan is a hybrid that neither the cast nor director Charles Repole seems sure what to do with. One has to respect Goodspeed for performing this story—about an American cheese mogul (played by Broadway veteran Ron Holgate) declaring war against Switzerland—with minimal revisions. While it's on safe ground with the two pairs of lovers (with fun performances by Emily Loesser and Jason Danieley), other characters refer to now-obscure comic conventions. The score, though, often soars . . ." *See*: **W27e**

B404. ". . . Revival 'Strike's' [sic] middle ground." *Herald Examiner* [Los Angeles], Aug. 8, 1988, pp. B1, B4.

While this reviewer liked some things about the production, his consensus was generally negative. ". . . Watching 'Strike Up the Band' gradually feels like an odd form of musical ancestor worship. You can almost sense Kaufman's ghost cringing in the Pasadena Civic, growling for one more chance to rewrite that second act. The lesson in Pasadena for musical scholars seems to be that you can restore, but you can't always resurrect." *See*: **W27d**

B405. O'CONNOR, Thomas. "'Band' strikes gold with restored songs but ultimately fails." *The Orange County* (CA) *Register*, Aug. 8, 1988, pp. F1, F3.

Review of the premiere of the production by the Pasadena California Music Theatre at the Pasadena Civic Auditorium, August, 1988. Although O'Conner liked the songs, this is generally a negative review. ". . . Even allowing for some B-minus production values, maybe this 'Strike Up the Band' comes to the plate with a couple of strikes already on it. Kaufman's book never reconciles the clunkiness of its story line . . . and marshalling those lovely Gershwin tunes in the service of satire might be beyond even a firmer, more imaginative production hand . . ." *See*: **W27d**

B406. WEBSTER, Daniel. "A promising debut for Phila. festival." *Philadelphia Inquirer*, July 15, 1984, entertainment/art section.

More a review of the entire American Music Theater Festival than of *Strike Up the Band*. ". . . [T]he production that played at the Walnut was a proof of the ingenuity and dedication of directors Eric Salzman and [Marjorie] Samoff . . ." *See*: **W27c**

W32. *STRIKE UP THE BAND* (1930)

B407. ATKINSON, J. Brooks. "The Play: In Ridicule of War." *NYTimes*, Jan. 15, 1930, p. 29.

Review of the first NY performance of the 1930 version. ". . . Promising as the satire is in its early moments, it becomes so involved and diffuse when it attacks the war spirit that the fun largely trickles out of it. The Gershwin's have done much better with it in their score and lyrics . . . In the other set pieces of musical comedy composition Mr. Gershwin has also managed to avoid tattered patterns . . . Mr. Gershwin avoids melody as if it were only a burgher's delight . . . After all, the scores for musical comedy should be simple and frankly popular at times. But with his oratorios and chorals and his satiric touches here and there he has made an original contribution to the comic musical stage . . ." *See*: **W32b**

B408. [**BEACH, Stewart**]. "The Editor Goes to the Play." *Theatre Magazine* 51 (March 1930), 44-48, 70, 72.

B409. BELLAMY, Francis R. "The Theatre: The Plays of the Week." *Outlook and Independent* 154/5 (Jan. 29, 1930): 191.
　　Review . ". . . As an antidote for things Russian we have hitherto been unable to think of anything better than Clark and McCullough in a new musical comedy by the Gershwin *freres* based on a libretto by George Kaufman. But after seeing *Strike Up the Band* we are not so enthusiastic . . . Of all things, to have Gershwin's music turn noisy, unoriginal and even reminiscent! . . ." *See*: **W32b**

B410. BENCHLEY, Robert. "Theatre." *New Yorker* 5 (Jan. 25, 1930): 27-28. *See*: **W32b**

B411. BROWN, John Mason. "'Strike Up the Band' at the Times Square . . . The Play: 'Strike Up the Band an Uproarious and Exceptional Musical Comedy in Which Clark and McCullough Return." *NY Evening Post*, Jan. 15, 1930, p. 14.
　　Review of the 1930 version in its NY opening, January 14, 1930. ". . . By no means least among its pleasures are the lyrics and the music that the Gershwins have supplied. Ira Gershwin's lyrics, especially in the chorus numbers, are ingenious in their rhymes, witty in their writing, and possessed of an uncommon felicity. While George Gershwin's score is not filled with melodies that are immediately hummable (if one excepts 'Strike Up the Band' and 'What's the Use of Hanging Around With Me') it is at all times pleasant and insinuating. And in its orchestration it is unusually effective . . ." *See*: **W32b**

B412. CLAUSEN, Bernard C. "Strike Up the Band!" *Christian Century* 48 (July 8, 1931): 899-901.

B413. GARLAND, Robert. "'Strike Up the Band:' War and Tired Business Man Targets of its Cutting Satire, Song-and-Dance Show Close to Being a Pair of Musical Comedies, Says Reviewer of Premiere—Jazzy and Jestful Tunes Abound in Long Performance." *NYTelegram*, Jan 15, 1930, p. 8. **[NN-L]**
　　Mixed review of the second version in its NY premiere. ". . . As for Mr. George Gershwin's music, it is better than Mr. Ira Gershwin's lyrics. 'Soon' has the real George Gershwin lilt. 'What's the Use of Hanging Around With You' and 'I've Got a Crush on You' are jazzy and jestful, and the scoring of 'Three Cheers for the Union' is too good to be true. On the whole, the composer has turned out a good Grade B score of which 'The Madamoiselle from New Rochelle' is the outstanding disappointment . . ." *See*: **W32b**

B414. "Heading for Broadway." *NYTimes*, Dec. 29, 1929, Section 8, p. 4. *See*: **W32a**

B415. LITTELL, Robert. "The New Play." *NY World*, Jan 15, 1930. **[NNMus]**
　　Glowing review in connection with the NY opening. ". . . 'Strike Up the Band' is the swellest phoenix that ever rose from the ashes . . . Last night was particularly memorable because the leader of the orchestra which played some of the best tunes he has ever written was George Gershwin himself . . ." *See*: **W32b**

W30. *TREASURE GIRL* (1928)

B416. LITTELL, Robert. "The Play: Gertrude Lawrence and Gershwin Music in the New Aarons and Freedley Show, 'Treasure Girl.'" *NYPost* **[NNMus]**, Nov. 9, 1928.

Review of the November 8, 1928, NY premiere, comparing it disadvantageously, to Noel Coward's *This Year of Grace* which opened, unfortunately, the night before. About the music: ". . . The bright spot was the music, though even here it must be said that George Gershwin has done better. Perhaps he has taught us to expect too much, and leaves us disappointed if all his tunes aren't as original and gifted as his best ones . . ." *See:* **W30a**

W26. *OH, KAY!* (1926)

B417. Adil. "Shows Out Of Town: Oh, Kay." *Variety* 291, July 26, 1978, p. 81.

Negative review of revival of *Oh, Kay!*, stemming from a tryout in Toronto (July 19) prior to Washington and then Broadway. *See:* **W26f**

B418. ATKINSON, J. Brooks. "The Play: Bootlegging Bedlam, OH, KAY!" *NYTimes* (*The NYTimes Theater Reviews*), Nov. 9, 1926.

Review of the NY premiere. ". . . Mr. Gershwin's score is woven closely into the fun of the comedy. Sometimes it is purely rhythmic as in 'Clap Yo' Hands' and 'Fidgety Feet'; sometimes it is capricious as in 'Do, Do, Do.' Mr. Gershwin also composes in the familiar romantic vein of 'Someone to Watch Over Me.' In this number Miss Lawrence embellishes the song with expressive turns on the stage . . ." *See:* **W26b**

B419. Burm. "Off-Broadway Reviews: Oh, Kay!." *Variety* 218, May 4, 1960, p. 60.

A positive review of this revival at the East 74th Street Playhouse in New York which opened in April of 1960. ". . . The virtue of the current production is that it doesn't pretend to be anything more than an honest recreation of a vintage musical. There's no spoofing or mugging to obscure the naivete of a musical diversion written before Freud became the rage . . . Five numbers from other G shows and films have been smoothly integrated into the current production . . ." "Little Jazz Bird" (from *Lady Be Good!*) and "Clap Yo' Hands" are two of these tunes. *See:* **W26e**

B420. HOLDEN, Stephen. "Reviews/Theater: A Gershwin-Wodehouse Spoof of Prohibition." Special to the *NYTimes* (dateline: East Haddam, CT, Oct. 29), Nov. 1, 1989.

Generally complimentary review. ". . . The relocation to Harlem makes sense . . . And much of the Gershwin's score . . . also has a Cotton Club ambiance . . ." *See:* **W26g**

B421. JASEN, David A. *The Theatre of P. G. Wodehouse.* London: B. T. Batsford, 1979.

This book covers a selection of Wodehouse's works for the theatre, among them *Oh, Kay!*, *Rosalie*, and the play version of *Damsel in Distress*, the latter from which the motion picture evolved. The coverage of *Oh, Kay!* is particularly interesting for its inclusion of Gertrude Lawrence's cast-autographed copy of the playbill of the original Broadway production (1926), and information on the Off-Broadway revival of April 1960. With the latter is a picture of the album cover from the original cast album (**D482**). *See:* **W26b, W26e, W29, F11**

B422. JOHNSON, Malcolm L. "Music, dance make 'Oh, Kay!' a winner." *The Hartford* [CT] *Courant* **[GOH]**, Oct. 23, 1989, p. ?

"From its jazzy overture in front of a glowing red hot and blue drop, right through to its last embrace, [this show] can brighten even the dreariest of rainy autumn nights . . ." *See*: **W26g**

B423. OLIVER, Edith. "The Theatre: Gershwins' Return." *New Yorker* (Nov. 12, 1990): 104-105.

A positive review. ". . . [T]he spirit and dancing and singing of the black company that David Merrick has assembled for his revival . . . are so glorious that it is nearer a crime than a pity that so many of the words are lost . . . in the damnable din of amplification . . . [T]he book is slapdash, but serviceable enough for one of the most joyous performances to be seen locally in years . . . A couple of numbers from the original score have been eliminated and replaced by . . . 'Slap That Bass' . . . and . . . 'Ask Me Again' . . ." *See*: **W26h**

B424. RATHBUN, Stephen. "'Oh, Kay!' Opens, Gertrude Lawrence Scores in Jolly Musical Show." *NYSun*, Nov. 9?, 1926.

". . . [T]he first night audience thundered its approval . . . The George Gershwin score is equal in quality to the 'Lady, Be Good' music, and several of the numbers will be popular in night clubs and wherever there is dancing . . ." *See*: **W26b**

B425. RICH, Frank. "Review/Theater: David Merrick Presents 'Oh, Kay!'" *NYTimes*, date ?, 1990, Section C, pp. 1, 5.

Like the Richards review, below, also damning. Pointing out that this production had "a mostly different cast" from that which was "well-received" at the Goodspeed Opera House in Connecticut during 1989, the reviewer found much fault with the show. Concerning the music, however, ". . . Certainly it's not necessary to sing Gershwin's praises at this late date, but it says much that 'Someone to Watch Over Me' still exerts a pull here, despite the fact that the muffled-sounding orchestration . . . is trashy and the singer (Ms. [Angela] Teek [in the lead role of Kay]) is strident of voice and mechanical of gesture . . ." *See*: **W26h, B429**

B426. RICHARDS, David. "Sunday View: The Gershwin's 'Oh, Kay!' Dances to Harlem, David Merrick's musical works hard . . ."*NYTimes*, Nov.11, 1990, Section H, pp. 5, 33.

A devastatingly negative review of this revival. The suggestion that this production is too "hard-working" pervades the entire review. ". . . A musical with no letup . . . can be a big letdown. As directed and choreographed by Dan Siretta, this one seems to be coming at you on a conveyor belt, jammed in forward gear and doomed to constant acceleration, so that the performers are all but thrust into the final production number . . ." *See*: **W26h, B429**

B427. SHIRLEY, Wayne. "Oh, Kay . . ." in the album *Oh, Kay!*, Smithsonian Collection R011.

An excellent set of informative program notes about the plot and music inserted in this album. *See*: **D483**

B428. SIMON, John. "Yo, Kay!" *New York* 23/44 (Nov. 12, 1990): 92.

A somewhat mixed review, although generally more complimentary than those in the *NYTimes* (**B425** and **B426**). ". . . Much of the sophisticated, class-conscious humor [of the original] had to be changed [to conform to the new script and all-black cast]; what was retained is now often out of place. You might say that the book has flip-flopped from okay to kayo . . . [T]here remain the music of George Gershwin and the lyrics of Ira, so most of the score is as joyous as—or, in these musically needy times, more joyous than—ever. Purists may have a point if they protest the Goodspeed Opera House (where the show originated) strategy of dropping inconvenient numbers and adding others from different shows by the same hands; anyone wishing to know what the songs really felt like in 1926 will be largely frustrated . . . Siretta's direction keeps things rolling along; you may not be bowled over by *Oh, Kay!*, but you surely won't feel gypped . . . ." *See*: **W26h**

B429. SOKOL, Fred. "'Oh, Kay!' a toe-tapper." *Union News* [Springfield, MA] **[GOH]**, Nov. 10, 1989, Arts and Entertainment Section, p. 49.
        Mixed review of the Dan Siretta revival. ". . . Conceptually innovative and uplifting in both tone and spirit, this high-energy play, with setting transformed from Long Island estate to Harlem nightclub [incomplete sentence in original] . . ." Sokol was critical of the singing voices. ". . . 'Oh, Kay!' is the type of old-fashioned yet not dated production rarely seen . . ." *See*: **W26h, B425, B426**

W34. *OF THEE I SING* (1931)

The entries here are presented by the year of production and alphabetically by author within the year. *See*: **B2170**

1931:

B430. ATKINSON, Brooks. "After Thinking It Over." *NYTimes*, Mar. 20, 1932, Section 8. *See*: **W34b**

B431. _____. "The Play: Fitting the Dunce's Cap on Politics in a Musical Merry-Go-Round by Kaufman, Ryskind and Gershwin." *NYTimes*, Dec. 28, 1931, p. 20.
        Review of the NY premiere. Although Atkinson found some fault with the book for the show, he praised the music highly: ". . . it has George Gershwin's most brilliant score to sharpen the humor and fantasticate the ideas . . . Whether it is satire, wit, doggerel or fantasy, Mr. Gershwin pours music out in full measure, and in many voices. Although the book is lively, Mr. Gershwin is exuberant. He has not only ideas but enthusiasm. He amplifies the show." *See*: **W34b**

B432. ATKINSON, Brooks. "Pulitzer Laurels, In Which the Play Committee Jumps Aboard the Band Wagon and Turns Its Back on the Drama." *NYTimes*, May 8, 1932, Section 8, p. 1.
        A long story in essay form announcing but disagreeing with the awarding of the Pulitzer Prize for drama for the book of OTIS in 1932. ". . . When the Pulitzer committee selects a musical comedy in preference to 'Mourning Becomes Electra' . . . its judgment, I think, is skittish . . ."

B433. _____. "Stinging Satire of National Politics in a Hilarious and Original Musical Comedy." *NYTimes*, Jan. 3, 1932, Section 8, p. 1. *See*: **W34b**

B434. BEEBE, Lucius. "Mr. Victor Moore, Vice-President, Considers the State of the Union." *NYHerald Tribune*, Jan. 3, 1932, Section 7, p. 2. *See*: **W34b**

B435. BENCHLEY, Robert. "Theatre." *New Yorker* 7 (Jan. 9, 1932): 28. *See*: **W34b**

B436. BLITZSTEIN, Mark. "Forecast and Review: Music and Theatre, 1932." *Modern Music* 9/4 (May-June 1932): 167.

Review comparing OTIS to Irving Berlin's *Face the Music*. The reviewer preferred *Face the Music* "in all other ways" excepting the music, where he preferred Gershwin's. Blitzstein also criticized the increasing sophistication of G's music, calling him "ambitious, in a misguided attempt to approach 'art' . . ."

B437. C., M. "Burleycue and Whimsy." *New Republic* 69 (Jan. 13, 1932), 243-244. *See:*
W34b

B438. CHATFIELD-TAYLOR, O. "The Latest Plays." *Outlook and Independent* 160/2 (Jan. 13, 1932): 54, 59.

In this very complimentary review of OTIS, Chatfield-Taylor referred to it as "an indubitable harbinger of our spiritual majority." ". . . *Of Thee I Sing* makes fun not only of politics but of the inevitable musical comedy formula as well . . ." *See:* **W34b**

B439. CORBIN, John. "George Kaufman." *The Saturday Review* 9/27 (Jan. 21, 1933): 385-386.

A lengthy discussion of Kaufman's contribution to OTIS, published concurrently with the closing of the show after a fifty-five week run on Broadway. The article is a critical appraisal of Kaufman and does not mention the music.

B440-449. (Numbers inadvertently omitted)

B450. DECASSERES, Benjamin. "Broadway to Date: The Passing Show Flattered, Flayed and Fumbled." *Arts and Decoration* 36 (Feb. 1932), 39, 56.

B451. _____. "Midsummer Stage Gayeties ; Has Broadway Gone Bowery?—The Inner Meaning of Two Musical Comedies and Two Plays—Open-Air Entertainment—Real Broadway Moves into the Country." *Arts and Decoration* 37 (Sept. 1932): 43, 58-59.

B452. "A 'Dunce Cap for Politics.'" *Literary Digest* 112 (Jan. 16, 1932): 18.

B453. EATON, Walter Pritchard. "Between Curtains, The Pulitzer Prize: What is a Play?" *Theatre Arts Monthly* 16 (July 1932): 593-596.

A substantial and convincing essay defending the Pulitzer prize jury for its choice of the book to OTIS for the 1931 prize. Critics of the choice were arguing that OTIS was not a play; Eaton, a jury member, countered that ". . . If a story is told coherently by the players, and this story is firm and strong enough to 'come through' whatever medium they employ to tell it, then you have a play. Call it a play with music, or a musical comedy, if you like. I don't care. But it is a play . . ." *See:* **W34b**

B454. FERGUSSON, Francis. "A Month of the Theatre; Comedies, Satirical and Sweet." *Bookman* 74/5 (Jan.-Feb. 1932): 561-562.

A review in essay form. ". . . For all its wealth of invention and singleness of intent, this is an extremely uneven show, for the reason that it lacks a consistent *form* . . ." *See:* **W34b**

B455. "Frothy Humor." *NYHerald Tribune Books*, May 22, 1932, p. 12.

B456. GARLAND, Robert. "Cast and Miscast: A Week-end with a Genius-Kissed Satire and a Sun-Kissed Bride." *NYWorld Telegram*, Dec 28, 1931. **[NNMus]**

Glowing review of the NY premiere. ". . . Gershwin's music is imaginative, fluent and as musician-like as anything the composer has so far done . . . For the time being suffice it to say that 'Of Thee I Sing' is an event in the history of the American theater. I must remember to tell my grandchildren that I was present at its opening . . ." *See*: **W34b**

B457. GOLDBERG, Isaac. "American Operetta Comes of Age: Annotations Upon 'Of Thee I Sing' and Its Merry Makers." *Disques* [Philadelphia] 3/1 (Mar. 1932): 7-12.
  A substantial essay about OTIS, with much attention given the music. Discussing the music for the finaletto in Act I, Goldberg commented: ". . . [I]t is excellent serio-comic music,—a sort of audible eye-winking at which George Gershwin is expert. Gershwin, even in his music for symphony orchestra, is a wit . . . The wit and melody and sound musicianship of Gershwin's score lie like a salve over the pertinent jibes that Kaufman and Ryskind have provided . . ." Goldberg found much to praise in the music and lyrics, e. g.: ". . . Take the entrance of the nine supreme court judges: George has them count themselves out to a whole-tone scale . . . This is humor *in tones* . . ." An excellent article for its assessment of the music.

B458. HAMMOND, Percy. "The Theater: Fault-Finding with One of the Best." *NY Herald Tribune*, Jan. 3, 1932, Section VII, p. 1. *See*: **W34b**

B459. HALE, Philip. "The Theatre." *Boston Herald American* ?, May 8, 1932.
  Announcement that the libretto for OTIS had been published by Alfred Knopf. Hale applauded the choice of the Pulitzer committee of OTIS for the prize over *Mourning Becomes Electra*. Hale felt that OTIS deserved the prize and that "future historians may quote from the text in their study of democracy in the United States." *See*: **B462**

B460. "Happy Birthday to 'Of Thee I Sing'; Broadway's Longest Run Show Has an Anniversary Cake and Eats It, Reminiscing the While." *NYTimes*, Dec. 18, 1932, Section 10, p. 5.

B461. "Harris Tells How He Came to Produce the Pulitzer Play." *NY Herald Tribune*, May 8, 1932, p. 2.

B462. KAUFMAN, George S., and **Morrie RYSKIND**. *Of Thee I Sing.* NY: A. A. Knopf, 1932.
  The script in book form. *See*: **B459**

B463. KRUTCH, Joseph Wood. "Drama: Treacle and Spice." *The Nation* 134/3479 (Mar. 9, 1932): 294.
  Review in the form of an essay which compares then current Broadway shows such as Irving Berlin's *Face the Music* to OTIS. ". . . [I]t is not nearly so good as 'Of Thee I Sing,' which it so obviously imitates . . ."

B464. _____. "Drama: Westchester and Washington [Review]." *The Nation* 134/3471 (Jan. 13, 1932): 56.
  Positive review of the New York Music Box production. ". . . [I]t is doubtful if there has ever been a time before when the general public would have found pleasing so raucously comtemptuous a treatment of the whole spectacle of our government . . ." *See*: **W34b**

B465. MANTLE, Burns, ed. *The Best Plays of 1931-32; And the Year Book of the Drama In America,* NY: Dodd, Mead, 1932.

B466. MURPHY, George, and **Victor LASKY.** *"Say. . . Didn't You Used To Be George Murphy?"* Bartholomew House, 1970, pp. 50, 109, 134.

Significant references to GG. A fourteen-page chapter titled "Of Thee I Sing" is an enlightening account of Murphy's auditioning for and subsequent role in the original cast of OTIS.

B467. "Musical Play Gets the Pulitzer Award; Mrs. Buck, Pershing, Duranty Honored." *NYTimes*, May 3, 1932, pp. 1, 16.

B468. NANNES, Casper H. *Politics in American Drama.* Washington: Catholic University of America Press, 1960, pp. 103-106.

Description of OTIS and Cake from the perspective of the Depression times. ". . . The play [OTIS], an immediate hit, is an angry satire . . . Throttlebottom alone draws the sympathy of the audience. And perhaps for the reason that everyone in the 1931 audience felt himself something of a Throttlebottom—confused, lost, and uncertain . . . It was a play attuned to the depression; in better days many of the barbs lose their satirical effectiveness . . ." *See*: **W34, W36**

B469. PARSONS, Geoffrey, Jr., "Holidays Bring Light to Dark Boston Stages, New Fred Stone Show, Shubert Operetta and 'Cloudy with Showers' Scheduled." *NY Herald Tribune*, Dec. 20, 1931, Section 7, p. 2. *See*: **W34a**

B470. RICHARDS, Stanley. *Ten Great Musicals of the American Theatre.* Radnor, PA: Chilton, 1973, pp. 1-74.

Libretto of OTIS.

B471. RUHL, Arthur. "'Of Thee I Sing'; Kaufman-Ryskind Musical Comedy Satire at the Music Box." *NYHerald Tribune*, Dec. 28, 1931, p. 9. *See*: **W34b**

B472. SCHUBERT, Gisela. „Zeitgeist im Glamour-Kostüm. George Gershwins Musicals: Von der Revue zur politischen Satire." *Neue Zeitschrift für Musik* (July-August 1991): 13-21.

Essay including discussion of OTIS and Cake, among others. *See*: **W34, W36**

B473. SKINNER, Richard Dana. "The Play." *Commonweal* 15 (Jan. 13, 1932): 301-302. *See*: **W34b**

B474. SMITH, Alfred E. "Books and Films . . . White Housekeeping: *The Diary of an ex-President* . . ." Nation 135/3502 (Aug. 17, 1932): 148.

Review of Morrie Ryskind's book written under the pseudonym John P. Wintergreen in the wake of OTIS. ". . . My personal opinion is that it should be made compulsory reading for every politician, campaigner, or political office-holder . . ."

B475. TEICHMANN, Howard. *George Kaufman: An Intimate Portrait.* New York: Atheneum, 1972, pp. 99, 100, 121, 140, 244, 248, 301, 326.

Concerning the genesis of OTIS: "In 1929, when there was a lot to talk about, Kaufman and Ryskind began discussing a new idea for a musical that was about as far away from the stock market crash and the musicals of the day as they could get . . ."

B476. TOOHEY, John L. *A History of the Pulitzer Prize Plays.* NY: Citadel Press, 1967,

94-104.

With quotes from reviews, Toohey devoted ten pages to his coverage of OTIS. The material is enhanced by the inclusion of caricatures of G and I by William Auerbach-Levy and Don Freeman, the latter, spread across two pages, of the Supreme Court Justices " getting into their robes in the incongruous hurly burly of backstage activity."

B477. "Two Incoming Musicals; 'Of Thee I Sing' Excites Boston—New Haven Sees the Fred Stone Show." *NYTimes*, Dec. 13, 1931, Section 8, p. 2. *See*: **W34a**

B478. "With a Hey, Nonny Nonny; Being a Selection from the Lyrics That They Sing in That Satire at the Music Box." *NYTimes* (Apr. 17, 1932), Section VIII, p. 3.

B479. WYATT, Euphemia Van Rensselaer. "The Drama: Wintergreen for President." *Catholic World* 134 (Feb. 1932), 587-588.

B480. YOUNG, Stark. "Town Notes." *New Republic* 70 (Mar. 9, 1932): 97-98.

Review obviously by a drama rather than a music critic, focusing on Kaufman's contribution, with no mention of the music.

1937:

B481. "Jones Beach Throng Sees 'Of Thee I Sing' . . ." *NYTimes* (dateline: Jones Beach, Long Island, NY, Aug. 9, 1937).

Running barely a month after GG's death, this review chronicles a run of OTIS. 10,000 people saw the premiere performance. *See*: **W34d, B923**

1952:

B482. ATKINSON, Brooks. "At the Theatre; 'Of Thee I Sing': Another Production from the Past Is Better than Most of the New Ones." *NYTimes,* May 6, 1952, p. 34.

Positive review. ". . . Nothing vital has been lost in the shuffle of the years. In fact, something may have been added. For George Gershwin's score has been played so constantly that it is now part of the musical language of the country. In Don Walker's orchestration . . . the score is played with gusto and crackle, and it is sung with spirit by Jack Carson and Betty Oakes . . ." *See*: **W34e**

B483. _____. "'Of Thee I Sing.'" *NYTimes (NYTimes Theater Reviews)*, May 11, 1952, Section 2, p. 1.

Review of the 1952 revival. ". . . In 1931 the United States was deep in the most profound economic depression of our history, and the theatre was beginning to come apart at the seems. But George Gershwin was at the peak of his powers, writing original and trenchant music in a wide range of moods . . . Being in high spirits Mr. Kaufman and Mr. Ryskind were contemptuous of the muddle and venality of national politics, possibly assuming that a new administration could sanitize the bureaucracy . . . After two years of Harding and six of Coolidge, Herbert Hoover and Charles Curtis were presiding over the destinies of the nation, and people were inclined to assume that the time had come to turn the Republican rascals out. While 'Of Thee I Sing' was entertaining American audiences, the Democratic rascals came in; but after almost twenty years of them, the devastatingly satiric point of view is still pertinent and popular. Things have come full circle . . . One reason why 'Of Thee I Sing' is still funny is the generality of its burlesque . . . It lampoons national government in general. It assumes that a national government is put in Washington by blatherskites and populated by knaves and imbeciles . . . Whether the current knaves are Democrats or Republicans is beside the point . . ." *See*: **W34e**

B484. BRACKER, Milton. "'Of Thee I Sing' in Modern Dress." *NYTimes*, May 4, 1952, Section II, pp. 1, 3. *See*: **W34e**

B485. BROWN, John Mason. "Seeing Things, Now—And Then." *Saturday Review of Literature* 35/21 (May 24, 1952): 30-32.
Review of the 1952 revival. Despite his misgivings, the reviewer found the first act of the revival satisfying, but the second act disappointing. He concluded: ". . . That it seems dated . . . is one way of measuring how much we and the world have changed since that memorable December night in 1931 when first it astonished and delighted us . . ." *See*: **W34e**

B486. CLURMAN, Harold. "The Monthly Critical Review: Revivals, Arrivals, and Quick Departures." *Theatre Arts* 36/7 (July 1952): 17, 82.
Referring to the revival, Clurman explained his negative criticism of it: ". . . It lacks the sparkle, the high-living muscular confidence of Bill Gaxton's spirit with its absurdly intemperate but infectious energy . . . As for the score, its presentation is so bad, and its songs so wretchedly rendered . . ." *See*: **W34e**

B487. GIBBS, Wolcott. "The Theatre: A Pair from the Past." *New Yorker* 28/13 (May 17, 1952): 79-80.
A negative review. The reviewer was critical both of the cast and the show itself: ". . . 'Of Thee I Sing' is strictly a product of an odd era in our national history, and it is hard to see how a contemporary audience under the age of forty-five [in 1952] can detect much humor or significance in it . . ." *See*: **W34e**

B488. HARPER, Mr. "After Hours: 'Of Thee I Sing' I Sing." *Harper's Magazine* 205 (July 1952): 92-93.
Having seen the original 1931 version, Harper could not avoid comparison, but generally liked the revival: ". . . For me it was 90-proof Fountain of Youth. I drank it straight . . ."

B489. KERR, Walter. "The Stage." *Commonweal* 56 (May 30, 1952), 196-197. *See*: **W34e**

B490. M., M. "Drama Note." *Nation* 174 (May 17, 1952): 486.

B491. "Theater; Revival: 'Of Thee I Sing.'" *Newsweek* 39 (May 19, 1952): 101. *See*: **W34e**

B492. "The Theatre: Old Musical in Manhattan." *Time* 59 (May 19, 1952): 83. *See*: **W34e**

B493. "Twenty Years After." *New Yorker* 28/13 (May 17, 1952): 26-27.
Commentary about the OTIS revival along with that of P&B. The article is based on Mr. and Mrs. Ira Gershwin's coming East for the opening of the OTIS revival, in what amounts to an interview of IG. *See*: **W34e**

B494. WYATT, Euphemia Van Rensselaer. "Theater: 'Of Thee I Sing.'" *Catholic World* 175 (July 1952): 310.

1969:

B495. BARNES, Clive. "Theater: 'Of Thee' Is Thirties, Baby: New Anderson Revival of Show Is Dated." *NYTimes*, Mar. 8, 1969.

At almost three columns, this is a negative review of the revival aiming mostly at the book. Concerning the music: ". . . George and Ira Gershwin remain as fresh as a daisy . . . They don't write musical scores like that anymore . . ." *See:* **W34g.1**

B496. DOVE, Ian. "'Of Thee I Sing' Returned in the Musical Style of the Thirties." *Billboard* 81 (Mar. 22, 1969 [dateline: NY]), p. 14.

Complimentary brief review of the revival at NY's Off-Broadway New Anderson Theater, based on the performance of March 7, 1969. *See:* **W34g.1**

1972 television production:

B497. O'CONNOR, John J. "TV: 'Of Thee I Sing'; C. B. S. Adaptation of '31 Musical Retains Basic Material for 9:30 Special." *NYTimes*, Oct. 22, 1972, p. 87. *See:* **W34h**

1984:

B498. METCALF, Steve. "Talented Youths Inject Life in Classic Gershwin." *Hartford* [CT] *Courant* (*Newsbank* PER 27-E8), Aug. 18, 1984.

Complimentary review of an *Of Thee I Sing* performance by the unusual Hartford Stage Company Youth Theater, on August 16, 1984. *See:* **W34i**

1987 revival at Brooklyn Academy of Music:

B499. HOLDEN, STEPHEN. "Two Classics by Gershwin in Brooklyn." *NYTimes*, March 20, 1987, pp. 19, 22.

Review of the premiere double bill performance, March 18, 1987, at the Brooklyn Academy of Music. This article reveals some elucidating information about the two political operettas. Until its discovery four years ago in a storage attic of the publisher Samuel French by John McGlinn, a conductor and Broadway musical scholar, and Ron Spiva . . . The original orchestral score for 'Of Thee I Sing' was thought to have been lost . . ." According to McGlinn, "[We] didn't even have a piano-vocal score for reference . . . All we had were the composer's sketches from the Library of Congress . . . I spent the summer working with microfilm to produce a detailed vocal score . . . Working from Mr. McGlinn's vocal score, Russell Warner constructed a new orchestration . . ." *See:* **W34c, W36d**

B500. KISSEL, Howard. "He Loves A Gershwin Tune!" *NYDaily News (Newsbank* PER 142:G10), Mar 20, 1987.

Complimentary review of the Brooklyn Academy of Music's production of OTIS and Cake. Kissel astutely pointed out the "especially savvy use of the clarinet" in Russell Warner's new orchestration for Cake. *See:* **W34c, W36d**

B501. OSBURNE, Charles. "America . . . New York." *Opera* 38/7 (July 1987): 765-766.

Brief descriptive review of the Brooklyn Academy of Music's March 22, 1987, performance of OTIS and Cake. *See:* **W34c, W36d**

B502. SCHLESINGER, Arthur M., Jr. "How History Upstaged the Gershwins." *NYTimes*,

Apr. 5, 1987, Section II, p. 6, 20.

This is a post-mortem article dealing with the productions of OTIS and Cake at the Broadway Academy of Music in March, 1987, from the perspective of the historian. Schlesinger compared the two shows in this excellent, reflective article. Schlesinger concluded that the Brooklyn Academy productions were a "public service," and despite the failure of Cake in its premiere presentations, ". . . both [operettas] leave a joyous heritage to posterity. . ." *See*: **W34c, W36d**

B503. STEARNS, David Patrick. "Michael Tilson Thomas: Let 'Em Sing Gershwin!"
Ovation 8/11 (December 1987): 12-14.

A general article on Tilson Thomas's then current involvement with Gershwin projects. Announcement was made of the November 27 and December 4, 1987, Public Broadcasting system telecasts "that capture the best moments of Thomas' multifaceted Gershwin gala at the Brooklyn Academy of Music last March [11th, 1987] and include studio performances of Gershwin he did with the London Symphony Orchestra shortly after." Tilson commented about G's music ". . . There's a deep, underlying confessional feeling in Gershwin's music . . . that is expressed in a certain kind of haunted loneliness we all feel in this confusing world of ours . . . The message of the Gershwins—in the harmonies, melodic lines and words—was a very heartfelt, specific, direct one . . ." Mention is also made of the March, 1987, revivals of OTIS AND Cake directed by Tilson Thomas at the BAM, and the CBS masterworks recording (#45222, **D467**) which resulted from those BAM performances. In the discussion of Cake, it is pointed out that one number, "Let 'Em Eat Caviar," "remains completely lost." *See*: **W34c, W36d**

B504. WILSON, John S. "Stage: Gershwin Duo In Concert Versions." *NYTimes,* March 22, 1987, p. 20.

Positive review of the March 18, 1987, commemorative revival of OTIS and Cake at the Brooklyn Academy of Music. Wilson gives a brief history of the works and summary of the plots. ". . . Although this concert presentation, with the principals and members of the New York Choral Artists in formal dress and with script books in hand, lacks the boisterous and colorful potential of the street parades, political rallies, [etc.] . . . that were written into the script, the Gershwins' principal songs are sung with vigor and polish by Maureen McGovern and Larry Kert . . ." *See:* **W34c**

B505. _____. "Stage: Political Satire, In Gershwin Double Bill." *NYTimes,* Mar. 27, 1987, section 1, p. 62.

A feature article on the BAM revivals of 1987. *See*: **W34c**

1990:

B506. KOZINN, Allan. "Gilbert and Sullivan Players Send an SOS to Gershwin." *NYTimes,* Mar. 29, 1990, p. C16.

Announcement of the forthcoming performances in NY by the Gilbert and Sullivan players, March 29 through April 15, 1990. *See*: **W34l**

W16. *OUR NELL* (original title: *HAYSEED*) (1922)

B507. "[Review]." *NYTimes,* December 5, 1922, 24:1.

"George Gershwin and William Daly have written some acceptable tunes . . . In brief, 'Our Nell' is an encouraging novelty so far as the musical comedy is concerned." *See*: **W16b**

W35. *PARDON MY ENGLISH* (1933)

B508. ATKINSON, Brooks. "The Play: Jack Pearl as a Germanic Commissioner of Police in 'Pardon My English.'" *NYTimes*, Jan. 21, 1933, p. 11. **[NNMus]**
Review of opening night of the NY run. ". . . 'Pardon My English' is a fast, well costumed musical comedy . . . For music there are a number of Mr. Gershwin's blaring cafe tunes, 'Dancing in the Streets' being the one best liked by this forum . . . on the whole, 'Pardon My English' is a little too gross for downright enjoyment." See: **W35b**

B509. CALDWELL, Cy. "To See or Not to See . . . Pardon My English." *New Outlook and Independent?* 161/6 (Mar. 1933): 48.
Brief negative review. ". . . It is by long odds the dullest, heaviest and most tiresome musical in town. A musical comedy that is short of both music and comedy is a sad affair, indeed. George Gershwin's music is nice and loud, and there are no discords in it, nor tunes to amount to much, either . . ."

B510. GARLAND, Robert. "'Pardon My English' Meets Big Audience in Debut at Majestic: Even Though Book, Lyrics and Music have Strong Pedigrees, Play is Old-Fashioned Piece of Mere Routine." *NY Telegram*, Jan 21, 1933, p. 10. **[NNMus]**
Garland reviewed the opening night in NY. His feelings were negative: "Maybe you'll like it. I wanted to most awfully . . . it should be something to cheer about. But, to my way of thinking, it isn't. From beginning to end it remains old-fashioned, lifeless routine. Devastating routine . . ." *See*: **W35b**

B511. HAMMOND, Percy. "The Theaters: 'Pardon My English,' a Rough and Pretty Operetta." *NY Herald Tribune*, Jan. 21, 1933, p. 8.
A generally positive review of the premiere, January 20, 1933. ". . . Mr. Gershwin's music is always good and important, even if you don't always like it, and in such less strident and dissonant numbers as 'So What?' and 'Lucky Man' there were pleasing chords and melodies . . ." *See*: **W35b**

B512. HOLDEN, Stephen. "Concert: Obscure Pair By the Young Gershwin." Special to *NYTimes*, dateline: Washington, May 16, 1987.
Important review of the resurrection and concert presentations of *Primrose* and *Pardon My English*, on March 15, 1987, at the Library of Congress. Concerning the latter: ". . . The score is typically early 30's Gershwin—propulsively jazzy, with many deft satirical flourishes . . ." Holden considered the tune *Naughty Baby* from *Pardon* to have the earmarks of "an overlooked masterpiece," comparing it to *Somebody Loves Me* and *'S Wonderful!*. The reviewer praised the cast and conductor and concluded: "These careful restorations of complete scores show that even the lighter side of Gershwin's oeuvre deserves to be scrutinized within a broadened concept of American classical tradition . . ." *See*: **W21b, W35c, B515**

B513. "Pearl Reviving 'Dutch' Comic of Early 1900s; Star of 'Pardon My English' Continues a Long Line of German Dialecticians." *NY Herald Tribune*, Jan. 22, 1933, Section 7, p. 4. *See*: **W35b**

B514. "Three New Shows in the Tryout Cities." *NYTimes*, Dec. 11, 1932, Section 9, p. 5.
Review of the premiere of the Philadelphia tryout, December 2, 1932, at the Garrick Theatre. The comments of Henry T. Murdock of the *Evening Public Ledger* were quoted in this article: ". . . George Gershwin has unbent a little from the cryptographic music of 'Of

Thee I Sing' and other of his recent shows, presenting several catchy tunes that one—after practice, perhaps—may whistle. Several of the tunes may be crooned in the privacy of one's bathroom without the assistance of a symphony orchestra that was slightly heavy in the muted brasses . . . Mix Jack Pearl . . . Miss Roberti . . . many Bavarian gangsters and Bavarian peasants, and an involved but entertaining evening results . . ." *See*: **W35a**

B515. TUCK, Lon. "The Gershwin Gold." *Washington Post,* May 16, 1987, Style section, p. G1.
Review of March 15, 1987, concert performances of *Primrose* and *Pardon My English* based on the scores discovered in 1982 at the Secaucus, New Jersey warehouse of Warner Brothers. "Last night at the Library of Congress there was—incredible as it may seem—the American debut of a musical by George and Ira Gershwin. The good news is that 's wonderful. Called 'Primrose,' it is no mere curiosity whose only claim to fame is its supremely distinguished pedigree. It is mature Gershwin, coming from 1924, the same year as no less a work than 'Rhapsody in Blue.' The music is spirited, and considerably less jazzy than most of Gershwin's show music. Its ballads are distinctly Kern-ish, and it is full of patter songs that sound quite English, which is not inappropriate because the musical was composed for staging in England, where it is said to have been a great success . . ." Tuck was particularly impressed with Ira G's lyrics for *Primrose*. "The other work on the library's delightful all-Gershwin program . . . is better known: 'Pardon My English,' which is from 1933, only two years before the Gershwin's masterpiece, 'Porgy and Bess.' It was the first time in many years that the songs from 'Pardon My English' were performed in their original, and long lost, orchestration . . . Apparently 'Primrose' was deemed too British for Broadway. In ways it brings to mind Noel Coward, both musically and dramatically, except that Coward would never have written so awkward and inane a book as the one done for the Gershwins by George Grossmith and Guy Bolton. Desmond Carter joined Ira in writing the lyrics . . . It may be a cliché, but the truth is that no one is writing stuff this good these days— '*Les Miserables*' very much included . . . ." *See*: **W21b, W35c, B512**

W37. *PORGY AND BESS* (1935)

General Bibliography

General Bibliography is presented first, followed by chronologically ordered bibliography.

B516. ALPERT, Hollis. *The Life and Times of Porgy and Bess.* New York: A. Knopf, 1990. 354 pp.
A substantial book, being a thoroughly researched attempt at the complete history of the opera and its performances throughout the world to 1990. *See*: **W37b, B550, B551, B1550**

B517. ARMITAGE, Merle. "George Gershwin," in his: *Accent on America* (NY: E. Weyhe, 1944): 289-98.
A chapter on P&B, pp. 163-66. Must reading for anyone interested in P&B.

B518. _____. *Accent on Life.* Ames, IA: Iowa State University Press, 1965, pp. 137-140, 186-202.
A series of essays by Armitage, including two chapters: "Porgy and Bess, Critics Called it a Failure" and "Gershwin, An American Original." The first is an account of Armitage's own West Coast revival (and its demise) in 1938. The second is a series of reminiscences on personal contacts and conversations Armitage had with G and his associates.

B519. *Avant-scène opéra* 103 (November 1987): Gershwin, Porgy and Bess. (Paris: Avant-scène, 1987) 119 p. Illustration, portrait, music examples, bibliography, discography. In French. ISSN 07642873.

The original libretto by **DuBose HEYWARD** and **Ira GERSHWIN** with French translation by **Annette BOUJU,** a commentary by **Christophe MOUDOT,** a discography by **Piotr KAMINSKI,** a bibliography by **Elisabeth GIULIANI,** and a chronology of the major productions by **Michel PAZDRO.** The following articles are abstracted in this issue: **Pierre BABIN,** Plus ou moins? [More or less?] (8302); **George GERSHWIN,** Rhapsodie a Catfish Row [Rhapsody on Catfish Row] (8397); **Denis JEAMBAR,** Gershwin, la rhapsodie d'un Américain [Gershwin: An American's rhapsody] (3657); **Alain LACOMBE,** Genèse d'un mythe-opéra: Porgy or not Heyward [Genesis of a myth-opera: Porgy or not Heyward] (3745); **Catherine LÉPRONT,** Porgy ou l'amour oblique [Porgy, or, Oblique love] (8465); **Laurine QUETIN,** Gershwin en quête de respectabilité parmi ses pairs [Gershwin and the quest for the respect of his peers] (3921). NOTES: edited by **Alain DUAULT**; Entry from DATABASE: *RILM ABSTRACTS OF MUSIC LITERATURE*

B520. BASKERVILLE, David. *Jazz Influence on Art Music to Mid-Century.* Ph. D. Dissertation: University of California at Los Angeles, 1965. 535 pp. *Dissertation Abstracts* 26/8 (Feb. 1966): 4710-A.

Contains a chapter on *Porgy and Bess. See*: Fuller entry under "Dissertations" at

B2154

B521. BRODY, Elaine. *Music in Opera: A Historical Anthology.* Englewood Cliffs, NJ: Prentice-Hall, 1970, pp. 539f.

In her anthology of excerpts from operas, Brody included "Damn you, give me dem bones" and "Good mornin' Mister Archdale" (the Buzzard's song), each with a brief commentary.

B522. BROWN, Thomas P. "Strawfiddle Antics." *Percussionist* 10/4 (1973): 130-133.

Suggestions for the performance of the Xylophone part to P&B.

B523. COOPER, John Webb. *A Comparative Study of Porgy, the Novel, Porgy, the Play, and Porgy and Bess, the Folk Opera.* Master's thesis, Columbia University, 1950.

Includes a good comparison between the play and libretto for the folk opera.

B524. CRAWFORD, Cheryl. *One Naked Individual: My Fifty Years in the Theatre.* Indianapolis & NY: Bobbs-Merrill, 1977, pp. 114-115.

In her autobiography, Crawford explained why she chose to revive P&B in 1941. ". . . When I knew the third season [at Maplewood, NJ] would have to come to an end because of gas rationing, I wanted to do something big, to close with a bang. My favorite popular composer was George Gershwin. For me his music and Ira's lyrics are real 'Amurrican,' hard, tough, joyful, bold, cheerful, affirmative, never self-pitying, never sentimentalized. The beat is relentless. They have the punch of a smack on the kisser, a three-base strike . . . Ira doesn't say, 'Oh, if my man would only come along and love me'; he says, 'Someday he'll *come* along—the man I love . . . When I had seen the 1932 [sic, 1935] production I had been critical of only one element, the recitatives . . . Smallens and I sat in the theatre [at Maplewood] and carefully cut recitatives we thought were out of place or unnecessary . . . The show became more of a piece . and flowed swiftly and tunefully . . ." *See*: **W37e**

B525. CRAWFORD, Richard. "Gershwin's Reputation: A Note on *Porgy and Bess."*
Musical Quarterly 65/2 (April 1979): 257-264.
An esteemed American musicologist looks at G and P&B in this thought provoking
article. Crawford makes a good argument for serious study of G, despite the fact that such
study has been previously "outside the sphere" of musicologists. In his concluding remarks,
Crawford stated: ". . . If we scholars worked to understand the significance of the many varied
roles that Gershwin's music fills—if we looked beyond the obvious commercialism and self-
aggrandizement which were so much a part of his career and that have put us off in the past—
we ourselves would be the ultimate gainers . . ."

B526. _____. "It Ain't Necessarily Soul: Gershwin's 'Porgy and Bess' as a Symbol."
Yearbook for Inter-American Musical Research 8 (1972): 17-38.
This article, earlier than the one by Crawford listed above, gives material on the genesis
of P&B which, according to Crawford, required a year and a half of G's " . . . concentrated
attention to a single work. In every way Porgy and Bess was his *magnum opus . . .*" Crawford's
purpose was to " . . . set forth four different perspectives from which *Porgy and Bess* has been
observed . . ," *viz.*, as "an American opera," as "American folklore," "as racial stereotype," and
"as cultural exploitation," and ". . . to demonstrate its potency as an effective symbol of
American cultural collision . . ." Crawford drew upon writings of Hall Johnson, Virgil
Thomson, Richard Dorson, Lorraine Hansberry, Era Bell Thompson, Harold Cruse, and Rudi
Blesh, to point out faults in *Porgy and Bess* as pertains to the four areas cited above, but
Crawford concluded ". . . Porgy and Bess remains a work of art—a work realized and
experienced only in performance . . ."

B527. DURHAM, Frank. *DuBose Heyward, the Man Who Wrote Porgy.*Columbia, SC:
University of South Carolina Press, 1954.
(A new bio of Heyward is projected for around 2000 from the University Press of
Mississippi).

B528. _____. *Dubose Heyward: The Southerner as Artist, A Critical and Biographical
Study.* Ph. D. dissertation, Columbia University, 1953. 451 pp.
See: Full entry under "Dissertations" at **B2160.**

B529. HEYWARD, Dorothy (Hartzell). "Porgy's Goat." *Harper's Magazine* 215/1291
(Dec. 1957): 37-41.

B530. JOHNSON, Harold Earle. *Operas on American Subjects.* NY: Coleman-Ross,
1964.

B531. KOLODIN, Irving. "Charleston Revisited." *Saturday Review* 34 (Sept. 24, 1951):
50-51.

B532. KONEN, Valentina Dzozefovna. "Dzordz Gersvin i ego opera." *Sovetskaya
Muzyka* 23/3 (Mar. 1959): 166-173.

B533. KOSTELANETZ, André. "George Gershwin—An American Composer."
Music Clubs Magazine 31/4 (May 1952): 4+.
Discussion of G works.

B534. LERNER, Alan J. *The Musical Theatre: A Celebration.* New York: McGraw-
Hill, 1987, 47,52, 60, 63, 130-135 [*P&B*], *et passim.*

Contains numerous references to G and IG, and to P&B.

B535. MURRAY, Martha M. *George Gershwin: Classical Composer*. Master's thesis (Music), Mississippi College [Clinton, MS], 1971. iii, 104 pp.

This paper includes a sixty-three page analysis of P&B ". . . in relation to the compositional idioms of traditional opera . . ." Conventional operatic terms such as "Recitative accompagnato, secco, arioso, parlando," e. g. are used in the analysis.

B536. NAUERT, Paul. "Theory and Practice in Porgy and Bess: The Gershwin-Schillinger Connection." *Musical Quarterly* 78/1 (Sept. 1994): 9-33.

This is a valuable and convincing study linking G's work with teacher Joseph Schillinger (1895–1943) to specific passages in *Porgy and Bess* and other works within the Gershwin oeuvre.

B537. RICHARDS, Stanley. *Ten Great Musicals of the American Theatre*. Radnor, PA: Chilton, 1973, pp. 75-113.

Includes libretto to P&B. *See:* **B582**

B538. SCHNEERSON, Grigoriy M. "Preface," in: *Porgy and Bess* (Moscow: State Publishers Music, 1965).

Preface to a Russian edition of the score.

B539. SEVERENS, Martha R. "Charleston in the Age of *Porgy and Bess*." *Southern Quarterly* (Special Issue, Visual Arts in the South) 28/1 (Fall 1989): 5-24.

What is unusual about this article is its inclusion of reproductions of art works, including *Jenkins Orphanage Band*, two views of Cabbage Row (one a photograph) which was in part inspiration for Catfish Row to DuBose Heyward. ". . . Actually Catfish Row was Heyward's synthesis of two blocks—Rainbow Row, an amalgam of structures near the wharves, and Cabbage Row, the structure just next door to the historic Heyward house . . ." Also included is Prentiss Taylor's *Experience Meeting, Massydony*, a lithograph from ca. 1935, which "created an image akin to George Gershwin's experiences [at Holy Rollers' meetings] during his visits to the Heywards at Folly Beach.

B540. SHIRLEY, Wayne D. "Porgy and Bess." *Quarterly Journal of the Library of Congress* 31/2 (Apr. 1974): 97-107.

Article consisting of probing discussion of the first-draft typescript libretto at the Library of Congress, along with tracing the evolution of P&B from play to opera. In the course of his well-informed essay, Shirley called attention to the number "Porgy" which pre-dated the Heyward-Gershwin version, in Lew Leslie's *Blackbirds of 1928*. Concerning the character, Porgy, in the Heyward novel: ". . . Although the character of Porgy was based on a familiar Charleston [SC] figure, the goat-cart beggar Samuel Smalls, Heyward was careful to disclaim his intent to write the biography of an actual person [in his novel *Porgy*] . . ." An interesting photograph of the "Slave Quarters" in Charleston, used by director Mamoulian for the stage set of the play *Porgy*, appears at the head of the article.

B541. _____. "Reconciliation on Catfish Row; Bess, Serena, and the Short Score of 'Porgy and Bess.'" *Quarterly Journal of the Library of Congress* 38 (Summer 1981): 144-165.

B542. SINGER, Barry. "On Hearing Her Sing, Gershwin Made 'Porgy' 'Porgy and Bess.'" NYTimes, Arts & Leisure section, Mar. 29, 1998.

Feature story concerning Anne Wiggins Brown, Gershwin's first Bess. Ms. Brown was in New York recently for a brief visit after a Gershwin Centennial celebration and symposium at the Library of Congress in Washington March 13-16. At age 85, Ms. Brown provided a description of her audition with GG for the role of Bess in 1935. Interesting first hand information. A typescript of the proceedings of the Washington symposium is being prepared by the LC. *See:* **W37b, B586**

B543.   SMITH, C. [Porgy and Bess] "Symphonic Percussion: *Porgy* and Me." *Perc Notes* 19/2 (1981): 65-68.

B544.   STARR, Lawrence. "Gershwin's 'Bess, You Is My Woman Now': The Sophistication and Subtlety of a Great Tune." *Musical Quarterly* 72/4 (1986): 429-448.
Distinguished American musicologist Starr provides an in-depth analysis of this single song from the opera. In this impressive article, Starr makes a strong case for Gershwin's place as an important twentieth-century composer, linking "him strongly to major lines of development in specifically American music, arts, and aesthetic thought."

B545.   STARR, Lawrence. "Toward a Reevaluation of Gershwin's *Porgy and Bess.*" *American Music* 2/2 (1984): 25-37.
A significant, substantial article, buttressed by analysis to substantiate Starr's realization of the value of P&B. "While *Porgy and Bess* is a work which certainly possesses some flaws and unevenness, one must remember that it was Gershwin's *first* attempt at composing grand opera. The measure of his accomplishment is that this first attempt does merit the most serious consideration and respect as part of the operatic tradition. I suspect that many who will come to know this work as Gershwin really wrote it will move, as I did, from a suspicious cynicism to a feeling toward this unique work that can best be described as a mingling of gratitude and awe . . . ."

B546.   SWAIN, Joseph P. *The Broadway Musical: A Critical and Musical Survey.* NY: Oxford University Press, 1990.
Has a chapter on P&B. Review in *Notes* Sept. 1992.

B547.   Twenty-Six Years on Catfish Row." *Theatre Arts* 37/5 (May 1953): 64-65.
Very brief, uninformative article on P&B. Pictures of the Catfish Row sets by Cleon Throckmorton (for the play *Porgy* of 1927), Herbert Andrews (Crawford revival of 1942), and Wolfgang Roth (1953 revival) are appended. *See:* **W37e, W37v**

B548.   WOLL, Allen. *Black Musical Theatre: From Coontown to Dreamgirls.* Baton Rouge and   London: Louisiana   State   University   Press,   1989,   154-175. (Republished 1992 Da Capo Press).
Woll devotes a chapter called "The Irony of *Porgy and Bess.*" Woll compared P&B to other black musicals, and considered that G's opera ". . . actually symbolizes the end of the black musical tradition that flourished in the early part of this century . . ."

B549.   WORBS, Hans Christoph. *Welterfolge der modernen Oper.* Berlin: Rembrandt, 1967.
P&B is discussed along with twenty-four other twentieth-century operas.

B550.   YOUNGREN, William. "Gershwin, Part IV, Porgy and Bess." *New Republic* (May 14, 1977): 23-26+.
Lengthy and informed essay on P&B. Among other points, Youngren points out the inadequacy of the published piano-vocal score: ". . . If you turn to page 197 . . . you will find

'I Got Plenty O' Nuttin' in the vocal part but in the piano staves you will see only the oom-pah accompaniment: there is no hint of the witty, enchanting woodwind writing that plays such an important role in the song's total effect . . . [and] several months of listening to the Maazel recording and studying Gershwin's manuscript score [from the Library of Congress] have brought me to the . . . firm conviction that *Porgy and Bess* is not only Gershwin's finest work but is also a fine opera, better than most both musically and dramatically . . ." This article should be required reading for all students of the evolution of P&B and its authentic performance practice. *See*: **B516**

1934-1936:

B551. ATKINSON, Brooks. "'Porgy and Bess.' Native Opera, Opens at the Alvin; Gershwin Work Based on Du Bose Heyward's Play: Dramatic Value of Community Legend Gloriously Transposed in New Form with Fine Regard for Its Verities." *NYTimes*, Oct. 11, 1935, p. 30.
Review of the premiere in NY by the Times' drama critic. A summary of the New York reviews appears in Hollis Alpert's book, **B516**, pp. 115-118. *See*: **W37b**

B552. BARRY, Edward. "'Porgy and Bess' Lends Opera Flavor to Guild's Season in City, Music Unites Themes of Manhattan and the Deep South." *Chicago Daily Tribune*, Feb. 18, 1936, p. 15.
Review of the first performance in Chicago of the post-Broadway tour, before an elite audience. *See*: **W37c**

B553. "Broadway in Review." *Theatre Arts Monthly* 19 (Dec. 1935): 893-894.
Short review of the original version. "*Porgy and Bess* is a fine show, one not to be missed . . . The union of music and story has not only served *Porgy* [the play] well, but has given Mr. Gershwin an opportunity, of which he has taken good advantage, for the enrichment and broadening of his customary musical material . . ." *See*: **W37b**

B554. DAVENPORT, Marcia, & Ruth Woodbury SEDGWICK. "Rhapsody in   Black." *Stage Magazine* 13/2 (Nov. 1935): 31-33.

B555. DOWNES, Olin. "'Porgy and Bess', Native Opera, Opens at the Alvin, Gershwin Work Based on Du Bose Heyward's Play: Exotic Richness of Negro Music and Color of Charleston, S.C., Admirably Conveyed in Score of Catfish Row Tragedy." *NYTimes*, Oct. 11, 1935, p. 30.
Review of the premiere by the Times' music critic. *See*: **W37b**

B556. _____. "When Critics Disagree: Amusing Dramatics and Musical Commentary Upon Gershwin's Porgy and Bess." *NYTimes*, Oct. 20, 1935, Section 10, p. 7. Also in: Irene DOWNES, ed. *Olin Downes on Music: A Selection from His Writings during the Half-Century* as: "Porgy and Bess and the Future of American Opera," pp. 208-211.

B557. "Drama: Dissenting Opinion." *The Nation* 66/3669 (Oct. 30, 1935): 518-519.

B558. FLATOW, S. "Premiere Porgy: Todd Duncan recalls the creation of Gershwin's opera." *Opera News* 49 (March 16, 1985): 34-35+

B559. GARLAND, Robert. "Negroes are Critical of 'Porgy and Bess.'" *New York*

World Telegram, Jan. 16, 1936, p. 14. *See*: **W37b**

B560. "Gershwin Back to Finish Work On New Opera; Manhattan Tone Poet Climbs Into His Cliff Dwelling Loaded With Negro Lore,Walked in Catfish Alley; Wants Robeson for 'Porgy' When Guild Produces It." *NY Herald Tribune* **[NN-L]**, Jan. 5, 1934.
General news story announcing G's return from Florida, his work on the "Six Variations on I Got Rhythm" for the upcoming tour with Leo Reisman, his stop in Charleston, SC on the way home, and the beginnings of his work on P&B.

B561. "Gershwin: Talented Composer Gave *Porgy* Life and Rhythm." *NewsWeek* 6/15 (Oct. 12, 1935): 22.
Review of the NY premiere. *See*: **W37b**

B562. "Gershwin's American Opera Puts Audience on Its Feet." *News-Week* 6/16 (Oct. 19, 1935): 23-24. *See*: **W37b**

B563. GILMAN, Lawrence. "George Gershwin's New Opera, Porgy and Bess, Produced by the Theatre Guild." *NY Herald Tribune*, Oct. 11, 1935.
Gilman's review of the NY premiere. *See*: **W37b**

B564. GOLDBERG, Isaac. "Score by George Gershwin: In the music for *Porgy and Bess* Mr. Gershwin richly expands and intensifies the original *Porgy*." *Stage Magazine* 13/3 (Dec. 1935): 37-38.
Lengthy and praiseworthy review of the Boston premiere. In essay form, the writing includes some musical analysis. *See*: **W37a**

B565. HAMM, Charles. "The Theatre Guild Production of *Porgy and Bess*." *Journal of the American Musicological Society* 40/3 (Fall 1987): 495-532.
In a very detailed scholarly article, Hamm traced the history of the original production under the auspices of the Theatre Guild, in Boston and New York. Hamm discussed G's and Mamoulian's roles in shaping that version. Five sources: (1, 2) at Harvard [2 scores], (3) the Music Division of the Library of Congress, (4) at the Billy Rose Theatre Collection in the New York Public Library, and (5) at Yale, were used as the basis for reconstructing the cuts made in the Boston and New York productions. At the time Hamm wrote this article he was not aware of a sixth source, the piano-vocal score held by the Millsaps College Library in Jackson, MS, the score which appears to have been used by Lehman Engel for his recording of P&B (Columbia, **D496**). Excellent bibliography. *See*: **W37a, W37b**

B566. HEYWARD, Dorothy & DuBose. *Porgy*. NY: Doubleday, Page, 1927.
The play version of the original 1925 novel.

B567. HEYWARD, DuBose. *Porgy* [the novel]. NY: Doran, 1925.

B568. _____, with color illustrations by **Alexander KING**. "Porgy and Bess: Return on Wings of Song," in **Merle Armitage,** ed. *George Gershwin*, reprinted by Da Capo Press, 1995, pp. 34-42. Original appeared in *Stage* 8/1 (Oct. 1935): 25-28.
Essay giving the genesis of the opera from the point of view of the librettist. Heyward also theorized: ". . . Statistics record the fact that there are 25,000,000 radios in America. Their contribution to the opera was indirect but important." *See*: **W37b**

B569. ISAACS, Edith J. R. "See America First: Broadway in Review." *Theatre Arts Monthly* 19/12 (Dec. 1935): 888-902.
Review of P&B, pp. 893-894. *See:* **W37b**

B570. JOHNSON, Hall. "Porgy and Bess—A Folk Opera: A Review." *Opportunity* (January 1936): 24-28.
A detailed evaluation from a review article. It concerns the Alvin Theatre production from the point of view of a "distinguished Negro musician." ". . . After having sat and stood through four performances of *Porgy and Bess*, I am certain that I do like it and that it is a good show . . ." However, Johnson also felt that the opera was not an authentic Negro work and found faults, including ". . . inexpert craftmanship in the manipuation of the variety element, the staging [about which he was particularly vehement] . . . the lack of story-telling qualities in the music; too little first-hand knowledge of his [G's] character-types and their real music; and the necessity (?) of perverting that little to satisfy Broadway tastes . . ."
See: **W37b**

B571. KOLODIN, Irving. "Porgy and Bess: American Opera in the Theatre." *Theatre Arts Monthly* 19 (1935): 853-865.
An appraisal of P&B based on Kolodin's extensive and theatrically astute observations of the July and August rehearsals prior to the September 20, 1935 world premiere in Boston. ". . . Whatever verdict may be returned regarding the details of this particular work, its large outlines and moments of climax mark it as the product of the first authentic talent in our musical theatre . . ." Kolodin pointed out what he considered to be faults in G's score, but concluded: ". . There is rarely a cessation in the flow of rich blood through the veins of the score; and both the vitality and fertility of the invention are qualities unique in our musical theatre. Gershwin has fairly accomplished his *Rienzi*—we wait to see and hear his *Lohengrin*, his *Tannhäuser*, and who knows but one day his *Meistersinger*.
See: **W37a & W37b**

B572. _____. "A Preface to the Premiere of 'Porgy and Bess': George Gershwin's First Opera Is Both Fulfillment and Promise." *Brooklyn Daily Eagle* **[NN-L]**, October 6, 1935.
"Speaking as one who has the opportunity of listening to the score from the composer's piano last Spring, and also observing the work of preparation from the earliest to the most recent stages, I am chiefly impressed with the manner in which 'Porgy and Bess' has fulfilled its early studio promise in the theater . . ." Kolodin found fault with G's writing in the love songs in P&B. *See:* **W37a**

B573. KRUTCH, Joseph Wood. "Drama: Dissenting Opinion." *The Nation* 141/3669 (Oct. 30, 1935): 518-519.
An unusual, negative review that would be a good candidate for inclusion in Nicolas Slonimsky's *Lexicon of Musical Invective*. ". . . Having no equipment for musical criticism [therefore giving an uninformed opinion] I speak with great diffidence, but to my lay ear Mr. Gershwin's music, though pretentious enough, seemed lacking in both memorable melodies [!] and real dramatic effect; most of it was obviously more or less in the idiom of the spiritual, but though this fact gave it a general character it never seemed to achieve much dramatic expressiveness capable of adding to the intensity of any particular situation. As for Mr. Mamoulian's production, I speak with more confidence. It was also very ambitious, but mechanical rather than imaginative . . ." *See:* **W37b**

B574. "Letters and Art: Charleston (and Gershwin) Provide Folk Opera. 'Porgy and Bess,'

Its Structure Intact, Furnishes a Rich, Brawling Theme for a Native Tale With Music, and Arouses Manhattan Cheers for Its Composer." *Literary Digest* 120/170-2375 (Oct. 26, 1935): 18.

One-page, but informative summary review of the NY premiere. "Drama- and music-critics, arm in arm, assigned themselves to the premiere of 'Porgy and Bess.' Only one New York play-critic has a musical background; the rest could not trust themselves to a true estimation of the score. The music critics were in similar case; they were ready and eager to appraise the music, unwilling to consider the dramatic aspects of the libretto. George Gershwin emerged from this duet of critical examination handsomely . . ." The article concludes with succinct quotes from New York newspaper critics W. J. Henderson, Gabriel, and Gilman. *See*: **W37b**

B575. MAMOULIAN, Rouben. "I Remember." in: **Merle ARMITAGE,** ed., *George Gershwin*, NY: Longmans, Green, 1938, pp. 47-57.

The first dramatic director of P&B reminisces about his experiences with G.

B576. MELLERS, Wilfrid. "From pop to art: opera, the musical and George Gershwin's "Porgy and Bess." in *Music in a New Found Land.* pp. 393-413.

A chapter of extensive musical analysis. The following passage, concerning the song "Gone, Gone, Gone," is typical: ". . . After the violent action of this scene [where Crown killed Robbins], the second scene of Act I is static. It begins with a lament for the dead Robbins, in which solo voices declaim the pentatonic ululations, based on observation of genuine gospel 'shouts.' The chorus intones the word 'gone' in a descending whole-tone progression, harmonized with unrelated diatonic concords. Each triad sounds like a thudding of earth-clods, while the chords' lack of harmonic relationship suggests disintegration, the opening of an abyss . . ."

B577. _____. "Music, Theatre, and Commerce: A Note on Gershwin, Menotti, and Marc Blitzstein." *The Score and I. M. A. Magazine* 12 (June 1955): 69-76.

Most of this article treats Blitzstein's "plays in music," but, in addition to commentary on Menotti's oeuvre and comparison of him to G, Mellers discussed P&B: "Significantly, G's only successful large-scale work is his opera, P&B. Here, the 'numbers,' as in the commercial musical, can be held together by the story: so it is comparatively unimportant that G's constructive technique is not much less rudimentary in his opera than in his symphonic pieces. Habitually, he resorts to *ostinato* basses, rhythmic patterns, alternations of two chords and mechanical sequences in order to keep the music going; in moments of excitement he unfailingly lapses into sliding chromatics. Yet *Porgy* is a moving, even impressive work; and it is so because, for all its sophisticated facilities, G's tunes have never been more spontaneous or more fetching . . ."

B578. "Music: Folk Opera." *Time* 26/17 (Oct. 21, 1935): 48.

Comparing it to the play, this is a review of the premiere production in NY. "A lullaby called *Summer Time* is likely to become a best-seller . . . *Porgy and Bess* is not 'grand,' is not intended for the musical few . . ." *See*: **W37b**

B579. "Music, Porgy into Opera." *Time* 26/4 (Sept. 30, 1935): 49-50.

Descriptive preview article, prior to the premiere opening in NY. *See*: **W37b**

B580. NATHAN, J. "The Theatre: Stanza IV." *Vanity Fair* 45 (Dec. 1935): 68.

Negative review. The critic could not accept *Porgy* even as a "folk opera." While admitting that P&B "contains some symptoms of hope for the aforesaid future," Nathan concluded about G's creative ability: ". . . But that his talent is equal to the demands of anything approaching true and genuine folk opera remains still for the future to answer . . ."*See*: **W37b**

B581. NORTON, Elliot. "Premiere of 'Porgy and Bess:' Opera at the Colonial Able and Brilliant Experiment." *Boston Post*, Oct. 1, 1935, p. 14.

Review of the premiere performance at the Boston tryout. Although Norton's review was mixed, he obviously was impressed and commented on the music: ". . . For Mr. Gershwin, the composer, the whole verdict cannot yet be read. This is neither dodging the question nor passing it along. What he has attempted is too big and too new to be completely and casually weighed . . . He has written much beautiful music: some it so melodic and inspired that it will positively be included in the best seller lists . . ." *See*: **W37a**

B582. "'Porgy:' the play that set the pattern." *Theatre Arts* 39/10 (Oct. 1955): 33-64.

Article including the complete text of *Porgy*, the 1927 play by DuBose and Dorothy Heyward, from which P&B was derived. This printing is easily accessible, and, with it, the reader can compare the original play script with the libretto for the opera as published in Stanley Richards' *Ten Great Musicals of the American Theatre* (**B537**).

B583. "Porgy Into Opera." *Time* 26/14 (Sept. 30, 1935): 49-50.

B584. SEDGWICK, Ruth W. "Two Adventures in Direction: Eight Years Ago Rouben Mamoulian made his Broadway debut as director of *Porgy*. Now, Back from Hollywood, he has directed the Gershwin-Heyward opera *Porgy and Bess*." *Stage* 13/1 (October 1935): 60-61.

Background material on Mamoulian's directing, first of the play *Porgy*, followed by his direction of the 1935 version of the opera. This interesting material was prepared before the premiere, and it includes a drawing of Mamoulian by Peggy Bacon, with a caption about him, also by Bacon. *See*: **W37b**

B585. SMITH, Warren Storey. "Premiere of 'Porgy and Bess:' Gershwin Starts Out Ambitiously and Music in First Act Shows Real Craftmanship—Thereafter Mixes His Styles—Singing, Excellent." *Boston Post*, Oct. 1, 1935, p. 14.

Review of the premiere performance at the Boston tryout, September 30, 1935. Generally this is a mixed appraisal. ". . . Musically speaking, in the first act, Mr. Gershwin, whatever his other shortcomings, did not mix his styles, an unforgivable offence in an operatic composer. Thereafter he did. More than once last evening the spectators, becoming confused as to the real nature of the piece, did not know whether they were to laugh or cry . . ." Smith compared P&B to Louis Gruenberg's *Emperor Jones* and Richard Strauss' *The Silent Woman*. *See*: **W37a**

B586. STANDIFER, James A. "Reminiscences of Black Musicians." *American Music* 4/2 (Summer 1986): 194-205.

Includes oral history interview of Todd Duncan and Anne Brown from the 1935 original cast. *See*: **W37b, B542**

B587. STEINERT, Alexander. "Porgy and Bess and Gershwin," in: **Merle ARMITAGE,** ed. *George Gershwin.* NY: Longmans, Green, 1938, pp. 43-46.
Comments by the vocal coach for the original production. *See*: **W37b**

B588. VERNON, Grenville. "The Play: Porgy and Bess." *The Commonweal* 22/26 (Oct. 25, 1935): 642.

In the review of the original NY production at the Alvin Theater, Vernon called P&B "a true music-drama." ". . . It is always interesting both musically and dramatically . . . Whether or not 'Porgy and Bess' is 'grand opera' is beside the point. Grand opera is a fluid term; its rules have never been defined and never will be . . . [Gershwin's] artistic integrity is impeccable, and never more so than in his spirituals . . ." *See:* **W37b**

B589. WATERS, Edward N. "Music." *The Library of Congress Quarterly Journal of Current Acquisitions* 18/1 (Nov. 1960): 13-39.

The gift of manuscript sketches for P&B is discussed.

B590. WALDAU, Roy Sandman. *The Theatre Guild's Middle Years—1928-1939.*

Ph.D. dissertation, New York University School of Education, 1966, pp. 288-300.

Concerns "the third production" of the Theatre Guild: the world premiere of P&B, and the "financial, casting, and rehearsal problems, among many others" the Guild endured in producing P&B. An informative discussion of the financing, the choice of the theatre, and the early offers for motion picture agreements are presented. A synopsis of the reviews for both the Boston and New York premieres is included. Problems with the Actors Equity and musicians labor unions encountered by the Guild are elaborated upon. By the end of the New York run, apparent financial difficulties caused the original 70-member cast to be reduced to 40. *See:* **W37**

B591. YOUNG, Stark. "Opera Blues: *Porgy and Bess* . . ." *New Republic* 84/1092 (Oct. 30, 1935): 338.

A mixed review of the NY premiere production at the Alvin by a non-musician, drama critic. ". . . I must say that I thought Mr. Gershwin's opera a real disappointment. It was too long, for one thing. It was curiously monotonous without creating any single compelling mood . . ." *See:* **W37b**

1940s:

B592. ATKINSON, Brooks. "Music in Catfish Row." *NYTimes* (*NYTimes Theater Reviews*), Feb. 1, 1942, section 9, p. 1.

A lengthy and positive review of the NY opening of Cheryl Crawford's revival of P&B at the Majestic Theater, January 22, 1942. Atkinson gave his reasons for why a favorable "change in public feeling came about" P&B, at the same time addressing himself to the question of the work as an opera. ". . . 'Porgy and Bess' has already outlived the drama, 'Porgy,' from which it was created. That is what the virtuoso songs and chorals by Gershwin have done for it." *See:* **W37g**

B593. _____. "Porgy and Bess." *NYTimes* (*New York Times Theater Reviews*), Jan. 23, 1942, section 2, p. 16.

Atkinson's first (of two) critical opinions of the Cheryl Crawford revival in its performance at NY's Majestic Theater on January 22, 1942. His second opinion is given above at **B592**. ". . . Some of the songs of 'Porgy and Bess.' like 'Summertime,' 'I Got Plenty O' Nuttin' and 'It Ain't Necessarily So,' have been played and sung constantly in concerts and over the radio and have become an authentic part of our musical heritage. Although the original production . . . ran only four months, its reputation has grown beyond that of any musical work produced in the theatre . . . Although he [G] respected opera as a form, he had a genius for songs. And what a playgoer can still enjoy with the most rhapsodic pleasure are the great songs he wrote for the lovable, free-hand sketch of the Negro community. *See*: **W37g**

B594. "Catfish Row in an Encore." *News-Week* 14/5 (Feb. 2, 1942): 55-57.
Review of the Crawford revival at NY's Majestic Theatre. *See*: **W37g**

B595. DOWNES, Olin. "'Porgy' Fantasy." *NYTimes*, Nov. 15, 1942, Section 8, p. 7.

B596. EWEN, David. "A Wartime 'Porgy.'" *NYTimes*, Oct. 9, 1955, Section I2, pp. 1, 3.
First European performance in 1943 in Nazi-occupied Denmark. *See*: **B598, W37k**

B597. GILDER, Rosamond. "Places and People: Broadway in Review." *Theatre Arts* 26/4 (Apr. 1942): 219-20.
Crawford's revival of P&B discussed favorably. *See*: **W37g**

B598. LAMB, G. "The Danish Porgy (Copenhagen, 1943)." *Opera* 42 (Feb. 1991): 169-170. *See*: **W37k, B596**

B599. NICHOLS, Lewis. "Porgy and Bess . . ." *NYTimes (NYTimes Theater Reviews)*, Sept. 14, 1943.
". . . Last evening [Sept. 13], before taking it out on another tour of the country, Cheryl Crawford brought . . .[P&B] . . . to the Forty-fourth Street Theatre, where it is to stay a few weeks to show those who have not seen it what they have missed and to show those who are going again what an unusually pleasant evening a repeat visit can provide . . ."
See: **W37i**

B600. NICHOLS. "'Porgy' in U. S. S. R." *NYTimes* (*NYTimes Theater Reviews*), June 17, 1945, Section 2, p. 4:3.
Review. "'Magnificent' was the word chosen by Dmitri Shostakovich to describe the first performance in Moscow of Gershwin's 'Porgy and Bess' last month . . ." *See*: **W37m**

B601. NICHOLS, Lewis. "Porgy is Back." *NYTimes*, Feb. 8, 1944, 13:2.
Effusive review of the Crawford revival on Feb. 7, 1944, the post-tour opening at the City Center, where it was to run for two weeks. Nichols gives the cast changes for this version, among them the fact that Todd Duncan was replaced as Porgy by William Franklin. Comparing this performance to the one in the fall of 1943, Nichols concluded "'Porgy and Bess' has become an institution—one of the best." *See*: **W37l**

B602. _____. "Porgy and Bess. . ." *NYTimes* (*NYTimes Theater Reviews*), Sept. 14, 1943, section 2, p. 26.
Review of the Cheryl Crawford revival in its NY premiere at the Forty-fourth Street Theatre. ". . . 'Porgy and Bess' has not staled and it is as fresh as when the [Theater] Guild first presented it and Miss Crawford made the first revival a year and a half ago . . . The opera has a high good humor and an excitement, it can be tender and tragic by turn and the music fits the mood. Between the first production and the revival some of the recitative was cut, a bit of editing which increased the speed without losing the character . . ." *See*: **W37i**

B603. *"Porgy and Bess* on Tour." *Theatre Arts* 27/11 (Nov. 1943): 677-678.
Discussion of the first year of the Cheryl Crawford tour. ". . . The response was enthusiastic, the potential audience barely sampled . . . As *Porgy and Bess* goes into its second year on the road, the only replacement since Etta Moten stepped into Anne Brown's shoes

during the New York run has been Alma Hubbard, who took over Serena's role after the death of Ruby Elzy . . ." *See*: **W37h**

B604. "Porgy in Maplewood," in **THOMSON, Virgil**. *The Musical Scene*. NY: Alfred A. Knopf, 1945, pp. 167-169.
Reprint of Thomson's review of the revival on opening night, in Maplewood, NJ on October 13, 1941, the review appearing in the October 19 *NYHerald Tribune*. ". . . Mr. Smallens [the conductor] has taken occasion to diminish the thickness of the instrumentation and to make some further musical cuts . . . [A] considerable number of these had been made, with Gershwin's consent, during the opera's original run. Others have been incorporated in this production, with the purpose of speeding up certain badly timed passages and with that of eliminating, where possible, the embarassments due to Gershwin's incredibly amatuerish way of writing recitative . . . It [P&B] remains, none the less, a beautiful piece of music and a deeply moving play for the lyric theater . . ." *See*: **W37e**

B605. VON STROBER, Mervin. "Letters (touring with Porgy and Bess in 1942-44)." *Opera News* 54 (Feb. 17, 1990): 43. *See*: **W37h**

B606. WYATT, Euphemia Van Rensselaer. "The Drama: American Opera." *Catholic World* 154/924 (Mar. 1942): 726-727.
Complimentary review of the 1942 revival of P&B. *See*: **W37g**

1950s:

B607. AHLER-BUUK, Margot, Malwine BLUNCK, and **Annette ZIEGLER,** with Introduction by **James HATCH.** "Black Musicians in Germany: Two Bibliographies . . . Reviews of *Porgy and Bess* in German Newspapers and Periodicals." *The Black Perspective in Music* 5/2 (Fall 1977): 161-172.
Translated excerpts from thirty-two reviews ranging from such sources as *Süddeutsche Zeitung*, November 23, 1952 (the first performance in Germany was on Sept. 17, 1952), to an article by H.W. Koch in *Opernwelt* (Heft8,S.54). *See*: **W37s**

B608. AMIS, John. "Opera: Mozart to Gershwin: 'Porgy and Bess.'" *Musical Times* 93 (Nov. 1952): 512-513.

B609. "The Arts, Music: Odyssey With Gershwin." *Newsweek* 47 (Jan. 9, 1956): 43-44.
Report about the Breen-Davis touring production written a week after the opera opened for a two-week run at the Leningrad Palace of Culture. ". . . 'Porgy and Bess' has played almost continuously, here and abroad, since it opened in Dallas on June 9, 1952. It has appeared in twenty cities in the U. S. and Canada, and in 37 in Europe, the Middle East, and Latin America. It has been seen by approximately 3 million people . . ." A translated quote from music critic Count Johannes Kalckreuth of the *Süddeutsche Zeitung* is included: ". . . To apply to 'Porgy' the rules for a perfect piece of art would never explain its success. The stunning brilliance of its presentation also does not explain it. What makes is so impressive is that it is a lucky crystallization of contemporary thought, just as were in their time 'Everyman' and the 'Beggars Opera' . . ." *See*: **W37jj**

B610. "Athens Applauds American Singers in 'Porgy and Bess.'" *Musical America* 75/3 (Feb. 1, 1955): 33. *See*: **W37aa**

B611. ATKINSON, Brooks. "Negro Folk Drama: Porgy and Bess Suitable for Production Before Audiences in European Capitals." *NYTimes,* Sept. 7, 1952, Section 2, p. 1.

B612. _____. "Return of a Classic: 'Porgy and Bess' Comes Home From Europe." *NYTimes,* Mar. 15, 1953, Section 2, p. 1, also to be found in: *NYTimes Theater Reviews* of Mar. 15, 1953.

Detailed story announcing the return of the Robert Breen production from its highly successful tour to Europe and England. Atkinson took this opportunity to slap the hands of those that opposed the tour in September of 1952, and to reaffirm his critical acceptance of the opera. ". . . [T]his is the best of the 'Porgy and Bess' productions we have had in New York since the Theatre Guild produced it in 1935 . . . In the present version [the director, Breen, and the conductor, Smallens] have restored a great deal of the operatic treatment, put music under scenes that used to be played as spoken drama and they have also introduced two songs that have never been used in New York before. The vocal and instrumental music now is not a comment on, or embellishment of, the story, but the fundamental tool of expression. And on these terms, 'Porgy and Bess' is a richer, more sensitive, more unified, more powerful piece of work . . ." *See:* **W37v, B551**

B613. ATKINSON, Brooks. "Porgy and Bess . . ." *NYTimes* (*NYTimes Theater Reviews*), Mar. 10, 1953, p. 25:5.

Effusive review of the opening, March 9, 1953, at NY's Ziegfeld, by the Breen-Davis touring company. ". . . It is the fifth 'Porgy and Bess' New York has had since the original opening in 1935. It is by odds the best and it is magnificent . . . George Gershwin, if he were alive today, would feel thoroughly vindicated. As a song show, 'Porgy and Bess' has been delightful during the intervening years. But as an opera with a brilliantly orchestrated score, with recitative and all the operatic mumbo-jumbo, it is a major work of art—a tumultous evocation of life among some high-spirited, poignant, admirable human beings. It is all Gershwin and it is gold . . ." *See:* **W37v**

B614. "Auld Lang Syne." *Musical America* 75/3 (Jan. 1, 1955): 9.
P&B in Belgrade and Zagreb. *See:* **W37z**

B615. "Austria." *Opera* 3/12 (Dec. 1952): 733.
Review. *See:* **W37r**

B616. B., G. "Opera, 'Porgy' Exotic and Exciting: Colourful Negro Opera." *Recorder* (England), October 18, 1952.
Review of the London run in 1952. ". . . P&B is a moving, colourful, exciting, uninhibited Negro opera which, because these very qualities are so rare in England today, may well run for a long time at the Stoll Theatre . . ." *See:* **W37t**

B617. BELLERBY, L. "Second Thoughts on Porgy and Bess." *Jazz Journal* 6/1 (Jan. 1953): 6.

B618. BERUTH, Fritzi. "Ein exotisches Lebensbild: ‚Porgy and Bess.' " *Wiener Zeitung,* 9 Sept. 1952. **[NNMus]**
Review of the first performance in at the Volksoper. *See:* **W37r**

B619. BLUTHNER, Hans. "'Porgy and Bess' in **Berlin**," trans. by **Jack CUNDALL.** *Jazz Journal* 5 (Nov. 1952): 12-13.

Article referring to the appearance of the Davis-Breen touring company at the Berlin Festival. Bluthner reported on the "after the theatre" musical activities of cast members, who frequented "The Bath Tub," Berlin's then best known jazz club, many of them sitting in with the local band. *See:* **W37s**

B620. BORNEMAN, Ernest. "Second Thoughts on Some Musical Sacrilege." *Melody Maker* 28/998 (Nov. 1, 1952): 8.
P&B criticized.

B621. BRENDEMÜHL, Rudolf. "Die Negeroper vom Bettler und der Dirne." *nachtedepesche*, 20 Sept. 1952.
Review of a Sept.1952 performance at the Titania-Palast in Berlin. *See:* **W37s**

B622. BUCHWALD, Art. "London After Dark: It Ain't Necessarily So." *NY Herald Tribune*, dateline London], October 13, 1952.
Brief review of the London premiere, October 9, 1952. *See:* **W37t**

B623. BURKE, Georgia. "The Porgy and Bess Story, 1952-53." *Equity* 38/5 (May 1953): 13-15.

B624. CALTA, Louis. "Stage Folk to See Preview of 'Porgy.'" *NYTimes*, Mar. 4, 1953, p. 21.

B625. CAPOTE, Truman. *The Muses Are Heard, an Account*. NY: Random House, 1956.
Capote's commentary on performances of P&B in Russia. *See:* **W37jj**

B626. CLURMAN, Harold. "Theater." *Nation* 176/13 (Mar. 28, 1953).
Brief review of the production of P&B at the Ziegfeld in New York in 1953. ". . . Gershwin's music has a certain smart sophistication, but its outstanding characteristic . . . is warm sentiment or a kind of yearning for sentiment. It is as if a skilful [sic] popular composer were trying to reach some area of feeling beyond the clatter and glister of 'Broadway's' surface, an area purer, richer, more tender than what others were satisfied with . . ." *See:* **W37v**

B627. COE, Richard. "Porgy at La Scala Just Another Wow Date; SRO Show Eyes Tent Setup." *Variety* 198, Mar. 9, 1955 (dateline: Milan, Mar. 1), pp. 2, 75.
Glowing review of the La Scala week-long run. According to this article, the touring company had returned to Europe at Venice the previous Fall (of 1954). Other scheduled stops were Genoa, Florence, and Rome. Previous stops mentioned were Alexandria, Egypt, Zagreb, and Belgrade. Cast members mentioned were: Leslie Scott and Gloria Davy who "were chosen to sing La Scala opening night," Fredye Marshall, Martha Flowers, La Verne Hutcherson, Irving Barnes, Lorenzo Fuller, Joseph Attles, Earl Jackson, John McCurray, and Paul Harris, with Alexander Smallens, conducting. *See:* **W37cc**

B628. _____. (The author was drama editor of the *Washington Post* and *Times-Herald*. "[Title?]." *Theatre Arts* 39/5 (May 1955): 66-67, 92-94.
Another review of the opera in its performance at Milan's Teatro della Scala. Regarding critical opinion by the local papers: ". . . The *Corriere's* chief critic, Franco Abbiati, wrote an essay that producer-director Breen might have written himself, urging such companies as this to revivify opera throughout the world . . . *L' Unita's* Rubens Tedeschi found *Porgy and Bess* 'Among the masterworks of lyric theatre . . . the excellence of performance so overwhelming

that the whole seems entirely spontaneous' . . ." ". . . [T]he *Porgy and Bess* company, in its travels abroad, has been doing much more than playing an opera. It has been acting . . . as an American ambassador . . ." *See:* **W37cc**

B629. "Congressman Attacks 'Porgy' Tour, Despite Show's Favorable Impact." *Variety* 201/2 (Dec. 14, 1955): 1+.

B630. COOKMAN, Anthony. "At the Theatre: 'Porgy and Bess' (Stoll)." *The Tatler and Bystander*, October 22, 1952.
Review of the 1952 Stoll Theatre production. ". . . There was the obvious risk that this audaciously close mingling of pictorial and human values would lead to a bewildering dispersion of interest. Too much might be happening in too many places at once. But, happily, this is not how it works [out] . . ." *See:* **W37t**

B631. DOLL, Bill. "Folk Opera Capacity in Washington: Heyward-Gershwin Work Will Go to Berlin, Vienna, London After a Successful Tour in This Country." Special to the *NYHerald Tribune* (dateline: Washington, Aug. 23, 1952), Aug. 24, 1952, Section 4, pp. 1, 3.
Lengthy article about the August 1952 run at Washington's National Theater. This story is of particular significance because it outlines director Robert Breen's version of the opera. ". . . His approach . . . was to wade carefully through the 750-page published score, also the abridged score from the [1942] Crawford production, and to familiarize himself with the version recorded by Columbia. Working with [Blevins] Davis, the new version took shape with many changes and additions that were not included in previous stage renditions. Breen has injected additional dialogue taken from the novel and the play, and by eliminating nine waits for scene changes, has managed to include more of the Gershwin score than has ever been used. He has injected 'Roll Dem Bones' into the first-act crap game, added 'I Ain't Got No Shame' to the picnic scene, and shifted 'Good Mornin' to make an immediate sharp contrast of mood following the killing of Crown. Throughout he has used bits and pieces of hitherto unused music to create bridges between scenes . . . He found for the first time a perfect spot for the inclusion of the much talked about 'Buzzard Song.' He uses it in the final act to create an air of foreboding before the citizenry of Catfish Row admit to Porgy that Bess has left him. Still revamping and improving, Breen will insert 'I Hate Your Struttin' Style' before the end of the local run . . ." *See:* **W37q**

B632. "Escenas del estreno de la opera Porgy and Bess de George Gershwin en la Staatsoper de Viena." *Boletin de Musica y Artes Visuales,* Pan American Union Nos. 36-37 (Feb.-Mar. 1953): 22-25.
Reviews a 1952 performance. *See:* **W37r**

B633. FREEDLEY, Vinton. "Porgy and Always the Best." *Saturday Review* 41 (Oct. 18, 1958): 14-15.

B634. FUNKE, Lewis. "News and Gossip of the Rialto: 'Porgy and Bess' Loses Official Support." *NYTimes,* Oct. 2, 1955, Section 2, p. 1.

B635. "'Gershwin's Music Subversive' Says Senator McCarthy." *Melody Maker* 29/1031 (June 13, 1953): 12.

B636. GRAF, Max. "Gershwins Meisterwerk: Erste Wiener Aufführung von 'Porgy and Bess' in der Wiener Volksoper." *Weltpresse*, Wien, 9 Sept. 1952. **[NNMus]**

Substantial two-column review of the first performance in Vienna at the Volksoper.
See: **W37r**

B637. _____. "Porgy and Bess Begins European Tour in Vienna." *Musical America*
72/12 (Oct. 1952 [dateline: Vienna]): 9.

Review of the opening performance, September 7, of the Davis-Breen 1952 troupe at
the Vienna Staatstheater. ". . . The performance was full of life and movement . . . William
Warfield [as Porgy] . . . made DuBose Heyward's character extraordinarily vivid, with his
warm personality and superb voice . . . Leontyne Price imbued the figure of Bess with
fascinating feminine charm. Not only did her voice sound beautiful, but she exerted an erotic
spell that gripped the audience . . ." *See*: **W37r**

B638.   HAJAS, Dezsö. "Der Gastspiel in der Volksoper: ,Porgy und Bess.'" *Der
Abend*, Wien, 8 Sept. 1952. **[NNMus]**

Article concerning the first performance in Vienna at the Volksoper. *See*: **W37r**

B639.   HANGEN, Welles. "'Porgy and Bess' in the U. S. S. R.: Gershwin-Heyward Work
Scores in Leningrad and Moscow." *NYTimes* (dateline: Moscow), Jan. 15, 1956,
section 2, p. 3.

Review of the Breen-Davis mid-fifties touring production. The article includes
observations on the impressions of the opera on the Russian populace. ". . . The Government
paper echoed general opinion when it extolled 'the ensemble harmony' of the production,
observing that the performance 'lives and breathes with one life' . . ." *See*: **W37jj & W37kk**

B640.   HAYES, Richard. "The Stage: Porgy & Bess." *Commonweal* 57/25 (Mar. 27, 1953):
624-625.

Mixed review of the Breen-Davis "most sumptuous revival yet" at NY's Ziegfeld
Theatre in 1953. While Hayes considered that ". . . [i]f opulence of sound and physical vivacity
were the essential stuff of opera, 'Porgy and Bess' would sweep all before it . . ." he
nonetheless found ". . . it impossible to speak of the work without some measure of
exasperation . . ." Labelling the work a folk opera, the reviewer concluded, ". . . Gershwin
could hold together the extraordinary efflorescence of his talent only with orchestration that
is either feeble or frantic, and with uninteresting recitative and dispirited connective material
. . ." *See*: **W37v.**

B641.   HUBALEK. "Kunst und Kultur: ,Porgy and Bess.'" *Arbeiter-Zeitung*. Wien, 9 Sept.,
1952. **[NNMus]**

Substantial two-column review of the first performance in at the Volksoper. *See*:
W37r

B642.   JONES, Max. "Gershwin could not have had a finer monument." *Melody Maker*,
October 18, 1952.

Review of one of the London Stoll Theatre performances. *See*: **W37t**

B643.   KOLODIN, Irving. "Music to My Ears: 'Porgy'—'Boris' with Siepi-Kubelik."
Saturday Review 36/13 (Mar. 28, 1953): 27-28.

Laudatory review of the opening of the 1953 revival. ". . . To be sure, it is something
of a rousing experience to come upon this score, 'live,' after four or five years away from it;
but . . . I'd still cite the present arrangement of Gershwin's materials . . . likewise those who
are giving them life, as superior to any previous combination . . ." Kolodin also listed the

changes made as a result of "evolutionary editorial work." *See*: **W37v**

B644. KONEN, Valentina Dzozefovna. "'Porgy i Bess' Spektaki amerikankoj ruppy 'Evrimen opera.'" *Sovetskaya Muzyka* 20/3 (Mar. 1956): 118-122.
See: **W37kk**

B645. KOVALYER, U. "Booked for Travel: The Russian Critic." *Saturday Review* 39/2 (Jan. 14, 1956): 38.
Review of a performance of the Breen-Davis touring company in Leningrad. Kovalyer seemed most taken by the dance in the performance, but concluded ". . . 'Porgy and Bess' presents one of the most interesting events of this theatrical season . . ." *See*: **W37jj**

B646. LEVIN, Sylvan. "So How's Your Embouchure? 'Porgy' Pickup Orchs O'Seas Quite a Problem to a Meticulous Maestro." *Variety*, Apr. 4, 1956, p. 2, 63.
A report of the problems encountered during the 1956 tour when trying to get the European orchestras, especially "pickup" groups, to play competently and in the uninhibited style dictated by P&B. See: **W37ll**

B647. LEYDI, Roberto. "George Gershwin e it 'Porgy and Bess.'" *Il Diapason* 5/1 (Jan. 1955): 15-23.

B648. "London Theatres: The Stoll." *The Stage* [London], October 16, 1952.
An unsigned and partially negative review of the October 9, 1952, opening at the Stoll. ". . . When the tragedy and pathos of the crippled Porgy call for musical expression, the composer's limitations, both orchestrally and vocally, are evident . . ." *See*: **W37t**

B649. LÜTTWITZ, Heinrich von. "Armeleutedramen-In Schwarz und Weiss." *Musica* 10/1 (Jan. 1956): 82-83.
Review of a performance at Düsseldorf. *See*: **W37ll**

B650. M., K. "Begeisterungsstürme um ‚Porgy und Bess' Gershwins Oper von amerikanischen Negerkünstlern in der Volksoper erstaufgeführt." *Wiener Kurier*, 8 Sept. 1952. **[NNMus]**
Very long article concerning the premiere performance in Vienna at the Volksoper. *See*: **W37r.**

B651. MALIPIERO, Riccardo. "Porgy and Bess." *La Biennale di Venezia* No. 22 (1954): 36-38. *See*: **W37x**

B652. MANNOCK, P. L. "It Was Worth Waiting 17 Years for Porgy." *Daily Herald* [London], October 10, 1952.
Review of the October 9, 1952, opening night of P&B in London. ". . . Vivid production brings to life the strange beauty of a tawdry community and the dusky cast, with immense vocal range and fierce gusto, do wonders. . ." *See*: **W37t**

B653. MCCORMAC, John. "'Porgy' Scores Hit At Bow In Vienna." *NYTimes* (Special to the Times) [dateline: Vienna, Sept. 7] (*NYTimes Theater Reviews*), Sept. 8, 1952, 18:2.
". . . [T]he artistic aspects of this performance in **Vienna** seemed to be successful . . . the cast received a dozen curtain calls . . ." at this, the European premiere. *See*: **W37r**

B654. MILA, Massimo. "Lettera da Venezia: 'Porgy and Bess' di Gershwin." *La Rassegna Musicale* 24/4 (Oct.-Dec. 1954): 349-351. *See:* **W37x**

B655. MONTAGU, George. "Musical Survey." *London Musical Events* 7/12 (Dec.1952): 37-38. *See:* **W37t**

B656. MONTSALVATGE, Xavier de. "Los conciertos en Barcelona." *Musica* [Madrid] 4/1 (Jan.-Mar. 1955): 107-108.
Review. *See:* **W37aa**

B657. "Music: Porgy Orgy." *Time* 60/16 (Oct. 20, 1952): 48.
Brief article referring to the London opening of the 1952 Breen-Davis touring company. Gives brief glowing quotes from reviews in the *Daily Mail, Daily Telegraph,* and *Daily Mirror,* and documents the problem of the British wanting a Briton to conduct rather than Alexander Smallens. *See:* **W37t**

B658. Myro. "Porgy and Bess, London, Oct. 10." *Variety*, October 15, 1952.
Review of one of the Stoll Theatre 1952 performances. ". . . With such able performances, the Gershwin score has a forceful, moving impact. William Warfield and Leontyne Price . . . sing and act with equal polish. Warfield's 'I Got Plenty O' Nuttin' and their two duets, together with Cab Calloway's 'It Ain't Necessarily So,' are among the musical highspots . . ." *See:* **W37t**

B659. "New Gershwin Melodies: 'Porgy and Bess' From Our London Music Critic."
Glasgow Herald, October 13, 1952.
Lengthy review of the London premiere, October 9, 1952: ". . . the vocal line in 'P&B' is natural, and frequently its beauty and expressiveness suggest a comparison with Puccini, from whom it would seem that G learned much. It is significant that the only serious lapse in the opera is the one orchestral section, which occurs during a change of scene in the second act. This interlude should have been rewritten, for it could hardly have sunk to a lower level of inspiration as regards both content and orchestration, or be more out of keeping with the rest of this otherwise utterly convincing work . . ." *See:* **W37t.**

B660. "Odyssey With Gershwin." *News-Week* 47/2 (Jan. 9, 1956): 43-44.

B661. OEHLMANN, Werner. "Porgy and Bess: Gershwins Negeroper im Titania-Palast." *Tagesspiegel,* 19 Sept. 1952. **[NN-L]**
Review of a 1952 performance at the Titania-Palast in Berlin. *See:* **W37s**

B662. ONNEN, Frank. "Georges Gershwins Opera 'Porgy and Bess.'" *Mens en Melodie* 8/4 (Apr. 1953): 117-19.

B663. ORMSBEE, Helen. "New Broadway Star: Leontyne Price's 'Bess' Caps Her Lucky Year." *NYHerald Tribune*, May 3, 1953, Section IV, p. 2.
See: **W37v**

B664. "Paris 'Porgy' Hung Just in Time After Channel Storm Delay for Boff Debut." *Variety,* Feb. 18, 1953, pp. 57-58. *See:* **W37u**

B665. PARMENTER, Ross. "Porgy Group Ends Its Recital Series." *NYTimes,* Aug. 31, 1953, p. 22.

B666. _____. "'Porgy' Singers Heard." *NYTimes,* July 20, 1953, p. 14.

B667. PERKINS, Francis D. "'Porgy' Singers Give Last Concert." *NY Herald Tribune,* Aug. 31, 1953, p. 7.

B668. PINCHERLE, Marc. "'Porgy and Bess' de Gershwin." *Les Annales* 62 [=No. 60] (1955): 25-34.

B669. POPOV, Innokenty. "Russian Report: 'Porgy and Bess.'" *Musical Courier* 153/4 (Mar. 1, 1956): 7+. *See:* **W37kk**

B670. "Porgy and Bess." *Mens en Melodie* 10/7 (July 1955): 223-224.

B671. "Porgy and Bess." *Music USA* 76/7 (July 1959): 35.

B672. "Porgy and Bess." *Musica* [Madrid] 2/1-2 (Jan.-June 1953): 148-149.

B673. "Porgy and Bess." *Opera* (London) 3/12 (Dec. 1952): 710-718. *See:* **W37t**

B674. "Porgy and Bess; Bethlehems nyinspelning." *Orkester Journal* (July-Aug. 1957): 42-43.

B675. "'Porgy and Bess,' Continuing Its Conquest Adds Rome to List of European Hearts." *NYTimes* (*NYTimes Theater Reviews*) (Special to the Times, dateline: Rome, April 21), Apr. 22, 1955, p. 20:6.
   Review of the Breen-Davis production, the performance of April 21, opening in Rome for a three-week run. ". . . In tomorrow's newspapers all the leading local critics will pay the highest tribute to the production . . . Since its opening in June, 1952, the operetta has given 1,200 performances in twelve countries. After the run in Rome it will end its European tour in Belgium and the Netherlands . . ." *See:* **W37ff**

B676. "'Porgy and Bess' Hailed at Rio Opening; Makes First Stop on South American Tour." *NYTimes* (*NYTimes Theater Reviews,* dateline: Rio de Janeiro, July 8), July 9, 1955, p. 9:5. *See:* **W37gg**

B677. "Porgy and Bess Hailed in Moscow." *Musical America* 76/2 (Jan. 15, 1956): 29.

B678. "'Porgy and Bess' in Moscow." *Etude* 74/3 (Mar. 1956): 14-15.
   A two-page spread of photographs taken during the Robert Breen tour of Soviet Russia. *See:* **W37kk**

B679. "'Porgy and Bess' Plays in Israel." *NYTimes* (dateline: Tel Aviv, Jan. 27, 1955), Jan. 28, 1955.
   Very brief notice of the production at the Habimah Theater (Breen-Davis tour). ". . . Eighty members of the American 'Porgy and Bess' troupe came here from Athens for the run."· *See:* **W37aa**

B680. "'Porgy & Bess' Praised in Spain." *NYTimes,* Feb. 8, 1955, p. 19. *See:* **W37aa**

B681. "Porgy and Bess Touring Europe." *Musical America* 76/4 (Feb. 15, 1956): 208.

B682. "Porgy and Bess Tours Behind Iron Curtain." *Musical Courier* 151/2 (Jan. 15, 1955): 33.

B683. "'Porgy' Bows In Venice: Folk Opera Has Italian Debut at International Music Fete."
NYTimes (*NYTimes Theater Reviews*) (Special to the Times, dateline: Venice, Sept. 22), Sept. 23, 1954, 42:6.
"'Porgy and Bess' scored a triumph in its Italian premiere here tonight . . . A capacity audience interrupted the playing frequently with enthusiastic applause and there were more than a dozen curtain calls . . ." *See:* **W37x**

B684. "'Porgy' Going Ahead with Russian Trip Plans Despite Lack of U.S. Coin Aid."
Variety 200/8, Oct. 26, 1955, p. 55+.

B685. "'Porgy' in Leningrad." *Time* 67/2 (Jan 9, 1956): 51. *See:* **W37jj**.

B686. "'Porgy' Is Cheered In La Scala Opening." *NYTimes* (*NYTimes Theater Reviews*)
(Special to the Times, dateline: Milan, Italy, Feb. 22), Feb. 23, 1955, p. 23:8.
Short, but very complimentary reference to the February 22nd, 1955, La Scala performance by the Breen-Davis touring company, ". . . the climax of a European tour . . . The Milanese are formidable opera fans but probably there is also more interest in jazz here than in any other Italian city . . . Local critics were unanimous in their praise of the performers . . ." *See:* **W37cc**

B687. "'Porgy' Makes a Hit With Athens Crowd." Special to the *NYTimes* (dateline: Athens, Jan. 20, 1955), Jan. 21, 1955.
Brief notice during the Breen-Davis tour. "'Porgy and Bess' brought laughter and tears to sophisticated Athenians tonight at the Royal Theatre, which was packed to capacity . . ." *See:* **W37aa**

B688. "Porgy Orgy." *Time* 60/16 (Oct. 20, 1952): 48.

B689. "Porgy Orgy (contd.)." *Time* 68/10 (Mar 7, 1955): 83.

B690. "'Porgy': the Play that Set a Pattern.*" Theatre Arts* 39/10 (Oct. 1955): 33-64.
Text of the play.

B691. "'Porgy' Production Is Staged In Naples." *NYTimes (NYTimes Theater Reviews)*
Special to the Times (dateline: Feb. 15), Feb. 16, 1955, p. 26: 4.
Review. ". . . The American production of 'Porgy and Bess' is touring Europe . . . and will move from Venice to Milan for climactic performances at La Scala. The audience gave the American troupe . . . a warm welcome . . . Some Neapolitan critics were more reserved . . ." *See:* **W37bb**

B692. "'Porgy' Tix on Black Market as Musical Wows Vienna." *Variety* 188/2 (Sept. 17, 1952): 2+. *See:* **W37r**

B693. "'Porgy' Trip to the USSR Delays 'Blues'; Will Tour Aussie and Later China." *Variety* 200/1 (Sept. 7, 1955): 65.

B694. "'Porgy' to TV for 112G; Two-Parter." *Variety* 205/4 (Dec. 26, 1956): 1+.

B695. PRAWY, Marcel. "Made in U.S.A." *Opera News* 17/7 (Dec. 15, 1952): 12-13.
Brief, but positive review of performance in Vienna. " . . . It is sincerely believed that these performances will leave traces here in Austria that will be felt in the field of musical creation, as well as in the realm of operatic stage design and direction . . ." *See:* **W37r**

B696. RAYMOND, Jack. "Berlin Acclaims Guests from Catfish Row." *NYTimes*, Sept. 28, 1952, Section 2, pp. 1, 3.
Review of a performance in Berlin. *See:* **W37s**

B697. _____. "Berlin Loves 'Bess' As Much As 'Porgy': Twenty-One Curtain Calls and Awed Reviews Make Negro Cast Feel Right At Home." *NYTimes (NYTimes Theater Reviews)* (Special to the Times, dateline: Sept. 17), Sept. 18, 1952, 36:5.
Review of the Sept. 17, 1952, opening night of the Breen-Davis touring group which "staggered an audience of Germans and Western Allies with its richness of music, story and acting, becoming, in the opinion of local critics the sensation of the month-long Cultural Festival." Quotes from the positive reviews of local critics Lothar Band, H. H. Stuckenschmidt, and Kurt Westphal were included. *See:* **W37s**

B698. _____. "'Porgy' Delights Belgrade Crowd: Residents of Catfish Row Are Seen as Goodwill Envoys—Opening is Festive." Special to the *NYTimes* (dateline: Belgrade, Yugoslavia, Dec. 16, 1954), Dec. 17, 1954.
" . . . The greatness of 'Porgy and Bess' was illustrated again tonight before an audience at the National Theatre that demanded thirteen curtain calls . . . The opening . . . inaugurated a tour of Yugoslavia, Greece and Egypt and possibly other Mediterranean countries . . ." *See:* **W37z**

B699. RICHARDS, Denby. "Music Review: Two Folk Operas." *Kensington News*, Oct. 24, 1952.
Review of a performance during the Davis-Breen 1952 tour to England. The reviewer singled out Cab Calloway: " . . . As the 'Devil's man, 'Sportin' Life, [he] is the most ebullient personality to hit the London stage for many a year. His general acting is nothing short of wonderful . . ." *See:* **W37t**

B700. RITTER, Heinz. "Ballade vom heissen Leben: Grosser Erfolg von Gershwins Volksoper ,Porgy and Bess' im Titania-Palast." *Die Grösste Berliner Tageszeitung*, 19 Sept. 1952. **[NN-L]**
Review of a 1952 performance at the Titania-Palast in Berlin. *See:* **W37s**

B701. ROSENFELD, John. "A New 'Porgy' in Dallas." *Saturday Review of Literature* 35/26 (June 28, 1952): 44. *See:* **W37p**

B702. SABIN, Robert. "Current Production of Porgy and Bess Justifies Its Success Here and Abroad." *Musical America* 73/6 (Apr. 15, 1953): 33.

B703. SCHAEFER, Theodore. "Gershwin Opera Heard in Capitol." *Musical America*
(dateline: Washington) 72/14 (Nov. 15, 1952): 23.
". . . As a whole, the performance was of overwhelming intensity . . ." *See:* **W37q**

B704. SCHERL, Adolph. "Gershwinova americká tragedie." *Divadlo* 7/4 (Apr. 1956):
343-346.

B705. SCHIRMER/REINHARD. "Porgy und Bess im Titania-Palast: Amerikanisches
Neger-Ensemble gastiert mit Georg Gershwins Volksoper." *Der Berliner Anzeiger,*
Sept. 19, 1952. **[NN-L]**
Review of a 1952 performance at the Titania-Palast in Berlin. *See:* **W37s**

B706. SCHROEDER, Juan German. "Porgy and Bess: Musica de George Gershwin,
Libreto du Bose Heyward." *Teatro; revista internacional de la escena*
No. 15 (Mar.-Apr. 1955): 24-28.

B707. SCULLY, Frank. "Scully's Scrapbook." *Variety* 201 (Feb. 15, 1956): 73.

B708. SELDEN-GOTH, Gisella. "Florence." *Musical Courier* 152/7 (May 1955): 31.
Positive mention of the performances in Florence, May 9–13, 1955. The large cast felt
that they had been received with unusual warmth in this Italian city. ". . . They made sold-out
houses at the 'Teatro Comunale' on six consecutive nights—an unheard-of record in this city
. . ." A recital was arranged for one of the leading members of this cast, Helen Thigpen. *See:*
W37ee

B709. SHANLEY, J. P. "Newcomer Takes Bess Role Tonight: Elizabeth Foster Listed
for Lead in Folk Opera During Urylee Leonardos' Vacation." *NYTimes*, Aug. 4,
1953, p. 15.
Announcement that Elizabeth Foster, twenty-one-year-old chorus member, will appear
as Bess on the performance of August 4, 1953 and three additional performances thereafter.
Leontyne Price will continue to alternate in the role.

B710. SHAWE-TAYLOR, Desmond. "The Arts and Entertainment: Three Operas." *The
New Statesman and Nation* 44/1128 (Oct. 18, 1952): 448.
A generally positive review of the 1952 production of P&B at the **Stoll** Theatre in
London. ". . . Two years ago, I saw *Porgy and Bess* given in German by a white company at
Zurich; and, perverse though it may seem to say so, the purely lyrical scenes sounded richer and
more affecting in that performance, because words and tune were strongly projected into the
house by good opera singers, and supported by the warm sound of an opera-house orchestra,
in contrast to the skinny tone produced by the anonymous players at the Stoll . . ." *See:* **W37t**

B711. SKORZENY, Fritz. ",Porgy and Bess' Sensationserfolg von Gershwins
amerikanischer Volksoper am Währinger Gürtel." *Neue Wiener Tageszeitung*, 9
Sept. 1952.
Review of the premiere performance in Vienna at the Volksoper. *See:* **W37r**

B712. STEWART, Ollie. "American Opera Conquers Europe." *Theatre Arts* 39/10 (Oct.
1955): 30-32, 93-94.
Chronicle of the Breen-Davis tours of Europe, beginning with the first performance in ·
Vienna, in September, 1952. *See:* **W37r**

B713. STUCKENSCHMIDT, H. H. *Der Neue Zeitung*, Sept. 19, 1952, Nummer 218.
    Review of the 1952 performance at the Titania-Palast in Berlin. *See*: **W37s**

B714. SUTTON, Horace. "Booked for Travel: From Catfish Row to the Kremlin." *Saturday Review* 39/2 (Jan. 14, 1956): 37-38.
    A very complimentary report on the Breen-Davis company's tour to Soviet Russia. The story is laced with human interest events happening to the group while in Russia, concluding that the trip served as an exemplary cultural exchange, positive in political purpose. *See*: **W37jj, W37kk**

B715. TARRAN, Geoffrey. "It Started 17 Years Ago, but . . . George Gershwin opera still rocks the stage." *Morning Advertiser* (London), October 18, 1952.
    Review of the Stoll Theatre production in 1952. "Nothing in the theatre this year has created more interest and provoked more praise that this strongly realistic drama of Negro life in Charleston, South Carolina . . ." *See*: **W37t**

B716. "The Theater: *Porgy* in Leningrad." *Time* 67/2 (Jan. 9, 1956): 51.
    Descriptive article about the Breen-Davis 1956 touring production's activities, social and otherwise, surrounding their fourteen-day performance at Leningrad's Palace of Cultural and Industrial Cooperatives, beginning December 26, 1956. It was also pointed out that "the Russians underwrote the tour themselves at a cost of $150,000 . . . *Porgy* shocked the Russians with its portrayal of life in the raw and sex in the open along Catfish Row . . . The audience reacted with gasps. But at the final curtain they rushed the stage and gave the cast a ten-minute ovation . . ." *See*: **W37jj, W37kk**

B717. THOMAS, Ernst. "America lebt in Strassen: Gershwins 'Porgy and Bess' in Frankfurt." *Neue Zeitschrift für Musik* 117/2 (Feb. 1956): 90. *See*: **W37ii**

B718. TORBERGS, Friedrich. "Post Scriptum, P. S. einem Theater-Ereignis." *Wiener Kurier*, Sept. 11, 1952. **[NNMus]**
    Review of its premiere performance at Vienna's Volksoper. *See*: **W37r**

B719. TREWIN, J. C. "At the Theatre." *The Sketch* (London), October 22, 1952.
    Review of the 1952 London premiere of P&B. ". . . Theatrical memories can be short; and many persons have forgotten, or have never heard of, the famous Cochran presentation of [the play] *Porgy* in 1929 . . . Gershwin's score is a superb musical interpretation . . . On the first night the audience nearly unroofed the theatre . . ." *See*: **W37t**

B720. W., E. G. "Eine amerikanische Volksoper: ,Porgy and Bess' von George Gershwin auf Europatournee." *Die Welt*, 19 Sept. 1952.
    Review of the 1952 performance at the Titania-Palast in Berlin. *See*: **W37s**

B721. WESTPHAL, Kurt. "Jubel um ,Porgy and Bess.'" *Der Kurier, Die Berliner Abendzeitung*, 18 Sept. 1952.
    Review of a 1952 performance at the Titania-Palast in Berlin. *See*: **W37s**

B722. _____. "Neue Musik in den Berliner Festwochen." *Melos* 19/11 (Nov. 1952): 322-324.

B723. *"Wiener Ereignisse:* ‚Porgy and Bess' in Wien, Jazz erneuert die Oper." *Die Presse,*
Wien, 13 Dec. 1952. **[NNMus]**
Substantial two-column review of the first performance in Vienna at the Volksoper.
See: **W37r**

B724. **WILTSHIRE, Maurice.** "SHOWPIECE: 'Porgy' Cheered After the Row." *Daily
Mail* [London], October 10, 1952.
Positive review of the 1952 Stoll Theatre London performance of P&B. ". . . It must
be many years since the London stage has known anything like it for verve, drama, and musical
delight . . ." *See:* **W37t**

B725. **WOLFERT, Ira.** "Ambassadors at Large: Porgy and Bess." *The Nation* 182/20
(May 19, 1956): 428-431.
Lengthy article by Wolfert, who made the tour, evaluating the political benefits of the
Bleen-Davis touring production and its visit to the Soviet Union and Eastern Europe. A list of
cities at which the opera was performed internationally during 1952-1956 is appended to the
essay.

B726. **Y.** "Gershwins ‚Porgy and Bess' in der Volksoper." *Neues Österreich,* Sept. 9, 1952.
Review of the first performance in Vienna at the Volksoper. *See:* **W37r**

B727. **ZOLOTOW, Sam.** "Tibbett Goes on July 15th as 'Porgy.'" *NYTimes,* June 24, 1953,
p. 29.

1960s:

B728. **ARDOIN, John.** "Music in New York: Warfield Outstanding in Porgy and Bess."
Musical America 81/7 (July 1961): 45.
In a review of the NY City Center's revival (opening night on May 17), Ardoin
emphatically called P&B an *opera,* not a "folk opera" or a "musical comedy." The reviewer
was particularly impressed with William Warfield's voice and performance, and felt that
". . . the remainder of the cast were not in Mr. Warfield's class and the production as a whole
lacked the pace and continuity of *Show Boat* and *South Pacific* . . ." *See:* **W37mm**

B729. **BORISOVA, S.** "Molodezh' derzhit ekzamen." *Sovetskaya Muzyka* 25/5 (May 1961):
53-57.

B730. **BROCK, Hella.** "Gershwins Oper *Porgy and Bess* in der Musikerziehung; zur
Eignung des Werkes für die Schulmusikerziehung. " *Musik in der Schule* 18/12
(Dec. 1967): 493-502.

B731. **CARR, Jay.** "Reports: U. S.: *Detroit." Opera News* 40/8 (Dec. 20-27, 1975): 32.
Mixed review of the Michigan Opera Theatre's production opening October 3, 1975,
at Detroit's Music Hall. *See:* **W37aaa**

B732. **CARUTHERS, Osgood.** "Catfish Row a la Soviet." *NYTimes* (dateline: Moscow),
May 28, 1961, section 2, p. 3.
Report on an unauthorized performance. ". . . The producer of the operetta, performed
in a tiny basement theatre, is Boris Aleksandrovich Pokrovsky, the chief sponsor of opera at
the Bolshoi Theatre. He has created a passable copy of the original . . . but one never quite

escapes the feeling that it is simply a performance by Russians in blackface and not the real thing . . ."

B733. "Casting Woes for Prawy's 'Porgy'; Sells Out Every Repeat Performance." *Variety* 256/11 (Dateline: Vienna, Oct.28, Oct. 29, 1969): 75.
Describes the woes director Marcel Prawy had in casting this version. *See*: **W37oo, B753**

B734. FIECHTNER, Helmut A. "Musica-Bericht: Gershwin's 'Porgy and Bess' (dateline: Vienna)." *Musica* 20/1 (Jan. 1966): 23-24.
Review of a performance in Vienna. *See*: **W37oo**

B735. FOSSUM, Knut. "Norway, Romantic 'Porgy' Oslo." *Opera* (Eng.) 19 (Jan. 1968): 62.
Review of a September 7, 1968, season opening performance in Oslo, produced by Anne Brown, who lives in Norway. ". . . Her production was at times slow, but Miss Brown showed us that at bottom this can be a romantic opera, not merely an opera about the hard and cruel life among the people in Catfish Row, and at least not a musical . . ." *See*: **W37rr**

B736. FRIEDRICH, Gotz. "Zwanzig Notizen zu einer Aufführungskonzeption von *Porgy and Bess.*" *Jahrbuch der Komischen Oper Berlin* 9 (1969): 153-162.

B737. GREEN, Benny. "Gershwin's 'Porgy and Bess.'" *Music and Musicians* 11 (Oct. 1962): 22-23.

B738. GRUNFELD, Fred. "The Great American Opera." *Opera News* 24/20 (Mar. 19, 1960): 6-9.

B739. HOHLWEG, Rudolf. "Strassburg: Besessen vom Spiel, Gershwin 'Porgy and Bess.'" *Opernwelt* 10/3 (March 1969): 44-45.
Review.

B740. KUZNETSOVA, Irina. "Pyat' i odna." *Sovetskaya Muzyka* 32/4 (Apr. 1968): 46-51.

B741. LITTLE, Stuart W. "'Porgy,' Lacking Negroes, Uses Whites to Fill Cast." *NY Herald Tribune*, May 7, 1964.
Very brief review of a 1964 revival at NY's City Center. The review focuses on the fact that the cast was not all black. *See*: **W37nn**, *See also*: Alan Rich, *NY Herald Tribune*, 5/7.

B742. MILLER, Mayne. "Er Komponierte 'Porgy and Bess.'" *Musikalische Jugend* 16/3 (1967): 14.

B743. "Norfolk: The Virginia Opera Association." *Opera Canada* 22/2 (1981): 31-32.

B744. "Revive 'Porgy & Bess' in Estonia; Producer Studied African Lore." *Variety*, Feb. 15, 1967 (dateline: Tallin, Estonia, Feb. 14), p. 22.
"Estonia Opera and Ballet Theatre here . . . has just revived Geoge Gershwin's 'Porgy and Bess' . . ." Udo Vilyoats (sp?) was stage director and George Ots sang Porgy, with Bess by Haili Sammelseld. Stage settings were by Lembit Rooz and the orchestra conducted by H. Neeme Yarvi. *See*: **W37qq**

B745. SARGENT, Winthrop. "Musical Events, Time on His Hands." *New Yorker* 38/8 (Apr. 14, 1962): 175-176.

Review of a performance on April 13, 1962, at NY's City Center, by the New York City Opera. "The performance I saw was by no means an entirely satisfactory one . . . To me, 'Porgy and Bess' remains a bastard product, in which the aggressiveness of the brasher type of old-fashioned musical show is mixed uneasily with some of the ingredients of a subtler art form. As a show, it has its points, and, again, the tunes are superb, but I cannot see it as what it is often called—America's great contribution to the opera . . ." *See*: **W37mm, B728**

B746. "Student Production of 'Porgy and Bess.'" *USSR* 57/6 (June 1961): 60-61.

B747. TAMUSSINO, Ursula. "Gershwin Triumphiert über Mozart." *Phono: Internationale Schallplatten-Zeitschrift* 12/2 (Mar.-Apr. 1965): 41+.

B748. THOMSON, Keith W., and **Frank DURHAM.** "The Impact of *Porgy and Bess* in New Zealand." *Mississippi Quarterly* 20/4 (Fall 1967): 207-216.

Report of performances in New Zealand and Australia. Regarding the cast: ". . . From America the company imported Ella Gerber as director, Dobbs Franks as musical director, Martha Flowers as Bess, John McCurry as Crown, and Delores Ivory as Serena . . . The rest of the cast and chorus were Maoris [i. e. Polynesians native to the area]. *See*: **W37pp**

B749. TSCHULIK, Norbert. "'Porgy and Bess' in der Volksoper." *Österreichische Musikzeitschrift* 20/11 (Nov. 1965): 599. *See*: **W37oo**

B750. TYNSON, Kh. "Geroi Gershvina na Estonskoy Stsene." *Sovetskaya Muzyka* 31/5 (May 1967): 45-48.

B751. WALLGREN, Olle. "Goteborg." *Opera News* 30/23 (Apr. 9, 1966): 33. Review.

B752. WATERS, Edward N. "Harvest of the Year: Selected Acquisitions of the Music Division." *Quarterly Journal of the Library of Congress* 24/1 (Jan 1967): 47-82.

On page 72, Waters documents receipt of gifts from IG in the form of commemorative medals, some in gold, and a Russian edition from 1965 of P&B.

B753. WECHSBERG, Joseph. "Austria: 'Porgy' Makes a Hit, **Vienna**." *Opera* 16/12 (Dec. 1965): 899-901.

Review of Marcel Prawy's production of P&B at Vienna's Volksoper during 1965, " . . in its original, legitimate form, as a tragic opera with sung recitatives . . . The production had the flavour of authenticity—it could almost have been in America . . ." *See*: **B733,W37oo**

B754. _____. "Vienna." *Opera News* 30/6 (Dec. 11, 1965): 32. *See*: **W37oo**

1970s:

B755. BECKER, Wolfgang. "Da Berlino." *Nuova Revista Musicale Italiana* 4/2 (Mar.-Apr., 1970): 343-44.

Contains a review of a Berlin performance. *See*: **W37ss**

B756. "Berlin." *Oper und Konzert* 9/6 (June 1971): 5.   Review. *See:* **W37xx**

B757. "Bregenzer Festspiele." *Oper und Konzert* 9/9 (Sep. 1971): 12, 58.
Review.

B758. BURLINA, E. "Zvuchit Muzyka Gershvina." *Sovetskaya Muzyka* No. 6 (June 1979):
36-38.

CARR, Jay. *See:* **B731**

B759. CONLY, J. "Houston 'Porgy and Bess' Exits L. A. for Bay Area." *Billboard,* June
25, 1977, pp. 38+. *See:* **W37eee**

B760. CONSTANT, D. "'Porgy and Bess'; ou L'impossible desir." *Jazz Magazine* no. 265
(June 1978): 36-39+; no. 266 (July-Aug. 1978): 46-49.

B761. DANNENBERG, Peter. "Gelsenkirchen: Nach fünfunddreissig Jahren [after thirty-
five years], Gershwin ,Porgy and Bess.'" *Opernwelt* 11/11 (Nov. 1970): 35-36.
A premiere performance in Gelsenkirchen, in what was then West Germany on October
3, 1970, brought this review. *See:* **W37uu**

B762.   ECKSTEIN, Pavel. "Gershwinuv 'Porgy a Bess.'" *Hudebni Rozhledy* 24/4
(Apr. 1971): 155.
Review of performance in Brno.

B763. FEINGOLD, Michael. "It's Heavy on Mythopoeia." *Village Voice,* October 18,
1974.
Review of the 1974 revival of P&B by the Houston Grand Opera and performed at the
Uris Theatre in New York, emphasizing the dramaturgy of the score, and concluding: ". . .
Gershwin, of course, did his work brilliantly on both opera and light-opera levels, which is why
P&B is a masterpiece, however schizoid. The songs are great, the concerted music and
recitative great in a different way . . ." *See:* **W37ggg**

B764. GILL, Brendan. "The Theatre: Open for Business." *New Yorker* 52/33 (Oct. 4,
1976): 77-78.
Brief, but complimentary review of P&B in its New York production at the Uris. *See:*
W37ggg

B765. "Graz." *Oper und Konzert* 14/11 (1976): 8-9.

B766. Hobe. "Shows on Broadway." *Variety,* Sept. 29, 1976, pp. 88-89.
Review of the Houston Grand Opera revival of 1976 (Uris Theatre in New York).
". . . Tonally, the performance is perhaps the best the opera has ever had, at least on Broadway.
The show's approximately three-hour running time is too long, however, while the staging
accents the theatricalism of the work, but frequently fails to indicate its meaning . . . Repeatedly
during the performance, the staging does not clarify the time element or the situation, and there
is nothing even remotely comparable to Rouben Mamoulian's originally directed sequence of
dawn in Catfish Row . . . The Davis-Breen version, staged by Breen and again conducted by
Smallens, had a 305-performance run at the old Ziegfeld Theatre, following an acclaimed tour
of Europe . . ." *See:* **W37ggg**

B767. JACOBSON, Robert. "Reports: U. S.: Philadelphia/Washington."*Opera News* 41/4 (Oct. 1976): 64.
Review of the Houston Grand Opera's touring company performing P&B in its 1976 revival at Philadelphia's Academy of Music, on July 30, 1976. ". . . This Porgy soared due to John DeMain's razor-sharp, idiomatic reading, which had throbbing emotional commitment as well as real feeling for jazz accents and expressive lyric line . . ." *See:* **W37fff**

B768. KADUCH, M. "Porgy a Bess." *Opus musicum* 9/4 (1977): 121-122.

B769. KERN, Heinz. "Internationales Theater, Im Spiegel unserer Korrespondentenberichte: Zürich: ‚Porgy und Bess.' *Bühne* 224 (May 1977): 23.
A revival performance in Zürich (Switzerland) resulted in this short, but informative article. *See:* **W37hhh**

B770. KERN, H. P. "Zürich." *Oper und Konzert* 15/5 (1977): 27-28. **W37hhh**

B771. KERTESZ, Istvan. "'Porgy es Bess'—Gershwin operájának bemutatója az Erkel Színházban." *Muzsika* 13/3 (Apr. 1970): 13-17.

B772. KLEIN, R. "Gershwin—Oper auf dem Bodensee." *Oesterreichische Musikzeitschrift* 26 (Sept. 1971): 518-519. *See:* **W37xx**

B773. KOLODZIEJSKA, D. "'Lancelot' w Berlinskiej Staatsoper ‚Porgy and Bess' w Komische Oper." *Ruch Muzyczny* 14/14 (1970): 10-11. *See:* **W37ss**

B774. LAAGE, J. von der. "Faszination in Schwarz (Houston Opera in Paris)." *Opernwelt* 19/4 (1978): 37.

B775. LEVINE, Jo Ann. "Fresh Portrait of Gershwin's Porgy." *Christian Science Monitor* 69 (Dec. 30, 1976): 18.
Article based on an interview of Abraham Lind-Oquendo who played Porgy in the triple-cast touring production by the Houston Grand Opera, during its run at the Mark Hellinger Theater in NY. *See:* **W37ggg**

B776. LUEDICKE, H. "‚Porgy'-Serie in Bregenz." *Musik und Gesellschaft* 21 (Nov. 1971): 698-699.

B777. LÜTTWITZ, Heinrich von. "Gelsenkirchen: ‚Porgy and Bess' Ohne Negerlarven." *Neue Zeitschrift für Musik* 132/8 (Aug. 1971): 439-441.
See: **W37uu**

B778. MILNES, Rodney. "In Concert: Porgy and Bess." *Opera* (English) 27 (May 1976): 488-489.
Review of a concert performance on March 17, 1976, at the Camden Festival, at St. Pancras Town Hall, by the Chelsea Opera Group (a mixed race cast). ". . . The vigor and total lack of inhibition that characterized both the orchestral playing and choral singing must be put down to Simon Rattle's inspired conducting . . ." *See:* **W37ddd**

B779. (Number inadvertently omitted)

B780. MOOR, Paul. "'Porgy' Comes to Germany." *High Fidelity/Musical America* 20/8 (dateline: East Berlin, Aug. 1970): 28-29.

Review of the 1970 Komische Oper production of P&B (not to be confused with the 1953 Davis-Breen touring company's performance). While praising this performance and production in a German translation, Moor was slightly critical of what he called a "flawed masterpiece." *See:***W37ss**

B781. "Muenchen." *Oper und Konzert* 9 (Apr. 1971): 19-20.

Review of performance in Munich.

B782. "Proben zu Gershwins ,Porgy and Bess' in der Berliner Komischen Oper." *Opernwelt* 11/3 (Mar. 1970): 8. *See:* **W37ss**

B783. P[ERDUE], R[oy]. "debuts & reappearances: Vienna, VA, Wolf Trap: 'Porgy and Bess.'" *Musical America* 26 (Dec. 1976): MA-25.

A generally favorable review of the performances by the Houston Opera's touring company at Wolf Trap in Virginia, August 24-28, 1976. *See:* **W37fff.1**

B784. PRAWY, Marcel. "Made in U. S. A.: American Opera Triumphs in Vienna." *Opera News* 17/7 (Dec. 15, 1952): 12-13.

Brief review of a performance by the Davis-Breen touring group at the Vienna *Volksoper. See:* **W37r**

B785. RADCLIFFE, Joe. "Broadway Review: 'Porgy and Bess' Revival Is a Major N. Y. Triumph." *Billboard* (Dateline NY, Oct. 9, 1976): 10.

Positive review of the revival, "the show is impeccable." *See:* **W37eee**

B786. RICHARDS, D. "Liverpool (Silver Jubilee Visit of the Queen)." *Music and Musicians* 26 (Nov. 1977): 56-57.

B787. S., H. J. "Musiktheater: ,Porgy und Bess' in der Komischen Oper Berlin." *Musik und Gesellschaft* 20/5 (May 1970): 325f. *See:* **W37ss**

B788. SAZANOV, Vladimir. "Leningrad." *Opera/Canada* 14/3 (1973): 41-42.

Inconsequential review of the performance by a Russian troupe in Leningrad. The musical director was Yury Termirkanov, with Emil Pasynkov as stage director. *See:* **W37yy**

B789. SCHAEFER, Hansjürgen. "Porgy und Bess in der Komischen Oper Berlin." *Musik und Gesellschaft* 20/5 (May 1970): 325-328. *See:* **W37ss**

B790. SCHONBERG, Harold. "A Minority Report on 'Porgy.'" *NYTimes*, October 17, 1976, Section 2, pp. 1, 19.

In this negative review of the revival by the Houston Opera at the Uris, Schonberg came down very hard on both P&B and G's music. He called *Rhapsody in Blue* and *American in Paris* junk music, concluding that a proposed 1976 performance of P&B at the Met "would have been a travesty." *See:* **W37ggg**

B791. SCHWINGER, Eckart. "Porgy and Bess." *Musica* 24/2 (Mar.-Apr. 1970): 148-149.

Review of a Berlin performance of the opera. *See:* **W37ss**

B792. SPINGEL, Hans Otto. "Die Leute von der Catfish Row." *Opernwelt* 11/4 (Apr. 1970): 14-15.
Review of performance at Berlin Komische Oper, Jan. 24, 1970. *See:* **W37ss**

B793. STEINMETZ, Karel. "Gershwinova Porgy A Bess V Ostravě." *Hudebni rozhledy* (Czech.) 30/5 (1977): 223-224.
Article concerning a performance in Czechoslovakia, which premiered on January 29, 1977. *See:* **W37ggg.1**

B794. STERRITT, David. "A Little Bit of Texas Comes to Broadway: Houston Grand Opera's 'Porgy.'" *Christian Science Monitor* (dateline: New York) 68 (Sept. 30, 1976): 22.
Review of the Houston Grand Opera version then running at the Uris in NY. "There is a touch of fairy tale to this palpably magical 'Porgy and Bess,' the sad kind where the hero never reaches the reward he deserves. There is a grittiness here, too, implicit in Gershwin's score and lustily celebrated on stage . . ." *See:* **W37ggg**

B795. STILES, Martha Bennett. "Porgy & Bess: The best art imitates nature . . ." *Stereo Review* 36 (Apr. 1976): 70-75.
While reminiscing about the creation of P&B through her mother's memories of happenings in Charleston, SC, in 1924, Stiles also reviewed the Michigan Opera Theatre's production of P&B during their 1975-1976 season. *See:* **W37zz**

B796. SUTCLIFFE, James Helme. "East Berlin." *Opera News* 34/20 (Mar. 14, 1970): 32-34.
Review of performance at the Komische Oper. *See:* **W37ss**

B797. _____. "West Berlin." *Opera* (Eng.) 22/6 (June 1971): 535-537.
Review. *See:* **W37xx**

B798. TAYLOR, N. E. "Wilhelmenia Fernandez Tackles Gershwin's Bess." *Christian Science Monitor* 69 (Apr. 4, 1977): 18.

B799. TEUTEBERG, Karin. "Gelsenkirchen." *Oper und Konzert* 8/11 (Nov. 1970): 9. *See:* **W37uu**

B800. TRAUBE, Leonard. "Charleston Gets Itself Plenty of Somethin' In Bow of 'Porgy and Bess.'" *Variety* 259/7, July 1, 1970 (dateline: Charleston, SC, June 30), p. 1, 53.
Review of the first performance in Charleston. ". . . Audience reaction at the premiere was one of continual and solid applause throughout—all but covering the music at some points . . ." What made this performance most unique was the use of an amateur cast with professional direction. *See:* **W37tt**

B801. WALDA, D. "Gershwin heute; ,Porgy and Bess' als Festpremiere in Karl-Marx-Stadt." *Musik und Gesellschaft* 21 (Sept. 1971): 589-590.

1980s:

B802. ARDOIN, John. "Porgy and Bess: The grand opera takes a bow in Dallas."

Dallas Morning News, May 8, 1987, Guide section, p. 28.

Announcement of the Houston Grand Opera-Dallas Opera production which ran in Dallas May 13-17, 1987. Includes a history and comparison of the productions between the first in Dallas in 1967 "by an *ad hoc* touring company" and the present "complete" version. *See*: **W37vvv, B803**

B803. _____. "'Porgy and Bess Returns to Dallas, Gershwin's Grand Opera Has
          Plenty of Everythin.'" *Dallas Morning News*, May 10, 1987, Today section, p. 1C.

Lengthy announcement article heralding the upcoming touring production and run of P&B at Dallas' Music Hall, May 13-17, and including the genesis of the play and opera. ". . . Porgy is an opera, a grand opera at that . . . If any further authentication were needed, it came last summer [1986] when Porgy became the hit of the European summer music festival circuit, in a landmark production by the Glyndebourne Festival Opera in England . . ." *See*: **B802, W37vvv, W37ooo (Glyndebourne)**

B804. "Ausbruch: George Gershwin: Porgy and Bess (Willard White, Cynthia Haymon,
          Damon Evans u.a.; Glyndebourne Chorus, London Philharmonic, Simon Rattle)."
          Neue Musikzeitung 38 (June-July 1989): 33. *See*: **W37ooo**

B805. BARRICELLI, Jean-Pierre. "It ain't necessarily, ain't necessarily so: Second
          review." *Press-Enterprise* [Riverside, CA] (*Newsbank* PER 125:B12), Feb. 14,
          1987.

A mixed review of the opening night performance, February 11, at the Orange County Performing Arts Center (Costa Mesa, California), by the Houston Grand Opera's 1987 touring company, in cooperation with Opera Pacific. *See*: **B818, W37rrr**

B806. "Berlin." *Oper und Konzert* 26 (July 1988): 13-14. *See*: **W37zzz**

B807. "Berlin (Theater des Westens)." *Oper Und Konzert* 27 (May 1989): 7. *See*: **W37cccc**

B808. BRANDT, E. "Berlin (Goetz Friedrichs Porgy-and-Bess Inszenierung)." *Das
          Orchester; Zeitschrift Fuer Orchesterkultur* 36 (Nov. 1988): 1154.

B809. CROUCH, S[tanley?]. "Theater: Catfish Immigrants (Radio City Music Hall)."
          Village Voice 28 (May 3, 1983): 108. *See*: **W37kkk**

B810. DEAN, W. and Stanley Sadie. "Gershwin 'Porgy and Bess' at Glyndebourne."
          Musical Times, 127/1723 (Sept. 1986): 508-509.

Review of a performance at Glyndebourne. *See*: **W37ooo**

B811. DIERKS, Donald. "The musical 'Porgy' had a delayed birth." *San Diego Union*
          (*Newsbank* PER 143:C13), Mar. 1, 1987.

Background article announcing the forthcoming opening of the Houston Grand Opera's production of P&B on tour, at San Diego's Civic Theatre, March 5, 1987. History of the opera since its original conception as a novel by DuBose Heyward is given. *See*: **B812, W37ttt**

B812. DIERKS, Donald. "Ah, 'Porgy and Bess': The cast is jumpin' and the quality's
          high." *San Diego Union* (*Newsbank* PER 143:D1), Mar. 7, 1987.

Positive review of every aspect of the production by the Houston Opera Company, which opened March 5, 1987, for a six performance run at San Diego's Civic Theatre. *See*:

W37ttt, B811

B813. DOLMETSCH, Carl. "Norfolk: The Virginia Opera Association." *Opera Canada* 22/2 (1981): 31-32.
Brief review of a regional premiere by a resident company in October and November, with six sold-out performances in Norfolk and two in Richmond. ". . . Sets, crisp costumes and Farrar's somewhat bowdlerized direction, however, tended to prettify Catfish Row and dissipate the work's naturalism . . ." *See*: **W37iii.1**

B814. FABIAN, I. "Musica triumphans. Carlos Kleiber dirigierte die Premiere von Verdis Traviata an der Met Ausserdem: Puccinis Trittico und Gershwins Porgy and Bess." *Opernwelt* 30 (Dec. 1989): 19.

B815. FARO, A. J. "Rio de Janeiro." *Opera* 38 (Feb. 1987): 182-183.

B816. FEDER, Susan. "New York." *Musical Times* 124 (July 1983): 444. *See*: **W37kkk**

B817. FORBES, E. "Roundup: Lewes: Glyndebourne Festival (Porgy and Bess; Incoronazione di Poppea; Don Giovanni)." *Opera Canada* 27/4 (1986): 39. *See*: **W37ooo**

B818. FOREMAN, T. E. "Two views: As an opera, 'Porgy' got plenty of nothin.'" *Press-Enterprise* [Riverside, CA] (*Newsbank* PER 125:B14), Feb. 14, 1987.
One of two reviews (*See*: **B805**, Barricelli) of the opening performance, February 11, at the Orange County Performing Arts Center (Costa Mesa, California), by the Houston Grand Opera's 1987 touring company in cooperation with Opera Pacific. The reviewer concentrated on the controversial question, "Is P&B an opera"? Foreman felt that P&B ". . . is not best served . . . with almost every line sung . . ." and that the dialogue is better spoken than sung. *See*: **W37rrr**

B819. GILL, Brendan. "The Theatre (at Radio City Music Hall)." *New Yorker* 59/9 (Apr. 18, 1983): 133.
Reminding the reader that Andrew Porter (then *New Yorker* music critic) "only last week" called P&B "one of the two great American operas (the other being Virgil Thomson's 'The Mother of Us All.')." This is a glowing review of the 1983 revival at Radio City Music Hall in NY. *See*: **W37kkk**

B820. "Glyndebourne (1986)." *Oper Und Konzert* 24/10 (1986): 7. *See*: **W37ooo**

B821. GOEPFERT,.P. H. "Berlin (Theater des Westens)." *Buehne: Das Oesterreichische Kulturmagazin* 358-9 (July-Aug. 1988):111+ *See*: **W37zzz**

B822. GONDA, J. "A Porgy es Bess felujitasa." *Muzsika* 25 (Mar. 1982): 25-27.

B823. GOODWIN, Noël. "In Review: from around the world, Among operas new to the Glyndebourne Festival in the last decade, none has been received with more enthusiasm than Porgy and Bess." *Opera News* 51/4 (October 1986): 54.
Positive review of the July 5, 1986, performance at Glyndebourne, England, conducted by Simon Rattle. *See*: **W37ooo**

B824. GREENFIELD, Edward. "*At Glyndebourne*: 'La Traviata' Cozy in Sight and
       Sound: Meanwhile 'Porgy and Bess' continues to captivate." *Musical America*
       108/1 (March 1988): 46-50.
    A general report on activities at Glyndebourne in Britain during the 1987 season.
Includes discussion of the 1987 production of P&B, "the first ever done by a British company."
Greenfield quoted from Damon Evans' (who played Porgy) statement in the program booklet:
". . . The dignity and integrity which I felt so strongly on the stage apparently came across to
the audience and gave the piece a new dimension. Gone were the unconciously racist minstrel
show traditions of American Theater. Gone was the condescending question of whether *Porgy
and Bess* was an opera or not. Gone was any question of the true genius of George Gershwin.
The British production . . . brought the opera to its full glory . . ." *See*: **W37ooo**

B825. HARRIS, D. "Roundup: New York: Metropolitan Opera." *Opera Canada* 26/2
       (1985): 34-35. *See*: **W37mmm**

B826. HENAHAN, Donal. "Music: Music View: A Good Deed, But a Disservice to
       Gershwin." *NYTimes*, March 10, 1985, p. H 21.
    In this review of the 1985 production of P&B at the Metropolitan, Henahan conceded:
". . . I am not at all reluctant to call 'Porgy' an opera; I merely suggest that it is not a very good
one . . . My own complaint against 'Porgy' is not . . . against its formal shape, but its failure,
at least in the Metropolitan version, to carry me along musically and dramatically in the way
I expect a lyric drama to do . . ." *See*: **W37mmm**

B827. HEYMONT, George. "Everybody's Porgy & Bess, This season's national tour
       brings 13 American opera companies together in a unique cooperative venture." *The
       Dallas Opera Magazine* 10/1 (1987 Spring Season): 18, 28-29.
    Informative article appearing in the magazine including the program for the May 13-17,
1987 performances in Dallas as part of the 1986-1987 national tour by the Houston Grand
Opera company. Background on how this tour, lasting from December 29, 1986 through July
5, 1987, came about is given. *See*: **W37vvv**

B828. JACOBS, A. "New York." *Opera* (Eng) 34 (July 1983): 742-744. *See*: **W37kkk**

B829. JACOBSON, R. "New York." *Opera News* 47 (June 1983): 46-47. *See*: **W37kkk**

B830. JALON, Allan. "She's Keeping Tabs on 'Porgy.' *LATimes*, Feb. 11, 1987
       [*Newsbank* NIN 164:B8].
    Review of the performance at the Orange County [CA] Performing Arts Center during
the 1987 Houston Grand Opera tour. "At 86, Ira Gershwin's widow scans the operatic
landscape. She says she loved the production the Houston Grand Opera gave 'Porgy and Bess,'
but wasn't happy that in a British version the crippled Porgy was made to stand up . . . She
blames a 'small heart attack' she suffered in 1985 on the production that year at the
Metropolitan . . . she [Mrs. Gershwin] plays a key role in granting performance rights. When
demand increased after the Met production, she worried that low standards might prevail. Her
worry prompted [the 1987 tour] . . . The sets are drawn from a production at Radio City Music
Hall [NY] in 1983 . . ." *See*: **W37rrr**

B831. JOHNSON, Harriett. "'Porgy & Bess' Comes Home." *NYPost*, Feb 8, 1985.
    A generally positive review of the 1985 revival of P&B at the Metropolitan Opera.
". . . Miss [Grace] Bumbry is a bit too mature for the role of the sexy girl [Bess]. . ." *See*:
W37mmm

B832. KELLOW, Brian. "In review: from around the world." *Opera News* 54/7(Dec. 23, 1989): 39.

A brief unapproving review. "[T]he return of *Porgy and Bess* to the Met . . . once again proved essentially unstageworthy. Since Gershwin's score is weighed down with DuBose Heyward's inadequate libretto, the best one usually hopes for are isolated moments of musical inspiration, but here they are in short supply . . . *See:* **W37mmm**

B833. KERNER, L. "Two Masterpieces, but Only One Success (at Radio City Music Hall)." *Village Voice* 28 (Apr. 19, 1983): 91. *See:* **W37kkk**

B834. _____. "Music: Porgy deluxe (Met's first production)." *Village Voice* 30 (Feb. 26, 1985): 78. *See:* **W37mmm**

B835. KOBE, R. "Im Berliner Theater des Westens: Porgy und Bess." *Jazz Podium* 37 (Aug. 1988): 31.

B836. KREBS, B. D. "[Porgy and Bess] Dayton." *Opera News* 47 (July 1982): 32.

B837. KRUGER, Debbie. "Melbourne-Spoleto fest strong; Porgy due for Sydney transfer." *Variety* 328 (Oct. 21, 1987): 545.

B838. MAHLKE, S. "Auf seinem Weg—zum Triumph: Gershwins Porgy and Bess im Berliner Theater des Westens". *Opernwelt* 29 (July 1988): 53-54.

B839. MANN, W. "Freude an Genua und Charleston (Glyndebourne)." *Opernwelt* 27/10 (1986): 25-27. *See:* **W37ooo**

B840. MCCUTCHAN, Ann. "Porgy Power: Gershwin Masterpiece brings Greatness to Performing Arts Center." *American-Statesman* [Austin, TX] (*Newsbank* PER 125:B9), Jan. 30, 1987.

An article previewing the opening of P&B on February 4 at Austin's Performing Arts Center to be given by the 1987 Houston Grand Opera's touring company. The interesting article includes background on G the composer, P&B, and quotes from the current conductor of this production, John DeMain. *See:* **W37qqq**

B841. MCGINN, Larry. "Production of 'Porgy' Takes Advantage of Splendid Voices." *Post-Standard* [Syracuse, NY], Apr. 22, 1989, "Living" section, p. B-1.

". . . The Syracuse version is judiciously cut and very operatic. And given the splendid voices of the cast, that's just the way it should be done . . ." *See:* **W37fff**

B841.1. MILNES, Rodney. "Glyndebourne—more daring?" *Opera* 38 (Autumn 1987): 14+ *See:* **W37ooo**

B842. MCPHAIL, Claire. "'Porgy and Bess' Warmly Received." *News and Courier* [Charleston, SC], Oct. 11, 1985.

Strong in details about the cast, this is a positive review of the opening night performance in Charleston of a ten-day run, October 10-20, 1985. *See:* **W37lll**

B843. Mor. "Shows Out of Town." *Variety* 310, (Dateline Chicago, Feb. 22) Feb. 23,

1983, pp. 102, 108.

A lengthy review, packed with information, of the 1983 HGO production of P&B during its *pre*-Radio City Music Hall run (opening in New York April 7), at the Arie Crown Theatre in Chicago. Article includes a history of previous productions along with information about how large this production is: there are 56 musicians in the pit and a cast of 80 singers and dancers, the names of whom are listed in this informative article. The reviewer liked the production: "...That it comes together at all is surprising, that it comes together so well is remarkable, and that it retains its intimacy and immediacy is miraculous . . . The cast is first-rate, although some are stronger than others . . ." *See*: **W37jjj**

B844. MORDDEN, Ethan C. "A Long Pull." *Opera News* (Mar. 16, 1985): 30-33, 46.

Essay inspired by P&B's arrival at the Met in 1985. A history of the major revivals is given, Mordden being critical only of Samuel Goldwyn's movie version of 1959. The writer concluded: "... The point is not how much of the score is given, how beautiful the production, or whether or not—can there be any doubt at this stage?—the piece is an opera . . . what is most impressive about *Porgy and Bess* is its imperishable innocence." This article includes a discography and critique of recordings available through the Cleveland/Maazel and Houston Grand Opera versions of 1976. The reviewer commented especially on a Music for Pleasure disc ". . . [the] disc is typical, its erratic vocalism enlivened by theater expertise, including a healthy selection of the traditional ad libs . . . the record does preserve a taste of Irving Barnes and Martha Flowers, a favorite lead team of the 1950s . . ." *See*: **W37mmm, W37h, W37v, F25**

B845. "Muenchen (Gastspiel eines New Yorker Ensembles)." *Oper und Konzert* 26 (June 1988): 7. *See*: **W37yyy**

B846. ONNEN, F. "George Gershwin's Opera 'Porgy and Bess.'" *Mens en Melodie* 8 (April 1983): 117-119.

B847. PINZAUTI, Florence. L. *Opera* 35/8 (June 1984): 667-668.

B848. POLLACK, Joe. "Review: 'Porgy and Bess' Makes a Rich Return." *St. Louis Post-Dispatch*, July 13, 1988, Section F, p. 8.

Generally positive review of the July 11, 1988, touring performance by the Houston Grand Opera at the Muny Theatre. A crowd of 7,987 was in attendance. Ivan Thomas played Crown, ". . . [he] displays a half-acre of muscular chest and, I'm sure, there are many who consider Bess foolish to even think of Porgy when this hunk . . . is on hand . . ." *See*: **W37bbbb**

B849. PORTER, Andrew. "A Long Pull to Get There," originally published in *The New Yorker*, February 25, 1985, reprinted in *Musical Events: A Chronicle, 1983-1986*. New York & London: Summit Books, 1989, pp. 262-266.

Review of the 1985 production at the Met. ". . . The Met production . . . was not altogether an unmixed delight. It raised old questions about the work which I thought had been laid to rest for me in a buoyant, stylish, and totally enjoyable performance by the Indiana University Opera Theatre five years ago" [Porter's review of which may be seen below, **B850**, and in his *Music of Three More Seasons, 1977-1980*, pp. 534-535]. *See*: **W37mmm**

B850. _____. "Musical Events: [Review of *Porgy and Bess* performance at Indiana University]." *New Yorker* 56 (Mar. 31, 1980): 96.

Porter was very positive about the performances at Indiana University in 1980:

"I thought it the most enjoyable and persuasive presentation of Gershwin's opera I've ever come across . . . The genre scenes built into a coherent whole . . . the sense of a linked community and of the individual sufferings and solaces of those within it was vividly conveyed. The Houston 'Porgy' that came to Broadway was less coherent though it gave some idea of what the opera might be . . . This Bloomington 'Porgy' is the first to make me add my voice to the chorus of those asking why neither New York house has Gershwin's opera in its regular repertory . . ." *See*: **W37iii**

B851. REICH, Howard. "Music - PORGY & BEST; Glyndebourne produces a definitive Gershwin classic." *Chicago Tribune,* August 20, 1989, final edition, arts p. 16. *See*: **W37ooo**

B852. ROCKWELL, John. "Opera: 'Porgy' Returns." *NYTimes,* Oct. 30, 1985, p. C17.
". . . When 'Porgy' returned to this season's Met repertory Monday night [October 28, 1985], it seemed to be happily accepted by the audience to fit right in with the company's regular repertory. Whatever this score is, and it certainly does have its flaws, this is still a great statement of musical Americana, and the Met's production, itself flawed, lets us savor that greatness . . . Mr. [James] Levine [the music director] treated this music with the seriousness it deserves, and, in the end, that dedication informed the entire performance." *See*: **W37mmm**

B853. ROSENTHAL, H. et al. "Glyndebourne welcomes Gershwin." *Opera* 37 (Autumn 1986):12-16. *See*: **W37ooo**

B854. SCHOLZ. D. D. "Gezappel und Getaenzel (Porgy and Bess)." *Neue Zeitschrift für Musik* 149 (July-Aug. 1988): 66-67.

B855. "Show on Broadway (Radio City Music Hall)." *Variety* 310 (Apr. 13 1983): 84.

B856. SMITH, CHARLES. "Symphonic percussion: Porgy and me." *Percussive Notes* 19/2 (1981): 65-68.
Anecdotes.

B857. SMITH, P. J. "Porgy at the Met." *Opera* 36 (May 1985): 498-502. *See*: **W37mmm**

B858. STORRER, W. A. "Charleston." *Opera* 37 (Feb. 1986): 166-167. David Stahl was conductor. *See*: **W37lll**

B859. SUTCLIFFE, James H. "Berlin (West)." *Opera* 39 (Nov. 1988): 1347-1348.

B860. TAKAHAMA, Valerie. "Gershwin's vision remains model for 'Porgy and Bess.'" *Long Beach Press Telegram* [CA] (*Newsbank* PER 125:B7), Feb. 15, 1987.
Article announcing the upcoming opening, February 19, of the Houston Grand Opera's touring production at the Wiltern Theater, under the aegis of the Los Angeles Music Center Opera. An interesting feature of the article is the explanation for the inclusion of the "Buzzard Song," often omitted: ". . . It's a song about superstition, basically. The buzzard is hovering, and if the buzzard lights on your door it means trouble . . . I have Bess witness the 'Buzzard Aria.' The process of falling in love with the anthesis of what you've loved before is a complicated and rather mature thing to do. I'm trying to make it clear to the audience how this woman who is Crown's Bess . . . how she can switch her allegiance so thoroughly to a crippled beggar and then switch back again . . ." Article is bristled with quotes giving perspectives on

the opera from then current director Jack O'Brien. *See:* **W37sss**

B861. TOEPEL, Michael. "Der Chor in Porgy and Bess." *Musik Und Bildung; Praxis Musikerziehung* 19 (Dec. 1987): 938-941.

B862. THORN, F. "Glyndebourne." *Buehne: Das Oesterreichische Kulturmagazin* 335 (Aug. 1986): 46. *See:* **W37ooo**

B863. WILSON, E. "On the Rialto: There's Life in Old Pearls Yet (Radio City Music Hall)." *Wall Street Journal* 63, Apr. 29 1983, p. 17. *See:* **W37kkk**

B864. ZAKARIASEN, Bill. ". . . In a dazzling performance." *NY Daily News*, Feb. 8, 1985.
        A very positive review of the performance at the Metropolitan Opera on February 6, 1985. ". . . G's complete score—particularly when played by an orchestra of the Met's size and expertise (to say nothing of James Levine's sweeping, probing and deeply committed conducting)——is an awesome revelation of his genius in instrumentation and theatrical power . . ." Zakariasen also had high praise for the cast and chorus. *See:* **W37mmm**

B865. _____. "Live appearances: New York (first time at the Met)." *Ovation* 6 (Apr. 1985): 26. *See:* **W37mmm**

1990s:

B866. "Berlin (Theater des Westens)." *Oper und Konzert* 28 (June 1990): 14. *See:* **W37gggg**

B867. BERNHEIMER, Martin. "It Ain't Necessarily Show: New 'Porgy and Bess' Production Veers From Hokum to Pathos." *Los Angeles Times*, June 9, 1995.
        Mixed review of the opening at the Chandler Pavilion, L. A. ". . . [Hope] Clarke's name [the stage director and choreographer] still appears in the program, but the . . . credits boast 'additional staging by Tazewell Thompson' and 'additional choreography by Julie Arenal.' Cutesy-fussy business often clutters the stage. So does hokey show business . . ." The Los Angeles area media responded plentifully to this production, and not always in a complimentary fashion. *See:* **W37nnnn**

B868. _____. "A New 'Porgy' That's Louder Than Life." *Los Angeles Times*,
        (dateline: San Diego), Mar. 10, 1995, Home Edition, Section: Calendar, p. 1 Pt. F.
        A lengthy, but mixed review of the 1995 HGO version of P&B based on its tour opening at San Diego, CA. The principal complaint was based on the amplification of the voices and orchestra. According to the reviewer ". . . [T]his 'Porgy' demeans the performers, insults the composer and assaults the listener with loudspeakers . . . This 'Porgy' is being presented around the country (and, later, in Japan) in association with eight other opera companies plus the Orange County Performing Arts Center . . . Hope Clarke, the first African American to stage a major production of Gershwin's opera, made a lot of fuss in numerous articles about some revisionist ideas. She said she wanted to avoid stereotypes, lend new dignity to the residents of Catfish Row and stress some tribal roots. As things have turned out, however, her 'Porgy' doesn't look drastically different from the excellent version directed 19 years ago by Jack O'Brien . . . The opening-night cast introduced Alvy Powell as a burly, dark-toned, sympathetic Porgy in the tradition of William Warfield, partnering Marquita Lister as a tough, poignant Bess who never made the mistake of confusing earthiness with glamour. Lester Lynch made Crown more bully than macho magnet. Luvenia Garner brought matriarchal

pride to the soaring plaints of Serena, and managed the glissandos of 'My Man's Gone Now' with heart-rending point. Kimberly Jones was all sweetness and light as Clara, but the sweetness never cloyed. Larry Fuller, the only holdover from the Houston casts of '76 and '87, proved that suave understatement still works best in the projection of Sportin' Life's disarming sleaze. Ann Duquesnay sang the music of Maria—including the restored 'Struttin' Style' rap—with a chesty torch-song contralto. A lapse or two notwithstanding, this performance bore signs of propulsive energy and enlightened sensitivity. 'Porgy' deserves nothing less. Unfortunately, the amplification came perilously close to making it plenty of nothing." *See*: **W37jjjj**

B869. BISS, R. "Microphones on Catfish Row: Porgy and Bess at the Mercury." *Music in New Zealand* 14 (Spring 1991): 43-45.

B870. BLOCK, Geoffrey. "Gershwin's buzzard and other mythological creatures." *The Opera Quarterly* 7/2 (1990): 74-82.

B871. BOTTAZZI, A. "Gershwin 'Porgy and Bess.'" *Opera* 45/9 (Sept. 1994): 1092-1093.
Performance review.

B872. CUNNINGHAM, Carl. "Three at Houston . . . Harvey *Milk* unveiled, with *Porgy* and Dido." *American Record Guide* (May/June 1995): 36-37.
A generally negative appraisal of what the reviewer called a "Broadway-oriented production." *See*: **W37hhhh**

B873. DUNCAN, Scott. "New staging makes this 'Porgy' better." *The Orange County Register*, Show Weekend Section, June 9, 1995.
Review of the premiere performance at Chandler Pavilion in L. A.. "The national tour . . . has improved, but the production still suffers from an underachieving cast . . ." Further evidence of mixed opinion about this version. *See*: **W37nnnn**

B874. GRITTEN, David. "Gershwins Were No Fans of Preminger's 'Porgy.'" *LA Times*, Jan. 19, 1993, Home Edition, Section: Calendar, p. 5 Pt. F Col. 3.
In re: the videotape of the Glyndebourne production: "Trevor Nunn's interpretation of the work has found favor with Gershwin's heirs. 'He's given the characters an emotional base in a way no one has done before,' said Michael Strunsky, nephew of Leonore Gershwin and sole trustee and executor of Ira Gershwin's estate, which has managed 'Porgy and Bess' for the last 40 years . . . Strunsky confirmed that this was only the second occasion that film rights for 'Porgy and Bess' had been granted. 'Ira and Leonore Gershwin,' he said, 'were unhappy with Otto Preminger's 1959 film of the work . . . That film was unfortunate . . . My aunt didn't want it distributed. She and my uncle felt it was a Hollywoodization of the piece. We (the estate) now acquire any prints we find and destroy them' . . ." *See*: **F25 (Preminger), F25.1 (Glyndebourne), W37ooo**

B875. HERMAN, Kenneth. "'Porgy' Gets a Cultural Makeover; Director Hope Clarke has added a historic African American flavor to Gershwin's classic characters on Catfish Row." *Los Angeles Times*, Mar. 5, 1995, Home Edition Calendar, p. 46.
A thorough assessment of the 1995 HGO production of P&B. ". . . 'The work had a Broadway stench to it,' explained Houston Grand Opera general director David Gockley in a recent phone interview . . . In January, Gockley and the Houston Grand Opera unveiled a new production of 'Porgy and Bess,' which will tour Southern California starting this week in San

Diego. This is the second time the Houston company has mounted Gershwin's work . . . But even as the American opera Establishment became more comfortable with 'Porgy and Bess,' [after successful performances around the world and in the United States culminating with performances at the Metropolitan Opera] cultural criticism of the work festered, especially among African Americans. Because the opera's hero was a beggar and his rival was a drug dealer, many perceived 'Porgy and Bess' as a catalogue of negative role models . . . For the new Houston production of 'Porgy and Bess,' Gockley selected Hope Clarke to be director and choreographer. The 52-year-old Clarke will enter the record books as the first African American to direct a professional U.S. staging of "Porgy and Bess." Clarke came to Gockley's attention through her work with New York City-based Opera Ebony productions of 'Porgy and Bess' in Brazil and Finland . . . With the choice of Clarke, Gockley hopes to overcome some of the remaining critical reservations about the opera. Clarke has brought out the African roots of the people who inhabit Gershwin's Catfish Row and has given its population a more positive, hopeful cast . . . Clarke has also made prominent use of drumming, a significant aspect of African culture. For example, at the big dance on Kittiwah Island, she has added an onstage drum and percussion ensemble. Clarke justified her African emphasis on the better understanding we now have of the Gullah community that inhabited the Sea Islands off the coast of the Carolinas and Charleston . . . Critical reaction to Clarke's approach has been positive . . . Gockley added that he has recently added a European extension to the 1996 tour, with performances at Milan's La Scala and the Paris Opera Bastille . . ." *See:* **W37nnnn**

B876. HASTINGS, S. "Gershwin 'Porgy and Bess.'" *Opera News* 56/17 (Jun. 1992): 57.
Review of a performance.

B877. HORN, David. "From Catfish Row to Granby Street; contesting meaning in Porgy and Bess." *Popular Music* 13/2 (1994): 165-174.
An long article of essay proportions concerning events surrounding proposed performances of P&B in Liverpool. ". . . As the opening event of its 1989–90 concert season, the Royal Liverpool Philharmonic Society planned two performances of *Porgy and Bess.* One was to be a concert performance involving international soloists . . . The second was to be a 'community' performance for which, in addition to the same performers, local choirs would be set up and rehearsed, and they would participate . . . in 'six or eight passages of suitable, familiar or exciting material.' The Philharmonic Hall was to be 'appropriately and atmosphereically decorated' by pupils from local primary schools, working with community artists . . . The idea came from the Society's newly appointed community outreach officer . . . The Society soon encountered opposition to its community performance proposal from a local black arts organisation, the Liverpool Anti-Racist and Community Arts Association, or LARCAA, who charged . . . that existing prejudices against black people in Liverpool would be reinforced by the work's depiction of blacks . . ." The ultimate result of the debate was that the community performance was cancelled; the concert performance was performed as planned. *See:* **W37dddd**

B878. KARRFALT, Wayne. "'Porgy and Bess' triumphs again in Tokyo." *The Japan Times,* February 4, 1996.
News story pertaining to the 1996 HGO tour and the performances in Toyko. "The Houston Opera Company's 'Porgy and Bess' is an indisputable success because all elements of the production have passion and precision . . ." *See:* **W37pppp**

B879. KOOPMAN, J. "Milwaukee." *Opera* 41 (July 1990): 838-839.

B880. SCHIFFMANN, Y. "Gershwin 'Porgy and Bess.'" *Opera* (Special issue, 1994):

107.
Review.

B881. STARKE., Amy Martinez. "Catfish Row throbs to life in grand Gershwin opera."
    Oregonian (Portland, OR), July 21, 1995.
    Overall, a complimentary review of the production in its last tour stop before going overseas. "In this two-cast production, the fascinating rhythms include more than the music. [Ex-] Director Hope Clark has extended them by adding African and Caribbean dance and rhythms to the crowd scenes . . ." *See:* **W37oooo**

B881.1. VOORHEES, John "This Is a 'Porgy And Bess' You Won't Want to Miss."
    Seattle Times (SE), October 4, 1993, Edition: FINAL, Section: TV, Page: F6.

B882. WARD, Charles. "'Porgy and Bess' HGO's third try has measure of charm."
    Houston Chronicle, Lifestyle and Entertainment Section, January 30, 1995.
    Positive review of this revisionist version of the opera. *See:* **W37hhhh**

W21. *PRIMROSE* (1924)

B883. GÄNZL, Kurt. *The British Musical Theatre,* Vol. II: 1915-1984. NY: Oxford
    University Press, 1986, pp. 226-227, 228 (*Tell Me More*), 234-235, 238 (*Primrose*),
    239 (*Tell Me More*), 353 (*Primrose*).
    There are four references to the premiere of *Primrose.* The following quote was chosen to illustrate the kind of information provided: ". . . It was all quite perfect for the Winter Garden [London], bright, light and modern, and Gershwin's music—his most substantial score to date—fitted the mood of the piece nicely. Five of the show's principal numbers he dug from his bottom drawer for Carter to fit with suitable new lyrics, and these provided the backbone of *Primrose's* score. 'Wait a Bit, Susie' was a lilting little tune with an anodyne lyric which provided the show with one of its principal song successes, while a duet for the hero and heroine, 'Naughty Baby' as sung by Joan in her 'vamp' metamorphosis, the pretty duet 'Some far away Someone,' and Pinkie's manhunting 'Man Wanted' were also well featured . . . [p. 226]" This is followed by two quotes from reviews, one each from *The Times* and *The Era.*
    See: **W21a, W23 (*Tell Me More*)**

W49. *REACHING FOR THE MOON* (derivative) **(1987)**

B884. HOLDEN, Stephen. "Stage: From Gershwin, 'Reaching for the Moon.'" *NYTimes,*
    Nov. 2, 1987, Section C, P. 16.
    Review of Eastman School of Music, NY opera theater's performance of the musical *Reaching for the Moon. See:* **W49a**

W29. *ROSALIE* (1928)

B884.1.   GELB, Arthur. "The Theatre: 'Rosalie;' 1928 Musical Revived in Central Park."
    NYTimes, June 26, 1957, 28:2.
    Negative review of this production. *See:* **W29c**

B884.2.   WOOLLCOTT, Alexander. "The Stage [Review of the premiere]." *NYWorld,*
    Jan. 12, 1928.
    A somewhat mixed review of the premiere, January 10th, 1928. Woollcott had praise

for Marilyn Miller, criticized Romberg's unmemorable music and conceded that "Brother Gershwin has written at least two jaunty songs which follow you further up the street [after the show]." *See*: **W29b**

W23. *TELL ME MORE* (1925)

B884.3. GÄNZL, Kurt. *The British Musical Theatre*, Vol. II: 1915-1984. NY: Oxford University Press, 1986, pp. 228, 239.

B885. "'Tell Me More' Is Bright Musical Play: A Lovely Score, Intelligent Lyrics, Fast Dancing and Ample Comedy in Gaiety's Show." *NYTimes (NYTimes Theater Reviews)*, Apr. 14, 1925, 27:3.

Positive review of a performance at NY's Gaiety theater. "George Gershwin has written a lovely score . . . There is, as in Lady Be Good, a book that will just about do . . ." *See*: **W23b**

PIANO MUSIC
(Works for Solo Piano)

W42. *PRELUDES FOR PIANO* (ca. 1923-1926)

B886. NILES, Abbe. "The Ewe Lamb of Widow Jazz." *The New Republic* XLIX/630 (Dec. 29, 1926): 164-166.

Significant mention of the five piano preludes premiered at the Marguerite D'Alvarez concert of December 4, 1926, by way of a review of that performance. "It is probable that the five new piano preludes which he [GG] played for the first time at the Roosevelt [Hotel] did not cost him an excessive amount of overtime, but were presented for what they are worth, recent by-products of his plenteous invention, and not to prove anything whatever. One was a frank tribute to Chopin; one criticized the crudity of the ragtime in Debussy's Golliwog's Cakewalk in just the way one clog-dancer would choose to criticize another's step; one was built on a theme written but not used for the famous blues movement of the Concerto in F; one might be a song deprived of its words; one started on the docks in New Orleans, to find itself shortly joyously footing it in Madrid. Yet every one should be published, none could have been written by another composer; the set exhibited the hard transparent surfaces, the fire-refracting facets and the cool blue depths of a circlet of well cut aquamarines and diamonds . . ." *See*: **W42a**

B887. B., H. "Other Music: Mme. d'Alvarez and George Gershwin." *NYEvening Post*, Dec. 6, 1926, p. 18.

Full transcript of this review may be seen in Robert Wyatt's thesis (**B899**). ". . . Mr. Gershwin played five new piano preludes for the first time, two of which at least are as fine as anything he has done in the idiom of modern American music, which bears no deep or vital relation to jazz, although it is still called by that somewhat doubtful name. The second prelude in particular has a great deal more than mere technical brilliance, and John Alden Carpenter is the only composer who can touch Mr. Gershwin in the original use of the idiom; it is full of feeling and should find its way to the programs of pianists who are not afraid of something new. The fourth is more directly in the blues tradition, a thoroughly fascinating bit . . ." *See*: **W42a**

B888. CHOTZINOFF, Samuel. "Gershwin and D'Alvarez." *The World*, Dec. 5, 1926, Sports Section, p. 26.

Full transcript of this review made be seen in Robert Wyatt's fine thesis (**B899**). "... Though all five [preludes] are interesting for their rhythmic treatment they left one with an impression of inconsequence, a feeling that the gifted composer was not propelled to write them down by anything of significance that took shape in his mind. The first prelude, in spite of an injection of a jazz rhythm in the accompaniment, was distinctly reminiscent of Chopin, and another came dangerously near to Mr. Gershwin's own song 'My Little Duckie.' In form and treatment this one was the freshest and most solid of the lot. The others sounded trifling and superficial as if they were dashed off in a hurry ..." *See:* **W42a**

B889.   G., R. R. "Mme. D'Alvarez, Gershwin Heard: Singer and Pianist Give Songs of Latter." *Boston Herald*, Jan. 17, 1927, p. 3.

Full transcript of this review may be seen in Wyatt's work (**B899**). "... As well as the rhapsody, Mr. Gershwin played five new preludes, music off the same piece, though one of them, perhaps the fourth, he allowed himself a certain prettiness ..." According to Jablonski, G played a sixth prelude at this concert. *See:* **W42b**

B890. "George Gershwin." *Etude* 47/3 (March 1929): 193-194.

A brief, unsigned biographical article, interesting only for the statement "... The *Six Piano Preludes, in the Style of Chopin* are more recent ..." *See:* **W42**

NILES, Abbe, *See:* **B886** above

B891.   P[ARKER], H[enry] T[aylor]. "Gershwin Variously: Concert and Composer, Week-end Concerts; Mr. Casella departs; Mr. Gershwin Enters; Mr. Gershwin Plain and Colored." *Boston Evening Transcript*, Jan. 17, 1927, p. 10.

Robert Wyatt provided a complete transcript of this lengthy review (**B899**). "... Not that the Five Preludes for Piano ... will add much to his reputation. They may land rather too often upon the common stock of such music a la Rakhmaninov [Rachmaninoff] ... they lack the freshness of the Rhapsody and the abundance of the Concerto ... he is quick with ingenuities ..." *See:* **W42b**

B892.   PERKINS, F. D. "Gershwin Gives His First Public Recital of Year: Pianist, With Mme. d'Alvarez, Wins Ovation for Pieces Combining Broadway with European Flavors. *NY Herald Tribune*, Dec. 5. 1926, Section 1, p. 20.

Full transcript of this review made be seen in Robert Wyatt's thesis (**B899**). "... A novelty of the program was a group of five piano pieces by Mr. Gershwin, played for the first time in public ... The Rhapsody in Blue ... proved, on the whole, effective in the two-piano version played yesterday by Mr. Gershwin and Isidor Gorn ... Mr. Gershwin's piano numbers proved to be skillfully written with the flavor of Broadway combined with various European flavors ... There was considerable liveliness in the group, though the fourth piece was a little languid and mostly French post-romantic in atmosphere. The fifth brought in a theme seemingly derived from the Rhapsody in Blue with a basic rhythm of Spanish savor in an interesting combination ..." *See:* **W42a**

B893.   R[OSENFELD], P[aul]. "George Gershwin at Symphony Hall: Composer and Prima Donna in Joint Recital." *Boston Globe*, Jan. 17, 1927, p. 7.

Review of the January 16, 1927, performance in Boston. Full transcript of this review may be seen in Robert Wyatt's thesis (**B899**). "... The five preludes are brief and sketchy, failing to establish a mood. The third is the most ingratiating of the set ... An audience of good size seemed much interested but seldom deeply stirred emotionally by the performance." *See:*

W42b

B894. S[MITH], C[arlton] S[prague]. "Music in Boston: d'Alvarez-Gershwin Recital."
Christian Science Monitor, Jan. 17, 1927, p. 4B.
Full transcript of this review may also be seen in Robert Wyatt's thesis (**B899**).
". . . [H]e played five of his own preludes, hitherto unheard in Boston. This music of
comparatively recent composition shows a clear advance in the composer's abilities. The first
exhibited clever manipulation of rhythms. The second proved unconvincing of anything. The
third of these pieces was a flashing, spirited bit, effectively contrived. Fourth came a brief
composition of amazing simplicity, yet widened scope. Last came a jerky, quivering musical
sketch, full of broken rhythms and syncopations of conventional jazz . . ." *See*: **W42b**

B895. SMITH, Moses. "Joint Recital Brings Jazz to the Fore." *Boston Evening American*,
Jan. 17, 1927, p. 22.
Full transcript of this review may be seen in Robert Wyatt's thesis (**B899**). ". . .
Gershwin's compositions, too, were puzzling. A snap judgement might be offered that he shot
his bolt with the 'Rhapsody,' that in it he said everything he knew. Certainly that piece stood
out head and shoulders above the preludes and that portion of the concerto which was offered
yesterday. The preludes, much anticipated, were disappointing. They gave the impression that
Gershwin is still groping . . ." *See*: **W42b**

B896. STOKES, Richard L. "Realm of Music." *NYEvening World*, Dec. 6, 1926, p. 15.
Full transcript of this review may be seen in Robert's thesis (**B899**). ". . . They [the
preludes] proved brief and glowing vignettes of New York life. The first was a vigorous bit of
syncopation, the second, lyrical in vein, resembled a nocturne; the third combined a jazz melody
with a rolling Chopinesque bass; the fourth was a blues variety, and the fifth stirred together
a Charleston for the left hand and a Spanish melody for the right. The melodic ideas of the
preludes appeared to me vivid, clever and original, but also unimportant and very seldom
beautiful . . ." *See*: **W42a**

B897. STOREY, Warren. "Jazz Recital Becomes Tame, Gershwin and Mme. d'Alvarez
in Symphony Hall." *Boston Post*, Jan. 17, 1927, p. 5.
Review of the concert with no mention of the preludes.

B898. WEIL, Irving. "High-Hatted Jazz, Some Imported Modernism and Harold Bauer."
NY Evening Journal, Dec. 6, 1926, p. 28.
Full transcript of this review may be seen in Robert Wyatt's thesis (**B899**). "The
reviewer's impressions of his week-end of music have to do with five new jazz preludes for
piano by George Gershwin, that youthful and redoubtable believer in dressing up jazz until it
perforce must find somewhere to go . . . but the whole of it seemed paltry and insignificant
beside the thing that the veteran pianist, Harold Bauer, created with the magic of his
interpretive art . . . It so happened that we slipped into Mr. Bauer's recital (as he began playing
the Mozart [A minor] sonata) just after listening to the Gershwin preludes. It was an ironic bit
of chance, and perhaps neither quite fair nor altogether apropos as a matter of juxtaposition—
but illuminating, nonetheless . . . [T]hey [the preludes] are nothing more than music to please
people who are not altogether grown up. Their ingredients of musical comedy, as it is known
on Broadway—a little commonplace melody and a great deal of obvious rhythmic excitation.
Some of the rhythmic counterpoint was interesting for the moment, but it meant nothing except
as a 'stunt' . . ." *See*: **W42a**

B899. WYATT, Robert. *The Piano Preludes of George Gershwin.* Doctor of Music treatise, Florida State University, Spring 1988. iv, 158 pp. Bib., pp. 87-102.

This paper is considerably more important to Gershwin scholarship than the label "treatise" implies. Indeed, it is a major contribution to Gershwin scholarship. Dr. Wyatt organized his study of the genesis and evolution of the piano preludes into four main chapters: II. The Story III. The Recitals, IV. The Music, and IV. Epilogue. An appendix provides full transcripts of the newspaper reviews of the New York and Boston d'Alvarez/Gershwin "Roosevelt Recitals" at which the preludes were premiered. After a painstaking job of research about the five piano preludes which were premiered on December 4, 1926, Wyatt concluded: ". . . Unfortunately, no one will ever know *exactly* what Gershwin played on the third segment of the recital. Historically, the two 'Novelettes' and the three published preludes have always been included on the program. But there is little doubt that 'Sleepless Night' was also performed as a prelude . . . The 1936 version of 'Sleepless Night' was finally published by the New World Music Corporation in 1984, a year after Ira died, but this edition is decidedly different from the original, found in the 1924 'Themes' notebook. If 'Sleepless Night' was played on either the New York or Boston recital (or both), Gershwin must have improvised an ending for the earlier version . . ." *See:* **B898**

B900. WYATT, Robert. "The Seven Jazz Preludes of George Gershwin: A Historical Narrative."*American Music* 7/1 (Spring 1989): 68-85.

Scott DeVeaux, editorial consultant for this special jazz issue of the journal, calls this article "an ingenious study" [p. 4.]. Derived from Wyatt's dissertation, above, the article provides easily accessible information, a wealth of detail, at the same time shedding light on the four preludes which were not published as piano preludes.

B901. ZIZZO, A[licia]. "The Gershwin 'Preludes.'" *Piano & Keyboard* 167 (Mar.-Apr. 1994): 29.

CHAMBER MUSIC

W38. *LULLABY (ca.* 1919-1920)

B902. "Larry Adler to Unveil Gershwin String Quartet at Edinburgh Festival." *Variety* 231, June 5, 1963 (dateline: Edinburgh, June 4), p. 43.

Announcement that Larry Adler, harmonica virtuoso, will premiere his adaptation of the string quartet "Lullaby" at the Edinburgh Festival on August 29. *See:* **W38a**

OTHER DERIVATIVE WORKS

W48. *MY ONE AND ONLY* (1983)

B903. BARNES, Clive. "Duncan, Correia: new two & only. *NY Post*, Dec 7, 1984. [*Newsbank* PER 65:G8]

Enthusiastic review of the version with Sandy Duncan and Don Correia at the Saint James in NY. ". . . What makes the whole vessel so seaworthy, virtually leakproof, are music and lyrics, respectively and respectfully, by George and Ira Gershwin."*See:* **W48b**

B904. BOWMAN, Harry. "'My One and Only': 'S Wonderful." *Dallas Morning News*, June 28, 1985 (*Newsbank* PER 7:E2).

A detailed review of this version which opened at Dallas' Music Hall in Fair Park on June 26, 1985. ". . . Happiness is a show called *My One and Only* . . . This musical . . . is so filled with bounding innocence and charming moments that what imperfections it has are energetically and decisively swept off the stage. Its intent to entertain is so pure that it insists on becoming a total delight . . ."

B905. "Director of 'Only' Gets Hub Heave-Ho; Tune, Walsh Step In."*Variety* (Dateline Boston, Feb. 1) 310, Feb 2, 1983, p. 117, 121.

Report of some of the pre-production problems in the 1983 musical *My One and Only*, which was based on *Funny Face* of 1927. The young director, Peter Sellars (25), was fired over "artistic differences," and replaced by Tommy Tune and Thommie Walsh as co-directors. *See:* **W48**

B906. DRAKE, Slyvie. "This Time, 'One, Only' Flies Right." *Los Angeles Times* (*Newsbank*), July 15, 1985.

Positive review of *My One and Only* at the Ahmanson in Los Angeles during July-August, 1985. With praise for all, Drake commented: ". . . This debonair show that barely got off the ground on Broadway two years ago soars . . ." *See:* **W48c**

B907. GERARD, Jeremy. "'My One and Only' remains endearing." *Dallas Morning News* (*Newsbank* PER 66:A2), dateline New York, Dec 22, 1984.

"Tommy Tune and Twiggy brought *My One and Only* to Broadway just in time for the 1983 Tony award nominations . . . [and it] won a slew of Tonys . . . Tune and Twiggy now [1984 cast] have been replaced by Sandy Duncan and Don Correia . . ." In a generally enthusiastic review, Gerard compared the performances of Tune/Twiggy to Duncan/Correia.

B908. HUMM. "Shows on Broadway: My One and Only." *Variety* 311, May 4, 1983, p. 534.

A detailed review of the run which opened May 1, 1983, at the St. James Theatre. Humm called the production a "mindless nostalgia bath." "High-tech musical staging, an abundance of expert performing talent and a gaggle of wonderful G songs should be enough to put 'My One and Only' over on Broadway. 'S far from a wonderful musical but it generally fulfills its steely-eyed intent of entertaining the audience . . . Tap is the primary terping motif and fanciers of that venerable show biz art will look upon the show as Valhalla . . ." *See:* **W48b**

B909. JAQUES, Damien. "Tommy and Twiggy put on a darling show." *Milwaukee Journal* (*Newsbank*) PER 15:G6), Dateline: New York, July 31, 1983.

Complimentary review of *My One and Only* at New York's St. James Theater during July, 1983. ". . . This is not a show for cynics and old cranks. It is a show for people who take a delight in clever, frothy, well-produced musicals, and it's a show that furthers a number of legends . . ." *See:* **W48b, B911**

B910. JONES, Welton. "Absence of 'One' hurts the rest." *San Diego [CA] Union* (*Newsbank* PER 17:B9), July 16, 1985.

A generally complimentary review of the show as performed at the Ahmanson Theater in Los Angeles for a limited run in July, 1985. Jones bemoans the absence of Twiggy in the leading girl's role, Twiggy having been replaced by Sandy Duncan, but indicates ". . . there's plenty of charm remaining . . ." *See:* **W48c**

B911. NOVICK, Julius. "Theater: Pretty Nice Work." *Village Voice* 28, May 10, 1983, p. 86.

Mixed review of *My One and Only* in a performance at the St. James Theater in NY. Includes history of the genesis of this version. ". . . *My One and Only* has emerged as a very polished, very clever, very professional, though somehow not overwhelmingly joyous, entertainment . . ." *See*: **W48b, B909**

B912. [My One and Only] "Thumbs Up, Thumbs Down: Theater." *Vanity Fair* 46 (July 1983): 20-21 *See*: **W48b**

B913. VIERTEL, Jack. "Gershwin music quickens your pulse." *Los Angeles Herald Examiner* (*Newsbank* PER 17:B11), July 15, 1985.
    Lengthy and generally positive review of *My One and Only* during its summer 1985 run at the Ahmanson Theatre in Los Angeles. *See*: **W48c**

B914. WEIL. "Shows Out of Town: My One and Only, Boston, Feb. 9." *Variety* 310, February 23, 1983, p. 108.
    Review of the Broadway-bound, Paramount Theatre Productions-Francine LeFrak & Kenneth Mark Productions presentation of *My One and Only*. This version of the show opened February 8, 1983, at the Colonial Theatre in Boston. ". . . The result is a disjointed, directionless jumble, well intentioned, certainly, a show that's pleasing enough to the ear and eye, but one that leaves the brain disengaged and fails to involve its audience . . ." The full cast is listed. *See*: **W48a**

B915. WILSON, E., and T. HALL. "*My One and Only* Opens on Broadway—After Losing Its Head in Boston (originally based on *Funny Face*)." *Wall Street Journal* 63, May 6, 1983, p. 19. *See*: **W48b**

W50. *CRAZY FOR YOU* (1992)
(*See*: **B298-B321**)

W52.1. *AT WIT'S END* (1987) (*See* below, **W52.1**)

MISCELLANEOUS PUBLICATIONS OF GERSHWIN MATERIAL

W53. WODEHOUSE, Artis. *Gershwin's Improvisations for Solo Piano transcribed from the 1926 and 1928 disc recordings.* Secaucus, NJ: **Warner Bros.** #PF0471, 1987.

B916. HALLMAN, Diana. "[Review]." *American Music* 7/1 (Spring 1989): 88-90.
    This informative review should be read by anyone planning to perform the "improvisations" from the Warner Bros. 1987 edition. Hallman points out the sparsity of available recordings of the original discs from 1926 and 1928. However, since Wodehouse had to have the originals to make the transcriptions, and since she had access to the Stanford University collection of 78 rpm recordings, I am assuming that they are available at that library.

B917. ORLEDGE, Robert. "[Review]." *Popular Music*, Great Britain 8/3 (October 1989): 353-354.

B918. SMITH, Joseph. "MUSIC REVIEWS: Keyboard Music, George Gershwin. Gershwin's Improvisations for solo piano . . ." M. L. A. *Notes* 45/4 (June 1989): 858.
    Well informed review of the Wodehouse transcriptions. Besides comparing this edition to the 1932 *Song-Book* by G himself, Smith commented: ". . . *Gershwin's Improvisations* offers. eight . . . recorded solos complete [from the ten recorded by G in London] (most containing three varied choruses plus verse) . . . this is an important publication that is sure to endure . . ."

W45. *SONG-BOOK* (1932)

B918.1. E[NGEL], C[arl]. "Views and Reviews." *Musical Quarterly* (1932): 646-652.
Review of the songbook. While not an admirer of RIB and Concerto, Engel stated ". . . [T]o us, Mr. Gershwin seems at his best in just the stuff his song-book is made of . . ." Regarding G's special arrangements of the songs, ". . . To Mr. Gershwin thanks are due for having herborized some specimens of the bloom and pressed and preserved them between the leaves of his 'song-book' . . ."

W52.1. *AT WIT'S END* (1987)

B918.2. DOLL. "Legit Review: At Wit's End." *Variety* (Daily), Feb. 19, 1989: 20.
Brief, but good review of *At Wit's End*.

B918.3. GALLO, Clifford. "Levant is at the soul of 'Wit's,' Play captures the composer's spirit." *LA Herald Examiner*, Feb. 15, 1989.
Descriptive review of *At Wit's End*, as played at the Coronet Theater in Los Angeles in 1989. ". . . During the first act, [Stan] Freeman [the star of the one-man show] deadpans his way through a variety of subjects ranging from mental illness . . . and his utter devotion to Gershwin . . ." *See*: **W52.1.bb, B1583**

B918.4. Irv. "At Wit's End: Oscar Levant 'live' in concert." *Miami Jewish World*, Oct. 24, 1987.
Review of the show in Florida. ". . . His [Levant's] real problem was that he wasn't born George Gershwin. He met Gershwin while still a young man, coming eventually both to befriend and to idolize him. He performed Gershwin's music even as he tried to emulate the man, down to George's manner of dress . . ." *See*: **W52.1.aa**

REVIEWS OF SELECTED PERFORMANCES
AND ALL-GERSHWIN CONCERTS

B919. G., G. "Gershwin Concert Has Record Crowd: More Than 20,000 in Lewisohn Stadium for Memorial to Modernistic Composer, Lehman and Mayor There; Music, With Chorus and Soloists, Covers Writer's Scope—Ethel Merman's Songs 'A Hit.'" *NYTimes* (Late editions), Aug. 11, 1937.
Review of the first New York Memorial concert at Lewisohn Stadium on August 9, 1937. *See*: **W3e, W54b, B923, B1709**

B920. GRITTEN, David. "'Gershwin' Not Up to Legend." *LAHerald-Examiner* **[AMPAS]**, Aug. 28, 1987.
"'George Gershwin Remembered' . . . is an oddly lifeless documentary about the legendary composer and his life. Part of the laudable 'American Masters' series on PBS, it faithfully records the stepping stones of Gershwin's career—but fails to give us much idea of the man or the nature of his prodigious talent . . . And we're left with a profile that fails to give us an insightful picture . . ." *See*: **F31**

B921. HARRIS, Radie. "Broadway Ballyhoo." *Hollywood Reporter* (dateline: NY) **[AMPAS]**, Feb. 9, 1987.
Announcement of the upcoming Gershwin Gala, March 11, 1987, at the Brooklyn Academy of Music. Also mentioned are the Gershwin family members expected to attend: Lee

Gershwin, Frankie Gershwin Godowsky and her twin daughters, Judy Gershwin, widow of Arthur, and her daughter-in-law and grandson (Marc's wife, Vicki, and son Alan). *See*: **W54m**

B922. LEVANT, Oscar. "'S Wonderful, 'S Marvelous, 'S Gershwin: A musical genius is recalled by a famous wit and pianist who knew him well." *TV Guide* (Jan. 15, 1972): 24-26.

Article announcing the January 17, 1972, Jack Lemmon NBC television special and including personal reminiscences by Levant. ". . . My first encounter with Gershwin came in 1925, after I had recorded 'Rhapsody in Blue' for Brunswick Records. That engagement had been an unexpected opportunity —the regular pianist with the orchestra failed to show up and I was called in as a last-minute substitute. When I completed the recording in one take (I was 18 and nerveless), it occurred to me they could pay me whatever they wanted for the job, even union scale, which they did . . ." *See*: **W1, D768, B1583**

B923. P., F. D. "Record Crowd Hears Concert For Gershwin: 20,223 Jam Stadium Where Composer Set High Mark for Attendance in 1932, Seats Filled by 7 P. M., Program Is Evenly Divided between Stage, Concert." *NYHerald Tribune*, Aug. 11, 1937.

Extensive review of the memorial concert held in Lewisohn Stadium in New York, on August 9, 1937. Mention is made in this article of a week long revival of OTIS at Jones Beach opening the same night, August 9th. *See*: **W54b, B481, B919, B1709, W34d**

BIBLIOGRAPHY ABOUT DISCOGRAPHY

Whenever possible, a symbol was assigned to the recorded performances discussed in these reviews. This system is based on the one used by Kurtz Myers in earlier issues of M. L. A. *Notes'* column *"Index to Record Reviews."* The symbols are:

[+] = Excellent

[adq] = adequate

[-] = inadequate

[*] = "a review of sufficient length and probity to warrant special attention."

GENERAL INFORMATION SOURCES ABOUT RECORDINGS

B924. BURTON, Jack. *The Blue Book of Hollywood Musicals: Songs from the Sound Tracks and the Stars Who Sang Them Since the Birth of the Talkies a Quarter-Century Ago.* Watkins Glen: Century House, 1953.

B925. ELLSWORTH, Ray. "Americans in Microgroove: Part II." *High Fidelity* 6/8 (Aug. 1956): 60-66.

Discussion of recordings of American composers of the mid-1950s including discussion of recordings of G's works then available.

B926. GREENFIELD, Edward, Robert LAYTON, and Ivan MARCH. *The Penguin Guide to Compact Discs, Cassettes, and LPs.* Harmondsworth, Middlesex, England & NY: Viking Penguin, 1986, pp. 351-360.

Twenty three recordings of G music are listed with evaluative and sometimes comparative annotations. *See*: **D65, D158, D355**

B927. HAMILTON, David. "Record reviews." *High Fidelity/Musical America* 26 (Dec. 1976): 100-102.

B928. _____. "Will We Be Ready for the Gershwin Centenary?" *High Fidelity* 24/7 (July 1974): 44-48.

This detailed article lists, describes, and evaluates Gershwiniana published during 1973. Among the many items covered are: the Monmouth-Evergreen *Lady Be Good* album; William Bolcom's "Song Book" album, which the reviewer labeled "virtuosic and stylish"; the albums issued by the Mark 56 label during 1973, including the *Second Rhapsody* in ". . . a private run-through Gershwin arranged for his own instruction just after the piece was finished . . . undeniably fascinating . . ." The "George Gershwin conducts excerpts from Porgy and Bess" Mark 56 album is discussed. About the Klavier KS 122 album of G performing his songs along with those of Kern and Walter Donaldson in piano roll versions, Hamilton observed: ". . . They cast additional light on Gershwin's keyboard style . . ." Also listed are the album of the London cast of *Tip-Toes* (Monmouth Evergreen MES 7052) "displaying a transatlantic dichotomy of style"; Gertrude Lawrence's songs from *Oh, Kay!* (Monmouth-Evergreen); ". . . [Fred] Astaire is the model for the style . . . and Columbia's recent reissue of songs from his films (SG 32472), including ten Gershwin numbers, is indispensable . . ." The article lists the Lehman Engel interpretation of P&B along with Goddard Lieberson's production of *Girl Crazy* (Columbia Special Products COS 2560). Among the books listed are those published during the years around 1973, the biographies of Jablonski and Stewart, Kimball and Simon, and Schwartz, e. g. *See:* **D583 (Bolcom), D461 *(Lady, Be Good!),* D716   (GG Conducts . . .), D717 *(Second Rhapsody),* D1137 (Klavier), D572 (Tip-toes), D481-D482 (Lawrence in *Oh, Kay!),* D496 (Engel, P&B), D453 (Lieberson, *Girl Crazy*)**

B929. HARRIS, D. S., "Berlin: Songs; Gershwin: Songs." *High Fidelity* 29 (Dec. 1979): 96-97.

B930. HOLDEN, Stephen. "The Pop Life: An exhaustive Gershwin recording project in the works . . ." *NYTimes,* May 24, 1989.

". . . [W]ork is to begin this fall [1989] on a six-album project to record George and Ira Gershwin's entire output for the musical theater . . . The first event of the project was a concert of Gershwin music, conducted by Robert Fisher, at the library's Coolidge Auditorium [Library of Congress] . . . The first show to be recorded in the project will be 'Girl Crazy' (1930) . . . Later releases are to include complete recordings of the Kurt Weill-Ira Gershwin show 'Lady in the Dark' (1941) . . . 'Pardon My English' (1933), both the 1927 and 1930 versions of the Gershwin brothers' 'Strike Up the Band,' and 'Primrose' . . . The albums will be followed by publication of a scholarly edition of the piano-vocal score for each show . . ." *See:* **W54u**

B931. JABLONSKI, Edward. "Gershwin at 80, Observations, discographical and other-wise, on the 80th anniversary of the birth of George Gershwin, American Composer. [part I] *American Record Guide* 41 (September 1978): 6-12, 58.

This is actually a discographical essay rich in material updating the discography in Jablonski and Stewart's biography published five years earlier in 1973. Extensive and informative annotations about fifteen recordings are given in two parts: "Historic Recordings" and "newly recorded 'serious' Gershwin." Jablonksi's discourse is informative, lively, and places a high priority on *musical* values. This article along with part II is must reading for collectors interested in Jablonski's opinions. [A copy of Judy Cimaglia's life-size portrait drawing of Gershwin serves as the cover for this issue].

B932. _____. "Gershwin at 80, Observations, discographical and otherwise, on the

80th anniversary of the birth of George Gershwin, American Composer. [part II] *American Record Guide* 41 (October 1978): 8-12, 57-59.

A less organized continuation of **B931**, above. Nevertheless, a wide range of recordings is covered including interpretations of the piano preludes, a reissue of the Toscanini/NBC disc of AiP, Frances G. Godowsky's recording of selected songs, and much more. The article concludes with mention of plans to publish the then unpublished songs: *Pay Some Attention to Me*, *Ask Me Again*, *Adored One*, and *Sleepless Night*. Like **B931** this is indispensable reading for collectors.

B933. JEPSON, Barbara. "Recordings View: The Flying Pianist and Other Wizards of the Keyboard." *NYTimes*, Arts & Leisure Section, Dec. 17, 1995, pp. 32-33.

A feature article focusing on Artis Wodehouse's then new project: a new CD reissue featuring Pauline Alpert, the first album in a series dubbed "Keyboard Wizards of the Gershwin Era." References are made to Wodehouse's previous successful effort, the best-selling Nonesuch reissue containing Gershwin playing Gershwin. *See*: **D1134**

B934. KOLODIN, Irving. "Mid-Month Recordings: From George to George with Love." *The Saturday Review* 42 (Oct. 17, 1959): 78-79.

B935. MCCLELLAN, Joseph. "Teaming Up With the Gershwins: Library of Congress & Elektra to Record Works." *Washington Post*, May 23, 1989, Final Edition, Style Section, p. D1.

Article in connection with the May 22 and 23, 1989, concerts held at the Library of Congress titled "Program of Music By George and Ira Gershwin Celebrating the Inauguration of the Leonore Gershwin/Library of Congress Recording and Publishing Project." In addition to discussing the concert, the article announced the inauguration of the Elektra/Nonesuch recording project which is to begin with an authentic revival recording of *Girl Crazy*, to be followed by such albums as "Michael Feinstein Sings Unpublished Gershwin"; "Lady in the Dark" (1941), IG's collaboration with Kurt Weill and Moss Hart; *Strike Up the Band* in both its 1927 and 1930 versions; *Pardon My English* and *Primrose*. Among those attending, Gershwin expert Robert Kimball was quoted: ". . . There are at least 15 shows that would be worth recording . . ." Mrs. Ira (Leonore) Gershwin, current Librarian of Congress James Billington, and James W. Pruett, Chief of the Music Division attended the concert. *See*: **W54u**

B935.1. OJA, Carol J. *American Music Recordings: A Discography of 20ʰ-Century U. S. Composers*, A project for the Institute for Studies in American Music for the Koussevitsky Foundation, Brooklyn: Institute for Studies in American Music, 1982, pp. 112-126.

This classic, meticulously prepared discography represents a thorough job on disc recordings prior to the CD era, having been published in 1982. Recordings issued between 1972 and 1979 are covered. Jazz, folk, or popular musics are not included.

B936. RIMLER, Walter. *A Gershwin Companion: A Critical Inventory & Discography, 1916-1984*. Ann Arbor, MI: Popular Culture, Ink., 1991.

Obviously a labor of love, this is an excellent inventory of works and discography to about 1984. Fine coverage of both serious and other works, but not including compact discs. *See*: **B146.1, B1787**

B937. ROSENBERG, Deena. "A Gershwin Musical Meant More Than Good Tunes." *NYTimes*, June 11, 1978.

A review of the Smithsonian record albums of *Lady, Be Good!* with Fred and Adele

Astaire, and *Oh, Kay!* in the London version with Gertrude Lawrence, and of Music Master's Arden and Ohman album. ". . . The new records are valuable . . . because they make available a number of Gershwin's piano accompaniments and arrangements which would otherwise have disappeared, to such songs as "So Am I," "I'd Rather Charleston" . . . and "Maybe" and "Someone to Watch Over Me . . ." Another important release is "Arden and Ohman (1925-1933)," the first LP issue of recordings by the duo-pianists, with period orchestra and vocalists . . ." Rosenberg emphasized the importance of these three recordings to the study of correct performance practice of the Gershwin music. *See*: **D459, D483 (*Lady*), D483 (*Oh, Kay!*)**

B938. ROSENBERG, Deena. "Mining America's gold: vintage musical theater albums." *High Fidelity/Musical America* 29 (March 1979): 104-106.

B939. RUST, Brian, with **Allen G. DEBUS.** *The Complete Entertainment Discography from the mid-1890s to 1942.* New Rochelle, NY: Arlington House, 1973, pp. 294-295. (Reprint ed. by Da Capo, 1988)
    Lists recordings made by G himself, the 1924 and 1927 recordings of RiB, e. g. This source is also valuable for its listing of other singles of G music released by many individual artists, among them Fred Astaire, Adele Astaire ('S Wonderful!/He Loves and She Loves), Judy Garland, and others.

B940. SMOLIAN, Steven. *A Handbook of Film, Theatre, and Television Music on Record, 1948-1969.* NY: The Record Undertaker, 1970. 2 vols.
    An American in Paris, Funny Face, Girl Crazy, Of Thee I Sing, Oh, Kay!, and *Porgy and Bess* on record receive coverage up to about 1969 in this edition.

B941. TODD, Arthur. "Theatre on the Disk: George Gershwin American Rhapsodist." *Theatre Arts* 36/7 (July 1952): 10, 93.
    Discography.

B942. YOUNGREN, William. "How Gershwin Played It." *The Atlantic* 257/5 (1986): 81-85.
    This is an informative article discussing a selection of currently available (1986) recordings, with a slant towards performance practice problems. Among other facts, Youngren points out that ". . . Warner Brothers . . . has just withdrawn the McBride score [of *Second Rhapsody*] from circulation, at the request of the Gershwin estate . . ." See: **W4**

ORCHESTRAL WORKS

W3. *AN AMERICAN IN PARIS* (1928)

B943. A., P. "GERSHWIN: An American in Paris; Porgy and Bess: A Symphonic Picture (arr. Robert Russell Bennett) . . ." *High Fidelity* 8/10 (Oct. 1958): 70. **[-]**
    Calling Antal Dorati's interpretation of AiP "raucous," this is a mixed review of the **Minneapolis Symphony Orchestra/Dorati recording (Mercury MG 50071)**. *See*: **D35, B948**

B944. _____. "Gershwin: An American in Paris; Rhapsody in Blue . . ." *High Fidelity* 9/3 (March 1959): 60. **[adq]**
    Mixed review of **Shefter/Warner Brothers Symphony/Heindorf (Warner Bros. B1243-BS1242)** recording. *See*: **D75, D345**

B945. _____ . "Gershwin: An American in Paris; Rhapsody in Blue . . ." *High Fidelity*
6/11 (Nov. 1959): 88. **[adq]**

Review of **Forum F 70008 with Joyce Hatto/Hamburg Pro Musica/George Byrd.**
"The young American conductor George Byrd has some very musicianly ideas about *An
American in Paris*, which he puts across rather convincingly . . . The same applies to Byrd's
joint efforts with Joyce Hatto in the *Rhapsody* though this work could profit by a little more
jazzlike freedom . . . Forum's . . . reproduction is not up to present high-fidelity standards
. . ."

B946. A., P. "[Review of Recordings] GERSHWIN: An American in Paris . . . Rhapsody
in Blue . . . Concerto for Piano and Orchestra, in F . . ." *High Fidelity* 8/11 (.): 60.

Review of five discs including the **List/Rochester Philharmonic/Hanson versions of
the Concerto and RiB (Mercury SR 90002), RCA Camden CAL 439/RCA Victor
Symphony   Orchestra/L.   Bernstein** and **Westminster   XWN   18687/Utah
Symphony/Abravanel** versions of AiP. *See*: Fuller entry at **B998** under **"Concerto."**

B947. AFFELDER, Paul. "Gershwin, George . . . An American in Paris. Copland: Billy
the Kid: Ballet Suite . . . RCA Camden CAL 439. LP." *Records in Review 1959
Edition.* Great Barrington, MA: Wyeth Press, p. 77. **[-]**

". . . Bernstein's recordings, made back in 78-rpm days, are completely out of the
running. The sound quality is not up to that of many other Camden reissues, and the
performances, while acceptable in most respects, are not distinctive enough to outweigh the
sonic shortcomings . . ." *See*: **D57**

B948. _____ . "Gershwin, George. An American in Paris; **[-]** Porgy and Bess: A
Symphonic Picture (arr. Robert Russell Bennett) . . . [Antal Dorati, cond.] Mercury
MG 50071. LP. **[adq]**" *Records in Review 1959 Edition.* Great Barrington, MA:
Wyeth Press, pp. 76-77.

"Gershwin made his musical visit to Paris during the roaring Twenties . . . but I doubt
he found the French capital quite as raucous as it appears in Dorati's blatant reading. The
conductor seems more at ease with the *Porgy* score . . ." *See*: **D35, B943**

B949. AFFELDER, Paul. "Gershwin, George . . . An American in Paris; Rhapsody in Blue;
Bert Shefter, piano . . . Warner Bros. Symphony Orchestra, Ray Heindorf, cond.
Warner Bros. B 1243. LP . . . BS 1243. SD." *Records in Review 1959 Edition.*
Great Barrington, MA: Wyeth Press, p. 77-78. **[adq]**

". . . Heindorf . . . plays everything quite loudly, with very few subtle nuances for relief.
He does have a lively conception of the music . . ." *See*: **D75, D345**

B950. _____ . "Gershwin, George . . . An American in Paris; Rhapsody in Blue . . .
Westminster XWN 18687.LP; Westminster WST 14002.SD. Concerto for Piano
and Orchestra, in F . . .Westminster XWN 18684.LP." *Records in Review 1959
Edition.* Great Barrington, MA: Wyeth Press, p. 77. **[adq]**

". . . From the technical standpoint, the performances by Abravanel, [Reid Nibley] and
the Utah Symphony are excellent. Interpretatively, however, the playing leaves something to
be desired—mainly a feeling of abandon, strangely missing from everything but the *Rhapsody
in Blue* and the last movement of the Concerto . . ." *See*: **D73, D323**

B951. _____ . "Gershwin, George . . . Concerto for Piano and Orchestra, in F; Rhapsody
in Blue . . . Mercury SR 90002.SD . . ." *Records in Review 1959 Edition.* Great
Barrington, MA: Wyeth Press, p. 77. **[+]**

"... Musically, Mercury's List-Hanson disc ... far outranks the Nibley-Abravanel efforts ..." *See:* **D309**

B952. A., V. "Gershwin: An American in Paris. Catfish Row (Suite from Porgy and Bess). Promenade ... [etc.] ... [Saint Louis Symphony, Slatkin] Moss Music MCD 10035 ..." *Fanfare* 10/4 (1986-1987): 135. **[adq]**

The reviewer took issue because Moss Music Group had "seen fit to release these adequate performances at full price and with less than maximum CD timings ... Recommended only if these performances have special meaning to you ..." *See:* **D63**

BENSON, Robert E. *See* **B1071** below under RiB

B953. BURWASSER, Peter. "Classical Recordings [Reviews] ... BBC Philharmonic Orchestra: conducted by Yan Pascal Tortelier CHANDOS CHAN 9325 **[DDD]** *Girl Crazy:* **Overture** (orch. Don Rose); *Variations on "I Got Rhythm"; An American in Paris.; Symphonic Suite: Catfish Row* (G's version); *Strike Up the Band:* Overture (orch. Don Rose) ..." *Fanfare* 18/5 (May/June 1995): 195.

"This is a beautifully played and recorded selection of orchestral Gershwin. Personally, I prefer my Gershwin with a bit more grit ..." *See:* Full entry at **B1322** under **"Overtures."**

B954. C., G. "[Review of *American in Paris*, Gershwin (CBS MK 42240)]." *Fanfare* 10/6 (1986-1987): 110.

B955. CARNOVALE, Norbert. "Reviews of Recordings ... George Gershwin ..." *Sonneck Society Bulletin* 14/3 (Fall 1988): 158. **[adq]**

Review of the digitally remastered CDs by Moss Music Group, MCD 10011 and MCD 10035, featuring the Saint Louis Symphony Orchestra under Leonard Slatkin. The discs include all of G's orchestral music, excepting *Cuban Overture.* I credited the St. Louis orchestra with being "grandiose and virtuosic in all sections," but I referred to these versions as being "at times ponderous." Furthermore, "... one has only to compare this recording of the *American* with that from 1929 by Nathaniel Shilkret and the RCA Victor Symphony Orchestra (RCA AVM1-1740) to note how far our American orchestras have come—especially in the quality of the wind players—in the last fifty-five years. The solo trumpet vibrato in the Shilkret version's blues theme section sounds straight out of Guy Lombardo, while Susan Slaughter of Saint Louis renders a gorgeously full, Germanic/American tone and tasteful vibrato. However, the wit and insouciance of Shilkret's reading conveys well much of what I believe was Gershwin's original intent ... Lovers of authenticity may therefore prefer the Shilkret [or Toscanini] recording." *See:* **D63, D101, D154, D349, D415**

B956. CHIEN, George. "Branching Out: New From Erato's Bonsai ... Gabriel Tacchino, piano ..." *Fanfare* 12/1 (Sept.-Oct. 1988): 61. **[+]**

Brief review of the **Erato ECD 55031** album. "... Erato hedged its bets by using a French pianist, who nevertheless seems quite at home in this American music. The recording is excellent ..." *See:* **D159**

B957. CHISLETT, W. A. "Nights At The Round Table [Review of recordings including Parlo PMC1026, Sondra Bianca, piano, with the Pro Musica Symphony, Hans-Jurgen Walther, conducting]." *Gramophone* (1955): 237. **[+]**

"... The *Rhapsody in Blue* is ... given a bravura performance which in swagger even rivals that of Paul Whiteman. In short if I wanted the latter alone I should buy the Whiteman but this record will chiefly be bought for the concerto [the other piece on the record] and those buying it need not hanker after any other record of the rhapsody . . ."

B958. DARRELL, R. D. "Gershwin, George . . . *Concerto for Piano and Orchestra in F*; *Rhapsody in Blue* . . . [Entremont/Philadelphia/Ormandy] . . . Columbia ML or MS 7013." *Records in Review 1968 Edition*. Great Barrington, MA: Wyeth Press, p. 146-147. **[-]**
      ". . . [T]he readings . . . are grimly serious, often ponderous or hurried, and self-conscious to an extreme when they attempt to be 'jazzy' . . ." *See*: **D112, D270**

B959. _____. "Gershwin, George . . . *An American in Paris*; *Porgy and Bess*: *Symphonic Picture* (arr. Bennett) . . . [Pittsburgh, Steinberg, cond.] Command CC 11037 . . ." *Records in Review 1968 Edition*, Great Barrington, MA: Wyeth Press, pp. 146-147. **[adq]**
      ". . . Whatever the Command process may be, the present recordings . . . achieve well-nigh ideal purity and balance . . . Steinberg's readings are just too careful and proper, lacking Gershwin's quintessential devil-may-care, thumb-at-nose spirit, but every scoring detail emerges here with gleaming pellucidity . . ." *See*: **D53, D241**

B960. _____. "Gershwin, George . . . *Concerto for Piano and Orchestra, in F*; *Rhapsody in Blue*; *Variations on 'I Got Rhythm'* . . . Philips 6500 118 . . . *Concerto for Piano and Orchestra, in F*; *Rhapsody in Blue*; *An American in Paris* . . . Angel S 36810." *Records in Review 1973 Edition*. Great Barrington, MA: Wyeth Press, pp. 131-132. *See*: Full entry under **"Concerto,"** and **D336**

B961. DARRELL, R. D. "Rhapsody in Blue; An American in Paris; Cuban Overture; Ivan Davis, piano . . . Cleveland Orchestra . . . London CS 6946 . . ." *Records in Review 1977 Edition*, p. 131. **[-]**
      Negative review of the record.

B962. _____. "Gershwin, George, *Concerto for Piano and Orchestra, in F* [Pyotr Pechersky & Alexander Tsvassman, pianos; Moscow Philharmonic Orchestra, Kiril Kondrashin, conducting & U. S. S. R. Symphony. . . Westminster Gold/ WG 8355." *Records in Review 1980 Edition*. Great Barrington, MA: Wyeth Press, pp. 142-143. **[adq]**
      Calling this performance a "non-foreign-accented reading," Darrell commented ". . . there's no real competition here for fully satisfactory American recordings . . . (I still stick with the 1960 Wild/Fiedler versions for RCA) . . ." *See*: **D141**

B963. DITSKY, John. "Gershwin: American in Paris; Katia and Marelle Lebèque . . . Angel DS-38130 . . ." *Fanfare* 8/3 (1984-1985): 168. **[+]**
      ". . . I find this album brilliantly played . . . and I recommend it highly . . . They deserve all manner of credit for restoring the original two-piano score to Gershwin's French ballet (as it inevitably became) to circulation . . . As for Grainger . . . this *Fantasy* is of no musical significance whatsever in terms of its *construction* . . . Anyone who cares for this music will [however] recognize how much Percy Grainger obviously did . . ." *See*: **D84**

B964. _____. "[Review of *American in Paris*, Lebèque (EMI CDC 7 47044 2)]." *Fanfare* 8/4 (1984-1985): 210. *See*: **D84**

B965. _____. "[Review of *American in Paris*, *Concerto*, Previn (EMI CDC 7 47161 2)]."

Fanfare 10/1 (1986-1987): 145. *See:* **D143**

B966. _____. "Classical Recordings: GERSHWIN: Concerto in F . . . An American
in Paris. Rhapsody in Blue . . . Jerome Lowenthal, piano, Utah Symphony . . .
EVERYMAN CLASSICS VBD-10017 . . ." *Fanfare* 12/2 (Nov.-Dec. 1988): 187-
188. **[+]**
    ". . . From a reviewer who has heard far more of this music over the past two years than
he cares to, then, comes this unreserved recommendation of this healthy portion of classic
Gershwiniana." *See:* **D135**

B967. F., A. "Gershwin: Rhapsody in Blue; An American in Paris . . ." *High Fidelity* 10/3
(Mar. 1960): 68. **[-]**
    Negative review of Bernstein/Columbia Symphony Orchestra/Bernstein (Columbia ML
5413) in AiP and Bernstein with the New York Philharmonic in RiB (same disc). *See:* Full entry
under **"Rhapsody in Blue."**

B968. "GERSHWIN 'Rhapsody in Blue', 'Cuban Overture', 'Porgy and Bess Suite', and
'American in Paris' - Deutsche-Grammophone 431-625-2 (Levine, James,
Chicago-Symphony Orchestra)." *American Heritage,* 45/6 (Oct. 1994): 104.
Review of the record. *See:* **D12, D176, D302**

B969. "Gershwin, of Sorts, GERSHWIN: Concerto in F . . . Rhapsody in Blue . . . An
American in Paris . . ." *Saturday Review* 41/17 (Apr. 26, 1958): 45. **[-] [*]**
See: Full text under **"Concerto."**

B970. GRUENINGER, Walter F. "Phonograph Records . . . *Rhapsody in Blue* . . . *An*
American in Paris . . ." *Consumer Bulletin* 43/4 (April 1960): 34. **[-]**
    Very brief review of Columbia MS 6091 (Columbia Symphony/ Bernstein on RiB and
New York Philharmonic/Bernstein on AiP). ". . . In the *Rhapsody*, Bernstein plays the solo part
in a staccato style that reveals feeling for the music, but lacks the . . . technical skill of many
full-time pianists . . ."

B971. _____. "Phonograph Records . . . Gershwin: *Rhapsody in Blue* and *An*
American in Paris . . ." *Consumer Bulletin* 43/5 (May 1960): 34. **[+]**
    This is the Wild/Boston Pops/Fiedler RCA Victor album (LSC 2367), about which the
reviewer exclaimed ". . . Stunning performances . . ." *See:* **D4**

B972. HAGGIN, Bernard H. "Music." *The Nation* 161/5 (Aug. 4, 1945): 115.
    In this essay, Haggin called AiP the best of G's ambitious works, at the same time
reviewing and comparing several albums which appeared to tie in with the release of the bio-
film RiB ". . . There is . . . more . . . muddy confusion on the recorded sound of 'An American
in Paris' with the New York Philharmonic Symphony ([Rodzinski] Columbia Set X-246) . . ."
See: **D47**

B973. INDCOX, J. F. "Rhapsody in Blue; Concerto for Piano and Orchestra, in F,
Julius Katchen, piano; orchestra, Montovani cond. London LL 1262 **[-]** . . .
Rhapsody in Blue; Concerto for Piano and Orchestra, in F, An American in Paris;
Suite from Porgy and Bess (arr. Morton Gould); Preludes for Piano; Piano Solo
from Porgy and Bess, Morton Gould, piano; orchestra, Morton Gould, cond. RCA
Victor LM 6033." *High Fidelity Record Annual,* ed. by Roland Gelatt (1956): 103.
[+] *See:* **D251 (Gould)**

B974. JABLONSKI, Edward. "Gershwin: . . . *An American in Paris*; [et al] Westminster
XWN-18684/7 [Nibley/Utah Symphony/Abravanel]. . ." *American Record Guide*
24/10 (June 1958): 427. **[+]**
"Long ago I had given up the possibility of ever hearing any Gershwin works 'as if for
the first time,' but these recordings come as a revelation . . ."

B975. JABLONSKI, Edward. "Gershwin: *An American in Paris*; *Porgy and Bess—*
A Symphonic Picture (Arr: Robert Russell Bennett) . . . Mercury   MG-50071
. . ." *American Record Guide* 25/1 (Sept. 1958): 32. **[adq]**
". . . Dorati and the Minneapolis men give us a vigorous account of the '*American*'
. . . For spirit I prefer the Gould version, and for the most faithful rendering of Gershwin's
orchestration the Abravanel is in a class all its own . . . In sum, the Minneapolis does its usual
excellent job, but others have done better." *See*: **D35, B948, B1130**

B976. JACQUES, Henry-. "Deux oeuvres de George Gershwin." *Disques* V   [=No. 45]
(Feb. 1952): 111.
Record reviews of AiP and RiB.

B977. KOLDYS, [Mark]. "Gershwin: *The Gershwin Collection: An Historical Treasury*
. . ." *American Record Guide* 51/2 (Mar.-Apr. 1988): 36. **[-] [*]** *See*: **D721**

B978. _____. "Gershwin: An American in Paris; Rhapsody in Blue . . . Chesky RC8
. . ." *American Record Guide* 51/2 (Mar.-Apr. 1988): 36. **[+] [*]**
"I have yet to hear one of Chesky's RCA 'Living Stereo' reissues that is not
demonstrably superior in sound quality to the equivalent RCA CD. If there are any doubters
this Gershwin LP will resolve the question once and for all . . . Fiedler and Wild have this music
in their blood, and their *Rhapsody in Blue* has snap, pizzaz, and suavity . . ." *See*: **D369**

B979. _____. "Gershwin: "Gershwin: *An American in Paris*; *Rhapsody in Blue* . . ."
American Record Guide 51/2 (Mar.-Apr. 1988): 36. **[+] [*]**
Review of the Wild/Fiedler/Boston Pops performance in a re-mastered version resulting
in Chesky RC8. . There was high praise of the engineering of this disc: "After almost thirty
years, these recordings still stand up musically; and sonically, they have a natural realism
lacking in many present-day digital wonders . . ." *See*: **D369**

B980. _____. "Gershwin: *Catfish Row*; *An American in Paris*; *Cuban Overture*;
Lullaby . . . Angel/EMI 49178" *American Record Guide* 51/2 (Mar.-Apr. 1988):
36-37. **[-] [*]**
This reviewer is especially informative because he relates the pressings to previous
recordings of the same material. Here he reviews the St. Louis/Slatkin CD version, Angel/EMI
49178. Koldys indicated a preference for the Morton Gould arrangement of the *Catfish Row*
suite over Gershwin's own, presented here. Koldys also opted for Slatkin's earlier recording
of all these concert works, on Vox 5132. ". . . This digitally-recorded CD sounds pretty good,
but it doesn't stand up to Slatkin's thirteen-year-old recordings, now on CD (Moss Music
Group 10035 [*q. v.* at **D62, B955**] . . . [T]he analog tapes from 1974 have a vibrant, realistic
excitement lacking in Angel's sound. In fact, MMG 10035 [**D101**] is one of the best recorded
CDs I have heard . . . [I]t is clearly the preferred recording . . ." *See*: **D416 (Vox 5132)**

B981. _____. "Gershwin: An American in Paris; Concerto in F; Rhapsody in Blue
Arabesque 6587. . ." *American Record Guide* 51/4 (July/Aug. 1988): 25. **[-]**
Because of several recent (as of 1988) reviews, it seems that Koldys is the *ARG*'s

resident G expert. Here he criticizes the David Golub/London Symphony/Mitch Miller CD release on Arabesque 6587. "... [T]he dilatory tempos employed in all of these works effectively suffocate the music ..." Recommendations: Siegel and Slatkin (MMG 10035 CD [**D100, D101**], or Wild and Fiedler (Chesky LPRC8, RCA CD 6519 [**D369**].

B982 . KOLODIN, Irving. "*Recordings* Reports I: Orchestral LPs . . . Gershwin: Concerto in F,'American in Paris,' 'Rhapsody in Blue,' 'Porgy' suite, etc. . . ." *Saturday Review* 38/44 (Oct. 29, 1955): 52. [adq]
    Review of Morton Gould playing and conducting (RCA Victor LM-6033). *See*: Full entry under **"Concerto"**

B983. KROEGER, Karl. "George Gershwin. AN AMERICAN IN PARIS. Samuel Barber. ADAGIO FOR STRINGS. Morton Gould. AMERICAN SALUTE ... Pro-Arte Records, SDS 627 . . ." *Sonneck Society Bulletin* 8/1 (Spring 1987): 33. [-]
    Brief, uncomplimentary review of this collection. "'. . . I can see no reason at all to buy Morton Gould's recording of Gershwin's *An American in Paris* . . ." *See*: **D38**

B984. LINKOWSKI, Allen. "Gershwin . . . Jerome Lewenthal; Utah Symphony . . .[AiP & Concerto] . . . Vanguard 10017 . . ." *American Record Guide* 52/1 (Jan.-Feb. 1989): 52-53. [-]
    "This disc is an unmitigated disaster. Not only are the performances undeniably substandard, but there are just too many technical flaws in the production. Jerome Lowenthal and Maurice Abravanel provide lackluster, slapdash performances in this collection that first appeared 21 years ago . . ." *See*: **D70**

B985. M. M. "Gershwin. An American in Paris. Porgy and Bess [Bennett Suite] . . . Mercury MMA 11004 . . ." *Gramophone* (1959): 403. [+]
    The reviewer called this disc "a first-class proposition in its field." His one carp was with the trumpet player's playing uneven eighth-notes during the latter part of the solo in the mid-section of AiP. Wisely, the reviewer dug out the "antique Gershwin-conducted [?] 78s" and found that the eighth-notes were played evenly. He also praised the Minneapolis orchestra in its performance of the Robert R. Bennett P&B Symphonic Picture.

B986. MARSH, Robert C. "Gershwin, George . . . *Orchestral Works* . . . Vox QSVBX 5132 . . ." *Records in Review 1976 Edition*, pp. 132-133. [adq]
    The reviewer was critical of Slatkin's performance practice on these discs. ". . . Banish once and for all the idea that a young American conductor of great talent [Slatkin] . . . automatically knows how to play Gershwin. The period is not part of his direct life experience . . . The *Promenade* [included here in an arrangement for full blown symphony orchestra], a most attractive little work, does not seem to be otherwise available [as of the Fall 1989 Schwann, it remains two of only three listings], and any serious Gershwin admirer will want it . . ." *See*: **D416**

B987. MCCOLLEY, Robert. "[Review of] **GERSHWIN: *An American in Paris.* *Concerto In F for Piano and Orchestra. Rhapsody in Blue.*** Mitch Miller conducting the London Symphony Orchestra; David Golub, piano . . . MITCH MILLER MUSIC MMM 14610 [DDD] . . . **GERSHWIN**: *Strike up the Baind*—Medley (arr. Don Rose). *Rhapsody In Blue. Girl Crazy*—Medley (arr. Don Rose). *An American in Paris. I Got Rhythm Variations* (arr. C. Schoenfeld). *Cuban Overture.* Wayne Marshall, piano, conducting the Aalborg Symphony Orchestra. VIRGIN CDM 5 61247 2 [DDD] . . ." *Fanfare* 19/3 (January-February

1996): 203-205. **[+] [*]**

"Both of these collections of Gershwin favorites are full of rewards for the serious listener; they are also strikingly different in performance style. A list of comparative timings [which the reviewer provides] will assist discussion of each; for further comparisons I have listed two outstanding bargains, London's *Gershwin Weekend* (436 570-2), and the Vox Box (CDX 5007) of nine Gershwin favorites featuring Leonard Slatkin conducting the St. Louis Symphony Orchestra . . . The other Wayne Marshall *Rhapsody in Blue,* in Ferde Grofe's original 1924 arrangement . . . appears on Virgin Classics VC 90766-2 (1989) . . . Finally, we have the 1976 Columbia recording (CBS 42516) of the 1924 version featuring George Gershwin's 1925 piano roll . . . The *Gershwin Weekend* performers are Julius Katchen, piano . . . [with] the London Symphony Orchestra . . ." and other performers and orchestras. The review which evaluates the performances is definitely worth reading. *See:* **D117 (M. Miller), D315 (Marshall on Virgin), D348 (Slatkin on Vox Box), D282 (piano roll on Columbia)**

B988. MCKELVEY, [John P]. "Guide to Records . . . GERSHWIN: *Concerto in F; Rhapsody in Blue; American in Paris; I Got Rhythm Variations* Earl Wild, Boston Pops, Arthur Fiedler RCA 6519 . . ." *American Record Guide* 55/2 (Mar./Apr. 1992): 62. **[+]**

This highly lauded recording (in a CD transfer) receives another affirmation here, the reviewer calling it "a recording that defines what Gershwin is all about." *See:* **D8, D164, D222, D368**

B989. NORTH, James H. "Bernstein: Arias and Barcôrolles . . . Barber: School for Scandal Overture . . . Gershwin: An American in Paris . . . Gerard Schwarz conducting the Seattle Symphony . . . Delos DE 3078." *Fanfare* 14/2 (Nov.-Dec. 1990): 176. [adq]

". . . Schwarz's performance is colorful yet warm and relaxed, fitting Gershwin's own verbal description of an American who 'strolls about the city' . . . It is lovely this way, but I miss the swagger . . ." *See:* **D66**

B990. "Recordings Reports I: Orchestral LPs . . . Rhapsody in Blue . . ." *Saturday Review* 49/22 (May 28, 1966): 56. RiB **[+]**; AiP **[adq].**

Brief assessment of the **Stanley Black/London Festival Orchestra** album including the RiB and AiP. ". . . [T]he standard of execution [of AiP] by such conductors as Bernstein and Rodzinski is higher in this work . . ." *See:* **D261**

B991. SALZMAN, Eric. "Milhaud, Darius: A Frenchman in New York; Gershwin: An American in Paris, Boston Pops Orchestra . . . RCA Victor LM 2702.LP. RCA Victor LSC 2702. SD." *Records in Review 1965 Edition.* Great Barrington, MA: Wyeth Press, pp. 76-77. **[+]**

". . . The Gershwin . . . gets a remarkable performance: exciting, almost frenetic in its energy and dash . . ." *See:* **D5**

B992. YOUNGREN, William. "[Review of *American in Paris,* Bernstein conducting (CBS MK 42264)]." *Fanfare* 10/6 (1986-1987): 110. *See:* **D42, D255**

B993. _____. "Gershwin, Part III: An American in Paris." *New Republic* (May 7, 1977): 23-26.

". . . The original 1929 recording by Nathaniel Shilkret and the RCA Victor Symphony Orchestra was the only complete version of a Gershwin work issued during his lifetime and was prepared under his supervision . . . Shilkret brings out the humor of the piece far more than conductors usually do today . . . and the four taxi horns are lower in pitch and more raucous than the ones usually heard in modern performances . . . Even finer is Toscanini's 1945 performance with the NBC Symphony . . . he gives the work a rhythmic vitality and a continuity that Shilkret cannot match and that have . . . remained unmatched ever since." Youngren also commented on the Tilson Thomas/New York Philharmonic (Columbia XM 34205), Edo de Waart/Monte Carlo Opera Orchestra (Philips 6500 290), and Leonard Slatkin/St. Louis Symphony (three record Vox set QSVBX 5132) versions, concluding that the latter was "the best recent recording." *See*: **D39 (Toscanini), D56 (Shilkret)**

W7. *CATFISH ROW SUITE* (1935-36)

B994. A., V. "[Review of *American in Paris, Catfish Row,* St. Louis orch., Slatkin conducting (Moss Music MCD 10035)]." *Fanfare* 10/4 (1986-1987): 135.
    See: Full entry at **B952** under **"AiP".**

B995. BURWASSER, Peter. "Classical Recordings [Reviews] . . . BBC Philharmonic Orchestra: conducted by Yan Pascal Tortelier CHANDOS CHAN 9325 **[DDD]** *Girl Crazy:* **Overture** (orch. Don Rose); *Variations on "I Got Rhythm"; An American in Paris.; Symphonic Suite: Catfish Row* (G's version); *Strike Up the Band:* Overture (orch. Don Rose) . . ." *Fanfare* 18/5 (May/June 1995): 195. *See*: Full entry at **B1322** under **"Overtures."**

B996. D., J. "[Review of *Catfish Row Suite* from *Porgy and Bess,* Weissenberg (Angel DS-38050)]." *Fanfare* 8/3 (1984-1985): 170. *See:* Full entry under **"Rhapsody in Blue."**

B997. JABLONSKI, Edward. "Gershwin's own Suite from 'Porgy and Bess'; An almost completely new work . . . [Nibley/Utah Symphony/Abravanel]" *American Record Guide* 25/12 (Aug. 1959): 848-849.
    "Westminster [XWN-18850] has come along with the most interesting Suite of all: this is Gershwin's *own* . . . Jablonski described the musical content of the suite in considerable detail, concluding: "Once and for all, perhaps, this suite will dissuade anyone from tampering with Gershwin's marvelous orchestrations . . ." Jablonski also discussed R. R. Bennett's and Morton Gould's (the latter on RCA Victor LM 2002, **D251**) suites of materials from P&B. ". . . [T]he Gershwin suite is significant for at least two reasons: first, because of the choice of material incorporated in it; second, for the brilliant orchestration . . ." *See*: **D103**

W2. *CONCERTO IN F* for Piano and Orchestra (1925)

B998. AFFELDER, Paul (A., P.) "[Review of Recordings] GERSHWIN: An American in Paris . . . Rhapsody in Blue . . . Concerto for Piano and Orchestra, in F . . ." *High Fidelity* 8/11 (Nov. 1958): 60.
    Review of five discs. The reviewer's choice was decidedly for the **List/Rochester Philharmonic/Hanson versions** of the Concerto and RiB (Mercury SR 90002) over that of **Nibley/Utah Symphony/Abravanel** (Westminster XWN 18684 & Westminster XWN 18687). *See*: **D72 (Utah), D309 (List/Hanson), D323 (Utah)**

B999. A., P. "GERSHWIN: Concerto for Piano and Orchestra, in F; Rhapsody in Blue . . ." *High Fidelity* 7/11: 68. **[+]**
    Very brief review of the performances by List/Eastman-Rochester Symphony/Hanson (Mercury MG 50138). ". . . [T]his felicitous coupling can take a high place among the

numerous disc versions of these popular works . . ." *See*: **D133**

B1000.   A., P. "Gershwin: Concerto in F; Rhapsody in Blue . . . Previn . . . Kostelanetz
[Columbia CL 1495] . . . Gershwin: Rhapsody in Blue; An American in Paris
. . . Sanromá. . . Pittsburgh . . . Steinberg [Everest SBDR 3067] . . ." *High
Fidelity* 10/11 (Nov. 1960): 84, 86. **[-]**
"Neither of these discs serves Gershwin as well as could have been expected
. . . Mercury's coupling of the Concerto and Rhapsody with Eugene List and the Eastman-
Rochester Symphony under Howard Hanson [SR 90002], is preferable in all respects . . ."
See: **D54, D343 (Sanromá/Pittsburgh), D144 (Previn/Kostelanetz), B1098**

B1001.   _____. "Gershwin: Concerto for Piano and Orchestra, in F [et al] . . ." *High
Fidelity* 12/4 (Apr. 1962): 70. **[+]**
Brief but glowing review of Earl Wild's performance with the Boston Pops on
RCA Victor LM 2586. *See*: **D165**

B1002.   _____. "Gershwin, George . . . Concerto for Piano and Orchestra, in F;
Rhapsody in Blue . . . Mercury SR 90002.SD . . ." *Records in Review* 1959
Edition. Great Barrington, MA: Wyeth Press, p. 77. **[adq]**
". . . Musically, Mercury's List-Hanson disc . . . far outranks the Nibley-Abravanel
efforts. Not only does every note come out with perfect clarity but both the soloist and
conductor infuse everything with a lively spirit, at the same time maintaining a judicious balance
between symphonic and jazz elements . . ." *See*: **D72, D309**

B1003.   _____. "Gershwin, George . . . Concerto for Piano and Orchestra, in F . . .
Westminster XWN 18684.LP . . ." *Records in Review 1959 Edition.* Great
Barrington, MA: Wyeth Press, p. 77. **[adq]**
". . . From the technical standpoint, the performances by Abravanel and the Utah
Symphony are excellent. Interpretatively, however, the playing leaves something to be desired
—mainly a feeling of abandon, strangely missing from everything but the *Rhapsody in Blue* and
the last movement of the Concerto . . . [T]here certainly could be more flash in his [Nibley's]
playing of the Concerto, which is positively sleepy in the second movement . . ."

B1004.   AFFELDER, Paul. "Gershwin, George . . . Concerto for Piano and Orchestra, in
F; Rhapsody in Blue . . . Mercury SR 90002.SD . . ." *Records in Review 1959
Edition.* Great Barrington, MA: Wyeth Press, p. 77. **[adq]**
". . . Musically, Mercury's List-Hanson disc . . . far outranks the Nibley-Abravanel
efforts. Not only does every note come out with perfect clarity but both the soloist and
conductor infuse everything with a lively spirit, at the same time maintaining a judicious balance
between symphonic and jazz elements . . ." *See*: **D133**

B1005.   _____. "Gershwin, George; Concerto for Piano and Orchestra, in F; Variations
on 'I Got Rhythm'; Cuban Overture; Earl Wild, piano; Boston Pops Orchestra
. . . RCA Victor LM 2586 . . ." *Records in Review 1963 Edition*, pp. 178-179.
[+]
". . . [T]he important work here is the Concerto, and it is treated importantly by Wild
and Fiedler. There is commanding style, warm lyricism, and a proper amount of nervous energy
in the pianist's interpretation . . . An old and respected hand at Gershwin, Fiedler provides ideal
orchestral collaboration on the two solo works and gives a rousing account of the overture
. . ." *See*: **D165**

B1006.   **ARDOIN, John.** "Welcome Revival: Gershwin: Piano Concerto in F [et al] . . ."
Musical America 82/2 (Mar. 1962): 25. **[+]**

Highly complimentary review. "What a welcome item, this new disc [RCA Victor LM 2586] by Earl Wild and Arthur Fiedler. Gershwin's marvelous set of Variations on *I Got Rhythm* has been absent from the catalogue . . ." *See:* **D165**

B1007.   **CARNOVALE, Norbert.** "Reviews of Recordings . . . George Gershwin . . .[St. Louis/Slatkin]." *Sonneck Society Bulletin* 14/3 (Fall 1988): 158. **[adq]**
See: Full entry at **B955** under **"AiP"** listing.

B1008.   "Comment in Brief." *NYTimes*, Sept. 4, 1955, p. 12 X. **[+]**

Very brief, but positive review of Alec Templeton's performance with the Cincinnati SO conducted by Thor Johnson (Remington R 199-184). *See:* **D160**

B1009.   **DARRELL, R. D.** Gershwin, George . . . *Concerto for Piano and Orchestra, in F; Rhapsody in Blue* . . . Columbia ML 6413 or MS 7013 [Entremont, piano; Philadelphia Orch.; Ormandy]." *Records in Review 1968 Edition.* Great Barrington, MA: Wyeth Press, pp. 146. **[-]**

". . . [T]he readings . . . are grimly serious, often ponderous or hurried, and self-conscious to an extreme when they attempt to be 'jazzy' . . ." *See:* **D270**

B1010.   _____. "Gershwin, George . . .[Werner Hass/Edo de Waart]: *Concerto for Piano and Orchestra, in F; Rhapsody in Blue; Variations on 'I Got Rhythm'* . . . Philips 6500 118 . . . [Previn]: *Concerto for Piano and Orchestra, in F; Rhapsody in Blue; An American in Paris* . . . Angel S 36810." *Records in Review 1973 Edition.* Great Barrington, MA: Wyeth Press, pp. 131-132.

Darrell gave a negative rating to the performance referred to above (Philips 6500 118). While he generally praised the Previn Angel disk, he concluded: ". . . But for myself, I'll stick with the Wild/Fiedler versions for RCA . . ." *See:* **D209, D293 (de Waart/Philips), D336 (Previn)**

B1011.   _____. "Gershwin, George, *Concerto for Piano and Orchestra, in F* . . . [Pyotr Pechersky & Alexander Tsvassman, pianos; with Soviet orchestras] Westminster Gold/Melodiya WG 8355." *Records in Review 1980 Edition.* Great Barrington, MA: Wyeth Press, pp. 142-143. **[adq]**

Calling this performance a "non-foreign-accented reading," Darrell commented ". . . there's no real competition here for fully satisfactory American recordings . . . (I still stick with the 1960 Wild/Fiedler versions for RCA) . . ." *See:* **D141, D327**

B1012.   **DITSKY, John.** "Classical Recordings: GERSHWIN: Concerto in F trans. Castagnetta). Three Preludes. Rhapsody in Blue (trans. Gershwin) . . . Stradivari Classics SCD-8000 (compact disc) . . . Norman Krieger, piano . . ." *Fanfare* 12/1 (Sept.-Oct. 1988): 155-156. **[+]**

Informative review of the above-named CD. "The solo piano version of Gershwin's piano concerto was prepared in 1945-46 by the pianist Grace Castagnetta—on a commission, following her broadcast of her improvised transcription of a single movement. A bit startling at first, the solo piano version is not a mere *reduction*, and there is no apparent formula by which certain orchestral colorations are assigned this or that piano value—or omitted. Lacking previous acquaintance with this transcription, I can only base my judgment that Norman Krieger [the piano soloist] is truly adept at the Gershwin idiom on the . . . Preludes, and also on the composer's own solo-piano version of the *Rhapsody in Blue* . . . this is a first-class release . . . I recommend this disc to all lovers of Gershwin . . ." *See:* **D170, D593, D626**

B1013.   ELBIN, Paul N. "New Records . . . Gershwin: Concerto in F for Piano and
　　　　　　Orchestra." *Etude* 73/11 (Nov. 1955): 47. **[+]**
　　　　"'Bang-up' is not too strong a term for describing the performance given this
Gershwin classic by Alec Templeton and the Cincinnati Orchestra . . . (Remington R 199-
184)." *See:* **D160**

B1014.   GERBER, Leslie. "Classical Recordings: GERSHWIN: Concerto in F . . .
　　　　　　RAVEL: Concerto in G . . . Andrew Litton, piano . . . Bournemouth Symph.
　　　　　　Virgin Classics SICS VC 90780-2 . . ." *Fanfare* 14/5 (May-June 1991): 174.
　　　　　　[adq]
　　　　"This is an apt coupling of two jazz-influenced concertos, marred by the obvious
stunt of conducting from the keyboard . . ." *See:* **D134**

B1015. "Gershwin, of Sorts, GERSHWIN: Concerto in F . . . Rhapsody in Blue . . . An
　　　　　　American in Paris . . ." *Saturday Review* 41/17 (Apr. 26, 1958): 45. **[-] [*]**
　　　　Review of two albums, Nibley/Utah Symphony/Abravanel's readings of *Concerto*
(Westminster XWN 18684) and RiB and AiP (Westminster XWN 18687). ". . . The beginning
of conductor Abravanel's trouble . . . is that he has no real sense of the jazz idiom, or what
Gershwin borrowed from it. Consequently tempi are distorted, outlines blurred and the
melodies shamefully sentimentalized . . ." *See:* **D73, D323**

B1016.   GRUENINGER, Walter F. "Phonograph Records . . . Gershwin: *Concerto
　　　　　　in F* and *Cuban Overture* and *"I Got Rhythm" Variations* . . . RCA Victor LSC
　　　　　　2586 . . ." *Consumer Bulletin* 45/6 (June 1962): 34. **[+]**
　　　　Very brief but effusive review of the recording by Wild/Boston Pops/Fiedler. *See:* **D165**

B1017.   HAGGIN, B. H. "Records." *Nation* 181/15 (Oct. 15, 1955): 330-331. **[+]**
　　　　Brief review of London LL-1262, Katchen/Mantovani's readings of Concerto and
RiB. *See:* **D34, D122, D300**

B1018.   HAVERSTOCK, Gwendolyn. "Classical Recordings: GERSHWIN: Concerto
　　　　　　in F for Piano and Orchestra . . . Alexander Cattarino, piano . . . OPUS LC 5969
　　　　　　. . ." *Fanfare* 12/2 (Nov.-Dec. 1988): 187. **[-, but worth reading]**
　　　　Review of this compact disc. ". . . Glasnost made one more believer last month,
when I found that the Gershwin craze has gone global. Not only has Gershwin's music become
widely available to citizens behind the iron curtain; now they are recording it and sending it
back to us . . . I recommend this, not for its musical merit (dubious indeed!), but for the
amusing statement it makes about east and west in this day and age." *See:* **D110**

B1019.   HERMAN, Justin R. "Lend an Ear . . . From One Serious Collector to Another."
　　　　　　Fanfare 12/1 (September/October 1988): 388. **[+]**
　　　　Complimentary review by an expert of the RPO Records MCAD-6229 release of
the **AiP** and **Concerto (Vakarelis and Royal Philharmonic)**. ". . . These standards are not
just razzle-dazzle, but have a high emotional content, and these readings, with their startlingly
different orchestral balances, give full reign to the nostalgic elements contained therein . . . If
you like Gershwin, and even if you have multiple versions of these works, this is a must . . ."
See: **D60, D162**

B1020. _____. "Guide to Records . . . Gershwin: Cuban . . . Concerto . . . Rhapsody in Blue . . . Zizzo . . . Charry . . . Pro Arte 514 . . ." *American Record Guide* 55/1 (Jan.-Feb. 1992): 55. **[*] [-]**

Herman detested this recording. "This is a recording that drives a critic to use every bit of invective at his disposal." See: **D167, D186, D374, D679**

B1021.   INDCOX, J. F. "Rhapsody in Blue; Concerto for Piano and Orchestra, in F Julius Katchen, piano; orchestra, Mantovani cond. London LL 1262 **[-]**. . . Rhapsody in Blue; Concerto for Piano and Orchestra, in F, An American in Paris; Suite from Porgy and Bess (arr. Morton Gould); Preludes for Piano; Piano Solo from Porgy and Bess, Morton Gould, piano; orchestra, Morton Gould, cond. RCA Victor LM 6033." *High Fidelity Record Annual*, ed. by Roland Gelatt (1956): 103. **[+]**

The reviewer thought the Mantovani performances atrocious. Comparing the performances to the Gould set, he stated: ". . . These are considerably more valid realizations, even though they expose the pianistic limitations of Gould as a Gershwin exponent . . ." *See:* **D34, D122, D300 (Mantovani); D24, D119, D251, D292, D623 (Gould)**

B1022.   ISACOFF, Stuart. "GERSHWIN . . . Alicia Zizzo/Charry/George Gershwin Festival Orch. . . Pro Arte CDD 514 . . . [&] . . . Earl Wild . . . Chesky CD 32 . . ." *Musical America* 111/3 (May 1991): 75. **[+] [*]**

A complimentary review of Zizzo's performances as well as the versions of the Concerto and RiB, which are "taken from manuscripts in the Library of Congress." Isacoff also highly praised Earl Wild's "pianistic prowess." *See:* **D167, D186, D374, D679 (Zizzo), D609 (Wild)**

B1023.   JABLONSKI, Edward. "Record Reviews: "Gershwin: *Concerto in F; Rhapsody in Blue;* Mercury MG-50138 . . ." *American Record Guide* 24/4 (Dec. 1957): 145. **[+]**

The reviewer liked **Eugene List** and **Howard Hansen's** interpretation and, at the time, considered this recording second only to "the superb Gould version." *See:* **D133**

B1024.   _____. ". . . *Concerto in F; [et al].*. . . Utah Symphony; Maurice Abravanel, conducting Westminster XWN-18684/7 . . ." *American Record Guide* 24/10 (June 1958): 427. **[+]**

". . . The Concerto, particularly, comes off very well . . . because of the piano interpretation of Reid Nibley . . ." See: **D323**

B1025.   JOHNSON, Carl. "Paul Whiteman's Recording of 'Concerto in F': A Double 'Who Done It?'" *Journal of Jazz Studies* 5/1 (1978): 91-97.

In re: Whiteman's September-October, 1928, recording of the *Concerto*, as specially arranged by Ferde Grofé for the Whiteman instrumentation, this is an article addressing two principal questions: "1. Which of the four men in the trumpet section [which included Bix Beiderbecke] played which of the four solos that are compelling features of the second movement?" and "2. Did Whiteman conduct his orchestra for this recording, or did he employ a stand-in [William Daly]?" No positive conclusions are drawn on either question, according to this interesting article. See: **D106, B223**

B1026.   KOLDYS, [Mark]. "Guide to Records . . . GERSHWIN: *Concerto in F; Rhapsody in Blue;* [and music by Enesco & Prokofieff] . . . Raymond Lewenthal, Oskar Danon . . . Chesky 56 . . ." *American Record Guide* 55/2 (Mar./Apr. 1992): 62. **[-]**

A negative review of the G works on this recording. *See:* **D307**

B1027. _____. "Guide to Records . . . GERSHWIN: *Piano Concerto in F; 3 Preludes*
. . . Peter Jablonski . . . Royal Philharmonic . . . London 430542
. . ." *American Record Guide* 55/2 (Mar./Apr. 1992): 61. **[adq]**
Although the reviewer considers this performance "one of the better Gershwin
Concertos around," he still considers "Earl Wild's affair on RCA definitive . . . Jablonski does
a fine job of the first two *Preludes* . . . but 3 is not extrovert enough . . ." *See:* **D743**

B1028. **KOLODIN, Irving.** "*Recordings* Reports I: Orchestral LPs . . . Gershwin
Rhapsody in Blue,' Concerto in F . . ." *Saturday Review* 38/39 (Sept. 24, 1955):
48. **[-]**
Review of Katchen/Montovani (London LL-1262). *See:* Full entry under
"Rhapsody in Blue."

B1029. _____. "*Recordings* Reports I: Orchestral LPs . . . Gershwin: Concerto in F
. . ." *Saturday Review* 38/44 (Oct. 29, 1955): 52. **[-]**
Review of **Templeton/Cincinnati Symphony/Johnson (Remington R 199-184)**.
The melodic essence of this work is well savored by Templeton . . . but the jazzy turns in it are
given a rather period 'quaintness' by the soloist's phrasing . . ." *See:* **D160**

B1030. _____. "*Recordings* Reports I: Orchestral LPs . . . Gershwin: Concerto in F.
'American in Paris,' 'Rhapsody in Blue,' 'Porgy' suite, etc. . . ."
Saturday Review 38/44 (Oct. 29, 1955): 52. **[adq]**
Review of **Morton Gould playing and conducting (RCA Victor LM-6033)**. "Gould
knows the idiom thoroughly with results that are persuasive in the orchestral works. However,
I am not convinced he is the best pianist RCA could have found for the solo parts on the
Concerto and Rhapsody . . ." *See:* **D251**

B1031. **L., J.** "[Record Reviews] Gershwin: Concerto in F . . ." *Musical America* 73/12
(Nov. 1953): 18.
For years Oscar Levant has had an LP monopoly on this apparently indestructible
work. Mr. **[Leonard] Pennario [Pittsburgh/Capitol LP P 8219]** is not heir to the same
traditions that his predecessor shared with the composer, but this recording inevitably supplants
the earlier one on all counts except authenticity meaning that Levant presumably knew how
Gershwin wanted it to go despite the implicit impossibility of capturing the jazz idiom in score
indications . . ."

B1032. **LINKOWSKI, Allen.** "Gershwin . . . Jerome Lowenthal; Utah Symphony . . .
[AiP & Concerto] . . . Vanguard 10017 . . ." *American Record Guide* 52/1 (Jan.-
Feb. 1989): 52-53. **[-]** *See* full entry at under **AiP**.

B1033. _____. "Guide to Records . . . GERSHWIN: *Concerto in F; Rhapsody in
Blue; Song-book* Peter Donohue . . . Simon Rattle—Angel/EMI 54280 [avail. in
CD, same no.] . . ." *American Record Guide* 55/2 (Mar./Apr. 1992): 61-62. **[+]**
Overall, Linkowski considers this "a wonderful record, highly recommended." *See:*
Full entry under **"Rhapsody in Blue."**

B1034. **MANILDI, Donald.** "[Review of] GERSHWIN: *Concerto in F* . . . Earl Wild,
piano . . . Chesky 98 . . ." *American Record Guide* 58/1 (Jan./Feb. 1995): 101.
Complimentary review. ". . . Wild's new account of the Gershwin will not totally

supplant his justly-famous earlier recording with Fiedler (RCA), but the soloist's high-spirited, high-powered pianism is combined with some discreet touching-up of the orchestral part to lend a remarkable freshness to the proceedings . . ." This recording includes 20 variations on Stephen Foster's *Camptown Races* (subtitled 'Doo-Dah Variations') covering the gamut from a barn dance to a blues to a revivalist march to a final Hollywood-cum-Rachmaninoff ending *See:* **D166**

B1035.   MCCOLLEY, Robert. "[Review of] **GERSHWIN:** *An American in Paris. Concerto In F for Piano and Orchestra. Rhapsody in Blue.* Mitch Miller conducting the London Symphony Orchestra; David Golub, piano . . . MITCH MILLER MUSIC MMM 14610 [DDD] . . . **GERSHWIN**: *Strike up the Band*—**Medley** (arr. Don Rose). *Rhapsody In Blue. Girl Crazy*—**Medley** (arr. Don Rose). *An American in Paris. I Got Rhythm Variations* (arr. C. Schoenfeld). *Cuban Overture.* Wayne Marshall, piano, conducting the Aalborg Symphony Orchestra. VIRGIN CDM 5 61247 2 [DDD] . . ." *Fanfare* 19/3 (January-February 1996): 203-205. [+] [*]
See: Full entry under **"AiP."**

B1036.   MCKELVEY, [John P]. "Guide to Records . . . GERSHWIN: *Concerto in F; Rhapsody in Blue; American in Paris; I Got Rhythm Variations* Earl Wild, Boston Pops, Arthur Fiedler RCA 6519 . . ." *American Record Guide* 55/2 (Mar./Apr. 1992): 62. [+]
See: **D8, D165, D222, D368**

B1037.   MILLER, Philip L. "Recorded Music: GERSHWIN: Concerto in F; Rhapsody in Blue . . ." *Library Journal* 83/3 (Feb. 1, 1958): 394. [+]
"Here are two extremely fine performances [by **Eugene List/Eastman-Rochester/Hanson on Mercury MG-50138]** . . . The rhapsody is by far the best currently available . . ." *See:* **D309**

B1038.   MONSON, Karen. "Ovation Record Review: Gershwin (arr. Grofé): Piano Concerto in F. Gershwin: Three Preludes; "Fascinatin' Rhythm; "The Man I Love"; "Somebody Loves Me." Russell Sherman, piano; Orchestra of St. Luke's, Gunther Schuller, cond. . . ." *Ovation* 8/9 (Oct 1987): 40-41.
Positive review of the Pro Arte PCD 244 recording. "The first recording in nearly sixty years of Ferde Grofé's early arrangement for Paul Whiteman's band of George Gershwin's Concerto in F gives a whole new face to the music. Gone—for the most part—are the symphonic pretensions . . ." *See:* **D151, D765**

B1039.   NORTH, James H. "Classical Recordings . . . GERSHWIN: Concerto in F. Three Preludes . . . Peter Jablonski, piano; Vladimir Ashkenazy conducting the Royal Philharmonic Orchestra. LONDON 430 542 . . ." *Fanfare* 15/4 (Mar./Apr. 1992): 192-193.
A negative opinion about the performance of the concerto, ". . . which is pure classical piano concerto, with all the jazz and blues filtered out . . . [The] three preludes are played with competence but no special insight . . ." *See:* **D743**

B1040.   RABINOWITZ, Peter J. "Classical Recordings: Gershwin: Blue Monday (arr. Bassman) . . . Leslie Stifelman, piano on Concerto, Marin Alsop, conducting . . . Angel CDC 7 54851 2 7 . . . Wild: Variations on An American Theme . . . Gershwin: Concerto . . . [with the] Des Moines Symphony Orchestra [on]

Chesky CD 98 . . ." *Fanfare* 17/1 (Sept.-Oct. 1993): 168-170. **[+] [*]**
A substantial review of the two above-named recordings. His comments about the Grofé arrangement of the Concerto (as used on the Angel record) are revealing: "The Grofé edition [arranged in 1928 for the Paul Whiteman band] is not an abridgement . . . It is, rather, a comprehensive (if not always comprehending) reorchestration, one that goes in spots beyond mere substitution of colors to a reconceptualization of the ways in which they relate to one another. Thus, gestures that are identically orchestrated in Gershwin's score are sometimes decked out with sharply contrasting timbres here, often creating the auditory illusion that the music itself has been changed. [Incidentally, One might wish to compare this recording to the version of the same arrangement as done by the Whiteman band, on Preamble PRCD 1785, **D106**]. Despite the somewhat negative comments above, Rabinowitz concluded "It's one of the few recordings [of the Concerto] in the catalog that can stand up to the classic Wild/Fiedler. Another challenge to the venerable Wild comes from Wild himself [in the Des Moines Symphony version, apparently using G's own original scoring]—who has revisited the concerto after thirty-odd years with surprisingly youthful results . . ." See: **D156 & D425** *(Blue Monday & Concerto)*, **D106 (Concerto arr. Grofé), D166, (Concerto, Wild)**

B1041. "Records in Brief." *Musical America* 75/14 (Nov. 5, 1955): 29.
". . . Of three new [in 1955] versions of Gershwin's Concerto in F, **Julius Katchen's** is the most imaginative **(London LL 1262)** . . . **Alec Templeton's** is the most comprehensive of the Gershwin idiom **(Remington R 199-184)** . . . **Sondra Bianca's (MGM 3237)** is the most intimate in the quasi-improvisations . . ." *See:* **D34 & D300 (Katchen), D160 (Templeton)**

B1042. **STEARNS, David Patrick.** "News & Views."*Gramophone* 66/769 (June 1987). Survey and brief reviews of recordings which came out during the commemorative year, 1987. Included are **CBS Masterworks S2M 42522: OTIS/Cake; Angel/EMI CDC 7 47454 2: "Kiri Sings Gershwin"; Reference RR-19: "Marni Nixon Sings Gershwin"; Musicmasters 40113 & 40114 (cassettes): "The Birth of the Rhapsody in Blue"; Pro Arte CDD 244: Russell Sherman/Orchestra of St. Luke's/Gunther Schuller**, about which he commented: ". . . Sherman makes the record worth buying. He isn't so tough and rhythmically eloquent as Oscar Levant . . . but this interpretation is an intelligent, expressive and unapologetic response to the piece [Concerto] by a musician who seems to come to Gershwin through Mozart . . ." *See:* **D463 (OTIS/Cake), D940 (Kiri), D908 (Marni Nixon), D266 (The Birth), D151, D765 (Pro Arte, w/ Sherman/Schuller)**

B1043. **WEIDNER, Dick,** ed. "Vivace." *ITG Journal* 13/3 (Feb. 1989): 33.
In response to a query, Bernard Adelstein, formerly principal trumpet with the Cleveland, OH orchestra, discussed performance practice on the second movement trumpet solo. ". . . I remember hearing a recording . . . with Oscar Levant as soloist. The beautiful trumpet solo in the second movement was played by Harry Glantz . . . Since then, it has been one of my favorites—the type solo in which a fine trumpeter can throw off the shackles that bind him, and play with a freedom and abandon seldom expressed . . . The solo should be played with some sort of felt hat (preferably with many holes in it) over the bell . . ." *See:* **D367**

B1044. **YOUNGREN, William.** "Gershwin, Part II, Concerto in F." *New Republic* (Apr. 30, 1977): 27-30.
A discussion of the concerto. The writer was especially pleased with a version of the second movement he heard played by Bix Beiderbecke (the opening of the second movement)

on a recording with Paul Whiteman from 1928 (this particular recording on the Joker label). He also noted differences in the orchestration from that heard in the usual orchestral version. Grofé did in fact orchestrate the concerto for Whiteman's jazz band, but according to this article, G was ". . . displeased by Grofés orchestration and by the fact that Whiteman's recording of it was the only available recording of the *Concerto*; incredibly, it seems never to have occurred to anyone to have Gershwin himself record it, and the original orchestration remained unrecorded until several years after his death . . ." *See*: **D104 (Whiteman recording)**, **D151 (Sherman/Schuller)**

W5. *CUBAN OVERTURE* (1932)

B1045.   **A., P.** "[Recordings Reviews] GERSHWIN: Cuban Overture; McBride: Mexican Rhapsody; Gould: Latin-American Symphonette . . ." *High Fidelity* 8/9 (Sept. 1958): 64. **[+]**

In a positive review of **Eastman-Rochester/Hanson's Mercury MG** 50166, the writer concluded: ". . . Like its companions on this bright sounding disc, the oft-neglected Gershwin piece emerges with appropriate dash and sparkle." *See*: **D183**

B1046.   _____."Gershwin, George; Concerto for Piano and Orchestra, in F; Variations on 'I Got Rhythm'; Cuban Overture; Earl Wild, piano; Boston Pops Orchestra . . . RCA Victor LM 2586 . . ." *Records in Review 1963 Edition*, pp. 178-179. **[+]**
See: Full entry at **B1005** under **"Concerto"**

B1047.   **DARRELL, R. D.** "Gershwin, George . . . Second Rhapsody; Variations on 'I Got Rhythm'; Cuban Overture (arr. McRitchie); Porgy and Bess: Medley (arr. McRitchie); Leonard Pennario, piano; Hollywood Bowl Symphony Orchestra . . . Capitol P 8581 . . ." *Records in Review 1963 Edition*, p. 179. **[+]**
See: Full entry under **"Second Rhapsody"** at **B1125.**

B1048.   "GERSHWIN 'Cuban Overture', 'Porgy and Bess Suite' et al . . . Deutsch-Grammophone-431-625-2 (Levine, James, Chicago-Symphony Orchestra)." *American Heritage*. 45/6 (Oct. 1994): 104.
Review of the record. *See*: **D176**

B1049.   **HERMAN, Justin R.** "Guide to Records . . . Gershwin: Cuban . . . Concerto . . . Rhapsody in Blue . . . Zizzo . . . Charry . . . Pro Arte 514 . . ." *American Record Guide* 55/1 (Jan.-Feb. 1992): 55. **[*] [-]**
Herman detested this recording. *See*: **D167, D186, D374, D679**

B1050.   **JABLONSKI, Edward.** "Record Reviews: GERSHWIN: Cuban Overture . . . Eastman-Rochester Symphony Orchestra . . . Hanson . . . Mercury MG-50166." *American Record Guide* 24/8 (Apr. 1958): 344. **[+]**
"Those Gershwinites who have been waiting for *the* recording of *Cuban Overture* . . . now have it. One fault or another afflicted the previous versions **[Kostelanetz: Columbia CL-783, Walther: MGM E-3307 (D612), and Whiteman: Coral 57021 (D220)]** . . . The piece was written because Gershwin was interested in utilizing the Cuban percussion instruments he had brought back with him from a vacation in Havana . . . On the autograph score . . . the composer literally sketched the Cuban instruments and specifies placement of them [in front of the orchestra, near the conductor's podium]. the full effect of the work is dependent upon that placement . . ." *See*: **D183 (Eastman/Hanson)**

B1051. "Recordings Reports I: Orchestral LPs, GERSHWIN: 'Second Rhapsody,' 'Cuban Overture,' 'Variations on I Got Rhythm,' and three Preludes [Bianca, piano, Pro Musica Symphony of Hamburg/Walther. MGM 3E-1]." *Saturday Review* 39/13 (Mar. 31, 1956): 50. **[-]**
Negative review. *See*: **D207**

W5. *"I GOT RHYTHM" VARIATIONS* (1934)

B1052. A., V. "[Review of *American in Paris, 'I Got Rhythm' Variations, J.* Siegel, piano, Slatkin conducting (Moss Music MCD 10035)]." *Fanfare* 10/4 (1986-1987): 135.
See: Full entry under **"AiP."**

B1053. **AFFELDER, Paul.** "George; Concerto for Piano and Orchestra, in F; Variations on 'I Got Rhythm'; Cuban Overture; Earl Wild, piano; Boston Pops Orchestra . . . RCA Victor LM 2586 . . ." *Records in Review 1963 Edition*, pp. 178-179. **[+]**
See: Full entry at **B1005** under **"Concerto."**

B1054. **ARDOIN, John.** "Welcome Revival: Gershwin: Piano Concerto in F; I Got Rhythm Variations [et al] [RCA Victor LM 2586 by Earl Wild/Fiedler] . . ." *Musical America* 82/2 (Mar. 1962): 25. **[+]** *See*: Full entry under **"Concerto."**

B1055. **BOOKSPAN, Martin.** "Basic Repertoire: Gershwin's Rhapsody in Blue." *Stereo Review* 37/1 (July 1976): 54.
Article reviewing the genesis of RiB, not I Got Rhythm Var.. *See*: Full entry at
B1071.

B1056. **BURWASSER, Peter.** "Classical Recordings [Reviews] . . . BBC Philharmonic Orchestra: conducted by Yan Pascal Tortelier CHANDOS CHAN 9325 **[DDD]** *Girl Crazy:* **Overture** (orch. Don Rose); *Variations on "I Got Rhythm"; An American in Paris; Symphonic Suite: Catfish Row* (G's version); *Strike Up the Band:* Overture (orch. Don Rose) . . ." *Fanfare* 18/5 (May/June 1995): 195.
See: Full entry at **B1322** under **"Overtures."**

B1057. **CARNOVALE, Norbert.** "Reviews of Recordings . . . George Gershwin . . .[St. Louis/Slatkin]." *Sonneck Society Bulletin* 14/3 (Fall 1988): 158. **[adq]**
See: Full entry at **B955** under **"AiP"** listing.

B1058. **DARRELL, R. D.** "Gershwin, George . . . Second Rhapsody; Variations on 'I Got Rhythm'; Cuban Overture (arr. McRitchie); Porgy and Bess: Medley (arr. McRitchie); Leonard Pennario, piano; Hollywood Bowl Symphony Orchestra . . . Capitol P 8581 . . ." *Records in Review 1963 Edition*, p. 179. **[+]**
See: **D187.** Full entry under **"Second Rhapsody,"** **B1125**.

B1059. _____. "Gershwin, George . . . *Concerto for Piano and Orchestra, in F; Rhapsody in Blue; Variations on 'I Got Rhythm'* . . . Philips 6500 118 . . . *Concerto for Piano and Orchestra, in F; Rhapsody in Blue; An American in Paris* . . . Angel S 36810." *Records in Review 1973 Edition*. Great Barrington, MA: Wyeth Press, pp. 131-132. *See*: Full entry under **"Concerto."**

B1060. **DARRELL, R. D.** "Rhapsody in Blue; An American in Paris; Cuban Overture;
Ivan Davis, piano . . . Cleveland Orchestra . . . London CS 6946 . . ." *Records
in Review 1977 Edition*, p. 131. **[-]**
Negative review of the record. *See:* **D15**

B1061. **DITSKY, John.** "[Review of 'I Got Rhythm' Variations, Donohoe (Angel DS-
38050)]." *Fanfare* 8/3 (1984-1985): 170. *See:* Full entry under **"RiB."**

B1062. **KOLDYS, Mark.** "Gershwin . . . Lincoln Mayorga; Moscow Philharmonic . . .
Sheffield Lab CD-28 . . ." *American Record Guide* 52/2 (Mar.-Apr. 1989): 36.
[-] *See:* Full entry under **"RiB."**

B1063. **MCKELVEY, [John P].** "Guide to Records . . . GERSHWIN: *Concerto in F;
Rhapsody in Blue; American in Paris; I Got Rhythm Variations* Earl Wild,
Boston Pops, Arthur Fiedler RCA 6519 . . ." *American Record Guide* 55/2
(Mar./Apr. 1992): 62. **[+]**
This highly lauded recording (in a CD transfer) receives another affirmation here, the
reviewer calling it "a recording that defines what Gershwin is all about." *See:* **D8, D164, D222,
D368**

W1. *RHAPSODY IN BLUE* (1924)

B1064. **A., P.** "Gershwin: An American in Paris; Rhapsody in Blue . . . 6/11 (Nov. 1959):
88. **[adq]**
Review of Forum F 70008 with Joyce Hatto/Hamburg Pro Musica/George Byrd.
See: Full entry under **"AiP."**

B1065. _____. "GERSHWIN: Concerto for Piano and Orchestra, in F; Rhapsody in
Blue . . .[List/Eastman-Rochester Symphony/Hanson (Mercury MG 50138)]."
High Fidelity 7/11 (Nov.1957): 68. **[+]**
See: Full entry under **"Concerto."**

B1066. **A., P.** "[Review of Recordings] GERSHWIN: An American in Paris . . . Rhapsody
in Blue . . . Concerto for Piano and Orchestra, in F . . ." *High Fidelity* 8/11 (Nov.
1958): 60.
See: Full entry under **"Concerto."**

B1067. _____. "GERSHWIN: An American in Paris; Rhapsody in Blue. . ." *High
Fidelity* 9/3 (March 1959): 60. **[adq]**
Mixed review of Shefter/Warner Brothers Symphony/Heindorf (Warner Bros.
B 1243-BS 1243) recording. The reviewer did like pianist Shefter's interpretation of the
rhapsody. *See:* **D75, D345**

B1068. _____. "Gershwin, George . . . An American in Paris; Rhapsody in Blue;
Bert Shefter, piano . . . Warner Bros. Symphony Orchestra, Ray Heindorf, cond.
Warner Bros. B 1243. LP . . . BS 1243. SD." *Records in Review 1959 Edition*.
Great Barrington, MA: Wyeth Press, p. 77-78. **[adq]**
". . . Heindorf . . . plays everything quite loudly, with very few subtle nuances for
relief. He does have a lively conception of the music, as does Shefter, who gives a fine account

of the piano solo in the *Rhapsody in Blue* . . ." *See:* **D75, D345**

B1069.   **BAUMAN, [Carl].** "Videos; The Great Video Roundup . . . Vol. 4: GERSHWIN:
Piano Concerto . . . RCA 60852; Vol 5: GERSHWIN: Rhapsody in Blue
. . . RCA 60853" *American Record Guide* 56/2 Mar.-Apr. 1993): 209-210.**[+]**
A positive review of these two laser discs.

B1070.   **BENSON, Robert E.** "Gershwin: Rhapsody in Blue; American in Paris. (George
Gershwin, Michael Tilson Thomas, Columbia Jazz Band, Buffalo
Philharmonic]_[record reviews]." *High Fidelity* 38 (Jan. 1988): 55.

B1071.   **BOOKSPAN, Martin.** "Basic Repertoire: Gershwin's Rhapsody in Blue."
Stereo Review 37/1 (July 1976): 54.
Article reviewing the genesis of RiB, along with the writer's stated preference of
recordings: **Eugene List/Samuel Adler/Berlin Symphony** (the jazz band version on
Turnabout TVS 34457), **Bernstein/New York Philharmonic (Columbia M 31804)**, and
Earl Wild/Fiedler/Boston Pops (RCA LSC 2367). *See:* **D312 (List/Adler), D40
(Bernstein), D4 (Wild/Fiedler)**

B1072.   **C., G.** "[Review of *Rhapsody in Blue*, Tilson Thomas/Columbia Jazz Band (CBS
42240)]." *Fanfare* 10/6 (1986-1987): 110. *See:* **D1090**

B1073.   **CARNOVALE, Norbert.** "Reviews of Recordings . . . George Gershwin . . .
[St. Louis/Slatkin]." *Sonneck Society Bulletin* 14/3 (Fall 1988): 158. **[adq]**
See: Full entry in **"AiP"** listing.

B1074.   "Composers and Lyricists Corner." *Show Music* 4/3 (Oct. 1986): 30-31. **[+]**
Review of **CBS Masterworks CBS IM 39699, "George Gershwin." Michael
Tilson Thomas**, who both performs and conducts.
See: Full entry in **"Second Rhapsody"** listing.

B1075.   **DARRELL, R. D.** "Gershwin, George . . . *Concerto for Piano and Orchestra,
in F; Rhapsody in Blue* . . . Columbia ML 6413 or MS 7013
[Entremont/Philadephia/Ormandy]." *Records in Review 1968 Edition*. Great
Barrington, MA: Wyeth Press, pp. 146. **[-]**
". . . [T]he readings . . . are grimly serious, often ponderous or hurried, and self-
conscious to an extreme when they attempt to be 'jazzy' . . ." *See:* **D112**

B1076.   _____. "Gershwin, George . . . *Concerto for Piano and Orchestra, in F;
Rhapsody in Blue; Variations on 'I Got Rhythm'* . . . Philips 6500 118 . . .
*Concerto for Piano and Orchestra, in F; Rhapsody in Blue; An American in
Paris* . . . Angel S 36810 [Previn, pa./London SO/Previn]." *Records in Review
1973 Edition*. Great Barrington, MA: Wyeth Press, pp. 131-132. *See* full entry
at **B1011** under **"Anthologies."**

B1077.   _____. "Rhapsody in Blue; An American in Paris; Cuban Overture; Ivan
Davis, piano . . . Cleveland Orchestra . . . London CS 6946 . . ." *Records in
Review 1977 Edition*, p. 131. **[-]**
Negative review of the record. *See:* **D178**

B1078.   **DARRELL, R. D.** "Gershwin, George . . . *Rhapsody in Blue* . . . [Pyotr

Pechersky & Alexander Tsvassman, pianos; Moscow Philharmonic Orchestra, Kiril Kondrashin, conducting] Westminster Gold/Melodiya WG 8355 [Russian pianists and orchestras]." *Records in Review 1980 Edition*, pp. 142-143. **[adq]**

". . . The appeal of this *Rhapsody in Blue* is mostly its enthusiasm . . . Both soloist **Alexander Tsvassman** and the orchestra are heavy-handed . . . But there's fine swaggering bravura here, and, miraculously, the fast andante moderato tune isn't as sentimentalized or inflated as it often is by American interpreters . . ." *See*: **D141, D327**

B1079. _____."Tapes . . . Rhapsody in Blue; Song Transcriptions: Someone to Watch Over Me, Liza, Love Walked In, Bidin' My Time, Maybe, I Got Rhythm, Roger Williams, piano; Symphony of the Air; Willis Page, cond. (in the Rhapsody); Orchestra, Marty Gold, cond. (in the Song Transcriptions) . . . Kapp KST 41008 . . ." *Records in Review 1960 Edition*. Great Barrington, MA: Wyeth Press, p. 424-425. **[+]** *See*: Full entry under **"Anthologies."**

B1080. **DITSKY, John**. "Gershwin: Rhapsody in Blue . . . [Catfish Row, I Got Rhythm Variations, etc.] . . . Weissenburg . . . Angel DS-38050 . . ." *Fanfare* 8/3 (1984-1985): 170. **[adq]**

". . . [T]his new Angel reading will probably never be a favorite of mine, but I am managing to get used to it fairly quickly. It brings bright digital sound to bear on what might otherwise have seemed a fairly stodgy traversal of the *Rhapsody* score . . . I have to conclude that **Ozawa's Berliners** . . . do take a big-band approach here that to some degree institutionalizes, if not quite mummifies, Gershwin's intrusion of jazz values into the concert hall. The elephant can be made to dance . . . but it remains an elephant dancing . . . Yet I would buy this disc if only for the *Catfish Row* suite made by Gershwin himself . . ." *See*: **D93, D361**

B1081. **DITSKY, John**. "[Review of *Rhapsody in Blue, Preludes*, etc. Tilson Thomas, piano and conductor; Los Angeles Philharmonic (CBS IM 39699 2)]." *Fanfare* 9/1 (1985-1986): 163. *See*: **D357, D417, D690, D773**

B1082. _____. "[Review of *Rhapsody in Blue*, Labèque (Philips 400 022-2)]." *Fanfare* 9/6 (1985-1986): 140. See: **D125**

B1083. _____. "[Review of *Rhapsody in Blue* for Two Pianos & Orch., [Cleveland Orch./R. Chailly] Labèque sisters (London 417 326-2)]." *Fanfare* 10/6 (1986-1987): 111.
See: **D177**

B1084. _____. "THE JAZZ ALBUM. Peter Donohue, piano; Michael Collins, clarinet; Harvey and the Wallbangers; London Sinfonietta conducted by Simon Rattle. EMI Angel CDC7 47991-2 . . ." *Fanfare* 11/5 (May/June 1988): 271-272. **[+, for the CD] [-, for RiB]**

Review of this unusual potpourri album. ". . . As conducted by Rattle, it [the RiB] strikes me as the revelation of a false prophet—altogether too raw, assertive, frenetic. Granted it's exciting and live, but is it Gershwin? Michael Tilson Thomas took a better measure of the original . . ." *See*: **D111, D268**

B1085. _____. "Classical Recordings: GERSHWIN: Concerto in F (trans. Castagnetta). Three Preludes. Rhapsody in Blue (trans. Gershwin) . . . Stradivari Classics SCD-8000 (compact disc) . . . Norman Krieger, piano . . ." *Fanfare* 12/1 (Sept.-Oct. 1988): 155-156. **[+]**

See: Full entry under **"Concerto," D170, D385, D593, D626**

B1086.   F., A. "Gershwin: Rhapsody in Blue; An American in Paris . . ." *High Fidelity*
10/3 (Mar. 1960): 68. **[-]**
Review of **Bernstein/Columbia Symphony Orchestra/Bernstein (Columbia ML
5413)** in AiP and Bernstein with the New York Philharmonic in RiB (same disc). ". . . None
of the present conductor's twenty-eight predecessors [in recorded performances] can possibly
have taken so many liberties with tempos and dynamics as he does in the *Rhapsody*, but his
liberties there are as nothing compared to what goes on overside, the modest, lighthearted
American in Paris is simply beaten to death . . ."

B1087.   FRENCH, Gilbert. "Gershwin: [7] *Preludes, Blue Monday [Piano Suite], Seven
Miniatures in Gershwin's Hand, Rhapsody in Blue* [for solo piano] Alicia Zizzo,
pa.—Carlton 6600052 (Allegro) . . ." *American Record Guide* 60/5 (Sept.-Oct.
1997): 133. *See*: Full entry at **B1223** under **"Piano Music"**

B1088.   GELATT, Roland. "Artsletter, Records—A Time of Revival." *Saturday
Review* 4/2 (Oct. 16, 1976): 31.
Includes a brief mention of two records of RiB: **CBS MK-42516 (Gershwin piano
roll/Columbia Jazz Band/Michael Tilson Thomas,** and **RCA "Victrola America" no. ?
Gershwin/Whiteman).** ". . . [These] two new records attempt to reproduce the piece as it
sounded, fresh-minted, on that historic occasion [the Aeolian Hall concert] . . ." *See*: **D282,
D646, D777, D1127**

B1089.   "GERSHWIN 'Rhapsody in Blue' [AiP, Catfish Row] . . . Deutsche-Grammophone-
431-625-2 (Levine, James, Chicago-Symphony Orchestra)." *American Heritage.*
45/6 (Oct. 1994): 104.
Review. *See*: **D12, D94, D176, D302**

B1090.   GRUENINGER, Walter F. "Phonograph Records . . . Gershwin: *Rhapsody in
Blue* and *An American in Paris* . . ." *Consumer Bulletin* 43/5 (May 1960): 34.
[+]
This is the **Wild/Boston Pops/Fiedler RCA Victor album (LSC 2367)**, about
which the reviewer exclaimed ". . . Stunning performances . . . Simply terrific is Earl Wild
. . ." *See*: **D4**

B1091.   H., M. "Gershwin. Piano Works. Los Angeles Philharmonic Orchestra/Michael
Tilson Thomas (pno). CBS Masterworks digital IM39669 . . ." *The Gramophone*
63/745 (June 1985): 37. **[+]**
Thomas used the original Grofé score of the first rhapsody and G's own manuscript
version of the second. The reviewer praised the authentication of the RiB and *Second
Rhapsody* by Thomas, and considered *Short Story, Sleepless Night,* and *Violin Piece,* to be
"characteristically attractive pieces." *See*: **D357, D417, D690, D773**

B1092.   HAGGIN, Bernard H. "Music." *The Nation* 161/5 (Aug. 4, 1945): 115. **[*]**
Along with value judgments about G's "serious" music, Haggin evaluated the
"flood" of recordings appearing in 1945, concurrent with the release of the movie RiB. The
reviewer compared **Oscar Levant's** version of the first rhapsody **(Columbia Set X-251 with
Philadelphia)** to that of Gershwin (Victor) referring to ". . . the deftness, lightness, and
precision of his [G's] playing . . . [I]n its simplicity of style the playing had an unfailing and
subtle continuity of rhythm and phrasing. As against this, Levant's playing astonishes me

. . . by its crude treatment of piano and phrase . . ." Concerning **Columbia's Set 572** performance by **Reiner/Pittsburgh of the Robert Russell Bennett suite from P&B** and **Victor Sevitzky's** interpretation of same with **Indianapolis (Columbia Set 999)**, ". . . Reiner's is the finer performance by miles; Sevitzky's the better recorded one by the same distance . . . There is even more . . . muddy confusion on the recorded sound of 'An American in Paris' with the **New York Philharmonic Symphony ([Rodzinski] Columbia Set X-246)** . . ." *See*: **D303 (Levant), D243 Reiner), D231 (Indianapolis), D774 (Rodzinski)**

B1093.   INDCOX, J. F. "Rhapsody in Blue; Concerto for Piano and Orchestra, in F Julius Katchen, piano; orchestra, Montovani cond. London LL 1262 [-] . . . Rhapsody in Blue; Concerto for Piano and Orchestra, in F, An American in Paris; Suite from Porgy and Bess (arr. Morton Gould); Preludes for Piano; Piano Solo from Porgy and Bess, Morton Gould, piano; orchestra, Morton Gould, cond. RCA Victor LM 6033." *High Fidelity Record Annual*, ed. by Roland Gelatt (1956): 103. [+]
See: Full entry under **"Concerto"**

B1094.   JABLONSKI, Edward. "Record Reviews: "Gershwin: *Concerto in F; Rhapsody in Blue*; Mercury MG-50138 . . ." *American Record Guide* 24/4 (Dec. 1957): 145. [+]
The reviewer liked **Eugene List** and **Howard Hansen's** interpretation and, at the time, considered this recording second only to "the superb Gould version." *See*: **D133, D309**

B1095.   _____. "Gershwin: *Rhapsody in Blue; Concerto in F; An American in Paris*; Westminster XWN-18684/7 [Reid Nibley/Utah/Abravanel]. . ." *American Record Guide* 24/10 (June 1958): 427. [+]
". . . The *Rhapsody* is given a delightful 'period' performance (you can hear the banjo plunking through), and again Reid's expressive, romantic playing does well by our George . . ." *See*: **D139**

B1096.   JABLONSKI, Edward. "Gershwin Plays Gershwin—Enjoy, Enjoy." *American Record Guide* 28 (Jan. 1962): 365. [+] *See*: **D277, D1150**

B1097.   JACQUES, Henry-. *See* under **"AiP"** above.

B1098.   KIPNIS, Igor. "Replacing a celebrated *Rhapsody in Blue* [Review of Everest Stereo LPBR-3067]." *American Record Guide* 27/2 (Oct. 1960): 134. [+]
"SANROMA has always been aclaimed [sic] for his *Rhapsody in Blue* . . . The new recording is, of course, much superior in sound . . . The pianist plays with his customary brilliance, though the orchestral performance is generally not so much jazzy as overly effervescent and there are a number of actual additions . . . and departures in terms of stretching tempi which to my taste lend little to the music . . . The *American in Paris* is extroverted but a little four-square, being neither as free in the jazz sense as Bernstein's version nor as dynamically controlled as Toscanini's controversial reading . . ." *See*: **D54, D343, B1000**

B1099. KOLDYS, Mark. "Gershwin . . . Lincoln Mayorga [D. Kitayenko, cond.] Sheffield Lab CD-28 . . ." *American Record Guide* 52/2 (Mar.-Apr. 1989): 36. [-]
". . . The Moscow Orchestra is impossibly stiff in this loose-jointed music, and while Mayorga's pianism is more fitting, the *Rhapsody* and the *Variations* just never got off

the ground . . ." *See*: **D676, D681, D753**

B1100. _____. "Guide to Records . . . GERSHWIN: *Concerto in F; Rhapsody in Blue;* [and music by Enesco & Prokofieff] . . . [Raymond Lewenthal/Metropolitan SO/Oskar Danon . . . Chesky 56 [an earlier LP version was by Quintessence]. . ." *American Record Guide* 55/2 (Mar./Apr. 1992): 62. [-]

A negative review of the G works on this recording. *See*: **D131, D308**

B1101. **KOLODIN, Irving.** "*Recordings* Reports I: Orchestral LPs . . . Gershwin 'Rhapsody in Blue,' Concerto in F . . ." *Saturday Review* 38/39 (Sept. 24, 1955): 48. [-]

Review of **Katchen/Mantovani (London LL-1262)**. "Katchen has technical facility in abundance . . . However, some of his tempi, especially in the phrasing of melodic matter, are exaggerated . . . [and] what of the really indefensible rearrangement of the 'Rhapsody,' in which the famous clarinet solo at the beginning becomes, almost immediately, an episode for strings?" *See*: **D34, D122, D300**

B1102. **LINKOWSKI, [Allen].** "Guide to Records . . . GERSHWIN: *Concerto in F; Rhapsody in Blue; Song-book* Peter Donohue . . . Simon Rattle—Angel/EMI 54280 [avail. in CD, same no.] . . ." *American Record Guide* 55/2 (Mar./Apr. 1992): 61-62. [+]

Decidedly a positive review by one who, until now, had felt that "nothing has challenged my allegiance to the Earl Wild/Arthur Fiedler collaboration in Gershwin's jazz-inspired concerto . . ." Overall, Linkowski considers this "a wonderful record, highly recommended." *See*: **D111, D268**

B1103. **MCCOLLEY, Robert.** "[Review of] **GERSHWIN: *An American in Paris. Concerto In F for Piano and Orchestra. Rhapsody in Blue.*** Mitch Miller conducting the London Symphony Orchestra; David Golub, piano . . . MITCH MILLER MUSIC MMM 14610 [DDD] . . . **GERSHWIN: *Strike up the Band*—Medley** (arr. Don Rose). ***Rhapsody In Blue. Girl Crazy*—Medley** (arr. Don Rose). ***An American in Paris. I Got Rhythm Variations*** (arr. C. Schoenfeld). ***Cuban Overture.*** Wayne Marshall, piano, conducting the Aalborg Symphony Orchestra. VIRGIN CDM 5 61247 2 [DDD] . . ." *Fanfare* 19/3 (January-February 1996): 203-205. [+] [*]

See: Full entry above under **"AiP."**

B1104. _____. "*Recordings* Reports I: Orchestral LPs . . . Gershwin: Concerto in F. 'American in Paris,' 'Rhapsody in Blue,' 'Porgy' suite, etc. . . ." *Saturday Review* 38/44 (Oct. 29, 1955): 52. [adq]

Review of **Morton Gould** playing and conducting **(RCA Victor LM-6033)**. *See*: Full entry at **B1022** under **"Concerto."**

B1105. **MCKELVEY, [John P].** "Guide to Records . . . GERSHWIN: *Concerto in F; Rhapsody in Blue; American in Paris; I Got Rhythm Variations* Earl Wild, Boston Pops, Arthur Fiedler RCA 6519 . . ." *American Record Guide* 55/2 (Mar./Apr. 1992): 62. [+] *See*: **D8, D164, D222, D368**

B1106. **MILLER, Philip L.** "Recorded Music: GERSHWIN: Concerto in F; Rhapsody in Blue . . .[List/Eastman-Rochester/Hanson]." *Library Journal* 83/3 (Feb. 1,

1958): 394. **[+]**
See: Full entry at **B1038** under **"Concerto."**

B1107.   MONSON, Karen. "Ovation Record Review: The Birth of *Rhapsody in Blue*,
Recording of Distinction, **MAURICE PERESS** . . . Music Masters MMD
20113X/14T . . ." *Ovation* (July 1987): 36.
Maurice Peress' "noble and exhaustive reconstruction" of the Aeolian Hall Paul
Whiteman concert of February 12, 1924, was selected as "Recording of Distinction" for the
July 1987 issue of *Ovation*. ". . . That it was a *wonderful* concert, elegantly programmed,
Peress proves with this recording, which is filled with spirit and color; You haven't heard a
slide whistle until you've heard Dave Bargeron's sail through 'Whispering' . . . There are
treasures of information in Peress' documentation for this album, but the conductor's remarks
simply make the reader and listener want to know more . . ." *See*: **D266**

B1108.   MOORE. "The Birth of Rhapsody in Blue . . ." *American Record Guide* 50/4
& 5 [double issue] (Fall 1987): 68-69. **[+] [*]**
Review of Maurice Peress' reconstruction of the Aeolian Hall concert in the
album Music-masters **MMD 20113X/14T**. ". . . We are in debt to Maurice Peress for
reconstructing it [the concert] with loving, tender care from the old Whiteman arrangements
and playing it with an immediacy that shows us what the excitement was all about . . ." In re:
Ivan Davis' performance of the RiB: ". . . [I]n some ways this performance feels even righter
than [Michael Tilson] Thomas'. . ." *See*: **D266**

B1109.   PHILLIPS, Wes, and **John ATKINSON.** "The Rhapsody Project. [Hyperion
Knight, pa. and cond.]." *Stereophile* 20/6 (June 1997): 70-81.
Detailed announcement of this new (1997) recording of the rhapsody in a new
arrangement. The album is thoroughly discussed, and, the article, because it appears in a sound
magazine, gives much information about the recording equipment used and the process. "The
combination of recording venue, microphone technique, and recording hardware makes
Rhapsody Stereophile's finest-sounding CD yet . . . (John Atkinson)." *See*: **D744, D301**

B1110.   "A Potpourri of Records of Interest." *Show Music* 5/3 (Apr. 1987): 69. **[+]**
Review of **MusicMasters** (not the shop formerly in NY) **MM 20113/4 "The Birth
of the Rhapsody in Blue" Maurice Peress** album. ". . . It is an altogether charming and
exciting recording, beautifully performed and digitally recorded . . . It's a beaut . . ." *See*: **D266**

B1111.   RABINOWITZ, Peter J. "New Port in New Bottles." *Fanfare* 11/4 (March/
April 1988): 51-51. **[-]**
Review of **Newport Classic 60042, "Rhapsody in Electric Blue,"** with the RiB
performed on synthesizer. ". . . Some of the performances are little more than electronic
paraphrases of Gershwin's original sounds—and, in that regard, seems even more pointless
. . ." *See*: **D78**

B1112.   _____. "Stravinsky: Three Movements from Petrouchka . . . Gershwin:
Rhapsody in Blue . . . Chandos Chan 873 . . ." *Fanfare* 13/3 (Jan.-Feb. 1990):
380-381. **[-]**
The performer here is pianist Louis Lortie. ". . . [T]he rhythmic distortions in the
Rhapsody are crudely self-indulgent . . ." *See*: **D388**

B1113.   "Record Reviews: George Gershwin Plays Rhapsody in Blue." *Jazz Journal* 30
(Apr. 1977): 29.

B1114.   "Recordings Reports I: Orchestral LPs . . . Rhapsody in Blue . . ." *Saturday Review* 49/22 (May 28, 1966): 56. RiB **[+]**; AiP **[adq].**

Brief assessment of the **Stanley Black/London Festival Orchesra** album including the RiB and AiP. ". . . He [pianist and conductor Black] produces a *Rhapsody* of outstanding qualities . . ." *See:* **D261**

B1115.   **STEARNS, David Patrick.** "News & Views." *Gramophone* 66/769 (June 1987).

Survey and brief reviews of recordings which came out during the commemorative year, 1987.

B1116.   **T., S.** "[Review] George Gershwin Plays . . . Columbia Masterworks . . ." *Jazz Journal* 30 (Apr. 1977): 29+

Review of the piano roll/jazz band version of RiB, and including AiP, by **Tilson Thomas (CBS MK-42240)** *See:* **D48, D283, D1127**

B1117.   **VROON, Donald R.** "Rachmaninoff: *Rhapsody on a Theme of Paganini*; Gershwin: *Rhapsody in Blue* . . . [Dorensky, pa., Dmitriyev, cond.] . . . Mobile Fidelity 866 . . ." *American Record Guide* 51/3 (May-June 1988): 53-54. **[adq].**

Review, mostly of the Rachmaninoff. The reviewer refers to the version of RiB: ". . . [T]his one's OK, even if it does begin *inside* the clarinet . . ." *See:* **D269**

B1118.   _____. "Gershwin: Rhapsody in Blue, Piano Concerto, excerpts from Catfish Row . . . Previn . . . Kostelanetz . . . CBS Odyssey 46270 [this version a CD, formerly Columbia CS 8286] . . ." *American Record Guide* 53/6 (Nov.-Dec. 1990): 59. **[+]**

Positive review by the editor of the *ARG* of this 1960 performance *See:* **D335**

B1119.   **WILSON, John S.** "Recordings: The Whiteman Concert of 1924 Lives On." *New York Times*, February 15, 1987, Arts and Leisure, section 2, pp. 25, 34.

A discussion of the February 12, 1924, Aeolian Hall concert along with a positive review and comparison of two recent recordings stemming from it. The recordings are the 1981 recorded reconstruction by the **Smithsonian Institution** (with Gershwin as soloist on *Rhapsody in Blue* and the Whiteman orchestra) and **Maurice Peress'** effort of 1985 for **MusicMasters.** *See:* **D266 (Peress)**

B1120.   **YOUNGREN, William7.** "Gershwin, Part I: Rhapsody in Blue." *New Republic* (Apr. 23, 1977): 21-24.

A very long article concerned primarily with the RiB, its genesis, the various versions of it, and performance practices related to those versions. A comparison of various recorded performances is also included. Among the recordings assayed are the **List/Adler/Berlin** performance on **Turnabout TV-S 34457, Gershwin (piano roll)-M.T. Thomas-Columbia Jazz Band on Columbia XM 34205, Gershwin (solo piano version) on Mark 56-641, Everest's Archives of Piano Music Series X-914,** another **Gershwin solo piano version; Gershwin's two recordings with Whiteman: Victrola AVM1-1740 (1924)** and **Victor Vintage Series LPV-555;** and the **Werner Haas-Edo de Waart-Monte Carlo Opera Orchestra** rendition on **Philips 6500 118.** In a comparison of the two arrangements of the work, Youngren observed: ". . . In the 1924 version . . . the [jazz] band enters after one of the piano interludes with the clarinet's opening tune played very sassily by soprano and baritone saxes, two octaves apart. But in the 1942 version the sassiness vanishes because instead of the two saxes we have an oboe and bassoon, instruments which of course have totally different associations and evocative powers . . ." Youngren concluded ". . . [A]lmost any move in the direction of lightness is a move in the right direction; it is the decades of increasingly overblown and heavy-handed symphonic performances that have made the work sound pretentious and silly, obscuring its true charm and wit." *See*: **D132, D312 (List/Adler), D646 (Thomas/Columbia Jazz Band), D717, D1140 (Mark 56), D1147 (Gershwin/Whiteman on Victrola and Victor)**

B1121.   YOUNGREN, William. "[Review of *Rhapsody in Blue*, Bernstein (CBS MK 42264)]."*Fanfare* 10/6 (1986-1987): 110. *See*: **D42, D255**

W4. *SECOND RHAPSODY* (1931)

B1122.   C., G. "Review of *Second Rhapsody*, Votapek (London 411 835-1)]." *Fanfare* 8/5 (1984-1985): 140. *See*: **D657**

B1123.   CARNOVALE, Norbert. "Reviews of Recordings . . . George Gershwin [St. Louis/Slatkin]. . ." *Sonneck Society Bulletin* 14/3 (Fall 1988): 158. **[adq]** *See*: Full entry under **"AiP."**

B1124.   "Composer's and Lyricist's Corner." *Show Music* 4/3 (Oct. 1986): 30-31. **[+]**
Review of CBS Masterworks CBS IM 39699, "George Gershwin." Michael Tilson Thomas, who both performs and conducts, ". . . also counts himself as a George Gershwin 'rescuer,' as his recording includes several melodies never before recorded or seldom done in their original versions . . ." *See*: **D357, D417, D690, D773**

B1125.   D[ARRELL], R. D. "Gershwin: Second Rhapsody; Variations on 'I Got Rhythm'; Cuban Overture (arr. McRitchie); Porgy and Bess: Medley (arr. McRitchie); Leonard Pennario, piano; Hollywood Bowl Symphony Orchestra
. . .Capitol P 8581 " *High Fidelity* 12/6 (May 1962): 58-59, also in *Records in Review 1963 Edition*, p. 179. **[+]**
"The first stereo edition of the Second Rhapsody [conducted here by Alfred Newman] is so dazzlingly played and recorded that this too often neglected showpiece can hardly fail to win a new popularity. Pennario . . . also brings enormous éclat, if less gusto than Earl Wild, to the diverting "*I Got Rhythm*" *Variations* [Wild on RCA Victor LM 2586]. But the real surprise here is the effectiveness of Greig McRitchie's concerto treatment of the *Cuban Overture*. *See*: **W5 (Re: *Cuban*), D165 (Wild), D187, D215, D411, D531**

B1126.   _____. "Gershwin, George . . . Orchestral Works: *Second Rhapsody for Piano and Orchestra* (arr. McBride); *Overtures* (orch. Rose): *Funny Face, Let 'Em Eat Cake, Oh, Kay!, & Girl Crazy; Wintergreen for President* parade number; [et al] . . . Ralph Votapek, piano; Boston Pops Orchestra; Arthur Fiedler, cond. London Phase-4 SPC 21185 . . ." *Records in Review 1980 Edition*, p. 143-144. **[+] [*]**
Praise was very high for this album, Fiedler's last. About Votapek's performance of the *Second Rhapsody* ". . . [It] is scarcely less steely-fingered and vital than the composer['s] as he remains in my memory . . . [This recording] takes a place of honor as a cornerstone of every Gershwinian album, along with the 1974 RCA "Great Gershwin" reissue collection of c. 1960-62 Fiedler/Pops recordings with Earl Wild . . ." *See*: **D420, D657, D703, D1089**

B1127.   H., M. "Gershwin. Piano Works. Los Angeles Philharmonic Orchestra/Michael Tilson Thomas (pno). CBS Masterworks digital IM39669 . . ." *The Gramophone* 63/745 (June 1985): 37. **[+]**

Thomas used G's own manuscript version of the second rhapsody. The reviewer praised the authentication of the RiB and *Second Rhapsody* by Thomas. *See:* **D773**

B1128.   KOLODIN, Irving. "*Recordings* Reports I: Orchestral LPs, GERSHWIN: 'Second Rhapsody,' 'Cuban Overture,' "Variations on I Got Rhythm,' and three Preludes . . ." *Saturday Review* 39/13 (Mar. 31, 1956): 50. **[-]**

Negative review of the **MGM E-3307** pressing of **Bianca/Pro Musica Symphony of Hamburg/Walther**. *See:* **D403, D615**

B1129.   MARSH, Robert C. "Gershwin, George . . . *Orchestral Works* . . . Vox QSVBX 5132 [St. Louis, Slatkin] . . ." *Records in Review 1976 Edition*, pp. 132-133. **[adq]**

The reviewer was critical of Slatkin's performance practice on these discs. ". . . Banish once and for all the idea that a young American conductor of great talent [Slatkin] automatically knows how to play Gershwin. The period is not part of his direct life experience . . . The *Promenade* [included here in an arrangement for full blown symphony orchestra], a most attractive little work, does not seem to be otherwise available and any serious Gershwin admirer will want it . . ." *See:* **D416, D348**

DERIVATIVE WORKS/ARRANGEMENTS

R. R. BENNETT. *PORGY AND BESS: A SYMPHONIC PICTURE*

B1130.   AFFELDER, Paul. "Gershwin, George. An American in Paris; **[-]** Porgy and Bess: A Symphonic Picture (arr. Robert Russell Bennett) . . . Minneapolis SO . . .Mercury MG 50071. LP." *Records in Review* 1959 Edition. Great Barrington, MA: Wyeth Press, pp. 76-77. **[adq]** *See:* **B975, D35**

B1131.   C., G. "[Review of *Porgy and Bess: A Symphonic Picture*, Ortiz [London SO, Previn] (EMI CDC 7 47021 2)]." *Fanfare* 9/1 (1985-1986): 157. *See:* **D190**

B1132.   "GERSHWIN 'Cuban Overture', 'Porgy and Bess Suite' et al . . . Deutsche-Grammophone 431-625-2 (Levine, James, Chicago Symphony Orchestra)." *American Heritage* 45/6 (Oct. 1994): 104. *See:* **D12, B94, D176, D302**

B1133.   HAGGIN, Bernard H. "Music." *The Nation* 161/5 (Aug. 4, 1945): 115. Comparison of several recordings. *See:* Full entry under **"RiB."**

B1134.   INDCOX, J. F. "Porgy and Bess—'A Symphonic Picture'; Tchaikovsky: The Queen of Spades . . . New York Philharmonic-Symphony . . . Columbia ML 4904 . . ." *High Fidelity Record Annual*, ed. by Roland Gelatt (1955): 112-113. **[+]**

". . . The artfully conceived Robert Russell Bennett arrangement of the better-known tunes is given a rousing performance . . ." conducted by André Kostelanetz. *See:* **D237**

B1135.   INDCOX, J. F. "An American in Paris; Porgy and Bess, Symphonic Suite (arr. Robert Russell Bennett) Philharmonia Orchestra of Hamburg, Jurgen Walther, cond. MGM E 3253." *High Fidelity Record Annual*, ed. by Roland Gelatt

(1956): 102. [+]

". . . A word should be added about the interesting liner notes concerning this recording and its part in the renascence of West Germany's interest in the music of Gershwin." *See*: **D236**

SUITE from PORGY AND BESS by Morton Gould

B1136.   INDCOX, J. F. "Rhapsody in Blue; Concerto for Piano and Orchestra, in F Julius Katchen, piano; orchestra, Montovani cond. London LL 1262 [-]. . . Rhapsody in Blue; Concerto for Piano and Orchestra, in F, An American in Paris; Suite from Porgy and Bess (arr. Morton Gould); Preludes for Piano; Piano Solo from Porgy and Bess, Morton Gould, piano; orchestra, Morton Gould, cond. RCA Victor LM 6033." *High Fidelity Record Annual*, ed. by Roland Gelatt (1956): 103
See: Full entry under **"Concerto."**

STAGE SHOWS
(In alphabetical order)

W15. *BLUE MONDAY*) (1922) [135th STREET]

B1137.   HAMILTON, David. "Gershwin . . . *Porgy and Bess* [Houston, 1976] . . . *Blue Monday* (*135th Street*). . ." *Records in Review: 1978 Edition*. Great Barrington, MA: Wyeth, pp. 147-148. **[adq] [*]**
A mixed review of the Turnabout TV-S 34638 recording of *Blue Monday* including some history of its performances. *See*: **D428**

B1138.   RABINOWITZ, Peter J. "Classical Recordings: Gershwin: Blue Monday . . . Concerto Marin Alsop, conducting . . . Angel CDC 7 54851 2 7 . . . Wild: Variations on An American Theme . . . Gershwin: Concerto . . . [with the] Des Moines Symphony Orchestra [on] Chesky CD 98 . . ." *Fanfare* 17/1 (Sept.-Oct. 1993): 168-170. **[+] [*]**
A substantial review of the two above-named recordings. Rabinowitz goes to considerable length to describe the early "miniature opera" *Blue Monday* in its various arrangements (by Will Vodery, Grofé, Gregg Smith, and in this version, George Bassman). The reviewer commented that conductor "Marin Alsop's performance is a knockout." See: **D156 (Alsop on Angel), D166 (Wild/Chesky)**

W50. *CRAZY FOR YOU* (derivative) (1992)

B1139.   MORDDEN, Ethan. "When the Go-Everywhere Song Grew Exclusive; The Gershwin style continues to develop as the new 'Crazy for You' and other recordings show." *NYTimes*, May 17, 1992, Arts & Leisure section, pp. 1, 8.
Extensive, informative article begun with discussion of the **Angel/EMI** original cast album of the show released May 1992. The article, at the same time, gives the reader a review of many recent developments in the Gershwin saga. Among the items discussed are the **Elektra/Nonesuch** albums of *Girl Crazy* and *Strike Up the Band*, the 1987 CBS pairings of **OTIS and Cake** (comparing the performance of OTIS unfavorably to the "old Capitol LP of the 1952 revival"), the **EMI John McGlinn "Gershwin Overtures"** album, **Philips' "The Gershwins in Hollywood" (John Mauceri)**, as well as those albums by **Barbara Hendricks** and the **Lebèque sisters**, the **Judy Kaye/William Sharp "He Loves and She Loves"** album,

and **Maureen McGovern's** highly musical collection entitled **"Naughty Baby."** This article also announces a then forthcoming biography of George by Joan Peyser, an edition of Ira's "complete" lyrics by Robert Kimball, and the fact that "the playwright John Guare is at work on a film biography . . . to be directed by Martin Scorsese." *See:* **D429** (*Crazy for You*), **D450** (*Girl Crazy*), **D564** (*Strike Up the Band*), **D467 (OTIS), D463 (Cake), D1095 (Overtures), D1122 (Hollywood), D857 (Hendricks/Lebèque), D877 (Judy Kaye/Sharp), D900 (McGovern)**

B1140.   "New Releases." *Show Music* 8/3 (Fall 1992): 6-7.
     Review of EMI/Broadway Angel's recording of *Crazy for You* (54618). ". . . The recording . . . effectively captures the occasionally giddy fun of the musical and will leave you with the desire to see it on stage . . ." (One should keep in mind that the 1992 London cast is also available from RCA, *See:* **D430**) In re: the Angel recording, *See:* **D429**

W28. *FUNNY FACE* (1927)

B1141.   SMOLIAN, Steven. *A Handbook of Film, Theatre, and Television Music on Record, 1948-1969.* NY: The Record Undertaker, 1970. 2 vols.
     Funny Face, among others on record, receive coverage up to about 1969 in this edition. *See:* **B940**

W33. *GIRL CRAZY* (1930)

B1142.   BLYTH, A. "Gershwin 'Girl Crazy' Elektra-Nonesuch-Warner-Classics-7559-79250-2 (Luft, Blazer, Lewis, Carroll, Gorshin, Garrison, Mauceri)." *Opera* 42/3 (1991): 359-360.
     Review of the album. *See:* **D450**
B1143.   DEUTSCH, Nicholas. "Classical Recordings: GERSHWIN: Girl Crazy . . . Elektra/Nonesuch 9 79250-2 . . ." *Fanfare* 14/5 (May-June 1991): 174. **[+] [*]**
     Yet another enthusiastic appraisal of the 1990 sixtieth-anniversary CD. The reviewer's only mixed reaction was to Lorna Luft: ". . . [She] has proven to be the only controversial choice [in the cast], partly because her three numbers have been transposed down, and partly because of doubts that a 'charm' singer can really deliver a 'belt' role. I enjoyed her work a lot . . . and she has plenty of brass in reserve for 'I Got Rhythm' . . ." *See:* **D450**

B1144.   GOODWIN, N. "Gershwin 'Girl Crazy' Elektra-Nonesuch-Warner-Classics-7559-79250-2 (Mauceri, Blazer, Carroll, Luft)." *Dance & Dancers*, (Nov. 1991): 28.
     Review of the album. *See:* **D450**
B1145.   "Popular music: *Girl Crazy* (recording)." *Stereo Review* 56 (Feb. 1991): 125. *See:* **D450**

B1146.   "Record reviews—*Gershwin: Girl Crazy* (Lorna Luft, David Carroll, Judy Blazer, Frank Gorshin; orchestra conducted by John Mauceri) (Nonesuch CD)." *Classical Music Magazine* 14/4 (1991): 38. *See:* **D450**

B1147.   "Record reviews: *Girl Crazy* (Elektra Nonesuch/Warner Classics)." *Opera* (Eng) 42 (Mar. 1991): 359-360. *See:* **D450**

B1148.   "Recordings (Blazer, Luft, Lewis; Carroll, Garrison, Gorshin; Mauceri) (Nonesuch)." *Opera News* 55 (May 1991): 49. *See:* **D450**

B1149.   "Retro-active: *Girl Crazy. Melody Maker* 67 (Mar. 2, 1991): 40. *See:* **D450**

B1150.   **SCHECTER, Scott A.** "Lorna Luft Records *Girl Crazy:* Who Could Ask for
         Anything More?" *Show Music* 7/1 (Spring 1991): 62-64.
         Schecter, who attended the recording sessions for the recent album
(Elektra/Nonesuch 9 79250-2), provided interesting details of the actual sessions along with
a tribute to Luft whom he claims "can belt like 'The Merm'." *See:* **D450**

B1151.   **SCHNEIDER, Wayne.** "Regarding recordings II: Bronco-busting Gershwin."
         Institute for Studies in American Music Newsletter 20/2 (May 1991): 14-15.
         See: next entry

B1152.   "Regarding Recordings II: Bronco-Busting Gershwin." *Newsletter* Institute for
         Studies in American Music 20/2 (May 1991): 14-15. **[+] [*]**
         Positive review of the first album in the Leonore Gershwin/Library of
Congress/Nonesuch-Roxbury Recording project (Elektra Nonesuch 9 79250-2). ". . . The
recording is a pip. There are pleasant surprises galore . . ." Schneider called for "a new, critical
edition of the score (in piano-vocal and full orchestra formats) and publication of the show's
book . . ." *See:* **D450**

B1153.   **SWAIN, Joseph P.** "Record Reviews: George Gershwin. **Girl Crazy** . . . Elektra
         Nonesuch 9 79250-2 Richard Rogers. **Babes in Arms** . . ." *American Music* 9/3
         (Fall 1991): 327-330. **[adq] [*]**
         A detailed and well thought out, descriptive review of the *Girl Crazy* album. ". . . Both
these discs serve a number of uses. For the historian, they begin to build a discography for two
empty decades of musical theater history, the 1920s and 1930s . . . For the lover of American
song, these discs are a small treasury of gems that can be heard in versions as close to the
originals as can be imagined . . ." *See:* **D450**

W22. *LADY, BE GOOD!* (1924)

B1154.   **GIDDINS, Gary.** "Reconstructing the Great White Way." *Village Voice* 23, Jan.
         9, 1978, p. 49.
         Review of a recording in the Smithsonian series, a resurrection of the 1920s
production of *Lady, Be Good!* ". . . Surveying the songs on these records, or any
comprehensive list of Tin Pan Alley outpourings, it would seem that those qualitites which
combine to make a song a standard are those that give it appeal to the improvising performer—
melodic suppleness and harmonic flow. Thus songs which may have been most effective in the
theater have not survived, while songs that lend themselves to personal interpretation have .
. ." *See:* **D456**

B1155.   **KRESH, Paul.** "Musical Comedy Archives." *Stereo Review* 40 (May 1978): 146-
         147, **[adq] [*]**
         Informative review of the Smithsonian's album of the 1926 version of *Lady, Be
Good!* (Smithsonian Collection R 008). ". . . The 'archival reconstruction' of George and Ira
Gershwin's *Lady, Be Good* . . . is full of pleasant moments. George Gershwin himself is at the
piano, limning *Fascinatin'* [sic] *Rhythm, So Am I, The Man I Love* . . . and *The Half Of It
Dearie Blues.* This material was culled from old radio airchecks, piano rolls, and thanks to a
happy custom instituted early on by English Columbia, the recorded scores of musicals as
performed by their original casts in London . . . The Astaires [Fred and Adele] are joined

several times at the piano by Gershwin, notably in the piquant and tricky *I'd Rather Charleston*
. . . Edward Jablonski's extensive notes are invaluable . . ." *See*: **D459**

B1156.   ROSENBERG, Deena. "A Gershwin Musical Meant More Than Good Tunes."
    NYTimes, June 11, 1978.
        A review of the Smithsonian record albums of *Lady, Be Good*! with Fred and Adele
Astaire, and *Oh, Kay*! in the London version with Gertrude Lawrence, and of Music Master's
Arden and Ohman album. ". . . The new records are valuable . . . because they make available
a number of Gershwin's piano accompaniments and arrangements which would otherwise have
disappeared, to such songs as 'So Am I,' 'I'd Rather Charleston' . . . and 'Maybe' and
'Someone to Watch Over Me' . . ." "Another important release is 'Arden and Ohman (1925-
1933),' the first LP issue of recordings by the duo-pianists, with period orchestra and vocalists
. . ." Rosenberg emphasized the importance of these three recordings to the study of correct
performance practice of the Gershwin music. *See*: **D459 (*Lady*), D482 (*Oh, Kay!*)**

B1157.   TRAUBNER, R. "Gershwin 'Lady, Be Good' - Elektra-Nonesuch-79308-2
    (Morrison, Austin, Teeter, Stern)." *Opera News* 57/13 (Mar. 13, 1993): 35.
        Generally positive, although mixed, review of this reconstruction of the 1924 show.
"If you expect merely a dancingly good '20s show with cute numbers that were not expected
to coalesce into a cohesive score, you'll be amply charmed." *See*: **D456**

B1158.   WATT, Douglas. "Popular Records: Charm." *New Yorker* 54/4 (Mar 13, 1978):
    126-133. In re: **These Charming People (RCA Victor ARL 1-2491** *See*: Full
    entry under **"Anthologies."**

W36. *LET 'EM EAT CAKE* (1933) and **W34. *OF THEE I SING*** (1931)

B1159.   DUCHAC, Joseph. "Ovation Record Review: Gershwin's Two 'Wintergreen'
    Shows Prove Evergreen!" Ovation 8/11 (Dec. 1987): 38.
        A rave review of the **CBS Masterworks 42522 album** which includes OTIS and
Cake. ". . . Clearly, enormous effort and care have gone into the preparation of these
performances, and the results should gladden the hearts of all lovers of the brothers Gershwin,
musical theater and good cheer . . ." *See*: **D463, D467**

B1160.   KART, Larry. "Recordings: Glories of Gershwin are captured in two forgotten
    works." *Chicago Tribune*, Oct. 18, 1987, Arts, Section 13, p. 20.
        Review in the form of an essay of the **CBS Masterworks Tilson/Thomas** recording
of OTIS and Cake. Comparing these performances to the McGlinn Library of Congress
revivals of *Primrose* and *Pardon My English*, the reviewer felt that the latter came off better,
more authentically. Kart concluded: ". . . So if CBS' 'Of Thee I Sing' and 'Let 'Em Eat Cake'
is not the 'dream' set one would have wished it to be, its virtues more than make up for its
flaws. Besides, given the difficulties involved in mounting such a project, it seems unlikely that
we will ever get another chance to find out what this wonderful music is like." *See*: **D463,
D467**

B1161.   ROCA, Octavia. "On Compact Disc [CBS CDS7 49347]: Gershwin's 'Of Thee
    I Sing': Embarrassment of riches." *Washington Times*, Washington Weekend
    Section, Jan. 7, 1988, M33. **[+]**
        The reviewer gave this recording by the BAM cast the maximum four-star rating for

both performance and sound. She had high praise for all aspects of the recording. *See*: **D467**

B1162.   STEARNS, David Patrick. "News & Views." *Gramophone* 66/769 (June 1987).
        Survey and brief reviews of recordings which came out during the commemorative
year, 1987.

B1163.   _____. "Gershwin Gems." *Gramophone* 65/775 (Dec. 1987): 876.
        Essay about the performances of OTIS and Cake at the Brooklyn Academy during
March 1987, and the CBS Masterworks recording which was made shortly thereafter.
Concerning G's orchestration, Kimball is quoted in the article: ". . . There's strong evidence
that . . . [GG's] first orchestrations date from 1922, with his song, *Naughty Baby* . . ." *See*:
D467

W26. *OH, KAY!* (1926)

B1164.   PREEO, Max O. "New Releases . . . [Review of Elektra-Nonesuch recording
        of *Oh, Kay!*]." *Show Music* 11/2 (Summer 1995): 58-59.
        Calling it "simply swell," this is a descriptive and complimentary review of the
recording, purported to be the last in the Roxbury series. *See*: **D490**

B1165.   ROSENBERG, Deena. "A Gershwin Musical Meant More Than Good Tunes.
        NYTimes, June 11, 1978. In re: Smithsonian recording of *Oh, Kay!* in the London
        version with Gertrude Lawrence, *See*: Full entry at **B1156**, above.

B1166.   TRAUBNER, R. "Gershwin 'Oh, Kay' - Nonesuch-79361 (Upshaw, Ollmann,
        Cassidy, Stern)." *Opera News* 60/2 (Aug. 1995): 37.
        Record review of the new Elektra-Nonesuch production. *See*: **D490**

B1167.   WILSON, John S. "Small-Show LP's: Adventurous Off-Broadway Musicals
        Preserved in Several New Albums." *NYTimes*, Sept. 25, 1960, p. 20 X.
        [+]
        In a lengthy review covering several albums, Wilson covered the 20th-Century Fox
cast album from the Off-Broadway revival of *Oh, Kay!* in the Spring of 1960. ". . . The
production has a lively period flavor (the addition of a banjo to the accompaniment on 'Do, Do,
Do' emphasizes its happy beat) and keeps alive several worthy Gershwin songs in addition to
the standouts that head the list . . ." *See*: **D485**

W37. *PORGY AND BESS* (1935)
Reviews of Recordings of the Opera

B1168.   BLYTH, Alan. "Here and There: Lorin Maazel." *Gramophone* 53/633 (Feb. 1976):
        1321.
        A talky interview with Maazel who had then just recorded the more complete (than
previous recordings) version of P&B with the **Cleveland Orchestra**. Maazel was critical of
the earlier 1953 Engel recording because of the number of cuts taken in it ". . . eliminating
about a half-hour of music, a very important half-hour—all the orchestra's connecting tissue,
and some arias such as the 'Buzzard Song' . . ." *See*: **D495**

B1169.   BOSE, Fritz. "'Porgy and Bess': die Negeroper erstmals auf Platten." *Musica
        Schallplatte* 3/3 (May 1960): 58-59.

B1170.   COHN, Arthur. *Recorded Classical Music: A Critical Guide to Compositions*

and Performances. New York: Schirmer Books, 1981, p. 677. **[+]**
   In re: **London 13116, Cleveland Orchestra**, "The performance is dramatic, beautifully colored, and the sound vivid . . . The cast's diction is of such clarity that one can cast the libretto aside . . . This release is a triumph." *See:* **D495**

B1171.   DAVIS, Peter G. "REPEAT PERFORMANCE: A Selective Guide to the Month's Reissues." *High Fidelity* 18/11 (Nov. 1968): 112. **[+]**
   Complimentary review of **Columbia D4SL 162, 1951, Lehman Engel's** version, made before the more complete ones of Cleveland and the Houston Grand Opera ". . . It's amazing how the over-all aura of the recording remains totally convincing and immediate . . ." *See:* **D496**

B1172.   DITSKY, John. "Classical Recordings . . . Gershwin: Porgy and Bess—Complete Opera . . . [Glyndebourne Festival production] . . ." *Fanfare* 13/2 (Nov.-Dec. 1989): 211-212.**[+] [*]**
   A very complimentary review of the Glyndebourne recording, comparing it to the earlier Cleveland/Maazel and Houston versions. ". . . It would be handy . . . if I could claim that Simon Rattle and his British musicians simply don't understand this music, but that is far from the case: Rattle conducts it suavely, endearingly, with the kind of affection I would expect from a Michael Tilson Thomas . . . The collector must make his . . . own choice . . . [T]his album's annotation, amply illustrated with color stills, is a model of its kind. . . ." *See:* **D497**

B1173.   ECKERT, JR., Thor. "All Stereo, All Black—All American."*Christian Science Monitor* 68 (July 15, 1976): 23. **[+] [*]**
   Review of **Lorin Maazel's Cleveland** version of P&B for **London (OSA 13116)**. ". . . Maazel has approached the work with the same dedication and conviction of, say, his 'Tosca" and 'La Traviata'—theatrical values, fine singing, dramatic cohesiveness, all in vibrant view. The case he makes for the work is unbelievably strong . . ." *See:* **D495**

B1174.   ELLSWORTH, Ray. "The RCA Victor 'Porgy and Bess.'" *American Record Guide* 30/3 (Nov. 1963): 196-99.

B1175.   HAMILTON, D[avid]. "[Porgy and Bess] Catfish Row Springs to Life (Turnabout and RCA recordings of 'Porgy and Bess')." *High Fidelity/Musical America* 27 (Sept. 1977): 92-94.

B1176.   _____. "Porgy and Bess . . . Cleveland Orchestra . . . London OSA 13116 . . ." *Records in Review 1977 Edition*, pp. 128-131. **[*]**
   Hamilton spent most of the space in this review criticizing the overall musical construction of P&B. A typical statement follows: ". . . After several hearings of London's new recording . . . I find myself troubled, not by the songs, but by what goes on in between . . . [P]oints of transition are bridged with chromatic scales, which turn out to be more than mere mannerism; by the end of the opera, it's hard to evade the conclusion that Gershwin simply didn't know any other way to splice things together . . ." However, in the end, Hamilton concluded about the opera: "Still and all, the tragedy of *Porgy* is not that it isn't good . . . The tragedy is that Gershwin never had a chance to write another opera . . . Whatever its flaws, *Porgy* lives, not many American operas can make that claim . . ." Hamilton praised the vocal performers and Cleveland players, yet felt that overall "it isn't quite right . . . For a work like *Porgy*, a concert performance . . . is probably not enough to establish the vivid interplay that we hear in the Odyssey [Lehman Engel, **D496**] set, not to mention the 1942 'original cast' recordings of the songs [**D508**]." *See:* **D495**

B1177.   HAMILTON, D[avid]. "Gershwin . . . Porgy and Bess [Houston, 1976] . . ."
Records in Review: 1978 Edition. Great Barrington, MA: Wyeth, pp. 146-147.
[+] [*]
Review comparing the Houston 1976 recording to the earlier version by Cleveland.
Clearly, Hamilton preferred the RCA set by Houston, claiming that "the stage experience shows
in the recording, and it's important . . ." *See:* **D499**

B1178.   HERMAN, Justin R. "[Review of EMI 77754, laser discs." *American Record
Guide* (Nov.-Dec. 1993): 266-267. [P&B, Glyndebourne] *See:* **D498**

B1179.   HOROWITZ, Is. "'Porgy & Bess' Reverts To An Opera." *Billboard* 88 (Dateline,
NY, Dec. 11, 1976): 5.
Article concerned with the 1976 RCA recording **(D499)** and costs of the sessions:
". . . 20 hours session time were used . . . at a total talent cost estimated at about $85,000
. . ."

B1180.   JABLONSKI, Edward. [Porgy and Bess] "Catfish Row Revisited (recordings)."
American Record Guide 40 (Sept. 1977): 10-15. *See:* **D499**

B1181.   _____. "Unlikely Corners . . . Porgy and Bess (Camden CAL-500) . . . [Helen
Jepson, soprano; Lawrence Tibbett, baritone]" *Fanfare* 26/1 (Sept. 1959): 77.
[+] [*]
"Not only is the album interesting because of the soloists, but also the fact that
Gershwin was present during the recording sessions endows the interpretations with some kind
of authority." *See:* **D511**

B1182.   KOEGLER, Horst. "Schallplatten . . . Sinkende Armut in CD-High-Fidelity,
Gershwins ‚Porgy and Bess' in der grossartigen Glyndebourne-Produktion . . .
EMI 7495682." *Opernwelt* 30/Nr. 8 (Aug. 1989): 64.
Four-column review of the **Glyndebourne** album. *See:* **D497**

B1183.   KOLODIN, Irving. "Charleston Revisited." *Saturday Review of Literature*
34/39 (Sept. 29, 1951): 50-51.
Review of a Porgy and Bess record.

B1184.   KRESH, Paul. "The Inexhaustible 'Porgy and Bess.'" *Stereo Review* 39 (Sept.
1977): 130. **[+] [*]**
Positive review of the **RCA ARL3-2109** recording by the **Houston Opera
Company**. Among other interesting details, the reviewer pointed out: ". . . Producer Thomas
Z. Shepard has brought in a children's chorus . . . for the *Good Morning, Sisters* number in the
final scene and restored an edited portion in one of Crown's big numbers. And with a theater
orchestra of only fifty, augmented by eight additional players and Dick Hyman at a deliberately
mistuned piano for the Jasbo Brown solo, music director John DeMain, with the help of an
ingenious engineering staff, has managed to get out of his enthusiastic forces a sound that belies
their small numbers . . ." *See:* **D499**

B1185.   M., J. "[Review of *Porgy and Bess*, Donnie Ray Albert, Clamma Dale, etc., w/
Houston Grand Opera (RCA Red Seal RCD3-2109)]." *Fanfare* 9/1 (1985-
1986): 157. *See:* **D499**

B1186.   MILLER, Philip L. "On the Record . . . GERSHWIN: *Porgy and Bess . . .* Engel, cond. . . ." *Library Journal* 94/2 (Jan. 15, 1969): 170. **[-]**

In this brief assessment of **Odyssey 32 36 0018**, a reissue of Columbia SL 162 from 1951, the writer does not recommend the new release because the sound is "raw," and because "the new issue does not include the libretto . . ." *See:* **D496**

B1187.   SALZMAN, Eric. "Porgy & Bess: A New London Recording." *Stereo Review* 36 (Apr. 1976): 74-75. **[+] [*]**

From twentieth-century music expert Salzman, a glowing review of the **Cleveland Orchestra's** recording of P&B **(London OSA 5-13116)**. ". . . The production—the choral singing, orchestral playing, London recording, and, above all, Lorin Maazel's firm direction— are straight, authentic *Urtext, Gesamtausgabe, echt* operatic, as much so as any Bayreuth *Ring of the Nibelung . . . Porgy* is not only Wagnerian in scope, it is Moussorgskian, Puccinian, Bergian, Ravelian, and Stravinskian as well . . ." *See:* **B495**

B1188.   SCHWARTZ, Sanford D. "Gershwin: Porgy and Bess . . . [Glyndebourne production] . . ." *American Record Guide* 52/6 (Nov.-Dec. 1989): 61.

". . . This recording from Glyndebourne is a fine effort, but it lacks theatrical excitement, especially when compared to the Houston recording [**D 499**]. It is hard to believe that this production was actually staged—all these singers sound so stiff. They all sound too much like ladies and gentlemen. *Porgy and Bess* should be earthier . . . In spite of these flaws this recording offers excellent singing and is well worth having . . . This recording would be my second choice, with the RCA [Houston] in first place . . . The Maazel [Cleveland-**D495**] is far behind . . ." *See:* **D497**

B1189.   STARR, Larry. "Record Reviews . . . George Gershwin, *Porgy and Bess . . .* Glyndebourne . . . EMI Records CDS 7 49568 . . ." *American Music* 8/4 (Winter 1990): 490-493. **[*]**

A mixed evaluation of the "first digital recording." With thought provoking and detailed comments, Starr praises the "sound quality [for] easily passing that found on any previous recording . . ." while, on the other hand, carefully articulating his questions about this performance's "ability to sustain long-range dramatic continuity . . ." *See:* **D497**

B1190.   WILSON, John S. "A Wide Variety of Porgys and Besses." *NYTimes,* May 24, 1959, Section II, p. 15.

Review of recordings available at that time.

Reviews of Recordings Inspired by the Opera (Including Excerpts Albums)

B1191.   A., J. "[Record Review]." *Musical America* 83/11 (Nov. 1963): 47.

Very brief, but highly complimentary review of the P&B highlights album conducted by **Skitch Henderson, RCA Victor LSC-2679.**

B1192.   BENNETT, Bill. "[Review of] Joe Henderson: *Porgy and Bess* Verve 314 539 046-2 . . ." *JazzTimes* (Dec. 1997): 146.

Positive review of the album. *See:* **D543**

B1193.   BOURGEOIS, Jacques. "Un disque d'extraits de Porgy and Bess." *Disques* VI (Feb.-Mar. 1953): 127.

B1194.   CARR, Ian. *Miles Davis.* NY: William Morrow, 1982, pp. 95-103.

This biography of Davis includes an interesting chapter (page nos. cited above) on the genesis of the recording of his P&B album. *See:* **B1208, D540**

B1195.   ELLSWORTH, Ray. "The RCA Victor 'Porgy and Bess'." *American Record*
            Guide 30 (Nov. 1963): 197-198. **[adq]**
            Review of the excerpts album by **RCA (LM-2679)**. Although he found some faults with this "highlights" album, he was very high on Leontyne Price's performance, saying she "is simply beyond praise."

B1196.   F., C. "Porgy and Bess." *Gramophone* (Oct. 1959): 202.
            Lengthy review of the spate of albums issued in the wake of the movie version. Concerning the sound-track album for the movie: ". . . "[T]he album is an enjoyable one, even if André Previn's score treats Gershwin's melodies a little too smoothly at some points . . ." The reviewer did not like **Lena Horne and Harry Belafonte's** coupling on **RCA SF-5039. Diahann Carroll,** who acts but does not sing in the film, shows that ". . . she has a warm, well-controlled voice, that she possesses a fine sense of dynamics, and that she is more of a legitimate than a jazz artist . . ." on her **London SAH-T6041.** On **Columbia SEG7913, Pearl Bailey's** performances are ". . . very free interpretations of the songs, close in spirit to the gutsy fashion in which one of the classic blues-singers might have launched into them . . ." The reviewer found the **101 strings** versions **(Pye Golden Guinea GGL008)** to be "capable performances of rather lush arrangements, tasteful but without any real character . . ." *See:* **D527 (Horne/Belafonte), D526 (Bailey), D1116 (P&B soundtrack)**

B1197.   FOGEL, Henry. "[Review of *Porgy and Bess* Scenes, Price/Warfield (RCA AGL
            1-5234)]." *Fanfare* 8/1 (1984-1985): 223. *See:* **D520**

B1198.   GREEN, Stanley. "Catfish Row in a 'Near Original'." *HiFi Review* 3/2 (Aug.
            1959): 40.
            Soundtrack of the film Porgy and Bess. *See:* **D1116**

B1199.   INDCOX, J. F. "Porgy and Bess (concert version) [**Porgy:** Brock Peters; **Bess:**
            Margaret Tynes] . . . Concert Hall CHS 1247 . . ." *High Fidelity Record Annual,*
            ed. by Roland Gelatt (1956): 102- 103. **[+]**
            ". . . Here on one twelve-inch disk can be found practically every major vocal portion of the work . . . An extremely able cast . . ." *See:* **D501**

B1200.   KUPFERBERG, Herbert. "The Record World: Some Varied Sides of Review
            Porgy and Bess." *NY Herald Tribune,* June 28,1959.
            Review of records released in the wake of the release of the movie version of P&B. Among those albums recommended by the reviewer were: the sound track album, **Columbia OS-2016, Sammy Davis, Jr.'s** album for Decca, the two-disk **Verve album (MGV-4011-2) by Ella Fitzgerald and Louis Armstrong, R.C.A. and Victor's album from 1935 (Tibbett/Jepson)** transferred to the **Camden label (CAL-500)**. Kupferberg also listed a number of jazz albums inspired by the music. In regard to the sound track album, the reviewer pointed out that Robert McFerrin and Adele Addison dubbed the voices for P&B, and that Cab Calloway sings the Sportin' Life role. The critic felt that the Fitzgerald-Armstrong album was ". . . the most spontaneous sounding of all the 'Porgy' records . . ." *See:* **D1116 (Soundtrack), D541 (Sammy Davis, Jr.), D542 (Fitzgerald/Armstrong), D511 (Camden)**

B1201.   M., J. "[Review of *Porgy and Bess* Excerpts, Roberta Alexander, Simon Estes, etc. (Philips 412 720-2)]." *Fanfare* 9/1 (1985-1986): 157. *See*: **D504**

B1202.   MALTIN. "Old Wine—New Bottles, Various Artists, Porgy and Bess, Bethlehem
BPB-1: complete score . . ." *Downbeat* 43/8 (April 22, 1976): 34-35. **[+]**
Review of this multi-artist album. "Bethlehem's ambitious recording of *Porgy and
Bess* . . . is the kind of work that demands a great deal of the listener, but pays off with an
unusual and rewarding musical experience. Amazingly, the many ingredients of this production
are interwoven in such a way that the finished work sounds like a unified performance and not
a potpourri . . . But the complexity of the recording and the necessity of following a
complicated libretto make *Porgy And Bess* the kind of record that demands careful listening
. . . to bring out its many rich qualities . . ." *See*: **D551**

B1203.   "New Releases." *Show Music* 4/2 (June 1985): n. p. **[-]**
Review of **Philips 412 720-1** recording of selections from **P&B**. The recording
features **Simon Estes** who sang Porgy in the 1985 Metropolitan Opera production. ". . . The
recording doesn't come close to the Houston Grand Opera version on RCA Red Seal . . ." *See*:
D504

B1204.   O[SBORNE], C[onrad] L. "[Record Reviews] Gershwin: Porgy and Bess
(selections)." *High Fidelity* 13/12 (Dec. 1963): 74. **[adq]**
A generally positive, although mixed, review of the selections album **RCA Victor
LM 2679**, conducted by **Skitch Henderson**. The reviewer was most upset by the "labeling of
the record" because it failed to point out ". . . that [Leontyne] Price sings not only Bess's
numbers, but 'Summertime' and 'My Man's Gone Now' as well. Nowhere is there a listing of
who, among the bit singers, sings what . . ." *See*: **D520**

B1205.   "Porgy and Bess; Bethlehems nyinspelning (recording)." *Orkester Journalen* 25
(July-August 1957): 42-43. *See*: **D551**

B1206.   "Recordings Reports II: Miscellaneous LPs." *Saturday Review* 46/39 (Sept. 28,
1963): 74.
Review of the selections album **RCA Victor LM 2679**, conducted by **Skitch
Henderson**. The reviewer did not like **Leontyne Price's** rendition of *Summertime*: ". . . Miss
Price's sound is overpowering for Gershwin's music and too arty for the lyrics . . ." *See*: **D520**

B1207.   REILLY, Peter. "A Performing Field Day and Musician's Ball With Gershwin
[Review of Ray Charles and Cleo Laine, RCA CPL2-1831]." *Stereo Review* 37/6
(Dec. 1976): 130. **[adq]**
Mixed review. ". . . Though there are other songs here—*It Ain't Necessarily So* or the
several variations on *Summertime*—that take beautifully and easily to the jazz approach,
something is absent from this skillful, consistently stylized production. That something is *heart*,
the humanely uncritical understanding of fallible humanity that fills the work . . ." *See*: **D545**

B1208.   "This Month's Jazz: Miles Davis: '*Porgy and Bess*' . . . Columbia CL-1274."
American Record Guide 25/8 (Apr. 1959): 555. **[+]**
"Seldom is such care lavished on a jazz package . . ." Referring to Gil Evans'
arrangements "for a nineteen piece orchestra: . . . They are marvels of intricate, subtle
sensitivity, written somehow with both justice to Gershwin and appreciation for the orchestra's
only soloist, Miles Davis . . . Davis dominates the album, and he does so in the manner of an
artist . . ." *See*: **D540, B1194**

B1209.   ULLMAN, Michael. "Porgy and Bess [Jim Cullum Jazz Band]_[record reviews]." *High Fidelity* 38 (July 1988): 58. *See*: **D539**

B1210.   WILSON, John S. "Louis and Ella and Ray and Cleo: Whether the stars are Louis Armstrong and Ella Fitzgerald or Ray Charles and Cleo Laine, Porgy and Bess Get Lost in the shuffle." *High Fidelity* 26 (Dec. 1976): 95. Armstrong/Fitzgerald: **[adq]**; Charles/Lane: **[-]**

Largely negative review of the **Verve VE 2-2507 (from VE 6040-2) Ella Fitzgerald and Louis Armstong excerpts from P&B album** and the two-disc **RCA Victor CPL 2-1831 Cleo Laine and Ray Charles** album of the same. ". . . The Armstrong/Fitzgerald set is a pleasant collection, the Charles/Lane set is essentially irritating. And Laine's atrocious performance of 'I Loves You, Porgy' . . . makes one acutely conscious of the absence of the female singer who could have played most provocatively opposite Charles: Nina Simone." *See*: **D542 (Armstrong/Fitzgerald), D545 (Laine/Charles)**

B1211.   _____. "A 'Porgy' for Jazz Band." *NYTimes*, June 28, 1988, Section C, p. 18. Wilson reviews the jazz rendition of P&B by **Jim Cullum's Jazz Band** at the 92d St. Y in New York City as part of JVC Jazz Festival. *See*: **D539**

B1212.   WILSON, John S. "A Wide Variety of Porgys and Besses." *NYTimes*, May 24, 1959, sction 2, p. 15.

A survey of recordings of selections intended to capitalize on the release of the film version. Included in the review were: **Louis Armstrong and Ella Fitzgerald (Verve)**, which Wilson called "the handsomest, most ambitious, and most rewarding set"; **Diahann Carroll and the André Previn Trio (United Artists); Sammy Davis, Jr. and Carmen McRae (Decca); Pearl Bailey (Roulette); Harry Belafonte and Lena Horne (Victor); Miles Davis (Columbia); Ralph Burns** with an eleven-piece group and smaller jazz ensemble **(Decca)**; **Monte Kelly's "Stereorchestrations" (Carlton); Mundell Lowe (Camden)**; and **Hank Jones (Capitol).** Wilson commented on all of the albums, seeming to be the least pleased with the Sammy Davis/McRae, Pearl Bailey, and Belafonte/Horne discs. *See*: **D542 (Armstrong/Fitzgerald), D541 (Davis/McRae), D526 (Bailey), D527 (Belafonte/Horne), D540 (Miles Davis), D546 (Mundell Lowe)**

B1213. "World of Entertainment: Here at Home, "Porgy and Bess." Recording from the film . . ." *High Fidelity* 9/8 (Aug. 8, 1959): 69.

Review of **Columbia OL 5410**, the sound track from the movie. ". . . The guiding hand behind this . . . belongs to **André Previn** . . . His musical emendations do not in any way change the spirit or intent of the composer's music, and the production is a most skillful accomplishment all round . . ." *See*: **D1116**

W27. *STRIKE UP THE BAND* (1927)

B1214.   HOLDEN, Stephen. "Recordings View: Ask Not Which Show Tunes Won the Tony." *NYTimes*, Feb. 2, 1992, Arts & Leisure Section, pp. 27, 35.

A lengthy article dealing with the cast albums for the current Broadway shows *The Will Rogers Follies* and *The Secret Garden*, and including information and a review of the recent (1991) **Elektra/Nonesuch/Roxbury** recording of the 1927 version of *Strike Up the Band*. ". . . In addition to its historical interest, there is a certain poignancy to the release of 'Strike Up the Band,' for it recalls a time when Broadway musicals were much closer to the heart of American popular culture than they are today . . ." *See*: **D564**

B1215.   TRAUBNER, [Richard]. "Classical Broadway PORTER: *Fifty Million Frenchmen* . . . GERSHWIN: *Strike Up the Band* . . . Nonesuch 79273 . . ." *American Record Guide* 55/2 (Mar./Apr. 1992): 220. **[adq]**
A brief and lukewarm review of the *Strike Up the Band* recording, focusing more on the inadequacies of the show itself rather than this recorded performance.
See: **D564**

W48. *MY ONE AND ONLY* (derivative) (1983)

B1216. "New Releases." *Show Music* 3/2 (Feb. 1984): n. p. **[-]**
Review of the **Atlantic 80110-1-E** album of *My One and Only*. ". . . [T]he whole enterprise has a flatness and lack of vitality that is most curious and disappointing for a show which features some of the Gershwins' most engaging songs . . ." *See*: **D465.1**

B1217.   REILLY, Peter. "My One and Only." *Stereo Review* 49/3 (Mar. 1984): 98. **[+]**
Positive review of the original cast album with **Tommy Tune and Twiggy (Atlantic 80110-1)**. ". . . When Twiggy sings *Boy Wanted* in counterpoint with Tune crooning *Soon*, the listener is catapulted right into the theater . . . It would be difficult to resist any musical that has, in superb new arrangements by Wally Harper, such immortal songs as *He Loves and She Loves*, *'S Wonderful!*, *Strike Up the Band*, *Nice Work if You Can Get It*, and *Funny Face*." *See*: **D465.1**

PIANO MUSIC

B1218.   DARRELL, R. D. "Classical Reviews: GERSHWIN: Works for Piano (29). Pennario . . . Angel EMI 4DS 37359 (D) . . ." *High Fidelity-Musical America Edition* 36/11 (Nov. 1986): 78.
Review of Leonard Pennario's recording of the *Song-book* and other piano pieces. While acknowledging Pennario's virtuosity, Darrell concluded: ". . . I feel that the 1973 Nonesuch versions by William Bolcom, while certainly exhibiting less bravura pianistically, capture more of the essential Gershwinian lilt and insouciance of these eternally haunting melodies . . ." *See*: **D601 (Pennario), D616 (Bolcom)**

B1219. _____. "Gershwin, George . . . Orchestral Works: *Second Rhapsody for Piano and Orchestra* (arr. McBride), *Three Preludes* (orch. Stone) [Overtures, et al] . . . Ralph Votapek, piano; Boston Pops Orchestra; Arthur Fiedler, cond. London Phase-4 SPC 21185 . . ." *Records in Review 1980 Edition*, p. 143-144. **[*]**
". . . The minor work is the set of three early preludes, blown up here in elaborate large-orchestra transcriptions . . . The arrangements can't dissuade me from the belief that the preludes are best left in their original form . . ." *See*: **D657, D1089**

B1220.   DITSKY, John. "American Piano Music. . . Eric Parkin, piano. PREAMBLE PRCD 1776 . . ." *Fanfare* 11/4 (March/April 1988): 253-254. **[+]**
Review of the above named CD. ". . . Let us note at the outset that this CD features idiomatically fine readings of American works, both familiar and relatively obscure, and in a variety of styles . . . Highly recommended and auspicious." *See*: **D635**

B1221. _____. "Classical Recordings: GERSHWIN: Concerto in F (trans. Castagnetta). Three Preludes. Rhapsody in Blue (trans. Gershwin) . . .

Stradivari Classics SCD-8000 (compact disc) . . . Norman Krieger, piano . . ."
Fanfare 12/1 (Sept.-Oct. 1988): 155-156. **[+]** *See:* Full entry under
"Concerto," D593

B1222.   **E., R. A.** "New Recordings: Miniatures, Preludes [KAPP LP 9029]. Perry O'Niel,
pianist." *Musical America* 79/8 (July 1959): 22. **[+]**
Review.

B1223.   **FRENCH, Gilbert.** "Gershwin: [7] *Preludes, Blue Monday [Piano Suite], Seven
Miniatures in Gershwin's Hand, Rhapsody in Blue* [for solo piano] Alicia Zizzo,
pa.—Carlton 6600052 (Allegro) . . ." *American Record Guide* 60/5 (Sept.-Oct.
1997): 133.
Generally a mixed review of this effort. ". . . Perhaps the final judgement must be
based on whether Zizzo the researcher [who is a musicologist] . . . wins out over Zizzo the
pianist—a tough call when so much of the material is not only preliminary by nature but blandly
performed." *See:* **D610**

B1224.   **HERMAN, Justin R.** "Lend an Ear . . . From One Serious Collector to Another."
Fanfare 12/1 (September/October 1988): 388. **[+]**
Brief review of the MCA Classics MCAD-6226 Richard and John Contiguglia album
of Percy Grainger transcriptions. ". . . The Contiguglias play as to the manner born, and MCA's
slightly overbright sonics are exciting . . ." *See:* **D584**

B1225.   **JABLONSKI, Edward.** "Unlikely Corners . . .George Gershwin at the Piano
(20th Fox 3013) . . ." *American Record Guide* 26/1 (Sept. 1959): 76.
Review of the album which includes a complete piano solo version of RiB. ". . . The
sound of these records is remarkable and the performances astonishingly realistic. There is no
doubt that Gershwin is playing, and only intermittently are you aware, because of the intrusion
of typical player-piano figurations . . . that you are listening to a piano roll rather than an actual
performance . . . [F]uture interpreters of the work [RiB] are referred to the composer's clean,
rhythmic, and unsentimental rendition to get an idea how it should really be done . . ." *See:*
D1153

B1226.   **KOLDYS, Mark.** "Guide to Records . . . Three Preludes; Six Songs . . . Naxos
8.550341 . . . Leon Bates, piano." *American Record Guide* 54/3 (May/June
1991): 59. **[adq]**
Brief review of this performance of the Preludes by Bates. *See:* **D612, D700**

B1227.   _____. "Guide to Records . . . GERSHWIN: *Piano Concerto in F; 3 Preludes*
. . . Peter Jablonski . . . Royal Philharmonic . . . London 430542
. . ." *American Record Guide* 55/2 (Mar./Apr. 1992): 61. **[adq]**
". . . Jablonski does a fine job of the first two *Preludes* . . . but 3 is not extrovert
enough . . ." *See:* **D743**

B1228.   _____. "[*Rhapsody in Electric Blue*] Gershwin: *Rhapsody in Blue; Three
Preludes; An American in Paris; Concerto in F;* Baker: *Tin Pan Hands (Homage
to George Gershwin)* . . . [Jeffrey Reid Baker, synthesizers] Newport Classic
60042 [CD]." *American Record Guide* 51/2 (Mar.-Apr. 1988): 37. **[adq]**
This version contains seventy-one minutes of music. ". . . There's little point in
debating the utility or even the propriety of this kind of electronic realization; either you like
this sort of thing or you don't. If you do, Baker's accomplishment is probably as good as any

you are likely to hear . . . Baker's own work, *Tin Pan Hands*, is . . . "a pleasant, inoffensive trifle, but to me it doesn't sound like Gershwin . . ." *See*: **D378**

B1229.   M., J. "[Review of *Song Book, Three Preludes, Promenade*, etc., Leonard Pennario (Angel DS-37359)]." *Fanfare* 10/1 (May 1986-1987): 146. *See*: **D601, D638**

B1230.   MILLER, P. "[Record Review] Gershwin . . . Leonard Pennario, piano . . ." *American Record Guide* 49/6 (Nov.-Dec. 1986): 13-14.
Appraisal of Angel EMI DS-37359 (Songbook, Preludes, and other piano music). After thorough coverage of the contents of Pennario's solo album, the reviewer indicated ". . . Pennario's earlier recording of the [piano] preludes (RCA 2731) is stricter and therefore preferred . . ." *See*: **D601, D638**

B1231.   NORTH, James H. "Classical Recordings . . . GERSHWIN: Concerto in F. Three Preludes . . . Peter Jablonski, piano; Vladimir Ashkenazy conducting the Royal Philharmonic Orchestra.   LONDON 430 542 . . ." *Fanfare* 15/4 (Mar./Apr. 1992): 192-193.
". . . [The] three preludes are played with competence but no special insight . . ." *See*: Full entry under **"Concerto."**

B1232.   PALMER, Richard. "Oscar Peterson: The George Gershwin Songbook." *Jazz Journal International* 38/12 (Dec 1985): 27.
A glowing review of Peterson's 1952 trio recording, re-mastered for Verve 823 249-1. *See*: **D1054**

B1233.   PFAFF, T. "Reproducer Software (the Elektra/Nonesuch 'Gershwin Plays Gershwin, the Piano Rolls')." *Piano & Keyboard* 172 (Jan.-Feb. 1995): 69. *See*: **D1134**

B1234.   RABINOWITZ, Peter J. "Classical Recordings . . . Gershwin . . . Leon Bates, piano. Naxos 8.550341 . . ." *Fanfare* 15/1 (Sept.-Oct. 1991): 223. **[+]**
Positive review of Bate's efforts on the Three Preludes, Corea, etc. *See*: **D612, D700**

B1235.   RABINOWITZ, Peter J. "[Review of] GERSHWIN: The Authentic George Gershwin, Volume 3: 1931–1937. Jack Gibbons, piano . . . WHL 2082 . . ." *Fanfare* (Jan.-Feb. 1995): 162-163.
Mixed review of this album. *See*: **D590**

B1236.   _____. "[Review of] GERSHWIN: Piano Music. Anna-Stella Schic, piano. Discques FY et du Solstice SoCD 114 . . ." *Fanfare* (Jan.-Feb. 1995): 163.
Negative review *See*: **D605**

B1237.   TEACHOUT, Terry. "Gershwin: Complete Works for Piano and Orchestra; Preludes for Piano [Oscar Levant, André Kostelanetz, Morton Gould, Eugene Ormandy, Philadelphia Orchestra]_MK42514 [record reviews]." *High Fidelity* 38 (July 1988): 57. *See*: **D129, D306, D630**

B1238.   VROON, Donald R. "Gershwin for Solo Piano . . . Dag Achatz—BIS 404 . . ." *American Record Guide* 52/3 (May-June 1989): 51.
"I didn't expect a Swedish to play Gershwin as idiomatically as André Watts does—

and he doesn't . . . Most Americans will respond more readily to Bolcom (Nonesuch 79151) or to Watts . . . For the Songbook, I have never heard better than Clive Lythgoe **[D595]** . . ."

B1239. _____."Guide to Records . . . Gershwin: Songbook . . . Lythgoe, piano, Concerto 0016 . . ." *American Record Guide* 53/2 (Mar./Apr. 1990): 53. **[+]**
". . . [The Songbook has been] recorded by pianists like Leonard Pennario and André Watts, but this is the best recording ever . . ." *See:* **D595**

B1240. WHEELER, Scott. "Classical Recordings . . . GERSHWIN: Three Preludes. Fascinatin' Rhythm. Somebody Loves Me. Liza. The Man I Love. I Got Rhythm. Strike Up the Band. COREA: Twenty Children's Songs . . . Leon Bates, piano. Naxos 8.550341 . . ." *Fanfare* 15/4 (Mar./Apr. 1992): 193-194. **[adq]**
With a recommendation to the two-disc set George Gershwin Plays George Gershwin (Pearl—GEMM CDS 9483), the reviewer's reaction to both Bate's arrangements and playing is mixed. ". . . Bates plays the first two preludes with elegance and sensitivity. In the third, he is overly aggressive—by over-dotting the swing eighths, he makes this jazzy piece sound Russian . . ." *See:* **D612, D700**

CHAMBER MUSIC

W38. *LULLABY FOR STRING QUARTET* (1919–1920)

B1241. SIMMONS, Walter. "[Review of *Lullaby,* perf. by the Dickerman String Quartet (Thor Capella MTH-275)]." *Fanfare* 9/3 (1985-1986): 111. *See:* **D668**

W47. *PROMENADE (Walking the Dog)* (1937)

B1242. A., V. "Gershwin: An American in Paris. Catfish Row (Suite from Porgy and Bess). Promenade . . . [etc.] . . . Moss Music MCD 10035 . . ." *Fanfare* 10/4 (1986-1987): 135. **[adq]**
See: Full entry under **"AiP."**

B1243. "Walking the Dog with Uncle Harry; Michael Tilson Thomas talks to Andrew Keener." *Gramophone* 63/745 (June 1985): 20-21.
A general article which, however, does elucidate about Thomas' **CBS Masterworks IM 39699** recording with the **Los Angeles Philharmonic.** ". . . Gershwin's own arrangement for chamber orchestra of the famous *Promenade [Walkin' the Dog]*, discovered seven years ago in a box of scoring material at the RKO studios warehouse . . ." was used for Thomas' version on this record. Gershwin purists may want to compare this performance with the original soundtrack available on the Music Masters album "The Gershwins in Hollywood, 1931-1964," as well as on the videocassette of the film *Shall We Dance?* (The Nostalgia Merchant NM 8077). *See:* **D773 (Tilson Thomas), D680, D1097 (Gershwins in Hollywood), F10 (Shall We Dance)**

ANTHOLOGIES

As pointed out earlier, the entries in this section include anthologies of Gershwin's classical and song production mixed in the same album, as well as compilations of works by Gershwin and other composers on the same recording. Gershwin songs *only* will be included under the sections **"Songs, vocal treatment"** and **"Songs, instrumental treatment."** Mixtures of vocal and instrumental treatment on the same album are included in this section.

Compilations of Gershwin's classical compositions will be found under their respective titles.

B1244.   BURWASSER, Peter. [Rv of NBC Symphony; Arturo Toscanini, conducting; RCA Victor Gold Seal 09026-60207-2]. *Fanfare* (Nov.-Dec. 1992): 242. Positive review. *See:* **D757**

B1245.   CONNELLY, Robert M. "Gershwin: *The Gershwin Collection: An Hisstorical Treasury . . .*" *American Record Guide* 51/2 (Mar.-Apr. 1988): 35-36. **[-] [*]**
The reviewer was very disappointed in this five-disc set, resulting in what I believe to be a rather too harsh assessment of this voluminous collection: ". . . Of all the archival material which exists in the vaults of MCA, RCA, CBS, and EMI, we have in this set only two selections [performed] by Mr. Gershwin himself . . . Diana Ross doing an up-tempo version of 'I loves you Porgy' is really awful . . ." After indicating his preferences for recordings of AiP and the Concerto, Connelly concluded: ". . . [T]his set cannot be recommended . . ." This item also reviewed in *ARG* 51/1 (Jan-Feb 88): 35, by Robert McConnell. *See:* **D721**

B1246.   D., R. D. "[Review of] JASCHA HEIFETZ: "Heiftetz Plays Gershwin and Music of France." *High Fidelity* 16/1 (Jan. 1966): 99.
A generally positive review of the **RCA Victor LM 2856** album. "While the present mélange of disarrangements might seem to be ridiculously antiquated nowadays, in actual hearing it is tantalizingly sugar-coated by Heifetz's ingenuities of transcription and his supreme executant skills. . ." *See:* **D738**

B1247.   DANKNER, Stephen. "[Review of] Music Masters 01612-67104-2, 'By George—Gershwin's Greatest Hits'" *Sonneck Society Bulletin* 20/3 (Fall 1994): 34. **[+]**
A complimentary review of this album by the **Atlantic Brass Quintet**. *See:* **D698**

B1248.   DARRELL, R. D. "Tapes . . . Rhapsody in Blue; Song Transcriptions: Someone to Watch Over Me, Liza, Love Walked In, Bidin' My Time, Maybe, I Got Rhythm Roger Williams, piano; Symphony of the Air; Willis Page, cond (in the Rhapsody); Orchestra, Marty Gold, cond. (in the Song Transcriptions) . . . Kapp KST 41008 . . ." *Records in Review 1960 Edition.* Great Barrington, MA: Wyeth Press, p. 424-425. **[+]**
". . . The Williams tape . . . is a wholly delightful sleeper—the first recorded performance of the *Rhapsody* by a popular pianist (other than Gershwin himself) which is entirely free from mannerisms, sentimentality, and overinflation. Williams himself plays with admirable straightforwardness and vivacity . . ." About the transcriptions of the songs for piano and orchestra: ". . . "[William's] *Liza*, both catchy and dazzlingly virtuosic, his highly original treatment of *I Got Rhythm*, his unnaccompanied nocturnelike *Love Walked In* [etc] . . . make this a tape that no Gershwinian can resist . . . ." *See:* **D782**

B1249.   DYER, Richard. "Marcus Roberts, Piano, Portraits in Blue: Music by Gershwin and James P. Johnson, Sony Classical." *Boston Globe,* Calendar Section, June 1996.
A typically astute review by Dyer in which he justifiably points out the problems with improvising on the RiB. "The real attraction [however] is a rare opportunity to hear James P. Johnson's 'Yamekraw' . . ." *See:* **D769**

B1250.   ERICSON, Raymond. "Recordings: Gershwin Stars in a Display of American

Musical Variety." *NYTimes,* Aug 18, 1985, p. H 19.

Review of four recorded albums of G's music. In re: Michael Tilson Thomas' album **(CBS Masterworks M 39699)**: ". . . If Mr. Thomas's handling of the 'Rhapsody' suggests Gershwin's original style, the piece gets what has become the more customary handling from **Misha Dichter,** piano, with the **Philharmonia Orchestra, Neville Marriner, conducting (Philips 411-123)**. ". . . Mr. Dichter treats the music more conventionally without sacrificing its jazzy elements, and Mr. Marriner brings an appropriate verve and grace to Grofe's symphonic last orchestration . . . Highlights from Gershwin's 'Porgy and Bess' are sung by **Roberta Alexander and Simon Estes on a Philips compact disk (412 720-2)** . . . here they appear with the **Berlin Radio Symphony** under **Leonard Slatkin.** Mr. Estes is first-class not only in Porgy's music but also in a couple of Sportin' Life's songs. Miss Alexander is equally fine in Bess's music but less at home in Clara's 'Summertime' and Serena's 'My Man's Gone Now' . . ." The fourth album reviewed is flutist **Pierre Rampal's "Fascinatin' Rampal."** ". . . The recording is attractive in its special way, but one wishes Mr. Rampal had kept to his simplest best, as in his lovely version of 'A Foggy Day' . . ." *See:* **D357, D773 (Thomas), D267 (Dichter/Marriner), D504 (Alexander/Estes), D87, D1060 (Rampal)**

B1251.   FRIEDWALD, Will. "The Dancing Man Who Also Sang Up a Storm: Two compilations of Astaire's recordings of many of his hits point up the importance of jazz in his swinging style." *NYTimes,* June 11, 1989, Arts/Leisure Section, p. H 29.

". . . The chance to reassess Astaire's singing in relation to its jazz influences comes with two double-CD reissues of his most important recordings, **'Starring Fred Astaire' (Columbia C2 44233)** . . . and **'The Astaire Story' (Polygram Verve 835 649-2** . . . [T]hese sessions [for Brunswick and Columbia] made between 1935 and 1940, feature the original commercial recordings of songs of Irving Berlin, George Gershwin, and Jerome Kern from the scores of all of Astaire's major 1930's musicals except 'The Gay Divorcee' . . . 'The Astaire Story' is an even more notable album, and constitutes Astaire's two finest hours as a recording artist . . . Recorded in December 1952, it consists of 34 vocals by Astaire and four instrumentals . . . In the 32-page color booklet that accompanies the set, Astaire writes, 'I'm grateful for the opportunity to become a sort of addition to the Jazz at the Philharmonic group . . .*" See:* **D796 (Columbia)**

B1252.   GANO, Peter. "Reviews of Recordings: George Gershwin Memorial Concert September 8, 1937 . . . Citadel Records CT 7025 . . ." *The Sonneck Society Bulletin* 14/1 (Spring 1988): 45-46. **[+]**

Review of the recording, finally released in 1981, of the September 8, 1937, Hollywood Bowl All-Gershwin Memorial concert. Calling the album "a collector's item," Gano pointed out that this is "the only recording of Otto Klemperer conducting Gershwin. The composer's *Second Prelude* is arranged by the conductor [Klemperer] in a funeral style specifically for this occasion. This is a most interesting piece . . ." The reviewer also commented on Lily Pons' appearance at the concert, calling her rendition of *Summertime* "fascinating." *See:* **D749, W54a**

B1253.   GRUENINGER, Walter F. "Phonograph Records: *Gershwin Wonderland* . . . Columbia CS 8933 [also CL 2133] . . ." *Consumer Bulletin* 47/6 (June 1964): 16. **[+]**

In a four-line review, Grueninger gave this album, based on André Kostelanetz' 1963 All-Gershwin concert at Lincoln Center, his highest "AA" rating. *See:* **D745**

B1254.   _____. "Phonograph Records: *Heifetz Plays Gershwin and Music of France*

. . ." *Consumer Bulletin* 49/1 (Jan. 1966): 12. **[-]**

Grueninger gave a positive review to the **Heifetz** album **(RCA Victor LM 2856)** which was panned later in *Saturday Review*. *See*: **D738**

B1255.   "[Heifetz Record review] Heifetz Plays Gershwin and Music of France . . . ." *Library Journal* 90/22 (Dec. 15, 1965): 5376. **[-]**

Caustic review of **RCA Victor LSC 2856**. ". . . [A] more dubious tribute [to GG] would be hard to imagine. What we are given here are sober, literal, 'square' transcriptions . . . The playing is faultless and without a trace of style . . ." *See*: **D738**

B1256.   JABLONSKI, Edward. "Unlikely Corners . . .George Gershwin at the Piano (20th Fox 3013) . . ." *American Record Guide* 26/1 (Sept. 1959): 76.

Review of the album which includes a complete piano solo version of RiB. ". . . The sound of these records is remarkable and the performances astonishingly realistic. There is no doubt that Gershwin is playing, and only intermittently are you aware, because of the intrusion of typical player-piano figurations . . . that you are listening to a piano roll rather than an actual performance . . . [F]uture interpreters of the work [RiB] are referred to the composer's clean, rhythmic, and unsentimental rendition to get an idea how it should really be done . . ." *See*: **D1153**

B1257.   . "Unlikely Corners . . . The George Gershwin Story . . . [Symphony of the Air] (Epic SN-6034, two records) . . ." *American Record Guide* 26/4 (Dec. 1959): 318. **[-]**

Jablonski reflected upon the album ". . . consisting of a medley of everything. Yes, even a medley of *Rhapsody in Blue*, *An American in Paris*, and the *Concerto in F*, all of which are of course presented in much-abbreviated form. Another medley is devoted to 'Porgy and Bess' (the Robert Russell Bennett arrangement), and one to 'Gershwin on Broadway,' and one to 'Gershwin in Hollywood.' This last has some interest because it includes the posthumous *Back Bay Polka* and *One, Two, Three* from 'The Shocking Miss Pilgrim' . . . [I]t all seems like a skimpy hodge-podge to me . . ." *See*: **D246, F17**

B1258.   JABLONSKI, Edward. "Unlikely Corners . . . Gershwin in Brass (Everest SDBR-1047) . . ." *American Record Guide* 26/2 (Oct. 1959): 150. **[+]**

". . . It is refreshing to hear these melodies without the usual strings for a change. And they are very well played, without distortion . . . A very worth-while experiment . . ." *See*: **D783, D1085**

B1259.   I., J. F. "[Record reviews] 'Frederick Fennell Conducts Gershwin' . . ." *High Fidelity* 12/1 (Jan. 1962): 92. **[-]**

Brief but very condemning review of **Mercury PPS 2006**. *See*: **D998**

B1260.   LINKOWSKI, [Allen]. "Guide to Records . . . GERSHWIN: *Concerto in F; Rhapsody in Blue; Song-book* Peter Donohue . . . Simon Rattle—Angel/EMI 54280 [avail. in CD, same no.] . . ." *American Record Guide* 55/2 (Mar./Apr. 1992): 61-62. **[+]**

Overall, Linkowski considers this "a wonderful record, highly recommended." *See*: Full entry under **"Rhapsody in Blue."**

B1261.   . "[Review of] The Authentic GERSHWIN: Volume 2: 1925-1930 . . . Jack Gibbons, piano P-ASV 2077 (Koch) . . ." *American Record Guide* 58/1 (Jan./Feb. 1995): 100-101.

Mixed review. "... [T]he unique spirit of the composer is missing. Gibbons is rather rhythmically stiff, lacking Gershwin's subtle flexibility. And though he plays almost everything at breakneck speed, that manic joy that is so much a part of the real thing is missing. Yet I enjoyed this record, in small doses; in its own way it is illuminating." *See*: **D589**

B1262.   "Miscellaneous—Recommended, Gershwin: Frederick Fennell Conducts . . ."
    Library Journal 87/3 (Feb. 1, 1962): 542. **[+]**
    In what seems to be a musically uninformed opinion, this brief review recommends **Mercury's PPS 2006**. *See*: **D998**

B1263.   "The New Recordings." *Harper's Magazine* 217 (Sept. 1958): 102.
    Review of **Dot DLP 3111, "The Masters Write Jazz (Stravinsky, Hindemith, Gershwin, Copland, Milhaud, Tansman)"** album. Without identifying the pieces on this album, the writer expressed the view that ". . . Gershwin aside, the music is not remotely to be classed as jazz . . . recognizable to a jazz specialist . . ." *See*: **D767**

B1264.   "Overview: American Composers." *American Record Guide* 58/4 (July/August 1995): 60-64.
    A helpful overview of currently available recordings of music of American composers that has been recorded more than once or twice. Recordings of AiP, Concerto (Slatkin, Bernstein, and Fiedler **[D8]**), and RiB (Bernstein **[D43]**, Previn **[D335]**) are covered in a comparative manner.

B1265.   "Recordings Reports II: Miscellaneous LPs." *Saturday Review* 48/44 (Oct. 30, 1965): 92. **[-]**
    In a review of **RCA Victor's LM 2856**, featuring **Jascha Heifetz**, the writer found that "[n]either Heifetz's tone nor his mode of musical thought are inherently helpful to the excerpts he has chosen for his transcriptions, the two together tend to prettify and make synthetic an order of expression which is, in its own terms, self-sufficient and genuine . . ." *See*: **D738**

B1266.   **SPOTO, Donald.** "Classic Gershwin: Various Artists, Columbia MK 42516, CD." *Audio* (Feb. 1988): 121-122. **[-]** *See*: **D552, D646, D777**

B1267.   **STEARNS, David Patrick.** in *USA TODAY*. **I Got Rhythm: The Music of George Gershwin (Smithsonian Recordings**, four CDs $59.96, tapes $54.96).
    This compilation is intelligently divided according to performance style: One CD for jazz performers (Billie Holiday, Benny Goodman), another for stage and screen performers (Gertrude Lawrence, Fred Astaire), another for pop singers (Lena Horne, Judy Garland) and one for the concert works, many performed by Gershwin himself. Rhapsody in Blue is heard in an early, swinging recording by the Paul Whiteman Orchestra. *See*: **D742**

B1268.   **TEACHOUT, Terry.** "Gershwin: Rhapsody in Blue; Selections from the Song-book; Gershwin-Kay: Who Cares? [Andrew Litton, Royal Philharmonic Orchestra]_[compact disc reviews]." *High Fidelity* 38 (July 1988): 57. *See*: **D313**

B1269.   _____. "Gershwin: Orchestral Works [Leonard Slatkin, St. Louis Symphony] _[compact disc reviews]." *High Fidelity* 38 (July 1988): 57. *See*: **D682**

B1270.   **ULLMAN, Michael.** "The Gershwin Collection (George Gershwin, André Previn, Leonard Bernstein, Nathaniel Shilkret, London Symphony Orchestra, New York Philharmonic, Paul Whiteman Concert Orchestra) [Teledisc USA TD 10]_[record reviews]." *High Fidelity* 38 (July 1988): 57. *See*: **D721**

B1271.   **WATT, Douglas.** "Popular Records: Charm." *New Yorker* 54/4 (Mar 13, 1978): 126-133.

Substantial review of recordings including Gershwin songs. "Coming across the restless, insistent, and absolutely first-rate George Gershwin tune 'Say So!' for the first time, on a new record called **'These Charming People' (RCA Victor ARL 1-2491),** was as pleasant as discovering . . . an unfamiliar turn of a path in Central Park . . ." Among other G tunes on this album, reviewed enthusiastically by Watt, are *These Charming People, The Half of It Dearie, Blues, Feeling I'm Falling, I Don't Think I'll Fall in Love Today, Hang On To Me,* and *The Babbitt and the Bromide.* Also included are the Smithsonian's "archival reconstructions" of *Lady, Be Good!* and the *Ziegfeld Follies of 1919.* Watts pointed out the duplications between these sets and the Monmouth-Evergreen recordings. *See*: **D942 (These Charming People), D459 (Lady, Be Good)**

B1272.   **WHEELER, Scott.** "Classical Recordings . . . GERSHWIN: Three Preludes. Fascinatin' Rhythm.   Somebody Loves Me. Liza. The Man I Love. I Got Rhythm. Strike Up the Band. COREA: Twenty Children's Songs . . . Leon Bates, piano. Naxos 8.550341 . . ." *Fanfare* 15/4 (Mar./Apr. 1992): 193-194. **[adq]**
See: Full entry under **"Piano Music."**

SONGS, VOCAL TREATMENT

B1273.   **ABEL.** "Album Reviews." *Variety* 200, Sept 7, 1955, 50.

Very complimentary review of **"The Popular Gershwin"** album, **RCA Victor LPM 6000.** Abel particularly liked the commentary by Arthur Schwartz on the enclosed kingsized booklet: ". . . [It] bespeaks authenticity in every detail . . ." *See*: **D913**

B1274.   **BROWN, Joe.** "Feinstein: Pop Crackles Again." *Washington Post,* May 15, 1987, Weekend section, p. 23.

Review of Feinstein's album **"Remember: Michael Feinstein Sings Irving Berlin" (Parnassus PR0-102)** with reference to his **"Pure Gershwin" album (Parnassus PR0-100).** ". . . As a singer, Feinstein has a somewhat uncertain baritone, with a tendency towards nasality. But his sincerity and affection for the songs is unquestionable . . ." In re: the "Pure Gershwin" album, ". . . This record displays his special affinity for G songs like 'Let's Call the Whole Thing Off' and 'They All Laughed' . . ." *See*: **D837**

B1275.   **C., G.** "[Review of Julia Migenes-Johnson Sings Gershwin (RCA ARL 1-5323)]." *Fanfare* 8/3 (1984-1985): 169-170. **[+]**

"Migenes comes across very well in her album, rather better than Fernandez . . . The big-band-style accompaniments are varied and imaginative . . . All told, a fine, entertaining disc . . ." *See*: **D905**

B1276.   **CAMNER, James.** Gershwin: He Loves and She Loves . . . Koch International Classics . . ." *Fanfare* 14/4 (Mar.-Apr. 1991): 217-218. **[adq]**

A mixed review praising Judy Kaye, soprano, but expressing the often stated view that "purists might object." *See*: **D877**

B1277.   "Composers and Lyricists Corner" *Show Music* 3/3 (June 1984): n. p. **[-]**
One-paragraph review of Pablo D 2312140, **"Nice work if you can get it: Ella Fitzgerald & André Previn do Gershwin"** album. ". . . Miss Fitzgerald's voice is, regretfully, showing the ravages of time, and we found parts of this recording painful to listen to . . ." *See:* **D839**

B1278.   "Composers' and Lyricists' Corner." *Show Music* 4/4 (Feb. 1986): 32. **[+]**
Complimentary review of **Audiophile Records AP-1, "Lee Wiley Sings the Songs of George & Ira Gershwin & Cole Porter."** "Lee Wiley may have been the first singer to do a series of albums devoted to composers over a period of several years . . . The first was done for Liberty Shop in 1939 and featured the songs of George Gershwin . . . The albums have been reissued on other labels . . . but never with the mono originals in the complete form in which they were initially released. This has been corrected [in this album] . . . Miss Wiley is sublime . . . [S]he was a truly unique vocalist who had a wonderfully smokey quality in her voice, and her phrasing was superb. She gets the most from every word in a song; even the most over-exposed lyric becomes something new in her treatment . . ." *See:* **D962**

B1279.   "Composers' and Lyricists' Corner." *Show Music* 4/4 (Feb. 1986): 33. **[+]**
This is a review of the CD release by **Polygram (three-disc package, no. 825 024-2)** of **"Ella Fitzgerald Sings the George and Ira Gershwin Song Book."** The review points out that the original five-record boxed set included a bonus 7-inch EP record with Nelson Riddle conducting Gershwin instrumental pieces *(Promenade, March of the Swiss Soldiers, Fidgety Feet,* and the piano preludes). This release doesn't include the music on the bonus record. The reviewer called Ella's version of *But Not for Me* "classic." *See:* **D840**

B1280.   "Composers' & Lyricists' Corner. *Show Music* 5/1 (June 1986): 30-31. **[+] [*]**
Descriptive review of **Reference Recordings RR 19, "Marni Nixon Sings Gershwin."** ". . . [This album] is her first excursion into the field of popular music for record, and it is delightful. . . Miss Nixon's program is similar to the recordings of Joan Morris, but the songs sung here are done with theatrical flair . . ." *See:* **D908**

B1281.   "Composers and Lyricists." *Show Music* 4/3 (Oct. 1986): 30. **[+]**
Calling the album "a delight and a treasure," this is quite a detailed review of Feinstein's **"Pure Gershwin," Parnassus PR 0100.** *See:* **D837**

B1282.   "Composers' & Lyricists' Corner." *Show Music* 5/4 (Fall 1987): 36-37. **[+]**
Review of **New Horizons NH 01:59:39 "Steve & Eydie and Friends Celebrate Gershwin."** ". . . This disc is . . . taken from a previously-issued analog recording, OUR LOVE IS HERE TO STAY, which is the title of a TV special from whence these tracks originated. The disc includes Steve & Eydie's exciting 'Gershwin Medley' (20 songs in just over 12 minutes) . . ." *See:* **D892**

B1283.   "Composers' & Lyricists' Corner." *Show Music* 5/4 (Fall 1987): 36.
Review of the two-record Milan A 249 & A250, **"Gershwin in the Movies."** ". . . If you don't mind the opera-overtones, a good collection representing Gershwin's music, but it should be noted that all the Fernandez tracks come from a previous Milan release . . . A 215, so you probably won't want these discs if you already have that album . . ." *See:* **D711**

B1284.   "Composers' & Lyricists' Corner." *Show Music* 5/4 (Fall 1987): 35. **[-] [*]**

Comparatively lengthy review of **Angel Records DS 47454, "Kiri Sings Gershwin."**
". . . The problem with this recording, and it's more a stylistic one than anything else, is its star, Dame Kiri . . . Yes, the lady sings well, she does make the *attempt* at musical theatre singing, but it's like . . . well, going to a *theatre* to hear Barbara Cook sing 'Them There Eyes' . . ."
See: **D940**

B1285.   DITSKY, John. "Collections . . . Cabaret Songs . . . Sarah Walker, mezzo-soprano . . . Meredian CDE 84167 . . ." *Fanfare* 12/6 (July/August 1989): 290. **[+]**
Brief review. ". . . What is exceptional about this release . . . is a) the sheer quantity of the music recorded here [61:09] and b) the quality of Sarah Walker's readings . . ." *See*: **D953**

B1286.   GALEWSKI, M. "He Loves to Rhyme (Ira Gershwin recordings)." *American Record Guide* 41 (Jan. 1978): 3-4.

B1287.   GREEN, Benny. "The Ella Fitzgerald/Norman Granz Songbooks: Locus Classicus of American Song." *High Fidelity/Musical America* 30 (Mar. 1980): 46-50. **[+] [*]**
Lengthy review including discussion of the songbook **Verve album VE 2-2525.**
". . . Ira Gershwin cooperated with Granz [the producer] from the beginning, expediting the presentation of obscure material and helping to select a mere fifty-three items from his late brother's vast reservoir of music. It is no doubt a measure of George Gershwin's stature that it required so many tracks even to hint at his range and fecundity . . ." *See*: **D840**

B1288.   GRUENINGER, Walter F. "Phonograph Records . . . 'The Gershwin Years' . . ." *Consumer Bulletin* 42/12 (Dec. 1959): 32. **[-]**
Review of **Decca's DXSZ 7160,** with **George Bassman** conducting and arranging.
". . . When it comes to performers, it impresses me as a low-budget job . . ." *See*: **D808**

B1289.   _____. "Phonograph Records: *Ella Fitzgerald Sings the George and Ira Gershwin Songbook.* Vol. 1 . . . Verve MGVS 6077 . . ." *Consumer Bulletin* 43/4 (Apr. 1960): 34. **[+]**
In a very brief evaluation, the reviewer said: "This is the way Gershwin should be sung! What a magnificent, understanding artist is Ella Fitzgerald . . . And the Riddle arrangements and accompanying band are as good as you can imagine . . ." *See*: **D840**

B1290.   HITCHCOCK, Wiley H. "Regarding Recordings." *Newsletter: Institute for Studies in American Music* 18/1 (Nov. 1987): 5. **[adq]**
". . . Two things are interesting about the fifteen songs on **Kiri Sings Gershwin** . . . One is their accompaniments' orchestrations, all but three carefully-researched and reconstructed originals . . . and beautifully prepared and conducted by John McGlinn. The other is the mixed blessing of Dame Kiri Te Kanawa's performances: in lustrous voice, she gives us, with extremely strange results, an amazing lesson in how to turn Gershwin into a clone of Victor Herbert and a composer of, I swear, turn-of-the-century operetta airs." *See*: **D940**

B1291.   J. "[Reviews] Vocal: Gershwin Songs. Wilhemenia Fernandez (s) . . ." *The New Records* 52/3 (May 1984): 12. **[+]**
In a very brief review of this album (**Milan A-215**), the reviewer found Fernandez' "smallish voice—just right for these evergreen Gershwin tunes . . ." *See*: **D838**

B1292.   JABLONSKI, Edward. "Unlikely Corners." *American Record Guide* 24/1
        (Sept. 1957): 34-35. **Vaughan: [adq], Conners: [-] [*]**
        Review of the two albums: **"Sarah Vaughn Sings George Gershwin" (Mercury
MGP-2-101)** and **"Chris Connor Sings the George Gershwin Almanac of Song" (Atlantic
2-601).** Jablonski points out that there are twenty-two songs in the Vaughan album, and thirty-
two by Conner, being quick to observe that "Conner omits the verse, which is like leaving out
half the song." The reviewer states that these are not items worthy of collections of purists, but
". . . [I]f it's beautiful (most of the time, that is) singing you want, then the Sarah Vaughan
album is a must . . . Miss Vaughan richly invests the Gershwin melodies with a voice of quality
. . ." Jablonski did not care for Conners' unauthentic, "jazz" renditions in her album. *See:* **D950
(Vaughan), D824 (Conner)**

B1293. _____. "Unlikely Corners . . . The Gershwin Years (Decca DX-160) . . ."
        Fanfare 26/1 (Sept. 1959): 76-77. **[+] [*]**
        The reviewer concluded: ". . . I think I can recommend this set without reservation
(not that I always agreed with every interpretation) for its full-dimensioned song portrait of
Gershwin . . ." See: **D808**

B1294. _____. "Popular: George Gershwin: A Birthday Garland, Three Treasurable
        New Albums to Mark the Composer's Seventy-fifth Anniversary."
        Stereo Review 31 (Dec. 1973): 88-89. **[+] [*].**
        Review of Frances Gershwin's **"For George and Ira" album (Monmouth
Evergreen MES 7060), Ronny Whyte/Travis Hudson's "We Like a Gershwin Tune"** also
on **Monmouth Evergreen (MES 7061),** and **Bobby Short's "K-ra-zy for Gershwin" album
(Atlantic CD2 608).** Concerning the Whyte/Huston pressing, the reviewer concluded, " . . .
this album is required listening for many reasons, not the least of which is the inclusion . . . of
several rarities . . ." Jablonski was high in praise of the Frankie Gershwin disc, calling it "The
Year's Most Endearing Album . . . in which we hear some twenty songs sweetly and
charmingly sung . . . Enough to say that there is a consistent rightness about the album that
makes it perfect and perfectly unique . . ." The reviewer raved about Short's album and the
second piano performance work of Kay Swift. *See:* **D851 (Frances Gershwin), D957
(Whyte/Hudson), D933 (Short)**

B1295.   KOLDYS. "Gershwin: *The Gershwin Collection: An Historical Treasury . . .*"
        American Record Guide 51/2 (Mar.-Apr. 1988): 36. **[-] [*]** *See:* **D721**

B1296.   KOLODIN, Irving. "Mid-Month Recordings: From George to George with
        Love." *Saturday Review* 42/42 (Oct 17, 1959): 78-79.
        Kolodin was particularly fond of the three LP set of songs selected, arranged,
coordinated, and conducted by **George Bassman, Decca DXSZ 7160.** Kolodin was less
enthusiastic about **Warner Brothers' LP BS 1243** of the **RiB and AiP, Bert Shefter, piano.**
". . . It . . . shows a keen striving for 'authenticity' in attempting to reproduce the spirit and
tempi that prevailed when the pieces were new . . . The result . . . is both archaic and a little
uncomfortable . . ." Also reviewed lukewarmly were **RCA Victor's LPM 2058** of the
rhapsody from GG's piano roll performance, and **Verve MG 2115, "Mitzi Gaynor Sings the
Lyrics of Ira Gershwin."** See: **D728, D808 (Bassman), D75 & D345 (Warner Bros.,
Shefter), D850 (Gaynor)**

B1297. "A Potpourri of Records of Interest." *Show Music* 3/2 (Feb. 1984): n. p. **[adq]**

Short review of the reissue via **EmArcy Jazz Series, Polygram 814 187-1, "Sarah Vaughan—The George Gershwin Songbook."** ". . . We had a love-hate relationship with this album, loving it when Miss Vaughan is at her simplest, and hating it when she changed Gershwin music to fit her style . . ."

B1298. "A Potpourri of Records of Interest." *Show Music* 3/2 (Feb. 1984): n. p. [+]
Review of **"Wilhelmenia Fernandez—Gershwin Songs"** (Milan A215, via RCA France). ". . . Miss Fernandez doesn't fall into the pit so many opera singers do who sing 'down' to popular music. Rather, she adapts her style to the songs . . . This is a charming album . . ." *See*: **D838**

B1299. **SCHNEIDER, Edward.** "Kiri Sings Gershwin (compact disc reviews)." *NYTimes*, Dec. 6, 1987, p. H29. *See*: **D940**

B1300. **SIMON, Bill.** "George Byron." *Saturday Review* (Oct. 25, 1952): 82. [+]
Complimentary review of baritone **George Byron's** album **"Rediscovered Songs by George and Ira Gershwin."** ". . . The Byron-Hyman collaboration on 'The Half of It Dearie Blues' . . . is worth the price of the entire disc." *See*: **D820**

B1301. **SPAETH, Sigmund.** "Theatre on Disc: Gershwin Rarities." *Theatre Arts* 38/6 (June 1954): 10. [+]
Positive review of the **Walden 302 "Gershwin Rarities, Vol. I"** album. ". . . [According to this writer], here are four songs never before recorded [as of 1954]: 'Kickin' the Clouds,' 'Stiff Upper Lip,' 'Funny Face,' and 'Seventeen and Twenty One' . . ." *See*: **D806**

B1302. **STEARNS, David Patrick.** "News & Views." *Gramophone* 66/769 (June 1987).
Survey and brief reviews of recordings which came out during the commemorative year, 1987. Includes Kiri and Marni Nixon albums. *See*: Full entry at **B1042.**

B1303. **TEACHOUT, Terry.** "Gershwin: Songs [Kiri Te Kanawa, John McGlinn, New Princess Theater Orchestra]_[record reviews]." *High Fidelity* 38 (July 1988): 56. *See*: **D940**

B1304. **UNTERMEYER, Louis, Edward Jablonski, and Miles Kreuger.** *The Gershwin Years.*
This twenty-four page booklet was included with the highly acclaimed three-disc set of the same title, **Decca DXZ 160 (D808)**. Untermeyer wrote on "Gershwin . . . and America," Jablonski, an essay titled "George Gershwin: 'Modern Romantic,' and Krueger provided a listing of Broadway musicals and Hollywood films in which G music was used. Excellent notes for every song in the album are also provided, along with many illustrations. *See*: **D808**

B1305. **WATT, Douglas.** "Popular Records: A Pair of Gershwins." *New Yorker* 35/44 (Dec. 19, 1959): 132-134, 137. **[Decca: +] [Verve: adq]**
Review of the albums **Decca DL 8910-8912 "The Gershwin Years"** and **Verve 2367 431-435 "Ella Fitzgerald Sings the George and Ira Gershwin Song Books."** About the Decca set: ". . . 'The Gershwin Years' . . . is the most comprehensive and most enjoyable collection of Gershwin pieces I have so far encountered . . ." Of the Fitzgerald set: ". . . [The songs] have been dressed up with a lingering, caressing vocalism and a juiced-up orchestral treatment that, in too many instances, contain within them the seeds of obsolescence . . ." *See*:

D808 (Decca), D840 (Fitzgerald)

B1306.   **WILSON, John S.** "Through the Years with Gershwin." *NYTimes*, October 4, 1959, Records-Hi-Fi, section 2, part 1, p. 24.
Review of albums including three Gershwin ones: **"The Gershwin Years" (Decca), "Mitzi Gaynor Sings the Lyrics of Ira Gershwin" (Verve),** and **"The George Gershwin Story" (Epic Records).** About the fifty-five songs in Decca's "Gershwin Years," Wilson commented perceptively that ". . . George Bassman has arranged and conducted them with obvious affection and understanding. He has managed to suggest the flavor appropriate to each song when it was first heard . . ." Wilson had praise for Gaynor's ". . . proper attention to the fine points of diction which an Ira Gershwin lyric demands . . ." and found the Epic Records album ". . . a rather inexplicable Gershwin set . . ." *See*: **D808 (Decca), D850 (M. Gaynor), D246 ("The George Gershwin Story")**

B1307.   _____."Ella Does Right by George." *NY Times*, Nov. 29, 1959, Section II, p. 19. *See*: **D840**

B1308.   _____. "Ella Meets the Gershwins, with an Assist from Nelson Riddle." *High Fidelity* 10/1 (Jan. 1960): 63-64. *See*: **D840**

B1309.   "World of Entertainment: Here at Home . . . 'The Gershwin Years' . . ." *High Fidelity* 9/11 (Nov. 1959): 105. **[-]**
With glowing praise for the booklet which accompanies **Decca's DXZ 160, with George Bassman** conducting and arranging, the reviewer at the same time found the performances not to his liking. He compared the album to previous sets: **RCA Camden CAL 177** "and the fine two-record set released by **Walden (Walden 302/3),**" considering the present volume "decidedly inferior to both the earlier issues." Other reviewers disagreed with this opinion. *See*: **D808 (Bassman), D927 (RCA Camden), D806, D807 (Walden 302/3)**

B1310.   **YOUNGREN, William.** "Classical Recordings . . . Naughty Baby: Maureen McGovern . . ." *Fanfare* 13/2 (Nov.-Dec. 1989): 211.**[-]**
An obviously opinionated review from an apparently extreme purist. Youngren, responsible for the excellent series of Gershwin articles in *The New Republic* (**B993, B1044, B1120**), took this opportunity to vent his sarcasm: ". . . McGovern and her ilk are the pop equivalent of those opera directors who insist on giving us *Don Giovanni* set in the ghetto . . ." Youngren recommends the two-disc "Starring Fred Astaire" album (**D796**) for the "real thing." Astaire is indeed vintage and authentic Gershwin, after all George *wrote* some of these songs with Fred in mind, *but* the superb artistry and musicianship that is Maureen McGovern has its place too. *See*: **D900**

SONGS, INSTRUMENTAL TREATMENT

B1311.   **C., G.** "[Review of 'Fascinatin' [sic] Rhythm' album, Davis (Fanfare DFL 6006)]." *Fanfare* 8/4 (1984-1985): 234.

B1312.   "Composers and Lyricists." *Show Music* 4/4 (Feb. 1986): 32. **[+]**
Positive review of the **"Fascinatin' [sic] Rhythm" album, Fanfare DFL 6006 & (C) DFC 6006.** The set "is a collection of Gershwin's melodies in rather unusual arrangements for flute, piano, guitar, vibraphone, piccolos, drums, and harpsichord . . . We found the

recording to be a delightful change of pace."

B1313. "Composers and Lyricists Corner." *Show Music* 4/4 (Feb. 1986): 33. **[+]**
Review of **Fanfare DFL 7007 & (C) DFC 7007, "The Unknown George Gershwin,"** performed by **Kevin Cole, piano.** ". . . The *Lady, Be Good!* and *Girl Crazy* overtures presented in this album are George Gershwin's own arrangements (and exciting to hear, too) . . . Terrific album which Gershwin collectors will want in their libraries . . ."
See: **D981**

B1314. **CORLEONIS, Adrian.** "Classical Recordings . . . Gershwin's Piano Improv-
isations . . . Stradivari Classics SCD-6039 . . [Paul Posnak, piano]." *Fanfare* 13/6 (July/Aug. 1990): 149. **[+] [*]**
A thoughtful and interesting review. ". . . The verdict? It's Gershwin and, by today's standards, well-played—you'll enjoy it . . . Meanwhile . . . Artis Wodehouse is converting some 120 Gershwin piano rolls to information capable of reproduction by a computer-activated player piano . . ." *See*: **D1056**

B1315. **GOODFRIEND, James.** "Stereo Review's Selection of Recordings of Special
Merit: Best of the Month, Classical. Is Gershwin Classical or Popular? *Stereo Review* 31 (Sept. 1973): 79-80. **[+] [*]**
Laudatory review of **William Bolcom's Nonesuch H 71284** recording of the Songbook. Speaking of Bolcolm's pianistic abilities, the reviewer said, "I would say he plays like Gershwin himself, but better." *See*: **D616**

B1316. **JABLONSKI, Edward..** "Unlikely Corners . . . 'But You've Never Heard
Gershwin With Bongos (Warner Bros. W-1360) . . .'" *American Record Guide* 26/7 (March 1960): 588. **[+]**
"Don Ralke's orchestra plays a dozen of the Gershwin standbys, spieced [sic] up with percussion, which lends them a piquancy unexpected in these days of mood music. The Gershwin affinity to rhythm comes through beautifully, but so do the ballads . . ."
See: **D1059**

B1317. **TUTTLE, Raymond.** "GERSHWIN PLAYS GERSHWIN: THE PIANO ROLLS
. . . (realized by Artis Wodehouse). ELEKTRA NONESUCH 9 79287-2 . . ." *Fanfare* 17/5 (May/June 1994): 149-150. [+], [*].
Positive review of Wodehouse's work with the piano rolls. *See*: **D1134**

B1318. **ULLMAN, Michael.** "Naughty Baby [Adam Makowicz, Charlie Haden]-[record
reviews]." *High Fidelity* 38 (July 1988): 58. *See*: **D389**

B1319. _____. "Gershwin by Guitar [John Holmquist, Daniel Estrem]-[record
reviews]." *High Fidelity* 38 (July 1988): 58. *See*: **D741**

B1320. **WOODARD J.** "The 'Gershwin Connection' - GRP-2005 (GRUSIN, Dave)."
Down Beat 59/1 (Jan. 1992): 33-34.
Review of the album. *See*: **D734**

B1321. **YOUNGREN, William.** "[Review of 'Unknown George Gershwin' album by
Kevin Cole (Fanfare DFL-7007)]." *Fanfare* 9/4 (1985-1986): 161. *See*: **D981**

OVERTURES TO MUSICALS

B1322. **BURWASSER, Peter.** "Classical Recordings [Reviews] . . . BBC Philharmonic Orchestra: conducted by Yan Pascal Tortelier CHANDOS CHAN 9325 **[DDD]** *Girl Crazy*: **Overture** (orch. Don Rose); *Variations on "I Got Rhythm"; An American in Paris*; *Symphonic Suite: Catfish Row* (G's version); *Strike Up the Band*: Overture (orch. Don Rose) . . ." *Fanfare* 18/5 (May/June 1995): 195.

"This is a beautifully played and recorded selection of orchestral Gershwin. Personally, I prefer my Gershwin with a bit more grit . . . If it is spit-and-polish big-band Gershwin that you seek, this slick production will fit the bill. For versions of this music with more pizzazz, you can't go wrong with the budget-priced Vox Box set with Slatkin and the St. Louis, which also includes the Gershwin version of music from Porgy." See: **D3, D1088**

B1323. **C., G.** "[Review of Broadway Overtures, Gershwin (CBS MK 42240)]." *Fanfare* 10/6 (1986-1987): 110. *See:* **D1090**

B1324. "Composers' & Lyricists' Corner." *Show Music* 5/4 (Fall 1987): 35-36.

Review of **Angel DS 47977, "Gershwin Overtures."** ". . . Many of the scores used for this recording have only recently been discovered after many years of lying in storage boxes in that infamous Warner Bros. music warehouse in Secaucus . . . In addition to the Broadway overtures, this album also includes a suite from the film *A Damsel in Distress* and the 'Funhouse Sequence' from the same picture, featuring the song 'Stiff Upper Lip' and using Robert Russell Bennett's original orchestrations . . . This last selection is particularly delightful as it recalls the nutty dance by Fred Astaire, George Burns and Gracie Allen as they coverted through a county fair funhouse . . ." *See:* **D1095**

B1325. **DARRELL, R. D.** "Gershwin, George . . . Orchestral Works: *Second Rhapsody for Piano and Orchestra* (arr. McBride); *Overtures* (orch. Rose): *Funny Face, Let 'Em Eat Cake, Oh, Kay!, & Girl Crazy; Wintergreen for President* parade number; [et al] . . . Ralph Votapek, piano; Boston Pops Orchestra; Arthur Fiedler, cond. London Phase-4 SPC 21185 . . ." *Records in Review 1980 Edition*, p. 143-144. **[+] [*]**

". . . [T]he pretentious orchestrations are a far cry in color, weight, and sheer sonic size from what was played by the original theater pit bands. But it's hard to complain, as one is swept away by the sumptuously sonorous settings of some of the finest tunes ever created for the Broadway stage . . ." *See:* **D420, D657, D703, D1089**

B1326. **HAMILTON, David.** "Gershwin, George . . . *Overtures* (arr. Rose) . . . [Columbia M 34542—Buffalo, Tilson Thomas]." *Records in Review 1979 Edition.* Barrington, MA: Wyeth, pp. 144-145. **[adq] [*]**

". . . What Don Rose has done [to the original scoring of the overtures] is to make full-symphony orchestra versions of six . . . overtures . . . Inevitably, the sound is lusher, the articulation less snappy than the originals must have been, but Rose has managed to retain the theatrical flavor within an orchestral layout similar to that of Gershwin's concert works . . ." *See:* **D1090**

B1327. **TEACHOUT, Terry.** "Gershwin: Overtures; Excerpts from "A Damsel in Distress." [John McGlinn, New Princess Theater Orchestra]_[record reviews]." *High Fidelity* 38 (July 1988): 57. *See:* **D1095**

MUSIC USED IN FILMS

F22. *Funny Face* (1957)

B1328.   J[ABLONSKI], E[dward]. "Unlikely Corners." *American Record Guide* 23/8
(May 1957): 131.
Review of the movie soundtrack (Verve MGV-15001). *See*: **D1104**

F25. *Porgy and Bess* (1959)

B1329.   GREEN, Stanley. "Catfish Row in a 'Near Original'." *HiFi Review* 3/2 (Aug.
1959): 40.
Soundtrack of the 1959 film of *Porgy and Bess. See*: **D1116**

RECORDINGS BY GERSHWIN

B1330.   COHN, Arthur. *Recorded Classical Music: A Critical Guide to the
Compositions and Performances.* New York: Schirmer Books, 1981, p. 675.
Re: **Klavier 124**: "This is an ear-opening performance that clears away all the
interpretative foliations that have smothered the work. Gershwin plays it [RiB] clean, plays it
straight, plays it as is." *See*: **D284, D1138**

B1331.   HAMILTON, David. "Gershwin, George: 'Gershwin Plays Gershwin' . . . RCA
Victrola AVM 1-1740 [+]. . . Piano Músic [André Watts] . . . Columbia M
34221 [-] . . . Rhapsody in Blue; An American in Paris [Tilson Thomas]. . .
Columbia M 34205 [-] . . . An American in Paris. GROFÉ: Grand Canyon Suite.
NBC Symphony . . . RCA Victrola AVM-1-1737 . . . [adq]" *Records in Review
1977 Edition*, pp. 124-128. [*]
This is an insightful, informative review of the four albums named above, in which,
among other things, Hamilton compared G's performances of the preludes to that of Watts:
". . . Even the composer nodded on occasion—for instance, the 1928 recording of the *Three
Preludes*, in which he conspicuously ignores his own dynamic markings. Still, anyone tempted
to moon over the second piece in this set—a category that includes Watts —to check out this
recording, which goes rather faster than the metronome marking. If you suspect, as I long did,
that Gershwin's tempo might have been conditioned by the exigencies of 78-rpm recordings,
then compare the air check on Mark 56 667; he really did mean it to go that way. [Further
proof of these thoughts exists: When Gershwin proofread a copyist's version in ink of the
original manuscript (at DLC, George and Ira Gershwin collection, Carton #2, Envelope #GIG-
33), it appears that he crossed through the original marking 'Slowly' and added the indication
'Andante con moto e poco rubato' in addition to the specific metronome marking of quarter
note = 88. Furthermore, the direction 'e poco rubato' appears to be an afterthought, since it
was added above a carat after the marking 'Andante con moto.'] Watts['] . . . rubato (decidedly
molto, rather than the specified poco) brings us closer to the world of the nocturne rather than
that of the blues . . ." Hamilton was critical of Watts' performances of the songs chosen from
the published songbook: "In many of Watts's performances, there is a tendency to moon . . .
The issue here isn't one of 'authenticity' . . . but effectiveness, coherence, continuity . . .
Bolcom's choices are ultimately preferable . . . The solo version of the *Rhapsody in Blue* [on
Watts' album] doesn't make a very satisfactory concert piece [in Watts' interpretation of it]
A more elaborate attempt at Gershwin rehabilitation comes from Columbia [M 34205, Tilson

Thomas] . . . [whose] effort, though note-complete, remains something of a curiosity—more fun than the piano roll alone, but something short of a convincing musical whole . . . Filling out these records, we have three performances of *An American in Paris* . . . Nathaniel Shilkret's was the first recording ever . . . [and] this is a lively and stylish performance . . ." In re: the Toscanini version of AiP, ". . . [T]he Italian conductor is suprisingly idiomatic: though there's no specification in the score, he allows his trumpeter [most likely Harry Glantz] to slide into the blues theme . . ." Hamilton concluded: ". . . The entire proceedings . . . are on the unrelenting side, for all the clarity and brilliance of execution . . . Finally, we have Michael Tilson Thomas' lively, apposite performance, which would have been still more enjoyable had there been less enthusiasm in the playing and or/recording of the percussion . . ." *See*: **D1147 (RCA Victor G Plays G), D400** and **D648 (Watts), D56 (Shilkret), D127 (Toscanini), D48 (Tilson Thomas)**

B1332.   KOLODIN, Irving. "Choosing Sides, Gershwin on Gershwin." *Stereo Review* (January 1974): 102-103. **[+] [*]**

Thought provoking review, in essay form, of the **Mark 56** two-disc album **"Gershwin by Gershwin"** and the **Klavier KS 122** piano roll album. In re: Mark 56 discs: "I found it [the album] to be a constantly entertaining, sometimes curious, and perhaps even spurious hour-plus with much more of the living Gershwin than most of us have re-experienced since his death . . ." Kolodin discussed the sources from which the album was derived and expressed his preference for the radio broadcasts over the piano roll performances. Despite the derivation from piano rolls, the "lavishly affectionate versions" of pieces on the Klavier album pleased the reviewer. Kolodin called the *I Got Rhythm Variations* (on Klavier) "possibly the best *composition* of all those he [G] wrote." *See*: **D717 ("Gershwin by Gershwin"), D1137 (Klavier album)**

B1333.   PFAFF, Timothy. "How Long Has This Been Going On?" *Piano & Keyboard* (Jan./Feb. 1995): 69, 72.

Review of **PianoSoft's** diskette of the Gershwin piano rolls researched, edited, and prepared by Artis Wodehouse. The diskette is intended to be reproduced on Yamaha's **Disklavier.** ". . . Adding to the value of the PianoSoft's release is the fact that its selections do not wholly duplicate those of the CD . . . ." *See*: **D1144**

OTHER GENERAL INFORMATION SOURCES ABOUT THE GERSHWINS

Biographies and Bibliographies about Biographies are given separate sections and are not listed here. This section includes materials concerned with treatments of the Gershwin brothers, one or the other or both, included within the references listed below.

B1334.   ADLER, Larry. *It Ain't Necessarily So: An Autobiography.* Grove Press, 1984.

B1335.   ALEXANDER, Shana. *Happy Days: My Mother, My Father, My Sister & Me.* Doubleday, 1995.

Alexander is Milton Ager's daughter, Ager was a composer friend of George's early in his career.

B1336.   ALTMAN, Rick. *The American Film Musical.* Bloomington, Indianapolis, IN & London: Indiana University Press, 1987, pp. 29, 38-40, 121, 175, 236, 283, 286, 299.

An erudite study of many American film musicals. Brief references to G and related films here and there as noted above. *See:* Full annotation under **"Bibliography about Filmography."**

B1337. **ANTHEIL, George.** *Bad Boy of Music.* Garden City, NY: Doubleday, Doran. 1945.

B1338. **ARDOIN, John.** "Discovered Treasures: Long-lost Broadway works fuel interest in America's musical past." *Dallas Morning News,* Section C, April 23, 1987, pp. 5-6.

"Long-forgotten songs by GG, Cole Porter, Richard Rodgers and Jerome Kern will make May 14 a grand night for singing in the nation's capitol. The music that will be performed at the annual awards evening of the National Institute for Music Theatre is part of a breathtaking cache of original manuscripts recently discovered in a warehouse in Secaucus, N. J. . . ." How were these precious scores found? "In that era, the music of most important Broadway compositions was published by Harms, a company that was bought in the mid-1920s by Warner Bros. . . . In the years that followed, Warner's relocated its offices several times, finally winding up in Secaucus. When the company was moving to its New Jersey facilities, it came across an extensive collection of manuscripts that it believed was primarily piano/vocal scores of old musicals prepared by in-house arrangers. A list was made of the holdings, and the manuscripts packed in 80 containers and stored in Warner's warehouse. What Warner's didn't realize was that the manuscripts were the composers' original scores, and in many instances the only extant, complete copies of entire shows. Unknowingly, Warner's had the mother lode of the American musical, including 70 [supposedly] 'lost' songs by G and IG, plus the original scores and orchestral parts of their musicals *Primrose* (1924), *Tip Toes* (1925), and *Pardon My English* (1933) . . . Beyond the music itself, the original orchestrations represent the greatest importance of this treasure trove. Although, as [Robert] Kimball has pointed out . . . many of these shows were not orchestrated by their composers, those who did the orchestrations—men such as Frank Saddler, Hans Spialek and Robert Russell Bennett [and Maurice DePackh]—created a distinctive Broadway sound that existed until it was massively altered by the amplification and sound enhancement of recent years . . ."

B1339. **ARMITAGE, Merle,** ed. *George Gershwin,* intro. by Edward Jablonski. 1ˢᵗ ed. published NY: Longmans, Green, 1938, Da Capo Press reprint ed. with new introduction by Edward Jablonski (1994): NY: Da Capo Press, 1995. ISBN: 0306806150 Includes work list, pp. 248-249. Discography, p. 250.

Essays in both editions are by **George Antheil,** "The Foremost American Composer"; **Harold Arlen,** "The Composer's Friend"; **Armitage,** Preface and "George Gershwin and His Time"; **Samuel Nathaniel Behrman,** "Profile"; **Irving Berlin,** "Poem"; **Henry A. Botkin,** "Painter and Collector"; **William Daly,** "George Gershwin as an Orchestrator"; **Walter Damrosch,** "Gershwin and the Concerto in F"; **Louis Dans,** "Gershwin and Schoenberg"; **Lester Donahue,** "Gershwin and the Social Scene"; **Olin Downes,** "Hail and Farewell"; **Todd Duncan,** "Memoirs of George Gershwin"; **David Ewen,** "Farewell to George Gershwin"; **Eva Gauthier,** "Personal Appreciation"; **George Gershwin,** "The Composer and the Machine Age"; **G. Gershwin,** "Rhapsody in Catfish Row"; **Ira Gershwin,** "My Brother"; **I. Gershwin,** "Works of George Gershwin"; **Isaac Goldberg,** "Homage to a Friend"; **Ferde Grofé,** "George Gershwin's Influence"; **Oscar Hammerstein II,** "To George Gershwin"; **Sam H. Harris,** "Gershwin and Golf"; **DuBose Heyward,** "Porgy and Bess Return on Wings of Song"; **Rosamond J. Johnson,** "Emancipator of American Idioms"; **Otto H. Kahn,** "George Gershwin and American Youth"; **Jerome Kern,** "Tribute"; **Serge Koussevitsky,** "Man and Musician"; **Nanette Kutner,** "Portrait in Our Time"; **Leonard Liebling,** "The George I Knew"; **Rouben Mamoulian,** "I Remember"; **Beverly Nichols,** "George Gershwin"; **Isamu**

Noguchi, "Portrait"; **Arnold Schoenberg,** "George Gershwin"; **Gilbert Seldes,** "The Gershwin Case"; **Albert Heink Sendrey,** "Tennis Game"; **Alexander Steinert,** "Porgy and Bess and Gershwin"; **Erma Taylor,** "George Gershwin—A Lament"; **Rudy Vallee,** "Troubadour"s Tribute"; **Paul Whiteman,** "George and the Rhapsody."

B1340. _____. "George Gershwin," in his: *Accent on America.* NY: E. Weyhe, 1944, pp. 289-98.

B1341. "Arts: Posthumous Exhibit Shows That Gershwin Knew Harmony on Canvas Also." *Newsweek* 10/25 (Dec. 20, 1937): 28.
Brief announcement of an exhibition of G's art work, held at the Marie Harriman Gallery in NY.

B1342. **ARVEY, Verna (Mrs. William Grant Still).** "George Gershwin Through the Eyes of a Friend." *Opera and Concert* 13/4 (Apr. 1948): 10-11, 27-28.
Discusses Kay Swift's friendship with Gershwin.

B1343. _____. "Afro-American Music Memo." *Music Journal* 27/9 (Nov. 1969): 36, 68-69.
Article reminiscing about the influence of the music of blacks on G and other classical composers. The article also discusses briefly William Grant Still's *Afro-American Symphony* (1930).

B1344. **ASSOCIATED PRESS.** "Kid Sister of the Gershwins Recalls Old Days on the Eve of a New Honor." *NYTimes*, June 6, 1983, p. C11.
". . . Last night the Gershwin brothers were honored at the 1983 Tony Awards presentations, when the name of Broadway's Uris Theater was changed to the Gershwin Theater and when a host of Broadway, Hollywood, and television personalities sang and danced to Gershwin words and music . . ."

B1345. **ASTAIRE, Fred.** *Steps in Time.* NY: Harper, 1959. 338 pp.
Includes some reminiscences by Astaire about his association with Gershwin.

B1346. **ATKINSON, Brooks.** *Broadway.* NY: Macmillan, 1970.

B1347. **AUSTIN, William W.** *Music in the 20th-Century: From Debussy through Stravinsky.* NY: W. W. Norton, 1966, pp. 48, 62, 192, 291, 384f, 502f, 504; in academic context, 441; and Debussy, 6; Delius, 89; Poulenc, 518; Prokofiev, 471; **Works:** AiP, 503; OTIS, P&B, Preludes, RiB, 502; Swanee, 191.
Brief references to G here and there as noted above. *Also See:* the Index.

B1348. **AUTHOR unknown. (Possibly Isaac GOLDBERG.)** "If Not Back to Bach, Then On to Lincoln; Hour with George Gershwin, His Mind Working All The Time." *Boston Evening Transcript* **[NN-L]**, May 10, 1930.
A lengthy and revealing, three-column interview. ". . . I found George listening to a Hindemith string quartet on his modernistic phonograph . . . [T]he Gilbert and Sullivan influence on Gershwin begins, not in 'Strike Up the Band' but in 'Primrose' . . . Gershwin, doing the piece within the shadow of the Savoy, could hardly withdraw himself from that influence . . . 'Primrose' is a jolly affair. It yields to the fascination that the mixed time of the six-eight bar has for the Londoner, and, as a result, has more of a lilt than most of his American scores . . . His latest ambition encompasses nothing less than a choric setting of Lincoln's

Gettysburg Address . . ." The following is a direct quote from what G told the interviewer: "'I am not interested . . . in the traditional choral setting. I don't see the famous speech as a solo and chorus in the regular manner, in which a tenor . . . will sing a line or so and then be backed up by an outburst from the sopranos, altos, tenor, and basses. That's too obvious. In fact, I don't see the chorus primarily as a musical chorus. They are Lincoln's listeners on the battlefield, as he delivers his historic speech, I don't even hear them . . . singing any definite words. I imagine a singer, let us say Lawrence Tibbett, as Lincoln, intoning the words of the address in a certain solemn, recitative-like manner. There are murmurs among the crowd—that is, the chorus. At first, indistinct murmurs, represented by subdued, barely audible harmonies. As the speech progresses, there is, in the chorus, a gradual, very gradual crescendo, in which the harmonies become somewhat more complicated as the voices rise. Until, at last, with the glorious finale of the Address itself, the chorus companions the voice of Lincoln in a climactic outburst . . .'" *See*: **W21 (Primrose)**

B1349. **BARAL, Robert.** "Irving Berlin's Oldtime Song Hits Most in Demand By Collectors." *Variety* 181/4 (Jan. 3, 1951): 219.

B1350. **BARRETT, Mary Ellin.** *Irving Berlin: A Daughter's Memoir.* NY: Simon & Schuster, 1994. pp. 77, 80, 155, *et passim.*
The index to this highly personal reminiscence lists several references to G, among the references is a description (p. 155) of a visit by G to the Berlin home not long before his death and (p. 158) a quote of the lines written by Berlin for G's memorial in 1938.

B1351. **BEHRMAN, Samuel Nathaniel.** *People in a Diary: Memoir.* Boston: Little, Brown, 1972, 239-58.
In a chapter titled "The Gershwin Years," the author reported on a concert he heard in Verona, Italy, in 1938, where RiB was performed. Besides other biographical details about G and IG, the chapter includes a first-hand and poignant account of the final days of G's life. There are five quotes from this book in Edward Jablonski's *Gershwin Remembered,* **B1563**.

B1352. _____. "Troubadour." *New Yorker* 5/14 (May 25, 1929): 27-29. Also as: "Profile," in: **Merle ARMITAGE,** ed. *George Gershwin.* NY: Longmans, Green, 1938, pp. 211-218.

B1353. "Belittling Gershwin." *Newsweek* (Aug. 20, 1945): 79.
Short article summarizing Barry Ulanov's critical article appearing in *Metronome.*

B1354. **BERGREEN, Laurence.** *As Thousands Cheer: The Life of Irving Berlin.* New York: Viking Penguin, 1990, pp. 191, 224-225, 304-305, 307, 311, 314, *et passim.*
Many references to G, some to G and Berlin (pp. 124-125, 164-165, 525). Excellent background reading to get a feel for the era. A review in the *New York Times Book Review* (by Gene Lees, July 1, 1990, pp. 1, 25) called it "a substantial contribution to our knowledge, not just of Irving Berlin but of American vernacular music."

B1355. **BERLIN, Irving.** "Poem," in: **Merle ARMITAGE,** ed. *George Gershwin.* NY: Longmans, Green, 1938, 78-80.

B1356. **BERNSTEIN, Leonard.** "A Nice Gershwin Tune." *Atlantic Monthly* 195/4 (Apr.

1955): 39-42.
This is the same essay cited below at **B1359.**

B1357. _____ . "Proc si nesednete a nenapisete takovou pisnicku jako Gershwin?" _Hudebni Rozhledy_ 18/16 (1965): 675-77.
Translated from Bernstein's book _The Joy of Music._

B1358. _____ . "Songwriter But Also Composer." _Saturday Review/World_ 1 (Oct. 9, 1973): 19.

B1359. _____ . "Why Don't You Run Upstairs and Write a Nice Gershwin Tune?" _Atlantic Monthly_ 195/4 (Apr. 1955): 39-42.—reprinted in Bernstein's _Joy of Music_, NY: Simon & Schuster, 1959.

B1360.   BILL. "Radio Reviews: Sound of Gershwin." _Variety_ 218 (May 25, 1960): 48.

B1361.   BLESH, Rudi, & Harriet JANIS. _They All Played Ragtime: The True Story of an American Music._ NY: A. A. Knopf, 1950, pp. 72, 204.
References to G.

B1362.   BLITZSTEIN, Marc. "Music and Theatre—1932." _Modern Music_ 9 (May-June 1932): 164-168.

B1363.   BLOOM, Ken. _American Song: The Complete Musical Theatre Companion,_ Vol. I (Vol. II is the index). NY & Oxford: Facts on File Publications, 1985.
This is a very detailed and important reference on American musicals. The title is misleading in that the subtitle should be the title, since the emphasis is clearly on the American musical theatre shows themselves. Titles of shows are arranged alphabetically. Sixty-three entries are cited under "Gershwin, George (Composer)" in the Index (Vol. II), and include everything from shows where one Gershwin piece was interpolated through those with all Gershwin music, as well as shows that were never produced such as _Ming Toy_ (_East is West_). Entries are quite complete including the NY opening date, the length of the run, names of the librettist, producer, drama director, choreographer, music director, orchestrator, set designer, song titles, and the names of the cast, though not the roles they played.

B1364.   BOLTON, Guy. "Musicals, Too, Were Memorable." _Theatre Arts_ 44 (Sept. 1960): 23-26, 69.

B1365.   BORDMAN, Gerald. _Days to be Happy, Years to be Sad: The Life and Music of Vincent Youmans._ NY & Oxford: Oxford University Press, 1982, 4, 16, 26-29, 33, 43, 46, 90, 94, _et passim._
Brief references to GG and his friends and associates are scattered throughout this biography. This book is helpful to a study of the milieu in which G worked, the two composers were born only one day apart, Youmans on September 27, and GG on September 26, 1898.

B1366.   BOTKIN, Henry. "Painter and Collector." in: **Merle ARMITAGE,** ed. _George Gershwin_ (NY: Longmans, Green, 1938), pp. 43.

B1367.   BOWEN, Meirion. "[Review]." _Musical Times_ 129/1749 (Nov. 1988): 599-602.
Review of a paperback reprint of _Lyrics on Several Occasions_ by Omnibus of London. _See:_ **B21**

B1368. **BRAGGIOTTI, Mario.** "Gershwin Is Here to Stay." *Etude* (Feb. 1953): 14, 63.

B1369. **BRIGGS, John.** "George Gershwin: A Reappraisal." *Tomorrow* 7 (July 1948): 20-24.

B1370. **BROWN, Royal S.** "An Interview with John McGlinn." *Fanfare* 12/2 (Nov.-Dec. 1988): 42-58.
A general interview which includes references to the Secaucus Warner Bros. "find" (p. 42) and Leonore Gershwin's work in helping to "preserve the legacy of her family." (p. 48) *See*: **D940, D1095**

B1371. **BUCHANAN, Charles L.** "Gershwin and Musical Snobbery." *The Outlook* 145/5 (Feb. 2, 1927): 146-48.

B1372. **BUONASSIS1, Vincenzo.** "Forse nella storia Gershwin." *La Scala* No. 114 (May 1959): 43-47, 77-78.

B1373. **BURTON, Jack.** "The Billboard Music Popularity Charts: The Honor Roll of Popular Songwriters, Part XII, No. 43—George Gershwin (Part I)." *Billboard* 61/47, Nov 19, 1949, p. 39.
Part of a series listing G's "Best Known Songs and Recordings Available." Arrangement is by the name of the musical or movie. This installment covers the period 1916 through 1923. *See*: **B1374, B1375, B1376**

B1374. _____. "The Billboard Music Popularity Charts: The Honor Roll of Popular Songwriters, Part XII, No. 43—George Gershwin (Part II)." *Billboard* 61/48, Nov. 26, 1949, p. 36.
Continuation of above, covering 1924 (*George White's Scandals of 1924*) through 1928 (*Rosalie*).

B1375. _____. "The Billboard Music Popularity Charts: The Honor Roll of Popular Songwriters, Part XII, No. 43—George Gershwin (Part III)." *Billboard* 61/49, Dec. 3, 1949, p. 38.
Continuation of above, from *Treasure Girl* of 1928 through RiB, and including the London Musicals, *Mayfair and Montmartre, Rainbow Revue, Primrose, Stop Flirting*, and *Shake Your Feet*.

B1376. _____. "The Billboard Music Popularity Charts: The Honor Roll of Popular Songwriters, Part XII, No. 43—George Gershwin (Part IV)." *Billboard* 61/50, Dec. 10, 1949, p. 40.
Final article in the series, covering from the Concerto (1925) through the movie, *The Shocking Miss Pilgrim* (1947, posthumous).

B1377. **BURTON, Jack.** *The Blue Book of Broadway Musicals.* Watkins Glen, NY: Century House, 1952, pp. 110, 179-182, 249-250, 306.

B1378. _____. "George Gershwin, 1898-1937," in his: *The Blue Book of Tin Pan Alley: A Human Interest Anthology of American Popular Music.* Watkins Glen,

NY: Century House, 1950 & 1965.

B1379. "'Buying American' in Music: Quest for a Native Rhythm Goes On While 'Bad Boys' Slip Into Obscurity Because Their Melodies Are Not Lasting." *Literary Digest* 118/26 (Dec. 29, 1934): 24.

Article concluding that "the poles of the modern conflict, and the struggle for a unified expression of the American spirit, are represented by George Gershwin, on the side of jazz, and John Alden Carpenter, on the side of austere classicism."

B1380. **CAMPBELL, Frank C.** "The Musical Scores of George Gershwin." *The Library of Congress Quarterly Journal of Current Acquisitions* 11/3 (May 1954): 127-139.

B1381. **CARP, L.** "George Gershwin—illustrious American composer: His Fatal Glioblastoma." *Am Journal Surg Pathol* 3(5) (Oct. 1979): 473-478.

B1381.1. *A Catalogue of the Exhibition: Gershwin George The Music/Ira The Words.* NY: The Museum of the City of New York, 1968.

A complete catalogue of the Exhibition held at the Museum May 6 through September 2, 1968. The museum is rich in holdings of Gershwiniana due to its collections of clippings files as well as sheet music, much of it in mint condition. *See:* **B1765**

B1382. **CERF, Bennett.** *Try and Stop Me: A Collection of Stories, Mostly Humorous.* NY: Simon & Schuster, 1944.

B1383. _____. "In Memory of George Gershwin." *Saturday Review of Literature* 26 (July 17, 1943): 14-16.

A revised version of this essay was included in Cerf's book *Try and Stop Me: A Collection of Stories, Mostly Humorous,* listed above.

B1384. **CHASE, Gilbert,** ed. *The American Composer Speaks: A Historical Anthology, 1770-1963.* Baton Rouge, LA: Louisiana State University Press, 1966, 3, 5, 13, 26, 139-40, 260.

Includes an introduction to Gershwin's article "The Composer in the Machine Age."

B1385. **CHASINS, Abram.** "Paradox in Blue." *Saturday Review* 39/8 (Feb. 26, 1956): 37, 39, 64-66.

B1386. **CHIRA, Susan.** "103d Street Celebrates Gershwin." *NYTimes,* June 20, 1982, Section 1, p. 34.

B1387. **CHRISTOPHER, Michael.** "Noguchi portraits. (Whitney Museum of American Art at Philip Morris, New York.)" *Sculpture Review* 38/3 (1989): 16-17+.

B1388. **CLAUSEN, Bernard C.** "Strike Up the Band." *Christian Century* 48/26 (July 8, 1931): 899-901.

B1389. **COEUROY, André.** *Panorama de la musique Contemporaine.* Paris: Les Documentaires, 1928, pp. 65, 70.

Remarks on Gershwin & jazz.

B1390.   **COE, Richard L.** "Ira: Alive and Well." *Washington Post* (dateline: Beverly Hills, CA) July 15, 1971, pp. K1, K5.

Detailed human interest story based on an interview with Ira. The article has many quotes from IG, among them the answer to the query "What about today's lyrics?": ". . . When the Beatles began I had to tune out and what followed was inevitable, more illiterate junk. But Stephen Sondheim made me feel better. He uses words with respect for their meanings . . ."

B1391.   "Composer of a Thousand Songs Finds Radio a Fast Pace-Maker." *NYTimes*, Mar. 4, 1934, Section 9, p. 11.

This unsigned article is based on an interview of George shortly after the Leo Reisman tour in 1934. In it Gershwin compares the rigors of performing four radio broadcasts in seven days with that of the Reisman tour. ". . . The activity during those twenty-eight days was more physical than mental . . . for while we covered 12,000 miles in less than a month, our program was unchanged in the various cities in which we played. But four broadcasts in a week is something else . . . it means preparing an entirely different program for each broadcast. At that rate it doesn't take long to exhaust even an extensive répertoire. The microphone is like a hungry lion the way it eats up material. It's really liable to prove something of a strain even to a composer who is in the habit of turning out melodies more or less on schedule . . . The concert tour, if it taught me nothing else, proved conclusively that radio has raised the tastes of the average man and woman and has educated them to a real appreciation and enjoyment of the best music has to offer . . ." The remainder of the interview of Gershwin reiterates this point in his own words. *See:* **Appendix A, T16-T43.**

B1392.   "A Composer's Pictures: George Gershwin, the Musician, Is a Collector of Modern Paintings." *Arts and Decoration* 40 (Jan. 1934): 48-50.

B1393.   **COPLAND, Aaron.** *Our New Music.* NY & London: Whittlesey House, McGraw-Hill, 1941, pp. 85, 99. Rev. ed. as: *The New Music, 1900-1960.*(NY: W. W. Norton, 1968), pp. 61, 70.
Brief passing remarks.

B1394.   _____. *What to Listen for in Music.* NY & London: Whittlesey House, McGraw-Hill, 1939, 1953.

B1395.   **CORBIN, John.** "George S. Kaufman." *Saturday Review of Literature* 9 (Jan. 21, 1933): 385-386.

B1396.   **CRAFT, Robert** and **Igor STRAVINSKY.** "Some Composers by Igor Stravinsky with Robert Craft." *Musical America* 82/6 (June 1961): 6-11.

In an interview with Craft, Stravinsky responded briefly to the question "What are your memories of George Gershwin?" In the response, Stravinsky dispelled the false story that Gershwin had asked him for lessons.

B1397.   **CROCE, Arlene.** *Afterimages.* NY: Alfred A. Knopf, 1977.

B1398.   _____. "Dancing: This Space and That Jazz and These Dancers." *New Yorker* 55 (Feb. 22, 1982): 99-103.

B1399.   **CROWNINSHIELD, Frank.** "Gershwin the Painter," in: *Rhapsody in Blue, the*

Jubilant Story of George Gershwin and His Music (Hollywood: Warner Bros. 1945), pp. 11-12.

B1400. _____. "Introduction," George Gershwin [Catalogue of the Gershwin Memorial Exhibition].

Exhibit catalogue for a posthumous exhibit of thirty-nine items including oil paintings, drawings and water colors, at the Marie Harriman Gallery, in New York, Dec. 18, 1937 through Jan. 4, 1938.

B1401.   DALY, William. "George Gershwin as Orchestrator," in: **Merle ARMITAGE**, ed. *George Gershwin* (NY: Longmans, Green, 1938), pp. 30-31. *See:* **B1614**

B1402 . _____. "Gershwin as Orchestrator; To the Music Editor." *NTTimes*, Jan. 15, 1933, Section 9, p. 8. *See:* **B1614**

B1403.   DAMROSCH, Walter. "Gershwin and His Music," in: *Rhapsody in Blue, The Jubilant Story of George Gershwin and His Music* (Hollywood: Warner Bros, 1945), pp. 7-8.

Pamphlet put together in connection with the film bio of 1945.

B1404.   DANUSER, Hermann. "Jazz und Kunstmusik: ihre Affinitat in den zwanziger Jahren [Jazz and Art Music: Their Affinity in the 1920s]." *Universitas* 38 (1983): 379-385.

According to this article, jazz played a vital role in European culture in the 1920s. The author cites G as an example of a musician who began as a popular composer/pianist and delved into "serious" music.

B1405.   DANZ, Louis. "Gershwin and Schoenberg," in: **Merle ARMITAGE,** ed. *George Gershwin* (NY: Longmans, Green, 1938), pp. 99-101.

B1406.   DASHIELL, Alan. "Foreword and Discography," in: **Isaac GOLDBERG,** *George Gershwin: A Study in American Music* (NY: Frederick Ungar, 1958), pp. xiii-xviii, 357-370.

B1407.   DAVENPORT, Marcia. *Too Strong for Fantasy.* NY: Charles Scribner's, 1967.

B1408.   DAVID, Hubert W. "Gershwin, The Man We Love." *Melody Maker* 30/1108 (Dec. 11,1954): 8.

B1409.   DAVIS, Lee. *Bolton and Wodehouse and Kern: The Men Who Made Musical Comedy.* NY: James H. Heineman, 1993.

B1410.   DAVIS, Ronald D. *A History of Music in American Life: The Modern Era, 1920-Present,* Vol III. Malabar, FL: Robert Krieger, 1981, pp. 121, 134-152, 160, 202, *et passim.*

A general book on this subject, written with the "undergraduate cultural history student and curious laymen in mind." Despite its ecumenical intent, the biographical detail and coverage of G's works in the book is detailed and thorough.

B1411. **DELONG, Thomas A.** *Pops: Paul Whiteman, King of Jazz.* Piscataway, NJ: New Century, 1983, pp. 3-6, 8-10, 50-51, 61-64, 66, 69-70, 76, *et passim.*
Biography of Whiteman.   The volume begins with a description of the Aeolian Hall premiere of the RiB in 1924, and has numerous references to the Gershwins. ". . . As Grofé turned more and more to arranging, his regular piano playing chores were turned over to a new musician, Harry Perrella . . . who performed the *Rhapsody* on the third tour—better than Gershwin himself, according to many who heard him . . ." [p. 79] [p. 93]: Paul's British fans were impatient to hear the *Rhapsody in Blue* . . ." Information about the genesis of the Whiteman Collection at Williams College in Williamstown, MA, is given on pp. 214-215, including information about Grofe's giving the original copy of the RiB score to the Library of Congress without Whiteman's permission. *See:* **W1a**

B1412. **DOERSCHUK, Robert L.** "Gershwin Goes MIDI." *Keyboard* 16/7 (July 1990): 64-72, 75, 78.
Explanation of Artis Wodehouse's fascinating project resurrecting Gershwin's piano roll performances for replay through disk on Yamaha's **Disklavier** and other hardware. *See:* **D1134, D1144**

B1413. **DOLL, Bill.** "Fan mail—after many years." *Theater Arts* 43/10 (Oct. 1959): 28-32, 84-85.
Article written to commemorate the twenty-second year after GG's death. Doll assembled a series of anecdotes about G's life; the vignettes were sent to Doll by IG, Sigmund Spaeth, Louise Dresser, Edward Kilenyi, Johnny Green, Lois Jacoby, Morton Gould, Rosamund Walling Tirana, John Chapman, Mrs. Serge Koussevitzky, Louis Sobol, Lillian Hellman, and Irving Berlin.

B1414. **DONAHUE, Lester.** "Gershwin and the Social Scene," in: **Merle ARMITAGE,** ed. *George Gershwin* (NY: Longmans, Green, 1938), pp. 170-77.

B1415. _____. "Gershwin Memorial: Retrospect of Rapid Rise of Composer and the Development of His Art." *NYTimes,* July 10, 1938, Section 9, p. 5.

B1416. **DOWNES, Olin.** "Hail & Farewell: Career & Position of George Gershwin in American Music." *NYTimes,* July 18, 1937, Section 10, p. 5. Also in **Merle ARMITAGE,** ed. *George Gershwin* (NY: Longmans, Green, 1938), pp. 219-224. Also titled "On the Passing of George Gershwin," in: **Irene DOWNES'** book.

B1417. _____. Papers. At University of Georgia, Athens.

B1418. **D[ÜRR], A[lfred].** "In Memoriam: George Gershwin (1898-1937)." *Musica* 11/1 (Jan.1957): 38-39.
German version of an article in *Harper's Magazine.*

B1419. **DUKE, Vernon.** "Gershwin, Schillinger, and Dukelsky—Some Reminiscences." *Musical Quarterly* 33/1 (Jan. 1947): 102-115.
Duke discusses his and Gershwin's studies with Schillinger.

B1420. _____. *Listen Here! A Critical Essay on Music Depreciation.* NY: Ivan Obolensky, 1963, pp. 7-8, 29, 36, 54-58, 63, 66, 73-74, 76-77, 118, 125, 139, *et passim.*

References to GG are scattered throughout. Among them, from the Preamble: ". . . Scoff if you must, but the first U. S.-made musical article to gain universal exposure was George Gershwin's *Rhapsody in Blue* . . . (p. 7)" Duke defended P&B against Virgil Thomson's negative writings about it: "Thomson's comments on the opera's *musical* substance are shot through with capricious ambiguity of the cattiest sort [p. 232] . . ." According to Charles Schwartz, this book is "A vitriolic assessment of music and musicians."

B1421. _____. *Passport to Paris.* Boston: Little, Brown, 1955.
Reminiscences about George and Ira Gershwin are included in this autobiography.

B1422. DUKELSKY, Vladimir. *See:* **DUKE, Vernon.**

B1423. DUMONT, Lou. "Historical Tape Recordings: Radio and TV." *Hobbies* 78/9 (Nov.1973): 54.
Partially biographical, this article also includes a textual transcription of an incomplete tape of the broadcast of the Hollywood Bowl Memorial Concert, September 8, 1937, presented by CBS radio, with Louis Whitten as master of ceremonies. *See:* **D510, W2h**

B1424. DUNCAN, Todd. "Memoirs of George Gershwin," in: **Merle ARMITAGE,** ed. *George Gershwin* (NY: Longmans, Green, 1938), pp.58-64.

B1425. DYER, Richard. "The Enduring George Gershwin, 50 Years After His Death, He Defies Categorization." *Boston Globe*, Arts & Film section, third edition, April 26, 1987.
A long article, much of it biographical and anecdotal, which attempts to assess G's contributions. Among other astute observations, Dyer noted ". . . The songs are frequently heard in glutinous orchestrations far removed from the spunky pit-band sound of the originals. Any recording of a Gershwin song, even the great ones by stylists like Sinatra and Ella Fitzgerald, immediately betrays its own period—only the song itself, as a kind of Platonic ideal, remains 'timeless.' Fortunately, this is beginning to change . . ."

B1426. ELLIOT, Susan. "Gershwin Crazy; Recently discovered scores are making possible a recorded revival of classic Broadway musicals." *Opera News* 54/2 (August 1989): 13-16, 36.
Detailed article about the Leonore Gershwin-Library of Congress Recording and Publishing Project. ". . . The Library of Congress . . . will supervise the preparation of the music and provide much of the historic material for the album packages . . . The library also will supervise preparation of piano-vocal scores, to be published by Warner-Chappell Music . . ." *See:* **D450 (*Girl Crazy*), D456 (*Lady, Be Good!*), D490 (*Oh, Kay!*), D492 (*Pardon My English*), D564 (*Strike Up the Band*)**

B1427. EDWARDS, Arthur C., & W. Thomas MARROCCO. *Music in the United States.* Dubuque, IA: Wm. C. Brown, 1968, pp. 105-107, 117, 154.

B1428. EELLS, George. *The Life That Late He Led: A Biography of Cole Porter.* NY: G. P. Putnam's Sons; London: W. H. Allen, 1967.

B1429. "Ein Phänomen der Musikgeschichte; Popularität zur Unsterblichkeit [George

Gershwin]." *Musikhandel* 6 (1955): 250.

ELISOFON, Eliot. *See:* **Arthur KNIGHT.**

B1430.   **E.[NGEL], C.[arl].** "Views and Reviews." *Musical Quarterly* 12 (1926): 299-314.

B1431.   **ENGEL, Lehman.** *The American Musical Theater*. NY: Macmillan, 1975.

B1432.   _____. *Words with Music*. NY: Macmillan, 1972.

B1433.   **EWEN, David,** ed. *The Book of Modern Composers,* 2nd ed., rev. & enlarged. NY: A. A. Knopf, 1942, 1950.

B1434.   _____. *Composers of Today*. NY: H. W. Wilson, 1934, pp. 85-86.

B1435.   _____. "George Gershwin, America's Musical Hope." *Gamut* (New York) 2/5 (Nov. 1929): 30-31.

B1436.   _____. "Gershwin Would Be Surprised." *Harper's Magazine* 120/1260 (May 1955): 68-69.
A two-page essay assessing the popularity of Gershwin's music *ca.* 1955.

B1437.   _____. "The King of Tin-Pan Alley; George Gershwin, Famous Creator of 'Rhapsody in Blue,' Is Quickly Becoming America's Most Popular Composer." *Jewish Tribune* 94/7 (Feb. 15, 1929): 2, 11.

B1438.   _____. *The Life and Death of Tin Pan Alley*. NY: Funk & Wagnalls, 1964.

B1439.   _____. "A Master of Symphonic Jazz; The Fourth Article in the Series 'The Jews in Music' Dealing with George Gershwin, Formerly of Tin Pan Alley." *Jewish Tribune* 91/15 (Oct. 7, 1927): 16.

B1440.   _____, ed. *Men of Popular Music*. Chicago/NY: Ziff-Davis, 1944.

B1441.   _____. "The Mighty Five of American Popular Music." *Theatre Arts* 35/12 (Dec. 1951): 42, 74-76.

B1442.   _____. "A New Gilbert and Sullivan on Broadway." *The American Hebrew* 121/17 (Sept. 2, 1927): 517, 522-530.
Concerning George S. Kaufman and GG.

B1443.   _____. "New Harmonists." *The American Hebrew* 123/16 (Aug. 24, 1928): 435, 441.
Significant twentieth-century composers GG, Louis Gruenberg, Aaron Copland, and Marion Bauer are discussed.

B1444.   _____. "The Stature of George Gershwin." *The American Mercury* 70/318 (June 1950): 716-724.

B1445.   _____. *The Story of America's Musical Theatre*. Philadelphia: Chilton, 1961,

1968, pp. 89-93, 112-120, 141-147, 167-168, *et passim*.

A history of the American musical with commentary on the musicals and P&B scattered throughout.

B1446. _____. "There'll Always Be a Gershwin." *Variety* 241/7 (Jan. 5, 1966): 207.

B1447. _____. *Twentieth-Century Composers*. NY: Thomas Y. Crowell, 1937.

B1448.   EWEN, David Collection, University of Miami, Coral Gables, FL.

The David Ewen Collection embodies Ewen's papers, including copies of his books and archival material such as newspaper and magazine clippings, photographs, pamphlets, brochures, etc. concerning composers, performers, and other subjects related to music. Of these, some eighteen folders concern the Gershwins, including one folder which contains thirty-one letters from Ira G. Fifteen copies of Ewen's books about Gershwin in various editions and translations are among the items in the collection. The collection is located in the Archives and Special Collections Department of the Otto G. Richter Library at the University of Miami, Coral Gables, FL, and may be consulted there. *See*: **B43**

B1449.   "Exhibit of Gershwiniana at . . . Museum [of the City of New York] Pulls Int'l Show Biz Crowd." *Variety* 250/12 (May 8, 1968): 241+.

B1450.   FABRICANT, Noah D., M.D. "George Gershwin's Fatal Headache." *The Eye, Ear, Nose and Throat Monthly* 37/5 (May 1958): 332-334.

B1451.   FARNESE, Harold. "Whither Is George Gershwin Going?" *Things Worth Knowing in Music and Art* 5 (July-Aug. 1929): 4-5.

B1452.   FARNSWORTH, Marjorie, with a foreword by **Billie Burke Ziegfeld.** *The Ziegfeld Follies*. London: Peter Davies, 1956, pp. 108, 116, 126, 165.

There are but four brief references to G in this volume, but for an understanding of the *personalities* of the era, Marilyn Miller and Helen Morgan among them, it is helpful.

B1453.   "Fear Complex Clutches Four Laughing Men; 'No Interpolations' Order Leaves Veteran Comedians in an Agitated Mental State." *NYHerald Tribune*, Apr. 10, 1932, Section 7, p. 2.

B1454.   FEATHER, Leonard. "Feather's Nest." *Down Beat* 23 (Apr. 18, 1956): 12.

B1455.   FEINSTEIN, Michael. *Nice Work If You Can Get It: My Life in Rhythm and Rhyme*. NY: Hyperion, 1995.

While this book discusses songwriters other than the Gershwins, it includes extensive information about both George and Ira, as can be traced through its Index. Because of Feinstein's close relationship with Ira, much inside Gershwin information can be gleaned from its pages. Feinstein's side of the so-called "Feinstein Affair" is also exposed. The book is must reading for anyone interested in the worlds of pop singing, songwriting, American musical theater, and the piano bar/cabaret scene. A review by James Gavin provides an astute assessment of this book. *See*: **B1469 (review), B1662, B1694**

B1456. _____. "The Gershwin Century." *The Dramatist* (Sept.-Oct. 1998).

B1456.1. "First Gershwin Festival." *Music Educators Journal* 57/1 (Sept. 1970): 176-179.

Also See: **W5d** and next entry:

B1457. "First World Festival—Gershwin Serious Music, Miami." *Pan Pipes of Sigma Alpha Iota* 63/2 (Jan. 1971): 35.

Report on the three-day Festival held at the University of Miami in Coral Gables, FL, October 27-29, 1970. *See*: **W2o, W4e, W5d, W6c, W1y**

B1458. **FORTE, Allen.** "Gershwin's Ballads," in *The American Popular Ballad of the Golden Era: 1924-1950.* Princeton, NJ: Princeton University Press, 1995, 147-176 (Chap. 11)

The book is an extraordinary, admirable *musical* treatment of the era. Schenkerian scholar Forte devotes a chapter of insightful comment to a "chronological spread" of G songs, excluding what he calls "arias" from P&B. In his introduction to the chapter, Forte rightfully, in my opinion, plays down the influence of Jerome Kern and Joseph Schillinger on G. Songs included by Forte complete with Schenkerian diagrams ("analytical sketches") are *Somebody Loves Me, Someone to Watch Over Me, How Long Has This Been Going On?, Embraceable You, A Foggy Day,* and *Nice Work if You Can Get It.*

B1459. **FREEMAN, J. W.** "Dagli Stati Uniti." *Nuova Rivista Musicale Italiana* 7/3-4 (1973): 472-474.

B1460. **FRUEH, Donald,** comp. *The Henry M. Katzman Collection: Gershwin Materials.* Typescript. Spencer Library, University of Kansas, April 15, 1972.

Henry Katzman was second pianist and organist for two series of radio programs featuring Gershwin. According to Katzman, the programs took place in the Fall of 1933 and 1934, each lasting for a twenty-six week season. The materials inventoried in this typescript were gifted to the University of Kansas by Katzman. ". . . This collection shows a variety of Gershwin works, including both large and small forms, his contribution of jazz to the concert stage and the theater stage . . ." Interestingly, the collection includes, e. g., an eight-part vocal arrangement of *Clap Yo' Hands* for SSAATTBB. The collection also includes manuscripts of songs by composers other than G: Herbert, Kern, R. Rodgers, Kay Swift (both *Can't We Be Friends* and *Fine and Dandy*); printed music by such as Arlen, Berlin, Rube Bloom, Carmichael, Confrey, Debussy, Porter, Romberg, etc., ample testament to George's promoting music by other composers on these radio shows.

B1461. **FULLER, Roy.** "The Persistence of Meter." *The Southern-Review* [Baton Rouge, LA] 17/1 (Jan., 1981): 3-16.

References are made to Ira's *Lyrics on Several Occasions* in this essay which its author calls "a commentary on quotations, a postscript to a series of pieces on prosody over some years." *See*: **B21 & B1602**

B1462. "Funds for Study with Schoenberg: Mrs. A. L. Filene and George Gershwin Aid Scholarships for Composer's Course; He Will Teach in Boston; Exile from Germany, He Will Join Staff of Newly Formed Malkin Conservatory." *NYTimes,* Sept. 26, 1933, p. 26.

B1463. **FURIA, Philip.** *Ira Gershwin: The Art of the Lyricist.* NY: Oxford University Press, 1996, vii, 278 pp.

Taking a chronological approach, English professor Furia discusses IG's life and lyrics from the earliest ones through those supplied for other composers after George's death. Readers may wish to use this book as a companion to Kimball's work (**B1602**) and Ira's own book on the subject (**B21**). *See:* **B53, B1657**

B1464. **GALEWSKI, Myron.** "Ira Gershwin: He Loves to Rhyme." *American Record Guide* 41 (Jan. 1978): 3-5.

B1465. **GAMMOND, Peter.** "Long Live the Duke." *Jazz Journal* 27 (July 1974): 5-6. Article which compares the music of G to that of Duke Ellington.

B1466. **GASSNER, John.** *The Theatre in Our Times: An Examination of the Men, Materials and Movements in the Modern Theatre.* NY: Crown, 1954.

B1467. **GAUTHIER, Eva.** "Personal Appreciation," in: **Merle ARMITAGE,** ed. *George Gershwin.* NY: Longmans, Green, 1938, pp. 193-202.

B1468. _____. "The Roaring Twenties." *Musical Courier* 151/3 (Feb. 1, 1955): 42-44. Gauthier's version of G's first encounter with Ravel at a party in her home.

B1469. **GAVIN, James.** "They Get a Kick Out Of Cole: Memoirs of cabaret life by Bobby Short and Michael Feinstein." *NYTimes Book Review*, Oct. 29, 1995, pp. 18-19. Cabaret scholar James Gavin provided an informative review of the books by "cabaret's two most celebrated singer-pianists" Short and Feinstein, both of whom have rendered interpretations of Gershwin songs. Gavin concluded his discussion of Feinstein's *Nice Work If You Can Get It* with the observation: ". . .It all adds up to a portrait of an Ohio boy who is still trying desperately to convince himself and everyone around him that he belongs in the spotlight." *See:* **B1455 (Feinstein's book), D836 & D837 (Feinstein), D933 (Short)**

B1470. "Geo. and Ira Gershwin Get Goodspeed Awards (First Annual Goodspeed Opera House Award for Excellence in Musical Theatre)." *Variety,* Aug. 26, 1981, p. 83.

B1471. "George Gershwin [1898-1937]." *Journal Musical Français* No. 155 (Mar. 1967): 41-42.

B1472. "George Gershwin's Son Reviving Foster Songs." *Variety* 259, July 1, 1970, p. 41. Announcement concerning Alan Gershwin, who claims to be G's illegitimate son, who ". . . is bringing out . . . a selection of religious songs by Stephen Foster, that until now have gone virtually unnoticed . . . Songs will be published by the Alpha and Omega Music Publishing Co. and there are now records in the offing by such artists as Tennessee Ernie Ford and Pat Boone.

B1473. **GERSHWIN, Alan.** "I am George Gershwin's Illegitimate Son." *Confidential* 6/6 (Feb. 1959): 10-13, 45-46. Joan Peyser devotes considerable space to the situation of George's alleged son Alan in her biography: *The Memory of All That* (1993). *See:* **B75, B143**

B1474.   "Gershwin Memorials." *Time* 32/4 (July 25, 1938): 33-34.
Review of the fifth All-Gershwin memorial concert held during 1937-1938, at NY's Lewisohn Stadium, July 12, 1938. *See:* **W3g**

B1475.   GERARD, Jeremy. "Neil Simon Writing Musical With Gershwin Songs." *NYTimes*, August 17, 1987, Section C, p. 13, col 1.
A long article about Neil Simon writing a play, *A Foggy Day*, to contain songs by IG and GG. To the best of my knowledge, the play did not materialize.

B1476.   "German Orchestra (U.S. Soloists) in First West German Tour with All-Gershwin Program." *Variety*, Aug. 31, 1955, p. 2+.

B1477.   "Gershwin Benefit Concert by Whiteman Tonight." *NYHerald Tribune*, Feb. 12, 1955, p. 8. *See:* **W1w**

B1478.   "Gershwin Concert Orchestra Filling 100 Dates on Tour." *Musical Courier* 147/4 (Feb. 15, 1953): 37.

B1479.   "Gershwin Considers $100,000 Offer By Fox, But Composer Denies Accepting Bid to Write Musical Show for Movietone." *NYTimes*, Aug. 15, 1928, section ?, p. 19.
"George Gershwin denied yesterday printed reports that he had accepted an offer from William Fox which would bring him $100,000 to supply the music for an original musical comedy to be reproduced by the Movietone process . . . The composer admitted, however, that he was still considering the offer . . . The composer added that he had received two additional offers from the Movietone people. One is to use his 'Rhapsody in Blue' as the basis of a story for talking pictures, which would have the music synchronized with the film . . ."

B1480.   "Gershwin Everywhere." *Time* 46/2 (July 9, 1945): 67.

B1481.   "Gershwin Festival Scheduled in October." *Music Clubs Magazine* 50/1 (Autumn 1970): 19.

B1482.   "Gershwin 50th Anniversary in ASCAP Celebrated in Miami Festival." *ASCAP Today* 5/1 (Mar. 1971): 20. *See:* **W6c**

B1483.   "Gershwin Has Musical Treat At Auditorium." *Seattle* [WA] *Daily Times*, Dec. 16, 1936, p. 18.
Review of the concert when G performed with the Seattle Symphony, December 15, 1936. "The songs were over but the melody lingered on in the humming of several thousand Seattle Symphony Orchestra patrons whom George Gershwin sent home last evening from the Civic Auditorium swaying to the tunes of 'I've Got Rhythm,' 'Man I Love,' and 'I Got Plenty O' Nuttin' . . . He played his 'Rhapsody in Blue,' and forever after thousands of Seattleites will be spoiled—they won't be able to bear hearing anyone else's fingers, however nimble, slip through the melody . . ." *See:* **B1551, W1o, W7b, W2e**

B1484.   "Gershwin im Sinfoniekonzert der Stuttgarter Philharmoniker." *Das Orchester* 12/9 (Sept. 1964): 295-96.

B1485.   "Gershwin Memorabilia." *Variety* 247/4 (June 14, 1967): 50.

Concerns Gershwin memorabilia in The Museum of the City of New York.

B1486.   "Gershwin Memorials." *Time* 32/4 (July 25, 1938): 33-34.

B1487.   "Gershwin Orchestra Tours 74 Cities." *Musical America* 74/2 (Jan. 15, 1954): 4.

B1488.   "Gershwin Service Here on Thursday." *NYTimes,* July 13, 1937, p. 20.

B1489.   "Gershwins Honored." *Variety* 243/2 (June 1, 1966): 45.

B1490.   **GIDDINS, Gary.** "Riffs: Reconstructing the Great White Way."*Village Voice* 23 (Jan. 9, 1978): 49.

B1491.   **GOLDBERG, Isaac.** "Homage to a Friend," in: **Merle ARMITAGE,** ed., *George Gershwin.* NY: Longmans, Green, 1938, pp. 161-167.

B1492.   _____. "In Memoriam: George Gershwin." *B'Nai B'rith Magazine* (Aug.-Sept. 1937): 8-9, 26.

B1493.   _____. "Jazzo-Analysis." *Disques* [Philadelphia] 1/9 (Nov. 1930): 394-98.

B1494.   _____. "Music in the Air: Schönberg-Gershwin—A New Phonographic Venture." *The Musical Record* 1/9 (Feb. 1934): 326-29.
Includes discussion of Gershwin's tour with the Reisman orchestra in 1934.

B1495.   _____**.** "Music by Gershwin." *Ladies Home Journal* 48/2 (Feb. 1931): 12-13, 149; 48/3 (Mar. 1931): 20+; 48/ 4 (Apr. 1931): 25+.
Three articles which were later incorporated into Goldberg's biography.

B1496.   **GOLDBERG, Isaac.** "Personal Note," in: **David EWEN,** ed., *The Book of Modern Composers,* 2nd ed. rev. & enlarged. NY: A. A. Knopf, 1950. 1st ed, 1942.

B1497.   _____. *Tin Pan Alley: A Chronicle of the American Popular Music Racket,* with an introduction by George Gershwin. NY: John Day, 1930, pp. vii-xi, 120, 172, 155-158, *et passim.* Reprint, with a supplement by **Edward Jablonski,** as: *Tin Pan Alley: A Chronicle of American Popular Music.* NY: Frederick Ungar, 1961.
An interesting account of the Alley *ca.* 1929 which includes an "introduction" supposedly written by GG and giving his thoughts on song writing. Brief references to G here and there throughout: ". . . 'Swanee,' the song that made G famous, sold, in phonographic form alone, over 2,250,000 . . . [p. 218]"

B1498.   _____**.** "What's Jewish in Gershwin's Music." *B'Nai B'rith Magazine* 50/7 (Apr. 1936): 226-227, 247.
Talk of Jewish elements in Gershwin's music.

B1499.   **GOLDSTEIN, Malcolm.** *The Political Stage: American Drama and Theater* *of the Great Depression.* NY: Oxford University Press, 1974.

B1500. _____. *Kaufman: His Life, His Theater.* NY: Oxford University Press, 1979.

B1501. **GORDON, Max, with Lewis FUNKE.** *Max Gordon Presents.* Bernard Geis
Associates, 1963.

B1502. **GOTTFRIED, Martin.** "Theater: Gershwin Revived and Well." *Saturday
Review* 5 (Sept.16, 1978): 35.
 A one-page article providing a worthwhile summary of G's accomplishments in the
American music theater, inspired by concurrent (1978) revivals of such shows as *Tip-Toes. See*:
W24d

B1503. _____. "Why Is Broadway Music So Bad?"*Music News* (Jan. 1971): 4-5.

B1504. **GRANT, W. Parks,** and **Edward JABLONSKI.** "Notes & Letters." *American
Record Guide* 42/2 (December 1978): 2.
 Letter to Jablonski from Grant along with Jablonski's reply. The letter claims
". . . that Gershwin once wrote a piano piece using quarter tones. I [Grant] was told this by
Hans Barth . . ." The letter also refers to a picture of Barth and Gershwin appearing on the
cover of *Keyboard* magazine, which Jablonski recalls having seen. Jablonski, however, claims
ignorance of the microtonal piano piece.

B1505. "The Great Songwriters and Records of Their Great Songs." *Billboard* 62/40
(Oct. 7, 1950): supplement, 79-81.

B1506. **GREEN, Abel,** and **Joe LAURIE, Jr.** *Show Biz from Vaude to Video.* NY:
Henry Holt, 1951.

B1507. **GREEN, Benny.** *P. G. Wodehouse: A Literary Biography.* NY: Rutledge
Press, 1981, 99, 103, 112, 123, 136, 176-179.
 This excellent biography is sprinkled through with references to G and IG. The
following quote about Ira is interesting: ". . . Until the end of his [Wodehouse's] life he
remained in postal touch with Ira, who treasured the cards and letters, not just because of the
whimsicality of their contents, nor even because the two men loved and admired each other so
much, but because the survival of each man was to the other a surety that their mutual past was
not yet lost . . . [p. 123]." Considerable attention is given to *A Damsel in Distress*: ". . . There
were a few redeeming features, all of them musical . . . Wodehouse was too modest ever to
point out that one of the lesser songs in the score, 'Stiff Upper Lip,' was Ira Gershwin's tribute
to his old friend. Ira, who has described his lyric for the song as an attempt to incorporate as
many Wodehouseanisms as possible, managed, among others, old fluff, chin up, old bean, dash
it all and pip-pip . . . [p. 178]" *See*: **F11**

B1508. **GREEN, Stanley.** *Broadway Musicals: Show By Show,* 4th ed. Rev. and up-
dated by Kay Green. Milwaukee, WI: Hal Leonard, 1994, (1st ed., 1985).
 Through its excellent index, one can find information about the best known
Gershwin brother's shows including *Crazy for You* from 1992.

B1509. _____. *Ring Bells! Sing Songs!* Broadway Musicals of the Thirties. New

Rochelle, NY: Arlington House, 1971, 17, 18, 22, 23, 32, 56, 59, *et passim.*
Reprint edition entitled *Broadway Musicals of the 30s.* NY: Da Capo Press,
1982.

G and IG receive considerable attention in this profusely illustrated work. The first
page of the first chapter of this book begins with a discussion of *Strike Up The Band,* and the
other G musicals of the '30s receive attention, presented in chronological order, here and there
throughout. Appendices include "Casts and Credits [and lists of songs] of Broadway Musicals
of the Thirties"; "List of London Productions"; "List of Film Versions"; and significant
bibliography and discography. *See:* **W32 (Strike Up the Band), W33 (Girl Crazy), W34
(OTIS), W36 (Cake), W35, (Pardon My English), W37 (Porgy & Bess)**

B1510.   _____. "A Songwriter by Any Other Name . . ." *Variety* 233/7 (Jan. 8, 1964):
195.

B1511.   _____. *The World of Musical Comedy: The story of the American musical
stage as told through the careers of its foremost composers and lyricists,* 3d. ed,
rev. & enlarged. Foreword by Deems Taylor. South Brunswick and New York:
A. S. Barnes, London: Thomas Yoseloff, 1960, 1968, 1974, pp. 109-128; 4th
ed. San Diego & NY: A. S. Barnes, 1980. Page & chapter nos. refer to the 3rd
ed.

Chapter Eight covers G and IG. The approach is, in part, biographical, and it
includes history and analysis of the musicals in which the G's were involved, from *La La
Lucille* through P&B, along with with plot descriptions and commentary about the outstanding
songs.

B1512.   **GREENHALGH, Richard S.** "When We Have Jazz Opera: An Interview with
Mr. George Gershwin." *Musical Canada* 6 (Oct. 1925): 13-14.

B1513.   **GREGSON, David.** "Gershwin . . . in words and music." *San Diego Union,*
July 10, 1984, pp. D-6, D-8.

Bristled with anecdotes, this is an announcement of the presentation "The Naked
Gershwin," conceived and directed by classical/jazz pianist Cecil Lytle, to be given on the
University of California's San Diego campus on July 11, 1984.

B1514.   **GROFÉ, Ferde.** "George Gershwin's Influence," in: **Merle ARMITAGE,** ed.
George Gershwin. NY: Longmans, Green, 1938: 27-29.

B1515.   **GUADAGNINO, Luigi.** "Conclusioni su 'Porgy and Bess'." *La Scala* No. 89
(Apr. 1957): 64-68. French, English & German summaries, 103A. **[NN-L]**

B1516.   **H., C.** "Gershwin's Music Jams the Stadium." *NYTimes,* July 8, 1949, p. 14. *See:*
W3i

B1517.   **HAGGIN, B. H.** "Gershwin and Our Music." *The Nation* 135/3509 (Oct. 5, 1932):
308-309.

A negative view of G as an American composer.

B1518.   **HAMM, Charles.** "Musical Theater." *New Grove Dictionary of American
Music,* ed. by H. Wiley Hitchcock and Stanley Sadie. London, Macmillan, 1986,

III, pp. 300-309.

Helpful encyclopedia survey article covering from the eighteenth century to *ca.* 1985. In a section titled "The Tin Pan Alley Era," G's work on Broadway including P&B, is assessed here and there.

B1519. _____. "Towards a new reading of Gershwin," in *Putting Popular Music in Its Place*. Cambridge & NY: Cambridge University Press, 1995, pp. 306-324.

Typical of Hamm's work, this is a thought provoking, pensive reassessment of Gershwin and his work.

B1520. _____. *Yesterdays: Popular Song in America*. NY: W. W. Norton, 1979, [paperback] 1983, pp. 346-352.

Includes a general discussion of GG. ". . . [G] brought more harmonic innovation and sophistication to his songs than any of his contemporary songwriters, even including Jerome Kern, and his harmonic experimentation helped expand the style of some of his peers . . . Equally distinctive . . . was his affinity for the music of blacks . . . He knew James Reese Europe . . ." Includes a rarely seen photograph of Al Jolson singing *Swanee* in the movie of RiB. *See:* **F16**

B1521. **HAGGIN, Bernard H.** "Gershwin and Our Music." *The Nation* 135/3509 (Oct. 5, 1932): 308-309.

B1522. _____. "Music." *The Nation* 161/5 (Aug. 4, 1945): 115.

B1523. **HAHN, K.** "The Journal Reviews, Books: THE NEW YORK TIMES GERSHWIN YEARS IN SONG . . ." *Music Journal* (Feb. 1974): 8.

Brief, but complimentary review of this spiral-bound collection. ". . . There is a sizable bonus in the back of the book which includes George's own piano arrangements of such evergreens as *The Man I Love, Fascinatin'* [*sic*] *Rhythm, 'S Wonderful*, and others . . ."

B1524. **HAINES, Charles.** "George Gershwin ovvero del musicista come eroe." *L 'Approdo musicale* 1/4 (Oct.-Dec. 1958): 3-23.

B1525. **HAMMERSTEIN, Oscar.** "Gershwin."*The Music Journal* 8/4 (Apr. 1955): 21.

B1526. **HAMMERSTEIN, Oscar, II.** "To George Gershwin," in: **Merle ARMITAGE,** ed. *George Gershwin* (NY: Longmans, Green, 1938), pp. 1-4. From The George Gershwin Memorial Concert Program: Hollywood Bowl, Sept. 6, 1937.

B1527. **HANDLIN, Oscar.** *The Uprooted*, 2nd ed., Boston: Little, Brown, 1973.

B1528. **HANDY, William C.** *Blues.* NY: A. & C. Boni, 1926.

B1529. **HANSON, Howard.** "Flowering of American Music." *The Saturday Review of Literature* 32/32 (Aug. 6, 1949): 157-164.

B1530. **HARRIS, Radie.** "Broadway Ballyhoo." *Hollywood Reporter* (dateline: NY) **[AMPAS]**, Feb. 9, 1987.

Announcement of the upcoming Gershwin Gala, March 11, 1987, at the Brooklyn

Academy of Music. The gala observed the fiftieth anniversary of Gs death. Also mentioned are the Gershwin family members expected to attend: Lee Gershwin, Frankie Gershwin Godowsky and her twin daughters, Judy Gershwin, widow of Arthur, and her daughter-in-law and grandson. *See*: **W54m**

B1531.   **HARRIS, Sam H.** "Gershwin and Golf," in: **Merle ARMITAGE,** ed. *George Gershwin* (NY: Longmans, Green, 1938, reprint Da Capo, 1995), pp. 168-69.

B1532.   **HAYAKAWA, S. I.** "Popular Songs vs. The Facts of Life," in **Bernard ROSENBERG** and **David Manning White,** eds., *Mass Culture: The Popular Arts in America.* Glencoe, IL: Free Press, 1957.

B1533.   **HEARST, James.** "Reminiscences." *North American Review* 259 (Fall 1974): 39-43.

B1534.   **HELM, Everett.** "To Talk of Many Things." *Musical America* 82/7 (July 1962): 46.

B1535.   **HIGHAM, Charles.** *Ziegfeld.* Chicago: Henry Regnery, 1972.

B1536.   **HILL, Richard S.** "Music." *Library of Congress Quarterly Journal of Current Acquisitions* 11 (Nov. 1953): 15-26.
              Documents Mother Rose Gershwin's gifts of scores to the Gershwin collection.

B1537.   _____. "Music." *Library of Congress Quarterly Journal of Current Acquisitions* 12 (Nov. 1954): 47. *See*: **B1828-B1842**

B1538.   **HISCHAK, Thomas S.** *Word Crazy: Broadway Lyricists from Cohan to Sondheim.* Westport, CT: Praeger Trade (Greenwood), 1991.
              Discussion of lyrics of songs from American musical theatre, including those of IG, Cohan, Berlin, Lerner, Sondheim, et al. *See*: **B21**

B1539.   **HITCHCOCK, H. Wiley.** *Music in the United States: A Historical Introduction,* 3rd. ed. Englewood Cliffs, NJ: Prentice-Hall, 1988, 1974, 1969, pp. 63, 190, 205-207, 237-239, 274, 286n, 289, 292.

B1540.   **HOGARTH, Basil.** "Strange Case of George Gershwin." *The Chesterian* 15 [=No. 115] (May-June 1934): 130-136.

B1541.   **HOLDEN, Stephen.** "Pop View: More Than Ever, Gershwin Songs Are Here to Stay." *NYTimes,* Jan. 17, 1988, Arts & Leisure section, pp. H23, H30.
              Substantial article giving an abundance of information. The article summarizes activities that transpired during the fiftieth anniversary year of 1987 and shortly thereafter. Among the facts listed are: that ". . . In mid-November, the earliest surviving notebook fetched $121,000 in an auction at Christie's. It was the highest price ever paid for an American musical manuscript; that the album "Kiri Sings Gershwin" **(D940)** . . . "is currently the country's best-selling 'classical crossover'"; that the writer, Holden, had the opportunity to investigate the materials found in Secaucus as "copied and presented" by Michael Feinstein, Robert Kimball, Tommy Krasker, and Dick Hyman; mention of the September, 1987, production by the

Eastman School of Music of an All-Gershwin tune musical titled *Reaching for the Moon* **(W49)**; about the Adam Makowicz trio album titled "Naughty Baby" **(D1043)** stemming from the Library of Congress production of *Primrose* in May, 1987; about the ballet being choreographed by Peter Martins for the New York City Ballet using previously unpublished Gershwin instrumental music; about the announced plans of EMI/Angel Records to record the Glyndebourne production of P&B; about Tommy Krasker's "reconstructing the 1927 show, 'Strike Up the Band,' for a production this August" **(W27d)** and, finally, the news that Irwin Winkler is preparing a new film biography of both George and Ira. Also included in this comprehensive article are the printed lyrics to three G songs: "I Don't Think I'll Fall in Love Today," "Gather Ye Rosebuds," and "Ask Me Again."

B1542. **HOLLERAN, Laura W.** "Gershwin 'S Wonderful for Students." *Clavier* 21/7 (Sept. 1982): 27-31.
A comprehensive and helpful article listing versions at various difficulty levels ("late intermediate," e. g.) of G's original piano music, and the many arrangements thereof. The author annotated the list, and provided a recommended list of recordings as well as appending *Impromptu in Two Keys* to the article.

B1543. **HOWARD, John Tasker.** *Our American Music: A Comprehensive History from 1620 to the Present*, 4th ed. NY: Thomas Y. Crowell, 1965, pp. 424-429, 797-798, *et passim*. 1st ed., 1931.

B1544. _____. "George Gershwin," in: **Oscar THOMPSON,** *The International Cyclopedia of Music and Musicians*, 4th. ed. NY: Dodd, Mead, 1964, 785-786. 1st ed., 1937.

B1545. _____. "George Gershwin," in: **David EWEN,** ed., *The Book of Modern Composers*, 2nd ed. rev. & enlarged. NY: A. A. Knopf, 1950. 1st ed. 1943.

B1546. _____. *Our Contemporary Composers*. NY: Thomas Y. Crowell, 1941, pp. 306-311, *et passim*. Also as: "George Gershwin," in: **Elie SIEGMEISTER,** ed. *The Music Lover's Handbook*. NY: William Morrow, 1943, pp. 453-457.

B1547. _____. *This Modern Music: A Guide for the Bewildered Listener*. NY: Thomas Y. Crowell, 1942, pp. 123, 185, 190-191.

B1548. **HOWARD, John Tasker, & George Kent BELLOWS.** "George Gershwin Symbolizes the Growth of Jazz," in their: *A Short History of Music in America*. NY: Thomas Y. Crowell, 1957, pp. 246-50, *et passim*.
Some discussion of OTIS, P&B, and RIB. *See:* **W34, W37, W1**

B1549. **HUNT, George W.** "Of many things." (George Gershwin) (column) *America* 157 (Dec. 12, 1987).

B1550. **IDEMA, James.** "Book reviews; *The Life and Times of Porgy and Bess . . . Hollis Alpert . . .*" *Smithsonian* 21/12 (Mar. 1991): 145-147.
A detailed and complimentary review, despite an error in fact in the first paragraph.
See: **B516**

B1551.   "If Gershwin's Mother Hadn't Bought a Piano—But She Did." *Seattle* [WA]
            Daily Times, Dec. 14, 1936.
            A human interest story based upon an interview of G held in connection with his
upcoming appearance with the Seattle Symphony, December 15, 1936. *See:* **W1o, B1483**

B1552.   "Inside Stuff—Music." *Variety* 202/5, Apr. 4, 1956, p. 49.
            "G's debt to the late Joseph Schillinger . . . is amplified by publicist Earl E. Ferris
who once handled publicity for a radio show, sponsored by a laxative chewing gum, on which
G appeared. Ferris writes: 'I know that with his mirrors and slide rules, Schillinger was helping
George a helluva lot on 'P&B.' . . . George said in my hearing that the only inspired melody
was 'Summertime' and that he worked out all the rest with algebraic formulae . . .
Unquestionably, G was a great man, but there is no reason to ignore . . . the great little
mathematics professor from Russia who got him away from ending each song a third up or a
third down . . ." *See:* **W37**

B1553.   "In Which Ira Gershwin Is Considered; The Tale of the Family Lyric-Writer,
            Who Devotes Himself to Fashioning the Words for George's Music." *NYTimes*,
            Jan. 19, 1930, Section 7, p. 2.

B1554.   "Ira Gershwin Donates $1,500 Annually to School Named for Brother George."
            Variety 236/5 (Sept. 23, 1964): 83.

B1555.   "Ira Gershwin, Gent." *ASCAP Today* 5 (Jan. 1972): 1, 4-7.

B1556.   **IRVIN, Marjory.** "It's George, Not Jazz: Gershwin's Influence in Piano Music."
            American Music Teacher 23 (Nov.-Dec. 1973): 31-34.

B1557.   **ISRAEL, Robert A.** "Great Man of Music." *Southwestern Musician* 19/5 (Jan.
            1953): 13+.

B1558.   **ITURBI, José.** "Gershwin Abroad," in: *Rhapsody in Blue*: the Jubilant Story
            of George Gershwin and His Music. Hollywood: Warner Bros., 1945, 9-10.

B1559.   **JABLONSKI, Edward.** "George Gershwin." *HiFi/Stereo Review* 18/5 (May
            1967): 49-61.

B1560.   _____. "Gershwin After 20 Years." *HiFi Music at Home* 3/3 (July-Aug.
            1956): 22-23, 52, 54, 56-58.

B1561.   _____. "Gershwin at 80; Observations, Discographical and Otherwise, on
            the 80th Anniversary of the Birth of George Gershwin, American Composer."
            American Record Guide 41 (Sept. 1978): 6-12, 58; (Oct. 1978): 8, 10-12, 57-59.

B1562.   _____. "Gershwin Plays Gershwin-Enjoy, Enjoy." *American Record Guide*
            28 (Jan. 1962): 365.
            Review of Distinguished Records 107 with G performing based on piano rolls.

B1563.   **JABLONSKI, Edward.** *Gershwin Remembered.* Portland, OR: Amadeus Press,
            1992.

A volume of memoirs written by persons who knew G., including his brother, Ira. The writings are arranged in chronological order, to fit G's life. There is also a chronology, incorporating "contemporary figures and events," as well as an Appendix containing some of George's writings on music.

B1564. _____. *Harold Arlen: Happy with the Blues,* Garden City, NY: Doubleday, 1961, pp. 17, 36, 45-46, 66-67, 88-89, 92-94, *et passim.*
Biography including numerous brief references to GG and IG.

B1565. _____. "Ira Gershwin—Reluctant Celebrity." *Listen* 1 (Mar.-Apr. 1964): 14-15.

B1566. _____. "Ira (Mr. Words) Gershwin." *Stereo Review* 32 (May 1974): 50-59.

B1567. _____. "The People and Time of George Gershwin." *The Reporter* 27 (July 19, 1962): 46-47.
Calling G "the first practicing *American* composer," this is an encomium coinciding with the twenty-fifth anniversary of his death. The central point of the article is that, despite the opinion of the music critics in 1937, ". . .who almost to a man predicted that his death would end the chapter on the 'serious' Gershwin . . . [G] . . . is today [1962] by far the most performed, the most recorded, the most renowned American composer on either side of the musical tracks, popular or serious."

B1568. _____. "Photo[s] by George Gershwin: A Portfolio of Originals." *American Record Guide* 28/11 (July 1962): 844-848.
A rare exposé of twelve photographs of friends taken personally by GG. Included here are shots of Andrea Swift Warburg and G (a mirror study), G with Irving Berlin (a time exposure), IG, Deems Taylor, Kay Swift, Gloria Braggiotti, E. Y. "Yip" Harburg, Emily Paley, Jerome Kern, David Siqueiros, Leopold Godowsky, and Ruby Elzy.

B1569. _____. "Piano 'Pounder' Extraordinaire: George Gershwin at the Keyboard." *Keyboard Classics* 4/1 (1984): 12, 20-26+
Excellent article emphasizing G's virtuosity as a pianist, with arrangements appended. A little known fact is pointed out by Jablonski: ". . . George took courses at Columbia University, with Rossetter G. Cole, one of which was in orchestration . . ." The arrangements included in this issue are: Jerome Kern's *Whip-Poor-Will* (Excerpt) unwritten arrangement for a piano roll recording by G, *I Got Rhythm* as performed by G on radio, February 19, 1934, transcribed by Dick Hyman, and G's special written arrangement of *I Got Rhythm* prepared for the *Gershwin Song Book.*

B1570. **JACOBI, Frederick.** "The Future of Gershwin." *Modern Music* 15/1 (Nov.-Dec. 1937): 2-7.
Critical evaluation of the composer. The central conclusion of Jacobi's (1891-1952) essay, full of ambivalence towards G, was that G's best work was as song writer, and that he lacked the skill to write effectively in the larger, serious forms. ". . . I believe that the *American in Paris* will live longer than either the *Rhapsody* or the *Concerto* and that, of the more pretentious works, *Porgy and Bess* will be the first to go . . ." Jacobi conceded that ". . . It is not in his 'larger' works that George will live. It is in the great number of songs, almost every one of which is a gem in its own way . . ." Steven Gilbert (*See* **B158**), among others, have provided ample evidence that Jacobi was mistaken.

B1571.   JACOBS, Tom. "Theater-Dance: Recalling the wit and worries of Levant."
[Reprint from the *Los Angeles Daily News*]. *Times Picayune* [New Orleans, LA],
(dateline: Los Angeles), Feb. 17, 1989, p. 12.

Story announcing the Los Angeles debut at the Coronet Theatre, of a then new play
At Wit's End, written by Joel Kimmel, and concerned with the life and music of Oscar Levant.
"The play, which had its premiere last year (1988) at the Burt Reynolds Theatre in Jupiter, FL,
is an imaginary recital Levant gave towards the end of his life . . ." Kimmel commented:
". . . There is almost as much music as there is dialogue . . . He [Levant] wanted to be the
world's greatest pianist and the world's greatest composer . . . He never achieved any of that.
His association with Gershwin made him realize he was not a genius . . ." *See:* **W52.1.bb,
B1583 (Bio of Levant)**

B1572.   JASEN, David A. *Tin Pan Alley, The Composers, the Songs, The Performers
and their Times: The Golden Age of American Popular Music from 1886 to
1956*. NY: Donald I. Fine, 1988, pp. 5, 63, 77, 100, 104, 133, 148, 157, 163-
173, *et passim*.

This excellent history of the Alley contains many references to GG, including a
biography (pp. 163-173), and many other peripherals which influenced his music and life.
Among other very interesting facts is an Appendix giving the complete history of the street
addresses of publishers, Jerome H. Remick among them. According to this list, it is interesting
to note that Jerome H. Remick moved to 219-221 West 46th Street in 1912. Since G went to
work as a song plugger for Remick in May of 1914, I theorize that is the 46th Street address
where he evidentally "pounded" rather than the West 28th location mentioned in other sources.
See: the Biography chapter, p. 4.

B1573. "Jazz Opera in View for Metropolitan: Otto H. Kahn Tells Berlin and Kern That
He Would Be Glad to Consider One. On Grand Opera Scale, Chairman's Interest
in Popular American Music Due to His Son's Successful Jazz Orchestra."
NYTimes, Nov. 18, 1924, section ?, p. 23

Article discussing Otto H. Kahn's wish that a "jazz opera" be composed for the
Metropolitan Opera House. Kahn was then chairman of the company that operated the Met.
". . . George Gershwin, whose orchestral piece, 'Rhapsody in Blue,' has been widely heard
. . . was mentioned as the man at the moment considered promising in music of the larger
orchestral and even operatic forms . . ."

B1574. "Jazzed Homesickness in Paris." *Literary Digest* 100/1 (Jan. 5, 1929): 22-23.

B1575.   JESSEL, George. *This Way, Miss;* foreword by **William SAROYAN.** NY:
Henry Holt, 1955.
Contains a tribute to GG.

B1576.   JEWELL, Edward Alden. "Art of Gershwin Put On Exhibition: Late Composer's
One Man Show Reveals Talent of Considerable Promise; Late Work the Feature
. . ." *NYTimes*, Dec. 21, 1937.

Review of the Marie Harriman Gallery's all-G showing of his paintings held during December of 1937. The review indicates that Frank Crowninshield provided a written
catalogue for the exhibition, which included "just short of forty items, seventeen of them oils
and the remaining works drawings and watercolors . . ."

B1577.   JOHNSON, J. Rosamond. "Emancipator of American Idioms," in: **Merle**

ARMITAGE, ed. *George Gershwin.* NY: Longmans, Green, 1938, pp. 65-71.

B1578. KAHN, Otto H. "George Gershwin and American Youth," in: **Merle ARMITAGE,** ed. *George Gershwin.* NY: Longmans, Green, 1938, pp. 126-128.

B1579. KANTER, Kenneth Aaron. *The Jews on Tin Pan Alley: The Jewish Contribution to American Popular Music, 1830-1940.* NY: KTAV Publishing House; Cincinnati, OH: American Jewish Archives, 1982, pp. 147-160. Part II, No. 12 is devoted to biography of GG. No new information here. Playbill for *Sinbad* (Al Jolson and *Swanee*) reproduced on book jacket.

B1580. KART, Larry. Article on unpublished songs and theater scores by George Gershwin, Jerome Kern, Cole Porter, other composers found in warehouse; performances at Library of Congress and Lincoln Center. *Chicago Tribune,* May 24, 1987, Section 13, p. 12.

B1581. (Number inadvertently omitted).

B1582. KASDAN, M.L. "The Final Days of George Gershwin, American Composer, September 26, 1898–July 11, 1937; 50th anniversary." *Journal Ky Med. Association* 85 (11, 1987): 649-652.

B1583. KASHNER, Sam, and Nancy SCHOENBERGER. *A Talent for Genius: The Life and Times of Oscar Levant* [1906-1972]. NY: Villard Books, 1994.
This excellent biography of George's friend Levant includes much anecdotal and factual information about Gershwin and the spirit of those times in the United States. *See:* **W2h.1,W2j, W3h, W4c & d,W52.1, W54d-g, D45, D126-130, D156, D211, D303-306, D367, D407, D425, D629-630, D746, D747, D1096, D1117, B106, B166, B918.2, B922, B1571, B1628-1632, B2077, F16, F18, F19**

B1584. KAUFMAN, George S. "Department of Amplification." *New Yorker* 22 (June 29, 1946): 51.

B1585. _____. "Jimmy the Well-Dressed Man: A Vaudeville Act with Music." *Nation* 134 (June 15, 1932): 676-677.

B1586. _____. "Music to My Ears." *Stage* 15 (Aug. 1938): 27-30.

B1587. _____. "Now It Can Be Told." *NY Herald Tribune,* June 17, 1945, Section 4, p.1.

B1588. _____. "The Tryout Blues (or Coos)." *NY Herald Tribune,* Sept. 29, 1957, Section 4, p. 1.

B1589. _____, and Morrie Ryskind. "Socratic Dialogue."*Nation* 136 (Apr. 12, 1933): 403.

B1590. KAUFMAN, Joanne. "Curious George; Did Gershwin's private life include an illegitimate son?" *People* (June 7, 1993): 129-133.
An article like this came about after the appearance of Joan Peyser's biography

in 1993. The article is based on an interview of Peyser by Kaufman, the result of which was to shore up the argument that Alan (Albert) Schneider is indeed the son of GG. *See*: **B75**

B1591.   **KAZIN, Alfred.** *On Native Grounds: An Interpretation of Modern American Prose Literature.* NY: Reynal & Hitchcock, 1942.

B1592.   **KELLER, Hans.** "Gershwin's Genius." *Musical Times* 103 [=No. 1437] (Nov. 1962): 763-764. *See*: **B1601**

B1593.   _____. "Rhythm: Gershwin and Stravinsky." *Score and I. M. A. Magazine* no. 20 (June 1957): 19-31.

B1594.   _____. "Truth and Music." *Music and Musicians* 16/2 (Oct. 1967): 16.

B1595.   **KELLNER, Bruce.** *Carl Van Vechten and the Irreverant Decades.* Norman: University of Oklahoma Press, 1968, pp. 186, 192-194, 197, 201, 281, 308, 313, Van Vechten's letter to GG, 193.
            This biography includes references to Van Vechten's relationship to the Gershwins. On pages 281-282, there is a description of the George Gershwin Memorial Collection of Music and Musical Literature which Van Vechten donated from his personal library to Fisk University, reasoning that ". . . If a Negro collection would draw Negro scholars to a white university [referring here to his collection donated to Yale University], why would a white collection not draw white scholars to a Negro University?. . ."

B1596.   **KERN, Jerome.** "Tribute," in: **Merle ARMITAGE,** ed., *George Gershwin.* NY: Longmans, Green, 1938, p. 120.

B1597.   **KHACHATURIAN, Aram.** "George Gershwin." *Uj zenei szemle* 6/l2 (Dec. 1955): 32-33.

B1598.   "Kid Sister of the Gershwins Recalls Old Days on the Eve of a New Honor." *NYTimes*, June 6, 1983, p. C11.

B1599.   **KILENYI, Edward, Sr.** *Gershwiniana: Recollections and Reminiscences of Times Spent with My Student George Gershwin.* Typescript, 1962-63 **[DLC].**

B1600.   _____. "George Gershwin As I Knew Him." *Etude* 68/10 (Oct. 1950): 11-12, 64.

B1601.   **KILLICK, John.** "An Open Letter to Hans Keller." *American Musical Digest* 1/5 (1970): 12-13. Reprinted from *The Listener* (Jan. 8, 1970).
            Negative comments about Keller's program of G songs held Dec. 29, 1969. *See*: **B1592**

B1602.   **KIMBALL, Robert.** *The Complete Lyrics of Ira Gershwin.* NY: Alfred A. Knopf, 1993. 414 pp.
            Anyone interested in G scholarship will want to examine this superb, cocktail table sized book, compare it to its predecessor *Lyrics on Several Occasions* (1959), **B21**, and read its informative Introduction and Chronology. Some insights into the G legend not seen before are presented by Kimball, who has good access to Ira's side of the family. He quotes IG liberally from the earlier *Lyrics*. The Kimball book organizes the IG lyrics/songs chronologically

by some twenty-seven shows and fifteen movies. IG's book grouped them together in various arbitrary categories devised by IG, such as "The Not Impossible He" which included *The Man I Love*, *Looking for a Boy*, *My Son-in-Law*, and *Sure Thing*, for example. According to Kimball in his introduction, ". . . There are more than seven hundred lyrics in this compilation . . . Nearly four hundred of the lyrics are being published for the first time . . ." *See:* **B1461**

B1603. **KIMBALL, Robert, and William BOLCOM.** *Reminiscing with Sissle and Blake.* NY: Viking Press, 1973.

B1604. **KINGMAN, Daniel.** *American Music: A Panorama.* NY: Schirmer Books, 1979.

B1605. **KIRBY, Fred.** "'Do It Again' Is Excellent Gershwin—But Disappoints." *Billboard* 83/10 (Mar. 6, 1971): 28.

B1606. **KNIGHT, Arthur.** "Musicals a la Mode." *Saturday Review* 40/15 (Apr. 13, 1957): 26.

B1607. _____ & **Eliot ELISOFON.** *The Hollywood Style.* NY: Macmillan, 1969.

B1608. **KNIGHT, Ellen.** "Charles Martin Loeffler and George Gershwin: A Forgotten Friendship." *American Music* (Winter 1985), 452-459.
Despite his being called "a proper Bostonian," Loeffler claimed he was "'frightfully addicted to jazz'" and hence was an ardent admirer of GG. Kay Swift, GG's close friend, studied composition with Loeffler. Among other interesting material, the article discusses correspondence between Loeffler and GG, including G's request for Loeffler to look at "part of the orchestration" for AiP. Knight discussed Loeffler's own *Partita* for violin and piano (1930), and concluded ". . . the Loeffler correspondence offers a number of expressions of genuine and enthusiastic admiration . . ." The correspondence is housed in the Gershwin Collection, Music Division, Library of Congress.

B1609. _____. "Choosing Sides: Gershwin on Gershwin." *Stereo Review* 32 (Jan. 1974): 102-103.

B1610. _____. "'The Gershwins' Two Astaires." *Saturday Review* 54/44 (Oct. 30, 1971): 70.

B1611. _____. "Jubilee in Blue; Fascinatin' Rhythm, Crackling Lyrics, and a New Musical Form Were the Gift of the Gershwins, Who Are Honored Today on the Seventy-Fifth Anniversary of George's Birth." *Saturday Review/World* 1 (Oct. 9, 1973): 16-18.

B1612. _____. "Paradox in Blue." *Saturday Review* 39/8 (Feb. 25, 1956): 37, 60-61.

B1613. **KOUSSEVITSKY, Serge.** "Man and Musician," in: **Merle ARMITAGE,** ed. *George Gershwin* (NY: Longmans, Green, 1938), pp. 13-14.

B1614. **KRAMER, A. Walter.** "I Do Not Think Jazz 'Belongs'"; American Composer Objects to Mr. Gershwin's Appraisal of 'Art'; Outspoken Comment on Broadway Music." *Singing* 1 (Sept. 1926): 13-14.
Kramer alleges that G didn't orchestrate the *Concerto in F. See:* **W2, B1401**

& **1402,** and GG's reply at **B2, B1619**

B1615.   KRASKER, Tommy, and **Robert KIMBALL.** *Catalog of the American*
Musical: Musicals of Irving Berlin, George & Ira Gershwin, Cole Porter,
Richard Rodgers & Lorenz Hart. National Institute for Opera and Musical
Theater, 1988.
A splendid work of research and documentation essential to the study of the
Gershwins. ". . . This first volume surveys the seventy-five book musicals of Irving Berlin,
George and Ira Gershwin, Cole Porter, and Richard Rodgers and Lorenz Hart, documenting
the location and completeness of all available original piano-vocal scores, lyrics and libretti, and
orchestra scores and parts . . . [from the Introduction]."

B1616.   KUTNER, Nanette. "Portrait in Our Time," in: **Merle ARMITAGE,** ed.
George Gershwin. NY: Longmans, Green, 1938, p. 235.

B1617.   LANCASTER, Albert. "George Gershwin." *Keynote* (Autumn 1946): 21-22.

B1618.   LANGLEY, Allan Lincoln. "The Gershwin Myth." *American Spectator* 1/2
(Dec. 1932): 1-2.

B1619.   _____."Gershwin, Daly and Langley." *NYTimes* [dateline, New York, Jan.
15], Jan. 22, 1933, Section 9, p. 8.
A letter to the music editor in response to William Daly's letter of Jan. 15, 1933, to
the *Times,* that letter in response to an article Langley wrote in *The Spectator* (**B1618**). The
gist of Langley's letter is defending the position he took in *The Spectator* article, namely that
William Daly was "connected in the capacity of a consultant with the Gershwin 'symphonic'
efforts . . ." *See*: **B2, B1614**

B1620.   LAURENTS, Arthur. "'Look, Girls, There's the Man with Our Tap Shoes!'"
NYTimes Magazine, Sept. 11, 1966, Section II, pp. 42-43, 48-50.

B1621.   LAWRENCE, Gertrude. *A Star Danced.* Garden City, NY: Doubleday, Doran,
1945.
The autobiography of a key player in the lives of George and Ira.

B1622.   LAWSON, Carol. "Kitty Carlisle Hart Ready for Return to Broadway." *NYTimes,*
June 14, 1983, p. C9.

B1623.   LAWTON, Dorothy. "Reading About Gershwin," in: *Rhapsody in Blue, the*
Jubilant Story of George Gershwin and His Music. Hollywood: Warner Bros.,
1945, p. 18.

B1624.   LAX, Roger, and Frederick SMITH. *The Great Song Thesaurus,* 2nd ed.,
Updated and Expanded. NY: Oxford University Press, 1989.
A curious reference book with lots of information, but strangely organized.

B1625.   LEDERER, Joseph. "Fred Astaire Remembers . . . Gershwin, Porter, Berlin,
Kern, and Youmans." *After Dark* (Oct. 1973): 54-59.
Reminiscences by Astaire. "'George came to Hollywood for *Shall We Dance* [not
accurate, it was for *Delicious* in 1931]. The producer knew that George suited my kind of
work, and I was happy they could get him. By then we were good friends. George and Ira tried

to write numbers that would be suitable for me. Very successfully, I'd say . . ."

B1626. LEISER, Erwin. "George Gershwin and the Jazz-Age." *Du-die Zeitschrift Der Kultur* 8 (1987): 54-57.

B1627. LERNER, Alan J. *The Musical Theatre: A Celebration.* NY: McGraw-Hill, 1987, 47, 52, 60, 63, 130-135 [P&B], *et passim.*
Contains numerous references to G and IG, and to P&B. *See:* **W37**

B1628. LEVANT, Oscar. *The Memoirs of an Amnesiac.* New York: G. P. Putnam's, 1965.
References to Gershwin and his music appear here and there throughout this interesting, rambling autobiographical work. *See:* **B1583**

B1629. _____. *A Smattering of Ignorance.* New York: Doubleday, Doran, 1940.
[Chapter: "My Life or The Story of George Gershwin"], pp. 147-210.
The first of three such works, it is a significant reference. Levant devoted an entire chapter to George, and to a lesser extent, to Ira. The material is in the form of an autobiographical essay and gives insights through Levant's perceptions of George the person, and his music. Levant concluded the chapter with a quotation from "so alien a musician as Schönberg:" ". . . Music to him [Gershwin] was the air he breathed, the food which nourished him, the drink that refreshed him. Music was what made him feel, and music was the feeling he expressed. Directness of this kind is given only to great men, and there is no doubt that he was a great composer. What he achieved was not only to the benefit of a national American music but also a contribution to the music of the whole world." *See:* **B1583**

B1630. _____. "'S Wonderful, 'S Marvelous, 'S Gershwin: A musical genius is re-called by a famous wit and pianist who knew him well." *TV Guide* (Jan. 15, 1972): 24-26.
Article announcing the January 17, 1972, Jack Lemmon NBC television special and including personal reminiscences by Levant. ". . . My first encounter with Gershwin came in 1925, after I had recorded 'Rhapsody in Blue' for Brunswick Records. That engagement had been an unexpected opportunity—the regular pianist with the orchestra failed to show up and I was called in as a last-minute substitute. When I completed the recording in one take (I was 18 and nerveless), it occurred to me they could pay me whatever they wanted for the job, even union scale, which they did . . ." *See:* **B1583**

B1631. _____. *The Unimportance of Being Oscar.* NY: G. P. Putnam's Sons, 1968, pp.41-44, 48, 103, 146, 149-151, 230.
The third and last of Levant's autobiographical books; it includes a few brief anecdotes about GG. *See:* **B1583**

B1632. _____. "Variations on a Gershwin Theme." *Town and Country* 94/4,206 (Nov. 1939): 58-61, 83-84.
Pure Levant with his typical wittiness. *See:* **B1583**

B1633. LEVIN, Floyd. "'Porgy and Bess' A Jazz Concert by the Jim Cullum Jazz Band, UCLA Center for the Performing Arts . . . September 30, 1988." *The Second Line* 41 (Winter 1989): 24-25.
Positive review of the concert at UCLA, the music based on that band's album of P&B music, **D539.**

B1634.   LEVINE, Henry. "Gershwin, Handy and the Blues." *Clavier* 9/7 (Oct. 1970): 10-20.

A lengthy and detailed discussion of various aspects of Rhapsody in Blue, including rhythm and piano fingering. *See:* **W1**

B1635.   LEVINGER, Henry W. "The Roaring Twenties: 1920-29." *Musical Courier* 151/3 (Feb. 1, 1955): 42-43.

Interview with mezzo-soprano Eva Gauthier, with whom G performed in the 1920s.

B1636.   LEWINE, Richard, and **Alfred SIMON.** *Encyclopedia of Theatre Music.* NY: Random House, 1961.

B1637.   LIBRARY OF CONGRESS. *The Gershwins and Their World,* presented by the Music Division and the Ira and Leonore Gershwin Trust for the Benefit of the Library of Congress, Robert Kimball and Elizabeth H. Auman, Coordinators, Coolidge Auditorium, March 13-16, 1998.

This is the printed program for this spectacular event held in Washington in March,1998. A transcript of the proceedings is in progress as of August, 1998. Gershwin scholar Robert Wyatt wrote a fine descriptive article concerning this event and its attendees, which appears in The Sonneck Society for American Music Bulletin 24/2 (Summer 1998): 40.

B1638.   "L[ibrary] of C[ongress] Gets George Gershwin Manuscripts." *Billboard* 65/10 (Mar. 7, 1953): 18.

B1639.   "Library of Congress receives Gershwin medals." *Coin World* (Aug. 24, 1988).

Announcement story concerning the bronze duplicates offered by the U. S. Mint of the congressional gold medal (Medal of the Congress 1985) honoring George and Ira which President Ronald Reagan presented to family members.

B1640.   LICHTMAN, Irv. "News Analysis:'New' Show Songs Raise Issues." *Billboard* 90, Dec 4, 1982 (dateline: NY), pp. 4, 60.

Article concerning the Secaucus discovery of "riches of American musical theatre" found at Warner Bros. warehouse in Secaucus, NJ. Don Rose, well-known arranger of G's music, found the 70 crates of manuscripts. The G materials are now [1987] at the Library of Congress. This article gives information on the publishing companies involved, Harms, in G's case, and points out that, under the terms of the new 1976 Copyright Act, Warner Bros. . . . "has been making termination deals with a number of the authors' estates . . . including . . . Gershwin . . ."

B1641.   LIEBLING, Leonard. "The George I Knew," in: **Merle ARMITAGE,** ed. *George Gershwin.* NY: Longmans, Green, 1938, pp. 123-25.

B1642.   LIPSKY, Leon. "George Gershwin, Jazz Glorified." *The American Hebrew* 118/2 (Nov. 20, 1925): 59, 67.

B1643.   LISKA, A. James. "Tormé, Urrams, Nero Play Gershwin." *Los Angeles Times,* Oct. 20, 1987, Section VI, p. 2.

Liska reviews jazz performance by Mel Tormé, Leslie Uggams, and Peter Nero of George Gershwin's music at UCLA's Royce Hall.

B1644. **LIST, Kurt.** "George Gershwin's Music: 'The Greatest American Composer —Alas!'" *Commentary* 1/2 (Dec. 1945): 27-34.
A lengthy, generalized critical assessment of G's music. List summarized his opinions in the concluding paragraphs: ". . . Gershwin made no contribution to serious music . . . But if Gershwin had been merely an improver and reformer in Tin Pan Alley his fame—and certainly his music—would have faded long ago. He was more than that, he was a part of America's social history transposed into music . . ."

B1645. "The Live Art of Music." *Outlook* 112/2 (Jan. 13, 1926): 47-48.

B1646. **LIVINGSTONE, William.** "GERSHWIN: The American composer George Gershwin died fifty years ago last month. Anniversary tributes are taking place in concerts, on TV, and on records." *Stereo Review* 52/8 (Aug. 1987): 63-66.
Lengthy tribute to G, in essay form. Much of the material is biographical but there is also an accounting of many of the commemorative performances that took place during 1987.

B1647. **LJUNGGREN, Bengt, M. D.** "The Case of George Gershwin." *Neurosurgery* 10/6, pt. I, (1982): 733-736.
Explanation using medical terminology of the brain tumor which caused G's death. Some biographical details are included.

B1648. "London Symphony Orchestra." *Musical Opinion* 81 [=No. 962] (Dec. 1957): 153.

B1649. **LONG, R.** "The Voice Before the Requiem: Immortals in Passing." *Fugue* 4 (June 1980): 15.

B1650. **LOWENS, Irving.** "Music." *Quarterly Journal of the Library of Congress* 21 (Jan. 1964): 23-24.

B1651. **MABIE, Janet.** "Rhapsody on Gershwin." *Christian Science Monitor* 27/219 (Aug. 14, 1935): 3, 14. (In Weekly Magazine Section.)

B1652. **MACADAM, B.** "Viva Gershwin (Collaboration with Siqueiros, David)." *ARTNEWS* 93/6 (Summer 1994): 29.

B1653. **MALKIEL, Henrietta.** "Scheherazade in West Virginia: Jazz Opera on Its Way." *Musical America* 42 (Apr. 25, 1925): 3, 26.

B1654. **MALMBERG, Helge.** "George Gershwin," in: *Sohlmans Musiklexicon*, 4 vols. Stockholm: Sohlmans Forlag, 1951-52, II, 542-543.

B1655. "The Man I Love." *New Republic* 91/1,181 (July 21, 1937): 293-294.
Obituary written less than a week after GG's death.

B1656. **MARROCCO, W. Thomas.** *See*: **Arthur C. EDWARDS, B1427.**

B1657. **MAST, Gerald.** *Can't Help Singin': The American Musical on Stage and Screen.* Woodstock, NY: Overlook Press, 1987, pp. 1, 3, 5, 10, 14, 24, 27-29, 35, *et passim*.
References to G throughout. While Chapter 6, titled "Pounding on Tin: George and

Ira Gershwin" includes a brief biography, it is also a clever analysis of the teamwork between the G brothers, with some insightful emphasis on the lyrics and their relationship to the music in selected songs. The chapter includes a clever assessment of Ira's work: ". . . George's driving piano may have kept the 'Gershwin Circle' spinning, but Ira was the affable social force at its center—a genial, casual elf who would rather play cards, play the horses, play word games, play with his cigars, play anything to avoid work. He was able to write only by turning his work into play, and no other lyricist was ever so insistently and consistently playful . . ." *See:* **B1463**

B1658.   "Master of Jazz." *The Commonweal* 26/13 (July 23, 1937): 316.

B1659.   MATES, Julian. *America's Musical Stage: Two Hundred Years of Musical Theatre.* Contributions in Drama and Theater Studies, Number 18. Westport, CT: Greenwood Press, 1985, pp. 37, 51, 61, 150, 152, 182-184, 186-188, 198.
While this source has few references to GG and IG, it does have quotes that put some of the G shows into perspective with other shows in the music theatre of the 1920s and 1930s in America. In re: OTIS, ". . . Probably the single most important change wrought by the 1930s musical is epitomized by *Of Thee I Sing* (1931) . . . This show . . . won the Pulitzer Prize (as best play!). More and more, people had begun to notice the musical, to become aware of its past and its potential. A certain pride in what seems to be a peculiarly American form was developing . . ." **W34**

B1660.   MATTHEWS, Peter. "Belittling Gershwin." *Newsweek* (Aug. 20, 1945): 79.
Short article summarizing Barry Ulanov's critical article which appeared in Metronome.

B1661.   MAXWELL, Elsa. *R. S. V. P.: Elsa Maxwell's Own Story.* Boston: Little, Brown, 1954.

B1662.   MCCLELLAN, Joseph. "Teaming Up With the Gershwins: Library of Congress & Elektra to Record Works." *Washington Post*, May 23, 1989, Final Edition, Style Section, p. D1.
Article in connection with the May 22 and 23, 1989, concerts held at the Library of Congress titled "A Program of Music By George and Ira Gershwin Celebrating the Inauguration of the Leonore Gershwin/Library of Congress Recording and Publishing Project." In addition to discussing the concert, the article announced the inauguration of the Elektra/Nonesuch recording project which is to begin with an authentic revival recording of *Girl Crazy*, to be followed by such albums as "Michael Feinstein Sings Unpublished Gershwin"; "Lady in the Dark" (1941), IG's collaboration with Kurt Weill and Moss Hart; *Strike Up the Band* in both its 1927 and 1930 versions; *Pardon My English* and *Primrose.* Among those attending, Gershwin expert Robert Kimball was quoted: ". . . There are at least 15 shows that would be worth recording . . . and we should be able to get them done before George Gershwin's centennial in 1998 . . ." Mrs. Ira (Leonore) Gershwin, current Librarian of Congress James Billington, and James W. Pruett, Chief of the Music Division attended the concert. *See:* **W54u, B1455 (explaining why Feinstein's album did not appear), B1694, D450, D564, D492 (*Pardon*)**

B1663.   MELLERS, Wilfrid. "Gershwin's Achievements." *Monthly Musical Record* 83 [=No. 943] (Jan. 1953): 13-16.

B1664.   MEL'NITSKAYA, M. "Kyubileyu Dzh. Gershvina." *Sovetskaja Muzyka* 38 (May

1974): 93-94.

B1665. **MEREDITH, Scott.** *George S. Kaufman and His Friends.* Garden City, NY: Doubleday, 1974. *See:* **W34, W36**

B1666. **MEYERSON, Harold, Ernie HARBURG, and Arthur PERLMAN.** *Who Put the Rainbow in The Wizard of Oz? Yip Harburg, Lyricist.* Ann Arbor: University of Michigan, 1993.

B1667. "Miami U's Gershwin Fest to Revue One-Act Opera '135th Street' & Other Works ." *Variety* 260/9 (Oct. 14, 1970): 58.
Announcement of Gershwin festival. *See:* **W54i**

B1668. **MILLIGAN, Spike.** "William McGonagall Meets George Gershwin." *Punch* 295 (Dec. 9, 1988): 66.

B1669. **MITCHELL, Donald.** "Concerts and Opera." *Musical Times* 97 (July 1956): 373-375.

B1670. **MONTGOMERY, Michael.** "George Gershwin Piano-Rollography." *Record Research* No. 42 (Mar.-Apr. 1962): 3-4.
Roll collector Montogomery compiled this list of 114 record rolls Gershwin made for different labels. Montgomery updated the list for Schneider, **B1735.1**, q. v.

B1671. **MOORE, Macdonald Smith.** *Yankee Blues: Musical Culture and American Identity.* Bloomington, IN: Indiana University Press, 1985, pp. 70-71, 94, 96, 98, 130-131, *et passim.*
Many references to Gershwin within this essay context. Biographical details are given and an assessment of the impact of RiB (pp. 136-138): ". . . In its first decade, *Rhapsody* earned Gershwin a quarter of a million dollars . . ." *See:* **W1**

B1672. **MORDDEN, Ethan.** *Better Foot Forward; The History of American Musical Theatre.* NY: Grossman, 1976.

B1673. _____. *Broadway Babies: The People Who Made the American Musical.* New York & Oxford: Oxford University Press, 1983, 34-36, 46, 62, 81-81, 87, 90-94, 97, *et passim.*
There are twenty-seven references to G in the index to this excellent survey. Among those references is this description of G: ". . . Gershwin is the first tricky composer. It was he who instituted 'blue' harmony, who redoubled syncopation, who sported a piano technique beyond any player's challenge and set the style into his published songs. He is the first composer whose arrangements for performance are so much a part of the tunes that to ignore them is to go out of style . . . (pp. 90-91)" The final chapter, "A Selective Discography," contains informed description of many of the well-known recordings of G songs, including, e. g., those by Ella Fitzgerald **(D840)**, Joan Morris/William Bolcom **(D907)**, Bobby Short **(D933)**, and Ben Bagley **(D803)**.

B1674. **MURPHY, George,** and **Victor LASKY.** *"Say. . . Didn't You Used To Be George Murphy?"* Bartholomew House, 1970, pp. 50, 109, 134.
Murphy played Sam Jenkins in the original cast of OTIS.

B1675. "Music: Gershwin Bros." *Time* 6/3 (July 20, 1925): 14.

In part biographical, this is the article which appeared in the issue which featured G at age 27, on its cover.

B1676. "Music: Music by Slide Rule." *Newsweek* 24/13 (Sept. 25, 1944): 80.

The anonymously written article which claimed that GG had gone to Joseph Schillinger "in desperation . . ."

B1677.   NANNES, Caspar H. *Politics in the American Drama.* Washington, DC: The Catholic University of America Press, 1960.

B1678.   NATHAN, George Jean. "The Lesson of Another Failure," in **Robert KIMBALL** and **William BOLCOM**, in *Reminiscing with Sissle and Blake.* NY: Viking Press, 1973.

B1679. "The New Etude Gallery of Musical Celebrities." *Etude* 47/3 (Mar. 1929): 193-194.

Portrait & brief biography.

B1680.   NEW YORK PUBLIC LIBRARY [NN-L]. Library Museum for the Performing Arts, Lincoln Center.

The NPL is rich in holdings about both George and Ira. It is the repository of the famous clippings files providing much newspaper commentary.

B1681.   NEWELL, George. "George Gershwin and Jazz." *The Outlook* 148/9 (Feb. 29, 1928): 342-343, 351.

Biographical article up to 1928.

B1682.   NICHOLS, Beverley. *Are They the Same at Home? Being a Series of Bouquets Diffidently Distributed.* NY: Doubleday, Doran, 1927. Also as: "George Gershwin," in: **Merle ARMITAGE,** ed. *George Gershwin.* NY: Longmans, Green, 1938, pp. 231-234.

Contains some information on G on the lighter side.

B1683.   NILES, Abbe. "The Ewe Lamb of Widow Jazz." *New Republic* 49/630 (Dec. 29, 1926), 164-166.

B1684. _____. "A Note on Gershwin." *Nation* 128 (Feb. 13, 1929): 193-194.

B1685.   NOGUCHI, Isamu. "George Gershwin (art reproduction)." *Du* No. 8 (1987): 13.

B1686. _____. "Portrait," in: **Merle ARMITAGE,** ed. *George Gershwin.* NY: Longmans, Green, 1938, pp. 209-210.

B1687. "Notes & Letters." *American Record Guide* 42 (Dec. 1978): 2.

B1688. "Notes and Quotes from Ira's Friends." *ASCAP Today* 5 (Jan. 1972): 7-9.

B1689.   NOVICK, J. "Theatre: Pretty Nice Work (St. James Theatre)." *Village Voice* 28 (May 10, 1983): 86.

B1690.   O'CONNOR, John J. "TV Reviews: Gershwin Is Lauded In Capitol."*NYTimes*, November 19, 1986, p. C33.

Review of the November 19, 1986, Gershwin tribute by means of a public telecast emanating from the White House, dubbed "In Performance at the White House." With obvious pleasure, the writer described the content of the show.

B1691.   O'HARA, John. "Entertainment Week: An American in Memoriam." *Newsweek* 16/3 (July 15, 1940): 34.

While announcing the annual All-Gershwin program at Lewisohn Stadium for 1940, O'Hara produced an anecdotal memorial, and containing the famous quote: "George died on July 11, 1937, but I don't have to believe that if I don't want to."

B1692.   OJA, Carol J. "Gershwin and American Modernists of the 1920s." *Musical Quarterly* 78/4 (Winter 1994): 646-668, (Reprint) CUNY Brooklyn College, Brooklyn, NY 11210.

A well documented, masterful article contributing much to Gershwin scholarship. The article compares G's position to that of others of "his American contemporaries," among them Aaron Copland. Among many interesting facts pointed out by Oja, she reminds us that Paul Whiteman's efforts "to foster a new American repertory" through his invitations and commissions to contribute new works have gone largely unrecognized, and, secondly, that during the 1920s "efforts were underway to fuse jazz with concert idioms." The latter activity predated Gunther Schuller's now well known Third Stream work of the late 1950s. The magnificent notes appended to this article along with the bibliographical information they reveal are themselves worth the effort taken to read the article. *See:* **B1722**

B1693.   OSGOOD, Henry Osborne. "The Jazz Bugaboo."*American Mercury* 6 (Nov. 1925): 328-330.

B1694.   O'TOOLE, Lawrence. "Ego, Paranoia and Power in the Land of Musical Rights." *NYTimes,* Arts & Leisure Section 2, May 30, 1993, pp. 1, 26.

An essay concerning some of the problems potential users have obtaining rights to songs from the heirs to songwriter's estates. G's name comes up more than once in this rather lengthy article, including reference to what the writer called "The Feinstein Affair." This concerned a planned recording by singer Michael Feinstein "that was to feature much unpublished Ira Gershwin material" but which never reached completion due to problems between Feinstein and the producer, John McClure, and between Feinstein and Michael Strunsky, nephew/estate representative of the deceased Leonore Gershwin. The master tapes of six of the eight planned sessions are stored by Roxbury Recordings. *See:* **B1662, B1455 (explains the "Feinstein Affair")**

B1695.   PABKIN, Gerald. *Drama and Commitment; Politics in the American Theatre of the Thirties.* Bloomington: Indiana University Press, 1964.

B1696.   PAGE, Tim. "Gershwin, Porter and Rodgers Scores Found." *NYTimes,* Nov. 20, 1982, pp. 1, 17.

Story about the Secaucus, NJ find of manuscripts.

B1697.   PERKINS, Francis D. "Concerts & Recitals: Paul Whiteman." NY *Herald Tribune,* Feb. 14, 1955, p. 9.

B1698.   PESTALOZZA, Luigi. "Il Mondo musicale di Gershwin." *L 'Approdo Musicale*

1/4 (Oct.-Dec. 1958): 24-45.

B1699. *Performing Arts: Music*, ed. by Iris Newsom. Washington: Library of Congress (avail. from U.S. Government Printing Office), 1995.
Eight essays on various aspects of American music ranging from G to Cole Porter to Jazz. The first essay "George Gershwin: A Presence in My Life" by David Raksin, composer of song *Laura*, includes interesting anecdotes about G not available elsewhere. Highly recommended.

B1700.   PEYSER, Joan. "His Fascinating Rhythms are Here to Stay." (George Gershwin) *TV Guide* 35 (Nov. 21, 1987): 9.

B1701.   _____. *Bernstein: A Biography.* New York: Beachtree Books, William Morrow, 1987, pp. 25, 46-47, 49-50, 63, 120, 130.
In this biography of Bernstein, written before Peyser's controversial bio of G, there are some interesting perspectives on G: "In 1983, when the Institute for Studies in American Music published a monograph consisting of articles and reviews from Minna Lederman's *Modern Music, The New York Times* interviewed Lederman . . . she prided herself on the fact that during her long tenure at the magazine she had never published an article by or about G. Hers was a serious journal, she said, and G 'was so popular; the attention he received was ridiculous' . . . The emphasis on intellect over emotion, on abstraction over representation, has had wide-ranging consequences for twentieth-century art . . . G suffered under the intellectual bias of the time . . ." Concerning the RiB and Concerto, Peyser commented: ". . . While there is much that is remarkable here—fresh and inventive melodies in profusion—the pieces themselves falter because of inherent structural weaknesses. It is in the songs that G left his greatest legacy. But because they were imbedded in Broadway shows with chorus lines and show-business hoopla, the critical establishment disregarded them. Schoenberg knew better. He told his friends that his greatest wish was to write tunes like Tchaikovsky's that people would whistle while leaving the hall. He knew that at least in this regard G would transcend him . . . (p. 50)"

B1702.   PFAFF, T. "Reproducer Software (The Elektra/Nonesuch 'Gershwin Plays Gershwin, the Piano Rolls')." *Piano & Keyboard,* 172 (Jan.-Feb.,1995): 69. *See*: **D1134**

B1703.   PINCHARD, Max. "La vocation irrestible de George Gershwin." *Musica* [Chaix] No. 80 (Nov. 1960): 25-29.

B1704.   PLEASANTS, Henry. *The Agony of Modern Music.* NY: Simon & Schuster, 1955.

B1705. "Plush Gershwin Festival Set for '53 Longhair Tour with Blessing of Family." *Variety* (Jan. 23, 1952): 1+.
The Gershwin Concert Orchestra goes on tour.

B1706. "Posthumous Exhibit Shows that Gershwin Knew Harmony on Canvas Also." *News-Week* 10/25 (Dec. 20, 1937): 28.
About a one-man show of Gershwin's paintings at the Marie Harriman Gallery in New York.

B1707.   POLLAK, Robert. "Gershwin." *The Magazine of Art* 30/9 (Sept. 1937): 531, 588.

The argument that G is not an American Mozart.

B1708. POOL, Rosey E. "Een nieuw lied voor Amerika." *Mens en Melodie* 8/1 (Jan. 1953): 28.

B1709. "Program Aug. 9 To Be Memorial For Gershwin: Special Stadium Event to Include 'Porgy and Bess' Choir With Philharmonic, 'Aristogenic' File Is Kept, Society Says It Has Record of His Characteristics." *NY Herald Tribune*, July ?, 1937.

Announcement of the Lewisohn Stadium memorial concert scheduled for August 9, 1937. Also of interest is the information included about the "Aristogenic" record of G: ". . . Scientists of the future will have access to records of the physical characteristics and personality of the late George Gershwin through data compiled by the Aristogenic Association, it was announced yesterday by Dr. C. Ward Crampton, president of the society. Dr. Crampton revealed for the first time that files of the association, which was founded eleven years ago to collect . . . scientific records of the . . . 'biologically best-born' Americans, contained data on Mr. Gershwin. He said that certain physical measurements of the composer, including X-rays of his head and hands, and other undisclosed information had been assembled several years ago. None of the material will be made available to the public for a least twenty-five years . . ." *See*: **W54b, B919, B923**

B1710. RAKSIN, David. "George Gershwin: A Presence in My Life." *See*: *Performing Arts: Music,* Full entry above, under **B1699.**

B1711. REYNA, Ferdinando. "Adesso anche a Parigi." *La Scala* No. 42 (May 1953): 38-42.

B1712. RICH, Alan. "The Lively Arts: George." *New York* (Sept. 10, 1973): 76-77.

An extended essay about G and some of his music, brought about by the 75th anniversary of his birth. Mention is made of the "little show" *The Gershwin Years* and its cast: Barbara Cook, Helen Gallagher, Julie Wilson, Harold Lang, Steve Ross, and Edward Morris. The show had a very successful tour during 1973. Rich expressed value judgments about Gershwin's music: ". . . The 'big' Gershwin works succeed because of the sheer vitality, the originality and high quality of the musical ideas they contain, but the working-out of these ideas—the moments in the *Concerto* for example, where a theme is developed to the point of hysteria—has to be an embarrassment to anyone who wants to derive a fair estimate of his abilities . . ." Rich also discussed the significance of Ira's lyrics as well as voicing his opinions about certain interpretations of the music: ". . . [W]e have to accept such banal misreadings as Balanchine's *Who Cares? . . .*" *See*: **W52**

B1713. _____. "The Arts: Music, Nice Work If You Can Get It; George Gershwin's magic extended from Tin Pan Alley to the concert hall. On the 50th anniversary of his death, New York offers a tribute." *Newsweek* 109/11 (March 16, 1987): 70-71.

Announcement article alluding to the then upcoming Gershwin Gala and performances of OTIS and Cake at the Brooklyn Academy of Music on March 11 and 18, 1987, respectively. Mention was also made of the Jack O'Brien ". . . exuberant 1976 Houston production . . ." of P&B and a current Houston production of a 17-city national tour, as well as the forthcoming summer 1987 British production of same. An unusual feature of this article is the appendage of an interesting photograph from OTIS showing the leading lady, Mary, holding her twin babies. Rich concluded: ". . . We haven't produced a better composer, and we probably never will, than GG. Color him, rhapsodically, blue. . . ." *See*: **W34c**

B1714.   RIPP, Allan. "Music By George, Words By Ira." *Horizon* 21 (Oct. 1978): 90-92.
An essay, including a chronicle of some of the events which transpired during 1978, including the film festival at the Metropolitan Museum of Art in New York. Ripp gave considerable attention to IG's lyric writing: ". . . A whole concordance could easily be compiled for Ira's lyrics, for which he managed to pull in references from literature, mythology, world history, the Bible, even nursery rhymes . . ."

B1715.   RISCHIN, Moses. *The Promised City: New York's Jews 1870-1914.* Cambridge: Harvard University Press, 1977.

B1716.   ROBBINS, R. J. "No Tribute to Gershwin (concert tribute)." *Crescendo International* 20 (Apr. 1982): 3.

B1717.   ROBINSON, Edward. "George Gershwin: a Punster Turned Poet." *The Fortnightly Musical Revue* 2/1 (Oct. 31, 1928): 3-4.

B1718.   ROCKWELL, John. "Capturing Gershwin's Genius." *NYTimes*, Apr. 18, 1982, Section II, pp. 23-24.

B1719.   _____. "The Genius of Gershwin Still Inspires Composers." *NYTimes,* Mar. 8, 1987, Section 2, pp. 23, 36.   [with cover photo of choreographer Dan Siretta and Baryshnikov].
Substantial article in anticipation of the March 11, 1987, all-star gala concert in connection with the 125th anniversary of the Brooklyn Academy of Music. ". . .The program will amount to an overview of the Gershwin era as well as a contemporary celebration of it, with an emphasis on unusual or reconstructed numbers and scenes . . ." In a window appended to the first page of the article, Rockwell added selected recommendations on recordings. ". . .The best complete recording of 'Porgy and Bess' remains the Houston Grand Opera version [as of the date of this article] . . ." *See*: **W54m**

B1720.   RODZINSKI, Artur. "George Gershwin," in: *Rhapsody in Blue: The Jubilant Story of George Gershwin and His Music.* Hollywood: Warner Bros., 1945, p. 15.

B1721.   ROLONTZ, Bob. "Gershwin Spec Misses Its Mark." *Billboard Music Week* 73/9 (Jan. 23, 1961): 8.

B1722.   ROSENFELD, Paul. "Aaron Copland: George Gershwin, in *An Hour with American Music.* Westport, CT: Hyperion Press, 1979, reprint of the 1929 edition published by J. P. Lippincott, Chap. VI, pp. 126-143.
Carol J. Oja quoted from this book in her article about the American Modernists of the 1920s. *See*: **B1692**

B1723.   ROSENFELD, Paul. "Gershwin," in his: *Discoveries of a Music Critic.* NY: Harcourt, Brace, Jovanovitch, 1936, 264-272, 384.
An essay in the form of predominantly negative value judgments about G's "serious" oeuvre. ". . . Gershwin's absolute and programmatic compositions are distinguished by their frequent, sometimes vivacious and adroit, at other times coarse and brutal, exploitations of the jazz idioms, rhythms, and colors . . ." Rosenfield considered the Concerto to be the "juiciest and most entertaining of G's concert works" and concluded ". . . We remain obliged to him

mostly for *Funny Face* and his other smart musical shows. His talent burgeons in them . . ."

B1724.   _____. "No Chabrier." *The New Republic* 73/944 (Jan. 4, 1933): 217-218.
Assessment of Gershwin.

B1725. ROSENWALD, Hans. "Speaking of Music." *Music News* 42/4 (Apr. 1950): 24.

B1726. "Rts. Issue In Gershwin Suit Vs. 'Let's Call.'" *Variety* (dateline Los Angeles,
March 11) 298/6 (March 12, 1980): 1, 108.
Report of a suit brought by Ira G. against The Whole Thing [production] Company
which had been performing a revue at the Westwood Theatre under the title *Let's Call the
Whole Thing Off*, The revue involved some fifty G. songs. The crux of the problem involved
grand vs. small rights (pertaining to copyright), an issue which became increasingly debatable
with the proliferation of revue-type productions.

B1727. RUBLOWSKY, John. "Gershwin and Ives: The Triumph of the Popular," in
his: *Music in America.* NY: Macmillan, 1967, pp. 146-155.

B1728.   _____. *Popular Music.* NY: Basic Books, 1967, pp. 56-57, 150.

B1729. SABLOSKY, Irving. *American Music.* Chicago: University of Chicago Press,
1969, pp. 149-151, 154-155.

B1730. SAERCHINGER, César. "Jazz." *Musikblätter des Anbruch: Monatsschrift für
moderne Musik* 7/4 (Apr. 1925): 205-210.
According to Charles Schwartz, ". . . this issue [is] devoted completely to jazz, [and]
the author writes about Paul Whiteman's contributions, with special attention to *Rhapsody in
Blue.*" *See:* **W1**

B1731. SANDOW, Hyman. "Silhouettes: A Play-Boy Turns Serious." *Musical Digest* 14
(Nov. 1929): 19, 37.

B1732. SCHAEFER, Theodore. "Gershwin Opera Heard in Capital." *Musical America*
72/14 (Nov. 15, 1952): 23.

B1733. SCHILLINGER, Frances. *Joseph Schillinger: A Memoir by His Wife.* NY:
Greenberg, 1949.
One would expect to read mention of Schillinger's star student, Gershwin.

B1734. SCHILLINGER, Joseph. *Kaleidophone: Pitch Scales in Relation to Chord
Structures.* NY: M. Witmark & Sons, 1940.

B1735. SCHNEIDER, Wayne. "Rediscovering Gershwin." *Humanities* 8/3 (May-June
1987): 10-13.
An important article by the writer of an excellent dissertation on *Of Thee I Sing* and
Let 'Em Eat Cake. In the article, Schneider made an appeal for restoration and preservation:
". . . efforts must continue to locate and preserve books, scores, and orchestral parts to shows
from the first Golden Age of Broadway lest our national heritage of musical theater disappear
forever . . ." That appeal has been heard as can be seen in several instances documented in this
book (The Library of Congress/Leonore Gershwin/Roxbury Recordings project and
Krasker/Kimball **[B1615]** to cite two examples).

B1735.1. _____, ed. *The Gershwin Style*: *New Looks at the Music of George Gershwin.* NY: Oxford University Press, 1998, 336 pp.

This is a fine series of essays by the current (1999), world's leading Gershwin experts, having been put together by eminent Gershwin scholar Schneider. The contents include: Introduction: *The Gershwin Style*, Wayne Schneider **[Part 1] Analysis and Manuscript Studies** *Toward a New Reading of Gershwin*, Charles Hamm; *Rotating Porgy and Bess*, Wayne D Shirley; *Gershwin's Operetta Overtures: Medley or Composition?*, Wayne Schneider; *Nice Work: Thoughts and Observations on Gershwins Last Songs*, Stephen E Gilbert; *Some Musings on 'Nice Gershwin* Tunes': Form, *and Harmony in the Concert Music of George Gershwin*, Larry Starr. **[Part 2] Reception** *Rhapsody in Blue: A Study in Hollywood Hagiography*, Charlotte Greenspan; *Gershwin on the Cover of Rolling Stone*, Susan Richardson; *George Gershwin and Jazz*, André Barbera **[Part 3] Performance Practice** *Tracing Gershwin's Piano Rolls*, Artis Wodehouse; *George Gershwin's Piano Rollography*, Michael Montgomery; *What About Ira?*, Edward Jablonski. Highly recommended. *See*: **B62**

B1736. **SCHÖNBERG, Arnold.** "A Self-Analysis." *Musical America* 73/3 (Feb. 1953): 14, 172.

Schönberg painted a portrait of G which is included here.

B1737. _____. "George Gershwin," in: **Merle ARMITAGE,** ed. *George Gershwin.* NY: Longmans, Green, 1938. pp. 97-98. Also in: **Sam MORGENSTERN,** ed. *Composers on Music: An Anthology of Composers' Writings from Palestrina to Copland.* NY: Pantheon, 1956, pp. 384-386.

B1738. "Schönberg über Gershwin." *Oesterreichische Musikzeitschrift* 35 (Feb. 1980): 66-67.

B1739. **SCHUBART, Mark A.** "George Gershwin-Song Writer," in: *Rhapsody in Blue; The Jubilant Story of George Gershwin and His Music.* Hollywood: Warner Bros., 1945, p .16.

B1740. **SCHUBERT, Gisela.** "George Gershwins Musicals: von der Revue zur politischen Satire." *Neue Zeitschrift für Musik* 152/7-8 (July/Aug. 1991): 13-21.

B1741. **SCHULLER, Gunther.** *Early Jazz: Its Roots and Musical Development,* Vol. I. NY: Oxford University Press, 1968, pp. 129n, 191, 192n, 273, 354.

G receives some attention in this masterly study of early jazz on the pages indicated. In regard to the footnote on page 192 (fn 21), Schuller has pointed out that he was in error concerning the statement that Chester Hazlett played the clarinet solo in the 1924 first Whiteman performance of the RiB, that it was in fact Ross Gorman, as documented in other sources.

B1742. **SCHWAB, Heinrich W.** "Zur Rezeption des Jazz in der komponierten Musik [Concerning the Reception of Jazz in Composed Music]." *Dansk aarbog for Musikforskning DK* 10 (1979): 127-178.

Using Gershwin and Milhaud among others as examples, the author of this substantial article "[t]races the history and reception of jazz in Europe in the early 20th c., focusing on its pervasive influence during the 1920s . . ." [from *RILM Abstracts* 14/1 (Jan.-Apr. 1980): 86]

B1743. **SCHWARTZ, Charles M.** *George Gershwin: A Selective Bibliography and Discography* (Bibliographies in American Music, No. 1). Detroit: Information Coordinators (for College Music Society), 1974.

This is an earlier attempt (1974) to bring the mass of Gershwin bibliography under control. It followed Schwartz's N. Y. U. dissertation on the orchestral works (1969-**B88**) and his major life and works of 1973 (**B86**). In addition to "Highlights of Gershwin's Life"—a chronology, the bibliography includes 654 citations, most of them not annotated. A comprehensive list of recordings to *ca.* 1973 arranged under titles of the works is included. Lists of musicals and movies of which recordings were made are appended. *See:* **B1864**

B1744. **SCHWARZ, Boris.** *Music and Musical Life in Soviet Russia, 1917-1970.* NY: W. W. Norton; London: Barrie & Jenkins, 1972, pp. 293, 357, 361, 443, 464.

B1745. **SCHWINGER, Wolfram.** "Notizen über Gershwin." *Musik und Gesellschaft* 10/5 (May 1960): 302-304.

SEDGWICK, Ruth Woodbury. *See:* **Marcia DAVENPORT, at B1407.**

B1746. `SELDES, Gilbert.** "The Gershwin Case," in: **Merle ARMITAGE,** ed. *George Gershwin.* NY: Longmans, Green, 1938, pp. 129-134.

B1747. _____. *The Seven Lively Arts.* NY & London: Harper & Brothers, 1924. Includes some discussion of G.

B1748. _____. "Toujours Jazz." *Dial* 75 (Aug. 1923): 151-166.

B1749. **SENDREY, Albert Heink.** "Tennis Game," in: **Merle ARMITAGE,** ed. *George Gershwin.* NY: Longmans, Green, 1938, pp. 102-112.

B1750. **SHALES, Tom.** "George Gershwin: Accepted by the Highbrows at Last." *Washington Post,* Entertainment, Gardens, Show section, Sept. 23, 1973, p. E1, E3.

Lengthy general article concurrent with George's seventy-fifth birthday. Shales interviewed Todd Duncan, then seventy, now deceased, and the article has some biographical details and anecdotes about Gershwin, some of the latter inaccurate.

B1751. "Shows on Broadway (St. James Theatre)." *Variety,* May 4, 1983, p. 534. *See:* **W48b**

B1752. **SHAW, Arnold.** "Gershwin, Arlen and the Blues," *Billboard* 79/25 (June 24, 1967), supplement, pp. 68-69.

B1753. **SHAWE-TAYLOR, Desmond.** "A Mini-Success." *American Musical Digest* 1/5 (1970): 12. Reprinted from the *London Sunday Times,* Jan. 4, 1970.

B1754. **SHEPARD, Richard F.** "Words and Music from the Days When Words and Music Reigned." (discovery of George Gershwin and Jerome Kern songs). *NYTimes,* Mar. 15, 1987, p. E26.

B1755. **SHIRLEY, Wayne D.** "Another American In Paris; George Antheil's Correspondence with Mary Curtis Bok." *Library of Congress Quarterly*

Journal 34 (Jan. 1977): 2-22.

B1756.   _____. "New Gershwin Acquisition." *Impromptu* No. 2 (Winter 1984): 1-3.

B1757.   SIEGMEISTER, Elie, ed. *The Music Lover's Handbook.* NY: William Morrow, 1943, pp. 728-729, 753-757, *et passim.*

B1758.   SINGER, Barry. *Black and Blue: The Life and Lyrics of Andy Razaf,* foreword by **Bobby SHORT.** NY: Schirmer Books, 1992, pp. 5, 23, 32-33, 140-141, 161, 274.
This biography of the composer of the lyrics to such great songs as "Ain't Misbehavin'." "Memories of You," "Honeysuckle Rose," and "Stompin' at the Savoy" provides some unique insights on G. ". . . By 1924, Gershwin was so intimately involved musically with Harlem that many of his piano playing friends on the rent strut circuit, including James P. Johnson and Willie 'The Lion' Smith, recalled the young pianist at this time often sitting cross-legged on the floor at rent struts, joyfully drinking in the music . . . (from p. 141)."

B1759.   SITWELL, Osbert. *Laughter in the Next Room.* Boston: Little, Brown, 1948.

B1760.   SLONIMSKY, Nicolas. "Musical Oddities." *Etude* 73/4 (Apr. 1955): 4-5.
According to Schwartz, includes an anecdote about Ravel and G.

B1761.   SMITH, Cecil M. *Musical Comedy in America.* NY: Theatre Arts Books, Robert M. MacGregor, 1950.

B1762.   SOBEL, Bernard. "Musical Comedy, Quo Vadis?" *Theatre Arts Monthly* 12 (Aug. 1928): 566-575.

B1763.   SOREL, Edward. "George Gershwin shows Fred Astaire how Fascinatin[g] Rhythm should be danced (art reproduction)." *Graphis* 42 (July/Aug. 1986): 50 col.

B1764.   SOREL, Nancy Caldwell. "Irving Berlin and George Gershwin (First Encounters)." *Atlantic* 261 (May 1988): 75.

B1765.   SORIA, Dorle J. "People and Places: Memorabilia to Go to Museum of the City of New York." *High Fidelity/Musical America* 17/9 (Sept. 1967): MA-5.
A useful catalog of the resulting Exposition sponsored by the museum was published by it in 1968. *See:* **B1381.1.**

B1776.   SPAETH, Sigmund. *The Facts of Life in Popular Song.* NY: Whittlesey House, 1934.

B1777.   _____. *A History of Popular Music in America.* NY: Random House, 1948.

B1778.   _____. "Our New Folk-Music," in his: *They Still Sing of Love.* NY: Horace Liveright, 1929, pp. 173-178.

B1779.   _____. "Theatre on the Disk." *Theatre Arts* 38/6 (June 1954): 10.

B1780.   _____. "Two Contemporary Americans: Gershwin and Hadley." *Scholastic*

3212 (Apr. 30, 1938): 23.

B1781. **SPENCE, K.** "Television." *Musical Times* 115 (Feb. 1974): 157-158.

B1782. **SPITALNY, Evelyn.** "First Gershwin Festival Rocks Miami U. Campus with Music, not Mayhem." *Variety* 260/13, (dateline: Miami, Nov. 10), Nov. 11, 1970: 46.
Review of the Festival. *See*: **W54i**

B1783. **Staff of the Division.** "Recent Acquisitions of the Music Division." *The Quarterly Journal of the Library of Congress* 31 (Jan. 1974): 32-33, 50, 57, 62-63. *See*: **B1842**

B1784. **STAMBLER, Irwin.** *Encyclopedia of Popular Music.* NY: St. Martin's Press, 1965, pp. 87-90, 185, et al.

B1785. **Stan.** "Shows Abroad." *Variety* 282, Mar 3, 1976 (dateline Melbourne, Australia, Feb. 22), pp. 89-90.
Review. "Described as a 'musical entertainment [actually a revue],' 'Gershwin' was first presented at . . . Fridays, a small suburban theatre . . . Restaged with the original cast, it has transferred to city centre in Melbourne [the Total Theatre] . . . A cast of four perform on an illuminated staircase and forestage . . . Each G stage show is dealt with, whilst his pix are dealt with in a montage segment of tunes . . ."

B1786. **STARR, Larry.** "Ives, Gershwin, and Copland: Reflections on the Strange History of American Music." *American Music* 12/2 (Summer 1994): 167-187.
A substantial and excellent article in which scholar Starr ". . . consider[ed] aspects of the music of [the] three [named] commanding and thoroughly distinctive composers of American art music . . . searching for their common ground rather than for the traits that make each composer separate and unique . . ." Starr suggests that these composers are ". . . undervalued by members of what we can call the critical and intellectual establishment . . ."

B1787. _____. "A Gershwin Companion - a Critical Inventory and Discography, 1916-1984 - Rimler, W. [**Book review**]." (Reprint) Univ. Washington, Seattle, WA. 98195, 1993. *See*: **B936**

B1788. **STEARNS, David Patrick.** "A Gershwin Evening (Library of Congress, Washington, D.C.) (concert reviews)." *Musical America* 107 (Nov. 1987): 30.

B1789. **STEARNS, Marshall and Jean.** *Jazz Dance: The Story of American Vernacular Dance.* NY: Schirmer Books, 1979.

B1790. "A Steichen Gallery." *Opera News* 31/9 (Dec. 24, 1966): 13.
Portrait of G in 1927.

B1791. **STEWART, Lawrence D.** *The Gershwins: Words Upon Music.* [Published in conjunction with the "Ellas Fitzgerald Sings The George and Ira Gershwin Song Books" Nelson Riddle album] Verve Records, Inc., 1959.
This book was intended to serve as an adjunct to the "Ella Fitzgerald Sings . . ." Verve album, cited at **D840**, and it serves well it that capacity. It includes biography and elucidating commentary on each of the pieces in the album, including their early performance

history and informative, analytical discussion of the lyrics of the songs. The book, interspersed with photographs and reproductions of Bernard Buffet drawings, stands as an excellent source for program notes on the works.

B1792.   STEVENSON, Ronald. "Last Week's Broadcast Music." *Listener* 83 (Jan. 8, 1970): 58.

B1793.   _____. "Plenty o' Sump'n." *American Musical Digest* 1/5 (1970): 12. Excerpt from *The Listener* 83/2,128 (Jan. 8, 1970): 58.
Review of a radio program of Dec. 29, 1969, involving G's music.

B1794. "Stop the Rhapsody, Mab Told." *Down Beat* 16/6 (Apr. 8, 1949): 1.
Charlie Barnet's big band had been playing an unauthorized arrangement of RiB. Harms took legal action to stop the use.

B1795.   STRAVINSKY, Igor, & Robert CRAFT. "Some Composers: by Igor Stravinsky with Robert Craft." *Musical America* 82/6 (June 1962): 6, 8.
G is discussed by Stravinsky.

B1796.   STRAVINSKY, Igor, & Robert CRAFT. *Dialogues and a Diary.* Garden City, NY: Doubleday, 1963. Includes the comments mentioned in **B1795.**

B1797.   SUSKIN, Steven. *Show Tunes: 1905-1985, The Songs, Shows and Careers of Broadway's Major Composers.* NY: Dodd, Mead & Co., 1986, pp. 104-137.
Suskin devoted a substantial section to a very complete and apparently well researched list of musicals in which G music was used. The lists of music published from each show seem to be accurate. The author claims to have gone through the copyright deposits at the Library of Congress (Preface, p. ix).

B1798.   SUTHERLAND, Sam. "Gershwin Push by Chappell & WB." Billboard 85, Mar. 3, 1973, p. 24.
Article noting the many activities taking place in celebration of the seventy-fifth anniversary of G's birth, in 1898 . . . for the 37 years since G's death, 'P&B' has accounted for 50 percent of the rental income for Chappell . . . The first G [television] project announced to date is a special documentary on the composition and production of 'P&B,' which BBC-TV is now tentatively scheduled to produce."

B1799.   SWIFT, Kay. "Remembering George Gershwin." *SR/World* 1/3 (Oct. 9, 1973): 18-21.
This article excerpted from Kimball and Simon's *The Gershwins*, is important for its reminiscences, many of them anecdotal. *See also:* Swift's "George Gershwin as duo pianist." *Crescendo International* 13 (Jan. 1975): 8.

B1800. "The Talk of the Town: Words and Music." *New Yorker* 52 (Nov. 8, 1976): 38-39.

B1801.   TAUBMAN, Howard. "After 20 Years: Gershwin Remains a Gifted Composer Who Cultivated a Specific Garden." *NYTimes,* July 7, 1957, Section II, p. 7.

B1802.   _____. "'Why Gershwin's Tunes Live On: His Gift Was That Out of Popular Themes He Could Arrive at Something Memorable." *NYTimes,* Sept. 28, 1952, Section VI (Magazine Section-Sunday Edition), p. 20.

B1803. **TAYLOR, Deems.** "Gershwin as Pioneer," in: *Rhapsody in Blue; The Jubilant Story of George Gershwin and His Music.* Hollywood: Warner Bros., 1945, pp. 13-14.

B1804. _____. *Of Men and Music.* NY: Simon & Schuster, 1937, pp. 144-153.
About the influential conductor Walter Damrosch and his influence on G.

B1805. _____. "Music and the Flag," in his: *Of Men and Music.* NY: Simon & Schuster, 1937, pp. 123-130.
Nationalism in American music, citing G.

B1806. **TAYLOR, Erma.** "George Gershwin —A Lament," in: **Merle ARMITAGE,** ed. *George Gershwin.* NY: Longmans, Green, 19738, pp. 178-192.

B1807. **TEICHMANN, Howard.** *George S. Kaufman: An Intimate Portrait.* NY: Atheneum, 1972.
Biography of Kaufman including anecdotes about the writer and G.

B1808. **TERPILOWSKI, Lech.** "'Trzeci nurt' a reminiscencje jazzowe w muzyce XX w." *Ruch Muzyczny* 6 [=No. 13] (July 1962): 11-13.

B1809. **THOMAS, Michael Tilson.** "Aspects of Gershwin." *Music and Musician's International* 35/10 (June 1987): 9-11.
An article which announces the June 1987 Gershwin Festival to be given at the Barbicon in London by the London Symphony Orchestra under newly appointed Principal Conductor Tilson Thomas. In this article, Thomas claimed that in Alban Berg's Violin Concerto and *Lulu*, one could ". . . hear a kind of chordal and harmonic sense which has similarities to . . . *Porgy and Bess* . . ." *See*: **W54n**

B1810. **THOMPSON, Oscar.** *The International Cyclopedia of Music and Musicians,* 9th ed. NY: Dodd, Mead, 1964, pp. 785-786.

B1811. **THOMSON, Virgil.** *American Music Since 1910,* with an introduction by Nicolas Nabokov. NY: Holt, Rinehart & Winston, 1971, pp. 62, 63, 146, *et al.*
References to G.

B1812. _____. *Music Right and Left.* NY: A. A. Knopf, 1951.
Reviews of G's work.

B1813. _____. *Virgil Thomson* NY: A. A. Knopf, 1967, pp. 151, 240, 242, 279, 405.
Gershwin's distinguished contemporary made numerous remarks about him in this autobiography.

TILSON THOMAS, Michael. "Aspects of Gershwin." *Music and Musician's International* 35/10 (June 1987): 9-11. *See*: **B1809**

B1814. **TISCHLER, Barbara L.** *An American Music: The Search for an American Musical Identity.* NY & Oxford: Oxford University Press, 1986, pp. 97-98, 102.
Very brief reference to G's serious orchestral pieces except the second rhapsody. There is also discussion of other composers' jazz-influenced pieces, Wallingford Riegger's *Triple Jazz*, e. g. (p. 103).

B1815. **TOBIN, Yann.** "L'autre Gershwin." *Positiv* 277 (March 1984): 16-17.

B1816. "Towards a new reading of Gershwin," in **Charles HAMM**, *Putting Popular Music in its Place.* Cambridge: Cambridge University Press, 1995, 306-324. A provocative, "must reading" essay by this distinguished scholar of popular music.

B1817. **T[RIMBLE], L[ester].** "Gershwin Night [at Hunter College]." *NY Herald Tribune*, Jan. 11, 1954, p. 10.

B1818. "Trunkfull of Tunes." *Newsweek* 63/9 (Mar. 2, 1964): 48. Coverage of some of the melodies left behind by G.

B1819. "Twenty Years After." *New Yorker* (May 17, 1952): 26-27. IG gets attention.

B1820. "U. S. 8-cent stamp to honor George Gershwin; Collections and crafts." *Christian Science Monitor*, Feb. 23, 1973.
Announcement of the February 28, 1973, issuance of the George Gershwin stamp, designed by Mark English of Georgetown, CT. An excellent picture of the stamp accompanied the article.

B1821. **UNIVERSITY OF GEORGIA.** Athens. Library, Department of Special Collections. Olin Downes Papers.
According to Charles Schwartz, the Georgia library holds "an extensive file of Olin Downes' reviews as well as other reviews from *The New York Times* and the *New York Herald Tribune.* Included among the materials is a folder marked 'George Gershwin,' which contains a variety of printed items, including clippings, sundry pamphlets & programs. [from p. 83, *George Gershwin: A Selective Bibliography . . .* Schwartz]"

B1822. "Unpublished Gershwin Songs to Be Released." *Variety* 233/13 (Feb. 19, 1964): 51. Conjectures that unpublished Gershwin tunes held by IG will eventually be released.

B1823. **VALLEE, Rudy.** "Troubadour's Tribute," in: **Merle ARMITAGE,** ed. *George Gershwin.* NY: Longmans, Green, 1938, pp. 135-136.

B1824. **VAN VECHTEN, Carl.** "George Gershwin: An American Composer Who Is Writing Notable Music in the Jazz Idiom." *Vanity Fair* 24 (Mar. 1925): 40, 78, 84.
Eva Gauthier's jazz concert and the RiB are discussed. *See:* **W1**

B1825. _____. "Introduction," in Edward Jablonski and Lawrence D. Stewart, *The Gershwin Years,* 2nd ed., Garden City: Doubleday, 1958, 1973.

B1826. **VILLIUS, Lars.** "Ålterblick på Gershwin." *Musikrevy* 8/2 (Feb. 1953): 49-50.

B1827. a cura di **VINAY, Gianfranco.** *Gershwin* / autori vari, in Series Biblioteca di cultura musicale. Autori e opere. Torino : EDT, 1992. Includes bibliographical references (p. 343-350), discography (p. 351-383), and index.

B1828. **WATERS, Edward N.** "Harvest of the Year: Selected Acquisitions of the Music

Division." *Quarterly Journal of the Library of Congress* 24 (Jan. 1967): 79.

B1829. _____. "In All Forms & For All Mediums; Music Division Acquisitions." *Quarterly Journal of the Library of Congress* 30 (Jan. 1973): 50.

B1830. _____. "Music." *Library of Congress Quarterly Journal of Current Acquisitions* 14 (Nov. 1956): 13.

B1831. _____. "Music." *Library of Congress Quarterly Journal of Current Acquisitions* 16 (Nov. 1958): 17.

B1832. _____. "Music." *Library of Congress Quarterly Journal of Current Acquisitions*17 (Nov. 1959): 23-24.

B1833. _____. "Music." *Library of Congress Quarterly Journal of Current Acquisitions*18 (Nov. 1960): 23.

B1834. _____. "Music." *Library of Congress Quarterly Journal of Current Acquisitions* 19 (Dec. 1961): 22-23.

B1835. _____. "Music." *Library of Congress Quarterly Journal of Current Acquisitions* 20 (Dec. 1962): 34-35, 60-61.

B1836. _____. "Music." *Quarterly Journal of the Library of Congress* 23 (Jan. 1966): 41, 43-45.

B1837. _____. "Notable Music Acquisitions." *The Quarterly Journal of The Library of Congress* 28/1 (Jan. 1971): 45-72.
   Lullaby for string quartet was gifted to the DLC, along with some sketches for P&B and drafts of IG's article for *The Saturday Review*, ". . . New York is a Nice Place . . . But I Wouldn't Want to Live There." On p. 46, there is description of gifts from IG: the draft for a short piece labeled *Lullaby*, written in piano solo form but intended for string quartet; ". . . a music notebook containing 23 pages of sketches and drafts, chiefly laid out for piano solo and including a first draft of *The Man I Love*; and ". . . a sheaf of 14 leaves bearing sketches of *Porgy and Bess* . . ." with identifications of the tunes by IG. *See*: **W38, W37**

B1838. **WATERS, Edward N.** "Notable Acquisitions of the Music Division." *Quarterly Journal of the Library of Congress* 29/1 (Jan. 1972): 48-76.
   Among the gifts from IG, documented in this article on page 49 are: ". . . a notebook containing pencil drafts and sketches for *Girl Crazy* . . . holograph sketches for *Of Thee I Sing* . . . and *Let 'Em Eat Cake* . . ." and pencil sketches of work on P&B; and a notebook containing themes and "early thoughts on *Rhapsody in Blue* and *Concerto in F*." On p. 61: the full manuscript score, written by orchestrator Will Vodery, of *135th Street* (*Blue Monday*). On p. 64, acknowledgment is made of the receipt of "25 gold coins . . . each representing a composer [one of which was Gershwin] . . ." Also described are the score of the *Catfish Row* suite, and a script from an interview conducted on March 13, 1933, over radio station WJZ. *See*: **W33, W34, W36, W37, W1, W2, W15, W7**

B1839. _____. "Paean to a Year of Plenty: Recent Acquisitions of the Music Division." *The Quarterly Journal of the Library of Congress* 26/1 (Jan. 1969): 21-47.

On page 22 there is a report on IG's gift of the "Red Tune Book," which includes ". . . Ira's valuable explanatory notes and identifications . . ." Page 37 documents receipt of ". . . a fine collection of correspondence and personal papers . . ." in the main, letters to and from IG. ". . . An important segment relates to the musical play *Lady in the Dark* [Kurt Weill-Ira Gershwin-Moss Hart] . . ."

B1840.   . "The Realm of Tone—Music." *Quarterly Journal of the Library of Congress* 22 (Jan. 1965): 56.

B1841.   . "Songs to Symphonies: Recent Acquisitions of the Music Division." *Quarterly Journal of the Library of Congress* 25/1 (Jan. 1968): 50-91.
       Mrs. Kay Swift Galloway donated the original manuscript to *The George Gershwin Songbook*, and this article describes (p. 53) that manuscript in its original form. ". . . The 18th and last song was arranged later, on February 10, 1932, and is not bound in with the preceding 17 . . ." Also included in the gift from Kay Swift is ". . . a folder which she has described as 'Mss. of George Gershwin (fragments) including a bit of "Cuban Overture," excerpt from "I Got Rhythm Variations" & a song lead sheet "Blue," excerpt from 3rd movement Concerto in F, etc.' [p. 54] . . ." A ". . . music sketch book" with sketches and drafts by Kay Swift and Gershwin is described (p. 54), as are IG's gifts of ". . . two exercises, playable as piano solos . . . [and] a short piece that Gershwin composed . . . in 1921 for clarinet, two bassoons, two horns, viola, cello, and double bass . . ." and titled "Figured Choral." Gershwin's literary outline for the variations on I Got Rhythm (p. 54), and three books of exercises of work with Joseph Schillinger (p. 55) are included. *See*: **W45, W5, W6, W2**

B1842.   . "Variations on a Theme: Recent Acquisitions of the Music Division." *The Quarterly Journal of the Library of Congress* 27/1 (Jan. 1970): 51-83.
       On p. 53, there is brief mention of the acquisition by gift from Arthur Gershwin of the exercise book from George's study with Edward Kilenyi, Sr. On p.77, there is documentation of Arthur's gift of the 560-page "thick black scrapbook" of stories, illness, and death notices, covering the period July 11-August 11, 1937. *See*: **B1783**

B1843.   **WATT, Douglas.** "Popular Records: A Pair of Gershwins. *New Yorker* 35/44 (Dec. 19, 1959): 132-134, 137.

B1844.   . "Records: Charm." *New Yorker* 54 (Mar. 13, 1978): 126-128, 131-133.

B1845.   **WHITEMAN, Paul,** and **Mary Margaret MCBRIDE.** *Jazz.* NY: J. H. Sears, 1926.

B1846.   **WHITESITT, Linda.** *The Life and Music of George Antheil, 1900-1959.* Ann Arbor: UMI Research Press, 1983.

B1847.   **WHITMAN, Alden.** "Paul Whiteman, 'the Jazz King' of the Jazz Age, Is Dead at 77."*NYTimes*, Dec. 30, 1967, Section I, p. 24.
       Obituary which summarizes Whiteman's career.

B1848.   **WIBORG, Mary Hoyt.** "The Three Emperors of Broadway: An Appreciation of the Composers of this Country Who Have Made Us Recognize the Musical Significance of Jazz." *Arts & Decoration* 23/1 (May 1925): 48, 66, 72.
       A tribute to Irving Berlin, Jerome Kern, and GG. High in her praise of native American jazz, the author made a plea for a jazz opera, inspired by Otto Kahn's hint that year

of one for the Metropolitan Opera.

B1849.   **WILDBIHLER, Hubert, and Sonja VÖLKLEIN.** *The Musical: An International Annotated Bibliography.* München, London, New York, Oxford, Paris: K. G. Saur, 1986, pp. 174-177.

This bibliography lists fifty-four references on GG, some duplicated elsewhere, but several not seen in other lists.

B1850.   **WILK, Max.** *They're Playing Our Song; The Stories Behind the Words and Music of Two Generations.* NY: Atheneum, 1973.

B1851.   **WILSON, Edmund.** *The Twenties, From Notebooks and Diaries of the Period,* ed. with an introduction by Leon Edel. NY: Farrar, Straus, and Giroux, 1975.

B1852.   **WILSON, John S.** "Misunderstood Pioneer: Whiteman's 'King of Jazz' Misnomer Obscured His Genuine Contribution." *NYTimes,* Dec. 30, 1967, Section II, p. 24.

A reassessment of Whiteman's contribution.

B1853.   _____. "A Plaque in Brooklyn to Mark George Gershwin's Birthplace." *NYTimes,* Sept. 23, 1963, p.31.

Article concerning the house in which G was born.

B1854.   _____. "Pop Music: Jazz Players Give Gershwin 'Portrait.'" *NY Times,* Jan. 18, 1974.

Complimentary review of the "Jazz Portrait of George Gershwin" presented January 14, at New York University's Loeb Student Center. The performers were Zoot Sims, Bucky Pizzarelli, Ellis Larkens, Al Hall, Cliff Leeman, and singer Teddi King.

B1855.   _____. "The Whiteman Concert of 1924 Lives On." *NYTimes,* Feb. 15, 1987, Section 2, p. 25.

Discussion of reproduction of original "Experiment in Modern Music" concert of 1924.

B1856.   **WODEHOUSE, Artis.** "George Gershwin, His Recordings, His Performance Style." Tape no. 83-5 [$5.00 plus 75 cents for mailing]. Ottawa, Ontario K1B 3A7: Association for Recorded Sound Collections, % Conference Tapes, 8 Woodburn Drive, 1983.

Tape of an excellent paper presented by Wodehouse at the 1983 ARSC Conference held in Nashville, TN. The main thrust of the talk is an analysis of the performances of *Fascinating Rhythm* and *The Man I Love* based on the radio broadcasts of the 1930s, and comparing these to the written transcriptions of his improvisations prepared by G for publication as the *Song Book* (1932). *See:* **W53**

B1857.   _____. "The Undiscovered Gershwin: His Solo Piano Improvisations." *Keyboard Classics* (Nov. 1987): 8-11.

Article concerned with G's ten electric record sides of solo piano improvisations made for Columbia in 1926 and 1928. ". . . [Wodehouse's] new transcriptions of eight of the ten improvisations (published by Warner Bros.) reveal Gershwin's remarkable artistic achievement as both virtuoso and piano composer . . . these improvisations may well be among Gershwin's most inventive and succinct works in terms of structure . . ." *See:* **W53**

B1858. _____ and **George Litterst.** "Gershwin—from Piano Roll to Score, Via Computer." *Newsletter* of the *Institute for Studies in American Music* 29/1 (Nov. 1989): 1-2.

The authors explain in detail Wodehouse's project to transcribe selected piano rolls both to disk for replay on Yamaha's Disklavier player piano and in notated form. *See:* **W53**

B1859. **WODEHOUSE, P. G.** *Performing Flea: A Self Portrait in Letters.* London: Herbert Jenkins, 1953, pp. 34, 37, 55, 92, 97, 213.

Brief references to GG on the pages cited, quoted from letters written by Wodehouse. So closely were G and F. Scott Fitzgerald associated in the minds of many people that S. N. Behrman wrote a play, *Let Me Hear the Melody*, based on his recollections of the two men. [Jablonski & Stewart, 1958, p. 236.]

B1860. _____ and **Guy R. BOLTON.** *Bring On The Girls!: The Improbable Story of Our Life in Musical Comedy* . . . New York: Simon & Schuster, 1953, pp. 86, 168-169, 190-191, 194-196, 198, 206, *et passim.*

"Plum" was Wodehouse's nickname. Autobiography of the two famous book writers with whom G worked so often. Brief references to the Gershwins here and there throughout.

B1861. **WOOLF, S. J.** "Finding in Jazz the Spirit of His Age; George Gershwin, a Product of New York's East Side, Holds Art Must Always Express the Contemporaneous." *NYTimes,* Jan. 20, 1929, Section V, p. 9.

B1862. **WOOLLCOTT, Alexander.** "George the Ingenuous." *Hearst's International-Cosmopolitan* 95/5 (Nov. 1933): 32-33, 122-23.

B1863. "Words and Music." *New Yorker* 52/38 (Nov. 8, 1976): 38-39.

Interesting description of the ceremony held for Ira on the occasion of the Graduate School of the City College of New York's awarding him its President's Medal. The article mentions that the Graduate Center on West Forty-second Street "got its start as Aeolian Hall." Among those present for the occasion are listed Harold Arlen, Yip Harburg, Burton Lane, Kay Swift, and Al Simon. The article is rich in anecdotes, including an impromtu speech rendered by Harburg in which he described being present when the piano was delivered to the Gershwin residence on Second Avenue. The speech was supposedly taped by Professor Barry Brook of the City College faculty.

B1864. **WYNAR, Christine L.** ". . . Schwartz, Charles. **George Gershwin: A Selective Bibliography and Discography . . ,**" in **WYNER, Bohdan, S.,** ed. *American Reference Books Annual 1976,* Vol. 7. Littleton, CO: Libraries Unlimited, 1976, p. 483.

Review of Schwartz's bibliography/discography. After describing the book's contents, Wynar concluded ". . . It is hoped that future issues in this series will do a better job of identifying the scope and intent of the bibliographies." *See:* **B1743**

B1865. _____ . "Gershwin's Genius." *Atlantic* 253 (Apr. 1984): 132-136.

B1866. **ZAKARIASEN, Bill.** "BAM's Gershwin Gala had just one sour note." *Daily News* (NY) (*Newsbank* PER 138:B11), Mar. 13, 1987.

Descriptive and complimentary review of the Gershwin Gala, March 11, 1987, at the Brooklyn Academy of Music. ". . . There was a world premiere . . . [of] 'Lonely Boy'—that was unaccountably cut from the original run of 'Porgy and Bess.' The only sour notes came from Bob Dylan, whose polytonal rendition of 'Soon' left most people in the audience bewildered . . ." *See*: **W54m**

B1867. ZAKARIASEN, W. "Pop Music by Classical Composers." *High Fidelity/Musical America* 24 (Jan. 1974): 96-100.

B1868. ZEPP, Arthur. "I Was There—A View from the Servant's Quarters." *Clavier* 10/2 (Feb. 1971): 12-18.

B1869. ZIMEL, Heyman. "George Gershwin." *Young Israel* 20/10 (June 1928): 10-11.

B1870. ZUCK, Barbara A. "A History of Musical Americanism." (Studies in Musicology No. 19) Ann Arbor, MI: University Microfilms International, 1980, 1978, pp. 78-86, 100, 108, 166, 250-251.

BIBLIOGRAPHY ABOUT FILMOGRAPHY

General Bibliography

B1871. **BURTON, Jack.** *The Blue Book of Hollywood Musicals. Songs from the Sound Tracks and the Stars Who Sang Them Since the Birth of the Talkies a Quarter-Century Ago.* Watkins Glen, NY: Century House, 1953.
Discusses: *Delicious,* 40; *A Damsel in Distress,* 94; *Shall We Dance?,* 97; *The Goldwyn Follies,* 109; *The Shocking Miss Pilgrim,* 232; *An American in Paris,* 263. *See*: **F7, F11, F10, F12, F17, F19.**

B1872. **CONNOR, Edward,** and **Edward JABLONSKI.** "The Sound Track." *Films in Review* 9/2 (February 1958): 96-98.

B1873. **CRAIG, Warren.** *The Great Songwriters of Hollywood.* San Diego & New York: A. S. Barnes; London: Tantivy Press, 1980, pp. 13, 176, 195-196, 198.
Very brief mentions of George. Ira, however, was given a four-page chapter including a chronological list of the "Film Songs of Ira Gershwin" along with the names of the films in which the songs were introduced (p. 198).

B1874. **KREUGER, Miles.** "Gershwin on Film: A retrospective of eleven motion pictures featuring the music of America's beloved composer." New York: *Playbill Magazine,* 1973. **[NNMus]**
Excellent program notes by eminent music theatre scholar Miles Kreuger, written for this retrospective sponsored by The New York Cultural Center, Fairleigh Dickinson University, and The Institute of the American Musical, Inc. One of the priceless contents of the collection at the Institute currently located in Los Angeles, is silent 16mm motion picture footage of over 150 Broadway musicals, actually filmed during theatrical performances from the *Ziegfeld Follies of 1931* to *A Little Night Music,* including filmed excerpts of the staged musicals from OTIS, CAKE, and *Pardon My English.* Most of the movies with Gershwin music are discussed. *See*: **W34b, W35b, W36b**

B1875. **HIRSCHHORN, Clive.** *The Hollywood Musical: Every Hollywood Musical from 1927 to the Present Day.* NY: Crown Publishers, 1981.

B1876. **JABLONSKI, Edward.** "George Gershwin." HiFi/Stereo Review 18/5 (May

1967): 49-61.
Lengthy article, largely biographical. Includes filmography.

B1877.   JABLONSKI, Edward, and **Milton A. CAINE.** "Gershwin's Movie Music." *Films in Review* 2//8 (October 1951): 23-28.

B1878.   KNIGHT, Arthur. *The Hollywood Style.* London: Macmillan Company, 1969.

B1879.   KOBAL, John. *A History of Movie Musicals: Gotta Sing, Gotta Dance.* NY: Exeter Books, 1971, 1983, pp. 33, 42, 131-132, 202, 204, *et passim* (under titles).
A lavishly illustrated general survey of movie musicals, including brief references to George's film music.

B1880.   *The Motion Picture Guide,* 10 vols., ed. by Robert NASH. Chicago: Cine Books, 1986 (Vol. X covers Silent Films).
A voluminous film research tool which includes listing of several of the motion pictures which use G music, among them four that are not widely known: *Lady Be Good,* 1928 silent **(F3)**; *Song of the Flame,* 1930 **(F6.1)**; and *Three for the Show,* 1955 **(F21)**. The plot descriptions are detailed, include "inside" information, and occasionally offer critical appraisals.

B1881.   MUELLER, John. *Astaire Dancing: The Musical Films.* NY: Alfred A. Knopf, 1985, Wings Books, 1991, pp. 4, 9, 15, 43, 101n, 116, 127, *passim.*
Profusely illustrated with frame enlargements and stills, this source provides pertinent comments about G and the use of his music in Astaire films, scattered about this remarkable scholarly achievement by film, dance, music, and political science scholar Mueller. The following quote in re: *A Damsel in Distress* is typical of Mueller's thoroughness and insight: ". . . The idea of making a movie out of the Wodehouse novel was George Gershwin's. RKO producer Pandro Berman purchased the film rights to the novel at Gershwin's urgings and then used this as part of an inducement package to bring the songwriting team to Hollywood. Wodehouse has suggested that Gershwin was attracted to the book simply because its hero is a successful American composer of popular songs named George. But the parallels are much deeper. As it happens, the novel's George was beset with the same unease as the real George . . ." Mueller gives a step-by-step description of the dance based on *The Babbit and the Bromide* (in *Ziegfeld Follies* [1945-46]) and the background for the use of the song in the film (pp. 248-250). In re: the *Funny Face* film of 1957, ". . . One of the splendid features of the film is the skill with which these thirty-year-old songs are blended into the script. They suit the situations so well that the lyrics seem a natural extension of the dialogue . . ." An indispensable reference. *See:* **F10, F11, F18, F23**

B1882.   RUBSAMEN, Walter H. "Music in the Cinema." *Arts and Architecture* 62/9 (September 1945): 20-21, 45.

B1883.   TRAUBNER, Richard. "Musical Film." *New Grove Dictionary of American Music,* ed. by H. Wiley Hitchcock and Stanley Sadie, 4 vols. London: Macmillan, 1986, III, 296-300.
In a survey of musical film, brief references are made to films employing G's music (*Delicious,* 1931, *e. g.*)

B1884.   VALLANCE, Tom. *The American Musical,* Screen Series. London: A. Zwemmer; NY: A. S. Barnes, 1970. 192 pp.

A biographical dictionary of the personalities involved in the American musical. Emphasis is on motion pictures, and titles are accessed through the index. No new information on G here.

B1885.   **WESCOTT, Steven D.**, compiler. *A Comprehensive Bibliography of Music for Film and Television*. Detroit: Detroit Studies in Music Bibliography, 1985, 1492, 2720, 3291-1394, 4854, 5218, *et passim*.

This bibliography lives up to its title, having 6340 references from a wide variety of sources from the literature of the film. The index lists seventeen references to G.

B1886.   **WOLL, Allen L**. *Songs from Hollywood Musical Comedies, 1927 to the Present: A Dictionary*. NY & London: Garland Publishing, 1976, nos. 17-18, 50, 208, 225, 312, 334-335, *et passim*.

Many references to both Gershwins. Includes chapters on the songs, the films, composers and lyricists, and a useful "Chronology of the Hollywood Musical," the latter including *Song of the Flame* **(F6.1)**.

Bibliography about Specific Movies
(By titles, alphabetized)

An American in Paris, F19.

B1887.   "American in Paris: Gershwin, Kelly, Modern Painters Create Colorful New Movie Dance." *Life* 55 (Apr. 23, 1951): 39.

Article with color pictures of the concluding ballet. ". . . The sequence features . . . the full diapason of Metro-Goldwyn-Mayer statistics: 120 dancers, 220 costumers, $450,000 total cost for the 17½-minute number . . ."

B1888.   "Cinema: The New Pictures, An American in Paris." *Time* 58 (Oct. 8, 1951): 108.

Positive review of the film. ". . . [The movie] is a production of many talents and a triumph of teamwork. Actress Caron, a young (19) French ballet dancer discovered by [Gene] Kelly, combines dancing skill with a fetching simplicity and the plump-cheeked freshness of a Renoir model . . ."

B1889.   **CROWTHER, Bosley.** "The Screen . . . 'An American in Paris' Arrival at Music Hall, Has Gene Kelly and Leslie Caron in Leads." *NYTimes*, Oct. 5, 1951, p. 24.

Review of the NY premiere. ". . . Count a bewitching French lassie by the name of Leslie Caron and a whoop-de-do ballet number, one of the finest ever put upon the screen, as the most commendable enchantments of the big, lavish musical film that Metro obligingly delivered to the Music Hall yesterday . . ."

B1890.   _____. "Americans in Paris: New Metro Film Affords a Fanciful Tour." *NYTimes*, Oct 14, 1951, Arts & Leisure section, p. 1.

Review of the film during its Radio City Music Hall run. ". . . Although 'An American in Paris,' which magnificent Metro has made with a prodigal liberality of production and George Gershwin songs, is about as romantically far-fetched as any such thing could possibly be, it is probably the absolute quintessence of most Americans' fond dreams of gay Paree. At least, it embraces completely the sublime and absurd images of that wonderfully rich and mellow city that have soap-bubbled through our dreams for years . . ." The reviewer was particularly impressed with the "fine closing ballet done to an excellent orchestration of

Gershwin melodies and his 'American in Paris'" and danced in a manner which "kindles this choreographic chef d'oeuvre with magic and emotional warmth" by Gene Kelly and Leslie Caron.

B1891.   HATCH, Robert. "Movies, Lack of Perspective . . . *An American in Paris.*"
    New Republic 125 (Oct. 22, 1951): 21-22.
    Mixed review of the film.

B1892.   JOHNSON, Julia. "An American in Paris." *Magill's Survey of Cinema,* First
    Series, Vol. I, Frank N. Magill, ed. Englewood Cliffs, NJ: Salem Press, 1980,
    1980, p. 60-63.
    Three-and-a-half page glowing description of the film, focusing more on the drama and dancing than on the music and allotting considerable space to the concluding ballet: ". . . The ballet is intended to dazzle and overwhelm us with its lights, movement, color, and variety of styles of costumes and decorations . . . [I]t is an ambitious, carefully crafted piece of work and is truly the high point of the film . . ."

B1893.   KNIGHT, Arthur. "SRL Goes to the Movies: Safe at First." *Saturday Review
    of Literature* 34 (Nov. 3, 1951): 28-29.
    Admitting this is a "minority report," the reviewer compared AiP to the Astaire/Rogers pictures, saying the former lacked the spontaneity of the latter. ". . . [E]verything about this picture is calculated to the last detail . . ." And about its stars, he concluded ". . . [O]nly Levant occasionally manages the proper irreverence for a good film musical . . ."

B1894.   LEWINE, R. "An American in Paris." *Film Music* 11 (Nov.-Dec. 1951):14-16.

B1895.   MINNELLI, Vincente with Hector Arce. *I Remember It Well*, foreword by
    Alan Jay Lerner. Garden City, NY: 1974., pp. 214-243.
    A chapter is devoted to AiP through the eyes of its director.

B1896.   PFAFF, William. "The Screen, All the Talent Money Can Buy." *Commonweal*
    55 (Oct. 19, 1951): 39.
    Review of the film. No mention of the music.

B1897.   "[Review]." *Commonweal* 55 (Oct. 19, 1951): 39.

B1898.   "[Review]." *Film Daily*, Aug. 28, 1951, p. 7.

B1899.   "[Review]." *Spectator* 187 (Aug. 17, 1951): 212.

B1900.   STAL. "An American in Paris . . . Gene Kelly starred in Gershwin calvalcade for
    sock grosses." *Variety Film Reviews* 8 (Aug. 29, 1951).
    Two-column, descriptive and complimentary review. The reviewer was particularly impressed with the concluding ballet. ". . . Gershwin's music gets boffo treatment throughout. While some 10 songs get special handling, true Gershwin fans will recognize strains of most of his other tunes in the background score . . ."

American Pop, F30.

B1901.   CANBY, Vincent. "Screen: 'American Pop' Grown-Up Animation." *NYTimes,*

Feb. 13, 1981, Section C, p. 5.
Review of the film, but no mention of the music used.

Barkleys of Broadway, F18.

B1902.   "'Barkleys,' Astaire, Rogers Triumph in Grand Reunion." *Hollywood Reporter*, April 11, 1949.
Glowing review of the musical. Brief mention of a GG and IG song. ". . . In a clever reprise of 'They Can't Take That Away from Me' Astaire and Rogers recall briefly their earlier triumphs . . ."

B1903.   **ENG, Frank.** "Film Review: 'The Barkleys of Broadway.'" *LA Daily News* [AMPAS], June 18, 1949.
Mixed review of the film. One must also keep in mind that the film uses only one G song: *They Can't Take That Away from Me*.

B1904.   **SLOAN, Lloyd L.** "'Barkleys' Film Wins Plaudits." *Hollywood Citizen-News* [AMPAS], June 18, 1949.
Generally a complimentary review of the comeback of Fred Astaire and Ginger Rogers in this film.

Damsel in Distress, F11.

B1905.   "A Damsel in Distress." *Time* 30 (Dec. 6, 1937): 49.
Review. ". . . Catchiest number: Nice Work If You Can Get It . . ."

B1906.   "'Damsel in Distress' A Bit British for Fred Astaire: Burns and Allen Comedy Great Aid . . ." *Hollywood Reporter*, Nov. 18, 1937, p. 3.
Review. ". . . There are . . . eight songs by the late George Gershwin, the most danceable of which is 'Nice Work if You Can Get It,' already made familiar on the air and 'Foggy Day in London Town' . . ."

B1907.   "Movie of the Week: Damsel in Distress." *Life* 3 (Nov. 29, 1937): 74-75.
No mention of the music.

B1908.   "[Review]." *Commonweal* 27 (Dec. 3, 1937): 160.

B1909.   "[Review]." *Film Daily*, Nov. 20, 1937, p. 7.

B1910.   "[Review]." *Motion Picture Herald*, Nov. 27, 1937, pp. 52, 54.

B1911.   "[Review]." *The Nation* 145 (Dec. 18, 1937): 697.

B1912.   "[Review]." *Time* 30 (Dec. 6, 1937): 49.

B1913.   **VANDOREN, Mark.** "A Damsel in Distress." *The Nation* 145 (Dec. 18, 1937): 697.
Short review with no mention of the songs.

B1914.   **WODEHOUSE, P. G.** *A Damsel in Distress*. London: Hutchinson, 1982.

Delicious, **F7.**

B1915.   **ATKINS, Irene Kahn.** *Source Music in Motion Pictures.* Rutherford, Madison,
& Teaneck, NJ: Fairleigh Dickinson University Press, 1983, pp. 100-108. *See:*
Full entry at **B280, W4**

B1916.   **Bige.** "Miniature Reviews: Delicious (With Songs)." *Variety [Variety Film
Reviews, 1930-1933],* Dec. 29, 1931.
Positive review. ". . . Music by George and Ira Gershwin helps to break up the plot
strain. The number from which the title was derived has commercial possibilities . . . a
Gershwin piano composition, which the composer is booked to play in concert shortly, is
mutilated as spotted in sections in this script. The title is 'New York Rhapsody' . . . Gershwin's
new rhapsody is cut in pieces when first used as the musical background in a studio scene, but
later gets into full play in a symbolic manner as Janet [Gaynor] wanders through the big city
in a daze . . ." *See:* **W4**

B1917.   **HALL, Mordaunt.** "The Screen: Janet Gaynor in a Sentimental Romance With
Musical Compositions by George Gershwin." *NYTimes [NYTimes Film Reviews]*
1, p. 784, Dec. 26, 1931, p. 15.
Reviewed at the premiere run at NY's Roxy. ". . . Mr. Gershwin's melodies are a help
to the scenes. There is the song 'Delicious' . . . Somebody from Somewhere . . . and 'New
York Rhapsody,' played [by Marvin Maazel] on the piano . . ." *See:* **W4**

B1918.   **HEMMING, Roy.** *The Melody Lingers On: The Great Songwriters and Their
Movie Musicals.* NY: Newmarket Press, 1986, pp. 61-62.
Includes a succinct but excellent description of the film.

B1919.   **PEET, Creighton.** "The New Movies: 'Delicious.'" *Outlook and Independent*
160 (Jan. 13, 1932): 55.
Review of the film, giving the story line and concluding: "The first weeks some
1,000,000,000 [?] people stood in line to see *Delicious.* Civilization hasn't had such a setback
since the Dark Ages."

B1920.   "[Review]." *Film Daily,* Dec. 27, 1931, p. 10.

B1921.   "[Review]." *Hollywood Reporter,* Dec. 1, 1931, p. 3.

B1922.   "[Review]." *Outlook and Independent* 160 (Jan. 13, 1932): 55.

B1923.   **WATTS, Richard, Jr.** "On the Screen: 'Delicious'—Roxy." *Herald Tribune,*
Dec. 25, 1931, p. 22.

Funny Face, **F23.**

B1924.   **Brog.** "Funny Face." *Variety [Variety Film Reviews, 1954-1957]* , Feb. 3, 1957.
Review based on a preview showing before the NY opening of March 28, 1957.
". . . Tunewise, there are six George and Ira Gershwin numbers from the stage musical and five
from producer Edens and scripter Gershe. All are either sung or used as backing for dance
numbers . . . All have a colorful dash, coupled with either humor, such as 'Clap Yo' Hands'
artfully done by Astaire and Kay Thompson, or with romance, as in the Astaire-Hepburn
church garden dancing to, first 'He Loves and She Loves' and later ''S Wonderful,'

the finale . . ."

B1925.   "Cinema: The New Pictures . . . Funny Face." *Time* 69 (Apr. 1, 1957): 94, 96.
Descriptive review which is critical of the script and which points out that the film cost nearly $9,000,000.

B1926.   **CROWTHER, Bosley.** "The Color Creator, New Contributor to the Fine Art of Films." *NYTimes*, Apr. 7, 1957, Section 2, p. 1.
Story focusing on the importance of "color consultants" in technicolor films.
". . . There's a scene that comes early. It's in a [Greenwich Village] bookshop, and Audrey Hepburn, a drab little clerk, has just been kissed by a fashion photographer, played by Fred Astaire. She sings her song, a plaintive little ditty, 'How Long Has This Been Going On,'—all in the dark, restricted colors of a bookish environment . . ."

B1927.   _____. "Funny Face [Review]." *NYTimes* [*NYTimes Film Reviews* 4], Mar. 29, 1957, 16:1.
". . . Let's begin with the songs of George and Ira Gershwin, which are from their musical comedy of the same title produced thirty years ago. That's the oldest thing in the picture, barring Mr. Astaire . . . Yet they have more lilt and frolic in them than if they had been written last year . . ."

B1928.   "Funny Face ." *Dance Magazine* 31 (May 1957): 16-22.
Six-page exposé of the film, with thirteen black and white still photographs. The article focuses mainly on the cinematography and how it was employed to enhance the filming of the dances, as well as the overall artistic merit of this motion picture.

B1929.   **HARTUNG, Philip T.** "The Screen: A Picture's Worth a Thousand Words." *Commonweal* 66 (Apr. 5, 1957): 16-17.
Complimentary, descriptive review, crediting *Harper's Bazaar* with technical assistance for the film..

B1930.   **KNIGHT, Arthur.** "SR Goes to the Movies: Musicals a la Mode." *Saturday Review* 40/15 (April 13, 1957): 26.
Highly complimentary review of the Paramount movie version of *Funny Face*.
". . . It is . . . one of the best musicals since 'Singin' in the Rain' and 'Seven Brides for Seven Brothers' . . . The studio has resurrected a good half-dozen of George Gershwin's most lilting tunes from the 1927 show of the same name (the only connection with the original) . . ."

B1931.   **MCCARTEN, John.** "The Current Cinema: Photographer's Holiday." *New Yorker* 33 (Apr. 6, 1957): 76.
Brief review of the film.

B1932.   **POWERS, James.** "'Funny Face' is a Smart Musical with Top Cast: Edens-Donen Film Geared for Big B. O. (Paramount) . . ." *The Hollywood Reporter* **[AMPAS],** Feb. 13, 1957.
Detailed, positive review. ". . . The current production has no connection with the former musical comedy of the same name . . . The most spectacular element of 'Funny Face' is the bold use of color and of screen techniques . . ."

B1933.   "[Review]." *Commonweal* 66 (Aug. 5, 1957): 16.

B1934.   "[Review]." *Dance Magazine* 31 (May 1957): 16-22.

B1935.   "[Review]." *Film Daily*, Feb. 13, 1957, p. 6.

B1936.   "[Review]." *New Yorker* 33 (Apr. 6, 1957): 76. (Same as McCarten article above)

B1937.   "[Review]." *Newsweek* 49 (Apr. 1, 1957): 106.

B1938.   **ROTH, Philip.** "Movies: Rescue from Philosophy." *New Republic* 36 (June 10, 1957): 22-23.
An intellectual discussion of the characters in the film, with no mention of the music.

B1939.   **SCHALLERT, Edwin.** "'Funny Face' Bright Flashy Film Event." *LA Times* **[AMPAS],** Apr. 18, 1957.
Review of the opening of the film, on April 17, 1957, at the Hollywood Paramount Theater. ". . . I won't go all the way in indulging in superlatives about this Paramount VistaVision . . . but enough to say that for nine-tenths of its distance it offers highly ingratiating entertainment . . . The French [Parisian] settings provide new atmosphere for many of the numbers . . ."

B1940.   **WILLIAMS, Judith A.** "Funny Face." *Magill's Survey of the Cinema* Second Series II—English language films, second series / edited by Frank N. Magill; associate editors, Stephen L. Hanson, Patricia King Hanson. Englewood Cliffs, NJ: Salem Press, c1981, pp. 859-861.
Three-page glowing description of the film, focusing more on the drama and dancing than on the music.

Girl Crazy (1932), F8 .

B1941.   **ABEL.** "Girl Crazy (With Songs)." *Variety* [*Variety Film Reviews* (1930-1933)], Mar. 29, 1932.
Negative review of the movie. " . . . The plentitude of people concerned in mixing this musical stew is the answer to why 'Girl Crazy,' on-screen, even under expert celluloid portrayal, can't hope to turn out for the best . . That Radio can't rush this one out fast enough becomes evident from the presentation musical tab vogue which the Gregory Ratoff condensation of 'Girl Crazy' has set. The Gershwin show tab has been around extensively and it may be capitalized to some degree in those sectors where the presentation prolog was exceptionally well received. But while it may be worth some ballyhoo that now they should see 'Girl Crazy' in its entirety, it's more of a certainty that, having seen the tab on-stage, the filmization, whether complete or not, can hold little added allure . . .Kitty Kelly has the tough assignment of 'Got Rhythm' which is the sole song outstander retained and spoiled by over-production . . ."

B1942.   "Girl Crazy." *Motion Picture Herald* **[AMPAS],** Apr. 2, 1932.
Positive review of the film based on attendance at the RKO Mayfair in NY. The review includes a detailed plot summary.

Girl Crazy (1943), F15.

B1943.   "Cinema, The New Pictures: Girl Crazy . . ." *Time* 42 (Dec. 27, 1943): 90.
Lengthy descriptive and positive review of the film. ". . . As sung by Cinemactress

Garland, *Embraceable You* and *Bidin' My Time* become hits all over again and the new *But Not For Me* sounds like another . . ."

B1944.   DONALDSON, Leslie. "Girl Crazy." *Magill's Survey of the Cinema*, First Series, Vol. 2, Frank N. Magill, ed. Englewood Cliffs, NJ: Salem Press, 1980, pp. 630-632.

Descriptive essay about the film. ". . . The filming of this variation on the familiar 'let's put on a show' plot is what sets *Girl Crazy* apart from earlier musicals . . . The difference in style becomes glaringly apparent in the final production number, 'I Got Rhythm,' which [director Bus] Berkeley shot before leaving the picture . . ."

B1945.   HARTUNG, Philip T. "In Mud We Die." *Commonweal* 39 (Dec. 17, 1943): 233.

". . . Whether you like 'Girl Crazy' or not depends on how much you like Mickey Rooney and Judy Garland . . . And then there are the music and lyrics by George and Ira Gershwin from the original musical comedy. Most of these deserve revival and merit billing as the film's major attraction . . ."

B1946.   "[Review]." *Film Review*, Aug. 3, 1943, p. 6.

B1947.   "[Review]." *Hollywood Reporter*, Aug. 3, 1943, p. 3.

B1948.   S., T. "The Screen in Review . . . At the Capitol, Girl Crazy . . ." *NYTimes*, Dec. 3, 1943, p. 27.

". . . With George Gershwin's music and plenty of elbow room for its twin stars [Rooney/Garland], 'Girl Crazy' is a funny, fast, and completely infectious entertainment."

B1949.   Scho. "Miniature Reviews: Girl Crazy (Musical)." Variety [*Variety Film Reviews, 1943-1948*], Aug. 4, 1943.

Review of the second film version of 1943, comparing it to the previous stage and film versions. ". . . The story thread [altered from previous scripts] is light, but enough to string together the George and Ira Gershwin songs . . . There's an added Gershwin starter in 'Fascinating Rhythm' which gives the [Tommy] Dorsey band a major inning with expert collaboration from Rooney at the piano. Latter doesn't look like dubbing, with Rooney known to be an okay ivory-tickler.

George Gershwin Remembered, F31.

B1950.   BUNCE, Alan. "[Review of 'American Masters: George Gershwin Remembered' on PBS]." *Christian Science Monitor*, Aug. 21, 1987, p. 19.

B1951.   CUTHBERT, David. "[Cuthbert reviews 'George Gershwin Remembered' TV show]."*Times-Picayune* (New Orleans, LA), Aug. 30, 1987, Section TV, p. 5.

B1952.   DE LORENZO, Ash. "Strike Up the Band: Celebrating Gershwin [George Gershwin, television program]." *Vogue* 177 (Dec. 1987): 100.

B1953.   O'CONNOR, John J. "Tribute to Gershwin, on Channel 13." *NYTimes,* Aug. 24, 1987, Section C, p. 18.

Review of the TV documentary "George Gershwin Remembered," part of "American Masters" series.

Goldwyn Follies, **F12** .

B1954. "The Current Cinema: Follies and Foibles." *New Yorker* 14 (Feb. 19, 1938): 58.
Complimentary review. ". . . [A] film enriched with four songs by George Gershwin and a crisp Menjou performance is also happy in some especially toothsome and candied ballets . . ."

B1955. "Entertainment: Technicolor Burgeons in Both Hemispheres, But with Some-what Varying Results." *Newsweek* 11 (FEb. 14, 1938: 25.
Review including *Goldwyn Follies*. Largely negative.

B1956. **Flin.** "Miniature Reviews: The Goldwyn Follies (Musical) (In Color)." *Variety* [*Variety Film Reviews, 1938-1942*], (dateline: Hollywood, CA, Jan. 26, 1938), Feb. 2, 1938.
A lengthy and positive review which gives abundant descriptive details of the musical.

B1957. **GALWAY, Peter.** "The Movies . . . 'The Goldwyn Follies,' at the Odeon . . ." *New Statesman and the Nation* 15 (Mar. 19, 1938): 479.
Brief, but positive review. No mention of the music.

B1958. "'Goldwyn Follies' Gorgeous: Spectacular Musical in Technicolor Blends Unique Beauty, Superb Ballet, Delightful Comedy and Fine Singing." *Hollywood Reporter*, Jan. 26, 1938, p. 3.
Complimentary review of the film. "Musically the picture has something of everything for everyone . . . All of the popular songs but one were composed by the late George Gershwin. There are at least two hits of the first rank in their four numbers . . . Best of the Gershwin songs is 'Love Walked In' . . . but the dancier 'I Was Doing All Right' . . . will run it close in popularity. [Kenny] Baker also has a good number in 'Love Is Here To Stay' . . . Alfred Newman's music direction is a notable addition . . . and Edward Powell's orchestrations are memorably interesting . . ."

B1959. "Movie of the Week: The Goldwyn Follies." *Life* 4 (Feb. 7, 1938): 20-23.
Typical *Life* pictorial with high praise for the film. ". . . In his search for a formula Samuel Goldwyn first paid three writers, including Dorothy Parker, $125,000. Then he tore up their script and hired Ben Hecht . . ."

B1960. "MOVIES: Sam Goldwyn gives us follies plus a ballet." *Literary Digest* 125/8 (Feb. 19, 1938): 23.
Descriptive review of the 1938 film. "Not a talent nor a ten-spot has been spared in *The Goldwyn Follies*, Sam Goldwyn's gift to gaiety-loving filmgoers. The fullness of his bounty is somewhat overpowering . . ." According to the unnamed reviewer ". . . Mr. Goldwyn presents ballet for the first time in the history of the screen . . ."

B1961. "Reviews of the New Films." *Film Daily*, Jan. 27, 1938, p. 5.
Review of a "special New York preview." ". . . Heralded as the initial feature to bear the Goldwyn name . . . the entire proceedings are worthy in every respect . . ." Mention is made of "the quality of the expertly fashioned musical score."

B1962. **NUGENT, Frank S.** "The Screen: 'The Goldwyn Follies,' A Typical Musical

Revue, Is Shown at the Rivoli . . ." *NYTimes*, Feb. 21, 1938, p. 15.
Negative opinion by the reviewer calling the movie a "hodgepodge."

B1963.   "[Review]." *Commonweal* 27 (Feb. 18, 1938): 468.

B1964.   "[Review]."*Film Daily*, Jan. 27, 1938, p. 5.

B1965.   "[Review]." *New Yorker* 14 (Feb. 19, 1938): 58.

B1966.   "[Review]." *New Statesman and the Nation* 15 (Mar. 19, 1938): 479.

B1967.   "[Review]." *Newsweek* 11 (Feb. 14, 1938): 25.

B1968.   "[Review]." *Time* 31 (Feb. 7, 1938): 58.

B1969.   "[Review]." *Variety*, Feb. 2, 1938, p. 15. (More detail at Flin review above, **B1956**)

King of Jazz, F6 .

B1970.   **HALL, Mordaunt.** "Murray Anderson's Sparkling Film: Pastel Shaded 'King of Jazz' Possesses Wonderful Photography and Smart Skits—Einstein's Old and New." *NYTimes*, May 11, 1930, p. 5.
     "It was a pleasant relief to find that 'The King of Jazz' was not an attempt to tell how Paul Whiteman reached his present popular position as a band leader, but a highly artistic and handsome audible Technicolor offering with a really keen sense of humor . . ." No mention of the rhapsody. *Also see*: p. 8.

B1971.   _____. "The Screen: A Sparkling Extravaganza." *NYTimes*, May 3, 1930, p. 23.
     Very complimentary review of the movie. ". . . An impressive conception of George Gershwin's 'Rhapsody in Blue' is set forth with much artistry. The primitive musical elements are registered by the rhythmic beating of a drum, and gradually this grows into the playing of jazz on the usual instruments . . ."

B1972.   **KOZARSKI, Richard, George LOBELL,** and **Richard CORLISS.** "Lost and Found: The King of Jazz (1930)." *Film Comment* (Spring 1971): 73-74.
     Review of the film. Brief reference to the appearance of the RiB in the picture: ". . . The limitations of the color process are readily apparent when 'Rhapsody in Blue' emerges in [bilious] shades of aqua . . ."

B1973.   **SIME.** "King of Jazz (Paul Whiteman) . . ." *Variety Film Reviews* 4 (May 7, 1930).
     Discerning review. ". . . If there is one big thing the Whiteman band is identified with . . . it is George Gershwin's 'Rhapsody in Blue.' The millions who have never heard the great Whiteman band play this biggest of all jazz melodies won't hear it here either. Mr. Anderson [the director] has seen fit to scramble it up with 'production'. . . [W]hat this picture muffed is a pity." (Author's note: I have seen the film and by today's standards, it is pitiful).

B1974.   "[Review]." *Commonweal* 12 (May 21, 1930): 80-81.

B1975.   "[Review]." *Life* 95 (May 30, 1930): 20.

B1976.   "[Review]." *The Nation* 130 (May 28, 1930): 632.

B1977.   "[Review]." *Photoplay* 38/1 (June 1930): 56.
Two-paragraph, surprisingly complimentary review. ". . . If you like revues—oh
boy!"

B1978.   "[Review]." *New Yorker* 6 (May 10, 1930): 101.

B1979.   "[Review]." *Outlook and Independent* 155 (May 14, 1930): 72.

B1980.   "[Review]." *Time* 15 (May 12, 1930): 64.

Kiss Me, Stupid, F26 .

B1981.   **HARTUNG, Philip T.** "The Screen, Dear Sir or Madame." *Commonweal* 81
(Dec. 18, 1964): 421-422.
"The best thing about the whole movie is its title." No mention of the music.

B1982.   **HERBSTMAN, Mandel.** "Reviews of New Films, 'Kiss Me, Stupid' . . ." *Film
Daily,* Dec. 17, 1964, p. 3.
The reviewer calls the film "adult comedy-drama with music. "

B1983.   **KAUFFMANN, Stanley.** "Kiss me, Stupid." *New Rupublic* 152 (Jan. 9, 1965): 26.
Negative review with no mention of the songs.

B1984.   "Mr. Billy Wilder Returns in his Best Farcical Form." *The Times* [London], Feb.
25, 1965, p. 16.
This reviewer liked the farce, noting that it included ". . . three notable new songs
from the Gershwin archive, one of them, 'All the livelong day,' worthy to stand with the best
. . ."

B1985.   "New Gershwin Tunes Featured in Movie." *Down Beat* (Apr. 23, 1964): 14-15.
About three posthumous Gershwin songs in Billy Wilder's movie *Kiss Me Stupid.*

B1986.   "An Oscar for Gershwin?" *Los Angeles Herald Examiner*, December 13, 1964
[AMPAS].
Short article indicating that the three new G tunes supplied with lyrics by Ira
("I'm a Poached Egg," "Sophia," and "All the Livelong Day") might be contenders for the
Oscar award.

B1987.   **PRY.** "Kiss Me Stupid: Lower grade Billy Wilder sex comedy with average to
good b. o. prospects." Variety [*Variety Film Reviews*, 1964-1967], Dec. 16,
1964.
Informative review of the movie. ". . . The score, which figures rather prominent-
ly as story motivation . . . carries the unusual credit of songs by Ira and George Gershwin.
Introed are three unpublished melodies by the long deceased composer to which brother Ira
has provided special lyrics. Numbers, pleasant but not especially impressive, are 'Sophia,'
'I'm A Poached Egg,' and 'All the Livelong Day' . . ."

B1988.   "[Review]." *Commonweal* 81 (Dec. 18, 1964): 144-145.

B1989. "[Review]." *Esquire* 63 (June 1965): 18, 20.

B1990. "[Review]." *Film Daily*, Dec. 17, 1964, p. 3.

B1991. "[Review]." *New Statesman* 69 (Feb. 26, 1965): 334.

B1992. "[Review]." *Newsweek* 64 (Dec. 28, 1964): 53-54.

B1993. "[Review]." *Playboy* 12 (Mar. 1965): 34.

B1994. "[Review]." *Saturday Review* 48 (Jan. 2, 1965): 31.

B1995. "[Review]." *The Spectator* 214 (Mar. 5, 1965): 298.

B1996. "[Review]." *Time* 85 (Jan. 1, 1965): 69.

B1997. "[Review]." *Village Voice* 10, Jan. 14, 1965, p. 14, 16.

B1998. WEILER, A. H. "[Review of] . . . Kiss Me, Stupid . . ." *NYTimes*, Dec. 23, 1964, p. 22.
Mr. [Dean] Martin sings three heretofore unpublished songs by the late George Gershwin and his brother, Ira . . . [T]hey are pleasant, if not memorable reminders of great talent. Little of that precious commodity is evident in Kiss Me, Stupid."

Lady, Be Good!, **F14.**

B1999. "At the Capitol: Lady Be Good." *NYTimes*, Sept. 19, 1941, p. 27.
Descriptive, negative review.

B2000. KUTNICK, Sam. "'Lady Be Good:' Plenty of Talent, But None of It Is Used." *People's World* **[AMPAS]**, Sept. 13, 1941.
"'Lady Be Good' is as concrete an example of inept writing, stupid direction and inexcusable waste of talent as anything Hollywood has done in many a discouraged moon."

B2001. "'Lady Be Good.'" *Hollywood Reporter* **[AMPAS]**, July 15, 1941, p. 3.
". . . MGM's 'Lady Be Good' is Entertainment Plus, a bright and sparkling, sentimental journey through Tin Pan Alley . . . [It] will be longest remembered for its magnificent use of music . . . The title song . . . is sold for a smash, with montages and varied use of vocal and instrumental effect . . ."

B2002. ". . . Lady, Be Good . . ." *NYTimes*, Sept. 21, 1941, Section 9, p. 3.
A very short notice about the film. ". . . Music, in part, by George Gershwin—and very suitable for whistling . . ."

B2003. "Lady Be Good (Musical)." *Variety* (July 15, 1941): 8.
Positive review.

B2004 . "[Review]." *Commonweal* 34 (Sept. 26, 1941): 548.

B2005. "[Reviews of films]." *Time* 38 (Sept. 29, 1941): 86.
According to this review, Winston Churchill liked this film. About Ann

Southern's rendition of *Lady, Be Good!*, ". . . her version . . . should please even a Prime Minister . . ." *See*: **D1085**

B2006.   "Reviews of New Films: 'Lady Be Good' . . . Gershwin Music Highlights a
          Tuneful But Longish Romantic Comedy." *Film Daily*, July 15, 1941, p. 7.
          "Featuring some good music . . . 'Lady Ge Good' should be well received by the
popular music devotees . . ."

B2007.   **Scho.** "Miniature Reviews: Lady Be Good (Musical)." Variety [*Variety Film
          Reviews*, 1938-1942], July 16, 1941.
          Negative review of the movie which points out that, beyond the title, there is no
similarity to the 1924 musical. ". . . With the exception of the title song and an orchestration
of 'Fascinating Rhythm,' danced by Eleanor Powell, the songs in this picture are likewise no
relation to the click [slick?] Gershwin score . . ."

Manhattan, F29.

B2008.   **CANBY, Vincent.** "The Screen: Woody Allen's 'Manhattan.'" *NYTimes*, Apr.
          25, 1979, p. C17.
          A very positive and excellently descriptive review of the film. ". . . There is a sense
of applied romance here, especially in the soundtrack use of some of the lushest melodies ever
written by George Gershwin . . ." *See*: **D1115**

B2009.   **GITTELSON, Natalie.** "The Maturing of Woody Allen." *Encyclopedia of
          Film*, Apr. 22, 1979.
          Lengthy review of the film, based on an interview with Allen. ". . . The score for
'Manhattan' is by George Gershwin. 'The Gershwin music fits in with Isaac's [lead male role
played by Allen] comprehension of the city . . . He *sees* Manhattan in black and white and
moving to the tunes of George Gershwin. The score helps to vibrate several themes in the
picture: the passing of time, the poignancy of where the city's gone, the fact that, in a sense,
Isaac's living in the past . . ."

B2010.   **KNIGHT, Arthur.** "Movie Review: Manhattan." *Hollywood Reporter*, Apr. 23,
          1979, p. 4.
          Probing, positive review. The reviewer considered the use of the Gershwin music
an enhancement.

B2011.   "[Review of Manhattan]." *Commonweal* 106 (Aug. 3, 1979): 438-439. (Details
          below at **B2020**).

B2012.   "[Review]." *Los Angeles Times*, Apr. 22, 1979, Calendar, p. 1.

B2013.   "[Review]." *The Nation* 228 (May 19, 1979): 580-581.

B2014.   "[Review]." *New Republic* 180 (May 19, 1979): 22-23.

B2015.   "[Review]." *New Yorker* 55 (Apr. 30, 1979): 110.

B2016.   "[Review]." *Newsweek* 93 (Apr. 30, 1979): 78.

B2017.   "[Review]." *Saturday Review* (July 7, 1979): 41.

B2018.   "[Review]." *Time* 113 (Apr. 30, 1979): 62-65, 68-69.

B2019.   "[Review]." *Variety* (Apr. 25, 1979): 18.

B2020.   **WESTERBECK, JR., Colin L.** "Screen: On the Town, A Visual Poem to New York City." *Commonweal* 106 (Aug. 3, 1979): 438-439.
Thoughtful review of the film with mention of the use of RiB and *Lady, Be Good!*

Mine, F34

B2021.   **BECK, Marilyn.** "Plans Coming Together for Film on Gershwins." *The Daily News of Los Angeles,* June 1, 1987, L. A. Life section, p. 18.
Short story pertaining to Irwin Winkler's plans to produce a new Gershwin film biography "by mid-1988. ". . . The story will focus on the relationship between the brothers [George and Ira] and the world of music 50 years ago . . ." As of 1987, Martin Scorsese was scheduled to direct and John Guare was to write a new screenplay. In an interview in 1989, Marc Gershwin indicated to me that such a production was (paraphrased) "a long way off." The film has not appeared as of 1999, but an announcement of it has appeared in a George and Ira Gershwin home page on the World Wide Web, tentatively titled *Mine*.

Porgy and Bess, F25 & F25.1

B2022.   "America's Classic Sings Anew: Music is superb in movie 'Porgy and Bess.'" *Life* 46/24 (June 15, 1959): 70-82.
Profusely illustrated, this article is particularly helpful because it gives the specifics concerning the voice dubbings in the movie version of P&B. The following details are given: ". . . All the music was recorded before the actors stepped before the cameras . . ." Robert McFerrin sang for Sidney Poitier as Porgy; Adele Addison sang for Dorothy Dandridge as Bess, but only after the rejection of an unnamed ghost; Inez Mathews ghosted for Ruth Attaway's Serena; Clara, acted by Diahann Carroll, was dubbed by ". . . a French-English white girl, Loulie Jean Norman . . . Pearl Bailey as Maria and Sammy Davis, Jr. as Sportin' Life both sing and act in the film. But in the sound-track LP, Davis has his singing done for him by Cab Calloway . . ." Incidentally, ". . . nearly 30 other *Porgy* albums in almost every possible version except harpsichord and hillbilly have appeared recently, all of them hoping to profit on the movie . . ." **W37, D1116**

B2023.   **ALTMAN, Rick.** *The American Film Musical.* Bloomington & Indianapolis, IN & London: Indiana University Press, 1987, pp. 29, 38-40, 121, 175, 236, 283, 286, 299.
An erudite study of the American film musical. The following excerpted quote [pp. 38-40] from the "folk [film] musical" P&B [1959] discussing the role of the duet, stands out: "['Bess, you is my woman now'] . . . one of George Gershwin's many outstanding contributions to the film musical, provides a particularly clear example of the multiple and subtle ways in which music contributes to the audience's overall impression of the film's sexual structure. Porgy begins with twelve bars in B major (a), followed by eight bars in F# major (b). Bess then takes up the words and melody which Porgy sings in (a), but she sings it in D major and reverses all the sexual designations (c); she too now modulates into F# major but this time keeps neither Porgy's words, his rhythm, his tempo, nor his accompaniment . . . The intriguing aspect of this duet . . . is not the rather pat antiphonal setup, but the tension beneath. The song's alternation serves to setup a sexual duality . . ."

B2024.   BOGLE, Donald. *Dorothy Dandridge: A Biography.* NY: Boulevard, 1997, pp. 125-126,147, 280, 313, 432-434, *et passim.*
References to the opera and the film in which Dandridge starred in the role of Bess.

B2025.   CROWTHER, Bosley. "Fitness of Folk Opera: A Rare Form in Films Is Exalted by Goldwyn's 'Porgy and Bess'." *NYTimes,* June 28, 1959, Sec. I2, p. 1.

B2026.   _____. "'Porgy and Bess' Again: Further Thoughts on a Second Look At the Filmed Folk Opera." *NYTimes,* Aug 2, 1959, section 2, p. 1.
Extensive observations based on a second viewing of the film. Crowther focused on the characterization of Sportin' Life by Sammy Davis, Jr., commenting: ". . . He's a comprehension of evil on an almost repulsive scale," in contrast to Cab Calloway's earlier rendition which ". . . made him flamboyantly wicked but not devoid of charm and sympathy . . . Notable, too, is the effective way the music evolves in an almost endless flow, so the melodic eloquence is persistent in the pattern of shifting action and moods . . ."

B2027.   CULLAZ, Maurice. "Porgy and Bess." *Jazz Hot* No. 226 (Dec. 1966): 7.

B2028.   "Dubbing In the Voices, Also a Big Production." *Life* 46/24 (June 15, 1954): pp. 79-82.

B2028.1.   "$5 Million Film Fire; Hint Race Row Arson." *LA Evening Mirror News,* July 2, 1958.

B2029.   GILBERT, Justin. "'Porgy and Bess' Is 21K Gold-wyn." *NY Mirror,* June 25, 1959, p. 27. **[NNMus]**
Review of the movie version of P&B at its Warner Theatre NY world premiere. Via Warner's Todd-AO screen, ". . . Heywood's fecund waterfront slum has been blown up to the proportions of a Coliseum . . . All in all, Goldwyn and Preminger have created a radiant and ringing photoplay . . ."

B2030.   HALE, Wanda. "'Porgy and Bess' a Screen Classic." *NY Daily News,* June 25, 1959, p. 68.
Review of the premiere at the Warner, on June 24, 1959. ". . . In screening the great American opera, Goldwyn has done the true music lovers of the world a great service. The production is superb, spreading vividly across a monumental screen . . . As 'Porgy and Bess' is an opera, voices of operatic quality were dubbed in for virtually everybody except Sammy Davis, Jr. and Pearl Bailey . . . Robert McFerrin signs for Poitier, Adele Addison for Dandridge, Loulie Jean Norman for Diahann Carroll, Inez Mathews for Ruth Attaway. The famous singer, Helen Thigpen, sings Strawberry Woman's role . . ."

B2031.   HARFORD, Margaret. "Preminger Tells Two Reasons 'Porgy' Summons Pleased Him." *LAMirror News* **[AMPAS]**, July 31, 1958.
Preminger cited his two reasons as "I like the story" and I'd like to see how he [Samuel Goldwyn, the producer] operates." Brief reference is made to the Goldwyn-Mamoulian schism.

B2032.   "Ira Gershwin Opposes Filming 'Porgy' Now." *Variety* 201/10 (Feb. 8, 1956): 1+.

B2033.   JONES, LeRoi. "Movie Review." *Jazz Review* 2/10 (Nov. 1959): 50-51.

An exceedingly negative review. "As a movie, *Porgy and Bess* is a complete failure. Otto Preminger and Sam Goldwyn with their usual passionate intensity have managed to suck out what few vital juices there are in the original 'operatic' version. They present it here as a kind of flat, uncinematic series of rather dull monologues, interrupted . . ."

B2034. KNIGHT, Arthur. "SR Goes to the Movies: Catfish Row in Todd-AO." *Saturday Review* 42/27 (July 4, 1957): 24-25.

A mixed review of the movie version. Although Knight conceded that ". . . the cast Mr. Goldwyn has assembled is, almost without exception, flawless . . . [but, he felt that] the dubbing of the singing voices is often painfully apparent . . . [and felt that the Gershwin opera] probably could not be translated properly to the [Todd-AO] screen under any circumstances . . ."

B2035. KOLODIN, Irving. "Catfish Row and Wilshire." *Saturday Review* 42/24 (June 13, 1959): 52.

B2036. KREUGER, Miles. "Porgy and Bess," in "Gershwin on Film." *Playbill* (1973): n. p.

A probing critical statement: ". . . Preminger's film version treats the material with a ponderous air of self-importance; it lumbers across the screen almost entirely void of spontaneity, lightness, or charm . . . [T]he internal fraudulence of casting big-name Negro stars instead of qualified singers for the leading roles stamps the work as a slick Hollywood product . . . But a film of this magnitude is bound to contain a few redeeming elements. Ruth Attaway's heartrending acting and Inez Matthews' dubbed singing of 'My Man's Gone Now' are chillingly moving; and Brock Peters' powerful performance . . . is a rare touch of the *Porgy and Bess* tradition. Also, one must applaud Ken Darby's superb choral work and many of the minor players, some of whom sing for themselves and offer intriguing vignettes within the muddled overall vision . . ."

B2037. LAND. "Film Reviews: Porgy and Bess . . ." *Variety*, July 1, 1959, p. 6.

A lengthy review. Gives history of the opera, along with a detailed analysis of the movie version including the acting, direction, editing, and costuming, e. g. ". . . Summing up, the two big come-on names here are Gershwin and Goldwyn. A classic has received the high-gloss treatment . . . Time alone can report whether the screening . . . adds up to a selective-appeal or a universal-appeal feature. The end result may fall between."

B2038. LUCRAFT, Howard. "Behind Music USA." *Music USA* 76/3 (Mar. 1959): 9.

B2039. NASH, Jay Robert, and Stanley Ralph ROSS. *The Motion Picture Guide* (1923-1983), Vol. VI. Chicago: Cinebooks, 1986, pp. 2431-2432.

Valuable information about the movie: "Given the talent and the material and the budget of over $6 million, why wasn't this classic American operetta a classic American movie? The fault has to lie in Goldwyn's decision to fire Mamoulian in favor of Preminger . . . Millions . . . were spent for advertising and promotion but the movie came nowhere close to recouping costs and stands as a financial disaster . . . Preminger's veteran cameraman, Shamroy, did a wonderful job and the art diection by Krizman and Wright was sensational . . . Ken Darby was listed as Associate Music Director [to André Previn] . . ."

B2040. PITMAN, Jack. "Lorraine Hansberry Deplores 'Porgy.'" *Variety*, May 27, 1959, p. ?

Story concerning a debate between Otto Preminger, director of the movie P&B, and black playwright Hansberry (*Raisin in the Sun*). Preminger and Hansberry had appeared on Irv Kupcinet's late night TV talk show from Chicago. Hansberry deemed the folklore of P&B "deplorable."

B2041. **PRYOR, Thomas M.** "Hollywood Dossier: 'Porgy and Bess' Heads for Films-Addenda." *NYTimes,* May 12, 1957, Section 2, p. 5.

B2042. _____. "Hollywood 'Porgy' Strife: Switch of Directors of Folk Opera Makes 'the Livin' A Little Uneasy—Anamorphic Lenses Unveiled." *NYTimes* (dateline: Hollywood), Aug. 3, 1958, section 2, p. 5.

Notice that producer Samuel Goldwyn had dismissed Rouben Mamoulian as director of the film, replacing him with Otto Preminger. Goldwyn explained: ". . . He [Mamoulian] and I could not see eye to eye on various matters . . ."

B2043. "[Review]." *Commonweal* 70 (Aug. 14, 1959): 424-425.

B2044. "[Review]." *Dance Magazine* 33 (Aug. 1959): 16-17.

B2045. "[Review]." *Film Daily* 115, (June 25, 1959), p. 25.

B2046. "[Review]." *Hollywood Reporter*, (June 25, 1959), p. 3.

B2047. "[Review]." *The Nation* 189 (July 4, 1959): 19.

B2048. "[Review]." *New Republic* 141 (July 13, 1959): 22.

B2049. "[Review]." *New Yorker* 35 (July 4, 1959): 65-66.

B2050. "[Review]." *Newsweek* 54 (July 6, 1959): 83.

B2051. "[Review]." *Saturday Review* 42 (July 4, 1959): 24-25.

B2052. "[Review]." *Time* 74 (July 6, 1959): 5.

B2053. **SCHEURER, Philip K.** "What Is Delaying 'Porgy and Bess?' Shot in Three Months, Opera Is Taking Six More to Finish." *LATimes,* Mar. 2, 1959.

Article bemoaning and explaining in careful detail, the delay in the completion of the movie. Despite the fact that the film "took slightly less than three months—from Sept. 22 last to Dec. 19 [1958]" to shoot, Scheurer detailed the problems with recording the sound track, screening in Todd-AO, opticals, color balance, post-scoring, redubbing, and re-recording.

B2054. **SCHUMACH, Murray.** "Hollywood Recall: Ira Gershwin Provides 'Notes' for 'Porgy.'" *NYTimes* (dateline: Hollywood), June 21, 1959, section 2, p.7.

Anecdotal interview of IG prior to the June 24, 1959, debut of the film.

B2055. **SWIFT, Kay.** "Gershwin and the Universal Touch." *Music of the West Magazine* (October 1959): 7, 24.

Complimentary review of the Samuel Goldwyn movie of P&B. ". . . In some aspects, the movie has added a dimension to the opera . . . there is the impact of seeing the nearness of the sea, its constant presence in the lives of the people of Catfish row. The sound of the sea colors all their singing; the motion of the waves is expressed in the way they move . . ."

B2056. **WAINRIGHT, Loudon.** "The One-Man Gang Is In Action Again: At 76 Sam Goldwyn Conquers Crisis After Crisis To Produce 'Porgy and Bess.'" *Life* 46/7 (Feb. 16, 1959): 103-116.

While providing a portrait of Samuel Goldwyn the man, this article discusses the many problems encountered in producing the movie version of P&B. Goldwyn got the rights to P&B by outbidding another studio which offered $1 million, with an offer of $650,000 as down payment "against a fat 10% of the receipts." Among other problems were: casting of the lead roles, a $2.5 million fire which destroyed the sets and costumes, and the firing of Rouben Mamoulian as director, precipitated by "a sudden upswing in publicity for Mamoulian. The director had been giving interviews in which he commented on a number of controversial matters in which his opinions did not coincide with Goldwyn's."

B2057. **WILLIAMS, Dick.** "Goldwyn Finishes 'Porgy and Bess.'" *Mirror-News* [LA] [AMPAS], Dec. 10, 1958.

Article announcing the completion of the filming of the movie version. ". . . Camera work began on Monday, Sept. 22, on Venice Island in the San Joaquin River near Stockton. Then it moved across the river to Tule Island, where the picnic and fish fry were filmed . . ." The article announced that IG was pleased with the film, that Bennett Cerf was writing the souvenir book, and that Goldwyn paid $650,000 cash plus a percentage of the gross receipts to the Gershwin and Heywood estates for the film property.

Porgy and Bess, videotape, F25.1.

B2058. **HERMAN, Justin R.** *American Record Guide* (Nov.-Dec. 1993): 266-267.

Review of EMI 77754, 3 laser discs or EMI 77757-3, 2 VHS videodiscs of P&B, Glyndebourne production. *See*: **W37ooo**

B2059. **GRITTEN, David.** "Gershwins Were No Fans of Preminger's 'Porgy.'" *Los Angeles Times*, Jan. 19, 1993, Home Edition, Section: Calendar, p. 5 Pt. F Col. 3

"Trevor Nunn's interpretation of the work has found favor with Gershwin's heirs. 'He's given the characters an emotional base in a way no one has done before,' said Michael Strunsky, nephew of Leonore Gershwin and sole trustee and executor of Ira Gershwin's estate, which has managed 'Porgy and Bess' for the last 40 years . . ." In regard to the Glyndebourne videotape, ". . . Strunsky confirmed that this was only the second occasion that film rights for 'Porgy and Bess' had been granted. Ira and Leonore Gershwin, he said, were unhappy with Otto Preminger's 1959 film of the work . . . That film was unfortunate, but typical of (social) attitudes of the time . . . My aunt didn't want it distributed. She and my uncle felt it was a Hollywoodization of the piece. We (the estate) now acquire any prints we find and destroy them . . . The impetus for this film began when my aunt went to see Trevor's production at Glyndebourne. She felt this was what 'Porgy and Bess' should be, emotionally, musically and intellectually." *See*: **F25.1, W37ooo**

B2059.1 **VOORHEES, John** "This Is a 'Porgy And Bess' You Won't Want to Miss."
Seattle Times (SE), October 4, 1993, Edition: FINAL, Section: TV, Page: F6.

This is a review of the video which was filmed for TV of the Glyndebourne production. *See*: **F25.1**

Rhapsody in Blue, F16.

B2060.   BARNES, Howard. "On The Screen." *NY Herald Tribune*, June 28, 1945, p. 16.
Review. ". . . As an anthology of wonderful tunes, this new film is something not to be missed. As the revelation of a strangely possessed musician, torn between the desire to join immortals and to compose Tin Pan Alley hits, it falters."

B2061.   BAUER, Marion. "The Gershwin Touch," in: *Rhapsody in Blue, The Jubilant Story of George Gershwin and His Music.* Hollywood: Warner Bros, 1945, p. 17.

B2062. "Cinema: The New Pictures, **Rhapsody in Blue.**" *Time* 46/1 (July 2, 1945): 85-86.
Complimentary, descriptive review. ". . . If *Rhapsody in Blue* fails to reveal in full the source and nature of the artistry that lay behind its hero's restless introspection, its music is ample compensation . . . With no story at all, this two-hour concert of Gershwin music would be well worth the price of admission . . ."

B2063.   CROWTHER, Bosley. "'Rhapsody in Blue,' a Picture in Music of George Gershwin, With Robert Alda in Role of Composer, at the Hollywood." *NYTimes* [*NYTimes Film Reviews* 3], June 28, 1945, 22:2.
Crowther found fault with the work as biography, but had high praise for the music: ". . . Throughout, the brilliant music . . . is spotted abundantly, and that is the best . . . And even though the symphonic premiére of the famous 'Rhapsody in Blue' is photographed in hackneyed orchestra framings, the sweep and melody of the work is eloquent . . ."

B2064.   FARBER, Manny. "Plenty of Nuthin'." *The New Republic* 113/4 (July 23, 1945).
Negative review of the movie. "'Rhapsody in Blue' is an interminable juvenilizing and denaturing of George Gershwin's person, career, friends, relatives and a period from about 1905 to 1937, which sacrifices biography even more extensively than did 'Wilson' to indifferent performances of songs . . ."

B2065. "Filming 'Rhapsody in Blue'," in: *Rhapsody in Blue; The Jubilant Story of George Gershwin and His Music.* (Hollywood: Warner Bros., 1945), pp. 19-20.

B2066.   KAUFMAN, George S. "Notes for a Film Biography." *New Yorker* 21 (Aug. 11, 1945): 26-27.
Unusual review of the film in that Kaufman liked it! ". . . I was struck by the fidelity with which it followed his life . . ."

B2067.   MANNERS, Dorothy. "Gershwin's Music Stars." *LA Examiner* **[AMPAS]**, Sept. 22, 1945.
An innocuous review of the movie. ". . . It could be said: 'That music—that divine Gershwin music can be heard in all its fascinating rhythm at the Warner theaters this week—that's all!' But that's enough! . . ."

B2068. "Movie of the Week: Rhapsody in Blue, George Gershwin, America's most famous composer, is the hero of a star-studded screen biography." *Life* 19/3 (July 16, 1945): 89-92.
Typical *Life* magazine story, replete with many photographs of scenes from the movie. ". . . [Gershwin's] rise from the slums of New York's lower East Side to the position of America's most famous composer has the elements of a fine psychological drama. In *Rhapsody in Blue* that drama is merely sketched, and its place is taken by large, beautifully served helpings of Gershwin's immortally ingratiating music. The result falls short of being a

great screen biography . . ."

B2069.   "Music: Gershwin Everywhere." *Time* 46/2 (July 9, 1945): 67.
General article coinciding with the release of the Warner Brothers film biography. Mother Rose Gershwin expressed her opinion of the movie, ". . . She was pretty scornful of the show's rags-to-riches theme: 'It's not the truth . . . There was always enough money for Georgie's lessons. Poppa had twelve restaurants. But [the film] is clean . . . you can take the children' . . ."

B2070.   **REDELINGS, Lowell E.** "Gershwin Music Wins Cheers in 'Rhapsody.'"
Citizen-News (Hollywood, CA), Sept. 15, 1945, p. 4.
Redelings found fault with "the wide departure from biographical facts," and the camera tricks used. ". . . The film story may not entertain you, but the music will . . ."

B2071.   "[Review]." *Commonweal* 42 (July 6, 1945): 286-287.

B2072.   "[Review]." *Film Daily*, June 27, 1945, p. 5.

B2073.   "[Review]." *Hollywood Reporter*, June 27, 1945, p. 3.

B2074.   "[Review]." *Life* 19 (July 16, 1945): 89-92. (Full entry at **B2068**, above).

B2075.   "[Review]." *New Yorker* 21 (July 21, 1945): p. 36.

B2076.   "[Review]." *Newsweek* 26 (July 9, 1945): 102.

B2077.   "Review." *Theatre Arts* 29 (Nov. 1945): 645.
One-paragraph negative review with high praise for Oscar Levant, accompanied by a picture of him at the piano. *See*: **B1583**

B2078.   "Reviews of New Films, 'Rhapsody in Blue' . . ." *Film Daily*, June 27, 1945, p. 5.
Glowing review of the film..

B2079.   *'Rhapsody in Blue', The Jubilant Story of George Gershwin and His Music.*
Hollywood: Warner Bros, 1945.
A promotional pamphlet about the movie containing short statements by **Marion BAUER, Frank CROWNINSHIELD, Walter DAMROSCH, José ITURBI, Dorothy LAWTON, Artur RODZINSKI, Mark A. SCHUBART, Deems TAYLOR,** and **Paul WHITEMAN.** Includes many still photographs from the movie.

B2080.   "Rhapsody in Blue." Screen play by Howard Koch and Elliot Paul, based on
original screen story by Sonya Levien, producer: Jesse L. Lasky. Hollywood:
Warner Bros. Pictures, 1945.151 leaves. **[NN-L]**
Shooting script of the movie with names of the cast included.

B2081.   **RUBSAMEN, Walter H.** "Music in the Cinema." *Arts and Architecture* 62/9
(Sept. 1945): 20-21, 45.
Lengthy review of the film. ". . .Gershwin had something that struck fire, something definable that emerges as one listens to the wide variety of music [no less than 29 compositions] contained in this film . . ." The article includes many biographical details.

B2082.   SHAW, Alexander. "The Cinema: 'Rhapsody in Blue.' At the Warner . . ."
Spectator 172 (Nov. 9, 1945): 435.
Uncomplimentary review of the run at London's Warner. ". . . In this long film which runs for over two hours not for one instant does the man or his surroundings come to life. It is a staggering and saddening thought that so much sheer hard work could have produced nothing except thousands of feet of celluloid with very dull pictures on them . . ."

B2083.   SPAETH, Sigmund. *Rhapsody in Blue (The Story of George Gershwin) A Musical Study Outline of the Motion Picture by Warner Bros. for Music Clubs and Classes.* New York: National Federation of Music Clubs, 1945.
A two-page study guide with superficial analysis of the music in the movie.

B2084.   ULANOV, Barry. "Gershwin Wasn't That Great: The current movie about him leads a questionable campaign to inflate his stature to fantastic size." *Metronome* (August 1945): 12, 22.
Review of the Warner Bros. movie. ". . . *Rhapsody in Blue* is disastrously full of anachronisms and serious distortions of fact . . ." which errors Ulanov lists in the article. Ulanov obviously thinks G is much over-rated and uses this article to make his point. A helpful feature of the article is a listing of then available recordings.

B2085.   WARNER BROTHERS. *Call Bureau Cast Service.* Los Angeles: Association of Motion Picture Producers, March 20, 1944. **[AMPAS]**
Complete list of the cast.

B2086.   WHITEBAIT, William. "The Movies: 'Burma Victory' . . . 'Rhapsody in Blue,' at Warner's." *The New Statesman and Nation* 30 (Nov. 3, 1945): 298.
"Now *Rhapsody in Blue*, a biography of Gershwin, does strike me as being stale beyond endurance. To have to listen once again, in a film lasting two and a half hours, to *two* performances of that Tin Pan Alley classic . . . is painful enough, but I could stand that if Gershwin weren't being continually hailed in this film as the equal of Brahms and Schubert. That Gershwin had talent I don't for a moment deny; he gave a tune to the extravagant vulgarity of his time and place . . ."

Shall We Dance?, F10.

B2087.   "Astaire-Rogers 'Shall We Dance' A Knockout, Sandrich Dir'n, Score, Cast Swell . . ." *Hollywood Reporter*, Apr. 27, 1937, p. 3.
Rave review of the film. ". . . Outstandingly interesting is a remarkably effective engine-room dance for Fred Astaire, the conception of Mark Sandrich, for which George Gershwin has written music of fascinating rhythm and sonority to express the pulse of the engines and which is accompanied by the dance and by the song, 'Slap That Bass' . . . George Gershwin's score contains some of the best things he has done. Its six songs are tuneful and lilting and will be widely played . . . One of the loveliest bits of musical writing in the picture is the instrumental accompaniment ot the deck stroll of the dog owners on a transatlantic liner [the *Walking the Dog* sequence] . . ." *See:* **W47**

B2088.   "Entertainment, Screen: Astaire and Rogers Set New Pace for Dance Fans." *Newsweek* 9 (May 15, 1937): 26.
No particular mention of G's music is given in this otherwise descriptive review.

B2089.   NUGENT, Frank S. "Shall We Dance." *NYTimes* [*NYTimes Film Reviews* 2],

May 14, 1937, 21: 1.
Review of the first run at Radio City Music Hall, NY. ". . . It has a grand score by George Gershwin . . ."

B2090.   "[Review]." *Commonweal* 26 (May 21, 1937): 104.

B2091.   "[Review]." *Film Daily*, Apr. 20, 1937, p. 9.

B2092.   "[Review]." *Journal of Popular Film and Television* 8 (Fall 1980): 15-24.

B2093.   "[Review]." *New Yorker* 13 (May 15, 1937): 86-87.

B2094.   "[Review]." *Newsweek* 9 (May 15, 1937): 26.(Details at **B2088,** above)

B2095.   "[Review]." *Scholastic* 30 (May 15, 1937): 26.

B2096.   "[Review]." *The Spectator* 158 (June 4, 1937): 1051.

B2097.   "[Review]." *The Tatler* 144 (May 26, 1937): 372.

B2098.   "Screen and Stage: Rogers, Roller-skates and Rhythm, Songs, Ballet and Funny
            Sayings in 'Shall We Dance?'" *Literary Digest* 123 (May 15, 1937): 20.
". . . There are those who will quibble daintily over the Gershwin score, holding that it has not the verve and enchantment found in previous musical jots fashioned for the singing and dancing of the RKO stars. Better or worse, it remains that it has three excellent numbers in 'Let's Call the Whole Thing Off,' 'Slap That Bass,' and 'They Can't Take That Away From Me' . . ."

The Shocking Miss Pilgrim, F17.

B2099.   **CROWTHER, Bosley.** "The Shocking Miss Pilgrim." *NYTimes* [*NYTimes Film
            Reviews* 3], Feb. 12, 1947, 34:2.
Brief review of the film as seen at NY's Roxy. ". . . There is considerable harmonizing by Miss Grable and Dick Haymes of some songs said to have been written but never published by George Gershwin . . . In a few a certain exuberance is momentarily achieved, but the bulk of the music is as sticky as toothpaste being squeezed out of a tube, especially the singing of the principals of the hit song 'For You, For Me, Forever More' . . ."

B2100.   **HARTUNG, Philip T.** "Everyman's Choice." *Commonweal* 45 (Feb. 7, 1947):
            424.
Brief review. ". . . Betty Grable . . . and Dick Haymes . . . gayly sing some George Gershwin songs that are now being heard for the first time. Even with lyrics by Ira, George's brother, they enhance the Gershwin reputation very little . . ."

B2101.   **Mike.** "Miniature Reviews: The Shocking Miss Pilgrim (Color-Songs)." *Variety*
            [*Variety Film Reviews, 1943-1948* (dateline: Hollywood, CA, Dec. 31, 1946)],
            Jan. 1, 1947.
". . . In stringing some George Gershwin tunes dug up out of the trunk a few years ago on a slim thread of a story, the William Perlberg-George Seaton team have gone about the whimsy in too heavy-handed a manner. As a result of which, except for a few flashes of the brilliant wit and tunefulness that inevitably made a show with a George and Ira Gershwin score

a standout in the past, 'The Shocking Miss Pilgrim' will have to rely on cast names . . . Music is standout, most hummable tunes being 'For You, For Me, Forever More' and 'Aren't You Kind of Glad We Did?' One that has all the flavor of the Gershwin freres' topmost sophisticated musicomedy stuff is 'But Not in Boston.' Others that listen well are 'Changing My Tune,' 'Stand Up and Fight,' and a fetching waltz . . ."

B2102.   "[Review]." *Commonweal* 45 (Feb. 7, 1947): 424.

B2103.   "[Review]." *Film Daily*, Jan. 2, 1947, p. 16.

B2104.   "[Review]." *New Republic* 116 (Feb. 17, 1947): 40.

B2105.   "[Review]." *Variety* (Jan. 1, 1947): 14. (Full entry at **B2101**, above).

B2106.   **SCHEUER, Philip K.** "Miss Gable Takes Boston." *Los Angeles Times*, Feb. 15, 1947.
    Positive descriptive review of the film. ". . . [T]his is ingratiatingly presented against a background of lilting tunes by the late George Gershwin—tunes hitherto unpublished, and set to new lyrics by brother Ira . . ."

Song of the Flame, F6.1.

B2107.   "Cinema: The New Pictures: Song of the Flame . . ." *Time* 15 (May 19, 1930): 62.
    Brief announcement. ". . . [E]laborate staging, good Gershwin tunes and 5,000 voices have been assembled in this reproduction of a Broadway operetta . . ."

B2108.   **HALL, Mordaunt.** "The Screen: A Vitaphone-Technicolor Operetta. Song of the Flame . . ." *NYTimes*, May 7, 1930, p. 24.
    Review including discussion of the songs. ". . . This picture, an expensive affair with a host of persons in its cast, is an adaptation of the operetta . . . [T]his is no more than has been done in several other musical screen offerings, only it has seldom been done as well . . . 'The Cossack Love Song' is a lilting melody that cannot fail to appeal to the spectator and as for as the 'Song of the Flame,' one could listen to it for longer than this picture lasts without becoming bored . . ."

B2109.   _____. "Murray Anderson's Sparkling Film: Pastel shaded 'King of Jazz' Possesses Wonderful Photography And Smart Skits—Einstein's Old and New . . . An Operetta . . ." *NYTimes*, May 11, 1930, p. 5.
    The "operetta" Hall referred to was *Song of the Flame*. He liked the singing of the principals and commented that ". . . The Gershwin-Stothart compositions are enjoyable, especially the widely played 'Song of the Flame' . . ."

Three for the Show, F21.

B2110.   **HIFT.** "Three for the Show . . . [review]." *Variety* [*Variety Film Reviews 1954-1958*] 9, Feb. 16, 1955.
    Lengthy review. ". . . [T]he music, including two George and Ira Gershwin numbers, is pleasant and well integrated . . ."

B2111.   "Three for the Show," in *Motion Picture Guide*, ed. by Stanley Ralph Ross.

Chicago: Cinebooks, VIII, p. 3413.
Descriptive coverage of the film. ". . . The Champions . . . do a wonderful piece to George and Ira Gershwin's beautiful song 'Someone to Watch Over Me' . . ."

When the Boys Meet the Girls, F27.

B2112. **HARFORD, Margaret.** "Dreary 'Meet the Girls' and 'My Success' Cloud Holidays." *LA Times*, Dec. 24, 1965.
Negative review of the film. ". . . Louis Armstrong does a wonderful jazz turn on Gershwin's 'I Got Rhythm' and the scene is momentarily brighter . . ."

B2113. **POWERS, James.** "Boys Me Musical, Katzman-Ganzer Film Exploitable." *Hollywood Reporter* **[AMPAS]**, Dec. 1, 1965.
"In addition to its other values, 'Boys' . . . has a gaggle of Gershwin standards . . There are six Gershwin tunes, plus six other songs by other composers . . ."

BIBLIOGRAPHY ABOUT ORCHESTRA TOURS

Bibliography About Whiteman Tours of 1924 and 1925

After the highly successful premiere of *Rhapsody in Blue* on February 12, 1924, Whiteman began booking many extensive tours, eventually covering from coast to coast of the United States as well as parts of Canada. The following bibliography gives contemporaneous accounts from selected cities on the tours. The reviews are presented by year and alphabetically by author's last name.

1924

B2114. **BOALS, L. R.** "Paul Whiteman's Concert Is an Uproarious Success; Offers Beautiful Tone, Versatility, and Comedy—But Paul Is an Entertainer, Not an Educator." *The Youngstown* [OH] *Daily Vindicator*, November 6, 1924, p. 2.
"Paul Whiteman and his orchestra were an uproaring success last evening (November 5, 1924) in the Rayen-Wood auditorium . . . The most pretentious number on the program, Gershwin's 'Rhapsody in Blue' had good moments, but not enough of them . . ." This biased and foolish critic predicted: ". . . When the styles of dancing changes, jazz is apt to die a natural death, though probably a lingering one . . ." *See:* **W1**

B2115. **D., G. B.** "Paul Whiteman And His Syncopaters, at the Post Wednesday Evening." *The Battle Creek* [MI] *Moon-Journal*, October 9, 1924, p. 9.
Lengthy review of the tour concert at the Post Theater on October 8, 1924. Concerning RiB, ". . . For the final number, a 'Rhapsody in Blues,' [!] a big Chickering was dragged out onto the stage and Harry Parella descended from the heights . . . to play what might be called a jazz symphony—a piano solo of strictly modern characteristics, yet reflective of the time-honored symphony, with orchestral background." *See:* **W1**

B2116. **DURNEY, Edward.** "Music in Buffalo: The Whiteman Concert." *Buffalo* [NY] *Evening News*, Sept. 29, 1924.
Review of the concert of September 28, a second appearance at Buffalo. The reviewer seemed prejudiced *against* the RiB. ". . . Among the musically pretentious, and perhaps least interesting, numbers of the evening were three novelties by Eastwood Lane, and

George Gershwin's rambling, dissonant [!] composition for piano and modern orchestra, 'Rhapsody in Blue,' which last named was more or less patiently endured last season. The composer played it at that time, and at last night's infliction Harry Parella was the dexterous performer . . ." *See*: **W1**

B2117.   GALLERY GOD. "Paul Whiteman Has Task in Closing His Program: Morton Downey's Lyric Tenor Voice Wins Outburst of Applause; Michael Pingatore Pleases in Banjo Numbers; Diversified Program Delights Capacity Audience." *Charleston* [WV] *Daily Mall*, Oct. 31, 1924.
   See: **[GREEN], Abel.** "Paul Whiteman's Concert." *Variety*, November 10, 1924 at **B2132.**

B2118.   MOORE, Edward. "Light Music at Its Best Given by Whiteman: His Orchestra Even Better than Expected." *Chicago Daily Tribune*, Oct. 20, 1924, p. 21.
   Review of the Whiteman Fall tour concert at the Studebaker on Oct. 19. ". . . [T]he 'Rhapsody in Blue' is something to hear, though it has not the fascinating thrill of some of the other pieces. Victor Herbert's 'Spanish Serenade' or the 'Russian Rose.' These were high spots, and I looked in vain for any trace of the famous vulgarity of jazz." *See*: **W1**

B2119. "Music: Whiteman's Orchestra." *Rochester* [NY] *Democrat and Chronicle*, May 16, 1924, p. 23.
   Review of the May 15, 1924, concert at Rochester's Convention Hall. ". . . The hall was practically filled, and the crowd was enthusiastic from first to last . . ." The reviewer praised Gershwin's performance highly, and commented on the rhapsody: ". . . This rhapsody starts with the queer label of jazz on it, but it soon carries the listener along through a finely constructed score, varied, supplied with lots of real themes, orchestrated with almost wizard-like success at conveying a clear notion of ideas . . ." *See*: **W1d, T1**

B2120.   PALMER, T. J. "Music: The Paul Whiteman Concert." *Ottawa Citizen*, October 1, 1924.
   Review of the concert the night before, September 30, 1924. ". . . The big item for the orchestra was the 'Rhapsody in Blue,' by Gershwin, with Milton Rettenberg as solo pianist. This work revealed clever thematic [sic] treatment, but is somewhat a burlesque on the piano concerto. The orchestration proved very rich but bizarre in tonal color. The piano part was most cleverly played and the Whiteman's ideal of the American orchestra was revealed in this number . . ." *See*: **W1**

B2121. "Paul Whiteman's Orchestra." *Decatur* [IL] *Review*, Oct. 17, 1924.
   ". . . Paul Whiteman attempted to demonstrate to a capacity audience in Lincoln Square last evening that jazz is to be taken seriously . . . George Gershwin's 'Rhapsody in Blue' for piano and orchestra was real symphonic music . . ." *See*: **W1**

B2122. "PLEASES LARGE AUDIENCE: Paul Whiteman's Orchestra Gives Varied and Spectacular Program of American Music." *The Wilkes-Barre Record*, Sept. 25, 1924, p.12.
   Generally complimentary commentary on the concert.

B2123.   ROGERS, James H. "Reception Awaits Whiteman Orchestra, Jazz King to be Greeted by Many at Depot Monday." *Cleveland Plain Dealer*, May 25, 1924, 6.
   An advance article announcing the May 26, 1924, concert to be held at Masonic Hall

in Cleveland. For obvious reasons, no critical opinion about the concert is given here. *See*: **T10**

B2124.   TRYON, Virginia V. "Ann Arbor's Social Realm: 'Perfect Program' Given By Whiteman and His Orchestra; Variety of Numbers and Their Excellent Rendition Please Large Audience." *Ann Arbor* [MI] *Times News*, Oct. 8, 1924.

Review of the October 7, 1924, afternoon concert in Hill auditorium. ". . . George Gershwin's 'Rhapsody in Blue,' as the final number on the program, is already known as a fascinating experiment, a composition of beauty and interest. In it Harry Parella was featured as soloist . . ." *See*: **W1**

B2125.   WHITWORTH, Walter. "Jazz Made Respectable by Whiteman's Orchestra." *Indianapolis News*, May 18, 1924.

Review of the tour concerts "at the Murat yesterday afternoon and night [May 17, 1924]." The reviewer liked the Whiteman band, but on the whole the review is negative. He was particularly critical of the Rhapsody: ". . . Heralded with a fanfare of trumpets and 'alarums,' one expected to listen to something more than a novelty, and one was disappointed at the lack of originality in the whole thing. It was little removed from the blatantly obvious, with no thematic development of any kind, with no incisiveness nor vigor and certainly no thought behind it . . . Nothing quite so revealed the paucity of thought in ragtime as Mr. Gershwin's work." *See*: **W1, T4**

B2126. "Whiteman's Music Receives Plaudits of Large Crowd." *The Post-Standard* [Syracuse, NY], September 28, 1924.

Brief review which corroborates that RiB was performed at both the afternoon and evening concerts. *See*: **W1**

1925

B2127.   AUGUR, Ruth M. " Whiteman Puts Pep in Concert: Audience Can Hardly Keep Feet From Stepping; Gets Enthusiastic Reception." *The El Paso Times*, Feb. 10, 1925, p.10.

A complimentary review of the concert even though the Liberty Hall stage was too small to accommodate the band and the piano required for the RiB. *See*: **W1**

B2128.   BLOOM, David, Jr. "Whiteman Plays to Record Audience Here: Master of 'American' Music Scores Huge success." *Commercial Appeal* [Memphis,TN] (Morning), Jan. 21, 1925, p. 12.

"Paul Whiteman came to Memphis last night and conquered the largest audience [5800] that has listened to a concert in the history of Memphis." A lengthy praiseworthy review of the concert, including the RiB. *See*: **W1**

B2129. "Concert By Whiteman Is A Tremendous Hit; Crowd Jams National Theater to Hear Attempt in Modern Music; Plenty of Jazz, Too." *Greensboro* [NC] *Daily News*, January 8, 1925, p. 15.

Lengthy review of the January 7, 1925, concert in Greensboro, NC. RiB is mentioned as is Leo Sowerby's *Synconata*. *See*: **W1**

B2130.   FLICKER, Felix. "Whiteman Gets Fine Reception and Scores Hit; Famous Phonograph Record Maker and His Orchestra Draw S. R. O. Crowd." *Greensboro* [NC] *Daily Record*, January 8, 1925, p. 5.

Review of Whiteman concert of January 7, 1925. "The . . . concert at the National theater last night was greeted by one of the largest audiences [nearly 2000] ever assembled in a local theater. Hundreds were turned away . . . Such a situation . . . has occurred in every city where the jazz master has played on his southern tour . . . The Whiteman renderation [?] was an art and his arranger George Gershwin [!] gets the credit . . ."

B2131.   "Given a Big Send-off; St. Joseph's Ovation to Raymond Turner and Whiteman; The Capacity Audience Heard the King of Jazz and His Orchestra at the Lyceum Theater—Lavishly Entertained." *The St. Joseph* [MO] *News-Press*, November 16, 1925.
Lengthy review of the concert by the Whiteman band in St. Joseph, Raymond Turner's hometown, during the Fall tour, November 15, 1925. ". . . Raymond Turner played the piano in the 'Rhapsody in Blue' . . . [Harry] Perrella usually plays the 'Rhapsody' . . . Turner gave the solo in the old home town, for the first time in public . . ." *See:* **W1**

B2132.   [GREEN], Abel. "Paul Whiteman's Concert." *Variety,* November 10, 1924.
Lengthy, one-column review of the private, invited performance preceding the Nov. 15 concert at Carnegie Hall. ". . . The program is almost entirely new . . . George Gershwin's famous 'Rhapsodie [sic] in Blue,' with the composer at the piano, and several of the unusual Whiteman arrangements of familiar classics and popular airs, are retained . . ." *See:* **W1g, B233**

B2133.   HARDING, Clarence W. "Whiteman." *South Bend* [IN] *Tribune*, October 21, 1925, p. 33.
Review of the Whiteman tour concert at South Bend's Blackstone Theater, October 21, 1925. ". . . Mr. Whiteman's experiment in American music is no longer an experiment, but a well founded bit of musical entertainment guaranteed to please the most fastidious . . . A request for George Gershwin's 'Rhapsody in Blue' placed this number on the program . . . The number combines all the tricks employed by the dance musician in the popular orchestra, with the piano predominating. The solo passages were played in excellent style last night by Harry Perrella . . ." *See:* **W1**

B2134.   "Jazz Has New Meaning with Paul's Advent; Famous Whiteman Orchestra Plays for Full House At Auditorium." *Waco* [TX] *Tribune-Herald*, February 1, 1925.
Glowing review of the January 31, 1925, Whiteman concert. ". . . The suit [sic] of serenades and the rhapsody in blue at the last all but closed a perfect program. Harry Perrella, pianist, led in the symphony of minor chords . . ." *See:* **W1**

B2135.   KARELL, Docia. "Music! Mad Music! Soul-Riot Melody, Whiteman Brings; How Can One Sit Down and Write About Such Gorgeous Tunes? Docia Pouts; Packed House Is Wild With Spent Delights; Leader's Charlestonette One Mad Climax to 'Jazz' and Considerably More, Winning Muskogee Audience." *Muskogee* [OK] *Daily Phoenix*, November 3, 1925, p. 1.
Review of the concert that opened the winter 1925 tour of the Whiteman group, November 2, 1925 at Muskogee's Orpheum Theatre. ". . . After the intermission the orchestra, with Harry Parrella, pianist, playing the solo part, played excerpts from George Gershwin's 'Rhapsody in Blue'—jazz, to be sure, but a thoroughly dignified piece of work none the less, with a well-defined theme and finely effective orchestration . . ." *See:* **W1**

B2136.   "'King of Jazz' Charms Crowd; Paul Whiteman and His Great Orchestra Acclaimed by Music Lovers." *Shreveport* [LA] *Times*, January 28, 1925, p. 13.

Review of the concert of January 27, 1925. "Paul Whiteman's interpretation of jazz music was a revelation to Shreveport music lovers. This was the unanimous opinion of more than 3,000 people who attended the concert at the Coliseum . . . and listened for three hours to a new voice in the music world . . ." No mention of RiB.

B2137.   "Many Request Re-Engagement of Whiteman: Cathedral Hall Filled to Overflow-
            ing with Audiences Whose Enthusiasm Knew No Bounds." *Houston* [TX]
            Chronicle, Jan. 31, 1925.

B2138.   **MARZONI, Pettersen.** "At the Theaters: American Has Music Distinctly Its
            Own, Whiteman Proves in Symphonic Syncopation at Auditorium Which
            Captures Almost Capacity Audience." *Birmingham* [AL] *News*, January 22,
            1925.
            Review of the Winter tour concert of January 21, 1925, at the municipal auditorium
in Birmingham. ". . . From the opening jangle of brass, reed, and kitchen utensils to Gershwin's
Rhapsody in Blue, running the entire scale of jazz, there was something that set the pulse to
leaping . . ." The paper pointed out that there were some 4000-5000 in attendance. *See:* **W1**

B2139.   "Memorial Hall is Jammed for Concert; Fully 3,200 Persons Are Entertained by
            Whiteman and His Jazz Orchestra." *Joplin* [MO] *Globe*, Nov. 11, 1925.
            While there was no mention of RiB, this article attests to the popularity of
Whiteman's group and the large number of persons that heard the work performed live.
". . . The audience was by far the largest ever assembled at any entertainment in this city. Every
seat in the house was sold, chairs were used and standing room was used, and many were
turned away . . ."

B2140.   "Paul Whiteman and His Orchestra Appear in Concert Here Tonight." *Joplin* [MO]
            Globe, November 10, 1925.

B2141.   **SMITH, George Boyt.** "Paul Whiteman and His Jazz Orchestra Scored Hit
            Here; Big Audience [over 2,000] Enjoyed Program Yesterday in Duval County—
            Orchestra Includes Splendid Musicians." *Times-Union* [Jacksonville, FL],
            January 12, 1925.
            Review of the January 11, 1925, concert by the Whiteman Orchestra in Jacksonville,
attended by 3,000. ". . . The Rhapsody in Blue, by Gershwin, much heralded and rather well
known through the phonograph records widely sold and played, was the great, big number of
the concert, and parts of it were very beautiful. The opening of the second part, suggesting a
Tschaikowsky valse, was perhaps the best illustration of the musical possibilities of the
organization, and could not fail to be appreciated by music lovers." *See:* **W1**

B2142.   Whiteman Heard By Large Crowd; Three Thousand Pack Armory to Hear Jazz
            Leader." *Jacksonville Journal*, Jan 12, 1925.
            ". . . Harry Parrella, at the piano, played more real music than any member of the
band, his interpretation of Gershwin's 'Rhapsody in Blue' being the hit of the afternoon. To
those who like jazz (for no matter what the critics say, it's that right on) the event yesterday
was a splendid affair, but one could not help sighing a bit over the fact that much good talent
is being expended to suit the needs of the hours for certain it is that no form of jazz can last
[!]." *See:* **W1**

B2143.   "Whiteman Opens Doors To New Possibilities." *The State* [Columbia, SC],
            January 11, 1925, p. 8.

"Mr. Whiteman's programs held two numbers of outstanding interest and promise. The 'Rhapsody in Blue' written by Harry Gershwin [sic!] for piano and orchestra, and the 'Syncopata,' [1924] by Leo Sowerby . . . [These pieces] are real music in conception and treatment, and Whiteman's musicians got into them rich, symphonic effects . . ." *See*: **W1**

B2144. "Whiteman Plays With Brilliance; Noted Orchestra Leader and His Men Reveal New beauties in Typically American Music." *The Lexington* [KY] *Leader*, Oct. 27, 1925.
Descriptive review of the October 26, 1925, concert at Woodland Auditorium. ". . . Harry Perrella . . . gave a remarkable performance of excerpts from George Gershwin's 'Rhapsody in Blue,' a syncopated composition that has reached such heights as to be played by leading symphony orchestras of the country . . ." *See*: **W1**

B2145. WIGGERS, Alvin S. "Paul Whiteman's Ear-Ticklers and More Serious Pieces Win Ovations; Jazz Orchestra Plays Before Crowded House at Auditorium . . ." *The Tennessean* [Nashville], January 20, 1925.
Review of the concert of January 19, 1925, at Ryman Auditorium. ". . . Young George Gershwin's 'Rhapsody in Blue' was a splendid part of the time and has one very good theme. Harry Perella played the difficult piano part well . . ." *See*: **W1**

Bibliography About Leo Reisman Tour of 1934

B2146. "'And You Were the Boy with the Horn?' George Gershwin Reminds Morton Downey of Time They Were in Whiteman's Orchestra; Melton Eggs Them On." *Sunday World Herald* [Omaha, NB], Jan. 28, 1934, p. 2.
Anecdotal article with kabitzing between Gershwin, Morton Downey, and tenor, James Melton. Complete with a picture of the three, with G at his practice keyboard, the trio was in town (Omaha, NB) for the concert the night before. *See*: **T29** and Borglum, below.

B2147. BORGLUM, August M. "Gershwin Delights Omaha, Glorifier of Jazz Finds Appreciative Audience Which Packs Tech High School." *Sunday World Herald* [Omaha, NB], Jan. 28, 1934, p. 4-A.
Review. "The Omaha Junior League, in presenting George Gershwin . . . and the Reisman Symphonic Orchestra . . . gave to an Omaha audience one of the most colorful musical and varied rhythmical performances in its history . . . The harmonies of the orchestra were especially glorious, while the variety of effects, tonal as well as rhythmic, were colorful, piquant, mocking, pleading—in fact representing the whole gamut of human emotions . . . The Rhapsody in Blue was played in Omaha by Mr. Gershwin with Paul Whiteman, some years ago. A second hearing brought out its beauty to a greater extent, fully justifying the reputation that he made with this, his first important work . . ." *See*: **T29** [No mention of the "*I Got Rhythm*" *Variations.*]

B2147.1. Boykin, Clarence. "The Theatre." *Times-Dispatch* (Richmond, VA), Feb.10, 1934, p. 2 (late ed.).
". . . [O]f personal preference was devoted to 'I Got Rhythm Variations' . . . In this . . . were revealed the most notable of the Gerhswinisms–'hot' rhythms in lavish display, minor chords on brilliant parade, leaping tempo in the manner of the revues–the music which is Gershwin, the melodies on which he built his reputation, the tunes which are in the intimate favor of the people known as Americans." *See*: **W6, T42**

B2147.2. ELWELL, Herbert. "Overflows Hall to Hear Gershwin; Crowd 'Gets Rhythm' from Master; Melton Wins Applause." *Cleveland* [OH] *Plain Dealer,* 21, 1934, p. 19.

". . . Critical consideration of such a program brings out a few significant points. For one thing, the orchestral portions seemed obligingly subdued, making the music very suitable for dinner and conversation. Of Mr. Gershwin's more 'serious' efforts, the 'Rhapsody in Blue' still stands out as his most important and most satisfactory achievement. And I would place his Variations next, for it displays great ingenuity in saying the same thing in different ways . . ." **W6a, T22**

B2148. "Gershwin Pleases Concert Audience. 'Rhapsody in Blue' Proves Still to Be Most Popular of His Works." *The Philadelphia Inquirer,* Feb. 8, 1934.

Review of the tour concert held at the Academy of Music, on February 7, 1934. ". . . The composer also offered some variations on the 'I Got Rhythm' theme which were described as new, indicating he has lost none of his daring. But it was [in] the 'Rhapsody in Blue,' whose 10th anniversary is being celebrated on the tour, that Gershwin admirers found the most satisfaction . . ." The reviewer noted that the concert lasted two hours. *See:* **W6, T40 (Variations) , W1 (RiB), T40**

B2148.1. LEIGHTON, George A. "Weekend Concerts . . .George Gershwin." *The Enquirer Cincinnati,* Feb. 5, 1934.

Lengthy two-column review of the concert at Taft Auditorium. In re: the Variations: "Barring a few obvious connecting epipodes, the variations are skillfully written and interesting in their treatment of the famous tune. Gershwin's delight in complex rhythms is to be noted throughout the work as well as his faculty of contrasting the 'blues' style with exuberant dance pulsations . . ."After his comments about the music, Leighton concluded: ". . . Altogether it was one of the pleasantest evenings we've had. The orchestra defies comparison in its classification . . ." *See:* **T36, W6a**

B2149.   MATTISON, Dorothy Boyd. "Gershwin and Melton Share Musical Honors: Audience of 2000 Enjoys All-American Program." *Worcester* [MA] *Daily Telegram,* Jan. 17, 1934.

Review of the concert in Worcester, sponsored by the Girl's League for Service. ". . . The ingenious rhythms of Mr. Gershwin have a lightsome spontaneity and wit which are not to be disassociated with the difficulty of their performance. Many believe his addition of the jazz element to the classical music form has given the folk touch considered necessary to the creation of a typical American music. As illustrative one might cite his variations of 'I Got Rhythm'. . ." *See:* **W6a, T18**

B2150.   MOORE, Edward. "Geo. Gershwin Concert Stirs Big Audience . . ." *Chicago Tribune,* Feb. 4, 1934.

In this short review, Moore had high praise for the program at its Reisman tour Chicago appearance, sponsored by the Red, White, and Blue Club. "Whether it is the Concerto in F, the 'Rhapsody in Blue,' his own new variations on his own 'I Got Rhythm,' or the pieces played by the orchestra, it is all vital, alert, nervous music, coming at high tension, presented in the brightest fashion imaginable . . ." *See:* **W2, W1, W6**

B2151.   MOTTE DE, Helen. "Gershwin Theme Still Is Rhythm: Compositions Since 'Rhapsody in Blue' Are Merely Repetitions." *Richmond [VA] News L eader,* Feb. 10, 1934 (All editions).

Review of the February 9, 1934, concert in Richmond. While the reviewer had much praise for RiB, she felt that G had "shot his bolt"with it and also noted that "The orchestra was effective and profited greatly by having John Corigliano as concertmeister." *See*: **W1, T42**

B2152. WISE, Herman. "Music: George Gershwin." *Detroit Free Press*, Jan. 22, 1934.
    Positive review of the Reisman tour concert of January 21, 1934, in Detroit, MI. "Everywhere the men [of the Reisman Symphonic Orchestra] have performed to sold-out houses; in each city there has been the utmost enthusiasm for the music of Mr. Gershwin. Apparently the name of Gershwin is like a magnet. Hundreds of persons who had never attended a concert were present Sunday . . . Sergei Rachmaninoff, the great Russian composer-pianist . . . joined in the applause with the rest . . . Members of the Detroit Symphony Orchestra and many other leading musicians in the City were profuse in their praises . . . If concerts like this one are what the public wants to hear, why not have more of them?" *See*: **T23**

BIBLIOGRAPHY ABOUT DISSERTATIONS AND THESES

B2153.   **BALS, Karen Elizabeth.** *The American Piano Concerto in the Mid-Twentieth Century.* DMA document, University of Kansas, 1982, pp. 27-30.
    Bals devotes three pages to an overview of the RiB and Concerto. *See*: **W1, W2**

B2154.   **BASKERVILLE, David R.** *Jazz Influence on Art Music to Mid-Century.* Ph.D. Dissertation: University of California at Los Angeles, 1965, pp. 449-503. 535 pp. *Dissertation Abstracts* 26/8 (Feb. 1966): 4710-A.
    Lengthy, sympathetic, and worthwhile discussion/analysis of G's classical oeuvre from the perspective of jazz influences on art music to *ca.* 1950. Musical analyses are provided for RiB, the Concerto, and P&B. In the discussion (p. 486), Baskerville pointed out the fact that Schoenberg has orchestrated the three preludes for piano. *See*: **W1, W2, W37, W42, B2168**

B2155.   **BESTOR, Charles Lemon.** *An Analysis of the 'Rhapsody in Blue' by George Gershwin.* Masters thesis (Music), University of Illinois, 1952. 183 pp.
    Includes a theoretical analysis of RiB. This thesis is especially valuable for a forty-one-page philosophical essay appended: "A General Survey of the Problems Involved in a Sociological, Cultural and Musical Discussion of the Jazz Idiom and the Attempt to Assign a Position to the Music of George Gershwin in Its Development." After presenting a considerable number of points of view, Bestor concluded: ". . . That Gershwin is America's greatest serious jazz composer [to date] is his claim virtually by default. That he is America's greatest serious composer per se is, at the very least, open to question, and that he is a serious composer at all one may grant him on the basis of his intentions while reserving judgment on the basis of his results . . . What Gershwin did for American serious music, in attempting to point the way along at least one path of the development of an indigenous national musical expression, was undoubtedly worth doing, even if it was a failure. It was worth doing even if the goal itself, the indigenous national expression, may not have been the highest toward which American music could aim . . . His failure, *if it was a failure* [italics mine], may have been the result of his creative limitations as a composer or may have been inherent in the attempt itself. . . ." *See*: **W1**

B2156. BLACK, Donald Fisher. *The Life and Work of Eva Jessye and Her Contributions to American Music.* Ph. D. dissertation, University of Michigan, 1986.
    A substantial study of Jessye and her choir. Jessye was the leader of the choir for the 1935 P&B production and the Everyman Opera Co. show of 1952. *See*: **W37b, W37p**

B2157. CHICURAL, Steven Robert. *George Gershwin's Songbook: Influences of*

Jewish Music, Ragtime, and Jazz. D. M. A. Dissertation, University of Kentucky, 1989, Abstract in *DAI* 1990.

Using the *Songbook* as a tool, Chicural looks at the Jewish, Ragtime, and Jazz influences contained therein *See:* **W45**

B2158.   CONRAD, Jon Alan. *Style and Structure in Songs by George Gershwin Published 1924-1938.* Ph. D. dissertation, Indiana University, 1985. xvii, 284 pp. UMI order no. 8602397.

In this carefully guided, and consequently excellent, music theory dissertation, Conrad organized his theoretical analyses of the songs under the chapter headings "Sectional Form of Refrains"; "Melody"; "Harmony"; "Verses"; and a final summary chapter titled "Unity." Conrad's approach is decidedly musical; there are 151 musical examples in the paper, and the lyrics are not considered. A set of eight tables provides much information about the songs in an easy-to-compare manner. An example of these tables can be seen in Conrad's No. 1, "Length and Form of Refrains," typified by the following entry on *I Got Rhythm,* from p. 35: "Length: 34, Form: A A B A1 (10)." All 132 songs studied by Conrad are given the same treatment. This dissertation is indispensable to anyone making a serious study of the musical content of the songs.

B2159.   COOPER, John Webb. *A Comparative Study of Porgy, the Novel, Porgy, the Play, and Porgy and Bess, the Folk Opera.* Master's thesis, Columbia University, 1950.

Includes a good comparison between the play and libretto for the opera. *See:* **W37**

B2160.   DURHAM, Francis Marion. *Dubose Heyward: The Southerner as Artist, A Critical and Biographical Study.* Ph. D. dissertation, Columbia University, 1953. 451 pp.

A very thorough doctoral study of Heyward's life and oeuvre. Includes probing analysis of the original novella by Heyward, *Porgy* (pp. 166ff), and its transmutation into a successful Broadway play (pp. 334ff), ultimately to become the opera P&B (pp. 364-389). *See:* **W37**

B2161.   FARRINGTON, James. *Ferde Grofé: An Investigation into His Musical Activities and Works.* Master of Music thesis. Tallahassee, FL: Florida State University, 1985, pp. 60-71. 193 pp.

This is a very good life and works approach to Grofé, and the above-cited pages contain specific information on the Rib and the Whiteman "Experiment." Farrington took advantage of the Ferde Grofé Tape Archive housed at Florida State University. The archive comprises 152 reel-to-reel tapes including pieces composed or arranged by Grofé, as well as interviews with Grofé. The collection was donated by Grofé's son, Ferde Jr., in November, 1983. According to Farrington, based on the Florida State tape no. 121, "Grofé was most influential in his advice to Gershwin concerning the inclusion of the E-major melody of the andante section" in the *Rhapsody. See:* **W1**

B2162.   GUTOWSKI, Lynda Diane. *George Gershwin's Relationship to the Search for an American Culture during the Nineteen-Twenties.* Master of Arts thesis, University of Maryland, 1967. iii, 124 pp.

In this American studies thesis, Gutowski summarized the focus of this paper well in her Introduction: ". . . I hope this study will prove helpful to anyone seeking an understanding of what was happening in the arts in America during the nineteen-twenties, and especially to anyone seeking to understand the relationship between George Gershwin and the artists in other fields . . . (p. 3)" Gutowski studied only the "serious" compositions. Among other artists of the Jazz Age, the writer compared Gershwin to F. Scott Fitzgerald (pp. 103-104). So closely were G and Fitzgerald associated in the minds of many people that S. N. Behrman wrote a play, *Let Me Hear the Melody,* based on his recollections of the two men (Jablonski & Stewart, *The Gershwin Years,* 1958, p. 236).

B2163.   HANSON, John Robert. *Macroforms in Selected Twentieth-Century Piano Concertos.* Ph.D. Dissertation. University of Rochester, Eastman School of Music, 1969. 404 pp. UM order no. 70-10,575.

The piano works with orchestra compared to thirty-three other works for piano. (RILM69) *See:* **W1, W2, W4, W6**

B2164.   HAWKINS, Roy Benton. *The Life and Works of Robert Russell Bennett.* Ph.D. dissertation. Texas Tech University, 1989. xii, 197 pp, pp. 56-57 (brief reference to *Girl Crazy),* 59-60, 66, 81.

References to G here and there throughout. Of interest: ". . . [I]n a reference to an otherwise undocumented work, a set of variations on *I Got Rhythm,* Marc Blitzstein wrote: 'Of all the jazz orchestrations of the last ten years, commend me to Russell Bennett's variations on *I Got Rhythm* . . . this surely is the high-water mark of a highly-developed, perfectly mature craft (*Modern Music,* Jan.-Feb. 1933, p. 102). This work does not appear in the works list of the article on Bennett in the *New Grove Dictionary of American Music,* 1ˢᵗ. ed., 1986. *See:* **W6 (IGR), W33 (Girl Crazy)**

B2165.   LOBALBO, Anthony Charles. *A Performance Guide to Selected Piano Music of George Gershwin.* Ph. D. dissertation. New York University, 1982. xxi, 338 pp. UMI Order No. 8307686.

The RiB, Concerto, Preludes for Piano, *Second Rhapsody,* and *"I Got Rhythm" Variations* were analyzed primarily from the point of view of a performer. ". . . After the analysis of each chapter [work], a performance guide is offered based on the evaluations and findings of the analysis presented. The performance guide consists of suggested fingerings, phrasing, and performance practices based on the writer's experience in performing Gershwin's piano music . . ." The following statement, from a discussion of "stride" piano performance is incorrect: ". . .Chronologically, the style was extremely popular in the early 1920s and certainly Gershwin, taking pride *in being a jazz musician himself* [italics mine], was aware of it . . . (p. 59)." GG was *not* a jazz musician, per se. Nevertheless, the author draws some well thought out conclusions and suggestions for further research in his final chapter. *See:* **W1, W2, W42, W4, W6**

B2166.   LOGAN, Charles G. *A Stylistic Analysis of George Gershwin's An American in Paris.* Master of Music thesis (Music theory), Texas Christian University, 1949. v, 149 pp.

Analysis of AiP, with comparisons to RiB, Concerto, and P&B. The harmonic analysis includes tables such as "Percentages of Chord Frequencies," "Table of 7th Chords," "Table of 9th Chords," and "Table of 11th Chords," each table breaking the types of chords down into frequencies of occurrence. Logan employed the same approach as part of his melodic analysis. Logan also subjected G's orchestration to analysis. Chapter six includes a comparison of AiP with RiB, Concerto, and P&B. Overall, although there are no profound revelations, this is a good master's study. *See:* **W3, W1, W2, W37**

B2167.   MAISEL, Arthur. *Talent and Technique: George Gershwin's* "Rhapsody in Blue." Ph.D dissertation., City University of New York, 1989, 191 pp. Order

Number: AAI9000045.

Description from *Dissertation Abstracts*: The dissertation consists of two parts, an analytical essay and a composition. The essay starts from the fact that the musical worth of the *Rhapsody in Blue* has often been questioned, despite its having been a fixture of the repertoire since its premiere. A close (Schenkerian) analysis shows the flaws of the piece in detail. It also reveals considerable structural coherence, however, comprising very sophisticated treatment of motives in the foreground and middleground, and, in the background, the unfolding of a tritone as the boundary of a tonic that is both B-flat major-minor and a whole-tone collection. Since Gershwin was mostly untrained at the time and the Rhapsody was his first large work, the question arises as to how he was able to achieve such sophistication. The answer proposed is that through improvisation he was able to tap his great talent . . . . *See*: **W1**

B2168.   MURRAY, Martha M. *George Gershwin: Classical Composer*. Masters thesis (Music), Mississippi College, 1971. iii, 104 pp.   ·
This paper includes a sixty-three page analysis of P&B ". . . in relation to the compositional idioms of traditional opera . . ." *See*: **W37, B2154**

B2169.   PERCONTI, William John. *A Comprehensive Performance Project in Saxophone Literature with an Essay Consisting of Selected Piano Works by George Gershwin transcribed for Saxophone Quartet*. D. M. A. Thesis, University of Iowa, 1986. iii, 69 pp.
Includes arrangements for quartet of soprano, alto, tenor, and baritone saxophones.

B2170.   SCHNEIDER, Wayne J. *George Gershwin's Political Operettas "Of Thee I Sing" (1931) and "Let 'Em Eat Cake" (1933), and Their Role in Gershwin's Musical and Emotional Maturing*, 2 vols. Ph. D. dissertation, Cornell University, 1985. 879 pp. UM order no. 8525755
A monumental, invaluable, detailed study of these two shows and many things on the periphery. This work is indispensable for anyone undertaking serious academic study of the Gershwins. *See*: **W34, W36**

B2171.   SCHWARTZ, Charles M. *The Life and Orchestral Works of George Gershwin*. Ph.D. dissertation. New York University, 1969. UMI no. 70-3105. *Dissertation Abstracts* 30/9 (Mar. 1970): 3977A.
This work, along with his Master's thesis listed below, preceded Schwartz' two books dealing with Gershwin. The dissertation includes considerable discussion of the orchestral pieces. *See*: Full annotation of the book at **B88, W1-W7**

B2172.   _____ . *Elements of Jewish Music in Gershwin's Melody*. M. A. Thesis. New York University, 1965.

B2173.   SMITH, Marian Monta. *Six Miles to Dawn: An Analysis of the Modern American Musical Comedy*. Ph.D. dissertation. Cornell University, 1971. 212 pp. UM: 71-17,133. *Dissertation Abstracts* 32/1 (July 1971), 587-A.
Limited discussion of OTIS and P&B. *See*: **W34, W37**

B2174.   TORNICK, Michael. "George Gershwin's Concerto in F for piano and orchestra: compositional style and structural cohesiveness." Reproduced from typescript. Thesis (M.M.)–NY: Manhattan School of Music, 1990. Vol. 2 contains a structural graph of Gershwin's Concerto in F. Includes bibliographical references (l. 217-219). *See:* **W2**

B2175.   WALDAU, Roy Sandman. *The Theatre Guild's Middle Years—1928-1939.*
Ph.D. dissertation, New York University School of Education, 1966, pp. 288-300.
Concerns "the third production" of the Theatre Guild: the world premiere of P&B, and the "financial, casting, and rehearsal problems, among many others" the Guild endured in producing P&B. An informative discussion of the financing, the choice of the theatre, early offers for motion picture agreements is presented. A synopsis of the reviews for both the Boston and New York premieres is included. Problems with the Actors Equity and musicians labor unions encountered by the Guild are elaborated upon. By the end of the New York run, apparent financial difficulties caused the original 70-member cast to be reduced to 40. *See:* **W37, W37a**

B2176.   WYATT, Robert. *The Piano Preludes of George Gershwin.* Doctor of Music treatise, Florida State University, Spring 1988. iv, 158 pp. Bib., pp. 87-102.
See: complete entry at **B899**

B2177.   YOUSLING, Richard S. *The Style of George Gershwin's Popular Songs.* Rochester, NY: Eastman School of Music, M. A. thesis, 1949. 116 pp.

Appendix A

Whiteman and Reisman Orchestra Tour Itineraries

The information here is derived largely from the Paul Whiteman Collection at Williams College, Williamstown, MA, through the kindness of Sylvia B. Kennick, curator. Whiteman took more tours than those given here, but discrepancies were found in the itineraries of orchestra tours after 1924, rendering those lists unreliable. The itineraries given are for the Spring 1924 Paul Whiteman Orchestra tour and the 1934 tour of Reisman's Symphonic Orchestra, conducted by Charles Previn. It should be noted here that bibliography (newspaper reviews) for cities from Whiteman's tour of 1925 was collected and can be seen beginning at page 551. However, I didn't consider the itinerary itself reliable enough to print below.

The tours of various versions of *Porgy and Bess* are not covered here because those dates are generally given under performances in the "Works and Performances" chapter. The Armitage tour of 1936 is covered at **W37d**; the Cheryl Crawford tour of 1942-1944 is lined out at **W37h**.

First tour after the premiere of *Rhapsody in Blue*, in Spring 1924

T1. 1924 (May 15–June 1): Paul Whiteman Spring tour, beginning on May 15
    in Rochester, NY; Convention Hall: *(See*: **B2119)**, and including:
T2. Buffalo, NY, Broadway Auditorium, May 16
T3. Pittsburg, PA, Syria Mosque, May 17
T4. Indianapolis, IN, Murat theatre, May 18 *See*: **B2125**
T5. Cincinnati, OH, Music Hall, May 20
T6. St. Louis, MO, Odeon Theatre, May 21
T7. Kansas City, MO, Convention Hall, May 22
T8. Milwaukee, WI, Auditorium, May 23
T9. Chicago, IL, Cohan's Grand, May 25
T10. Cleveland, OH, Masonic Hall, May 26 *See*: **B2123**
    Cleveland, OH, City Auditorium, May 27
T11. Toledo, OH, Coliseum, May 28
T12. Detroit, MI, Arcadia Auditorium, May 29
T13. Toronto, Canada, Arena Theater, May 30
T14. Ottawa, Canada, May 31
T15. Montreal, St. Dennis Theater, June 1

Gershwin's Tour with the Leo Reisman Orchestra of 1934
(*See*: **B1391** for interview of GG regarding the tour)

T16. Boston, MA, Symphony Hall, Jan. 14 *See*: **W6a**
T17. Portland, ME, City Hall Auditorium, Jan. 15
T18. Worcester, MA, Memorial Auditorium, Jan. 16 *See*: **B2149**
T19. Springfield, MA, City Auditorium, Jan. 17
T20. Syracuse, NY, Lincoln Auditorium (H. S.), Jan. 18
T21. Toronto, Canada, Massey Hall, Jan. 19
T22. Cleveland, OH, Music Hall, Jan.20 *See*: **B2147.2.**
T23. Detroit, MI, Orchestra Hall, Jan. 21 *See*: **B2152**
T24. Ft. Wayne, IN, Shrine Theater, Jan. 22
T25. Milwaukee, WI, Auditorium, Jan. 23
T26. Madison, WI, West H.S. Auditorium, Jan. 24
T27. St. Paul, MN, Auditorium, Jan. 25
T28. Sioux Falls, SD, The Coliseum, Jan. 26
T29. Omaha, NE, Tech. H.S., Jan. 27 *See*: **B2146, B2147**
T30. Kansas City, KS, Convention Hall, Jan. 28
T31. Des Moines, IA, Shrine Auditorium, Jan. 29
T32. Davenport, IA, Masonic Auditorium, Jan. 30
T33. St. Louis, MO, The Odeon, Jan. 31
T34. Indianapolis, IN, English Opera House, Feb. 1
T35. Louisville, KY, Memorial Auditorium, Feb. 2
T36. Cincinnati, OH, Taft Auditorium, Feb. 3 *See*: **B2148.1**
T37. Chicago, IL, Auditorium Theater, Feb. 4
T38. Dayton, OH, Memorial Hall, Feb. 5
T39. Pittsburgh, PA, Syria Mosque, Feb. 6
T40. Philadelphia, PA, Academy of Music, Feb. 7 *See*: **B2148**
T41. Washington, DC, Constitution Hall, Feb. 8
T42. Richmond, VA, Mosque Auditorium, Feb. 9 *See*: **B2147.1, B2151**
T43. Brooklyn, NY, Academy of Music, Feb. 10

Index

References within each index citation are presented as follows: Arabic numerals, e.g., 10, refer to page numbers in the "Brief Biography." Other cross references are to the "Works and Performances" section, e.g., **W10**, the "Discography," e.g., **D10**, the "Filmography," e.g., **F10**, the various bibliography sections, e.g., **B10**, and the tour cities, e.g., **T10**.

About the Author

NORBERT CARNOVALE is Professor Emeritus of Music and formerly Chairman of the Music Department at University of Southern Mississippi. He is Series Adviser for the Greenwood Press series, Jazz Companions, and author of *Gunther Schuller: A Bio-Bibliography* (Greenwood, 1987). Presently, he writes for the *All Music Guide.*